The Middle Ages · SIMPSON

The Sixteenth Century · GREENBLATT / LOGAN

The Early Seventeenth Century

MAUS

The Restoration and the Eighteenth Century

NOGGLE

The Romantic Period · LYNCH

The Victorian Age · ROBSON

The Twentieth and Twenty-First Centuries

RAMAZANI

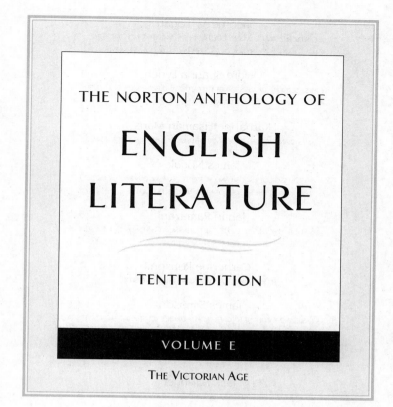

THE NORTON ANTHOLOGY OF

ENGLISH

LITERATURE

TENTH EDITION

VOLUME E

THE VICTORIAN AGE

THE NORTON ANTHOLOGY OF

ENGLISH

LITERATURE

TENTH EDITION

Stephen Greenblatt, *General Editor*
COGAN UNIVERSITY PROFESSOR OF THE HUMANITIES
HARVARD UNIVERSITY

VOLUME E

THE VICTORIAN AGE

Catherine Robson

W · W · NORTON & COMPANY

NEW YORK · LONDON

W. W. Norton & Company has been independent since its founding in 1923, when William Warder Norton and Mary D. Herter Norton first published lectures delivered at the People's Institute, the adult education division of New York City's Cooper Union. The firm soon expanded its program beyond the Institute, publishing books by celebrated academics from America and abroad. By midcentury, the two major pillars of Norton's publishing program— trade books and college texts—were firmly established. In the 1950s, the Norton family transferred control of the company to its employees, and today—with a staff of four hundred and a comparable number of trade, college, and professional titles published each year—W. W. Norton & Company stands as the largest and oldest publishing house owned wholly by its employees.

Editors: Julia Reidhead and Marian Johnson
Assistant Editor, Print: Rachel Taylor
Manuscript Editors: Michael Fleming, Katharine Ings, Candace Levy
Media Editor: Carly Fraser Doria
Assistant Editor, Media: Ava Bramson
Marketing Manager, Literature: Kimberly Bowers
Managing Editor, College Digital Media: Kim Yi
Production Manager: Sean Mintus
Text design: Jo Anne Metsch
Art director: Rubina Yeh
Photo Editor: Nelson Colon
Permissions Manager: Megan Jackson Schindel
Permissions Clearing: Nancy J. Rodwan
Cartographer: Adrian Kitzinger
Composition: Westchester Book Company
Manufacturing: LSC Crawfordsville

ISBN: 978-0-393-60306-4

W. W. Norton & Company, Inc., 500 Fifth Avenue, New York, NY 10110
wwnorton.com

W. W. Norton & Company Ltd., 15 Carlisle Street, London W1D 3BS

5 6 7 8 9 0

Contents*

The Victorian Age (1830–1901)

* Additional readings are available on the NAEL Archive (digital.wwnorton.com/englishlit10def).

Appendixes A1

Preface to the Tenth Edition

For centuries the study of literature has occupied a central place in the Humanities curriculum. The power of great literature to reach across time and space, its exploration of the expressive potential of language, and its ability to capture the whole range of experiences from the most exalted to the everyday have made it an essential part of education. But there are significant challenges to any attempt to derive the full measure of enlightenment and pleasure from this precious resource. In a world in which distraction reigns, savoring works of literature requires quiet focus. In a society in which new media clamor for attention, attending to words on the page can prove difficult. And in a period obsessed with the present at its most instantaneous, it takes a certain effort to look at anything penned earlier than late last night.

The Norton Anthology of English Literature is designed to meet these challenges. It is deeply rewarding to enter the sensibility of a different place, to hear a new voice, to be touched by an unfamiliar era. It is critically important to escape the narrow boundaries of our immediate preoccupations and to respond with empathy to lives other than our own. It is moving, even astonishing, to feel that someone you never met is speaking directly to you. But for any of this to happen requires help. The overarching goal of the Norton Anthology—as it has been for over fifty-five years and ten editions—is to help instructors energize their classrooms, engage their students, and bring literature to life.* At a time when the Humanities are under great pressure, we are committed to facilitating the special joy that comes with encountering significant works of art.

The works anthologized in these six volumes generally form the core of courses designed to introduce students to English literature. The selections reach back to the earliest moments of literary creativity in English, when the language itself was still molten, and extend to some of the most recent experiments, when, once again, English seems remarkably fluid and open. That openness—a recurrent characteristic of a language that has never been officially regulated and that has constantly renewed itself—helps to account for the sense of freshness that characterizes the works brought together here.

One of the joys of literature in English is its spectacular abundance. Even within the geographical confines of England, Scotland, Wales, and Ireland, where the majority of texts in this collection originated, one can find more

---

* For more on the help we offer and how to access it, see "Additional Resources for Instructors and Students," p. xxiv.

than enough distinguished and exciting works to fill the pages of this anthology many times over. But English literature is not confined to the British Isles; it is a global phenomenon. This border-crossing is not a consequence of modernity alone. It is fitting that among the first works here is *Beowulf*, a powerful epic written in the Germanic language known as Old English about a singularly restless Scandinavian hero. *Beowulf*'s remarkable translator in *The Norton Anthology of English Literature*, Seamus Heaney, was one of the great contemporary masters of English literature—he was awarded the Nobel Prize for Literature in 1995—but it would be potentially misleading to call him an "English poet" for he was born in Northern Ireland and was not in fact English. It would be still more misleading to call him a "British poet," as if the British Empire were the most salient fact about the language he spoke and wrote in or the culture by which he was shaped. What matters is that the language in which Heaney wrote is English, and this fact links him powerfully with the authors assembled in these volumes, a linguistic community that stubbornly refuses to fit comfortably within any firm geographical or ethnic or national boundaries. So too, to glance at other authors and writings in the anthology, in the twelfth century, the noblewoman Marie de France wrote her short stories in an Anglo-Norman dialect at home on both sides of the channel; in the sixteenth century William Tyndale, in exile in the Low Countries and inspired by German religious reformers, translated the New Testament from Greek and thereby changed the course of the English language; in the seventeenth century Aphra Behn touched readers with a story that moves from Africa, where its hero is born, to South America, where Behn herself may have witnessed some of the tragic events she describes; and early in the twentieth century Joseph Conrad, born in Ukraine of Polish parents, wrote in eloquent English a celebrated novella whose ironic vision of European empire gave way by the century's end to the voices of those over whom the empire, now in ruins, had once hoped to rule: the Caribbean-born Claude McKay, Louise Bennett, Derek Walcott, Kamau Brathwaite, V. S. Naipaul, and Grace Nichols; the African-born Chinua Achebe, J. M. Coetzee, Ngũgĩ Wa Thiong'o, and Chimamanda Ngozi Adichie; and the Indian-born A. K. Ramanujan and Salman Rushdie.

A vital literary culture is always on the move. This principle was the watchword of M. H. Abrams, the distinguished literary critic who first conceived *The Norton Anthology of English Literature*, brought together the original team of editors, and, with characteristic insight, diplomacy, and humor, oversaw seven editions. Abrams wisely understood that new scholarly discoveries and the shifting interests of readers constantly alter the landscape of literary history. To stay vital, the anthology, therefore, would need to undergo a process of periodic revision, guided by advice from teachers, as well as students, who view the anthology with a loyal but critical eye. As with past editions, we have benefited from detailed information on the works actually assigned and suggestions for improvements from 273 reviewers. Their participation has been crucial as the editors grapple with the task of strengthening the selection of more traditional texts while adding texts that reflect the expansion of the field of English studies.

With each edition, *The Norton Anthology of English Literature* has offered a broadened canon without sacrificing major writers and a selection of complete longer texts in which readers can immerse themselves. Perhaps the most emblematic of these great texts are the epics *Beowulf* and *Paradise Lost*. Among the many other complete longer works in the Tenth Edition are *Sir Gawain and the Green Knight* (in Simon Armitage's spectacular translation), Sir Thomas More's *Utopia*, Sir Philip Sidney's *Defense of Poesy*, William Shakespeare's *Twelfth Night* and *Othello*, Samuel Johnson's *Rasselas*, Aphra Behn's *Oroonoko*, Jonathan Swift's *Gulliver's Travels*, Laurence Sterne's *A Sentimental Journey through France and Italy*, Charles Dickens's *A Christmas Carol*, Robert Louis Stevenson's *The Strange Case of Dr. Jekyll and Mr. Hyde*, Rudyard Kipling's *The Man Who Would Be King*, Joseph Conrad's *Heart of Darkness*, Virginia Woolf's *Mrs. Dalloway*, James Joyce's *Portrait of the Artist as a Young Man*, Samuel Beckett's *Waiting for Godot*, Harold Pinter's *The Dumb Waiter*, and Tom Stoppard's *Arcadia*. To augment the number of complete longer works instructors can assign, and—a special concern—better to represent the achievements of novelists, the publisher is making available the full list of Norton Critical Editions, more than 240 titles, including such frequently assigned novels as Jane Austen's *Pride and Prejudice*, Mary Shelley's *Frankenstein*, Charles Dickens's *Hard Times*, and Chinua Achebe's *Things Fall Apart*. A Norton Critical Edition may be included with either package (volumes A, B, C and volumes D, E, F) or any individual volume at a discounted price (contact your Norton representative for details).

We have in this edition continued to expand the selection of writing by women in several historical periods. The sustained work of scholars in recent years has recovered dozens of significant authors who had been marginalized or neglected by a male-dominated literary tradition and has deepened our understanding of those women writers who had managed, against considerable odds, to claim a place in that tradition. The First Edition of the Norton Anthology included 6 women writers; this Tenth Edition includes 84, of whom 13 are newly added and 10 are reselected or expanded. Poets and dramatists whose names were scarcely mentioned even in the specialized literary histories of earlier generations—Aemilia Lanyer, Lady Mary Wroth, Margaret Cavendish, Mary Leapor, Anna Letitia Barbauld, Charlotte Smith, Letitia Elizabeth Landon, Mary Elizabeth Coleridge, Mina Loy, and many others—now appear in the company of their male contemporaries. There are in addition four complete long prose works by women—Aphra Behn's *Oroonoko*, Eliza Haywood's *Fantomina*, Jane Austen's *Love and Friendship*, and Virginia Woolf's *Mrs. Dalloway*—along with selections from such celebrated fiction writers as Maria Edgeworth, Jean Rhys, Katherine Mansfield, Doris Lessing, Margaret Atwood, Kiran Desai, Zadie Smith, and new authors Hilary Mantel and Chimamanda Ngozi Adichie.

Building on an innovation introduced in the First Edition, the editors have expanded the array of topical clusters that gather together short texts illuminating the cultural, historical, intellectual, and literary concerns of each of the periods. We have designed these clusters with three aims: to make them lively and accessible, to ensure that they can be taught effectively in a class meeting or two, and to make clear their relevance to the surrounding works of literature. Hence, for example, in the Sixteenth Century, a new cluster, "The Wider World," showcases the English fascination with narratives of adventure, exploration, trade, and reconnaissance. New in the Eighteenth Century, "Print Culture and the Rise of the Novel"

offers statements on the emergence of what would become English literature's most popular form as well as excerpts from *Robinson Crusoe* and
Evelina. And in the Romantic Period, a new cluster on "The Romantic
Imagination and the 'Oriental Nations'" joins contemporary discussion of the
literature of those nations with selections from William Beckford's *Vathek*
and Byron's *The Giaour*, among other texts. Across the volumes the clusters
provide an exciting way to broaden the field of the literary and to set masterpieces in a wider cultural, social, and historical framework

Now, as in the past, cultures define themselves by the songs they sing
and the stories they tell. But the central importance of visual media in contemporary culture has heightened our awareness of the ways in which songs
and stories have always been closely linked to the images that societies have
fashioned and viewed. The Tenth Edition of *The Norton Anthology of English
Literature* features fifty-six pages of color plates (in seven color inserts) and
more than 120 black-and-white illustrations throughout the volumes, including six new maps. In selecting visual material—from the Sutton Hoo treasure of the seventh century to Yinka Shonibare's *Nelson's Ship in a Bottle* in
the twenty-first century—the editors sought to provide images that conjure
up, whether directly or indirectly, the individual writers in each section; that
relate specifically to individual works in the anthology; and that shape and
illuminate the culture of a particular literary period. We have tried to choose
visually striking images that will interest students and provoke discussion,
and our captions draw attention to important details and cross-reference
related texts in the anthology.

Period-by-Period Revisions

The Middle Ages. Edited by James Simpson, this period, huge in its scope
and immensely varied in its voices, continues to offer exciting surprises.
The heart of the Anglo-Saxon portion is the great epic *Beowulf*, in the
acclaimed translation by Seamus Heaney. Now accompanied by a map of
England at the time, the Anglo-Saxon texts include the haunting poems
"Wulf and Eadwacer" and "The Ruin" as well as an intriguing collection of
Anglo-Saxon riddles. These new works join verse translations of the *Dream
of the Rood*, the *Wanderer*, and *The Wife's Lament*. An Irish Literature
selection features a tale from *The Tain* and a group of ninth-century lyrics.
The Anglo-Norman section—a key bridge between the Anglo-Saxon period
and the time of Chaucer—offers a new pairing of texts about the tragic
story of Tristan and Ysolt; an illuminating cluster on the Romance, with
three stories by Marie de France (in award-winning translations); and *Sir
Orfeo*, a comic version of the Orpheus and Eurydice story. The Middle
English section centers, as always, on Chaucer, with a generous selection of
tales and poems glossed and annotated so as to heighten their accessibility.
Simon Armitage's brilliant verse translation of *Sir Gawain and the Green
Knight* appears once again, and we offer newly modernized versions both of
Thomas Hoccleve's *My Complaint*, a startlingly personal account of the
speaker's attempt to reenter society after a period of mental instability, and
of the playfully ironic and spiritually moving *Second Shepherds' Play*. "Talking Animals," a delightful new cluster, presents texts by Marie de France,

Chaucer, and Robert Henryson that show how medieval writers used animals in stories that reveal much about humankind.

The Sixteenth Century, edited by Stephen Greenblatt and George Logan, features eight extraordinary longer texts in their entirety: More's *Utopia* (with two letters from More to Peter Giles); Book 1 of Spenser's *Faerie Queene* and, new to this edition, the posthumously published *Mutabilitie Cantos,* which arguably offer some of Spenser's finest poetry; Marlowe's *Hero and Leander* and *Doctor Faustus,* Sidney's *Defense of Poesy*; and Shakespeare's *Twelfth Night* and *Othello,* which has been added to the Tenth Edition by instructor request. Two exciting new topical clusters join the section. "An Elizabethan Miscellany" is a full, richly teachable grouping of sixteenth-century poems in English, by writers from George Gascoigne to Michael Drayton to Thomas Campion, among others, and provides access the period's explosion of lyric genius. "The Wider World" showcases the English Renaissance fascination with narratives of adventure, exploration, trade, and reconnaissance. Ranging from Africa to the Muslim East to the New World, the texts are compelling reading in our contemporary global context and offer particularly suggestive insights into the world of Shakespeare's *Othello.*

The Early Seventeenth Century. At the heart of this period, edited by Katharine Eisaman Maus, is John Milton's *Paradise Lost,* presented in its entirety. New to the Tenth Edition are the Arguments to each book, which are especially helpful for students first reading this magnificent, compelling epic. Along with Milton's "Lycidas" and *Samson Agonistes,* which is new to this edition, other complete longer works include John Donne's *Satire 3* and *The Anatomy of the World: The First Anniversary;* Aemilia Lanyer's country-house poem "The Description of Cookham"; Ben Jonson's *Volpone* and the moving Cary-Morison ode; and John Webster's tragedy *The Duchess of Malfi.* Generous selections from Donne, Mary Wroth, George Herbert, Katherine Philips, Andrew Marvell, and others, as well as the clusters "Inquiry and Experience," "Gender Relations," and "Crisis of Authority," together make for an exciting and thorough representation of the period.

The Restoration and the Eighteenth Century. The impressive array of complete longer texts in this period, edited by James Noggle, includes Dryden's *Absalom and Achitophel* and *MacFlecknoe*; Aphra Behn's *Oroonoko* (now with its dedicatory epistle); Congreve's comedy *The Way of the World;* Swift's *Gulliver's Travels* (newly complete, with illustrations from the first edition); Pope's *Essay on Criticism, The Rape of the Lock,* and *Epistle to Dr. Arbuthnot*; Gay's *Beggar's Opera*; Eliza Haywood's novella of sexual role-playing, *Fantomina*; Hogarth's graphic satire "Marriage A-la-Mode"; Johnson's *Vanity of Human Wishes* and *Rasselas*; Laurence Sterne's *A Sentimental Journey through France and Italy* (new to this edition); Gray's "Elegy Written in a Country Churchyard"; and Goldsmith's "The Deserted Village." An exciting new topical cluster, "Print Culture and the Rise of the Novel," with selections by Daniel Defoe, Henry Fielding, Samuel Richardson, Frances Burney, Clara Reeve, and others, enables readers to explore the origins of English literature's most popular form.

The Romantic Period. Edited by Deidre Shauna Lynch, this period again offers many remarkable additions. Chief among them are two topical clusters: "Romantic Literature and Wartime," which, through texts by Godwin, Wordsworth, Coleridge, Barbauld, Byron, De Quincey, and others, explores the varied ways in which war's violence came home to English literature; and "The Romantic Imagination and the 'Oriental Nations,'" which shows how English writers of the late eigththeenth and early nineteenth centuries looked eastward for new, often contradictory themes of cultural identity and difference and for "exotic" subjects that were novel and enticing to the English audience. Also new to this period are poems by Barbauld, Robinson, Charlotte Smith, Wordsworth, Shelley, Hemans, and Landon. We are excited to include an excerpt from *The History of Mary Prince, a West Indian Slave*—the first slave narrative by a woman. John Clare, the increasingly appreciated "natural poet," receives four new texts.

The Victorian Age, edited by Catherine Robson, offers an impressive array of complete longer works. New to the prose selections is Charles Dickens's *A Christmas Carol,* complete with its original illustrations. Dickens's celebrated tale, which entertains at the same time that it deals brilliantly with matters social, economic, and spiritual, joins Robert Louis Stevenson's *The Strange Case of Dr. Jekyll and Mr. Hyde,* Arthur Conan Doyle's *The Speckled Band,* Elizabeth Gaskell's *The Old Nurse's Story,* and Rudyard Kipling's *The Man Who Would Be King.* Authors with significant longer poems include Elizabeth Barrett Browning, Alfred, Lord Tennyson, Robert Browning, Dante Gabriel Rossetti, Christina Rossetti, Algernon Charles Swinburne, and Gerard Manley Hopkins. Plays include Oscar Wilde's *The Importance of Being Earnest* and George Bernard Shaw's controversial drama on prostitution, *Mrs Warren's Profession.* And, continuing the tradition of enabling readers to grapple with the period's most resonant and often fiercely contentious issues, the Tenth Edition offers an exciting new cluster, "Beacons of the Future? Education in Victorian Britain," which brings together powerful reflections by John Stuart Mill and others, government reports on the nature of education, and illuminating excerpts from *Hard Times, Alice's Adventures in Wonderland, Tom Brown's School Days,* and *Jude the Obscure.*

The Twentieth and Twenty-First Centuries. The editor, Jahan Ramazani, continues his careful revision of this, the most rapidly changing period in the anthology. Once again its core is three modernist masterpieces: Virginia Woolf's *Mrs. Dalloway,* James Joyce's *Portrait of the Artist as a Young Man,* and Samuel Beckett's *Waiting for Godot,* all complete. These works are surrounded by a dazzling array of other fiction and drama. New to the Tenth Edition are the recent recipient of the Nobel Prize for Literature, Kazuo Ishiguro, along with Hilary Mantel, Caryl Phillips, and Chimamanda Ngozi Adichie. Their works join Joseph Conrad's *Heart of Darkness,* Harold Pinter's *The Dumb Waiter,* Tom Stoppard's *Arcadia,* and stories by D. H. Lawrence, Katherine Mansfield, Jean Rhys, Doris Lessing, Nadine Gordimer, Kiran Desai, and Zadie Smith. A generous representation of poetry centers on substantial selections from Thomas Hardy, William Butler Yeats, and T. S. Eliot, and extends out to a wide range of other poets, from A. E. Housman, Wilfred Owen, and W. H. Auden to Philip Larkin, Derek Walcott, and Seamus Heaney. Two new poets, frequently requested by our readers, join the anthology: Anne Carson and Simon Armitage; and there are new poems by Yeats, Heaney, Geoffrey Hill, and Carol Ann Duffy. Visual aids have proved very helpful in teaching this period, and new ones include facsimile manuscript pages of poems by Isaac Rosenberg and Wilfred Owen, plus five new maps, which illustrate, among other things, the dramatic changes in the British Empire from 1891 to the late twentieth century, the movement of peoples to and from England during this time, and the journeys around London of the central characters in Woolf's *Mrs. Dalloway*. Linton Kwesi Johnson, Bernardine Evaristo, Patience Agbabi, and Daljit Nagra join Claude McKay, Louise Bennett, Kamau Brathwaite, Ngũgĩ Wa Thiong'o, M. NourbeSe Philip, Salman Rushdie, and Grace Nichols in the much-praised cluster "Nation, Race, and Language"—together they bear witness to the global diffusion of English, the urgency of issues of nation and identity, and the rich complexity of literary history.

Editorial Procedures and Format

The Tenth Edition adheres to the principles that have always characterized *The Norton Anthology of English Literature*. Period introductions, headnotes, and annotations are designed to enhance students' reading and, without imposing an interpretation, to give students the information they need to understand each text. The aim of these editorial materials is to make the anthology self-sufficient, so that it can be read anywhere—in a coffeeshop, on a bus, under a tree.

The Norton Anthology of English Literature prides itself on both the scholarly accuracy and the readability of its texts. To ease students' encounter with some works, we have normalized spelling and capitalization in texts up to and including the Romantic period—for the most part they now follow the conventions of modern English. We leave unaltered, however, texts in which such modernizing would change semantic or metrical qualities. From the Victorian period onward, we have used the original spelling and punctuation. We continue other editorial procedures that have proved useful in the past. After each work, we cite the date of first publication on the right; in some instances, this date is followed by the date of a revised edition for which the author was responsible. Dates of composition, when they differ from those of publication and when they are known, are provided on the left. We use square brackets to indicate titles supplied by the editors for the convenience of readers. Whenever a portion of a text is omitted, we indicate that omission with three asterisks. If the omitted portion is important for following the plot or argument, we provide a brief summary within the text or in a footnote. Finally, we have reconsidered annotations throughout and increased the number of marginal glosses for archaic, dialect, or unfamiliar words.

The Tenth Edition includes the useful "Literary Terminology" appendix, a quick-reference alphabetical glossary with examples from works in the anthology. We have also updated the General Bibliography that appears in the print volumes, as well as the period and author bibliographies, which appear online, where they can be easily searched and updated.

Additional Resources for Instructors and Students

The idea that a vital literary culture is always on the move applies not only to the print anthology but also to the resources that accompany it. For the Tenth Edition, we have added exciting new resources and improved and updated existing resources to make them more useful and easy to find.

We are pleased to launch the new NAEL Archive site, found at digital. wwnorton.com/englishlit10abc (for volumes A, B, C) and digital.wwnorton .com/englishlit10def (for volumes D, E, F). This searchable and sortable site contains thousands of resources for students and instructors in one centralized place at no additional cost. Following are some highlights:

- A series of twenty brand-new video modules designed to enhance classroom presentation of the literary works. These videos, conceived of and narrated by the anthology editors, bring various texts from the anthology to life by providing a closer look at a rarely seen manuscript, visiting a place of literary significance, or offering a conversation with a living writer.
- Over 1,000 additional readings from the Middle Ages to the turn of the twentieth century, edited, glossed, and annotated to the scholarly standards and with the sensitivity to classroom use for which the Norton Anthology is renowned. Teachers who wish to add to the selections in the print anthology will find numerous exciting works, including Wycherley's *The Country Wife*, Joanna Baillie's "A Mother to Her Waking Infant," and Edward Lear's "The Jumblies." In addition, there are many fascinating topical clusters—"The First Crusade: Sanctifying War," "Genius," and "The Satanic and Byronic Hero," to name only a few— all designed to draw readers into larger cultural contexts and to expose them to a wide spectrum of voices.
- Hundreds of images—maps, author portraits, literary places, and manuscripts—available for student browsing or instructor download for in-class presentation.
- Several hours of audio recordings.
- Annotated bibliographies for all periods and authors in the anthology.

The NAEL Archive also provides a wealth of teaching resources that are unlocked on instructor log-in:

- "Quick read" summaries, teaching notes, and discussion questions for every work in the anthology, from the much-praised *Teaching with* The Norton Anthology of English Literature: *A Guide for Instructors* by Naomi Howell (University of Exeter), Philip Schwyzer (University of Exeter), Judyta Frodyma (University of Northern British Columbia), and Sondra Archimedes (University of California–Santa Cruz).
- Downloadable PowerPoints featuring images and audio for in-class presentation

In addition to the wealth of resources in the NAEL Archive, Norton offers a downloadable coursepack that allows instructors to easily add high-quality Norton digital media to online, hybrid, or lecture courses—all at no cost. Norton Coursepacks work within existing learning management systems; there's no new system to learn, and access is free and easy. Content is customizable and includes over seventy-four reading-comprehension quizzes, short-answer questions with suggested answers, links to the video modules, and more.

The editors are deeply grateful to the hundreds of teachers worldwide who have helped us to improve *The Norton Anthology of English Literature*. A list of the instructors who replied to a detailed questionnaire follows, under Acknowledgments. The editors would like to express appreciation for their assistance to Jessica Berman (University of Maryland Baltimore County), Lara Bovilsky (University of Oregon), Gordon Braden (University of Virginia), Bruce Bradley (Clongowes Wood College), Dympna Callaghan (Syracuse University), Ariel Churchill (Harvard University), Joseph Connors (Harvard University), Taylor Cowdery (University of North Carolina at Chapel Hill), Maria Devlin (Harvard University), Lars Engel (University of Tulsa), James Engel (Harvard University), Aubrey Everett (Harvard University), Anne Fernald (Fordham University), Kevis Goodman (University of California, Berkeley), Alexander Gourlay (Rhode Island School of Design), John Hale (University of Otago), Stephen Hequembourg (University of Virginia), Seth Herbst (United States Military Academy, West Point), Rhema Hokama (Singapore University of Technology and Design), Jean Howard (Columbia University), Robert Irvine (University of Edinburgh), Thomas Keirstead (University of Toronto), Margaret Kelleher (University College Dublin), Cara Lewis (Indiana University Northwest), Mario Menendez (Harvard University), Tara Menon (New York University), John Miller (University of Virginia), Peter Miller (University of Virginia), A. J. Odasso (Wellesley College), Declan O'Keeffe (Clongowes Wood College), Juan Christian Pellicer (University of Oslo), Robert Pinsky (Boston University), Will Porter (Harvard University), Mark Rankin (James Madison University), Josephine Reece (Harvard University), Jessica Rosenberg (University of Miami), Suparna Roychoudhury (Mount Holyoke College), Peter Sacks (Harvard University), Ray Siemens (University of Victoria), Kim Simpson (University of Southampton), Bailey Sincox (Harvard University), Ramie Targoff (Brandeis University), Misha Teramura (Reed College), Gordon Teskey (Harvard University), Katie Trumpener (Yale University), Paul Westover (Brigham Young University), Katy Woodring (Harvard University), and Faye Zhang (Harvard University).

We also thank the many people at Norton, an employee-owned publishing house with a commitment to excellence, who contributed to the Tenth Edition. In planning this edition, Julia Reidhead served, as she has done in the past, as our wise and effective collaborator. In addition, we are now working with Marian Johnson, literature editor and managing editor for college books, a splendid new collaborator who has helped us bring the Tenth Edition to fruition. With admirable equanimity and skill, Carly Frasier Doria, electronic media editor and course guide editor, fashioned the new video modules and brought together the dazzling array of web resources and other pedagogical aids. We also have debts of gratitude to Katharine Ings, Candace Levy, and Michael Fleming, manuscript editors; Sean Mintus, senior production manager; Kimberly Bowers, marketing manager for literature; Megan Jackson Schindel and Nancy Rodwan, permissions; Jo Anne Metsch, designer; Nelson Colon, photo editor; and Rachel Taylor and Ava Bramson, assistant editor and assistant media editor, respectively. All these friends provided the editors with indispensable help in meeting the challenge of representing the unparalleled range and variety of English literature.

STEPHEN GREENBLATT

Acknowledgments

The editors would like to express appreciation and thanks to the hundreds of teachers who provided reviews:

Michel Aaij (Auburn University at Montgomery), Jerry J. Alexander (Presbyterian College), Sarah Alexander (The University of Vermont), Marshall N. Armintor (University of North Texas), Marilyn Judith Atlas (Ohio University), Alison Baker (California State Polytechnic University, Pomona), Reid Barbour (University of North Carolina, Chapel Hill), Jessica Barnes-Pietruszynski (West Virginia State University), Jessica Barr (Eureka College), Chris Barrett (Louisiana State University), Craig Barrette (Brescia University), Carol Beran (St. Mary's College), Peter Berek (Amherst College), David Bergman (Towson University), Scott Black (University of Utah), William R. "Beau" Black III (Weatherford College), Justin Blessinger (Dakota State University), William E. Bolton (La Salle University), Wyatt Bonikowski (Suffolk University), Rebecca Bossie (University of Texas at El Paso), Bruce Brandt (South Dakota State University), Heather Braun (University of Akron), Mark Brown (University of Jamestown), Logan D. Browning (Rice University), Monica Brzezinski Potkay (College of William and Mary), Rebecca Bushnell (University of Pennsylvania), Claire Busse (La Salle University), Thomas Butler (Eastern Kentucky University), Jim Casey (Arcadia University), Susan P. Cerasano (Colgate University), Maria Chappell (University of Georgia), Brinda Charry (Keene State College), Susannah Chewning (Union County College), Lin Chih-hsin (National Chengchi University), Kathryn Chittick (Trent University), Rita Colanzi (Immaculata University), Nora Corrigan (Mississippi University for Women), David Cowart (University of South Carolina), Catherine Craft-Fairchild (University of St. Thomas), Susan Crisafulli (Franklin College), Jenny Crisp (Dalton State College), Ashley Cross (Manhattan College), James P. Crowley (Bridgewater State University), Susie Crowson (Del Mar College), Rebecca Crump (Louisiana State University), Cyrus Mulready (SUNY New Paltz), Lisa Darien (Hartwick College), Sean Dempsey (University of Arkansas), Anthony Ding (Grossmont Community College), Lorraine Eadie (Hillsdale College), Schuyler Eastin (San Diego Christian College), Gary Eddy (Winona State University), J. Craig Eller (Louisburg College), Robert Ellison (Marshall University), Nikolai Endres (Western Kentucky University), Robert Epstein (Fairfield University), Richard Erable (Franklin College), Simon C. Estok (Sungkyunkwan University), Michael Faitell (Mohawk Valley Community College), Jonathan Farina (Seton Hall University), Tyler Farrell

(Marquette University), Jennifer Feather (The University of North Carolina Greensboro), Annette Federico (James Madison University), Kerstin Feindert (Cosumnes River College), Maryanne Felter (Cayuga Community College), Benjamin Fischer (Northwest Nazarene University), Matthew Fisher (University of California, Los Angeles), Chris Fletcher (North Central University), Michael J. Flynn (The University of North Dakota), James E. Foley (Worcester State University), Walter C. Foreman (University of Kentucky), Ann Frank Wake (Elmhurst College), Michael D. Friedman (University of Scranton), Lee Garver (Butler University), Paul L. Gaston (Kent State University), Sara E. Gerend (Aurora University), Avilah Getzler (Grand View University), Edward Gieskes (University of South Carolina), Elaine Glanz (Immaculata University), Adam Golaski (Brown University), Rachel Goldberg (Northeastern CPS), Augusta Gooch (University of Alabama–Huntsville), Nathan Gorelick (Utah Valley University), Robert Gorsch (Saint Mary's College of California), Carey Goyette (Clinton Community College), Richard J. Grande Pennsylvania State University–Abington, David A. Grant (Columbus State Community College), Sian Griffiths (Weber State University), Ann H. Guess (Alvin Community College), Audley Hall (NorthWest Arkansas Community College), Jenni Halpin (Savannah State University), Brian Harries (Concordia University Wisconsin), Samantha Harvey (Boise State University), Raychel Haugrud Reiff (University of Wisconsin–Superior), Erica Haugtvedt (The Ohio State University), Mary Hayes (University of Mississippi), Joshua R. Held (Indiana University, Bloomington), Roze Hentschell (Colorado State University), Erich Hertz (Siena College), Natalie Hewitt (Hope International University), Lisa Hinrichsen (University of Arkansas), Lorretta Holloway (Framingham State University), Catherine Howard (University of Houston), Chia-Yin Huang (Chinese Culture University), Sister Marie Hubert Kealy (Immaculata University), Elizabeth Hutcheon (Huntingdon College), Peter Hyland (Huron University College, Western University), Eileen Jankowski (Chapman University), Alan Johnson (Idaho State University), Brian Jukes (Yuba College), Kari Kalve (Earlham College), Parmita Kapadia (Northern Kentucky University), Deborah Kennedy (Saint Mary's University), Mark Kipperman (Northern Illinois University), Cindy Klestinec (Miami University–Ohio), Neal W. Kramer (Brigham Young University), Kathryn Laity (College of Saint Rose), Jameela Lares (University of Southern Mississippi), Caroline Levine (University of Wisconsin–Madison), Melinda Linscott (Idaho State University), Janet Madden (El Camino College), Gerald Margolis (Temple University), Elizabeth Mazzola (The City College of New York), Keely McCarthy (Chestnut Hill College), Cathryn McCarthy Donahue (College of Mount Saint Vincent), Mary H. McMurran (University of Western Ontario), Josephine A. McQuail (Tennessee Technological University), Brett Mertins (Metropolitan Community College), Christian Michener (Saint Mary's University), Brook Miller (University of Minnesota, Morris), Kristine Miller (Utah State University), Jacqueline T. Miller (Rutgers University), Richard J. Moll (University of Western Ontario), Lorne Mook (Taylor University), Rod Moore (Los Angeles Valley College), Rory Moore (University of California, Riverside), Grant Moss (Utah Valley University), Nicholas D. Nace (Hampden-Sydney College), Jonathan Naito (St. Olaf College), Mary Nelson (Dallas Baptist University), Mary Anne Nunn (Central Connecticut State University), John O'Brien (University of

Virginia), Onno Oerlemans (Hamilton College), Michael Oishi (Leeward Community College), Sylvia Pamboukian (Robert Morris University), Adam Parkes (University of Georgia), Michelle Parkinson (University of Wisconsin–River Falls), Geoffrey Payne (Macquarie University), Anna Peak (Temple University), Dan Pearce (Brigham Young University–Idaho), Christopher Penna (University of Delaware), Zina Petersen (Brigham Young University), Kaara L. Peterson (Miami University of Ohio), Keith Peterson (Brigham Young University–Hawaii), Professor Maggie Piccolo (Rowan University), Ann Pleiss Morris (Ripon College), Michael Pogach (Northampton Community College), Matthew Potolsky (The University of Utah), Miguel Pogach (Northampton Community College), Matthew Potolsky (The University of Utah), Miguel Powers (Fullerton College), Gregory Priebe (Harford Community College), Jonathan Purkiss (Pulaski Technical College), Kevin A. Quarmby (Oxford College of Emory University), Mark Rankin (James Madison University), Tawnya Ravy (The George Washington University), Joan Ray (University of Colorado, Colorado Springs), Helaine Razovsky (Northwestern State University of Louisiana), Vince Redder (Dakota Wesleyan University), Elizabeth Rich (Saginaw Valley State University), Patricia Rigg (Acadia University), Albert J. Rivero (Marquette University), Phillip Ronald Stormer (Culver-Stockton College), Kenneth Rooney (University College Cork, Ireland), David Ruiter (University of Texas at El Paso), Kathryn Rummell (California Polytechnic State University), Richard Ruppel (Chapman University), Jonathan Sachs (Concordia University), David A. Salomon (Russell Sage College), Abigail Scherer (Nicholls State University), Roger Schmidt (Idaho State University), William Sheldon (Hutchinson Community College), Christian Sheridan (Bridgewater College), Nicole Sidhu (East Carolina University), Lisa Siefker Bailey (Indiana University–Purdue University Columbus), Samuel Smith (Messiah College), Cindy Soldan (Lakehead University), Diana Solomon (Simon Fraser University), Vivasvan Soni (Northwestern University), Timothy Spurgin (Lawrence University), Felicia Jean Steele (The College of New Jersey), Carole Lynn Stewart (Brock University), Judy Suh (Duquesne University), Dean Swinford (Fayetteville State University), Allison Symonds (Cecil College), Brenda Tuberville (Rogers State University), Verne Underwood (Rogue Community College), Janine Utell (Widener University), Paul Varner (Abilene Christian University), Deborah Vause (York College of Pennsylvania), Nicholas Wallerstein (Black Hills State University), Rod Waterman (Central Connecticut State University), Eleanor Welsh (Chesapeake College), Paul Westover (Brigham Young University), Christopher Wheatley (The Catholic University of America), Miranda Wilcox (Brigham Young University), Brett D. Wilson (College of William & Mary), Lorraine Wood (Brigham Young University), Nicholas A. Wright (Marist College), Michael Wutz (Weber State University).

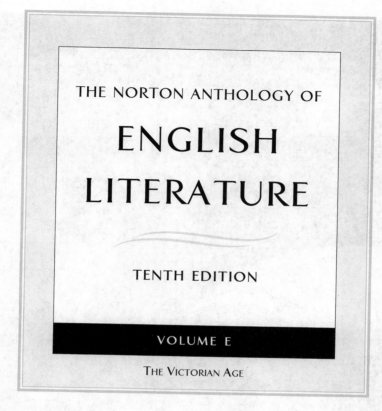

THE NORTON ANTHOLOGY OF

ENGLISH LITERATURE

TENTH EDITION

VOLUME E

THE VICTORIAN AGE

The Victorian Age
1830–1901

1832:   The First Reform Bill
1837:   Victoria becomes queen
1846:   The Corn Laws repealed
1850:   Tennyson succeeds Wordsworth as
           poet laureate
1851:   The Great Exhibition in London
1859:   Charles Darwin's *Origin of Species*
           published
1870–71:   Franco-Prussian War
1901:   Death of Victoria

In 1897 Mark Twain was visiting London during the Diamond Jubilee celebrations honoring the sixtieth anniversary of Queen Victoria's coming to the throne. "British history is two thousand years old," Twain observed, "and yet in a good many ways the world has moved farther ahead since the Queen was born than it moved in all the rest of the two thousand put together." And if the whole world had "moved" during that long lifetime and reign of Victoria's, it was in her own country itself that the change was most marked and dramatic, a change that brought Britain to its highest point of development as a world power.

In the eighteenth century the pivotal city of Western civilization had been Paris; by the second half of the nineteenth century this center of influence had shifted to London, a city that expanded from about two million inhabitants when Victoria came to the throne to six and a half million at the time of her death. The rapid growth of London is one of the many indications of the most important development of the age: the shift from a way of life based on the ownership of land to a modern urban economy based on trade and manufacturing. "We have been living, as it were, the life of three hundred years in thirty" was the impression formed by

Work (detail), Ford Madox Brown, 1852. For more information about this image, see the color insert in this volume.

3

Dr. Thomas Arnold during the early stages of Britain's industrialization. By the end of the century—after the resources of steam power had been more fully exploited for fast railways and iron ships, looms, printing presses, and farmers' combines, and after the introduction of the telegraph, intercontinental cable, photography, anesthetics, and universal compulsory education—a late Victorian could look back with astonishment on these developments during his or her lifetime. Walter Besant, one of these late Victorians, observed that so completely transformed were "the mind and habits of the ordinary Englishman" by 1897, "that he would not, could he see him, recognize his own grandfather." (Besant's use of the term *Englishman*, we might note, is symptomatic. The United Kingdom of Great Britain came into being in 1707, the date of the Act of Union between the kingdoms of Scotland and England [plus the principality of Wales, subjugated to England since the late middle ages]; the Act of Union linking Great Britain to Ireland was passed in 1800–01. Despite this history, many in England, the most populous and politically dominant member of the union, used *English* as a synonym for *British*. This error—still common today—was rarely made by those from Scotland, Wales, or Ireland.)

Because Britain was the first country to become industrialized, its transformation was an especially painful one: it experienced a host of social and economic problems consequent to rapid and unregulated industrialization. Britain also experienced an enormous increase in wealth. An early start enabled Britain to capture markets all over the globe. Cotton and other manufactured products were exported in British ships, a merchant fleet whose size was without parallel in other countries. The profits gained from trade led also to extensive capital investments in all continents. After Britain had become the world's workshop, London became, from 1870 on, the world's banker. Britain gained particular profit from the development of its own colonies, which, by 1890, comprised more than a quarter of all the territory on the surface of the earth; one in four people was a subject of Queen Victoria. By the end of the century Britain was the world's foremost imperial power.

The reactions of Victorian writers to the fast-paced expansion of Britain were various. Thomas Babington Macaulay (1800–1859) relished the spectacle with enthusiasm. During the prosperous 1850s Macaulay's essays and histories, with their recitations of the statistics of industrial growth, constituted a Hymn to Progress as well as a celebration of the superior qualities of the British people—"the greatest and most highly civilized people that ever the world saw." Other writers felt that leadership in commerce and industry was being paid for at a terrible price in human happiness, that a so-called progress had been gained only by abandoning traditional rhythms of life and traditional patterns of human relationships. The melancholy poetry of Matthew Arnold often strikes this note:

> For what wears out the life of mortal men?
> 'Tis that from change to change their being rolls;
> 'Tis that repeated shocks, again, again,
> Exhaust the energy of strongest souls.

Although many Victorians shared a sense of satisfaction in the industrial and political preeminence of Britain during the period, they also suffered from an anxious sense of something lost, a sense too of being displaced persons in a world made alien by technological changes that had been exploited too quickly for the adaptive powers of the human psyche. In concert with the era's profound challenges to the security of traditional religious beliefs, these changes tempered the triumphalism of the Victorian spirit with, at times, an anxious and self-questioning melancholy.

QUEEN VICTORIA AND THE VICTORIAN TEMPER

Queen Victoria's long reign, from 1837 to 1901, defines the historical period that bears her name. The question naturally arises whether the distinctive character of those years justifies the adjective *Victorian*. In part Victoria herself encouraged her own identification with the qualities we associate with the adjective—earnestness, moral responsibility, domestic propriety. As a young wife, as the mother of nine children, and as the black-garbed Widow of Windsor in the forty years after her husband's death in 1861, Victoria represented the domestic fidelities her citizens embraced. After her death Henry James wrote, "I mourn the safe and motherly old middle-class queen, who held the nation warm under the fold of her big, hideous Scotch-plaid shawl." Changes in the reproduction of visual images aided in making her the icon she became. She is the first British monarch of whom we have photographs. These pictures, and the ease and cheapness with which they were reproduced, facilitated her representing her country's sense of itself during her reign.

Victoria came to the throne in a decade that does seem to mark a different historical consciousness among Britain's writers. In 1831 John Stuart Mill asserts, "we are living in an age of transition." In the same year Thomas Carlyle writes, "The Old has passed away, but alas, the New appears not in its stead; the Time is still in pangs of travail with the New." Although the historical changes that created the Britain of the 1830s had been in progress for many decades, writers of the thirties shared a sharp new sense of modernity, of a break with the past, of historical self-consciousness. They responded to their sense of the historical moment with a call to action that they self-consciously distinguished from the attitude of the previous generation.

In 1834 Carlyle urged his contemporaries, "Close thy *Byron*; open thy *Goethe*." He was saying, in effect, to abandon the introspection of the Romantics and to turn to the higher moral purpose that he found in Goethe. The popular novelist Edward Bulwer-Lytton in his *England and the English* (1833) made a similar judgment. "When Byron passed away," he wrote, ". . . we turned to the actual and practical career of life: we awoke from the morbid, the dreaming, 'the moonlight and dimness of the mind,' and by a natural reaction addressed ourselves to the active and daily objects which lay before us." This sense of historical self-consciousness, of strenuous social enterprise, and of growing national achievement led writers as early as the 1850s and 1860s to define their age as Victorian. The very fact that Victoria reigned for so long sustained the concept of a distinctive historical period that writers defined even as they lived it.

When Queen Victoria died, a reaction developed against many of the achievements of the previous century; this reinforced the sense that the Victorian age was a distinct period. In the earlier decades of the twentieth century, writers took pains to separate themselves from the Victorians. It was then the fashion for most literary critics to treat their Victorian predecessors as

The Royal Family, Francis Xavier Winterhalter, 1846.

somewhat absurd creatures, stuffily complacent prigs with whose way of life they had little in common. Writers of the Georgian period (1911–36) took great delight in puncturing overinflated Victorian balloons, as Lytton Strachey, a member of Virginia Woolf's circle, did in *Eminent Victorians* (1918). A subtler example occurs in Woolf's *Orlando* (1928), a fictionalized survey of English literature from Elizabethan times to 1928, in which the Victorians are presented in terms of dampness, rain, and proliferating vegetation:

> Ivy grew in unparalleled profusion. Houses that had been of bare stone were smothered in greenery. . . . And just as the ivy and the evergreen rioted in the damp earth outside, so did the same fertility show itself within. The life of the average woman was a succession of childbirths. . . . Giant cauliflowers towered deck above deck till they rivaled . . . the elm trees themselves. Hens laid incessantly eggs of no special tint. . . . The whole sky itself as it spread wide above the British Isles was nothing but a vast feather bed.

This witty description not only identifies a distinguishing quality of Victorian life and literature—a superabundant energy—but reveals the author's distaste for its smothering profusion. Woolf was the daughter of Sir Leslie Stephen (1832–1904), an eminent Victorian. In her later life, when assessing her father's powerful personality, Woolf recorded in her diary that she could never have become a writer if he had not died when he did. Growing up under such towering shadows, she and her generation mocked their predecessors to make them less intimidating. In his reminiscences *Portraits from Life* (1937), the novelist Ford Madox Ford recalled his feelings of terror when he confronted the works of Carlyle and Ruskin, which he likened to an overpowering range of high mountains. The mid-Victorians, he wrote, were "a childish nightmare to me."

The Georgians' reaction against immediate predecessors was responsible in part for the low estimation of Victorian literature that persisted for many years in academic literary studies; its aftereffects can also be felt when the term *Victorian* is employed in an exclusively pejorative sense, as prudish or old-fashioned. Contemporary historians and critics find the Victorian period a richly complex example of a society struggling with the issues and problems we identify with modernism. But to give the period the single designation *Victorian* reduces its complexity. Because it is a period of almost seventy years, we can hardly expect generalizations to be uniformly applicable. It is, therefore, helpful to subdivide the age into three phases: early Victorian (1830–48), mid-Victorian (1848–70), and late Victorian (1870–1901). It is also helpful to consider the final decade, the nineties, as a bridge between two centuries.

THE EARLY PERIOD (1830–48): A TIME OF TROUBLES

In the early 1830s two historical events occurred of momentous consequence for Britain. In 1830 the Liverpool and Manchester Railway opened, becoming the first steam-powered public railway line in the world. The next decade witnessed Railway Mania: more than six thousand miles of railway line were built as a result of projects initiated between 1844 and 1846 alone. By 1897 the country as a whole had 21,429 lines of track and an underground railway system beneath London. The train transformed Britain's landscape, supported the growth of its commerce, and shrank the distance between its cities. The opening of the first railway coincided with the opening of the country's Reform Parliament. The railway had increased the pressure for parliamentary reform. "Parliamentary reform must follow soon after the opening of this road," a Manchester man observed in 1830. "A million of persons will pass over it in the course of this year, and see that hitherto unseen village of Newton; and they must be convinced of the absurdity of its sending two members to Parliament while Manchester sends none." Despite the growth of manufacturing cities consequent to the Industrial Revolution, Britain was still governed by an archaic electoral system whereby some of the new industrial cities were unrepresented in Parliament while "rotten boroughs" (communities that had become depopulated) elected the nominees of the local squire to Parliament.

By 1830 a time of economic distress had brought the country close to revolution. Manufacturing interests, who refused to tolerate their exclusion from the political process any longer, led working men in agitating for reform. Fearing the kind of revolution it had seen in Europe, Parliament passed a Reform Bill in 1832 that transformed the existing class structure. This extended the right to vote to all males owning property worth £10 or more in annual rent in England and Wales; a Scottish Reform Act also passed in 1832, which generally made the same move. In effect the voting public thereafter included the lower middle classes but not the working classes, who did not obtain the vote until 1867, when a second Reform Bill was passed. Even more important than the extension of the franchise was the virtual abolition of the rotten boroughs and the redistribution of parliamentary representation. Because it broke up the monopoly of power that the conservative landowners had so long enjoyed (the Tory Party had been in office almost continuously from 1783 to 1830), the Reform Bill represents the beginning of a new age, in which middle-class economic interests gained increasing power.

Yet even the newly constituted Parliament was unable to find legislative solutions to the problems facing the nation. The economic and social difficulties attendant on industrialization were so severe that the 1830s and 1840s became known as the Time of Troubles. After a period of prosperity from 1832 to 1836, a crash in 1837, followed by a series of bad harvests, produced a period of unemployment, desperate poverty, and rioting. Conditions in the new industrial and coal-mining areas were terrible. Workers and their families in the slums of such cities as Manchester lived in horribly crowded, unsanitary housing; and the conditions under which men, women, and children toiled in mines and factories were unimaginably brutal. Elizabeth Barrett's poem "The Cry of the Children" (1843) expresses her horrified response to an official report on child labor that described five-year-olds sitting alone in darkness to open and close ventilation doors, and twelve-year-olds dragging heavy tubs of coal through low-ceilinged mine passages for sixteen hours a day.

The owners of mines and factories regarded themselves as innocent of blame for such conditions, for they were wedded to an economic theory of laissez-faire, which assumed that unregulated working conditions would ultimately benefit everyone. A sense of the seemingly hopeless complexity of the situation during the Hungry Forties is provided by an entry for 1842 in the diary of the statesman Charles Greville, an entry written at the same time that Carlyle was making his contribution to the "Condition of England Question," *Past and Present*. Conditions in the north of England, Greville reports, were "appalling."

> There is an immense and continually increasing population, no adequate demand for labor, . . . no confidence, but a universal alarm, disquietude, and discontent. Nobody can sell anything. . . . Certainly I have never seen . . . so serious a state of things as that which now stares us in the face; and this after thirty years of uninterrupted peace, and the most ample scope afforded for the development of all our resources. . . . One remarkable feature in the present condition of affairs is that nobody can account for it, and nobody pretends to be able to point out any remedy.

In reality many remedies were proposed. One of the most striking was put forward by the Chartists, a large organization of workers. In 1838 the organization drew up a "People's Charter" advocating the extension of the right to vote, the use of secret balloting, and other legislative reforms. For ten years the Chartist leaders engaged in agitation to have their program adopted by Parliament. Their fiery speeches, delivered at conventions designed to collect signatures for petitions to Parliament, created fears of revolution. In "Locksley Hall" (1842), Alfred, Lord Tennyson seems to have had the Chartist demonstrations in mind when he wrote: "Slowly comes a hungry people, as a lion, creeping nigher, / Glares at one that nods and winks behind a slowly-dying fire." Although the Chartist movement had fallen apart by 1848, it succeeded in creating an atmosphere open to reform. One of the most important reforms was the abolition of the high tariffs on imported grains, tariffs known as the Corn Laws (the word *corn* in Britain refers to wheat and other grains). These high tariffs had been established to protect British

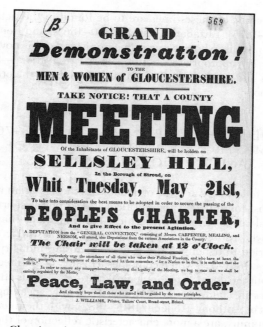

Chartism. Announcement of a Chartist meeting in Gloucestershire, 1839.

farm products from having to compete with low-priced products imported from abroad. Landowners and farmers fought to keep these tariffs in force so that high prices for their wheat would be ensured; but the rest of the population suffered severely from the exorbitant price of bread or, in years of bad crops, from scarcity of food. In 1845 serious crop failures in Britain and the outbreak of potato blight in Ireland convinced Sir Robert Peel, the Tory prime minister, that traditional protectionism must be abandoned. In 1846 the Corn Laws were repealed by Parliament, and the way was paved for the introduction of a system of free trade whereby goods could be imported with the payment of only minimal tariff duties. Although free trade did not eradicate the slums of Manchester, it worked well for many years and helped relieve the major crisis of the Victorian economy. In 1848, when revolutions were breaking out all over Europe, Britain was relatively unaffected. A large Chartist demonstration in London seemed to threaten violence, but it came to nothing. The next two decades were relatively calm and prosperous.

This Time of Troubles left its mark on some early Victorian literature. "Insurrection is a most sad necessity," Carlyle writes in his *Past and Present*, "and governors who wait for that to instruct them are surely getting into the fatalest courses." A similar refrain runs through Carlyle's history *The French Revolution* (1837). Memories of the French Reign of Terror lasted longer than memories of British victories over Napoleon at Trafalgar and Waterloo, memories freshened by later outbreaks of civil strife, "the red fool-fury of the Seine" as Tennyson described one of the violent overturnings of government in France. The most marked response to the industrial and political scene, however, comes in the "Condition of England" novels of the 1840s and early

1850s. Vivid records of these times are to be found in the fiction of Charles Kingsley (1819–1875); Elizabeth Gaskell (1810–1865); and Benjamin Disraeli (1804–1881), a novelist who became prime minister. For his novel *Sybil* (1845), Disraeli chose an appropriate subtitle, *The Two Nations*—a phrase that pointed out the line dividing the Britain of the rich from the other nation, the Britain of the poor.

THE MID-VICTORIAN PERIOD (1848–70): ECONOMIC PROSPERITY, THE GROWTH OF EMPIRE, AND RELIGIOUS CONTROVERSY

In the decades following the Time of Troubles some Victorian writers, such as Charles Dickens, continued to make critical attacks on the shortcomings of the Victorian social scene. Even more critical and indignant than Dickens was John Ruskin, who turned from a purely moral and aesthetic criticism of art during this period to denounce the evils of Victorian industry, as in his *The Stones of Venice* (1851–53), which combines a history of architecture with stern prophecies about the doom of technological culture, or in his attacks on laissez-faire economics in *Unto This Last* (1862). Generally speaking, however, the realistic novels of Anthony Trollope (1815–1882), with their comfortable toler-ance and equanimity, are a more characteristic reflection of the mid-Victorian attitude toward the social and political scene than are Ruskin's lamentations. Overall, this second phase of the Victorian period had many harassing prob-lems, but it was a time of prosperity. On the whole its institutions worked well. Even the badly bungled war against Russia in the Crimea (1854–56) did not seriously affect the growing sense of satisfaction that the challenging difficul-ties of the 1840s had been solved or would be solved by British wisdom and energy. The monarchy was proving its worth in a modern setting. The queen and her husband, Prince Albert, were models of middle-class domesticity and devotion to duty. The aristocracy was discovering that free trade was enrich-ing rather than impoverishing their estates; agriculture flourished together with trade and industry. And through a succession of Factory Acts in Parliament, which restricted child labor and limited hours of employment, the condition of the working classes was also being gradually improved. When we speak of Victorian complacency or stability or optimism, we are usually refer-ring to this mid-Victorian phase—"The Age of Improvement," as the historian Asa Briggs has called it. "Of all the decades in our history," writes G. M. Young, "a wise man would choose the eighteen-fifties to be young in."

In 1851 Prince Albert opened the Great Exhibition in Hyde Park, where a gigantic glass greenhouse, the Crystal Palace, had been erected to display the exhibits of modern industry and science. The Crystal Palace was one of the first buildings constructed according to modern architectural principles in which materials such as glass and iron are employed for purely functional ends (much late Victorian furniture, on the other hand, with its fantastic and irrelevant ornamentation, was constructed according to the opposite principle). The building, as well as the exhibits, symbolized the triumphant feats of Victorian technology. As Benjamin Disraeli wrote to a friend in 1862: "It is a privilege to live in this age of rapid and brilliant events. What an error to consider it a utilitarian age. It is one of infinite romance."

The Medieval Court, Joseph Nash (1809–1878), from *Dickinson's Comprehensive Pictures of the Great Exhibition of 1851* (1854).

Britain's technological progress led to an enormous expansion of the country's operations around the globe. These activities had incalculably devastating effects on the territories Britain conquered and controlled, not least the destruction of many indigenous industries. For Britain the economic boost was astounding: annual exports of goods nearly trebled in value between 1850 and 1870. Not only the export of goods but that of people and capital increased. Between 1853 and 1880 2,466,000 emigrants left Britain, many bound for British colonies. By 1870 British capitalists had invested £800 million abroad; in 1850 the total had been only £300 million. This investment, of people, money, and technology, created the British Empire. Important building blocks of the empire were put in place in the mid-Victorian period. In the 1850s and 1860s there was large-scale immigration to Australia; in 1867 Parliament unified the Canadian provinces into the Dominion of Canada. Following the brutal suppression of an uprising of Indian troops and peasantry in 1857, Parliament took over the government of India from the private East India Company and started to put a civil service into place. In 1876 Queen Victoria was named empress of India. Although the competitive scramble for African colonies did not take place until the final decades of the century, the model of empire was created earlier, made possible by technological revolution in communication and transportation. Much as Rome had built roads through Europe in the years of the Roman Empire, Britain built railways and strung telegraph wires. It also put in place a framework for education and government that preserves British influence, for good or ill, in former colonies even today. Britain's motives, in creating its empire, were many. It sought wealth, markets for manufactured goods, sources for raw materials, and world power and influence. Many British people also saw the expansion of empire as a moral responsibility—what Rudyard Kipling, in another context, termed "the White Man's burden." Queen Victoria stated that the imperial mission was "to protect the poor natives and advance civilization." Missionary societies flourished, spreading Christianity in India, Asia, and Africa.

At the same time that the British missionary enterprise was expanding, there was increasing debate about religious belief. By the mid-Victorian period the Church of England had evolved into three major divisions: Evangelical, or Low Church; Broad Church; and High Church. The Evangelicals emphasized spiritual transformation of the individual by conversion and a strictly moral Christian life. Zealously dedicated to good causes (they were responsible for the emancipation of all slaves in the British Empire in 1833), advocates of a strict Puritan code of morality, and righteously censorious of worldliness in others, the Evangelicals became a powerful and active minority in the early part of the nineteenth century. Much of the power of the Evangelicals depended on the fact that their view of life and religion was virtually identical with that of a much larger group external to the Church of England: the Nonconformists, or Dissenters—that is, Baptists, Methodists, Congregationalists, and other Protestant denominations. The High Church was also associated with a group external to the Church of England; it was the "Catholic" side of the Church, emphasizing the importance of tradition, ritual, and authority. In the 1830s a High Church movement took shape, known both as the Oxford movement, because it originated at Oxford University, and as Tractarianism, because its leaders developed their arguments in a series of pamphlets or tracts. Led by John Henry Newman, who later converted to Roman Catholicism, Tractarians argued that the Church could maintain its power and authority only by resisting liberal tendencies and holding to its original traditions. The Broad Church resisted the doctrinal and ecclesiastical controversies that separated the High Church and Evangelical divisions. Open to modern advances in thought, its adherents emphasized the broadly inclusive nature of the Church.

Some rationalist challenges to religious belief that developed before the Victorian period maintained their influence. The most significant was Utilitarianism, also known as Benthamism or Philosophical Radicalism. Utilitarianism derived from the thought of Jeremy Bentham (1748–1832) and his disciple James Mill (1773–1836), the father of John Stuart Mill. Bentham believed that all human beings seek to maximize pleasure and minimize pain. The criterion by which we should judge a morally correct action, therefore, is the extent to which it provides the greatest pleasure to the greatest number. Measuring religion by this moral arithmetic, Benthamites concluded that it was an outmoded superstition; it did not meet the rationalist test of value. Utilitarianism was widely influential in providing a philosophical basis for political and social reforms, but it aroused considerable opposition on the part of those who felt it failed to recognize people's spiritual needs. Raised according to strict utilitarian principles by his father, John Stuart Mill came to be critical of them. In the mental and spiritual crisis portrayed in his *Autobiography* (1873), Mill describes his realization that his utilitarian upbringing had left him no power to feel. In *Sartor Resartus* (1833–34) Carlyle describes a similar spiritual crisis in which he struggles to rediscover the springs of religious feeling in the face of his despair at the specter of a universe governed only by utilitarian principles. Later both Dickens, in his portrayal of Thomas Gradgrind in *Hard Times* (1854), "a man of facts and calculations" who is "ready to weigh and measure any parcel of human nature," and Ruskin, in his *Unto This Last*, attack utilitarianism.

In mid-Victorian Britain, however, the challenge to religious belief gradually shifted from the Utilitarians to some of the leaders of science, in particular to Thomas Henry Huxley, who popularized the theories of Charles Darwin. Although many British scientists were themselves individuals of strong religious convictions, the impact of their scientific discoveries seemed consistently damaging to established faiths. Complaining in 1851 about the "flimsiness" of his own religious faith, Ruskin exclaimed: "If only the Geologists would let me alone, I could do very well, but those dreadful hammers! I hear the clink of them at the end of every cadence of the Bible verses."

The damage lamented by Ruskin was effected in two ways. First the scientific attitude of mind was applied toward a study of the Bible. This kind of investigation, developed especially in Germany, was known as the Higher Criticism. Instead of treating the Bible as a sacredly infallible document, scientifically minded scholars examined it as a mere text of history and presented evidence about its composition that believers, especially in Protestant countries, found disconcerting, to say the least. A noteworthy example of such Higher Criticism studies was David Friedrich Strauss's *Das Leben Jesu*, which was translated by George Eliot in 1846 as *The Life of Jesus*. The second kind of damage was effected by the view of humanity implicit in the discoveries of geology and astronomy, the new and "Terrible Muses" of literature, as Tennyson called them in a late poem. Geology, by extending the history of the earth backward millions of years, reduced the stature of the human species in time. John Tyndall, an eminent physicist, said in an address at Belfast in 1874 that in the eighteenth century people had an "unwavering trust" in the "chronology of the Old Testament" but in Victorian times they had to become accustomed to

> the idea that not for six thousand, nor for sixty thousand, nor for six thousand thousand, but for aeons embracing untold millions of years, this earth has been the theatre of life and death. The riddle of the rocks has been read by the geologist and paleontologist, from sub-Cambrian depths to the deposits thickening over the sea bottoms of today. And upon the leaves of that stone book are . . . stamped the characters, plainer and surer than those formed by the ink of history, which carry the mind back into abysses of past time.

The discoveries of astronomers, by extending a knowledge of stellar distances to dizzying expanses, were likewise disconcerting. Carlyle's friend John Sterling remarked in a letter of 1837 how geology "gives one the same sort of bewildering view of the abysmal extent of Time that Astronomy does of Space." To Tennyson's speaker in *Maud* (1855) the stars are "innumerable" tyrants of "iron skies." They are "Cold fires, yet with power to burn and brand / His nothingness into man."

In the mid-Victorian period biology reduced humankind even further into "nothingness." Darwin's great treatise *The Origin of Species* (1859) was interpreted by the nonscientific public in a variety of ways. Some chose to assume that evolution was synonymous with progress, but most readers recognized that Darwin's theory of natural selection conflicted not only with the concept of creation derived from the Bible but also with long-established assumptions of the values attached to humanity's special role in the world. Darwin's later treatise *The Descent of Man* (1871) raised more explicitly the haunting question of our identification with the animal kingdom. If the principle of survival of the fittest was accepted, there remained the inquiry: fittest for what? As John Fowles writes in his 1968 novel about Victorian England, *The French Lieutenant's Woman*, Darwin's theories made the Victorians feel "infinitely isolated." "By the 1860s the great iron structures of their philosophies, religions, and social stratifications were already beginning to look dangerously corroded."

Disputes about evolutionary science, like the disputes about religion, are a reminder that beneath the placidly prosperous surface of the mid-Victorian age there were serious conflicts and anxieties. In the same year as the Great Exhibition, with its celebration of the triumphs of trade and industry, Charles Kingsley wrote, "The young men and women of our day are fast parting from their parents and each other; the more thoughtful are wandering either towards Rome, towards sheer materialism, or towards an unchristian and unphilosophic spiritualism."

THE LATE PERIOD (1870–1901): DECAY OF VICTORIAN VALUES

The third phase of the Victorian age is more difficult to categorize. At first glance its point of view seems merely an extension of mid-Victorianism, whose golden glow lingered on through the Jubilee years of 1887 and 1897 (years celebrating the fiftieth and sixtieth anniversaries of the queen's accession) down to 1914. For many affluent Victorians, this final phase of the century was a time of serenity and security, the age of house parties and long weekends in the country. In the amber of Henry James's prose is immortalized a sense of the comfortable pace of these pleasant, food-filled gatherings. Life in London, too, was for many an exhilarating heyday. In *My Life and Loves* the Irish-American Frank Harris (1854–1931), often a severe critic of the English scene, records his recollections of the gaiety of London in the 1880s: "London: who would give even an idea of its varied delights: London, the center of civilization, the queen city of the world without a peer in the multitude of its attractions, as superior to Paris as Paris is to New York." The exhilarating sense of London's delights reflects in part the proliferation of things: commodities, inventions, products that were changing the texture of modern life. Britain had become committed not only to continuing technological change but also to a culture of consumerism, generating new products for sale.

The wealth of Britain's empire provided the foundation on which its economy was built. The final decades of the century saw the apex of British imperialism. Although most Britons rarely considered the plight inflicted on subjugated peoples across the globe, many started to question the costs of empire to their own countrymen. These seemed increasingly apparent in rebellions, massacres, and bungled wars, such as the uprising of Indian troops and peasantry in the "mutiny" of 1857; the Jamaica Rebellion in 1865; the massacre of General Gordon and his soldiers at Khartoum, in the Sudan, in 1885, where he had been sent to evacuate the British in the face of a religiously inspired revolt; and two Anglo-Boer wars at the end of the century, in which Britain engaged in a long, bloody, and unpopular struggle to annex two independent republics in the south of Africa controlled by Dutch settlers called Boers. In addition the "Irish Ques-

Piccadilly Circus, ca. 1893, in the center of London.

tion," as it was called, grew especially divisive in the 1880s, when home rule for Ireland became a topic of heated debate—a proposed reform that was unsuccessfully advocated by Prime Minister Gladstone and other leaders. And outside the British Empire, other developments challenged Victorian stability and security. The sudden emergence of Bismarck's Germany after the defeat of France in 1871 was progressively to confront Britain with powerful threats to its naval and military position and also to its preeminence in trade and industry. The recovery of the United States after the Civil War likewise provided new and serious competition not only in industry but also in agriculture. As the westward expansion of railroads in the United States and Canada opened up the vast, grain-rich prairies, the typical British farmer had to confront lower grain prices and a dramatically different scale of productivity, which Britain could not match. In 1873 and 1874 such severe economic depressions occurred that the rate of emigration rose to an alarming degree. Another change in the mid-Victorian balance of power was the growth of labor as a political and economic force. In 1867, under Disraeli's guidance, a second Reform Bill had been passed that extended the right to vote to sections of the working classes; the increasing educational opportunities that opened up for the poor over the course of the century also served to heighten political awareness and activity. These factors, together with the subsequent development of trade unions, made labor a powerful political force that included a wide variety of kinds of socialism. Some labor leaders were disciples of the Tory-socialism of John Ruskin and shared his idealistic conviction that the middle-class economic and political system, with its distrust of state interference, was irresponsible and immoral. Other labor leaders had been influenced instead by the revolutionary theories of Karl Marx and Friedrich Engels as expounded in their *Communist Manifesto* of 1847 and in Marx's *Das Kapital* (1867, 1885, 1895). The first British author of note to embrace Marxism was the poet and painter William Morris, who shared with Marx a conviction that utopia could be achieved only after the working classes had, by revolution, taken control of government and industry.

In much of the literature of this final phase of Victorianism we can sense an overall change of attitudes. Some of the late Victorian writers expressed the change openly by simply attacking the major mid-Victorian idols. Samuel Butler, for example, set about demolishing Darwin, Tennyson, and Prime Minister Gladstone, figures whose aura of authority reminded him of his own father. For the more worldly and casual-mannered Prime Minister Disraeli, on the other hand, Butler could express considerable admiration: "Earnestness was his greatest danger, but if he did not quite overcome it (as who indeed can? it is the last enemy that shall be subdued), he managed to veil it with a fair amount of success." In his novel *The Way of All Flesh* (1903), much of which was written in the 1870s, Butler satirized family life, in particular the tyrannical self-righteousness of a Victorian father, his own father (a clergyman) serving as his model. In a different vein Walter Pater and his followers concluded that the striving of their predecessors was ultimately pointless, that the answers to our problems are not to be found, and that our role is to enjoy the fleeting moments of beauty in "this short day of frost and sun."

THE NINETIES

The changes in attitude that had begun cropping up in the 1870s became much more conspicuous in the final decade of the century and give the nineties a special aura of notoriety. Of course the changes were not in evidence everywhere. At the empire's outposts in India and Africa, the British were building railways and administering governments with the same strenuous energy as in the mid-Victorian period. The stories of Kipling and Joseph Conrad variously record the struggles of such people. Also embodying the task of sustaining an empire were the soldiers and sailors who fought in various colonial wars, most notably in the war against the Boers in South Africa (1899–1902). But back in Britain, Victorian standards were breaking down on several fronts. One colorful embodiment of changing values was Victoria's son and heir, Edward, Prince of Wales, who was entering his fiftieth year as the nineties began. A pleasure-seeking easygoing person, Edward was the antithesis of his father, Prince Albert, an earnest-minded intellectual who had devoted his life to hard work and to administrative responsibilities. Edward's carryings-on were a favorite topic for newspaper articles, one of which noted how this father of five children "openly maintained scandalous relations with ballet dancers and chorus singers."

Much of the writing of the decade illustrates a breakdown of a different sort. Melancholy, not gaiety, is characteristic of its spirit. Artists of the nineties, representing the aesthetic movement, were very much aware of living at the end of a great century and often cultivated a deliberately fin de siècle ("end-of-century") pose. A studied languor, a weary sophistication, a search for new ways of titillating jaded palates can be found in both the poetry and the prose of the period. *The Yellow Book,* a periodical that ran from 1894 to 1897, is generally taken to represent the aestheticism of the nineties. The startling black-and-white drawings and designs of its art editor, Aubrey Beardsley, the prose of George Moore and Max Beerbohm, and the poetry of Ernest Dowson illustrate different aspects of the movement. Writings of the era that embraced other values and attracted broader readerships nevertheless

Oscar Wilde. One of the photographic portraits of Wilde taken by Napoleon Sarony (1821–1896) in 1882.

shared aestheticism's perspective that a distinctly new spirit was at large, at least in the metropolis. Sir Arthur Conan Doyle's hugely popular Sherlock Holmes stories, for instance, present both a hero who simultaneously embodies and polices the city's cosmopolitan decadence and his bluff sidekick Dr. Watson, to whom London is "that great cesspool into which all the loungers and idlers of the Empire are irresistibly drained." In 1893 the Austrian critic Max Nordau summed up what seemed to him to be happening, in a book that was as sensational as its title: *Degeneration*.

From our perspective, however, it is easy to see in the nineties the beginning of the modernist movement in literature; a number of the great writers of the twentieth century—Yeats, Hardy, Conrad, Shaw—were already publishing.

In Dickens's *David Copperfield* (1850) the hero affirms: "I have always been thoroughly in earnest." Forty-five years later Oscar Wilde's comedy *The Importance of Being Earnest* (1895) turns the typical mid-Victorian word *earnest* into a pun, a key joke in this comic spectacle of earlier Victorian values being turned upside down. As Richard Le Gallienne (a novelist of the nineties) remarked in *The Romantic Nineties* (1926): "Wilde made dying Victorianism laugh at itself, and it may be said to have died of the laughter."

THE ROLE OF WOMEN

Political and legal reforms in the course of the Victorian period had given citizens many rights. In 1844 Friedrich Engels observed: "England is unquestionably the freest—that is the least unfree—country in the world, North America not excepted." The country as a whole had indeed done much to extend its citizens' liberties, but women did not share in these freedoms. They could not vote or hold political office. (Although petitions to Parliament advocating women's suffrage were introduced as early as the 1840s, women did not get the vote until 1918.) Until the passage of the Married Women's Property Acts (1870–1908), married women could not own or handle their own property. While men could divorce their wives for adultery, wives could divorce their husbands only if adultery were combined with cruelty, bigamy, incest, or bestiality. Educational and employment opportunities for women were limited. These inequities stimulated a spirited debate about women's roles known as the "Woman Question." Some of the social changes that such discussion helped foster eventually affected the lives of all, or many, of the country's female population; nevertheless, it is important to recognize that this Victorian debate, despite the inclusive claims of its title was, with a few exceptions, conducted by the middle classes about middle-class women.

Arguments for women's rights were based on the same libertarian principles that had formed the basis of extended rights for men. In Hardy's last novel, *Jude the Obscure* (1895), his heroine justifies leaving her husband by quoting a passage from Mill's *On Liberty* (1859). She might have quoted another work by Mill, *The Subjection of Women* (1869), which, like Mary Wollstonecraft's *A Vindication of the Rights of Woman* (1792), challenges long-established assumptions about women's role in society. Legislative measures over the course of the nineteenth century gradually brought about changes in a number of areas.

The Custody Act of 1839 gave a mother the right to petition the court for access to her minor children and custody of children under seven (raised to sixteen in 1878). The Divorce and Matrimonial Causes Act of 1857 established a civil divorce court (divorce previously could be granted only by an ecclesiastical court) and provided a deserted wife the right to apply for a protection order that would allow her rights to her property. Although divorce remained so expensive as to be available only to the very rich, these changes in marriage and divorce laws, together with the Married Women's Property Acts, began to establish a basis for the rights of women in marriage.

In addition to pressuring Parliament for legal reform, feminists worked to enlarge female educational opportunities. In 1837 none of the country's universities was open to women. Tennyson's long poem *The Princess* (1847), with its fantasy of a women's college from whose precincts all males are excluded, was inspired by contemporary discussions of the need for women to obtain an education more advanced than that provided by the popular finishing schools ("Miss Pinkerton's Academy" in William Makepeace Thackeray's *Vanity Fair* [1847–48] is a good parody of one of these institutions). Although by the end of the poem Princess Ida has repented of her Amazonian scheme, she and the prince look forward to a future in which man will be "more of woman, she of man." The poem reflects a climate of opinion that led in 1848 to the establishment of the first women's college in London, an example later recommended by Thomas Henry Huxley, a strong advocate of advanced education for women. By the end of Victoria's reign, women could take degrees at twelve universities or university colleges and could study, although not earn a degree, at Oxford and Cambridge.

There was also agitation for improved employment opportunities for women. Writers as diverse as Charlotte Brontë, Elizabeth Barrett Browning, and

Florence Nightingale complained that women from middle- and upper-class homes were taught trivial accomplishments to fill up days in which there was nothing important to do. Had they been aware of such complaints, women from the majority lower-class population might have found it hard to show sympathy: the working lives of poor British women had always been strenuous, inside and outside the house, but industrial society brought unprecedented pressures. Although the largest proportion of working women labored as servants in the homes of the more affluent, the explosive growth of mechanized industries, especially in the textile trade, created new and grueling forms of paid employment. Hundreds of thousands of lower-class women worked at factory jobs under appalling conditions, while the need for coal to fuel England's industrial development brought women into the mines for the first time. A series of Factory Acts (1802–78) gradually regulated the conditions of labor in mines and factories, eventually reducing the sixteen-hour day and banning women from mine work altogether; but even with such changes, the lot of the country's poorest women, whether factory operatives or housemaids, seamstresses or field laborers, was undoubtedly hard. Bad working conditions and underemployment drove thousands of women into prostitution, which in the nineteenth century became increasingly professionalized—and the subject of an almost obsessive public concern, whose manifestations included frequent literary and artistic representation.

For the most part, prostitution was a trade for working-class women, but there was considerable anxiety about the possible fates of what contemporary journalists called the "surplus" or "redundant" women of the middle classes—that is, women who remained unmarried because of the imbalance in numbers between the sexes. Such women (of whom there were approximately half a million in mid-Victorian Britain) had few employment opportunities, none of them attractive or profitable. Emigration was frequently proposed as a solution to the problem, but the number of single female emigrants was never high enough to affect the population imbalance significantly. The only occupation at which an unmarried middle-class woman could earn a living and maintain some claim to gentility was that of a governess, but a governess could expect no security of employment, only minimal wages, and an ambiguous status, somewhere between servant and family member, that isolated her within the household. Perhaps because the governess so clearly indicated the precariousness of the unmarried middle-class woman's status in Victorian Britain, the governess novel, of which the most famous examples are *Jane Eyre* (1847) and *Vanity Fair*, became a popular genre through which to explore women's roles in society.

As such novels indicate, Victorian society was preoccupied not only with legal and economic limitations on women's lives but with the very nature of woman. In *The Subjection of Women*, John Stuart Mill argues that "what is now called the nature of women is eminently an artificial thing—the result of forced repression in some directions, unnatural stimulation in others." In Tennyson's *The Princess* the king voices a more traditional view of male and female roles, a view that has come to be known as the doctrine of "separate spheres":

> Man for the field and woman for the hearth:
> Man for the sword and for the needle she:
> Man with the head and woman with the heart:
> Man to command and woman to obey.

The king's relegation of women to the hearth and heart reflects an ideology that claimed that woman had a special nature peculiarly fit for her domestic role. Most aptly epitomized by the title of Coventry Patmore's immensely popular poem *The Angel in the House* (1854–62), this concept of womanhood stressed woman's purity and selflessness. Protected and enshrined within the home, her role was to create a place of peace where man could take refuge from the difficulties of modern life. In "Of Queens' Gardens" (1865), John Ruskin writes:

> This is the true nature of home—it is the place of Peace; the shelter, not only from all injury, but from all terror, doubt, and division. In so far as it is not this, it is not home; so far as the anxieties of the outer life penetrate into it, and the inconsistently-minded, unknown, unloved, or hostile society of the outer world is allowed either by husband or wife to cross the threshold, it ceases to be home; it is then only a part of that outer world which you have roofed over, and lighted fire in. But so far as it is a sacred place, a vestal temple, a temple of the hearth watched over by Household Gods, . . . so far it vindicates the name, and fulfills the praise, of home.

Such an exalted conception of home placed great pressure on the woman who ran it to be, in Ruskin's words, "enduringly, incorruptibly good; instinctively, infallibly wise—wise, not for self-development, but for self-renunciation." It is easy to recognize the oppressive aspects of this domestic ideology. Paradoxically, however, it was used not only by antifeminists, eager to keep woman in her place, but by some feminists as well, in justifying the special contribution that woman could make to public life.

In his preface to *The Portrait of a Lady* (1881) Henry James writes: "Millions of presumptuous girls, intelligent or not intelligent, daily affront their destiny, and what is it open to their destiny to *be*, at the most, that we should make an ado about it?" Every major Victorian novelist makes the "ado" that James describes in addressing the question of woman's vocation; by the 1890s the "New Woman," an emerging form of emancipated womanhood, was endlessly debated in a wave of fiction and magazine articles. Ultimately, as Victorian texts illustrate, the basic problem was not only political, economic, and educational. It was how women were regarded, and regarded themselves, as members of a society.

LITERACY, PUBLICATION, AND READING

Literacy increased significantly during the Victorian period, although precise figures are difficult to calculate. In 1837 about half of the adult male population could read and write to some extent; by the end of the century, basic literacy was almost universal, the product in large part of compulsory national education, required by 1880 to the age of ten. There was also an explosion of things to read. Because of technological changes in printing—presses powered by steam, paper made from wood pulp rather than rags, and toward the end of the century, typesetting machines—publishers could bring out more printed material more cheaply than ever before. The number of newspapers, periodicals, and books increased exponentially during the Victorian period.

Books remained fairly expensive, and most readers borrowed them from commercial lending libraries. (There were few public libraries until the final decades of the century.) After the repeal of the stamp tax and duties on advertisements just after midcentury, an extensive popular press developed.

The most significant development in publishing from the point of view of literary culture was the growth of the periodical. In the first thirty years of the Victorian period, 170 new periodicals were started in London alone. There were magazines for every taste: cheap and popular magazines, like the "penny dread-fuls" that published sensational tales; religious monthlies; weekly newspapers; satiric periodicals noted for their political cartoons (the most famous of these was *Punch*); women's magazines; monthly miscellanies publishing fiction, poetry, and articles on current affairs; and reviews and quarterlies, ostensibly reviewing new books but using the reviews, which were always unsigned, as occasions for essays on the subjects in question. The chief reviews and monthly magazines had a great deal of power and influence; they defined issues in public affairs, and they made and broke literary reputations. They also published the major writers of the period: the fiction of Dickens, Thackeray, Eliot, Trollope, Gaskell, and Hardy; the essays of Carlyle, Mill, Arnold, and Ruskin; and the poetry of Tennyson and the Brownings all appeared in monthly magazines.

The circumstances of periodical publication exerted a shaping force on literature. Novels and long works of nonfiction prose were often published in serial form. Although serial publication of works began in the late eighteenth century, it was the publication of Dickens's *Pickwick Papers* (1836–37) in individual numbers that established the popularity of the serial form. All of Dickens's novels and many of those of his contemporaries were published in this manner. Readers therefore read these works in relatively short, discrete installments over a period that could extend more than a year, with time for reflection and interpretation in between. Serial publication encouraged a certain kind of plotting and pacing and allowed writers to take account of their readers' reactions as they constructed subsequent installments. Writers created a continuing world, punctuated by the ends of installments, which served to stimulate the curiosity that would keep readers buying subsequent issues. Serial publication also created a distinctive sense of a community of readers, a sense encouraged by the practice of reading aloud in family gatherings.

As the family reading of novels suggests, the middle-class reading public enjoyed a common reading culture. Poets such as Tennyson and Elizabeth Barrett Browning and anthologies such as Palgrave's *Golden Treasury* (1861) appealed to a large body of readers; prose writers such as Carlyle, Arnold, and Ruskin achieved a status as sages; and the major Victorian novelists were popular writers. Readers shared the expectation that literature would not only delight but instruct, that it would be continuous with the lived world, and that it would illuminate social problems. "Tennyson," one of his college friends warned him, "we cannot live in Art." These expectations weighed more heavily on some writers than others. Tennyson wore his public mantle with considerable ambivalence; Arnold abandoned the private mode of lyric poetry to speak about public issues in lectures and essays.

By the 1870s the sense of a broad readership, with a shared set of social concerns, had begun to dissolve. Some writers had begun to define themselves in opposition to a general public; poets like the Pre-Raphaelites pursued art for art's sake, doing exactly what Tennyson's friend had warned against; other writers consciously catered to the new and diverse markets springing up within the increasing ranks of the literate. By the end of Victoria's reign, writers could no longer assume a unified reading public.

SHORT FICTION AND THE NOVEL

Fiction flourished in a variety of forms in the Victorian period. A staple of the era's thriving periodical culture, short works were extremely popular and demonstrated considerable ingenuity in genre; the series of Christmas stories Dickens wrote in the wake of the huge success he enjoyed with *A Christmas Carol* (1843) offers a good case in point. The last two decades of the century saw some of the most celebrated achievements in short fiction, such as Stevenson's thrilling novella *The Strange Case of Dr. Jekyll and Mr. Hyde*, Kipling's colonial tales, and the detective adventures of Sherlock Holmes, but there is a rich archive for the entire period. It is, however, the novel that has come to be seen as the era's preeminent literary triumph. Initially published, for the most part, in serial form, novels subsequently appeared in three-volume editions, or "three-deckers." "Large loose baggy monsters," Henry James called them, reflecting his dissatisfaction with their sprawling panoramic expanse. As their size suggests, Victorian novels seek to represent a large and comprehensive social world, with the variety of classes and social settings that constitute a community. They contain a multitude of characters and a number of plots, setting in motion the kinds of patterns that reveal the author's vision of the deep structures of the social world—how, in George Eliot's words, "the mysterious mixture behaves under the varying experiments of Time." They present themselves as realistic—that is, as representing a social world that shares the features of the one we inhabit. The French novelist Stendhal (1783–1842) called the novel "a mirror wandering down a road," but the metaphor of the mirror is somewhat deceptive because it implies that writers exert no shaping force on their material. It would be more accurate to speak not of realism but of realisms because each novelist presents a specific vision of reality whose representational force he or she seeks to persuade us to acknowledge through a variety of techniques and conventions. The worlds of Dickens, of Trollope, of Eliot, of the Brontës hardly seem continuous with each other, but their authors share the attempt to convince us that the characters and events they imagine resemble those we experience in actual life.

The experience that Victorian novelists most frequently depict is the set of social relationships in the middle-class society developing around them. It is a society where the material conditions of life indicate social position, where money defines opportunity, where social class enforces a powerful sense of stratification, yet where chances for class mobility exist. Pip can aspire to the great expectations that provide the title for Dickens's novel; Jane Eyre can marry her employer, a landed gentleman. Most Victorian novels focus on a protagonist whose effort to define his or her place in society is the main concern of the plot. The novel thus constructs a tension between surrounding social conditions and the aspiration of the hero or heroine, whether it be for love, social position, or a life adequate to his or her imagination. This tension makes the novel the natural form to use in portraying woman's struggle for self-realization in the context of the constraints imposed on her. For both men and women writers, the heroine is often, therefore, the representative protagonist whose search for fulfillment emblematizes the human condition. The great heroines of Victorian fiction—Jane Eyre, Maggie Tulliver, Dorothea Brooke, Isabel Archer, Tess of the d'Urbervilles, even Becky Sharp—all seem in some way to illustrate George Eliot's judgment, voiced in the Prelude to *Middlemarch* (1871–72), of "a certain spiritual grandeur ill-matched with meanness of opportunity."

From the beginning of the nineteenth century, the novel was more than a fertile medium for the portrayal of women; women writers were, for the first time, not figures on the margins but major authors. Jane Austen, the Brontës, Elizabeth Gaskell, George Eliot—all helped define the genre. When Charlotte Brontë screwed up her courage to write to the poet laureate, Robert Southey, to ask his advice about a career as a writer, he warned her, "Literature cannot be the business of a woman's life, and it ought not to be." Charlotte Brontë put this letter, with one other from Southey, in an envelope, with the inscription "Southey's advice to be kept forever. My twenty-first birthday." Brontë's ability ultimately to depart from this advice derived in part from how amenable the novel was to women writers. It concerned the domestic life that women knew well—courtship, family relationships, marriage. It was a popular form whose market women could enter easily. It did not carry the burden of an august tradition as poetry did, nor did it build on the learning of a university education. In his essay "The Lady Novelists" (1852) George Henry Lewes declared, "The advent of female literature promises woman's view of life, woman's experience." His common-law wife, George Eliot, together with many of her sister novelists, fulfilled his prophecy.

Whether written by women or men, the Victorian novel was extraordinarily various. It encompassed a wealth of styles and genres from the extravagant comedy of Dickens to the Gothic romances of the Brontë sisters; from the satire of Thackeray to the probing psychological fiction of Eliot; from the social and political realism of Trollope to the sensation novels of Wilkie Collins; and from the grim naturalism of Gissing to the rural tragedies of Hardy. For the Victorians the novel was both a principal form of entertainment and a spur to social sympathy. There was no social topic that the novel did not address. Dickens, Gaskell, and many other novelists tried to stimulate efforts for social reform through their depiction of social problems. Writing at the beginning of the twentieth century, Joseph Conrad defined the novel in a way that could speak for the Victorians: "What is a novel if not a conviction of our fellow-men's existence strong enough to take upon itself a form of imagined life clearer than reality and whose accumulated verisimilitude of selected episodes puts to shame the pride of documentary history?"

POETRY

Although today we generally consider the novel as not only the most distinctive but also the most important literary form of the Victorian era, nineteenth-century readers would have disagreed; for them, poetry represented literature's highest pinnacle. Some made even loftier claims. The most famous of these appeared in Matthew Arnold's book *The Study of Poetry* (1880):

> More and more mankind will discover that we have to turn to poetry to interpret life for us, to console us, to sustain us. Without poetry, our science will appear incomplete; and most of what now passes with us for religion and philosophy will be replaced by poetry.

Arnold, whose lifetime activities encompassed the composition of poetry, the writing of influential books and articles on poetry, and, as part of his duties as a governmental official and inspector of schools, the institutionalization of poetry within the nation's elementary curriculum, did all a man could do to bring about such a state of affairs. And demographically speaking, poetry became part of the lives of more people than ever before in the Victorian period, inasmuch as poems were printed in the pages of every kind of newspaper and periodical, regularly heard in domestic and public settings alike, and, from the late 1870s onward, repeatedly recited in the nation's growing network of schools for the masses. But this pervasive presence and democratization of poetry proved in many ways to be its downfall, at least from the point of view of the influential criticism of the first half of the twentieth century, from which literary studies in later years inherited certain engrained opinions. Long deemed sentimental and anti-intellectual, popular poetry reading in the Victorian period is however now beginning to receive serious attention.

To a degree, this denigration of the era's poetic culture extended itself not only to how people read poems in the Victorian period but also to how they wrote them; Victorian poetry has often been treated as if it languished in an uninspired dip between the twin peaks of Romantic and Modernist achievement. Yet this is a perspective that requires careful examination so that we can better understand the special qualities of Victorian poetry. Influenced by the vibrancy and formal advances of the novel in this period, poets devised new ways of telling stories in verse; examples include Tennyson's *Maud*, Elizabeth Barrett Browning's *Aurora Leigh* (1857), Robert Browning's *The Ring and the Book* (1868–69), and Arthur Hugh Clough's *Amours de Voyage* (1857–58). Poets and critics debated what the appropriate subjects of such long narrative poems should be. Some, like Matthew Arnold, held that poets should use the heroic materials of the past; others, like Elizabeth Barrett Browning, felt that poets should represent "their age, not Charlemagne's." Poets also experimented with character and perspective. *Amours de Voyage* is a long epistolary poem that tells the story of a failed romance through letters written by its various characters; *The Ring and the Book* presents its plot—an old Italian murder story—through ten different perspectives.

Undeniably innovative, Victorian poetry was nevertheless deeply affected by the shadow of Romanticism. By 1837, when Victoria ascended the throne, all the major Romantic poets, save William Wordsworth, were dead, but they had died young, and many readers consequently still regarded them as their contemporaries. Not even twenty years separated the birth dates of Tennyson and Browning from that of John Keats, but they lived more than three times as long as he did. All the Victorian poets show the strong influence of the Romantics, but they cannot sustain the confidence that the Romantics felt in the power of the imagination. The Victorians often rewrite Romantic poems with a sense of belatedness and distance. When, in his poem "Resignation," Arnold addresses his sister upon revisiting a landscape, much as Wordsworth had addressed his sister in "Tintern Abbey," he tells her the rocks and sky "seem to bear rather than rejoice." Tennyson frequently represents his muse as an embowered woman, cut off from the world and doomed to death. The speakers of Browning's poems, who embrace the visions that their imaginations present, are madmen. When Hardy writes "The Darkling Thrush," in December 1900, Keats's nightingale has become "an aged thrush, frail, gaunt, and small."

Victorian poets build on this sense of belated Romanticism in a number of ways. Some poets writing in the second half of the century, like Dante Gabriel Rossetti and Algernon Charles Swinburne, embrace an attenuated Romanticism, art pursued for its own sake. Reacting against what he sees as the insufficiency of an allegory of the state of one's own mind as the basis of poetry, Arnold seeks an objective basis for poetic emotion and finally gives up writing poems altogether when he decides that the present age lacks the culture necessary to support great poetry. The more fruitful reaction to the subjectivity of Romantic poetry, however, was not Arnold's but Robert Browning's. Turning from the mode of his early poetry, modeled on Percy Bysshe Shelley, Browning began writing dramatic monologues—poems, he said, that are "Lyric in expression" but "Dramatic in principle, and so many utterances of so many imaginary persons, not mine." Tennyson simultaneously developed a more lyric form of the dramatic monologue. The idea of creating a lyric poem in the voice of a speaker ironically distinct from the poet is the great achievement of Victorian poetry, one developed extensively in the twentieth century. In *Poetry and the Age* (1953), the modernist poet and critic Randall Jarrell acknowledges this fact: "The dramatic monologue, which once had depended for its effect upon being a departure from the norm of poetry, now became in one form or other the norm."

The formal experimentation of Victorian poetry, both in long narrative and in the dramatic monologue, may make it seem eclectic, but Victorian poetry shares a number of characteristics. It tends to be pictorial, using detail to construct visual images that represent the emotion or situation the poem concerns. In his review of Tennyson's first volume of poetry, Arthur Henry Hallam defines this kind of poetry as "picturesque," as combining visual impressions in such a way that they create a picture that carries the dominant emotion of the poem. This aesthetic brings poets and painters close together. Contemporary artists frequently illustrated Victorian poems, and poems themselves often present paintings. Victorian poetry also uses sound in a distinctive way. Whether it be the mellifluousness of Tennyson or Swinburne, with its emphasis on beautiful cadences, alliteration, and vowel sounds, or the roughness of Browning or Gerard Manley Hopkins, a roughness adopted in part in reaction against Tennyson, the sound of Victorian poetry reflects an attempt to use poetry as a medium with a presence almost independent of sense. The resulting style can become so syntactically elaborate that it is easy to parody, as in Hopkins's description of Browning as a man "bouncing up from table with his mouth full of bread and cheese" or T. S. Eliot's criticism of Swinburne's poetry, where "meaning is merely the hallucination of meaning." Yet it is important to recognize that these poets use sound to convey meaning, to quote Hallam's review of Tennyson once more, "where words would not." "The tone becomes the sign of the feeling." In all of these developments—the experimentation with narrative and perspective, the dramatic monologue, the use of visual detail and sound—Victorian poets seek to represent psychology in a different way. Their most distinctive achievement is a poetry of mood and character.

They therefore sat in uneasy relationship to the public expectation that poets be sages with something to teach. Tennyson, Browning, and Arnold showed varying discomfort with this public role; poets beginning to write in the second half of the century distanced themselves from their public by embracing an identity as bohemian rebels. Women poets encountered a different set of difficulties in developing their poetic voice. When, in Barrett Browning's epic about the growth of a woman poet, Aurora Leigh's cousin Romney discourages her poetic ambitions by telling her that women are "weak for art" but "strong for life and duty," he articulates the prejudice of an age. Women poets in this era frequently viewed their vocation in the context of the constraints on and expectations of their sex.

PROSE

Although Victorian poets felt ambivalent about the didactic mission the public expected of literary figures, writers of nonfictional prose aimed specifically to instruct. Although the term *nonfictional prose* is clumsy and not quite exact (the Victorians themselves referred instead to history, biography, theology, criticism, political economy, and so forth), it has its uses not only to distinguish these prose writers from the novelists but also to indicate the centrality of argument and persuasion to Victorian intellectual life. The growth of the periodical press, described earlier, provided the vehicle and marketplace for nonfictional prose. It reflects a vigorous sense of shared intellectual life and the public urgency of social and moral issues. On a wide range of controversial topics—religious, political, and aesthetic—writers seek to convince their readers to share their convictions and values. Such writers seem at times almost secular priests. Indeed, in the fifth lecture of *On Heroes, Hero-Worship, and the Heroic in History* (1841), Carlyle defines the writer precisely in these terms: "Men of Letters are a perpetual Priesthood, from age to age, teaching all Men that God is still present in their life. . . . In the true Literary Man, there is thus ever, acknowledged or not by the world, a sacredness." The modern man of letters, Carlyle argues, differs from his earlier counterpart in that he writes for money. "Never, till about a hundred years ago, was there seen any figure of a Great Soul living apart in that anomalous manner; endeavouring to speak forth the inspiration that was in him by Printed Books, and find place and subsistence by what the world would please him for doing that." This combination, of a new market position for nonfictional writing and an exalted sense of the didactic function of the writer, produces a quintessential Victorian form.

On behalf of nonfictional prose, Walter Pater argued in his essay "Style" (1889) that it was "the special and opportune art of the modern world." He believed not that it was superior to verse but that it more readily conveys the "chaotic variety and complexity" of modern life, the "incalculable" intellectual diversity of the "master currents of the present time." Pater's characterization of prose helps us understand what its writers were attempting to do. Despite the diversity of styles and subjects, Victorian prose writers were engaged in shaping belief in a bewilderingly complex and changing world. Their modes of persuasion differ. Mill and Huxley rely on clear reasoning, logical argument, and the kind of lucid style favored by essayists of the eighteenth century.

Carlyle and Ruskin write a prose that is more Romantic in character, that seeks to move readers as well as convince them. Whatever the differences in their rhetorical techniques, however, they share an urgency of exposition. Not only by what they said but by how they said it, Victorian prose writers were claiming a place for literature in a scientific and materialistic culture. Arnold and Pater share this as an explicit aim. Each in his own way argues that culture—the intensely serious appreciation of great works of literature—provides the kind of immanence and meaning that people once found in religion. For Arnold this is an intensely moral experience; for Pater it is aesthetic. Together they develop the basis for the claims of modern literary criticism.

DRAMA AND THEATER

The plays written and performed in the Victorian age, apart from those in the final decade of the century, have until recently received relatively little scholarly attention. Yet the theater, throughout the period, was a flourishing and popular institution, which staged not merely conventional dramas but a rich variety of theatrical entertainments, many with lavish spectacular effects—burlesques, extravaganzas, highly scenic and altered versions of Shakespeare's plays, melodramas, pantomimes, and musicals. Robert Corrigan gives figures that suggest the extent of the popularity of such entertainment: "In the decade between 1850 and 1860 the number of theaters built throughout the country was doubled, and in the middle of the sixties, in London alone, 150,000 would be attending the theater on any given day." The popularity of theatrical entertainment made it a powerful influence on other genres. Dickens was devoted to the theater and composed many of the scenes of his novels with theatrical techniques. Thackeray represents himself as the puppet master of his characters in *Vanity Fair* and employs the stock gestures and expressions of melodramatic acting in his illustrations for the novel. Tennyson, Browning, and Henry James tried their hands at writing plays, though with no commercial success. Successful plays on stage were written by such figures as Dion Boucicault (1820–1890) and Henry Arthur Jones (1851–1921), prolific dramatists of the period. The comic operas of W. S. Gilbert (1836–1911) and Arthur Sullivan (1842–1900) were also hugely popular. Their satire of Victorian values and institutions, what Gilbert called their "topsyturvydom," and their grave and quasi-respectful treatment of the ridiculous not only make them delightful in themselves but anticipate the techniques of two great figures of British theater from this period, the Irishmen George Bernard Shaw and Oscar Wilde. Around 1890, when the socially controversial plays of the Norwegian dramatist Henrik Ibsen (1828–1906) became known in England, Arthur Pinero (1855–1934) and Shaw began writing "problem plays," which addressed difficult social issues. In the 1890s Shaw and Wilde transformed British theater with their comic masterpieces. Although they did not like each other's work, they both created a kind of comedy that took aim at Victorian pretense and hypocrisy.

The Victorian Age

TEXTS	CONTEXTS
1830 Alfred Lord Tennyson, *Poems, Chiefly Lyrical*	**1830** Opening of Liverpool and Manchester Railway
1832 Sir Charles Lyell, *Principles of Geology*	**1832** First Reform Bill
1833 Thomas Carlyle, *Sartor Resartus*	**1833** Factory Act. Abolition of Slavery Act. Beginning of Oxford Movement
1836 Charles Dickens, *Pickwick Papers*	**1836** First train in London
1837 Carlyle, *The French Revolution*	**1837** Victoria becomes queen
	1838 "People's Charter" issued by Chartist Movement
	1840 Queen marries Prince Albert
1842 Tennyson, *Poems*. Robert Browning, *Dramatic Lyrics*	**1842** Chartist Riots. Copyright Act. Mudie's Circulating Library
1843 John Ruskin, *Modern Painters* (vol. 1). Dickens, *A Christmas Carol*.	
	1845–46 Potato famine in Ireland. Mass emigration to North America
1846 George Eliot, *The Life of Jesus* (translation)	**1846** Repeal of Corn Laws.
1847 Charlotte Brontë, *Jane Eyre*. Emily Brontë, *Wuthering Heights*	**1847** Ten Hours Factory Act
1848 Elizabeth Gaskell, *Mary Barton*. William Makepeace Thackeray, *Vanity Fair*	**1848** Revolution on the Continent. Second Republic established in France. Founding of Pre-Raphaelite Brotherhood
1850 Tennyson, *In Memoriam*. William Wordsworth, *The Prelude* (posthumous publication)	**1850** Tennyson succeeds Wordsworth as Poet Laureate
1851 Ruskin, *Stones of Venice*	**1851** Great Exhibition of science and industry at the Crystal Palace
1853 Matthew Arnold, *Poems*	
1854 Dickens, *Hard Times*	**1854** Crimean War. Florence Nightingale organizes nurses to care for sick and wounded
1855 Robert Browning, *Men and Women*	
1857 Elizabeth Barrett Browning, *Aurora Leigh*	**1857** Indian "Mutiny," or Uprising. Matrimonial Causes Act
1859 Charles Darwin, *Origin of Species*. John Stuart Mill, *On Liberty*. Tennyson, *Idylls of the King* (books 1–4)	
1860 Dickens, *Great Expectations*. Eliot, *The Mill on the Floss*	**1860** Italian unification
	1861 Death of Prince Albert
	1861–65 American Civil War
1862 Christina Rossetti, *Goblin Market*	
1864 R. Browning, *Dramatis Personae*	
1865 Lewis Carroll, *Alice's Adventures in Wonderland*	**1865** Jamaica Rebellion

TEXTS	CONTEXTS
1866 Algernon Charles Swinburne, *Poems and Ballads*	
1867 Karl Marx, *Das Kapital*	1867 Second Reform Bill
	1868 Opening of Suez Canal
1869 Arnold, *Culture and Anarchy*. Mill, *The Subjection of Women*	
	1870 Married Women's Property Act. Victory in Franco-Prussian War makes Germany a world power. Elementary Education Act
1871 Darwin, *Descent of Man*	1871 Newnham College (first women's Oxbridge college) founded at Cambridge
1872 Eliot, *Middlemarch*	
1873 Walter Pater, *Studies in the History of the Renaissance*	
	1877 Queen Victoria made empress of India.
	1878 Electric street lighting in London
1885 W. S. Gilbert and Arthur Sullivan, *The Mikado*	1885 Massacre of General Gordon and his forces and fall of Khartoum
1886 Robert Louis Stevenson, *Doctor Jekyll and Mr. Hyde*	
1888 Rudyard Kipling, *Plain Tales from the Hills*	
1889 William Butler Yeats, *Crossways*	
	1890 First subway line in London
1891 Thomas Hardy, *Tess of the D'Urbervilles*. Bernard Shaw, *The Quintessence of Ibsenism*. Oscar Wilde, *The Picture of Dorian Grey*. Arthur Conan Doyle, *Adventures of Sherlock Holmes*	1891 Free elementary education
1893 Shaw, *Mrs. Warren's Profession*	1893 Independent Labour Party
1895 Wilde, *The Importance of Being Earnest*. Hardy, *Jude the Obscure*	1895 Oscar Wilde arrested and imprisoned for homosexuality
1896 A. E. Housman, *A Shropshire Lad*	
1898 Hardy, *Wessex Poems*	1898 Discovery of radium
	1899 Irish Literary Theatre founded in Dublin
	1899–1902 Anglo-Boer War
1900 Joseph Conrad, *Lord Jim*	
	1901 Death of Queen Victoria; succession of Edward VII

THOMAS CARLYLE
1795–1881

W. B. Yeats once asked William Morris which writers had inspired the socialist movement of the 1880s, and Morris replied: "Oh, Ruskin and Carlyle, but somebody should have been beside Carlyle and punched his head every five minutes." Morris's mixed feelings of admiration and exasperation are typical of the response Thomas Carlyle evokes in many readers. Anyone approaching his prose for the first time should expect to be sometimes bewildered. Like George Bernard Shaw, Carlyle discovered, early in life, that exaggeration can be a highly effective way of gaining the attention of an audience. But it can also be a way of distracting an audience unfamiliar with the idiosyncrasies of his rhetoric and unprepared for the distinctive enjoyments his writings can provide.

One of the idiosyncrasies of his prose is that it is meant to be read aloud. "His paragraphs," as Ralph Waldo Emerson observes, "are all a sort of splendid conversation." As a talker Carlyle was as famous in his day as Samuel Johnson in his. Charles Darwin testified that he was "the best worth listening to of any man I know." Johnson's talk was recorded by Boswell, his biographer, but no Boswell was needed for Carlyle, whose prose adopts the rhythm, idiosyncrasy, and spontaneity of the spoken voice. It is a noisy and emphatic voice, startling on a first reading.

Carlyle was forty-one years old when Victoria became queen of England. He had been born in the same year as John Keats, yet he is rarely grouped with his contemporaries among the Romantic writers. Instead his name is linked with younger men such as Charles Dickens, Robert Browning, and John Ruskin, the early generation of Victorian writers, for whom he became (according to Elizabeth Barrett Browning) "the great teacher of the age." The classification is fitting, for it was Carlyle's role to foresee the problems that were to preoccupy the Victorians and to report on his experiences in confronting these problems. After 1837 his loud voice began to attract an audience; and he soon became one of the most influential figures of the age, affecting the attitudes of scientists, statesmen, and especially of writers. His wife once complained that Emerson had no ideas (except mad ones) that he had not derived from Carlyle. "'But pray, Mrs. Carlyle,' replied a friend, 'who has?'"

Carlyle was born in Ecclefechan, a village in Scotland, the eldest child of a large family. His mother, at the time of her marriage, was illiterate. His father, James Carlyle, a stonemason and later a farmer, was proudly characterized by his son as a peasant. The key to the character of James Carlyle was the Scottish Calvinism that he instilled into the members of his household. Frugality, hard work, a tender but undemonstrative family loyalty, and a peculiar blend of self-denial and self-righteousness were characteristic features of Carlyle's childhood home.

With his father's aid the young Carlyle was educated at Annan Academy and at Edinburgh University, the subject of his special interest being mathematics; he left without taking a degree. It was his parents' hope that their son would become a clergyman, but in this respect Thomas made a severe break with his ancestry. He was a prodigious reader, and his exposure to such skeptical writers as David Hume, Voltaire, and Edward Gibbon had undermined his faith. Gibbon's *Decline and Fall of the Roman Empire* (1776–88), he told Emerson, was "the splendid bridge from the old world to the new." By the time he was twenty-three Carlyle had crossed the bridge and had abandoned his Christian faith and his proposed career as a clergyman.

During the period in which he was thinking through his religious position, he supported himself by teaching school in Scotland and, later, by tutoring private pupils; but from 1824 to the end of his life he relied exclusively on his writings for his livelihood. His early writings consisted of translations, biographies, and critical studies of Johann Wolfgang von Goethe and other German authors, to whose view of life he was deeply attracted. The German Romantics (loosely grouped by Carlyle under the label "Mystics") were the second most important influence on his life and character, exceeded only by his early family experiences. Aided by the writings of these German poets and philosophers, he arrived finally at a faith in life that served as a substitute for the Christian faith he had lost.

His most significant early essay, "Characteristics," appeared in *The Edinburgh Review* in 1831. A year earlier he had begun writing *Sartor Resartus,* an account of the life and opinions of an imaginary philosopher, Professor Diogenes Teufelsdröckh, a work he had great difficulty in persuading anyone to publish. In book form *Sartor* first appeared in America in 1836, where Carlyle's follower Emerson had prepared an enthusiastic audience for this unusual work. His American following (which was later to become a vast one) did little at first, however, to relieve the poverty in which he still found himself after fifteen years of writing. In 1837 the tide at last turned when he published *The French Revolution.* "O it has been a great success, dear," his wife assured him, but her husband, embittered by the long struggle, was incredulous that the sought-for recognition had at last come to him.

It was in character for his wife, Jane Welsh Carlyle, to be less surprised by his success than he was. That Thomas Carlyle was a genius had been an article of faith to her from her first meeting with him in 1821. A witty, intelligent, and intellectually ambitious young woman, the daughter of a doctor of good family, Jane Welsh had many suitors. When in 1826 she finally accepted Carlyle, her family and friends were shocked. This peasant's son, of no fixed employment, seemed a preposterous choice. Subsequent events seemed to confirm her family's verdict. Not long after marriage Carlyle insisted on their retiring to a remote farm at Craigenputtock, where for six years (1828–34) this sociable woman was obliged to live in isolation and loneliness. After they moved to London in 1834 and settled in a house on Cheyne Walk in Chelsea, Jane Carlyle was considerably happier and enjoyed her role at the center of the intellectual and artistic circle that surrounded her husband. Her husband, however, remained a difficult man to live with. His stomach ailments, irascible nerves, and preoccupation with his writings, as well as the lionizing to which he was subjected, left him with little inclination for domestic amenities or for encouraging his wife's considerable intellectual talents. As a young girl she had wanted to be a writer; her letters, some of the most remarkable of the century, show that she had considerable literary talent.

This marriage of the Carlyles has aroused almost as much interest as that of the Brownings. Their friend the Reverend W. H. Brookfield (whose marriage was an unhappy one) once said cynically that marrying is "dipping into a pitcher of snakes for the chance of an eel," and some biographers have argued that Jane Welsh Carlyle drew a snake instead of an eel. Yet if we study her letters, it is evident that she wanted to marry a man of genius who would change the world. Despite the years she endured of comparative poverty, poor health, and loneliness, she had the satisfaction of recognizing her husband's triumph when the peasant's son she had chosen returned to Scotland to deliver his inaugural address as lord rector of Edinburgh University. While he was away, to Carlyle's great grief, she died.

During the first thirty years of his residence in London Carlyle wrote extensive historical works and many pamphlets concerning contemporary issues. After *The French Revolution* he edited, in 1845, the *Letters and Speeches of Oliver Cromwell,* a Puritan leader of heroic dimensions in Carlyle's eyes, and later wrote a full-length biography, *The History of Friedrich II of Prussia, Called Frederick the Great* (1858–65). Carlyle's pamphleteering is seen at its best in *Past and Present* (1843) and in its most violent phase in his *Latter-Day Pamphlets* (1850). Following the death of his wife, he wrote very little. For the remaining fifteen years of his life, he confined himself to reading or to talking to the stream of visitors who called at Cheyne Walk to listen to the "Sage of Chelsea," as he came to be called. In 1874 he accepted the Prussian Order of Merit from Bismarck, the German chancellor, but declined an English baronetcy offered by Prime Minister Disraeli. In 1881 he died and was buried near his family in Ecclefechan churchyard.

To understand Carlyle's role as historian, biographer, and social critic, it is essential to understand his attitude toward religion. Like many Victorians, Carlyle underwent a crisis of religious belief. By the time he was twenty-three, he had been shorn of his faith in Christianity. At this stage, as Carlyle observed with dismay, many people seemed content simply to stop or, worse, to adopt antispiritual ideas. A Utilitarian such as James Mill or some of his commonsensical professors at the University of Edinburgh regarded society and the universe as machines. To such thinkers the machines might sometimes seem complex, but they were not mysterious, for machines are subject to humankind's control and understanding through reason and observation. To Carlyle, and to many others, life without a sense of the divine was a meaningless nightmare. In the first part of "The Everlasting No," a chapter of *Sartor Resartus*, he memorably depicts the horrors of such a soulless world that drove him in 1822 to thoughts of suicide. The eighteenth-century Enlightenment had left him not in light but in darkness.

In developing his views of religion, Carlyle used the metaphor of the "Clothes Philosophy." The naked individual seeks clothing for protection. One solution, represented by Coleridge and his followers, was to repudiate the skepticism of Voltaire and Hume and to return to the protective beliefs and rituals of the Christian Church. To Carlyle such a return was pointless. The traditional Christian coverings were worn out—"Hebrew Old Clothes," he called them. His own solution, described in "The Everlasting Yea," was to tailor a new suit of beliefs from German philosophy, shreds of Scottish Calvinism, and his own observations. The following summarizes his basic religious attitude: "Gods die with the men who have conceived them. But the god-stuff roars eternally, like the sea. . . . Even the gods must be born again. We must be born again." Although this passage is from *The Plumed Serpent* (1926) by D. H. Lawrence (a writer who resembles Carlyle at many points), it might have come from any one of Carlyle's own books—most especially from *Sartor Resartus*, in which he describes his being born again—his "Fire-baptism"—into a new secular faith. Carlyle was thus in many ways the quintessential nineteenth-century mystic; yet at the same time, many contemporary critics note, his writings also gesture toward postmodernism. Certainly his self-aware, genre-defying, and often contradictory prose exposes the inherent difficulty of assuming that literature or philosophy can ever achieve a unified, foundational truth.

Nevertheless, Carlyle often talked like a *vitalist*—that is, as though the presence of energy in the world were, in itself, a sign of the godhead. Carlyle therefore judges everything in terms of the presence or absence of some vital spark. The minds of people, books, societies, churches, or even landscapes are rated as alive or dead, dynamic or merely mechanical. The government of Louis XVI, for example, was obviously moribund, doomed to be swept away by the dynamic forces of the French Revolution. The government of Victorian England seemed likewise to be doomed unless infused with vital energies of leadership and an awareness of the real needs of humankind. When an editor complained that his essay "Characteristics" was "inscrutable," Carlyle remarked: "My own fear was that it might be too *scrutable*; for it indicates decisively enough that Society (in my view) is utterly condemned to destruction, and even now beginning its long travail-throes of Newbirth."

In his inquiry into the principles of government and social order, Carlyle, like many of his contemporaries, is seeking to understand a world of great social unrest and historical change. This preoccupation with revolution and the destruction of the old orders suggests that Carlyle's politics were radical, but his position is bewilderingly difficult to classify. During the Hungry Forties he was one of the most outspoken critics of middle-class bunglings and of the economic theory of laissez-faire that, in his opinion, was ultimately responsible for those bunglings. He worked strenuously on behalf of the millions of people suffering from the miseries attendant on a major breakdown of industry and agriculture. At other times, because of his insistence on strong and heroic leadership, Carlyle appears to be a violent conservative or, as some have argued, virtually a fascist. He had no confidence that democratic institutions could work efficiently. A few individuals in every age are, in his view, leaders; the rest are followers and are happy only as followers. Society should be organized so that these gifted leaders can have scope to govern effectively. Such leaders are, for Carlyle, heroes. George Bernard Shaw, who learned much from Carlyle, would call them "supermen." Liberals and democrats, however, might call them dictators. Although Carlyle was aware that the Western world was committed to a faith in a system of balloting and of legislative debate, he was confident that the system would eventually break down. The democratic assumption that all voters are equally capable of choice and the assumption that people value liberty more than they value order seemed to him nonsense. Carlyle's authoritarianism intensified as he grew older. When the governor of Jamaica violently repressed a rebellion of black plantation workers, Carlyle served as chair of his defense fund, arguing that England owed the governor honor and thanks for his defense of civilization.

Carlyle's prose style reflects the intensity of his views. At the time he began to write, the essayists of the eighteenth century, Samuel Johnson in particular, were the models of good prose. Carlyle recognized that their style, however admirable an instrument for reasoning, analysis, and generalized exposition, did not suit his purposes. Like a poet, he wanted to convey the sense of experience itself. Like a preacher or prophet, he wanted to exhort or inspire his readers rather than to develop a chain of logical argument. Like a psychoanalyst, he wanted to explore the unconscious and irrational levels of human life, the hidden nine-tenths of the iceberg rather than the conscious and rational fraction above the surface. To this end he developed his highly individual manner of writing, with its vivid imagery of fire and barnyard and zoo, its mixture of biblical rhythms and explosive talk, and its inverted and unorthodox syntax. Classicists may complain, as Walter Savage Landor did, that the result is not English. Carlyle would reply that it is not eighteenth-century English but that his style was appropriate for a Victorian who reports of revolutions in society and in thought. In reply to a friend who had protested about his stylistic experiments, Carlyle exclaimed: "Do you reckon this really a time for Purism of Style? I do not: with whole ragged battalions of Scott's Novel Scotch, with Irish, German, French, and even Newspaper Cockney . . . storming in on us, and the whole structure of our Johnsonian English breaking up from its foundations—revolution *there* as visible as anywhere else?" George Eliot wrote (in an essay of 1855) that Carlyle was "more of an artist than a philosopher." As she said: "No novelist has made his creations live for us more thoroughly." Carlyle is best regarded, that is, as a man of letters, the inventor of a distinctive and extremely effective prose medium, and one who strove tirelessly to create a new spiritual and political philosophy adequate to the age.

Sartor Resartus

Sartor Resartus is a combination of novel, autobiography, and essay. To present some of his own experiences, Carlyle invented a hero, Professor Diogenes Teufelsdröckh of Germany, whose name (meaning "God-Begotten Devil's Dreck") suggests the grotesque humor that Carlyle uses to expound a serious treatise. Teufelsdröckh tells the story of his unhappiness in love and of his difficulties in religion. He also airs his opinions on a variety of subjects. Interspersed between the professor's words (which are in quotation marks) are the remarks of an editor, also imaginary, who has the task of putting together the story from assorted documents written by Teufelsdröckh. The title, meaning "The Tailor Retailored," refers to the editor's role of patching the story together. The title also refers to Carlyle's so-called Clothes Philosophy, which is expounded by the hero in many chapters of *Sartor*. In effect this Clothes Philosophy is an attempt to demonstrate the difference between the appearances of things and their reality. The appearance of an individual depends on the costume he or she wears; the reality of that individual is the body underneath the costume. By analogy Carlyle suggests that institutions, such as churches or governments, are like clothes. They may be useful "visible emblems" of the spiritual forces that they cover, but they wear out and have to be replaced by new clothes. The Christian Church, for example, which once expressed humanity's permanent religious desires, is, in Carlyle's terms, worn out and must be discarded. But the underlying religious spirit must be recognized and kept alive at all costs. Carlyle also uses the clothes analogy to describe the relationship between the material and spiritual worlds. Clothes hide the body just as the world of nature cloaks the reality of God and as the body itself cloaks the reality of the soul. The discovery of these realities behind the appearances is, for Carlyle and for his hero, the initial stage of a solution to the dilemmas of life. As contemporary critics have pointed out, the Clothes Philosophy, as well as the unusual form of the book, suggests that Carlyle is also concerned with fundamental problems of language and representation. Implicitly, and sometimes explicitly, his text often questions whether a biographer or autobiographer can ever capture the "essence" of his or her subject.

Teufelsdröckh's religious development, as described in the following chapters, may be contrasted with J. S. Mill's account of his own crisis of spirit in his *Autobiography*. These selections are chapters 7 to 9 of book 2.

From Sartor Resartus

The Everlasting No

Under the strange nebulous envelopment, wherein our Professor has now shrouded himself, no doubt but his spiritual nature is nevertheless progressive, and growing: for how can the "Son of Time," in any case, stand still? We behold him, through those dim years, in a state of crisis, of transition: his mad Pilgrimings, and general solution[1] into aimless Discontinuity, what is all this but a mad Fermentation; wherefrom, the fiercer it is, the clearer product will one day evolve itself?

Such transitions are ever full of pain: thus the Eagle when he moults is sickly; and, to attain his new beak, must harshly dash-off the old one upon rocks. What Stoicism soever our Wanderer, in his individual acts and motions, may affect, it is clear that there is a hot fever of anarchy and misery raging within; coruscations of which flash out: as, indeed, how could there be other? Have we not seen him disappointed, bemocked of Destiny, through long years? All that the young heart might desire and pray for has been denied; nay, as in the last worst instance, offered and then snatched away. Ever an "excellent Passivity"; but of useful, reasonable Activity, essential to the former as Food to Hunger, nothing granted: till at length, in this wild Pilgrimage, he must forcibly seize for himself an Activity, though useless,

---

1. Dissolution.

unreasonable. Alas, his cup of bitterness, which had been filling drop by drop, ever since that first "ruddy morning" in the Hinterschlag Gymnasium, was at the very lip; and then with that poison-drop, of the Towgood-and-Blumine[2] business, it runs over, and even hisses over in a deluge of foam.

He himself says once, with more justice than originality: "Man is, properly speaking, based upon Hope, he has no other possession but Hope; this world of his is emphatically the Place of Hope." What, then, was our Professor's possession? We see him, for the present, quite shut-out from Hope; looking not into the golden orient, but vaguely all round into a dim copper firmament, pregnant with earthquake and tornado.

Alas, shut-out from Hope, in a deeper sense than we yet dream of! For, as he wanders wearisomely through this world, he has now lost all tidings of another and higher. Full of religion, or at least of religiosity, as our Friend has since exhibited himself, he hides not that, in those days, he was wholly irreligious: "Doubt had darkened into Unbelief," says he; "shade after shade goes grimly over your soul, till you have the fixed, starless, Tartarean[3] black." To such readers as have reflected, what can be called reflecting, on man's life, and happily discovered, in contradiction to much Profit-and-loss Philosophy, speculative and practical, that Soul is *not* synonymous with Stomach; who understand, therefore, in our Friend's words, "that, for man's well-being, Faith is properly the one thing needful;[4] how, with it, Martyrs, otherwise weak, can cheerfully endure the shame and the cross; and without it, Worldlings puke-up their sick existence, by suicide, in the midst of luxury": to such it will be clear that, for a pure moral nature, the loss of his religious Belief was the loss of everything. Unhappy young man! All wounds, the crush of long-continued Destitution, the stab of false Friendship and of false Love, all wounds in thy so genial heart, would have healed again, had not its life-warmth been withdrawn. Well might he exclaim, in his wild way: "Is there no God, then; but at best an absentee God, sitting idle, ever since the first Sabbath, at the outside of his Universe, and *seeing* it go? Has the word Duty no meaning; is what we call Duty no divine Messenger and Guide, but a false earthly Fantasm, made-up of Desire and Fear, of emanations from the Gallows and from Dr. Graham's Celestial-Bed?[5] Happiness of an approving Conscience! Did not Paul of Tarsus, whom admiring men have since named Saint, feel that *he* was 'the chief of sinners';[6] and Nero of Rome, jocund in spirit (*wohlgemuth*), spend much of his time in fiddling?[7] Foolish Word-monger and Motive-grinder, who in thy Logic-mill hast an earthly mechanism for the Godlike itself, and wouldst fain grind me out Virtue from the husks of Pleasure,[8]—I tell thee, Nay! To the unregenerate Prometheus Vinctus[9] of a man, it is ever the bitterest aggravation

---

2. A woman loved by Teufelsdröckh who had married his friend Towgood. His distress is pictured in the preceding chapter, titled "Sorrows of Teufelsdröckh." "Hinterschlag Gymnasium": "Smack-bottom" high school, a fake German name invented by Carlyle.
3. Of Tartarus, the lowest region of the classical underworld, where the wicked were punished.
4. Luke 10.42.
5. James Graham (1745–1794), a quack doctor, had invented an elaborate bed that was supposed to cure sterility in couples using it. In this passage, the bed is apparently a symbol of sexual desires.
6. Paraphrase of 1 Timothy 1.15.

7. Nero (37–68 C.E.; Roman emperor, 54–68) was rumored to have recited his poems and played his lyre during a great fire in 64 C.E. that destroyed much of Rome; thus the saying "Nero fiddled while Rome burned."
8. Here, as in his earlier reference to "Profit-and-loss Philosophy," Carlyle attacks the Utilitarian concepts of Jeremy Bentham (1748–1832), who argued that the good is whatever brings the greatest happiness (or pleasure) to the greatest number of people.
9. I.e., Prometheus Bound; this is also the title of a play by Aeschylus depicting the sufferings of a hero who defied Zeus.

of his wretchedness that he is conscious of Virtue, that he feels himself the victim not of suffering only, but of injustice. What then? Is the heroic inspiration we name Virtue but some Passion; some bubble of the blood, bubbling in the direction others *profit* by? I know not; only this I know, If what thou namest Happiness be our true aim, then are we all astray. With Stupidity and sound Digestion man may front much. But what, in these dull unimaginative days, are the terrors of Conscience to the diseases of the Liver! Not on Morality, but on Cookery, let us build our stronghold: there brandishing our frying-pan, as censer, let us offer sweet incense to the Devil, and live at ease on the fat things *he* has provided for his Elect!"

Thus has the bewildered Wanderer to stand, as so many have done, shouting question after question into the Sibyl-cave of Destiny,[1] and receive no Answer but an Echo. It is all a grim Desert, this once-fair world of his; wherein is heard only the howling of wild-beasts, or the shrieks of despairing, hate-filled men; and no Pillar of Cloud by day, and no Pillar of Fire by night,[2] any longer guides the Pilgrim. To such length has the spirit of Inquiry carried him. "But what boots it (*was thut's*)?" cries he: "it is but the common lot in this era. Not having come to spiritual majority prior to the *Siècle de Louis Quinze*,[3] and not being born purely a Loghead (*Dummkopf*), thou hast no other outlook. The whole world is, like thee, sold to Unbelief, their old Temples of the Godhead, which for long have not been rainproof, crumble down; and men ask now: Where is the Godhead; our eyes never saw him?"

Pitiful enough were it, for all these wild utterances, to call our Diogenes wicked. Unprofitable servants as we all are,[4] perhaps at no era of his life was he more decisively the Servant of Goodness, the Servant of God, than even now when doubting God's existence. "One circumstance I note," says he: "after all the nameless woe that Inquiry, which for me, what it is not always, was genuine Love of Truth, had wrought me, I nevertheless still loved Truth, and would bate no jot[5] of my allegiance to her. 'Truth!' I cried, 'though the Heavens crush me for following her: no Falsehood! though a whole celestial Lubberland[6] were the price of Apostasy.' In conduct it was the same. Had a divine Messenger from the clouds, or miraculous Handwriting on the wall, convincingly proclaimed to me *This thou shalt do,* with what passionate readiness, as I often thought, would I have done it, had it been leaping into the infernal Fire. Thus, in spite of all Motive-grinders, and Mechanical Profit-and-Loss Philosophies, with the sick ophthalmia and hallucination they had brought on, was the Infinite nature of Duty still dimly present to me: living without God in the world, of God's light I was not utterly bereft; if my as yet sealed eyes, with their unspeakable longing, could nowhere see Him, nevertheless in my heart He was present, and His heaven-written Law still stood legible and sacred there."

Meanwhile, under all these tribulations, and temporal and spiritual destitutions, what must the Wanderer, in his silent soul, have endured! "The painfullest feeling," writes he, "is that of your own Feebleness (*Unkraft*); ever, as the English Milton says, to be weak is the true misery.[7] And yet of your

---

1. An allusion to Virgil's *Aeneid* 6.36ff.; there Aeneas questions the Cumaean Sibyl, who foretells the future.
2. Exodus 13.21.
3. The Century of Louis XV (French), allusion to *Précis du Siècle de Louis* XV (1768), Voltaire's history of the skeptical and inquiring spirit of 18th-century France during the reign of Louis

XV (1715–74).
4. An allusion to Matthew 25.20 and Luke 17.7–10.
5. Would hold back no part.
6. Land of Plenty.
7. *Paradise Lost* 1.157: "Fallen cherub, to be weak is miserable."

Strength there is and can be no clear feeling, save by what you have prospered in, by what you have done. Between vague wavering Capability and
fixed indubitable Performance, what a difference! A certain inarticulate Self-
consciousness dwells dimly in us; which only our Works can render articulate
and decisively discernible. Our Works are the mirror wherein the spirit first
sees its natural lineaments. Hence, too, the folly of that impossible Precept,
Know thyself;[8] till it be translated into this partially possible one, *Know what
thou canst work at.*

"But for me, so strangely unprosperous had I been, the net-result of my
Workings amounted as yet simply to—Nothing. How then could I believe in
my Strength, when there was as yet no mirror to see it in? Ever did this agitating, yet, as I now perceive, quite frivolous question, remain to me insoluble:
Hast thou a certain Faculty, a certain Worth, such even as the most have not;
or art thou the completest Dullard of these modern times? Alas! the fearful
Unbelief is unbelief in yourself; and how could I believe? Had not my first,
last Faith in myself, when even to me the Heavens seemed laid open, and I
dared to love, been all-too cruelly belied? The speculative Mystery of Life
grew ever more mysterious to me: neither in the practical Mystery[9] had I
made the slightest progress, but been everywhere buffeted, foiled, and contemptuously cast-out. A feeble unit in the middle of a threatening Infinitude,
I seemed to have nothing given me but eyes, whereby to discern my own
wretchedness. Invisible yet impenetrable walls, as of Enchantment, divided
me from all living: was there, in the wide world, any true bosom I could press
trustfully to mine? O Heaven, No, there was none! I kept a lock upon my lips:
why should I speak much with that shifting variety of so-called Friends, in
whose withered, vain and too-hungry souls Friendship was but an incredible
tradition? In such cases, your resource is to talk little, and that little mostly
from the Newspapers. Now when I look back, it was a strange isolation I then
lived in. The men and women around me, even speaking with me, were but
Figures; I had, practically, forgotten that they were alive, that they were not
merely automatic. In midst of their crowded streets and assemblages, I
walked solitary; and (except as it was my own heart, not another's, that I kept
devouring) savage also, as the tiger in his jungle. Some comfort it would have
been, could I, like a Faust,[1] have fancied myself tempted and tormented of
the Devil; for a Hell, as I imagine, without Life, though only diabolic Life,
were more frightful: but in our age of Down-pulling and Disbelief, the very
Devil has been pulled down, you cannot so much as believe in a Devil. To me
the Universe was all void of Life, of Purpose, of Volition, even of Hostility: it
was one huge, dead, immeasurable Steam-engine, rolling on, in its dead
indifference, to grind me limb from limb. O, the vast, gloomy, solitary Golgotha,[2] and Mill of Death! Why was the Living banished thither companionless, conscious? Why, if there is no Devil; nay, unless the Devil is your God?"

A prey incessantly to such corrosions, might not, moreover, as the worst
aggravation to them, the iron constitution even of a Teufelsdröckh threaten
to fail? We conjecture that he has known sickness; and, in spite of his loco-

---

8. This maxim was inscribed in the temple of
Apollo at Delphi.
9. A profession or practical occupation.
1. Both Christopher Marlowe and Goethe wrote
plays about the temptations of Johann Faust (ca.

1480–ca. 1540), a German teacher and magician who became the subject of many stories and
folktales.
2. Calvary, the place where Jesus was crucified.

motive habits, perhaps sickness of the chronic sort. Hear this, for example: "How beautiful to die of broken-heart, on Paper! Quite another thing in practice; every window of your Feeling, even of your Intellect, as it were, begrimed and mud-bespattered, so that no pure ray can enter; a whole Drugshop in your inwards; the fordone soul drowning slowly in quagmires of Disgust!"

Putting all which external and internal miseries together, may we not find in the following sentences, quite in our Professor's still vein, significance enough? "From Suicide a certain aftershine (*Nachschein*) of Christianity withheld me: perhaps also a certain indolence of character; for, was not that a remedy I had at any time within reach? Often, however, was there a question present to me: Should some one now, at the turning of that corner, blow thee suddenly out of Space, into the other World, or other No-World, by pistol-shot,—how were it? On which ground, too, I have often, in sea-storms and sieged cities and other death-scenes, exhibited an imperturbability, which passed, falsely enough, for courage.

"So had it lasted," concludes the Wanderer, "so had it lasted, as in bitter protracted Death-agony, through long years. The heart within me, unvisited by any heavenly dewdrop, was smouldering in sulphurous, slow-consuming fire. Almost since earliest memory I had shed no tear; or once only when I, murmuring half-audibly, recited Faust's Deathsong, that wild *Selig der den er im Siegesglanze findet* (Happy whom *he* finds in Battle's splendour),[3] and thought that of this last Friend even I was not forsaken, that Destiny itself could not doom me not to die. Having no hope, neither had I any definite fear, were it of Man or of Devil: nay, I often felt as if it might be solacing, could the Arch-Devil himself, though in Tartarean terrors, but rise to me, that I might tell him a little of my mind. And yet, strangely enough, I lived in a continual, indefinite, pining fear; tremulous, pusillanimous, apprehensive of I knew not what: it seemed as if all things in the Heavens above and the Earth beneath would hurt me; as if the Heavens and the Earth were but boundless jaws of a devouring monster, wherein I, palpitating, waited to be devoured.

"Full of such humour,[4] and perhaps the miserablest man in the whole French Capital or Suburbs, was I, one sultry Dogday, after much perambulation, toiling along the dirty little *Rue Saint-Thomas de l'Enfer*,[5] among civic rubbish enough, in a close atmosphere, and over pavements hot as Nebuchadnezzar's Furnace;[6] whereby doubtless my spirits were little cheered; when, all at once, there rose a Thought in me, and I asked myself: 'What *art* thou afraid of? Wherefore, like a coward, dost thou forever pip and whimper, and go cowering and trembling? Despicable biped! what is the sum-total of the worst that lies before thee? Death? Well, Death; and say the pangs of Tophet[7] too, and all that the Devil and Man may, will or can do against thee! Hast thou not a heart; canst thou not suffer whatsoever it be; and, as a Child of Freedom, though outcast, trample Tophet itself under thy feet, while it consumes thee? Let it come, then; I will meet it and defy it!' And as I so

3. Adapted from Goethe's *Faust* (1808) 1.4.1573–76.
4. State of mind.
5. St. Thomas-of-Hell Street (French). In later life Carlyle admitted that this incident was based on his own experience during a walk in Edinburgh (rather than in Paris). "Dogday": i.e., in the dog days, a hot and unwholesome summer period coinciding with the prominence of Sirius, the Dog Star.
6. Cf. Daniel 3: the Babylonian king Nebuchadnezzar erected a golden idol and threw those who refused to fall down and worship it into a fiery furnace.
7. Hell.

thought, there rushed like a stream of fire over my whole soul; and I shook base Fear away from me forever. I was strong, of unknown strength; a spirit, almost a god. Ever from that time, the temper of my misery was changed: not Fear or whining Sorrow was it, but Indignation and grim fire-eyed Defiance.

"Thus had the EVERLASTING No[8] (*das ewige Nein*) pealed authoritatively through all the recesses of my Being, of my ME; and then was it that my whole ME stood up, in native God-created majesty, and with emphasis recorded its Protest. Such a Protest, the most important transaction in Life, may that same Indignation and Defiance, in a psychological point of view, be fitly called. The Everlasting No had said: 'Behold, thou art fatherless, outcast, and the Universe is mine (the Devil's)'; to which my whole Me now made answer: '*I* am not thine, but Free, and forever hate thee!'

"It is from this hour that I incline to date my Spiritual Newbirth, or Baphometic Fire-baptism,[9] perhaps I directly thereupon began to be a Man."

Centre of Indifference

Though, after this "Baphometic Fire-baptism" of his, our Wanderer signifies that his Unrest was but increased; as indeed, "Indignation and Defiance," especially against things in general, are not the most peaceable inmates; yet can the Psychologist surmise that it was no longer a quite hopeless Unrest; that henceforth it had at least a fixed centre to revolve round. For the fire-baptised soul, long so scathed and thunder-riven, here feels its own Freedom, which feeling is its Baphometic Baptism: the citadel of its whole kingdom it has thus gained by assault, and will keep in-expugnable; outwards from which the remaining dominions, not indeed without hard battling, will doubtless by degrees be conquered and pacificated. Under another figure, we might say, if in that great moment, in the *Rue Saint-Thomas de l'Enfer,* the old inward Satanic School was not yet thrown out of doors, it received peremptory judicial notice to quit;—whereby, for the rest, its howl-chantings, Ernulphuscursings,[1] and rebellious gnashings of teeth, might, in the meanwhile, become only the more tumultuous, and difficult to keep secret.

Accordingly, if we scrutinise these Pilgrimings well, there is perhaps discernible henceforth a certain incipient method in their madness. Not wholly as a Spectre does Teufelsdröckh now storm through the world; at worst as a spectre-fighting Man, nay who will one day be a Spectre-queller. If pilgriming restlessly to so many "Saints' Wells,"[2] and ever without quenching of his thirst, he nevertheless finds little secular wells, whereby from time to time some alleviation is ministered. In a word, he is now, if not ceasing, yet intermitting to "eat his own heart"; and clutches round him outwardly on

8. This phrase does not signify the hero's protest; it represents the sum of all the forces that had denied meaning to life. These negative forces, which had hitherto held the hero in bondage, are repudiated by his saying no to the "Everlasting No."
9. A transformation by a flash of spiritual illumination. The term may derive from Baphomet, an idol that the Knights Templar in the 14th century were accused of worshipping as part of their initiation ceremony.
1. Curse devised by Ernulf (1040–1124), bishop of Rochester, when sentencing persons to excommunication. "Satanic School": term coined by Robert Southey (1774–1843) to characterize the self-assertive and rebellious temper of the poetry of Byron and Shelley.
2. Holy fountains or wells, the waters of which were reputed to restore health.

the NOT-ME for wholesomer food. Does not the following glimpse exhibit him in a much more natural state?

"Towns also and Cities, especially the ancient, I failed not to look upon with interest. How beautiful to see thereby, as through a long vista, into the remote Time; to have as it were, an actual section of almost the earliest Past brought safe into the Present, and set before your eyes! There, in that old City, was a live ember of Culinary Fire put down, say only two-thousand years ago; and there, burning more or less triumphantly, with such fuel as the region yielded, it has burnt, and still burns, and thou thyself seest the very smoke thereof. Ah! and the far more mysterious live ember of Vital Fire was then also put down there; and still miraculously burns and spreads; and the smoke and ashes thereof (in these Judgment-Halls and Churchyards), and its bellows-engines (in these Churches), thou still seest; and its flame, looking out from every kind countenance, and every hateful one, still warms thee or scorches thee.

"Of Man's Activity and Attainment the chief results are aeriform, mystic, and preserved in Tradition only: such are his Forms of Government, with the Authority they rest on; his Customs, or Fashions both of Cloth-habits and of Soul-habits; much more his collective stock of Handicrafts, the whole Faculty he has acquired of manipulating Nature: all these things, as indispensable and priceless as they are, cannot in any way be fixed under lock and key, but must flit, spirit-like, on impalpable vehicles, from Father to Son; if you demand sight of them, they are nowhere to be met with. Visible Plowmen and Hammermen there have been, ever from Cain and Tubalcain[3] downwards: but where does your accumulated Agricultural, Metallurgic, and other Manufacturing SKILL lie warehoused? It transmits itself on the atmospheric air, on the sun's rays (by Hearing and by Vision); it is a thing aeriform, impalpable, of quite spiritual sort. In like manner, ask me not, Where are the LAWS; where is the GOVERNMENT? In vain wilt thou go to Schönbrunn, to Downing Street, to the Palais Bourbon:[4] thou findest nothing there but brick or stone houses, and some bundles of Papers tied with tape. Where, then, is that same cunningly-devised almighty GOVERNMENT of theirs to be laid hands on? Everywhere, yet nowhere: seen only in its works, this too is a thing aeriform, invisible; or if you will, mystic and miraculous. So spiritual (*geistig*) is our whole daily Life: all that we do springs out of Mystery, Spirit, invisible Force; only like a little Cloud-image, or Armida's Palace,[5] air-built, does the Actual body itself forth from the great mystic Deep.

"Visible and tangible products of the Past, again, I reckon-up to the extent of three. Cities, with their Cabinets and Arsenals; then tilled Fields, to either or to both of which divisions Roads with their Bridges, may belong; and thirdly—Books. In which third truly, the last invented, lies a worth far surpassing that of the two others. Wondrous indeed is the virtue of a true Book. Not like a dead city of stones, yearly crumbling, yearly needing repair; more like a tilled field, but then a spiritual field: like a spiritual tree, let me rather say, it stands from year to year, and from age to age (we have Books that already number some hundred-and-fifty human ages); and yearly comes its

---

3. Descendant of Cain, son of Adam and Eve (Genesis 4.1–22).
4. Headquarters of government in Vienna, London, and Paris, respectively.
5. The magic palace of a beautiful enchantress in Torquato Tasso's *Jerusalem Delivered* (1581).

new produce of leaves (Commentaries, Deductions, Philosophical, Political Systems; or were it only Sermons, Pamphlets, Journalistic Essays), every one of which is talismanic and thaumaturgic,[6] for it can persuade men. O thou who art able to write a Book, which once in the two centuries or oftener there is a man gifted to do, envy not him whom they name City-builder, and inexpressibly pity him whom they name Conqueror or City-burner! Thou too art a Conqueror and Victor; but of the true sort, namely over the Devil: thou too hast built what will outlast all marble and metal, and be a wonder-bringing City of the Mind, a Temple and Seminary and Prophetic Mount, whereto all kindreds of the Earth will pilgrim.—Fool! why journeyest thou wearisomely, in thy antiquarian fervour, to gaze on the stone pyramids of Geeza, or the clay ones of Sacchara?[7] These stand there, as I can tell thee, idle and inert, looking over the Desert, foolishly enough, for the last three-thousand years: but canst thou not open thy Hebrew BIBLE, then, or even Luther's Version[8] thereof?"

No less satisfactory is his sudden appearance not in Battle, yet on some Battle-field; which, we soon gather, must be that of Wagram;[9] so that here, for once, is a certain approximation to distinctiveness of date. Omitting much, let us impart what follows:

"Horrible enough! A whole Marchfeld[1] strewed with shell-splinters, cannon-shot, ruined tumbrils, and dead men and horses; stragglers still remaining not so much as buried. And those red mould heaps: ay, there lie the Shells of Men, out of which all the Life and Virtue has been blown; and now are they swept together, and crammed-down out of sight, like blown Egg-shells!—Did Nature, when she bade the Donau bring down his mould-cargoes from the Carinthian and Carpathian Heights, and spread them out here into the softest, richest level,—intend thee, O Marchfeld, for a corn-bearing Nursery, whereon her children might be nursed; or for a Cockpit, wherein they might the more commodiously be throttled and tattered? Were thy three broad Highways, meeting here from the ends of Europe, made for Ammunition-wagons, then? Were thy Wagrams and Stillfrieds but so many ready-built Casemates,[2] wherein the house of Hapsburg might batter with artillery, and with artillery be battered? König Ottokar, amid yonder hillocks, dies under Rodolf's truncheon; here Kaiser Franz falls a-swoon under Napoleon's: within which five centuries, to omit the others, how has thy breast, fair Plain, been defaced and defiled! The greensward is torn-up and trampled-down; man's fond care of it, his fruit-trees, hedge-rows, and pleasant dwellings, blown away with gunpowder; and the kind seedfield lies a desolate, hideous Place of Sculls.[3]—Nevertheless, Nature is at work; neither shall these Powder-Devilkins with their utmost devilry gainsay[4] her: but all that gore and carnage will be shrouded-in, absorbed into manure; and next year the Marchfeld will be green, nay greener. Thrifty unwearied Nature,

6. Miracle working.
7. I.e., Giza and Saqqara, near Cairo.
8. The German translation by Martin Luther (1483–1546).
9. A village in Austria; site of Napoleon's victory over the Austrians, July 1809.
1. A fertile plain in Austria whose soil (according to Teufelsdröckh) was brought down from the Carpathian Mountains by the Danube

("Donau") River.
2. Fortified chambers. Stillfried was the site of a battle in which Ottokar, king ("König") of Bohemia, was killed by the forces of Rudolph of Hapsburg in 1278. The Hapsburg armies at Wagram were led by Emperor Francis ("Franz") I.
3. Translation of Golgotha (Aramaic); where Jesus was crucified.
4. Contradict.

ever out of our great waste educing some little profit of thy own,—how dost thou, from the very carcass of the Killer, bring Life for the Living!

"What, speaking in quite unofficial language, is the net-purport and upshot of war? To my own knowledge, for example, there dwell and toil, in the British village of Dumdrudge,[5] usually some five-hundred souls. From these, by certain 'Natural Enemies'[6] of the French, there are successively selected, during the French war, say thirty able-bodied men: Dumdrudge, at her own expense, has suckled and nursed them: she has, not without difficulty and sorrow, fed them up to manhood, and even trained them to crafts, so that one can weave, another build, another hammer, and the weakest can stand under thirty stone[7] avoirdupois. Nevertheless, amid much weeping and swearing, they are selected; all dressed in red; and shipped away, at the public charges, some two-thousand miles, or say only to the south of Spain;[8] and fed there till wanted. And now to that same spot, in the south of Spain, are thirty similar French artisans, from a French Dumdrudge, in like manner wending: till at length, after infinite effort, the two parties come into actual juxtaposition; and Thirty stands fronting Thirty, each with a gun in his hand. Straightway the word 'Fire!' is given: and they blow the souls out of one another; and in place of sixty brisk useful craftsmen, the world has sixty dead carcasses, which it must bury, and anew shed tears for. Had these men any quarrel? Busy as the Devil is, not the smallest! They lived far enough apart; were the entirest strangers; nay, in so wide a Universe, there was even, unconsciously, by Commerce, some mutual helpfulness between them. How then? Simpleton! their Governors had fallen-out; and, instead of shooting one another, had the cunning to make these poor blockheads shoot.—Alas, so is it in Deutschland, and hitherto in all other lands; still as of old, 'what devilry soever Kings do, the Greeks must pay the piper!'[9]—In that fiction of the English Smollett,[1] it is true, the final Cessation of War is perhaps prophetically shadowed forth; where the two Natural Enemies, in person, take each a Tobacco-pipe, filled with Brimstone; light the same, and smoke in one another's faces, till the weaker gives in: but from such predicted Peace-Era, what blood-filled trenches, and contentious centuries, may still divide us!"

Thus can the Professor, at least in lucid intervals, look away from his own sorrows, over the many-coloured world, and pertinently enough note what is passing there. We may remark, indeed, that for the matter of spiritual culture, if for nothing else, perhaps few periods of his life were richer than this. Internally, there is the most momentous instructive Course of Practical Philosophy, with Experiments, going on; towards the right comprehension of which his Peripatetic[2] habits, favourable to Meditation, might help him rather than hinder. Externally, again, as he wanders to and fro, there are, if for the longing heart little substance, yet for the seeing eye sights enough: in these so boundless Travels of his, granting that the Satanic School was even partially kept down, what an incredible knowledge of our Planet, and its

5. An imaginary location.
6. Term often used in English newspapers to account for the frequency of wars between the English and French.
7. I.e., 420 pounds.
8. Where British armies fought against Napoleon (1808–14).

9. Horace's *Epistles* 1.2.14.
1. Tobias Smollett (1721–1771), *The Adventures of Ferdinand Count Fathom* (1753), chap. 41.
2. Walking about, after the manner of Aristotle, who delivered his lectures while walking in the Lyceum.

Inhabitants and their Works, that is to say, of all knowable things, might not Teufelsdröckh acquire!

"I have read in most Public Libraries," says he, "including those of Constantinople and Samarcand: in most Colleges, except the Chinese Mandarin ones, I have studied, or seen that there was no studying. Unknown Languages have I oftenest gathered from their natural repertory, the Air, by my organ of Hearing; Statistics, Geographies, Topographies came, through the Eye, almost of their own accord. The ways of Man, how he seeks food, and warmth, and protection for himself, in most regions, are ocularly known to me. Like the great Hadrian, I meted-out much of the terraqueous Globe with a pair of Compasses[3] that belonged to myself only.

"Of great Scenes why speak? Three summer days, I lingered reflecting, and even composing (*dichtete*), by the Pine-chasms of Vaucluse; and in that clear Lakelet[4] moistened my bread. I have sat under the Palm-trees of Tadmor;[5] smoked a pipe among the ruins of Babylon. The great Wall of China I have seen; and can testify that it is of gray brick, coped and covered with granite, and shows only second-rate masonry.—Great Events, also, have not I witnessed? Kings sweated-down (*ausgemergelt*) into Berlin-and-Milan Customhouse-Officers;[6] the World well won, and the World well lost oftener than once a hundred-thousand individuals shot (by each other) in one day. All kindreds and peoples and nations dashed together, and shifted and shovelled into heaps, that they might ferment there, and in time unite. The birthpangs of Democracy,[7] wherewith convulsed Europe was groaning in cries that reached Heaven, could not escape me.

"For great Men I have ever had the warmest predilection; and can perhaps boast that few such in this era have wholly escaped me. Great Men are the inspired (speaking and acting) Texts of that divine BOOK OF REVELATION, whereof a Chapter is completed from epoch to epoch, and by some named HISTORY; to which inspired Texts your numerous talented men, and your innumerable untalented men, are the better or worse exegetic Commentaries, and wagonload of too-stupid, heretical or orthodox, weekly Sermons. For my study, the inspired Texts themselves! Thus did not I, in very early days, having disguised me as tavern-waiter, stand behind the field-chairs, under that shady Tree at Treisnitz by the Jena Highway;[8] waiting upon the great Schiller and greater Goethe; and hearing what I have not forgotten. For—"

—But at this point the Editor recalls his principle of caution, some time ago laid down, and must suppress much. Let not the sacredness of Laurelled,[9] still more, of Crowned Heads, be tampered with. Should we, at a future day, find circumstances altered, and the time come for Publication, then may these glimpses into the privacy of the Illustrious be conceded; which for the present were little better than treacherous, perhaps traitorous Eavesdroppings. Of Lord Byron, therefore, of Pope Pius, Emperor Tarakwang, and

---

3. Legs. Hadrian (76–138 c.e.), Roman emperor who traveled extensively throughout his empire.
4. A pool at the base of a mountain in Vaucluse in southern France, one of Petrarch's favorite haunts.
5. Palmyra in Syria.
6. Napoleon reduced some of Europe's kings to the status of mere tax collectors for his regime.

7. As manifested in the revolutionary outbreaks in France (1789 and 1830) and in the agitations in England preceding the Reform Bill of 1832.
8. Where Goethe (1749–1832) and Schiller (1759–1805) met during the 1790s when they were collaborating on their writings.
9. I.e., poets, whose excellence is recognized with a crown of laurel.

the "White Water-roses"[1] (Chinese Carbonari) with their mysteries, no notice here! Of Napoleon himself we shall only, glancing from afar, remark that Teufelsdröckh's relation to him seems to have been of very varied character. At first we find our poor Professor on the point of being shot as a spy; then taken into private conversation, even pinched on the ear, yet presented with no money; at last indignantly dismissed, almost thrown out of doors, as an "Ideologist." "He himself," says the Professor, "was among the completest Ideologists, at least Ideopraxists:[2] in the Idea (in der Idee) he lived, moved and fought. The man was a Divine Missionary, though unconscious of it; and preached, through the cannon's throat, that great doctrine, La carrière ouverte aux talens[3] (The Tools to him that can handle them), which is our ultimate Political Evangel,[4] wherein alone can liberty lie. Madly enough he preached, it is true, as Enthusiasts[5] and first Missionaries are wont, with imperfect utterance, amid much frothy rant; yet as articulately perhaps as the case admitted. Or call him, if you will, an American Backwoodsman, who had to fell unpenetrated forests, and battle with innumerable wolves, and did not entirely forbear strong liquor, rioting, and even theft; whom, notwithstanding, the peaceful Sower will follow, and, as he cuts the boundless harvest, bless."

More legitimate and decisively authentic is Teufelsdröckh's appearance and emergence (we know not well whence) in the solitude of the North Cape, on that June Midnight. He has a "light-blue Spanish cloak" hanging round him, as his "most commodious, principal, indeed sole upper-garment"; and stands there, on the World-promontory, looking over the infinite Brine, like a little blue Belfry (as we figure), now motionless indeed, yet ready, if stirred, to ring quaintest changes.

"Silence as of death," writes he; "for Midnight, even in the Arctic latitudes, has its character: nothing but the granite cliffs ruddy-tinged, the peaceable gurgle of that slow-heaving Polar Ocean, over which in the utmost North the great Sun hangs low and lazy, as if he too were slumbering. Yet is his cloud-couch wrought of crimson and cloth-of-gold; yet does his light stream over the mirror of waters, like a tremulous fire-pillar, shooting downwards to the abyss, and hide itself under my feet. In such moments, Solitude also is invaluable; for who would speak, or be looked on, when behind him lies all Europe and Africa, fast asleep, except the watchmen; and before him the silent Immensity, and Palace of the Eternal, whereof our Sun is but a porch-lamp?

"Nevertheless, in this solemn moment comes a man, or monster, scrambling from among the rock-hollows; and, shaggy, huge as the Hyperborean[6] Bear, hails me in Russian speech: most probably, therefore, a Russian Smuggler. With courteous brevity, I signify my indifference to contraband trade, my humane intentions, yet strong wish to be private. In vain: the monster, counting doubtless on his superior stature, and minded to make sport for

1. In China a secret revolutionary society (and therefore like the early-19th-century Carbonari in Italy, France, and Spain) during the regime of Emperor Tarakwang (Tao-kuang, 1821–50). George Gordon, Lord Byron (1788–1824), English poet and champion of liberty. Pope Pius VII (1742–1823; pope, 1800–23) crowned Napoleon in 1804 but later came to oppose him; he also

suppressed the Carbonari.
2. Those who put ideas into practice.
3. Literally, the career open to talent (French), a maxim associated with Napoleon.
4. Gospel; good news.
5. Religious fanatics.
6. From the far North.

himself, or perhaps profit, were it with murder, continues to advance; ever assailing me with his importunate train-oil[7] breath; and now has advanced, till we stand both on the verge of the rock, the deep Sea rippling greedily down below. What argument will avail? On the thick Hyperborean, cherubic reasoning, seraphic eloquence were lost. Prepared for such extremity, I, deftly enough, whisk aside one step; draw out, from my interior reservoirs, a sufficient Birmingham Horse-pistol, and say, 'Be so obliging as retire, Friend (*Er ziehe sich zurück, Freund*), and with promptitude!' This logic even the Hyperborean understands: fast enough, with apologetic, petitionary growl, he sidles off; and, except for suicidal as well as homicidal purposes, need not return.

"Such I hold to be the genuine use of Gunpowder: that it makes all men alike tall.[8] Nay, if thou be cooler, cleverer than I, if thou have more *Mind*, though all but no *Body* whatever, then canst thou kill me first, and are the taller. Hereby, at last, is the Goliath powerless, and the David resistless;[9] savage Animalism is nothing, inventive Spiritualism is all.

"With respect to Duels, indeed, I have my own ideas. Few things, in this so surprising world, strike me with more surprise. Two little visual Spectra of men, hovering with insecure enough cohesion in the midst of the UNFATHOM-ABLE, and to dissolve therein, at any rate, very soon,—make pause at the distance of twelve paces asunder; whirl round; and, simultaneously by the cunningest mechanism, explode one another into Dissolution; and off-hand become Air, and Nonextant! Deuce on it (*verdammt*), the little spitfires!—Nay, I think with old Hugo von Trimberg:[1] 'God must needs laugh outright, could such a thing be, to see his wondrous Manikins here below.'"

But amid these specialties, let us not forget the great generality, which is our Chief guest here: How prospered the inner man of Teufelsdröckh under so much outward shifting? Does Legion[2] still lurk in him, though repressed; or has he exorcised that Devil's Brood? We can answer that the symptoms continue promising. Experience is the grand spiritual Doctor; and with him Teufelsdröckh has been long a patient, swallowing many a bitter bolus.[3] Unless our poor Friend belong to the numerous class of Incurables, which seems not likely, some cure will doubtless be effected. We should rather say that Legion, or the Satanic School, was now pretty well extirpated and cast out, but next to nothing introduced in its room; whereby the heart remains, for the while, in a quiet but no comfortable state.

"At length, after so much roasting," thus writes our Autobiographer, "I was what you might name calcined. Pray only that it be not rather, as is the more frequent issue, reduced to a *caputmortuum*![4] But in any case, by mere dint of practice, I had grown familiar with many things. Wretchedness was still wretched; but I could now partly see through it, and despise it. Which highest mortal, in this inane Existence, had I not found a Shadow-hunter, or Shadow-hunted; and, when I looked through his brave garnitures, miserable enough? Thy wishes have all been sniffed aside, thought I: but what, had they ever been all granted! Did not the Boy Alexander weep because he had

---

7. Whale oil.
8. Brave; strong.
9. For the fight between Goliath, the huge champion of the Philistines, and the young Israelite David, who killed him with a slingshot,

see 1 Samuel 17.
1. Medieval poet (1260–1309).
2. Unclean spirits (Mark 5.9).
3. Large pill.
4. Death's head (Latin).

not two Planets to conquer;[5] or a whole Solar System; or after that, a whole Universe? *Ach Gott*,[6] when I gazed into these Stars, have they not looked-down on me as if with pity, from their serene spaces; like Eyes glistening with heavenly tears over the little lot of man! Thousands of human generations, all as noisy as our own, have been swallowed-up of[7] Time, and there remains no wreck[8] of them any more; and Arcturus and Orion and Sirius and the Pleiades are still shining in their courses, clear and young, as when the Shepherd first noted them in the plain of Shinar.[9] Pshaw! what is this paltry little Dog-cage[1] of an Earth; what art thou that sittest whining there? Thou art still Nothing, Nobody: true; but who, then, is Something, Somebody? For thee the Family of Man has no use; it rejects thee; thou art wholly as a dissevered limb: so be it; perhaps it is better so!"

Too-heavy-laden Teufelsdröckh! Yet surely his bands are loosening: one day he will hurl the burden far from him, and bound forth free and with a second youth.

"This," says our Professor, "was the CENTRE OF INDIFFERENCE I had now reached; through which whoso travels from the Negative Pole to the Positive must necessarily pass."

The Everlasting Yea

"Temptations in the Wilderness!"[2] exclaims Teufelsdröckh: "Have we not all to be tried with such? Not so easily can the old Adam, lodged in us by birth, be dispossessed. Our Life is compassed round with Necessity; yet is the meaning of Life itself no other than Freedom, than Voluntary Force: thus have we a warfare; in the beginning, especially, a hard-fought battle. For the God-given mandate, *Work thou in Welldoing*, lies mysteriously written, in Promethean[3] Prophetic Characters, in our hearts; and leaves us no rest, night or day, till it be deciphered and obeyed; till it burn forth, in our conduct, a visible, acted Gospel of Freedom. And as the clay-given mandate, *Eat thou and be filled*, at the same time persuasively proclaims itself through every nerve,—must not there be a confusion, a contest, before the better Influence can become the upper?

"To me nothing seems more natural than that the Son of Man, when such God-given mandate first prophetically stirs within him, and the Clay must now be vanquished, or vanquish,—should be carried of the spirit into grim Solitudes, and there fronting the Tempter do grimmest battle with him; defiantly setting him at naught, till he yield and fly. Name it as we choose: with or without visible Devil, whether in the natural Desert of rocks and sands, or in the populous moral Desert of selfishness and baseness,—to such Temptation are we all called. Unhappy if we are not! Unhappy if we are but Half-men, in whom that divine handwriting has never blazed forth, all-subduing,

---

5. According to tradition, when Alexander the Great (356–323 B.C.E.) realized that he had subjugated the known world he wept because he had no worlds left to conquer.
6. Alas God (German).
7. By.
8. Remnant cast ashore from a shipwreck.
9. In the Sumerian region (now in Iraq). "Shepherd": probably Abraham, who was commanded by the Lord to "tell the stars, if thou be able to

number them" (Genesis 15.5).
1. A drum-shaped cage that turns when a dog runs inside the cylinder. This dog-powered device, attached to a kitchen spit, was used to turn roasting joints of meat.
2. Paraphrase of Matthew 4.1.
3. Fiery or fiery-spirited, an allusion to Prometheus, the defiant Titan who brought the secret of fire-making to humanity.

in true sun-splendour; but quivers dubiously amid meaner lights: or smoulders, in dull pain, in darkness, under earthly vapours!—Our Wilderness is the wide World in an Atheistic Century; our Forty Days[4] are long years of suffering and fasting: nevertheless, to these also comes an end. Yes, to me also was given, if not Victory, yet the consciousness of Battle, and the resolve to persevere therein while life or faculty is left. To me also, entangled in the enchanted forests, demon-peopled, doleful of sight and of sound, it was given, after weariest wanderings, to work out my way into the higher sunlit slopes—of that Mountain which has no summit, or whose summit is in Heaven only!"

He says elsewhere, under a less ambitious figure; as figures are, once for all, natural to him: "Has not thy Life been that of most sufficient men (*tüchtigen Männer*) thou hast known in this generation? An outflush of foolish young Enthusiasm, like the first fallow-crop, wherein are as many weeds as valuable herbs: this all parched away, under the Droughts of practical and spiritual Unbelief, as Disappointment, in thought and act, often-repeated gave rise to Doubt, and Doubt gradually settled into Denial! If I have had a second-crop, and now see the perennial greensward, and sit under umbrageous[5] cedars, which defy all Drought (and Doubt); herein too, be the Heavens praised, I am not without examples, and even exemplars."

So that, for Teufelsdröckh also, there has been a "glorious revolution":[6] these mad shadow-hunting and shadow-hunted Pilgrimings of his were but some purifying "Temptation in the Wilderness," before his Apostolic work (such as it was) could begin; which Temptation is now happily over, and the Devil once more worsted! Was "that high moment in the *Rue de l'Enfer*," then, properly the turning-point of the battle; when the Fiend said, *Worship me or be torn in shreds*; and was answered valiantly with an *Apage Satana*?[7]— Singular Teufelsdröckh, would thou hadst told thy singular story in plain words! But it is fruitless to look there, in those Paper-bags,[8] for such. Nothing but innuendoes, figurative crotchets:[9] a typical Shadow, fitfully wavering, prophetic-satiric; no clear logical Picture. "How paint to the sensual eye," asks he once, "what passes in the Holy-of-Holies of Man's Soul; in what words, known to these profane times, speak even afar-off of the unspeakable?" We ask in turn: Why perplex these times, profane as they are, with needless obscurity, by omission and by commission? Not mystical only is our Professor, but whimsical; and involves himself, now more than ever, in eyebewildering *chiaroscuro*.[1] Successive glimpses, here faithfully imparted, our more gifted readers must endeavour to combine for their own behoof.

He says: "The hot Harmattan wind[2] had raged itself out; its howl went silent within me; and the long-deafened soul could now hear. I paused in my wild wanderings; and sat me down to wait, and consider; for it was as if the hour of change drew nigh. I seemed to surrender, to renounce utterly, and say: Fly, then, false shadows of Hope; I will chase you no more, I will believe you no more. And ye too, haggard spectres of Fear, I care not for you; ye too are all shadows and a lie. Let me rest here: for I am way-weary and

4. The length of time that Jesus spent fasting in the wilderness (Matthew 4.2).
5. Shady.
6. The overthrow of James II of England in 1688.
7. Get thee hence, Satan (Greek; Matthew 4.10).

8. Bags containing documents and writings by Teufelsdröckh.
9. Perverse notions.
1. Light and shade (Italian).
2. A hot and dry wind in Africa.

life-weary; I will rest here, were it but to die: to die or to live is alike to me; alike insignificant."—And again: "Here, then, as I lay in that CENTRE OF INDIFFERENCE; cast, doubtless by benignant upper Influence, into a healing sleep, the heavy dreams rolled gradually away, and I awoke to a new Heaven and a new Earth.[3] The first preliminary moral Act, Annihilation of Self (*Selbst-tödtung*), had been happily accomplished; and my mind's eyes were now unsealed, and its hands ungyved."[4]

Might we not also conjecture that the following passage refers to his Locality, during this same "healing sleep"; that his Pilgrim-staff lies cast aside here, on "the high table-land"; and indeed that the repose is already taking wholesome effect on him? If it were not that the tone, in some parts, has more of riancy,[5] even of levity, than we could have expected! However, in Teufelsdröckh, there is always the strangest Dualism: light dancing, with guitar-music, will be going on in the fore-court, while by fits from within comes the faint whimpering of woe and wail. We transcribe the piece entire:

"Beautiful it was to sit there, as in my skyey Tent, musing and meditating; on the high table-land, in front of the Mountains; over me, as roof, the azure Dome, and around me, for walls, four azure-flowing curtains,—namely, of the Four azure winds, on whose bottom-fringes also I have seen gilding. And then to fancy the fair Castles that stood sheltered in these Mountain hollows; with their green flower-lawns, and white dames and damosels, lovely enough: or better still, the straw-roofed Cottages, wherein stood many a Mother baking bread, with her children round her:—all hidden and protectingly folded-up in the valley-folds; yet there and alive, as sure as if I beheld them. Or to see, as well as fancy, the nine Towns and Villages, that lay round my mountain-seat, which, in still weather, were wont to speak to me (by their steeple-bells) with metal tongue; and, in almost all weather, proclaimed their vitality by repeated Smoke-clouds; whereon, as on a culinary horologe,[6] I might read the hour of the day. For it was the smoke of cookery, as kind housewives at morning, midday, eventide, were boiling their husband's kettles; and ever a blue pillar rose up into the air, successively or simultaneously, from each of the nine, saying, as plainly as smoke could say: Such and such a meal is getting ready here. Not uninteresting! For you have the whole Borough, with all its love-makings and scandal-mongeries, contentions and contentments, as in miniature, and could cover it all with your hat.—If, in my wide Wayfarings, I had learned to look into the business of the World in its details, here perhaps was the place for combining it into general propositions, and deducing inferences therefrom.

"Often also could I see the black Tempest marching in anger through the Distance: round some Schreckhorn,[7] as yet grim-blue, would the eddying vapour gather, and there tumultuously eddy, and flow down like a mad witch's hair; till, after a space, it vanished, and, in the clear sunbeam, your Schreckhorn stood smiling grim-white, for the vapour had held snow. How thou fermentest and elaboratest, in thy great fermenting-vat and laboratory of an Atmosphere, of a World, O Nature!—Or what is Nature? Ha! why do I not name thee GOD? Art not thou the 'Living Garment of God'?[8] O Heavens, is it,

---

3. Revelation 21.1.
4. Unfettered.
5. Gaiety.
6. Clock.

7. Peak of Terror (German); a mountain in Switzerland.
8. Goethe, *Faust* 1.509.

in very deed, HE, then, that ever speaks through thee; that lives and loves in thee, that lives and loves in me?

"Fore-shadows, call them rather fore-splendours, of that Truth, and Beginning of Truths, fell mysteriously over my soul. Sweeter than Dayspring to the Shipwrecked in Nova Zembla;[9] ah, like the mother's voice to her little child that strays bewildered, weeping, in unknown tumults; like soft streamings of celestial music to my too-exasperated heart, came that Evangel. The Universe is not dead and demoniacal, a charnel-house with spectres; but godlike, and my Father's!

"With other eyes, too, could I now look upon my fellow man; with an infinite Love, an infinite Pity. Poor, wandering, wayward man! Art thou not tired, and beaten with stripes, even as I am? Ever, whether thou bear the royal mantle or the beggar's gabardine, art thou not so weary, so heavy-laden; and thy Bed of Rest is but a Grave. O my Brother, my Brother, why cannot I shelter thee in my bosom, and wipe away all tears from thy eyes! Truly, the din of many-voiced Life, which, in this solitude, with the mind's organ, I could hear, was no longer a maddening discord, but a melting one; like inarticulate cries, and sobbings of a dumb creature, which in the ear of Heaven are prayers. The poor Earth, with her poor joys, was now my needy Mother, not my cruel Stepdame; man, with his so mad Wants and so mean Endeavours, had become the dearer to me; and even for his sufferings and his sins, I now first named him Brother. Thus I was standing in the porch of that 'Sanctuary of Sorrow';[1] by strange, steep ways had I too been guided thither; and ere long its sacred gates would open, and the 'Divine Depth of Sorrow' lie disclosed to me."

The Professor says, he here first got eye on the Knot that had been strangling him, and straightway could unfasten it, and was free. "A vain interminable controversy," writes he, "touching what is at present called Origin of Evil, or some such thing, arises in every soul, since the beginning of the world; and in every soul, that would pass from idle Suffering into actual Endeavouring, must first be put an end to. The most, in our time, have to go content with a simple, incomplete enough Suppression of this controversy; to a few some Solution of it is indispensable. In every new era, too, such Solution comes-out in different terms; and ever the Solution of the last era has become obsolete, and is found unserviceable. For it is man's nature to change his Dialect from century to century; he cannot help it though he would. The authentic *Church-Catechism* of our present century has not yet fallen into my hands: meanwhile, for my own private behoof, I attempt to elucidate the matter so. Man's Unhappiness, as I construe, comes of his Greatness; it is because there is an Infinite in him, which with all his cunning[2] he cannot quite bury under the Finite. Will the whole Finance Ministers and Upholsterers and Confections of modern Europe undertake, in joint-stock company, to make one Shoeblack HAPPY? They cannot accomplish it, above an hour or two; for the Shoeblack also has a Soul quite other than his Stomach; and would require, if you consider it, for his permanent satisfaction and saturation, simply this allotment, no more, and no less: *God's infinite Universe altogether to himself,* therein to enjoy infi-

9. A Dutch sea captain, whose ship was wrecked off the island of Nova Zembla in the Arctic in 1596, recorded in his journal his thankfulness at the coming of daylight.

1. Adapted from Goethe's *Wilhelm Meister* (1821–29).
2. Skill.

nitely, and fill every wish as fast as it rose. Oceans of Hochheimer, a Throat like that of Ophiuchus:[3] speak not of them; to the infinite Shoeblack they are as nothing. No sooner is your ocean filled, than he grumbles that it might have been of better vintage. Try him with half of a Universe, of an Omnipotence, he sets to quarrelling with the proprietor of the other half, and declares himself the most maltreated of men.—Always there is a black spot in our sunshine: it is even as I said, the *Shadow of Ourselves.*

"But the whim we have of Happiness is somewhat thus. By certain valuations, and averages, of our own striking, we come upon some sort of average terrestrial lot; this we fancy belongs to us by nature, and of indefeasible right. It is simple payment of our wages, of our deserts; requires neither thanks nor complaint; only such *overplus* as there may be do we account Happiness; any *deficit* again is Misery. Now consider that we have the valuation of our own deserts ourselves, and what a fund of Self-conceit there is in each of us,—do you wonder that the balance should so often dip the wrong way, and many a Blockhead cry: See there, what a payment; was ever worthy gentleman so used!—I tell thee, Blockhead, it all comes of thy Vanity; of what thou *fanciest* those same deserts of thine to be. Fancy that thou deservest to be hanged (as is most likely), thou wilt feel it happiness to be only shot: fancy that thou deservest to be hanged in a hair-halter, it will be a luxury to die in hemp.[4]

"So true is it, what I then say, that *the Fraction of Life can be increased in value not so much by increasing your Numerator as by lessening your Denominator.* Nay, unless my Algebra deceive me, *Unity* itself divided by *Zero* will give *Infinity.* Make thy claim of wages a zero, then; thou hast the world under thy feet. Well did the Wisest of our time write: 'It is only with Renunciation (*Entsagen*) that Life, properly speaking, can be said to begin.'[5]

"I asked myself: What is this that, ever since earliest years, thou hast been fretting and fuming, and lamenting and self-tormenting, on account of? Say it in a word: is it not because thou art not HAPPY? Because the THOU (sweet gentleman) is not sufficiently honoured, nourished, soft-bedded, and lovingly cared for? Foolish soul! What Act of Legislature was there that *thou* shouldst be Happy? A little while ago thou hadst no right to *be* at all. What if thou wert born and predestined not to be Happy, but to be Unhappy! Art thou nothing other than a Vulture, then, that fliest through the Universe seeking after somewhat to *eat;* and shrieking dolefully because carrion enough is not given thee? Close thy *Byron;* open thy *Goethe.*"

"*Es leuchtet mir ein,*[6] I see a glimpse of it!" cries he elsewhere: "there is in man a HIGHER than Love of Happiness: he can do without Happiness, and instead thereof find Blessedness! Was it not to preach-forth this same HIGHER that sages and martyrs, the Poet and the Priest, in all times, have spoken and suffered; bearing testimony, through life and through death, of the Godlike that is in Man, and how in the Godlike only has he Strength and Freedom? Which God-inspired Doctrine art thou also honoured to be taught; O Heavens! and broken with manifold merciful Afflictions, even till thou become contrite, and learn it! O, thank thy Destiny for these; thankfully bear

3. The constellation also known as the Serpent Holder. "Hochheimer": Rhine wine or hock from Hochheim.
4. A hangman's noose made of hemp, which has a texture similar to linen, is smoother than one made of horsehair.
5. Adapted from *Wilhelm Meister* by Goethe ("wisest of our time").
6. An exclamation of Wilhelm Meister's (German).

what yet remain: thou hadst need of them; the Self in thee needed to be anni-
hilated. By benignant fever-paroxysms is Life rooting out the deep-seated
chronic Diseases, and triumphs over Death. On the roaring billows of Time,
thou art not engulfed, but borne aloft into the azure of Eternity. Love not
Pleasure; love God.[7] This is the EVERLASTING YEA wherein all contradiction is
solved: wherein whoso walks and works, it is well with him."

And again: "Small is it that thou canst trample the Earth with its injuries
under thy feet, as old Greek Zeno[8] trained thee: thou canst love the Earth
while it injures thee, and even because it injures thee; for this a Greater than
Zeno was needed, and he too was sent. Knowest thou that *'Worship of Sorrow'*?[9] the Temple thereof, founded some eighteen centuries ago, now lies in
ruins, overgrown with jungle, the habitation of doleful creatures:[1] nevertheless, venture forward; in a low crypt, arched out of falling fragments, thou
findest the Altar still there, and its sacred Lamp perennially burning."

Without pretending to comment on which strange utterances, the Editor
will only remark, that there lies beside them much of a still more questionable character; unsuited to the general apprehension; nay wherein he himself does not see his way. Nebulous disquisitions on Religion, yet not without
bursts of splendour; on the "perennial continuance of Inspiration"; on Prophecy; that there are "true Priests, as well as Baal-Priests,[2] in our own day":
with more of the like sort. We select some fractions, by way of finish to this
farrago.

"Cease, my much-respected Herr von Voltaire,"[3] thus apostrophises the
Professor: "shut thy sweet voice; for the task appointed thee seems finished.
Sufficiently has thou demonstrated this proposition, considerable or otherwise: That the Mythus of the Christian Religion looks not in the eighteenth
century as it did in the eighth. Alas, were thy six-and-thirty quartos, and the
six-and-thirty thousand other quartos and folios, and flying sheets or reams,
printed before and since on the same subject, all needed to convince us of so
little! But what next? Wilt thou help us to embody the divine Spirit of that
Religion in a new Mythus, in a new vehicle and vesture, that our Souls, otherwise too like perishing, may live? What! thou hast no faculty in that kind?
Only a torch for burning, no hammer for building? Take our thanks, then,
and—thyself away.

"Meanwhile what are antiquated Mythuses to me? Or is the God present,
felt in my own heart, a thing which Herr von Voltaire will dispute out of me;
or dispute into me? To the *'Worship of Sorrow'* ascribe what origin and genesis
thou pleasest, *has* not that Worship originated, and been generated; is it not
here? Feel it in thy heart, and then say whether it is of God! This is Belief; all
else is Opinion,—for which latter whoso will let him worry and be worried."

"Neither," observes he elsewhere, "shall ye tear-out one another's eyes,
struggling over 'Plenary Inspiration,'[4] and suchlike: try rather to get a little

---

7. Adapted from 2 Timothy 3.4.
8. Stoic philosopher (3rd century B.C.E.), who,
after being injured in a fall, is reputed to have
struck the earth with his hand as if the earth were
responsible for his injury. Afterward he committed suicide. Hence he is said to "trample the
Earth."
9. Christianity.
1. Isaiah 34.13–15.

2. False priests, mentioned in 1 Kings 18.17–40.
3. French philosopher, satirist, and encyclope-
dist (1694–1778), famously hostile to superstition, injustice, and organized religion.
4. Doctrine that all statements in the Bible are
supernaturally inspired and authoritative. Voltaire had sought to demonstrate that this doctrine was absurd.

even Partial Inspiration, each of you for himself. One BIBLE I know, of whose Plenary Inspiration doubt is not so much as possible; nay with my own eyes I saw God's-Hand writing it: thereof all other Bibles are but leaves,—say, in Picture-Writing to assist the weaker faculty."

Or, to give the wearied reader relief, and bring it to an end, let him take the following perhaps more intelligible passage:

"To me, in this our life," says the Professor, "which is an internecine warfare with the Time-spirit, other warfare seems questionable. Hast thou in any way a Contention with thy brother, I advise thee, think well what the meaning thereof is. If thou gauge it to the bottom, it is simply this: 'Fellow, see! thou art taking more than thy share of Happiness in the world, something from *my* share: which, by the Heavens, thou shalt not; nay I will fight thee rather.'—Alas, and the whole lot to be divided is such a beggarly matter, truly a 'feast of shells,'[5] for the substance has been spilled out: not enough to quench one Appetite; and the collective human species clutching at them!—Can we not, in all such cases, rather say: 'Take it, thou too-ravenous individual; take that pitiful additional fraction of a share, which I reckoned mine, but which thou so wantest; take it with a blessing: would to Heaven I had enough for thee!'—If Fichte's *Wissenschaftslehre*[6] be, 'to a certain extent, Applied Christianity,' surely to a still greater extent, so is this. We have here not a Whole Duty of Man,[7] yet a Half Duty, namely the Passive half: could we but do it, as we can demonstrate it!

"But indeed Conviction, were it never so excellent, is worthless till it convert itself into Conduct. Nay properly Conviction is not possible till then; inasmuch as all Speculation is by nature endless, formless, a vortex amid vortices: only by a felt indubitable certainty of Experience does it find any centre to revolve round, and so fashion itself into a system. Most true is it, as a wise man teaches us, that 'Doubt of any sort cannot be removed except by Action.' On which ground, too, let him who gropes painfully in darkness or uncertain light, and prays vehemently that the dawn may ripen into day, lay this other precept well to heart, which to me was of invaluable service: '*Do the Duty which lies nearest thee*,'[8] which thou knowest to be a Duty! Thy second Duty will already have become clearer.

"May we not say, however, that the hour of Spiritual Enfranchisement is even this: When your Ideal World, wherein the whole man has been dimly struggling and inexpressibly languishing to work, becomes revealed, and thrown open; and you discover, with amazement enough, like the Lothario in *Wilhelm Meister*, that your 'America is here or nowhere'? The Situation that has not its Duty, its Ideal, was never yet occupied by man. Yes here, in this poor, miserable, hampered, despicable Actual, wherein thou even now standest, here or nowhere is thy Ideal: work it out therefrom; and working, believe, live, be free. Fool! the Ideal is in thyself, the impediment too is in thyself: thy Condition is but the stuff thou art to shape that same Ideal out of: what matters whether such stuff be of this sort or that, so the Form thou

---

5. Empty eggshells. The phrase appears in both James Macpherson's *Fingal* (1761) and Byron's imitation of it, "The Death of Calmer and Orla" (1806).
6. The doctrine of knowledge (German); the shortened title of the 1798 work by Johann Gottlieb Fichte (1762–1814), German philosopher.
7. Title of an anonymous book of religious instruction first published in 1659. The phrase is from Ecclesiastes 12.13.
8. This and the previous quotation are from Goethe's *Wilhelm Meister*.

give it be heroic, be poetic? O thou that pinest in the imprisonment of the Actual, and criest bitterly to the gods for a kingdom wherein to rule and create, know this of a truth: the thing thou seekest is already with thee, 'here or nowhere,' couldst thou only see!

"But it is with man's Soul as it was with Nature: the beginning of Creation is—Light.[9] Till the eye have vision, the whole members are in bonds.[1] Divine moment, when over the tempest-tost Soul, as once over the wild-weltering Chaos, it is spoken: Let there be Light! Ever to the greatest that has felt such moment, is it not miraculous and God-announcing; even as, under simpler figures, to the simplest and least. The mad primeval Discord is hushed; the rudely-jumbled conflicting elements bind themselves into separate Firmaments: deep silent rock-foundations are built beneath; and the skyey vault with its everlasting Luminaries above: instead of a dark wasteful Chaos, we have a blooming, fertile, heaven-encompassed World.

"I too could now say to myself: Be no longer a Chaos, but a World, or even Worldkin.[2] Produce! Produce! Were it but the pitifullest infinitesimal fraction of a Product, produce it, in God's name! 'Tis the utmost thou hast in thee: out with it, then. Up, up! Whatsoever thy hand findeth to do, do it with thy whole might. Work while it is called Today; for the Night cometh, wherein no man can work."[3]

1830–31

1833–34

From Past and Present[1]

From Democracy

If the Serene Highnesses and Majesties do not take note of that,[2] then, as I perceive, *that* will take note of itself! The time for levity, insincerity, and idle babble and play-acting, in all kinds, is gone by; it is a serious, grave time. Old long-vexed questions, not yet solved in logical words or parliamentary laws, are fast solving themselves in facts, somewhat unblessed to behold! This largest of questions, this question of Work and Wages, which ought, had we heeded Heaven's voice, to have begun two generations ago or more, cannot

9. Cf. Genesis 1.3: "And God said, Let there be light: and there was light."
1. Cf. Matthew 6.22: "The light of the body is the eye."
2. A little world, a microcosm.
3. Adapted from Ecclesiastes 9.10 and John 9.4.
1. In 1843 there were reputedly one and a half million unemployed in England (out of a population of eighteen million). The closing of factories and the reduction of wages led to severe rioting in the manufacturing districts. Bread-hungry protesters (as well as the Chartist demonstrators who demanded political reforms) caused many observers to dread that a large-scale revolution was imminent. Carlyle was so appalled by the plight of the industrial workers that he postponed his research into the life and times of Cromwell to air his views on the contemporary crisis. *Past and Present*, a book written in seven weeks, was a call for heroic leadership. Cromwell and other historic

leaders are cited, but the principal example from the past is Abbot Samson, a medieval monk who established order in the monasteries under his charge. Carlyle hoped that the "Captains of Industry" might provide a comparable leadership in 1843. He was aware that the spread of democracy was inevitable, but he had little confidence in it as a method of producing leaders. Nor did he have any confidence, at this time, in the landed aristocracy, who seemed to him preoccupied with foxhunting, preserving their game, and upholding the tariffs on grain (Corn Laws). In place of a "Do-nothing Aristocracy" there was need for a "Working Aristocracy." This first selection is from book 3, chap. 13.
2. The previous chapter, "Reward," had urged that English manufacturers needed the help of everyone and that Parliament should remove the tariffs (Corn Laws) restricting the growth of trade and industry.

be delayed longer without hearing Earth's voice. "Labour" will verily need to be somewhat "organized," as they say,—God knows with what difficulty. Man will actually need to have his debts and earnings a little better paid by man; which, let Parliaments speak of them, or be silent of them, are eternally his due from man, and cannot, without penalty and at length not without death-penalty,[3] be withheld. How much ought to cease among us straightway; how much ought to begin straightway, while the hours yet are!

Truly they are strange results to which this of leaving all to "Cash"; of quietly shutting up the God's Temple, and gradually opening wide-open the Mammon's Temple, with "Laissez-faire, and Every man for himself,"[4]—have led us in these days! We have Upper, speaking Classes, who indeed do "speak" as never man spake before;[5] the withered flimsiness, godless baseness and barrenness of whose Speech might of itself indicate what kind of Doing and practical Governing went on under it! For Speech is the gaseous element out of which most kinds of Practice and Performance, especially all kinds of moral Performance, condense themselves, and take shape; as the one is, so will the other be. Descending, accordingly, into the Dumb Class in its Stockport Cellars and Poor-Law Bastilles,[6] have we not to announce that they are hitherto unexampled in the History of Adam's Posterity?

Life was never a May-game for men: in all times the lot of the dumb millions born to toil was defaced with manifold sufferings, injustices, heavy burdens, avoidable and unavoidable; not play at all, but hard work that made the sinews sore and the heart sore. As bond-slaves, *villani, bordarii, sochemanni,*[7] nay indeed as dukes, earls and kings, men were often-times made weary of their life; and had to say, in the sweat of their brow[8] and of their soul, Behold, it is not sport, it is grim earnest, and our back can bear no more! Who knows not what massacrings and harryings there have been; grinding, long-continuing, unbearable injustices,—till the heart had to rise in madness, and some "*Eu Sachsen, nimith euer sachses,* You Saxons, out with your gully-knives, then!" You Saxons, some "arrestment," partial "arrestment of the Knaves and Dastards" has become indispensable!—The page of Dryasdust[9] is heavy with such details.

And yet I well venture to believe that in no time, since the beginnings of Society, was the lot of those same dumb millions of toilers so entirely unbearable as it is even in the days now passing over us. It is not to die, or even to die of hunger, that makes a man wretched; many men have died; all men must die,—the last exit of us all is in a Fire-Chariot of Pain.[1] But it is to live miserable we know not why; to work sore and yet gain nothing; to be heartworn, weary, yet isolated, unrelated, girt-in with a cold universal Laissez-faire: it is to die slowly all our life long, imprisoned in a deaf, dead, Infinite Injustice, as in the accursed iron belly of a Phalaris' Bull![2] This is and remains for ever

---

3. I.e., by the outbreak of a revolution, as in France.
4. The pursuit of wealth (Mammon is the devil of covetousness) under a noninterventionist economic policy. *Laissez-faire* literally means "let it be" (French).
5. John 7.46.
6. I.e., workhouses for the unemployed. "Stockport Cellars": in a cellar in the slum district of Stockport, an industrial town near Manchester, three children were poisoned by their starving

parents, who wanted to collect insurance benefits from a burial society.
7. Three categories of feudal tenants, from lowest in status to highest (Latin).
8. Genesis 3.19.
9. An imaginary author of dull histories.
1. 2 Kings 2.11.
2. Phalaris was a Sicilian tyrant (6th century B.C.E.) whose victims were roasted alive by being confined inside the brass figure of a bull under which a fire was lit.

intolerable to all men whom God has made. Do we wonder at French Revolutions, Chartisms, Revolts of Three Days?[3] The times, if we will consider them, are really unexampled.

Never before did I hear of an Irish Widow reduced to "prove her sisterhood by dying of typhus-fever and infecting seventeen persons,"—saying in such undeniable way, "You *see*, I was your sister!"[4] Sisterhood, brotherhood, was often forgotten; but not till the rise of these ultimate Mammon and Shotbelt Gospels[5] did I ever see it so expressly denied. If no pious Lord or *Law-ward* would remember it, always some pious Lady (*"Hlaf-dig,"* Benefactress, *"Loaf-giveress,"* they say she is,—blessings on her beautiful heart!) was there, with mild mother-voice and hand, to remember it; some pious thoughtful *Elder*, what we now call "Prester," *Presbyter* or "Priest," was there to put all men in mind of it, in the name of the God who had made all.

Not even in Black Dahomey[6] was it ever, I think, forgotten to the typhus-fever length. Mungo Park,[7] resourceless, had sunk down to die under the Negro Village-Tree, a horrible White object in the eyes of all. But in the poor Black Woman, and her daughter who stood aghast at him, whose earthly wealth and funded capital consisted of one small calabash of rice, there lived a heart richer than *"Laissez-faire"*: they, with a royal munificence, boiled their rice for him; they sang all night to him, spinning assiduous on their cotton distaffs, as he lay to sleep: "Let us pity the poor white man; no mother has he to fetch him milk, no sister to grind him corn!" Thou poor black Noble One,—thou *Lady* too: did not a God make thee too; was there not in thee too something of a God!—

Gurth,[8] born thrall of Cedric the Saxon, has been greatly pitied by Dryasdust and others. Gurth, with the brass collar round his neck, tending Cedric's pigs in the glades of the wood, is not what I call an exemplar of human felicity: but Gurth, with the sky above him, with the free air and tinted boscage and umbrage round him, and in him at least the certainty of supper and social lodging when he came home; Gurth to me seems happy, in comparison with many a Lancashire and Buckinghamshire man, of these days, not born thrall of anybody! Gurth's brass collar did not gall him: Cedric *deserved* to be his Master. The pigs were Cedric's, but Gurth too would get his parings of them. Gurth had the inexpressible satisfaction of feeling himself related indissolubly, though in a rude brass-collar way, to his fellow-mortals in this Earth. He had superiors, inferiors, equals.—Gurth is now "emancipated" long since; has what we call "Liberty." Liberty, I am told, is a Divine thing. Liberty when it becomes the "Liberty to die by starvation" is not so divine!

Liberty? The true liberty of a man, you would say, consisted in his finding out, or being forced to find out, the right path, and to walk thereon. To learn, or to be taught, what work he actually was able for; and then by permission, persuasion, and even compulsion, to set about doing of the same! That is his true blessedness, honour, "liberty" and maximum of wellbeing: if liberty be not that, I for one have small care about liberty. You do not allow

---

3. The 1830 revolution in France (July 27–29).
4. An incident referred to several times in *Past and Present*. Dickens in *Bleak House* (1851) also showed how indifference to the lack of sanitation in London slums led to the spread of disease to other parts of the city.
5. The attitudes of land-owning aristocracy who were committed to preserving their exclusive right to shoot game birds and animals.
6. A state in west Africa where human sacrifice and cannibalism persisted.
7. Explorer and author (1771–1806); he was killed by Africans.
8. A swineherd described in Scott's *Ivanhoe* (1819).

a palpable madman to leap over precipices; you violate his liberty, you that are wise; and keep him, were it in strait-waistcoats, away from the precipices! Every stupid, every cowardly and foolish man is but a less palpable madman: his true liberty were that a wiser man, that any and every wiser man, could, by brass collars, or in whatever milder or sharper way, lay hold of him when he was going wrong, and order and compel him to go a little righter. O, if thou really art my *Senior*, Seigneur, my *Elder*, Presbyter or Priest,—if thou art in very deed my *Wiser*, may a beneficent instinct lead and impel thee to "conquer" me, to command me! If thou do know better than I what is good and right, I conjure[9] thee in the name of God, force me to do it; were it by never such brass collars, whips and handcuffs, leave me not to walk over precipices! That I have been called, by all the Newspapers, a "free man" will avail me little, if my pilgrimage have ended in death and wreck. O that the Newspapers had called me slave, coward, fool, or what it pleased their sweet voices to name me, and I had attained not death, but life!—Liberty requires new definitions.

A conscious abhorrence and intolerance of Folly, of Baseness, Stupidity, Poltroonery and all that brood of things, dwells deep in some men: still deeper in others an *un*conscious abhorrence and intolerance, clothed moreover by the beneficent Supreme Powers in what stout appetites, energies, egoisms so-called, are suitable to it;—these latter are your Conquerors, Romans, Normans, Russians, Indo-English; Founders of what we call Aristocracies. Which indeed have they not the most "divine right" to found;—being themselves very truly *Aristoi*, Bravest, Best; and conquering generally a confused rabble of Worst, or at lowest, clearly enough, of Worse? I think their divine right, tried, with affirmatory verdict, in the greatest Law-Court known to me, was good! A class of men who are dreadfully exclaimed against by Dryasdust; of whom nevertheless beneficent Nature has oftentimes had need; and may, alas, again have need.

When, across the hundredfold poor scepticisms, trivialisms, and constitutional cobwebberies of Dryasdust, you catch any glimpse of a William the Conqueror, a Tancred of Hauteville[1] or such like,—do you not discern veritably some rude outline of a true God-made King; whom not the Champion of England[2] cased in tin, but all Nature and the Universe were calling to the throne? It is absolutely necessary that he get thither. Nature does not mean her poor Saxon children to perish, of obesity, stupor or other malady, as yet: a stern Ruler and Line of Rulers therefore is called in,—a stern but most beneficent *perpetual House-Surgeon* is by Nature herself called in, and even the appropriate *fees* are provided for him! Dryasdust talks lamentably about Hereward and the Fen Counties; fate of earl Waltheof;[3] Yorkshire and

9. Solemnly charge.
1. Norman hero of the First Crusade (1095–99). King William I of England (ca. 1028–1087; reigned 1066–87), surnamed *the Conqueror* after the Battle of Hastings in 1066. Being an illegitimate son, he also bore the surname of William the Bastard. Although some historians condemn William as a ruthless ruler, he is ranked by Carlyle as a hero because of his strong and efficient government. William fulfilled the requirements of the kingly hero described by Carlyle in his lectures *On Heroes*: a man fittest "to *command* over

us . . . to tell us what we are to *do*."
2. An official who goes through a formality, at coronation ceremonies, of demanding whether anyone challenges the right of the monarch to ascend the throne. He wears full armor ("cased in tin") and is a symbol of outworn feudal customs.
3. His execution in 1075, on a supposedly trumped-up charge, is cited as a blot on William's record as king. Hereward the Wake was an outlaw whose exploits against William the Conqueror made him seem a romantic figure like Robin Hood.

the North reduced to ashes; all of which is undoubtedly lamentable. But even Dryasdust apprises me of one fact: "A child, in this William's reign, might have carried a purse of gold from end to end of England." My erudite friend, it is a fact which outweighs a thousand! Sweep away thy constitutional, sentimental, and other cobwebberies; look eye to eye, if thou still have any eye, in the face of this big burly William Bastard: thou wilt see a fellow of most flashing discernment, of most strong lion-heart;—in whom, as it were, within a frame of oak and iron, the gods have planted the soul of "a man of genius"! Dost thou call that nothing? I call it an immense thing!—Rage enough was in this Willelmus Conquaestor, rage enough for his occasions;—and yet the essential element of him, as of all such men, is not scorching *fire*, but shining illuminative *light*. Fire and light are strangely interchangeable; nay, at bottom, I have found them different forms of the same most godlike "elementary substance" in our world: a thing worth stating in these days. The essential element of this Conquaestor is, first of all, the most sun-eyed perception of what *is* really what on this God's-Earth;—which, thou wilt find, does mean at bottom "Justice," and "Virtues" not a few: *Conformity* to what the Maker has seen good to make; that, I suppose, will mean Justice and a Virtue or two?—

Dost thou think Willelmus Conquaestor would have tolerated ten years' jargon, one hour's jargon, on the propriety of killing Cotton-manufactures by partridge Corn-Laws?[4] I fancy, this was not the man to knock out of his night's-rest with nothing but a noisy bedlamism in your mouth![5] "Assist us still better to bush the partridges; strangle Plugson who spins the shirts?"— *"Par la Splendeur de Dieu!"*[6]—Dost thou think Willelmus Conquaestor, in this new time, with Steam-engine Captains of Industry on one hand of him, and Joe-Manton Captains of Idleness[7] on the other, would have doubted which *was* really the BEST; which did deserve strangling, and which not?

I have a certain indestructible regard for Willelmus Conquaestor. A resident House-Surgeon, provided by Nature for her beloved English People, and even furnished with the requisite fees, as I said; for he by no means felt himself doing Nature's work, this Willelmus, but his own work exclusively! And his own work withal it was; informed *"par la Splendeur de Dieu."*—I say, it is necessary to get the work out of such a man, however harsh that be! When a world, not yet doomed for death, is rushing down to ever-deeper Baseness and Confusion, it is a dire necessity of Nature's to bring in her ARISTOCRACIES, her BEST, even by forcible methods. When their descendants or representatives cease entirely to *be* the Best, Nature's poor world will very soon rush down again to Baseness; and it becomes a dire necessity of Nature's to cast them out. Hence French Revolutions, Five-point Charters,[8] Democracies, and a mournful list of *Etceteras*, in these our afflicted times.

* * *

4. See p. 53, notes 1–2 to this selection.
5. I.e., not the man to disturb with your mad ravings. Bedlam, the hospital of St. Mary in Bethlehem, was London's most famous lunatic asylum.
6. By the splendor of God! (French): one of William's oaths. Plugson of Undershot was Carlyle's fictive representative of the new class of industrial leaders. This imaginary speech ("Assist us . . .") sums up the pleas of the High Tariff lobby in Parliament. "Keep the Corn Laws intact

so that the aristocratic landlords may continue to enjoy shooting partridges on their estates; subdue the manufacturing leaders by preventing trade."
7. The idle aristocracy who wasted time shooting partridges with guns made by Joseph Manton, a London gunsmith.
8. The Chartist movement for political reform called first for six, then for five major changes to the existing system of parliamentary democracy.

Democracy, the chase of Liberty in that direction, shall go its full course; unrestrained by him of Pferdefuss-Quacksalber,[9] or any of *his* household. The Toiling Millions of Mankind, in most vital need and passionate instinctive desire of Guidance, shall cast away False-Guidance; and hope, for an hour, that No-Guidance will suffice them: but it can be for an hour only. The smallest item of human Slavery is the oppression of man by his Mock-Superiors; the palpablest, but I say at bottom the smallest. Let him shake off such oppression, trample it indignantly under his feet; I blame him not, I pity and commend him. But oppression by your Mock-Superiors well shaken off, the grand problem yet remains to solve: That of finding government by your Real-Superiors! Alas, how shall we ever learn the solution of that, benighted, bewildered, sniffing, sneering, godforgetting unfortunates as we are? It is a work for centuries; to be taught us by tribulations, confusions, insurrections, obstructions; who knows if not by conflagration and despair! It is a lesson inclusive of all other lessons; the hardest of all lessons to learn.

Captains of Industry[1]

If I believed that Mammonism with its adjuncts was to continue henceforth the one serious principle of our existence, I should reckon it idle to solicit remedial measures from any Government, the disease being insusceptible of remedy. Government can do much, but it can in no wise do all. Government, as the most conspicuous object in Society, is called upon to give signal of what shall be done; and, in many ways, to preside over further, and command the doing of it. But the Government cannot do, by all its signalling and commanding, what the Society is radically indisposed to do. In the long-run every Government is the exact symbol of its People, with their wisdom and unwisdom; we have to say, Like People like Government.—The main substance of this immense Problem of Organizing Labour, and first of all of Managing the Working Classes, will, it is very clear, have to be solved by those who stand practically in the middle of it; by those who themselves work and preside over work. Of all that can be enacted by any Parliament in regard to it, the germs must already lie potentially extant in those two Classes, who are to obey such enactment. A Human Chaos *in* which there is no light, you vainly attempt to irradiate by light shed *on* it: order never can arise there.

But it is my firm conviction that the "Hell of England" will *cease* to be that of "not making money"; that we shall get a nobler Hell and a nobler Heaven! I anticipate light *in* the Human Chaos, glimmering, shining more and more; under manifold true signals from without That light shall shine. Our deity no longer being Mammon,—O Heavens, each man will then say to himself: "Why such deadly haste to make money? I shall not go to Hell, even if I do not make money! There is another Hell, I am told!" Competition, at railway-speed, in all branches of commerce and work will then abate:—good felt-hats for the head, in every sense, instead of seven-feet lath-and-plaster hats on wheels,[2] will then be discoverable! Bubble-periods,[3] with their panics and commercial crises, will again become infrequent; steady modest industry will take the place of gambling speculation. To be a noble Master, among

9. Horse foot quack doctor (a fake German name invented by Carlyle).
1. From book 4, chap. 4.

2. A London hatter's mode of advertising.
3. Periods of violent fluctuation in the stock market caused by unsound speculating.

noble Workers, will again be the first ambition with some few; to be a rich Master only the second. How the Inventive Genius of England, with the whirr of its bobbins and billy-rollers[4] shoved somewhat into the backgrounds of the brain, will contrive and devise, not cheaper produce exclusively, but fairer distribution of the produce at its present cheapness! By degrees, we shall again have a Society with something of Heroism in it, something of Heaven's Blessing on it; we shall again have, as my German friend[5] asserts, "instead of Mammon-Feudalism with unsold cotton-shirts and Preservation of the Game, noble just Industrialism and Government by the Wisest!"

It is with the hope of awakening here and there a British man to know himself for a man and divine soul, that a few words of parting admonition, to all persons to whom the Heavenly Powers have lent power of any kind in this land, may now be addressed. And first to those same Master-Workers, Leaders of Industry; who stand nearest, and in fact powerfullest, though not most prominent, being as yet in too many senses a Virtuality rather than an Actuality.

The Leaders of Industry, if Industry is ever to be led, are virtually the Captains of the World; if there be no nobleness in them, there will never be an Aristocracy more. But let the Captains of Industry consider: once again, are they born of other clay than the old Captains of Slaughter; doomed for ever to be not Chivalry, but a mere gold-plated *Doggery,*—what the French well name *Canaille,* "Doggery" with more or less gold carrion at its disposal? Captains of Industry are the true Fighters, henceforth recognizable as the only true ones: Fighters against Chaos, Necessity and the Devils and Jötuns;[6] and lead on Mankind in that great, and alone true, and universal warfare; the stars in their courses fighting for them, and all Heaven and all Earth saying audibly, Well done! Let the Captains of Industry retire into their own hearts, and ask solemnly, If there is nothing but vulturous hunger for fine wines, valet reputation and gilt carriages, discoverable there? Of hearts made by the Almighty God I will not believe such a thing. Deep-hidden under wretchedest god-forgetting Cants, Epicurisms, Dead-Sea Apisms;[7] forgotten as under foullest fat Lethe[8] mud and weeds, there is yet, in all hearts born into this God's-World, a spark of the Godlike slumbering. Awake, O nightmare sleepers; awake, arise, or be for ever fallen![9] This is not playhouse poetry; it is sober fact. Our England, our world cannot live as it is. It will connect itself with a God again, or go down with nameless throes and fire-consummation to the Devils. Thou who feelest aught of such a Godlike stirring in thee, any faintest intimation of it as through heavy-laden dreams, follow *it,* I conjure thee. Arise, save thyself, be one of those that save thy country.

Bucaniers,[1] Chactaw Indians, whose supreme aim in fighting is that they may get the scalps, the money, that they may amass scalps and money; out of such came no Chivalry, and never will! Out of such came only gore and

---

4. Machines used to prepare cotton or wool for spinning.
5. Teufelsdröckh, the hero of *Sartor Resartus* (1833–34).
6. Giants of Scandinavian mythology.
7. A reference to a Muslim story in which members of a tribe living near the Dead Sea were transformed into apes because they had ignored the prophecies of Moses.
8. The river of forgetfulness in the classical underworld.
9. Satan's appeal to the devils in Milton's *Paradise Lost* 1.330.
1. Buccaneers.

wreck, infernal rage and misery; desperation quenched in annihilation. Behold it, I bid thee, behold there, and consider! What is it that thou have a hundred thousand-pound bills laid up in thy strong-room, a hundred scalps hung up in thy wigwam? I value not them or thee. Thy scalps and thy thousand-pound bills are as yet nothing, if no nobleness from within irradiate them; if no Chivalry, in action, or in embryo ever struggling towards birth and action, be there.

Love of men cannot be bought by cash-payment; and without love, men cannot endure to be together. You cannot lead a Fighting World without having it regimented, chivalried: the thing, in a day, becomes impossible; all men in it, the highest at first, the very lowest at last, discern consciously, or by a noble instinct, this necessity. And can you any more continue to lead a Working World unregimented, anarchic? I answer, and the Heavens and Earth are now answering, No! The thing becomes not "in a day" impossible; but in some two generations it does. Yes, when fathers and mothers, in Stockport hunger-cellars, begin to eat their children, and Irish widows have to prove their relationship by dying of typhus-fever; and amid Governing "Corporations of the Best and Bravest," busy to preserve their game by "bushing," dark millions of God's human creatures start up in mad Chartisms, impracticable Sacred-Months, and Manchester Insurrections;[2]—and there is a virtual Industrial Aristocracy as yet only half-alive, spell-bound amid money-bags and ledgers; and an actual Idle Aristocracy seemingly near dead in somnolent delusions, in trespasses and double-barrels,[3] "sliding," as on inclined-planes, which every new year they *soap* with new Hansard's-jargon under God's sky, and so are "sliding" ever faster, towards a "scale"[4] and balance-scale whereon is written *Thou art found Wanting;*[5]—in such days, after a generation or two, I say, it does become, even to the low and simple, very palpably impossible! No Working World, any more than a Fighting World, can be led on without a noble Chivalry of Work, and laws and fixed rules which follow out of that,—far nobler than any Chivalry of Fighting was. As an anarchic multitude on mere Supply-and-demand, it is becoming inevitable that we dwindle in horrid suicidal convulsion, and self-abrasion, frightful to the imagination, into *Chactaw* Workers. With wigwams and scalps,—with palaces and thousand-pound bills; with savagery, depopulation, chaotic desolation! Good Heavens, will not one French Revolution and Reign of Terror suffice us, but must there be two? There will be two if needed; there will be twenty if needed; there will be precisely as many as needed. The Laws of Nature will have themselves fulfilled. That is a thing certain to me.

Your gallant battle-hosts and work-hosts, as the others did, will need to be made loyally yours; they must and will be regulated, methodically secured in their just share of conquest under you;—joined with you in veritable brotherhood, sonhood, by quite other and deeper ties than those of temporary day's wages! How would mere redcoated regiments, to say nothing of chival-

2. In 1819 a large open-air labor meeting in Manchester was broken up by charging cavalry. Thirteen men and women were massacred, and many others were wounded. "Bushing": protecting game from poachers who use nets, by positioning bushes or branches on the grounds.
3. I.e., the only concern of the landed aristocrats is to keep trespassers off their game preserves

and reserve shooting rights to themselves.
4. The "sliding scale" refers to the system of variable tariffs within the Corn Laws that benefited the aristocratic landlords. "Hansard's-jargon": parliamentary oratory, as in Hansard's printed record of debates in the Houses of Parliament.
5. The message of the miraculous writing on the wall in Daniel 5.

ries, fight for you, if you could discharge them on the evening of the battle, on payment of the stipulated shillings,—and they discharge you on the morning of it! Chelsea Hospitals,[6] pensions, promotions, rigorous lasting covenant on the one side and on the other, are indispensable even for a hired fighter. The Feudal Baron, much more,—how could he subsist with mere temporary mercenaries round him, at sixpence a day; ready to go over to the other side, if sevenpence were offered? He could not have subsisted;—and his noble instinct saved him from the necessity of even trying! The Feudal Baron had a Man's Soul in him; to which anarchy, mutiny, and the other fruits of temporary mercenaries, were intolerable: he had never been a Baron otherwise, but had continued a Chactaw and Bucanier. He felt it precious, and at last it became habitual, and his fruitful enlarged existence included it as a necessity, to have men round him who in heart loved him; whose life he watched over with rigour yet with love; who were prepared to give their life for him, if need came. It was beautiful; it was human! Man lives not otherwise, nor can live contented, anywhere or anywhen. Isolation is the sum-total of wretchedness to man. To be cut off, to be left solitary: to have a world alien, not your world; all a hostile camp for you; not a home at all, of hearts and faces who are yours, whose you are! It is the frightfullest enchantment; too truly a work of the Evil One. To have neither superior, nor inferior, nor equal, united manlike to you. Without father, without child, without brother. Man knows no sadder destiny. "How is each of us," exclaims Jean Paul,[7] "so lonely in the wide bosom of the All!" Encased each as in his transparent "ice-palace"; our brother visible in his, making signals and gesticulations to us;—visible, but for ever unattainable: on his bosom we shall never rest, nor he on ours. It was not a God that did this; no!

Awake, ye noble Workers, warriors in the one true war: all this must be remedied. It is you who are already half-alive, whom I will welcome into life; whom I will conjure in God's name to shake off your enchanted sleep, and live wholly! Cease to count scalps, goldpurses; not in these lies your or our salvation. Even these, if you count only these, will not be left. Let bucaniering be put far from you; alter, speedily abrogate all laws of the bucaniers, if you would gain any victory that shall endure. Let God's justice, let pity, nobleness and manly valour, with more gold-purses or with fewer, testify themselves in this your brief Life-transit to all the Eternities, the Gods and Silences. It is to you I call; for ye are not dead, ye are already half-alive: there is in you a sleepless dauntless energy, the prime-matter of all nobleness in man. Honour to you in your kind. It is to you I call: ye know at least this, That the mandate of God to His creature man is: Work! The future Epic of the World rests not with those that are near dead, but with those that are alive, and those that are coming into life.

Look around you. Your world-hosts are all in mutiny, in confusion, destitution; on the eve of fiery wreck and madness! They will not march farther for you, on the sixpence a day and supply-and-demand principle; they will not; nor ought they, nor can they. Ye shall reduce them to order, begin reducing them. To order, to just subordination; noble loyalty in return for noble guidance. Their souls are driven nigh mad; let yours be sane and ever saner.

6. Homes for disabled veterans.
7. Jean Paul Richter (1763–1825), German humorist.

Not as a bewildered bewildering mob; but as a firm regimented mass, with real captains over them, will these men march any more. All human interests, combined human endeavours, and social growths in this world, have, at a certain stage of their development, required organizing: and Work, the grandest of human interests, does now require it.

God knows, the task will be hard: but no noble task was ever easy. This task will wear away your lives, and the lives of your sons and grandsons: but for what purpose, if not for tasks like this, were lives given to men? Ye shall cease to count your thousand-pound scalps, the noble of you shall cease! Nay, the very scalps, as I say, will not long be left if you count on these. Ye shall cease wholly to be barbarous vulturous Chactaws, and become noble European Nineteenth-Century Men. Ye shall know that Mammon, in never such gigs[8] and flunkey "respectabilities," is not the alone God; that of himself he is but a Devil, and even a Brute-god.

Difficult? Yes, it will be difficult. The short-fibre cotton; that too was difficult. The waste cotton-shrub, long useless, disobedient, as the thistle by the wayside,—have ye not conquered it; made it into beautiful bandana webs; white woven shirts for men; bright-tinted air-garments wherein flit goddesses? Ye have shivered mountains asunder, made the hard iron pliant to you as soft putty: the Forest-giants, Marsh-jötuns bear sheaves of golden grain; Aegir the Seademon[9] himself stretches his back for a sleek highway to you, and on Fire-horses and Windhorses ye career. Ye are most strong. Thor red-bearded, with his blue sun-eyes, with his cheery heart and strong thunder-hammer, he and you have prevailed. Ye are most strong, ye Sons of the icy North, of the far East,—far marching from your rugged Eastern Wildernesses, hitherward from the grey Dawn of Time! Ye are Sons of the *Jötun-land*; the land of Difficulties Conquered. Difficult? You must try this thing. Once try it with the understanding that it will and shall have to be done. Try it as ye try the paltrier thing, making of money! I will bet on you once more, against all Jötuns, Tailor-gods,[1] Double-barrelled Law-wards, and Denizens of Chaos whatsoever.

1843   1843

8. Light carriages; to own one was a sign of respectability.

9. From Scandinavian mythology.
1. False gods.

JOHN HENRY CARDINAL NEWMAN
1801–1890

Like Thomas Carlyle, John Henry Newman powerfully affected the thinking of his contemporaries, whether they agreed or disagreed with him. According to Martin Svaglic, Newman has long attracted both "apotheosizers" and "calumniators" who praise or blame him "as an unusually compelling spokesman for what some consider eternal verities and others regressive myths." During his long lifetime Newman frequently found himself at the center of some of the most intense disputes that stirred Victorian England, disputes in which he himself emerged as a controversialist of great skill—engagingly persuasive in defense of his position and devastatingly effective in disposing of opponents. Thomas Hardy, whose position was at the opposite extreme from Newman's, paid him a high compliment when he noted in his diary: "Worked at J. H. Newman's *Apologia* which we have all been talking about lately. . . . Style charming and his logic really human, being based not on syllogisms but on converging probabilities. Only—and here comes the fatal catastrophe—there is no first link to his excellent chain of reasoning, and down you come headlong."

Newman was born in London, the son (like Robert Browning) of a banker. In his spiritual autobiography, *Apologia Pro Vita Sua* (in effect, his vindication of his life, 1864–65), he traces the principal stages of his religious development from the strongly Protestant period of his youth to his conversion to Roman Catholicism in 1845. Along the way, after being elected to a fellowship at Oriel College in Oxford and becoming an Anglican clergyman, he was attracted briefly into the orbit of religious liberalism. Gradually coming to realize, however, that liberalism, with its reliance on human reason, would be powerless to defend traditional religion from attack, Newman shifted over into the new High Church wing of the Anglican Church. He soon was recognized as the leading figure of what was known as the Oxford movement, which pressed for the reinstatement of some older Christian traditions within church practices. During the 1830s he built up a large and influential following by his sermons at Oxford and also by his writing of tracts—that is, appeals, in pamphlet form, on behalf of a cause. In these publications he developed arguments about the powers of church versus state and other issues of deep concern to his High Church colleagues—or Tractarians, as they were also called. Newman's own efforts to demonstrate the true catholicity of the Church of England provoked increasing opposition as his position grew closer to Roman Catholicism. Distressed by constant denunciations, he withdrew into isolation and silence. After much reflection he took the final step. At the age of forty-four he entered the Roman Catholic priesthood and moved to Birmingham, where he spent the rest of his life. In 1879 he was created cardinal. In 1991, at the instigation of Pope John Paul II, his title became The Venerable John Henry Cardinal Newman, marking the first of three stages toward sainthood.

In view of this development, Newman's response to a woman who had spoken of him as a saint is touching. In some distress he wrote to her: "Saints are not literary men, they do not love the classics, they do not write Tales."

Although the story of Newman's development seems to emphasize change, certain features remain constant. His sense of God's guidance is especially evident. Characteristic is a poem written in Italy in 1834, following a severe illness, which opens with the line "Lead, kindly light" and concludes with this stanza:

> So long Thy power hath blest me, sure it still
> > Will lead me on,
> O'er moor and fen, o'er crag and torrent, till
> > The night is gone;
> And with the morn those angel faces smile
> Which I have loved long since, and lost awhile.

Set to music, Newman's poem became one of the most popular hymns ever written.

The writing of verse, however, was a subordinate task for Newman; most of his writings are prose, and it is noteworthy that despite his mastery of prose style, Newman found the act of composition to be even more painfully difficult than most of us do. During his years at Birmingham, he was nevertheless prompted to write several books, including works of religious poetry and fiction. Of particular interest are Newman's lectures on the aims of education, which were delivered in Dublin at the newly founded Catholic University of Ireland, a university he led for a few years as rector. These lectures, published in 1852 and later titled *The Idea of a University,* are a classic statement of the value of "the disciplined intellect" that can be developed by a liberal education rather than by a technical training. Like the later lectures of Matthew Arnold and T. H. Huxley, *The Idea of a University* shows the Victorian engagement with the role of education in society. Moreover, its exploration of the qualities of the ideal gentleman (see the excerpt from *Discourse* 8 below) also speaks to a concern of his time: this classic definition is essential reading for those interested in debates about Victorian gender roles.

It should be noted that Newman's view of a liberal education is largely independent of his religious position. Such an education, he said, could form the minds of profligates and anticlericals as well as of saints and priests of the Church. In considerable measure, his view reflects his admiration for the kind of intellectual enlargement he had himself enjoyed as an undergraduate at Trinity College, Oxford. One of the most moving passages in Newman's autobiography is the account of his farewell to an Oxford friend, in February 1846, as he was preparing his final departure from the precincts of the university he loved:

> In him I took leave of my first College, Trinity, which was so dear to me. . . . There used to be much snapdragon growing on the walls opposite my freshman's rooms there, and I had taken it as the emblem of my perpetual residence even unto death in my University.
>
> On the morning of the 23rd I left the Observatory. I have never seen Oxford since, excepting its spires, as they are seen from the railway.

From The Idea of a University

From *Discourse 5. Knowledge Its Own End*

6

Now bear with me, Gentlemen, if what I am about to say has at first sight a fanciful appearance. Philosophy, then, or Science, is related to Knowledge in this way: Knowledge is called by the name of Science or Philosophy, when it is acted upon, informed, or if I may use a strong figure, impregnated by Reason. Reason is the principle of that intrinsic fecundity of Knowledge, which, to those who possess it, is its especial value, and which dispenses with the necessity of their looking abroad for any end to rest upon external to itself. Knowledge, indeed, when thus exalted into a scientific form, is also power; not only is it excellent in itself, but whatever such excellence may be, it is something more, it has a result beyond itself. Doubtless; but that is a further consideration, with which I am not concerned. I only say that, prior to its being a power, it is a good; that it is, not only an instrument, but an end. I know well it may resolve itself into an art, and terminate in a mechanical process, and in tangible fruit; but it also may fall back upon that Reason which informs it, and resolve itself into Philosophy. In one case it is called Useful Knowledge, in the other Liberal. The same person may cultivate it in both ways at once; but this again is a matter foreign to my subject; here I do but say that there are two ways of using Knowledge, and in matter of fact those who use it in one way are not likely to use it in the other, or at least in a very limited measure. You see, then, here are two methods of Education; the end of the one is to be philosophical, of the other to be mechanical; the one rises towards general ideas, the other is exhausted upon what is particular and external. Let me not be thought to deny the necessity, or to decry the benefit, of such attention to what is particular and practical, as belongs to the useful or mechanical arts; life could not go on without them; we owe our daily welfare to them; their exercise is the duty of the many, and we owe to the many a debt of gratitude for fulfilling that duty. I only say that Knowledge, in proportion as it tends more and more to be particular, ceases to be Knowledge. It is a question whether Knowledge can in any proper sense be predicated of the brute creation; without pretending to metaphysical exactness of phraseology, which would be unsuitable to an occasion like this, I say, it seems to me improper to call that passive sensation, or perception of things, which brutes seem to possess, by the name of Knowledge. When I speak of Knowledge, I mean something intellectual, something which grasps what it perceives through the senses; something which takes a view of things; which sees more than the senses convey; which reasons upon what it sees, and while it sees; which invests it with an idea. It expresses itself, not in a mere enunciation, but by an enthymeme:[1] it is of the nature of science from the first, and in this consists its dignity. The principle of real dignity in Knowledge, its worth, its desirableness, considered irrespectively of its results, is this germ within it of a scientific or a philosophical process. This is how it comes to be an end in itself; this is why it admits of being called Liberal. Not to know the relative disposition of things is the state of slaves or children; to have mapped out the Universe is the boast, or at least the ambition, of Philosophy.

Moreover, such knowledge is not a mere extrinsic or accidental advantage, which is ours today and another's tomorrow, which may be got up from a book, and easily forgotten again, which we can command or communicate at our pleasure, which we can borrow for the occasion, carry about in our hand, and take into the market; it is an acquired illumination, it is a habit, a personal possession, and an inward endowment. And this is the reason why it is more correct, as well as more usual, to speak of a University as a place of education than of instruction, though, when knowledge is concerned, instruction would at first sight have seemed the more appropriate word. We are instructed, for instance, in manual exercises, in the fine and useful arts, in trades, and in ways of business; for these are methods, which have little or no effect upon the mind itself, are contained in rules committed to memory, to tradition, or to use, and bear upon an end external to themselves. But education is a higher word; it implies an action upon our mental nature, and the formation of a character; it is something individual and permanent, and is commonly spoken of in connection with religion and virtue. When, then, we speak of the communication of Knowledge as being Education, we thereby really imply that that Knowledge is a state or condition of mind; and since cultivation of mind is surely worth seeking for its own sake, we are thus brought once more to the conclusion, which the word "Liberal" and the word "Philosophy" have already suggested, that there is a Knowledge, which is desirable, though nothing come of it, as being of itself a treasure, and a sufficient remuneration of years of labor.

---

1. A syllogism in which one of the premises is understood but not stated.

From *Discourse 7. Knowledge Viewed in Relation
to Professional Skill*

1

I have been insisting, in my two preceding Discourses,[2] first, on the cultivation of the intellect, as an end which may reasonably be pursued for its own sake; and next, on the nature of that cultivation, or what that cultivation consists in. Truth of whatever kind is the proper object of the intellect; its cultivation then lies in fitting it to apprehend and contemplate truth. Now the intellect in its present state, with exceptions which need not here be specified, does not discern truth intuitively, or as a whole. We know, not by a direct and simple vision, not at a glance, but, as it were, by piecemeal and accumulation, by a mental process, by going round an object, by the comparison, the combination, the mutual correction, the continual adaptation, of many partial notions, by the employment, concentration, and joint action of many faculties and exercises of mind. Such a union and concert of the intellectual powers, such an enlargement and development, such a comprehensiveness, is necessarily a matter of training. And again, such a training is a matter of rule; it is not mere application, however exemplary, which introduces the mind to truth, nor the reading many books, nor the getting up[3] many subjects, nor the witnessing many experiments, nor the attending many lectures. All this is short of enough; a man may have done it all, yet be lingering in the vestibule of knowledge: he may not realize what his mouth utters; he may not see with his mental eye what confronts him; he may have no grasp of things as they are; or at least he may have no power at all of advancing one step forward of himself, in consequence of what he has already acquired, no power of discriminating between truth and falsehood, of sifting out the grains of truth from the mass, of arranging things according to their real value, and, if I may use the phrase, of building up ideas. Such a power is the result of a scientific formation of mind; it is an acquired faculty of judgment, of clearsightedness, of sagacity, of wisdom, of philosophical reach of mind, and of intellectual self-possession and repose—qualities which do not come of mere acquirement. The bodily eye, the organ for apprehending material objects, is provided by nature; the eye of the mind, of which the object is truth, is the work of discipline and habit.

This process of training, by which the intellect, instead of being formed or sacrificed to some particular or accidental purpose, some specific trade or profession, or study or science, is disciplined for its own sake, for the perception of its own proper object, and for its own highest culture, is called Liberal Education; and though there is no one in whom it is carried as far as is conceivable, or whose intellect would be a pattern of what intellects should be made, yet there is scarcely anyone but may gain an idea of what real training is, and at least look towards it, and make its true scope and result, not something else, his standard of excellence; and numbers there are who may submit themselves to it, and secure it to themselves in good measure. And to set forth the right standard, and to train according to it, and to help forward all students toward it according to their various capacities, this I conceive to be the business of a University.

2. Discourse 6 (not included here) is titled "Knowledge Viewed in Relation to Learning."
3. Studying.

2

Now this is what some great men are very slow to allow; they insist that Education should be confined to some particular and narrow end, and should issue in some definite work, which can be weighed and measured. They argue as if every thing, as well as every person, had its price; and that where there has been a great outlay, they have a right to expect a return in kind. This they call making Education and Instruction "useful," and "Utility" becomes their watchword. With a fundamental principle of this nature, they very naturally go on to ask what there is to show for the expense of a University; what is the real worth in the market of the article called "a Liberal Education," on the supposition that it does not teach us definitely how to advance our manufactures, or to improve our lands, or to better our civil economy; or again, if it does not at once make this man a lawyer, that an engineer, and that a surgeon; or at least if it does not lead to discoveries in chemistry, astronomy, geology, magnetism, and science of every kind.

* * *

5

* * *

This is the obvious answer which may be made to those who urge upon us the claims of Utility in our plans of Education;[4] but I am not going to leave the subject here: I mean to take a wider view of it. Let us take "useful," as Locke[5] takes it, in its proper and popular sense, and then we enter upon a large field of thought, to which I cannot do justice in one Discourse, though today's is all the space that I can give to it. I say, let us take "useful" to mean, not what is simply good, but what *tends* to good, or is the *instrument* of good; and in this sense also, Gentlemen, I will show you how a liberal education is truly and fully a useful, though it be not a professional, education. "Good" indeed means one thing, and "useful" means another; but I lay it down as a principle, which will save us a great deal of anxiety, that, though the useful is not always good, the good is always useful. Good is not only good, but reproductive of good; this is one of its attributes; nothing is excellent, beautiful, perfect, desirable for its own sake, but it overflows, and spreads the likeness of itself all around it. Good is prolific; it is not only good to the eye, but to the taste; it not only attracts us, but it communicates itself; it excites first our admiration and love, then our desire and our gratitude, and that, in proportion to its intenseness and fullness in particular instances. A great good will impart great good. If then the intellect is so excellent a portion of us, and its cultivation so excellent, it is not only beautiful, perfect, admirable, and noble in itself, but in a true and high sense it must be useful to the possessor and to all around him; not useful in any low, mechanical, mercantile sense, but as diffusing good, or as a blessing, or a gift, or power, or a treasure, first to the owner, then through him to the world. I say then, if a liberal education be good, it must necessarily be useful too.

good = useful

4. The Utilitarians argued that a useful education would be one that trained the mind in the "habit of pushing things up to their first principles." Newman had earlier pointed out that a liberal education does exactly that and is hence useful.
5. John Locke (1632–1704), whose treatise *Some Thoughts Concerning Education* (1693) advocated a utilitarian concept of education.

6

You will see what I mean by the parallel of bodily health. Health is a good in itself, though nothing came of it, and is especially worth seeking and cherishing; yet, after all, the blessings which attend its presence are so great, while they are so close to it and so redound back upon it and encircle it, that we never think of it except as useful as well as good, and praise and prize it for what it does, as well as for what it is, though at the same time we cannot point out any definite and distinct work or production which it can be said to effect. And so as regards intellectual culture, I am far from denying utility in this large sense as the end of Education, when I lay it down that the culture of the intellect is a good in itself and its own end; I do not exclude from the idea of intellectual culture what it cannot but be, from the very nature of things; I only deny that we must be able to point out, before we have any right to call it useful, some art, or business, or profession, or trade, or work, as resulting from it, and as its real and complete end. The parallel is exact: As the body may be sacrificed to some manual or other toil, whether moderate or oppressive, so may the intellect be devoted to some specific profession; and I do not call *this* the culture of the intellect. Again, as some member or organ of the body may be inordinately used and developed, so may memory, or imagination, or the reasoning faculty; and *this* again is not intellectual culture. On the other hand, as the body may be tended, cherished, and exercised with a simple view to its general health, so may the intellect also be generally exercised in order to its perfect state; and this *is* its cultivation.

Again, as health ought to precede labor of the body, and as a man in health can do what an unhealthy man cannot do, and as of this health the properties are strength, energy, agility, graceful carriage and action, manual dexterity, and endurance of fatigue, so in like manner general culture of mind is the best aid to professional and scientific study, and educated men can do what illiterate cannot; and the man who has learned to think and to reason and to compare and to discriminate and to analyze, who has refined his taste, and formed his judgment, and sharpened his mental vision, will not indeed at once be a lawyer, or a pleader, or an orator, or a statesman, or a physician, or a good landlord, or a man of business, or a soldier, or an engineer, or a chemist, or a geologist, or an antiquarian, but he will be placed in that state of intellect in which he can take up any one of the sciences or callings I have referred to, or any other for which he has a taste or special talent, with an ease, a grace, a versatility, and a success, to which another is a stranger. In this sense then, and as yet I have said but a very few words on a large subject, mental culture is emphatically *useful*.

If then I am arguing, and shall argue, against Professional or Scientific knowledge as the sufficient end of a University Education, let me not be supposed, Gentlemen, to be disrespectful towards particular studies, or arts, or vocations, and those who are engaged in them. In saying that Law or Medicine is not the end of a University course, I do not mean to imply that the University does not teach Law or Medicine. What indeed can it teach at all, if it does not teach something particular? It teaches *all* knowledge by teaching all *branches* of knowledge, and in no other way. I do but say that there will be this distinction as regards a Professor of Law, or of Medicine, or of Geology, or of Political Economy, in a University and out of it, that out of a

University he is in danger of being absorbed and narrowed by his pursuit, and of giving Lectures which are the Lectures of nothing more than a lawyer, physician, geologist, or political economist; whereas in a University he will just know where he and his science stand, he has come to it, as it were, from a height, he has taken a survey of all knowledge, he is kept from extravagance by the very rivalry of other studies, he has gained from them a special illumination and largeness of mind and freedom and self-possession, and he treats his own in consequence with a philosophy and a resource, which belongs not to the study itself, but to his liberal education.

This then is how I should solve the fallacy, for so I must call it, by which Locke and his disciples would frighten us from cultivating the intellect, under the notion that no education is useful which does not teach us some temporal calling, or some mechanical art, or some physical secret. I say that a cultivated intellect, because it is a good in itself, brings with it a power and a grace to every work and occupation which it undertakes, and enables us to be more useful, and to a greater number. There is a duty we owe to human society as such, to the state to which we belong, to the sphere in which we move, to the individuals towards whom we are variously related, and whom we successively encounter in life; and that philosophical or liberal education, as I have called it, which is the proper function of a University, if it refuses the foremost place to professional interest, does but postpone them to the formation of the citizen, and, while it subserves the larger interests of philanthropy, prepares also for the successful prosecution of those merely personal objects which at first sight it seems to disparage.

* * *

10

But I must bring these extracts[6] to an end. Today I have confined myself to saying that that training of the intellect, which is best for the individual himself, best enables him to discharge his duties to society. The Philosopher, indeed, and the man of the world differ in their very notion, but the methods, by which they are respectively formed, are pretty much the same. The Philosopher has the same command of matters of thought, which the true citizen and gentleman has of matters of business and conduct. If then a practical end must be assigned to a University course, I say it is that of training good members of society. Its art is the art of social life, and its end is fitness for the world. It neither confines its views to particular professions on the one hand, nor creates heroes or inspires genius on the other. Works indeed of genius fall under no art; heroic minds come under no rule; a University is not a birthplace of poets or of immortal authors, of founders of schools, leaders of colonies, or conquerors of nations. It does not promise a generation of Aristotles or Newtons, of Napoleons or Washingtons, or Raphaels or Shakespeares,[7] though such miracles of nature it has before now contained within its precincts. Nor is it content on the other hand with

6. Quotations cited from other authorities on education.
7. I.e., of natural philosophers, such as Aristotle (384–322 B.C.E.) and Sir Isaac Newton (1642–1727); of leaders of armies and nations, such as George Washington (1732–1799) and Napoleon Bonaparte (1769–1821); and of masters of the creative arts, such as Raphael (1483–1520) and William Shakespeare (1546–1616).

forming the critic or the experimentalist, the economist or the engineer, though such too it includes within its scope. But a University training is the great ordinary means to a great but ordinary end; it aims at raising the intellectual tone of society, at cultivating the public mind, at purifying the national taste, at supplying true principles to popular enthusiasm and fixed aims to popular aspiration, at giving enlargement and sobriety to the ideas of the age, at facilitating the exercise of political power, and refining the intercourse of private life. It is the education which gives a man a clear conscious view of his own opinions and judgments, a truth in developing them, an eloquence in expressing them, and a force in urging them. It teaches him to see things as they are, to go right to the point, to disentangle a skein of thought, to detect what is sophistical, and to discard what is irrelevant. It prepares him to fill any post with credit, and to master any subject with facility. It shows him how to accommodate himself to others, how to throw himself into their state of mind, how to bring before them his own, how to influence them, how to come to an understanding with them, how to bear with them. He is at home in any society, he has common ground with every class; he knows when to speak and when to be silent; he is able to converse, he is able to listen; he can ask a question pertinently, and gain a lesson seasonably, when he has nothing to impart himself; he is ever ready, yet never in the way; he is a pleasant companion, and a comrade you can depend upon; he knows when to be serious and when to trifle, and he has a sure tact which enables him to trifle with gracefulness and to be serious with effect. He has the repose of a mind which lives in itself, while it lives in the world, and which has resources for its happiness at home when it cannot go abroad. He has a gift which serves him in public, and supports him in retirement,[8] without which good fortune is but vulgar, and with which failure and disappointment have a charm. The art which tends to make a man all this is in the object which it pursues as useful as the art of wealth or the art of health, though it is less susceptible of method, and less tangible, less certain, less complete in its result.

From Discourse 8. Knowledge Viewed in Relation to Religion

10

Hence it is that it is almost a definition of a gentleman to say he is one who never inflicts pain. This description is both refined and, as far as it goes, accurate. He is mainly occupied in merely removing the obstacles which

8. In a later work, *The Grammar of Assent* (1870), Newman enlarges on this aspect of his subject in a passage describing the impact that classical literature may have on us at different ages of our lives, a passage admired by James Joyce.

> Let us consider, too, how differently young and old are affected by the words of some classic author, such as Homer or Horace. Passages, which to a boy are but rhetorical commonplaces, neither better nor worse than a hundred others which any clever writer might supply, which he gets by heart and thinks very fine, and imitates, as he thinks, successfully, in his own flowing versification, at length come home to him, when long years have passed, and he has had experience of life, and pierce him, as if he had never before known them, with their sad earnestness and vivid exactness. Then he comes to understand how it is that lines, the birth of some chance morning or evening at an Ionian festival, or among the Sabine hills, have lasted generation after generation, for thousands of years, with a power over the mind, and a charm, which the current literature of his own day, with all its obvious advantages, is utterly unable to rival. Perhaps this is the reason of the medieval opinion about Virgil, as if a prophet or magician; his single words and phrases, his pathetic half lines, giving utterance, as the voice of Nature herself, to that pain and weariness, yet hope of better things, which is the experience of her children in every time.

hinder the free and unembarrassed action of those about him; and he concurs with their movements rather than takes the initiative himself. His benefits may be considered as parallel to what are called comforts or conveniences in arrangements of a personal nature: like an easy chair or a good fire, which do their part in dispelling cold and fatigue, though nature provides both means of rest and animal heat without them. The true gentleman in like manner carefully avoids whatever may cause a jar or a jolt in the minds of those with whom he is cast;—all clashing of opinion, or collision of feeling, all restraint, or suspicion, or gloom, or resentment; his great concern being to make every one at their ease and at home. He has his eyes on all his company; he is tender towards the bashful, gentle towards the distant, and merciful towards the absurd; he can recollect to whom he is speaking; he guards against unseasonable allusions, or topics which may irritate; he is seldom prominent in conversation, and never wearisome. He makes light of favours while he does them, and seems to be receiving when he is conferring. He never speaks of himself except when compelled, never defends himself by a mere retort, he has no ears for slander or gossip, is scrupulous in imputing motives to those who interfere with him, and interprets every thing for the best. He is never mean or little in his disputes, never takes unfair advantage, never mistakes personalities or sharp sayings for arguments, or insinuates evil which he dare not say out. From a long-sighted prudence, he observes the maxim of the ancient sage, that we should ever conduct ourselves towards our enemy as if he were one day to be our friend. He has too much good sense to be affronted at insults, he is too well employed to remember injuries, and too indolent to bear malice. He is patient, forbearing, and resigned, on philosophical principles; he submits to pain, because it is inevitable, to bereavement, because it is irreparable, and to death, because it is his destiny. If he engages in controversy of any kind, his disciplined intellect preserves him from the blundering discourtesy of better, perhaps, but less educated minds; who, like blunt weapons, tear and hack instead of cutting clean, who mistake the point in argument, waste their strength on trifles, misconceive their adversary, and leave the question more involved than they find it. He may be right or wrong in his opinion, but he is too clear-headed to be unjust; he is as simple as he is forcible, and as brief as he is decisive. Nowhere shall we find greater candour, consideration, indulgence: he throws himself into the minds of his opponents, he accounts for their mistakes. He knows the weakness of human reason as well as its strength, its province and its limits. If he be an unbeliever, he will be too profound and large-minded to ridicule religion or to act against it; he is too wise to be a dogmatist or fanatic in his infidelity. He respects piety and devotion; he even supports institutions as venerable, beautiful, or useful, to which he does not assent; he honours the ministers of religion, and it contents him to decline its mysteries without assailing or denouncing them. He is a friend of religious toleration, and that, not only because his philosophy has taught him to look on all forms of faith with an impartial eye, but also from the gentleness and effeminacy[9] of feeling, which is the attendant on civilization.

Not that he may not hold a religion too, in his own way, even when he is not a Christian. In that case his religion is one of imagination and sentiment;

9. Tenderness.

it is the embodiment of those ideas of the sublime, majestic, and beautiful, without which there can be no large philosophy. Sometimes he acknowledges the being of God, sometimes he invests an unknown principle or quality with the attributes of perfection. And this deduction of his reason, or creation of his fancy, he makes the occasion of such excellent thoughts, and the starting-point of so varied and systematic a teaching, that he even seems like a disciple of Christianity itself. From the very accuracy and steadiness of his logical powers, he is able to see what sentiments are consistent in those who hold any religious doctrine at all, and he appears to others to feel and to hold a whole circle of theological truths, which exist in his mind no otherwise than as a number of deductions.

1852, 1873

JOHN STUART MILL
1806–1873

In many American colleges the writings of J. S. Mill are studied in courses in government or in philosophy, and it may therefore be asked why they should also have a place in the study of literature. It may seem that Mill is less literary than other Victorian prose writers. His analytic mind is preoccupied with abstractions rather than with the concrete details that are the concern of the more typical writer; his self-effacing manner and his relatively transparent style are the marks of an author whose value lies in generalizations from personal experience rather than in the rendering of particular experiences for their own sake. Yet a knowledge of Mill's writings is essential to our understanding of Victorian literature. He is one of the leading figures in the intellectual history of his century, a thinker whose honest grappling with the political and religious problems of his age was to have a profound influence on writers as diverse as Matthew Arnold, Algernon Charles Swinburne, and Thomas Hardy.

Mill was educated at home in London under the direction of his father, James Mill, a leader of the Utilitarians. James Mill believed that ordinary schooling fails to develop our intellectual capacities early enough, and he demonstrated his point by the extraordinary results he achieved in training his son. As a child John Stuart Mill read Greek and Latin; and as a boy he could carry on intelligent discussions of problems in mathematics, philosophy, and economics. By the time he was fourteen, as he reports in his *Autobiography* (1873) his intensive education enabled him to start his career "with an advantage of a quarter of a century" over his contemporaries.

Mill worked in the office of the East India Company for many years and also served a term in Parliament in the 1860s; but his principal energies were devoted to his writings on such subjects as logic and philosophy, political principles, and economics. His *System of Logic* (1843) earned him the position of the most respected philosopher in mid-Victorian England. He began as a disciple of the Utilitarian theories of his father and of Jeremy Bentham but became gradually dissatisfied with the narrowness of their conception of human motives. Working in the empiricist tradition, Utilitarians attempted to show that most traditional views of politics, ethics, and psychology were based on nothing more than long-standing superstition and habit, and that superstition and habit generally stood in the way of progress. Most famously, they challenged the idea that human beings functioned according to God-given intuitions and drives, arguing that the mind worked on the physical process of the association of feelings. According to the Utilitarians, then, individuals were ultimately motivated not by an innate sense of right and wrong but by the simple desire to find pleasure and avoid pain. Politically, the Utilitarians thus lobbied for whatever would bring the greatest pleasure (or happiness) to the greatest number. Though Mill was raised in this no-nonsense, reforming tradition, his honesty and open-mindedness enabled him to appreciate the values of such anti-Utilitarians as Samuel Taylor Coleridge and Thomas Carlyle and, whenever possible, to incorporate some of these values into the Utilitarian system. In part this sympathy was gained by the lesson he learned through experiencing a nervous breakdown during his early twenties. This painful event, described in a chapter of his *Autobiography,* taught him that the lack of concern for people's affections and emotions characteristic of the Utilitarian system of thought (and typified by his own education) was a fatal flaw in that system. His tribute to the therapeutic value of art (because of its effect on human emotions), both in his *Autobiography* and in his early essay "What Is Poetry?" (1833) would have astonished Mill's master, Bentham, who had equated poetry with pushpin, an idle pastime.

Mill's emotional life was also broadened by his love for Harriet Taylor, a married woman who shared his intellectual interests and eventually became his wife, in 1851, after the death of her husband. Little that Taylor wrote was published under her own name during her life, but her contribution to Mill's work should not be underestimated; Mill later described her as "the inspirer, and in part the author, of all that is best in my writings." They shared a commitment to the cause of female emancipation, one of several unpopular movements to which Mill was dedicated. Throughout human history, as he saw it, the role of a husband has always been legally that of a tyrant, and the object of his farseeing essay *The Subjection of Women* (1869) was to change law and public opinion so that half the human race might be liberated from slavery and regarded as equals. The subjection of women was, however, only one aspect of the tyranny against which he fought. His fundamental concern was to prevent the subjection of individuals in a democracy. His classic treatise *On Liberty* (1859) is not a traditional liberal attack against tyrannical kings or dictators; it is an attack against tyrannical majorities. Mill foresaw that in democracies such as the United States the pressure toward conformity might crush all individualists (intellectual individualists in particular) to the level of what he called a "collective mediocrity." Throughout all of his writings, even in his discussions of the advantages of socialism, Mill is concerned with demonstrating that the individual is more important than institutions such as church or state. In *On Liberty* we find a characteristic example of the process of his reasoning; but here, where the theme of individualism is central, his logic is charged with eloquence.

A similar eloquence is evident in a passage from his *Principles of Political Economy* (1848), a prophetic comment on the fate of the individual in an overpopulated world:

> There is room in the world, no doubt, and even in old countries, for a great increase of population, supposing the arts of life go on improving, and capital to increase. But even if innocuous, I confess I see very little reason for desiring it. . . . It is not good for a man to be kept perforce at all times in the presence of his species. A world from which solitude is extirpated, is a very poor ideal. Solitude, in the sense of being often alone, is essential to any depth of meditation or of character: and solitude in the presence of natural beauty and grandeur, is the cradle of thoughts and aspirations which are not only good for the individual, but which society could ill do without. Nor is there much satisfaction in contemplating the world with nothing left to the spontaneous activity of nature; with every rood of land brought into cultivation, which is capable of growing food for human beings; every flowery waste or natural pasture ploughed up, all quadrupeds or birds which are not domesticated for man's use

exterminated as his rivals for food, every hedgerow or superfluous tree rooted out, and scarcely a place left where a wild shrub or flower could grow without being eradicated as a weed in the name of improved agriculture. If the earth must lose that great portion of its pleasantness which it owes to things that the unlimited increase of wealth and population would extirpate from it, for the mere purpose of enabling it to support a larger, but not a better or happier population, I sincerely hope, for the sake of posterity, that they will be content to be stationary, long before necessity compels them to it.

What Is Poetry?

It has often been asked, What Is Poetry? And many and various are the answers which have been returned. The vulgarest of all—one with which no person possessed of the faculties to which poetry addresses itself can ever have been satisfied—is that which confounds poetry with metrical composition; yet to this wretched mockery of a definition many have been led back by the failure of all their attempts to find any other that would distinguish what they have been accustomed to call poetry from much which they have known only under other names.

That, however, the word "poetry" imports something quite peculiar in its nature; something which may exist in what is called prose as well as in verse; something which does not even require the instrument of words, but can speak through the other audible symbols called musical sounds, and even through the visible ones which are the language of sculpture, painting, and architecture—all this, we believe, is and must be felt, though perhaps indistinctly, by all upon whom poetry in any of its shapes produces any impression beyond that of tickling the ear. The distinction between poetry and what is not poetry, whether explained or not, is felt to be fundamental; and, where every one feels a difference, a difference there must be. All other appearances may be fallacious; but the appearance of a difference is a real difference. Appearances too, like other things, must have a cause; and that which can cause anything, even an illusion, must be a reality. And hence, while a half-philosophy disdains the classifications and distinctions indicated by popular language, philosophy carried to its highest point frames new ones, but rarely sets aside the old, content with correcting and regularizing them. It cuts fresh channels for thought, but does not fill up such as it finds ready-made: it traces, on the contrary, more deeply, broadly, and distinctly, those into which the current has spontaneously flowed.

Let us then attempt, in the way of modest inquiry, not to coerce and confine Nature within the bounds of an arbitrary definition, but rather to find the boundaries which she herself has set, and erect a barrier round them; not calling mankind to account for having misapplied the word "poetry," but attempting to clear up the conception which they already attach to it, and to bring forward as a distinct principle that which, as a vague feeling, has really guided them in their employment of the term.

The object of poetry is confessedly to act upon the emotions; and therein is poetry sufficiently distinguished from what Wordsworth affirms to be its logical opposite;[1] namely, not prose but matter of fact, or science. The one

---

1. In his "Preface" to *Lyrical Ballads* (1800).

addresses itself to the belief; the other, to the feelings. The one does its work by convincing or persuading; the other, by moving. The one acts by presenting a proposition to the understanding; the other, by offering interesting objects of contemplation to the sensibilities.

This, however, leaves us very far from a definition of poetry. This distinguishes it from one thing; but we are bound to distinguish it from everything. To bring thoughts or images before the mind, for the purpose of acting upon the emotions, does not belong to poetry alone. It is equally the province (for example) of the novelist: and yet the faculty of the poet and that of the novelist are as distinct as any other two faculties; as the faculties of the novelist and of the orator, or of the poet and the metaphysician. The two characters may be united, as characters the most disparate may; but they have no natural connection.

Many of the greatest poems are in the form of fictitious narratives; and, in almost all good serious fictions, there is true poetry. But there is a radical distinction between the interest felt in a story as such, and the interest excited by poetry; for the one is derived from incident, the other from the representation of feeling. In one, the source of the emotion excited is the exhibition of a state or states of human sensibility; in the other, of a series of states of mere outward circumstances. Now, all minds are capable of being affected more or less by representations of the latter kind, and all, or almost all, by those of the former; yet the two sources of interest correspond to two distinct and (as respects their greatest development) mutually exclusive characters of mind.

At what age is the passion for a story, for almost any kind of story, merely as a story, the most intense? In childhood. But that also is the age at which poetry, even of the simplest description, is least relished and least understood; because the feelings with which it is especially conversant are yet undeveloped, and, not having been even in the slightest degree experienced, cannot be sympathized with. In what stage of the progress of society, again, is storytelling most valued, and the storyteller in greatest request and honor? In a rude state like that of the Tartars and Arabs at this day, and of almost all nations in the earliest ages. But, in this state of society, there is little poetry except ballads, which are mostly narrative—that is, essentially stories— and derive their principal interest from the incidents. Considered as poetry, they are of the lowest and most elementary kind: the feelings depicted, or rather indicated, are the simplest our nature has; such joys and griefs as the immediate pressure of some outward event excites in rude minds, which live wholly immersed in outward things, and have never, either from choice or a force they could not resist, turned themselves to the contemplation of the world within. Passing now from childhood, and from the childhood of society, to the grown-up men and women of this most grown-up and unchildlike age, the minds and hearts of greatest depth and elevation are commonly those which take greatest delight in poetry: the shallowest and emptiest, on the contrary, are, at all events, not those least addicted to novel-reading. This accords, too, with all analogous experience of human nature. The sort of persons whom not merely in books, but in their lives, we find perpetually engaged in hunting for excitement from without, are invariably those who do not possess, either in the vigor of their intellectual powers or in the depth of their sensibilities, that which would enable them to find ample excitement nearer home. The most idle and frivolous persons take a natural delight in fictitious narrative: the excitement it affords is of the kind which comes from without. Such persons are rarely lovers of poetry, though they may fancy themselves so because they relish novels in verse. But poetry, which is the delineation of the deeper and more secret workings of human emotion, is interesting only to those to whom it recalls what they have felt, or whose imagination it stirs up to conceive what they could feel, or what they might have been able to feel, had their outward circumstances been different.

Poetry, when it is really such, is truth; and fiction also, if it is good for anything, is truth: but they are different truths. The truth of poetry is to paint the human soul truly: the truth of fiction is to give a true picture of life. The two kinds of knowledge are different, and come by different ways, come mostly to different persons. Great poets are often proverbially ignorant of life. What they know has come by observation of themselves: they have found within them one highly delicate and sensitive specimen of human nature, on which the laws of emotion are written in large characters, such as can be read off without much study. Other knowledge of mankind, such as comes to men of the world by outward experience, is not indispensable to them as poets: but, to the novelist, such knowledge is all in all; he has to describe outward things, not the inward man; actions and events, not feelings; and it will not do for him to be numbered among those, who, as Madame Roland said of Brissot,[2] know man, but not *men*.

All this is no bar to the possibility of combining both elements, poetry and narrative or incident, in the same work, and calling it either a novel or a poem; but so may red and white combine on the same human features or on the same canvas. There is one order of composition which requires the union of poetry and incident, each in its highest kind—the dramatic. Even there, the two elements are perfectly distinguishable, and may exist of unequal quality and in the most various proportion. The incidents of a dramatic poem may be scanty and ineffective, though the delineation of passion and character may be of the highest order, as in Goethe's admirable "Torquato Tasso";[3] or, again, the story as a mere story may be well got up for effect, as is the case with some of the most trashy productions of the Minerva Press:[4] it may even be, what those are not, a coherent and probable series of events, though there be scarcely a feeling exhibited which is not represented falsely, or in a manner absolutely commonplace. The combination of the two excellences is what renders Shakespeare so generally acceptable, each sort of readers finding in him what is suitable to their faculties. To the many, he is great as a storyteller; to the few, as a poet.

In limiting poetry to the delineation of states of feeling, and denying the name where nothing is delineated but outward objects, we may be thought to have done what we promised to avoid—to have not found, but made, a definition in opposition to the usage of language, since it is established by common consent that there is a poetry called descriptive. We deny the charge. Description is not poetry because there is descriptive poetry, no more than science is poetry because there is such a thing as a didactic poem. But an object which admits of being described, or a truth which may fill a place in a

---

2. Jacques-Pierre Brissot (1754–1793), a leading reformer during the French Revolution, is characterized in the *Mémoires* of Jeanne-Manon Roland (1754–1793).

3. A play (1790) based on the life of this 16th-century Italian poet.
4. An early 19th-century publishing house that fostered the production of sentimental novels.

scientific treatise, may also furnish an occasion for the generation of poetry, which we thereupon choose to call descriptive or didactic. The poetry is not in the object itself, nor in the scientific truth itself, but in the state of mind in which the one and the other may be contemplated. The mere delineation of the dimensions and colors of external objects is not poetry, no more than a geometrical ground-plan of St. Peter's or Westminster Abbey is painting. Descriptive poetry consists, no doubt, in description, but in description of things as they appear, not as they are; and it paints them, not in their bare and natural lineaments, but seen through the medium and arrayed in the colors of the imagination set in action by the feelings. If a poet describes a lion, he does not describe him as a naturalist would, nor even as a traveler would, who was intent upon stating the truth, the whole truth, and nothing but the truth. He describes him by imagery, that is, by suggesting the most striking likenesses and contrasts which might occur to a mind contemplating a lion, in the state of awe, wonder, or terror, which the spectacle naturally excites, or is, on the occasion, supposed to excite. Now, this is describing the lion professedly, but the state of excitement of the spectator really. The lion may be described falsely or with exaggeration and the poetry be all the better: but, if the human emotion be not painted with scrupulous truth, the poetry is bad poetry, i.e., is not poetry at all, but a failure.

Thus far, our progress towards a clear view of the essentials of poetry has brought us very close to the last two attempts at a definition of poetry which we happen to have seen in print, both of them by poets, and men of genius. The one is by Ebenezer Elliott, the author of "Corn-law Rhymes," and other poems of still greater merit. "Poetry," says he, "is impassioned truth."[5] The other is by a writer in "Blackwood's Magazine," and comes, we think, still nearer the mark. He defines poetry, "man's thoughts tinged by his feelings." There is in either definition a near approximation to what we are in search of. Every truth which a human being can enunciate, every thought, even every outward impression, which can enter into his consciousness, may become poetry, when shown through any impassioned medium; when invested with the coloring of joy, or grief, or pity, or affection, or admiration, or reverence, or awe, or even hatred or terror; and, unless so colored, nothing, be it as interesting as it may, is poetry. But both these definitions fail to discriminate between poetry and eloquence. Eloquence, as well as poetry, is impassioned truth; eloquence, as well as poetry, is thoughts colored by the feelings. Yet common apprehension and philosophic criticism alike recognize a distinction between the two: there is much that everyone would call eloquence, which no one would think of classing as poetry. A question will sometimes arise, whether some particular author is a poet; and those who maintain the negative commonly allow, that, though not a poet, he is a highly eloquent writer. The distinction between poetry and eloquence appears to us to be equally fundamental with the distinction between poetry and narrative, or between poetry and description, while it is still farther from having been satisfactorily cleared up than either of the others.

Poetry and eloquence are both alike the expression or utterance of feeling: but, if we may be excused the antithesis, we should say that eloquence is *heard*; poetry is *overheard*. Eloquence supposes an audience. The peculiarity

5. In the "Preface" to *Corn-Law Rhymes* (1828), by Elliott (1781–1849).

of poetry appears to us to lie in the poet's utter unconsciousness of a listener. Poetry is feeling confessing itself to itself in moments of solitude, and embodying itself in symbols which are the nearest possible representations of the feeling in the exact shape in which it exists in the poet's mind. Eloquence is feeling pouring itself out to other minds, courting their sympathy, or endeavoring to influence their belief, or move them to passion or to action.

All poetry is of the nature of soliloquy. It may be said that poetry which is printed on hot-pressed paper, and sold at a bookseller's shop, is a soliloquy in full dress and on the stage. It is so; but there is nothing absurd in the idea of such a mode of soliloquizing. What we have said to ourselves we may tell to others afterwards; what we have said or done in solitude we may voluntarily reproduce when we know that other eyes are upon us. But no trace of consciousness that any eyes are upon us must be visible in the work itself. The actor knows that there is an audience present: but, if he act as though he knew it, he acts ill. A poet may write poetry, not only with the intention of printing it, but for the express purpose of being paid for it. That it should *be* poetry, being written under such influences, is less probable, not, however, impossible; but no otherwise possible than if he can succeed in excluding from his work every vestige of such lookings-forth into the outward and every-day world, and can express his emotions exactly as he has felt them in solitude, or as he is conscious that he should feel them, though they were to remain for ever unuttered, or (at the lowest) as he knows that others feel them in similar circumstances of solitude. But when he turns round, and addresses himself to another person; when the act of utterance is not itself the end, but a means to an end—viz., by the feelings he himself expresses, to work upon the feelings, or upon the belief or the will of another; when the expression of his emotions, or of his thoughts tinged by his emotions, is tinged also by that purpose, by that desire of making an impression upon another mind—then it ceases to be poetry, and becomes eloquence.

Poetry, accordingly, is the natural fruit of solitude and meditation; eloquence, of intercourse with the world. The persons who have most feeling of their own, if intellectual culture has given them a language in which to express it, have the highest faculty of poetry: those who best understand the feelings of others are the most eloquent. The persons and the nations who commonly excel in poetry are those whose character and tastes render them least dependent upon the applause or sympathy or concurrence of the world in general. Those to whom that applause, that sympathy, that concurrence, are most necessary, generally excel most in eloquence. And hence, perhaps, the French, who are the least poetical of all great and intellectual nations, are among the most eloquent; the French also being the most sociable, the vainest, and the least self-dependent.

If the above be, as we believe, the true theory of the distinction commonly admitted between eloquence and poetry, or even though it be not so, yet if, as we cannot doubt, the distinction above stated be a real bona fide distinction, it will be found to hold, not merely in the language of words, but in all other language, and to intersect the whole domain of art.

Take, for example, music. We shall find in that art, so peculiarly the expression of passion, two perfectly distinct styles—one of which may be called the poetry, the other the oratory, of music. This difference, being seized, would put an end to much musical sectarianism. There has been much contention whether the music of the modern Italian school, that of Rossini,[6] and his successors, be impassioned or not. Without doubt, the passion it expresses is not the musing, meditative tenderness or pathos or grief of Mozart or Beethoven; yet it is passion, but garrulous passion, the passion which pours itself into other ears, and therein the better calculated for dramatic effect, having a natural adaptation for dialogue. Mozart also is great in musical oratory; but his most touching compositions are in the opposite style, that of soliloquy. Who can imagine "Dove sono"[7] *heard*? We imagine it *overheard*.

Purely pathetic music commonly partakes of soliloquy. The soul is absorbed in its distress and, though there may be bystanders, it is not thinking of them. When the mind is looking within, and not without, its state does not often or rapidly vary; and hence the even, uninterrupted flow, approaching almost to monotony, which a good reader or a good singer will give to words or music of a pensive or melancholy cast. But grief, taking the form of a prayer or of a complaint, becomes oratorical: no longer low and even and subdued, it assumes a more emphatic rhythm, a more rapidly returning accent; instead of a few slow, equal notes, following one after another at regular intervals, it crowds note upon note, and often assumes a hurry and bustle like joy. Those who are familiar with some of the best of Rossini's serious compositions, such as the air "Tu che i miseri conforti,"[8] in the opera of "Tancredi," or the duet "Ebben per mia memoria,"[9] in "La Gazza Ladra," will at once understand and feel our meaning. Both are highly tragic and passionate: the passion of both is that of oratory, not poetry. The like may be said of that most moving invocation in Beethoven's "Fidelio,"

> "Komm, Hoffnung, lass das letzte Stern
> Der Müde nicht erbleichen"—[1]

in which Madame Schröder Devrient exhibited such consummate powers of pathetic expression. How different from Winter's beautiful "Paga fui,"[2] the very soul of melancholy exhaling itself in solitude! fuller of meaning, and therefore more profoundly poetical, than the words for which it was composed; for it seems to express, not simple melancholy, but the melancholy of remorse.

If from vocal music we now pass to instrumental, we may have a specimen of musical oratory in any fine military symphony or march; while the poetry of music seems to have attained its consummation in Beethoven's "Overture to Egmont," so wonderful in its mixed expression of grandeur and melancholy.

6. Gioacchino Rossini (1792–1868), composer of operas.
7. Where are fled [the lovely moments?] (Italian); soprano aria from act 3 of *The Marriage of Figaro* (1786), by the Austrian composer Wolfgang Amadeus Mozart (1756–1791).
8. You, who give comfort to the wretched (Italian); soprano aria from Rossini's *Tancredi* (1813).
9. Indeed according to my memory (Italian); soprano aria from Rossini's *La Gazza Ladra* (1817).
1. Come, Hope, let not the weary person's last star fade out (German); aria from *Fidelio* (1805), by the German composer Ludwig van Beethoven (1770–1827). Mill seems to be quoting from memory. The passage should read: "Komm, Hoffnung, lass den letzten Stern / Der Müden nicht erbleichen."
2. I have been contented (Italian); aria from the once-popular opera *Il Ratto di Proserpina*, by Peter Winter (1754–1825), first performed in London in 1804.

In the arts which speak to the eye, the same distinctions will be found to hold, not only between poetry and oratory, but between poetry, oratory, narrative, and simple imitation or description.

Pure description is exemplified in a mere portrait or a mere landscape, productions of art, it is true, but of the mechanical rather than of the fine arts; being works of simple imitation, not creation. We say, a mere portrait or a mere landscape; because it is possible for a portrait or a landscape, without ceasing to be such, to be also a picture, like Turner's landscapes, and the great portraits by Titian or Vandyke.[3]

Whatever in painting or sculpture expresses human feeling—or character, which is only a certain state of feeling grown habitual—may be called, according to circumstances, the poetry or the eloquence of the painter's or the sculptor's art: the poetry, if the feeling declares itself by such signs as escape from us when we are unconscious of being seen; the oratory, if the signs are those we use for the purpose of voluntary communication.

The narrative style answers to what is called historical painting, which it is the fashion among connoisseurs to treat as the climax of the pictorial art. That it is the most difficult branch of the art, we do not doubt, because, in its perfection, it includes the perfection of all the other branches; as, in like manner, an epic poem, though, in so far as it is epic (i.e., narrative), it is not poetry at all, is yet esteemed the greatest effort of poetic genius, because there is no kind whatever of poetry which may not appropriately find a place in it. But an historical picture as such, that is, as the representation of an incident, must necessarily, as it seems to us, be poor and ineffective. The narrative powers of painting are extremely limited. Scarcely any picture, scarcely even any series of pictures, tells its own story without the aid of an interpreter. But it is the single figures, which, to us, are the great charm even of an historical picture. It is in these that the power of the art is really seen. In the attempt to narrate, visible and permanent signs are too far behind the fugitive audible ones, which follow so fast one after another; while the faces and figures in a narrative picture, even though they be Titian's, stand still. Who would not prefer one "Virgin and Child" of Raphael to all the pictures which Rubens,[4] with his fat, frouzy Dutch Venuses, ever painted?—though Rubens, besides excelling almost everyone in his mastery over the mechanical parts of his art, often shows real genius in *grouping* his figures, the peculiar problem of historical painting. But then, who, except a mere student of drawing and coloring, ever cared to look twice at any of the figures themselves? The power of painting lies in poetry, of which Rubens had not the slightest tincture, not in narrative, wherein he might have excelled.

The single figures, however, in an historical picture, are rather the eloquence of painting than the poetry. They mostly (unless they are quite out of place in the picture) express the feelings of one person as modified by the presence of others. Accordingly, the minds whose bent leads them rather to eloquence than to poetry rush to historical painting. The French painters, for instance, seldom attempt, because they could make nothing of, single heads,

3. Sir Anthony Van Dyck (1599–1641), Flemish painter who produced more than five hundred portraits. J. M. W. Turner (1775–1851), British landscape painter. Titian (Tiziano Vicelli, ca. 1488–1576), master painter of the Venetian school.

4. Peter Paul Rubens (1577–1640), Flemish painter (and Van Dyck's teacher). Raphael (Raffaello Sanzio, 1483–1520), Italian painter of the high Renaissance.

like those glorious ones of the Italian masters with which they might feed themselves day after day in their own Louvre.[5] They must all be historical; and they are, almost to a man, attitudinizers. If we wished to give any young artist the most impressive warning our imagination could devise against that kind of vice in the pictorial which corresponds to rant in the histrionic art, we would advise him to walk once up and once down the gallery of the Luxembourg.[6] Every figure in French painting or statuary seems to be showing itself off before spectators. They are not poetical, but in the worst style of corrupted eloquence.

1833, 1859

From On Liberty
From Chapter 3. Of Individuality as One of the Elements of Well-Being

* * *

Few persons, out of Germany, even comprehend the meaning of the doctrine which Wilhelm von Humboldt, so eminent both as a savant and as a politician, made the text of a treatise—that "the end of man, or that which is prescribed by the eternal or immutable dictates of reason, and not suggested by vague and transient desires, is the highest and most harmonious development of his powers to a complete and consistent whole"; that, therefore, the object "towards which every human being must ceaselessly direct his efforts, and on which especially those who design to influence their fellow men must ever keep their eyes, is the individuality of power and development"; that for this there are two requisites, "freedom, and variety of situations"; and that from the union of these arise "individual vigor and manifold diversity," which combine themselves in "originality."[1]

Little, however, as people are accustomed to a doctrine like that of Von Humboldt, and surprising as it may be to them to find so high a value attached to individuality, the question, one must nevertheless think, can only be one of degree. No one's idea of excellence in conduct is that people should do absolutely nothing but copy one another. No one would assert that people ought not to put into their mode of life, and into the conduct of their concerns, any impress whatever of their own judgment, or of their own individual character. On the other hand, it would be absurd to pretend that people ought to live as if nothing whatever had been known in the world before they came into it; as if experience had as yet done nothing towards showing that one mode of existence, or conduct, is preferable to another. Nobody denies that people should be so taught and trained in youth, as to know and benefit by the ascertained results of human experience. But it is the privilege and proper condition of

---

5. A palace in Paris, opened as a public museum in 1793. The Italian Renaissance paintings originally owned by Francis I are the core of its collection.
6. A palace in Paris, where paintings of scenes from French history were exhibited.

1. From *The Sphere and Duties of Government,* by Baron Wilhelm von Humboldt (1767–1835), Prussian statesman and man of letters. Originally written in 1791, the treatise was first published in Germany in 1852 and was translated into English in 1854.

a human being, arrived at the maturity of his faculties, to use and interpret experience in his own way. It is for him to find out what part of recorded experience is properly applicable to his own circumstances and character. The traditions and customs of other people are, to a certain extent, evidence of what their experience has taught *them;* presumptive evidence, and as such, have a claim to his deference: but, in the first place, their experience may be too narrow; or they may not have interpreted it rightly. Secondly, their interpretation of experience may be correct, but unsuitable to him. Customs are made for customary circumstances, and customary characters; and his circumstances or his character may be uncustomary. Thirdly, though the customs be both good as customs, and suitable to him, yet to conform to custom, merely *as* custom, does not educate or develop in him any of the qualities which are the distinctive endowment of a human being. The human faculties of perception, judgment, discriminative feeling, mental activity, and even moral preference are exercised only in making a choice. He who does anything because it is the custom makes no choice. He gains no practice either in discerning or in desiring what is best. The mental and moral, like the muscular powers, are improved only by being used. The faculties are called into no exercise by doing a thing merely because others do it, no more than by believing a thing only because others believe it. If the grounds of an opinion are not conclusive to the person's own reason, his reason cannot be strengthened, but is likely to be weakened, by his adopting it: and if the inducements to an act are not such as are consentaneous[2] to his own feelings and character (where affection, or the rights of others, are not concerned) it is so much done towards rendering his feelings and character inert and torpid, instead of active and energetic.

He who lets the world, or his own portion of it, choose his plan of life for him has no need of any other faculty than the apelike one of imitation. He who chooses his plan for himself employs all his faculties. He must use observation to see, reasoning and judgment to foresee, activity to gather materials for decision, discrimination to decide, and when he has decided, firmness and self-control to hold to his deliberate decision. And these qualities he requires and exercises exactly in proportion as the part of his conduct which he determines according to his own judgment and feelings is a large one. It is possible that he might be guided in some good path, and kept out of harm's way, without any of these things. But what will be his comparative worth as a human being? It really is of importance, not only what men do, but also what manner of men they are that do it. Among the works of man, which human life is rightly employed in perfecting and beautifying, the first in importance surely is man himself. Supposing it were possible to get houses built, corn grown, battles fought, causes tried, and even churches erected and prayers said, by machinery—by automatons in human form—it would be a considerable loss to exchange for these automatons even the men and women who at present inhabit the more civilized parts of the world, and who assuredly are but starved specimens of what nature can and will produce. Human nature is not a machine to be built after a model, and set to do exactly the work prescribed for it, but a tree, which requires to grow and

2. Agreeable.

develop itself on all sides, according to the tendency of the inward forces which make it a living thing.

It will probably be conceded that it is desirable people should exercise their understandings, and that an intelligent following of custom, or even occasionally an intelligent deviation from custom, is better than a blind and simply mechanical adhesion to it. To a certain extent it is admitted that our understanding should be our own: but there is not the same willingness to admit that our desires and impulses should be our own likewise; or that to possess impulses of our own, and of any strength, is anything but a peril and a snare. Yet desires and impulses are as much a part of a perfect human being, as beliefs and restraints: and strong impulses are only perilous when not properly balanced; when one set of aims and inclinations is developed into strength, while others, which ought to coexist with them, remain weak and inactive. It is not because men's desires are strong that they act ill; it is because their consciences are weak. There is no natural connection between strong impulses and a weak conscience. The natural connection is the other way. To say that one person's desires and feelings are stronger and more various than those of another is merely to say that he has more of the raw material of human nature, and is therefore capable, perhaps of more evil, but certainly of more good. Strong impulses are but another name for energy. Energy may be turned to bad uses; but more good may always be made of an energetic nature than of an indolent and impassive one. Those who have most natural feeling are always those whose cultivated feelings may be made the strongest. The same strong susceptibilities which make the personal impulses vivid and powerful are also the source from whence are generated the most passionate love of virtue, and the sternest self-control. It is through the cultivation of these that society both does its duty and protects its interests: not by rejecting the stuff of which heroes are made, because it knows not how to make them. A person whose desires and impulses are his own— are the expression of his own nature, as it has been developed and modified by his own culture—is said to have a character. One whose desires and impulses are not his own, has no character, no more than a steam engine has a character. If, in addition to being his own, his impulses are strong, and are under the government of a strong will, he has an energetic character. Whoever thinks that individuality of desires and impulses should not be encouraged to unfold itself must maintain that society has no need of strong natures—is not the better for containing many persons who have much character—and that a high general average of energy is not desirable.

In some early states of society, these forces might be, and were, too much ahead of the power which society then possessed of disciplining and controlling them. There has been a time when the element of spontaneity and individuality was in excess, and the social principle had a hard struggle with it. The difficulty then was to induce men of strong bodies or minds to pay obedience to any rules which require them to control their impulses. To overcome this difficulty, law and discipline, like the Popes struggling against the Emperors, asserted a power over the whole man, claiming to control all his life in order to control his character—which society had not found any other sufficient means of binding. But society has now fairly got the better of individuality; and the danger which threatens human nature is not the excess, but the deficiency, of personal impulses and preferences. Things are vastly changed, since the passions of those who were strong by station or by personal endowment were in a state of habitual rebellion against laws and ordinances, and required to be rigorously chained up to enable the persons within their reach to enjoy any particle of security. In our times, from the highest class of society down to the lowest, everyone lives as under the eye of a hostile and dreaded censorship. Not only in what concerns others, but in what concerns only themselves, the individual or the family do not ask themselves—what do I prefer? or, what would suit my character and disposition? or, what would allow the best and highest in me to have fair play, and enable it to grow and thrive? They ask themselves, what is suitable to my position? what is usually done by persons of my station and pecuniary circumstances? or (worse still) what is usually done by persons of a station and circumstances superior to mine? I do not mean that they choose what is customary, in preference to what suits their own inclination. It does not occur to them to have any inclination, except for what is customary. Thus the mind itself is bowed to the yoke: even in what people do for pleasure, conformity is the first thing thought of; they like in crowds; they exercise choice only among things commonly done: peculiarity of taste, eccentricity of conduct, are shunned equally with crimes: until by dint of not following their own nature, they have no nature to follow: their human capacities are withered and starved: they become incapable of any strong wishes or native pleasures, and are generally without either opinions or feelings of home growth, or properly their own. Now is this, or is it not, the desirable condition of human nature?

It is so, on the Calvinistic theory. According to that, the one great offense of man is self-will. All the good of which humanity is capable is comprised in obedience. You have no choice; thus you must do, and no otherwise: "whatever is not a duty is a sin." Human nature being radically corrupt, there is no redemption for anyone until human nature is killed within him. To one holding this theory of life, crushing out any of the human faculties, capacities, and susceptibilities is no evil: man needs no capacity but that of surrendering himself to the will of God: and if he uses any of his faculties for any other purpose but to do that supposed will more effectually, he is better without them. This is the theory of Calvinism; and it is held, in a mitigated form, by many who do not consider themselves Calvinists; the mitigation consisting in giving a less ascetic interpretation to the alleged will of God; asserting it to be his will that mankind should gratify some of their inclinations; of course not in the manner they themselves prefer, but in the way of obedience, that is, in a way prescribed to them by authority; and, therefore, by the necessary conditions of the case, the same for all.

In some such insidious form there is at present a strong tendency to this narrow theory of life, and to the pinched and hidebound type of human character which it patronizes. Many persons, no doubt, sincerely think that human beings thus cramped and dwarfed are as their Maker designed them to be; just as many have thought that trees are a much finer thing when clipped into pollards,[3] or cut out into figures of animals, than as nature made them. But if it be any part of religion to believe that man was made by a good Being, it is more consistent with that faith to believe that this Being gave all

3. Trees that acquire an artificial shape by being cut back to produce a mass of dense foliage.

human faculties that they might be cultivated and unfolded, not rooted out and consumed, and that he takes delight in every nearer approach made by his creatures to the ideal conception embodied in them, every increase in any of their capabilities of comprehension, of action, or of enjoyment. There is a different type of human excellence from the Calvinistic; a conception of humanity as having its nature bestowed on it for other purposes than merely to be abnegated. "Pagan self-assertion" is one of the elements of human worth, as well as "Christian self-denial."[4] There is a Greek ideal of self-development, which the Platonic and Christian ideal of self-government blends with, but does not supersede. It may be better to be a John Knox than an Alcibiades, but it is better to be a Pericles[5] than either, nor would a Pericles, if we had one in these days, be without anything good which belonged to John Knox.

It is not by wearing down into uniformity all that is individual in themselves, but by cultivating it and calling it forth, within the limits imposed by the rights and interests of others, that human beings become a noble and beautiful object of contemplation; and as the works partake the character of those who do them, by the same process human life also becomes rich, diversified, and animating, furnishing more abundant aliment to high thoughts and elevating feelings, and strengthening the tie which binds every individual to the race, by making the race infinitely better worth belonging to. In proportion to the development of his individuality, each person becomes more valuable to himself, and is therefore capable of being more valuable to others. There is a greater fullness of life about his own existence, and when there is more life in the units there is more in the mass which is composed of them. As much compression as is necessary to prevent the stronger specimens of human nature from encroaching on the rights of others cannot be dispensed with; but for this there is ample compensation even in the point of view of human development. The means of development which the individual loses by being prevented from gratifying his inclinations to the injury of others are chiefly obtained at the expense of the development of other people. And even to himself there is a full equivalent in the better development of the social part of his nature, rendered possible by the restraint put upon the selfish part. To be held to rigid rules of justice for the sake of others develops the feelings and capacities which have the good of others for their object. But to be restrained in things not affecting their good, by their mere displeasure, develops nothing valuable, except such force of character as may unfold itself in resisting the restraint. If acquiesced in, it dulls and blunts the whole nature. To give any fair play to the nature of each, it is essential that different persons should be allowed to lead different lives. In proportion as this latitude has been exercised in any age, has that age been noteworthy to posterity. Even despotism does not produce its worst effects, so long as individuality exists under it; and whatever crushes individuality is despotism, by whatever name it may be called, and whether it professes to be enforcing the will of God or the injunctions of men.

4. From the *Essays* (1848) of John Sterling (1806–1844), a writer and friend of Carlyle's.
5. A model statesman in Athens (495–429 B.C.E.).

Knox (1514–1572), a stern Scottish Calvinist reformer. Alcibiades (450–404 B.C.E.), a brilliant but dissolute Athenian commander.

Having said that Individuality is the same thing with development, and that it is only the cultivation of individuality which produces, or can produce, well-developed human beings, I might here close the argument: for what more or better can be said of any condition of human affairs than that it brings human beings themselves nearer to the best thing they can be? or what worse can be said of any obstruction to good than that it prevents this? Doubtless, however, these considerations will not suffice to convince those who most need convincing; and it is necessary further to show that these developed human beings are of some use to the undeveloped—to point out to those who do not desire liberty, and would not avail themselves of it, that they may be in some intelligible manner rewarded for allowing other people to make use of it without hindrance.

In the first place, then, I would suggest that they might possibly learn something from them. It will not be denied by anybody, that originality is a valuable element in human affairs. There is always need of persons not only to discover new truths, and point out when what were once truths are true no longer, but also to commence new practices, and set the example of more enlightened conduct, and better taste and sense in human life. This cannot well be gainsaid by anybody who does not believe that the world has already attained perfection in all its ways and practices. It is true that this benefit is not capable of being rendered by everybody alike: there are but few persons, in comparison with the whole of mankind, whose experiments, if adopted by others, would be likely to be any improvement on established practice. But these few are the salt of the earth; without them, human life would become a stagnant pool. Not only is it they who introduce good things which did not before exist; it is they who keep the life in those which already existed. If there were nothing new to be done, would human intellect cease to be necessary? Would it be a reason why those who do the old things should forget why they are done, and do them like cattle, not like human beings? There is only too great a tendency in the best beliefs and practices to degenerate into the mechanical; and unless there were a succession of persons whose ever-recurring originality prevents the grounds of those beliefs and practices from becoming merely traditional, such dead matter would not resist the smallest shock from anything really alive, and there would be no reason why civilization should not die out, as in the Byzantine Empire. Persons of genius, it is true, are, and are always likely to be, a small minority; but in order to have them, it is necessary to preserve the soil in which they grow. Genius can only breathe freely in an *atmosphere* of freedom. Persons of genius are, *ex vi termini*,[6] *more* individual than any other people—less capable, consequently, of fitting themselves, without hurtful compression, into any of the small number of molds which society provides in order to save its members the trouble of forming their own character. If from timidity they consent to be forced into one of these molds, and to let all that part of themselves which cannot expand under the pressure remain unexpanded, society will be little the better for their genius. If they are of a strong character, and break their fetters, they become a mark for the society which has not succeeded in reducing them to commonplace, to point at with solemn warning as "wild,"

6. By force of the term (Latin); i.e., by definition.

"erratic," and the like; much as if one should complain of the Niagara River for not flowing smoothly between its banks like a Dutch canal.

I insist thus emphatically on the importance of genius, and the necessity of allowing it to unfold itself freely both in thought and in practice, being well aware that no one will deny the position in theory, but knowing also that almost everyone, in reality, is totally indifferent to it. People think genius a fine thing if it enables a man to write an exciting poem, or paint a picture. But in its true sense, that of originality in thought and action, though no one says that it is not a thing to be admired, nearly all, at heart, think that they can do very well without it. Unhappily this is too natural to be wondered at. Originality is the one thing which unoriginal minds cannot feel the use of. They cannot see what it is to do for them: how should they? If they could see what it would do for them, it would not be originality. The first service which originality has to render them is that of opening their eyes: which being once fully done, they would have a chance of being themselves original. Meanwhile, recollecting that nothing was ever yet done which someone was not the first to do, and that all good things which exist are the fruits of originality, let them be modest enough to believe that there is something still left for it to accomplish, and assure themselves that they are more in need of originality, the less they are conscious of the want.

In sober truth, whatever homage may be professed, or even paid, to real or supposed mental superiority, the general tendency of things throughout the world is to render mediocrity the ascendant power among mankind. In ancient history, in the middle ages, and in a diminishing degree through the long transition from feudality to the present time, the individual was power in himself; and if he had either great talents or a high social position, he was a considerable power. At present individuals are lost in the crowd. In politics it is almost a triviality to say that public opinion now rules the world. The only power deserving the name is that of masses, and of governments while they make themselves the organ of the tendencies and instincts of masses. This is as true in the moral and social relations of private life as in public transactions. Those whose opinions go by the name of public opinion, are not always the same sort of public: in America they are the whole white population; in England, chiefly the middle class. But they are always a mass, that is to say, collective mediocrity. And what is a still greater novelty, the mass do not now take their opinions from dignitaries in Church or State, from ostensible leaders, or from books. Their thinking is done for them by men much like themselves, addressing them or speaking in their name, on the spur of the moment, through the newspapers. I am not complaining of all this. I do not assert that anything better is compatible, as a general rule, with the present low state of the human mind. But that does not hinder the government of mediocrity from being mediocre government. No government by a democracy or a numerous aristocracy, either in its political acts or in the opinions, qualities, and tone of mind which it fosters, ever did or could rise above mediocrity, except in so far as the sovereign Many have let themselves be guided (which in their best times they always have done) by the counsels and influence of a more highly gifted and instructed One or Few. The initiation of all wise or noble things, comes and must come from individuals; generally at first from some one individual. The honor and glory of the average man is that he is capable of following that initiative; that he can respond internally to wise and noble things, and be led to them with his eyes open. I am not countenancing the sort of "hero worship" which applauds the strong man of genius for forcibly seizing on the government of the world and making it do his bidding in spite of itself.[7] All he can claim is freedom to point out the way. The power of compelling others into it is not only inconsistent with the freedom and development of all the rest, but corrupting to the strong man himself. It does seem, however, that when the opinions of masses of merely average men are everywhere become or becoming the dominant power, the counterpoise and corrective to that tendency would be the more and more pronounced individuality of those who stand on the higher eminences of thought. It is in these circumstances most especially that exceptional individuals, instead of being deterred, should be encouraged in acting differently from the mass. In other times there was no advantage in their doing so, unless they acted not only differently, but better. In this age, the mere example of nonconformity, the mere refusal to bend the knee to custom, is itself a service. Precisely because the tyranny of opinion is such as to make eccentricity a reproach, it is desirable, in order to break through that tyranny, that people should be eccentric. Eccentricity has always abounded when and where strength of character has abounded; and the amount of eccentricity in a society has generally been proportional to the amount of genius, mental vigor, and moral courage which it contained. That so few now dare to be eccentric marks the chief danger of the time.

* * *

There is one characteristic of the present direction of public opinion, peculiarly calculated to make it intolerant of any marked demonstration of individuality. The general average of mankind are not only moderate in intellect, but also moderate in inclinations: they have no tastes or wishes strong enough to incline them to do anything unusual, and they consequently do not understand those who have, and class all such with the wild and intemperate whom they are accustomed to look down upon. Now, in addition to this fact which is general, we have only to suppose that a strong movement has set in towards the improvement of morals, and it is evident what we have to expect. In these days such a movement has set in; much has actually been effected in the way of increased regularity of conduct, and discouragement of excesses; and there is a philanthropic spirit abroad, for the exercise of which there is no more inviting field than the moral and prudential improvement of our fellow creatures. These tendencies of the times cause the public to be more disposed than at most former periods to prescribe general rules of conduct, and endeavor to make everyone conform to the approved standard. And that standard, express or tacit, is to desire nothing strongly. Its ideal of character is to be without any marked character; to maim by compression, like a Chinese lady's foot,[8] every part of human nature which stands out prominently, and tends to make the person markedly dissimilar in outline to commonplace humanity.

7. As advocated by Thomas Carlyle in *On Heroes, Hero-Worship, and the Heroic in History* (1841).
8. The practice of foot binding, which aimed to make women's feet only three inches long, was widespread in China from the 10th century until its formal prohibition in 1911.

As is usually the case with ideals which exclude one half of what is desirable, the present standard of approbation produces only an inferior imitation of the other half. Instead of great energies guided by vigorous reason, and strong feelings strongly controlled by a conscientious will, its result is weak feelings and weak energies, which therefore can be kept in outward conformity to rule without any strength either of will or reason. Already energetic characters on any large scale are becoming merely traditional. There is now scarcely any outlet for energy in this country except business. The energy expended in this may still be regarded as considerable. What little is left from that employment, is expended on some hobby; which may be a useful, even a philanthropic hobby, but is always some one thing, and generally a thing of small dimensions. The greatness of England is now all collective: individually small, we only appear capable of anything great by our habit of combining; and with this our moral and religious philanthropies are perfectly contented. But it was men of another stamp than this that made England what it has been; and men of another stamp will be needed to prevent its decline.

The despotism of custom is everywhere the standing hindrance to human advancement, being in unceasing antagonism to that disposition to aim at something better than customary, which is called, according to circumstances, the spirit of liberty, or that of progress or improvement. The spirit of improvement is not always a spirit of liberty, for it may aim at forcing improvements on an unwilling people; and the spirit of liberty, in so far as it resists such attempts, may ally itself locally and temporarily with the opponents of improvement; but the only unfailing and permanent source of improvement is liberty, since by it there are as many possible independent centers of improvement as there are individuals. The progressive principle, however, in either shape, whether as the love of liberty or of improvement, is antagonistic to the sway of Custom, involving at least emancipation from that yoke; and the contest between the two constitutes the chief interest of the history of mankind. The greater part of the world has, properly speaking, no history, because the depotism of Custom is complete. This is the case over the whole East. Custom is there, in all things, the final appeal; justice and right mean conformity to custom; the argument of custom no one, unless some tyrant intoxicated with power, thinks of resisting. And we see the result. Those nations must once have had originality; they did not start out of the ground populous, lettered, and versed in many of the arts of life; they made themselves all this, and were then the greatest and most powerful nations of the world. What are they now? The subjects or dependants of tribes whose forefathers wandered in the forests when theirs had magnificent palaces and gorgeous temples, but over whom custom exercised only a divided rule with liberty and progress. A people, it appears, may be progressive for a certain length of time, and then stop: when does it stop? When it ceases to possess individuality. If a similar change should befall the nations of Europe, it will not be in exactly the same shape: the despotism of custom with which these nations are threatened is not precisely stationariness. It proscribes singularity, but it does not preclude change, provided all change together. We have discarded the fixed costumes of our forefathers; everyone must still dress like other people, but the fashion may change once or twice a year. We thus take care that when there is change it shall be for change's sake, and not from any idea of beauty or convenience; for the same idea of beauty or convenience would not strike all the world at the same moment, and be simultaneously thrown aside by all at another moment. But we are progressive as well as changeable: we continually make new inventions in mechanical things, and keep them until they are again superseded by better; we are eager for improvement in politics, in education, even in morals, though in this last our idea of improvement chiefly consists in persuading or forcing other people to be as good as ourselves. It is not progress that we object to; on the contrary, we flatter ourselves that we are the most progressive people who ever lived. It is individuality that we war against: we should think we had done wonders if we had made ourselves all alike; forgetting that the unlikeness of one person to another is generally the first thing which draws the attention of either to the imperfection of his own type, and the superiority of another, or the possibility, by combining the advantages of both, of producing something better than either. We have a warning example in China—a nation of much talent, and, in some respects, even wisdom, owing to the rare good fortune of having been provided at an early period with a particularly good set of customs, the work, in some measure, of men to whom even the most enlightened European must accord, under certain limitations, the title of sages and philosophers. They are remarkable, too, in the excellence of their apparatus for impressing, as far as possible, the best wisdom they possess upon every mind in the community, and securing that those who have appropriated most of it shall occupy the posts of honor and power. Surely the people who did this have discovered the secret of human progressiveness, and must have kept themselves steadily at the head of the movement of the world. On the contrary, they have become stationary—have remained so for thousands of years; and if they are ever to be farther improved, it must be by foreigners. They have succeeded beyond all hope in what English philanthropists are so industriously working at—in making a people all alike, all governing their thoughts and conduct by the same maxims and rules; and these are the fruits. The modern regime of public opinion is, in an unorganized form, what the Chinese educational and political systems are in an organized; and unless individuality shall be able successfully to assert itself against this yoke, Europe, notwithstanding its noble antecedents and its professed Christianity, will tend to become another China.

* * *

1859

The Subjection of Women
After its 1869 publication in England and America, Mill's *The Subjection of Women* was quickly adopted by the leaders of the suffrage movement as the definitive analysis of the position of women in society. American suffragists sold copies of the book at their conventions; at the age of seventy-nine, American reformer Sarah Grimké went door to door in her hometown to sell one hundred copies.

The book had its roots in a tradition of libertarian thought and writing dating from the late eighteenth century. Out of this context came the first major work of feminist theory, Mary Wollstonecraft's *A Vindication of the Rights of Woman* (1792). (Wollstonecraft's reputation was so scandalous that Mill avoided referring to her work.) In the early decades of the nineteenth century, there was much discussion of women's rights in the Unitarian and radical circles inhabited by Mill and his wife, Harriet Taylor, who wrote her own essay on women's suffrage. By the middle of the century, the "Woman Question," as the Victorians called it, had become a frequent subject of writing and debate; and an organized feminist movement had begun to develop. Early reform efforts focused on the conditions of women's work, particularly in mines and factories; access to better jobs and to higher education; and married women's property rights. Women's suffrage started attracting support in the 1860s. Mill himself introduced the first parliamentary motion extending the franchise to women in 1866.

From The Subjection of Women

From *Chapter 1*

The object of this Essay is to explain as clearly as I am able, the grounds of an opinion which I have held from the very earliest period when I had formed any opinions at all on social or political matters, and which, instead of being weakened or modified, has been constantly growing stronger by the progress of reflection and the experience of life: That the principle which regulates the existing social relations between the two sexes—the legal subordination of one sex to the other—is wrong in itself, and now one of the chief hindrances to human improvement; and that it ought to be replaced by a principle of perfect equality, admitting no power or privilege on the one side, nor disability on the other.

* * *

Some will object, that a comparison cannot fairly be made between the government of the male sex and the forms of unjust power[1] which I have adduced in illustration of it, since these are arbitrary, and the effect of mere usurpation, while it on the contrary is natural. But was there ever any domination which did not appear natural to those who possessed it? There was a time when the division of mankind into two classes, a small one of masters and a numerous one of slaves, appeared, even to the most cultivated minds, to be a natural, and the only natural, condition of the human race. No less an intellect, and one which contributed no less to the progress of human thought, than Aristotle, held this opinion without doubt or misgiving; and rested it on the same premises on which the same assertion in regard to the dominion of men over women is usually based, namely that there are different natures among mankind, free natures, and slave natures; that the Greeks were of a free nature, the barbarian races of Thracians and Asiatics of a slave nature. But why need I go back to Aristotle? Did not the slaveowners of the Southern United States maintain the same doctrine, with all the fanaticism with which men cling to the theories that justify their passions and legitimate their personal interests? Did they not call heaven and earth to witness that the dominion of the white man over the black is natural, that the black race

1. As examples of unjust power Mill had cited the forceful control of slaves by slave owners or of nations by military despots.

is by nature incapable of freedom, and marked out for slavery? some even going so far as to say that the freedom of manual laborers is an unnatural order of things anywhere. Again, the theorists of absolute monarchy have always affirmed it to be the only natural form of government; issuing from the patriarchal, which was the primitive and spontaneous form of society, framed on the model of the paternal, which is anterior to society itself, and, as they contend, the most natural authority of all. Nay, for that matter, the law of force itself, to those who could not plead any other, has always seemed the most natural of all grounds for the exercise of authority. Conquering races hold it to be Nature's own dictate that the conquered should obey the conquerors, or, as they euphoniously paraphrase it, that the feebler and more unwarlike races should submit to the braver and manlier. The smallest acquaintance with human life in the middle ages, shows how supremely natural the dominion of the feudal nobility over men of low condition appeared to the nobility themselves, and how unnatural the conception seemed, of a person of the inferior class claiming equality with them, or exercising authority over them. It hardly seemed less so to the class held in subjection. The emancipated serfs and burgesses, even in their most vigorous struggles, never made any pretension to a share of authority; they only demanded more or less of limitation to the power of tyrannizing over them. So true is it that unnatural generally means only uncustomary, and that everything which is usual appears natural. The subjection of women to men being a universal custom, any departure from it quite naturally appears unnatural. But how entirely, even in this case, the feeling is dependent on custom, appears by ample experience. Nothing so much astonishes the people of distant parts of the world, when they first learn anything about England, as to be told that it is under a queen: the thing seems to them so unnatural as to be almost incredible. To Englishmen this does not seem in the least degree unnatural, because they are used to it; but they do feel it unnatural that women should be soldiers or members of Parliament. In the feudal ages, on the contrary, war and politics were not thought unnatural to women, because not unusual; it seemed natural that women of the privileged classes should be of manly character, inferior in nothing but bodily strength to their husbands and fathers. The independence of women seemed rather less unnatural to the Greeks than to other ancients, on account of the fabulous Amazons[2] (whom they believed to be historical), and the partial example afforded by the Spartan women; who, though no less subordinate by law than in other Greek states, were more free in fact, and being trained to bodily exercises in the same manner with men, gave ample proof that they were not naturally disqualified for them. There can be little doubt that Spartan experience suggested to Plato, among many other of his doctrines, that of the social and political equality of the two sexes.[3]

But, it will be said, the rule of men over women differs from all these others in not being a rule of force: it is accepted voluntarily; women make no complaint, and are consenting parties to it. In the first place, a great number of women do not accept it. Ever since there have been women able to make their sentiments known by their writings (the only mode of publicity which

2. A mythical race of woman warriors.
3. Plato's *Republic*, book 5. Plato was Athenian.

society permits to them), an increasing number of them have recorded protests against their present social condition: and recently many thousands of them, headed by the most eminent women known to the public, have petitioned Parliament for their admission to the Parliamentary Suffrage.[4] The claim of women to be educated as solidly, and in the same branches of knowledge, as men, is urged with growing intensity, and with a great prospect of success; while the demand for their admission into professions and occupations hitherto closed against them, becomes every year more urgent. Though there are not in this country, as there are in the United States, periodical Conventions[5] and an organized party to agitate for the Rights of Women, there is a numerous and active Society organized and managed by women, for the more limited object of obtaining the political franchise. Nor is it only in our own country and in America that women are beginning to protest, more or less collectively, against the disabilities under which they labor. France, and Italy, and Switzerland, and Russia now afford examples of the same thing. How many more women there are who silently cherish similar aspirations, no one can possibly know; but there are abundant tokens how many *would* cherish them, were they not so strenuously taught to repress them as contrary to the proprieties of their sex. It must be remembered, also, that no enslaved class ever asked for complete liberty at once. When Simon de Montfort[6] called the deputies of the commons to sit for the first time in Parliament, did any of them dream of demanding that an assembly, elected by their constituents, should make and destroy ministries, and dictate to the king in affairs of state? No such thought entered into the imagination of the most ambitious of them. The nobility had already these pretensions; the commons pretended to nothing but to be exempt from arbitrary taxation, and from the gross individual oppression of the king's officers. It is a political law of nature that those who are under any power of ancient origin, never begin by complaining of the power itself, but only of its oppressive exercise. There is never any want of women who complain of ill usage by their husbands. There would be infinitely more, if complaint were not the greatest of all provocatives to a repetition and increase of the ill usage. It is this which frustrates all attempts to maintain the power but protect the woman against its abuses. In no other case (except that of a child) is the person who has been proved judicially to have suffered an injury, replaced under the physical power of the culprit who inflicted it. Accordingly wives, even in the most extreme and protracted cases of bodily ill usage, hardly ever dare avail themselves of the laws made for their protection: and if, in a moment of irrepressible indignation, or by the interference of neighbors, they are induced to do so, their whole effort afterward is to disclose as little as they can, and to beg off their tyrant from his merited chastisement.

All causes, social and natural, combine to make it unlikely that women should be collectively rebellious to the power of men. They are so far in a position different from all other subject classes, that their masters require

4. As a member of the House of Commons, Mill had introduced a petition for women's suffrage in 1866.
5. Such as the Women's Rights Convention held at Worcester, Massachusetts, in October 1850, which had occasioned an essay by Mill's wife

titled "Enfranchisement of Women" (1851).
6. English nobleman and statesman (ca. 1208–1265), who assembled a parliament in 1265 that has been called the basis of the modern House of Commons.

something more from them than actual service. Men do not want solely the obedience of women, they want their sentiments. All men, except the most brutish, desire to have, in the woman most nearly connected with them, not a forced slave but a willing one, not a slave merely, but a favorite. They have therefore put everything in practice to enslave their minds. The masters of all other slaves rely, for maintaining obedience, on fear; either fear of themselves, or religious fears. The masters of women wanted more than simple obedience, and they turned the whole force of education to effect their purpose. All women are brought up from the very earliest years in the belief that their ideal of character is the very opposite to that of men; not self-will, and government by self-control, but submission, and yielding to the control of others. All the moralities tell them that it is the duty of women, and all the current sentimentalities that it is their nature, to live for others; to make complete abnegation of themselves, and to have no life but in their affections. And by their affections are meant the only ones they are allowed to have—those to the men with whom they are connected, or to the children who constitute an additional and indefeasible tie between them and a man. When we put together three things—first, the natural attraction between opposite sexes; secondly, the wife's entire dependence on the husband, every privilege or pleasure she has being either his gift, or depending entirely on his will; and lastly, that the principal object of human pursuit, consideration, and all objects of social ambition, can in general be sought or obtained by her only through him, it would be a miracle if the object of being attractive to men had not become the polar star of feminine education and formation of character. And, this great means of influence over the minds of women having been acquired, an instinct of selfishness made men avail themselves of it to the utmost as a means of holding women in subjection, by representing to them meekness, submissiveness, and resignation of all individual will into the hands of a man, as an essential part of sexual attractiveness. Can it be doubted that any of the other yokes which mankind have succeeded in breaking, would have subsisted till now if the same means had existed, and had been as sedulously used, to bow down their minds to it? If it had been made the object of the life of every young plebeian to find personal favor in the eyes of some patrician, of every young serf with some seigneur; if domestication with him, and a share of his personal affections, had been held out as the prize which they all should look out for, the most gifted and aspiring being able to reckon on the most desirable prizes; and if, when this prize had been obtained, they had been shut out by a wall of brass from all interests not centering in him, all feelings and desires but those which he shared or inculcated; would not serfs and seigneurs, plebeians and patricians, have been as broadly distinguished at this day as men and women are? and would not all but a thinker here and there, have believed the distinction to be a fundamental and unalterable fact in human nature?

The preceding considerations are amply sufficient to show that custom, however universal it may be, affords in this case no presumption, and ought not to create any prejudice, in favor of the arrangements which place women in social and political subjection to men. But I may go farther, and maintain that the course of history, and the tendencies of progressive human society, afford not only no presumption in favor of this system of inequality of rights, but a strong one against it; and that, so far as the whole course of human improvement up to this time, the whole stream of modern tendencies, warrants any inference on the subject, it is, that this relic of the past is discordant with the future, and must necessarily disappear.

For, what is the peculiar character of the modern world—the difference which chiefly distinguishes modern institutions, modern social ideas, modern life itself, from those of times long past? It is, that human beings are no longer born to their place in life, and chained down by an inexorable bond to the place they are born to, but are free to employ their faculties, and such favourable chances as offer, to achieve the lot which may appear to them most desirable.

* * *

The social subordination of women thus stands out an isolated fact in modern social institutions; a solitary breach of what has become their fundamental law; a single relic of an old world of thought and practice exploded in everything else, but retained in the one thing of most universal interest; as if a gigantic dolmen,[7] or a vast temple of Jupiter Olympius, occupied the site of St. Paul's[8] and received daily worship, while the surrounding Christian churches were only resorted to on fasts and festivals. This entire discrepancy between one social fact and all those which accompany it, and the radical opposition between its nature and the progressive movement which is the boast of the modern world, and which has successively swept away everything else of an analogous character, surely affords, to a conscientious observer of human tendencies, serious matter for reflection. It raises a *primâ facie* presumption on the unfavorable side, far outweighing any which custom and usage could in such circumstances create on the favorable; and should at least suffice to make this, like the choice between republicanism and royalty, a balanced question.

The least that can be demanded is, that the question should not be considered as prejudged by existing fact and existing opinion, but open to discussion on its merits, as a question of justice and expediency: the decision on this, as on any of the other social arrangements of mankind, depending on what an enlightened estimate of tendencies and consequences may show to be most advantageous to humanity in general, without distinction of sex. And the discussion must be a real discussion, descending to foundations, and not resting satisfied with vague and general assertions. It will not do, for instance, to assert in general terms, that the experience of mankind has pronounced in favor of the existing system. Experience cannot possibly have decided between two courses, so long as there has only been experience of one. If it be said that the doctrine of the equality of the sexes rests only on theory, it must be remembered that the contrary doctrine also has only theory to rest upon. All that is proved in its favor by direct experience, is that mankind have been able to exist under it, and to attain the degree of improvement and prosperity which we now see; but whether that prosperity has been attained sooner, or is now greater, than it would have been under the other system, experience does not say. On the other hand, experience does say, that every step in improvement has been so invariably accompanied by a step made in raising the social position of women, that historians

7. Prehistoric stone monument, here associated with pagan religious rites. 8. The cathedral in the city of London.

and philosophers have been led to adopt their elevation or debasement as on the whole the surest test and most correct measure of the civilization of a people or an age. Through all the progressive period of human history, the condition of women has been approaching nearer to equality with men. This does not of itself prove that the assimilation must go on to complete equality; but it assuredly affords some presumption that such is the case.

Neither does it avail anything to say that the *nature* of the two sexes adapts them to their present functions and position, and renders these appropriate to them. Standing on the ground of common sense and the constitution of the human mind, I deny that any one knows, or can know, the nature of the two sexes, as long as they have only been seen in their present relation to one another. If men had ever been found in society without women, or women without men, or if there had been a society of men and women in which the women were not under the control of the men, something might have been positively known about the mental and moral differences which may be inherent in the nature of each. What is now called the nature of women is an eminently artificial thing—the result of forced repression in some directions, unnatural stimulation in others. It may be asserted without scruple, that no other class of dependents have had their character so entirely distorted from its natural proportions by their relation with their masters; for, if conquered and slave races have been, in some respects, more forcibly repressed, whatever in them has not been crushed down by an iron heel has generally been let alone, and if left with any liberty of development, it has developed itself according to its own laws; but in the case of women, a hot-house[9] and stove cultivation has always been carried on of some of the capabilities of their nature, for the benefit and pleasure of their masters. Then, because certain products of the general vital force sprout luxuriantly and reach a great development in this heated atmosphere and under this active nurture and watering, while other shoots from the same root, which are left outside in the wintry air, with ice purposely heaped all round them, have a stunted growth, and some are burnt off with fire and disappear; men, with that inability to recognize their own work which distinguishes the unanalytic mind, indolently believe that the tree grows of itself in the way they have made it grow, and that it would die if one half of it were not kept in a vapour bath and the other half in the snow.

Of all difficulties which impede the progress of thought, and the formation of well-grounded opinions on life and social arrangements, the greatest is now the unspeakable ignorance and inattention of mankind in respect to the influences which form human character. Whatever any portion of the human species now are, or seem to be, such, it is supposed, they have a natural tendency to be: even when the most elementary knowledge of the circumstances in which they have been placed, clearly points out the causes that made them what they are. Because a cottier[1] deeply in arrears to his landlord is not industrious, there are people who think that the Irish are naturally idle. Because constitutions can be overthrown when the authorities appointed to execute them turn their arms against them, there are people who think the French incapable of free government. Because the Greeks cheated the Turks, and the Turks only plundered the Greeks, there are per-

---

9. A heated greenhouse.   1. Tenant cottager on a small Irish farm.

sons who think that the Turks are naturally more sincere: and because women, as is often said, care nothing about politics except their personalities, it is supposed that the general good is naturally less interesting to women than to men. History, which is now so much better understood than formerly, teaches another lesson: if only by showing the extraordinary susceptibility of human nature to external influences, and the extreme variableness of those of its manifestations which are supposed to be most universal and uniform. But in history, as in traveling, men usually see only what they already had in their own minds; and few learn much from history, who do not bring much with them to its study.

Hence, in regard to that most difficult question, what are the natural differences between the two sexes—a subject on which it is impossible in the present state of society to obtain complete and correct knowledge—while almost everybody dogmatizes upon it, almost all neglect and make light of the only means by which any partial insight can be obtained into it. This is, an analytic study of the most important department of psychology, the laws of the influence of circumstances on character. For, however great and apparently ineradicable the moral and intellectual differences between men and women might be, the evidence of their being natural differences could only be negative. Those only could be inferred to be natural which could not possibly be artificial—the residuum, after deducting every characteristic of either sex which can admit of being explained from education or external circumstances. The profoundest knowledge of the laws of the formation of character is indispensable to entitle any one to affirm even that there is any difference, much more what the difference is, between the two sexes considered as moral and rational beings; and since no one, as yet, has that knowledge (for there is hardly any subject which, in proportion to its importance, has been so little studied), no one is thus far entitled to any positive opinion on the subject. Conjectures are all that can at present be made; conjectures more or less probable, according as more or less authorized by such knowledge as we yet have of the laws of psychology, as applied to the formation of character.

Even the preliminary knowledge, what the differences between the sexes now are, apart from all question as to how they are made what they are, is still in the crudest[2] and most incomplete state. Medical practitioners and physiologists have ascertained, to some extent, the differences in bodily constitution; and this is an important element to the psychologist: but hardly any medical practitioner is a psychologist. Respecting the mental characteristics of women; their observations are of no more worth than those of common men. It is a subject on which nothing final can be known, so long as those who alone can really know it, women themselves, have given but little testimony, and that little, mostly suborned. It is easy to know stupid women. Stupidity is much the same all the world over. A stupid person's notions and feelings may confidently be inferred from those which prevail in the circle by which the person is surrounded. Not so with those whose opinions and feelings are an emanation from their own nature and faculties. It is only a man here and there who has any tolerable knowledge of the character even of the women of his own family. I do not mean, of their capabilities; these

2. Roughest, least refined.

nobody knows, not even themselves, because most of them have never been called out. I mean their actually existing thoughts and feelings. Many a man thinks he perfectly understands women, because he has had amatory relations with several, perhaps with many of them. If he is a good observer, and his experience extends to quality as well as quantity, he may have learnt something of one narrow department of their nature—an important department, no doubt. But of all the rest of it, few persons are generally more ignorant, because there are few from whom it is so carefully hidden. The most favorable case which a man can generally have for studying the character of a woman, is that of his own wife: for the opportunities are greater, and the cases of complete sympathy not so unspeakably rare. And in fact, this is the source from which any knowledge worth having on the subject has, I believe, generally come. But most men have not had the opportunity of studying in this way more than a single case: accordingly one can, to an almost laughable degree, infer what a man's wife is like, from his opinions about women in general. To make even this one case yield any result, the woman must be worth knowing, and the man not only a competent judge, but of a character so sympathetic in itself, and so well adapted to hers, that he can either read her mind by sympathetic intuition, or has nothing in himself which makes her shy of disclosing it. Hardly anything, I believe, can be more rare than this conjunction. It often happens that there is the most complete unity of feeling and community of interests as to all external things, yet the one has as little admission into the internal life of the other as if they were common acquaintance. Even with true affection, authority on the one side and subordination on the other prevent perfect confidence. Though nothing may be intentionally withheld, much is not shown. In the analogous relation of parent and child, the corresponding phenomenon must have been in the observation of every one. As between father and son, how many are the cases in which the father, in spite of real affection on both sides, obviously to all the world does not know, nor suspect, parts of the son's character familiar to his companions and equals. The truth is, that the position of looking up to another is extremely unpropitious to complete sincerity and openness with him. The fear of losing ground in his opinion or in his feelings is so strong, that even in an upright character, there is an unconscious tendency to show only the best side, or the side which, though not the best, is that which he most likes to see: and it may be confidently said that thorough knowledge of one another hardly ever exists, but between persons who, besides being intimates, are equals. How much more true, then, must all this be, when the one is not only under the authority of the other, but has it inculcated on her as a duty to reckon everything else subordinate to his comfort and pleasure, and to let him neither see nor feel anything coming from her, except what is agreeable to him. All these difficulties stand in the way of a man's obtaining any thorough knowledge even of the one woman whom alone, in general, he has sufficient opportunity of studying. When we further consider that to understand one woman is not necessarily to understand any other woman; that even if he could study many women of one rank, or of one country, he would not thereby understand women of other ranks or countries; and even if he did, they are still only the women of a single period of history; we may safely assert that the knowledge which men can acquire of women, even as they have been and are, without reference to what they might be, is wretchedly imperfect and superficial, and always will be so, until women themselves have told all that they have to tell.

And this time has not come; nor will it come otherwise than gradually. It is but of yesterday that women have either been qualified by literary accomplishments, or permitted by society, to tell anything to the general public. As yet very few of them dare tell anything, which men, on whom their literary success depends, are unwilling to hear. Let us remember in what manner, up to a very recent time, the expression, even by a male author, of uncustomary opinions, or what are deemed eccentric feelings, usually was, and in some degree still is, received; and we may form some faint conception under what impediments a woman, who is brought up to think custom and opinion her sovereign rule, attempts to express in books anything drawn from the depths of her own nature. The greatest woman who has left writings behind her sufficient to give her an eminent rank in the literature of her country, thought it necessary to prefix as a motto to her boldest work, "Un homme peut braver l'opinion; une femme doit s'y soumettre."[3] The greater part of what women write about women is mere sycophancy to men. In the case of unmarried women, much of it seems only intended to increase their chance of a husband. Many, both married and unmarried, overstep the mark, and inculcate a servility beyond what is desired or relished by any man, except the very vulgarest. But this is not so often the case as, even at a quite late period, it still was. Literary women are becoming more freespoken, and more willing to express their real sentiments. Unfortunately, in this country especially, they are themselves such artificial products, that their sentiments are compounded of a small element of individual observation and consciousness, and a very large one of acquired associations. This will be less and less the case, but it will remain true to a great extent, as long as social institutions do not admit the same free development of originality in women which is possible to men. When that time comes, and not before, we shall see, and not merely hear, as much as it is necessary to know of the nature of women, and the adaptation of other things to it.

* * *

One thing we may be certain of—that what is contrary to women's nature to do, they never will be made to do by simply giving their nature free play. The anxiety of mankind to interfere in behalf of nature, for fear lest nature should not succeed in effecting its purpose, is an altogether unnecessary solicitude. What women by nature cannot do, it is quite superfluous to forbid them from doing. What they can do, but not so well as the men who are their competitors, competition suffices to exclude them from; since nobody asks for protective duties and bounties in favor of women; it is only asked that the present bounties and protective duties in favor of men should be recalled. If women have a greater natural inclination for some things than for others, there is no need of laws or social inculcation to make the majority of them do the former in preference to the latter. Whatever women's services are most wanted for, the free play of competition will hold out the strongest

3. A man can defy what is thought; a woman must submit to it (French); the epigraph to *Delphine* (1802) by Mme de Staël (1766–1817).

inducements to them to undertake. And, as the words imply, they are most wanted for the things for which they are most fit; by the apportionment of which to them, the collective faculties of the two sexes can be applied on the whole with the greatest sum of valuable result.

The general opinion of men is supposed to be, that the natural vocation of a woman is that of a wife and mother. I say, is supposed to be, because, judging from acts—from the whole of the present constitution of society— one might infer that their opinion was the direct contrary. They might be supposed to think that the alleged natural vocation of women was of all things the most repugnant to their nature; insomuch that if they are free to do anything else—if any other means of living, or occupation of their time and faculties, is open, which has any chance of appearing desirable to them—there will not be enough of them who will be willing to accept the condition said to be natural to them. If this is the real opinion of men in general, it would be well that it should be spoken out. I should like to hear somebody openly enunciating the doctrine (it is already implied in much that is written on the subject)—"It is necessary to society that women should marry and produce children. They will not do so unless they are compelled. Therefore it is necessary to compel them." The merits of the case would then be clearly defined. It would be exactly that of the slaveholders of South Carolina and Louisiana. "It is necessary that cotton and sugar should be grown. White men cannot produce them. Negroes will not, for any wages which we choose to give. *Ergo* they must be compelled." An illustration still closer to the point is that of impressment.[4] Sailors must absolutely be had to defend the country. It often happens that they will not voluntarily enlist. Therefore there must be the power of forcing them. How often has this logic been used! and, but for one flaw in it, without doubt it would have been suc- cessful up to this day. But it is open to the retort—First pay the sailors the honest value of their labor. When you have made it as well worth their while to serve you, as to work for other employers, you will have no more difficulty than others have in obtaining their services. To this there is no logical answer except "I will not:" and as people are now not only ashamed, but are not desirous, to rob the laborer of his hire, impressment is no longer advocated. Those who attempt to force women into marriage by closing all other doors against them, lay themselves open to a similar retort. If they mean what they say, their opinion must evidently be, that men do not render the married condition so desirable to women, as to induce them to accept it for its own recommendations. It is not a sign of one's thinking the boon one offers very attractive, when one allows only Hobson's choice,[5] "that or none." And here, I believe, is the clue to the feelings of those men, who have a real antipathy to the equal freedom of women. I believe they are afraid, not lest women should be unwilling to marry, for I do not think that any one in reality has that apprehension; but lest they should insist that marriage should be on equal conditions; lest all women of spirit and capacity should prefer doing almost anything else, not in their own eyes degrading, rather than marry, when marrying is giving themselves a master, and a master too of all their

---

4. The practice of seizing men and forcing them into service as sailors.

5. A choice without an alternative, so called in reference to the practice of Thomas Hobson (1544–1630), who rented out horses and required every customer to take the horse nearest the door.

earthly possessions. And truly, if this consequence were necessarily incident to marriage, I think that the apprehension would be very well founded. I agree in thinking it probable that few women, capable of anything else, would, unless under an irresistible *entrainement*,[6] rendering them for the time insensible to anything but itself, choose such a lot, when any other means were open to them of filling a conventionally honorable place in life: and if men are determined that the law of marriage shall be a law of despotism, they are quite right, in point of mere policy, in leaving to women only Hobson's choice. But, in that case, all that has been done in the modern world to relax the chain on the minds of women, has been a mistake. They never should have been allowed to receive a literary education. Women who read, much more women who write, are, in the existing constitution of things, a contradiction and a disturbing element: and it was wrong to bring women up with any acquirements but those of an odalisque, or of a domestic servant.

1860

1869

From Autobiography

From *Chapter 5. A Crisis in My Mental History.*
One Stage Onward

For some years after this time[1] I wrote very little, and nothing regularly, for publication: and great were the advantages which I derived from the intermission. It was of no common importance to me, at this period, to be able to digest and mature my thoughts for my own mind only, without any immediate call for giving them out in print. Had I gone on writing, it would have much disturbed the important transformation in my opinions and character, which took place during those years. The origin of this transformation, or at least the process by which I was prepared for it, can only be explained by turning some distance back.

From the winter of 1821, when I first read Bentham,[2] and especially from the commencement of the *Westminster Review*, I had what might truly be called an object in life; to be a reformer of the world. My conception of my own happiness was entirely identified with this object. The personal sympathies I wished for were those of fellow laborers in this enterprise. I endeavored to pick up as many followers as I could by the way; but as a serious and permanent personal satisfaction to rest upon, my whole reliance was placed on this; and I was accustomed to felicitate myself on the certainty of a happy life which I enjoyed, through placing my happiness in something durable and distant, in which some progress might be always making, while it could never be exhausted by complete attainment. This did very well for several years, during which the general improvement going on in the world and the idea of myself as engaged with others in struggling to promote it, seemed enough to fill up an interesting and animated existence. But the time came

6. Rapture (French).
1. I.e., 1828. Mill had been contributing articles to the *Westminster Review*, a respected monthly periodical.

2. Jeremy Bentham (1748–1832), founder of Utilitarianism and a co-founder of the *Westminster Review*.

when I awakened from this as from a dream. It was in the autumn of 1826.
I was in a dull state of nerves, such as everybody is occasionally liable to;
unsusceptible to enjoyment or pleasurable excitement; one of those moods
when what is pleasure at other times becomes insipid or indifferent; the
state, I should think, in which converts to Methodism usually are, when
smitten by their first "conviction of sin." In this frame of mind it occurred to
me to put the question directly to myself: "Suppose that all your objects in
life were realized; that all the changes in institutions and opinions which you
are looking forward to could be completely effected at this very instant: would
this be a great joy and happiness to you?" And an irrepressible self-
consciousness distinctly answered, "No!" At this my heart sank within me:
the whole foundation on which my life was constructed fell down. All my
happiness was to have been found in the continual pursuit of this end. The
end had ceased to charm, and how could there ever again be any interest in
the means? I seemed to have nothing left to live for.

At first I hoped that the cloud would pass away of itself; but it did not. A
night's sleep, the sovereign remedy for the smaller vexations of life, had no
effect on it. I awoke to a renewed consciousness of the woeful fact. I carried
it with me into all companies, into all occupations. Hardly anything had
power to cause me even a few minutes' oblivion of it. For some months the
cloud seemed to grow thicker and thicker. The lines in Coleridge's *Dejection*—I was not then acquainted with them—exactly describe my case:

> A grief without a pang, void, dark and drear,
> A drowsy, stifled, unimpassioned grief,
> Which finds no natural outlet or relief
> In word, or sigh, or tear.[3]

In vain I sought relief from my favorite books; those memorials of past
nobleness and greatness from which I had always hitherto drawn strength
and animation. I read them now without feeling, or with the accustomed
feeling minus all its charm; and I became persuaded that my love of mankind, and of excellence for its own sake, had worn itself out. I sought no
comfort by speaking to others of what I felt. If I had loved anyone sufficiently
to make confiding my griefs a necessity, I should not have been in the condition I was. I felt, too, that mine was not an interesting, or in any way respectable distress. There was nothing in it to attract sympathy. Advice, if I had
known where to seek it, would have been most precious. The words of Macbeth to the physician[4] often occurred to my thoughts. But there was no one
on whom I could build the faintest hope of such assistance. My father, to
whom it would have been natural to me to have recourse in any practical
difficulties, was the last person to whom, in such a case as this, I looked for
help. Everything convinced me that he had no knowledge of any such mental state as I was suffering from, and that even if he could be made to understand it, he was not the physician who could heal it. My education, which
was wholly his work, had been conducted without any regard to the possibility of its ending in this result; and I saw no use in giving him the pain of
thinking that his plans had failed, when the failure was probably irremedia-

---

3. "Dejection: An Ode" (1802), lines 21–24.
4. Shakespeare's *Macbeth* 5.3.42: "Canst thou not minister to a mind diseased . . . ?"

ble, and, at all events, beyond the power of *his* remedies. Of other friends, I had at that time none to whom I had any hope of making my condition intelligible. It was however abundantly intelligible to myself; and the more I dwelt upon it, the more hopeless it appeared.

My course of study had led me to believe that all mental and moral feelings and qualities, whether of a good or of a bad kind, were the results of association; that we love one thing, and hate another, take pleasure in one sort of action or contemplation, and pain in another sort, through the clinging of pleasurable or painful ideas to those things, from the effect of education or of experience. As a corollary from this, I had always heard it maintained by my father, and was myself convinced, that the object of education should be to form the strongest possible associations of the salutary class; associations of pleasure with all things beneficial to the great whole, and of pain with all things hurtful to it. This doctrine appeared inexpugnable;[5] but it now seemed to me, on retrospect, that my teachers had occupied themselves but superficially with the means of forming and keeping up these salutary associations. They seemed to have trusted altogether to the old familiar instruments, praise and blame, reward and punishment. Now, I did not doubt that by these means, begun early, and applied unremittingly, intense associations of pain and pleasure, especially of pain, might be created, and might produce desires and aversions capable of lasting undiminished to the end of life. But there must always be something artificial and casual in associations thus produced. The pains and pleasures thus forcibly associated with things are not connected with them by any natural tie; and it is therefore, I thought, essential to the durability of these associations that they should have become so intense and inveterate as to be practically indissoluble, before the habitual exercise of the power of analysis had commenced. For I now saw, or thought I saw, what I had always before received with incredulity—that the habit of analysis has a tendency to wear away the feelings: as indeed it has, when no other mental habit is cultivated, and the analyzing spirit remains without its natural complements and correctives. The very excellence of analysis (I argued) is that it tends to weaken and undermine whatever is the result of prejudice; that it enables us mentally to separate ideas which have only casually clung together: and no associations whatever could ultimately resist this dissolving force, were it not that we owe to analysis our clearest knowledge of the permanent sequences in nature; the real connections between Things, not dependent on our will and feelings; natural laws, by virtue of which, in many cases, one thing is inseparable from another in fact; which laws, in proportion as they are clearly perceived and imaginatively realized, cause our ideas of things which are always joined together in Nature to cohere more and more closely in our thoughts. Analytic habits may thus even strengthen the associations between causes and effects, means and ends, but tend altogether to weaken those which are, to speak familiarly, a *mere* matter of feeling. They are therefore (I thought) favorable to prudence and clear-sightedness, but a perpetual worm at the root both of the passions and of the virtues; and, above all, fearfully undermine all desires, and all pleasures, which are the effects of association, that is, according to the theory I held, all except the purely physical and organic; of the entire

5. Unconquerable.

insufficiency of which to make life desirable, no one had a stronger conviction than I had. These were the laws of human nature, by which, as it seemed to me, I had been brought to my present state. All those to whom I looked up were of opinion that the pleasure of sympathy with human beings, and the feelings which made the good of others, and especially of mankind on a large scale, the object of existence, were the greatest and surest sources of happiness. Of the truth of this I was convinced, but to know that a feeling would make me happy if I had it, did not give me the feeling. My education, I thought, had failed to create these feelings in sufficient strength to resist the dissolving influence of analysis, while the whole course of my intellectual cultivation had made precocious and premature analysis the inveterate habit of my mind. I was thus, as I said to myself, left stranded at the commencement of my voyage, with a well-equipped ship and a rudder, but no sail; without any real desire for the ends which I had been so carefully fitted out to work for: no delight in virtue, or the general good, but also just as little in anything else. The fountains of vanity and ambition seemed to have dried up within me, as completely as those of benevolence. I had had (as I reflected) some gratification of vanity at too early an age: I had obtained some distinction, and felt myself of some importance, before the desire of distinction and of importance had grown into a passion: and little as it was which I had attained, yet having been attained too early, like all pleasures enjoyed too soon, it had made me *blasé* and indifferent to the pursuit. Thus neither selfish nor unselfish pleasures were pleasures to me. And there seemed no power in nature sufficient to begin the formation of my character anew, and create in a mind now irretrievably analytic, fresh associations of pleasure with any of the objects of human desire.

These were the thoughts which mingled with the dry heavy dejection of the melancholy winter of 1826–7. During this time I was not incapable of my usual occupations. I went on with them mechanically, by the mere force of habit. I had been so drilled in a certain sort of mental exercise that I could still carry it on when all the spirit had gone out of it. I even composed and spoke several speeches at the debating society, how, or with what degree of success, I know not. Of four years continual speaking at that society, this is the only year of which I remember next to nothing. Two lines of Coleridge, in whom alone of all writers I have found a true description of what I felt, were often in my thoughts, not at this time (for I had never read them), but in a later period of the same mental malady:

> Work without hope draws nectar in a sieve,
> And hope without an object cannot live.[6]

In all probability my case was by no means so peculiar as I fancied it, and I doubt not that many others have passed through a similar state; but the idiosyncrasies of my education had given to the general phenomenon a special character, which made it seem the natural effect of causes that it was hardly possible for time to remove. I frequently asked myself if I could, or if I was bound to go on living, when life must be passed in this manner. I generally answered to myself, that I did not think I could possibly bear it beyond a year. When, however, not more than half that duration of time had elapsed,

6. The last two lines of Coleridge's short poem "Work without Hope" (1828).

a small ray of light broke in upon my gloom. I was reading, accidentally, Marmontel's *Mémoires*,[7] and came to the passage which relates his father's death, the distressed position of the family, and the sudden inspiration by which he, then a mere boy, felt and made them feel that he would be everything to them—would supply the place of all that they had lost. A vivid conception of that scene and its feelings came over me, and I was moved to tears. From this moment my burden grew lighter. The oppression of the thought that all feeling was dead within me was gone. I was no longer hopeless: I was not a stock or a stone. I had still, it seemed, some of the material out of which all worth of character, and all capacity for happiness, are made. Relieved from my ever present sense of irremediable wretchedness, I gradually found that the ordinary incidents of life could again give me some pleasure; that I could again find enjoyment, not intense, but sufficient for cheerfulness, in sunshine and sky, in books, in conversation, in public affairs; and that there was, once more, excitement, though of a moderate kind, in exerting myself for my opinions, and for the public good. Thus the cloud gradually drew off, and I again enjoyed life: and though I had several relapses, some of which lasted many months, I never again was as miserable as I had been.

The experiences of this period had two very marked effects on my opinions and character. In the first place, they led me to adopt a theory of life, very unlike that on which I had before acted, and having much in common with what at that time I certainly had never heard of, the anti-self-consciousness theory of Carlyle.[8] I never, indeed, wavered in the conviction that happiness is the test of all rules of conduct, and the end of life. But I now thought that this end was only to be attained by not making it the direct end. Those only are happy (I thought) who have their minds fixed on some object other than their own happiness; on the happiness of others, on the improvement of mankind, even on some art or pursuit, followed not as a means, but as itself an ideal end. Aiming thus at something else, they find happiness by the way. The enjoyments of life (such was now my theory) are sufficient to make it a pleasant thing, when they are taken *en passant*,[9] without being made a principal object. Once make them so, and they are immediately felt to be insufficient. They will not bear a scrutinizing examination. Ask yourself whether you are happy, and you cease to be so. The only chance is to treat, not happiness, but some end external to it, as the purpose of life. Let your self-consciousness, your scrutiny, your self-interrogation exhaust themselves on that; and if otherwise fortunately circumstanced you will inhale happiness with the air you breathe, without dwelling on it or thinking about it, without either forestalling it in imagination, or putting it to flight by fatal questioning. This theory now became the basis of my philosophy of life. And I still hold to it as the best theory for all those who have but a moderate degree of sensibility[1] and of capacity for enjoyment, that is, for the great majority of mankind.

The other important change which my opinions at this time underwent was that I, for the first time, gave its proper place, among the prime necessities

7. Published in 1804. Jean-François Marmontel (1723–1799), French dramatist and critic.
8. See "The Everlasting Yea" (p. 46), of Carlyle's

Sartor Resartus (1833–34).
9. In passing (French).
1. Sensitivity.

of human well-being, to the internal culture of the individual. I ceased to attach almost exclusive importance to the ordering of outward circumstances, and the training of the human being for speculation and for action.

I had now learnt by experience that the passive susceptibilities needed to be cultivated as well as the active capacities, and required to be nourished and enriched as well as guided. I did not, for an instant, lose sight of, or undervalue, that part of the truth which I had seen before; I never turned recreant to intellectual culture, or ceased to consider the power and practice of analysis as an essential condition both of individual and of social improvement. But I thought that it had consequences which required to be corrected, by joining other kinds of cultivation with it. The maintenance of a due balance among the faculties now seemed to me of primary importance. The cultivation of the feelings became one of the cardinal points in my ethical and philosophical creed. And my thoughts and inclinations turned in an increasing degree toward whatever seemed capable of being instrumental to that object.

I now began to find meaning in the things which I had read or heard about the importance of poetry and art as instruments of human culture. But it was some time longer before I began to know this by personal experience. The only one of the imaginative arts in which I had from childhood taken great pleasure was music; the best effect of which (and in this it surpasses perhaps every other art) consists in exciting enthusiasm; in winding up to a high pitch those feelings of an elevated kind which are already in the character, but to which this excitement gives a glow and a fervor, which, though transitory at its utmost height, is precious for sustaining them at other times. This effect of music I had often experienced; but like all my pleasurable susceptibilities it was suspended during the gloomy period. I had sought relief again and again from this quarter, but found none. After the tide had turned, and I was in process of recovery, I had been helped forward by music, but in a much less elevated manner. I at this time first became acquainted with Weber's *Oberon*,[2] and the extreme pleasure which I drew from its delicious melodies did me good, by showing me a source of pleasure to which I was as susceptible as ever. The good, however, was much impaired by the thought that the pleasure of music (as is quite true of such pleasure as this was, that of mere tune) fades with familiarity, and requires either to be revived by intermittence, or fed by continual novelty. And it is very characteristic both of my then state, and of the general tone of my mind at this period of my life, that I was seriously tormented by the thought of the exhaustibility of musical combinations. The octave consists only of five tones and two semitones, which can be put together in only a limited number of ways, of which but a small proportion are beautiful: most of these, it seemed to me, must have been already discovered, and there could not be room for a long succession of Mozarts and Webers, to strike out, as these had done, entirely new and surpassingly rich veins of musical beauty. This source of anxiety may, perhaps, be thought to resemble that of the philosophers of Laputa,[3] who feared lest the sun should be burnt out. It was, however, connected with the best feature in my character, and the only good point to be

2. A romantic opera (1826) composed by Carl Maria von Weber (1786–1826).
3. In part 3 of *Gulliver's Travels* (1726) by Jonathan Swift (1667–1745).

found in my very unromantic and in no way honorable distress. For though my dejection, honestly looked at, could not be called other than egotistical, produced by the ruin, as I thought, of my fabric of happiness, yet the destiny of mankind in general was ever in my thoughts, and could not be separated from my own. I felt that the flaw in my life must be a flaw in life itself; that the question was whether, if the reformers of society and government could succeed in their objects, and every person in the community were free and in a state of physical comfort, the pleasures of life, being no longer kept up by struggle and privation, would cease to be pleasures. And I felt that unless I could see my way to some better hope than this for human happiness in general, my dejection must continue; but that if I could see such an outlet, I should then look on the world with pleasure; content as far as I was myself concerned, with any fair share of the general lot.

This state of my thoughts and feelings made the fact of my reading Wordsworth for the first time (in the autumn of 1828), an important event in my life. I took up the collection of his poems from curiosity, with no expectation of mental relief from it, though I had before resorted to poetry with that hope. In the worst period of my depression, I had read through the whole of Byron (then new to me), to try whether a poet, whose peculiar department was supposed to be that of the intenser feelings, could rouse any feeling in me. As might be expected, I got no good from this reading, but the reverse. The poet's state of mind was too like my own. His was the lament of a man who had worn out all pleasures, and who seemed to think that life, to all who possess the good things of it, must necessarily be the vapid, uninteresting thing which I found it. His Harold and Manfred had the same burden on them which I had; and I was not in a frame of mind to derive any comfort from the vehement sensual passion of his Giaours, or the sullenness of his Laras.[4] But while Byron was exactly what did not suit my condition, Wordsworth was exactly what did. I had looked into The Excursion[5] two or three years before, and found little in it; and I should probably have found as little had I read it at this time. But the miscellaneous poems, in the two-volume edition of 1815 (to which little of value was added in the latter part of the author's life), proved to be the precise thing for my mental wants at that particular juncture.

In the first place, these poems addressed themselves powerfully to one of the strongest of my pleasurable susceptibilities, the love of rural objects and natural scenery; to which I had been indebted not only for much of the pleasure of my life, but quite recently for relief from one of my longest relapses into depression. In this power of rural beauty over me, there was a foundation laid for taking pleasure in Wordsworth's poetry; the more so, as his scenery lies mostly among mountains, which, owing to my early Pyrenean excursion,[6] were my ideal of natural beauty. But Wordsworth would never have had any great effect on me, if he had merely placed before me beautiful pictures of natural scenery. Scott[7] does this still better than Wordsworth,

4. The heroes of some of Byron's early poems were gloomy and self-preoccupied. Mill refers here to Childe Harold's Pilgrimage (1812–18), Manfred (1817), The Giaour (1813), and Lara (1814).
5. A long meditative poem by Wordsworth, published in 1814.

6. At fifteen Mill had been deeply affected by the landscape of the Pyrenees in Spain, a mountainous region that also made a strong impression on Tennyson.
7. Sir Walter Scott (1771–1832), Scottish poet and novelist.

and a very second-rate landscape does it more effectually than any poet. What made Wordsworth's poems a medicine for my state of mind, was that they expressed, not mere outward beauty, but states of feeling, and of thought colored by feeling, under the excitement of beauty. They seemed to be the very culture of the feelings, which I was in quest of. In them I seemed to draw from a source of inward joy, of sympathetic and imaginative pleasure, which could be shared in by all human beings; which had no connection with struggle or imperfection, but would be made richer by every improvement in the physical or social condition of mankind. From them I seemed to learn what would be the perennial sources of happiness, when all the greater evils of life shall have been removed. And I felt myself at once better and happier as I came under their influence. There have certainly been, even in our own age, greater poets than Wordsworth; but poetry of deeper and loftier feeling could not have done for me at that time what his did. I needed to be made to feel that there was real, permanent happiness in tranquil contemplation. Wordsworth taught me this, not only without turning away from, but with a greatly increased interest in the common feelings and common destiny of human beings. And the delight which these poems gave me proved that with culture of this sort, there was nothing to dread from the most confirmed habit of analysis. At the conclusion of the Poems came the famous *Ode*, falsely called Platonic, *Intimations of Immortality*: in which, along with more than his usual sweetness of melody and rhythm, and along with the two passages of grand imagery but bad philosophy so often quoted, I found that he too had had similar experience to mine; that he also had felt that the first freshness of youthful enjoyment of life was not lasting; but that he had sought for compensation, and found it, in the way in which he was now teaching me to find it. The result was that I gradually, but completely, emerged from my habitual depression, and was never again subject to it. I long continued to value Wordsworth less according to his intrinsic merits than by the measure of what he had done for me. Compared with the greatest poets, he may be said to be the poet of unpoetical natures, possessed of quiet and contemplative tastes. But unpoetical natures are precisely those which require poetic cultivation. This cultivation Wordsworth is much more fitted to give than poets who are intrinsically far more poets than he.

* * *

1873

ELIZABETH BARRETT BROWNING
1806–1861

During her lifetime Elizabeth Barrett Browning was one of England's most famous poets. Passionately admired by contemporaries as diverse as John Ruskin, Algernon Charles Swinburne, and Emily Dickinson for her moral and emotional ardor and her energetic engagement with the issues of her day, she was better known than her husband, Robert Browning, at the time of her death. Her work fell into disrepute with the modernist reaction against what was seen as the inappropriate didacticism and rhetorical excess of Victorian poetry; but recently scholars interested in her exploration of what it means to be a woman poet and in her response to social and political events have restored her status as a major writer.

Barrett Browning was born into a family that derived much of its considerable wealth, on both her mother's and her father's sides, from slave-owning plantations in Jamaica. After the abolition of slavery in 1833 and numerous lawsuits, her father lost a great deal of money and was forced to sell Hope End, the opulent estate in the Malvern Hills in Herefordshire where Barrett Browning had grown up. Although the family was by no means poor after this event, its members were haunted by the fall and the fear that they might have to move to the West Indies.

The education that Barrett Browning received was unusual for a woman of her time. Availing herself of her brother's tutor, she studied Latin and Greek; she also learned how to read Hebrew. She read voraciously in history, philosophy, and literature and began to write poetry from an early age—her first volume of poetry was published when she was thirteen. But as her intellectual and literary powers matured, her personal life became increasingly circumscribed both by ill health and by her father; tyrannically protective, he had forbidden any of his eleven children to marry. By the age of thirty-nine, Elizabeth Barrett was a prominent woman of letters who lived in semiseclusion as an invalid in her father's house in Wimpole Street in the center of London; here she occasionally received visitors in her room. One of these visitors was Robert Browning, who, moved by his admiration of her poetry, wrote to tell her "I do as I say, love these books with all my heart—and I love you too." He thereby initiated a courtship that culminated in 1846 in their secret marriage and elopement to Italy, for which her father never forgave her. In Italy Barrett Browning regained much health and strength, bearing and raising a son, Pen, to whom she was ardently devoted, and becoming deeply involved in Italian nationalist politics. She and her husband made their home in Florence, at the house called Casa Guidi, where she died in 1861.

Barrett Browning's poetry is characterized by a fervent moral sensibility. In her early work she tended to use the visionary modes of Romantic narrative poetry, but she turned increasingly to contemporary topics, particularly to liberal causes of her day. For example, in 1843, when government investigations exposed the exploitation of children employed in coal mines and factories, she wrote "The Cry of the Children," a powerful indictment of the appalling use of child labor. Like Harriet Beecher Stowe in *Uncle Tom's Cabin* (1851–52), Barrett Browning uses literature as a tool of social protest and reform, lending her voice, for example, to the cause of American abolitionism in "The Runaway Slave at Pilgrim's Point." In later poems she took up the cause of the *risorgimento,* the movement to unify Italy as a nation-state, in which Italy's struggle for freedom and identity found resonance with her own.

For many years Elizabeth Barrett Browning was best-known for her *Sonnets from the Portuguese* (1850), a sequence of forty-four sonnets presented under the guise of a translation from the Portuguese language, in which she recorded the stages of her love for Robert Browning. But increasingly, her verse novel *Aurora Leigh* (1857) has attracted critical attention. The poem depicts the growth of a woman poet; although not the first work in English by a woman writer in which the heroine herself is an author (this accolade goes to Jane Barker's *Love Intrigues* of 1713), it nevertheless represents a fascinating and extensive investigation of the trials facing a female artist. When Barrett Browning first envisioned the poem, she wrote, "My chief *intention* just now is the writing of a sort of novel-poem . . . running into the midst of our conventions, and rushing into drawing-rooms and the like 'where angels fear to tread'; and so, meeting face to face and without mask the Humanity of the age, and speaking the truth as I conceive of it out plainly." The poem is a portrait of the artist as a young woman committed to a socially inclusive realist art. It is a daring work both in its presentation of social issues concerning women and in its claims for Aurora's poetic vocation; on her twentieth birthday, to pursue her career as a poet, Aurora refuses a proposal of marriage from her cousin Romney, who wants her to be his helpmate in the liberal causes he has embraced. Later in the poem, she rescues a fallen woman and takes her to Italy, where they settle together and confront a chastened Romney.

Immensely popular in its own day, *Aurora Leigh* had extravagant admirers (like Ruskin, who asserted that it was the greatest poem written in English) and critics who found fault with both its poetry and its morality. With its crowded canvas and melodramatic plot, it seems closer to the novel than to poetry, but it is important to view the poem in the context of the debate about appropriate poetic subject matter that engaged other Victorian poets. Unlike Matthew Arnold, who believed that the present age had not produced actions heroic enough to be the subject of great poetry, and unlike Alfred, Lord Tennyson, who used Arthurian legend to represent contemporary concerns, Barrett Browning felt that the present age contained the materials for an epic poetry. Virginia Woolf writes that "Elizabeth Barrett was inspired by a flash of true genius when she rushed into the drawing-room and said that here, where we live and work, is the true place for the poet." *Aurora Leigh* succeeds in giving us what Woolf describes as "a sense of life in general, of people who are unmistakably Victorian, wrestling with the problems of their own time, all brightened, intensified, and compacted by the fire of poetry. . . . Aurora Leigh, with her passionate interest in social questions, her conflict as artist and woman, her longing for knowledge and freedom, is the true daughter of her age."

The Cry of the Children[1]

"Φεῦ, φεῦ, τί προσδέρκεσθέ μ' ὄμμασιν, τέκνα;"
—*Medea*[2]

Do ye hear the children weeping, O my brothers,
    Ere the sorrow comes with years?
They are leaning their young heads against their mothers,
    And *that* cannot stop their tears.
5 The young lambs are bleating in the meadows,
    The young birds are chirping in the nest,
The young fawns are playing with the shadows,

1. Barrett Browning wrote "The Cry of the Children" in response to the report of a parliamentary commission, to which her friend R. H. Horne contributed, on the labor of children in mines and factories. Many of the details of Barrett Browning's poem derive from the report. See "Industrialism: Progress or Decline?" on p. 633.
2. Alas, my children, why do you look at me? (Greek), from Euripides' tragedy *Medea*. Medea speaks these lines before killing her children in vengeance against her husband, who has taken a new wife. (The poem's title is spoken by the chorus.)

The young flowers are blowing toward the west—
But the young, young children, O my brothers,
10   They are weeping bitterly!
They are weeping in the playtime of the others,
        In the country of the free.

Do you question the young children in the sorrow
        Why their tears are falling so?
15 The old man may weep for his to-morrow
        Which is lost in Long Ago;
The old tree is leafless in the forest,
        The old year is ending in the frost,
The old wound, if stricken, is the sorest,
20   The old hope is hardest to be lost:
But the young, young children, O my brothers,
        Do you ask them why they stand
Weeping sore° before the bosoms of their mothers,   *bitterly*
        In our happy Fatherland?

25 They look up with their pale and sunken faces,
        And their looks are sad to see,
For the man's hoary anguish draws and presses
        Down the cheeks of infancy;
"Your old earth," they say, "is very dreary,"
30   "Our young feet," they say, "are very weak;
Few paces have we taken, yet are weary—
        Our grave-rest is very far to seek:
Ask the aged why they weep, and not the children,
        For the outside earth is cold,
35 And we young ones stand without, in our bewildering,
        And the graves are for the old."

"True," say the children, "it may happen
        That we die before our time:
Little Alice died last year, her grave is shapen
40   Like a snowball, in the rime.°   *frost*
We looked into the pit prepared to take her:
        Was no room for any work in the close clay!
From the sleep wherein she lieth none will wake her,
        Crying, 'Get up, little Alice! it is day.'
45 If you listen by that grave, in sun and shower,
        With your ear down, little Alice never cries;
Could we see her face, be sure we should not know her,
        For the smile has time for growing in her eyes:
And merry go her moments, lulled and stilled in
50   The shroud by the kirk° chime.   *church*
It is good when it happens," say the children,
        "That we die before our time."

Alas, alas, the children! they are seeking
        Death in life, as best to have:
55 They are binding up their hearts away from breaking,
        With a ceremen° from the grave.   *shroud*

Go out, children, from the mine and from the city,
    Sing out, children, as the little thrushes do;
Pluck your handfuls of the meadow-cowslips pretty,
60   Laugh aloud, to feel your fingers let them through!
But they answer, "Are your cowslips of the meadows
    Like our weeds anear the mine?[3]
Leave us quiet in the dark of the coal-shadows,
    From your pleasures fair and fine!

65 "For oh," say the children, "we are weary,
    And we cannot run or leap;
If we cared for any meadows, it were merely
    To drop down in them and sleep.
Our knees tremble sorely in the stooping,
70   We fall upon our faces, trying to go;
And, underneath our heavy eyelids drooping,
    The reddest flower would look as pale as snow.
For, all day, we drag our burden tiring
    Through the coal-dark, underground;
75 Or, all day, we drive the wheels of iron
    In the factories, round and round.

"For, all day, the wheels are droning, turning;
    Their wind comes in our faces,
Till our hearts turn, our heads with pulses burning,
80   And the walls turn in their places:
Turns the sky in the high window blank and reeling,
    Turns the long light that drops adown the wall,
Turn the black flies that crawl along the ceiling,
    All are turning, all the day, and we with all.
85 And all day, the iron wheels are droning,
    And sometimes we could pray,
'O ye wheels,' (breaking out in a mad moaning)
    'Stop! be silent for to-day!'"

Ay, be silent! Let them hear each other breathing
90   For a moment, mouth to mouth!
Let them touch each other's hands, in a fresh wreathing
    Of their tender human youth!
Let them feel that this cold metallic motion
    Is not all the life God fashions or reveals:
95 Let them prove their living souls against the notion
    That they live in you, or under you, O wheels!
Still, all day, the iron wheels go onward,
    Grinding life down from its mark;
And the children's souls, which God is calling sunward,
100   Spin on blindly in the dark.

Now tell the poor young children; O my brothers,
    To look up to Him and pray;

---

3. A commissioner mentions the fact of weeds being thus confounded with the idea of flowers [Barrett Browning's note].

So the blessed One who blesseth all the others,
    Will bless them another day.
105 They answer, "Who is God that He should hear us,
    While the rushing of the iron wheels is stirred?
When we sob aloud, the human creatures near us
    Pass by, hearing not, or answer not a word.
And *we* hear not (for the wheels in their resounding)
110   Strangers speaking at the door:
Is it likely God, with angels singing round Him,
    Hears our weeping any more?

Two words, indeed, of praying we remember,
    And at midnight's hour of harm,
115 'Our Father,' looking upward in the chamber,
    We say softly for a charm.
We know no other words except 'Our Father.'
    And we think that, in some pause of angels' song,
God may pluck them with the silence sweet to gather,
120   And hold both within His right hand which is strong.
'Our Father!' If He heard us, He would surely
    (For they call Him good and mild)
Answer, smiling down the steep world very purely,
    'Come and rest with me, my child.'

125 "But, no!" say the children, weeping faster,
    "He is speechless as a stone:
And they tell us, of His image is the master
    Who commands us to work on.
Go to!" say the children,—"up in Heaven,
130   Dark, wheel-like, turning clouds are all we find.
Do not mock us; grief has made us unbelieving:
We look up for God, but tears have made us blind."
Do you hear the children weeping and disproving,
    O my brothers, what ye preach?
135 For God's possible is taught by His world's loving,[4]
    And the children doubt of each.

And well may the children weep before you!
    They are weary ere they run;
They have never seen the sunshine, nor the glory
140   Which is brighter than the sun.
They know the grief of man, without its wisdom;
    They sink in man's despair, without its calm;
Are slaves, without the liberty in Christdom,
    Are martyrs, by the pang without the palm:[5]
145 Are worn as if with age, yet unretrievingly
    The harvest of its memories cannot reap,—
Are orphans of the earthly love and heavenly.
    Let them weep! let them weep!

4. I.e., we gain our sense of the possibilities of God's love from our experience of love in the world.
5. Palm branch, symbol of victory.

They look up with their pale and sunken faces,
150   And their look is dread to see,
For they mind you of their angels in high places,
          With eyes turned on Deity.
"How long," they say, "how long, O cruel nation,
    Will you stand, to move the world, on a child's heart,—
155 Stifle down with a mailed heel its palpitation,
          And tread onward to your throne amid the mart?
Our blood splashes upward, O gold-heaper,
          And your purple[6] shows your path!
But the child's sob in the silence curses deeper
160   Than the strong man in his wrath."

                                                1843

To George Sand[1]

A Desire

Thou large-brained woman and large-hearted man,
Self-called George Sand! whose soul, amid the lions
Of thy tumultuous senses, moans defiance
And answers roar for roar, as spirits can:
5 I would some mild miraculous thunder ran
Above the applauded circus,[2] in appliance
Of thine own nobler nature's strength and science,
Drawing two pinions, white as wings of swan,
From thy strong shoulders, to amaze the place
10 With holier light! that thou to woman's claim
And man's, mightst join beside the angel's grace
Of a pure genius sanctified from blame,
Till child and maiden pressed to thine embrace
To kiss upon thy lips a stainless fame.

                                                1844

To George Sand

A Recognition

True genius, but true woman! dost deny
The woman's nature with a manly scorn,
And break away the gauds° and armlets worn   *ornaments*

6. Color associated with royalty and (in poetry) with blood.
1. Pen name of the French Romantic novelist Amandine-Aurore-Lucile Dudevant (1804–1876), famous for her unconventional ideas and behavior. Barrett Browning discovered Sand's writing while an invalid, "a prisoner," and asserts that Sand, together with Balzac, "kept the colour in my life." A defender of Sand's genius to less-sympathetic friends critical of Sand's morality, Barrett Browning writes to her friend Mary Russell Mitford (a novelist and dramatist) that Sand "is eloquent as a fallen angel . . . A true woman of genius!—but of a womanhood tired of itself, and scorned by *her,* while she bears it burning above her head."
2. A Roman spectacle that might include such entertainment as fights between humans and lions.

By weaker women in captivity?
5   Ah, vain denial! that revolted cry
Is sobbed in by a woman's voice forlorn,—
Thy woman's hair, my sister, all unshorn
Floats back dishevelled strength in agony,
Disproving thy man's name: and while before
10 The world thou burnest in a poet-fire,
We see thy woman-heart beat evermore
Through the large flame. Beat purer, heart, and higher,
Till God unsex thee on the heavenly shore
Where unincarnate° spirits purely aspire!   *disembodied*

1844

From Sonnets from the Portuguese

21

Say over again, and yet once over again,
That thou dost love me. Though the word repeated
Should seem "a cuckoo song,"[1] as thou dost treat it,
Remember, never to the hill or plain,
5   Valley and wood, without her cuckoo strain
Comes the fresh Spring in all her green completed.
Belovèd, I, amid the darkness greeted
By a doubtful spirit voice, in that doubt's pain
Cry, "Speak once more—thou lovest!" Who can fear
10 Too many stars, though each in heaven shall roll,
Too many flowers, though each shall crown the year?
Say thou dost love me, love me, love me—toll
The silver iterance!°—only minding, Dear,   *repetition*
To love me also in silence with thy soul.

22

When our two souls stand up erect and strong,
Face to face, silent, drawing nigh and nigher,
Until the lengthening wings break into fire
At either curvèd point—what bitter wrong
5   Can the earth do to us, that we should not long
Be here contented? Think. In mounting higher,
The angels would press on us and aspire
To drop some golden orb of perfect song
Into our deep, dear silence. Let us stay
10 Rather on earth, Belovèd,—where the unfit
Contrarious moods of men recoil away
And isolate pure spirits, and permit

1. The cuckoo has a repeating call.

A place to stand and love in for a day,
With darkness and the death-hour rounding it.

32

The first time that the sun rose on thine oath
To love me, I looked forward to the moon
To slacken all those bonds which seemed too soon
And quickly tied to make a lasting troth.
5 Quick-loving hearts, I thought, may quickly loathe;
And, looking on myself, I seemed not one
For such man's love!—more like an out-of-tune
Worn viol, a good singer would be wroth
To spoil his song with, and which, snatched in haste,
10 Is laid down at the first ill-sounding note.
I did not wrong myself so, but I placed
A wrong on *thee*. For perfect strains may float
'Neath master-hands, from instruments defaced—
And great souls, at one stroke, may do and dote.

43

How do I love thee? Let me count the ways.
I love thee to the depth and breadth and height
My soul can reach, when feeling out of sight
For the ends of Being and ideal Grace.
5 I love thee to the level of everyday's
Most quiet need, by sun and candlelight.
I love thee freely, as men strive for Right;
I love thee purely, as they turn from Praise.
I love thee with the passion put to use
10 In my old griefs, and with my childhood's faith.
I love thee with a love I seemed to lose
With my lost saints—I love thee with the breath,
Smiles, tears, of all my life!—and, if God choose,
I shall but love thee better after death.

1845–47   1850

The Runaway Slave at Pilgrim's Point[1]

I

I stand on the mark beside the shore
    Of the first white pilgrim's bended knee,
Where exile turned to ancestor,
    And God was thanked for liberty.

---

1. Plymouth Rock, Massachusetts, where the Pilgrims landed in November 1620.

5 I have run through the night, my skin is as dark,
  I bend my knee down on this mark:
   I look on the sky and the sea.

II

 O pilgrim-souls, I speak to you!
  I see you come proud and slow
10 From the land of the spirits pale as dew
  And round me and round me ye go.
 O pilgrims, I have gasped and run
 All night long from the whips of one
  Who in your names works sin and woe!

III

15 And thus I thought that I would come
  And kneel here where ye knelt before,
 And feel your souls around me hum
  In undertone to the ocean's roar;
 And lift my black face, my black hand,
20 Here, in your names, to curse this land
  Ye blessed in freedom's, evermore.

IV

 I am black, I am black,
  And yet God made me, they say:
 But if He did so, smiling back
25 He must have cast his work away
 Under the feet of his white creatures,
 With a look of scorn, that the dusky features
  Might be trodden again to clay.

V

 And yet He has made dark things
30 To be glad and merry as light:
 There's a little dark bird sits and sings,
  There's a dark stream ripples out of sight,
 And the dark frogs chant in the safe morass,°   *marsh*
 And the sweetest stars are made to pass
35 O'er the face of the darkest night.

VI

 But *we* who are dark, we are dark!
  Ah God, we have no stars!
 About our souls in care and cark°   *anxiety*
  Our blackness shuts like prison-bars:
40 The poor souls crouch so far behind
 That never a comfort can they find
  By reaching through the prison-bars.

VII

Indeed we live beneath the sky,
   That great smooth Hand of God stretched out
45 On all His children fatherly,
   To save them from the dread and doubt
Which would be if, from this low place,
All opened straight up to His face
   Into the grand eternity.

VIII

50 And still God's sunshine and His frost,
   They make us hot, they make us cold,
As if we were not black and lost;
   And the beasts and birds, in wood and fold,
Do fear and take us for very men:
55 Could the whip-poor-will or the cat of the glen°   *bobcat*
   Look into my eyes and be bold?

IX

I am black, I am black!
   But, once, I laughed in girlish glee,
For one of my colour stood in the track
60   Where the drivers drove, and looked at me,
And tender and full was the look he gave—
Could a slave look *so* at another slave?—
   I look at the sky and the sea.

X

And from that hour our spirits grew
65   As free as if unsold, unbought:
Oh, strong enough, since we were two,
   To conquer the world, we thought.
The drivers drove us day by day;
We did not mind, we went one way,
70   And no better a freedom sought.

XI

In the sunny ground between the canes,°   *sugar canes*
   He said "I love you" as he passed;
When the shingle-roof rang sharp with the rains,
   I heard how he vowed it fast:
75 While others shook he smiled in the hut,
As he carved me a bowl of the cocoa-nut
   Through the roar of the hurricanes.

XII

I sang his name instead of a song,
  Over and over I sang his name,
80 Upward and downward I drew it along
  My various notes,—the same, the same!
I sang it low, that the slave-girls near
Might never guess, from aught they could hear,
  It was only a name—a name.

XIII

85 I look on the sky and the sea.
  We were two to love, and two to pray:
Yes, two, O God, who cried to Thee,
  Though nothing didst Thou say!
Coldly Thou sat'st behind the sun:
90 And now I cry who am but one,
  Thou wilt not speak to-day.

XIV

We were black, we were black,
  We had no claim to love and bliss,
What marvel if each went to wrack?°   *ruin*
95   They wrung my cold hands out of his,
They dragged him—where? I crawled to touch
His blood's mark in the dust . . . not much,
  Ye pilgrim-souls, though plain as *this*!

XV

Wrong, followed by a deeper wrong!
100   Mere grief's too good for such as I:
So the white men brought the shame ere long
  To strangle the sob of my agony.
They would not leave me for my dull
Wet eyes!—it was too merciful
105   To let me weep pure tears and die.

XVI

I am black, I am black!
  I wore a child upon my breast,
An amulet that hung too slack,
  And, in my unrest, could not rest:
110 Thus we went moaning, child and mother,
One to another, one to another,
  Until all ended for the best.

XVII

For hark! I will tell you low, low,
   I am black, you see,—
115 And the babe who lay on my bosom so,
   Was far too white, too white for me;
As white as the ladies who scorned to pray
Beside me at church but yesterday,
   Though my tears had washed a place for my knee.

XVIII

120 My own, own child! I could not bear
   To look in his face, it was so white;
I covered him up with a kerchief there,
   I covered his face in close and tight:
And he moaned and struggled, as well might be,
125 For the white child wanted his liberty—
   Ha, ha! he wanted the master-right.

XIX

He moaned and beat with his head and feet,
   His little feet that never grew;
He struck them out, as it was meet,
130   Against my heart to break it through:
I might have sung and made him mild,
But I dared not sing to the white-faced child
   The only song I knew.

XX

I pulled the kerchief very close:
135   He could not see the sun, I swear,
More, then, alive, than now he does
   From between the roots of the mango . . . where?
I know where. Close! A child and mother
Do wrong to look at one another
140   When one is black and one is fair.

XXI

Why, in that single glance I had
   Of my child's face, . . . I tell you all,
I saw a look that made me mad!
   The *master's* look, that used to fall
145 On my soul like his lash . . . or worse!
And so, to save it from my curse,
   I twisted it round in my shawl.

XXII

And he moaned and trembled from foot to head,
   He shivered from head to foot;
150 Till after a time, he lay instead
   Too suddenly still and mute.
I felt, beside, a stiffening cold:
I dared to lift up just a fold,
   As in lifting a leaf of the mango-fruit.

XXIII

155 But *my* fruit . . . ha, ha!—there, had been
   (I laugh to think on 't at this hour!)
Your fine white angels (who have seen
   Nearest the secret of God's power)
And plucked my fruit to make them wine,
160 And sucked the soul of that child of mine
   As the humming-bird sucks the soul of the flower.

XXIV

Ha, ha, the trick of the angels white!
   They freed the white child's spirit so.
I said not a word, but day and night
165   I carried the body to and fro,
And it lay on my heart like a stone, as chill.
—The sun may shine out as much as he will:
   I am cold, though it happened a month ago.

XXV

From the white man's house, and the black man's hut,
170   I carried the little body on;
The forest's arms did round us shut,
   And silence through the trees did run:
They asked no question as I went,
They stood too high for astonishment,
175   They could see God sit on His throne.

XXVI

My little body, kerchiefed fast,
   I bore it on through the forest, on;
And when I felt it was tired at last,
   I scooped a hole beneath the moon:
180 Through the forest-tops the angels far,
With a white sharp finger from every star,
   Did point and mock at what was done.

XXVII

Yet when it was all done aright,—
   Earth, 'twixt me and my baby, strewed,—
185 All, changed to black earth,—nothing white,—
   A dark child in the dark!—ensued
Some comfort, and my heart grew young;
I sate down smiling there and sung
   The song I learnt in my maidenhood.

XXVIII

190 And thus we two were reconciled,
   The white child and black mother, thus;
For as I sang it soft and wild,
   The same song, more melodious,
Rose from the grave whereon I sate:
195 It was the dead child singing that,
   To join the souls of both of us.

XXIX

I look on the sea and the sky.
   Where the pilgrims' ships first anchored lay
The free sun rideth gloriously,
200   But the pilgrim-ghosts have slid away
Through the earliest streaks of the morn:
My face is black, but it glares with a scorn
   Which they dare not meet by day.

XXX

Ha!—in their stead, their hunter sons!
205   Ha, ha! they are on me—they hunt in a ring!
Keep off! I brave you all at once,
   I throw off your eyes like snakes that sting!
You have killed the black eagle at nest, I think:
Did you ever stand still in your triumph, and shrink
210   From the stroke of her wounded wing?

XXXI

(Man, drop that stone you dared to lift!—)
   I wish you who stand there five abreast,
Each, for his own wife's joy and gift,
   A little corpse as safely at rest
215 As mine in the mangoes! Yes, but *she*
May keep live babies on her knee,
   And sing the song she likes the best.

XXXII

I am not mad: I am black.
  I see you staring in my face—
220 I know you staring, shrinking back,
    Ye are born of the Washington-race,[2]
And this land is the free America,
And this mark on my wrist—(I prove° what I say)   *demonstrate*
  Ropes tied me up here to the flogging-place.

XXXIII

225 You think I shrieked then? Not a sound!
    I hung, as a gourd hangs in the sun;
I only cursed them all around
    As softly as I might have done
My very own child: from these sands
230 Up to the mountains, lift your hands,
    O slaves, and end what I begun!

XXXIV

Whips, curses; these must answer those!
    For in this UNION you have set
Two kinds of men in adverse rows,
235   Each loathing each; and all forget
The seven wounds in Christ's body fair,
While HE sees gaping everywhere
    Our countless wounds that pay no debt.

XXXV

Our wounds are different. Your white men
240   Are, after all, not gods indeed,
Nor able to make Christs again
    Do good with bleeding. *We* who bleed
(Stand off!) we help not in our loss!
We are too heavy for our cross,
245   And fall and crush you and your seed.

XXXVI

I fall, I swoon! I look at the sky.
    The clouds are breaking on my brain;
I am floated along, as if I should die
    Of liberty's exquisite pain.
250 In the name of the white child waiting for me
In the death-dark where we may kiss and agree,
White men, I leave you all curse-free
    In my broken heart's disdain!

1846
                                           1848, 1850

2. I.e., the white race (the race of George Washington, the first president of the United States).

From Aurora Leigh

From *Book 1*

[THE EDUCATION OF AURORA LEIGH][1]

Then, land!—then, England! oh, the frosty cliffs[2]
Looked cold upon me. Could I find a home
Among those mean red houses through the fog?
And when I heard my father's language first
255 From alien lips which had no kiss for mine
I wept aloud, then laughed, then wept, then wept,
And some one near me said the child was mad
Through much sea-sickness. The train swept us on:
Was this my father's England? the great isle?
260 The ground seemed cut up from the fellowship
Of verdure, field from field,[3] as man from man;
The skies themselves looked low and positive,
As almost you could touch them with a hand,
And dared to do it they were so far off
265 From God's celestial crystals;[4] all things blurred
And dull and vague. Did Shakespeare and his mates
Absorb the light here?—not a hill or stone
With heart to strike a radiant colour up
Or active outline on the indifferent air.

270 I think I see my father's sister stand
Upon the hall-step of her country-house
To give me welcome. She stood straight and calm,
Her somewhat narrow forehead braided tight
As if for taming accidental thoughts
275 From possible pulses;[5] brown hair pricked with gray
By frigid use of life (she was not old,
Although my father's elder by a year),
A nose drawn sharply, yet in delicate lines;
A close mild mouth, a little soured about
280 The ends, through speaking unrequited loves
Or peradventure niggardly° half-truths;   *miserly*
Eyes of no colour,—once they might have smiled,
But never, never have forgot themselves
In smiling; cheeks, in which was yet a rose
285 Of perished summers, like a rose in a book,
Kept more for ruth° than pleasure,—if past bloom,   *remorse*
Past fading also.
                        She had lived, we'll say,
A harmless life, she called a virtuous life,

---

1. Aurora Leigh, the only child of an Italian mother and an English father, is raised in Italy by her father after her mother's death when Aurora is four years old. When she is thirteen her father also dies, and the orphaned girl is sent to live in England with her father's sister, who is to be responsible for the girl's education.

2. The white chalk cliffs at Dover.
3. English fields were separated from each other by hedgerows.
4. Perhaps a reference to the ancient notion that the sky was composed of several crystalline spheres orbiting the earth.
5. I.e., pulsation in her temples from excitement.

A quiet life, which was not life at all
290 (But that, she had not lived enough to know),
Between the vicar and the county squires,
The lord-lieutenant[6] looking down sometimes
From the empyrean° to assure their souls   *highest heaven*
Against chance vulgarisms, and, in the abyss,
295 The apothecary,[7] looked on once a year
To prove their soundness of humility.
The poor-club[8] exercised her Christian gifts
Of knitting stockings, stitching petticoats,
Because we are of one flesh, after all,
300 And need one flannel[9] (with a proper sense
Of difference in the quality)—and still
The book-club, guarded from your modern trick
Of shaking dangerous questions from the crease,[1]
Preserved her intellectual.° She had lived   *intellectual gifts*
305 A sort of cage-bird life, born in a cage,
Accounting that to leap from perch to perch
Was act and joy enough for any bird.
Dear heaven, how silly are the things that live
In thickets, and eat berries!
                          I, alas,
310 A wild bird scarcely fledged, was brought to her cage,
And she was there to meet me. Very kind.
Bring the clean water, give out the fresh seed.

She stood upon the steps to welcome me,
Calm, in black garb. I clung about her neck,—
315 Young babes, who catch at every shred of wool
To draw the new light closer, catch and cling
Less blindly. In my ears my father's word
Hummed ignorantly, as the sea in shells,
"Love, love, my child." She, black there with my grief,
320 Might feel my love—she was his sister once—
I clung to her. A moment she seemed moved,
Kissed me with cold lips, suffered me to cling,
And drew me feebly through the hall into
The room she sat in.
                    There, with some strange spasm
325 Of pain and passion, she wrung loose my hands
Imperiously, and held me at arm's length,
And with two grey-steel naked-bladed eyes
Searched through my face,—ay, stabbed it through and through,
Through brows and cheeks and chin, as if to find
330 A wicked murderer in my innocent face,
If not here, there perhaps. Then, drawing breath,

---

6. Governor of the county.
7. Pharmacist, who in England at the time could prescribe as well as sell medicine.
8. Club devoted to making things for the poor.
9. I.e., flannel petticoat.

1. The fold between two pages of a book, which had to be cut to open the pages. Presumably, modern books were more apt to reveal dangerous material when the crease was cut.

She struggled for her ordinary calm—
And missed it rather,—told me not to shrink,
As if she had told me not to lie or swear,—
335 "She loved my father and would love me too
As long as I deserved it." Very kind.

I understood her meaning afterward;
She thought to find my mother in my face,
And questioned it for that. For she, my aunt,
340 Had loved my father truly, as she could,
And hated, with the gall of gentle souls,
My Tuscan[2] mother who had fooled away
A wise man from wise courses, a good man
From obvious duties, and, depriving her,
345 His sister, of the household precedence,
Had wronged his tenants, robbed his native land,
And made him mad, alike by life and death,
In love and sorrow. She had pored° for years   *pored over*
What sort of woman could be suitable
350 To her sort of hate, to entertain it with,
And so, her very curiosity
Became hate too, and all the idealism
She ever used in life was used for hate,
Till hate, so nourished, did exceed at last
355 The love from which it grew, in strength and heat,
And wrinkled her smooth conscience with a sense
Of disputable virtue (say not, sin)
When Christian doctrine was enforced at church.

And thus my father's sister was to me
360 My mother's hater. From that day she did
Her duty to me (I appreciate it
In her own word as spoken to herself),
Her duty, in large measure, well pressed out
But measured always. She was generous, bland,
365 More courteous than was tender, gave me still
The first place,—as if fearful that God's saints
Would look down suddenly and say "Herein
You missed a point, I think, through lack of love."
Alas, a mother never is afraid
370 Of speaking angerly to any child,
Since love, she knows, is justified of love.
And I, I was a good child on the whole,
A meek and manageable child. Why not?
I did not live, to have the faults of life:
375 There seemed more true life in my father's grave
Than in all England. Since *that* threw me off
Who fain would cleave (his latest will, they say,

2. From Tuscany, a region in central Italy.

Consigned me to his land), I only thought
Of lying quiet there where I was thrown
380   Like sea-weed on the rocks, and suffering her
To prick me to a pattern with her pin,[3]
Fibre from fibre, delicate leaf from leaf,
And dry out from my drowned anatomy
The last sea-salt left in me.
                So it was.
385   I broke the copious curls upon my head
In braids, because she liked smooth-ordered hair.
I left off saying my sweet Tuscan words
Which still at any stirring of the heart
Came up to float across the English phrase
390   As lilies (*Bene* or *Che che*[4]), because
She liked my father's child to speak his tongue.
I learnt the collects[5] and the catechism,
The creeds, from Athanasius back to Nice,[6]
The Articles, the Tracts *against* the times[7]
395   (By no means Buonaventure's "Prick of Love"[8]),
And various popular synopses of
Inhuman doctrines never taught by John,[9]
Because she liked instructed piety.
I learnt my complement of classic French
400   (Kept pure of Balzac and neologism[1])
And German also, since she liked a range
Of liberal education,—tongues,° not books.   *languages*
I learnt a little algebra, a little
Of the mathematics,—brushed with extreme flounce[2]
405   The circle of the sciences, because
She misliked women who are frivolous.
I learnt the royal genealogies
Of Oviedo,[3] the internal laws
Of the Burmese empire,—by how many feet
410   Mount Chimborazo outsoars Teneriffe,[4]
What navigable river joins itself
To Lara,[5] and what census of the year five
Was taken at Klagenfurt,[6]—because she liked

---

3. As in embroidery.
4. No, no, indeed (Italian). "*Bene*": it is well (Italian).
5. Seasonal opening prayers in the Anglican Church service.
6. Articles of Christian faith such as those proclaimed by Athanasius, an Egyptian theologian of the 4th century C.E., and at the early Church council held at Nicaea in the same era.
7. In the 1830s leaders of the conservative High Church party, such as John Henry Newman, had published *Tracts for the Times*, which expounded arguments against efforts by liberals to modernize the Anglican Church. Aurora's version of the title is hence ironic. "Articles": the thirty-nine articles are the principles of faith of the Church of England.

8. St. Bonaventure's doctrine that the power of the heart to love leads to higher illumination than the power of the mind to reason.
9. I.e., the author of the Gospel.
1. A new word or expression. Honoré de Balzac (1799–1850), a French novelist whose realism made him improper reading for a young English lady of the 19th century.
2. An ornamental edge to a skirt. "Extreme": outermost.
3. Spanish historian (16th century), who wrote a book on the genealogies of Spanish noblemen.
4. A mountain in the Canary Islands. Mount Chimborazo is one of the highest peaks of the Andes.
5. A town in Spain on the river Arlanza.
6. A town in Austria.

A general insight into useful facts.
415 I learnt much music,—such as would have been
As quite impossible in Johnson's day[7]
As still it might be wished—fine sleights of hand
And unimagined fingering, shuffling off
The hearer's soul through hurricanes of notes
420 To a noisy Tophet;° and I drew . . . costumes   *hell*
From French engravings, nereids° neatly draped   *sea nymphs*
(With smirks of simmering godship): I washed in[8]
Landscapes from nature (rather say, washed out).
I danced the polka and Cellarius,[9]
425 Spun glass, stuffed birds, and modeled flowers in wax,
Because she liked accomplishments in girls.
I read a score of books on womanhood
To prove, if women do not think at all,
They may teach thinking (to a maiden aunt
430 Or else the author),—books that boldly assert
Their right of comprehending husband's talk
When not too deep, and even of answering
With pretty "may it please you," or "so it is,"—
Their rapid insight and fine aptitude,
435 Particular worth and general missionariness,
As long as they keep quiet by the fire
And never say "no" when the world says "ay,"
For that is fatal,—their angelic reach
Of virtue, chiefly used to sit and darn,
440 And fatten household sinners,—their, in brief,
Potential faculty in everything
Of abdicating power in it: she owned
She liked a woman to be womanly,
And English women, she thanked God and sighed
445 (Some people always sigh in thanking God),
Were models to the universe. And last
I learnt cross-stitch,[1] because she did not like
To see me wear the night with empty hands
A-doing nothing. So, my shepherdess
450 Was something after all (the pastoral saints
Be praised for't), leaning lovelorn with pink eyes
To match her shoes, when I mistook the silks;
Her head uncrushed by that round weight of hat
So strangely similar to the tortoise shell
Which slew the tragic poet.[2]
455   By the way,
The works of women are symbolical.
We sew, sew, prick our fingers, dull our sight,

---

7. Allusion to the story about Samuel Johnson (1709–1784), who, when informed of the difficulty of a piece of music a young lady was playing, replied, "I would it had been impossible."
8. As in painting with watercolors.
9. A kind of waltz.

1. I.e., embroidery.
2. According to tradition, the Greek playwright Aeschylus was killed by an eagle who, mistaking his bald head for a stone, dropped a tortoise on it to break the shell.

Producing what? A pair of slippers, sir,
To put on when you're weary—or a stool
460 To stumble over and vex you . . . "curse that stool!"
Or else at best, a cushion, where you lean
And sleep, and dream of something we are not
But would be for your sake. Alas, alas!
This hurts most, this—that, after all, we are paid
The worth of our work, perhaps.
465   In looking down
Those years of education (to return)
I wonder if Brinvilliers suffered more
In the water-torture[3] . . . flood succeeding flood
To drench the incapable throat and split the veins . . .
470 Than I did. Certain of your feebler souls
Go out° in such a process; many pine   *die*
To a sick, inodorous light; my own endured:
I had relations in the Unseen, and drew
The elemental nutriment and heat
475 From nature, as earth feels the sun at nights,
Or as a babe sucks surely in the dark.
I kept the life thrust on me, on the outside
Of the inner life with all its ample room
For heart and lungs, for will and intellect,
480 Inviolable by conventions. God,
I thank thee for that grace of thine!
                                          At first
I felt no life which was not patience,—did
The thing she bade me, without heed to a thing
Beyond it, sat in just the chair she placed,
485 With back against the window, to exclude
The sight of the great lime-tree on the lawn,[4]
Which seemed to have come on purpose from the woods
To bring the house a message,—ay, and walked
Demurely in her carpeted low rooms,
490 As if I should not, harkening my own steps,
Misdoubt° I was alive. I read her books,   *doubt*
Was civil to her cousin, Romney Leigh,
Gave ear to her vicar, tea to her visitors,
And heard them whisper, when I changed a cup
495 (I blushed for joy at that),—"The Italian child,
For all her blue eyes and her quiet ways,
Thrives ill in England: she is paler yet
Than when we came the last time; she will die."

3. Marie Marguerite, Marquise de Brinvilliers, a celebrated criminal who was beheaded in 1676, was tortured by having water forced down her throat.
4. Cf. Coleridge's "This Lime-Tree Bower My Prison" (1800), in which the lime tree becomes the vehicle of a realization that Nature never deserts the wise and pure even when they seem to be cut off from her most beautiful vistas.

From *Book 2*

[AURORA'S ASPIRATIONS][5]

Times followed one another. Came a morn
I stood upon the brink of twenty years,
And looked before and after, as I stood
Woman and artist,—either incomplete,
5   Both credulous of completion. There I held
The whole creation in my little cup,
And smiled with thirsty lips before I drank
"Good health to you and me, sweet neighbour mine,
And all these peoples."
                I was glad, that day;
10   The June was in me, with its multitudes
Of nightingales all singing in the dark,
And rosebuds reddening where the calyx[6] split.
I felt so young, so strong, so sure of God!
So glad, I could not choose be very wise!
15   And, old at twenty, was inclined to pull
My childhood backward in a childish jest
To see the face of't once more, and farewell!
In which fantastic mood I bounded forth
At early morning,—would not wait so long
20   As even to snatch my bonnet by the strings,
But, brushing a green trail across the lawn
With my gown in the dew, took will and away
Among the acacias of the shrubberies,
To fly my fancies in the open air
25   And keep° my birthday, till my aunt awoke   *observe*
To stop good dreams. Meanwhile I murmured on
As honeyed bees keep humming to themselves,
"The worthiest poets have remained uncrowned
Till death has bleached their foreheads to the bone;
30   And so with me it must be unless I prove
Unworthy of the grand adversity,
And certainly I would not fail so much.
What, therefore, if I crown myself to-day
In sport, not pride, to learn the feel of it,
35   Before my brows be numbed as Dante's own
To all the tender pricking of such leaves?
Such leaves! what leaves?"
                I pulled the branches down
To choose from.
        "Not the bay![7] I choose no bay
(The fates deny us if we are overbold),

---

5. Stifled by her aunt's oppressive conventionality, Aurora has found three sources of comfort and inspiration: poetic aspirations, fostered by the discovery of her father's library; the beauty of the natural world; and the intellectual companionship of her cousin Romney Leigh, an idealistic young man troubled by the misery of the poor and inspired by contemporary notions of social reform.
6. The protective outer leaves covering a flower or bud.
7. Laurel, associated with poetry and prophecy by the ancient Greeks, who also crowned the athletic victors in the Pythian games with a laurel wreath.

40 Nor myrtle—which means chiefly love; and love
Is something awful which one dares not touch
So early o' mornings. This verbena strains
The point of passionate fragrance; and hard by,
This guelder-rose,° at far too slight a beck   *cranberry bush*
45 Of the wind, will toss about her flower-apples.
Ah—there's my choice,—that ivy on the wall,
That headlong ivy! not a leaf will grow
But thinking of a wreath. Large leaves, smooth leaves,
Serrated like my vines, and half as green.
50 I like such ivy, bold to leap a height
'Twas strong to climb; as good to grow on graves
As twist about a thyrsus;[8] pretty too
(And that's not ill) when twisted round a comb."
Thus speaking to myself, half singing it,
55 Because some thoughts are fashioned like a bell
To ring with once being touched, I drew a wreath
Drenched, blinding me with dew, across my brow,
And fastening it behind so, turning faced
. . . My public!—cousin Romney—with a mouth
Twice graver than his eyes.
60   I stood there fixed,—
My arms up, like the caryatid,[9] sole
Of some abolished temple, helplessly
Persistent in a gesture which derides
A former purpose. Yet my blush was flame,
As if from flax, not stone.
65   "Aurora Leigh,
The earliest of Auroras!"[1]
                     Hand stretched out
I clasped, as shipwrecked men will clasp a hand,
Indifferent to the sort of palm. The tide
Had caught me at my pastime, writing down
70 My foolish name too near upon the sea
Which drowned me with a blush as foolish. "You,
My cousin!"
           The smile died out in his eyes
And dropped upon his lips, a cold dead weight,
For just a moment, "Here's a book I found!
75 No name writ on it—poems, by the form;
Some Greek upon the margin,—lady's Greek
Without the accents.[2] Read it? Not a word.
I saw at once the thing had witchcraft in't,
Whereof the reading calls up dangerous spirits:
I rather bring it to the witch."
80   "My book.
You found it" . . .
       "In the hollow by the stream

---

8. Staff twined with ivy that was carried, according to Greek myth, by Dionysus, god of wine and fertility.
9. Classical column in the form of a draped female figure.

1. Dawns; from Aurora, Roman goddess of the dawn.
2. Romney is gently mocking Aurora for her apparent ignorance of the complex rules of classical Greek accentuation.

That beech leans down into—of which you said
The Oread in it has a Naiad's[3] heart
And pines for waters."
                                "Thank you."
                                        "Thanks to *you*
85 My cousin! that I have seen you not too much
Witch, scholar, poet, dreamer, and the rest,
To be a woman also."
                        With a glance
The smile rose in his eyes again and touched
The ivy on my forehead, light as air.
90 I answered gravely "Poets needs must be
Or° men or women—more's the pity."   *either*
                                        "Ah,
But men, and still less women, happily,
Scarce need be poets. Keep to the green wreath,
Since even dreaming of the stone and bronze
95 Brings headaches, pretty cousin, and defiles
The clean white morning dresses."
                                "So you judge!
Because I love the beautiful I must
Love pleasure chiefly, and be overcharged
For ease and whiteness! well, you know the world,
100 And only miss your cousin, 'tis not much.
But learn this; I would rather take my part
With God's Dead, who afford to walk in white
Yet spread His glory, than keep quiet here
And gather up my feet from even a step
105 For fear to soil my gown in so much dust.
I choose to walk at all risks.—Here, if heads
That hold a rhythmic thought, must ache perforce,
For my part I choose headaches,—and to-day's
My birthday,"
                    "Dear Aurora, choose instead
To cure them. You have balsams."°   *soothing cures*
110   "I perceive.
The headache is too noble for my sex.
You think the heartache would sound decenter,
Since that's the woman's special, proper ache,
And altogether tolerable, except
115 To a woman."

[AURORA'S REJECTION OF ROMNEY][4]

                    There he glowed on me
With all his face and eyes. "No other help?"

3. Water nymph's. "Oread": tree nymph.
4. Romney and Aurora have been arguing about whether art, particularly a young woman's poetry, is useful in a world that, according to Romney, is full of human suffering. Romney claims that women have no ability to generalize from their personal experiences and are, there-fore, doomed to be trivial poets and ineffectual social reformers. Aurora is quick to agree that to be merely an inferior poet would be intolerable to her, but while she admires Romney's lofty concern for humanity, she remains untempted to join forces with him.

Said he—"no more than so?"
₃₄₅   "What help?" I asked.
"You'd scorn my help,—as Nature's self, you say,
Has scorned to put her music in my mouth
Because a woman's. Do you now turn round
And ask for what a woman cannot give?"

₃₅₀ "For what she only can, I turn and ask,"
He answered, catching up my hands in his,
And dropping on me from his high-eaved brow
The full weight of his soul,—"I ask for love,
And that, she can; for life in fellowship
₃₅₅ Through bitter duties—that, I know she can;
For wifehood—will she?"
                   "Now," I said, "may God
Be witness 'twixt us two!" and with the word,
Meeseemed[5] I floated into a sudden light
Above his stature,—"am I proved too weak
₃₆₀ To stand alone, yet strong enough to bear
Such leaners on my shoulder? poor to think,
Yet rich enough to sympathise with thought?
Incompetent to sing, as blackbirds can,
Yet competent to love, like HIM?"
                      I paused;
₃₆₅ Perhaps I darkened, as the lighthouse will
That turns upon the sea. "It's always so.
Anything does for a wife."
                "Aurora, dear,
And dearly honoured,"—he pressed in at once
With eager utterance,—"you translate me ill.
₃₇₀ I do not contradict my thought of you
Which is most reverent, with another thought
Found less so. If your sex is weak for art
(And I, who said so, did but honour you
By using truth in courtship), it is strong
₃₇₅ For life and duty. Place your fecund heart
In mine, and let us blossom for the world
That wants love's colour in the grey of time.
My talk, meanwhile, is arid to you, ay,
Since all my talk can only set you where
₃₈₀ You look down coldly on the arena-heaps
Of headless bodies, shapeless, indistinct!
The Judgment-Angel scarce would find his way
Through such a heap of generalised distress
To the individual man with lips and eyes,
₃₈₅ Much less Aurora. Ah, my sweet, come down,
And hand in hand we'll go where yours shall touch
These victims, one by one! till, one by one,
The formless, nameless trunk of every man
Shall seem to wear a head with hair you know,

5. It seemed to me.

390 And every woman catch your mother's face
To melt you into passion."
                              "I am a girl,"
I answered slowly; "you do well to name
My mother's face. Though far too early, alas,
God's hand did interpose 'twixt it and me,
395 I know so much of love as used to shine
In that face and another. Just so much;
No more indeed at all. I have not seen
So much love since, I pray you pardon me,
As answers even to make a marriage with
400 In this cold land of England. What you love
Is not a woman, Romney, but a cause:
You want a helpmate, not a mistress, sir,
A wife to help your ends,—in her no end.
Your cause is noble, your ends excellent,
405 But I, being most unworthy of these and that,
Do otherwise conceive of love. Farewell."

"Farewell, Aurora? you reject me thus?"
He said.
            "Sir, you were married long ago.
You have a wife already whom you love,
410 Your social theory. Bless you both, I say.
For my part, I am scarcely meek enough
To be the handmaid of a lawful spouse.
Do I look a Hagar,⁶ think you?"
                                  "So you jest."

"Nay, so, I speak in earnest," I replied.
415 "You treat of° marriage too much like, at least,   *talk about*
A chief apostle: you would bear with you
A wife . . . a sister . . . shall we speak it out?
A sister of charity."
                        "Then, must it be
Indeed farewell? And was I so far wrong
420 In hope and in illusion, when I took
The woman to be nobler than the man,
Yourself the noblest woman, in the use
And comprehension of what love is,—love,
That generates the likeness of itself
425 Through all heroic duties? so far wrong,
In saying bluntly, venturing truth on love,
'Come, human creature, love and work with me,'—
Instead of 'Lady, thou art wondrous fair,
'And, where the Graces⁷ walk before, the Muse
430 'Will follow at the lightning of their eyes,
'And where the Muse walks, lovers need to creep:
'Turn round and love me, or I die of love.'"

6. In Genesis 16 Sarah's maidservant, who bore a child, Ishmael, by Sarah's husband, Abraham.

7. In classical mythology goddesses who personified beauty and charm.

With quiet indignation I broke in.
"You misconceive the question like a man,
435   Who sees a woman as the complement
Of his sex merely. You forget too much
That every creature, female as the male,·
Stands single in responsible act and thought
As also in birth and death. Whoever says
440   To a loyal woman, 'Love and work with me,'
Will get fair answers if the work and love,
Being good themselves, are good for her—the best
She was born for. Women of a softer mood,
Surprised by men when scarcely awake to life,
445   Will sometimes only hear the first word, love,
And catch up with it any kind of work,
Indifferent, so that dear love go with it.
I do not blame such women, though, for love,
They pick much oakum;[8] earth's fanatics make
450   Too frequently heaven's saints. But *me* your work
Is not the best for,—nor your love the best,
Nor able to commend the kind of work
For love's sake merely. Ah, you force me, sir,
To be overbold in speaking of myself:
455   I too have my vocation,—work to do,
The heavens and earth have set me since I changed
My father's face for theirs, and, though your world
Were twice as wretched as you represent,
Most serious work, most necessary work
460   As any of the economists'. Reform,
Make trade a Christian possibility,
And individual right no general wrong;
Wipe out earth's furrows of the Thine and Mine,
And leave one green for men to play at bowls,[9]
465   With innings for them all! . . . What then, indeed,
If mortals are not greater by the head
Than any of their prosperities? what then,
Unless the artist keep up open roads
Betwixt the seen and unseen,—bursting through
470   The best of your conventions with his best,
The speakable, imaginable best
God bids him speak, to prove what lies beyond
Both speech and imagination? A starved man
Exceeds a fat beast: we'll not barter, sir,
475   The beautiful for barley.—And, even so,
I hold you will not compass your poor ends
Of barley-feeding and material ease,
Without a poet's individualism
To work your universal. It takes a soul,
480   To move a body: it takes a high-souled man,
To move the masses, even to a cleaner stye:

8. Fiber derived by untwisting (picking) old rope, a task frequently assigned to workhouse inmates.

9. A game of skill played on a smooth lawn with weighted wooden balls.

It takes the ideal, to blow a hair's-breadth off
The dust of the actual.—Ah, your Fouriers[1] failed,
Because not poets enough to understand
485   That life develops from within.——For me,
Perhaps I am not worthy, as you say,
Of work like this: perhaps a woman's soul
Aspires, and not creates: yet we aspire,
And yet I'll try out your perhapses, sir,
490   And if I fail . . . why, burn me up my straw[2]
Like other false works—I'll not ask for grace;
Your scorn is better, cousin Romney. I
Who love my art, would never wish it lower
To suit my stature. I may love my art.
495   You'll grant that even a woman may love art,
Seeing that to waste true love on anything
Is womanly, past question."

From *Book 5*

[POETS AND THE PRESENT AGE]

The critics say that epics have died out
140   With Agamemnon and the goat-nursed gods;[3]
I'll not believe it. I could never deem,
As Payne Knight[4] did (the mythic mountaineer
Who travelled higher than he was born to live,
And showed sometimes the goitre[5] in his throat
145   Discoursing of an image seen through fog),
That Homer's heroes measured twelve feet high.
They were but men:—his Helen's hair turned grey
Like any plain Miss Smith's who wears a front;[6]
And Hector's infant whimpered at a plume[7]
150   As yours last Friday at a turkey-cock.
All actual heroes are essential men,
And all men possible heroes: every age,
Heroic in proportions, double-faced,
Looks backward and before, expects a morn
And claims an epos.°   *epic poem*
155   Ay, but every age
Appears to souls who live in't (ask Carlyle)[8]
Most unheroic. Ours, for instance, ours:
The thinkers scout it,° and the poets abound   *dismiss it scornfully*

---

1. I.e., Utopian thinkers. François-Marie-Charles Fourier (1772–1837) was a French political theorist who advocated communal property as a basis for social harmony.
2. I.e., destroy my poetry. See 1 Corinthians 3.12–15.
3. Zeus, the ruler of the ancient Greek gods, was nursed by a goat. Agamemnon was the commander of the Greeks in the Trojan War.
4. Richard Payne Knight (1750–1824), a classical philologist who claimed that Lord Elgin had wasted his labor taking the marble friezes from the Parthenon in Greece to England because the

marbles were not all Greek.
5. A disease often contracted in high mountain areas because of the low iodine content of the water.
6. A piece of false hair worn over the forehead by women.
7. In the *Iliad*, book 6, the Trojan hero Hector reaches for his infant son, but the child clings to his nurse, frightened of his father's helmet and crest.
8. In *Heroes, Hero-Worship, and the Heroic in History* (1841), Carlyle argues that the present age needs a renewed perception of the heroic.

Who scorn to touch it with a finger-tip:
160   A pewter age,[9]—mixed metal, silver-washed;
An age of scum, spooned off the richer past,
An age of patches for old gaberdines,°   *coats*
An age of mere transition,[1] meaning nought
Except that what succeeds° must shame it quite   *follows*
165   If God please. That's wrong thinking, to my mind,
And wrong thoughts make poor poems.
                             Every age,
Through being beheld too close, is ill-discerned
By those who have not lived past it. We'll suppose
Mount Athos carved, as Alexander schemed,
170   To some colossal statue of a man.[2]
The peasants, gathering brushwood in his ear,
Had guessed as little as the browsing goats
Of form or feature of humanity
Up there,—in fact, had travelled five miles off
175   Or ere the giant image broke on them,
Full human profile, nose and chin distinct,
Mouth, muttering rhythms of silence up the sky
And fed at evening with the blood of suns;
Grand torso,—hand, that flung perpetually
180   The largesse of a silver river down
To all the country pastures. 'Tis even thus
With times we live in,—evermore too great
To be apprehended near.
                      But poets should
Exert a double vision; should have eyes
185   To see near things as comprehensively
As if afar they took their point of sight,
And distant things as intimately deep
As if they touched them. Let us strive for this.
I do distrust the poet who discerns
190   No character or glory in his times,
And trundles back his soul five hundred years,
Past moat and drawbridge, into a castle-court,
To sing—oh, not of lizard or of toad
Alive i' the ditch there,—'twere excusable,
195   But of some black chief, half knight, half sheep-lifter,°   *sheep stealer*
Some beauteous dame, half chattel and half queen,
As dead as must be, for the greater part,
The poems made on their chivalric bones;
And that's no wonder: death inherits death.

---

9. Allusion to the convention, which originates in Hesiod (Greek poet, ca. 8th century B.C.E), of describing civilization's decline through a succession of ages named for increasingly less precious materials: i.e., the Golden Age, the Silver Age, the Bronze Age.
1. In *The Spirit of the Age* (1831), John Stuart Mill calls the present age "an age of transition."

2. Deinocrates, a Macedonian architect (4th century B.C.E.), is said to have suggested to Alexander the Great that Mount Athos be carved into the statue of a conqueror with a city in his left hand and a basin in his right, where all the waters of the region could be collected and used to water the pasturelands below.

200 Nay, if there's room for poets in this world
    A little overgrown (I think there is),
    Their sole work is to represent the age,
    Their age, not Charlemagne's,[3]—this live, throbbing age,
    That brawls, cheats, maddens, calculates, aspires,
205 And spends more passion, more heroic heat,
    Betwixt the mirrors of its drawing-rooms,
    Than Roland[4] with his knights at Roncesvalles.
    To flinch from modern varnish, coat or flounce,
    Cry out for togas and the picturesque,
210 Is fatal,—foolish too. King Arthur's self
    Was commonplace to Lady Guenever;
    And Camelot to minstrels seemed as flat
    As Fleet Street[5] to our poets.
                       Never flinch,
    But still, unscrupulously epic, catch
215 Upon the burning lava of a song
    The full-veined, heaving, double-breasted Age:
    That, when the next shall come, the men of that
    May touch the impress° with reverent hand, and say   *impression*
    "Behold,—behold the paps° we all have sucked!   *breasts*
220 This bosom seems to beat still, or at least
    It sets ours beating: this is living art,
    Which thus presents and thus records true life."

1853–56   1857

Mother and Poet[1]

(*Turin, After News from Gaeta, 1861*)

1

DEAD! One of them shot by the sea in the east,
    And one of them shot in the west by the sea.
Dead! both my boys! When you sit at the feast
    And are wanting a great song for Italy free,
5   Let none look at *me*!

2

Yet I was a poetess only last year,
    And good at my art, for a woman, men said;
But *this* woman, *this*, who is agonised here,

---

3. Frankish conqueror (742–814), who created a European empire.
4. Legendary medieval hero, whose adventures are told in the epic poem *Chanson de Roland* (11th century); his last battle is fought at Roncesvalles, a Spanish village.
5. A center for book shops and newspaper and publishing offices in London.
1. The speaker is the Italian poet and patriot Laura Savio of Turin, both of whose sons were killed in the struggle for the unification of Italy—one in the attack on the fortress at Ancona, the other at the siege of Gaeta, the last stronghold of the Neapolitan government.

—The east sea and west sea rhyme on in her head
10   For ever instead.

3

What art can a woman be good at? Oh, vain!
   What art *is* she good at, but hurting her breast
With the milk-teeth of babes, and a smile at the pain?
   Ah boys, how you hurt! you were strong as you pressed,
15   And I proud, by that test.

4

What art's for a woman? To hold on her knees
   Both darlings! to feel all their arms round her throat,
Cling, strangle a little! to sew by degrees
   And 'broider the long-clothes° and neat little coat;   *infant's clothing*
20   To dream and to doat.

5

To teach them . . . It stings there! *I* made them indeed
   Speak plain the word *country*. *I* taught them, no doubt,
That a country's a thing men should die for at need.
   I prated of liberty, rights, and about
25   The tyrant cast out.

6

And when their eyes flashed . . . O my beautiful eyes! . . .
   I exulted; nay, let them go forth at the wheels
Of the guns, and denied not. But then the surprise
   When one sits quite alone! Then one weeps, then one kneels!
30   God, how the house feels!

7

At first, happy news came, in gay letters moiled°   *moistened*
   With my kisses,—of camp-life and glory, and how
They both loved me; and, soon coming home to be spoiled
   In return would fan off every fly from my brow
35   With their green laurel-bough.[2]

8

Then was triumph at Turin: "Ancona was free!"
   And some one came out of the cheers in the street,
With a face pale as stone, to say something to me.
   My Guido was dead! I fell down at his feet,
40   While they cheered in the street.

2. A laurel crown is the conventional mark of a poet's fame.

9

I bore it; friends soothed me; my grief looked sublime
    As the ransom of Italy. One boy remained
To be leant on and walked with, recalling the time
    When the first grew immortal, while both of us strained
45   To the height he had gained.

10

And letters still came, shorter, sadder, more strong,
    Writ now but in one hand, "I was not to faint,—
One loved me for two—would be with me ere long:
    And *Viva l'Italia!*—*he* died for, our saint,
50   Who forbids our complaint."

11

My Nanni would add, "he was safe, and aware
    Of a presence that turned off the balls,°—was imprest   *cannonballs*
It was Guido himself, who knew what I could bear,
    And how 'twas impossible, quite dispossessed
55   To live on for the rest."[3]

12

On which, without pause, up the telegraph line
    Swept smoothly the next news from Gaeta:—*Shot.*
Tell his mother. Ah, ah, "his," "their" mother,—not "mine,"
    No voice says "*My* mother" again to me. What!
60   You think Guido forgot?

13

Are souls straight° so happy that, dizzy with Heaven,   *immediately*
    They drop earth's affections, conceive not of woe?
I think not. Themselves were too lately forgiven
    Through THAT Love and Sorrow which reconciled so
65   The Above and Below.

14

O Christ of the five wounds, who look'dst through the dark
    To the face of thy mother! consider, I pray,
How we common mothers stand desolate, mark,
    Whose sons, not being Christs, die with eyes turned away
70   And no last word to say!

15

Both boys dead? but that's out of nature. We all
    Have been patriots, yet each house must always keep one.

---

3. I.e., that she could survive if both sons died.

'Twere imbecile, hewing out roads to a wall;
    And, when Italy's made, for what end is it done
75   If we have not a son?

16

Ah, ah, ah! when Gaeta's taken, what then?
    When the fair wicked queen[4] sits no more at her sport
Of the fire-balls of death crashing souls out of men?
    When the guns of Cavalli[5] with final retort
80   Have cut the game short?

17

When Venice and Rome keep their new jubilee,[6]
    When your flag takes all heaven for its white, green, and red,
When *you* have your country from mountain to sea,
    When King Victor has Italy's crown on his head,
85   (And *I* have my Dead)—

18

What then? Do not mock me. Ah, ring your bells low,
    And burn your lights faintly! *My* country is *there,*
Above the star pricked by the last peak of snow:
    My Italy's THERE, with my brave civic Pair,
90   To disfranchise despair!

19

Forgive me. Some women bear children in strength,
    And bite back the cry of their pain in self-scorn;
But the birth-pangs of nations will wring us at length
    Into wail such as this—and we sit on forlorn
95   When the man-child is born.

20

Dead! One of them shot by the sea in the east,
    And one of them shot in the west by the sea.
Both! both my boys! If in keeping the feast
    You want a great song for your Italy free,
100   Let none look at *me!*

1861   1862

4. Maria of Bavaria, wife of Francis II, the last ruler of the Neapolitan government, who retreated to Gaeta.
5. The general commanding the siege of Gaeta.
6. The celebration when they too will have been united with the rest of Italy under King Victor Emmanuel II (1820–1878; reigned, 1861–78). In 1861, when the poem was written, they were the two cities that were still independent of the new state.

ALFRED, LORD TENNYSON
1809–1892

In his own lifetime Tennyson was the most popular of poets; his works, from 1850 onward, occupied a significant space on the bookshelves of almost every family of readers in England and the United States. Such popularity inevitably provoked a reaction in the decades following his death. In the course of repudiating their Victorian predecessors, the Edwardians and Georgians established the fashion of making fun of Tennyson's achievements. Samuel Butler (1835–1902), who anticipated early-twentieth-century tastes, has a characteristic entry in his *Notebooks:* "Talking it over, we agreed that Blake was no good because he learnt Italian at sixty in order to study Dante, and we knew Dante was no good because he was so fond of Virgil, and Virgil was no good because Tennyson ran [followed] him, and as for Tennyson—well, Tennyson goes without saying." Butler's flippant dismissal expresses an attitude that is no longer fashionable: Tennyson's stature as one of the major poets of the English language seems uncontroversial today.

Like his poetry, Tennyson's life and character have been reassessed in recent times. To many of his contemporaries he seemed a remote wizard secure in his laureate's robes, a man whose life had been sheltered, marred only by the loss of his best friend in youth. During much of his career Tennyson may have been isolated, but his was not a sheltered life in the real sense of the word. His childhood home, a parsonage, was a household dominated by frictions and loyalties and broodings over ancestral inheritances, in which the children showed marked strains of instability and eccentricity.

Alfred Tennyson was the fourth son in a family of twelve children. One of his brothers had to be confined to an insane asylum for life; another was long addicted to opium; another had violent quarrels with his father, the Reverend Dr. George Tennyson. This father, a man of considerable learning, had been born the eldest son of a wealthy landowner and had, therefore, expected to be heir to his family's estates. Instead he was disinherited in favor of his younger brother and had to make his own livelihood by joining the clergy, a profession that he disliked. After George Tennyson had settled in a small rectory in Somersby, his brooding sense of dissatisfaction led to increasingly violent bouts of drunkenness; he was nevertheless able to act as his sons' tutor in classical and modern languages to prepare them for entering the university.

Before leaving this strange household for Cambridge, Tennyson had already demonstrated a flair for writing verse—precocious exercises in the manner of John Milton or Byron or the Elizabethan dramatists. He had even published a volume in 1827, in collaboration with his brother Charles, *Poems by Two Brothers*. This feat drew him to the attention of a group of gifted undergraduates at Cambridge, "the Apostles," who encouraged him to devote his life to poetry. Up until that time the young man had known scarcely anyone outside the circle of his own family. Despite his massive frame and powerful physique, he was painfully shy, and the friendships he found at Cambridge as well as the intellectual and political discussions in which he participated gave him confidence and widened his horizons as a poet. The most important of these friendships was with Arthur Hallam, a leader of the Apostles, who later became engaged to Tennyson's sister Emily. Hallam's sudden death, in 1833, seemed an overwhelming calamity to his friend. Not only the long elegy *In Memoriam* (1850) but many of Tennyson's other poems are tributes to this early friendship.

Tennyson's career at Cambridge was interrupted and finally broken off in 1831 by family dissensions and financial need, and he returned home to study and practice the craft of poetry. His early volumes (1830 and 1832) were attacked as "obscure" or "affected" by some of the reviewers. Tennyson suffered acutely under hostile criticism, but he also profited from it. His 1842 volume demonstrated a remarkable leap forward, and in 1850 he at last attained fame and full critical recognition with *In Memoriam*. In the same year he became poet laureate in succession to William Wordsworth. The struggle during the previous twenty years had been made especially painful by the long postponement of his marriage to Emily Sellwood, whom he had loved since 1836 but could not marry, because of poverty, until 1850.

His life thereafter was a comfortable one. He was as popular as Byron had been, and the earnings from his poetry (sometimes exceeding £10,000 a year) enabled him to purchase a house in the country and to enjoy the kind of seclusion he liked. His notoriety was enhanced, like that of George Bernard Shaw and Walt Whitman, by his colorful appearance. Huge and shaggy in cloak and broad-brimmed hat, gruff in manner, he impressed everyone as what is called a "character." The pioneering photographer Julia Cameron, who took magnificent portraits of him, called him "the most beautiful old man on earth." Like Dylan Thomas in the twentieth century, Tennyson had a booming voice that electrified listeners when he read his poetry, "mouthing out his hollow o's and a's, / Deep-chested music," as he would covertly describe himself in an early version of his Arthurian epic. Moreover, for many Victorian readers, he seemed not only a great poetical phrase maker and a striking individual but also a wise man whose occasional pronouncements on politics or world affairs represented the national voice itself. In 1884 he accepted a peerage. In 1892 he died and was buried in Westminster Abbey.

It is often said that success was bad for Tennyson and that after *In Memoriam* his poetic power seriously declined. That in his last forty-two years certain of his mannerisms became accentuated is true. One of the difficulties of his dignified blank verse was, as he said himself, that it is hard to describe commonplace objects and "at the same time to retain poetical elevation." This difficulty is evident, for example, in *Enoch Arden* (1864), a long blank verse narrative of everyday life in a fishing village, in which a basketful of fish is ornately described as "Enoch's ocean spoil / In ocean-smelling osier." In his later poems dealing with national affairs, there is also an increased shrillness of tone—a mannerism accentuated by Tennyson's realizing that he, like Charles Dickens, had a vast public behind him to back up his pronouncements.

It would be unwise, however, to ignore all of Tennyson's later productions. In 1855 he published his experimental monologue *Maud*, in which he presents an alienated hero who feels great bitterness toward society. In 1859 appeared four books of his *Idylls of the King*, a large-scale epic that occupied most of his energies in the second half of his career. The *Idylls* uses the body of Arthurian legend to construct a vision of civilization's rise and fall. In this civilization women both inspire men's highest efforts and sow the seeds of those efforts' destruction. The *Idylls* provides Tennyson's most extensive social vision, one that typifies much social thought of the age in its concern with medieval ideals of social community, heroism, and courtly love and in its despairing sense of the cycles of historical change.

W. H. Auden stated that Tennyson had "the finest ear, perhaps, of any English poet." The interesting point is that Tennyson did not "have" such an ear: he developed it. Studies of the original versions of his poems in the 1830 and 1832 volumes demonstrate how hard he worked at his craftsmanship. Like Geoffrey Chaucer or Alexander Pope or John Keats, Tennyson studied his predecessors assiduously to perfect his technique. Anyone wanting to learn the traditional craft of English verse can study profitably the various stages of revision that poems such as "The

Lotos-Eaters" were subjected to by this painstaking and artful poet. Some lines written in 1988 by the American poet Karl Shapiro effectively characterize Tennyson's accomplishments in these areas:

> Long-lived, the very image of English Poet,
> Whose songs still break out tears in the generations,
> Whose poetry for practitioners still astounds,
> Who crafted his life and letters like a watch.

Tennyson's early poetry shows other skills as well. One of these was a capacity for linking scenery to states of mind. As early as 1835 J. S. Mill identified the special kind of scene painting to be found in poems such as "Mariana" (1830): "not the power of producing that rather vapid species of composition usually termed descriptive poetry . . . but the power of *creating* scenery, in keeping with some state of human feeling so fitted to it as to be the embodied symbol of it, and to summon up the state of feeling itself, with a force not to be surpassed by anything but reality."

The state of feeling to which Tennyson was most intensely drawn was a melancholy isolation, often portrayed through the consciousness of an abandoned woman, as in "Mariana." Tennyson's absorption with such emotions in his early poetry evoked considerable criticism. His friend R. C. Trench warned him, "Tennyson, we cannot live in Art," and Mill urged him to "cultivate, and with no half devotion, philosophy as well as poetry." Advice of this kind Tennyson was already predisposed to heed. The death of Hallam and the religious uncertainties that he had himself experienced, together with his own extensive study of writings by geologists, astronomers, and biologists, led him to confront many of the religious issues that bewildered his and later generations. The result was *In Memoriam*, a long elegy written over a period of seventeen years, embodying the poet's reflections on the relation of human beings to God and to nature.

Tennyson's exploration of these vast subjects prompted some readers, such as T. H. Huxley, to consider him an intellectual giant, a thinker who had mastered the scientific thought of his century and fully confronted the issues it raised. Others dismissed Tennyson, in this phase, as a lightweight. Auden went so far as to call him the "stupidest" of English poets. He added, "There was little about melancholia that he didn't know; there was little else that he did." Perhaps T. S. Eliot's evaluation of *In Memoriam* is the more thought-provoking: the poem, he wrote, is remarkable not "because of the quality of its faith but because of the quality of its doubt." Tennyson's mind was slow, ponderous, brooding; for the composition of *In Memoriam* such qualities of mind were assets, not liabilities. Very different are the poems Tennyson writes of events of the moment over which his thoughts and feelings have had no time to brood. Several of these are what he himself called "newspaper verse." They are letters to the editor in effect, with the heat we expect of such productions. "The Charge of the Light Brigade" (1854), inspired by a report in the London *Times* of a cavalry charge at Balaclava during the Crimean War, is one of the most fascinating of his productions in this category.

Tennyson's poems of contemporary events were inevitably popular in his own day. So too were those poems in which, as in "Locksley Hall" (1842), he dipped into the future. The technological changes wrought by Victorian inventors and engineers fascinated him, sometimes giving him an exultant assurance of human progress. At other times the horrors of industrialism's by-products in the slums, the persistence of barbarity and bloodshed, and the greed of the newly rich destroyed his hopes that humanity was evolving upward. In the final book of *Idylls of the King* (1869), Arthur laments that his "realm / Reels back into the beast": Tennyson was similarly haunted by the possibility of retrogression.

For despite Tennyson's fascination with technological developments, he was essentially a poet of the countryside, a man whose whole being was conditioned by the recurring rhythms of rural rather than urban life. He had the country dweller's awareness of traditional roots and sense of the past. It is appropriate that so many of his poems are about the past, not about the present or future. Tennyson said that "the words 'far, far away' had always a strange charm" for him, even in his childhood; he was haunted by what he called "the passion of the past." The past became his great theme, whether it be his own past (such as the times he shared with Hallam), his country's past (as in *Idylls of the King*), or the past of the world itself, as expressed in these lines from *In Memoriam*:

> There rolls the deep where grew the tree.
> O earth, what changes hast thou seen!
> There where the long street roars hath been
> The stillness of the central sea.

Though Tennyson more often is inspired by the recorded past of humankind, he is the first major writer to express this awareness of the vast extent of geological time that has haunted human consciousness since Victorian scientists exposed the history of the earth's crust.

Mariana[1]

"Mariana in the moated grange."
—*Measure for Measure*

With blackest moss the flower-plots
  Were thickly crusted, one and all;
The rusted nails fell from the knots
  That held the pear to the gable wall.
5 The broken sheds looked sad and strange:
  Unlifted was the clinking latch;
  Weeded° and worn the ancient thatch   *full of weeds*
Upon the lonely moated grange.
      She only said, "My life is dreary,
10   He cometh not," she said;
      She said, "I am aweary, aweary,
      I would that I were dead!"

Her tears fell with the dews at even;
  Her tears fell ere the dews were dried;
15 She could not look on the sweet heaven,
  Either at morn or eventide.
After the flitting of the bats,
  When thickest dark did trance° the sky,   *cross*
  She drew her casement curtain by,
20 And glanced athwart° the glooming flats.[2]   *across*
      She only said, "The night is dreary,
      He cometh not," she said;
      She said, "I am aweary, aweary,
      I would that I were dead!"

---

1. Mariana, in Shakespeare's *Measure for Measure* 3.1.255, waits in a grange (an outlying farmhouse) for her lover, who has deserted her.
2. An area of low, level ground.

₂₅ Upon the middle of the night,
 Waking she heard the nightfowl crow;
The cock sung out an hour ere light;
 From the dark fen° the oxen's low   *marshland*
Came to her; without hope of change,
₃₀ In sleep she seemed to walk forlorn,
 Till cold winds woke the gray-eyed morn
About the lonely moated grange.
  She only said, "The day is dreary,
   He cometh not," she said;
₃₅ She said, "I am aweary, aweary,
   I would that I were dead!"

About a stonecast° from the wall   *stone's throw*
 A sluice with blackened waters slept,
And o'er it many, round and small,
₄₀ The clustered marish-mosses³ crept.
Hard° by a poplar shook alway,   *close*
 All silver-green with gnarlèd bark:
For leagues no other tree did mark
The level waste, the rounding gray.
₄₅ She only said, "My life is dreary,
   He cometh not," she said;
  She said, "I am aweary, aweary,
   I would that I were dead!"

And ever when the moon was low,
₅₀ And the shrill winds were up and away,
In the white curtain, to and fro,
 She saw the gusty shadow sway.
But when the moon was very low,
 And wild winds bound within their cell,⁴
₅₅ The shadow of the poplar fell
Upon her bed, across her brow.
  She only said, "The night is dreary,
   He cometh not," she said;
  She said, "I am aweary, aweary,
₆₀   I would that I were dead!"

All day within the dreamy house,
 The doors upon their hinges creaked;
The blue fly sung in the pane; the mouse
 Behind the moldering wainscot° shrieked, *wooden paneling*
₆₅ Or from the crevice peered about.
  Old faces glimmered through the doors,
  Old footsteps trod the upper floors,
 Old voices called her from without.
  She only said, "My life is dreary,
₇₀   He cometh not," she said;

3. The little marsh-moss lumps that float on the surface of water [Tennyson's note].

4. According to Virgil, Aeolus, god of winds, kept the winds imprisoned in a cave (*Aeneid* 1.50–59).

She said, "I am aweary, aweary,
I would that I were dead!"

The sparrow's chirrup on the roof,
  The slow clock ticking, and the sound
75 Which to the wooing wind aloof
  The poplar made, did all confound
Her sense; but most she loathed the hour
  When the thick-moted sunbeam lay
  Athwart the chambers, and the day
80 Was sloping toward his western bower.
    Then, said she, "I am very dreary,
      He will not come," she said;
    She wept, "I am aweary, aweary,
      Oh God, that I were dead!"

1830

The Lady of Shalott[1]

Part 1

On either side the river lie
Long fields of barley and of rye,
That clothe the wold° and meet the sky;   *rolling plain*
And through the field the road runs by
5   To many-towered Camelot;
And up and down the people go,
Gazing where the lilies blow°   *bloom*
Round an island there below,
  The island of Shalott.

10 Willows whiten, aspens quiver,
Little breezes dusk and shiver
Through the wave that runs forever
By the island in the river
  Flowing down to Camelot.
15 Four gray walls, and four gray towers,
Overlook a space of flowers,
And the silent isle imbowers
  The Lady of Shalott.

By the margin, willow-veiled,
20 Slide the heavy barges trailed
By slow horses; and unhailed

1. The story of the Lady of Shalott is a version of the tale of "Elaine the fair maid of Astolat," which appears in book 18 of *Morte Darthur* (1470) by Sir Thomas Malory (ca. 1405–1471). Tennyson, however, claimed he did not know Malory's version when he wrote his draft in 1832, identifying his source as a 14th-century tale about "la Damigella di Scalot": "I met the story first in some Italian *novelle*: but the web, mirror, island, etc., were my own. Indeed, I doubt whether I should ever have put it in that shape if I had been aware of the Maid of Astolat in *Morte d'Arthur*." Tennyson subjected this poem to numerous revisions over the years.

The shallop° flitteth silken-sailed   *light open boat*
  Skimming down to Camelot:
But who hath seen her wave her hand?
25 Or at the casement seen her stand?
Or is she known in all the land,
  The Lady of Shalott?

Only reapers, reaping early
In among the bearded barley,
30 Hear a song that echoes cheerly
From the river winding clearly,
  Down to towered Camelot;
And by the moon the reaper weary,
Piling sheaves in uplands airy,
35 Listening, whispers "'Tis the fairy
  Lady of Shalott."

Part 2

There she weaves by night and day
A magic web with colors gay.
She has heard a whisper say,
40 A curse is on her if she stay°   *pause*
  To look down to Camelot.
She knows not what the curse may be,
And so she weaveth steadily,
And little other care hath she,
45 The Lady of Shalott.

And moving through a mirror clear[2]
That hangs before her all the year,
Shadows of the world appear.
There she sees the highway near
50 Winding down to Camelot;
There the river eddy whirls,
And there the surly village churls,°   *peasants*
And the red cloaks of market girls,
  Pass onward from Shalott.

55 Sometimes a troop of damsels glad,
An abbot on an ambling pad,°   *easy-paced horse*
Sometimes a curly shepherd lad,
Or long-haired page in crimson clad,
  Goes by to towered Camelot;
60 And sometimes through the mirror blue
The knights come riding two and two:
She hath no loyal knight and true,
  The Lady of Shalott.

---

2. Weavers used mirrors, placed facing their looms, to see the progress of their work.

But in her web she still delights
65 To weave the mirror's magic sights,
For often through the silent nights
A funeral, with plumes and lights
    And music, went to Camelot;
Or when the moon was overhead,
70 Came two young lovers lately wed:
"I am half sick of shadows," said
    The Lady of Shalott.

Part 3

A bowshot from her bower eaves,
He rode between the barley sheaves,
75 The sun came dazzling through the leaves,
And flamed upon the brazen greaves[3]
    Of bold Sir Lancelot.
A red-cross knight forever kneeled
To a lady in his shield,
80 That sparkled on the yellow field,
    Beside remote Shalott.

The gemmy bridle glittered free,
Like to some branch of stars we see
Hung in the golden Galaxy.
85 The bridle bells rang merrily
    As he rode down to Camelot;
And from his blazoned baldric[4] slung
A mighty silver bugle hung,
And as he rode his armor rung,
90   Beside remote Shalott.

All in the blue unclouded weather
Thick-jeweled shone the saddle leather,
The helmet and the helmet-feather
Burned like one burning flame together,
95   As he rode down to Camelot;
As often through the purple night,
Below the starry clusters bright,
Some bearded meteor, trailing light,
    Moves over still Shalott.

100 His broad clear brow in sunlight glowed;
On burnished hooves his war horse trode;
From underneath his helmet flowed
His coal-black curls as on he rode,
    As he rode down to Camelot.
105 From the bank and from the river
He flashed into the crystal mirror,

---

3. Armor protecting the leg below the knee.
4. A belt worn diagonally from one shoulder to the opposite hip, supporting a sword or bugle. "Blazoned": painted with a heraldic device.

"Tirra lirra,"[5] by the river
    Sang Sir Lancelot.

She left the web, she left the loom,
110   She made three paces through the room,
She saw the water lily bloom,
She saw the helmet and the plume,
    She looked down to Camelot.
Out flew the web and floated wide;
115   The mirror cracked from side to side;
"The curse is come upon me," cried
    The Lady of Shalott.

Part 4

In the stormy east wind straining,
The pale yellow woods were waning,
120   The broad stream in his banks complaining,
Heavily the low sky raining
    Over towered Camelot;
Down she came and found a boat
Beneath a willow left afloat,
125   And round about the prow she wrote
    The Lady of Shalott.

And down the river's dim expanse
Like some bold seër in a trance,
Seeing all his own mischance—
130   With a glassy countenance
    Did she look to Camelot.
And at the closing of the day
She loosed the chain, and down she lay;
The broad stream bore her far away,
135   The Lady of Shalott.

Lying, robed in snowy white
That loosely flew to left and right—
The leaves upon her falling light—
Through the noises of the night
140   She floated down to Camelot;
And as the boat-head wound along
The willowy hills and fields among,
They heard her singing her last song,
    The Lady of Shalott.

145   Heard a carol, mournful, holy,
Chanted loudly, chanted lowly,
Till her blood was frozen slowly,
And her eyes were darkened wholly,[6]

---

5. Cf. Autolycus's song in Shakespeare's *The Winter's Tale* 4.3.9: "The lark, that tirra-lirra chants."
6. In the 1832 version this line read: "And her smooth face sharpened slowly." George Eliot informed Tennyson that she preferred the earlier version.

The Lady of Shalott. This 1857 engraving, created by Dante Gabriel Rossetti for publisher Edward Moxon's illustrated collection of Tennyson's poetry, shows Lancelot musing "a little space" on the Lady in her boat.

Turned to towered Camelot.

150   For ere she reached upon the tide
    The first house by the waterside,
    Singing in her song she died,
The Lady of Shalott.

    Under tower and balcony,
155   By garden wall and gallery,
    A gleaming shape she floated by,
    Dead-pale between the houses high,
Silent into Camelot.
    Out upon the wharfs they came,
160   Knight and burgher, lord and dame,
    And round the prow they read her name,
The Lady of Shalott.

    Who is this? and what is here?
    And in the lighted palace near
165   Died the sound of royal cheer;

And they crossed themselves for fear,
    All the knights at Camelot:
But Lancelot mused a little space;
He said, "She has a lovely face;
170 God in his mercy lend her grace,
    The Lady of Shalott."

1831–32   1832, 1842

The Lotos-Eaters[1]

"Courage!" he[2] said, and pointed toward the land,
"This mounting wave will roll us shoreward soon."
In the afternoon they came unto a land[3]
In which it seemèd always afternoon.
5 All round the coast the languid air did swoon,
Breathing like one that hath a weary dream.
Full-faced above the valley stood the moon;
And, like a downward smoke, the slender stream
Along the cliff to fall and pause and fall did seem.

10 A land of streams! some, like a downward smoke,
Slow-dropping veils of thinnest lawn,° did go;   *fine thin linen*
And some through wavering lights and shadows broke,
Rolling a slumbrous sheet of foam below.
They saw the gleaming river seaward flow
15 From the inner land; far off, three mountaintops
Three silent pinnacles of aged snow,
Stood sunset-flushed; and, dewed with showery drops,
Up-clomb° the shadowy pine above the woven copse.   *climbed up*

The charmèd sunset lingered low adown
20 In the red West; through mountain clefts the dale
Was seen far inland, and the yellow down[4]
Bordered with palm, and many a winding vale
And meadow, set with slender galingale;[5]
A land where all things always seemed the same!
25 And round about the keel with faces pale,

---

1. Based on a short episode from the *Odyssey* (9.82–97) in which the weary Greek veterans of the Trojan War are tempted by a desire to abandon their long voyage homeward. As Odysseus later reported: "On the tenth day we set foot on the land of the lotos-eaters who eat a flowering food. . . . I sent forth certain of my company [who] . . . mixed with the men of the lotos-eaters who gave . . . them of the lotos to taste. Now whosoever of them did eat the honey-sweet fruit of the lotos had no more wish to bring tidings nor to come back, but there he chose to abide . . . forgetful of his homeward way."
Tennyson expands Homer's brief account into an elaborate picture of weariness and the desire for rest and death. The descriptions in the first stanzas are similar to Spenser's *The Faerie Queene* (1590) 2.6 and employ the same stanza form. The final section derives, in part, from Lucretius's conception of the gods in *De Rerum Natura* (ca. 55 B.C.E.).
2. Odysseus (or Ulysses).
3. The repetition of "land" from line 1 was deliberate; Tennyson said that this "no rhyme" was "lazier" in its effect. This technique of repeating words, phrases, and sounds continues; cf. "afternoon" (lines 3–4) and the rhyming of "adown" and "down" (lines 19 and 21).
4. An open plain on high ground.
5. A plant resembling tall coarse grass.

Dark faces pale against that rosy flame,
The mild-eyed melancholy Lotos-eaters came.

Branches they bore of that enchanted stem,
Laden with flower and fruit, whereof they gave
30 To each, but whoso did receive of them
And taste, to him the gushing of the wave
Far far away did seem to mourn and rave
On alien shores; and if his fellow spake,
His voice was thin, as voices from the grave;
35 And deep-asleep he seemed, yet all awake,
And music in his ears his beating heart did make.

They sat them down upon the yellow sand,
Between the sun and moon upon the shore;
And sweet it was to dream of Fatherland,
40 Of child, and wife, and slave; but evermore
Most weary seemed the sea, weary the oar,
Weary the wandering fields of barren foam,
Then some one said, "We will return no more";
And all at once they sang, "Our island home°   *Ithaca*
45 Is far beyond the wave; we will no longer roam."

Choric Song[6]

1

There is sweet music here that softer falls
Than petals from blown roses on the grass,
Or night-dews on still waters between walls
Of shadowy granite, in a gleaming pass;
50 Music that gentlier on the spirit lies,
Than tired[7] eyelids upon tired eyes;
Music that brings sweet sleep down from the blissful skies.
Here are cool mosses deep,
And through the moss the ivies creep,
55 And in the stream the long-leaved flowers weep,
And from the craggy ledge the poppy hangs in sleep.

2

Why are we weighed upon with heaviness,
And utterly consumed with sharp distress,
While all things else have rest from weariness?
60 All things have rest: why should we toil alone,
We only toil, who are the first of things,
And make perpetual moan,
Still from one sorrow to another thrown;
Nor ever fold our wings,

---

6. Sung by the mariners.
7. Tennyson wanted the word to be pronounced as *tie-yerd* rather than *tier'd* or *tire-èd*, thus

"making the word neither monosyllable or disyllabic, but a dreamy child of the two."

65 And cease from wanderings,
Nor steep our brows in slumber's holy balm;
Nor harken what the inner spirit sings,
"There is no joy but calm!"—
Why should we only toil, the roof and crown of things?[8]

3

70 Lo! in the middle of the wood,
The folded leaf is wooed from out the bud
With winds upon the branch, and there
Grows green and broad, and takes no care,
Sun-steeped at noon, and in the moon
75 Nightly dew-fed; and turning yellow
Falls, and floats adown the air.
Lo! sweetened with summer light,
The full-juiced apple, waxing over-mellow,
Drops in a silent autumn night.
80 All its allotted length of days
The flower ripens in its place,
Ripens and fades, and falls, and hath no toil,
Fast-rooted in the fruitful soil.

4

Hateful is the dark blue sky,
85 Vaulted o'er the dark blue sea.
Death is the end of life; ah, why
Should life all labor be?
Let us alone. Time driveth onward fast,
And in a little while our lips are dumb.
90 Let us alone. What is it that will last?
All things are taken from us, and become
Portions and parcels of the dreadful past.
Let us alone. What pleasure can we have
To war with evil? Is there any peace
95 In ever climbing up the climbing wave?
All things have rest, and ripen toward the grave
In silence—ripen, fall, and cease:
Give us long rest or death, dark death, or dreamful ease.[9]

5

How sweet it were, hearing the downward stream,
100 With half-shut eyes ever to seem
Falling asleep in a half-dream!
To dream and dream, like yonder amber light,
Which will not leave the myrrh-bush[1] on the height;

8. Cf. *The Faerie Queene* 2.6.17: "Why then dost thou, O man, that of them all / Art Lord, and eke of nature Sovereaine, / Wilfully . . . wast thy joyous houres in needlesse paine?"
9. Cf. *The Faerie Queen* 1.9.40: "Sleepe after toyle, port after stormie seas, / Ease after warre, death after life does greatly please."
1. Myrrh, a resin used in perfume and incense, is associated with sweetness and comfort.

To hear each other's whispered speech;
105 Eating the Lotos day by day,
To watch the crisping° ripples on the beach,   *curling*
And tender curving lines of creamy spray;
To lend our hearts and spirits wholly
To the influence of mild-minded melancholy;
110 To muse and brood and live again in memory,
With those old faces of our infancy
Heaped over with a mound of grass,
Two handfuls of white dust, shut in an urn of brass!

6

Dear is the memory of our wedded lives,
115 And dear the last embraces of our wives
And their warm tears; but all hath suffered change;
For surely now our household hearths are cold,
Our sons inherit us,° our looks are strange,   *succeed us as our heirs*
And we should come like ghosts to trouble joy.
120 Or else the island princes[2] overbold
Have eat our substance, and the minstrel sings
Before them of the ten years' war in Troy,
And our great deeds, as half-forgotten things.
Is there confusion in the little isle?
125 Let what is broken so remain.
The Gods are hard to reconcile;
'Tis hard to settle order once again.
There *is* confusion worse than death,
Trouble on trouble, pain on pain,
130 Long labor unto aged breath,
Sore tasks to hearts worn out by many wars
And eyes grown dim with gazing on the pilot-stars.

7

But, propped on beds of amaranth and moly,[3]
How sweet—while warm airs lull us, blowing lowly—
135 With half-dropped eyelid still,
Beneath a heaven dark and holy,
To watch the long bright river drawing slowly
His waters from the purple hill—
To hear the dewy echoes calling
140 From cave to cave through the thick-twined vine—
To watch the emerald-colored water falling
Through many a woven acanthus[4] wreath divine!
Only to hear and see the far-off sparkling brine,
Only to hear were sweet, stretched out beneath the pine.

2. The suitors of Penelope, Odysseus's wife; during his long absence they have settled themselves as guests in his hall as they pressure her to remarry.

3. A flower with magical properties mentioned by Homer. "Amaranth": a legendary unfading flower.
4. A plant resembling a thistle. Its leaves were the model for ornaments on Corinthian columns.

8

145 The Lotos blooms below the barren peak,
The Lotos blows by every winding creek;
All day the wind breathes low with mellower tone;
Through every hollow cave and alley lone
Round and round the spicy downs the yellow Lotos dust is blown.
150 We have had enough of action, and of motion we,
Rolled to starboard, rolled to larboard, when the surge was seething free,
Where the wallowing monster spouted his foam-fountains in the sea.
Let us swear an oath, and keep it with an equal mind,
In the hollow Lotos land to live and lie reclined
155 On the hills like Gods together, careless of mankind.
For they lie beside their nectar, and the bolts° are hurled   *thunderbolts*
Far below them in the valleys, and the clouds are lightly curled
Round their golden houses, girdled with the gleaming world;
Where they smile in secret, looking over wasted lands,
160 Blight and famine, plague and earthquake, roaring deeps and fiery sands,
Clanging fights, and flaming towns, and sinking ships, and praying hands.
But they smile, they find a music centred in a doleful song
Steaming up, a lamentation and an ancient tale of wrong,
Like a tale of little meaning though the words are strong;
165 Chanted from an ill-used race of men that cleave the soil,
Sow the seed, and reap the harvest with enduring toil,
Storing yearly little dues of wheat, and wine and oil;
Till they perish and they suffer—some, 'tis whispered—down in hell
Suffer endless anguish, others in Elysian valleys dwell,
170 Resting weary limbs at last on beds of asphodel.[5]
Surely, surely, slumber is more sweet than toil, the shore
Than labor in the deep mid-ocean, wind and wave and oar;
O, rest ye, brother mariners, we will not wander more.

1832, 1842

Ulysses[1]

It little profits that an idle king,
By this still hearth, among these barren crags,
Matched with an aged wife, I mete and dole
Unequal laws[2] unto a savage race,

---

5. A yellow lilylike flower supposed to grow in Elysium—in classical mythology a paradise for heroes favored by the gods.
1. According to Dante, after the fall of Troy, Ulysses never returned to his island home of Ithaca. Instead he persuaded some of his followers to seek new experiences by a voyage of exploration westward out beyond the Strait of Gibraltar. In his inspiring speech to his aging crew he said: "Consider your origin: you were not made to live as brutes, but to pursue virtue and knowledge" (*Inferno* 26). Tennyson modified

Dante's 14th-century version by combining it with Homer's account (*Odyssey* 19–24). Thus Tennyson has Ulysses make his speech in Ithaca some time after he has returned home; reunited with his wife, Penelope, and his son, Telemachus; and, presumably, resumed his administrative responsibilities involved in governing his kingdom.
Tennyson stated that this poem expressed his own "need of going forward and braving the struggle of life" after the death of Arthur Hallam.
2. Measure out rewards and punishments.

5 That hoard, and sleep, and feed,[3] and know not me.
  I cannot rest from travel; I will drink
 Life to the lees. All times I have enjoyed
 Greatly, have suffered greatly, both with those
 That loved me, and alone; on shore, and when
10 Through scudding drifts the rainy Hyades[4]
 Vexed the dim sea. I am become a name;
 For always roaming with a hungry heart
 Much have I seen and known—cities of men
 And manners, climates, councils, governments,
15 Myself not least, but honored of them all—
 And drunk delight of battle with my peers,
 Far on the ringing plains of windy Troy,
 I am a part of all that I have met;
 Yet all experience is an arch wherethrough
20 Gleams that untraveled world whose margin fades
 Forever and forever when I move.
 How dull it is to pause, to make an end,
 To rust unburnished, not to shine in use![5]
 As though to breathe were life! Life piled on life
25 Were all too little, and of one to me
 Little remains; but every hour is saved
 From that eternal silence, something more,
 A bringer of new things; and vile it were
 For some three suns to store and hoard myself,
30 And this gray spirit yearning in desire
 To follow knowledge like a sinking star,
 Beyond the utmost bound of human thought.

  This is my son, mine own Telemachus,
 To whom I leave the scepter and the isle—
35 Well-loved of me, discerning to fulfill
 This labor, by slow prudence to make mild
 A rugged people, and through soft degrees
 Subdue them to the useful and the good.
 Most blameless is he, centered in the sphere
40 Of common duties, decent not to fail
 In offices of tenderness, and pay
 Meet° adoration to my household gods,   *suitable, fitting*
 When I am gone. He works his work, I mine.

  There lies the port; the vessel puffs her sail;
45 There gloom the dark, broad seas. My mariners,
 Souls that have toiled, and wrought, and thought with me—
 That ever with a frolic welcome took
 The thunder and the sunshine,[6] and opposed

---

3. Cf. Shakespeare's *Hamlet* 4.4.9.23–25: "What is a man / If his chief good . . . Be but to sleep and feed?—a beast, no more."
4. A group of stars (literally, "rainy ones") in the constellation Taurus; their heliacal rising and setting generally coincided with the season of heavy rains. "Scudding drifts": driving showers of spray and rain.
5. Cf. Ulysses' speech in Shakespeare's *Troilus and Cressida* 3.3.144–47: "Perseverance, dear my lord, / Keeps honour bright. To have done is to hang / Quite out of fashion, like a rusty mail / In monumental mock'ry."
6. I.e., varying fortunes.

Free hearts, free foreheads°—you and I are old;   *confidence*
50 Old age hath yet his honor and his toil.
Death closes all; but something ere the end,
Some work of noble note, may yet be done,
Not unbecoming men that strove with Gods.
The lights begin to twinkle from the rocks;
55 The long day wanes; the slow moon climbs; the deep
Moans round with many voices. Come, my friends,
'Tis not too late to seek a newer world.
Push off, and sitting well in order smite
The sounding furrows; for my purpose holds
60 To sail beyond the sunset, and the baths[7]
Of all the western stars, until I die.
It may be that the gulfs will wash us down;
It may be we shall touch the Happy Isles,[8]
And see the great Achilles,[9] whom we knew.
65 Though much is taken, much abides; and though
We are not now that strength which in old days
Moved earth and heaven, that which we are, we are—
One equal temper of heroic hearts,
Made weak by time and fate, but strong in will
70 To strive, to seek, to find, and not to yield.

1833   1842

Tithonus[1]

The woods decay, the woods decay and fall,
The vapors weep their burthen to the ground,
Man comes and tills the field and lies beneath,
And after many a summer dies the swan.[2]
5   Me only cruel immortality
Consumes; I wither slowly in thine arms,[3]
Here at the quiet limit of the world,
A white-haired shadow roaming like a dream
The ever-silent spaces of the East,
10 Far-folded mists, and gleaming halls of morn.
Alas! for this gray shadow, once a man—
So glorious in his beauty and thy choice,
Who madest him thy chosen, that he seemed

---

7. The outer ocean or river that the Greeks believed surrounded the flat circle of the earth; the stars descended into it.
8. In Greek myth the Islands of the Blessed, a paradise of perpetual summer, located in the far-western ocean, where the virtuous and heroes dwell forever after death (often identified with Elysium).
9. The greatest of the Greek warriors at Troy,
where he was killed.
1. A Trojan prince loved by the goddess of the dawn, Eos or Aurora, who obtained for him the gift of living forever but neglected to ask for the gift of everlasting youth.
2. Some species of swans live for at least fifty years.
3. Aurora's arms.

To his great heart none other than a God!
15 I asked thee, "Give me immortality."
Then didst thou grant mine asking with a smile,
Like wealthy men who care not how they give.
But thy strong Hours indignant worked their wills,
And beat me down and marred and wasted me,
20 And though they could not end me, left me maimed
To dwell in presence of immortal youth,
Immortal age beside immortal youth,
And all I was in ashes. Can thy love,
Thy beauty, make amends, though even now,
25 Close over us, the silver star,[4] thy guide,
Shines in those tremulous eyes that fill with tears
To hear me? Let me go; take back thy gift.
Why should a man desire in any way
To vary from the kindly race of men,
30 Or pass beyond the goal of ordinance[5]
Where all should pause, as is most meet for all?
   A soft air fans the cloud apart; there comes
A glimpse of that dark world where I was born.
Once more the old mysterious glimmer steals
35 From thy pure brows, and from thy shoulders pure,
And bosom beating with a heart renewed.
Thy cheek begins to redden through the gloom,
Thy sweet eyes brighten slowly close to mine,
Ere yet they blind the stars, and the wild team[6]
40 Which love thee, yearning for thy yoke, arise,
And shake the darkness from their loosened manes,
And beat the twilight into flakes of fire.
   Lo! ever thus thou growest beautiful
In silence, then before thine answer given
45 Departest, and thy tears are on my cheek.
   Why wilt thou ever scare me with thy tears,
And make me tremble lest a saying learnt,
In days far-off, on that dark earth, be true?
"The Gods themselves cannot recall their gifts."
50   Ay me! ay me! with what another heart
In days far-off, and with what other eyes
I used to watch—if I be he that watched—
The lucid outline forming round thee; saw
The dim curls kindle into sunny rings;
55 Changed with thy mystic change, and felt my blood
Glow with the glow that slowly crimsoned all
Thy presence and thy portals, while I lay,
Mouth, forehead, eyelids, growing dewy-warm
With kisses balmier than half-opening buds
60 Of April, and could hear the lips that kissed
Whispering I knew not what of wild and sweet,

---

4. The morning star that precedes the dawn.
5. What is decreed or ordained as human destiny.

6. The horses that draw Aurora's chariot into the sky at daybreak.

Like that strange song I heard Apollo sing,
While Ilion like a mist rose into towers.[7]
    Yet hold me not forever in thine East;
65 How can my nature longer mix with thine?
Coldly thy rosy shadows bathe me, cold
Are all thy lights, and cold my wrinkled feet
Upon thy glimmering thresholds, when the steam
Floats up from those dim fields about the homes
70 Of happy men that have the power to die,
And grassy barrows° of the happier dead.   *burial mounds*
Release me, and restore me to the ground.
Thou seest all things, thou wilt see my grave;
Thou wilt renew thy beauty morn by morn,
75 I earth in earth forget these empty courts,
And thee returning on thy silver wheels.

1833, 1859   1860

Break, Break, Break

Break, break, break,
  On thy cold gray stones, O Sea!
And I would that my tongue could utter
  The thoughts that arise in me.

5 O, well for the fisherman's boy,
  That he shouts with his sister at play!
O, well for the sailor lad,
  That he sings in his boat on the bay!

And the stately ships go on
10   To their haven under the hill;
But O for the touch of a vanished hand,
  And the sound of a voice that is still!

Break, break, break,
  At the foot of thy crags, O Sea!
15 But the tender grace of a day that is dead
  Will never come back to me.

1834   1842

---

7. The walls of Troy ("Ilion") were supposed to have been built to the strains of the god Apollo's music.

From The Epic[1]
[Morte d'Arthur]

At Francis Allen's on the Christmas eve—
The game of forfeits done—the girls all kissed
Beneath the sacred bush° and passed° away—   mistletoe / gone
The parson Holmes, the poet Everard Hall,
5   The host, and I sat round the wassail-bowl,[2]
Then halfway ebbed; and there we held a talk,
How all the old honor had from Christmas gone,
Or gone or dwindled down to some odd games
In some odd nooks like this; till I, tired out
10 With cutting eights° that day upon the pond,   figure eights
Where, three times slipping from the outer edge,
I bumped the ice into three several stars,
Fell in a doze; and half-awake I heard
The parson taking wide and wider sweeps,
15 Now harping on the church-commissioners,[3]
Now hawking at geology and schism;
Until I woke, and found him settled down
Upon the general decay of faith
Right through the world: "at home was little left,
20 And none abroad; there was no anchor, none,
To hold by." Francis, laughing, clapped his hand
On Everard's shoulder, with "I hold by him."
"And I," quoth Everard, "by the wassail-bowl."
"Why yes," I said, "we knew your gift that way
25 At college; but another which you had—
I mean of verse (for so we held it then),
What came of that?" "You know," said Frank, "he burnt
His epic, his King Arthur, some twelve books"—
And then to me demanding why: "O, sir,
30 He thought that nothing new was said, or else
Something so said 'twas nothing—that a truth
Looks freshest in the fashion of the day;
God knows; he has a mint of reasons; ask.
It pleased *me* well enough." "Nay, nay," said Hall,
35 "Why take the style of those heroic times?
For nature brings not back the mastodon,
Nor we those times; and why should any man
Remodel models? these twelve books of mine

1. At age twenty-four Tennyson proposed to write a long epic on King Arthur. Five years later he had completed one book of the twelve, the story of Arthur's death, which he published in 1842 under the title "Morte d'Arthur." In this early version the story is given a framework, "The Epic," which consists of a short introductory section (fifty-one lines) and an epilogue (thirty lines), describing a party on Christmas Eve in modern times, at which the poet ("Everard Hall") reads "Morte d'Arthur" to his friends. In 1869 Tennyson incorporated "Morte d'Arthur" into his long narrative poem *Idylls of the King*; it appears there as the twelfth book, *The Passing of Arthur*. At that time the "Epic" framework was discarded and some lines added. The 1842 version can be reconstructed from *The Passing of Arthur*, which incorporates "Morte d'Arthur" (lines 170–440; only two lines are modified).
2. A vessel containing a spiced alcoholic drink, traditionally drunk during the festive season.
3. Commissioners appointed by the government in 1835 to regulate the finances of the Anglican Church.

Were faint Homeric echoes,[4] nothing-worth,
40 Mere chaff and draff,° much better burnt." "But I," *bits of straw*
Said Francis, "picked the eleventh from this hearth,
And have it; keep a thing, its use will come.
I hoard it as a sugarplum for Holmes."
He laughed, and I, though sleepy, like a horse
45 That hears the corn-bin open, pricked my ears;
For I remembered Everard's college fame
When we were Freshmen. Then at my request
He brought it; and the poet, little urged,
But with some prelude of disparagement,
50 Read, mouthing out his hollow o's and a's,
Deep-chested music, and to this result.[5]

＊ ＊ ＊

Here ended Hall, and our last light, that long
325 Had winked and threatened darkness, flared and fell;
At which the parson, sent to sleep with sound,
And waked with silence, grunted "Good!" but we
Sat rapt: it was the tone with which he read—
Perhaps some modern touches here and there
330 Redeemed it from the charge of nothingness—
Or else we loved the man, and prized his work;
I know not; but we sitting, as I said,
The cock crew loud, as at that time of year
The lusty bird takes every hour for dawn.[6]
335 Then Francis, muttering like a man ill-used,
"There now—that's nothing!" drew a little back,
And drove his heel into the smoldered log,
That sent a blast of sparkles up the flue.
And so to bed, where yet in sleep I seemed
340 To sail with Arthur under looming shores,
Point after point; till on to dawn, when dreams
Begin to feel the truth and stir of day,
To me, methought, who waited with the crowd,
There came a bark° that, blowing forward, bore *small ship*
345 King Arthur, like a modern gentleman
Of stateliest port;° and all the people cried, *deportment*
"Arthur is come again: he cannot die."
Then those that stood upon the hills behind
Repeated—"Come again, and thrice as fair";
350 And, further inland, voices echoed—"Come
With all good things, and war shall be no more."
At this a hundred bells began to peal,
That with the sound I woke, and heard indeed
The clear church bells ring in the Christmas morn.

1833–38   1842

4. After reading "Morte d'Arthur" in manuscript, Walter Savage Landor commented: "It is more Homeric than any poem of our time, and rivals some of the noblest parts of the Odyssey."
5. Here followed the 271 lines of "Morte d'Arthur"

in 1842 (see *The Passing of Arthur*, lines 170–440, pp. 238–44). "The Epic" then continued as follows.
6. See Shakespeare's *Hamlet* 1.1.138–41, on the legend of the cock's crowing "all night long" in the season of Jesus' birth.

Locksley Hall[1]

Comrades, leave me here a little, while as yet 'tis early morn;
Leave me here, and when you want me, sound upon the bugle horn.

'Tis the place, and all around it, as of old, the curlews call,
Dreary gleams[2] about the moorland flying over Locksley Hall;

5 Locksley Hall, that in the distance overlooks the sandy tracts,
And the hollow ocean-ridges roaring into cataracts.

Many a night from yonder ivied casement, ere I went to rest,
Did I look on great Orion sloping slowly to the west.

Many a night I saw the Pleiads,[3] rising through the mellow shade,
10 Glitter like a swarm of fireflies tangled in a silver braid.

Here about the beach I wandered, nourishing a youth sublime
With the fairy tales of science, and the long result of time;

When the centuries behind me like a fruitful land reposed;
When I clung to all the present for the promise that it closed°   *enclosed*

15 When I dipped into the future far as human eye could see,
Saw the vision of the world and all the wonder that would be.—

In the spring a fuller crimson comes upon the robin's breast;
In the spring the wanton lapwing gets himself another crest;

In the spring a livelier iris changes on the burnished dove;[4]
20 In the spring a young man's fancy lightly turns to thoughts of love.

Then her cheek was pale and thinner than should be for one so young,
And her eyes on all my motions with a mute observance hung.

And I said, "My cousin Amy, speak, and speak the truth to me,
Trust me, cousin, all the current of my being sets to thee."

25 On her pallid cheek and forehead came a color and a light,
As I have seen the rosy red flushing in the northern night.

1. The situation in this poem—of a young man's being jilted by a woman who chose to marry a wealthy landowner—may have been suggested to Tennyson by the experience of his brother Frederick, a hot-tempered man who had fallen in love with his cousin Julia Tennyson and who was similarly unsuccessful. It may also have been inspired by Tennyson's own frustrated courtship of Rosa Baring, who rejected the young poet in favor of a wealthy suitor. Concerning the ranting tone of the speaker (a tone accentuated by the heavily marked trochaic meter), Tennyson said: "The whole poem represents young life, its good side, its deficiencies, and its yearnings."
2. Tennyson stated that the noun "gleams" refers not to "curlews" flying but to streaks of light.
3. Or the Pleiades, seven stars in the constellation Taurus.
4. The rainbowlike colors of a dove's throat plumage are intensified in the mating season.

And she turned—her bosom shaken with a sudden storm of sighs—
All the spirit deeply dawning in the dark of hazel eyes—

Saying, "I have hid my feelings, fearing they should do me wrong";
30 Saying, "Dost thou love me, cousin?" weeping, "I have loved thee long."

Love took up the glass of Time, and turned it in his glowing hands;
Every moment, lightly shaken, ran itself in golden sands.

Love took up the harp of Life, and smote on all the chords with might;
Smote the chord of Self, that, trembling, passed in music out of sight.

35 Many a morning on the moorland did we hear the copses ring,
And her whisper thronged my pulses with the fullness of the spring.

Many an evening by the waters did we watch the stately ships,
And our spirits rushed together at the touching of the lips.

O my cousin, shallow-hearted! O my Amy, mine no more!
40 O the dreary, dreary moorland! O the barren, barren shore!

Falser than all fancy fathoms, falser than all songs have sung,
Puppet to a father's threat, and servile to a shrewish tongue!

Is it well to wish thee happy?—having known me—to decline
On a range of lower feelings and a narrower heart than mine!

45 Yet it shall be; thou shalt lower to his level day by day,
What is fine within thee growing coarse to sympathize with clay.

As the husband is, the wife is; thou art mated with a clown,°   *boor*
And the grossness of his nature will have weight to drag thee down.

He will hold thee, when his passion shall have spent its novel force,
50 Something better than his dog, a little dearer than his horse.

What is this? his eyes are heavy; think not they are glazed with wine.
Go to him, it is thy duty; kiss him, take his hand in thine.

It may be my lord is weary, that his brain is overwrought;
Soothe him with thy finer fancies, touch him with thy lighter thought.

55 He will answer to the purpose, easy things to understand—
Better thou wert dead before me, though I slew thee with my hand!

Better thou and I were lying, hidden from the heart's disgrace,
Rolled in one another's arms, and silent in a last embrace.

Cursed be the social wants that sin against the strength of youth!
60 Cursed be the social lies that warp us from the living truth!

Cursed be the sickly forms that err from honest Nature's rule!
Cursed be the gold that gilds the straitened° forehead of the fool!   *narrowed*

Well—'tis well that I should bluster!—Hadst thou less unworthy proved—
Would to God—for I had loved thee more than ever wife was loved.

65 Am I mad, that I should cherish that which bears but bitter fruit?
I will pluck it from my bosom, though my heart be at the root.

Never, though my mortal summers to such length of years should come
As the many-wintered crow⁵ that leads the clanging rookery home.

Where is comfort? in division of the records of the mind?
70 Can I part her from herself, and love her, as I knew her, kind?

I remember one that perished; sweetly did she speak and move;
Such a one do I remember, whom to look at was to love.

Can I think of her as dead, and love her for the love she bore?
No—she never loved me truly; love is love for evermore.

75 Comfort? comfort scorned of devils! this is truth the poet⁶ sings,
That a sorrow's crown of sorrow is remembering happier things.

Drug thy memories, lest thou learn it, lest thy heart be put to proof,
In the dead unhappy night, and when the rain is on the roof.

Like a dog, he hunts in dreams, and thou art staring at the wall,
80 Where the dying night-lamp flickers, and the shadows rise and fall.

Then a hand shall pass before thee, pointing to his drunken sleep,
To thy widowed⁷ marriage-pillows, to the tears that thou wilt weep.

Thou shalt hear the "Never, never," whispered by the phantom years.
And a song from out the distance in the ringing of thine ears;

85 And an eye shall vex thee, looking ancient kindness on thy pain.
Turn thee, turn thee on thy pillow; get thee to thy rest again.

Nay, but Nature brings thee solace; for a tender voice will cry.
'Tis a purer life than thine, a lip to drain thy trouble dry.

Baby lips will laugh me down; my latest rival brings thee rest.
90 Baby fingers, waxen touches, press me from the mother's breast.

O, the child too clothes the father with a dearness not his due.
Half is thine and half is his; it will be worthy of the two.

---

5. A rook, a long-lived bird.
6. Dante; see *Inferno* 5.121–23: "There is no greater sorrow / Than to be mindful of the happy time in misery" [Longfellow's translation].
7. Presumably figurative. Her marriage having become a mockery, she is widowed.

O, I see thee old and formal, fitted to thy petty part,
With a little hoard of maxims preaching down a daughter's heart.

95   "They were dangerous guides the feelings—she herself was not
      exempt—
Truly, she herself had suffered"—Perish in thy self-contempt!

Overlive it—lower yet—be happy! wherefore should I care?
I myself must mix with action, lest I wither by despair.

What is that which I should turn to, lighting upon days like these?
100   Every door is barred with gold, and opens but to golden keys.

Every gate is thronged with suitors, all the markets overflow.
I have but an angry fancy; what is that which I should do?

I had been content to perish, falling on the foeman's ground,
When the ranks are rolled in vapor, and the winds are laid with
     sound.[8]

105   But the jingling of the guinea helps the hurt that Honor feels,
And the nations do but murmur, snarling at each other's heels.

Can I but relive in sadness? I will turn that earlier page.
Hide me from my deep emotion, O thou wondrous Mother-Age![9]

Make me feel the wild pulsation that I felt before the strife,
110   When I heard my days before me, and the tumult of my life;

Yearning for the large excitement that the coming years would yield,
Eager-hearted as a boy when first he leaves his father's field,

And at night along the dusky highway near and nearer drawn,
Sees in heaven the light of London flaring like a dreary dawn;

115   And his spirit leaps within him to be gone before him then,
Underneath the light he looks at, in among the throngs of men;

Men, my brothers, men the workers, ever reaping something new;
That which they have done but earnest° of the things that they   *pledge*
     shall do.

For I dipped into the future, far as human eye could see,
120   Saw the Vision of the world, and all the wonder that would be;

Saw the heavens fill with commerce, argosies of magic sails,[1]
Pilots of the purple twilight, dropping down with costly bales;

---

8. It was once believed that the firing of artillery stilled the winds.
9. A happier past at life's beginning, which generated a more confident anticipation of the future (see also line 185).
1. Probably airships, such as balloons. "Argosies": merchant vessels.

Heard the heavens fill with shouting, and there rained a ghastly dew
From the nations' airy navies grappling in the central blue;

125 Far along the world-wide whisper of the south wind rushing warm,
With the standards of the peoples plunging through the thunderstorm;

Till the war drum throbbed no longer, and the battle flags were furled
In the Parliament of man, the Federation of the world.

There the common sense of most shall hold a fretful realm in awe,
130 And the kindly earth shall slumber, lapped in[2] universal law.

So I triumphed ere my passion sweeping through me left me dry,
Left me with the palsied heart, and left me with the jaundiced eye;

Eye, to which all order festers, all things here are out of joint.
Science moves, but slowly, slowly, creeping on from point to point;

135 Slowly comes a hungry people, as a lion, creeping nigher,
Glares at one that nods and winks behind a slowly-dying fire.

Yet I doubt not through the ages one increasing purpose runs,
And the thoughts of men are widened with the process of the suns.

What is that to him that reaps not harvest of his youthful joys,
140 Though the deep heart of existence beat forever like a boy's?

Knowledge comes, but wisdom lingers, and I linger on the shore,
And the individual withers, and the world is more and more.

Knowledge comes, but wisdom lingers, and he bears a laden breast,
Full of sad experience, moving toward the stillness of his rest.

145 Hark, my merry comrades call me, sounding on the bugle horn,
They to whom my foolish passion were a target for their scorn.

Shall it not be scorn to me to harp on such a moldered string?
I am shamed through all my nature to have loved so slight a thing.

Weakness to be wroth with weakness! woman's pleasure, woman's pain—
150 Nature made them blinder motions bounded in a shallower brain.

Woman is the lesser man, and all thy passions, matched with mine,
Are as moonlight unto sunlight, and as water unto wine—

Here at least, where nature sickens, nothing. Ah, for some retreat
Deep in yonder shining Orient, where my life began to beat.

155 Where in wild Mahratta-battle[3] fell my father evil-starred—
I was left a trampled orphan, and a selfish uncle's ward.

2. "Lapped in": encompassed by.
3. Reference to wars waged by a Hindu confeder- acy against the British East India Company (1803 and 1817).

Or to burst all links of habit—there to wander far away,
On from island unto island at the gateways of the day.

160　Larger constellations burning, mellow moons and happy skies,
Breadths of tropic shade and palms in cluster, knots of Paradise.

Never comes the trader, never floats an European flag,
Slides the bird o'er lustrous woodland, swings the trailer° from the　　*vine*
　　crag;

Droops the heavy-blossomed bower, hangs the heavy-fruited tree—
Summer isles of Eden lying in dark purple spheres of sea.

165　There methinks would be enjoyment more than in this march of mind,
In the steamship, in the railway, in the thoughts that shake mankind.

There the passions cramped no longer shall have scope and breathing
　　space;
I will take some savage woman, she shall rear my dusky race.

170　Iron-jointed, supple-sinewed, they shall dive, and they shall run,
Catch the wild goat by the hair, and hurl their lances in the sun;

Whistle back the parrot's call, and leap the rainbows of the brooks,
Not with blinded eyesight poring over miserable books—

Fool, again the dream, the fancy! but I *know* my words are wild,
But I count the gray barbarian lower than the Christian child.

175　I, to herd with narrow foreheads, vacant of our glorious gains,
Like a beast with lower pleasures, like a beast with lower pains!

Mated with a squalid savage—what to me were sun or clime?
I the heir of all the ages, in the foremost files of time—

I that rather held it better men should perish one by one,
180　Than that earth should stand at gaze like Joshua's moon in Ajalon![4]

Not in vain the distance beacons. Forward, forward let us range,
Let the great world spin forever down the ringing grooves[5] of change.

Through the shadow of the globe we sweep into the younger day;
Better fifty years of Europe than a cycle of Cathay.[6]

185　Mother-Age—for mine I knew not—help me as when life begun;
Rift the hills, and roll the waters, flash the lightnings, weigh the sun.

---

4. At Joshua's command the sun and moon stood still while the Israelites completed the slaughter of their enemies in the valley of Ajalon (Joshua 10.12–13).
5. Railroad tracks. Tennyson at one time had the impression that train wheels ran in grooved rails.
6. China, regarded in the 19th century as a static, unprogressive country. Cf. Mill, *On Liberty* (1859), p. 81.

O, I see the crescent promise of my spirit hath not set.
Ancient founts of inspiration well through all my fancy yet.

Howsoever these things be, a long farewell to Locksley Hall!
190   Now for me the woods may wither, now for me the roof-tree fall.

Comes a vapor from the margin,° blackening over heath and   *riverbank*
   holt,°   *wood*
Cramming all the blast before it, in its breast a thunderbolt.

Let it fall on Locksley Hall, with rain or hail, or fire or snow;
For the mighty wind arises, roaring seaward, and I go.

1837–38   1842

*F*ROM THE PRINCESS[1]

Tears, Idle Tears[2]

Tears, idle tears, I know not what they mean,
Tears from the depth of some divine despair
Rise in the heart, and gather to the eyes,
In looking on the happy autumn-fields,
5   And thinking of the days that are no more.

Fresh as the first beam glittering on a sail,
That brings our friends up from the underworld,
Sad as the last which reddens over one
That sinks with all we love below the verge;
10   So sad, so fresh, the days that are no more.

Ah, sad and strange as in dark summer dawns
The earliest pipe of half-awakened birds
To dying ears, when unto dying eyes
The casement slowly grows a glimmering square;
15   So sad, so strange, the days that are no more.

Dear as remembered kisses after death,
And sweet as those by hopeless fancy feigned
On lips that are for others; deep as love,
Deep as first love, and wild with all regret;
20   O Death in Life, the days that are no more!

1847

1. *The Princess* (1847), a long narrative poem, contains interludes in which occasional songs are sung. Several of these songs, two of which are printed here, have been set to music by various composers.
2. Tennyson commented: "This song came to me on the yellowing autumn-tide at Tintern Abbey, full for me of its bygone memories." This locale would be for him associated both with Words- worth's "Tintern Abbey" (1798) and with memories of Arthur Hallam, who was buried across the Bristol Channel in this area. "It is what I have always felt even from a boy, and what as a boy I called the 'passion of the past.' And it is so always with me now; it is the distance that charms me in the landscape, the picture and the past, and not the immediate today in which I move."

Now Sleeps the Crimson Petal

Now sleeps the crimson petal, now the white;
Nor waves the cypress in the palace walk;
Nor winks the gold fin in the porphyry font.
The firefly wakens; waken thou with me.

5 Now droops the milk-white peacock like a ghost,
And like a ghost she glimmers on to me.

Now lies the Earth all Danaë[1] to the stars,
And all thy heart lies open unto me.

Now slides the silent meteor on, and leaves
10 A shining furrow, as thy thoughts in me.

Now folds the lily all her sweetness up,
And slips into the bosom of the lake.
So fold thyself, my dearest, thou, and slip
Into my bosom and be lost in me.

1847

["The woman's cause is man's"][1]

"Blame not thyself too much," I said, "nor blame
240 Too much the sons of men and barbarous laws;
These were the rough ways of the world till now.
Henceforth thou hast a helper, me, that know
The woman's cause is man's: they rise or sink
Together, dwarfed or godlike, bond or free:
245 For she that out of Lethe[2] scales with man
The shining steps of Nature, shares with man
His nights, his days, moves with him to one goal,
Stays all the fair young planet in her hands—
If she be small, slight-natured, miserable,

1. A Greek princess, whose father confined her in a brazen chamber after hearing the oracle that her son would kill him. But Zeus came to her in the form of a shower of gold, and she bore the hero Perseus.
1. *The Princess* was Tennyson's attempt to address the contemporary debate over woman's proper role. It tells the story of a prince who courts the young and beautiful Princess Ida. She has vowed she will never marry and has established a women's university from which men are excluded. The prince and his two companions dress themselves up in women's clothes to gain entrance to the university. When a battle ensues—in which King Gama, the prince's father,

invades the university to rescue his son and force Ida to marry him—the university is turned into a hospital and the princess is persuaded of the error of her ways. The prince's final vision, from book 7 (reprinted here), in which he imagines a future of gradual change, by which men and women adopt the strengths of the other while maintaining their distinct natures, has been a key text in debates about Victorian constructions of masculinity and femininity. In the operetta *Princess Ida* (1884), W. S. Gilbert and Arthur Sullivan parody Tennyson's poem and satirize feminism.
2. In the classical underworld, the river of forgetfulness.

250 How shall men grow? but work no more alone!
Our place is much: as far as in us lies
We two will serve them both in aiding her—
Will clear away the parasitic forms
That seem to keep her up but drag her down—
255 Will leave her space to burgeon out of all
Within her—let her make herself her own
To give or keep, to live and learn and be
All that not harms distinctive womanhood.
For woman is not undevelopt man,
260 But diverse: could we make her as the man,
Sweet Love were slain: his dearest bond is this,
Not like to like, but like in difference.
Yet in the long years liker must they grow;
The man be more of woman, she of man;
265 He gain in sweetness and in moral height,
Nor lose the wrestling thews that throw the world;
She mental breadth, nor fail in childward care,
Nor lose the childlike in the larger mind;
Till at the last she set herself to man,
270 Like perfect music unto noble words;
And so these twain, upon the skirts of Time,
Sit side by side, full-summed in all their powers,
Dispensing harvest, sowing the To-be,
Self-reverent each and reverencing each,
275 Distinct in individualities,
But like each other even as those who love.
Then comes the statelier Eden back to men:
Then reign the world's great bridals, chaste and calm:
Then springs the crowning race of humankind.
May these things be!"
280   Sighing she spoke "I fear
They will not."
                    "Dear, but let us type° them now   *model*
In our own lives, and this proud watchword rest
Of equal; seeing either sex alone
Is half itself, and in true marriage lies
285 Nor equal, nor unequal: each fulfils
Defect in each, and always thought in thought,
Purpose in purpose, will in will, they grow,
The single pure and perfect animal,
The two-celled heart beating, with one full stroke,
Life."
290   And again sighing she spoke: "A dream
That once was mine! what woman taught you this?"

1839–47   1847

In Memoriam A. H. H.

When Arthur Hallam died suddenly at the age of twenty-two, probably of a stroke, Tennyson felt that his life had been shattered. Hallam was not only Tennyson's closest friend, and his sister's fiancé, but a critic and champion of his poetry. Widely regarded as the most promising young man of his generation, Hallam had written a review of Tennyson's first book of poetry that is still one of the best assessments of it. When Tennyson lost Hallam's love and support, he was overwhelmed with doubts about his own life and vocation and about the meaning of the universe and humankind's place in it, doubts reinforced by his study of geology and other sciences. To express the variety of his feelings and reflections, he began to compose a series of lyrics. Tennyson later arranged these "short swallow-flights of song," as he called them, written at intervals over a period of seventeen years, into one long elegy. Although the resulting poem has many affinities with traditional elegies like Milton's "Lycidas" (1638) and Shelley's *Adonais* (1821), its structure is strikingly different. It is made up of individual lyric units that are seemingly self-contained but take their full meaning from their place in the whole. As T. S. Eliot has written, "It is unique: it is a long poem made by putting together lyrics, which have only the unity and continuity of a diary, the concentrated diary of a man confessing himself." Though intensely personal, the elegy expressed the religious doubts of his age. It is also a love poem. Like Shakespeare's sonnets, to which the poem alludes, *In Memoriam* vests its most intense emotion in male relationships.

The sections of the poem record a progressive development from despair to some sort of hope. Some of the early sections of the poem resemble traditional pastoral elegies, including those portraying the voyage during which Hallam's body was brought to England for burial (sections 9 to 15 and 19). Other early sections portraying the speaker's loneliness, in which even Christmas festivities seem joyless (sections 28 to 30), are more distinctive. The poem's internal chronology covers a span of around three years, and with the passage of time, indicated by anniversaries and by recurring changes of the seasons, the speaker comes to accept the loss and to assert his belief in life and in an afterlife. In particular the recurring Christmases (sections 28, 78, 104) indicate the stages of his development, yet the pattern of progress in the poem is not a simple unimpeded movement upward. Dramatic conflicts recur throughout. Thus the most intense expression of doubt occurs not at the beginning of *In Memoriam* but as late as sections 54, 55, and 56.

The quatrain form in which the whole poem is written is usually called the "*In Memoriam* stanza," although it had been occasionally used by earlier poets. So rigid a form taxed Tennyson's ingenuity in achieving variety, but it is one of several means by which the diverse parts of the poem are knitted together.

The introductory section, consisting of eleven stanzas, is commonly referred to as the "Prologue," although Tennyson did not assign a title to it. It was written in 1849 after the rest of the poem was complete.

From In Memoriam A. H. H.

OBIIT MDCCCXXXIII[1]

Strong Son of God, immortal Love,
    Whom we, that have not seen thy face,
    By faith, and faith alone, embrace,
Believing where we cannot prove;[2]

5   Thine are these orbs[3] of light and shade;
    Thou madest Life in man and brute;
    Thou madest Death; and lo, thy foot
Is on the skull which thou hast made.

Thou wilt not leave us in the dust:
10   Thou madest man, he knows not why,
    He thinks he was not made to die;
And thou hast made him: thou art just.

Thou seemest human and divine,
    The highest, holiest manhood, thou.
15   Our wills are ours, we know not how;
Our wills are ours, to make them thine.

Our little systems[4] have their day;
    They have their day and cease to be;
    They are but broken lights of thee,
20   And thou, O Lord, art more than they.

We have but faith: we cannot know,
    For knowledge is of things we see;
    And yet we trust it comes from thee,
A beam in darkness: let it grow.

25   Let knowledge grow from more to more,
    But more of reverence in us dwell;
    That mind and soul, according well,
May make one music as before,[5]

But vaster. We are fools and slight;
30   We mock thee when we do not fear:
    But help thy foolish ones to bear;
Help thy vain worlds to bear thy light.

Forgive what seemed my sin in me,
    What seemed my worth since I began;
35   For merit lives from man to man,
And not from man, O Lord, to thee.

1. He died 1833 (Latin).
2. Cf. John 20.24–29, in which Jesus rebukes Thomas for his doubts concerning the Resurrection: "Blessed are they that have not seen, and yet have believed."

3. The sun and moon (according to Tennyson's note).
4. Of religion and philosophy.
5. As in the days of fixed religious faith.

Forgive my grief for one removed,
   Thy creature, whom I found so fair.
   I trust he lives in thee, and there
40 I find him worthier to be loved.

Forgive these wild and wandering cries,
   Confusions of a wasted° youth;   *desolated*
   Forgive them where they fail in truth,
And in thy wisdom make me wise.

1849

1

I held it truth, with him who sings
   To one clear harp in divers tones,[6]
   That men may rise on stepping stones
Of their dead selves to higher things.

5 But who shall so forecast the years
   And find in loss a gain to match?
   Or reach a hand through time to catch
The far-off interest of tears?

Let Love clasp Grief lest both be drowned,
10   Let darkness keep her raven gloss.
   Ah, sweeter to be drunk with loss,
To dance with Death, to beat the ground,

Than that the victor Hours should scorn
   The long result of love, and boast,
15   "Behold the man that loved and lost,
But all he was is overworn."

2

Old yew, which graspest at the stones
   That name the underlying dead,
   Thy fibres net the dreamless head,
Thy roots are wrapped about the bones.

5 The seasons bring the flower again,
   And bring the firstling to the flock;
   And in the dusk of thee the clock
Beats out the little lives of men.

O, not for thee the glow, the bloom,
10   Who changest not in any gale,

---

6. Identified by Tennyson as the German poet Johann Wolfgang von Goethe (1749–1832).

Nor branding summer suns avail
To touch thy thousand years of gloom[7]

And gazing on thee, sullen tree,
   Sick for° thy stubborn hardihood,   *envying*
15   I seem to fail from out my blood
And grow incorporate into thee.

3

O Sorrow, cruel fellowship,
   O Priestess in the vaults of Death,
   O sweet and bitter in a breath,
What whispers from thy lying lip?

5   "The stars," she whispers, "blindly run;
   A web is woven across the sky;
   From out waste places comes a cry,
And murmurs from the dying sun;

"And all the phantom, Nature, stands—
10   With all the music in her tone,
   A hollow echo of my own—
A hollow form with empty hands."

And shall I take a thing so blind,
   Embrace her° as my natural good;   *Sorrow*
15   Or crush her, like a vice of blood,
Upon the threshold of the mind?

4

To Sleep I give my powers away;
   My will is bondsman to the dark;
   I sit within a helmless bark,
And with my heart I muse and say:

5   O heart, how fares it with thee now,
   That thou should fail from thy desire,
   Who scarcely darest to inquire,
"What is it makes me beat so low?"

Something it is which thou hast lost,
10   Some pleasure from thine early years.
   Break thou deep vase of chilling tears,
That grief hath shaken into frost![8]

---

7. The ancient yew tree, growing in the grounds near the clock tower and church where Hallam was to be buried, seems neither to blossom in spring nor to change from its dark mournful color in summer. "Thousand years": cf. Book of Common Prayer, Psalm 90: "For a thousand years in Thy sight are but as yesterday when it is past, and as a watch in the night."
8. Water can be brought below freezing-point and not turn into ice—if it be kept still; but if it be moved suddenly it turns into ice and may break a vase [Tennyson's note].

Such clouds of nameless trouble cross
　　All night below the darkened eyes;
15　　With morning wakes the will, and cries,
"Thou shalt not be the fool of loss."

5

I sometimes hold it half a sin
　　To put in words the grief I feel;
　　For words, like Nature, half reveal
And half conceal the Soul within.

5　But, for the unquiet heart and brain,
　　A use in measured language lies;
　　The sad mechanic exercise,
Like dull narcotics, numbing pain.

In words, like weeds,° I'll wrap me o'er,　　*mourning garments*
10　　Like coarsest clothes against the cold;
　　But that large grief which these enfold
Is given in outline and no more.

6

One writes, that "Other friends remain,"
　　That "Loss is common to the race"—
　　And common is the commonplace,
And vacant chaff° well meant for grain.　　*husks*

5　That loss is common would not make
　　My own less bitter, rather more:
　　Too common! Never morning wore
To evening, but some heart did break.

O father, wheresoe'er thou be,
10　　Who pledgest° now thy gallant son;　　*toasts*
　　A shot, ere half thy draft be done,
Hath stilled the life that beat from thee.

O mother, praying God will save
　　Thy sailor—while thy head is bowed,
15　　His heavy-shotted° hammock-shroud　　*heavily weighted*
Drops in his vast and wandering grave.[9]

Ye know no more than I who wrought
　　At that last hour to please him well;[1]
　　Who mused on all I had to tell,
20　And something written, something thought;

---

9. Sailors buried at sea were often wrapped in their own hammocks.
1. According to his son, Tennyson discovered that he had been writing a letter to Hallam during the very hour in which his friend died.

Expecting still his advent home;
   And ever met him on his way
   With wishes, thinking, "here today,"
Or "here tomorrow will he come."

25 O somewhere, meek, the unconscious dove,
   That sittest ranging° golden hair;   *arranging*
   And glad to find thyself so fair,
Poor child, that waitest for thy love!

For now her father's chimney glows
30   In expectation of a guest;
   And thinking "this will please him best,"
She takes a riband or a rose;

For he will see them on tonight;
   And with the thought her color burns;
35   And, having left the glass, she turns
Once more to set a ringlet right;

And, even when she turned, the curse
   Had fallen, and her future Lord
   Was drowned in passing through the ford,
40 Or killed in falling from his horse.

O what to her shall be the end?
   And what to me remains of good?
   To her, perpetual maidenhood,
And unto me no second friend.

7

Dark house,[2] by which once more I stand
   Here in the long unlovely street,
   Doors, where my heart was used to beat
So quickly, waiting for a hand,

5 A hand that can be clasped no more—
   Behold me, for I cannot sleep,
   And like a guilty thing I creep
At earliest morning to the door.

He is not here; but far away
10   The noise of life begins again,
   And ghastly through the drizzling rain
On the bald street breaks the blank day.

2. The house on Wimpole Street, in London, where Hallam had lived.

8

A happy lover who has come
　To look on her that loves him well,
　Who 'lights° and rings the gateway bell,　　　　　*alights*
And learns her gone and far from home;

5　He saddens, all the magic light
　Dies off at once from bower and hall,
　And all the place is dark, and all
The chambers emptied of delight:

So find I every pleasant spot
10　In which we two were wont to meet,
　The field, the chamber, and the street,
For all is dark where thou art not.

Yet as that other, wandering there
　In those deserted walks, may find
15　A flower beat with rain and wind,
Which once she fostered up with care;

So seems it in my deep regret,
　O my forsaken heart, with thee
　And this poor flower of poesy
20　Which little cared for fades not yet.

But since it pleased a vanished eye,[3]
　I go to plant it on his tomb,
　That if it can it there may bloom,
Or dying, there at least may die.

9

Fair ship, that from the Italian shore[4]
　Sailest the placid ocean-plains
　With my lost Arthur's loved remains,
Spread thy full wings, and waft him o'er.

5　So draw him home to those that mourn
　In vain; a favorable speed
　Ruffle thy mirrored mast, and lead
Through prosperous floods his holy urn.

All night no ruder air perplex
10　Thy sliding keel, till Phosphor,° bright　　　　*morning star*
　As our pure love, through early light
Shall glimmer on the dewy decks.

---

3. Hallam expressed enthusiasm for Tennyson's
early poetry in a review written in 1831.

4. Hallam's body was conveyed back to England
by ship from Trieste, Italy.

Sphere all your lights around, above;
   Sleep, gentle heavens, before the prow;
15   Sleep, gentle winds, as he sleeps now,
My friend, the brother of my love;

My Arthur, whom I shall not see
   Till all my widowed race be run;
   Dear as the mother to the son,
20   More than my brothers are to me.

10

I hear the noise about thy keel;
   I hear the bell struck in the night;
   I see the cabin window bright;
I see the sailor at the wheel.

5   Thou bring'st the sailor to his wife,
   And traveled men from foreign lands;
   And letters unto trembling hands;
And, thy dark freight, a vanished life.

So bring him; we have idle dreams;
10   This look of quiet flatters thus
   Our home-bred fancies. O, to us,
The fools of habit, sweeter seems

To rest beneath the clover sod,
   That takes the sunshine and the rains,
15   Or where the kneeling hamlet drains
The chalice of the grapes of God;[5]

Than if with thee the roaring wells
   Should gulf him fathom-deep in brine,
   And hands so often clasped in mine,
20   Should toss with tangle° and with shells.   *seaweed*

11

Calm is the morn without a sound,
   Calm as to suit a calmer grief,
   And only through the faded leaf
The chestnut pattering to the ground;

5   Calm and deep peace on this high wold,°   *open countryside*
   And on these dews that drench the furze,
   And all the silvery gossamers
That twinkle into green and gold;

---

5. Reference to a burial inside a church building rather than in the churchyard.

Calm and still light on yon great plain
10   That sweeps with all its autumn bowers,
     And crowded farms and lessening towers,
To mingle with the bounding main;°   *open sea*

Calm and deep peace in this wide air,
     These leaves that redden to the fall,
15   And in my heart, if calm at all,
If any calm, a calm despair;

Calm on the seas, and silver sleep,
     And waves that sway themselves in rest,
     And dead calm in that noble breast
20   Which heaves but with the heaving deep.

12

Lo, as a dove when up she springs
     To bear through Heaven a tale of woe,
     Some dolorous message knit below
The wild pulsation of her wings;

5 Like her I go; I cannot stay;
     I leave this mortal ark behind,
     A weight of nerves without a mind,
And leave the cliffs, and haste away

O'er ocean-mirrors rounded large,
10   And reach the glow of southern skies,
     And see the sails at distance rise,
And linger weeping on the marge,°   *shore*

And saying; "Comes he thus, my friend?
     Is this the end of all my care?"
15   And circle moaning in the air:
"Is this the end? Is this the end?"

And forward dart again, and play
     About the prow, and back return
     To where the body sits, and learn
20 That I have been an hour away.

13

Tears of the widower, when he sees
     A late-lost form that sleep reveals,
     And moves his doubtful arms, and feels
Her place is empty, fall like these;

5 Which weep a loss forever new,
     A void where heart on heart reposed;

And, where warm hands have pressed and closed,
    Silence, till I be silent too;

    Which weep the comrade of my choice,
10   An awful thought, a life removed,
      The human-hearted man I loved,
    A Spirit, not a breathing voice.

    Come, Time, and teach me, many years,
      I do not suffer in a dream;
15   For now so strange do these things seem,
    Mine eyes have leisure for their tears,

    My fancies time to rise on wing,
      And glance about the approaching sails,
      As though they brought but merchants' bales,
20   And not the burthen that they bring.

14

If one should bring me this report,
    That thou° hadst touched the land today,   *the ship*
    And I went down unto the quay;[6]
    And found thee lying in the port;

5   And standing, muffled round with woe,
      Should see thy passengers in rank
      Come stepping lightly down the plank
    And beckoning unto those they know;

    And if along with these should come
10   The man I held as half divine,
      Should strike a sudden hand in mine,
    And ask a thousand things of home;

    And I should tell him all my pain,
      And how my life had drooped of late,
15   And he should sorrow o'er my state
    And marvel what possessed my brain;

    And I perceived no touch of change,
      No hint of death in all his frame,
      But found him all in all the same,
20   I should not feel it to be strange.

15

Tonight the winds begin to rise
    And roar from yonder dropping day;

6. By 1850 the accepted pronunciation of "quay" would rhyme with *key*, but Tennyson reverts to an earlier pronunciation, *kay*.

The last red leaf is whirled away,
The rooks are blown about the skies;

5 The forest cracked, the waters curled,
  The cattle huddled on the lea;
  And wildly dashed on tower and tree
The sunbeam strikes along the world:

And but for fancies, which aver
10 That all thy motions gently pass
  Athwart a plane of molten glass,[7]
I scarce could brook the strain and stir

That makes the barren branches loud;
  And but for fear it is not so,
15 The wild unrest that lives in woe
Would dote and pore on yonder cloud

That rises upward always higher,
  And onward drags a laboring breast,
  And topples round the dreary west,
20 A looming bastion fringed with fire.

    * * *

19

The Danube to the Severn[8] gave
  The darkened heart that beat no more;
  They laid him by the pleasant shore,
And in the hearing of the wave.

5 There twice a day the Severn fills;
  The salt sea water passes by,
  And hushes half the babbling Wye,[9]
And makes a silence in the hills.

The Wye is hushed nor moved along,
10 And hushed my deepest grief of all,
  When filled with tears that cannot fall,
I brim with sorrow drowning song.

The tide flows down, the wave again
  Is vocal in its wooded walls;[1]
15 My deeper anguish also falls,
And I can speak a little then.

    * * *

7. I.e., a calm sea.
8. Hallam died at Vienna on the river Danube. His burial place is on the banks of the Severn, a tidal river in the southwest of England.
9. A tributary of the Severn.

1. The water of the Wye River is dammed up as the tide flows in, and its sound is silenced until, with the turn of the tide, its "wave" once more becomes "vocal"; these stanzas were written at Tintern Abbey in the Wye valley.

21

I sing to him that rests below
    And, since the grasses round me wave,
    I take the grasses of the grave,[2]
And make them pipes whereon to blow.

5   The traveler hears me now and then,
    And sometimes harshly will he speak:
    "This fellow would make weakness weak,
And melt the waxen hearts of men."

Another answers: "Let him be,
10   He loves to make parade of pain,
    That with his piping he may gain
The praise that comes to constancy."

A third is wroth: "Is this an hour
    For private sorrow's barren song,
15   When more and more the people throng
The chairs and thrones of civil power?

"A time to sicken and to swoon,
    When Science reaches forth her arms[3]
    To feel from world to world, and charms
20 Her secret from the latest moon?"[4]

Behold, ye speak an idle thing;
    Ye never knew the sacred dust.
    I do but sing because I must,
And pipe but as the linnets sing:

25 And one is glad; her note is gay,
    For now her little ones have ranged;
    And one is sad; her note is changed,
Because her brood is stolen away.

22

The path by which we twain did go,
    Which led by tracts that pleased us well,
    Through four sweet years arose and fell,
From flower to flower, from snow to snow;

5   And we with singing cheered the way,
    And, crowned with all the season lent,
    From April on to April went,
And glad at heart from May to May.

2. The poet assumes that the burial was in the churchyard; in fact, on January 3, 1834, at St. Andrews in Clevedon, Somersetshire, Hallam's body was interred in a vault inside the church.

3. Astronomical instruments, such as telescopes.
4. Probably alluding to the discovery in 1846 of the planet Neptune and one of its moons.

But where the path we walked began
    To slant the fifth autumnal slope,[5]
    As we descended following Hope,
There sat the Shadow feared of man;

Who broke our fair companionship,
    And spread his mantle dark and cold,
    And wrapped thee formless in the fold,
And dulled the murmur on thy lip,

And bore thee where I could not see
    Nor follow, though I walk in haste,
    And think that somewhere in the waste
The Shadow sits and waits for me.

23

Now, sometimes in my sorrow shut,
    Or breaking into song by fits,
    Alone, alone, to where he sits,
The Shadow cloaked from head to foot,

Who keeps the keys of all the creeds,
    I wander, often falling lame,
    And looking back to whence I came,
Or on to where the pathway leads;

And crying, How changed from where it ran
    Through lands where not a leaf was dumb,
    But all the lavish hills would hum
The murmur of a happy Pan;[6]

When each by turns was guide to each,
    And Fancy light from Fancy caught,
    And Thought leapt out to wed with Thought
Ere Thought could wed itself with Speech;

And all we met was fair and good,
    And all was good that Time could bring,
    And all the secret of the Spring
Moved in the chambers of the blood;

And many an old philosophy
    On Argive[7] heights divinely sang,
    And round us all the thicket rang
To many a flute of Arcady.[8]

---

5. Hallam died just before the beginning of autumn (September 15, 1833) in the fifth year of the friendship.
6. In Greek mythology the god of woods and pastures.
7. Of Argos, an ancient city-state in the northeastern Peloponnesus; more generally, Greek.
8. A sheep-raising region in Greece associated with pastoral poetry.

24

And was the day of my delight
   As pure and perfect as I say?
   The very source and fount of day
Is dashed with wandering isles of night.[9]

5 If all was good and fair we met,
   This earth had been the Paradise
   It never looked to human eyes
Since our first sun arose and set.

And is it that the haze of grief
10   Makes former gladness loom so great?
   The lowness of the present state,
That sets the past in this relief?

Or that the past will always win
   A glory from its being far,
15   And orb into the perfect star
We saw not when we moved therein?[1]

25

I know that this was Life—the track
   Whereon with equal feet we fared;
   And then, as now, the day prepared
The daily burden for the back.

5 But this it was that made me move
   As light as carrier birds in air;
   I loved the weight I had to bear,
Because it needed help of Love;

Nor could I weary, heart or limb,
10   When mighty Love would cleave in twain
   The lading° of a single pain,   *burden*
And part it, giving half to him.

26

Still onward winds the dreary way;
   I with it, for I long to prove
   No lapse of moons can canker Love,
Whatever fickle tongues may say.

5 And if that eye which watches guilt
   And goodness, and hath power to see

---

9. Moving spots on the sun.
1. The poet wonders whether Earth would have the deceptive appearance of being a perfect orb if viewed from afar, on another planet.

Within the green the mouldered tree,
And towers fallen as soon as built—

O, if indeed that eye foresee
10   Or see—in Him is no before—
In more of life true life no more
And Love the indifference to be,

Then might I find, ere yet the morn
    Breaks hither over Indian seas,
15   That Shadow waiting with the keys,
To shroud me from my proper scorn.[2]

27

I envy not in any moods
    The captive void of noble rage,
    The linnet born within the cage,
That never knew the summer woods;

5 I envy not the beast that takes
    His license in the field of time,
    Unfettered by the sense of crime,
To whom a conscience never wakes;

Nor, what may count itself as blest,
10   The heart that never plighted troth
    But stagnates in the weeds of sloth;
Nor any want-begotten rest.[3]

I hold it true, whate'er befall;
    I feel it, when I sorrow most;
15   'Tis better to have loved and lost
Than never to have loved at all.

28

The time draws near the birth of Christ.[4]
    The moon is hid, the night is still;
    The Christmas bells from hill to hill
Answer each other in the mist.

5 Four voices of four hamlets round,
    From far and near, on mead and moor,
    Swell out and fail, as if a door
Were shut between me and the sound;

---

2. The Deity, being outside time, sees (rather than foresees) whether or not the rest of life ("more of life," line 11) will be pointless. If pointless, then the way for the speaker to deal with his self-scorn ("proper scorn") might be to seek death.

3. Complacency resulting from some deficiency ("want").

4. The first Christmas after Hallam's death (1833); the setting is Tennyson's family home in Lincolnshire.

Each voice four changes[5] on the wind,
10   That now dilate, and now decrease,
    Peace and goodwill, goodwill and peace,
Peace and goodwill, to all mankind.

This year I slept and woke with pain,
    I almost wished no more to wake,
15   And that my hold on life would break
Before I heard those bells again;

But they my troubled spirit rule,
    For they controlled me when a boy;
    They bring me sorrow touched with joy,
20 The merry, merry bells of Yule.

29

With such compelling cause to grieve
    As daily vexes household peace,
    And chains regret to his decease,
How dare we keep our Christmas eve;

5 Which brings no more a welcome guest
    To enrich the threshold of the night
    With showered largess of delight
In dance and song and game and jest?

Yet go, and while the holly boughs
10   Entwine the cold baptismal font,
    Make one wreath more for Use and Wont,[6]
That guard the portals of the house;

Old sisters of a day gone by,
    Gray nurses, loving nothing new;
15   Why should they miss their yearly due
Before their time? They too will die.

30

With trembling fingers did we weave
    The holly round the Christmas hearth;
    A rainy cloud possessed the earth,
And sadly fell our Christmas eve.

5 At our old pastimes in the hall
    We gamboled, making vain pretense
    Of gladness, with an awful sense
Of one mute Shadow watching all.

5. Different sequences in which church bells are pealed.
6. Personifying the spirits who expect custom-ary observances of the Christmas season to be followed.

We paused: the winds were in the beech;
10   We heard them sweep the winter land;
    And in a circle hand-in-hand
Sat silent, looking each at each.

Then echo-like our voices rang;
   We sung, though every eye was dim,
15   A merry song we sang with him
Last year; impetuously we sang.

We ceased; a gentler feeling crept
   Upon us: surely rest is meet.°   *proper, appropriate*
   "They rest," we said, "their sleep is sweet,"
20 And silence followed, and we wept.

Our voices took a higher range;
   Once more we sang: "They do not die
   Nor lose their mortal sympathy,
Nor change to us, although they change;

25 "Rapt from[7] the fickle and the frail
   With gathered power, yet the same,
   Pierces the keen seraphic flame
From orb to orb, from veil[8] to veil."

Rise, happy morn, rise, holy morn,
30   Draw forth the cheerful day from night:
   O Father, touch the east, and light
The light that shone when Hope was born.

*   *   *

34

My own dim life should teach me this,
   That life shall live forevermore,
   Else earth is darkness at the core,
And dust and ashes all that is;

5 This round of green, this orb of flame,
   Fantastic beauty; such as lurks
   In some wild poet, when he works
Without a conscience or an aim.

What then were God to such as I?
10   'Twere hardly worth my while to choose
   Of things all mortal, or to use
A little patience ere I die;

7. Carried away from.
8. An image representing the boundary between different worlds, especially that between Earth and heaven (cf. section 56, line 28). "From orb to orb": the angelic spirit ("flame") of the dead moves from star to star.

'Twere best at once to sink to peace,
  Like birds the charming serpent[9] draws,
15   To drop head-foremost in the jaws
Of vacant darkness and to cease.

35

Yet if some voice that man could trust
  Should murmur from the narrow house,
  "The cheeks drop in, the body bows;
Man dies, nor is there hope in dust";

5 Might I not say? "Yet even here,
  But for one hour, O Love, I strive
  To keep so sweet a thing alive."
But I should turn mine ears and hear

The moanings of the homeless sea,
10   The sound of streams that swift or slow
  Draw down Aeonian[1] hills, and sow
The dust of continents to be;

And Love would answer with a sigh,
  "The sound of that forgetful shore[2]
15   Will change my sweetness more and more,
Half-dead to know that I shall die."

O me, what profits it to put
  An idle case? If Death were seen
  At first as Death, Love had not been,
20 Or been in narrowest working shut,

Mere fellowship of sluggish moods,
  Or in his coarsest Satyr-shape[3]
  Had bruised the herb and crushed the grape,
And basked and battened° in the woods.[4]   *grown fat*

* * *

39

Old warder of these buried bones,
  And answering now my random stroke
  With fruitful cloud and living smoke,
Dark yew, that graspest at the stones

---

9. Some snakes are reputed to capture their prey
by hypnotizing it.
1. Eons old, seemingly everlasting.
2. I.e., of Lethe, the river in the classical underworld whose water caused forgetfulness.
3. In Greek mythology satyrs were half-man,

half-beast (goat or horse) in appearance, desires,
and behavior.
4. Lines 18–24 may be paraphrased: if we knew
death to be final and that no afterlife were possible, love could not exist except on a primitive or
bestial level.

5 And dippest toward the dreamless head,
  To thee too comes the golden hour
  When flower is feeling after flower;[5]
 But Sorrow—fixed upon the dead,

 And darkening the dark graves of men—
10 What whispered from her lying lips?
  Thy gloom is kindled at the tips,[6]
 And passes into gloom again.

* * *

47

That each, who seems a separate whole,
 Should move his rounds,[7] and fusing all
 The skirts[8] of self again, should fall
Remerging in the general Soul,

5 Is faith as vague as all unsweet.
  Eternal form shall still divide
  The eternal soul from all beside;
 And I shall know him when we meet;

 And we shall sit at endless feast,
10 Enjoying each the other's good.
  What vaster dream can hit the mood
Of Love on earth? He seeks at least

 Upon the last and sharpest height,
  Before the spirits fade away,
15 Some landing place, to clasp and say,
 "Farewell! We lose ourselves in light."[9]

48

If these brief lays, of Sorrow born,
 Were taken to be such as closed
 Grave doubts and answers here proposed,
Then these were such as men might scorn.

5 Her° care is not to part and prove;   *Sorrow's*
 She takes, when harsher moods remit,
 What slender shade of doubt may flit,
 And makes it vassal unto love;

5. The ancient yew tree in the graveyard was described in section 2 as never changing. Now the poet discovers that in the flowering season, if the tree is struck ("my random stroke"), it gives off a cloud of golden pollen.
6. Only the tips of the yew branches are in flower.
7. I.e., go through the customary circuit of life.

8. Outer edges or fringes.
9. These lines express the hope that, as Tennyson wrote, "individuality lasts after death, and we are not utterly absorbed into the Godhead. If we are to be finally merged into the Universal Soul, Love asks to have at least one more parting before we lose ourselves."

And hence, indeed, she sports with words,
10   But better serves a wholesome law,
    And holds it sin and shame to draw
The deepest measure from the chords;

Nor dare she trust a larger lay,°   *song*
    But rather loosens from the lip
15   Short swallow-flights of song, that dip
Their wings in tears, and skim away.

* * *

50

Be near me when my light is low,
    When the blood creeps, and the nerves prick
    And tingle; and the heart is sick,
And all the wheels of being slow.

5 Be near me when the sensuous frame
    Is racked with pangs that conquer trust;
    And Time, a maniac scattering dust,
And Life, a Fury slinging flame.

Be near me when my faith is dry,
10   And men the flies of latter spring,
    That lay their eggs, and sting and sing
And weave their petty cells and die.

Be near me when I fade away,
    To point the term of human strife,
15   And on the low dark verge of life
The twilight of eternal day.

* * *

54

O, yet we trust that somehow good
    Will be the final goal of ill,
    To pangs of nature, sins of will,
Defects of doubt, and taints of blood;

5 That nothing walks with aimless feet;
    That not one life shall be destroyed,
    Or cast as rubbish to the void,
When God hath made the pile complete;

That not a worm is cloven in vain;
10   That not a moth with vain desire
    Is shriveled in a fruitless fire,
Or but° subserves another's gain.   *only*

Behold, we know not anything;
   I can but trust that good shall fall
15   At last—far off—at last, to all,
And every winter change to spring.

So runs my dream; but what am I?
   An infant crying in the night;
   An infant crying for the light,
20   And with no language but a cry.

55

The wish, that of the living whole
   No life may fail beyond the grave,
   Derives it not from what we have
The likest God within the soul?[1]

5   Are God and Nature then at strife,
   That Nature lends such evil dreams?
   So careful of the type she seems,
So careless of the single life,

That I, considering everywhere
10   Her secret meaning in her deeds,
   And finding that of fifty seeds
She often brings but one to bear,

I falter where I firmly trod,
   And falling with my weight of cares
15   Upon the great world's altar-stairs
That slope through darkness up to God,

I stretch lame hands of faith, and grope,
   And gather dust and chaff, and call
   To what I feel is Lord of all,
20   And faintly trust the larger hope.[2]

56

"So careful of the type?" but no.
   From scarpèd[3] cliff and quarried stone
   She° cries, "A thousand types are gone;   *Nature*
I care for nothing, all shall go.

5   "Thou makest thine appeal to me:
   I bring to life, I bring to death;
   The spirit does but mean the breath:
I know no more." And he, shall he,

---

1. According to Tennyson, the "inner conscience—the divine in man."

2. As expressed in lines 1 and 2.
3. Cut away so that the strata are exposed.

Man, her last work, who seemed so fair,
10   Such splendid purpose in his eyes,
        Who rolled the psalm to wintry skies,
        Who built him fanes° of fruitless prayer,   *temples*

        Who trusted God was love indeed
        And love Creation's final law—
15   Though Nature, red in tooth and claw
        With ravine, shrieked against his creed—

        Who loved, who suffered countless ills,
        Who battled for the True, the Just,
        Be blown about the desert dust,
20   Or sealed within the iron hills?[4]

        No more? A monster then, a dream,
        A discord. Dragons of the prime,°   *primeval age*
        That tare° each other in their slime,   *tore (archaic)*
        Were mellow music matched with° him.   *compared to*

25   O life as futile, then, as frail!
        O for thy voice to soothe and bless!
        What hope of answer, or redress?
        Behind the veil, behind the veil.

                              57

        Peace; come away: the song of woe
        Is after all an earthly song.
        Peace; come away: we do him wrong
        To sing so wildly: let us go.

5   Come; let us go: your cheeks are pale;
        Methinks my friend is richly shrined;
        But half my life I leave behind.
        But I shall pass, my work will fail.

        Yet in these ears, till hearing dies,
10   One set slow bell will seem to toll
        The passing of the sweetest soul
        That ever looked with human eyes.

        I hear it now, and o'er and o'er,
        Eternal greetings to the dead;
15   And "Ave,° Ave, Ave," said,   *Hail (Latin)*
        "Adieu, adieu," forevermore.

---

4. Preserved like fossils in rock.

58

In those sad words I took farewell.
  Like echoes in sepulchral halls,
  As drop by drop the water falls
In vaults and catacombs, they fell;

5 And, falling, idly broke the peace
  Of hearts that beat from day to day,
  Half-conscious of their dying clay,
And those cold crypts where they shall cease.

The high Muse answered: "Wherefore grieve
10 Thy brethren with a fruitless tear?
  Abide a little longer here,
And thou shalt take a nobler leave."

59

O Sorrow, wilt thou live with me
  No casual mistress, but a wife,
  My bosom friend and half of life;
As I confess it needs must be?

5 O Sorrow, wilt thou rule my blood,
  Be sometimes lovely like a bride,
  And put thy harsher moods aside,
If thou wilt have me wise and good?

My centered passion cannot move,
10 Nor will it lessen from today;
  But I'll have leave at times to play
As with the creature of my love;

And set thee forth, for thou art mine,
  With so much hope for years to come,
15 That, howsoe'er I know thee, some
Could hardly tell what name were thine.

* * *

64

Dost thou look back on what hath been,
  As some divinely gifted man,
  Whose life in low estate began
And on a simple village green;

5 Who breaks his birth's invidious bar,
  And grasps the skirts of happy chance,
  And breasts the blows of circumstance,
And grapples with his evil star;

5. Badges of high public office.

Who makes by force his merit known
10   And lives to clutch the golden keys,[5]
        To mold a mighty state's decrees,
And shape the whisper of the throne;

And moving up from high to higher,
        Becomes on Fortune's crowning slope
15   The pillar of a people's hope,
The centre of a world's desire;

Yet feels, as in a pensive dream,
        When all his active powers are still,
        A distant dearness in the hill,
20   A secret sweetness in the stream,

The limit of his narrower fate,
        While yet beside its vocal springs
        He played at counselors and kings,
With one that was his earliest mate;

25   Who plows with pain his native lea
        And reaps the labour of his hands,
        Or in the furrow musing stands:
"Does my old friend remember me?"

*   *   *

67

When on my bed the moonlight falls,
        I know that in thy place of rest
        By that broad water[6] of the west
There comes a glory on the walls:

5   Thy marble bright in dark appears,
        As slowly steals a silver flame
        Along the letters of thy name,
And o'er the number of thy years.

The mystic glory swims away,
10   From off my bed the moonlight dies;
        And closing eaves of wearied eyes
I sleep till dusk is dipped in gray;

And then I know the mist is drawn
        A lucid veil from coast to coast,
15   And in the dark church like a ghost
Thy tablet glimmers to the dawn.

*   *   *

6. The Severn River.

70

I cannot see the features right,
    When on the gloom I strive to paint
    The face I know; the hues are faint
And mix with hollow masks of night;

5   Cloud-towers by ghostly masons wrought,
    A gulf that ever shuts and gapes,
    A hand that points, and pallèd shapes
In shadowy thoroughfares of thought;

And crowds that stream from yawning doors,
10   And shoals of puckered faces drive;
    Dark bulks that tumble half alive,
And lazy lengths on boundless shores;

Till all at once beyond the will
    I hear a wizard music roll,
15   And through a lattice on the soul
Looks thy fair face and makes it still.

71

Sleep, kinsman thou to death and trance
    And madness, thou has forged at last
    A night-long present of the past
In which we went through summer France.[7]

5   Hadst thou such credit with the soul?
    Then bring an opiate trebly strong,
    Drug down the blindfold sense of wrong,
That so my pleasure may be whole;

While now we talk as once we talked
10   Of men and minds, the dust of change,
    The days that grow to something strange,
In walking as of old we walked

Beside the river's wooded reach,
    The fortress, and the mountain ridge,
15   The cataract flashing from the bridge,
The breaker breaking on the beach.

72

Risest thou thus, dim dawn, again,[8]
    And howlest, issuing out of night,
    With blasts that blow the poplar white,
And lash with storm the streaming pane?

7. In the summer of 1830 Hallam and Tennyson
went through southern France en route to Spain.

8. September 15, 1834, the first anniversary of
Hallam's death.

5   Day, when my crowned estate[9] begun
     To pine in that reverse of doom,[1]
     Which sickened every living bloom,
  And blurred the splendor of the sun;

  Who usherest in the dolorous hour
10   With thy quick tears that make the rose
     Pull sideways, and the daisy close
  Her crimson fringes to the shower;

  Who mightst have heaved a windless flame
     Up the deep East, or, whispering, played
15   A checker-work of beam and shade
  Along the hills, yet looked the same,

  As wan, as chill, as wild as now;
     Day, marked as with some hideous crime,
     When the dark hand struck down through time,
20 And canceled nature's best: but thou,

  Lift as thou mayst thy burthened brows
     Through clouds that drench the morning star,
     And whirl the ungarnered sheaf afar,
  And sow the sky with flying boughs,

25 And up thy vault with roaring sound
     Climb thy thick noon, disastrous day;
     Touch thy dull goal of joyless gray,
  And hide thy shame beneath the ground.

*　*　*

75

  I leave thy praises unexpressed
     In verse that brings myself relief,
     And by the measure of my grief
  I leave thy greatness to be guessed.

5 What practice howsoe'er expert
     In fitting aptest words to things,
     Or voice the richest-toned that sings,
  Hath power to give thee as thou wert?

  I care not in these fading days
10   To raise a cry that lasts not long,
     And round thee with the breeze of song
  To stir a little dust of praise.

9. State of happiness.
1. The reversal or disaster that doom brought upon him when Hallam died.

Thy leaf has perished in the green,
  And, while we breathe beneath the sun,
15   The world which credits what is done
Is cold to all that might have been.

So here shall silence guard thy fame;
  But somewhere, out of human view,
  Whate'er thy hands are set to do
20 Is wrought with tumult of acclaim.

* * *

78

Again at Christmas[2] did we weave
  The holly round the Christmas hearth;
  The silent snow possessed the earth,
And calmly fell our Christmas eve.

5 The yule clog° sparkled keen with frost,   *log*
  No wing of wind the region swept,
  But over all things brooding slept
The quiet sense of something lost.

As in the winters left behind,
10   Again our ancient games had place,
  The mimic picture's[3] breathing grace,
And dance and song and hoodman-blind.[4]

Who showed a token of distress?
  No single tear, no mark of pain—
15   O sorrow, then can sorrow wane?
O grief, can grief be changed to less?

O last regret, regret can die!
  No—mixed with all this mystic frame,
  Her deep relations are the same,
20 But with long use her tears are dry.

* * *

82

I wage not any feud with Death
  For changes wrought on form and face;
  No lower life that earth's embrace
May breed with him can fright my faith.

2. The second Christmas (1834) after Hallam's death.
3. A game in which the participants pose in the manner of some famous statue or painting and the spectators try to guess what work of art is being portrayed.
4. The player in the game of blindman's buff who wears a blindfold or hood.

5   Eternal process moving on,
     From state to state the spirit walks;
     And these are but the shattered stalks,
  Or ruined chrysalis of one.

  Nor blame I Death, because he bare
10   The use of virtue out of earth;
     I know transplanted human worth
  Will bloom to profit, otherwhere.

  For this alone on Death I wreak
     The wrath that garners in my heart:
15   He put our lives so far apart
  We cannot hear each other speak.

83

  Dip down upon the northern shore,
     O sweet new-year° delaying long;   *spring 1835*
     Thou doest expectant Nature wrong;
  Delaying long, delay no more.

5   What stays thee from the clouded noons,
     Thy sweetness from its proper place?
     Can trouble live with April days,
  Or sadness in the summer moons?

  Bring orchis, bring the foxglove spire,
10   The little speedwell's° darling blue,   *spring flower*
     Deep tulips dashed with fiery dew,
  Laburnums, dropping-wells of fire.

  O thou, new-year, delaying long,
     Delayest the sorrow in my blood,
15   That longs to burst a frozen bud
  And flood a fresher throat with song.

84

  When I contemplate all alone
     The life that had been thine below,
     And fix my thoughts on all the glow
  To which thy crescent would have grown,

5   I see thee sitting crowned with good,
     A central warmth diffusing bliss
     In glance and smile, and clasp and kiss,
  On all the branches of thy blood;

  Thy blood, my friend, and partly mine;
10   For now the day was drawing on,

When thou shouldst link thy life with one
   Of mine own house, and boys of thine

   Had babbled "Uncle" on my knee;
     But that remorseless iron hour
15   Made cypress of her orange flower,[5]
   Despair of hope, and earth of thee.

   I seem to meet their least desire,
     To clap their cheeks, to call them mine.
     I see their unborn faces shine
20   Beside the never-lighted fire.

   I see myself an honored guest,
     Thy partner in the flowery walk
     Of letters, genial table talk,
   Or deep dispute, and graceful jest;

25   While now thy prosperous labor fills
     The lips of men with honest praise,
     And sun by sun the happy days
   Descend below the golden hills

   With promise of a morn as fair;
30   And all the train of bounteous hours
     Conduct, by paths of growing powers,
   To reverence and the silver hair;

   Till slowly worn her earthly robe,
     Her lavish mission richly wrought,
35   Leaving great legacies of thought,
   Thy spirit should fail from off the globe;

   What time mine own might also flee,
     As linked with thine in love and fate,
     And, hovering o'er the dolorous strait
40   To the other shore, involved in thee,

   Arrive at last the blessed goal,
     And He that died in Holy Land
     Would reach us out the shining hand,
   And take us as a single soul.

45   What reed was that on which I leant?
     Ah, backward fancy, wherefore wake
     The old bitterness again, and break
   The low beginnings of content?

* * *

---

5. Orange blossoms are associated with brides—here the poet's sister Emily Tennyson, to whom Hallam had been engaged. Cypress branches are associated with funerals.

86

Sweet after showers, ambrosial air,
  That rollest from the gorgeous gloom
  Of evening over brake° and bloom   *thicket*
And meadow, slowly breathing bare

5   The round of space,[6] and rapt below
  Through all the dewy-tasseled wood,
  And shadowing down the hornèd flood[7]
In ripples, fan my brows and blow

The fever from my cheek, and sigh
10   The full new life that feeds thy breath
  Throughout my frame, till Doubt and Death,
Ill brethren, let the fancy fly

From belt to belt of crimson seas
  On leagues of odor streaming far,
15   To where in yonder orient star
A hundred spirits whisper "Peace."

87

I passed beside the reverend walls[8]
  In which of old I wore the gown;
  I roved at random through the town,
And saw the tumult of the halls;

5   And heard once more in college fanes°   *chapels*
  The storm their high-built organs make,
  And thunder-music, rolling, shake
The prophet blazoned on the panes;

And caught once more the distant shout,
10   The measured pulse of racing oars
  Among the willows; paced the shores
And many a bridge, and all about

The same gray flats[9] again, and felt
  The same, but not the same; and last
15   Up that long walk of limes I passed
To see the rooms in which he dwelt.

Another name was on the door.
  I lingered; all within was noise
  Of songs, and clapping hands, and boys
20   That crashed the glass and beat the floor;

6. The "ambrosial air" is slowly clearing the
clouds from the sky.
7. Between two promontories [Tennyson's note].

8. Of Trinity College, Cambridge University.
9. Areas of low, level ground.

Where once we held debate, a band
   Of youthful friends,[1] on mind and art,
   And labor, and the changing mart,
And all the framework of the land;

25   When one would aim an arrow fair,
   But send it slackly from the string;
   And one would pierce an outer ring,
And one an inner, here and there;

And last the master bowman, he,
30   Would cleave the mark. A willing ear
   We lent him. Who but hung to hear
The rapt oration flowing free

From point to point, with power and grace
   And music in the bounds of law,
35   To those conclusions when we saw
The God within him light his face,

And seem to lift the form, and glow
   In azure orbits heavenly-wise;
   And over those ethereal eyes
40   The bar of Michael Angelo?[2]

88

Wild bird,[3] whose warble, liquid sweet,
   Rings Eden through the budded quicks,°   *hawthorn hedges*
   O tell me where the senses mix,
   O tell me where the passions meet,

5   Whence radiate: fierce extremes employ
   Thy spirits in the darkening leaf,
   And in the midmost heart of grief
Thy passion clasps a secret joy;

And I—my harp would prelude woe—
10   I cannot all command the strings;
   The glory of the sum of things
Will flash along the chords and go.

89

Witch elms that counterchange the floor
   Of this flat lawn with dusk and bright;[4]

---

1. The Apostles, an undergraduate club to which Tennyson and Hallam had belonged.
2. Hallam, like the Italian artist Michelangelo (1475–1564), had a prominent ridge of bone above his eyes.
3. Probably a nightingale.
4. Shadows of the elm tree checker the lawn at Somersby, the Tennysons' country home.

And thou, with all thy breadth and height
Of foliage, towering sycamore;

5 How often, hither wandering down,
  My Arthur found your shadows fair,
  And shook to all the liberal air
The dust and din and steam of town!

He brought an eye for all he saw;
10 He mixed in all our simple sports;
  They pleased him, fresh from brawling courts
And dusty purlieus° of the law.[5]   *regions*

O joy to him in this retreat,
  Immantled in ambrosial dark,
15 To drink the cooler air, and mark
The landscape winking through the heat!

O sound to rout the brood of cares,
  The sweep of scythe in morning dew,
  The gust that round the garden flew,
20 And tumbled half the mellowing pears!

O bliss, when all in circle drawn
  About him, heart and ear were fed
  To hear him, as he lay and read
The Tuscan poets[6] on the lawn!

25 Or in the all-golden afternoon
  A guest, or happy sister, sung,
  Or here she brought the harp and flung
A ballad to the brightening moon.

Nor less it pleased in livelier moods,
30 Beyond the bounding hill to stray,
  And break the livelong summer day
With banquet in the distant woods;

Whereat we glanced from theme to theme,
  Discussed the books to love or hate,
35 Or touched the changes of the state,
Or threaded some Socratic dream;[7]

But if I praised the busy town,
  He loved to rail against it still,
  For "ground in yonder social mill
40 We rub each other's angles down,

---

5. Hallam became a law student in London after leaving Cambridge.
6. A group of 13th- and 14th-century poets in central Italy (Tuscany); the best-known of them are Dante and Petrarch.
7. I.e., worked our way through some discourse of Socrates (as recorded by Plato).

"And merge," he said, "in form and gloss
   The picturesque of man and man."
   We talked: the stream beneath us ran,
The wine-flask lying couched in moss,

45   Or cooled within the glooming wave;
   And last, returning from afar,
   Before the crimson-circled star[8]
Had fallen into her father's[9] grave,

And brushing ankle-deep in flowers,
50   We heard behind the woodbine veil
   The milk that bubbled in° the pail,   *into*
And buzzings of the honeyed hours.

* * *

91

When rosy plumelets tuft the larch,
   And rarely° pipes the mounted thrush,   *exquisitely*
   Or underneath the barren bush
Flits by the sea-blue bird° of March;   *kingfisher*

5   Come, wear the form by which I know
   Thy spirit in time among thy peers;
   The hope of unaccomplished years
Be large and lucid round thy brow.

When summer's hourly-mellowing change
10   May breathe, with many roses sweet,
   Upon the thousand waves of wheat
That ripple round the lowly grange,°   *outlying farmhouse*

Come; not in watches of the night,
   But where the sunbeam broodeth warm,
15   Come, beauteous in thine after form,
And like a finer light in light.

* * *

93

I shall not see thee. Dare I say
   No spirit ever brake the band
   That stays him from the native land
Where first he walked when clasped in clay?[1]

5   No visual shade of someone lost,
   But he, the Spirit himself, may come

---

8. Venus, which will sink into the west as the Sun has done.
9. According to the nebular hypothesis, planets condensed out of the sun's atmosphere; in this sense the Sun is the "father" of planets.
1. I.e., when he was alive and in fleshly form.

Where all the nerve of sense is numb,
　Spirit to Spirit, Ghost to Ghost.

Oh, therefore from thy sightless° range　　　　　　*invisible*
10　　With gods in unconjectured bliss,
　　Oh, from the distance of the abyss
Of tenfold-complicated change,

Descend, and touch, and enter; hear
　The wish too strong for words to name,
15　　That in this blindness of the frame°　　　　*human body*
My Ghost may feel that thine is near.

94

How pure at heart and sound in head,
　With what divine affections bold
　Should be the man whose thought would hold
An hour's communion with the dead.

5　In vain shalt thou, or any, call
　The spirits from their golden day,
　Except, like them, thou too canst say,
My spirit is at peace with all.

They haunt the silence of the breast,
10　　Imaginations calm and fair,
　　The memory like a cloudless air,
The conscience as a sea at rest;

But when the heart is full of din,
　And doubt beside the portal waits,
15　　They can but listen at the gates,
And hear the household jar° within.　　　　　　*noise*

95

By night we lingered on the lawn,
　For underfoot the herb was dry;
　And genial warmth; and o'er the sky
The silvery haze of summer drawn;

5　And calm that let the tapers burn
　　Unwavering: not a cricket chirred;
　　The brook alone far off was heard,
And on the board the fluttering urn.[2]

And, bats went round in fragrant skies,
10　　And wheeled or lit the filmy shapes[3]

---

2. Vessel for boiling water for tea or coffee, heated by a fluttering flame.

3. The white-winged night moths called ermine moths.

That haunt the dusk, with ermine capes
And woolly breasts and beaded eyes;

While now we sang old songs that pealed
From knoll to knoll, where, couched at ease,
15   The white kine° glimmered, and the trees   *cows*
Laid their dark arms[4] about the field.

But when those others, one by one,
Withdrew themselves from me and night,
And in the house light after light
20 Went out, and I was all alone,

A hunger seized my heart; I read
Of that glad year which once had been,
In those fallen leaves which kept their green,
The noble letters of the dead.

25   And strangely on the silence broke
The silent-speaking words, and strange
Was love's dumb cry defying change
To test his worth; and strangely spoke

The faith, the vigor, bold to dwell
30   On doubts that drive the coward back,
And keen through wordy snares to track
Suggestion to her inmost cell.

So word by word, and line by line,
The dead man touched me from the past,
35   And all at once it seemed at last
The[5] living soul was flashed on mine.

And mine in this was wound, and whirled
About empyreal° heights of thought,   *heavenly*
And came on that which is, and caught
40 The deep pulsations of the world,

Aeonian music[6] measuring out
The steps of Time—the shocks of Chance—
The blows of Death. At length my trance
Was canceled, stricken through with doubt.[7]

4. Cast the shadows of their branches.
5. "His" in the 1st edition. Also in the 1st edition, line 37 read: "And mine in his was wound."
6. Music of the universe, which has pulsated for eons.
7. In a letter of 1874, replying to an inquiry about his experience of mystical trances, Tennyson wrote: "A kind of waking trance I have frequently had, quite up from boyhood, when I have been all alone. This has generally come upon me through repeating my own name two or three times to myself silently, till all at once, as it were out of the intensity of the consciousness of individuality, the individuality itself seemed to dissolve and fade away into boundless being, and this not a con-fused state, but the clearest of the clearest, the surest of the surest, the weirdest of the weirdest, utterly beyond words, where death was an almost laughable impossibility, the loss of personality (if so it were) seeming no extinction but the only true life. . . . This might . . . be the state which St. Paul describes, 'Whether in the body I cannot tell, or whether out of the body I cannot tell.' . . . I am ashamed of my feeble description. Have I not said the state is utterly beyond words? But in a moment, when I come back to my normal state of 'sanity,' I am ready to fight for *mein liebes Ich* [my dear self], and hold that it will last for aeons of aeons" (*Alfred Lord Tennyson, A Memoir*, 1897, vol. 1, 320).

45   Vague words! but ah, how hard to frame
       In matter-molded forms of speech,
       Or even for intellect to reach
    Through memory that which I became.

    Till now the doubtful dusk revealed
50   The knolls once more where, couched at ease,
       The white kine glimmered, and the trees
    Laid their dark arms about the field;

    And sucked from out the distant gloom
       A breeze began to tremble o'er
55   The large leaves of the sycamore,
    And fluctuate all the still perfume,

    And gathering freshlier overhead,
       Rocked the full-foliaged elms, and swung
       The heavy-folded rose, and flung
60   The lilies to and fro, and said,

    "The dawn, the dawn," and died away;
       And East and West, without a breath,
       Mixed their dim lights, like life and death,
    To broaden into boundless day.

96

    You say, but with no touch of scorn,
       Sweet-hearted, you,[8] whose light blue eyes
       Are tender over drowning flies,
    You tell me, doubt is Devil-born.

5   I know not: one indeed I knew
       In many a subtle question versed,
       Who touched a jarring lyre at first,
    But ever strove to make it true;

    Perplexed in faith, but pure in deeds,
10   At last he beat his music out.
       There lives more faith in honest doubt,
    Believe me, than in half the creeds.

    He fought his doubts and gathered strength,
       He would not make his judgment blind,
15   He faced the specters of the mind
    And laid them; thus he came at length

    To find a stronger faith his own,
       And Power was with him in the night,

8. A woman of simple faith.

Which makes the darkness and the light,
20 And dwells not in the light alone,

But in the darkness and the cloud,
As over Sinaï's peaks of old,
While Israel made their gods of gold,
Although the trumpet blew so loud.[9]

* * *

99

Risest thou thus, dim dawn, again,[1]
So loud with voices of the birds,
So thick with lowings of the herds,
Day, when I lost the flower of men;

5 Who tremblest through thy darkling red
On yon swollen brook that bubbles fast[2]
By meadows breathing of the past,
And woodlands holy to the dead;

Who murmurest in the foliage eaves
10 A song that slights the coming care,[3]
And Autumn laying here and there
A fiery finger on the leaves;

Who wakenest with thy balmy breath
To myriads on the genial° earth,   *generative*
15 Memories of bridal, or of birth,[4]
And unto myriads more, of death.

Oh, wheresoever those[5] may be,
Betwixt the slumber of the poles,
Today they count as kindred souls;
20 They know me not, but mourn with me.

* * *

103

On that last night before we went
From out the doors where I was bred,[6]
I dreamed a vision of the dead,
Which left my after-morn content.

---

9. After veiling Mount Sinai in a "thick cloud" and signifying the divine presence by "the voice of the trumpet" (Exodus 19.16), God addresses Moses from the "thick darkness" (20.21). Meanwhile Aaron made, and the Israelites worshiped, a golden calf (32.1–6).
1. September 15, 1835, the second anniversary of Hallam's death.
2. I.e., reflections of the clouded red light of dawn quiver on the surface of the fast-moving water.

3. I.e., that disregards future events such as death or the coming of autumn.
4. Cf. "Epilogue," lines 117–28 (p. 220).
5. I.e., the many who remember death.
6. In 1837 Tennyson and his family moved away from their home in Lincolnshire, which had been closely associated with his friendship with Hallam. In section 104 the move seems to occur in 1835, the year of the third Christmas after Hallam's death.

5 Methought I dwelt within a hall,
    And maidens with me; distant hills
    From hidden summits fed with rills
A river sliding by the wall.

The hall with harp and carol rang.
10   They sang of what is wise and good
    And graceful. In the center stood
A statue veiled, to which they sang;

And which, though veiled, was known to me,
    The shape of him I loved, and love
15   Forever. Then flew in a dove
And brought a summons from the sea;

And when they learnt that I must go,
    They wept and wailed, but led the way
    To where the little shallop° lay   *light open boat*
20 At anchor in the flood below;

And on by many a level mead,°   *meadow*
    And shadowing bluff that made the banks,
    We glided winding under ranks
Of iris and the golden reed;

25 And still as vaster grew the shore
    And rolled the floods in grander space,
    The maidens gathered strength and grace
And presence, lordlier than before;

And I myself, who sat apart
30   And watched them, waxed° in every limb;   *grown*
    I felt the thews of Anakim,[7]
The pulses of a Titan's[8] heart;

As one would sing the death of war,
    And one would chant the history
35   Of that great race which is to be,[9]
And one the shaping of a star;

Until the forward-creeping tides
    Began to foam, and we to draw
    From deep to deep, to where we saw
40 A great ship lift her shining sides.[1]

---

7. Plural of *Anak;* a reference to the giant sons of Anak (see Numbers 13.33).
8. Giant of Greek mythology.
9. See the account of the "crowning race" in "Epilogue," lines 128–44.
1. Cf. *The Passing of Arthur,* lines 361–469, in which Bedivere is left behind as Arthur's barge, the ship of death, sails away. In the present dream vision the speaker is taken aboard, as are his companions, who represent the creative arts of this world—"all the human powers and talents that do not pass with life but go along with it," as Tennyson said of this passage.

The man we loved was there on deck,
    But thrice as large as man he bent
    To greet us. Up the side I went,
And fell in silence on his neck;

45   Whereat those maidens with one mind
    Bewailed their lot; I did them wrong:
    "We served thee here," they said, "so long,
And wilt thou leave us now behind?"

So rapt° I was, they could not win   *entranced*
50   An answer from my lips, but he
    Replying, "Enter likewise ye
And go with us:" they entered in.

And while the wind began to sweep
    A music out of sheet and shroud,
55   We steered her toward a crimson cloud
That landlike slept along the deep.

104

The time draws near the birth of Christ;[2]
    The moon is hid, the night is still;
    A single church below the hill
Is pealing, folded in the mist.

5   A single peal of bells below,
    That wakens at this hour of rest
    A single murmur in the breast,
That these are not the bells I know.

Like strangers' voices here they sound,
10   In lands where not a memory strays,
    Nor landmark breathes of other days,
But all is new unhallowed ground.

105

Tonight ungathered let us leave
    This laurel, let this holly stand:[3]
    We live within the stranger's land,
And strangely falls our Christmas eve.

5   Our father's dust is left alone
    And silent under other snows:
    There in due time the woodbine blows,°   *blooms*
The violet comes, but we are gone.

2. The third Christmas (1835) after Hallam's death.
3. Cf. section 29, in which the family in their former home still continued to gather holly. In the new home the customary observances lapse.

No more shall wayward grief abuse
10   The genial hour with mask and mime;
    For change of place, like growth of time,
Has broke the bond of dying use.

Let cares that petty shadows cast,
    By which our lives are chiefly proved,
15   A little spare the night I loved,
And hold it solemn to the past.

But let no footstep beat the floor,
    Nor bowl of wassail mantle warm;[4]
    For who would keep an ancient form
20 Through which the spirit breathes no more?

Be neither song, nor game, nor feast;
    Nor harp be touched, nor flute be blown;
    No dance, no motion, save alone
What lightens in the lucid east

25 Of rising worlds[5] by yonder wood.
    Long sleeps the summer in the seed;
    Run out your measured arcs, and lead
The closing cycle rich in good.

106

Ring out, wild bells, to the wild sky,
    The flying cloud, the frosty light:
    The year is dying in the night;
Ring out, wild bells, and let him die.

5 Ring out the old, ring in the new,
    Ring, happy bells, across the snow:
    The year is going, let him go;
Ring out the false, ring in the true.

Ring out the grief that saps the mind,
10   For those that here we see no more;
    Ring out the feud of rich and poor,
Ring in redress to all mankind.

Ring out a slowly dying cause,
    And ancient forms of party strife;
15   Ring in the nobler modes of life,
With sweeter manners, purer laws.

Ring out the want, the care, the sin,
    The faithless coldness of the times:

4. I.e., let no bowl of hot punch warm the mantelpiece.

5. The scintillating motion of the stars that rise [Tennyson's note].

Ring out, ring out my mournful rhymes,
20   But ring the fuller minstrel in.

Ring out false pride in place and blood,
    The civic slander and the spite;
    Ring in the love of truth and right,
Ring in the common love of good.

25   Ring out old shapes of foul disease;
    Ring out the narrowing lust of gold;
    Ring out the thousand wars of old,
Ring in the thousand years of peace.

Ring in the valiant man and free,
30   The larger heart, the kindlier hand;
    Ring out the darkness of the land,
Ring in the Christ that is to be.[6]

107

It is the day when he was born.°   *February 1*
    A bitter day that early sank
    Behind a purple-frosty bank
Of vapor, leaving night forlorn.

5   The time admits not flowers or leaves
    To deck the banquet. Fiercely flies
    The blast of North and East, and ice
Makes daggers at the sharpened eaves,

And bristles all the brakes° and thorns   *thickets*
10   To yon hard crescent, as she hangs
    Above the wood which grides[7] and clangs
Its leafless ribs and iron horns

Together, in the drifts[8] that pass
    To darken on the rolling brine
15   That breaks the coast. But fetch the wine,
Arrange the board and brim the glass;

Bring in great logs and let them lie,
    To make a solid core of heat;
    Be cheerful-minded, talk and treat
20   Of all things even as he were by;

We keep the day. With festal cheer,
    With books and music, surely we

6. These allusions to the second coming of Christ and to the millennium are derived from Revelation 20, but Tennyson has interpreted the biblical account in his own way. He once told his son of his conviction that "the forms of Christian religion would alter; but that the spirit of Christ would still grow from more to more."
7. Clashes with a strident noise.
8. Either cloud drifts or clouds of snow.

Will drink to him, whate'er he be,
And sing the songs he loved to hear.

108

I will not shut me from my kind,
 And, lest I stiffen into stone,
 I will not eat my heart alone,
Nor feed with sighs a passing wind:

5 What profit lies in barren faith,
 And vacant yearning, though with might
 To scale the heaven's highest height,
Or dive below the wells of Death?

What find I in the highest place,
10 But mine own phantom chanting hymns?
 And on the depths of death there swims
The reflex of a human face.°   *his own face*

I'll rather take what fruit may be
 Of sorrow under human skies:
15 'Tis held that sorrow makes us wise,
Whatever wisdom sleep with thee.°   *Hallam*

109

Heart-affluence in discursive talk
 From household fountains never dry;
 The critic clearness of an eye
That saw through all the Muses' walk;[9]

5 Seraphic intellect and force
 To seize and throw the doubts of man;
 Impassioned logic, which outran
The hearer in its fiery course;

High nature amorous of the good,
10 But touched with no ascetic gloom;
 And passion pure in snowy bloom
Through all the years of April blood;

A love of freedom rarely felt,
 Of freedom in her regal seat
15 Of England; not the schoolboy heat,
The blind hysterics of the Celt;[1]

And manhood fused with female grace
 In such a sort, the child would twine

---

9. The realm of art and literature.
1. From the 18th century onward, the word *Celtic* had been used as a descriptor of the family of languages that included Welsh, Cornish, Irish, and Gaelic. In the spurious slippage from language to ethnicity or "race" that was common in the 19th and 20th centuries, the term *Celt* was frequently applied to anyone who spoke (or was descended from those who spoke) a Celtic language. Tennyson here uses it as a synonym for "Irish." Cf. Arnold's description of the Irish temperament as "Celtic" in *On the Study of Celtic Literature*.

A trustful hand, unasked, in thine,
20 And find his comfort in thy face;

All these have been, and thee mine eyes
Have looked on: if they looked in vain,
My shame is greater who remain,
Nor let thy wisdom make me wise.

* * *

115

Now fades the last long streak of snow,
Now burgeons every maze of quick°   *hawthorn hedge*
About the flowering squares,° and thick   *fields*
By ashen roots the violets blow.

5   Now rings the woodland loud and long,
The distance takes a lovelier hue,
And drowned in yonder living blue
The lark becomes a sightless song.

Now dance the lights on lawn and lea,
10   The flocks are whiter down the vale,
And milkier every milky sail
On winding stream or distant sea;

Where now the seamew° pipes, or dives   *seabird*
In yonder greening gleam, and fly
15   The happy birds, that change their sky
To build and brood, that live their lives

From land to land; and in my breast
Spring wakens too, and my regret
Becomes an April violet,
20   And buds and blossoms like the rest.

* * *

118

Contèmplate all this work of Time,
The giant laboring in his youth;
Nor dream of human love and truth,
As dying Nature's earth and lime;[2]

5   But trust that those we call the dead
Are breathers of an ampler day
For ever nobler ends. They° say,   *Scientists*
The solid earth whereon we tread

2. Two of the perishable organic ingredients of the human body.

In tracts of fluent heat began,
10   And grew to seeming-random forms,
    The seeming prey of cyclic storms,
Till at the last arose the man;

Who throve and branched from clime to clime,
    The herald of a higher race,
15   And of himself in higher place
If so he type[3] this work of time

Within himself, from more to more;
    Or, crowned with attributes of woe
    Like glories, move his course, and show
20 That life is not as idle ore,

But iron dug from central gloom,
    And heated hot with burning fears,
    And dipped in baths of hissing tears,
And battered with the shocks of doom

25 To shape and use. Arise and fly
    The reeling Faun,[4] the sensual feast;
    Move upward, working out the beast,
And let the ape and tiger die.

119

Doors,[5] where my heart was used to beat
    So quickly, not as one that weeps
    I come once more; the city sleeps;
I smell the meadow in the street;

5   I hear a chirp of birds; I see
    Betwixt the black fronts long-withdrawn
    A light blue lane of early dawn,
And think of early days and thee,

And bless thee, for thy lips are bland,°   *gentle*
10   And bright the friendship of thine eye;
    And in my thoughts with scarce a sigh
I take the pressure of thine hand.

120

I trust I have not wasted breath:
    I think we are not wholly brain,
    Magnetic mockeries;[6] not in vain,
Like Paul[7] with beasts, I fought with Death;

3. Emulate, prefigure as a type.
4. In Roman mythology a half-human, half-beast deity of the woods and mountains.
5. The doors of Hallam's house on London's Wimpole Street. Cf. section 7.
6. Mechanisms operated by responses to electrical forces.
7. 1 Corinthians 15.32.

5 Not only cunning° casts in clay: *skillful*
  Let Science prove we are, and then
  What matters Science unto men,
At least to me? I would not stay.

 Let him, the wiser man who springs
10 Hereafter, up from childhood shape
  His action like the greater ape,
But I was *born* to other things.

121

Sad Hesper° o'er the buried sun   *evening star*
  And ready, thou, to die with him,
  Thou watchest all things ever dim
And dimmer, and a glory done.

5 The team is loosened from the wain,°   *hay wagon*
  The boat is drawn upon the shore;
  Thou listenest to the closing door,
And life is darkened in the brain.

Bright Phosphor,° fresher for the night,   *morning star*
10 By thee the world's great work is heard
  Beginning, and the wakeful bird;
Behind thee comes the greater light.[8]

The market boat is on the stream,
  And voices hail it from the brink;
15 Thou hear'st the village hammer clink,
And see'st the moving of the team.

Sweet Hesper-Phosphor, double name[9]
  For what is one, the first, the last,
  Thou, like my present and my past,
20 Thy place is changed; thou art the same.

      * * *

123

There rolls the deep where grew the tree.
  O earth, what changes hast thou seen!
  There where the long street roars hath been
The stillness of the central sea.[1]

8. Cf. Genesis 1.16: "the greater light to rule the day."
9. The planet Venus, named for the Roman goddess of love, is both the evening star and the morning star (visible at different times in different seasons).
1. In a passage from *The Principles of Geology* (1832), a book well known to Tennyson, Sir Charles Lyell discusses the "interchange of sea and land" that has occurred "on the surface of our globe": "In the Mediterranean alone, many flourishing inland towns and a still greater number of ports now stand where the sea rolled its waves since the era when civilized nations first grew in Europe."

5   The hills are shadows, and they flow
      From form to form, and nothing stands;
      They melt like mist, the solid lands,
    Like clouds they shape themselves and go.

    But in my spirit will I dwell,
10   And dream my dream, and hold it true;
      For though my lips may breathe adieu,
    I cannot think the thing farewell.

124

That which we dare invoke to bless;
    Our dearest faith; our ghastliest doubt;
    He, They, One, All; within, without;
The Power in darkness whom we guess—

5   I found Him not in world or sun,
      Or eagle's wing, or insect's eye,[2]
      Nor through the questions men may try,
The petty cobwebs we have spun.

If e'er when faith had fallen asleep,
10   I heard a voice, "believe no more,"
      And heard an ever-breaking shore
That tumbled in the Godless deep,

A warmth within the breast would melt
    The freezing reason's colder part,
15   And like a man in wrath the heart
Stood up and answered, "I have felt."[3]

No, like a child in doubt and fear:
    But that blind clamor made me wise;
    Then was I as a child that cries,
20   But, crying, knows his father near;

And what I am beheld again
    What is, and no man understands;
    And out of darkness came the hands
That reach through nature, molding men.

* * *

126

Love is and was my lord and king,
    And in his presence I attend
    To hear the tidings of my friend,
Which every hour his couriers bring.

2. He does not discover satisfactory proof of God's existence in the 18th-century argument that because objects in nature are designed there must exist a designer.
3. Cf. Carlyle's *Sartor Resartus* (1833–34), "The Everlasting No" (p. 34).

5 Love is and was my king and lord,
      And will be, though as yet I keep
      Within the court on earth, and sleep
   Encompassed by his faithful guard,

   And hear at times a sentinel
10   Who moves about from place to place,
      And whispers to the worlds of space,
   In the deep night, that all is well.

127

   And all is well, though faith and form[4]
      Be sundered in the night of fear;
      Well roars the storm to those that hear
   A deeper voice across the storm,

5 Proclaiming social truth shall spread,
      And justice, even though thrice again
      The red fool-fury of the Seine[5]
   Should pile her barricades with dead.[6]

   But ill for him that wears a crown,
10   And him, the lazar,[7] in his rags!
      They tremble, the sustaining crags;
   The spires of ice are toppled down,

   And molten up, and roar in flood;
      The fortress crashes from on high,
15   The brute earth lightens[8] to the sky,
   And the great Aeon[9] sinks in blood,

   And compassed by the fires of hell,
      While thou, dear spirit, happy star,
      O'erlook'st the tumult from afar,
20 And smilest, knowing all is well.

                  *   *   *

129

   Dear friend, far off, my lost desire,
      So far, so near in woe and weal,°   *happiness*
      O loved the most, when most I feel
   There is a lower and a higher;

---

4. Traditional institutions through which faith was formerly expressed, such as the Church.
5. The river that runs through Paris.
6. Reference to revolutionary uprisings in France, in each of which a king lost his throne (line 9): in 1789 against Louis XVI, in 1830 against Charles X, and in 1848 against Louis-Philippe. If, as Tennyson recollected, section 127 was finished at a date earlier than 1848, the reference to three revolutions (line 6) was prophetic.
7. Pauper suffering from disease.
8. Is lit up by fire.
9. A vast tract of time, here perhaps modern Western civilization.

5   Known and unknown, human, divine;
      Sweet human hand and lips and eye;
      Dear heavenly friend that canst not die,
    Mine, mine, forever, ever mine;

    Strange friend, past, present, and to be;
10   Loved deeplier, darklier understood;
      Behold, I dream a dream of good,
    And mingle all the world with thee.

130

    Thy voice is on the rolling air
      I hear thee where the waters run;
      Thou standest in the rising sun,
    And in the setting thou art fair.

5   What art thou then? I cannot guess;
      But though I seem in star and flower
      To feel thee some diffusive power,
    I do not therefore love thee less.

    My love involves the love before;
10   My love is vaster passion now;
      Tho' mix'd with God and Nature thou,
    I seem to love thee more and more.

    Far off thou art, but ever nigh;
      I have thee still, and I rejoice;
15   I prosper, circled with thy voice;
    I shall not lose thee tho' I die.

131

    O living will[1] that shalt endure
      When all that seems shall suffer shock,
      Rise in the spiritual rock,[2]
    Flow through our deeds and make them pure,

5   That we may lift from out of dust
      A voice as unto him that hears,
      A cry above the conquered years
    To one that with us works, and trust,

    With faith that comes of self-control,
10   The truths that never can be proved
      Until we close with all we loved,
    And all we flow from, soul in soul.

1. Tennyson later commented that he meant here the moral will of humankind.
2. Christ. Cf. 1 Corinthians 10.4: "And did all drink the same spiritual drink: for they drank of that spiritual Rock that followed them: and that Rock was Christ."

From Epilogue[3]

* * *

And rise, O moon, from yonder down,
110   Till over down and over dale
    All night the shining vapor sail
And pass the silent-lighted town,

The white-faced halls, the glancing rills,
    And catch at every mountain head,
115   And o'er the friths[4] that branch and spread
Their sleeping silver through the hills;

And touch with shade the bridal doors,
    With tender gloom the roof, the wall;
    And breaking let the splendor fall
120 To spangle all the happy shores

By which they rest, and ocean sounds,
    And, star and system rolling past,
    A soul shall draw from out the vast
And strike his being into bounds,

125 And, moved through life of lower phase,
    Result in man,[5] be born and think,
    And act and love, a closer link
Betwixt us and the crowning race

Of those that, eye to eye, shall look
130   On knowledge; under whose command
    Is Earth and Earth's, and in their hand
Is Nature like an open book;

No longer half-akin to brute,
    For all we thought and loved and did,
135   And hoped, and suffered, is but seed
Of what in them is flower and fruit;

Whereof the man that with me trod
    This planet was a noble type°   *model, example*
    Appearing ere the times were ripe,
140 That friend of mine who lives in God,

3. The Epilogue describes the wedding day of Tennyson's sister Cecilia to Edmund Lushington. At the conclusion (printed here) the speaker reflects on the moonlit wedding night and the kind of offspring that will result from their union.
4. Inlets of the sea.

5. A child will be conceived and will develop in embryo through various stages. This development is similar to human evolution from the animal to the human level and perhaps to a future higher stage of development.

That God, which ever lives and loves,
One God, one law, one element,
And one far-off divine event,
To which the whole creation moves.

1833–50   1850

The Charge of the Light Brigade[1]

1

Half a league,[2] half a league,
Half a league onward,
All in the valley of Death
Rode the six hundred.[3]
5 "Forward the Light Brigade!
Charge for the guns!" he said.
Into the valley of Death[4]
Rode the six hundred.

2

"Forward, the Light Brigade!"
10 Was there a man dismayed?
Not though the soldier knew
Someone had blundered.
Theirs not to make reply,
Theirs not to reason why,
15 Theirs but to do and die.
Into the valley of Death
Rode the six hundred.

3

Cannon to right of them,
Cannon to left of them,
20 Cannon in front of them
Volleyed and thundered;
Stormed at with shot and shell,
Boldly they rode and well,
Into the jaws of Death,
25 Into the mouth of hell
Rode the six hundred.

1. During the Crimean War (1854–56), owing to confusion of orders, a brigade of British cavalry charged some entrenched batteries of Russian artillery. This blunder cost the lives of three-quarters of the six hundred horsemen engaged (see Cecil Woodham-Smith, *The Reason Why*, 1954). Tennyson rapidly composed his "ballad" (as he called the poem) after reading an account of the battle in a newspaper.
2. About a mile and a half.
3. In the recording Tennyson made of this poem, *hundred* sounds like "hunderd"—a Lincolnshire pronunciation that reinforces the rhyme with *thundered*, etc.
4. See Psalms 23.4: "Yea, though I walk through the valley of the shadow of death."

4

Flashed all their sabers bare,
Flashed as they turned in air
Sab'ring the gunners there,
30   Charging an army, while
        All the world wondered.
Plunged in the battery smoke
Right through the line they broke;
Cossack and Russian
35   Reeled from the saber stroke
        Shattered and sundered.
Then they rode back, but not,
        Not the six hundred.

5

Cannon to right of them,
40   Cannon to left of them,
Cannon behind them
        Volleyed and thundered;
Stormed at with shot and shell,
While horse and hero fell.
45   They that had fought so well
Came through the jaws of Death,
Back from the mouth of hell,
All that was left of them,
        Left of six hundred.

6

50   When can their glory fade?
O the wild charge they made!
        All the world wondered.
Honor the charge they made!
Honor the Light Brigade,
55   Noble six hundred!

1854   1854

Idylls of the King

Idylls of the King   When John Milton was considering subjects suitable for an epic poem, one of those he entertained was the story of the British king Arthur, a semilegendary leader from about 500 C.E. who fought off the Saxon invaders who had swarmed into Britain after the withdrawal of the Roman legions. Tennyson likewise saw that the Arthurian story had epic potential and selected it for his lifework as "the greatest of all poetical subjects." At intervals, during a period of fifty years, he labored over the twelve books that make up his *Idylls of the King*, completing the work in 1888.

The principal source of Tennyson's stories of Arthur and his knights was Sir Thomas Malory's *Morte Darthur*, a version that Malory translated into English prose from French sources in 1470. As Talbot Donaldson suggested, one basis of the appeal of the Arthurian stories, like the legends of Robin Hood and stories of the

American West, is that they represent the struggle of individuals to restore order when chaos and anarchy are ascendant, a task performed in the face of seemingly overwhelming odds. The individual stories in Tennyson's *Idylls* have the same basic appeal, but the overall design of the whole poem is more ambitious and impressive. The epic represents the rise and fall of a civilization, and its underlying theme is that after two thousand years of Christianity, Western civilization may be going through a cycle in which it must confront the possibilities of a renewal in the future or an apocalyptic extinction. The first book, *The Coming of Arthur*, introduces the basic myth of a springtime hero transforming a wasteland and inspiring faith and hope in the highest values of civilized life among his devoted followers, the knights of his Round Table. Succeeding books move through summer and autumn and culminate in the bleak wintry scene of Arthur's last battle in which his order perishes in a civil war; the leader of the enemy forces is his own nephew, Sir Modred.

Throughout the later books of the *Idylls* the forces of opposition grow in strength, and discontent and resentment infect leading figures of the Round Table itself. The most glaring example is the adulterous relationship between Guinevere, Arthur's "sumptuous" queen (as Tennyson once described her), and the king's chief lieutenant and friend, Sir Lancelot. Many other fallings away subsequently come to light, such as the deceitful betrayal by Sir Gawain in the ninth book, *Pelleas and Ettarre*, and the cynical conduct of Sir Tristram, whose story is told in the bitter tenth book, *The Last Tournament*. Even Merlin, Arthur's trusted magician and counselor, becomes corrupted and can perform no further offices for the king (*Merlin and Vivien*). *The Passing of Arthur* depicts the apocalyptic end of this long process of disintegration and decay.

From Idylls of the King

The Coming of Arthur

Leodogran, the King of Cameliard,
Had one fair daughter, and none other child;
And she was fairest of all flesh on earth,
Guinevere, and in her his one delight.

5   For many a petty king ere Arthur came
Ruled in this isle, and ever waging war
Each upon other, wasted all the land;
And still from time to time the heathen host
Swarm'd overseas, and harried° what was left.   *ravaged*
10   And so there grew great tracts of wilderness,
Wherein the beast was ever more and more,
But man was less and less, till Arthur came.
For first Aurelius[1] lived and fought and died,
And after him King Uther fought and died,
15   But either fail'd to make the kingdom one.
And after these King Arthur for a space,
And thro' the puissance° of his Table Round,   *power*
Drew all their petty princedoms under him,
Their king and head, and made a realm, and reign'd.

1. Brother of King Uther.

20   And thus the land of Cameliard was waste,
       Thick with wet woods, and many a beast therein,
       And none or few to scare or chase the beast;
       So that wild dog, and wolf and boar and bear
       Came night and day, and rooted° in the fields,   *dug for food*
25   And wallow'd in the gardens of the King.
       And ever and anon the wolf would steal
       The children and devour, but now and then,
       Her own brood lost or dead, lent her fierce teat
       To human sucklings; and the children, housed
30   In her foul den, there at their meat would growl,
       And mock their foster-mother on four feet,
       Till, straighten'd, they grew up to wolf-like men,
       Worse than the wolves. And King Leodogran
       Groan'd° for the Roman legions here again,   *yearned*
35   And Caesar's eagle:[2] then his brother king,
       Urien, assail'd him: last a heathen horde,
       Reddening the sun with smoke and earth with blood,
       And on the spike that split the mother's heart
       Spitting° the child, brake on him, till, amazed,   *impaling*
40   He knew not whither he should turn for aid.

       But—for he heard of Arthur newly crown'd,
       Tho' not without an uproar made by those
       Who cried, "He is not Uther's son"—the King
       Sent to him, saying, "Arise, and help us thou!
45   For here between the man and beast we die."

       And Arthur yet had done no deed of arms,
       But heard the call, and came: and Guinevere
       Stood by the castle walls to watch him pass;
       But since he neither wore on helm or shield
50   The golden symbol of his kinglihood,[3]
       But rode a simple knight among his knights,
       And many of these in richer arms than he,
       She saw him not, or mark'd not, if she saw,
       One among many, tho' his face was bare.
55   But Arthur, looking downward as he past,
       Felt the light of her eyes into his life
       Smite on the sudden, yet rode on, and pitch'd
       His tents beside the forest. Then he drave°   *drove away*
       The heathen; after, slew the beast, and fell'd
60   The forest, letting in the sun, and made
       Broad pathways for the hunter and the knight
       And so return'd.

                    For while he linger'd there,
       A doubt that ever smoulder'd in the hearts
       Of those great Lords and Barons of his realm
65   Flash'd forth and into war: for most of these,

---

2. I.e., imperial protection.   3. The golden dragon [Tennyson's note].

Colleaguing with a score of petty kings,
Made head against him, crying, "Who is he
That he should rule us? who hath proven him
King Uther's son? for lo! we look at him,
70 And find nor face nor bearing, limbs nor voice,
Are like to those of Uther whom we knew.
This is the son of Gorloïs, not the King;
This is the son of Anton, not the King."

    And Arthur, passing thence to battle, felt
75 Travail, and throes and agonies of the life,
Desiring to be join'd with Guinevere;
And thinking as he rode, "Her father said
That there between the man and beast they die.
Shall I not lift her from this land of beasts
80 Up to my throne, and side by side with me?
What happiness to reign a lonely king,
Vext—O ye stars that shudder over me,
O earth that soundest hollow under me,
Vext with waste dreams? for saving° I be join'd   *unless*
85 To her that is the fairest under heaven,
I seem as nothing in the mighty world,
And cannot will my will, nor work my work
Wholly, nor make myself in mine own realm
Victor and lord. But were I join'd with her,
90 Then might we live together as one life,
And reigning with one will in everything
Have power on this dark land to lighten it,
And power on this dead world to make it live."

    Thereafter—as he speaks who tells the tale—
95 When Arthur reach'd a field-of-battle bright
With pitch'd pavilions of his foe, the world
Was all so clear about him, that he saw
The smallest rock far on the faintest hill,
And even in high day the morning star,
100 So when the King had set his banner broad,
At once from either side, with trumpet-blast,
And shouts, and clarions shrilling unto blood,
The long-lanced battle let their horses run.
And now the Barons and the kings prevail'd,
105 And now the King, as here and there that war
Went swaying; but the Powers who walk the world
Made lightnings and great thunders over him,
And dazed all eyes, till Arthur by main might,
And mightier of his hands with every blow,
110 And leading all his knighthood threw° the kings   *defeated*
Carádos, Urien, Cradlemont of Wales,
Claudias, and Clariance of Northumberland,
The King Brandagoras of Latangor,
With Anguisant of Erin, Morganore,
115 And Lot of Orkney. Then, before a voice

As dreadful as the shout of one who sees
To one who sins, and deems himself alone
And all the world asleep, they swerved and brake

Flying, and Arthur call'd to stay the brands°   *swords*
120 That hack'd among the flyers, "Ho! they yield!"
So like a painted battle the war stood
Silenced, the living quiet as the dead,
And in the heart of Arthur joy was lord.
He laugh'd upon his warrior° whom he loved   *Lancelot*
125 And honour'd most. "Thou dost not doubt me King,
So well thine arm hath wrought for me to-day."
"Sir and my liege," he cried, "the fire of God
Descends upon thee in the battle-field:
I know thee for my King!" Whereat the two,
130 For each had warded° either in the fight,   *guarded*
Sware on the field of death a deathless love.
And Arthur said, "Man's word is God in man:
Let chance what will, I trust thee to the death."

Then quickly from the foughten field he sent
135 Ulfius, and Brastias, and Bedivere,
His new-made knights, to King Leodogran,
Saying, "If I in aught have served thee well,
Give me thy daughter Guinevere to wife."

Whom when he heard, Leodogran in heart
140 Debating—"How should I that am a king,
However much he holp° me at my need,   *helped*
Give my one daughter saving to a king,
And a king's son?"—lifted his voice, and call'd
A hoary man, his chamberlain, to whom
145 He trusted all things, and of him required
His counsel: "Knowest thou aught of Arthur's birth?"

Then spake the hoary chamberlain and said,
"Sir King, there be but two old men that know:
And each is twice as old as I; and one
150 Is Merlin, the wise man that ever served
King Uther thro' his magic art; and one
Is Merlin's master (so they call him) Bleys,
Who taught him magic; but the scholar ran
Before the master, and so far, that Bleys
155 Laid magic by, and sat him down, and wrote
All things and whatsoever Merlin did
In one great annal-book, where after-years
Will learn the secret of our Arthur's birth."

To whom the King Leodogran replied,
160 "O friend, had I been holpen half as well
By this King Arthur as by thee to-day,
Then beast and man had had their share of me:

But summon here before us yet once more
Ulfius, and Brastias, and Bedivere."

165   Then, when they came before him, the King said,
"I have seen the cuckoo chased by lesser fowl,
And reason in the chase: but wherefore now
Do these your lords stir up the heat of war,
Some calling Arthur born of Gorloïs,
170 Others of Anton? Tell me, ye yourselves,
Hold ye this Arthur for King Uther's son?"

    And Ulfius and Brastias answer'd, "Ay."
Then Bedivere, the first of all his knights
Knighted by Arthur at his crowning, spake—
175 For bold in heart and act and word was he,
Whenever slander breathed against the King—

    "Sir, there be many rumours on this head:°   *subject*
For there be those who hate him in their hearts,
Call him baseborn, and since his ways are sweet,
180 And theirs are bestial, hold him less than man:
And there be those who deem him more than man,
And dream he dropt from heaven: but my belief
In all this matter—so ye care to learn—
Sir, for ye know that in King Uther's time
185 The prince and warrior Gorloïs, he that held
Tintagil castle by the Cornish sea,
Was wedded with a winsome wife, Ygerne:
And daughters had she borne him,—one whereof,
Lot's wife, the Queen of Orkney, Bellicent,
190 Hath ever like a loyal sister cleaved
To Arthur,—but a son she had not borne.
And Uther cast upon her eyes of love:
But she, a stainless wife to Gorloïs,
So loathed the bright dishonour of his love,
195 That Gorloïs and King Uther went to war:
And overthrown was Gorloïs and slain.
Then Uther in his wrath and heat besieged
Ygerne within Tintagil, where her men,
Seeing the mighty swarm about their walls,
200 Left her and fled, and Uther enter'd in,
And there was none to call to but himself.
So, compass'd by the power of the King,
Enforced she was to wed him in her tears,
And with a shameful swiftness: afterward,
205 Not many moons, King Uther died himself,
Moaning and wailing for an heir to rule
After him, lest the realm should go to wrack.°   *ruin*
And that same night, the night of the new year,
By reason of the bitterness and grief
210 That vext his mother, all before his time
Was Arthur born, and all as soon as born

Deliver'd at a secret postern-gate
To Merlin, to be holden far apart
Until his hour should come; because the lords
215   Of that fierce day were as the lords of this,
Wild beasts, and surely would have torn the child
Piecemeal among them, had they known; for each
But sought to rule for his own self and hand,
And many hated Uther for the sake
220   Of Gorloïs. Wherefore Merlin took the child,
And gave him to Sir Anton, an old knight
And ancient friend of Uther; and his wife
Nursed the young prince, and rear'd him with her own;
And no man knew. And ever since the lords
225   Have foughten like wild beasts among themselves,
So that the realm has gone to wrack: but now,
This year, when Merlin (for his hour had come)
Brought Arthur forth, and set him in the hall,
Proclaiming, 'Here is Uther's heir, your king,'
230   A hundred voices cried, 'Away with him!
No king of ours! a son of Gorloïs he,
Or else the child of Anton, and no king,
Or else baseborn.' Yet Merlin thro' his craft,
And while the people clamour'd for a king,
235   Had Arthur crown'd; but after, the great lords
Banded, and so brake out in open war."

    Then while the King debated with himself
If Arthur were the child of shamefulness,
Or born the son of Gorloïs, after death,
240   Or Uther's son, and born before his time,
Or whether there were truth in anything
Said by these three, there came to Cameliard,
With Gawain and young Modred, her two sons,
Lot's wife, the Queen of Orkney, Bellicent;
245   Whom as he could, not as he would, the King
Made feast for, saying, as they sat at meat,

    "A doubtful throne is ice on summer seas.
Ye come from Arthur's court. Victor his men
Report him! Yea, but ye—think ye this king—
250   So many those that hate him, and so strong,
So few his knights, however brave they be—
Hath body enow° to hold his foemen down?"   *enough*

    "O King," she cried, "and I will tell thee: few,
Few, but all brave, all of one mind with him;
255   For I was near him when the savage yells
Of Uther's peerage died, and Arthur sat
Crown'd on the daïs, and his warriors cried,
'Be thou the king, and we will work thy will
Who love thee.' Then the King in low deep tones,
260   And simple words of great authority,

Bound them by so strait° vows to his own self,   *strict*
That when they rose, knighted from kneeling, some
Were pale as at the passing of a ghost,
Some flush'd, and others dazed, as one who wakes
265   Half-blinded at the coming of a light.

"But when he spake and cheer'd his Table Round
With large, divine, and comfortable words,
Beyond my tongue to tell thee—I beheld
From eye to eye thro' all their Order flash
270   A momentary likeness of the King:
And ere it left their faces, thro' the cross
And those around it and the Crucified,
Down from the casement over Arthur, smote
Flame-colour, vert° and azure, in three rays,   *green*
275   One falling upon each of three fair queens,
Who stood in silence near his throne, the friends
Of Arthur, gazing on him, tall, with bright
Sweet faces, who will help him at his need.

"And there I saw mage° Merlin, whose vast wit   *magician*
280   And hundred winters are but as the hands
Of loyal vassals toiling for their liege.

"And near him stood the Lady of the Lake,[4]
Who knows a subtler magic than his own—
Clothed in white samite,[5] mystic, wonderful.
285   She gave the King his huge cross-hilted sword,
Whereby to drive the heathen out: a mist
Of incense curl'd about her, and her face
Wellnigh was hidden in the minster° gloom;   *church*
But there was heard among the holy hymns
290   A voice as of the waters,[6] for she dwells
Down in a deep; calm, whatsoever storms
May shake the world, and when the surface rolls,
Hath power to walk the waters like our Lord.

"There likewise I beheld Excalibur
295   Before him at his crowning borne, the sword
That rose from out the bosom of the lake,
And Arthur row'd across and took it—rich
With jewels, elfin° Urim,[7] on the hilt,   *elflike*
Bewildering heart and eye—the blade so bright
300   That men are blinded by it—on one side,
Graven in the oldest tongue of all this world,
'Take me,' but turn the blade and ye shall see,
And written in the speech ye speak yourself,
'Cast me away!' And sad was Arthur's face

4. The Lady of the Lake in the old legends is the
Church [Tennyson's note].
5. A rich silk fabric.
6. Cf. Revelation 14.2: "And I heard a voice from
heaven, as the voice of many waters."
7. Mentioned numerous times in the Old Testament, this is a device of precious stones worn by
priests and used in prophesying.

305 Taking it, but old Merlin counsell'd him,
'Take thou and strike! the time to cast away
Is yet far-off.' So this great brand the king
Took, and by this will beat his foemen down."

Thereat Leodogran rejoiced, but thought
310 To sift his doubtings to the last, and ask'd,
Fixing full eyes of question on her face,
"The swallow and the swift are near akin,
But thou art closer to this noble prince,
Being his own dear sister;" and she said,
315 "Daughter of Gorloïs and Ygerne am I;"
"And therefore Arthur's sister?" ask'd the King
She answer'd, "These be secret things," and sign'd
To those two sons to pass, and let them be.
And Gawain went, and breaking into song
320 Sprang out, and follow'd by his flying hair
Ran like a colt, and leapt at all he saw:
But Modred laid his ear beside the doors,
And there half-heard; the same that afterward
Struck for the throne, and striking found his doom.

325 And then the Queen made answer, "What know I?
For dark my mother was in eyes and hair,
And dark in hair and eyes am I; and dark
Was Gorloïs, yea and dark was Uther too,
Wellnigh to blackness; but this King is fair
330 Beyond the race of Britons and of men.
Moreover, always in my mind I hear
A cry from out the dawning of my life,
A mother weeping, and I hear her say,
'O that ye had some brother, pretty one,
335 To guard thee on the rough ways of the world.'

"Ay," said the King, "and hear ye such a cry?
But when did Arthur chance upon thee first?"

"O King!" she cried, "and I will tell thee true:
He found me first when yet a little maid:
340 Beaten I had been for a little fault
Whereof I was not guilty; and out I ran
And flung myself down on a bank of heath,
And hated this fair world and all therein,
And wept, and wish'd that I were dead; and he—
345 I know not whether of himself he came,
Or brought by Merlin, who, they say, can walk
Unseen at pleasure—he was at my side,
And spake sweet words, and comforted my heart,
And dried my tears, being a child with me.
350 And many a time he came, and evermore
As I grew greater grew with me; and sad
At times he seem'd, and sad with him was I,

Stern too at times, and then I loved him not,
But sweet again, and then I loved him well.
355 And now of late I see him less and less,
But those first days had golden hours for me,
For then I surely thought he would be king.

"But let me tell thee now another tale:
For Bleys, our Merlin's master, as they say,
360 Died but of late, and sent his cry to me,
To hear him speak before he left his life.
Shrunk like a fairy changeling[8] lay the mage;
And when I enter'd told me that himself
And Merlin ever served about the King,
365 Uther, before he died; and on the night
When Uther in Tintagil past away
Moaning and wailing for an heir, the two
Left the still King, and passing forth to breathe,
Then from the castle gateway by the chasm
370 Descending thro' the dismal night—a night
In which the bounds of heaven and earth were lost—
Beheld, so high upon the dreary deeps
It seem'd in heaven, a ship, the shape thereof
A dragon wing'd, and all from stem to stern
375 Bright with a shining people on the decks,
And gone as soon as seen. And then the two
Dropt to the cove, and watch'd the great sea fall,
Wave after wave, each mightier than the last,
Till last, a ninth one, gathering half the deep
380 And full of voices, slowly rose and plunged
Roaring, and all the wave was in a flame:
And down the wave and in the flame was borne
A naked babe, and rode to Merlin's feet,
Who stoopt and caught the babe, and cried 'The King!
385 Here is an heir for Uther!' And the fringe
Of that great breaker, sweeping up the strand,
Lash'd at the wizard as he spake the word,
And all at once all round him rose in fire,
So that the child and he were clothed in fire.
390 And presently thereafter follow'd calm,
Free sky and stars: 'And this same child,' he said,
'Is he who reigns; nor could I part in peace
Till this were told.' And saying this the seer
Went thro' the strait° and dreadful pass of death,   *narrow*
395 Not ever to be question'd any more
Save on the further side; but when I met
Merlin, and ask'd him if these things were truth—
The shining dragon and the naked child
Descending in the glory of the seas—
400 He laugh'd as is his wont,° and answer'd me   *custom*
In riddling triplets of old time, and said:

8. Child secretly substituted for another.

"'Rain, rain, and sun! a rainbow in the sky!
A young man will be wiser by and by;
An old man's wit may wander ere he die.
405 Rain, rain, and sun! a rainbow on the lea!
And truth is this to me, and that to thee;
And truth or clothed or naked let it be.
Rain, sun, and rain! and the free blossom blows:
Sun, rain, and sun! and where is he who knows?
410 From the great deep to the great deep he goes.'

"So Merlin riddling anger'd me; but thou
Fear not to give this King thine only child,
Guinevere: so great bards of him will sing
Hereafter; and dark sayings from of old
415 Ranging and ringing thro' the minds of men,
And echo'd by old folk beside their fires
For comfort after their wage-work is done,
Speak of the King; and Merlin in our time
Hath spoken also, not in jest, and sworn
420 Tho' men may wound him that he will not die,
But pass, again to come; and then or now
Utterly smite the heathen underfoot,
Till these and all men hail him for their king."

She spake and King Leodogran rejoiced,
425 But musing "Shall I answer yea or nay?"
Doubted, and drowsed, nodded and slept, and saw,
Dreaming, a slope of land that ever grew,
Field after field, up to a height, the peak
Haze-hidden, and thereon a phantom king,
430 Now looming, and now lost; and on the slope
The sword rose, the hind° fell, the herd was driven,   *peasant*
Fire glimpsed;° and all the land from roof and rick,[9]   *glimmered*
In drifts of smoke before a rolling wind,
Stream'd to the peak, and mingled with the haze
435 And made it thicker; while the phantom king
Sent out at times a voice; and here or there
Stood one who pointed toward the voice, the rest
Slew on and burnt, crying, "No king of ours,
No son of Uther, and no king of ours;"
440 Till with a wink his dream was changed, the haze
Descended, and the solid earth became
As nothing, but the King stood out in heaven,
Crown'd. And Leodogran awoke, and sent
Ulfius, and Brastias and Bedivere,
445 Back to the court of Arthur answering yea.

Then Arthur charged his warrior whom he loved
And honour'd most, Sir Lancelot, to ride forth

---

9. Stacks of grain.

And bring the Queen;—and watch'd him from the gates:
And Lancelot past away among the flowers,
450 (For then was latter April) and return'd
Among the flowers, in May, with Guinevere.
To whom arrived, by Dubric the high saint,
Chief of the church in Britain, and before
The stateliest of her altar-shrines, the King
455 That morn was married, while in stainless white,
The fair beginners of a nobler time,
And glorying in their vows and him, his knights
Stood round him, and rejoicing in his joy.
Far shone the fields of May thro' open door,
460 The sacred altar blossom'd white with May,
The Sun of May descended on their King,
They gazed on all earth's beauty in their Queen,
Roll'd incense, and there past along the hymns
A voice as of the waters, while the two
465 Sware at the shrine of Christ a deathless love:
And Arthur said, "Behold, thy doom° is mine.   *destiny*
Let chance what will, I love thee to the death!"
To whom the Queen replied with drooping eyes,
"King and my lord, I love thee to the death!"
470 And holy Dubric spread his hands and spake,
"Reign ye, and live and love, and make the world
Other, and may thy Queen be one with thee,
And all this Order of thy Table Round
Fulfil the boundless purpose of their King!"
475 So Dubric said; but when they left the shrine
Great Lords from Rome before the portal stood,
In scornful stillness gazing as they past;
Then while they paced a city all on fire
With sun and cloth of gold, the trumpets blew,
480 And Arthur's knighthood sang before the King:—

"Blow trumpet, for the world is white with May;
Blow trumpet, the long night hath roll'd away!
Blow thro' the living world—'Let the King reign.'

"Shall Rome or Heathen rule in Arthur's realm?
485 Flash brand and lance, fall battleaxe upon helm,
Fall battleaxe, and flash brand! Let the King reign.
"Strike for the King and live! his knights have heard.
That God hath told the King a secret word.
Fall battleaxe, and flash brand! Let the King reign.

490 "Blow trumpet! he will lift us from the dust.
Blow trumpet! live the strength and die the lust!
Clang battleaxe, and clash brand! Let the King reign.

"Strike for the King and die! and if thou diest,
The King is King, and ever wills the highest.
495 Clang battleaxe, and clash brand! Let the King reign.

"Blow, for our Sun is mighty in his May!
Blow, for our Sun is mightier day by day!
Clang battleaxe, and clash brand! Let the King reign.

"The King will follow Christ, and we the King
500   In whom high God hath breathed a secret thing.
Fall battleaxe, and flash brand! Let the King reign."

So sang the knighthood, moving to their hall.
There at the banquet those great Lords from Rome,
The slowly-fading mistress of the world,
505   Strode in, and claim'd their tribute as of yore.
But Arthur spake, "Behold, for these have sworn
To wage my wars, and worship me their King;
The old order changeth, yielding place to new;
And we that fight for our fair father Christ,
510   Seeing that ye be grown too weak and old
To drive the heathen from your Roman wall,
No tribute will we pay:" so those great lords
Drew back in wrath, and Arthur strove with Rome.

And Arthur and his knighthood for a space
515   Were all one will, and thro' that strength the King
Drew in the petty princedoms under him,
Fought, and in twelve great battles overcame
The heathen hordes, and made a realm and reign'd.

1869   1869

The Passing of Arthur[1]

That story which the bold Sir Bedivere,[2]
First made and latest left of all the knights,
Told, when the man was no more than a voice
In the white winter of his age, to those
5   With whom he dwelt, new faces, other minds.

For on their march to westward, Bedivere,
Who slowly paced among the slumbering host,
Heard in his tent the moanings of the King:

"I found Him in the shining of the stars,
10   I marked Him in the flowering of His fields,

---

1. On the composition of this final idyll and its relation to Tennyson's *Morte d'Arthur* of 1842, see p. 161, n.1. The principal source is Malory's *Morte Darthur* 21.4–5. Preceding the action of this idyll, Arthur has been in France with his nephew Gawain, fighting against the forces of Lancelot. Learning at that time of the gathering of an army against him in England, under the leadership of his nephew, Modred, Arthur returns there to engage in his last battle. Upon landing at Dover, Gawain is slain.

2. A knight who has long been close to the king, described in *The Coming of Arthur*, lines 173–74: "Bedivere, the first of all his knights / Knighted by Arthur at his crowning."

But in His ways with men I find Him not.
I waged His wars, and now I pass and die.
O me! for why is all around us here
As if some lesser god had made the world,
15　But had not force to shape it as he would,
Till the High God behold it from beyond,
And enter it, and make it beautiful?
Or else as if the world were wholly fair,
But that these eyes of men are dense and dim,
20　And have not power to see it as it is:
Perchance, because we see not to the close;—
For I, being simple, thought to work His will,
And have but stricken with the sword in vain;
And all whereon I leaned in wife and friend
25　Is traitor to my peace, and all my realm
Reels back into the beast, and is no more.
My God, thou hast forgotten me in my death:[3]
Nay—God my Christ—I pass but shall not die."

　　Then, ere that last weird battle in the west,
30　There came on Arthur sleeping, Gawain killed
In Lancelot's war, the ghost of Gawain blown
Along a wandering wind, and past his ear
Went shrilling. "Hollow, hollow all delight!
Hail, King! tomorrow thou shalt pass away.
35　Farewell! there is an isle of rest for thee.
And I am blown along a wandering wind,
And hollow, hollow, hollow all delight."
And fainter onward, like wild birds that change
Their season in the night and wail their way
40　From cloud to cloud, down the long wind the dream
Shrilled; but in going mingled with dim cries
Far in the moonlit haze among the hills,
As of some lonely city sacked by night,
When all is lost, and wife and child with wail
45　Pass to new lords; and Arthur woke and called,
"Who spake? A dream. O light upon the wind,
Thine, Gawain, was the voice—are these dim cries
Thine? or doth all that haunts the waste and wild
Mourn, knowing it will go along with me?"

50　　This heard the bold Sir Bedivere and spake:
"O me, my King, let pass whatever will,
Elves, and the harmless glamour of the field;[4]
But in their stead thy name and glory cling
To all high places like a golden cloud
55　Forever: but as yet thou shalt not pass.
Light was Gawain in life, and light in death

---

3. Cf. Jesus's cry in Matthew 27.46: "My God, my God, why hast thou forsaken me?"
4. Tennyson said the reference is to "the legends which cluster round the King's name." One legend told of the elves' bestowing gifts on Arthur as a child.

Is Gawain, for the ghost is as the man;
And care not thou for dreams from him, but rise—
I hear the steps of Modred in the west,
60 And with him many of thy people, and knights
Once thine, whom thou hast loved, but grosser grown
Than heathen, spitting at their vows and thee.
Right well in heart they know thee for the King.
Arise, go forth and conquer as of old."

65   Then spake King Arthur to Sir Bedivere:
"Far other is this battle in the west
Whereto we move, than when we strove in youth,
And brake the petty kings, and fought with Rome,
Or thrust the heathen from the Roman wall,[5]
70 And shook him through the north. Ill doom° is mine   *destiny*
To war against my people and my knights.
The king who fights his people fights himself.
And they my knights, who loved me once, the stroke
That strikes them dead is as my death to me.
75 Yet let us hence, and find or feel a way
Through this blind haze, which ever since I saw
One lying in the dust at Almesbury,[6]
Hath folded in the passes of the world."

Then rose the King and moved his host by night,
80 And ever pushed Sir Modred, league by league,
Back to the sunset bound of Lyonnesse[7]—
A land of old upheaven from the abyss
By fire, to sink into the abyss again;
Where fragments of forgotten peoples dwelled,
85 And the long mountains ended in a coast
Of ever-shifting sand, and far away
The phantom circle of a moaning sea.
There the pursuer could pursue no more,
And he that fled no further fly the King;
90 And there, that day when the great light of heaven
Burned at his lowest in the rolling year,
On the waste sand by the waste sea they closed.
Nor ever yet had Arthur fought a fight
Like this last, dim, weird battle of the west.
95 A deathwhite mist slept over sand and sea:
Whereof the chill, to him who breathed it, drew
Down with his blood, till all his heart was cold
With formless fear; and even on Arthur fell
Confusion, since he saw not whom he fought.
100 For friend and foe were shadows in the mist,

5. Hadrian's Wall, built in northern Britain, by the 2nd-century Roman emperor Hadrian as a defense against invaders from the north.
6. The convent to which Guinevere withdraws in the eleventh idyll; during the king's farewell visit to her there, she lies in the dust at his feet.
7. Legendary land, extending west from Cornwall, that sank into the sea.

And friend slew friend not knowing whom he slew;[8]
And some had visions out of golden youth,
And some beheld the faces of old ghosts
Look in upon the battle; and in the mist
105 Was many a noble deed, many a base,
And chance and craft and strength in single fights,
And ever and anon with host to host
Shocks, and the splintering spear, the hard mail hewn,
Shield-breakings, and the clash of brands,° the crash   *swords*
110 Of battleaxes on shattered helms, and shrieks
After the Christ, of those who falling down
Looked up for heaven, and only saw the mist;
And shouts of heathen and the traitor knights,
Oaths, insult, filth, and monstrous blasphemies,
115 Sweat, writhings, anguish, laboring of the lungs
In that close mist, and cryings for the light,
Moans of the dying, and voices of the dead.

    Last, as by some one deathbed after wail
Of suffering, silence follows, or through death
120 Or deathlike swoon, thus over all that shore,
Save for some whisper of the seething seas,
A dead hush fell; but when the dolorous day
Grew drearier toward twilight falling, came
A bitter wind, clear from the North, and blew
125 The mist aside, and with that wind the tide
Rose, and the pale King glanced across the field
Of battle: but no man was moving there;
Nor any cry of Christian heard thereon,
Nor yet of heathen; only the wan wave
130 Brake in among dead faces, to and fro
Swaying the helpless hands, and up and down
Tumbling the hollow helmets of the fallen,
And shivered brands that once had fought with Rome,
And rolling far along the gloomy shores
135 The voice of days of old and days to be.

    Then spake King Arthur to Sir Bedivere,
And whiter than the mist that all day long
Had held the field of battle was the King:

    "Hearest thou this great voice that shakes the world,
140 And wastes the narrow realm whereon we move,
And beats upon the faces of the dead,
My dead, as though they had not died for me?—
O Bedivere, for on my heart hath fallen

---

8. Cf. the description of a battle by the Greek writer Thucydides (ca. 455–ca. 400 B.C.E.) in his *History of the Peloponnesian War* (7.44), in which the invaders become confused by darkness and slaughter many of their own men, and Matthew Arnold's 1851 reworking of this scene in "Dover Beach," lines 35–37 (p. 434).

Confusion, till I know not what I am,
145 Nor whence I am, nor whether I be King.
Behold, I seem but King among the dead."

Then spake the bold Sir Bedivere: "My King,
King everywhere! and so the dead have kings,
There also will I worship thee as King.
150 Yet still thy life is whole, and still I live
Who love thee; but who hates thee, he that brought
The heathen back among us, yonder stands,
Modred, unharmed, the traitor of thine house."

Then spake the King: "My house hath been my doom.
155 But call not thou this traitor of my house
Who hath but dwelled beneath one roof with me.
My house are rather they who sware my vows,
Yea, even while they brake them, owned° me King.   *acknowledged*
And well for thee, saying in my dark hour,
160 When all the purport of my throne hath failed,
That quick or dead thou holdest me for King.
King am I, whatsoever be their cry;
And one last act of kinghood shalt thou see
Yet, ere I pass." And uttering this the King
165 Made at the man: then Modred smote his liege
Hard on that helm which many a heathen sword
Had beaten thin; while Arthur at one blow,
Striking the last stroke with Excalibur,
Slew him, and all but slain himself, he fell.

170 So all day long the noise of battle rolled
Among the mountains by the winter sea;
Until King Arthur's Table, man by man,
Had fallen in Lyonnesse about their lord,
King Arthur. Then, because his wound was deep,
175 The bold Sir Bedivere uplifted him,
And bore him to a chapel nigh the field,
A broken chancel with a broken cross,
That stood on a dark strait of barren land:
On one side lay the Ocean, and on one
180 Lay a great water, and the moon was full.

Then spake King Arthur to Sir Bedivere:
"The sequel of today unsolders all
The goodliest fellowship of famous knights
Whereof this world holds record. Such a sleep
185 They sleep—the men I loved. I think that we
Shall never more, at any future time,
Delight our souls with talk of knightly deeds,
Walking about the gardens and the halls
Of Camelot, as in the days that were.
190 I perish by this people which I made,—
Though Merlin sware that I should come again

To rule once more;[9] but, let what will be, be,
I am so deeply smitten through the helm
That without help I cannot last til morn.
195   Thou therefore take my brand Excalibur,
Which was my pride: for thou rememberest how
In those old days, one summer noon, an arm
Rose up from out the bosom of the lake,
Clothed in white samite,[1] mystic, wonderful,
200   Holding the sword—and how I rowed across
And took it, and have worn it, like a king;
And, wheresoever I am sung or told
In aftertime, this also shall be known:
But now delay not: take Excalibur,
205   And fling him far into the middle mere:°   *middle of the lake*
Watch what thou seëst, and lightly° bring me word."   *quickly*

To him replied the bold Sir Bedivere:
"It is not meet,° Sir King, to leave thee thus,   *fitting*
Aidless, alone, and smitten through the helm—
210   A little thing may harm a wounded man;
Yet I thy hest° will all perform at full,   *command*
Watch what I see, and lightly bring thee word."

So saying, from the ruined shrine he stepped,
And in the moon athwart° the place of tombs,   *across*
215   Where lay the mighty bones of ancient men,
Old knights, and over them the sea-wind sang
Shrill, chill, with flakes of foam. He, stepping down
By zigzag paths, and juts of pointed rock,
Came on the shining levels of the lake.

220   There drew he forth the brand Excalibur,
And o'er him, drawing it, the winter moon,
Brightening the skirts of a long cloud, ran forth
And sparkled keen with frost against the hilt:
For all the haft° twinkled with diamond sparks,   *hilt*
225   Myriads of topaz-lights, and jacinth°-work   *red gem*
Of subtlest jewelry. He gazed so long
That both his eyes were dazzled as he stood,
This way and that dividing the swift mind,
In act to throw: but at the last it seemed
230   Better to leave Excalibur concealed
There in the many-knotted waterflags,
That whistled stiff and dry about the marge.°   *shore*
So strode he back slow to the wounded King.

Then spake King Arthur to Sir Bedivere:
235   "Hast thou performed my mission which I gave?
What is it thou hast seen? or what hast heard?"

9. Cf. Malory, *Morte Darthur* 21.7: "Some men yet say in many parts of England that King Arthur is not dead, but by the will of our Lord in another place. And men say that he will come again."
1. A rich silk fabric.

And answer made the bold Sir Bedivere:
"I heard the ripple washing in the reeds,
And the wild water lapping on the crag."

240 To whom replied King Arthur, faint and pale:
"Thou hast betrayed thy nature and thy name.
Not rendering true answer, as beseemed
Thy fëalty, nor like a noble knight:
For surer sign had followed, either hand,
245 Or voice, or else a motion of the mere.
This is a shameful thing for men to lie.
Yet now, I charge thee, quickly go again,
As thou art lief° and dear, and do the thing   *beloved*
I bade thee, watch, and lightly bring me word."

250 Then went Sir Bedivere the second time
Across the ridge, and paced beside the mere,
Counting the dewy pebbles, fixed in thought;
But when he saw the wonder of the hilt,
How curiously° and strangely chased,° he smote   *skillfully / decorated*
255 His palms together, and he cried aloud:

"And if indeed I cast the brand away,
Surely a precious thing, one worthy note,
Should thus be lost forever from the earth,
Which might have pleased the eyes of many men.
260 What good should follow this, if this were done?
What harm, undone? Deep harm to disobey,
Seeing obedience is the bond of rule.
Were it well to obey then, if a king demand
An act unprofitable, against himself?
265 The King is sick, and knows not what he does.
What record, or what relic of my lord
Should be to aftertime, but empty breath
And rumors of a doubt? But were this kept,
Stored in some treasure-house of mighty kings,
270 Some one might show it at a joust of arms,
Saying, 'King Arthur's sword, Excalibur,
Wrought by the lonely maiden of the Lake.
Nine years she wrought it, sitting in the deeps
Upon the hidden bases of the hills.'
275 So might some old man speak in the aftertime
To all the people, winning reverence.
But now much honor and much fame were lost."

So spake he, clouded with his own conceit,[2]
And hid Excalibur the second time,
280 And so strode back slow to the wounded king.

Then spoke King Arthur, breathing heavily:
"What is it thou hast seen? or what hast heard?"

2. Vain and foolish fancies.

And answer made the bold Sir Bedivere:
"I heard the water lapping on the crag,
285 And the long ripple washing in the reeds."

To whom replied King Arthur, much in wrath:
"Ah, miserable and unkind, untrue,
Unknightly, traitor-hearted! Woe is me!
Authority forgets a dying king,
290 Laid widowed of the power in his eye
That bowed the will. I see thee what thou art,
For thou, the latest-left of all my knights,
In whom should meet the offices of all,
Thou wouldst betray me for the precious hilt;
295 Either from lust of gold, or like a girl
Valuing the giddy pleasure of the eyes.
Yet, for a man may fail in duty twice,
And the third time may prosper, get thee hence:
But, if thou spare to fling Excalibur,
300 I will arise and slay thee with my hands."

Then quickly rose Sir Bedivere, and ran,
And, leaping down the ridges lightly, plunged
Among the bullrush beds, and clutched the sword,
And strongly wheeled and threw it. The great brand
305 Made lightnings in the splendor of the moon,
And flashing round and round and whirled in an arch,
Shot like a streamer of the northern morn,°   *northern lights*
Seen where the moving isles of winter shock[3]
By night, with noises of the Northern Sea.
310 So flashed and fell the brand Excalibur:
But ere he dipped the surface, rose an arm
Clothed in white samite, mystic, wonderful,
And caught him by the hilt, and brandished him
Three times, and drew him under in the mere.
315 And lightly went the other to the King.

Then spoke King Arthur, drawing thicker breath:
"Now see I by thine eyes that this is done.
Speak out: what is it thou hast heard, or seen?"

And answer made the bold Sir Bedivere:
320 "Sir King, I closed mine eyelids, lest the gems
Should blind my purpose, for I never saw,
Nor shall see, here or elsewhere, till I die,
Not though I live three lives of mortal men,
So great a miracle as yonder hilt.
325 Then with both hands I flung him, wheeling him;
But when I looked again, behold an arm,
Clothed in white samite, mystic, wonderful,
That caught him by the hilt, and brandished him
Three times, and drew him under in the mere."

3. Where the icebergs collide.

330　　And answer made King Arthur, breathing hard:
　　"My end draws nigh; 'tis time that I were gone.
　　Make broad thy shoulders to receive my weight,
　　And bear me to the margin; yet I fear
　　My wound hath taken cold, and I shall die."

335　　So saying, from the pavement he half rose,
　　Slowly, with pain, reclining on his arm,
　　And looking wistfully with wide blue eyes
　　As in a picture. Him Sir Bedivere
　　Remorsefully regarded through his tears,
340　　And would have spoken, but he found not words;
　　Then took with care, and kneeling on one knee,
　　O'er both his shoulders drew the languid hands,
　　And rising bore him through the place of tombs.

　　But, as he walked, King Arthur panted hard,
345　　Like one that feels a nightmare on his bed
　　When all the house is mute. So sighed the King,
　　Muttering and murmuring at his ear, "Quick, quick!
　　I fear it is too late, and I shall die."
　　But the other swiftly strode from ridge to ridge,
350　　Clothed with his breath, and looking, as he walked,
　　Larger than human on the frozen hills.
　　He heard the deep behind him, and a cry
　　Before. His own thought drove him like a goad.
　　Dry clashed his harness in the icy caves
355　　And barren chasms, and all to left and right
　　The bare black cliff clanged round him, as he based
　　His feet on juts of slippery crag that rang
　　Sharp-smitten with the dint of armèd heels—
　　And on a sudden, lo! the level lake,
360　　And the long glories of the winter moon.

　　Then saw they how there hove a dusky barge,
　　Dark as a funeral scarf from stem to stern,
　　Beneath them; and descending they were ware°　　　　　　*aware*
　　That all the decks were dense with stately forms,
365　　Black-stoled, black-hooded, like a dream—by these
　　Three Queens with crowns of gold: and from them rose
　　A cry that shivered to the tingling stars,
　　And, as it were one voice, an agony
　　Of lamentation, like a wind that shrills
370　　All night in a waste land, where no one comes,
　　Or hath come, since the making of the world.

　　Then murmured Arthur, "Place me in the barge."
　　So to the barge they came. There those three Queens
　　Put forth their hands, and took the King, and wept.
375　　But she, that rose the tallest of them all
　　And fairest, laid his head upon her lap,
　　And loosed the shattered casque,° and chafed his hands,　　　*helmet*

And called him by his name, complaining loud,
And dropping bitter tears against a brow
380 Striped with dark blood: for all his face was white
And colorless, and like the withered moon
Smote by the fresh beam of the springing east;
And all his greaves and cuisses[4] dashed with drops
Of onset;[5] and the light and lustrous curls—
385 That made his forehead like a rising sun
High from the daïs-throne—were parched with dust;
Or, clotted into points and hanging loose,
Mixed with the knightly growth that fringed his lips.
So like a shattered column lay the King;
390 Not like that Arthur who, with lance in rest,
From spur to plume a star of tournament,
Shot through the lists at Camelot, and charged
Before the eyes of ladies and of kings.

Then loudly cried the bold Sir Bedivere:
395 "Ah! my Lord Arthur, whither shall I go?
Where shall I hide my forehead and my eyes?
For now I see the true old times are dead,
When every morning brought a noble chance,
And every chance brought out a noble knight.
400 Such times have been not since the light[6] that led
The holy Elders with the gift of myrrh.
But now the whole Round Table is dissolved
Which was an image of the mighty world,
And I, the last, go forth companionless,
405 And the days darken round me, and the years,
Among new men, strange faces, other minds."

And slowly answered Arthur from the barge:
"The old order changeth, yielding place to new,
And God fulfills himself in many ways,
410 Lest one good custom should corrupt the world.
Comfort thyself: what comfort is in me?
I have lived my life, and that which I have done
May He within himself make pure! but thou,
If thou shouldst never see my face again,
415 Pray for my soul. More things are wrought by prayer
Than this world dreams of. Wherefore, let thy voice
Rise like a fountain for me night and day.
For what are men better than sheep or goats
That nourish a blind life within the brain,
420 If, knowing God, they lift not hands of prayer
Both for themselves and those who call them friend?
For so the whole round earth is every way
Bound by gold chains about the feet of God.
But now farewell. I am going a long way

4. Armor to protect the front of the thighs. "Greaves": armor to protect the leg below the knee.
5. Blood from battle.
6. I.e., the star that guided the three kings ("Elders") to the infant Jesus at Bethlehem. See Matthew 2.1–12.

425   With these thou seëst—if indeed I go
     (For all my mind is clouded with a doubt)—
     To the island-valley of Avilion;[7]
     Where falls not hail, or rain, or any snow,
     Nor ever wind blows loudly: but it lies
430   Deep-meadowed, happy, fair with orchard lawns
     And bowery hollows crowned with summer sea,
     Where I will heal me of my grievous wound."

     So said he, and the barge with oar and sail
     Moved from the brink, like some full-breasted swan
435   That, fluting a wild carol ere her death,
     Ruffles her pure cold plume, and takes the flood
     With swarthy webs.° Long stood Sir Bedivere   *webbed feet*
     Revolving many memories, till the hull
     Looked one black dot against the verge of dawn,
440   And on the mere the wailing died away.

     But when that moan had passed for evermore,
     The stillness of the dead world's winter dawn
     Amazed him, and he groaned, "The King is gone."
     And therewithal came on him the weird rhyme,[8]
445   "From the great deep to the great deep he goes."

     Whereat he slowly turned and slowly clomb
     The last hard footstep of that iron crag;
     Thence marked the black hull moving yet, and cried,
     "He passes to be King among the dead,
450   And after healing of his grievous wound
     He comes again; but—if he come no more—
     O me, be yon dark Queens in yon black boat,
     Who shrieked and wailed, the three whereat we gazed
     On that high day, when, clothed with living light,
455   They stood before his throne in silence, friends
     Of Arthur, who should help him at his need?"[9]

     Then from the dawn it seemed there came, but faint
     As from beyond the limit of the world,
     Like the last echo born of a great cry,
460   Sounds, as if some fair city were one voice
     Around a king returning from his wars.

     Thereat once more he moved about, and clomb
     Even to the highest he could climb, and saw,
     Straining his eyes beneath an arch of hand,
465   Or thought he saw, the speck that bare the King,
     Down that long water opening on the deep

---

7. Or Avalon; in Celtic mythology and medieval romance, the Vale of the Blessed where heroes enjoyed life after death.
8. In *The Coming of Arthur*, Merlin speaks a mysterious prophecy, in verse, concerning Arthur's birth; see lines 402–10 (p. 232).
9. In *The Coming of Arthur*, Arthur's half-sister Bellicent describes his coronation. See lines 275–78 (p. 229).

Somewhere far off, pass on and on, and go
From less to less and vanish into light.
And the new sun rose bringing the new year.

1833–69   1869

Crossing the Bar[1]

Sunset and evening star,
    And one clear call for me!
And may there be no moaning of the bar,[2]
    When I put out to sea,

5   But such a tide as moving seems asleep,
    Too full for sound and foam,
When that which drew from out the boundless deep
    Turns again home.

Twilight and evening bell,
10   And after that the dark!
And may there be no sadness of farewell,
    When I embark;

For though from out our bourne° of Time and Place   *boundary*
    The flood may bear me far,
15   I hope to see my Pilot face to face
    When I have crossed the bar.

1889   1889

1. Although not the last poem written by Tennyson, "Crossing the Bar" appears, at his request, as
the final poem in all collections of his work.

2. Mournful sound of the ocean beating on a
sand bar at the mouth of a harbor.

ELIZABETH GASKELL
1810–1865

It is ironic that the writer whom contemporaries and future generations knew as
"Mrs. Gaskell" once instructed her sister-in-law that it was "a silly piece of bride-
like affectation not to sign yourself by your proper name." Despite the wifely identity
that the name Mrs. Gaskell connotes, Elizabeth Gaskell, as she always signed herself,
wrote fiction on contemporary social topics that stimulated considerable controversy.
Her first novel, *Mary Barton* (1848), presents a sympathetic picture of the hardships
and the grievances of the working class. Another early novel, *Ruth* (1853), portrays
the seduction and rehabilitation of an unmarried mother.

Elizabeth Cleghorn Gaskell was born in 1810 in Chelsea, on the outskirts of London, to a family that followed Unitarianism, a Christian movement that rejected the doctrine of the Trinity and advocated religious tolerance. Her mother died when Gaskell was one, and the girl was sent to rural Knutsford, in Cheshire, to be raised by her aunt. At the age of twenty-one, she met and married William Gaskell, a Unitarian minister whose chapel was in the industrial city of Manchester. For the first ten years of her marriage, she led the life of a minister's wife, bearing five children, keeping a house, and helping her husband serve his congregation. When her fourth child and only son, William, died at the age of one year, Gaskell became depressed. Her husband encouraged her to write as a way of allaying her grief, and so she produced *Mary Barton*, subtitled *A Tale of Manchester Life*. In the preface to the novel, she wrote that she was inspired by thinking "how deep might be the romance in the lives of some of those who elbowed me daily in the busy streets of the town in which I resided. I had always felt a deep sympathy with the careworn men, who looked as if doomed to struggle through their lives in strange alternations between work and want." Observing the mutual distrust of the rich and the poor, and their accompanying resentments, Gaskell hoped that her novel would help create within her middle-class readership understanding and sympathy for the working classes.

Anonymously published, the novel was widely reviewed and discussed. Gaskell was soon identified as the author; she subsequently developed a wide acquaintance in literary circles. She wrote five more novels and about thirty short stories, many of which were published in Charles Dickens's journal *Household Words* and its successor, *All the Year Round*. The contrasting experiences Gaskell's existence had given her of two ways of life, of rural Knutsford and industrial Manchester, defined the poles of her fiction. Her second novel, *Cranford* (1853), presents a delicate picture of the small events of country village life, a subject to which she returns with greater range and psychological depth in her last novel, *Wives and Daughters* (1866). In *North and South* (1855), Gaskell brings together the two worlds of her fiction in the story of Margaret Hale, a young woman from a village in the south of England who moves to a factory town in the north.

One of the writers Gaskell's literary fame led her to know was Charlotte Brontë, with whom she became friends. When Brontë died in 1855, Gaskell was approached by Patrick Brontë to write the story of his daughter's life. Gaskell's *Life of Charlotte Brontë* (1857) is a masterpiece of English biography and one of her finest portrayals of character. Her focus in the *Life* on the relationship between Brontë's identity as a writer and her role as daughter, sister, and wife reflects the balance Gaskell herself sought between the stories she wove and the people she cared for. Referred to by Dickens as "my dear Scheherazade," Gaskell wrote not just to entertain but also to critique society and to promote social reform.

The Old Nurse's Story[1]

You know, my dears, that your mother was an orphan, and an only child; and I dare say you have heard that your grandfather was a clergyman up in Westmoreland, where I come from. I was just a girl in the village school, when, one day, your grandmother came in to ask the mistress if there was any scholar there who would do for a nurse-maid; and mighty proud I was, I can tell ye, when the mistress called me up, and spoke to my being a good girl at my needle, and a steady honest girl, and one whose parents were very

1. Originally published anonymously in the 1852 Christmas number of Dickens's journal *Household Words*; it was later republished in Gaskell's *Lizzie Leigh, and Other Tales* (1855).

respectable, though they might be poor. I thought I should like nothing better than to serve the pretty young lady, who was blushing as deep as I was, as she spoke of the coming baby, and what I should have to do with it. However, I see you don't care so much for this part of my story, as for what you think is to come, so I'll tell you at once I was engaged,[2] and settled at the parsonage before Miss Rosamond (that was the baby, who is now your mother) was born. To be sure, I had little enough to do with her when she came, for she was never out of her mother's arms, and slept by her all night long; and proud enough was I sometimes when missis trusted her to me. There never was such a baby before or since, though you've all of you been fine enough in your turns; but for sweet winning ways, you've none of you come up to your mother. She took after her mother, who was a real lady born; a Miss Furnivall, a granddaughter of Lord Furnivall's in Northumberland. I believe she had neither brother nor sister, and had been brought up in my lord's family till she had married your grandfather, who was just a curate, son to a shopkeeper in Carlisle—but a clever fine gentleman as ever was—and one who was a right-down hard worker in his parish, which was very wide, and scattered all abroad over the Westmoreland Fells. When your mother, little Miss Rosamond, was about four or five years old, both her parents died in a fortnight—one after the other. Ah! that was a sad time. My pretty young mistress and me was looking for another baby, when my master came home from one of his long rides, wet and tired, and took the fever he died of; and then she never held up her head again, but just lived to see her dead baby, and have it laid on her breast before she sighed away her life. My mistress had asked me, on her death-bed, never to leave Miss Rosamond; but if she had never spoken a word, I would have gone with the little child to the end of the world.

The next thing, and before we had well stilled our sobs, the executors and guardians came to settle the affairs. They were my poor young mistress's own cousin, Lord Furnivall, and Mr. Esthwaite, my master's brother, a shopkeeper in Manchester; not so well to do then, as he was afterwards, and with a large family rising about him. Well! I don't know if it were their settling, or because of a letter my mistress wrote on her death-bed to her cousin, my lord; but somehow it was settled that Miss Rosamond and me were to go to Furnivall Manor House, in Northumberland, and my lord spoke as if it had been her mother's wish that she should live with his family, and as if he had no objections, for that one or two more or less could make no difference in so grand a household. So, though that was not the way in which I should have wished the coming of my bright and pretty pet to have been looked at—who was like a sunbeam in any family, be it never so grand—I was well pleased that all the folks in the Dale should stare and admire, when they heard I was going to be young lady's maid at my Lord Furnivall's at Furnivall Manor.

But I made a mistake in thinking we were to go and live where my lord did. It turned out that the family had left Furnivall Manor House fifty years or more. I could not hear that my poor young mistress had ever been there, though she had been brought up in the family; and I was sorry for that, for I should have liked Miss Rosamond's youth to have passed where her mother's had been.

2. Hired.

My lord's gentleman, from whom I asked as many questions as I durst, said that the Manor House was at the foot of the Cumberland Fells, and a very grand place; that an old Miss Furnivall, a great-aunt of my lord's, lived there, with only a few servants; but that it was a very healthy place, and my lord had thought that it would suit Miss Rosamond very well for a few years, and that her being there might perhaps amuse his old aunt.

I was bidden by my lord to have Miss Rosamond's things ready by a certain day. He was a stern, proud man, as they say all the Lord Furnivalls were; and he never spoke a word more than was necessary. Folk did say he had loved my young mistress; but that, because she knew that his father would object, she would never listen to him, and married Mr. Esthwaite; but I don't know. He never married at any rate. But he never took much notice of Miss Rosamond; which I thought he might have done if he had cared for her dead mother. He sent his gentleman with us to the Manor House, telling him to join him at Newcastle that same evening; so there was no great length of time for him to make us known to all the strangers before he, too, shook us off; and we were left, two lonely young things (I was not eighteen), in the great old Manor House. It seems like yesterday that we drove there. We had left our own dear parsonage very early, and we had both cried as if our hearts would break, though we were travelling in my lord's carriage, which I had thought so much of once. And now it was long past noon on a September day, and we stopped to change horses for the last time at a little smoky town, all full of colliers and miners. Miss Rosamond had fallen asleep, but Mr. Henry told me to waken her, that she might see the park and the Manor House as we drove up. I thought it rather a pity; but I did what he bade me, for fear he should complain of me to my lord. We had left all signs of a town or even a village, and were then inside the gates of a large wild park—not like the parks here in the south, but with rocks, and the noise of running water, and gnarled thorn-trees, and old oaks, all white and peeled with age.

The road went up about two miles, and then we saw a great and stately house, with many trees close around it, so close that in some places their branches dragged against the walls when the wind blew; and some hung broken down; for no one seemed to take much charge of the place;—to lop the wood, or to keep the moss-covered carriage-way in order. Only in front of the house all was clear. The great oval drive was without a weed; and neither tree nor creeper was allowed to grow over the long, many-windowed front; at both sides of which a wing projected, which were each the ends of other side fronts; for the house, although it was so desolate, was even grander than I expected. Behind it rose the Fells, which seemed unenclosed and bare enough; and on the left hand of the house as you stood facing it, was a little old-fashioned flower-garden, as I found out afterwards. A door opened out upon it from the west front; it had been scooped out of the thick dark wood for some old Lady Furnivall; but the branches of the great forest trees had grown and overshadowed it again, and there were very few flowers that would live there at that time.

When we drove up to the great front entrance, and went into the hall I thought we should be lost—it was so large, and vast, and grand. There was a chandelier all of bronze, hung down from the middle of the ceiling; and I had never seen one before, and looked at it all in amaze. Then, at one end of the hall, was a great fire-place, as large as the sides of the houses in my country, with massy andirons and dogs[3] to hold the wood; and by it were heavy old-fashioned sofas. At the opposite end of the hall, to the left as you went in—on the western side—was an organ built into the wall, and so large that it filled up the best part of that end. Beyond it, on the same side, was a door; and opposite, on each side of the fire-place, were also doors leading to the east front; but those I never went through as long as I stayed in the house, so I can't tell you what lay beyond.

The afternoon was closing in, and the hall, which had no fire lighted in it, looked dark and gloomy; but we did not stay there a moment. The old servant who had opened the door for us bowed to Mr. Henry, and took us in through the door at the further side of the great organ, and led us through several smaller halls and passages into the west drawing-room, where he said that Miss Furnivall was sitting. Poor little Miss Rosamond held very tight to me, as if she were scared and lost in that great place, and, as for myself, I was not much better. The west drawing-room was very cheerful-looking, with a warm fire in it, and plenty of good comfortable furniture about. Miss Furnivall was an old lady not far from eighty, I should think, but I do not know. She was thin and tall, and had a face as full of fine wrinkles as if they had been drawn all over it with a needle's point. Her eyes were very watchful, to make up, I suppose, for her being so deaf as to be obliged to use a trumpet.[4] Sitting with her, working at the same great piece of tapestry, was Mrs. Stark, her maid and companion, and almost as old as she was. She had lived with Miss Furnivall ever since they both were young, and now she seemed more like a friend than a servant; she looked so cold and grey, and stony, as if she had never loved or cared for any one; and I don't suppose she did care for any one, except her mistress; and, owing to the great deafness of the latter, Mrs. Stark treated her very much as if she were a child. Mr. Henry gave some message from my lord, and then he bowed good-bye to us all,—taking no notice of my sweet little Miss Rosamond's out-stretched hand—and left us standing there, being looked at by the two old ladies through their spectacles.

I was right glad when they rung for the old footman who had shown us in at first, and told him to take us to our rooms. So we went out of that great drawing-room, and into another sitting-room, and out of that, and then up a great flight of stairs, and along a broad gallery—which was something like a library, having books all down one side, and windows and writing-tables all down the other—till we came to our rooms, which I was not sorry to hear were just over the kitchens; for I began to think I should be lost in that wilderness of a house. There was an old nursery, that had been used for all the little lords and ladies long ago, with a pleasant fire burning in the grate, and the kettle boiling on the hob, and tea things spread out on the table; and out of that room was the night-nursery, with a little crib for Miss Rosamond close to my bed. And old James called up Dorothy, his wife, to bid us welcome; and both he and she were so hospitable and kind, that by-and-by Miss Rosamond and me felt quite at home; and by the time tea was over, she was sitting on Dorothy's knee, and chattering away as fast as her little tongue could go. I

3. Large decorative fireplace supports.
4. A horn-shaped device used by the hard of hearing to amplify sound.

soon found out that Dorothy was from Westmoreland, and that bound her and me together, as it were; and I would never wish to meet with kinder people than were old James and his wife. James had lived pretty nearly all his life in my lord's family, and thought there was no one so grand as they. He even looked down a little on his wife; because, till he had married her, she had never lived in any but a farmer's household. But he was very fond of her, as well he might be. They had one servant under them, to do all the rough work. Agnes they called her; and she and me, and James and Dorothy, with Miss Furnivall and Mrs. Stark, made up the family; always remembering my sweet little Miss Rosamond! I used to wonder what they had done before she came, they thought so much of her now. Kitchen and drawing-room, it was all the same. The hard, sad Miss Furnivall, and the cold Mrs. Stark, looked pleased when she came fluttering in like a bird, playing and pranking hither and thither, with a continual murmur, and pretty prattle of gladness. I am sure, they were sorry many a time when she flitted away into the kitchen, though they were too proud to ask her to stay with them, and were a little surprised at her taste; though, to be sure, as Mrs. Stark said, it was not to be wondered at, remembering what stock her father had come of. The great, old rambling house, was a famous[5] place for little Miss Rosamond. She made expeditions all over it, with me at her heels; all, except the east wing, which was never opened, and whither we never thought of going. But in the western and northern part was many a pleasant room; full of things that were curiosities to us, though they might not have been to people who had seen more. The windows were darkened by the sweeping boughs of the trees, and the ivy which had overgrown them: but, in the green gloom, we could manage to see old China jars and carved ivory boxes, and great heavy books, and, above all, the old pictures!

Once, I remember, my darling would have Dorothy go with us to tell us who they all were; for they were all portraits of some of my lord's family, though Dorothy could not tell us the names of every one. We had gone through most of the rooms, when we came to the old state drawing-room over the hall, and there was a picture of Miss Furnivall; or, as she was called in those days, Miss Grace, for she was the younger sister. Such a beauty she must have been! but with such a set, proud look, and such scorn looking out of her handsome eyes, with her eyebrows just a little raised, as if she wondered how any one could have the impertinence to look at her; and her lip curled at us, as we stood there gazing. She had a dress on, the like of which I had never seen before, but it was all the fashion when she was young; a hat of some soft white stuff like beaver, pulled a little over her brows, and a beautiful plume of feathers sweeping round it on one side; and her gown of blue satin was open in front to a quilted white stomacher.[6]

"Well, to be sure!" said I, when I had gazed my fill. "Flesh is grass,[7] they do say; but who would have thought that Miss Furnivall had been such an out-and-out beauty, to see her now?"

"Yes," said Dorothy. "Folks change sadly. But if what my master's father used to say was true, Miss Furnivall, the elder sister, was handsomer than

---

5. Exciting, wonderful.
6. Ornamental covering for the front of the body. "Beaver": felted wool.
7. Cf. 1 Peter 1.24: "For all flesh is as grass, and all the glory of men as the flower of grass. The grass withereth, and the flower thereof falleth away."

Miss Grace. Her picture is here somewhere; but, if I show it you, you must never let on, even to James, that you have seen it. Can the little lady hold her tongue, think you?" asked she.

I was not so sure, for she was such a little sweet, bold, open-spoken child, so I set her to hide herself; and then I helped Dorothy to turn a great picture, that leaned with its face towards the wall, and was not hung up as the others were. To be sure, it beat Miss Grace for beauty; and, I think, for scornful pride, too, though in that matter it might be hard to choose. I could have looked at it an hour, but Dorothy seemed half frightened of having shown it to me, and hurried it back again, and bade me run and find Miss Rosamond, for that there were some ugly places about the house, where she should like ill for the child to go. I was a brave, high-spirited girl, and thought little of what the old woman said, for I liked hide-and-seek as well as any child in the parish; so off I ran to find my little one.

As winter drew on, and the days grew shorter, I was sometimes almost certain that I heard a noise as if some one was playing on the great organ in the hall. I did not hear it every evening; but, certainly, I did very often; usually when I was sitting with Miss Rosamond, after I had put her to bed, and keeping quite still and silent in the bedroom. Then I used to hear it booming and swelling away in the distance. The first night, when I went down to my supper, I asked Dorothy who had been playing music, and James said very shortly that I was a gowk to take the wind soughing[8] among the trees for music; but I saw Dorothy look at him very fearfully, and Bessy, the kitchen-maid, said something beneath her breath, and went quite white. I saw they did not like my question, so I held my peace till I was with Dorothy alone, when I knew I could get a good deal out of her. So, the next day, I watched my time, and I coaxed and asked her who it was that played the organ; for I knew that it was the organ and not the wind well enough, for all I had kept silence before James. But Dorothy had had her lesson, I'll warrant, and never a word could I get from her. So then I tried Bessy, though I had always held my head rather above her, as I was evened[9] to James and Dorothy, and she was little better than their servant. So she said I must never, never tell; and, if I ever told, I was never to say *she* had told me; but it was a very strange noise, and she had heard it many a time, but most of all on winter nights, and before storms; and folks did say, it was the old lord playing on the great organ in the hall, just as he used to do when he was alive; but who the old lord was, or why he played, and why he played on stormy winter evenings in particular, she either could not or would not tell me. Well! I told you I had a brave heart; and I thought it was rather pleasant to have that grand music rolling about the house, let who would be the player; for now it rose above the great gusts of wind, and wailed and triumphed just like a living creature, and then it fell to a softness most complete; only it was always music and tunes, so it was nonsense to call it the wind. I thought, at first, it might be Miss Furnivall who played, unknown to Bessy; but, one day when I was in the hall by myself, I opened the organ and peeped all about it, and around it, as I had done to the organ in Crosthwaite Church once before, and I saw it was all broken and destroyed inside, though it looked so brave[1] and fine; and then, though it was

---

8. Moaning. "Shortly": curtly. "Gowk": fool.
9. Of equal status.

1. Excellent.

noon-day, my flesh began to creep a little, and I shut it up, and ran away pretty quickly to my own bright nursery; and I did not like hearing the music for some time after that, any more than James and Dorothy did. All this time Miss Rosamond was making herself more and more beloved. The old ladies liked her to dine with them at their early dinner; James stood behind Miss Furnivall's chair, and I behind Miss Rosamond's, all in state; and, after dinner, she would play about in a corner of the great drawing-room, as still as any mouse, while Miss Furnivall slept, and I had my dinner in the kitchen. But she was glad enough to come to me in the nursery afterwards; for, as she said, Miss Furnivall was so sad, and Mrs. Stark so dull; but she and I were merry enough; and, by-and-by, I got not to care for that weird rolling music, which did one no harm, if we did not know where it came from.

That winter was very cold. In the middle of October the frosts began, and lasted many, many weeks. I remember, one day at dinner, Miss Furnivall lifted up her sad, heavy eyes, and said to Mrs. Stark, "I am afraid we shall have a terrible winter," in a strange kind of meaning way. But Mrs. Stark pretended not to hear, and talked very loud of something else. My little lady and I did not care for the frost;—not we! As long as it was dry we climbed up the steep brows, behind the house, and went up on the Fells, which were bleak and bare enough, and there we ran races in the fresh, sharp air; and once we came down by a new path that took us past the two old gnarled holly-trees, which grew about half-way down by the east side of the house. But the days grew shorter and shorter; and the old lord, if it was he, played away more and more stormily and sadly on the great organ. One Sunday afternoon,—it must have been towards the end of November—I asked Dorothy to take charge of little Missey when she came out of the drawing-room, after Miss Furnivall had had her nap; for it was too cold to take her with me to church, and yet I wanted to go. And Dorothy was glad enough to promise, and was so fond of the child that all seemed well; and Bessy and I set off very briskly, though the sky hung heavy and black over the white earth, as if the night had never fully gone away; and the air, though still, was very biting and keen.

"We shall have a fall of snow," said Bessy to me. And sure enough, even while we were in church, it came down thick, in great large flakes, so thick it almost darkened the windows. It had stopped snowing before we came out, but it lay soft, thick and deep beneath our feet, as we tramped home. Before we got to the hall the moon rose, and I think it was lighter then,—what with the moon, and what with the white dazzling snow—than it had been when we went to church, between two and three o'clock. I have not told you that Miss Furnivall and Mrs. Stark never went to church: they used to read the prayers together, in their quiet gloomy way; they seemed to feel the Sunday very long without their tapestry-work to be busy at. So when I went to Dorothy in the kitchen, to fetch Miss Rosamond and take her up-stairs with me, I did not much wonder when the old woman told me that the ladies had kept the child with them, and that she had never come to the kitchen, as I had bidden her, when she was tired of behaving pretty in the drawing-room. So I took off my things and went to find her, and bring her to her supper in the nursery. But when I went into the best drawing-room, there sat the two old ladies, very still and quiet, dropping out a word now and then, but looking as if nothing so bright and merry as Miss Rosamond had ever been near them. Still I thought she might be hiding from me; it was one of her pretty ways;

and that she had persuaded them to look as if they knew nothing about her; so I went softly peeping under this sofa, and behind that chair, making believe I was sadly frightened at not finding her.

"What's the matter, Hester?" said Mrs. Stark sharply. I don't know if Miss Furnivall had seen me, for, as I told you, she was very deaf, and she sat quite still, idly staring into the fire, with her hopeless face. "I'm only looking for my little Rosy-Posy," replied I, still thinking that the child was there, and near me, though I could not see her.

"Miss Rosamond is not here," said Mrs. Stark. "She went away more than an hour ago to find Dorothy." And she too turned and went on looking into the fire.

My heart sank at this, and I began to wish I had never left my darling. I went back to Dorothy and told her. James was gone out for the day, but she and me and Bessy took lights, and went up into the nursery first and then we roamed over the great large house, calling and entreating Miss Rosamond to come out of her hiding place, and not frighten us to death in that way. But there was no answer; no sound.

"Oh!" said I at last, "Can she have got into the east wing and hidden there?"

But Dorothy said it was not possible, for that she herself had never been in there; that the doors were always locked, and my lord's steward had the keys, she believed; at any rate, neither she nor James had ever seen them: so, I said I would go back and see if, after all, she was not hidden in the drawing-room, unknown to the old ladies; and if I found her there, I said, I would whip her well for the fright she had given me; but I never meant to do it. Well, I went back to the west drawing-room, and I told Mrs. Stark we could not find her anywhere, and asked for leave to look all about the furniture there, for I thought now, that she might have fallen asleep in some warm hidden corner; but no! we looked, Miss Furnivall got up and looked, trembling all over, and she was no where there; then we set off again, every one in the house, and looked in all the places we had searched before, but we could not find her. Miss Furnivall shivered and shook so much, that Mrs. Stark took her back into the warm drawing-room; but not before they had made me promise to bring her to them when she was found. Well-a-day! I began to think she never would be found, when I bethought me to look out into the great front court, all covered with snow. I was up-stairs when I looked out; but, it was such clear moonlight, I could see quite plain two little footprints, which might be traced from the hall door, and round the corner of the east wing. I don't know how I got down, but I tugged open the great, stiff hall door; and, throwing the skirt of my gown over my head for a cloak, I ran out. I turned the east corner, and there a black shadow fell on the snow; but when I came again into the moonlight, there were the little footmarks going up— up to the Fells. It was bitter cold; so cold that the air almost took the skin off my face as I ran, but I ran on, crying to think how my poor little darling must be perished[2] and frightened. I was within sight of the holly-trees, when I saw a shepherd coming down the hill, bearing something in his arms wrapped in his maud.[3] He shouted to me, and asked me if I had lost a bairn;[4] and, when

2. Extremely cold.
3. A shawl of gray plaid used by shepherds in the

region.
4. Child.

I could not speak for crying, he bore towards me, and I saw my wee bairnie lying still, and white, and stiff, in his arms, as if she had been dead. He told me he had been up the Fells to gather in his sheep, before the deep cold of night came on, and that under the holly-trees (black marks on the hill-side, where no other bush was for miles around) he had found my little lady—my lamb—my queen—my darling—stiff and cold, in the terrible sleep which is frost-begotten. Oh! the joy, and the tears of having her in my arms once again! for I would not let him carry her; but took her, maud and all, into my own arms, and held her near my own warm neck and heart, and felt the life stealing slowly back again into her little gentle limbs. But she was still insensible when we reached the hall, and I had no breath for speech. We went in by the kitchen door.

"Bring the warming-pan," said I; and I carried her up-stairs and began undressing her by the nursery fire, which Bessy had kept up. I called my little lammie all the sweet and playful names I could think of,—even while my eyes were blinded by my tears; and at last, oh! at length she opened her large blue eyes. Then I put her into her warm bed, and sent Dorothy down to tell Miss Furnivall that all was well; and I made up my mind to sit by my darling's bedside the live-long night. She fell away into a soft sleep as soon as her pretty head had touched the pillow, and I watched by her till morning light; when she wakened up bright and clear—or so I thought at first—and, my dears, so I think now.

She said, that she had fancied that she should like to go to Dorothy, for that both the old ladies were asleep, and it was very dull in the drawing-room; and that, as she was going through the west lobby, she saw the snow through the high window falling—falling—soft and steady; but she wanted to see it lying pretty and white on the ground; so she made her way into the great hall; and then, going to the window, she saw it bright and soft upon the drive; but while she stood there, she saw a little girl, not so old as she was, "but so pretty," said my darling, "and this little girl beckoned to me to come out; and oh, she was so pretty and so sweet, I could not choose but go." And then this other little girl had taken her by the hand, and side by side the two had gone round the east corner.

"Now you are a naughty little girl, and telling stories," said I. "What would your good mamma, that is in heaven, and never told a story in her life, say to her little Rosamond, if she heard her—and I dare say she does—telling stories!"

"Indeed, Hester," sobbed out my child; "I'm telling you true. Indeed I am."

"Don't tell me!" said I, very stern. "I tracked you by your foot-marks through the snow; there were only yours to be seen: and if you had had a little girl to go hand-in-hand with you up the hill, don't you think the foot-prints would have gone along with yours?"

"I can't help it, dear, dear Hester," said she, crying, "if they did not; I never looked at her feet, but she held my hand fast and tight in her little one, and it was very, very cold. She took me up the Fell-path, up to the holly trees; and there I saw a lady weeping and crying; but when she saw me, she hushed her weeping, and smiled very proud and grand, and took me on her knees, and began to lull me to sleep; and that's all, Hester—but that is true; and my dear mamma knows it is," said she, crying. So I thought the child was in a fever, and pretended to believe her, as she went over her story—over and over again, and always the same. At last Dorothy knocked at the door with Miss Rosamond's breakfast; and she told me the old ladies were down in the eating-parlour, and that they wanted to speak to me. They had both been into the night-nursery the evening before, but it was after Miss Rosamond was asleep; so they had only looked at her—not asked me any questions.

"I shall catch it," thought I to myself, as I went along the north gallery. "And yet," I thought, taking courage, "it was in their charge I left her; and it's they that's to blame for letting her steal away unknown and unwatched." So I went in boldly, and told my story. I told it all to Miss Furnivall, shouting it close to her ear; but when I came to the mention of the other little girl out in the snow, coaxing and tempting her out, and willing her up to the grand and beautiful lady by the Holly-tree, she threw her arms up—her old and withered arms—and cried aloud, "Oh! Heaven, forgive! Have mercy!"

Mrs. Stark took hold of her; roughly enough, I thought; but she was past Mrs. Stark's management, and spoke to me, in a kind of wild warning and authority.

"Hester! keep her from that child! It will lure her to her death! That evil child! Tell her it is a wicked, naughty child." Then, Mrs. Stark hurried me out of the room; where, indeed, I was glad enough to go; but Miss Furnivall kept shrieking out, "Oh! have mercy! Wilt Thou never forgive! It is many a long year ago——"

I was very uneasy in my mind after that. I durst never leave Miss Rosamond, night or day, for fear lest she might slip off again, after some fancy or other; and all the more, because I thought I could make out that Miss Furnivall was crazy, from their odd ways about her; and I was afraid lest something of the same kind (which might be in the family, you know) hung over my darling. And the great frost never ceased all this time; and, whenever it was a more stormy night than usual, between the gusts, and through the wind, we heard the old lord playing on the great organ. But, old lord, or not, wherever Miss Rosamond went, there I followed; for my love for her, pretty helpless orphan, was stronger than my fear for the grand and terrible sound. Besides, it rested with me to keep her cheerful and merry, as beseemed her age. So we played together, and wandered together, here and there, and everywhere; for I never dared to lose sight of her again in that large and rambling house. And so it happened, that one afternoon, not long before Christmas day, we were playing together on the billiard-table in the great hall (not that we knew the right way of playing, but she liked to roll the smooth ivory balls with her pretty hands, and I liked to do whatever she did); and, by-and-bye, without our noticing it, it grew dusk indoors, though it was still light in the open air, and I was thinking of taking her back into the nursery, when, all of a sudden, she cried out:

"Look, Hester! look! there is my poor little girl out in the snow!"

I turned towards the long narrow windows, and there, sure enough, I saw a little girl, less than my Miss Rosamond—dressed all unfit to be out-of-doors such a bitter night—crying, and beating against the window-panes, as if, she wanted to be let in. She seemed to sob and wail, till Miss Rosamond could bear it no longer, and was flying to the door to open it, when, all of a sudden, and close upon us, the great organ pealed out so loud and thundering, it fairly made me tremble; and all the more, when I remembered me that, even in the stillness of that dead-cold weather, I had heard no sound of little battering hands upon the window-glass, although the Phantom Child had seemed to put forth all its force; and, although I had seen it wail and cry, no faintest touch of sound had fallen upon my ears. Whether I remembered all this at the very moment, I do not know; the great organ sound had so stunned me into terror; but this I know, I caught up Miss Rosamond before she got the hall-door opened, and clutched her, and carried her away, kicking and screaming, into the large bright kitchen, where Dorothy and Agnes were busy with their mince-pies.

"What is the matter with my sweet one?" cried Dorothy, as I bore in Miss Rosamond, who was sobbing as if her heart would break.

"She won't let me open the door for my little girl to come in; and she'll die if she is out on the Fells all night. Cruel, naughty Hester," she said, slapping me; but she might have struck harder, for I had seen a look of ghastly terror on Dorothy's face, which made my very blood run cold.

"Shut the back kitchen door fast, and bolt it well," said she to Agnes. She said no more; she gave me raisins and almonds to quiet Miss Rosamond: but she sobbed about the little girl in the snow, and would not touch any of the good things. I was thankful when she cried herself to sleep in bed. Then I stole down to the kitchen, and told Dorothy I had made up my mind. I would carry my darling back to my father's house in Applethwaite; where, if we lived humbly, we lived at peace. I said I had been frightened enough with the old lord's organ-playing; but now, that I had seen for myself this little moaning child, all decked out as no child in the neighborhood could be, beating and battering to get in, yet always without any sound or noise—with the dark wound on its right shoulder; and that Miss Rosamond had known it again for the phantom that had nearly lured her to her death (which Dorothy knew was true); I would stand it no longer.

I saw Dorothy change color once or twice. When I had done, she told me she did not think I could take Miss Rosamond with me, for that she was my lord's ward, and I had no right over her; and she asked me, would I leave the child that I was so fond of, just for sounds and sights that could do me no harm; and that they had all had to get used to in their turns? I was all in a hot, trembling passion; and I said it was very well for her to talk, that knew what these sights and noises betokened, and that had, perhaps, had something to do with the Spectre-child while it was alive. And I taunted her so, that she told me all she knew, at last; and then I wished I had never been told, for it only made me more afraid than ever.

She said she had heard the tale from old neighbors, that were alive when she was first married; when folks used to come to the hall sometimes, before it had got such a bad name on the country side: it might not be true, or it might, what she had been told.

The old lord was Miss Furnivall's father—Miss Grace, as Dorothy called her, for Miss Maude was the elder, and Miss Furnivall by rights. The old lord was eaten up with pride. Such a proud man was never seen or heard of; and his daughters were like him. No one was good enough to wed them, although they had choice enough; for they were the great beauties of their day, as I had seen by their portraits, where they hung in the state drawing-room. But, as the old saying is, "Pride will have a fall;" and these two haughty beauties fell in love with the same man, and he no better than a foreign musician, whom their father had down from London to play music with him at the Manor

House. For, above all things, next to his pride, the old lord loved music. He could play on nearly every instrument that ever was heard of; and it was a strange thing it did not soften him; but he was a fierce dour old man, and had broken his poor wife's heart with his cruelty, they said. He was mad after music, and would pay any money for it. So he got this foreigner to come; who made such beautiful music, that they said the very birds on the trees stopped their singing to listen. And, by degrees, this foreign gentleman got such a hold over the old lord, that nothing would serve him but that he must come every year; and it was he that had the great organ brought from Holland and built up in the hall, where it stood now. He taught the old lord to play on it; but many and many a time, when Lord Furnivall was thinking of nothing but his fine organ, and his finer music, the dark foreigner was walking abroad in the woods with one of the young ladies; now Miss Maude, and then Miss Grace.

Miss Maude won the day and carried off the prize, such as it was; and he and she were married, all unknown to any one; and before he made his next yearly visit, she had been confined of[5] a little girl at a farm-house on the Moors, while her father and Miss Grace thought she was away at Doncaster Races. But though she was a wife and a mother, she was not a bit softened, but as haughty and as passionate as ever; and perhaps more so, for she was jealous of Miss Grace, to whom her foreign husband paid a deal of court—by way of blinding her—as he told his wife. But Miss Grace triumphed over Miss Maude, and Miss Maude grew fiercer and fiercer, both with her husband and with her sister; and the former—who could easily shake off what was disagreeable, and hide himself in foreign countries—went away a month before his usual time that summer, and half threatened that he would never come back again. Meanwhile, the little girl was left at the farm-house, and her mother used to have her horse saddled and gallop wildly over the hills to see her once every week, at the very least—for where she loved, she loved; and where she hated, she hated. And the old lord went on playing—playing on his organ; and the servants thought the sweet music he made had soothed down his awful temper, of which (Dorothy said) some terrible tales could be told. He grew infirm too, and had to walk with a crutch; and his son—that was the present Lord Furnivall's father—was with the army in America, and the other son at sea; so Miss Maude had it pretty much her own way, and she and Miss Grace grew colder and bitterer to each other every day; till at last they hardly ever spoke, except when the old lord was by. The foreign musician came again the next summer, but it was for the last time; for they led him such a life with their jealousy and their passions, that he grew weary, and went away, and never was heard of again. And Miss Maude, who had always meant to have her marriage acknowledged when her father should be dead, was left now a deserted wife—whom nobody knew to have been married—with a child that she dared not own, although she loved it to distraction; living with a father whom she feared, and a sister whom she hated. When the next summer passed over and the dark foreigner never came, both Miss Maude and Miss Grace grew gloomy and sad; they had a haggard look about them, though they looked handsome as ever. But by and by Miss Maude brightened; for her father grew more and more infirm, and more than

5. Given birth to.

ever carried away by his music; and she and Miss Grace lived almost entirely apart, having separate rooms, the one on the west side—Miss Maude on the east—those very rooms which were now shut up. So she thought she might have her little girl with her, and no one need ever know except those who dared not speak about it, and were bound to believe that it was, as she said, a cottager's child she had taken a fancy to. All this, Dorothy said, was pretty well known; but what came afterwards no one knew, except Miss Grace, and Mrs. Stark, who was even then her maid, and much more of a friend to her than ever her sister had been. But the servants supposed, from words that were dropped, that Miss Maude had triumphed over Miss Grace, and told her that all the time the dark foreigner had been mocking her with pretended love—he was her own husband; the colour left Miss Grace's cheek and lips that very day for ever, and she was heard to say many a time that sooner or later she would have her revenge; and Mrs. Stark was for ever spying about the east rooms.

One fearful night, just after the New Year had come in, when the snow was lying thick and deep, and the flakes were still falling—fast enough to blind any one who might be out and abroad—there was a great and violent noise heard, and the old lord's voice above all, cursing and swearing awfully,—and the cries of a little child,—and the proud defiance of a fierce woman,—and the sound of a blow,—and a dead stillness,—and moans and wailings dying away on the hill-side! Then the old lord summoned all his servants, and told them, with terrible oaths, and words more terrible, that his daughter had disgraced herself, and that he had turned her out of doors,—her, and her child,—and that if ever they gave her help,—or food—or shelter,—he prayed that they might never enter Heaven. And, all the while, Miss Grace stood by him, white and still as any stone; and when he had ended <u>she heaved a great sigh, as much as to say her work was done, and her end was accomplished</u>. But the old lord never touched his organ again, and died within the year; and no wonder! for, on the morrow of that wild and fearful night, the shepherds, coming down the Fell side, found Miss Maude sitting, all crazy and smiling, under the holly-trees, nursing a dead child,—with a terrible mark on its right shoulder. "But that was not what killed it," said Dorothy; "it was the frost and the cold—every wild creature was in its hole, and every beast in its fold,— while the child and its mother were turned out to wander on the Fells! And now you know all! and I wonder if you are less frightened now?"

I was more frightened than ever; but I said I was not. I wished Miss Rosamond and myself well out of that dreadful house for ever; but I would not leave her, and I dared not take her away. But oh! how I watched her, and guarded her! We bolted the doors, and shut the window-shutters fast, an hour or more before dark, rather than leave them open five minutes too late. But my little lady still heard the weird child crying and mourning; and not all we could do or say, could keep her from wanting to go to her, and let her in from the cruel wind and the snow. All this time, I kept away from Miss Furnivall and Mrs. Stark, as much as ever I could; for I feared them—I knew no good could be about them, with their grey hard faces, and their dreamy eyes, looking back into the ghastly years that were gone. But, even in my fear, I had a kind of pity—for Miss Furnivall, at least. Those gone down to the pit[6] can hardly have a more hopeless look than that which

6. Hell.

was ever on her face. At last I even got so sorry for her—who never said a word but what was quite forced from her—that I prayed for her; and I taught Miss Rosamond to pray for one who had done a deadly sin; but often when she came to those words, she would listen, and start up from her knees, and say, "I hear my little girl plaining[7] and crying very sad—Oh! let her in, or she will die!"

One night—just after New Year's Day had come at last, and the long winter had taken a turn as I hoped—I heard the west drawing-room bell ring three times, which was the signal for me. I would not leave Miss Rosamond alone, for all she was asleep—for the old lord had been playing wilder than ever—and I feared lest my darling should waken to hear the spectre child; see her I knew she could not, I had fastened the windows too well for that. So, I took her out of her bed and wrapped her up in such outer clothes as were most handy, and carried her down to the drawing-room, where the old ladies sat at their tapestry work as usual. They looked up when I came in, and Mrs. Stark asked, quite astounded, "Why did I bring Miss Rosamond there, out of her warm bed?" I had begun to whisper, "Because I was afraid of her being tempted out while I was away, by the wild child in the snow," when she stopped me short (with a glance at Miss Furnivall) and said Miss Furnivall wanted me to undo some work she had done wrong, and which neither of them could see to unpick. So, I laid my pretty dear on the sofa, and sat down on a stool by them, and hardened my heart against them as I heard the wind rising and howling.

Miss Rosamond slept on sound, for all the wind blew so; and Miss Furnivall said never a word, nor looked round when the gusts shook the windows. All at once she started up to her full height, and put up one hand as if to bid us listen.

"I hear voices!" said she. "I hear terrible screams—I hear my father's voice!"

Just at that moment, my darling wakened with a sudden start: "My little girl is crying, oh, how she is crying!" and she tried to get up and go to her, but she got her feet entangled in the blanket, and I caught her up; for my flesh had begun to creep at these noises, which they heard while we could catch no sound. In a minute or two the noises came, and gathered fast, and filled our ears; we, too, heard voices and screams, and no longer heard the winter's wind that raged abroad. Mrs. Stark looked at me, and I at her, but we dared not speak. Suddenly Miss Furnivall went towards the door, out into the anteroom, through the west lobby, and opened the door into the great hall. Mrs. Stark followed, and I durst not be left, though my heart almost stopped beating for fear. I wrapped my darling tight in my arms, and went out with them. In the hall the screams were louder than ever; they sounded to come from the east wing—nearer and nearer—close on the other side of the locked-up doors—close behind them. Then I noticed that the great bronze chandelier seemed all alight, though the hall was dim, and that a fire was blazing in the vast hearth-place, though it gave no heat; and I shuddered up with terror, and folded my darling closer to me. But as I did so, the east door shook, and she, suddenly struggling to get free from me, cried, "Hester! I must go! My little girl is there; I hear her; she is coming! Hester, I must go!"

7. Lamenting.

I held her tight with all my strength; with a set will, I held her. If I had died, my hands would have grasped her still; I was so resolved in my mind. Miss Furnivall stood listening, and paid no regard to my darling, who had got down to the ground, and whom I, upon my knees now, was holding with both my arms clasped round her neck; she still striving and crying to get free.

All at once, the east door gave way with a thundering crash, as if torn open in a violent passion, and there came into that broad and mysterious light, the figure of a tall old man, with grey hair and gleaming eyes. He drove before him, with many a relentless gesture of abhorrence, a stern and beautiful woman, with a little child clinging to her dress.

"Oh Hester! Hester!" cried Miss Rosamond. "It's the lady! the lady below the holly-trees; and my little girl is with her. Hester! Hester! let me go to her; they are drawing me to them. I feel them—I feel them. I must go!"

Again she was almost convulsed by her efforts to get away; but I held her tighter and tighter; till I feared I should do her a hurt; but rather that than let her go towards those terrible phantoms. They passed along towards the great hall-door, where the winds howled and ravened for their prey; but before they reached that, the lady turned; and I could see that she defied the old man with a fierce and proud defiance; but then she quailed—and then she threw up her arms wildly and piteously to save her child—her little child—from a blow from his uplifted crutch.

And Miss Rosamond was torn as by a power stronger than mine, and writhed in my arms, and sobbed (for by this time the poor darling was growing faint).

"They want me to go with them on to the Fells—they are drawing me to them. Oh, my little girl! I would come, but cruel, wicked Hester holds me very tight." But when she saw the uplifted crutch she swooned away, and I thanked God for it. Just at this moment—when the tall old man, his hair streaming as in the blast of a furnace, was going to strike the little shrinking child—Miss Furnivall, the old woman by my side, cried out, "Oh, father! father! spare the little innocent child!" But just then I saw—we all saw—another phantom shape itself, and grow clear out of the blue and misty light that filled the hall; we had not seen her till now, for it was another lady who stood by the old man, with a look of relentless hate and triumphant scorn. That figure was very beautiful to look upon, with a soft white hat drawn down over the proud brows, and a red and curling lip. It was dressed in an open robe of blue satin. I had seen that figure before. It was the likeness of Miss Furnivall in her youth; and the terrible phantoms moved on, regardless of old Miss Furnivall's wild entreaty,—and the uplifted crutch fell on the right shoulder of the little child, and the younger sister looked on, stony and deadly serene. But at that moment, the dim lights, and the fire that gave no heat, went out of themselves, and Miss Furnivall lay at our feet stricken down by the palsy—death-stricken.

Yes! she was carried to her bed that night never to rise again. She lay with her face to the wall, muttering low but muttering alway: "Alas! alas! what is done in youth can never be undone in age! What is done in youth can never be undone in age!"

1852

ghosts re-enact the pivotal moment, crux of Ms. Furnivall's sinful youth

CHARLES DICKENS
1812–1870

Charles Dickens was Victorian England's most beloved and distinctive novelist. In the words of the eulogy that the classicist Benjamin Jowett spoke at his funeral service, Dickens "occupied a greater space than any other writer during the last thirty-five years. We read him, talked about him, acted him; we laughed with him, we were roused by him to a consciousness of the misery of others, and to a pathetic [i.e., emotional] interest in human life."

Dickens was born the second of eight children in the coastal town of Portsmouth in southern England. His father, a clerk in the Naval Pay Office, found it difficult to keep his family out of debt. Plagued by financial insecurity, the family moved from place to place, to increasingly poorer lodgings, finally ending up in London. In an effort to help the family out, a friend of his father's offered Charles a job at a blacking warehouse, an enterprise that produced shoe polish. Two days before his twelfth birthday, Charles began work, labeling bottles for six shillings a week. Two weeks later his father was arrested and sent to the Marshalsea Prison for debt. His family went to live in prison with him, as was the custom; they decided that Charles should remain outside, continuing to work and living with a woman who took in young lodgers.

Some thirty-five years after this period, Dickens told his friend and eventual biographer John Forster that the recollection of these times "haunted him and made him miserable, even to that hour." He began to compose an autobiographical account for Forster but soon abandoned it to write instead his most personal novel, *David Copperfield*, in which the titular character undergoes a similar class fall into menial employment at the age of twelve. It has long been a scholarly and popular commonplace that this early experience constituted a trauma that accounts for the emotional concerns of Dickens's fiction, particularly its pronounced sympathy for the figure of the abused or abandoned child. Critics now counter that the suffering of the blacking factory period may have been retrospectively, if unconsciously, shaped by the middle-aged novelist to provide himself with an explanatory primal scene for his subsequent psychological development. Either way, the topic of childhood is unquestionably important throughout Dickens's novels and stories; their attention to this stage of life marked a new and influential emphasis in British fiction.

Dickens's father was able to leave debtors prison after three months, upon receipt of a legacy from his mother. He removed Charles from the factory and sent him to school. At fifteen Dickens began work as a junior clerk at a law office; eighteen months later he became a freelance journalist, reporting court proceedings and then debates in the House of Commons. Reporting led him to other kinds of writing. He began publishing literary sketches, at first anonymously and then under the pseudonym "Boz." In 1836, on his twenty-fourth birthday, he published the collection *Sketches by Boz*. The success of the volume led to a commission from the publishers Chapman & Hall to provide amusing text to accompany serial installments of a set of illustrations of hunting, shooting, and sporting scenes. The result, *Pickwick Papers* (1836–37), brought Dickens fame and prosperity. This picaresque novel, relating the adventures of Mr. Pickwick and his friends as they travel around England, set the pattern of illustrated serial publication that was to define Dickens's writing career and to shape the reading habits of his generation. Families would wait in suspense for the next installment of a novel to be issued, which they would read aloud as an evening's entertainment. Successes followed quickly: *Oliver Twist* (1838), *Nicholas Nickleby* (1838–39), and *The Old Curiosity Shop* (1840–41).

Through the 1840s and 1850s Dickens continued to write novels at an intense pace, producing *Barnaby Rudge* (1841), *Martin Chuzzlewit* (1843–44), *Dombey and Son* (1846–48), *David Copperfield* (1849–50), *Bleak House* (1852–53), *Hard Times* (1854), *Little Dorrit* (1855–57), and *A Tale of Two Cities* (1859). He also became deeply involved in a number of other activities, including traveling, working for charities, and acting. During this time he founded and edited the weekly magazine *Household Words* (incorporated in 1859 into *All the Year Round*), which published fiction by Elizabeth Gaskell, Wilkie Collins, Dickens himself, and other novelists as well as opinion pieces about political and social issues. And he began a series of Christmas books, the first of which was the phenomenally successful tale, *A Christmas Carol* (1843). Almost as beloved as the text are its illustrations: *A Christmas Carol* featured four hand-colored etchings and four black-and-white engravings by the artist John Leech (1817–1864). All eight are included in the text below.

At the time of *Pickwick's* completion, Dickens had married Catherine Hogarth, the daughter of a fellow journalist, and had begun a family; they eventually had ten children. Domestic chaos would come increasingly to frustrate him. Dickens left his wife in 1858; his response to rumors about the separation was to publish a denial in *Household Words*, subsequently reprinted in other newspapers, that provided little by way of clarification and was followed by another statement suggesting that it was only through the efforts of Catherine's sister Georgina that the household had been kept together as long as it had. In truth Dickens was secretly involved with Ellen Ternan, an actress some twenty-seven years his junior. Ostensibly alone, he took up residence at Gad's Hill, a gentleman's house in Kent. Dickens now abandoned amateur theatricals to embark on a series of lucrative professional readings, which were so emotionally and physically exhausting his doctor finally instructed him to stop. He slowed the pace of his writing, publishing only two novels in the 1860s: *Great Expectations* (1860–61) and *Our Mutual Friend* (1864–65). He died suddenly in 1870, leaving his last novel, *The Mystery of Edwin Drood* (1870), unfinished.

The popularity of Dickens's writings with general readers coupled with their many film and television adaptations has given his work a broad and continuous cultural afterlife. Back in 1870, fellow novelist Anthony Trollope observed that no other writer except Shakespeare has left so many "characters which are known by their names familiarly as household words, and which bring to our minds vividly and at once, a certain well-understood set of ideas, habits, phrases and costumes, making together a man, or woman, or child, whom we know at a glance and recognize at a sound, as we do our own intimate friends." But the scale of Dickens's achievement is by no means limited to his ability to construct memorably distinctive human beings. A master-plotter, a writer of extraordinarily evocative prose, and a keen observer of his developing country, he also created fictions shot through with fierce social criticism; as the playwright George Bernard Shaw wrote in 1937, "Dickens never regarded himself as a revolutionist, though he certainly was one." Dickens's early novels often concern specific abuses—the workhouses in which pauper children were confined in *Oliver Twist*, abusive and fraudulent schools in *Nicholas Nickleby*—but, as his career progressed, he felt an increasing urgency to mount a broader attack, demonstrating how the acts of powerful institutions and individuals alike belied the tenets of the compassionate religion they claimed to embrace.

Dickens hoped his stories would trigger the moral regeneration of his readers and thus work to counteract the uncaring tendencies of a highly inequitable era. *A Christmas Carol* is perhaps the most famous example of a Dickens fiction that propelled enduring characters into the world: Scrooge with his anti-Christmas refrain "Bah! Humbug!" is the archetype of a life-denying miser; crippled Tiny Tim and his words "God bless us every one!" provide the epitome of a saintly suffering child. And in its desire, in Dickens's words, to "awaken some loving and forebearing thoughts, never out of season in a Christian land," *A Christmas Carol* connects directly to the novelist's campaign to bring about the transformation of the individual human heart and assert the values of hearth and home.

Mr. Fezziwig's Ball

See n. 1 on p. 264 for identification of this image.

A Christmas Carol

Stave[1] One

MARLEY'S GHOST

Marley was dead: to begin with. There is no doubt whatever about that. The register of his burial was signed by the clergyman, the clerk, the undertaker, and the chief mourner. Scrooge signed it: and Scrooge's name was good upon 'Change,[2] for anything he chose to put his hand to. Old Marley was as dead as a door-nail.

Mind! I don't mean to say that I know, of my own knowledge, what there is particularly dead about a door-nail. I might have been inclined, myself, to regard a coffin-nail as the deadest piece of ironmongery in the trade. But the wisdom of our ancestors is in the simile; and my unhallowed hands shall not disturb it, or the Country's done for. You will therefore permit me to repeat, emphatically, that Marley was as dead as a door-nail.

Scrooge knew he was dead? Of course he did. How could it be otherwise? Scrooge and he were partners for I don't know how many years. Scrooge was his sole executor, his sole administrator, his sole assign, his sole residuary legatee, his sole friend, and sole mourner. And even Scrooge was not so dreadfully cut up by the sad event, but that he was an excellent man of business on the very day of the funeral, and solemnised it with an undoubted bargain.

The mention of Marley's funeral brings me back to the point I started from. There is no doubt that Marley was dead. This must be distinctly understood, or nothing wonderful can come of the story I am going to relate. If we were not perfectly convinced that Hamlet's Father died before the play began, there would be nothing more remarkable in his taking a stroll at night, in an easterly wind, upon his own ramparts, than there would be in any other middle-aged gentleman rashly turning out after dark in a breezy spot—say Saint Paul's Churchyard for instance—literally to astonish his son's weak mind.

Scrooge never painted out Old Marley's name. There it stood, years afterwards, above the warehouse door: Scrooge and Marley. The firm was known as Scrooge and Marley. Sometimes people new to the business called Scrooge Scrooge, and sometimes Marley, but he answered to both names. It was all the same to him.

Oh! But he was a tight-fisted hand at the grindstone, Scrooge! a squeezing, wrenching, grasping, scraping, clutching, covetous old sinner! Hard and sharp as flint, from which no steel had ever struck out generous fire; secret, and self-contained, and solitary as an oyster. The cold within him froze his old features, nipped his pointed nose, shrivelled his cheek, stiffened his gait; made his eyes red, his thin lips blue; and spoke out shrewdly in his grating voice. A frosty rime was on his head, and on his eyebrows, and his wiry chin. He carried his own low temperature always about with him; he iced his office in the dog-days;[3] and didn't thaw it one degree at Christmas.

---

1. Staff (archaic); a stanza of a song or poem. This term extends the idea that the story is a Christmas carol in prose. The illustration on page 263, of Mr. Fezziwig's Ball, appeared as the volume's frontispiece when the story was first published.

2. I.e., that Scrooge had good credit at the Royal Exchange, the center of London's financial world.
3. From July 3 to August 11, often the hottest days of the year, when the Dog Star, Sirius, rises and sets with the sun.

External heat and cold had little influence on Scrooge. No warmth could warm, nor wintry weather chill him. No wind that blew was bitterer than he, no falling snow was more intent upon its purpose, no pelting rain less open to entreaty. Foul weather didn't know where to have him. The heaviest rain, and snow, and hail, and sleet, could boast of the advantage over him in only one respect. They often "came down" handsomely, and Scrooge never did.

Nobody ever stopped him in the street to say, with gladsome looks, "My dear Scrooge, how are you? when will you come to see me?" No beggars implored him to bestow a trifle, no children asked him what it was o'clock, no man or woman ever once in all his life inquired the way to such and such a place, of Scrooge. Even the blindmen's dogs appeared to know him; and when they saw him coming on, would tug their owners into doorways and up courts; and then would wag their tails as though they said, "no eye at all is better than an evil eye, dark master!"

But what did Scrooge care! It was the very thing he liked. To edge his way along the crowded paths of life, warning all human sympathy to keep its distance, was what the knowing ones call "nuts" to Scrooge.[4]

Once upon a time—of all the good days in the year, on Christmas Eve— old Scrooge sat busy in his counting-house. It was cold, bleak, biting weather: foggy withal: and he could hear the people in the court outside go wheezing up and down, beating their hands upon their breasts, and stamping their feet upon the pavement-stones to warm them. The city clocks had only just gone three, but it was quite dark already: it had not been light all day: and candles were flaring in the windows of the neighbouring offices, like ruddy smears upon the palpable brown air. The fog came pouring in at every chink and keyhole, and was so dense without, that although the court was of the narrowest, the houses opposite were mere phantoms. To see the dingy cloud come drooping down, obscuring everything, one might have thought that Nature lived hard by, and was brewing on a large scale.

The door of Scrooge's counting-house was open that he might keep his eye upon his clerk, who in a dismal little cell beyond, a sort of tank, was copying letters. Scrooge had a very small fire, but the clerk's fire was so very much smaller that it looked like one coal. But he couldn't replenish it, for Scrooge kept the coal-box in his own room; and so surely as the clerk came in with the shovel, the master predicted that it would be necessary for them to part. Wherefore the clerk put on his white comforter, and tried to warm himself at the candle; in which effort, not being a man of a strong imagination, he failed.

"A merry Christmas, uncle! God save you!" cried a cheerful voice. It was the voice of Scrooge's nephew, who came upon him so quickly that this was the first intimation he had of his approach.

"Bah!" said Scrooge, "Humbug!"[5]

He had so heated himself with rapid walking in the fog and frost, this nephew of Scrooge's, that he was all in a glow; his face was ruddy and handsome; his eyes sparkled, and his breath smoked again.

"Christmas a humbug, uncle!" said Scrooge's nephew. "You don't mean that, I am sure."

---

4. Agreeable or pleasing to Scrooge (slang).
5. Deceptive, or hypocritical, talk or behavior (slang).

"I do," said Scrooge. "Merry Christmas! what right have you to be merry? what reason have you to be merry? You're poor enough."

"Come, then," returned the nephew gaily. "What right have you to be dismal? what reason have you to be morose? You're rich enough."

Scrooge having no better answer ready on the spur of the moment, said, "Bah!" again; and followed it up with "Humbug."

"Don't be cross, uncle," said the nephew.

"What else can I be" returned the uncle, "when I live in such a world of fools as this? Merry Christmas! Out upon merry Christmas! What's Christmas time to you but a time for paying bills without money; a time for finding yourself a year older, and not an hour richer; a time for balancing your books and having every item in 'em through a round dozen of months presented dead against you? If I could work my will," said Scrooge, indignantly, "every idiot who goes about with 'Merry Christmas,' on his lips, should be boiled with his own pudding, and buried with a stake of holly through his heart. He should!"

"Uncle!" pleaded the nephew.

"Nephew!" returned the uncle, sternly, "keep Christmas in your own way, and let me keep it in mine."

"Keep it!" repeated Scrooge's nephew. "But you don't keep it."

"Let me leave it alone, then," said Scrooge. "Much good may it do you! Much good it has ever done you!"

"There are many things from which I might have derived good, by which I have not profited, I dare say," returned the nephew: "Christmas among the rest. But I am sure I have always thought of Christmas time, when it has come round—apart from the veneration due to its sacred name and origin, if anything belonging to it can be apart from that—as a good time: a kind, forgiving, charitable, pleasant time: the only time I know of, in the long calendar of the year, when men and women seem by one consent to open their shut-up hearts freely, and to think of people below them as if they really were fellow-passengers to the grave, and not another race of creatures bound on other journeys. And therefore, uncle, though it has never put a scrap of gold or silver in my pocket, I believe that it *has* done me good, and *will* do me good; and I say, God bless it!"

The clerk in the tank involuntarily applauded: becoming immediately sensible of the impropriety, he poked the fire, and extinguished the last frail spark for ever.

"Let me hear another sound from *you*" said Scrooge, "and you'll keep your Christmas by losing your situation. You're quite a powerful speaker, sir," he added, turning to his nephew. "I wonder you don't go into Parliament."

"Don't be angry, uncle. Come! Dine with us to-morrow."

Scrooge said that he would see him—yes, indeed he did. He went the whole length of the expression, and said that he would see him in that extremity first.[6]

"But why?" cried Scrooge's nephew. "Why?"

"Why did you get married?" said Scrooge.

"Because I fell in love."

"Because you fell in love!" growled Scrooge, as if that were the only one thing in the world more ridiculous than a merry Christmas. "Good afternoon!"

6. That is, Scrooge said he would see him damned or in hell.

"Nay, uncle, but you never came to see me before that happened. Why give it as a reason for not coming now?"

"Good afternoon," said Scrooge.

"I want nothing from you; I ask nothing of you; why cannot we be friends?"

"Good afternoon," said Scrooge.

"I am sorry, with all my heart, to find you so resolute. We have never had any quarrel, to which I have been a party. But I have made the trial in homage to Christmas, and I'll keep my Christmas humour to the last. So A Merry Christmas, uncle!"

"Good afternoon!" said Scrooge.

"And A Happy New Year!"

"Good afternoon!" said Scrooge.

His nephew left the room without an angry word, notwithstanding. He stopped at the outer door to bestow the greetings of the season on the clerk, who, cold as he was, was warmer than Scrooge; for he returned them cordially.

"There's another fellow," muttered Scrooge; who overheard him: "my clerk, with fifteen shillings a-week, and a wife and family, talking about a merry Christmas. I'll retire to Bedlam."[7]

This lunatic, in letting Scrooge's nephew out, had let two other people in. They were portly gentlemen, pleasant to behold, and now stood, with their hats off, in Scrooge's office. They had books and papers in their hands, and bowed to him.

"Scrooge and Marley's, I believe," said one of the gentlemen, referring to his list. "Have I the pleasure of addressing Mr. Scrooge, or Mr. Marley?"

"Mr. Marley has been dead these seven years," Scrooge replied. "He died seven years ago, this very night."

"We have no doubt his liberality is well represented by his surviving partner," said the gentleman, presenting his credentials.

It certainly was; for they had been two kindred spirits. At the ominous word "liberality," Scrooge frowned, and shook his head, and handed the credentials back.

"At this festive season of the year, Mr. Scrooge," said the gentleman, taking up a pen, "it is more than usually desirable that we should make some slight provision for the Poor and destitute, who suffer greatly at the present time. Many thousands are in want of common necessaries; hundreds of thousands are in want of common comforts, sir."

"Are there no prisons?" asked Scrooge.

"Plenty of prisons," said the gentleman, laying down the pen again.

"And the Union workhouses?" demanded Scrooge. "Are they still in operation?"

---

7. I.e., Bethlehem, the shortened name of the country's most famous asylum for the insane, London's Hospital of St. Mary of Bethlehem. The term became a synonym for *madhouse*.

8. Funded by local taxation and intended to give financial and material help to those unable to provide for themselves, first instituted in the 16th century. A supposedly rationalizing and cost-cutting Poor Law Amendment Act (known as the "New Poor Law") had been passed in 1834; Dickens wrote *Oliver Twist* (1837) in part as a protest against the severity of some of its measures. Fore-most among these was the replacement of parish "outrelief" (assistance from the local administrative district that had allowed the needy to continue living in their own homes) by "Union workhouses": applicants for help now had to move into large centralized institutions run by newly created unions of parishes. "Treadmill": a method of criminal punishment, first introduced in London's Brixton Prison in 1821, in which prisoners were forced to walk on the steps of a large revolving wheel to power a grain mill.

"They are. Still," returned the gentleman, "I wish I could say they were not."

"The Treadmill and the Poor Law[8] are in full vigour, then?" said Scrooge.

"Both very busy, sir."

"Oh! I was afraid, from what you said at first, that something had occurred to stop them in their useful course," said Scrooge. "I'm very glad to hear it."

"Under the impression that they scarcely furnish Christian cheer of mind or body to the multitude," returned the gentleman, "a few of us are endeavouring to raise a fund to buy the Poor some meat and drink, and means of warmth. We choose this time, because it is a time, of all others, when Want is keenly felt, and Abundance rejoices. What shall I put you down for?"

"Nothing!" Scrooge replied.

"You wish to be anonymous?"

"I wish to be left alone," said Scrooge. "Since you ask me what I wish, gentlemen, that is my answer. I don't make merry myself at Christmas, and I can't afford to make idle people merry. I help to support the establishments I have mentioned: they cost enough: and those who are badly off must go there."

"Many can't go there; and many would rather die."

"If they would rather die," said Scrooge, "they had better do it, and decrease the surplus population.[9] Besides—excuse me—I don't know that."

"But you might know it," observed the gentleman.

"It's not my business," Scrooge returned. "It's enough for a man to understand his own business, and not to interfere with other people's. Mine occupies me constantly. Good afternoon, gentlemen!"

Seeing clearly that it would be useless to pursue their point, the gentlemen withdrew. Scrooge resumed his labours with an improved opinion of himself, and in a more facetious temper than was usual with him.

Meanwhile the fog and darkness thickened so, that people ran about with flaring links,[1] proffering their services to go before horses in carriages, and conduct them on their way. The ancient tower of a church, whose gruff old bell was always peeping slily down at Scrooge out of a gothic window in the wall, became invisible, and struck the hours and quarters in the clouds, with tremulous vibrations afterwards, as if its teeth were chattering in its frozen head up there. The cold became intense. In the main street, at the corner of the court, some labourers were repairing the gas-pipes, and had lighted a great fire in a brazier, round which a party of ragged men and boys were gathered: warming their hands and winking their eyes before the blaze in rapture. The water-plug[2] being left in solitude, its overflowing sullenly congealed, and turned to misanthropic ice. The brightness of the shops where holly sprigs and berries crackled in the lamp-heat of the windows, made pale faces ruddy as they passed. Poulterers' and grocers' trades became a splendid joke: a glorious pageant, with which it was next to impossible to believe that such dull principles as bargain and sale had anything to do. The Lord Mayor, in the stronghold of the mighty Mansion House,[3] gave orders to his fifty cooks and

9. A reference to the famous *Essay on the Principle of Population* (1803) by the political economist Thomas Robert Malthus (1766–1834), which predicts that population, if left unchecked, increases more rapidly than the supply of food. The "surplus," in Malthus's opinion, is made up of those who cannot be supported by their parents and whose labor is unwanted by society; a man in this condition, he writes, "has no claim of *right* to the smallest portion of food, and, in fact, has no business to be where he is."
1. Torches made of cloth dipped in tar.
2. Fire hydrant.
3. The official residence of the Lord Mayor in the City, London's commercial and financial district.

butlers to keep Christmas as a Lord Mayor's household should; and even the little tailor, whom he had fined five shillings on the previous Monday for being drunk and blood-thirsty in the streets, stirred up to-morrow's pudding in his garret, while his lean wife and the baby sallied out to buy the beef.

Foggier yet, and colder! Piercing, searching, biting cold. If the good Saint Dunstan had but nipped the Evil Spirit's nose with a touch of such weather as that, instead of using his familiar weapons,[4] then indeed he would have roared to lusty purpose. The owner of one scant young nose, gnawed and mumbled by the hungry cold as bones are gnawed by dogs, stooped down at Scrooge's keyhole to regale him with a Christmas carol: but at the first sound of

> "God bless you merry gentleman!
> May nothing you dismay!"

Scrooge seized the ruler with such energy of action, that the singer fled in terror, leaving the keyhole to the fog and even more congenial frost.

At length the hour of shutting up the counting-house arrived. With an ill-will Scrooge dismounted from his stool, and tacitly admitted the fact to the expectant clerk in the Tank, who instantly snuffed his candle out, and put on his hat.

"You'll want all day to-morrow, I suppose?' said Scrooge.

"If quite convenient, Sir."

"It's not convenient," said Scrooge, "and it's not fair. If I was to stop half-a-crown for it,[5] you'd think yourself ill used, I'll be bound?"

The clerk smiled faintly.

"And yet," said Scrooge, "you don't think *me* ill-used, when I pay a day's wages for no work."

The clerk observed that it was only once a year.

"A poor excuse for picking a man's pocket every twenty-fifth of December!" said Scrooge, buttoning his great-coat to the chin. "But I suppose you must have the whole day. Be here all the earlier next morning!"

The clerk promised that he would; and Scrooge walked out with a growl. The office was closed in a twinkling, and the clerk, with the long ends of his white comforter dangling below his waist (for he boasted no great-coat), went down a slide on Cornhill, at the end of a lane of boys, twenty times, in honour of its being Christmas-eve, and then ran home to Camden Town as hard as he could pelt, to play at blindman's-buff.[6]

Scrooge took his melancholy dinner in his usual melancholy tavern; and having read all the newspapers, and beguiled the rest of the evening with his banker's-book, went home to bed. He lived in chambers which had once belonged to his deceased partner. They were a gloomy suite of rooms, in a lowering pile of building up a yard, where it had so little business to be, that one could scarcely help fancying it must have run there when it was a young house, playing at hide-and-seek with other houses, and have forgotten the way out again. It was old enough now, and dreary enough, for nobody lived

---

4. According to legend, the devil once leaned through Dunstan's workshop window to try to tempt him away from his labor. Dunstan, patron saint of armor makers, blacksmiths, goldsmiths, locksmiths, and musicians, responded by seizing the devil's nose with red-hot pincers.
5. Two shillings and sixpence, one sixth of Cratchit's weekly salary.
6. A popular parlor game, in which one person is blindfolded and then must catch another player and guess whom he or she has caught. Cornhill is a major street in the City. Camden Town is a district in inner northeast London.

in it but Scrooge, the other rooms being all let out as offices. The yard was so dark that even Scrooge, who knew its every stone, was fain to grope with his hands. The fog and frost so hung about the black old gateway of the house, that it seemed as if the Genius of the Weather sat in mournful meditation on the threshold.

Now, it is a fact, that there was nothing at all particular about the knocker on the door, except that it was very large. It is also a fact, that Scrooge had seen it night and morning during his whole residence in that place; also that Scrooge had as little of what is called fancy about him as any man in the City of London, even including—which is a bold word—the corporation, aldermen, and livery.[7] Let it also be borne in mind that Scrooge had not bestowed one thought on Marley, since his last mention of his seven-years' dead partner that afternoon. And then let any man explain to me, if he can, how it happened that Scrooge, having his key in the lock of the door, saw in the knocker, without its undergoing any intermediate process of change: not a knocker, but Marley's face.

Marley's face. It was not in impenetrable shadow as the other objects in the yard were, but had a dismal light about it, like a bad lobster in a dark cellar. It was not angry or ferocious, but looked at Scrooge as Marley used to look: with ghostly spectacles turned up upon its ghostly forehead. The hair was curiously stirred, as if by breath or hot-air; and though the eyes were wide open, they were perfectly motionless. That, and its livid colour, made it horrible; but its horror seemed to be, in spite of the face and beyond its control, rather than a part of its own expression.

As Scrooge looked fixedly at this phenomenon, it was a knocker again.

To say that he was not startled, or that his blood was not conscious of a terrible sensation to which it had been a stranger from infancy, would be untrue. But he put his hand upon the key he had relinquished, turned it sturdily, walked in, and lighted his candle.

He *did* pause, with a moment's irresolution, before he shut the door; and he *did* look cautiously behind it first, as if he half-expected to be terrified with the sight of Marley's pigtail sticking out into the hall. But there was nothing on the back of the door, except the screws and nuts that held the knocker on; so he said "Pooh, pooh!" and closed it with a bang.

The sound resounded through the house like thunder. Every room above, and every cask in the wine-merchant's cellars below, appeared to have a separate peal of echoes of its own. Scrooge was not a man to be frightened by echoes. He fastened the door, and walked across the hall, and up the stairs: slowly too: trimming his candle[8] as he went.

You may talk vaguely about driving a coach-and-six up a good old flight of stairs, or through a bad young Act of Parliament;[9] but I mean to say you might have got a hearse up that staircase, and taken it broadwise, with the splinter-bar[1] towards the wall, and the door towards the balustrades: and

7. The administrative body ("corporation") of the City of London consisted at that time of the mayor; twenty-six "aldermen," each representing a ward or district; and 206 councilmen; all of whom were required to belong to one of London's professional guilds or companies, many of which had special clothing ("livery") that members were entitled to wear.
8. Scrooge is carrying a dip, a length of wick dipped several times in melted animal fat.

Cheaper than wax candles, they had to be repeatedly "trimmed" to stop the burned section from dropping to the ground.
9. The Irish political leader Daniel O'Connell (1775–1847) apparently used to boast that he could drive a coach and six horses through English laws because they were so loosely worded.
1. The crossbar at the front of a coach, supporting the springs.

done it easy. There was plenty of width for that, and room to spare; which is perhaps the reason why Scrooge thought he saw a locomotive hearse going on before him in the gloom. Half a dozen gas-lamps out of the street wouldn't have lighted the entry too well, so you may suppose that it was pretty dark with Scrooge's dip.

Up Scrooge went, not caring a button for that: darkness is cheap, and Scrooge liked it. But before he shut his heavy door, he walked through his rooms to see that all was right. He had just enough recollection of the face to desire to do that.

Sitting-room, bed-room, lumber-room. All as they should be. Nobody under the table, nobody under the sofa; a small fire in the grate; spoon and basin ready; and the little saucepan of gruel (Scrooge had a cold in his head) upon the hob. Nobody under the bed; nobody in the closet; nobody in his dressing-gown, which was hanging up in a suspicious attitude against the wall. Lumber-room as usual. Old fire-guard, old shoes, two fish-baskets, washing-stand on three legs, and a poker.

Quite satisfied, he closed his door, and locked himself in; double-locked himself in, which was not his custom. Thus secured against surprise, he took off his cravat; put on his dressing-gown and slippers, and his night-cap; and sat down before the fire to take his gruel.

It was a very low fire indeed; nothing on such a bitter night. He was obliged to sit close to it, and brood over it, before he could extract the least sensation of warmth from such a handful of fuel. The fire-place was an old one, built by some Dutch merchant long ago, and paved all round with quaint Dutch tiles, designed to illustrate the Scriptures. There were Cains and Abels; Pharaoh's daughters, Queens of Sheba, Angelic messengers descending through the air on clouds like feather-beds, Abrahams, Belshazzars, Apostles putting off to sea in butter-boats, hundreds of figures, to attract his thoughts; and yet that face of Marley, seven years dead, came like the ancient Prophet's rod,[2] and swallowed up the whole. If each smooth tile had been a blank at first, with power to shape some picture on its surface from the disjointed fragments of his thoughts, there would have been a copy of old Marley's head on every one.

"Humbug!" said Scrooge; and walked across the room.

After several turns, he sat down again. As he threw his head back in the chair, his glance happened to rest upon a bell, a disused bell, that hung in the room, and communicated for some purpose now forgotten with a chamber in the highest story of the building. It was with great astonishment, and with a strange, inexplicable dread, that as he looked, he saw this bell begin to swing. It swung so softly in the outset that it scarcely made a sound; but soon it rang out loudly, and so did every bell in the house.

This might have lasted half a minute, or a minute, but it seemed an hour. The bells ceased as they had begun, together. They were succeeded by a clanking noise, deep down below; as if some person were dragging a heavy chain over the casks in the wine-merchant's cellar. Scrooge then remembered to have heard that ghosts in haunted houses were described as dragging chains.

---

2. Aaron's staff, transformed into a snake by God, swallows up all of the Egyptians' rods, which have been turned into snakes by magicians (Exodus 7.8–12).

The cellar-door flew open with a booming sound, and then he heard the noise much louder, on the floors below; then coming up the stairs; then coming straight towards his door.

"It's humbug still!" said Scrooge. "I won't believe it."

His colour changed though, when, without a pause, it came on through the heavy door, and passed into the room before his eyes. Upon its coming in, the dying flame leaped up, as though it cried "I know him! Marley's Ghost!" and fell again.

Marley's Ghost

The same face: the very same. Marley in his pig-tail, usual waistcoat, tights,[3] and boots; the tassels on the latter bristling, like his pigtail, and his coat-skirts, and the hair upon his head. The chain he drew was clasped about his middle. It was long, and wound about him like a tail; and it was made (for Scrooge observed it closely) of cash-boxes, keys, padlocks, ledgers, deeds, and heavy purses wrought in steel. His body was transparent:

3. Tight-fitting breeches.

so that Scrooge, observing him, and looking through his waistcoat, could see the two buttons on his coat behind.

Scrooge had often heard it said that Marley had no bowels, but he had never believed it until now.[4]

No, nor did he believe it even now. Though he looked the phantom through and through, and saw it standing before him; though he felt the chilling influence of its death-cold eyes; and marked the very texture of the folded kerchief bound about its head and chin, which wrapper he had not observed before; he was still incredulous, and fought against his senses.

"How now!" said Scrooge, caustic and cold as ever. "What do you want with me?"

"Much!"—Marley's voice, no doubt about it.

"Who are you?"

"Ask me who I *was*."

"Who *were* you then?" said Scrooge, raising his voice. "You're particular— for a shade." He was going to say "*to* a shade,"[5] but substituted this, as more appropriate.

"In life I was your partner, Jacob Marley."

"Can you—can you sit down?" asked Scrooge, looking doubtfully at him.

"I can."

"Do it then."

Scrooge asked the question, because he didn't know whether a ghost so transparent might find himself in a condition to take a chair; and felt that in the event of its being impossible, it might involve the necessity of an embarrassing explanation. But the ghost sat down on the opposite side of the fireplace, as if he were quite used to it.

"You don't believe in me," observed the Ghost.

"I don't," said Scrooge.

"What evidence would you have of my reality, beyond that of your senses?"

"I don't know," said Scrooge.

"Why do you doubt your senses?"

"Because," said Scrooge, "a little thing affects them. A slight disorder of the stomach makes them cheats. You may be an undigested bit of beef, a blot of mustard, a crumb of cheese, a fragment of an underdone potato. There's more of gravy than of grave about you, whatever you are!"

Scrooge was not much in the habit of cracking jokes, nor did he feel, in his heart, by any means waggish then. The truth is, that he tried to be smart, as a means of distracting his own attention, and keeping down his terror; for the spectre's voice disturbed the very marrow in his bones.

To sit, staring at those fixed, glazed eyes, in silence for a moment, would play, Scrooge felt, the very deuce with him. There was something very awful, too, in the spectre's being provided with an infernal atmosphere of its own. Scrooge could not feel it himself, but this was clearly the case; for though the Ghost sat perfectly motionless, its hair, and skirts, and tassels, were still agitated as by the hot vapour from an oven.

---

4. A joke, playing on the alignment of the figurative and literal conditions of having no bowels. Bowels were traditionally believed to be the seat of compassion in the human body; corpses are disemboweled before burial to slow down the process of decomposition.
5. Scrooge resists a pun. "For a shade": for a ghost. "To a shade": to a degree.

"You see this toothpick?" said Scrooge, returning quickly to the charge, for the reason just assigned; and wishing, though it were only for a second, to divert the vision's stony gaze from himself.

"I do," replied the Ghost.

"You are not looking at it," said Scrooge.

"But I see it," said the Ghost, "notwithstanding."

"Well!" returned Scrooge. "I have but to swallow this, and be for the rest of my days persecuted by a legion of goblins, all of my own creation. Humbug, I tell you; humbug!"

At this, the spirit raised a frightful cry, and shook its chain with such a dismal and appalling noise, that Scrooge held on tight to his chair, to save himself from falling in a swoon. But how much greater was his horror, when the phantom taking off the bandage round its head, as if it were too warm to wear in-doors, its lower jaw dropped down upon its breast!

Scrooge fell upon his knees, and clasped his hands before his face.

"Mercy!" he said. "Dreadful apparition, why do you trouble me?"

"Man of the worldly mind!" replied the Ghost, "do you believe in me or not?"

"I do," said Scrooge. "I must. But why do spirits walk the earth, and why do they come to me?"

"It is required of every man," the Ghost returned, "that the spirit within him should walk abroad among his fellow-men, and travel far and wide; and if that spirit goes not forth in life, it is condemned to do so after death. It is doomed to wander through the world—oh, woe is me!—and witness what it cannot share, but might have shared on earth, and turned to happiness!"

Again the spectre raised a cry, and shook its chain, and wrung its shadowy hands.

"You are fettered," said Scrooge, trembling. "Tell me why?"

"I wear the chain I forged in life," replied the Ghost. "I made it link by link, and yard by yard; I girded it on of my own free will, and of my own free will I wore it. Is its pattern strange to *you?*"

Scrooge trembled more and more.

"Or would you know," pursued the Ghost, "the weight and length of the strong coil you bear yourself? It was full as heavy and as long as this, seven Christmas Eves ago. You have laboured on it, since. It is a ponderous chain!"

Scrooge glanced about him on the floor, in the expectation of finding himself surrounded by some fifty or sixty fathoms of iron cable: but he could see nothing.

"Jacob," he said, imploringly. "Old Jacob Marley, tell me more. Speak comfort to me, Jacob."

"I have none to give," the Ghost replied. "It comes from other regions, Ebenezer Scrooge, and is conveyed by other ministers, to other kinds of men. Nor can I tell you what I would. A very little more, is all permitted to me. I cannot rest, I cannot stay, I cannot linger anywhere. My spirit never walked beyond our counting-house—mark me!—in life my spirit never loved beyond the narrow limits of our money-changing hole; and weary journeys lie before me!"

It was a habit with Scrooge, whenever he became thoughtful, to put his hands in his breeches pockets. Pondering on what the Ghost had said, he did so now, but without lifting up his eyes, or getting off his knees.

"You must have been very slow about it, Jacob," Scrooge observed, in a business-like manner, though with humility and deference.

"Slow!" the Ghost repeated.

"Seven years dead," mused Scrooge. "And travelling all the time?"

"The whole time," said the Ghost. "No rest, no peace. Incessant torture of remorse."

"You travel fast?" said Scrooge.

"On the wings of the wind," replied the Ghost.

"You might have got over a great quantity of ground in seven years," said Scrooge.

The Ghost, on hearing this, set up another cry, and clanked its chain so hideously in the dead silence of the night, that the Ward[6] would have been justified in indicting it for a nuisance.

"Oh! captive, bound, and double-ironed," cried the phantom, "not to know, that ages of incessant labour by immortal creatures, for this earth must pass into eternity before the good of which it is susceptible is all developed. Not to know that any Christian spirit working kindly in its little sphere, whatever it may be, will find its mortal life too short for its vast means of usefulness. Not to know that no space of regret can make amends for one life's opportunities misused! Yet such was I! Oh! Such was I!"

"But you were always a good man of business, Jacob," faultered Scrooge, who now began to apply this to himself.

"Business!" cried the Ghost, wringing its hands again. "Mankind was my business. The common welfare was my business; charity, mercy, forbearance, and benevolence, were, all, my business. The dealings of my trade were but a drop of water in the comprehensive ocean of my business!"

It held up its chain at arm's length, as if that were the cause of all its unavailing grief, and flung it heavily upon the ground again.

"At this time of the rolling year," the spectre said, "I suffer most. Why did I walk through crowds of fellow-beings with my eyes turned down, and never raise them to that blessed Star which led the Wise Men to a poor abode?[7] Were there no poor homes to which its light would have conducted *me!*"

Scrooge was very much dismayed to hear the spectre going on at this rate, and began to quake exceedingly.

"Hear me!" cried the Ghost. "My time is nearly gone."

"I will," said Scrooge. "But don't be hard upon me! Don't be flowery, Jacob! Pray!"

"How it is that I appear before you in a shape that you can see, I may not tell. I have sat invisible beside you many and many a day."

It was not an agreeable idea. Scrooge shivered, and wiped the perspiration from his brow.

"That is no light part of my penance," pursued the Ghost. "I am here tonight to warn you, that you have yet a chance and hope of escaping my fate. A chance and hope of my procuring, Ebenezer."

"You were always a good friend to me," said Scrooge. "Thank'ee!"

"You will be haunted," resumed the Ghost, "by Three Spirits."

---

6. The night watchman of the ward, or district.
7. The three wise men, or kings, were led by a star to Jesus's birthplace in a stable (Matthew 2.1–12).

Scrooge's countenance fell almost as low as the Ghost's had done.

"Is that the chance and hope you mentioned, Jacob?" he demanded, in a faultering voice.

"It is."

"I—I think I'd rather not," said Scrooge.

"Without their visits," said the Ghost, "you cannot hope to shun the path I tread. Expect the first to-morrow, when the bell tolls One."

"Couldn't I take'em all at once, and have it over, Jacob?" hinted Scrooge.

"Expect the second on the next night at the same hour. The third upon the next night when the last stroke of Twelve has ceased to vibrate. Look to see me no more; and look that, for your own sake, you remember what has passed between us!"

When it had said these words, the spectre took its wrapper from the table, and bound it round its head, as before. Scrooge knew this, by the smart sound its teeth made, when the jaws were brought together by the bandage. He ventured to raise his eyes again, and found his supernatural visitor confronting him in an erect attitude, with its chain wound over and about its arm.

The apparition walked backward from him; and at every step it took, the window raised itself a little, so that when the spectre reached it, it was wide open. It beckoned Scrooge to approach, which he did. When they were within two paces of each other, Marley's Ghost held up its hand, warning him to come no nearer. Scrooge stopped.

Not so much in obedience, as in surprise and fear: for on the raising of the hand, he became sensible of confused noises in the air; incoherent sounds of lamentation and regret; wailings inexpressibly sorrowful and self-accusatory. The spectre, after listening for a moment, joined in the mournful dirge; and floated out upon the bleak, dark night.

Scrooge followed to the window: desperate in his curiosity. He looked out.

The air was filled with phantoms, wandering hither and thither in restless haste, and moaning as they went. Every one of them wore chains like Marley's Ghost; some few (they might be guilty governments) were linked together; none were free. Many had been personally known to Scrooge in their lives. He had been quite familiar with one old ghost, in a white waistcoat, with a monstrous iron safe attached to its ancle, who cried piteously at being unable to assist a wretched woman with an infant, whom it saw below, upon a door-step. The misery with them all was, clearly, that they sought to interfere, for good, in human matters, and had lost the power for ever.

Whether these creatures faded into mist, or mist enshrouded them, he could not tell. But they and their spirit voices faded together; and the night became as it had been when he walked home.

Scrooge closed the window, and examined the door by which the Ghost had entered. It was double-locked, as he had locked it with his own hands, and the bolts were undisturbed. He tried to say "Humbug!" but stopped at the first syllable. And being, from the emotion he had undergone, or the fatigues of the day, or his glimpse of the Invisible World, or the dull conversation of the Ghost, or the lateness of the hour, much in need of repose; went straight to bed, without undressing, and fell asleep upon the instant.

Stave Two

THE FIRST OF THE THREE SPIRITS

When Scrooge awoke, it was so dark, that looking out of bed, he could scarcely distinguish the transparent window from the opaque walls of his chamber. He was endeavouring to pierce the darkness with his ferret eyes, when the chimes of a neighbouring church struck the four quarters. So he listened for the hour.

To his great astonishment the heavy bell went on from six to seven, and from seven to eight, and regularly up to twelve; then stopped. Twelve! It was past two when he went to bed. The clock was wrong. An icicle must have got into the works. Twelve!

He touched the spring of his repeater, to correct this most preposterous clock. Its rapid little pulse beat twelve; and stopped.

"Why, it isn't possible," said Scrooge, "that I can have slept through a whole day and far into another night. It isn't possible that anything has happened to the sun, and this is twelve at noon!"

The idea being an alarming one, he scrambled out of bed, and groped his way to the window. He was obliged to rub the frost off with the sleeve of his dressing-gown before he could see anything; and could see very little then. All he could make out was, that it was still very foggy and extremely cold, and that there was no noise of people running to and fro, and making a great stir, as there unquestionably would have been if night had beaten off bright day, and taken possession of the world. This was a great relief, because "three days after sight of this First of Exchange pay to Mr. Ebenezer Scrooge or his order,"[8] and so forth, would have become a mere United States' security[9] if there were no days to count by.

Scrooge went to bed again, and thought, and thought, and thought it over and over and over, and could make nothing of it. The more he thought, the more perplexed he was; and the more he endeavoured not to think, the more he thought. Marley's Ghost bothered him exceedingly. Every time he resolved within himself, after mature inquiry, that it was all a dream, his mind flew back again, like a strong spring released, to its first position, and presented the same problem to be worked all through, "Was it a dream or not?"

Scrooge lay in this state until the chimes had gone three quarters more, when he remembered, on a sudden, that the Ghost had warned him of a visitation when the bell tolled one. He resolved to lie awake until the hour was past; and, considering that he could no more go to sleep than go to Heaven, this was perhaps the wisest resolution in his power.

The quarter was so long, that he was more than once convinced he must have sunk into a doze unconsciously, and missed the clock. At length it broke upon his listening ear.

"Ding, dong!"

"A quarter past," said Scrooge, counting.

"Ding, dong!"

"Half past!" said Scrooge.

"Ding, dong!"

"A quarter to it," said Scrooge.

"Ding dong!"

"The hour itself," said Scrooge, triumphantly, "and nothing else!"

He spoke before the hour bell sounded, which it now did with a deep, dull, hollow, melancholy ONE. Light flashed up in the room upon the instant, and the curtains of his bed were drawn.

The curtains of his bed were drawn aside, I tell you, by a hand. Not the curtains at his feet, nor the curtains at his back, but those to which his face was addressed. The curtains of his bed were drawn aside; and Scrooge, starting up into a half-recumbent attitude, found himself face to face with the unearthly visitor who drew them: as close to it as I am now to you, and I am standing in the spirit at your elbow.

8. The technical wording of a bill of exchange for a debt or credit.
9. After the financial crisis of 1837, a number of U.S. states that had borrowed money from European sources to finance public works were unable to pay their debts.

It was a strange figure—like a child: yet not so like a child as like an old man, viewed through some supernatural medium, which gave him the appearance of having receded from the view, and being diminished to a child's proportions. Its hair, which hung about its neck and down its back, was white as if with age; and yet the face had not a wrinkle in it, and the tenderest bloom was on the skin. The arms were very long and muscular; the hands the same, as if its hold were of uncommon strength. Its legs and feet, most delicately formed, were, like those upper members, bare. It wore a tunic of the purest white; and round its waist was bound a lustrous belt, the sheen of which was beautiful. It held a branch of fresh green holly in its hand; and, in singular contradiction of that wintry emblem, had its dress trimmed with summer flowers. But the strangest thing about it was, that from the crown of its head there sprung a bright clear jet of light, by which all this was visible; and which was doubtless the occasion of its using, in its duller moments, a great extinguisher for a cap, which it now held under its arm.

Even this, though, when Scrooge looked at it with increasing steadiness, was *not* its strangest quality. For as its belt sparkled and glittered now in one part and now in another, and what was light one instant, at another time was dark, so the figure itself fluctuated in its distinctness: being now a thing with one arm, now with one leg, now with twenty legs, now a pair of legs without a head, now a head without a body: of which dissolving parts, no outline would be visible in the dense gloom wherein they melted away. And in the very wonder of this, it would be itself again; distinct and clear as ever.

"Are you the Spirit, sir, whose coming was foretold to me?" asked Scrooge.

"I am!"

The voice was soft and gentle. Singularly low, as if instead of being so close beside him, it were at a distance.

"Who, and what are you?" Scrooge demanded.

"I am the Ghost of Christmas Past."

"Long past?" inquired Scrooge: observant of its dwarfish stature.

"No. Your past."

Perhaps, Scrooge could not have told anybody why, if anybody could have asked him; but he had a special desire to see the Spirit in his cap; and begged him to be covered.

"What!" exclaimed the Ghost, "would you so soon put out, with worldly hands, the light I give? Is it not enough that you are one of those whose passions made this cap, and force me through whole trains of years to wear it low upon my brow!"

Scrooge reverently disclaimed all intention to offend, or any knowledge of having wilfully "bonneted" the Spirit at any period of his life. He then made bold to inquire what business brought him there.

"Your welfare!" said the Ghost.

Scrooge expressed himself much obliged, but could not help thinking that a night of unbroken rest would have been more conducive to that end. The Spirit must have heard him thinking, for it said immediately:

"Your reclamation, then. Take heed!"

It put out its strong hand as it spoke, and clasped him gently by the arm. "Rise! And walk with me!"

It would have been in vain for Scrooge to plead that the weather and the hour were not adapted to pedestrian purposes; that bed was warm, and the thermometer a long way below freezing; that he was clad but lightly in his slippers, dressing-gown, and nightcap; and that he had a cold upon him at that time. The grasp, though gentle as a woman's hand, was not to be resisted. He rose: but finding that the Spirit made towards the window, clasped its robe in supplication.

"I am a mortal," Scrooge remonstrated, "and liable to fall."

"Bear but a touch of my hand *there*," said the Spirit, laying it upon his heart, "and you shall be upheld in more than this!"

As the words were spoken, they passed through the wall, and stood upon an open country road, with fields on either hand. The city had entirely vanished. Not a vestige of it was to be seen. The darkness and the mist had vanished with it, for it was a clear, cold, winter day, with snow upon the ground.

"Good Heaven!" said Scrooge, clasping his hands together, as he looked about him. "I was bred in this place. I was a boy here!"

The Spirit gazed upon him mildly. Its gentle touch, though it had been light and instantaneous, appeared still present to the old man's sense of feeling. He was conscious of a thousand odours floating in the air, each one connected with a thousand thoughts, and hopes, and joys, and cares long, long, forgotten!

"Your lip is trembling," said the Ghost. "And what is that upon your cheek?"

Scrooge muttered, with an unusual catching in his voice, that it was a pimple; and begged the Ghost to lead him where he would.

"You recollect the way?" inquired the Spirit.

"Remember it!" cried Scrooge with fervour. "I could walk it blindfold."

"Strange to have forgotten it for so many years!" observed the Ghost. "Let us go on."

They walked along the road; Scrooge recognizing every gate, and post, and tree; until a little market-town appeared in the distance, with its bridge, its church, and winding river. Some shaggy ponies now were seen trotting towards them with boys upon their backs, who called to other boys in country gigs and carts, driven by farmers. All these boys were in great spirits, and shouted to each other, until the broad fields were so full of merry music, that the crisp air laughed to hear it.

"These are but shadows of the things that have been," said the Ghost. "They have no consciousness of us."

The jocund travelers came on; and as they came, Scrooge knew and named them every one. Why was he rejoiced beyond all bounds to see them! Why did his cold eye glisten, and his heart leap up as they went past! Why was he filled with gladness when he heard them give each other Merry Christmas, as they parted at cross-roads and bye-ways, for their several homes! What was merry Christmas to Scrooge? Out upon merry Christmas! What good had it ever done to him?

"The school is not quite deserted," said the Ghost. "A solitary child, neglected by his friends, is left there still."

Scrooge said he knew it. And he sobbed.

They left the high-road, by a well remembered lane, and soon approached a mansion of dull red brick, with a little weathercock-surmounted cupola, on the roof, and a bell hanging in it. It was a large house, but one of broken fortunes; for the spacious offices were little used, their walls were damp and mossy, their windows broken, and their gates decayed. Fowls clucked and strutted in the stables; and the coach-houses and sheds were over-run with grass. Nor was it more retentive of its ancient state, within; for entering the dreary hall, and glancing through the open doors of many rooms, they found them poorly furnished, cold, and vast. There was an earthy savour in the air, a chilly bareness in the place, which associated itself somehow with too much getting up by candle-light, and not too much to eat.

They went, the Ghost and Scrooge, across the hall, to a door at the back of the house. It opened before them, and disclosed a long, bare, melancholy room, made barer still by lines of plain deal forms[1] and desks. At one of these a lonely boy was reading near a feeble fire; and Scrooge sat down upon a form, and wept to see his poor forgotten self as he had used to be.

Not a latent echo in the house, not a squeak and scuffle from the mice behind the panneling, not a drip from the half-thawed water-spout in the dull yard behind, not a sigh among the leafless boughs of one despondent poplar, not the idle swinging of an empty store-house door, no, not a clicking in the fire, but fell upon the heart of Scrooge with softening influence, and gave a freer passage to his tears.

The Spirit touched him on the arm, and pointed to his younger self, intent upon his reading. Suddenly a man, in foreign garments: wonderfully real and distinct to look at: stood outside the window, with an axe stuck in his belt, and leading an ass laden with wood by the bridle.

"Why, it's Ali Baba!"[2] Scrooge exclaimed in ecstacy. "It's dear old honest Ali Baba! Yes, yes, I know! One Christmas time, when yonder solitary child was left here all alone, he *did* come, for the first time, just like that. Poor boy! And Valentine," said Scrooge, "and his wild brother, Orson;[3] there they go! And what's his name, who was put down in his drawers, asleep, at the Gate of Damascus;[4] don't you see him! And the Sultan's Groom turned upside-down by the Genii; there he is upon his head! Serve him right. I'm glad of it. What business had *he* to be married to the Princess!"

To hear Scrooge expending all the earnestness of his nature on such subjects, in a most extraordinary voice between laughing and crying; and to see his heightened and excited face; would have been a surprise to his business friends in the city, indeed.

"There's the Parrot!" cried Scrooge. "Green body and yellow tail, with a thing like a lettuce growing out of the top of his head; there he is! Poor Robin Crusoe,[5] he called him, when he came home again after sailing round the island. 'Poor Robin Crusoe, where have you been, Robin Crusoe?' The man thought he was dreaming, but he wasn't. It was the Parrot, you know. There goes Friday, running for his life to the little creek! Halloa! Hoop! Halloo!"

Then, with a rapidity of transition very foreign to his usual character, he said, in pity for his former self, "Poor boy!" and cried again.

---

1. Long unpainted school benches made of pine ("deal").
2. A reference to "Ali Baba and the Forty Thieves," from the *Arabian Nights*, a popular children's book in Britain.
3. A reference to *The History of two Valyannte Brethren, Valentyne and Orson*, a 15th-century

French romance, which had become a popular children's story in Britain.
4. A reference to "Noureddin Ali of Cairo and His Son Bedreddin Hassan," from the *Arabian Nights*.
5. Scrooge recounts episodes from Daniel Defoe's *Life and Adventures of Robinson Crusoe* (1719).

"I wish," Scrooge muttered, putting his hand in his pocket, and looking about him, after drying his eyes with his cuff: "but it's too late now."

"What is the matter?" asked the Spirit.

"Nothing," said Scrooge. "Nothing. There was a boy singing a Christmas Carol at my door last night. I should like to have given him something: that's all."

The Ghost smiled thoughtfully, and waved its hand: saying as it did so, "Let us see another Christmas!"

Scrooge's former self grew larger at the words, and the room became a little darker and more dirty. The panels shrunk, the windows cracked; fragments of plaster fell out of the ceiling, and the naked laths were shown instead; but how all this was brought about, Scrooge knew no more than you do. He only knew that it was quite correct; that everything had happened so; that there he was, alone again, when all the other boys had gone home for the jolly holidays.

He was not reading now, but walking up and down despairingly. Scrooge looked at the Ghost, and with a mournful shaking of his head, glanced anxiously towards the door.

It opened; and a little girl, much younger than the boy, came darting in, and putting her arms about his neck, and often kissing him, addressed him as her "Dear, dear brother."

"I have come to bring you home, dear brother!" said the child, clapping her tiny hands, and bending down to laugh. "To bring you home, home, home!"

"Home, little Fan?" returned the boy.

"Yes!" said the child, brimful of glee. "Home, for good and all. Home, for ever and ever. Father is so much kinder than he used to be, that home's like Heaven! He spoke so gently to me one dear night when I was going to bed, that I was not afraid to ask him once more if you might come home; and he said Yes, you should; and sent me in a coach to bring you. And you're to be a man!" said the child, opening her eyes, "and are never to come back here; but first, we're to be together all the Christmas long, and have the merriest time in all the world."

"You are quite a woman, little Fan!" exclaimed the boy.

She clapped her hands and laughed, and tried to touch his head; but being too little, laughed again, and stood on tiptoe to embrace him. Then she began to drag him, in her childish eagerness, towards the door; and he, nothing loth to go, accompanied her.

A terrible voice in the hall cried, "Bring down Master Scrooge's box, there!" and in the hall appeared the schoolmaster himself, who glared on Master Scrooge with a ferocious condescension, and threw him into a dreadful state of mind by shaking hands with him. He then conveyed him and his sister into the veriest old well of a shivering best-parlour that ever was seen, where the maps upon the wall, and the celestial and terrestrial globes in the windows, were waxy with cold. Here he produced a decanter of curiously light wine, and a block of curiously heavy cake, and administered instalments of those dainties to the young people: at the same time, sending out a meagre servant to offer a glass of "something" to the postboy, who answered that he thanked the gentleman, but if it was the same tap as he had tasted before, he had rather not. Master Scrooge's trunk being by this time tied on to the top of the chaise, the children bade the schoolmaster good-bye right willingly; and getting into it, drove gaily down the garden-sweep: the quick wheels dashing the hoar-frost and snow from off the dark leaves of the evergreens like spray.

"Always a delicate creature, whom a breath might have withered," said the Ghost. "But she had a large heart!"

"So she had," cried Scrooge. "You're right. I will not gainsay it, Spirit. God forbid!"

"She died a woman," said the Ghost, "and had, as I think, children."

"One child," Scrooge returned.

"True," said the Ghost. "Your nephew!"

Scrooge seemed uneasy in his mind; and answered briefly, "Yes."

Although they had but that moment left the school behind them, they were now in the busy thoroughfares of a city, where shadowy passengers passed and repassed; where shadowy carts and coaches battled for the way, and all the strife and tumult of a real city were. It was made plain enough, by the dressing of the shops, that here too it was Christmas time again; but it was evening, and the streets were lighted up.

The Ghost stopped at a certain warehouse door, and asked Scrooge if he knew it.

"Know it!" said Scrooge. "Was I apprenticed here!"

They went in. At sight of an old gentleman in a Welch wig,[6] sitting behind such a high desk, that if he had been two inches taller he must have knocked his head against the ceiling, Scrooge cried in great excitement:

"Why, it's old Fezziwig! Bless his heart; it's Fezziwig alive again!"

Old Fezziwig laid down his pen, and looked up at the clock, which pointed to the hour of seven. He rubbed his hands; adjusted his capacious waistcoat; laughed all over himself, from his shoes to his organ of benevo-lence;[7] and called out in a comfortable, oily, rich, fat, jovial voice:

"Yo ho, there! Ebenezer! Dick!"

Scrooge's former self, now grown a young man, came briskly in, accompanied by his fellow-'prentice.

"Dick Wilkins, to be sure!" said Scrooge to the Ghost. "Bless me, yes. There he is. He was very much attached to me, was Dick. Poor Dick! Dear, dear!"

"Yo ho, my boys!" said Fezziwig. "No more work to-night. Christmas Eve, Dick. Christmas, Ebenezer! Let's have the shutters up," cried old Fezziwig, with a sharp clap of his hands, "before a man can say, Jack Robinson!"[8]

You wouldn't believe how those two fellows went at it! They charged into the street with the shutters—one, two, three—had 'em up in their places—four, five, six—barred 'em and pinned 'em—seven, eight, nine—and came back before you could have got to twelve, panting like race-horses.

"Hilli-ho!" cried old Fezziwig, skipping down from the high desk, with wonderful agility. "Clear away, my lads, and let's have lots of room here! Hilli-ho, Dick! Chirrup, Ebenezer!"

6. A woolen or worsted cap, originally made in Montgomery, Wales.
7. According to phrenology, a popular 19th-century pseudoscience in which the shape of the skull determined character, the area at the top of the forehead reveals the degree to which an individual possesses, or lacks, feelings of benevolence.
8. I.e., in an instant; from a comic song of the late 17th century.

Clear away! There was nothing they wouldn't have cleared away, or couldn't have cleared away, with old Fezziwig looking on. It was done in a minute. Every movable was packed off, as if it were dismissed from public life for evermore; the floor was swept and watered, the lamps were trimmed, fuel was heaped upon the fire; and the warehouse was as snug, and warm, and dry, and bright a ball-room, as you would desire to see upon a winter's night.

In came a fiddler with a music-book, and went up to the lofty desk, and made an orchestra of it, and tuned like fifty stomach-aches. In came Mrs. Fezziwig, one vast substantial smile. In came the three Miss Fezziwigs, beaming and loveable. In came the six young followers whose hearts they broke. In came all the young men and women employed in the business. In came the housemaid, with her cousin, the baker. In came the cook, with her brother's particular friend, the milkman. In came the boy from over the way, who was suspected of not having board enough from his master; trying to hide himself behind the girl from next door but one, who was proved to have had her ears pulled by her Mistress. In they all came, one after another; some shyly, some boldly, some gracefully, some awkwardly, some pushing, some pulling; in they all came, anyhow and everyhow. Away they all went, twenty couple at once, hands half round and back again the other way; down the middle and up again; round and round in various stages of affectionate grouping; old top couple always turning up in the wrong place; new top couple starting off again, as soon as they got there; all top couples at last, and not a bottom one to help them. When this result was brought about, old Fezziwig, clapping his hands to stop the dance, cried out, "Well done!" and the fiddler plunged his hot face into a pot of porter,[9] especially provided for that purpose. But scorning rest upon his reappearance, he instantly began again, though there were no dancers yet, as if the other fiddler had been carried home, exhausted, on a shutter; and he were a bran-new man resolved to beat him out of sight, or perish.

There were more dances, and there were forfeits, and more dances, and there was cake, and there was negus, and there was a great piece of Cold Roast, and there was a great piece of Cold Boiled,[1] and there were mince-pies, and plenty of beer. But the great effect of the evening came after the Roast and Boiled, when the fiddler (an artful dog, mind! The sort of man who knew his business better than you or I could have told it him!) struck up "Sir Roger de Coverley."[2] Then old Fezziwig stood out to dance with Mrs. Fezziwig. Top couple too; with a good stiff piece of work cut out for them; three or four and twenty pair of partners; people who were not to be trifled with; people who *would* dance, and had no notion of walking.

But if they had been twice as many: ah, four times: old Fezziwig would have been a match for them, and so would Mrs. Fezziwig. As to *her*, she was worthy to be his partner in every sense of the term. If that's not high praise, tell me higher, and I'll use it. A positive light appeared to issue from Fezziwig's calves. They shone in every part of the dance like moons. You couldn't have predicted, at any given time, what would become of 'em next. And when old Fezziwig and Mrs. Fezziwig had gone all through the dance; advance and retire, hold hands

9. A dark, bitter, beer.
1. I.e., boiled beef, and roast beef, both served cold. "Negus": a mixture of fortified wine, such as port or sherry, with hot water, sugar, lemon juice, and nutmeg and other spices.
2. A popular, if complex, country dance or reel.

with your partner; bow and curtsey; corkscrew; thread-the-needle, and back again to your place; Fezziwig "cut"—cut so deftly, that he appeared to wink with his legs, and came upon his feet again without a stagger.[3]

When the clock struck eleven, this domestic ball broke up. Mr. and Mrs. Fezziwig took their stations, one on either side the door, and shaking hands with every person individually as he or she went out, wished him or her a Merry Christmas. When everybody had retired but the two 'prentices, they did the same to them; and thus the cheerful voices died away, and the lads were left to their beds; which were under a counter in the back-shop.

During the whole of this time, Scrooge had acted like a man out of his wits. His heart and soul were in the scene, and with his former self. He corroborated everything, remembered everything, enjoyed everything, and underwent the strangest agitation. It was not until now, when the bright faces of his former self and Dick were turned from them, that he remembered the Ghost, and became conscious that it was looking full upon him, while the light upon its head burnt very clear.

"A small matter," said the Ghost, "to make these silly folks so full of gratitude."

"Small!" echoed Scrooge.

The Spirit signed to him to listen to the two apprentices, who were pouring out their hearts in praise of Fezziwig: and when he had done so, said,

"Why! Is it not? He has spent but a few pounds of your mortal money: three or four, perhaps. Is that so much that he deserves this praise?"

"It isn't that," said Scrooge, heated by the remark, and speaking unconsciously like his former, not his latter, self. "It isn't that, Spirit. He has the power to render us happy or unhappy; to make our service light or burdensome; a pleasure or a toil. Say that his power lies in words and looks; in things so slight and insignificant that it is impossible to add and count 'em up: what then? The happiness he gives, is quite as great as if it cost a fortune."

He felt the Spirit's glance, and stopped.

"What is the matter?" asked the Ghost.

"Nothing particular," said Scrooge.

"Something, I think?" the Ghost insisted.

"No," said Scrooge, "No. I should like to be able to say a word or two to my clerk just now! That's all."

His former self turned down the lamps as he gave utterance to the wish; and Scrooge and the Ghost again stood side by side in the open air.

"My time grows short," observed the Spirit. "Quick!"

This was not addressed to Scrooge, or to any one whom he could see, but it produced an immediate effect. For again Scrooge saw himself. He was older now; a man in the prime of life. His face had not the harsh and rigid lines of later years; but it had begun to wear the signs of care and avarice. There was an eager, greedy, restless motion in the eye, which showed the passion that had taken root, and where the shadow of the growing tree would fall.

He was not alone, but sat by the side of a fair young girl in a mourning-dress: in whose eyes there were tears, which sparkled in the light that shone out of the Ghost of Christmas Past.

---

3. I.e., executed a dance step that involves a rapid crossing of the feet in midair.

"It matters little," she said, softly. "To you, very little. Another idol has displaced me; and if it can cheer and comfort you in time to come, as I would have tried to do, I have no just cause to grieve."

"What Idol has displaced you?" he rejoined.

"A golden one."

"This is the even-handed dealing of the world!" he said. "There is nothing on which it is so hard as poverty; and there is nothing it professes to condemn with such severity as the pursuit of wealth!"

"You fear the world too much," she answered, gently. "All your other hopes have merged into the hope of being beyond the chance of its sordid reproach. I have seen your nobler aspirations fall off one by one, until the master-passion, Gain, engrosses you. Have I not?"

"What then?" he retorted. "Even if I have grown so much wiser, what then? I am not changed towards you."

She shook her head.

"Am I?"

"Our contract is an old one. It was made when we were both poor and content to be so, until, in good season, we could improve our worldly fortune by our patient industry. You *are* changed. When it was made, you were another man."

"I was a boy," he said impatiently.

"Your own feeling tells you that you were not what you are," she returned. "I am. That which promised happiness when we were one in heart, is fraught with misery now that we are two. How often and how keenly I have thought of this, I will not say. It is enough that I *have* thought of it, and can release you."

"Have I ever sought release?"

"In words. No. Never."

"In what, then?"

"In a changed nature; in an altered spirit; in another atmosphere of life; another Hope as its great end. In everything that made my love of any worth or value in your sight. If this had never been between us," said the girl, looking mildly, but with steadiness, upon him; "tell me, would you seek me out and try to win me now? Ah, no!"

He seemed to yield to the justice of this supposition, in spite of himself. But he said, with a struggle, "You think not."

"I would gladly think otherwise if I could," she answered, "Heaven knows! When *I* have learned a Truth like this, I know how strong and irresistible it must be. But if you were free to-day, to-morrow, yesterday, can even I believe that you would choose a dowerless girl—you who, in your very confidence with her, weigh everything by Gain: or, choosing her, if for a moment you were false enough to your one guiding principle to do so, do I not know that your repentance and regret would surely follow? I do; and I release you. With a full heart, for the love of him you once were."

He was about to speak; but with her head turned from him, she resumed.

"You may—the memory of what is past half makes me hope you will—have pain in this. A very, very brief time, and you will dismiss the recollection of it, gladly, as an unprofitable dream, from which it happened well that you awoke. May you be happy in the life you have chosen!"

She left him; and they parted.

"Spirit!" said Scrooge, "show me no more! Conduct me home. Why do you delight to torture me?"

"One shadow more!" exclaimed the Ghost.

"No more!" cried Scrooge. "No more. I don't wish to see it. Show me no more!"

But the relentless Ghost pinioned him in both his arms, and forced him to observe what happened next.

They were in another scene and place: a room, not very large or handsome, but full of comfort. Near to the winter fire sat a beautiful young girl, so like the last that Scrooge believed it was the same, until he saw *her*, now a comely matron, sitting opposite her daughter. The noise in this room was perfectly tumultuous, for there were more children there, than Scrooge in his agitated state of mind could count; and, unlike the celebrated herd in the poem,[4] they were not forty children conducting themselves like one, but every child was conducting itself like forty. The consequences were uproarious beyond belief; but no one seemed to care; on the contrary, the mother and daughter laughed heartily, and enjoyed it very much; and the latter, soon beginning to mingle in the sports, got pillaged by the young brigands most ruthlessly. What would I not have given to be one of them! Though I never could have been so rude, no, no! I wouldn't for the wealth of all the world have crushed that braided hair, and torn it down; and for the precious little shoe, I wouldn't have plucked it off, God bless my soul ! to save my life. As to measuring her waist in sport, as they did, bold young brood, I couldn't have done it; I should have expected my arm to have grown round it for a punishment, and never come straight again. And yet I should have dearly liked, I own, to have touched her lips; to have questioned her, that she might have opened them; to have looked upon the lashes of her downcast eyes, and never raised a blush; to have let loose waves of hair, an inch of which would be a keepsake beyond price: in short, I should have liked, I do confess, to have had the lightest licence of a child, and yet been man enough to know its value.

But now a knocking at the door was heard, and such a rush immediately ensued that she with laughing face and plundered dress was borne towards it the centre of a flushed and boisterous group, just in time to greet the father, who, came home attended by a man laden with Christmas toys and presents. Then the shouting and the struggling, and the onslaught that was made on the defenceless porter! The scaling him, with chairs for ladders, to dive into his pockets, despoil him of brown-paper parcels, hold on tight by his cravat, hug him round the neck, pommel his back, and kick his legs in irrepressible affection! The shouts of wonder and delight with which the development of every package was received! The terrible announcement that the baby had been taken in the act of putting a doll's frying-pan into his mouth, and was more than suspected of having swallowed a fictitious turkey, glued on a wooden platter! The immense relief of finding this a false alarm! The joy, and gratitude, and ecstacy! They are all indescribable alike. It is enough that by degrees the children and their emotions got out of the parlour and by one stair at a time, up to the top of the house; where they went to bed, and so subsided.

---

4. From William Wordsworth's "Written in March" (1802): "The cattle are grazing, / Their heads never raising; / There are forty feeding like one!"

And now Scrooge looked on more attentively than ever, when the master of the house, having his daughter leaning fondly on him, sat down with her and her mother at his own fireside; and when he thought that such another creature, quite as graceful and as full of promise, might have called him father, and been a spring-time in the haggard winter of his life, his sight grew very dim indeed.

"Belle," said the husband, turning to his wife with a smile, "I saw an old friend of yours this afternoon."

"Who was it?"

"Guess!"

"How can I? Tut, don't I know," she added in the same breath, laughing as he laughed. "Mr. Scrooge."

"Mr. Scrooge it was. I passed his office window; and as it was not shut up, and he had a candle inside, I could scarcely help seeing him. His partner lies upon the point of death, I hear; and there he sat alone. Quite alone in the world, I do believe."

"Spirit!" said Scrooge in a broken voice, "remove me from this place."

"I told you these were shadows of the things that have been," said the Ghost. "That they are what they are, do not blame me!"

"Remove me!" Scrooge exclaimed. "I cannot bear it!"

He turned upon the Ghost, and seeing that it looked upon him with a face, in which in some strange way there were fragments of all the faces it had shown him, wrestled with it.

"Leave me! Take me back. Haunt me no longer!"

In the struggle, if that can be called a struggle in which the Ghost with no visible resistance on its own part was undisturbed by any effort of its adversary, Scrooge observed that its light was burning high and bright; and dimly connecting that with its influence over him, he seized the extinguisher-cap, and by a sudden action pressed it down upon its head.

The Spirit dropped beneath it, so that the extinguisher covered its whole form; but though Scrooge pressed it down with all his force, he could not hide the light: which streamed from under it, in an unbroken flood upon the ground.

He was conscious of being exhausted, and overcome by an irresistible drowsiness; and, further, of being in his own bedroom. He gave the cap a parting squeeze, in which his hand relaxed; and had barely time to reel to bed, before he sank into a heavy sleep.

Stave Three

THE SECOND OF THE THREE SPIRITS

Awaking in the middle of a prodigiously tough snore, and sitting up in bed to get his thoughts together, Scrooge had no occasion to be told that the bell was again upon the stroke of One. He felt that he was restored to consciousness in the right nick of time, for the especial purpose of holding a conference with the second messenger dispatched to him through Jacob Marley's intervention. But finding that he turned uncomfortably cold when he began to wonder which of his curtains this new spectre would draw back, he put them every one aside with his own hands; and lying down again, established a sharp look-out all round the bed. For he wished to challenge the

Spirit on the moment of its appearance, and did not wish to be taken by surprise and made nervous.

Gentlemen of the free-and-easy sort, who plume themselves on being acquainted with a move or two, and being usually equal to the time-of-day, express the wide range of their capacity for adventure by observing that they are good for anything from pitch-and-toss[5] to manslaughter; between which opposite extremes, no doubt, there lies a tolerably wide and comprehensive range of subjects. Without venturing for Scrooge quite as hardily as this, I don't mind calling on you to believe that he was ready for a good broad field of strange appearances, and that nothing between a baby and a rhinoceros would have astonished him very much.

Now, being prepared for almost anything, he was not by any means prepared for nothing; and, consequently, when the Bell struck One, and no shape appeared, he was taken with a violent fit of trembling. Five minutes, ten minutes, a quarter of an hour went by, yet nothing came. All this time, he lay upon his bed, the very core and centre of a blaze of ruddy light, which

5. A street gambling game, in which coins are thrown at a target; the player whose coin is closest tosses the other coins in the air, and keeps all those that land heads-up.

streamed upon it when the clock proclaimed the hour; and which being only light, was more alarming than a dozen ghosts, as he was powerless to make out what it meant, or would be at; and was sometimes apprehensive that he might be at that very moment an interesting case of spontaneous combustion, without having the consolation of knowing it. At last, however, he began to think—as you or I would have thought at first; for it is always the person not in the predicament who knows what ought to have been done in it, and would unquestionably have done it too—at last, I say, he began to think that the source and secret of this ghostly light might be in the adjoining room: from whence, on further tracing it, it seemed to shine. This idea taking full possession of his mind, he got up softly and shuffled in his slippers to the door.

The moment Scrooge's hand was on the lock, a strange voice called him by his name, and bade him enter. He obeyed.

It was his own room. There was no doubt about that. But it had undergone a surprising transformation. The walls and ceiling were so hung with living green, that it looked a perfect grove, from every part of which, bright gleaming berries glistened. The crisp leaves of holly, mistletoe, and ivy reflected back the light, as if so many little mirrors had been scattered there; and such a mighty blaze went roaring up the chimney, as that dull petrifaction of a hearth had never known in Scrooge's time, or Marley's, or for many and many a winter season gone. Heaped up upon the floor, to form a kind of throne, were turkeys, geese, game, poultry, brawn, great joints of meat, sucking-pigs, long wreaths of sausages, mince-pies, plum-puddings, barrels of oysters, red-hot chestnuts, cherry-cheeked apples, juicy oranges, luscious pears, immense twelfth-cakes,[6] and seething bowls of punch, that made the chamber dim with their delicious steam. In easy state upon this couch, there sat a jolly Giant, glorious to see; who bore a glowing torch, in shape not unlike Plenty's horn,[7] and held it up, high up, to shed its light on Scrooge, as he came peeping round the door.

"Come in!" exclaimed the Ghost. "Come in! and know me better, man!"

Scrooge entered timidly, and hung his head before this Spirit. He was not the dogged Scrooge he had been; and though its eyes were clear and kind, he did not like to meet them.

"I am the Ghost of Christmas Present," said the Spirit. "Look upon me!"

Scrooge reverently did so. It was clothed in one simple deep green robe, or mantle, bordered with white fur. This garment hung so loosely on the figure, that its capacious breast was bare, as if disdaining to be warded or concealed by any artifice. Its feet, observable beneath the ample folds of the garment, were also bare; and on its head it wore no other covering than a holly wreath set here and there with shining icicles. Its dark brown curls were long and free: free as its genial face, its sparkling eye, its open hand, its cheery voice, its unconstrained demeanour, and its joyful air. Girded round its middle was an antique scabbard; but no sword was in it, and the ancient sheath was eaten up with rust.

"You have never seen the like of me before!" exclaimed the Spirit.

"Never," Scrooge made answer to it.

6. Large pastries, traditionally served on Twelfth Night (January 6).
7. The horn of plenty (or cornucopia), overflowing with produce, flowers, or nuts, is an ancient classical symbol of abundance and nourishment.

Scrooge's third Visitor.

"Have never walked forth with the younger members of my family; meaning (for I am very young) my elder brothers born in these later years?" pursued the Phantom.

"I don't think I have," said Scrooge. "I am afraid I have not. Have you had many brothers, Spirit?"

"More than eighteen hundred," said the Ghost.

"A tremendous family to provide for!" muttered Scrooge.

The Ghost of Christmas Present rose.

"Spirit," said Scrooge submissively, "conduct me where you will. I went forth last night on compulsion, and I learnt a lesson which is working now. To-night, if you have aught to teach me, let me profit by it."

"Touch my robe!"

Scrooge did as he was told, and held it fast.

Holly, mistletoe, red berries, ivy, turkeys, geese, game, poultry, brawn, meat, pigs, sausages, oysters, pies, puddings, fruit, and punch, all vanished instantly. So did the room, the fire, the ruddy glow, the hour of night, and they stood in the city streets on Christmas morning, where (for the weather was severe) the people made a rough, but brisk and not unpleasant kind of music, in scraping the snow from the pavement in front of their dwellings, and from the tops of their houses: whence it was mad delight to the boys to see it come plumping down into the road below, and splitting into artificial little snowstorms.

The house fronts looked black enough, and the windows blacker, contrasting with the smooth white sheet of snow upon the roofs, and with the dirtier snow upon the ground; which last deposit had been ploughed up in deep furrows by the heavy wheels of carts and wagons; furrows that crossed and recrossed each other hundreds of times where the great streets branched off; and made intricate channels, hard to trace, in the thick yellow mud and icy water. The sky was gloomy, and the shortest streets were choked up with a dingy mist, half thawed half frozen, whose heavier particles descended in a shower of sooty atoms, as if all the chimneys in Great Britain had, by one consent, caught fire, and were blazing away to their dear hearts' content. There was nothing very cheerful in the climate or the town, and yet was there an air of cheerfulness abroad that the clearest summer air and brightest summer sun might have endeavoured to diffuse in vain.

For the people who were shovelling away on the house-tops were jovial and full of glee; calling out to one another from the parapets, and now and then exchanging a facetious snowball—better-natured missile far than many a wordy jest—laughing heartily if it went right, and not less heartily if it went wrong. The poulterers' shops were still half open, and the fruiterers' were radiant in their glory. There were great, round, pot-bellied baskets of chestnuts, shaped like the waistcoats of jolly old gentlemen, lolling at the doors, and tumbling out into the street in their apoplectic opulence. There were ruddy, brown-faced, broad-girthed Spanish Onions, shining in the fatness of their growth like Spanish Friars; and winking from their shelves in wanton slyness at the girls as they went by, and glanced demurely at the hung-up mistletoe. There were pears and apples, clustered high in blooming pyramids; there were bunches of grapes, made, in the shopkeepers' benevolence, to dangle from conspicuous hooks, that people's mouths might water gratis as they passed; there were piles of filberts, mossy and brown, recalling, in their fragrance, ancient walks among the woods, and pleasant shufflings ankle deep through withered leaves; there were Norfolk Biffins,[8] squab and swarthy, setting off the yellow of the oranges and lemons, and, in the great compactness of their juicy persons, urgently entreating and beseeching to be

---

8. A variety of cooking apple.

carried home in paper bags and eaten after dinner. The very gold and silver fish,[9] set forth among these choice fruits in a bowl, though members of a dull and stagnant-blooded race, appeared to know that there was something going on; and, to a fish, went gasping round and round their little world in slow and passionless excitement.

The Grocers'! oh the Grocers'! nearly closed, with perhaps two shutters down, or one; but through those gaps such glimpses! It was not alone that the scales descending on the counter made a merry sound, or that the twine and roller parted company so briskly, or that the canisters were rattled up and down like juggling tricks, or even that the blended scents of tea and coffee were so grateful to the nose, or even that the raisins were so plentiful and rare, the almonds so extremely white, the sticks of cinnamon so long and straight, the other spices so delicious, the candied fruits so caked and spotted with molten sugar as to make the coldest lookers-on feel faint and subsequently bilious. Nor was it that the figs were moist and pulpy, or that the French plums blushed in modest tartness from their highly-decorated boxes, or that everything was good to eat and in its Christmas dress: but the customers were all so hurried and so eager in the hopeful promise of the day, that they tumbled up against each other at the door, crashing their wicker baskets wildly, and left their purchases upon the counter, and came running back to fetch them, and committed hundreds of the like mistakes in the best humour possible; while the Grocer and his people were so frank and fresh that the polished hearts with which they fastened their aprons behind might have been their own, worn outside for general inspection, and for Christmas daws[1] to peck at if they chose.

But soon the steeples called good people all, to church and chapel, and away they came, flocking through the streets in their best clothes, and with their gayest faces. And at the same time there emerged from scores of bye streets, lanes, and nameless turnings, innumerable people, carrying their dinners to the bakers' shops.[2] The sight of these poor revelers appeared to interest the Spirit very much, for he stood with Scrooge beside him in a baker's doorway, and taking off the covers as their bearers passed, sprinkled incense on their dinners from his torch. And it was a very uncommon kind of torch, for once or twice when there were angry words between some dinner-carriers who had jostled with each other, he shed a few drops of water on them from it, and their good humour was restored directly. For they said, it was a shame to quarrel upon Christmas Day. And so it was! God love it, so it was!

In time the bells ceased, and the bakers' were shut up; and yet there was a genial shadowing forth of all these dinners and the progress of their cooking, in the thawed blotch of wet above each baker's oven; where the pavement smoked as if its stones were cooking too.

"Is there a peculiar flavour in what you sprinkle from your torch?" asked Scrooge.

"There is. My own."

9. Members of the carp family, sold in glass bowls by London street traders at that time.
1. Jackdaws, a type of crow. Cf. Shakespeare, *Othello* 1.1.64–65: "For I will wear my heart upon my sleeve / For daws to peck at."

2. In that period, most cooking in the homes of the poor was done over an open fire; bakers, prohibited from baking on Sundays and Christmas Day, allowed people to use their ovens for a small charge on those days.

"Would it apply to any kind of dinner on this day?" asked Scrooge.

"To any kindly given. To a poor one most."

"Why to a poor one most?" asked Scrooge.

"Because it needs it most."

"Spirit," said Scrooge, after a moment's thought, "I wonder you, of all the beings in the many worlds about us, should desire to cramp these people's opportunities of innocent enjoyment."

"I!" cried the Spirit.

"You would deprive them of their means of dining every seventh day, often the only day on which they can be said to dine at all," said Scrooge. "Wouldn't you?"

"I!" cried the Spirit.

"You seek to close these places on the Seventh Day?"[3] said Scrooge. "And it comes to the same thing."

"*I* seek?" exclaimed the Spirit.

"Forgive me if I am wrong. It has been done in your name, or at least in that of your family," said Scrooge.

"There are some upon this earth of yours," returned the Spirit, "who lay claim to know us, and who do their deeds of passion, pride, ill-will, hatred, envy, bigotry, and selfishness in our name; who are as strange to us and all our kith and kin, as if they had never lived. Remember that, and charge their doings on themselves, not us."

Scrooge promised that he would; and they went on, invisible, as they had been before, into the suburbs of the town. It was a remarkable quality of the Ghost (which Scrooge had observed at the baker's) that notwithstanding his gigantic size, he could accommodate himself to any place with ease; and that he stood beneath a low roof quite as gracefully and like a supernatural creature, as it was possible he could have done in any lofty hall.

And perhaps it was the pleasure the good Spirit had in showing off this power of his, or else it was his own kind, generous, hearty nature, and his sympathy with all poor men, that led him straight to Scrooge's clerk's; for there he went, and took Scrooge with him, holding to his robe; and on the threshold of the door the Spirit smiled, and stopped to bless Bob Cratchit's dwelling with the sprinklings of his torch. Think of that! Bob had but fifteen "Bob"[4] a-week himself; he pocketed on Saturdays but fifteen copies of his Christian name; and yet the Ghost of Christmas Present blessed his four-roomed house!

Then up rose Mrs. Cratchit, Cratchit's wife, dressed out but poorly in a twice-turned gown, but brave in ribbons, which are cheap and make a goodly show for sixpence; and she laid the cloth, assisted by Belinda Cratchit, second of her daughters, also brave in ribbons; while Master Peter Cratchit plunged a fork into the saucepan of potatoes, and getting the corners of his monstrous shirt-collar (Bob's private property, conferred upon his son and heir in honour of the day) into his mouth, rejoiced to find himself so gallantly attired, and yearned to show his linen in the fashionable Parks.[5] And

---

3. These exchanges connect to the Sabbatarianism movement, active from the 1830s, which sought to close the bakeries and limit the entertainments of the poor on Sundays. Dickens was strenuously opposed.

4. A shilling (slang).
5. I.e., one of the Royal Parks in central London, such as St. James's Park, Green Park, and Hyde Park.

now two smaller Cratchits, boy and girl, came tearing in, screaming that outside the baker's they had smelt the goose, and known it for their own; and basking in luxurious thoughts of sage-and-onion, these young Cratchits danced about the table, and exalted Master Peter Cratchit to the skies, while he (not proud, although his collars nearly choked him) blew the fire, until the slow potatoes bubbling up, knocked loudly at the saucepan-lid to be let out and peeled.

"What has ever got your precious father then," said Mrs. Cratchit. "And your brother, Tiny Tim! And Martha warn't as late last Christmas Day by half-an-hour!"

"Here's Martha, mother!" said a girl, appearing as she spoke.

"Here's Martha, mother!" cried the two young Cratchits. "Hurrah! There's *such* a goose, Martha!"

"Why, bless your heart alive, my dear, how late you are!" said Mrs. Cratchit, kissing her a dozen times, and taking off her shawl and bonnet for her, with officious zeal.

"We'd a deal of work to finish up last night," replied the girl, "and had to clear away this morning, mother!"

"Well! Never mind so long as you are come," said Mrs. Cratchit. "Sit ye down before the fire, my dear, and have a warm, Lord bless ye!"

"No no! There's father coming," cried the two young Cratchits, who were everywhere at once. "Hide Martha, hide!"

So Martha hid herself, and in came little Bob, the father, with at least three feet of comforter exclusive of the fringe, hanging down before him; and his thread-bare clothes darned up and brushed, to look seasonable; and Tiny Tim upon his shoulder. Alas for Tiny Tim, he bore a little crutch, and had his limbs supported by an iron frame!

"Why, where's our Martha?" cried Bob Cratchit looking round.

"Not coming," said Mrs. Cratchit.

"Not coming!" said Bob, with a sudden declension in his high spirits; for he had been Tim's blood horse[6] all the way from church, and had come home rampant. "Not coming upon Christmas Day!"

Martha didn't like to see him disappointed, if it were only in joke; so she came out prematurely from behind the closet door, and ran into his arms, while the two young Cratchits hustled Tiny Tim, and bore him off into the wash-house, that he might hear the pudding singing in the copper.[7]

"And how did little Tim behave?" asked Mrs. Cratchit, when she had rallied Bob on his credulity and Bob had hugged his daughter to his heart's content.

"As good as gold," said Bob, "and better. Somehow he gets thoughtful, sitting by himself so much, and thinks the strangest things you ever heard. He told me, coming home, that he hoped the people saw him in the church, because he was a cripple, and it might be pleasant to them to remember upon Christmas Day, who made lame beggars walk and blind men see."[8]

Bob's voice was tremulous when he told them this, and trembled more when he said that Tiny Tim was growing strong and hearty.

---

6. A thoroughbred, particularly a racehorse.
7. A large vessel, made of copper or cast iron, used primarily for boiling laundry.

8. See John 5.1–9 for the account of Jesus's healing of the lame man, and Mark 8.22–25, for the restoration of the blind man's vision.

His active little crutch was heard upon the floor, and back came Tiny Tim before another word was spoken, escorted by his brother and sister to his stool beside the fire; and while Bob, turning up his cuffs—as if, poor fellow, they were capable of being made more shabby—compounded some hot mixture in a jug with gin and lemons, and stirred it round and round and put it on the hob to simmer; Master Peter and the two ubiquitous young Cratchits went to fetch the goose, with which they soon returned in high procession.

Such a bustle ensued that you might have thought a goose the rarest of all birds; a feathered phenomenon, to which a black swan was a matter of course: and in truth it was something very like it in that house. Mrs. Cratchit made the gravy (ready beforehand in a little saucepan) hissing hot; Master Peter mashed the potatoes with incredible vigour; Miss Belinda sweetened up the apple-sauce; Martha dusted the hot plates; Bob took Tiny Tim beside him in a tiny corner at the table; the two young Cratchits set chairs for everybody, not forgetting themselves, and mounting guard upon their posts, crammed spoons into their mouths, lest they should shriek for goose before their turn came to be helped. At last the dishes were set on, and grace was said. It was succeeded by a breathless pause, as Mrs. Cratchit, looking slowly all along the carving-knife, prepared to plunge it in the breast; but when she did, and when the long expected gush of stuffing issued forth, one murmur of delight arose all round the board, and even Tiny Tim, excited by the two young Cratchits, beat on the table with the handle of his knife, and feebly cried Hurrah!

There never was such a goose. Bob said he didn't believe there ever was such a goose cooked. Its tenderness and flavor, size and cheapness, were the themes of universal admiration. Eked out by the apple-sauce and mashed potatoes, it was a sufficient dinner for the whole family; indeed, as Mrs. Cratchit said with great delight (surveying one small atom of a bone upon the dish), they hadn't ate it all at last! Yet every one had had enough, and the youngest Cratchits in particular, were steeped in sage and onion to the eyebrows! But now, the plates being changed by Miss Belinda, Mrs. Cratchit left the room alone—too nervous to bear witnesses—to take the pudding up, and bring it in.

Suppose it should not be done enough! Suppose it should break in turning out! Suppose somebody should have got over the wall of the back-yard, and stolen it, while they were merry with the goose: a supposition at which the two young Cratchits became livid! All sorts of horrors were supposed.

Hallo! A great deal of steam! The pudding was out of the copper. A smell like a washing-day! That was the cloth. A smell like an eating-house, and a pastry cook's next door to each other, with a laundress's next door to that! That was the pudding. In half a minute Mrs. Cratchit entered: flushed, but smiling proudly: with the pudding, like a speckled cannon-ball, so hard and firm, blazing in half of half-a-quartern of ignited brandy, and bedight with Christmas holly stuck into the top.

Oh, a wonderful pudding! Bob Cratchit said, and calmly too, that he regarded it as the greatest success achieved by Mrs. Cratchit since their marriage. Mrs. Cratchit said that now the weight was off her mind, she would confess she had had her doubts about the quantity of flour. Everybody had something to say about it, but nobody said or thought it was at all a small pudding for a large family. It would have been flat heresy to do so. Any Cratchit would have blushed to hint at such a thing.

At last the dinner was all done, the cloth was cleared, the hearth swept, and the fire made up. The compound in the jug being tasted and considered perfect, apples and oranges were put upon the table, and a shovel-full of chesnuts on the fire. Then all the Cratchit family drew round the hearth, in what Bob Cratchit called a circle, meaning half a one; and at Bob Cratchit's elbow stood the family display of glass; two tumblers, and a custard-cup without a handle.

These held the hot stuff from the jug, however, as well as golden goblets would have done; and Bob served it out with beaming looks, while the chesnuts on the fire sputtered and crackled noisily. Then Bob proposed:

"A Merry Christmas to us all, my dears. God bless us!"

Which all the family re-echoed.

"God bless us every one!" said Tiny Tim, the last of all.

He sat very close to his father's side, upon his little stool. Bob held his withered little hand in his, as if he loved the child, and wished to keep him by his side, and dreaded that he might be taken from him.

"Spirit," said Scrooge, with an interest he had never felt before, "tell me if Tiny Tim will live."

"I see a vacant seat," replied the Ghost, "in the poor chimney corner, and a crutch without an owner, carefully preserved. If these shadows remain unaltered by the Future, the child will die."

"No, no," said Scrooge. "Oh no, kind Spirit! say he will be spared."

"If these shadows remain unaltered by the Future, none other of my race," returned the Ghost, "will find him here. What then? If he be like to die, he had better do it, and decrease the surplus population."

Scrooge hung his head to hear his own words quoted by the Spirit, and was overcome with penitence and grief.

"Man," said the Ghost, "if man you be in heart, not adamant, forbear that wicked cant until you have discovered What the surplus is, and Where it is. Will you decide what men shall live, what men shall die? It may be, that in the sight of Heaven, you are more worthless and less fit to live than millions like this poor man's child. Oh God! to hear the Insect on the leaf pronouncing on the too much life among his hungry brothers in the dust!"

Scrooge bent before the Ghost's rebuke, and trembling cast his eyes upon the ground. But he raised them speedily, on hearing his own name.

"Mr. Scrooge!" said Bob; "I'll give you Mr. Scrooge, the Founder of the Feast!"

"The Founder of the Feast indeed!" cried Mrs. Cratchit, reddening. "I wish I had him here. I'd give him a piece of my mind to feast upon, and I hope he'd have a good appetite for it."

"My dear," said Bob, "the children; Christmas Day."

"It should be Christmas Day, I am sure," said she, "on which one drinks the health of such an odious, stingy, hard, unfeeling man as Mr. Scrooge. You know he is, Robert! Nobody knows it better than you do, poor fellow!"

"My dear," was Bob's mild answer, "Christmas Day."

"I'll drink his health for your sake and the Day's," said Mrs. Cratchit, "not for his. Long life to him! A merry Christmas and a happy new year! He'll be very merry and very happy, I have no doubt!"

The children drank the toast after her. It was the first of their proceedings which had no heartiness in it. Tiny Tim drank it last of all, but he didn't care twopence for it. Scrooge was the Ogre of the family. The mention of his name cast a dark shadow on the party, which was not dispelled for full five minutes.

After it had passed away, they were ten times merrier than before, from the mere relief of Scrooge the Baleful being done with. Bob Cratchit told them how he had a situation in his eye for Master Peter, which would bring in, if obtained, full five-and-sixpence weekly. The two young Cratchits laughed tremendously at the idea of Peter's being a man of business; and Peter himself looked thoughtfully at the fire from between his collars, as if he were deliberating what particular investments he should favour when he came into the receipt of that bewildering income. Martha, who was a poor apprentice at a milliner's, then told them what kind of work she had to do, and how many hours she worked at a stretch, and how she meant to lie a-bed to-morrow morning for a good long rest; to-morrow being a holiday she passed at home. Also how she had seen a countess and a lord some days before, and how the lord "was much about as tall as Peter;" at which Peter pulled up his collars so high that you couldn't have seen his head if you had been there. All this time the chesnuts and the jug went round and round; and bye and bye they had a song, about a lost child travelling in the snow, from Tiny Tim; who had a plaintive little voice, and sang it very well indeed.

There was nothing of high mark in this. They were not a handsome family; they were not well dressed; their shoes were far from being waterproof; their clothes were scanty; and Peter might have known, and very likely did, the inside of a pawnbroker's. But they were happy, grateful, pleased with one another, and contented with the time; and when they faded, and looked happier yet in the bright sprinklings of the Spirit's torch at parting, Scrooge had his eye upon them, and especially on Tiny Tim, until the last.

By this time it was getting dark, and snowing pretty heavily; and as Scrooge and the Spirit went along the streets, the brightness of the roaring fires in kitchens, parlours, and all sorts of rooms, was wonderful. Here, the flickering of the blaze showed preparations for a cosy dinner, with hot plates baking through and through before the fire, and deep red curtains, ready to be drawn, to shut out cold and darkness. There, all the children of the house were running out into the snow to meet their married sisters, brothers, cousins, uncles, aunts, and be the first to greet them. Here, again, were shadows on the window-blind of guests assembling; and there a group of handsome girls, all hooded and fur-booted, and all chattering at once, tripped lightly off to some near neighbour's house; where, wo upon the single man who saw them enter—artful witches: well they knew it—in a glow!

But if you had judged from the numbers of people on their way to friendly gatherings, you might have thought that no one was at home to give them welcome when they got there, instead of every house expecting company, and piling up its fires half-chimney high. Blessings on it, how the Ghost exulted! How it bared its breadth of breast, and opened its capacious palm, and floated on, outpouring, with a generous hand, its bright and harmless mirth on everything within its reach! The very lamplighter, who ran on before, dotting the dusky street with specks of light, and who was dressed to spend the evening somewhere, laughed out loudly as the Spirit passed: though little kenned the lamp-lighter that he had any company but Christmas!

And now, without a word of warning from the Ghost, they stood upon a bleak and desert moor, where monstrous masses of rude stone were cast about, as though it were the burial-place of giants;[9] and water spread itself wheresoever it listed; or would have done so, but for the frost that held it prisoner; and nothing grew but moss and furze, and coarse, rank grass. Down in the west the setting sun had left a streak of fiery red, which glared upon the desolation for an instant, like a sullen eye, and frowning lower, lower, lower yet, was lost in the thick gloom of darkest night.

"What place is this?" asked Scrooge.

"A place where Miners live, who labour in the bowels of the earth," returned the Spirit. "But they know me. See!"

A light shone from the window of a hut, and swiftly they advanced towards it. Passing through the wall of mud and stone, they found a cheerful company assembled round a glowing fire. An old, old man and woman, with their children and their children's children, and another generation beyond that, all decked out gaily in their holiday attire. The old man, in a voice that seldom rose above the howling of the wind upon the barren waste, was singing them a Christmas song; it had been a very old song when he was a boy; and from time to time they all joined in the chorus. So surely as they raised their voices, the old man got quite blithe and loud; and so surely as they stopped, his vigour sank again.

The Spirit did not tarry here, but bade Scrooge hold his robe, and passing on above the moor, sped whither? Not to sea? To sea. To Scrooge's horror, looking back, he saw the last of the land, a frightful range of rocks, behind them; and his ears were deafened by the thundering of water, as it rolled, and roared, and raged among the dreadful caverns it had worn, and fiercely tried to undermine the earth.

Built upon a dismal reef of sunken rocks, some league or so from shore, on which the waters chafed and dashed, the wild year through, there stood a solitary lighthouse. Great heaps of sea-weed clung to its base, and storm-birds—born of the wind one might suppose, as sea-weed of the water—rose and fell about it, like the waves they skimmed.

But even here, two men who watched the light had made a fire, that through the loophole in the thick stone wall shed out a ray of brightness on the awful sea. Joining their horny hands over the rough table at which they sat, they wished each other Merry Christmas in their can of grog; and one of them: the elder, too, with his face all damaged and scarred with hard weather, as the figure-head of an old ship might be: struck up a sturdy song that was like a Gale in itself.

Again the Ghost sped on, above the black and heaving sea—on, on—until, being far away, as he told Scrooge, from any shore, they lighted on a ship. They stood beside the helmsman at the wheel, the look-out in the bow, the officers who had the watch; dark, ghostly figures in their several stations; but every man among them hummed a Christmas tune, or had a Christmas thought, or spoke below his breath to his companion of some bygone Christmas Day, with homeward hopes belonging to it. And every man on board,

9. Cornwall, in the far southwest of Great Britain, is the traditional setting of the children's story "Jack the Giant Killer." In the vision that follows, Dickens is drawing on a visit he made to the county in 1842 to see the appalling conditions experienced by child laborers in the Cornish tin and copper mines.

waking or sleeping, good or bad, had had a kinder word for another on that day than on any day in the year; and had shared to some extent in its festivities; and had remembered those he cared for at a distance, and had known that they delighted to remember him.

It was a great surprise to Scrooge, while listening to the moaning of the wind, and thinking what a solemn thing it was to move on through the lonely darkness over an unknown abyss, whose depths were secrets as profound as Death: it was a great surprise to Scrooge, while thus engaged, to hear a hearty laugh. It was a much greater surprise to Scrooge to recognize it as his own nephew's, and to find himself in a bright, dry, gleaming room, with the Spirit standing smiling by his side, and looking at that same nephew with approving affability!

"Ha, ha!" laughed Scrooge's nephew. "Ha, ha, ha!"

If you should happen, by any unlikely chance, to know a man more blest in a laugh than Scrooge's nephew, all I can say is, I should like to know him too. Introduce him to me, and I'll cultivate his acquaintance.

It is a fair, even-handed, noble adjustment of things, that while there is infection in disease and sorrow, there is nothing in the world so irresistibly contagious as laughter and good-humour. When Scrooge's nephew laughed in this way: holding his sides, rolling his head, and twisting his face into the most extravagant contortions: Scrooge's niece, by marriage, laughed as heartily as he. And their assembled friends being not a bit behindhand, roared out, lustily.

"Ha, ha! Ha, ha, ha, ha!"

"He said that Christmas was a humbug, as I live!" cried Scrooge's nephew. "He believed it too!"

"More shame for him, Fred!" said Scrooge's niece, indignantly. Bless those women; they never do anything by halves. They are always in earnest.

She was very pretty: exceedingly pretty. With a dimpled, surprised-looking, capital face; a ripe little mouth, that seemed made to be kissed—as no doubt it was; all kinds of good little dots about her chin, that melted into one another when she laughed; and the sunniest pair of eyes you ever saw in any little creature's head. Altogether she was what you would have called provoking, you know; but satisfactory, too. Oh, perfectly satisfactory!

"He's a comical old fellow," said Scrooge's nephew, "that's the truth; and not so pleasant as he might be. However, his offences carry their own punishment, and I have nothing to say against him."

"I'm sure he is very rich, Fred," hinted Scrooge's niece. "At least you always tell *me* so."

"What of that, my dear!" said Scrooge's nephew. "His wealth is of no use to him. He don't do any good with it. He don't make himself comfortable with it. He hasn't the satisfaction of thinking—ha, ha, ha!—that he is ever going to benefit Us with it."

"I have no patience with him," observed Scrooge's niece. Scrooge's niece's sisters, and all the other ladies, expressed the same opinion.

"Oh, I have!" said Scrooge's nephew. "I am sorry for him; I couldn't be angry with him if I tried. Who suffers by his ill whims? Himself, always. Here, he takes it into his head to dislike us, and he won't come and dine with us. What's the consequence? He don't lose much of a dinner."

"Indeed, I think he loses a very good dinner," interrupted Scrooge's niece. Everybody else said the same, and they must be allowed to have been competent judges, because they had just had dinner; and, with the dessert upon the table, were clustered round the fire, by lamplight.

"Well! I am very glad to hear it," said Scrooge's nephew, "because I haven't any great faith in these young housekeepers. What do *you* say, Topper?"

Topper had clearly got his eye upon one of Scrooge's niece's sisters, for he answered that a bachelor was a wretched outcast, who had no right to express an opinion on the subject. Whereat Scrooge's niece's sister—the plump one with the lace tucker:[1] not the one with the roses—blushed.

"Do go on, Fred," said Scrooge's niece, clapping her hands. "He never finishes what he begins to say! He is such a ridiculous fellow!"

Scrooge's nephew reveled in another laugh, and as it was impossible to keep the infection off; though the plump sister tried hard to do it with aromatic vinegar; his example was unanimously followed.

"I was only going to say," said Scrooge's nephew, "that the consequence of his taking a dislike to us, and not making merry with us, is, as I think, that he loses some pleasant moments, which could do him no harm. I am sure he loses pleasanter companions than he can find in his own thoughts, either in his mouldy old office, or his dusty chambers. I mean to give him the same chance every year, whether he likes it or not, for I pity him. He may rail at Christmas till he dies, but he can't help thinking better of it—I defy him—if he finds me going there, in good temper, year after year, and saying Uncle Scrooge, how are you? If it only puts him in the vein to leave his poor clerk fifty pounds, *that's* something; and I think I shook him, yesterday."

It was their turn to laugh now, at the notion of his shaking Scrooge. But being thoroughly good-natured, and not much caring what they laughed at, so that they laughed at any rate, he encouraged them in their merriment, and passed the bottle, joyously.

After tea, they had some music. For they were a musical family, and knew what they were about, when they sung a Glee or Catch,[2] I can assure you: especially Topper, who could growl away in the bass like a good one, and never swell the large veins in his forehead, or get red in the face over it. Scrooge's niece played well upon the harp; and played among other tunes a simple little air (a mere nothing: you might learn to whistle it in two minutes), which had been familiar to the child who fetched Scrooge from the boarding-school, as he had been reminded by the Ghost of Christmas Past. When this strain of music sounded, all the things that Ghost had shown him, came upon his mind; he softened more and more; and thought that if he could have listened to it often, years ago, he might have cultivated the kindnesses of life for his own happiness with his own hands, without resorting to the sexton's spade that buried Jacob Marley.

But they didn't devote the whole evening to music. After a while they played at forfeits[3]; for it is good to be children sometimes, and never better

---

1. A piece of lace or linen worn at the top of a bodice or as an insert at the front of a low-cut dress.
2. A comic song for numerous voices, in which, after the first singer has finished a line, the second begins, or "catches" the words just sung, and so on. "Glee": a song for multiple voices, with distinct harmonizing parts for each.
3. A popular parlor game. One player (the judge) leaves the room; the others each place a small personal item in a bag or box. The judge returns, picks out an item, and describes it; its owner must do something amusing or embarrassing (pay a forfeit) to win it back.

than at Christmas, when its mighty Founder was a child himself. Stop! There was first a game at blindman's buff. Of course there was. And I no more believe Topper was really blind than I believe he had eyes in his boots. My opinion is, that it was a done thing between him and Scrooge's nephew; and that the Ghost of Christmas Present knew it. The way he went after that plump sister in the lace tucker, was an outrage on the credulity of human nature. Knocking down the fire-irons, tumbling over the chairs, bumping up against the piano, smothering himself among the curtains, wherever she went, there went he. He always knew where the plump sister was. He wouldn't catch anybody else. If you had fallen up against him, as some of them did, and stood there; he would have made a feint of endeavouring to seize you, which would have been an affront to your understanding; and would instantly have sidled off in the direction of the plump sister. She often cried out that it wasn't fair; and it really was not. But when at last, he caught her; when, in spite of all her silken rustlings, and her rapid fluttering past him, he got her into a corner whence there was no escape; then his conduct was the most execrable. For his pretending not to know her; his pretending that it was necessary to touch her head-dress, and further to assure himself of her identity by pressing a certain ring upon her finger, and a certain chain about her neck; was vile, monstrous! No doubt she told him her opinion of it, when, another blind-man being in office, they were so very confidential together, behind the curtains.

Scrooge's niece was not one of the blind-man's buff party, but was made comfortable with a large chair and a footstool, in a snug corner, where the Ghost and Scrooge were close behind her. But she joined in the forfeits, and loved her love to admiration with all the letters of the alphabet.[4] Likewise at the game of How, When, and Where,[5] she was very great, and to the secret joy of Scrooge's nephew, beat her sisters hollow: though they were sharp girls too, as Topper could have told you. There might have been twenty people there, young and old, but they all played, and so did Scrooge; for, wholly forgetting in the interest he had in what was going on, that his voice made no sound in their ears, he sometimes came out with his guess quite loud, and very often guessed right, too; for the sharpest needle, best Whitechapel, warranted not to cut in the eye,[6] was not sharper than Scrooge: blunt as he took it in his head to be.

The Ghost was greatly pleased to find him in this mood, and looked upon him with such favour that he begged like a boy to be allowed to stay until the guests departed. But this the Spirit said could not be done.

"Here is a new game," said Scrooge. "One half hour, Spirit, only one!"

It was a Game called Yes and No, where Scrooge's nephew had to think of something, and the rest must find out what; he only answering to their questions yes or no as the case was. The brisk fire of questioning to which he was exposed, elicited from him that he was thinking of an animal, a live animal, rather a disagreeable animal, a savage animal, an animal that

---

4. A word game, in which each player must complete a series of statements with words beginning with A, and then B, and so forth.
5. A word game, in which players ask one of their number "How do you like it?" "When do you like it?" and "Where do you like it?" to try to establish

the mystery entity of which he or she is thinking.
6. The eye of a well-made needle has smooth edges so it will not cut the cotton threaded through it. Whitechapel, a poor district east of the City of London, was then the site of needle-making workshops.

growled and grunted sometimes, and talked sometimes, and lived in London, and walked about the streets, and wasn't made a show of, and wasn't led by anybody, and didn't live in a menagerie, and was never killed in a market, and was not a horse, or an ass, or a cow, or a bull, or a tiger, or a dog, or a pig, or a cat, or a bear. At every fresh question that was put to him, this nephew burst into a fresh roar of laughter; and was so inexpressibly tickled, that he was obliged to get up off the sofa and stamp. At last the plump sister, falling into a similar state, cried out:

"I have found it out! I know what it is, Fred! I know what it is!"

"What is it?" cried Fred.

"It's your Uncle Scro-o-o-o-oge!"

Which it certainly was. Admiration was the universal sentiment, though some objected that the reply to "Is it a bear?" ought to have been "Yes;" inasmuch as an answer in the negative was sufficient to have diverted their thoughts from Mr. Scrooge, supposing they had ever had any tendency that way.

"He has given us plenty of merriment, I am sure," said Fred, "and it would be ungrateful not to drink his health. Here is a glass of mulled wine ready to our hand at the moment; and I say 'Uncle Scrooge!'"

"Well! Uncle Scrooge!" they cried.

"A Merry Christmas and a happy New Year to the old man, whatever he is!" said Scrooge's nephew. "He wouldn't take it from me, but may he have it, nevertheless. Uncle Scrooge!"

Uncle Scrooge had imperceptibly become so gay and light of heart, that he would have pledged the unconscious company in return, and thanked them in an inaudible speech, if the Ghost had given him time. But the whole scene passed off in the breath of the last word spoken by his nephew; and he and the Spirit were again upon their travels.

Much they saw, and far they went, and many homes they visited, but always with a happy end. The Spirit stood beside sick beds, and they were cheerful; on foreign lands, and they were close at home; by struggling men, and they were patient in their greater hope; by poverty, and it was rich. In almshouse, hospital, and jail, in misery's every refuge, where vain man in his little brief authority[7] had not made fast the door, and barred the Spirit out, he left his blessing, and taught Scrooge his precepts.

It was a long night, if it were only a night; but Scrooge had his doubts of this, because the Christmas Holidays appeared to be condensed into the space of time they passed together. It was strange, too, that while Scrooge remained unaltered in his outward form, the Ghost grew older, clearly older. Scrooge had observed this change, but never spoke of it, until they left a children's Twelfth Night party, when, looking at the Spirit as they stood together in an open place, he noticed that its hair was gray.

"Are spirits' lives so short?" asked Scrooge.

"My life upon this globe, is very brief," replied the Ghost. "It ends to-night."

"To-night!" cried Scrooge.

"To-night at midnight. Hark! The time is drawing near."

The chimes were ringing the three quarters past eleven at that moment.

---

7. Cf. Shakespeare, *Measure for Measure* 2.2.120–22: "But man, proud man, / Dressed in a little brief authority, / Most ignorant of what he's most assured."

"Forgive me if I am not justified in what I ask," said Scrooge, looking intently at the Spirit's robe, "but I see something strange, and not belonging to yourself, protruding from your skirts. Is it a foot or a claw!"

"It might be a claw, for the flesh there is upon it," was the Spirit's sorrowful reply. "Look here."

From the folding of its robe, it brought two children; wretched, abject, frightful, hideous, miserable. They knelt down at its feet, and clung upon the outside of its garment.

"Oh, Man! look here. Look, look, down here!" exclaimed the Ghost.

They were a boy and girl. Yellow, meagre, ragged, scowling, wolfish; but prostrate, too, in their humility. Where graceful youth should have filled their features out, and touched them with its freshest tints, a stale and shrivelled hand, like that of age, had pinched, and twisted them, and pulled them into shreds. Where angels might have sat enthroned, devils lurked, and glared out menacing. No change, no degradation, no perversion of humanity, in any grade, through all the mysteries of wonderful creation, has monsters half so horrible and dread.

Scrooge started back, appalled. Having them shown to him in this way, he tried to say they were fine children, but the words choked themselves, rather than be parties to a lie of such enormous magnitude.

"Spirit! are they yours?" Scrooge could say no more.

"They are Man's," said the Spirit, looking down upon them. "And they cling to me, appealing from their fathers. This boy is Ignorance. This girl is Want. Beware them both, and all of their degree, but most of all beware this boy, for on his brow I see that written which is Doom, unless the writing be erased. Deny it!" cried the Spirit, stretching out its hand towards the city. "Slander those who tell it ye! Admit it for your factious purposes, and make it worse! And bide the end!"

"Have they no refuge or resource?" cried Scrooge.

"Are there no prisons?" said the Spirit, turning on him for the last time with his own words. "Are there no workhouses?"

The bell struck twelve.

Scrooge looked about him for the Ghost, and saw it not. As the last stroke ceased to vibrate, he remembered the prediction of old Jacob Marley, and lifting up his eyes, beheld a solemn Phantom, draped and hooded, coming, like a mist along the ground, towards him.

Stave Four

THE LAST OF THE SPIRITS

The Phantom slowly, gravely, silently, approached. When it came near him, Scrooge bent down upon his knee; for in the very air through which this Spirit moved it seemed to scatter gloom and mystery.

It was shrouded in a deep black garment, which concealed its head, its face, its form, and left nothing of it visible save one outstretched hand. But for this it would have been difficult to detach its figure from the night, and separate it from the darkness by which it was surrounded.

He felt that it was tall and stately when it came beside him, and that its mysterious presence filled him with a solemn dread. He knew no more, for the Spirit neither spoke nor moved.

"I am in the presence of the Ghost of Christmas Yet To Come?" said Scrooge.

The Spirit answered not, but pointed onward with its hand.

"You are about to show me shadows of the things that have not happened, but will happen in the time before us," Scrooge pursued. "Is that so, Spirit?"

The upper portion of the garment was contracted for an instant in its folds, as if the Spirit had inclined its head. That was the only answer he received.

Although well used to ghostly company by this time, Scrooge feared the silent shape so much that his legs trembled beneath him, and he found that he could hardly stand when he prepared to follow it. The Spirit paused a moment, as observing his condition, and giving him time to recover.

But Scrooge was all the worse for this. It thrilled him with a vague uncertain horror, to know that behind the dusky shroud, there were ghostly eyes intently fixed upon him, while he, though he stretched his own to the utmost, could see nothing but a spectral hand and one great heap of black.

"Ghost of the Future!" he exclaimed, "I fear you more than any Spectre I have seen. But, as I know your purpose is to do me good, and as I hope to live to be another man from what I was, I am prepared to bear you company, and do it with a thankful heart. Will you not speak to me?"

It gave him no reply. The hand was pointed straight before them.

"Lead on!" said Scrooge. "Lead on! The night is waning fast, and it is precious time to me, I know. Lead on, Spirit!"

The Phantom moved away as it had come towards him. Scrooge followed in the shadow of its dress, which bore him up, he thought, and carried him along.

They scarcely seemed to enter the city; for the city rather seemed to spring up about them, and encompass them of its own act. But there they were, in the heart of it; on 'Change, amongst the merchants; who hurried up and down, and chinked the money in their pockets, and conversed in groups, and looked at their watches, and trifled thoughtfully with their great gold seals;[8] and so forth, as Scrooge had seen them often.

The Spirit stopped beside one little knot of business men. Observing that the hand was pointed to them, Scrooge advanced to listen to their talk.

"No," said a great fat man with a monstrous chin, "I don't know much about it, either way. I only know he's dead."

"When did he die?" inquired another.

"Last night, I believe."

"Why, what was the matter with him?" asked a third, taking a vast quantity of snuff out of a very large snuff-box. "I thought he'd never die."

"God knows," said the first, with a yawn.

"What has he done with his money?" asked a red-faced gentleman with a pendulous excrescence on the end of his nose, that shook like the gills of a turkey-cock.

"I haven't heard," said the man with the large chin, yawning again. "Left it to his Company, perhaps. He hasn't left it to *me*. That's all I know."

This pleasantry was received with a general laugh.

"It's likely to be a very cheap funeral," said the same speaker; "for upon my life I don't know of anybody to go to it. Suppose we make up a party and volunteer?"

"I don't mind going if a lunch is provided," observed the gentleman with the excrescence on his nose. "But I must be fed, if I make one."

Another laugh.

"Well, I am the most disinterested among you, after all," said the first speaker, "for I never wear black gloves,[9] and I never eat lunch. But I'll offer to go, if anybody else will. When I come to think of it, I'm not at all sure that I wasn't his most particular friend; for we used to stop and speak whenever we met. Bye, bye!"

Speakers and listeners strolled away, and mixed with other groups. Scrooge knew the men, and looked towards the Spirit for an explanation.

The Phantom glided on into a street. Its finger pointed to two persons meeting. Scrooge listened again, thinking that the explanation might lie here.

He knew these men, also, perfectly. They were men of business: very wealthy, and of great importance. He had made a point always of standing well in their esteem: in a business point of view, that is; strictly in a business point of view.

8. Men of business carried seals, in the form of medallions or rings, so that they could impress their own distinctive marks into the wax used to close or authenticate documents.
9. It was customary to present mourners at a funeral with a pair of black gloves.

"How are you?" said one.

"How are you?" returned the other.

"Well!" said the first. "Old Scratch[1] has got his own at last, hey?"

"So I am told," returned the second. "Cold, isn't it?"

"Seasonable for Christmas time. You're not a skaiter, I suppose?"

"No. No. Something else to think of. Good morning!"

Not another word. That was their meeting, their conversation, and their parting.

Scrooge was at first inclined to be surprised that the Spirit should attach importance to conversations apparently so trivial; but feeling assured that they must have some hidden purpose, he set himself to consider what it was likely to be. They could scarcely be supposed to have any bearing on the death of Jacob, his old partner, for that was Past, and this Ghost's province was the Future. Nor could he think of any one immediately connected with himself, to whom he could apply them. But nothing doubting that to whomsoever they applied they had some latent moral for his own improvement, he resolved to treasure up every word he heard, and everything he saw; and especially to observe the shadow of himself when it appeared. For he had an expectation that the conduct of his future self would give him the clue he missed, and would render the solution of these riddles easy.

He looked about in that very place for his own image; but another man stood in his accustomed corner, and though the clock pointed to his usual time of day for being there, he saw no likeness of himself among the multitudes that poured in through the Porch. It gave him little surprise, however; for he had been revolving in his mind a change of life, and thought and hoped he saw his new-born resolutions carried out in this.

Quiet and dark, beside him stood the Phantom, with its outstretched hand. When he roused himself from his thoughtful quest, he fancied from the turn of the hand, and its situation in reference to himself, that the Unseen Eyes were looking at him keenly. It made him shudder, and feel very cold.

They left the busy scene, and went into an obscure part of the town, where Scrooge had never penetrated before, although he recognised its situation, and its bad repute. The ways were foul and narrow; the shops and houses wretched; the people half-naked, drunken, slipshod, ugly. Alleys and archways, like so many cesspools, disgorged their offences of smell, and dirt, and life, upon the straggling streets; and the whole quarter reeked with crime, with filth, and misery.

Far in this den of infamous resort, there was a low-browed, beetling[2] shop, below a pent-house roof, where iron, old rags, bottles, bones, and greasy offal, were bought. Upon the floor within, were piled up heaps of rusty keys, nails, chains, hinges, files, scales, weights, and refuse iron of all kinds. Secrets that few would like to scrutinise were bred and hidden in mountains of unseemly rags, masses of corrupted fat, and sepulchres of bones. Sitting in among the wares he dealt in, by a charcoal-stove, made of old bricks, was a gray-haired rascal, nearly seventy years of age; who had screened himself from the cold air without, by a frousy curtaining of miscellaneous tatters, hung upon a line; and smoked his pipe in all the luxury of calm retirement.

1. The devil (slang).   2. Projecting, overhanging.

Scrooge and the Phantom came into the presence of this man, just as a woman with a heavy bundle slunk into the shop. But she had scarcely entered, when another woman, similarly laden, came in too; and she was closely followed by a man in faded black, who was no less startled by the sight of them, than they had been upon the recognition of each other. After a short period of blank astonishment, in which the old man with the pipe had joined them, they all three burst into a laugh.

"Let the charwoman alone to be the first!" cried she who had entered first. "Let the laundress alone to be the second; and let the undertaker's man alone to be the third. Look here, old Joe, here's a chance! If we haven't all three met here without meaning it!"

"You couldn't have met in a better place," said old Joe, removing his pipe from his mouth. "Come into the parlour. You were made free of it long ago, you know; and the other two an't strangers. Stop till I shut the door of the shop. Ah! How it skreeks! There an't such a rusty bit of metal in the place as its own hinges, I believe; and I'm sure there's no such old bones here, as mine. Ha, ha! We're all suitable to our calling, we're all suitable to our calling, we're well matched. Come into the parlour. Come into the parlour."

The parlour was the space behind the screen of rags. The old man raked the fire together with an old stair-rod, and having trimmed his smoky lamp (for it was night), with the stem of his pipe, put it in his mouth again.

While he did this, the woman who had already spoken threw her bundle on the floor and sat down in a flaunting manner on a stool; crossing her elbows on her knees, and looking with a bold defiance at the other two.

"What odds then! What odds, Mrs. Dilber?" said the woman. "Every person has a right to take care of themselves. *He* always did!"

"That's true, indeed!" said the laundress. "No man more so."

"Why, then, don't stand staring as if you was afraid, woman; who's the wiser? We're not going to pick holes in each other's coats, I suppose?"

"No, indeed!" said Mrs. Dilber and the man together. "We should hope not."

"Very well, then!" cried the woman. "That's enough. Who's the worse for the loss of a few things like these? Not a dead man, I suppose."

"No, indeed," said Mrs. Dilber, laughing.

"If he wanted to keep 'em after he was dead, a wicked old screw," pursued the woman, "why wasn't he natural in his lifetime? If he had been, he'd have had somebody to look after him when he was struck with Death, instead of lying gasping out his last there, alone by himself."

"It's the truest word that ever was spoke," said Mrs. Dilber. "It's a judgment on him."

"I wish it was a little heavier judgment," replied the woman; "and it should have been, you may depend upon it, if I could have laid my hands on anything else. Open that bundle, old Joe, and let me know the value of it. Speak out plain. I'm not afraid to be the first, nor afraid for them to see it. We knew pretty well that we were helping ourselves, before we met here, I believe. It's no sin. Open the bundle, Joe."

But the gallantry of her friends would not allow of this; and the man in faded black, mounting the breach first, produced *his* plunder. It was not extensive. A seal or two, a pencil-case, a pair of sleeve-buttons, and a brooch of no great value, were all. They were severally examined and appraised by old Joe, who chalked the sums he was disposed to give for each, upon the wall, and added them up into a total when he found that there was nothing more to come.

"That's your account," said Joe, "and I wouldn't give another sixpence, if I was to be boiled for not doing it. Who's next?"

Mrs. Dilber was next. Sheets and towels, a little wearing apparel, two old-fashioned silver teaspoons, a pair of sugar-tongs, and a few boots. Her account was stated on the wall in the same manner.

"I always give too much to ladies. It's a weakness of mine, and that's the way I ruin myself," said old Joe. "That's your account. If you asked me for another penny, and made it an open question, I'd repent of being so liberal, and knock off half-a-crown."

"And now undo *my* bundle, Joe," said the first woman.

Joe went down on his knees for the greater convenience of opening it, and having unfastened a great many knots, dragged out a large and heavy roll of some dark stuff.

"What do you call this?" said Joe. "Bed-curtains!"

"Ah!" returned the woman, laughing and leaning forward on her crossed arms. "Bed-curtains!"

"You don't mean to say you took 'em down, rings and all, with him lying there?" said Joe.

"Yes I do," replied the woman. "Why not?"

"You were born to make your fortune," said Joe, "and you'll certainly do it."

"I certainly shan't hold my hand, when I can get anything in it by reaching it out, for the sake of such a man as He was, I promise you, Joe," returned the woman coolly. "Don't drop that oil upon the blankets, now."

"His blankets?" asked Joe.

"Whose else's do you think?" replied the woman. "He isn't likely to take cold without 'em, I dare say."

"I hope he didn't die of anything catching? Eh?" said old Joe, stopping in his work, and looking up.

"Don't you be afraid of that," returned the woman. "I an't so fond of his company that I'd loiter about him for such things, if he did. Ah! You may look through that shirt till your eyes ache; but you won't find a hole in it, nor a thread-bare place. It's the best he had, and a fine one too. They'd have wasted it, if it hadn't been for me."

"What do you call wasting of it?" asked old Joe.

"Putting it on him to be buried in, to be sure," replied the woman with a laugh. "Somebody was fool enough to do it, but I took it off again. If calico an't good enough for such a purpose, it isn't good enough for anything. It's quite as becoming to the body. He can't look uglier than he did in that one."

Scrooge listened to this dialogue in horror. As they sat grouped about their spoil, in the scanty light afforded by the old man's lamp, he viewed them with a detestation and disgust, which could hardly have been greater, though they had been obscene demons, marketing the corpse itself.

"Ha, ha!" laughed the same woman, when old Joe, producing a flannel bag with money in it, told out their several gains upon the ground. "This is the end of it, you see! He frightened every one away from him when he was alive, to profit us when he was dead! Ha, ha, ha!"

"Spirit!" said Scrooge, shuddering from head to foot. "I see, I see. The case of this unhappy man might be my own. My life tends that way, now. Merciful Heaven, what is this!"

He recoiled in terror, for the scene had changed, and now he almost touched a bed: a bare, uncurtained bed: on which, beneath a ragged sheet, there lay a something covered up, which, though it was dumb, announced itself in awful language.

The room was very dark, too dark to be observed with any accuracy, though Scrooge glanced round it in obedience to a secret impulse, anxious to know what kind of room it was. A pale light, rising in the outer air, fell straight upon the bed; and on it, plundered and bereft, unwatched, unwept, uncared for, was the body of this man.

Scrooge glanced towards the Phantom. Its steady hand was pointed to the head. The cover was so carelessly adjusted that the slightest raising of it, the motion of a finger upon Scrooge's part, would have disclosed the face. He thought of it, felt how easy it would be to do, and longed to do it; but had no more power to withdraw the veil than to dismiss the spectre at his side.

Oh cold, cold, rigid, dreadful Death, set up thine altar here, and dress it with such terrors as thou hast at thy command: for this is thy dominion! But of the loved, revered, and honoured head, thou canst not turn one hair to thy dread purposes, or make one feature odious. It is not that the hand is heavy and will fall down when released; it is not that the heart and pulse are still; but that the hand was open, generous, and true; the heart brave, warm, and tender; and the pulse a man's. Strike, Shadow, strike! And see his good deeds springing from the wound, to sow the world with life immortal!

No voice pronounced these words in Scrooge's ears, and yet he heard them when he looked upon the bed. He thought, if this man could be raised up now, what would be his foremost thoughts? Avarice, hard dealing, griping cares? They have brought him to a rich end, truly!

He lay, in the dark empty house, with not a man, a woman, or a child, to say he was kind to me in this or that, and for the memory of one kind word I will be kind to him. A cat was tearing at the door, and there was a sound of gnawing rats beneath the hearth-stone. What *they* wanted in the room of death, and why they were so restless and disturbed, Scrooge did not dare to think.

"Spirit!" he said, "this is a fearful place. In leaving it, I shall not leave its lesson, trust me. Let us go!"

Still the Ghost pointed with an unmoved finger to the head.

"I understand you," Scrooge returned, "and I would do it, if I could. But I have not the power, Spirit. I have not the power."

Again it seemed to look upon him.

"If there is any person in the town, who feels emotion caused by this man's death," said Scrooge quite agonized, "show that person to me, Spirit, I beseech you!"

The phantom spread its dark robe before him for a moment, like a wing; and withdrawing it, revealed a room by daylight, where a mother and her children were.

She was expecting some one, and with anxious eagerness; for she walked up and down the room; started at every sound; looked out from the window; glanced at the clock; tried, but in vain, to work with her needle; and could hardly bear the voices of the children in their play.

At length the long-expected knock was heard. She hurried to the door, and met her husband; a man whose face was care-worn and depressed, though he was young. There was a remarkable expression in it now; a kind of serious delight of which he felt ashamed, and which he struggled to repress.

He sat down to the dinner that had been hoarding for him by the fire; and when she asked him faintly what news (which was not until after a long silence), he appeared embarrassed how to answer.

"Is it good," she said, "or bad?"—to help him.

"Bad," he answered.

"We are quite ruined?"

"No. There is hope yet, Caroline."

"If *he* relents," she said, amazed, "there is! Nothing is past hope, if such a miracle has happened."

"He is past relenting," said her husband. "He is dead."

She was a mild and patient creature if her face spoke truth; but she was thankful in her soul to hear it, and she said so, with clasped hands. She prayed forgiveness the next moment, and was sorry; but the first was the emotion of her heart.

"What the half-drunken woman whom I told you of last night, said to me, when I tried to see him and obtain a week's delay; and what I thought was a mere excuse to avoid me; turns out to have been quite true. He was not only very ill, but dying, then."

"To whom will our debt be transferred?"

"I don't know. But before that time we shall be ready with the money; and even though we were not, it would be bad fortune indeed to find so merciless a creditor in his successor. We may sleep to-night with light hearts, Caroline!"

Yes. Soften it as they would, their hearts were lighter. The children's faces, hushed and clustered round to hear what they so little understood, were brighter; and it was a happier house for this man's death! The only emotion that the Ghost could show him, caused by the event, was one of pleasure.

"Let me see some tenderness connected with a death," said Scrooge; "or that dark chamber, Spirit, which we left just now, will be for ever present to me."

The Ghost conducted him through several streets familiar to his feet; and as they went along, Scrooge looked here and there to find himself, but nowhere was he to be seen. They entered poor Bob Cratchit's house; the dwelling he had visited before; and found the mother and the children seated round the fire.

Quiet. Very quiet. The noisy little Cratchits were as still as statues in one corner, and sat looking up at Peter, who had a book before him. The mother and her daughters were engaged in sewing. But surely they were very quiet!

"'And He took a child, and set him in the midst of them.'"[3]

Where had Scrooge heard those words? He had not dreamed them. The boy must have read them out, as he and the Spirit crossed the threshold. Why did he not go on?

The mother laid her work upon the table, and put her hand up to her face.

---

3. Matthew 18.2 and Mark 9.36.

"The colour hurts my eyes," she said.

The colour? Ah, poor Tiny Tim!

"They're better now again," said Cratchit's wife. "It makes them weak by candle-light; and I wouldn't show weak eyes to your father when he comes home, for the world. It must be near his time."

"Past it rather," Peter answered, shutting up his book. "But I think he has walked a little slower than he used, these few last evenings, mother."

They were very quiet again. At last she said, and in a steady cheerful voice, that only faultered once:

"I have known him walk with—I have known him walk with Tiny Tim upon his shoulder, very fast indeed."

"And so have I," cried Peter. "Often."

"And so have I!" exclaimed another. So had all.

"But he was very light to carry," she resumed, intent upon her work, "and his father loved him so, that it was no trouble: no trouble. And there is your father at the door!"

She hurried out to meet him; and little Bob in his comforter—he had need of it, poor fellow—came in. His tea was ready for him on the hob, and they all tried who should help him to it most. Then the two young Cratchits got upon his knees and laid, each child a little cheek, against his face, as if they said, "Don't mind it, father. Don't be grieved!"

Bob was very cheerful with them, and spoke pleasantly to all the family. He looked at the work upon the table, and praised the industry and speed of Mrs. Cratchit and the girls. They would be done long before Sunday he said.

"Sunday! You went to-day then, Robert?" said his wife.

"Yes, my dear," returned Bob. "I wish you could have gone. It would have done you good to see how green a place it is. But you'll see it often. I promised him that I would walk there on a Sunday. My little, little child!" cried Bob. "My little child!"

He broke down all at once. He couldn't help it. If he could have helped it, he and his child would have been farther apart perhaps than they were.

He left the room, and went up stairs into the room above, which was lighted cheerfully, and hung with Christmas. There was a chair set close beside the child, and there were signs of some one having been there, lately. Poor Bob sat down in it, and when he had thought a little and composed himself, he kissed the little face. He was reconciled to what had happened, and went down again quite happy.

They drew about the fire, and talked; the girls and mother working still. Bob told them of the extraordinary kindness of Mr. Scrooge's nephew, whom he had scarcely seen but once, and who, meeting him in the street that day, and seeing that he looked a little—"just a little down you know" said Bob, enquired what had happened to distress him. "On which," said Bob, "for he is the pleasantest-spoken gentleman you ever heard, I told him. 'I am heartily sorry for it, Mr. Cratchit,' he said, 'and heartily sorry for your good wife.' By the bye, how he ever knew *that*, I don't know."

"Knew what, my dear?"

"Why, that you were a good wife," replied Bob.

"Everybody knows that!" said Peter.

"Very well observed, my boy!" cried Bob. "I hope they do. 'Heartily sorry,' he said, 'for your good wife. If I can be of service to you in any way,' he said, giving me his card, 'that's where I live. Pray come to me.' Now, it wasn't," cried Bob, "for the sake of anything he might be able to do for us, so much as for his kind way, that this was quite delightful. It really seemed as if he had known our Tiny Tim, and felt with us."

"I'm sure he's a good soul!" said Mrs. Cratchit.

"You would be surer of it, my dear," returned Bob, "if you saw and spoke to him. I shouldn't be at all surprised, mark what I say, if he got Peter a better situation."

"Only hear that, Peter," said Mrs. Cratchit.

"And then," cried one of the girls, "Peter will be keeping company with some one, and setting up for himself."

"Get along with you!" retorted Peter, grinning.

"It's just as likely as not," said Bob, "one of these days; though there's plenty of time for that, my dear. But however and whenever we part from one another, I am sure we shall none of us forget poor Tiny Tim—shall we— or this first parting that there was among us?"

"Never, father!" cried they all.

"And I know," said Bob, "I know, my dears, that when we recollect how patient and how mild he was; although he was a little, little child; we shall not quarrel easily among ourselves, and forget poor Tiny Tim in doing it."

"No, never, father!" they all cried again.

"I am very happy," said little Bob, "I am very happy!"

Mrs. Cratchit kissed him, his daughters kissed him, the two young Cratchits kissed him, and Peter and himself shook hands. Spirit of Tiny Tim, thy childish essence was from God!

"Spectre," said Scrooge, "something informs me that our parting moment is at hand. I know it, but I know not how. Tell me what man that was whom we saw lying dead?"

The Ghost of Christmas Yet To Come conveyed him, as before—though at a different time, he thought: indeed, there seemed no order in these latter visions, save that they were in the Future—into the resorts of business men, but showed him not himself. Indeed, the Spirit did not stay for anything, but went straight on, as to the end just now desired, until besought by Scrooge to tarry for a moment.

"This court," said Scrooge, "through which we hurry now, is where my place of occupation is, and has been for a length of time. I see the house. Let me behold what I shall be, in days to come."

The Spirit stopped; the hand was pointed elsewhere.

"The house is yonder," Scrooge exclaimed.

"Why do you point away?"

The inexorable finger underwent no change.

Scrooge hastened to the window of his office, and looked in. It was an office still, but not his. The furniture was not the same, and the figure in the chair was not himself. The Phantom pointed as before.

He joined it once again, and wondering why and whither he had gone, accompanied it until they reached an iron gate. He paused to look round before entering.

A churchyard. Here, then, the wretched man whose name he had now to learn, lay underneath the ground. It was a worthy place. Walled in by houses; overrun by grass and weeds, the growth of vegetation's death, not life; choked up with too much burying; fat with repleted appetite. A worthy place!

The Spirit stood among the graves, and pointed down to One. He advanced towards it trembling. The Phantom was exactly as it had been, but he dreaded that he saw new meaning in its solemn shape.

"Before I draw nearer to that stone to which you point," said Scrooge, "answer me one question. Are these the shadows of the things that Will be, or are they shadows of the things that May be, only?"

Still the Ghost pointed downward to the grave by which it stood.

"Men's courses will foreshadow certain ends, to which, if persevered in, they must lead," said Scrooge. "But if the courses be departed from, the ends will change. Say it is thus with what you show me!"

The Spirit was immovable as ever.

Scrooge crept towards it, trembling as he went; and following the finger, read upon the stone of the neglected grave his own name, EBENEZER SCROOGE.

The Last of the Spirits.

"Am *I* that man who lay upon the bed?" he cried, upon his knees.

The finger pointed from the grave to him, and back again.

"No, Spirit! Oh no, no!"

The finger still was there.

"Spirit!" he cried, tight clutching at its robe, "hear me! I am not the man I was. I will not be the man I must have been but for this intercourse. Why show me this, if I am past all hope?"

For the first time the hand appeared to shake.

"Good Spirit," he pursued, as down upon the ground he fell before it: "Your nature intercedes for me, and pities me. Assure me that I yet may change these shadows you have shown me, by an altered life!"

The kind hand trembled.

"I will honour Christmas in my heart, and try to keep it all the year. I will live in the Past, the Present, and the Future. The Spirits of all Three shall strive within me. I will not shut out the lessons that they teach. Oh, tell me I may sponge away the writing on this stone!"

In his agony, he caught the spectral hand. It sought to free itself, but he was strong in his entreaty, and detained it. The Spirit, stronger yet, repulsed him.

Holding up his hands in one last prayer to have his fate reversed, he saw an alteration in the Phantom's hood and dress. It shrunk, collapsed, and dwindled down into a bedpost.

Stave Five

THE END OF IT

Yes! and the bedpost was his own. The bed was his own, the room was his own. Best and happiest of all, the Time before him was his own, to make amends in!

"I will live in the Past, the Present, and the Future!" Scrooge repeated, as he scrambled out of bed. "The Spirits of all Three shall strive within me. Oh Jacob Marley! Heaven, and the Christmas Time be praised for this! I say it on my knees, old Jacob; on my knees!"

He was so fluttered and so glowing with his good intentions, that his broken voice would scarcely answer to his call. He had been sobbing violently in his conflict with the Spirit, and his face was wet with tears.

"They are not torn down," cried Scrooge, folding one of his bed-curtains in his arms, "they are not torn down, rings and all. They are here: I am here: the shadows of the things that would have been, may be dispelled. They will be. I know they will!"

His hands were busy with his garments all this time: turning them inside out, putting them on upside down, tearing them, mislaying them, making them parties to every kind of extravagance.

"I don't know what to do!" cried Scrooge, laughing and crying in the same breath; and making a perfect Laocoön[4] of himself with his stockings. "I am as light as a feather, I am as happy as an angel, I am as merry as a school-boy.

---

4. A Trojan priest who, according to Virgil (*Aeneid* 2.130), so offended the goddess Athena by warning his people about the Greeks' wooden horse trick that she sent two giant sea serpents to strangle him and his two sons. His struggle with the snakes is the subject of a famous classical sculpture.

I am as giddy as a drunken man. A merry Christmas to everybody! A happy New Year to all the world. Hallo here! Whoop! Hallo!"

He had frisked into the sitting-room, and was now standing there: perfectly winded.

"There's the saucepan that the gruel was in!" cried Scrooge, starting off again, and going round the fire-place. "There's the door, by which the Ghost of Jacob Marley entered! There's the corner where the Ghost of Christmas Present, sat! There's the window where I saw the wandering Spirits! It's all right, it's all true, it all happened. Ha ha ha!"

Really, for a man who had been out of practice for so many years, it was a splendid laugh, a most illustrious laugh. The father of a long, long, line of brilliant laughs!

"I don't know what day of the month it is!" said Scrooge. "I don't know how long I've been among the Spirits. I don't know anything. I'm quite a baby. Never mind. I don't care. I'd rather be a baby. Hallo! Whoop! Hallo here!"

He was checked in his transports by the churches ringing out the lustiest peals he had ever heard. Clash, clang, hammer, ding, dong, bell. Bell, dong, ding, hammer, clang, clash! Oh, glorious, glorious!

Running to the window, he opened it, and put out his head. No fog, no mist; clear, bright, jovial, stirring, cold; cold, piping for the blood to dance to; Golden sunlight; Heavenly sky; sweet fresh air; merry bells. Oh, glorious. Glorious!

"What's to-day?" cried Scrooge, calling downward to a boy in Sunday clothes, who perhaps had loitered in to look about him.

"Eh?" returned the boy, with all his might of wonder.

"What's to-day, my fine fellow?" said Scrooge.

"To-day!" replied the boy. "Why, CHRISTMAS DAY."

"It's Christmas Day!" said Scrooge to himself.

"I haven't missed it. The Spirits have done it all in one night. They can do anything they like. Of course they can. Of course they can. Hallo, my fine fellow!"

"Hallo!" returned the boy.

"Do you know the Poulterer's, in the next street but one, at the corner?" Scrooge inquired.

"I should hope I did," replied the lad.

"An intelligent boy!" said Scrooge. "A remarkable boy! Do you know whether they've sold the prize Turkey that was hanging up there? Not the little prize Turkey: the big one?"

"What, the one as big as me?" returned the boy.

"What a delightful boy!" said Scrooge. "It's a pleasure to talk to him. Yes, my buck!"

"It's hanging there now," replied the boy.

"Is it?" said Scrooge. "Go and buy it."

"Walk-ER!"[5] exclaimed the boy.

"No, no," said Scrooge, "I am in earnest. Go and buy it, and tell 'em to bring it here, that I may give them the direction where to take it. Come

---

5. An expression of surprise, ridicule, or incredulity (London slang, of uncertain origin).

back with the man, and I'll give you a shilling. Come back with him in less than five minutes, and I'll give you half-a-crown!"

The boy was off like a shot. He must have had a steady hand at a trigger who could have got a shot off half so fast.

"I'll send it to Bob Cratchit's!" whispered Scrooge, rubbing his hands, and splitting with a laugh. "He sha'n't know who sends it. It's twice the size of Tiny Tim. Joe Miller never made such a joke[6] as sending it to Bob's will be!"

The hand in which he wrote the address was not a steady one, but write it he did, somehow, and went down stairs to open the street door, ready for the coming of the poulterer's man. As he stood there, waiting his arrival, the knocker caught his eye.

"I shall love it, as long as I live!" cried Scrooge, patting it with his hand. "I scarcely ever looked at it before. What an honest expression it has in its face! It's a wonderful knocker!—Here's the Turkey. Hallo! Whoop! How are you! Merry Christmas!"

It *was* a Turkey! He never could have stood upon his legs, that bird. He would have snapped 'em short off in a minute, like sticks of sealing-wax.

"Why, it's impossible to carry that to Camden Town," said Scrooge. "You must have a cab."

The chuckle with which he said this, and the chuckle with which he paid for the Turkey, and the chuckle with which he paid for the cab, and the chuckle with which he recompensed the boy, were only to be exceeded by the chuckle with which he sat down breathless in his chair again, and chuckled till he cried.

Shaving was not an easy task, for his hand continued to shake very much; and shaving requires attention, even when you don't dance while you are at it. But if he had cut the end of his nose off, he would have put a piece of sticking-plaister over it, and been quite satisfied.

He dressed himself "all in his best," and at last got out into the streets. The people were by this time pouring forth, as he had seen them with the Ghost of Christmas Present; and walking with his hands behind him, Scrooge regarded every one with a delighted smile. He looked so irresistibly pleasant, in a word, that three or four good-humoured fellows said, "Good morning, sir! A merry Christmas to you!" And Scrooge said often afterwards, that of all the blithe sounds he had ever heard, those were the blithest in his ears.

He had not gone far, when coming on towards him he beheld the portly gentleman, who had walked into his counting-house the day before and said, "Scrooge and Marley's, I believe?" It sent a pang across his heart to think how this old gentleman would look upon him when they met; but he knew what path lay straight before him, and he took it.

"My dear sir," said Scrooge, quickening his pace, and taking the old gentleman by both his hands. "How do you do? I hope you succeeded yesterday. It was very kind of you. A merry Christmas to you, sir!"

"Mr. Scrooge?"

"Yes," said Scrooge. "That is my name, and I fear it may not be pleasant to you. Allow me to ask your pardon. And will you have the goodness"— here Scrooge whispered in his ear.

6. The supposed jokes of Joe Miller (1684–1738), a comic actor, were collected in the popular *Jest-Book*, first published in 1739.

"Lord bless me!" cried the gentleman, as if his breath were gone. "My dear Mr. Scrooge, are you serious?"

"If you please," said Scrooge. "Not a farthing less. A great many back-payments are included in it, I assure you. Will you do me that favour?"

"My dear sir," said the other, shaking hands with him. "I don't know what to say to such munifi—"

"Don't say anything, please," retorted Scrooge. "Come and see me. Will you come and see me?"

"I will!" cried the old gentleman. And it was clear he meant to do it.

"Thank 'ee," said Scrooge. "I am much obliged to you. I thank you fifty times. Bless you!"

He went to church, and walked about the streets, and watched the people hurrying to and fro, and patted children on the head, and questioned beggars, and looked down into the kitchens of houses, and up to the windows; and found that everything could yield him pleasure. He had never dreamed that any walk—that anything—could give him so much happiness. In the afternoon, he turned his steps towards his nephew's house.

He passed the door a dozen times, before he had the courage to go up and knock. But he made a dash, and did it:

"Is your master at home, my dear?" said Scrooge to the girl. Nice girl! Very.

"Yes, sir."

"Where is he, my love?" said Scrooge.

"He's in the dining-room, sir, along with mistress. I'll show you up stairs, if you please."

"Thank 'ee. He knows me," said Scrooge, with his hand already on the dining-room lock. "I'll go in here, my dear."

He turned it gently, and sidled his face in, round the door. They were looking at the table (which was spread out in great array); for these young housekeepers are always nervous on such points, and like to see that everything is right.

"Fred!" said Scrooge.

Dear heart alive, how his niece by marriage started! Scrooge had forgotten, for the moment, about her sitting in the corner with the footstool, or he wouldn't have done it, on any account.

"Why bless my soul!" cried Fred, "who's that?"

"It's I. Your uncle Scrooge. I have come to dinner. Will you let me in, Fred?"

Let him in! It is a mercy he didn't shake his arm off. He was at home in five minutes. Nothing could be heartier. His niece looked just the same. So did Topper when *he* came. So did the plump sister, when *she* came. So did every one when *they* came. Wonderful party, wonderful games, wonderful unanimity, won-der-ful happiness!

But he was early at the office next morning. Oh he was early there. If he could only be there first, and catch Bob Cratchit coming late! That was the thing he had set his heart upon.

And he did it; yes he did! The clock struck nine. No Bob. A quarter past. No Bob. He was full eighteen minutes and a half, behind his time. Scrooge sat with his door wide open, that he might see him come into the Tank.

His hat was off, before he opened the door; his comforter too. He was on his stool in a jiffy; driving away with his pen, as if he were trying to overtake nine o'clock.

"Hallo!" growled Scrooge, in his accustomed voice as near as he could feign it. "What do you mean by coming here at this time of day?"

"I am very sorry, sir," said Bob. "I *am* behind my time."

"You are?" repeated Scrooge. "Yes. I think you are. Step this way, if you please."

"It's only once a year, sir," pleaded Bob, appearing from the Tank. "It shall not be repeated. I was making rather merry yesterday, sir."

"Now, I'll tell you what, my friend," said Scrooge, "I am not going to stand this sort of thing any longer. And therefore," he continued, leaping from his stool, and giving Bob such a dig in the waistcoat that he staggered back into the Tank again: "and therefore I am about to raise your salary!"

Bob trembled, and got a little nearer to the ruler. He had a momentary idea of knocking Scrooge down with it; holding him; and calling to the people in the court for help and a strait-waistcoat.[7]

"A merry Christmas, Bob!" said Scrooge, with an earnestness that could not be mistaken, as he clapped him on the back. "A merrier Christmas, Bob, my good fellow, than I have given you, for many a year! I'll raise your salary, and endeavour to assist your struggling family, and we will discuss your affairs this very afternoon, over a Christmas bowl of smoking bishop,[8] Bob! Make up the fires, and buy another coal-scuttle before you dot another i, Bob Cratchit!"

Scrooge was better than his word. He did it all, and infinitely more; and to Tiny Tim, who did NOT die, he was a second father. He became as good a friend, as good a master, and as good a man, as the good old city knew, or any other good old city, town, or borough, in the good old world. Some people laughed to see the alteration in him, but he let them laugh, and little heeded them; for he was wise enough to know that nothing ever happened on this globe, for good, at which some people did not have their fill of laughter in the outset; and knowing that such as these would be blind anyway, he thought it quite as well that they should wrinkle up their eyes in grins, as have the malady in less attractive forms. His own heart laughed: and that was quite enough for him.

He had no further intercourse with Spirits, but lived upon the Total Abstinence Principle,[9] ever afterwards; and it was always said of him, that he knew how to keep Christmas well, if any man alive possessed the knowledge. May that be truly said of us, and all of us! And so, as Tiny Tim observed, God Bless Us, Every One!

THE END.

1843

---

7. Used, like a straitjacket, to subdue violent prisoners or patients by binding their arms to their bodies.

8. A popular Christmas drink, made by combining red wine or port with sugar, spices, and oranges and called "bishop" because of its purple color.

9. I.e., teetotalism; the watchword of an extreme temperance movement of the 1830s, which encouraged individuals to pledge never to drink intoxicating beverages again. Dickens here puns on *spirits*, which can indicate "alcohol" or "ghosts."

ROBERT BROWNING
1812–1889

During the years of his marriage, Robert Browning was sometimes referred to as "Mrs. Browning's husband." Elizabeth Barrett was at that time a famous poet, whereas her husband was a relatively unknown experimenter whose poems were greeted with misunderstanding or indifference. Not until the 1860s did he at last gain a public and become recognized as the rival or equal of Alfred, Lord Tennyson. In the twentieth century his reputation persisted but in an unusual way: his poetry was admired by two groups of readers widely different in tastes. To one group, among whom were the Browning societies that flourished in England and America, Browning was a wise philosopher and religious teacher who resolved the doubts that troubled Matthew Arnold and Tennyson. The second group of readers enjoyed Browning less for his attempt to solve problems of religious doubt than for his attempt to solve the problems of how poetry should be written. Poets such as Ezra Pound and Robert Lowell argued that more than any other nineteenth-century poet, it was Browning who energetically hacked through a trail that subsequently became the main road of twentieth-century poetry. In *Poetry and the Age* (1953) Randall Jarrell remarked that "the dramatic monologue, which once had depended for its effect upon being a departure from the norm of poetry, now became in one form or another the norm."

A simple definition of a dramatic monologue runs as follows: a poem that presents itself as a speech delivered by a created character. Some take the form of soliloquies, uttered by the speaker to himself or herself; others are addressed to another character or characters who remain silent. As Browning uses it, the dramatic monologue separates the speaker from the poet in such a way that the reader must work through the words of the speaker to discover the meaning of the poet. For example, in the well-known early monologue "My Last Duchess" (1842), we listen to the duke as he speaks of his dead wife. From his one-sided conversation we piece together the situation, both past and present, and we infer what sort of woman the duchess really was and what sort of man the duke is. Ultimately, we may also infer what the poet himself thinks of the speaker he has created. In this instance it is fairly easy to reach such a judgment; the pleasure of the poem results from our reconstruction of a story quite different from the one the duke thinks he is telling. Many of Browning's poems are far less stable, and it is difficult to discern the relationship of the poet to his speaker. In "'Childe Roland to the Dark Tower Came'" (1855), for example, is the speaker describing a phantasmagoric landscape of his own paranoid imagining, or is the poem a fable of courage and defiance in a modern wasteland?

In addition to his experiments with the dramatic monologue, Browning also experimented with language and syntax. The grotesque rhymes and jaw-breaking diction that he often employs have been repugnant to some critics; George Santayana, for instance, dismissed him as a clumsy barbarian. But to those who appreciate Browning, the incongruities of language are a humorous and appropriate counterpart to an imperfect world. Ezra Pound's tribute to "Old Hippety-Hop o' the accents," as he addresses Browning, is both affectionate and memorable:

> Heart that was big as the bowels of Vesuvius
> Words that were winged as her sparks in eruption,
> Eagled and thundered as Jupiter Pluvius
> Sound in your wind past all signs o' corruption.

Robert Browning was born in Camberwell, a London suburb. His father, a bank clerk, was a learned man with an extensive library. His mother was a kindly, religious-minded woman, interested in music, whose love for her brilliant son was warmly reciprocated. Until the time of his marriage, at the age of thirty-four, Browning was rarely absent from his parents' home. He attended a boarding school near Camber-well, traveled a little (to Russia and Italy), and was a student at the University of London for a short period, but he preferred to pursue his education at home, where he was tutored in foreign languages, music, boxing, and horsemanship and where he read omnivorously. From this unusual education he acquired a store of knowledge on which to draw for the background of his poems.

The "obscurity" of which his contemporaries complained in his earlier poetry may be partly accounted for by the circumstances of Browning's education, but it also reflects his anxious desire to avoid exposing himself too explicitly before his readers. His first poem, *Pauline* (1833), published when he was twenty-one, had been modeled on the example of Percy Bysshe Shelley, the most personal of poets. When an other-wise admiring review by John Stuart Mill noted that the young author was afflicted with an "intense and morbid self-consciousness," Browning was overwhelmed with embarrassment. He resolved to avoid confessional writings thereafter.

One way of reducing the personal element in his poetry was to write plays instead of soul-searching narratives or lyrics. In 1836, encouraged by the actor W. C. Mac-ready, Browning began work on his first play, *Strafford*, a historical tragedy that lasted only four nights when it was produced in London in 1837. For ten years the young writer struggled to write for the theater, but all his stage productions remained fail-ures. Nevertheless, writing dialogue for actors led him to explore another form more congenial to his genius. His first collection of dramatic monologues, *Dramatic Lyrics*, appeared in 1842; but it received no more critical enthusiasm than did his plays.

Browning's resolution to avoid the subjective manner of Shelley did not preclude his being influenced by the earlier poet in other ways. At fourteen, when he first discovered Shelley's works, he became an atheist and liberal. Although he grew away from the atheism, after a struggle, and also the extreme phases of his liberalism, he retained from Shelley's influence something permanent and more difficult to define: an ardent dedication to ideals (often undefined ideals) and an energetic striving toward goals (often undefined goals).

Browning's ardent romanticism also found expression in his love affair with Eliza-beth Barrett, which had the dramatic ingredients of Browning's own favorite story of St. George rescuing the maiden from the dragon. Few would have forecast the out-come when Browning met Elizabeth Barrett in 1845. She was six years older than he was, and a semi-invalid, jealously guarded by her possessively tyrannical father. But love, as the poet was to say later, is best; and love swept aside all obstacles. After their elopement to Italy, the former semi-invalid was soon enjoying far better health and a full life. The husband likewise seemed to thrive during the years of this remarkable marriage. His most memorable volume of poems, *Men and Women* (1855), reflects his enjoyment of Italy: its picturesque landscapes and lively street scenes as well as its monuments from the past—its Renaissance past in particular.

The happy fifteen-year sojourn in Italy ended in 1861 with Elizabeth's death. The widower returned to London with his son. During the twenty-eight years remaining to him, he continued to produce large quantities of verse. *Dramatis Personae* (1864) is a volume containing some of his most intriguing monologues, such as "Caliban upon Setebos." And in 1868 he published his longest and most significant single poem, *The Ring and the Book*, which was inspired by his discovery of an old book of legal records concerning a murder trial in seventeenth-century Rome. His poem tells the story of a brutally sadistic husband, Count Guido Franceschini. The middle-aged Guido grows dissatisfied with his young wife, Pompilia, and accuses her of having adulterous rela-tions with a handsome priest who, like St. George, had tried to rescue her from the appalling situation in which her husband confined her. Eventually Guido stabs his wife to death and is himself executed. In a series of twelve books, Browning retells this tale of violence, presenting it from the contrasting points of view of participants and spectators. Because of its vast scale, *The Ring and the Book* is like a Victorian novel, but in its experiments with multiple points of view it anticipates later works such as Joseph Conrad's novel *Lord Jim* (1900) and Akira Kurosawa's film *Rashōmon* (1950).

After *The Ring and the Book* several more volumes appeared. In general, Browning's writings during the last two decades of his life exhibit a certain mechanical repetition of mannerism and an excess of argumentation—tendencies into which he may have been led by the unqualified enthusiasm of his admirers, for it was during this period that he gained his great following. When he died, in 1889, he was buried in Westminster Abbey.

During the London years Browning became extremely fond of social life. He dined at the homes of friends and at clubs, where he enjoyed port wine and conversation. He would talk loudly and emphatically about many topics—except his own poetry, about which he was usually reticent. Despite his bursts of outspokenness, Browning's character seemed, in Thomas Hardy's words, "*the* literary puzzle of the nineteenth century." Like William Butler Yeats, he was a poet preoccupied with masks. On the occasion of his burial, his friend Henry James reflected that many oddities and many great writers have been buried in Westminster Abbey, "but none of the odd ones have been so great and none of the great ones been so odd."

Just as Browning's character is hard to identify so also are his poems difficult to relate to the age in which they were written. Bishops and painters of the Renaissance, an inmate of a Spanish monastery, Shakespeare's "man-monster" on a distant isle—as we explore this gallery of talking portraits we seem to be in remote times or places, far from the world of steam engines and disputes about human beings' descent from the ape. Yet our first impression is misleading. Many of these portraits explore problems that confronted Browning's contemporaries, especially problems of faith and doubt, of good and evil, and of the function of the artist in modern life. "Caliban upon Setebos," for example, is a highly topical critique of Darwinism and of natural (as opposed to supernatural) religions. Browning's own attitude toward these topics is partially concealed because of his use of speakers and of settings from earlier ages, yet we do encounter certain recurrent religious assumptions that we can safely assign to the poet himself. The most recurrent is that God has created an imperfect world as a kind of testing ground, a "vale of soul-making," as John Keats had said. It followed, for Browning's purposes, that the human soul must be immortal and that heaven itself be perfect. Armed with such a faith, Browning sometimes gives the impression that he was himself untroubled by the doubts that gnawed at the hearts of Tennyson, Arnold, and other figures in the mid-Victorian period. Yet Browning's apparent optimism is consistently being tested by his bringing to light the evils of human nature. His gallery of villains—murderers, sadistic husbands, mean and petty manipulators—is an extraordinary one. Few writers, in fact, seem to have been more aware of the existence of evil.

A second aspect of Browning's poetry that separates it from the Victorian age is its style. The most representative Victorian poets such as Tennyson and Dante Gabriel Rossetti write in the manner of Keats, John Milton, and Edmund Spenser, and of classical poets such as Virgil. Theirs is the central stylistic tradition in English poetry, one that favors smoothly polished texture, elevated diction and subjects, and pleasing liquidity of sound. Browning draws from a different tradition, more colloquial and discordant, a tradition that includes the poetry of John Donne, the soliloquies of William Shakespeare, and certain features of the narrative style of Geoffrey Chaucer. Of most significance are Browning's affinities with Donne. Both poets sacrifice, on occasion, the pleasures of harmony and of a consistent elevation of tone by using a harshly discordant style and unexpected juxtapositions that startle us into an awareness of a world of everyday realities and trivialities. Readers who dislike this kind of poetry in Browning or in Donne argue that it suffers from prosiness. Oscar Wilde once described the novelist George Meredith as "a prose Browning." And so, he added, was

Browning. Wilde's joke may help us understand Browning's relationship to the writers of his era. For if Browning seems out of step with other Victorian poets, he is by no means out of step with his contemporaries in prose. The grotesque, which plays such a prominent role in the style and subject matter of Carlyle and Dickens and in the aesthetic theories of John Ruskin, is equally prominent in Browning's verse:

> Fee, faw, fum! bubble and squeak!
> Blessedest Thursday's the fat of the week.
> Rumble and tumble, sleek and rough,
> Stinking and savory, smug and gruff.

Like Thomas Carlyle's *Sartor Resartus* (1833–34), these lines from "Holy-Cross Day" (1855) present a situation of grave seriousness with noisy jocularity. It was fitting that Browning and Carlyle remained good friends, even though the elder writer kept urging Browning to give up verse in favor of prose.

The link between Browning and the Victorian prose writers is not limited to style. With the later generation of Victorian novelists, George Eliot, George Meredith, and Henry James, Browning shares a central preoccupation. Like Eliot in particular, he was interested in exposing the devious ways in which our minds work and the complexity of our motives. "My stress lay on incidents in the development of a human soul," he wrote; "little else is worth study." His psychological insights can be readily detected in poems such as "The Bishop Orders His Tomb" (1845) and "Andrea del Sarto" (1855). Although these are spoken monologues, not inner monologues in the manner of James Joyce, the insight into the workings of the mind is similarly acute. As in reading Joyce, we must follow the rapid shifts of the speaker's mental processes as jumps are made from one cluster of associations to another. A further challenge for the reader of Browning is to identify what has been left out. As was remarked in a letter by the 1890s poet Ernest Dowson, Browning's "masterpieces in verse" demonstrate both "subtlety" and "the tact of omission." "My Last Duchess," he added, "is pure Henry James."

But Browning's role as a forerunner of twentieth-century literature should not blind us to his essential Victorianism. Energy is the most characteristic aspect of his writing and of the man (Ivan Turgenev compared Browning's handshake to an electric shock). Gerard Manley Hopkins described Browning as "a man bouncing up from table with his mouth full of bread and cheese and saying that he meant to stand no blasted nonsense." This buoyancy imparts a creative vitality to all of Browning's writings.

Porphyria's Lover[1]

> The rain set early in tonight,
>   The sullen wind was soon awake,
> It tore the elm-tops down for spite,
>   And did its worst to vex the lake:
> 5   I listened with heart fit to break.
> When glided in Porphyria; straight
>   She shut the cold out and the storm,
> And kneeled and made the cheerless grate
>   Blaze up, and all the cottage warm;
> 10   Which done, she rose, and from her form

---

1. One of a pair of monologues originally published as "Madhouse Cells," a title that emphasized the speaker's abnormal state of mind.

Withdrew the dripping cloak and shawl,
  And laid her soiled gloves by, untied
Her hat and let the damp hair fall,
  And, last, she sat down by my side
15 And called me. When no voice replied,
She put my arm about her waist,
  And made her smooth white shoulder bare,
And all her yellow hair displaced,
  And, stooping, made my cheek lie there,
20 And spread, o'er all, her yellow hair,
Murmuring how she loved me—she
  Too weak, for all her heart's endeavor,
To set its struggling passion free
  From pride, and vainer ties dissever,
25 And give herself to me forever.
But passion sometimes would prevail,
  Nor could tonight's gay feast restrain
A sudden thought of one so pale
  For love of her, and all in vain:
30 So, she was come through wind and rain.
Be sure I looked up at her eyes
  Happy and proud; at last I knew
Porphyria worshiped me: surprise
  Made my heart swell, and still it grew
35 While I debated what to do.
That moment she was mine, mine, fair,
  Perfectly pure and good: I found
A thing to do, and all her hair
  In one long yellow string I wound
40 Three times her little throat around,
And strangled her. No pain felt she;
  I am quite sure she felt no pain.
As a shut bud that holds a bee,
  I warily oped her lids: again
45 Laughed the blue eyes without a stain.
And I untightened next the tress
  About her neck; her cheek once more
Blushed bright beneath my burning kiss:
  I propped her head up as before,
50 Only, this time my shoulder bore
Her head, which droops upon it still:
  The smiling rosy little head,
So glad it has its utmost will,
  That all it scorned at once is fled,
55 And I, its love, am gained instead!
Porphyria's love: she guessed not how
  Her darling one wish would be heard.
And thus we sit together now,
  And all night long we have not stirred,
60 And yet God has not said a word!

1834   1836, 1842

Soliloquy of the Spanish Cloister

1

Gr-r-r—there go, my heart's abhorrence!
    Water your damned flowerpots, do!
If hate killed men, Brother Lawrence,
    God's blood,[1] would not mine kill you!
5 What? your myrtle bush wants trimming?
    Oh, that rose has prior claims—
Needs its leaden vase filled brimming?
    Hell dry you up with its flames!

2

At the meal we sit together:
10   *Salve tibi!*[2] I must hear
Wise talk of the kind of weather,
    Sort of season, time of year:
Not a plenteous cork crop: scarcely
    Dare we hope oak-galls,[3] *I doubt:*
15 *What's the Latin name for "parsley"?*
    What's the Greek name for Swine's Snout?[4]

3

Whew! We'll have our platter burnished,
    Laid with care on our own shelf!
With a fire-new spoon we're furnished,
20   And a goblet for ourself,
Rinsed like something sacrificial
    Ere 'tis fit to touch our chaps°   *jaws*
Marked with L. for our initial!
    (He-he! There his lily snaps!)

4

25 *Saint*, forsooth! While brown Dolores
    Squats outside the Convent bank
With Sanchicha, telling stories,
    Steeping tresses in the tank,
Blue-black, lustrous, thick like horsehairs,
30   —Can't I see his dead eye glow,
Bright as 'twere a Barbary corsair's?[5]
    (That is, if he'd let it show!)

---

1. An oath (archaic).
2. Hail to thee! (Latin); i.e., "your health!" This and other speeches in italics in this stanza are the words of Brother Lawrence.
3. Abnormal outgrowths on oak trees, used for tanning.
4. Dandelion (19th-century use).
5. Pirate of the Barbary Coast of northern Africa, renowned for fierceness and lechery.

5

When he finishes refection,°   *dinner*
    Knife and fork he never lays
35 Cross-wise, to my recollection,
    As do I, in Jesu's praise.
I the Trinity illustrate,
    Drinking watered orange pulp—
In three sips the Arian[6] frustrate;
40   While he drains his at one gulp.

6

Oh, those melons? If he's able
    We're to have a feast! so nice!
One goes to the Abbot's table,
    All of us get each a slice.
45 How go on your flowers? None double?
    Not one fruit-sort can you spy?
Strange!—And I, too, at such trouble,
    Keep them close-nipped on the sly!

7

There's a great text in Galatians,[7]
50   Once you trip on it, entails
Twenty-nine distinct damnations,
    One sure, if another fails:
If I trip him just a-dying,
    Sure of heaven as sure can be,
55 Spin him round and send him flying
    Off to hell, a Manichee?[8]

8

Or, my scrofulous French novel
    On gray paper with blunt type!
Simply glance at it, you grovel
60   Hand and foot in Belial's° gripe: *the devil's*
If I double down its pages
    At the woeful sixteenth print,
When he gathers his greengages,
    Ope a sieve and slip it in't?

9

65 Or, there's Satan!—one might venture
    Pledge one's soul to him, yet leave

---

6. Heretical follower of Arius (256–336 C.E.), who denied the doctrine of the Trinity.
7. The speaker hopes to obtain Lawrence's damnation by luring him into a heresy when he may prove unable to interpret Galatians in an unswervingly orthodox way. In Galatians 5.15–23 St. Paul specifies an assortment of "works of the flesh" that lead to damnation, which could make up a total of "twenty-nine" (line 51).
8. A heretic, a follower of Mani (3rd century), Persian religious leader.

Such a flaw in the indenture
    As he'd miss till, past retrieve,
Blasted lay that rose-acacia[9]
70   We're so proud of! *Hy, Zy, Hine*[1]
'St, there's Vespers![2] *Plena gratiâ*
    Ave, Virgo![3] Gr-r-r—you swine!

ca. 1839   1842

My Last Duchess[1]

Ferrara

That's my last Duchess painted on the wall,
Looking as if she were alive. I call
That piece a wonder, now: Frà Pandolf's[2] hands
Worked busily a day, and there she stands.
5   Will't please you sit and look at her? I said
"Frà Pandolf" by design, for never read
Strangers like you that pictured countenance,
The depth and passion of its earnest glance,
But to myself they turned (since none puts by
10   The curtain I have drawn for you, but I)
And seemed as they would ask me, if they durst,
How such a glance came there; so, not the first
Are you to turn and ask thus. Sir, 'twas not
Her husband's presence only, called that spot
15   Of joy into the Duchess' cheek: perhaps
Frà Pandolf chanced to say "Her mantle laps
Over my lady's wrist too much," or "Paint
Must never hope to reproduce the faint
Half-flush that dies along her throat": such stuff
20   Was courtesy, she thought, and cause enough
For calling up that spot of joy. She had
A heart—how shall I say?—too soon made glad,
Too easily impressed; she liked whate'er
She looked on, and her looks went everywhere.
25   Sir, 'twas all one! My favor at her breast,
The dropping of the daylight in the West,
The bough of cherries some officious fool
Broke in the orchard for her, the white mule
She rode with round the terrace—all and each

9. The speaker would pledge his own soul to Satan in return for blasting Lawrence and his "rose-acacia," but the pledge would be so cleverly worded that the speaker would not have to pay his debt to Satan. There would be an escape clause ("flaw in the indenture") for himself.
1. Perhaps the opening of a mysterious curse against Lawrence.
2. Evening prayers.
3. Full of grace, Hail, Virgin! (Latin). The speaker's state of mind may be reflected in his mixed-up version of the prayer to Mary: "*Ave, Maria, gratia plena.*"
1. The poem is based on incidents in the life of Alfonso II, Duke of Ferrara in Italy, whose first wife, Lucrezia, a young woman, died in 1561 after three years of marriage. Following her death, the duke negotiated through an agent to marry a niece of the Count of Tyrol. Browning represents the duke as addressing this agent.
2. Friar Pandolf, an imaginary painter.

30   Would draw from her alike the approving speech,
     Or blush, at least. She thanked men—good! but thanked
     Somehow—I know not how—as if she ranked
     My gift of a nine-hundred-years-old name
     With anybody's gift. Who'd stoop to blame
35   This sort of trifling? Even had you skill
     In speech—(which I have not)—to make your will
     Quite clear to such an one, and say, "Just this
     Or that in you disgusts me; here you miss,
     Or there exceed the mark"—and if she let
40   Herself be lessoned so, nor plainly set
     Her wits to yours, forsooth, and made excuse
     —E'en then would be some stooping; and I choose
     Never to stoop. Oh sir, she smiled, no doubt,
     Whene'er I passed her; but who passed without
45   Much the same smile? This grew; I gave commands;
     Then all smiles stopped together. There she stands
     As if alive. Will 't please you rise? We'll meet
     The company below, then. I repeat,
     The Count your master's known munificence
50   Is ample warrant that no just pretense
     Of mine for dowry will be disallowed;
     Though his fair daughter's self, as I avowed
     At starting, is my object. Nay, we'll go
     Together down, sir. Notice Neptune, though,
55   Taming a sea horse, thought a rarity,
     Which Claus of Innsbruck[3] cast in bronze for me!

1842   1842

The Lost Leader[1]

1

Just for a handful of silver he left us,[2]
     Just for a riband[3] to stick in his coat—
Found the one gift of which fortune bereft us,
     Lost all the others she lets us devote;
5   They, with the gold to give, doled him out silver,
     So much was theirs who so little allowed:
How all our copper had gone for his service!
     Rags—were they purple, his heart had been proud!
We that had loved him so, followed him, honored him,
10   Lived in his mild and magnificent eye,

3. An unidentified or imaginary sculptor. The Count of Tyrol had his capital at Innsbruck.
1. William Wordsworth, who had been an ardent liberal in his youth, had become a political conservative in later years. In old age, when he accepted a grant of money from the government and the office of poet laureate, he alienated some of his young admirers such as Browning, whose liberalism was then as passionate as Wordsworth's had once been.
2. Browning here alludes to the "thirty pieces of silver" for which Judas betrayed Jesus (Matthew 26.14–16).
3. Symbol of the office of poet laureate.

Learned his great language, caught his clear accents,
    Made him our pattern to live and to die!
Shakespeare was of us, Milton was for us,
    Burns, Shelley, were with us—they watch from their graves!
15 He alone breaks from the van[4] and the freemen
    —He alone sinks to the rear and the slaves!

2

We shall march prospering—not through his presence;
    Songs may inspirit us—not from his lyre;
Deeds will be done—while he boasts his quiescence,
20   Still bidding crouch whom the rest bade aspire:
Blot out his name, then, record one lost soul more,
    One task more declined, one more footpath untrod,
One more devils'-triumph and sorrow for angels,
    One wrong more to man, one more insult to God!
25 Life's night begins: let him never come back to us!
    There would be doubt, hesitation and pain,
Forced praise on our part—the glimmer of twilight,
    Never glad confident morning again!
Best fight on well, for we taught him—strike gallantly,
30   Menace our heart ere we master his own;
Then let him receive the new knowledge and wait us,
    Pardoned in heaven, the first by the throne!

1843   1845

How They Brought the Good News
from Ghent to Aix[1]

(16—)

1

I sprang to the stirrup, and Joris, and he;
I galloped, Dirck galloped, we galloped all three;
"Good speed!" cried the watch, as the gate-bolts undrew;
"Speed!" echoed the wall to us galloping through;
5 Behind shut the postern,° the lights sank to rest,   *side door*
And into the midnight we galloped abreast.

2

Not a word to each other; we kept the great pace
Neck by neck, stride by stride, never changing our place;
I turned in my saddle and made its girths tight,

---

4. Vanguard of the army of liberalism.
1. The distance between Ghent, in Flanders, and Aix-la-Chapelle (now Aachen, in Germany) is about one hundred miles. Browning said that the incident, occurring during the wars between

Flanders and Spain, was an imaginary one. In 1889 Thomas Edison prepared a cylinder recording of Browning's recitation of the opening lines of this poem.

10 Then shortened each stirrup, and set the pique° right,   *spur or pommel*
Rebuckled the cheek-strap, chained slacker the bit,
Nor galloped less steadily Roland a whit.

3

'Twas moonset at starting; but while we drew near
Lokeren, the cocks crew and twilight dawned clear;
15 At Boom, a great yellow star came out to see;
At Düffeld, 'twas morning as plain as could be;
And from Mecheln church-steeple we heard the half-chime,
So, Joris broke silence with, "Yet there is time!"

4

At Aershot, up leaped of a sudden the sun,
20 And against him the cattle stood black every one,
To stare through the mist at us galloping past,
And I saw my stout galloper Roland at last,
With resolute shoulders, each butting away
The haze, as some bluff river headland its spray:

5

25 And his low head and crest, just one sharp ear bent back
For my voice, and the other pricked out on his track;
And one eye's black intelligence—ever that glance
O'er its white edge at me, his own master, askance!
And the thick heavy spume-flakes which ay and anon
30 His fierce lips shook upwards in galloping on.

6

By Hasselt, Dirck groaned; and cried Joris, "Stay spur!
Your Roos galloped bravely, the fault's not in her,
We'll remember at Aix"—for one heard the quick wheeze
Of her chest, saw the stretched neck and staggering knees,
35 And sunk tail, and horrible heave of the flank
As down on her haunches she shuddered and sank.

7

So, we were left galloping, Joris and I,
Past Looz and past Tongres, no cloud in the sky;
The broad sun above laughed a pitiless laugh,
40 Neath our feet broke the brittle bright stubble like chaff;
Till over by Dalhem a dome-spire sprang white,
And "Gallop," gasped Joris, "for Aix is in sight!"

8

"How they'll greet us!"—and all in a moment his roan
Rolled neck and croup° over, lay dead as a stone;   *rump*
45 And there was my Roland to bear the whole weight

Of the news which alone could save Aix from her fate,
With his nostrils like pits full of blood to the brim,
And with circles of red for his eye-sockets' rim.

9

Then I cast loose my buffcoat, each holster let fall,
50   Shook off both my jack boots, let go belt and all,
Stood up in the stirrup, leaned, patted his ear,
Called my Roland his pet name, my horse without peer;
Clapped my hands, laughed and sang, any noise, bad or good,
Till at length into Aix Roland galloped and stood.

10

55   And all I remember is—friends flocking round
As I sat with his head 'twixt my knees on the ground;
And no voice but was praising this Roland of mine,
As I poured down his throat our last measure of wine,
Which (the burgesses voted by common consent)
60   Was no more than his due who brought good news from Ghent.

ca. 1844   1845

The Bishop Orders His Tomb at
Saint Praxed's Church[1]

Rome, 15—

Vanity, saith the preacher, vanity![2]
Draw round my bed: is Anselm keeping back?
Nephews—sons mine . . . ah God, I know not! Well—
She, men would have to be your mother once,
5   Old Gandolf envied me, so fair she was!
What's done is done, and she is dead beside,
Dead long ago, and I am Bishop since,
And as she died so must we die ourselves,
And thence ye may perceive the world's a dream.
10   ife, how and what is it? As here I lie

1. In "Fra Lippo Lippi" (p. 346), Browning represents the dawn of the Renaissance in Italy, with its fresh zest for human experiences in this world. In this monologue he portrays a later stage of the Renaissance when such worldliness, full-blown, had infected some of the leading clergy of Italy. Browning's portrait of the dying bishop is, however, not primarily a satire against corruption in the church. It is a brilliant exposition of the workings of a mind, a mind that has been conditioned by special historical circumstances. The Victorian historian of art John Ruskin said of this poem:

    I know of no other piece of modern English, prose or poetry, in which there is so much told,

as in these lines, of the Renaissance spirit—its worldliness, inconsistency, pride, hypocrisy, ignorance of itself, love of art, of luxury, and of good Latin. It is nearly all that I have said of the central Renaissance in thirty pages of the *Stones of Venice*, put into as many lines, Browning's also being the antecedent work.

    St. Praxed's Church was named in honor of St. Praxedes, a Roman virgin of the 2nd century who gave her riches to poor Christians. Both the bishop and his predecessor, Gandolf, are imaginary persons.
2. Cf. Ecclesiastes 1.2: "Vanity of vanities; all is vanity."

In this state chamber, dying by degrees,
Hours and long hours in the dead night, I ask
"Do I live, am I dead?" Peace, peace seems all.
Saint Praxed's ever was the church for peace;
15   And so, about this tomb of mine. I fought
With tooth and nail to save my niche, ye know:
—Old Gandolf cozened° me, despite my care;   *cheated*
Shrewd was that snatch from out the corner south
He graced his carrion with,³ God curse the same!
20   Yet still my niche is not so cramped but thence
One sees the pulpit o' the epistle side,⁴
And somewhat of the choir, those silent seats,
And up into the aery dome where live
The angels, and a sunbeam's sure to lurk:
25   And I shall fill my slab of basalt⁵ there,
And 'neath my tabernacle⁶ take my rest,
With those nine columns round me, two and two,
The odd one at my feet where Anselm stands:
Peach-blossom marble all, the rare, the ripe
30   As fresh-poured red wine of a mighty pulse.⁷
—Old Gandolf with his paltry onion-stone,⁸
Put me where I may look at him! True peach,
Rosy and flawless: how I earned the prize!
Draw close: that conflagration of my church
35   —What then? So much was saved if aught were missed!
My sons, ye would not be my death? Go dig
The white-grape vineyard where the oil-press stood,
Drop water gently till the surface sink,
And if ye find . . . Ah God, I know not, I! . . .
40   Bedded in store of rotten fig leaves soft,
And corded up in a tight olive-frail,⁹
Some lump, ah God, of *lapis lazuli*,¹
Big as a jew's head cut off at the nape,²
Blue as a vein o'er the Madonna's breast . . .
45   Sons, all have I bequeathed you, villas, all,
That brave Frascati³ villa with its bath,
So, let the blue lump poise between my knees,
Like God the Father's globe on both his hands
Ye worship in the Jesu Church⁴ so gay,
50   For Gandolf shall not choose but see and burst!

---

3. Bishop Gandolf shrewdly chose a prize spot in the southern corner of the church for his burial place. The tomb that the speaker is ordering will also be inside the church, as was common for important people in this era.
4. The Epistles of the New Testament are read from the right-hand side of the altar (as one faces it).
5. Dark-colored igneous rock.
6. Stone canopy or tentlike roof, presumably supported by the "nine columns" under which the sculptured effigy of the bishop would lie on the "slab of basalt."
7. A pulpy mash of fermented grapes from which

a strong wine might be poured off.
8. An inferior marble that peels in layers.
9. Basket for holding olives.
1. Valuable bright blue stone.
2. Perhaps a reference to the head of John the Baptist, cut off at Salomé's request (Matthew 14.6–11).
3. Suburb of Rome, used as a resort by wealthy Italians.
4. Il Gesù, a Jesuit church in Rome. In a chapel in this church the figure of an angel (rather than God) holds a huge lump of lapis lazuli in his hands.

Swift as a weaver's shuttle fleet our years:[5]
Man goeth to the grave, and where is he?
Did I say basalt for my slab, sons? Black°—   *black marble*
'Twas ever antique-black I meant! How else
55   Shall ye contrast my frieze[6] to come beneath?
The bas-relief[7] in bronze ye promised me,
Those Pans and Nymphs ye wot° of, and perchance   *know*
Some tripod, thyrsus, with a vase or so,
The Saviour at his sermon on the mount,
60   Saint Praxed in a glory, and one Pan
Ready to twitch the Nymph's last garment off,
And Moses with the tables[8] . . . but I know
Ye mark° me not! What do they whisper thee,   *heed*
Child of my bowels, Anselm? Ah, ye hope
65   To revel down my villas while I gasp
Bricked o'er with beggar's moldy travertine°   *Italian limestone*
Which Gandolf from his tomb-top chuckles at!
Nay, boys, ye love me—all of jasper, then!
'Tis jasper ye stand pledged to, lest I grieve
70   My bath must needs be left behind, alas!
One block, pure green as a pistachio nut,
There's plenty jasper somewhere in the world—
And have I not Saint Praxed's ear to pray
Horses for ye, and brown Greek manuscripts,
75   And mistresses with great smooth marbly limbs?
—That's if ye carve my epitaph aright,
Choice Latin, picked phrase, Tully's[9] every word,
No gaudy ware like Gandolf's second line—
Tully, my masters? Ulpian[1] serves his need!
80   And then how I shall lie through centuries,
And hear the blessed mutter of the mass,
And see God made and eaten all day long,[2]
And feel the steady candle flame, and taste
Good strong thick stupefying incense-smoke!
85   For as I lie here, hours of the dead night,
Dying in state and by such slow degrees,
I fold my arms as if they clasped a crook,°   *bishop's staff*
And stretch my feet forth straight as stone can point,
And let the bedclothes, for a mortcloth,[3] drop
90   Into great laps and folds of sculptor's-work:

5. Cf. Job 7.6: "My days are swifter than a weaver's shuttle."
6. Continuous band of sculpture.
7. Sculpture in which the figures do not project far from the background surface.
8. The sculpture would consist of a mixture of pagan and Christian iconography. "Tripod": seat on which the Oracle of Delphi made prophecies. "Thyrsus": a staff twined with ivy that was carried, according to Greek mythology, by Dionysus, god of wine and fertility. "Glory": halo. "Tables": the stone tablets on which the Ten Commandments were written. Such intermingling of pagan

and Christian traditions, characteristic of the Renaissance, had been attacked in 1841 in *Contrasts*, a book on architecture by A. W. Pugin, a Roman Catholic.
9. I.e., Marcus Tullius Cicero (106–43 B.C.E.), orator and statesman who was one of the great stylists of classical Latin prose.
1. Late Latin author of legal commentaries (d. 228 C.E.); not a model of good style.
2. Reference to the doctrine of transubstantiation.
3. Rich cloth spread over a dead body or coffin.

And as yon tapers dwindle, and strange thoughts
Grow, with a certain humming in my ears,
About the life before I lived this life,
And this life too, popes, cardinals, and priests,
95 Saint Praxed at his sermon on the mount,[4]
Your tall pale mother with her talking eyes,
And new-found agate urns as fresh as day,
And marble's language, Latin pure, discreet
—Aha, ELUCESCEBAT[5] quoth our friend?
100 No Tully, said I, Ulpian at the best!
Evil and brief hath been my pilgrimage.[6]
All *lapis*, all, sons! Else I give the Pope
My villas! Will ye ever eat my heart?
Ever your eyes were as a lizard's quick,
105 They glitter like your mother's for my soul,
Or ye would heighten my impoverished frieze,
Piece out its starved design, and fill my vase
With grapes, and add a vizor and a Term,[7]
And to the tripod ye would tie a lynx[8]
110 That in his struggle throws the thyrsus down,
To comfort me on my entablature[9]
Whereon I am to lie till I must ask
"Do I live, am I dead?" There, leave me, there!
For ye have stabbed me with ingratitude
115 To death—ye wish it—God, ye wish it! Stone—
Gritstone,° a-crumble! Clammy squares   coarse sandstone
  which sweat
As if the corpse they keep were oozing through—
And no more *lapis* to delight the world!
Well go! I bless ye. Fewer tapers there,
120 But in a row: and, going, turn your backs
—Aye, like departing altar-ministrants,
And leave me in my church, the church for peace,
That I may watch at leisure if he leers—
Old Gandolf, at me, from his onion-stone,
125 As still he envied me, so fair she was!

1844   1845

---

4. The bishop is confusing St. Praxed (a woman) with Jesus—an indication that his mind is wandering.
5. He was illustrious (Latin); word from Gandolf's epitaph. The bishop considers the form of the verb to be in "gaudy" bad taste (line 78). If the epitaph had been copied from Cicero instead of from Ulpian, the word would have been *elucebat*.
6. Cf. Genesis 47.9: "few and evil have the days

of the years of my life been."
7. Statue of Terminus, the Roman god of boundaries, usually represented without arms. "Vizor": part of a helmet, often represented in sculpture.
8. An animal that traditionally accompanied Bacchus.
9. Horizontal platform supporting a statue or effigy.

A Toccata of Galuppi's[1]

1

Oh, Galuppi, Baldassaro, this is very sad to find!
I can hardly misconceive you; it would prove me deaf and blind;
But although I take your meaning, 'tis with such a heavy mind!

2

Here you come with your old music, and here's all the good it brings.
5   What, they lived once thus at Venice where the merchants were the kings,
Where Saint Mark's is, where the Doges used to wed the sea with rings?[2]

3

Aye, because the sea's the street there; and 'tis arched by . . . what you call
. . . Shylock's bridge[3] with houses on it, where they kept the carnival:
I was never out of England—it's as if I saw it all.

4

10   Did young people take their pleasure when the sea was warm in May?
Balls and masks° begun at midnight, burning ever to midday,   *masquerades*
When they made up fresh adventures for the morrow, do you say?

5

Was a lady such a lady, cheeks so round and lips so red—
On her neck the small face buoyant, like a bellflower on its bed,
15   O'er the breast's superb abundance where a man might base his head?

6

Well, and it was graceful of them—they'd break talk off and afford
—She, to bite her mask's black velvet—he, to finger on his sword,
While you sat and played toccatas, stately at the clavichord?[4]

7

What? Those lesser thirds so plaintive, sixths diminished, sigh on sigh,
20   Told them something? Those suspensions, those solutions—"Must we die?"
Those commiserating sevenths[5]—"Life might last! we can but try!"

1. For the main speaker of this poem, Browning invents a 19th-century English scientist, who is listening to music by the Italian composer Baldassaro Galuppi (1706–1785). The music evokes for the scientist visions of 18th-century Venice, including an imaginary scene of a party at which Galuppi performs his composition for an audience. From line 20 onward we hear snippets of conversation from members of this audience as they respond to the different moods of the piece, and then, in lines 35–43, Galuppi's own imagined musings. "Toccata": according to *Grove's Dictionary of Music*, a "touch-piece, or a composition intended to exhibit the touch and execution of the performer." The same authority states that "no particular composition was taken as the basis of the poem."
2. An annual ceremony in which the doge, the Venetian chief magistrate, threw a ring into the water to symbolize the bond between his city, with its maritime empire, and the sea.
3. The Rialto, a bridge over the Grand Canal.
4. A keyboard instrument whose strings are struck by metal hammers. Its mechanism resembles that of a piano, but its sound is more like that of a harpsichord.
5. "Sevenths," "sixths," and "thirds": intervals in musical pitch.

8

"Were you happy?"—"Yes."—"And are you still as happy?"—"Yes. And you?"
—"Then, more kisses!"—"Did *I* stop them, when a million seemed so few?"
Hark, the dominant's persistence till it must be answered to!

9

25 So, an octave struck the answer.[6] Oh, they praised you, I dare say!
"Brave Galuppi! that was music; good alike at grave and gay!
I can always leave off talking when I hear a master play!"

10

Then they left you for their pleasure: till in due time, one by one,
Some with lives that came to nothing, some with deeds as well undone,
30 Death stepped tacitly and took them where they never see the sun.

11

But when I sit down to reason, think to take my stand nor swerve,
While I triumph o'er a secret wrung from nature's close reserve,
In you come with your cold music till I creep through every nerve.

12

Yes, you, like a ghostly cricket, creaking where a house was burned:
35 "Dust and ashes, dead and done with, Venice spent what Venice earned.
The soul, doubtless, is immortal—where a soul can be discerned.

13

"Yours for instance: you know physics, something of geology,
Mathematics are your pastime; souls shall rise in their degree;
Butterflies may dread extinction—you'll not die, it cannot be!

14

40 "As for Venice and her people, merely born to bloom and drop,
Here on earth they bore their fruitage, mirth and folly were the crop:
What of soul was left, I wonder, when the kissing had to stop?

15

"Dust and ashes!" So you creak it, and I want° the heart to scold.   *lack*
Dear dead women, with such hair, too—what's become of all the gold
45 Used to hang and brush their bosoms? I feel chilly and grown old.

ca. 1847   1855

---

6. The terms in these lines refer to the technical
devices used by Galuppi to produce alternating
moods in his music, conflict in each instance being
resolved into harmony. Thus the "dominant" (the
fifth note of the scale), after being persistently
sounded, is answered by a resolving chord (lines
24–25).

Love among the Ruins

1

Where the quiet-colored end of evening smiles,
    Miles and miles
On the solitary pastures where our sheep
    Half-asleep
5   Tinkle homeward through the twilight, stray or stop
    As they crop—
Was the site once of a city great and gay
    (So they say),
Of our country's very capital, its prince
10   Ages since
Held his court in, gathered councils, wielding far
    Peace or war.

2

Now—the country does not even boast a tree,
    As you see,
15 To distinguish slopes of verdure, certain rills
    From the hills
Intersect and give a name to (else they run
    Into one),
Where the domed and daring palace shot its spires
20   Up like fires
O'er the hundred-gated circuit of a wall
    Bounding all,
Made of marble, men might march on nor be pressed,
    Twelve abreast.

3

25 And such plenty and perfection, see, of grass
    Never was!
Such a carpet as, this summertime, o'erspreads
    And embeds
Every vestige of the city, guessed alone,
30   Stock or stone—
Where a multitude of men breathed joy and woe
    Long ago;
Lust of glory pricked their hearts up, dread of shame
    Struck them tame;
35 And that glory and that shame alike, the gold
    Bought and sold.

4

Now—the single little turret that remains
    On the plains,
By the caper overrooted, by the gourd
40   Overscored,

While the patching houseleek's[1] head of blossom winks
　　　Through the chinks—
Marks the basement whence a tower in ancient time
　　　Sprang sublime,
45 And a burning ring, all round, the chariots traced
　　　As they raced,
And the monarch and his minions and his dames
　　　Viewed the games.

5

And I know, while thus the quiet-colored eve
50 　　　Smiles to leave
To their folding, all our many-tinkling fleece
　　　In such peace,
And the slopes and rills in undistinguished gray
　　　Melt away—
55 That a girl with eager eyes and yellow hair
　　　Waits me there
In the turret whence the charioteers caught soul
　　　For the goal,
When the king looked, where she looks now, breathless, dumb
60 　　　Till I come.

6

But he looked upon the city, every side,
　　　Far and wide,
All the mountains topped with temples, all the glades'
　　　Colonnades,
65 All the causeys,[2] bridges, aqueducts—and then,
　　　All the men!
When I do come, she will speak not, she will stand,
　　　Either hand
On my shoulder, give her eyes the first embrace
70 　　　Of my face,
Ere we rush, ere we extinguish sight and speech
　　　Each on each.

7

In one year they sent a million fighters forth
　　　South and north,
75 And they built their gods a brazen° pillar high　　　　　　　*brass*
　　　As the sky,
Yet reserved a thousand chariots in full force—
　　　Gold, of course.
Oh heart! oh blood that freezes, blood that burns!
80 　　　Earth's returns
For whole centuries of folly, noise, and sin!

---

1. Common European plant with petals clustered in the shape of rosettes.
2. Causeways or roads raised above low ground.

Shut them in,
With their triumphs and their glories and the rest!
Love is best.

1853   1855

"Childe Roland to the Dark Tower Came"[1]

(See Edgar's Song in "Lear")

1

My first thought was, he lied in every word,
   That hoary cripple, with malicious eye
   Askance° to watch the working of his lie   *squinting sideways*
On mine, arid mouth scarce able to afford
5 Suppression of the glee, that pursed and scored
   Its edge, at one more victim gained thereby.

2

What else should he be set for, with his staff?
   What, save to waylay with his lies, ensnare
   All travelers who might find him posted there,
10 And ask the road? I guessed what skull-like laugh
Would break, what crutch 'gin° write my epitaph   *would begin to*
   For pastime in the dusty thoroughfare,

3

If at his counsel I should turn aside
   Into that ominous tract which, all agree,
15   Hides the Dark Tower. Yet acquiescingly
I did turn as he pointed: neither pride
Nor hope rekindling at the end descried,
   So much as gladness that some end might be.

4

For, what with my whole world-wide wandering,
20   What with my search drawn out through years, my hope

---

1. Browning stated that this poem "came upon me as a kind of dream," and that it was written in one day. Although the poem was among those of his own writings that pleased him most, he was reluctant to explain what the dream (or nightmare) signified. He once agreed with a friend's suggestion that the meaning might be expressed in the statement: "He that endureth to the end shall be saved" (cf. Matthew 24.13). Most readers have responded to the poem in this way, finding in the story of Roland's quest an inspiring expression of defiance and courage. Other readers find that the poem expresses despair more than enduring hope, and it is at least true that the landscape is as grim and nightmarelike as in 20th-century writings such as T. S. Eliot's "The Hollow Men" (1925) or Franz Kafka's "In the Penal Colony" (1919).

The lines from Shakespeare's *King Lear* 3.4 (lines 158–60), from which the title is taken, are spoken when Lear is about to enter a hovel on the heath, and Edgar, feigning madness, chants the fragment of a song reminiscent of quests and challenges in fairy tales: "Child Roland to the dark tower come, / His word was still, 'Fie, fo, and fum; / I smell the blood of a British man.'" "Childe": a youth of noble birth, usually a candidate for knighthood.

Dwindled into a ghost not fit to cope
With that obstreperous joy success would bring,
I hardly tried now to rebuke the spring
   My heart made, finding failure in its scope.

5

25 As when a sick man very near to death
   Seems dead indeed, and feels begin and end
   The tears and takes the farewell of each friend,
And hears one bid the other go, draw breath
Freelier outside ("since all is o'er," he saith,
30   "And the blow fallen no grieving can amend"),

6

While some discuss if near the other graves
   Be room enough for this, and when a day
   Suits best for carrying the corpse away,
With care about the banners, scarves and staves:[2]
35 And still the man hears all, and only craves
   He may not shame such tender love and stay.

7

Thus, I had so long suffered in this quest,
   Heard failure prophesied so oft, been writ
   So many times among "The Band"—to wit,
40 The knights who to the Dark Tower's search addressed
Their steps—that just to fail as they, seemed best,
   And all the doubt was now—should I be fit?

8

So, quiet as despair, I turned from him,
   That hateful cripple, out of his highway
45   Into the path he pointed. All the day
Had been a dreary one at best, and dim
Was settling to its close, yet shot one grim
   Red leer to see the plain catch its estray.[3]

9

For mark! no sooner was I fairly found
50   Pledged to the plain, after a pace or two,
   Than, pausing to throw backward a last view
O'er the safe road, 'twas gone; gray plain all round:
Nothing but plain to the horizon's bound.
   I might go on; naught else remained to do.

2. The trappings of an imagined funeral.
3. Literally, a domestic animal that has strayed away from its home.

10

55 So, on I went. I think I never saw
        Such starved ignoble nature; nothing throve:
        For flowers—as well expect a cedar grove!
    But, cockle, spurge,[4] according to their law
    Might propagate their kind, with none to awe,
60   You'd think; a burr had been a treasure trove.

11

    No! penury, inertness and grimace,
        In some strange sort, were the land's portion. "See
        Or shut your eyes," said Nature peevishly,
    "It nothing skills:[5] I cannot help my case;
65   Tis the Last Judgment's fire must cure this place,
        Calcine[6] its clods and set my prisoners free."

12

    If there pushed any ragged thistle stalk
        Above its mates, the head was chopped; the bents[7]
        Were jealous else. What made those holes and rents
70   In the dock's° harsh swarth leaves, bruised as to balk   *coarse plant*
    All hope of greenness? 'tis a brute must walk
        Pashing° their life out, with a brute's intents.   *smashing*

13

    As for the grass, it grew as scant as hair
        In leprosy; thin dry blades pricked the mud
75   Which underneath looked kneaded up with blood.
    One stiff blind horse, his every bone a-stare,
    Stood stupefied, however he came there:
        Thrust out past service from the devil's stud!

14

    Alive? he might be dead for aught I know,
80   With that red gaunt and colloped° neck a-strain,   *ridged*
        And shut eyes underneath the rusty mane;
    Seldom went such grotesqueness with such woe;
    I never saw a brute I hated so;
        He must be wicked to deserve such pain.

15

85   I shut my eyes and turned them on my heart.
        As a man calls for wine before he fights,
        I asked one draught of earlier, happier sights,

---

4. A bitter-juiced weed. "Cockle": a weed that
bears burrs.
5. I.e., it is no use.

6. Turn to powder by heat.
7. Coarse stiff grasses.

Ere fitly I could hope to play my part.
Think first, fight afterwards—the soldier's art:
90   One taste of the old time sets all to rights.

16

Not it! I fancied Cuthbert's reddening face
Beneath its garniture of curly gold,
Dear fellow, till I almost felt him fold
An arm in mine to fix me to the place,
95 That way he used. Alas, one night's disgrace!
Out went my heart's new fire and left it cold.

17

Giles then, the soul of honor—there he stands
Frank as ten years ago when knighted first.
What honest man should dare (he said) he durst.
100 Good—but the scene shifts—faugh! what hangman hands
Pin to his breast a parchment? His own bands
Read it. Poor traitor, spit upon and cursed!

18

Better this present than a past like that;
Back therefore to my darkening path again!
105   No sound, no sight as far as eye could strain.
Will the night send a howlet° or a bat?   *owl*
I asked: when something on the dismal flat
Came to arrest my thoughts and change their train.

19

A sudden little river crossed my path
110   As unexpected as a serpent comes.
No sluggish tide congenial to the glooms;
This, as it frothed by, might have been a bath
For the fiend's glowing hoof—to see the wrath
Of its black eddy bespate° with flakes and spumes.   *bespattered*

20

115 So petty yet so spiteful! All along,
Low scrubby alders kneeled down over it;
Drenched willows flung them headlong in a fit
Of mute despair, a suicidal throng:
The river which had done them all the wrong,
120   Whate'er that was, rolled by, deterred no whit.

21

Which, while I forded—good saints, how I feared
To set my foot upon a dead man's cheek,
Each step, or feel the spear I thrust to seek

For hollows, tangled in his hair or beard!
125 —It may have been a water rat I speared,
    But, ugh! it sounded like a baby's shriek.

22

Glad was I when I reached the other bank.
    Now for a better country. Vain presage!
    Who were the strugglers, what war did they wage,
130 Whose savage trample thus could pad the dank
    Soil to a plash?° Toads in a poisoned tank,   *puddle*
    Or wild cats in a red-hot iron cage—

23

The fight must so have seemed in that fell cirque.°   *dreadful arena*
    What penned them there, with all the plain to choose?
135   No footprint leading to that horrid mews,[8]
None out of it. Mad brewage set to work
Their brains, no doubt, like galley slaves the Turk
    Pits for his pastime, Christians against Jews.

24

And more than that—a furlong on—why, there!
140   What bad use was that engine for, that wheel,
    Or brake,[9] not wheel—that harrow fit to reel
Men's bodies out like silk? with all the air
Of Tophet's° tool, on earth left unaware,   *hell's*
    Or brought to sharpen its rusty teeth of steel.

25

145 Then came a bit of stubbed ground, once a wood,
    Next a marsh, it would seem, and now mere earth
    Desperate and done with; (so a fool finds mirth,
Makes a thing and then mars it, till his mood
Changes and off he goes!) within a rood[1]
150   Bog, clay and rubble, sand and stark black dearth.

26

Now blotches rankling, colored gay and grim,
    Now patches where some leanness of the soil's
    Broke into moss or substances like boils;
Then came some palsied oak, a cleft in him
155 Like a distorted mouth that splits its rim
    Gaping at death, and dies while it recoils.

8. Enclosed stable yard.   torture.
9. A toothed machine used for separating the   1. I.e., a short distance (6–8 yards).
fibers of flax or hemp; here an instrument of

27

And just as far as ever from the end!
  Naught in the distance but the evening, naught
  To point my footstep further! At the thought,
160 A great black bird, Apollyon's[2] bosom friend,
  Sailed past, nor beat his wide wing dragon-penned[3]
  That brushed my cap—perchance the guide I sought.

28

For, looking up, aware I somehow grew,
  'Spite of the dusk, the plain had given place
165 All round to mountains—with such name to grace
Mere ugly heights and heaps now stolen in view.
How thus they had surprised me—solve it, you!
  How to get from them was no clearer case.

29

Yet half I seemed to recognize some trick
170 Of mischief happened to me, God knows when—
  In a bad dream perhaps. Here ended, then,
Progress this way. When, in the very nick
Of giving up, one time more, came a click
  As when a trap shuts—you're inside the den!

30

175 Burningly it came on me all at once,
  This was the place! those two hills on the right,
  Crouched like two bulls locked horn in horn in fight;
While to the left, a tall scalped mountain . . . Dunce,
Dotard, a-dozing at the very nonce,°   *moment*
180 After a life spent training for the sight!

31

What in the midst lay but the Tower itself?
  The round squat turret, blind as the fool's heart,[4]
  Built of brown stone, without a counterpart
In the whole world. The tempest's mocking elf
185 Points to the shipman thus the unseen shelf
  He strikes on, only when the timbers start.° *separate; come loose*

32

Not see? because of night perhaps?—why, day
  Came back again for that! before it left,
  The dying sunset kindled through a cleft:

2. In Revelation 9.11 Apollyon is "the angel of the bottomless pit." In *The Pilgrim's Progress* (1678) by John Bunyan (1628–1688) he is a hideous "monster"; "he had wings like a dragon."

3. With wings or pinions like those of a dragon.
4. Cf. Psalms 14.1: "The fool hath said in his heart, There is no God."

190 The hills, like giants at a hunting, lay,
    Chin upon hand, to see the game at bay—
      "Now stab and end the creature—to the heft!"[5]

33

Not hear? when noise was everywhere! it tolled
    Increasing like a bell. Names in my ears
195   Of all the lost adventurers my peers—
How such a one was strong, and such was bold,
And such was fortunate, yet each of old
      Lost, lost! one moment knelled the woe of years.

34

There they stood, ranged along the hillsides, met
200   To view the last of me, a living frame
      For one more picture! in a sheet of flame
I saw them and I knew them all. And yet
Dauntless the slug-horn[6] to my lips I set,
      And blew. *"Childe Roland to the Dark Tower came."*

1852   1855

Fra Lippo Lippi[1]

I am poor brother Lippo, by your leave!
You need not clap your torches to my face.
Zooks,[2] what's to blame? you think you see a monk!
What, 'tis past midnight, and you go the rounds,
5 And here you catch me at an alley's end
Where sportive ladies leave their doors ajar?
The Carmine's[3] my cloister: hunt it up,
Do—harry out, if you must show your zeal,
Whatever rat, there, haps on his wrong hole,
10 And nip each softling of a wee white mouse,
Weke, weke, that's crept to keep him company!
Aha, you know your betters! Then, you'll take
Your hand away that's fiddling on my throat,
And please to know me likewise. Who am I?
15 Why, one, sir, who is lodging with a friend

5. Handle of dagger or sword.
6. The war cry or slogan of a clan about to engage in battle (Scottish). In 1770, however, the poet Thomas Chatterton was misled into using it to mean a kind of trumpet or horn. Browning followed Chatterton's example, although the original meaning would also be relevant here.
1. This monologue portrays the dawn of the Renaissance in Italy at a point when the medieval attitude toward life and art was about to be displaced by a fresh appreciation of earthly pleasures. It was from Giorgio Vasari's *Lives of the*

Painters (1550) that Browning derived most of his information about the life of the Florentine painter and friar Lippo Lippi (1406–1469), but the theory of art propounded by Lippi in the poem was developed by the poet.
2. A shortened version of *Gadzooks,* a mild oath now obscure in meaning but perhaps resembling a phrase still in use: "God's truth."
3. Santa Maria del Carmine, a church and cloister of the Carmelite order of friars to which Lippi belonged.

Three streets off—he's a certain . . . how d'ye call?
Master—a . . . Cosimo of the Medici,[4]
I' the house that caps the corner. Boh! you were best!
Remember and tell me, the day you're hanged,
20   How you affected such a gullet's gripe![5]
But you,[6] sir, it concerns you that your knaves
Pick up a manner nor discredit you:
Zooks, are we pilchards,° that they sweep the streets   *small fish*
And count fair prize what comes into this net?
25   He's Judas to a tittle,° that man is![7]   *to a tee*
Just such a face! Why, sir, you make amends.
Lord, I'm not angry! Bid your hangdogs go
Drink out this quarter-florin[8] to the health
Of the munificent House that harbors me
30   (And many more beside, lads! more beside!)
And all's come square again. I'd like his face—
His, elbowing on his comrade in the door
With the pike and lantern—for the slave that holds
John Baptist's head a-dangle by the hair
35   With one hand ("Look you, now," as who should say)
And his weapon in the other, yet unwiped!
It's not your chance to have a bit of chalk,
A wood-coal° or the like? or you should see!   *piece of charcoal*
Yes, I'm the painter, since you style me so.
40   What, brother Lippo's doings, up and down,
You know them and they take you? like enough!
I saw the proper twinkle in your eye—
'Tell you, I liked your looks at very first.
Let's sit and set things straight now, hip to haunch.
45   Here's spring come, and the nights one makes up bands
To roam the town and sing out carnival,[9]
And I've been three weeks shut within my mew,°   *private den*
A-painting for the great man, saints and saints
And saints again. I could not paint all night—
50   Ouf! I leaned out of window for fresh air.
There came a hurry of feet and little feet,
A sweep of lute-strings, laughs, and whifts of song—
Flower o' the broom,
Take away love, and our earth is a tomb!
55   *Flower o' the quince,*
I let Lisa go, and what good in life since?[1]
Flower o' the thyme—and so on. Round they went.
Scarce had they turned the corner when a titter
Like the skipping of rabbits by moonlight—three slim shapes,
60   And a face that looked up . . . zooks, sir, flesh and blood,

That's all I'm made of! Into shreds it went,
Curtain and counterpane and coverlet,
All the bed-furniture—a dozen knots,
There was a ladder! Down I let myself,
65   Hands and feet, scrambling somehow, and so dropped,
And after them. I came up with the fun
Hard by° Saint Laurence,[2] hail fellow, well met—   *next to*
Flower o' the rose,
If I've been merry, what matter who knows!
70   And so as I was stealing back again
To get to bed and have a bit of sleep
Ere I rise up tomorrow and go work
On Jerome knocking at his poor old breast
With his great round stone to subdue the flesh,[3]
75   You snap me of the sudden. Ah, I see!
Though your eye twinkles still, you shake your head—
Mine's shaved—a monk, you say—the sting's in that!
If Master Cosimo announced himself,
Mum's the word naturally; but a monk!
80   Come, what am I a beast for? tell us, now!
I was a baby when my mother died
And father died and left me in the street.
I starved there, God knows how, a year or two
On fig skins, melon parings, rinds and shucks,
85   Refuse and rubbish. One fine frosty day,
My stomach being empty as your hat,
The wind doubled me up and down I went.
Old Aunt Lapaccia trussed me with one hand
(Its fellow° was a stinger as I knew),   *her other hand*
90   And so along the wall, over the bridge,
By the straight cut to the convent. Six words there,
While I stood munching my first bread that month:
"So, boy, you're minded," quoth the good fat father
Wiping his own mouth, 'twas refection time°—   *mealtime*
95   "To quit this very miserable world?
Will you renounce" . . . "the mouthful of bread?" thought I;
By no means! Brief, they made a monk of me;
I did renounce the world, its pride and greed,
Palace, farm, villa, shop, and banking house,
100   Trash, such as these poor devils of Medici
Have given their hearts to—all at eight years old.
Well, sir, I found in time, you may be sure,
'Twas not for nothing—the good bellyful,
The warm serge and the rope[4] that goes all round,
105   And day-long blessed idleness beside!
"Let's see what the urchin's fit for"—that came next.
Not overmuch their way, I must confess.
Such a to-do! They tried me with their books:

2. San Lorenzo, a church in Florence.
3. A picture of Saint Jerome (ca. 340–420), whose ascetic observances were hardly a conge-

nial subject for a painter such as Lippi.
4. The material ("serge") and belt ("rope") of a monk's clothing.

Lord, they'd have taught me Latin in pure waste!
110 *Flower o' the clove,*
All the Latin I construe is "amo," I love!
But, mind you, when a boy starves in the streets
Eight years together, as my fortune was,
Watching folk's faces to know who will fling
115 The bit of half-stripped grape bunch he desires,
And who will curse or kick him for his pains—
Which gentleman processional and fine,
Holding a candle to the Sacrament,
Will wink and let him lift a plate and catch
120 The droppings of the wax to sell again,
Or holla for the Eight° and have him whipped—   *Florentine magistrates*
How say I?—nay, which dog bites, which lets drop
His bone from the heap of offal in the street—
Why, soul and sense of him grow sharp alike,
125 He learns the look of things, and none the less
For admonition from the hunger-pinch.
I had a store of such remarks, be sure,
Which, after I found leisure, turned to use.
I drew men's faces on my copybooks,
130 Scrawled them within the antiphonary's marge,[5]
Joined legs and arms to the long music-notes,
Found eyes and nose and chin for A's and B's,
And made a string of pictures of the world
Betwixt the ins and outs of verb and noun,
135 On the wall, the bench, the door. The monks looked black.
"Nay," quoth the Prior,[6] "turn him out, d' ye say?
In no wise. Lose a crow and catch a lark.
What if at last we get our man of parts,°   *skill, genius*
We Carmelites, like those Camaldolese
140 And Preaching Friars,[7] to do our church up fine
And put the front on it that ought to be!"
And hereupon he bade me daub away.
Thank you! my head being crammed, the walls a blank,
Never was such prompt disemburdening.
145 First, every sort of monk, the black and white,
I drew them, fat and lean: then, folk at church,
From good old gossips waiting to confess
Their cribs° of barrel droppings, candle ends—   *petty thefts*
To the breathless fellow at the altar-foot,
150 Fresh from his murder, safe[8] and sitting there
With the little children round him in a row
Of admiration, half for his beard and half
For that white anger of his victim's son
Shaking a fist at him with one fierce arm,
155 Signing himself with the other because of Christ
(Whose sad face on the cross sees only this

5. Margin of a music book used for choral singing.
6. Head of a Carmelite convent.
7. Benedictine and Dominican religious orders, respectively.
8. Having claimed sanctuary in the church.

After the passion° of a thousand years)   *sufferings*
Till some poor girl, her apron o'er her head
(Which the intense eyes looked through), came at eve
160 On tiptoe, said a word, dropped in a loaf,
Her pair of earrings and a bunch of flowers
(The brute took growling), prayed, and so was gone.
I painted all, then cried "'Tis ask and have;
Choose, for more's ready!"—laid the ladder flat,
165 And showed my covered bit of cloister wall.
The monks closed in a circle and praised loud
Till checked, taught what to see and not to see,
Being simple bodies—"That's the very man!
Look at the boy who stoops to pat the dog!
170 That woman's like the Prior's niece who comes
To care about his asthma: it's the life!"
But there my triumph's straw-fire flared and funked;[9]
Their betters took their turn to see and say:
The Prior and the learned pulled a face
175 And stopped all that in no time. "How? what's here?
Quite from the mark of painting, bless us all!
Faces, arms, legs and bodies like the true
As much as pea and pea! it's devil's game!
Your business is not to catch men with show,
180 With homage to the perishable clay,
But lift them over it, ignore it all,
Make them forget there's such a thing as flesh.
Your business is to paint the souls of men—
Man's soul, and it's a fire, smoke . . . no, it's not . . .
185 It's vapor done up like a newborn babe—
(In that shape when you die it leaves your mouth)
It's . . . well, what matters talking, it's the soul!
Give us no more of body than shows soul!
Here's Giotto,[1] with his Saint a-praising God,
190 That sets us praising—why not stop with him?
Why put all thoughts of praise out of our head
With wonder at lines, colors, and what not?
Paint the soul, never mind the legs and arms!
Rub all out, try at it a second time.
195 Oh, that white smallish female with the breasts,
She's just° my niece . . . Herodias,[2] I would say— *exactly like*
Who went and danced and got men's heads cut off!
Have it all out!" Now, is this sense, I ask?
A fine way to paint soul, by painting body
200 So ill, the eye can't stop there, must go further
And can't fare worse! Thus, yellow does for white
When what you put for yellow's simply black,
And any sort of meaning looks intense

9. Went up in smoke.
1. Great Florentine painter (1276–1337) whose stylized pictures of religious subjects were admired as models of pre-Renaissance art.
2. I.e., Salomé (her mother was Herodias, the sister-in-law of King Herod). Because John the Baptist had aroused her mother's displeasure, Salomé asked for his head on a platter after she danced (Matthew 14.6–11).

When all beside itself means and looks naught.
205 Why can't a painter lift each foot in turn,
Left foot and right foot, go a double step,
Make his flesh liker and his soul more like,
Both in their order? Take the prettiest face,
The Prior's niece . . . patron-saint—is it so pretty
210 You can't discover if it means hope, fear,
Sorrow or joy? won't beauty go with these?
Suppose I've made her eyes all right and blue,
Can't I take breath and try to add life's flash,
And then add soul and heighten them threefold?
215 Or say there's beauty with no soul at all—
(I never saw it—put the case the same—)
If you get simple beauty and naught else,
You get about the best thing God invents:
That's somewhat: and you'll find the soul you have missed,
220 Within yourself, when you return him thanks.
"Rub all out!" Well, well, there's my life, in short,
And so the thing has gone on ever since.
I'm grown a man no doubt, I've broken bounds:
You should not take a fellow eight years old
225 And make him swear to never kiss the girls.
I'm my own master, paint now as I please—
Having a friend, you see, in the Corner-house![3]
Lord, it's fast holding by the rings in front—
Those great rings serve more purposes than just
230 To plant a flag in, or tie up a horse!
And yet the old schooling sticks, the old grave eyes
Are peeping o'er my shoulder as I work,
The heads shake still—"It's art's decline, my son!
You're not of the true painters, great and old;
235 Brother Angelico's the man, you'll find;
Brother Lorenzo[4] stands his single peer:
Fag on° at flesh, you'll never make the third!"   *work hard*
Flower o' the pine,
You keep your mistr . . . manners, and I'll stick to mine!
240 I'm not the third, then: bless us, they must know!
Don't you think they're the likeliest to know,
They with their Latin? So, I swallow my rage,
Clench my teeth, suck my lips in tight, and paint
To please them—sometimes do and sometimes don't;
245 For, doing most, there's pretty sure to come
A turn, some warm eve finds me at my saints—
A laugh, a cry, the business of the world—
(Flower o' the peach,
Death for us all, and his own life for each!)
250 And my whole soul revolves, the cup runs over,
The world and life's too big to pass for a dream,
And I do these wild things in sheer despite,

3. The Medici palace.
4. Fra Angelico (1387–1455) and Lorenzo Monaco

(1370–1425), whose paintings were in the approved traditional manner.

And play the fooleries you catch me at,
In pure rage! The old mill-horse, out at grass
255　After hard years, throws up his stiff heels so,
Although the miller does not preach to him
The only good of grass is to make chaff.°   *straw*
What would men have? Do they like grass or no[5]—
May they or mayn't they? all I want's the thing
260　Settled forever one way. As it is,
You tell too many lies and hurt yourself:
You don't like what you only like too much,
You do like what, if given you at your word,
You find abundantly detestable.
265　For me, I think I speak as I was taught;
I always see the garden[6] and God there
A-making man's wife: and, my lesson learned,
The value and significance of flesh,
I can't unlearn ten minutes afterwards.

270　　You understand me: I'm a beast, I know.
But see, now—why, I see as certainly
As that the morning star's about to shine,
What will hap some day. We've a youngster here
Comes to our convent, studies what I do,
275　Slouches and stares and lets no atom drop:
His name is Guidi[7]—he'll not mind the monks—
They call him Hulking Tom, he lets them talk—
He picks my practice up—he'll paint apace,
I hope so—though I never live so long,
280　I know what's sure to follow. You be judge!
You speak no Latin more than I, belike;
However, you're my man, you've seen the world
—The beauty and the wonder and the power,
The shapes of things, their colors, lights and shades,
285　Changes, surprises—and God made it all!
—For what? Do you feel thankful, aye or no,
For this fair town's face, yonder river's line,
The mountain round it and the sky above,
Much more the figures of man, woman, child,
290　These are the frame to? What's it all about?
To be passed over, despised? or dwelt upon,
Wondered at? oh, this last of course!—you say.
But why not do as well as say—paint these
Just as they are, careless what comes of it?
295　God's works—paint any one, and count it crime
To let a truth slip. Don't object, "His works

---

5. I.e., while horses are allowed to enjoy playing in the grass, human beings are taught by the Church that physical experience is valuable only in its relation to their future condition in the afterlife. The biblical text "all flesh is as grass" (1 Peter 1.24) lurks within Lippi's question.
6. I.e., Eden.
7. Guidi or Masaccio (1401–1428), a painter who may have been Lippi's master rather than his pupil, although Browning, in a letter to the press in 1870, argued that Lippi had been born earlier. Like Lippi, Masaccio was in revolt against the medieval theory of art. His frescoes in the chapel of Santa Maria del Carmine are considered his masterpiece.

Are here already; nature is complete:
Suppose you reproduce her—(which you can't)
There's no advantage! You must beat her, then."
300 For, don't you mark?° we're made so that we love   *observe*
First when we see them painted, things we have passed
Perhaps a hundred times nor cared to see;
And so they are better, painted—better to us,
Which is the same thing. Art was given for that;
305 God uses us to help each other so,
Lending our minds out. Have you noticed, now,
Your cullion's° hanging face? A bit of chalk,   *rascal's*
And trust me but you should, though! How much more,
If I drew higher things with the same truth!
310 That were to take the Prior's pulpit-place,
Interpret God to all of you! Oh, oh,
It makes me mad to see what men shall do
And we in our graves! This world's no blot for us,
Nor blank; it means intensely, and means good:
315 To find its meaning is my meat and drink.
"Aye, but you don't so instigate to prayer!"
Strikes in the Prior: "when your meaning's plain
It does not say to folk—remember matins,
Or, mind you fast next Friday!" Why, for this
320 What need of art at all? A skull and bones,
Two bits of stick nailed crosswise, or, what's best,
A bell to chime the hour with, does as well.
I painted a Saint Laurence[8] six months since
At Prato, splashed the fresco[9] in fine style:
325   "How looks my painting, now the scaffold's down?"
I ask a brother: "Hugely," he returns—
"Already not one phiz° of your three slaves   *face*
Who turn the Deacon off his toasted side,
But it's scratched and prodded to our heart's content,
330 The pious people have so eased their own
With coming to say prayers there in a rage:
We get on fast to see the bricks beneath.
Expect another job this time next year,
For pity and religion grow i' the crowd—
335 Your painting serves its purpose!" Hang the fools!

      —That is—you'll not mistake an idle word
Spoke in a huff by a poor monk, God wot,°   *knows*
Tasting the air this spicy night which turns
The unaccustomed head like Chianti wine!
340 Oh, the church knows! don't misreport me, now!
It's natural a poor monk out of bounds
Should have his apt word to excuse himself:
And hearken how I plot to make amends.

---

8. A scene representing the fiery martyrdom of St. Laurence (or Lawrence).
9. Painted on a freshly plastered surface. It must be painted quickly before the plaster dries. Prato is a town near Florence.

I have bethought me: I shall paint a piece
345 . . . There's for you! Give me six months, then go, see
Something in Sant' Ambrogio's![1] Bless the nuns!
They want a cast o' my office.[2] I shall paint
God in the midst, Madonna and her babe,
Ringed by a bowery flowery angel brood,
350 Lilies and vestments and white faces, sweet
As puff on puff of grated orris-root[3]
When ladies crowd to Church at midsummer.
And then i' the front, of course a saint or two—
Saint John, because he saves the Florentines,
355 Saint Ambrose, who puts down in black and white
The convent's friends and gives them a long day,
And Job,[4] I must have him there past mistake,
The man of Uz (and Us without the z,
Painters who need his patience). Well, all these
360 Secured at their devotion, up shall come
Out of a corner when you least expect,
As one by a dark stair into a great light,
Music and talking, who but Lippo! I!—
Mazed,° motionless and moonstruck—I'm the man!   confused
365 Back I shrink—what is this I see and hear?
I, caught up with my monk's things by mistake,
My old serge gown and rope that goes all round,
I, in this presence, this pure company!
Where's a hole, where's a corner for escape?
370 Then steps a sweet angelic slip of a thing
Forward, puts out a soft palm—"Not so fast!"
—Addresses the celestial presence, "nay—
He made you and devised you, after all,
Though he's none of you! Could Saint John there draw—
375 His camel-hair[5] make up a painting-brush?
We come to brother Lippo for all that,
Iste perfecit opus!"[6] So, all smile—
I shuffle sideways with my blushing face
Under the cover of a hundred wings
380 Thrown like a spread of kirtles° when you're gay   skirts
And play hot cockles,[7] all the doors being shut,
Till, wholly unexpected, in there pops
The hothead husband! Thus I scuttle off
To some safe bench behind, not letting go
385 The palm of her, the little lily thing
That spoke the good word for me in the nick,
Like the Prior's niece . . . Saint Lucy, I would say.

---

1. A convent church in Florence.
2. Sample of my work. The completed painting, which Browning saw in Florence, is Lippi's *Coronation of the Virgin* (1441).
3. A powder (like talcum) made from sweet-smelling roots of a flower.
4. The prosperous man who endured immense suffering without once questioning God's will

(see the book of Job).
5. Cf. Mark 1.6: "And John was clothed with camel's hair."
6. This man made the work! (Latin). In this painting, as later completed, these words appear beside a figure that Browning took to be Lippi's self-portrait.
7. A game in which a player wears a blindfold.

And so all's saved for me, and for the church
A pretty picture gained. Go, six months hence!
390   Your hand, sir, and good-by: no lights, no lights!
The street's hushed, and I know my own way back,
Don't fear me! There's the gray beginning. Zooks!

ca. 1853   1855

Andrea del Sarto[1]

(called "The Faultless Painter")

But do not let us quarrel any more,
No, my Lucrezia; bear with me for once:
Sit down and all shall happen as you wish.
You turn your face, but does it bring your heart?
5   I'll work then for your friend's friend, never fear,
Treat his own subject after his own way,
Fix his own time, accept too his own price,
And shut the money into this small hand
When next it takes mine. Will it? tenderly?
10   Oh, I'll content him—but tomorrow, Love!
I often am much wearier than you think,
This evening more than usual, and it seems
As if—forgive now—should you let me sit
Here by the window with your hand in mine
15   And look a half-hour forth on Fiesole,[2]
Both of one mind, as married people use,°   usually are
Quietly, quietly the evening through,
I might get up tomorrow to my work
Cheerful and fresh as ever. Let us try.
20   Tomorrow, how you shall be glad for this!
Your soft hand is a woman of itself,
And mine the man's bared breast she curls inside.
Don't count the time lost, neither; you must serve
For each of the five pictures we require:
25   It saves° a model. So! keep looking so—   saves the expense of
My serpentining beauty, rounds on rounds![3]
—How could you ever prick those perfect ears,
Even to put the pearl there! oh, so sweet—

1. This portrait of Andrea del Sarto (1486–1531) was derived from a biography written by his pupil Giorgio Vasari, author of *The Lives of the Painters* (1550). Vasari's account seeks to explain why his Florentine master, one of the most skillful painters of the Renaissance, never altogether fulfilled the promise he had shown early in his career and why he had never arrived (in Vasari's opinion) at the level of such artists as Raphael. Vasari noted that Andrea suffered from "a certain timidity of mind . . . which rendered it impossible that those evidences of ardor and animation, which are proper to the more exalted character, should ever appear in him."
    Browning also follows Vasari's account of Andrea's marriage to a beautiful widow, Lucrezia, "an artful woman who made him do as she pleased in all things." Vasari reports that Andrea's "immoderate love for her soon caused him to neglect the studies demanded by his art" and that this infatuation had "more influence over him than the glory and honor towards which he had begun to make such hopeful advances."
2. A suburb on the hills overlooking Florence.
3. Coils of hair like the coils of a serpent.

My face, my moon, my everybody's moon,
30 Which everybody looks on and calls his,
And, I suppose, is looked on by in turn,
While she looks—no one's: very dear, no less.[4]
You smile? why, there's my picture ready made,
There's what we painters call our harmony!
35 A common grayness silvers everything[5]—
All in a twilight, you and I alike
—You, at the point of your first pride in me
(That's gone you know)—but I, at every point;
My youth, my hope, my art, being all toned down
40 To yonder sober pleasant Fiesole.
There's the bell clinking from the chapel top;
That length of convent wall across the way
Holds the trees safer, huddled more inside;
The last monk leaves the garden; days decrease,
45 And autumn grows, autumn in everything.
Eh? the whole seems to fall into a shape
As if I saw alike my work and self
And all that I was born to be and do,
A twilight-piece. Love, we are in God's hand.
50 How strange now, looks the life he makes us lead;
So free we seem, so fettered fast we are!
I feel he laid the fetter: let it lie!
This chamber for example—turn your head—
All that's behind us! You don't understand
55 Nor care to understand about my art,
But you can hear at least when people speak:
And that cartoon,° the second from the door   *drawing*
—It is the thing, Love! so such things should be—
Behold Madonna!—I am bold to say.
60 I can do with my pencil what I know,
What I see, what at bottom of my heart
I wish for, if I ever wish so deep—
Do easily, too—when I say, perfectly,
I do not boast, perhaps: yourself are judge,
65 Who listened to the Legate's[6] talk last week,
And just as much they used to say in France.
At any rate 'tis easy, all of it!
No sketches first, no studies, that's long past:
I do what many dream of, all their lives,
70 —Dream? strive to do, and agonize to do,
And fail in doing. I could count twenty such
On twice your fingers, and not leave this town,
Who strive—you don't know how the others strive
To paint a little thing like that you smeared
75 Carelessly passing with your robes afloat—

4. Her affections are centered on no one person, not even on her husband, yet she is nevertheless dear to him.

5. The predominant color in many of Andrea's paintings is silver gray.
6. A deputy of the pope.

Yet do much less, so much less, Someone[7] says
(I know his name, no matter)—so much less!
Well, less is more, Lucrezia: I am judged.
There burns a truer light of God in them,
80 In their vexed beating stuffed and stopped-up brain,
Heart, or whate'er else, than goes on to prompt
This low-pulsed forthright craftsman's hand of mine.
Their works drop groundward, but themselves, I know,
Reach many a time a heaven that's shut to me,
85 Enter and take their place there sure enough,
Though they come back and cannot tell the world.
My works are nearer heaven, but I sit here.
The sudden blood of these men! at a word—
Praise them, it boils, or blame them, it boils too.
90 I, painting from myself and to myself,
Know what I do, am unmoved by men's blame
Or their praise either. Somebody remarks
Morello's[8] outline there is wrongly traced,
His hue mistaken; what of that? or else,
95 Rightly traced and well ordered; what of that?
Speak as they please, what does the mountain care?
Ah, but a man's reach should exceed his grasp,
Or what's a heaven for? All is silver-gray
Placid and perfect with my art: the worse!
100 I know both what I want and what might gain,
And yet how profitless to know, to sigh
"Had I been two, another and myself,
Our head would have o'erlooked the world!" No doubt.
Yonder's a work now, of that famous youth
105 The Urbinate[9] who died five years ago.
('Tis copied,[1] George Vasari sent it me.)
Well, I can fancy how he did it all,
Pouring his soul, with kings and popes to see,
Reaching, that heaven might so replenish him,
110 Above and through his art—for it gives way;
That arm is wrongly put—and there again—
A fault to pardon in the drawing's lines,
Its body, so to speak: its soul is right,
He means right—that, a child may understand.
115 Still, what an arm! and I could alter it:
But all the play, the insight and the stretch—
Out of me, out of me! And wherefore out?
Had you enjoined them on me, given me soul,
We might have risen to Rafael, I and you!
120 Nay, Love, you did give all I asked, I think—
More than I merit, yes, by many times.
But had you—oh, with the same perfect brow,

---

7. Probably the artist Michelangelo (1475–1564).
8. A mountain peak outside Florence.
9. Raphael (1483–1520), or Raffaello Sanzio, born at Urbino.

1. In saying that the painting is a copy, Andrea may perhaps be concerned to prevent Lucrezia from selling it.

And perfect eyes, and more than perfect mouth,
And the low voice my soul hears, as a bird
125 The fowler's pipe,[2] and follows to the snare—
Had you, with these the same, but brought a mind!
Some women do so. Had the mouth there urged
"God and the glory! never care for gain.
The present by the future, what is that?
130 Live for fame, side by side with Agnolo!°   *Michelangelo*
Rafael is waiting: up to God, all three!"
I might have done it for you. So it seems:
Perhaps not. All is as God overrules.
Beside, incentives come from the soul's self;
135 The rest avail not. Why do I need you?
What wife had Rafael, or has Agnolo?
In this world, who can do a thing, will not;
And who would do it, cannot, I perceive:
Yet the will's somewhat°—somewhat, too, the power—   *of some importance*
140 And thus we half-men struggle. At the end,
God, I conclude, compensates, punishes.
'Tis safer for me, if the award be strict,
That I am something underrated here.
Poor this long while, despised, to speak the truth.
145 I dared not, do you know, leave home all day,
For fear of chancing on the Paris lords.
The best is when they pass and look aside;
But they speak sometimes; I must bear it all.
Well may they speak! That Francis,[3] that first time,
150 And that long festal year at Fontainebleau!
I surely then could sometimes leave the ground,
Put on the glory, Rafael's daily wear,
In that humane great monarch's golden look—
One finger in his beard or twisted curl
155 Over his mouth's good mark that made the smile,
One arm about my shoulder, round my neck,
The jingle of his gold chain in my ear,
I painting proudly with his breath on me,
All his court round him, seeing with his eyes,
160 Such frank French eyes, and such a fire of souls
Profuse, my hand kept plying by those hearts—
And, best of all, this, this, this face beyond,
This in the background, waiting on my work,
To crown the issue with a last reward!
165 A good time, was it not, my kingly days?
And had you not grown restless . . . but I know—

---

2. Whistle or call used by hunters to lure wild fowl into range.
3. King Francis I of France (1494–1547; reigned 1515–47) had invited Andrea to his court at Fontainebleau and warmly encouraged him in his painting. On returning to Florence, however, Andrea is reputed to have stolen some funds entrusted to him by Francis; and to please Lucrezia he built a house with the money. Now he is afraid of being insulted by "Paris lords" on the streets.

'Tis done and past; 'twas right, my instinct said;
Too live the life grew, golden and not gray,
And I'm the weak-eyed bat no sun should tempt
170 Out of the grange° whose four walls make his world.   *farmhouse*
How could it end in any other way?
You called me, and I came home to your heart.
The triumph was—to reach and stay there; since
I reached it ere the triumph, what is lost?
175 Let my hands frame your face in your hair's gold,
You beautiful Lucrezia that are mine!
"Rafael did this, Andrea painted that;
The Roman's is the better when you pray,
But still the other's Virgin was his wife—"
180 Men will excuse me. I am glad to judge
Both pictures in your presence; clearer grows
My better fortune, I resolve to think.
For, do you know, Lucrezia, as God lives,
Said one day Agnolo, his very self,
185 To Rafael . . . I have known it all these years . . .
(When the young man was flaming out his thoughts
Upon a palace wall for Rome to see,
Too lifted up in heart because of it)
"Friend, there's a certain sorry little scrub
190 Goes up and down our Florence, none cares how,
Who, were he set to plan and execute
As you are, pricked on by your popes and kings,
Would bring the sweat into that brow of yours!"
To Rafael's—And indeed the arm is wrong.
195 I hardly dare . . . yet, only you to see,
Give the chalk here—quick, thus the line should go!
Aye, but the soul! he's Rafael! rub it out!
Still, all I care for, if he spoke the truth,
(What he? why, who but Michel Agnolo?
200 Do you forget already words like those?)
If really there was such a chance, so lost—
Is, whether you're—not grateful—but more pleased.
Well, let me think so. And you smile indeed!
This hour has been an hour! Another smile?
205 If you would sit thus by me every night
I should work better, do you comprehend?
I mean that I should earn more, give you more.
See, it is settled dusk now; there's a star;
Morello's gone, the watch-lights show the wall,
210 The cue-owls[4] speak the name we call them by.
Come from the window, love—come in, at last,
Inside the melancholy little house
We built to be so gay with. God is just.
King Francis may forgive me: oft at nights

---

4. Scops owls; the term is Browning's coinage from the Italian *chiù* or *ciù*, a name that imitates their cry.

215　When I look up from painting, eyes tired out,
　　The walls become illumined, brick from brick
　　Distinct, instead of mortar, fierce bright gold,
　　That gold of his I did cement them with!
　　Let us but love each other. Must you go?
220　That Cousin here again? he waits outside?
　　Must see you—you, and not with me? Those loans?
　　More gaming debts to pay?⁵ you smiled for that?
　　Well, let smiles buy me! have you more to spend?
　　While hand and eye and something of a heart
225　Are left me, work's my ware, and what's it worth?
　　I'll pay my fancy. Only let me sit
　　The gray remainder of the evening out,
　　Idle, you call it, and muse perfectly
　　How I could paint, were I but back in France,
230　One picture, just one more—the Virgin's face,
　　Not yours this time! I want you at my side
　　To hear them—that is, Michel Agnolo—
　　Judge all I do and tell you of its worth.
　　Will you? Tomorrow, satisfy your friend.
235　I take the subjects for his corridor,
　　Finish the portrait out of hand—there, there,
　　And throw him in another thing or two
　　If he demurs; the whole should prove enough
　　To pay for this same Cousin's freak.° Beside,　　　　　*whim*
240　What's better and what's all I care about,
　　Get you the thirteen scudi° for the ruff!　　　　　*Italian coins*
　　Love, does that please you? Ah, but what does he,
　　The Cousin! What does he to please you more?

　　　　I am grown peaceful as old age tonight.
245　I regret little, I would change still less.
　　Since there my past life lies, why alter it?
　　The very wrong to Francis!—it is true
　　I took his coin, was tempted and complied,
　　And built this house and sinned, and all is said.
250　My father and my mother died of want.⁶
　　Well, had I riches of my own? you see
　　How one gets rich! Let each one bear his lot.
　　They were born poor, lived poor, and poor they died:
　　And I have labored somewhat in my time
255　And not been paid profusely. Some good son
　　Paint my two hundred pictures—let him try!
　　No doubt, there's something strikes a balance. Yes,
　　You loved me quite enough, it seems tonight.
　　This must suffice me here. What would one have?

5. Lucrezia's "Cousin" (or lover or friend) owes gambling debts to a creditor. Andrea has already contracted (lines 5–10) to pay off these debts by painting some pictures according to the creditor's specifications. Now he agrees to pay off further debts.

6. According to Vasari, Andrea's infatuation with Lucrezia prompted him to stop supporting his poverty-stricken parents.

260 In heaven, perhaps, new chances, one more chance—
Four great walls in the New Jerusalem,[7]
Meted on each side by the angel's reed,°   *measuring rod*
For Leonard,[8] Rafael, Agnolo and me
To cover—the three first without a wife,
265 While I have mine! So—still they overcome
Because there's still Lucrezia—as I choose.

Again the Cousin's whistle! Go, my Love.

ca. 1853   1855

Caliban upon Setebos Shakespeare's *Tempest* provided Browning with

the idea for his speaker (Caliban is Prospero's brutish slave, half-man, half-beast)
and the subject of his musings (Setebos is briefly referred to in the play as the god
of Caliban's mother, the witch Sycorax). From these beginnings Browning wrote a
poem that reflects on two closely related controversies of the Victorian period.
The first concerned the nature of God and God's responsibility for the existence
of pain in the world. The second debate, stimulated by the publication of Darwin's
Origin of Species (1859), focused on humanity's origins and our relation to other
beings.

As the poem's epigraph reveals, Browning is interested in the idea that the human
conception of the divine is conditioned by our own limitations, or by our understanding of ourselves. Caliban, a lower being, draws his notion of the god who he
believes dictates his fortunes from three main sources: his observations of life on
the island, his own character, and his experiences with Prospero, his master. The
first of these, his knowledge of the behavior and sufferings of animal life, gives rise
to his "natural theology"—that is, his tendency to understand the character of his
god from evidences provided by nature rather than from the evidence of supernatural revelation. From his perceptions of his own motivations and the conduct of
his earthly ruler comes Caliban's conception of Setebos's willful power. Caliban
admires power and thinks of his god as a being who selects at random some creatures who are to be saved and others who are condemned to suffer. His musings
thus connect in complex ways with key and pressing issues for the religious and
scientific communities of the Victorian era: through the lens of this most unlikely
philosopher, Browning raises the topics both of eternal salvation and of natural
selection. Significantly, Caliban feels the need to posit a higher divine being, or presence, that exists "over Setebos": puzzling about this other deity, "the Quiet," Browning's speaker delves into fundamental questions of origin and the construction of
myth.

An obstacle for the reader is Caliban's use of the third-person pronoun to refer to
himself. Thus "'Will sprawl" means "Caliban will sprawl" (an apostrophe before the
verb usually indicates that Caliban is the implied subject). Setebos is also referred to
in the third person but with an initial capital letter ("He").

7. Cf. Revelation 21.10–21, which gives a descrip- 8. Leonardo da Vinci (1452–1519).
tion of "that great city, the holy Jerusalem."

Caliban upon Setebos

Or Natural Theology in the Island

"Thou thoughtest that I was altogether such a one as thyself."[1]

['Will sprawl, now that the heat of day is best,
Flat on his belly in the pit's much mire,
With elbows wide, fists clenched to prop his chin.
And, while he kicks both feet in the cool slush,
5   And feels about his spine small eft-things°   *water lizards*
Run in and out each arm, and make him laugh:
And while above his head a pompion° plant,   *pumpkin*
Coating the cave-top as a brow its eye,
Creeps down to touch and tickle hair and beard,
10   And now a flower drops with a bee inside,
And now a fruit to snap at, catch and crunch—
He looks out o'er yon sea which sunbeams cross
And recross till they weave a spider web
(Meshes of fire, some great fish breaks at times)
15   And talks to his own self, howe'er he please,
Touching that other, whom his dam° called God.   *mother*
Because to talk about Him, vexes—ha,
Could He but know! and time to vex is now,
When talk is safer than in wintertime.
20   Moreover Prosper and Miranda[2] sleep
In confidence he drudges at their task,
And it is good to cheat the pair, and gibe,°   *insult them*
Letting the rank tongue blossom into speech.]

Setebos, Setebos, and Setebos!
25   'Thinketh, He dwelleth i' the cold o' the moon.

'Thinketh He made it, with the sun to match,
But not the stars; the stars came otherwise;
Only made clouds, winds, meteors, such as that:
Also this isle, what lives and grows thereon,
30   And snaky sea which rounds and ends the same.

'Thinketh, it came of being ill at ease:
He hated that He cannot change His cold,
Nor cure its ache. 'Hath spied an icy fish
That longed to 'scape the rock-stream where she lived,
35   And thaw herself within the lukewarm brine
O' the lazy sea her stream thrusts far amid,
A crystal spike 'twixt two warm walls of wave;[3]
Only, she ever sickened, found repulse
At the other kind of water, not her life,
40   (Green-dense and dim-delicious, bred o' the sun)
Flounced back from bliss she was not born to breathe,

---

1. Psalms 50.21. The speaker is God.
2. Prospero's daughter.

3. I.e., the thin stream of cold water that is driven
into the warm ocean like a spike between walls.

And in her old bounds buried her despair,
Hating and loving warmth alike: so He.

'Thinketh, He made thereat the sun, this isle,
45 Trees and the fowls here, beast and creeping thing.
Yon otter, sleek-wet, black, lithe as a leech;
Yon auk,° one fire-eye in a ball of foam,   *seabird*
That floats and feeds; a certain badger brown
He hath watched hunt with that slant white-wedge eye
50 By moonlight; and the pie° with the long tongue   *magpie*
That pricks deep into oakwarts for a worm,
And says a plain word when she finds her prize,
But will not eat the ants; the ants themselves
That build a wall of seeds and settled stalks
55 About their hole—He made all these and more,
Made all we see, and us, in spite: how else?
He could not, Himself, make a second self
To be His mate; as well have made Himself:
He would not make what he mislikes or slights,
60 An eyesore to Him, or not worth His pains:
But did, in envy, listlessness, or sport,
Make what Himself would fain,° in a manner, be—   *gladly*
Weaker in most points, stronger in a few,
Worthy, and yet mere playthings all the while,
65 Things He admires and mocks too—that is it.
Because, so brave, so better though they be,
It nothing skills if He begin to plague.[4]
Look now, I melt a gourd-fruit into mash,
Add honeycomb and pods, I have perceived,
70 Which bite like finches when they bill and kiss—
Then, when froth rises bladdery,° drink up all,   *bubbly*
Quick, quick, till maggots scamper through my brain;
Last, throw me on my back i' the seeded thyme,
And wanton, wishing I were born a bird.
75 Put case, unable to be what I wish,
I yet could make a live bird out of clay:
Would not I take clay, pinch my Caliban
Able to fly?—for, there, see, he hath wings,
And great comb like the hoopoe's[5] to admire,
80 And there, a sting to do his foes offense,
There, and I will that he begin to live,
Fly to yon rock-top, nip me off the horns
Of griggs° high up that make the merry din,   *grasshoppers*
Saucy through their veined wings, and mind me not.
85 In which feat, if his leg snapped, brittle clay,
And he lay stupid-like—why, I should laugh;
And if he, spying me, should fall to weep,
Beseech me to be good, repair his wrong,
Bid his poor leg smart less or grow again—

4. I.e., the superior virtues of Setebos's crea-   them.
tures are no help to them if he decides to torture   5. Bird with bright plumage.

90   Well, as the chance were, this might take or else
      Not take my fancy: I might hear his cry,
      And give the mankin° three sound legs for one,   *little man*
      Or pluck the other off, leave him like an egg,
      And lessoned° he was mine and merely clay.   *thus taught*
95   Were this no pleasure, lying in the thyme,
      Drinking the mash, with brain become alive,
      Making and marring clay at will? So He.
      'Thinketh, such shows nor right nor wrong in Him,
      Nor kind, nor cruel: He is strong and Lord.
100 'Am strong myself compared to yonder crabs
      That march now from the mountain to the sea;
      'Let twenty pass, and stone the twenty-first,
      Loving not, hating not, just choosing so.
      'Say, the first straggler that boasts purple spots
105 Shall join the file, one pincer twisted off;
      'Say, this bruised fellow shall receive a worm,
      And two worms he whose nippers end in red;
      As it likes me each time, I do: so He.

      Well then, 'supposeth He is good i' the main,
110 Placable if His mind and ways were guessed,
      But rougher than His handiwork, be sure!
      Oh, He hath made things worthier than Himself,
      And envieth that, so helped, such things do more
      Than He who made them! What consoles but this?
115 That they, unless through Him, do naught at all,
      And must submit: what other use in things?
      'Hath cut a pipe of pithless elder-joint
      That, blown through, gives exact the scream o' the jay
      When from her wing you twitch the feathers blue:
120 Sound this, and little birds that hate the jay
      Flock within stone's throw, glad their foe is hurt:
      Put case such pipe could prattle and boast forsooth,
      "I catch the birds, I am the crafty thing,
      I make the cry my maker cannot make
125 With his great round mouth; he must blow through mine!"
      Would not I smash it with my foot? So He.

      But wherefore rough, why cold and ill at ease?
      Aha, that is a question! Ask, for that,
      What knows—the something over Setebos
130 That made Him, or He, may be, found and fought,
      Worsted, drove off and did to nothing,[6] perchance.
      There may be something quiet o'er His head,
      Out of His reach, that feels nor° joy nor grief,   *neither*
      Since both derive from weakness in some way.
135 I joy because the quails come; would not joy
      Could I bring quails here when I have a mind:
      This Quiet, all it hath a mind to, doth.

6. "Did to nothing": completely overcame.

'Esteemeth° stars the outposts of its couch,   *he believes*
But never spends much thought nor care that way.
140   It may look up, work up—the worse for those
It works on! 'Careth but for Setebos[7]
The many-handed as a cuttlefish,
Who, making Himself feared through what He does,
Looks up, first, and perceives he cannot soar
145   To what is quiet and hath happy life;
Next looks down here, and out of very spite
Makes this a bauble-world to ape yon real,
These good things to match those as hips[8] do grapes.
'Tis solace making baubles, aye, and sport.
150   Himself peeped late, eyed Prosper at his books
Careless and lofty, lord now of the isle:
Vexed, 'stitched a book of broad leaves, arrow-shaped,
Wrote thereon, he knows what, prodigious words;
Has peeled a wand and called it by a name;
155   Weareth at whiles for an enchanter's robe
The eyed skin of a supple oncelot;[9]
And hath an ounce[1] sleeker than youngling mole,
A four-legged serpent he makes cower and couch,
Now snarl, now hold its breath and mind his eye,
160   And saith she is Miranda and my wife:
'Keeps for his Ariel[2] a tall pouch-bill crane
He bids go wade for fish and straight° disgorge;   *immediately*
Also a sea beast, lumpish, which he snared,
Blinded the eyes of, and brought somewhat tame,
165   And split its toe-webs, and now pens the drudge
In a hole o' the rock and calls him Caliban;
A bitter heart that bides its time and bites.
'Plays thus at being Prosper in a way,
Taketh his mirth with make-believes: so He.
170   His dam held that the Quiet made all things
Which Setebos vexed only: 'holds not so.
Who made them weak, meant weakness He might vex.
Had He meant other, while His hand was in,
Why not make horny eyes no thorn could prick,
175   Or plate my scalp with bone against the snow,
Or overscale my flesh 'neath joint and joint,
Like an orc's° armor? Aye—so spoil His sport!   *sea monster's*
He is the One now: only He doth all.

'Saith, He may like, perchance, what profits Him.
180   Aye, himself loves what does him good; but why?
'Gets good no otherwise. This blinded beast
Loves whoso places flesh-meat on his nose,
But, had he eyes, would want no help, but hate

7. Caliban's concern is to appease only Setebos,
not the other deity—the Quiet.
8. Hard fruits produced by some roses.
9. Browning may have invented this term from
the Spanish *oncela* or from the French *ocelot*

(i.e., a leopard or spotted wildcat).
1. A lynx or other wild feline of moderate size or
a snow leopard.
2. In *The Tempest* a spirit who serves Prospero.

Or love, just as it liked him: He hath eyes.
185 Also it pleaseth Setebos to work,
Use all His hands, and exercise much craft,
By no means for the love of what is worked.
'Tasteth, himself, no finer good i' the world
When all goes right, in this safe summertime,
190 And he wants little, hungers, aches not much,
Than trying what to do with wit and strength.
'Falls to make something: 'piled yon pile of turfs,
And squared and stuck there squares of soft white chalk,
And, with a fish-tooth, scratched a moon on each,
195 And set up endwise certain spikes of tree,
And crowned the whole with a sloth's skull a-top,
Found dead i' the woods, too hard for one to kill.
No use at all i' the work, for work's sole sake;
'Shall some day knock it down again: so He.

200 'Saith He is terrible: watch His feats in proof!
One hurricane will spoil six good months' hope.
He hath a spite against me, that I know,
Just as He favors Prosper, who knows why?
So it is, all the same, as well I find.
205 'Wove wattles half the winter, fenced them firm
With stone and stake to stop she-tortoises
Crawling to lay their eggs here: well, one wave,
Feeling the foot of Him upon its neck,
Gaped as a snake does, lolled out its large tongue,
210 And licked the whole labor flat; so much for spite.
'Saw a ball° flame down late (yonder it lies)   *meteorite*
Where, half an hour before, I slept i' the shade:
Often they scatter sparkles: there is force!
'Dug up a newt He may have envied once
215 And turned to stone, shut up inside a stone.
Please Him and hinder this?—What Prosper does?[3]
Aha, if He would tell me how! Not He!
There is the sport: discover how or die!
All need not die, for of the things o' the isle
220 Some flee afar, some dive, some run up trees;
Those at His mercy—why, they please Him most
When . . . when . . . well, never try the same way twice!
Repeat what act has pleased, He may grow wroth.
You must not know His ways, and play Him off,
225 Sure of the issue.° 'Doth the like himself: *outcome*
'Spareth a squirrel that it nothing fears
But steals[4] the nut from underneath my thumb,
And when I threat, bites stoutly in defense:
'Spareth an urchin° that contrariwise   *hedgehog*
230 Curls up into a ball, pretending death
For fright at my approach: the two ways please.

---

3. I.e., shall I please Setebos, as Prospero does, and thus prevent my being punished as the newt was punished?

4. I.e., that is fearless enough to steal.

But what would move my choler more than this,
That either creature counted on its life
Tomorrow and next day and all days to come,
235 Saying, forsooth, in the inmost of its heart,
"Because he did so yesterday with me,
And otherwise with such another brute,
So must he do henceforth and always."—Aye?
Would teach the reasoning couple what "must" means!
240 'Doth as he likes, or wherefore Lord? So He.

'Conceiveth all things will continue thus,
And we shall have to live in fear of Him
So long as He lives, keeps His strength: no change,
If He have done His best, make no new world
245 To please Him more, so leave off watching this—
If He surprise not even the Quiet's self
Some strange day—or, suppose, grow into it
As grubs grow butterflies: else, here are we,
And there is He, and nowhere help at all.
250 'Believeth with the life, the pain shall stop.
His dam held different, that after death
He both plagued enemies and feasted friends:
Idly!⁵ He doth His worst in this our life,
Giving just respite lest we die through pain,
255 Saving last pain for worst—with which, an end.
Meanwhile, the best way to escape His ire
Is, not to seem too happy. 'Sees, himself,
Yonder two flies, with purple films and pink,
Bask on the pompion°-bell above: kills both.   *pumpkin*
260 'Sees two black painful beetles roll their ball
On head and tail as if to save their lives:
Moves them the stick away they strive to clear.

Even so, 'would have Him misconceive, suppose
This Caliban strives hard and ails no less,
265 And always, above all else, envies Him;
Wherefore he mainly dances on dark nights,
Moans in the sun, gets under holes to laugh,
And never speaks his mind save housed as now:
Outside, 'groans, curses. If He caught me here,
270 O'erheard this speech, and asked "What chucklest at?"
'Would, to appease Him, cut a finger off,
Or of my three kid yearlings burn the best,
Or let the toothsome apples rot on tree,
Or push my tame beast for the orc to taste:
275 While myself lit a fire, and made a song
And sung it, *"What I hate, be consecrate*
To celebrate Thee and Thy state, no mate
For Thee; what see for envy in poor me?"
Hoping the while, since evils sometimes mend,

5. I.e., Caliban thinks his mother's opinion was wrong or idle. Setebos's sport with his creatures is confined to this world: there is no afterlife.

280 Warts rub away and sores are cured with slime,
    That some strange day, will either the Quiet catch
    And conquer Setebos, or likelier He
    Decrepit may doze, doze, as good as die.

    ———————————

    [What, what? A curtain o'er the world at once!
285 Crickets stop hissing; not a bird—or, yes,
    There scuds His raven[6] that has told Him all!
    It was fool's play this prattling! Ha! The wind
    Shoulders the pillared dust, death's house o' the move,[7]
    And fast invading fires begin! White blaze—
290 A tree's head snaps—and there, there, there, there, there,
    His thunder follows! Fool to gibe at Him!
    Lo! 'Lieth flat and loveth Setebos!
    'Maketh his teeth meet through his upper lip,
    Will let those quails fly, will not eat this month
295 One little mess of whelks,° so he may 'scape!]   *shellfish*

ca. 1860   1864

Rabbi Ben Ezra[1]

1

            Grow old along with me!
            The best is yet to be,
    The last of life, for which the first was made:
            Our times are in His hand
5   Who saith, "A whole I planned,
    Youth shows but half; trust God: see all nor be afraid!"

2

            Not that, amassing flowers,
            Youth sighed, "Which rose make ours,
    Which lily leave and then as best recall?"
10   Not that, admiring stars,
            It yearned, "Nor Jove, nor Mars;
    Mine be some figured flame which blends, transcends them all!"

3

            Not for such hopes and fears
            Annulling youth's brief years,
15 Do I remonstrate: folly wide the mark!
            Rather I prize the doubt

6. In Norse mythology ravens brought the daily
news to Odin, the most powerful god.
7. The whirlwind stirs up a column of dust that
Caliban associates with a house of death.
1. The speaker, Abraham Ibn Ezra (ca. 1092–
1167), was an eminent biblical scholar of Spain,
but Browning makes little attempt to present him
as a distinct individual or to relate him to the age
in which he lived. Unlike the more characteristic
monologues, "Rabbi Ben Ezra" presents a meditation on a theme, not an individual in the grip of a
dramatic situation.

Low kinds exist without,
Finished and finite clods, untroubled by a spark.

4

Poor vaunt of life indeed,
20   Were man but formed to feed
On joy, to solely seek and find and feast:
      Such feasting ended, then
      As sure an end to men;
Irks care the crop-full bird? Frets doubt the maw-crammed beast?[2]

5

25   Rejoice we are allied
      To That which doth provide
And not partake, effect and not receive!
      A spark disturbs our clod;
      Nearer we hold of God
30 Who gives, than of His tribes that take, I must believe.

6

Then, welcome each rebuff
      That turns earth's smoothness rough,
Each sting that bids nor sit nor stand but go!
      Be our joys three parts pain!
35   Strive, and hold cheap the strain;
Learn, nor account the pang; dare, never grudge the throe!°   *anguish*

7

For thence—a paradox
      Which comforts while it mocks—
Shall life succeed in that it seems to fail:
40   What I aspired to be,
      And was not, comforts me:
A brute I might have been, but would not sink i' the scale.

8

What is he but a brute
      Whose flesh has soul to suit,
45 Whose spirit works lest arms and legs want play?
      To man, propose this test—
      Thy body at its best,
How far can that project thy soul on its lone way?

9

Yet gifts should prove their use:
50   I own the Past profuse

---

2. I.e., does care disturb a bird whose gullet ("crop") is full of food? Does doubt trouble an animal whose stomach ("maw") is full?

Of power each side, perfection every turn:
    Eyes, ears took in their dole,
    Brain treasured up the whole;
Should not the heart beat once, "How good to live and learn"?

10

55   Not once beat, "Praise be Thine!
    I see the whole design,
I, who saw power, see now love perfect too:
    Perfect I call Thy plan:
    Thanks that I was a man!
60 Maker, remake, complete—I trust what Thou shalt do!"

11

    For pleasant is this flesh;
    Our soul, in its rose-mesh[3]
Pulled ever to the earth, still yearns for rest;
    Would we some prize might hold
65   To match those manifold
Possessions of the brute—gain most, as we did best!

12

    Let us not always say,
    "Spite of this flesh today
I strove, made head, gained ground upon the whole!"
70   As the bird wings and sings,
    Let us cry, "All good things
Are ours, nor soul helps flesh more, now, than flesh helps soul!"

13

    Therefore I summon age
    To grant youth's heritage,
75 Life's struggle having so far reached its term:
    Thence shall I pass, approved
    A man, for aye removed
From the developed brute; a god though in the germ.

14

    And I shall thereupon
80   Take rest, ere I be gone
Once more on my adventure brave and new;[4]
    Fearless and unperplexed,
    When I wage battle next,
What weapons to select, what armor to indue.°   *put on*

---

3. The body, which holds the soul in its net.   4. In the next life.

15

85   Youth ended, I shall try
       My gain or loss thereby;
Leave the fire ashes,[5] what survives is gold:
       And I shall weigh the same,
       Give life its praise or blame:
90 Young, all lay in dispute; I shall know, being old.

16

       For note, when evening shuts,
       A certain moment cuts
The deed off, calls the glory from the gray:
       A whisper from the west
95   Shoots—"Add this to the rest,
Take it and try its worth: here dies another day."

17

       So, still within this life,
       Though lifted o'er its strife,
Let me discern, compare, pronounce at last,
100   "This rage was right i' the main,
       That acquiescence vain:
The Future I may face now I have proved the Past."

18

       For more is not reserved
       To man, with soul just nerved
105 To act tomorrow what he learns today:
       Here, work enough to watch
       The Master work, and catch
Hints of the proper craft, tricks of the tool's true play.

19

       As it was better, youth
110   Should strive, through acts uncouth,
Toward making, than repose on aught found made:
       So, better, age, exempt
       From strife, should know, than tempt°   *attempt*
Further. Thou waitedst age: wait death nor° be afraid!   *and do not*

20

115   Enough now, if the Right
       And Good and Infinite
Be named here, as thou callest thy hand thine own,
       With knowledge absolute,

---

5. If the fire leaves ashes.

Subject to no dispute
120 From fools that crowded youth, nor let thee feel alone.

21

Be there, for once and all,
Severed great minds from small,
Announced to each his station in the Past!
Was I, the world arraigned,[6]
125 Were they, my soul disdained,
Right? Let age speak the truth and give us peace at last!

22

Now, who shall arbitrate?
Ten men love what I hate,
Shun what I follow, slight what I receive;
130 Ten, who in ears and eyes
Match me: we all surmise,
They this thing, and I that: whom shall my soul believe?

23

Not on the vulgar° mass   common
Called "work," must sentence pass,
135 Things done, that took the eye and had the price;
O'er which, from level stand,
The low world laid its hand,
Found straightway to its mind, could value in a trice:

24

But all, the world's coarse thumb
140 And finger failed to plumb,[7]
So passed in making up the main account;
All instincts immature,
All purposes unsure,
That weighed not as his work, yet swelled the man's amount:

25

145 Thoughts hardly to be packed
Into a narrow act,
Fancies that broke through language and escaped;
All I could never be,
All, men ignored in me,
150 This, I was worth to God, whose wheel the pitcher shaped.[8]

---

6. I.e., was I, whom the world arraigned.
7. Allusion to a merchant or buyer feeling fabric to determine its price or value.
8. The speaker's highest qualities of soul were shaped on a potting wheel into an enduring "pitcher" or vessel by God. Cf. Isaiah 64.8: "Lord, thou art our father; we are the clay, and thou our potter; and we all are the work of thy hand."

26

Aye, note that Potter's wheel,
That metaphor! and feel
Why time spins fast, why passive lies our clay—
Thou, to whom fools propound,[9]
155   When the wine makes its round,
"Since life fleets, all is change; the Past gone, seize today!"

27

Fool! All that is, at all,
Lasts ever, past recall;
Earth changes, but thy soul and God stand sure:
160   What entered into thee,
That was, is, and shall be:
Time's wheel runs back or stops: Potter and clay endure.

28

He fixed thee 'mid this dance
Of plastic° circumstance,   *molded*
165 This Present, thou, forsooth, wouldst fain arrest:[1]
    Machinery just meant
    To give thy soul its bent,
Try thee and turn thee forth, sufficiently impressed.

29

What though the earlier grooves
170   Which ran the laughing loves[2]
Around thy base,[3] no longer pause and press?
    What though, about thy rim,
    Skull-things in order grim
Grow out, in graver mood, obey the sterner stress?

30

175   Look not thou down but up!
    To uses of a cup,
The festal board, lamp's flash, and trumpet's peal,
    The new wine's foaming flow,
    The Master's lips a-glow!
180 Thou, heaven's consummate cup, what need'st thou with earth's wheel?

31

But I need, now as then,
Thee, God, who moldest men;

---

9. Perhaps addressed to the Persian philosopher Omar Khayyám (1048–1131), whose poem, *The Rubáiyát*, urged men to eat, drink, and be merry.
1. I.e., you would be glad to stop ("arrest") time at this present point of your life.
2. May refer to figures of cherublike boys, often featured in Renaissance art.
3. Of the clay pitcher.

And since, not even while the whirl was worst,
  Did I—to the wheel of life
185   With shapes and colors rife,
Bound dizzily—mistake my end, to slake Thy thirst:

32

  So, take and use Thy work:
  Amend what flaws may lurk,
What strain o' the stuff, what warpings past the aim!
190   My times be in Thy hand!
  Perfect the cup as planned!
Let age approve of youth, and death complete the same!

ca. 1862   1864

EMILY BRONTË
1818–1848

E mily Brontë spent most of her life in a stone parsonage in the small village of Haworth on the wild and bleak Yorkshire moors. She was the fifth of Patrick and Maria Brontë's six children. Her father was a clergyman; her mother died when she was two. At the age of six, she was sent away to a school for the daughters of poor clergy with her three elder sisters; within a year, the two oldest girls had died, in part the result of the school's harsh and unhealthy conditions, which Charlotte Brontë was later to portray in *Jane Eyre* (1847). Mr. Brontë brought his two remaining daughters home, where, together with their brother and younger sister, he educated them himself. Emily was the most reclusive and private of the children; she shunned the company of those outside her family and suffered acutely from homesickness in her few short stays away from the parsonage.

Despite the isolation of Haworth, the Brontë family shared a rich literary life. Mr. Brontë discussed poetry, history, and politics with his children, and the children themselves created an extraordinary fantasy world together. When Mr. Brontë gave his son a box of wooden soldiers, each child excitedly seized one and named it. The soldiers became for them the centers of an increasingly elaborate set of stories that they first acted out in plays and later recorded in a series of book-length manuscripts, composed for the most part by Charlotte and her brother, Branwell. The two younger children, Emily and Anne, later started a separate series, a chronicle about an imaginary island called Gondal.

In 1850 Charlotte Brontë told the story of how she and her sisters came to write for publication. One day when she accidentally came upon a manuscript volume of verse in Emily's handwriting, she was struck by the conviction "that these were not common effusions, nor at all like the poetry women generally write." With some difficulty, Charlotte persuaded her intensely private sister to publish some of her poems in a selection of poetry by all three Brontë sisters. Averse to personal publicity and afraid that "authoresses are liable to be looked on with prejudice," Charlotte, Emily, and Anne adopted the pseudonyms of Currer, Ellis, and Acton Bell. Although the

1846 book sold only two copies, its publication inspired each of the Brontë sisters to begin work on a novel; Emily's was *Wuthering Heights* (1847). She began work on a second novel, but a year after the publication of *Wuthering Heights*, she died of tuberculosis.

Many of Emily's poems—"Remembrance" and "The Prisoner," for example—were written for the Gondal saga and express its preoccupation with political intrigue, passionate love, rebellion, war, imprisonment, and exile. Brontë also wrote personal lyrics unconnected with the Gondal stories; but both groups of poems share a drive to break through the constrictions of ordinary life, whether by the transfigurative power of the imagination, by union with another, or by death itself. Like Catherine and Heathcliff in *Wuthering Heights*, the speakers of Brontë's poems yearn for a fuller, freer world of spirit, transcending the forms and limits of mortal life. Her concern with a visionary world links her to the Romantic poets, particularly to Byron and Percy Bysshe Shelley; but her hymnlike stanzas have a haunting quality that distinguishes her individual voice.

I'm happiest when most away

I'm happiest when most away
I can bear my soul from its home of clay
On a windy night when the moon is bright
And the eye can wander through worlds of light—
5   When I am not and none beside—
Nor earth nor sea nor cloudless sky—
But only spirit wandering wide
Through infinite immensity.

1838   1910

The Night-Wind

In summer's mellow midnight,
A cloudless moon shone through
Our open parlour window
And rosetrees wet with dew.

5   I sat in silent musing,
The soft wind waved my hair:
It told me Heaven was glorious.
And sleeping Earth was fair.

I needed not its breathing
10 To bring such thoughts to me,
But still it whispered lowly,
"How dark the woods will be!

"The thick leaves in my murmur
Are rustling like a dream,

15 And all their myriad voices
   Instinct° with spirit seem."   *imbued*

I said, "Go, gentle singer,
   Thy wooing voice is kind,
But do not think its music
20 Has power to reach my mind.

"Play with the scented flower,
   The young tree's supple bough,
And leave my human feelings
   In their own course to flow."

25 The wanderer would not leave me;
   Its kiss grew warmer still—
"O come," it sighed so sweetly,
   "I'll win thee 'gainst thy will.

"Have we not been from childhood friends?
30 Have I not loved thee long?
As long as thou hast loved the night
   Whose silence wakes my song.

"And when thy heart is laid at rest
   Beneath the church-yard stone
35 I shall have time enough to mourn
   And thou to be alone."

1840   1850

Remembrance[1]

Cold in the earth, and the deep snow piled above thee!
Far, far removed, cold in the dreary grave!
Have I forgot, my Only Love, to love thee,
Severed at last by Time's all-wearing wave?

5 Now, when alone, do my thoughts no longer hover
Over the mountains, on that northern shore;
Resting their wings where heath and fern-leaves cover
Thy noble heart for ever, ever more?

Cold in the earth, and fifteen wild Decembers
10 From those brown hills have melted into spring—
Faithful indeed is the spirit that remembers
After such years of change and suffering!

---

1. Titled in manuscript "R. Alcona to J. Breznaida," this poem was originally composed as a lament by the heroine of the Gondal saga for the hero's death.

Sweet Love of youth, forgive if I forget thee
While the World's tide is bearing me along:
15 Other desires and other hopes beset me,
Hopes which obscure but cannot do thee wrong.

No later light has lightened up my heaven,
No second morn has ever shone for me:
All my life's bliss from thy dear life was given—
20 All my life's bliss is in the grave with thee.

But when the days of golden dreams had perished
And even Despair was powerless to destroy,
Then did I learn how existence could be cherished,
Strengthened and fed without the aid of joy;

25 Then did I check the tears of useless passion,
Weaned my young soul from yearning after thine;
Sternly denied its burning wish to hasten
Down to that tomb already more than mine!

And even yet, I dare not let it languish,
30 Dare not indulge in Memory's rapturous pain;
Once drinking deep of that divinest anguish,
How could I seek the empty world again?

1845   1846

Stars

Ah! why, because the dazzling sun
Restored our earth to joy
Have you departed, every one,
And left a desert sky?

5 All through the night, your glorious eyes
Were gazing down in mine,
And with a full heart's thankful sighs
I blessed that watch divine!

I was at peace, and drank your beams
10 As they were life to me
And revelled in my changeful dreams
Like petrel° on the sea.   *small dark seabirds*

Thought followed thought—star followed star
Through boundless regions on,
15 While one sweet influence, near and far,
Thrilled through and proved us one.

Why did the morning dawn to break
So great, so pure a spell,

And scorch with fire the tranquil cheek
20 Where your cool radiance fell?

Blood-red he rose, and arrow-straight
His fierce beams struck my brow:
The soul of Nature sprang elate,
But mine sank sad and low!

25 My lids closed down—yet through their veil
I saw him blazing still;
And steep in gold the misty dale
And flash upon the hill.

I turned me to the pillow then
30 To call back Night, and see
Your worlds of solemn light, again
Throb with my heart and me!

It would not do—the pillow glowed
And glowed both roof and floor,
35 And birds sang loudly in the wood,
And fresh winds shook the door.

The curtains waved, the wakened flies
Were murmuring round my room,
Imprisoned there, till I should rise
40 And give them leave to roam.

O Stars and Dreams and Gentle Night;
O Night and Stars return!
And hide me from the hostile light
That does not warm, but burn—

45 That drains the blood of suffering men;
Drinks tears, instead of dew:
Let me sleep through his blinding reign,
And only wake with you!

1845   1846

The Prisoner. A Fragment[1]

In the dungeon crypts idly did I stray,
Reckless of the lives wasting there away;
"Draw the ponderous bars; open, Warder stern!"
He dare not say me nay—the hinges harshly turn.

1. An excerpt from a poem in the Gondal manuscript, "Julian M. and A. G. Rochelle," describing an event unplaced in the story, this poem was printed as "The Prisoner: A Fragment" in *Poems* (1846) by the Brontë sisters. The speaker, a man, is visiting a dungeon in his father's castle.

5   "Our guests are darkly lodged," I whispered, gazing through
The vault whose grated eye showed heaven more grey than blue.
(This was when glad spring laughed in awaking pride.)
"Aye, darkly lodged enough!" returned my sullen guide.

10 Then, God forgive my youth, forgive my careless tongue!
I scoffed, as the chill chains on the damp flagstones rung;
"Confined in triple walls, art thou so much to fear,
That we must bind thee down and clench thy fetters here?"

The captive raised her face; it was as soft and mild
As sculptured marble saint or slumbering, unweaned child;
15 It was so soft and mild, it was so sweet and fair,
Pain could not trace a line nor grief a shadow there!

The captive raised her hand and pressed it to her brow:
"I have been struck," she said, "and I am suffering now;
Yet these are little worth, your bolts and irons strong;
20 And were they forged in steel they could not hold me long."

Hoarse laughed the jailor grim: "Shall I be won to hear;
Dost think, fond° dreaming wretch, that *I* shall grant thy prayer?   *foolish*
Or, better still, wilt melt my master's heart with groans?
Ah, sooner might the sun thaw down these granite stones!

25 "My master's voice is low, his aspect bland and kind,
But hard as hardest flint the soul that lurks behind;
And I am rough and rude, yet not more rough to see
Than is the hidden ghost which has its home in me!"

About her lips there played a smile of almost scorn:
30 "My friend," she gently said, "you have not heard me mourn;
When you my kindred's lives—*my* lost life, can restore
Then may I weep and sue—but *never*, Friend, before!

"Still, let my tyrants know, I am not doomed to wear
Year after year in gloom and desolate despair;
35 A messenger of Hope comes every night to me,
And offers, for short life, eternal liberty.

"He comes with western winds, with evening's wandering airs,
With that clear dusk of heaven that brings the thickest stars;
Winds take a pensive tone, and stars a tender fire,
40 And visions rise and change that kill me with desire—

"Desire for nothing known in my maturer years
When joy grew mad with awe at counting future tears;
When, if my spirit's sky was full of flashes warm,
I knew not whence they came, from sun or thunderstorm;

45 "But first a hush of peace, a soundless calm descends;
The struggle of distress and fierce impatience ends;

Mute music soothes my breast—unuttered harmony
That I could never dream till earth was lost to me.

"Then dawns the Invisible, the Unseen its truth reveals;
50 My outward sense is gone, my inward essence feels—
Its wings are almost free, its home, its harbour found;
Measuring the gulf it stoops and dares the final bound!

"Oh, dreadful is the check—intense the agony
When the ear begins to hear and the eye begins to see;
55 When the pulse begins to throb, the brain to think again,
The soul to feel the flesh and the flesh to feel the chain!

"Yet I would lose no sting, would wish no torture less;
The more that anguish racks the earlier it will bless;
And robed in fires of Hell, or bright with heavenly shine,
60 If it but herald Death, the vision is divine."[2]

She ceased to speak, and we, unanswering turned to go—
We had no further power to work the captive woe;
Her cheek, her gleaming eye, declared that man had given
A sentence unapproved, and overruled by Heaven.

1845   1846

No coward soul is mine[1]

No coward soul is mine
No trembler in the world's storm-troubled sphere
I see Heaven's glories shine
And Faith shines equal arming me from Fear

5 O God within my breast
Almighty ever-present Deity
Life, that in me hast rest
As I Undying Life, have power in Thee

Vain are the thousand creeds
10 That move men's hearts, unutterably vain,
Worthless as withered weeds
Or idlest froth amid the boundless main

To waken doubt in one
Holding so fast by thy infinity
15 So surely anchored on
The steadfast rock of Immortality

2. Cf. the words of the dying Catherine in *Wuthering Heights* (1847), chap. 15: "The thing that irks me most is this shattered prison [my body]. . . . I'm tired, tired of being enclosed here. I'm wearying to escape into that glorious world, and to be always there. . . . I shall be incomparably beyond and above you all."
1. According to Charlotte Brontë, these are the last lines her sister wrote.

With wide-embracing love
Thy spirit animates eternal years
Pervades and broods above,
20 Changes, sustains, dissolves, creates and rears

Though Earth and moon were gone
And suns and universes ceased to be
And thou wert left alone
Every Existence would exist in thee

25 There is not room for Death
Nor atom that his might could render void
Since thou art Being and Breath
And what thou art may never be destroyed.

1846   1850

JOHN RUSKIN
1819–1900

John Ruskin was both the leading Victorian critic of art and an important critic of society. These two roles can be traced back to two important influences of his childhood. His father, a wealthy wine merchant, enjoyed travel, and on tours of the Continent he introduced his son to landscapes, architecture, and art. From this exposure Ruskin acquired a zest for beauty that animates even the most theoretical of his discussions of aesthetics. In his tranquil autobiography (titled *Praeterita*, 1885–89, or, as he said, "Past things"), composed in the penultimate decade of a turbulent life, Ruskin reflected on the profound experience of his first view of the Swiss Alps at sunset. For his fourteen-year-old self, he writes, "the seen walls of lost Eden could not have been more beautiful":

> It is not possible to imagine, in any time of the world, a more blessed entrance into life, for a child of such a temperament as mine. True, the temperament belonged to the age: a very few years,—within the hundred,—before that, no child could have been born to care for mountains, or for the men that lived among them, in that way. Till Rousseau's time, there had been no "sentimental" love of nature; and till Scott's, no such apprehensive love of "all sorts and conditions of men," not in the soul merely, but in the flesh . . . I went down that evening from the garden-terrace of Schaffhausen with my destiny fixed in all of it that was to be sacred and useful.

Such a rapturous response to the beauties of nature was later to be duplicated by his response to the beauties of architecture and art. During a tour of "this Holy Land of Italy" (as he called it), he visited Venice and recorded in his diary (May 6, 1841) his response to Saint Mark's cathedral square in that city: "Thank God I am here! It is the Paradise of cities and there is moon enough to make half the sanities of earth lunatic, striking its pure flashes of light against the grey water before the window; and I am happier than I have been these five years. . . . I feel fresh and young when my foot is on these pavements."

Ruskin's choice of phrase in these accounts of how beauty affected him reflects the second influence in his life, often at odds with the first: his daily Bible readings under the direction of his mother, a devout Evangelical Christian. From this biblical indoctrination Ruskin derived some elements of his lush and highly rhythmical prose style but more especially his sense of prophecy and mission as a critic of modern society.

Ruskin's life was spent in traveling, lecturing, and writing. His prodigious literary output can be roughly divided into three phases. At first he was preoccupied with problems of art. *Modern Painters* (1843–60), which he began writing at the age of twenty-three after his graduation from Oxford, was a defense of the English landscape painter J. M. W. Turner (1775–1851). This defense (which was to extend to five volumes) involved Ruskin in problems of truth in art (as in his chapter "Pathetic Fallacy") and in the ultimate importance of imagination (as in his discussion of Turner's painting *The Slave Ship*).

During the 1850s Ruskin's principal interest shifted from art to architecture, especially to the problem of determining what kind of society is capable of producing great buildings. His enthusiasm for Gothic architecture was infectious, and he has sometimes been blamed for the prevalence of Gothic buildings on college campuses in America. A study of *The Stones of Venice* (1851–53), however (especially the chapter printed here), will show that merely to revive the Gothic style was not his concern. What he wanted to revive was the kind of society that had produced such architecture, a society in which the individual workers could express themselves and enjoy what Ruskin's disciple William Morris called "work-pleasure." A mechanized production-line society, such as Ruskin's or our own, could produce not Gothic architecture but only imitations of its mannerisms. Ruskin's concern was to change industrial society, not to decorate concrete towers with gargoyles.

This interest in the stultifying effects of industrialism led Ruskin gradually into economics. After 1860 the critic of art became (like the writer he most greatly admired, Thomas Carlyle) an outspoken critic of laissez-faire, or noninterventionist, economics. His conception of the responsibilities of employers toward their workers, as expounded in *Unto This Last* (1860), was dismissed by his contemporaries as an absurdity. What he was laboring to show was that self-seeking business relationships could be reconfigured on the principle of dedicated service, taking as a model the learned professions and the military. The soldier, however unrefined, is more highly regarded by society than the capitalist, Ruskin said, "for the soldier's trade . . . is not slaying, but being slain." Although his position was essentially conservative in the proper sense of the word (he styled himself "a violent Tory of the old school;—Walter Scott's school"), he was regarded as a radical eccentric. It was many years before his social criticism gained a following among writers as diverse as William Morris, Bernard Shaw, and D. H. Lawrence, and in particular among the founders of the British Labour Party, his influence was to be profound and lasting.

Ruskin's realization, after 1860, that despite his fame he was becoming isolated and that the world was continuing to move in directions opposite from those to which he pointed may have contributed to the recurrent mental breakdowns from which he suffered between 1870 and 1900. As he reports in *Fors Clavigera* (1880): "The doctors said I went mad, this time two years ago, from overwork," but he had not then been working harder than usual. "I went mad because nothing came of my work . . . because after I got [my manuscripts] published, nobody believed a word of them." Also contributing to his breakdowns may have been his unhappiness in his relations with women. His marriage to Effie Gray in 1848 was a disaster. After six years of living together, an annulment was arranged on the grounds that the marriage had not been consummated. Ruskin testified that he had not found his wife's person physically attractive, although by others she was considered a great beauty. One of these admirers was the Pre-Raphaelite painter John Millais, who fell in love with her at a time when he was painting her husband's portrait; shortly after the annulment he married her. (Given the spectacular failure of Ruskin's marriage and subsequent romantic relationships, it is ironic that he was to produce a highly influential, and frequently reprinted, description of the ideal characters of man and woman, husband and wife, in an 1864 lecture, "Of Queens' Gardens." See "The 'Woman Question'" on, p. 661.) In later years Ruskin fell in love with a young Irish girl, Rose La Touche, whom he first met when he was nearly forty and she was a child of nine. They were divided not only by the gap of age but by religious differences. She was an intensely pious believer, and for several years after Ruskin proposed marriage to her, when she was eighteen, she tried unsuccessfully to persuade him to return to the Evangelical faith that he had abandoned. In 1875, after herself experiencing bouts of mental illness, La Touche died at the age of twenty-five. In his autobiography Ruskin commented: "I wonder mightily what sort of creature I should have turned out, if instead of the distracting and useless pain, I had had the joy of approved love, and the untellable, incalculable motive of its sympathy and praise. It seems to me such things are not allowed in the world. The men capable of the highest imaginative passion are always tossed on fiery waves by it."

Despite both the despair that he suffered following La Touche's death and the recurring attacks of mental illness that blighted the last thirty-five years of his life, Ruskin remained active and productive up until his final silent decade of the 1890s. His publications during his active period included six volumes of his lectures on art that he had delivered as Slade Professor of Fine Arts at Oxford and his letters to laborers, *Fors Clavigera* (1871–84). One topic that becomes especially prominent in these later writings is pollution of air and water—an ideal subject for Ruskin's eloquence. In discussing it he combines his lifelong love for beautiful landscape and landscape painting with his later acquired conviction that modern industrial leadership was woefully irresponsible. A letter by A. E. Housman, who was an undergraduate at Oxford in 1877, provides a vivid record of how effective Ruskin could be:

> This afternoon Ruskin gave us a great outburst against modern times. He had got a picture of Turner's, framed and glassed, representing Leicester and the Abbey in the distance at sunset, over a river. He read the account of Wolsey's death out of *Henry VIII.* Then he pointed to the picture as representing Leicester when Turner had drawn it. Then he said, "You, if you like, may go to Leicester to see what it is like now. I never shall. But I can make a pretty good guess." Then he caught up a paintbrush. "These stepping-stones of course have been done away with, and are replaced by a be-au-ti-ful iron bridge." Then he dashed in the iron bridge on the glass of the picture. "The color of the stream is supplied on one side by the indigo factory." Forthwith one side of the stream became indigo. "On the other side by the soap factory." Soap dashed in. "They mix in the middle—like curds," he said, working them together with a sort of malicious deliberation. "This field, over which you see the sun setting behind the abbey, is now occupied in a *proper* manner." Then there went a flame of scarlet across the picture, which developed itself into windows and roofs and red brick, and rushed up into a chimney. "The atmosphere is supplied—thus!" A puff and cloud of smoke all over Turner's sky: and then the brush thrown down, and Ruskin confronting modern civilization amidst a tempest of applause, which he always elicits now, as he has this term become immensely popular, his lectures being crowded, whereas of old he used to prophesy to empty benches.

From Modern Painters

[A DEFINITION OF GREATNESS IN ART][1]

Painting, or art generally, as such, with all its technicalities, difficulties, and particular ends, is nothing but a noble and expressive language, invaluable as the vehicle of thought, but by itself nothing. He who has learned what is commonly considered the whole art of painting, that is, the art of representing any natural object faithfully, has as yet only learned the language by which his thoughts are to be expressed. He has done just as much towards being that which we ought to respect as a great painter, as a man who has learnt how to express himself grammatically and melodiously has towards being a great poet. The language is, indeed, more difficult of acquirement in the one case than in the other, and possesses more power of delighting the sense, while it speaks to the intellect; but it is, nevertheless, nothing more than language, and all those excellences which are peculiar to the painter as such, are merely what rhythm, melody, precision, and force are in the words of the orator and the poet, necessary to their greatness, but not the tests of their greatness. It is not by the mode of representing and saying, but by what is represented and said, that the respective greatness either of the painter or the writer is to be finally determined.

* * *

So that, if I say that the greatest picture is that which conveys to the mind of the spectator the greatest number of the greatest ideas, I have a definition which will include as subjects of comparison every pleasure which art is capable of conveying. If I were to say, on the contrary, that the best picture was that which most closely imitated nature, I should assume that art could only please by imitating nature; and I should cast out of the pale[2] of criticism those parts of works of art which are not imitative, that is to say, intrinsic beauties of color and form, and those works of art wholly, which, like the Arabesques of Raffaelle in the Loggias,[3] are not imitative at all. Now, I want a definition of art wide enough to include all its varieties of aim. I do not say, therefore, that the art is greatest which gives most pleasure, because perhaps there is some art whose end is to teach, and not to please. I do not say that the art is greatest which teaches us most, because perhaps there is some art whose end is to please, and not to teach. I do not say that the art is greatest which imitates best, because perhaps there is some art whose end is to create and not to imitate. But I say that the art is greatest which conveys to the mind of the spectator, by any means whatsoever, the greatest number of the greatest ideas; and I call an idea great in proportion as it is received by a higher faculty of the mind, and as it more fully occupies, and in occupying, exercises and exalts, the faculty by which it is received.

If this, then, be the definition of great art, that of a great artist naturally follows. He is the greatest artist who has embodied, in the sum of his works, the greatest number of the greatest ideas.

---

1. From vol. 1, part 1, section 1, chap. 2.
2. Beyond the notice or attention.
3. The arabesques in the Loggia of the Vatican, designed by the Italian painter Raphael (1483–

1520), were decorative wall paintings that featured a complex pattern of leaves, animals, and human figures.

["THE SLAVE SHIP"][4]

But I think the noblest sea that Turner has ever painted, and, if so, the noblest certainly ever painted by man, is that of "The Slave Ship," the chief Academy[5] picture of the exhibition of 1840. It is a sunset on the Atlantic after prolonged storm; but the storm is partially lulled, and the torn and streaming rain clouds are moving in scarlet lines to lose themselves in the hollow of the night. The whole surface of sea included in the picture is divided into two ridges of enormous swell, not high, nor local, but a low, broad heaving of the whole ocean, like the lifting of its bosom by deep-drawn breath after the torture of the storm. Between these two ridges the fire of the sunset falls along the trough of the sea, dyeing it with an awful but glorious light, the intense and lurid splendor which burns like gold and bathes like blood. Along this fiery path and valley the tossing waves by which the swell of the sea is restlessly divided lift themselves in dark, indefinite, fantastic forms, each casting a faint and ghastly shadow behind it along the illumined foam. They do not rise everywhere, but three or four together in wild groups, fitfully and furiously, as the under-strength of the swell compels or permits them; leaving between them treacherous spaces of level and whirling water, now lighted with green and lamplike fire, now flashing back the gold of the declining sun, now fearfully shed from above with the indistinguishable images of the burning clouds, which fall upon them in flakes of crimson and scarlet and give to the reckless waves the added motion of their own fiery being. Purple and blue, the lurid shadows of the hollow breakers are cast upon the mist of night, which gathers cold and low, advancing like the shadow of death upon the guilty ship as it labors amidst the lightning of the sea, its thin masts written upon the sky in lines of blood, girded with condemnation in that fearful hue which signs the sky with horror, and mixes its flaming flood with the sunlight, and, cast far along the desolate heave of the sepulchral waves, incarnadines the multitudinous sea.[6]

I believe, if I were reduced to rest Turner's immortality upon any single work, I should choose this. Its daring conception—ideal in the highest sense of the word—is based on the purest truth, and wrought out with the concentrated knowledge of a life; its color is absolutely perfect, not one false or morbid hue in any part or line, and so modulated that every square inch of canvas is a perfect composition; its drawing as accurate as fearless; the ship buoyant, bending, and full of motion; its tones as true as they are wonderful; and the whole picture dedicated to the most sublime of subjects and impressions—completing thus the perfect system of all truth which we have shown to be formed by Turner's works—the power, majesty, and deathfulness of the open, deep, illimitable Sea.

1843

---

4. From vol. 1, part 2, section 5, chap. 3.
5. The Royal Academy of Arts, founded in London in 1768. The painting (included in this volume's color insert) is by the great British landscapist J. M. W. Turner (1775–1851) and was originally titled "Slavers Throwing Overboard the Dead and Dying—Typhoon Coming On." Turner was inspired to paint it after reading about the slave ship *Zong* in Thomas Clarkson's *History and Abolition of the Slave Trade* (1808). In 1781, the *Zong's* captain ordered 133 sick and dying slaves thrown overboard so that insurance money available only for slaves "lost at sea" could be collected. The painting was given to Ruskin by his father as a New Year's present in 1844 and hung in the Ruskin household for a number of years until Ruskin decided to sell it because he found its subject "too painful to live with." It now hangs in the Museum of Fine Arts in Boston.
6. Cf. Shakespeare's *Macbeth* 2.2.60: "this my hand will rather / The multitudinous seas incarnadine." "Incarnadines": reddens.

From *Of the Pathetic Fallacy*[7]

* * *

Now therefore, putting these tiresome and absurd words[8] quite out of our way, we may go on at our ease to examine the point in question—namely, the difference between the ordinary, proper, and true appearances of things to us; and the extraordinary, or false appearances, when we are under the influence of emotion, or contemplative fancy; false appearances, I say, as being entirely unconnected with any real power of character in the object, and only imputed to it by us.

For instance—

> The spendthrift crocus, bursting through the mold
> Naked and shivering, with his cup of gold.[9]

This is very beautiful, and yet very untrue. The crocus is not a spendthrift, but a hardy plant; its yellow is not gold, but saffron. How is it that we enjoy so much the having it put into our heads that it is anything else than a plain crocus?

It is an important question. For, throughout our past reasonings about art, we have always found that nothing could be good or useful, or ultimately pleasurable, which was untrue. But here is something pleasurable in written poetry, which is nevertheless *un*true. And what is more, if we think over our favorite poetry, we shall find it full of this kind of fallacy, and that we like it all the more for being so.

It will appear also, on consideration of the matter, that this fallacy is of two principal kinds. Either, as in this case of the crocus, it is the fallacy of willful fancy, which involves no real expectation that it will be believed; or else it is a fallacy caused by an excited state of the feelings, making us, for the time, more or less irrational. Of the cheating of the fancy we shall have to speak presently; but, in this chapter, I want to examine the nature of the other error, that which the mind admits when affected strongly by emotion. Thus, for instance, in *Alton Locke*—

> They rowed her in across the rolling foam—
> The cruel, crawling foam.[1]

The foam is not cruel, neither does it crawl. The state of mind which attributes to it these characters of a living creature is one in which the reason is unhinged by grief. All violent feelings have the same effect. They produce in us a falseness in all our impressions of external things, which I would generally characterize as the "pathetic fallacy."

---

7. From vol. 3, part 4, chap. 12. In this celebrated chapter Ruskin shifts from discussing problems of truth and realism in art to the same problems in literature. The term *pathetic* refers not to something feebly ineffective but to the emotion (pathos) with which a writer invests highlighting of objects and to the distortion (fallacy) that may result. Poets such as Tennyson protested that Ruskin was being unfairly rigorous in highlighting

the fallacy, and Ruskin himself falls into it often. See, e.g., his reference to "the guilty ship" in his discussion of Turner's *The Slave Ship* (p. 385).
8. The metaphysical terms *objective* and *subjective* as applied to kinds of truth.
9. From "Astraea" (1850), a poem by Oliver Wendell Holmes (1809–1894).
1. From chap. 26 of the novel *Alton Locke* (1850) by Charles Kingsley (1819–1875).

Now we are in the habit of considering this fallacy as eminently a character of poetical description, and the temper of mind in which we allow it, as one eminently poetical, because passionate. But, I believe, if we look well into the matter, that we shall find the greatest poets do not often admit this kind of falseness—that it is only the second order of poets who much delight in it.

Thus, when Dante describes the spirits falling from the bank of Acheron "as dead leaves flutter from a bough,"[2] he gives the most perfect image possible of their utter lightness, feebleness, passiveness, and scattering agony of despair, without, however, for an instant losing his own clear perception that *these* are souls, and *those* are leaves: he makes no confusion of one with the other. But when Coleridge speaks of

> The one red leaf, the last of its clan,
> That dances as often as dance it can,[3]

he has a morbid, that is to say, a so far false, idea about the leaf: he fancies a life in it, and will, which there are not; confuses its powerlessness with choice, its fading death with merriment, and the wind that shakes it with music. Here, however, there is some beauty, even in the morbid passage; but take an instance in Homer and Pope. Without the knowledge of Ulysses, Elpenor, his youngest follower, has fallen from an upper chamber in the Circean palace, and has been left dead, unmissed by his leader or companions, in the haste of their departure. They cross the sea to the Cimmerian land; and Ulysses summons the shades from Tartarus.[4] The first which appears is that of the lost Elpenor. Ulysses, amazed, and in exactly the spirit of bitter and terrified lightness which is seen in Hamlet, addresses the spirit with the simple, startled words: "Elpenor! How earnest thou under the shadowy darkness? Hast thou come faster on foot than I in my black ship?"[5] Which Pope renders thus:

> O, say, what angry power Elpenor led
> To glide in shades, and wander with the dead?
> How could thy soul, by realms and seas disjoined,
> Outfly the nimble sail, and leave the lagging wind?

I sincerely hope the reader finds no pleasure here, either in the nimbleness of the sail, or the laziness of the wind! And yet how is it that these conceits[6] are so painful now, when they have been pleasant to us in the other instances?

For a very simple reason. They are not a *pathetic* fallacy at all, for they are put into the mouth of the wrong passion—a passion which never could possibly have spoken them—agonized curiosity. Ulysses wants to know the facts of the matter; and the very last thing his mind could do at the moment would be to pause, or suggest in anywise what was *not* a fact. The delay in the first three lines, and conceit in the last, jar upon us instantly, like the most frightful discord in music. No poet of true imaginative power would possibly have written the passage.

---

2. *Inferno* 3.112, by Dante Alighieri (1265–1321). Acheron is a river of the classical underworld.
3. *Christabel* (1816), 49–50, by Samuel Taylor Coleridge (1772–1834).
4. In classical mythology the lowest region of the underworld.
5. *Odyssey* (8th century B.C.E.) 11.51. The translation by Alexander Pope (1688–1744) was published in 1715–20.
6. Extended poetic devices.

Therefore, we see that the spirit of truth must guide us in some sort, even in our enjoyment of fallacy. Coleridge's fallacy has no discord in it, but Pope's has set our teeth on edge. * * *

1856

From The Stones of Venice

[THE SAVAGENESS OF GOTHIC ARCHITECTURE][1]

I am not sure when the word "Gothic" was first generically applied to the architecture of the North; but I presume that, whatever the date of its original usage, it was intended to imply reproach, and express the barbaric character of the nations among whom that architecture arose. It never implied that they were literally of Gothic lineage, far less that their architecture had been originally invented by the Goths themselves; but it did imply that they and their buildings together exhibited a degree of sternness and rudeness,[2] which, in contradistinction to the character of Southern and Eastern nations, appeared like a perpetual reflection of the contrast between the Goth and the Roman in their first encounter. And when that fallen Roman, in the utmost impotence of his luxury, and insolence of his guilt, became the model for the imitation of civilized Europe,[3] at the close of the so-called Dark Ages, the word Gothic became a term of unmitigated contempt, not unmixed with aversion. From that contempt, by the exertion of the antiquaries and architects of this century, Gothic architecture has been sufficiently vindicated; and perhaps some among us, in our admiration of the magnificent science of its structure, and sacredness of its expression, might desire that the term of ancient reproach should be withdrawn, and some other, of more apparent honorableness, adopted in its place. There is no chance, as there is no need, of such a substitution. As far as the epithet was used scornfully, it was used falsely; but there is no reproach in the word, rightly understood; on the contrary, there is a profound truth, which the instinct of mankind almost unconsciously recognizes. It is true, greatly and deeply true, that the architecture of the North is rude and wild; but it is not true that, for this reason, we are to condemn it, or despise. Far otherwise: I believe it is in this very character that it deserves our profoundest reverence.

The charts of the world which have been drawn up by modern science have thrown into a narrow space the expression of a vast amount of knowledge, but I have never yet seen any one pictorial enough to enable the spectator to imagine the kind of contrast in physical character which exists between Northern and Southern countries. We know the differences in detail, but we have not that broad glance and grasp which would enable us to feel them in their fullness. We know that gentians grow on the Alps, and olives on

---

1. From vol. 2, chap. 6.
2. Lack of refinement, roughness. "Goths": a Germanic people who by the 3rd century C.E. had settled north of the Black Sea.
3. Renaissance architecture, based on imitating classical buildings, was distasteful to Ruskin. He later stated that his aim in *The Stones of Venice*

had been "to show that the Gothic architecture of Venice had risen out of . . . a state of pure national faith and domestic virtue; and that its Renaissance architecture had arisen out of . . . a state of concealed national infidelity and domestic corruption."

the Apennines; but we do not enough conceive for ourselves that variegated mosaic of the world's surface which a bird sees in its migration, that difference between the district of the gentian and of the olive which the stork and the swallow see far off, as they lean upon the sirocco wind.[4] Let us, for a moment, try to raise ourselves even above the level of their flight, and imagine the Mediterranean lying beneath us like an irregular lake, and all its ancient promontories sleeping in the sun: here and there an angry spot of thunder, a gray stain of storm, moving upon the burning field; and here and there a fixed wreath of white volcano smoke, surrounded by its circle of ashes; but for the most part a great peacefulness of light, Syria and Greece, Italy and Spain, laid like pieces of a golden pavement into the sea-blue, chased, as we stoop nearer to them, with bossy[5] beaten work of mountain chains, and glowing softly with terraced gardens, and flowers heavy with frankincense, mixed among masses of laurel, and orange, and plumy palm, that abate with their gray-green shadows the burning of the marble rocks, and of the ledges of porphyry sloping under lucent sand. Then let us pass farther towards the north, until we see the orient colors change gradually into a vast belt of rainy green, where the pastures of Switzerland, and poplar valleys of France, and dark forests of the Danube and Carpathians stretch from the mouths of the Loire to those of the Volga, seen through clefts in gray swirls of rain cloud and flaky veils of the mist of the brooks, spreading low along the pasture lands: and then, farther north still, to see the earth heave into mighty masses of leaden rock and heathy moor, bordering with a broad waste of gloomy purple that belt of field and wood, and splintering into irregular and grisly islands amidst the northern seas, beaten by storm, and chilled by ice drift, and tormented by furious pulses of contending tide, until the roots of the last forests fail from among the hill ravines, and the hunger of the north wind bites their peaks into barrenness; and, at last, the wall of ice, durable like iron, sets, deathlike, its white teeth against us out of the polar twilight. And, having once traversed in thought this gradation of the zoned iris of the earth in all its material vastness, let us go down nearer to it, and watch the parallel change in the belt of animal life: the multitudes of swift and brilliant creatures that glance in the air and sea, or tread the sands of the southern zone; striped zebras and spotted leopards, glistening serpents, and birds arrayed in purple and scarlet. Let us contrast their delicacy and brilliancy of color, and swiftness of motion, with the frost-cramped strength, and shaggy covering, and dusky plumage of the northern tribes; contrast the Arabian horse with the Shetland,[6] the tiger and leopard with the wolf and bear, the antelope with the elk, the bird of paradise with the osprey: and then, submissively acknowledging the great laws by which the earth and all that it bears are ruled throughout their being, let us not condemn, but rejoice in the expression by man of his own rest in the statutes of the lands that gave him birth. Let us watch him with reverence as he sets side by side the burning gems, and smooths with soft sculpture the jasper pillars, that are to reflect a ceaseless sunshine, and rise into a cloudless sky: but not with less reverence let us stand by him, when, with rough strength and hurried stroke, he smites an uncouth animation out of the rocks which he has torn from among the moss of the moorland, and heaves into the darkened air the pile of

4. Hot wind from the southern Mediterranean.
5. Ornamental, or embossed. "Chased": decorated.

6. A breed of pony from the Shetland Isles.

iron buttress and rugged wall, instinct with[7] work of an imagination as wild and wayward as the northern sea; creations of ungainly shape and rigid limb, but full of wolfish life; fierce as the winds that beat, and changeful as the clouds that shade them.

There is, I repeat, no degradation, no reproach in this, but all dignity and honorableness: and we should err grievously in refusing either to recognize as an essential character of the existing architecture of the North, or to admit as a desirable character in that which it yet may be, this wildness of thought, and roughness of work; this look of mountain brotherhood between the cathedral and the Alp; this magnificence of sturdy power, put forth only the more energetically because the fine finger-touch was chilled away by the frosty wind, and the eye dimmed by the moor mist, or blinded by the hail; this outspeaking of the strong spirit of men who may not gather redundant fruitage from the earth, nor bask in dreamy benignity of sunshine, but must break the rock for bread, and cleave the forest for fire, and show, even in what they did for their delight, some of the hard habits of the arm and heart that grew on them as they swung the ax or pressed the plow.

If, however, the savageness of Gothic architecture, merely as an expression of its origin among Northern nations, may be considered, in some sort, a noble character, it possesses a higher nobility still, when considered as an index, not of climate, but of religious principle.

In the 13th and 14th paragraphs of Chapter XXI of the first volume of this work, it was noticed that the systems of architectural ornament, properly so called, might be divided into three: (1) Servile ornament, in which the execution or power of the inferior workman is entirely subjected to the intellect of the higher; (2) Constitutional ornament, in which the executive inferior power is, to a certain point, emancipated and independent, having a will of its own, yet confessing its inferiority and rendering obedience to higher powers; and (3) Revolutionary ornament, in which no executive inferiority is admitted at all. I must here explain the nature of these divisions at somewhat greater length.

Of Servile ornament, the principal schools are the Greek, Ninevite, and Egyptian; but their servility is of different kinds. The Greek master-workman was far advanced in knowledge and power above the Assyrian or Egyptian. Neither he nor those for whom he worked could endure the appearance of imperfection in anything; and, therefore, what ornament he appointed to be done by those beneath him was composed of mere geometrical forms—balls, ridges, and perfectly symmetrical foliage—which could be executed with absolute precision by line and rule, and were as perfect in their way, when completed, as his own figure sculpture. The Assyrian and Egyptian, on the contrary, less cognizant of accurate form in anything, were content to allow their figure sculpture to be executed by inferior workmen, but lowered the method of its treatment to a standard which every workman could reach, and then trained him by discipline so rigid that there was no chance of his falling beneath the standard appointed. The Greek gave to the lower workman no subject which he could not perfectly execute. The Assyrian gave him subjects which he could only execute imperfectly, but fixed a legal standard for his imperfection. The workman was, in both systems, a slave.

7. Imbued with as an animating force.

But in the medieval, or especially Christian, system of ornament, this slavery is done away with altogether; Christianity having recognized, in small things as well as great, the individual value of every soul. But it not only recognizes its value; it confesses its imperfection, in only bestowing dignity upon the acknowledgment of unworthiness. That admission of lost power and fallen nature, which the Greek or Ninevite felt to be intensely painful, and, as far as might be, altogether refused, the Christian makes daily and hourly, contemplating the fact of it without fear, as tending, in the end, to God's greater glory. Therefore, to every spirit which Christianity summons to her service, her exhortation is: Do what you can, and confess frankly what you are unable to do; neither let your effort be shortened for fear of failure, nor your confession silenced for fear of shame. And it is, perhaps, the principal admirableness of the Gothic schools of architecture, that they thus receive the results of the labor of inferior minds; and out of fragments full of imperfection, and betraying that imperfection in every touch, indulgently raise up a stately and unaccusable whole.

But the modern English mind has this much in common with that of the Greek, that it intensely desires, in all things, the utmost completion or perfection compatible with their nature. This is a noble character in the abstract, but becomes ignoble when it causes us to forget the relative dignities of that nature itself, and to prefer the perfectness of the lower nature to the imperfection of the higher; not considering that as, judged by such a rule, all the brute animals would be preferable to man, because more perfect in their functions and kind, and yet are always held inferior to him, so also in the works of man, those which are more perfect in their kind are always inferior to those which are, in their nature, liable to more faults and shortcomings. For the finer the nature, the more flaws it will show through the clearness of it; and it is a law of this universe that the best things shall be seldomest seen in their best form. The wild grass grows well and strongly, one year with another; but the wheat is, according to the greater nobleness of its nature, liable to the bitterer blight. And therefore, while in all things that we see, or do, we are to desire perfection, and strive for it, we are nevertheless not to set the meaner[8] thing, in its narrow accomplishment, above the nobler thing, in its mighty progress; not to esteem smooth minuteness above shattered majesty; not to prefer mean victory to honorable defeat; not to lower the level of our aim, that we may the more surely enjoy the complacency of success. But above all, in our dealings with the souls of other men, we are to take care how we check, by severe requirement or narrow caution, efforts which might otherwise lead to a noble issue; and, still more, how we withhold our admiration from great excellencies, because they are mingled with rough faults. Now, in the make and nature of every man, however rude or simple, whom we employ in manual labor, there are some powers for better things: some tardy imagination, torpid capacity of emotion, tottering steps of thought, there are, even at the worst; and in most cases it is all our own fault that they *are* tardy or torpid. But they cannot be strengthened, unless we are content to take them in their feebleness, and unless we prize and honor them in their imperfection above the best and most perfect manual skill. And this is what we have to do with all our laborers; to look for the *thoughtful* part

8. Lesser.

of them, and get that out of them, whatever we lose for it, whatever faults and errors we are obliged to take with it. For the best that is in them cannot manifest itself, but in company with much error. Understand this clearly: You can teach a man to draw a straight line, and to cut one; to strike a curved line, and to carve it; and to copy and carve any number of given lines or forms, with admirable speed and perfect precision; and you find his work perfect of its kind: but if you ask him to think about any of those forms, to consider if he cannot find any better in his own head, he stops; his execution becomes hesitating; he thinks, and ten to one he thinks wrong; ten to one he makes a mistake in the first touch he gives to his work as a thinking being. But you have made a man of him for all that. He was only a machine before, an animated tool.

And observe, you are put to stern choice in this matter. You must either make a tool of the creature, or a man of him. You cannot make both. Men were not intended to work with the accuracy of tools, to be precise and perfect in all their actions. If you will have that precision out of them, and make their fingers measure degrees like cogwheels, and their arms strike curves like compasses, you must unhumanize them. All the energy of their spirits must be given to make cogs and compasses of themselves. All their attention and strength must go to the accomplishment of the mean act. The eye of the soul must be bent upon the finger point, and the soul's force must fill all the invisible nerves that guide it, ten hours a day, that it may not err from its steely precision, and so soul and sight be worn away, and the whole human being be lost at last—a heap of sawdust, so far as its intellectual work in this world is concerned; saved only by its Heart, which cannot go into the form of cogs and compasses, but expands, after the ten hours are over, into fireside humanity. On the other hand, if you will make a man of the working creature, you cannot make a tool. Let him but begin to imagine, to think, to try to do anything worth doing; and the engine-turned precision is lost at once. Out come all his roughness, all his dullness, all his incapability; shame upon shame, failure upon failure, pause after pause: but out comes the whole majesty of him also; and we know the height of it only, when we see the clouds settling upon him. And, whether the clouds be bright or dark, there will be transfiguration behind and within them.

And now, reader, look around this English room of yours, about which you have been proud so often, because the work of it was so good and strong, and the ornaments of it so finished. Examine again all those accurate mold-ings, and perfect polishings, and unerring adjustments of the seasoned wood and tempered steel. Many a time you have exulted over them, and thought how great England was, because her slightest work was done so thoroughly. Alas! if read rightly, these perfectnesses are signs of a slavery in our England a thousand times more bitter and more degrading than that of the scourged African, or helot[9] Greek. Men may be beaten, chained, tormented, yoked like cattle, slaughtered like summer flies, and yet remain in one sense, and the best sense, free. But to smother their souls within them, to blight and hew into rotting pollards[1] the suckling branches of their human intelligence, to make the flesh and skin which, after the worm's work on it, is to see God,[2]

---

9. A class of serfs in ancient Sparta.
1. Trees with top branches cut back to the trunk.

2. Cf. Job 19.26: "And though after my skin worms destroy this body, yet in my flesh shall I see God."

into leathern thongs to yoke machinery with—this it is to be slave-masters indeed; and there might be more freedom in England, though her feudal lords' lightest words were worth men's lives, and though the blood of the vexed husbandman dropped in the furrows of her fields, than there is while the animation of her multitudes is sent like fuel to feed the factory smoke, and the strength of them is given daily to be wasted into the fineness of a web, or racked into the exactness of a line.

And, on the other hand, go forth again to gaze upon the old cathedral front, where you have smiled so often at the fantastic[3] ignorance of the old sculptors: examine once more those ugly goblins, and formless monsters, and stern statues, anatomiless[4] and rigid; but do not mock at them, for they are signs of the life and liberty of every workman who struck the stone; a freedom of thought, and rank in scale of being, such as no laws, no charters, no charities can secure; but which it must be the first aim of all Europe at this day to regain for her children.

Let me not be thought to speak wildly or extravagantly. It is verily this degradation of the operative into a machine, which, more than any other evil of the times, is leading the mass of the nations everywhere into vain, incoherent, destructive struggling for a freedom of which they cannot explain the nature to themselves. Their universal outcry against wealth, and against nobility, is not forced from them either by the pressure of famine, or the sting of mortified pride. These do much, and have done much in all ages; but the foundations of society were never yet shaken as they are at this day. It is not that men are ill fed, but that they have no pleasure in the work by which they make their bread, and therefore look to wealth as the only means of pleasure. It is not that men are pained by the scorn of the upper classes, but they cannot endure their own; for they feel that the kind of labor to which they are condemned is verily a degrading one, and makes them less than men. Never had the upper classes so much sympathy with the lower, or charity for them, as they have at this day, and yet never were they so much hated by them: for, of old, the separation between the noble and the poor was merely a wall built by law; now it is a veritable difference in level of standing, a precipice between upper and lower grounds in the field of humanity, and there is pestilential air at the bottom of it. I know not if a day is ever to come when the nature of right freedom will be understood, and when men will see that to obey another man, to labor for him, yield reverence to him or to his place, is not slavery. It is often the best kind of liberty—liberty from care. The man who says to one, Go, and he goeth, and to another, Come, and he cometh,[5] has, in most cases, more sense of restraint and difficulty than the man who obeys him. The movements of the one are hindered by the burden on his shoulder; of the other, by the bridle on his lips: there is no way by which the burden may be lightened; but we need not suffer from the bridle if we do not champ at it. To yield reverence to another, to hold ourselves and our lives at his disposal, is not slavery; often, it is the noblest state in which a man can live in this world. There is, indeed, a reverence which is servile, that is to say irrational or selfish: but there is also noble reverence, that is to say, reasonable and loving; and a man is never so noble as when he is reverent

3. Fanciful, imaginative.
4. Devoid of anatomy (Ruskin's coinage).

5. Matthew 8.9.

in this kind; nay, even if the feeling pass the bounds of mere reason, so that it be loving, a man is raised by it. Which had, in reality, most of the serf nature in him—the Irish peasant who was lying in wait yesterday for his landlord, with his musket muzzle thrust through the ragged hedge; or that old mountain servant, who, 200 years ago, at Inverkeithing, gave up his own life and the lives of his seven sons for his chief?[6]—as each fell, calling forth his brother to the death, "Another for Hector!" And therefore, in all ages and all countries, reverence has been paid and sacrifice made by men to each other, not only without complaint, but rejoicingly; and famine, and peril, and sword, and all evil, and all shame, have been borne willingly in the causes of masters and kings; for all these gifts of the heart ennobled the men who gave not less than the men who received them, and nature prompted, and God rewarded the sacrifice. But to feel their souls withering within them, unthanked, to find their whole being sunk into an unrecognized abyss, to be counted off into a heap of mechanism, numbered with its wheels, and weighed with its hammer strokes—this nature bade not—this God blesses not—this humanity for no long time is able to endure.

We have much studied and much perfected, of late, the great civilized invention of the division of labour; only we give it a false name. It is not, truly speaking, the labour that is divided; but the men: Divided into mere segments of men—broken into small fragments and crumbs of life; so that all the little piece of intelligence that is left in a man is not enough to make a pin, or a nail, but exhausts itself in making the point of a pin, or the head of a nail. Now it is a good and desirable thing, truly, to make many pins in a day; but if we could only see with what crystal sand their points were polished—sand of human soul, much to be magnified before it can be discerned for what it is—we should think there might be some loss in it also. And the great cry that rises from all our manufacturing cities, louder than their furnace blast, is all in very deed for this—that we manufacture everything there except men; we blanch cotton, and strengthen steel, and refine sugar, and shape pottery; but to brighten, to strengthen, to refine, or to form a single living spirit, never enters into our estimate of advantages. And all the evil to which that cry is urging our myriads can be met only in one way: not by teaching nor preaching, for to teach them is but to show them their misery, and to preach to them, if we do nothing more than preach, is to mock at it. It can be met only by a right understanding, on the part of all classes, of what kinds of labour are good for men, raising them, and making them happy; by a determined sacrifice of such convenience, or beauty, or cheapness as is to be got only by the degradation of the workman; and by equally determined demand for the products and results of healthy and ennobling labour.

And how, it will be asked, are these products to be recognized, and this demand to be regulated? Easily: by the observance of three broad and simple rules:

1. Never encourage the manufacture of any article not absolutely necessary, in the production of which *Invention* has no share.

2. Never demand an exact finish for its own sake, but only for some practical or noble end.

6. An incident described in the preface to the novel *The Fair Maid of Perth* (1828) by Sir Walter Scott (1771–1832). Inverkeithing is a town in Fife, Scotland.

3. Never encourage imitation or copying of any kind, except for the sake of preserving record of great works.

The second of these principles is the only one which directly rises out of the consideration of our immediate subject; but I shall briefly explain the meaning and extent of the first also, reserving the enforcement of the third for another place.

1. Never encourage the manufacture of anything not necessary, in the production of which invention has no share.

For instance. Glass beads are utterly unnecessary, and there is no design or thought employed in their manufacture. They are formed by first drawing out the glass into rods; these rods are chopped up into fragments of the size of beads by the human hand, and the fragments are then rounded in the furnace. The men who chop up the rods sit at their work all day, their hands vibrating with a perpetual and exquisitely timed palsy, and the beads dropping beneath their vibration like hail. Neither they, nor the men who draw out the rods or fuse the fragments, have the smallest occasion for the use of any single human faculty; and every young lady, therefore, who buys glass beads is engaged in the slave trade, and in a much more cruel one than that which we have so long been endeavouring to put down.[7]

But glass cups and vessels may become the subjects of exquisite invention; and if in buying these we pay for the invention, that is to say for the beautiful form, or color, or engraving, and not for mere finish of execution, we are doing good to humanity.

So, again, the cutting of precious stones, in all ordinary cases, requires little exertion of any mental faculty; some tact and judgment in avoiding flaws, and so on, but nothing to bring out the whole mind. Every person who wears cut jewels merely for the sake of their value is, therefore, a slave driver.

But the working of the goldsmith, and the various designing of grouped jewelry and enamel-work, may become the subject of the most noble human intelligence. Therefore, money spent in the purchase of well-designed plate, of precious engraved vases, cameos, or enamels, does good to humanity; and, in work of this kind, jewels may be employed to heighten its splendor; and their cutting is then a price paid for the attainment of a noble end, and thus perfectly allowable.

I shall perhaps press this law farther elsewhere, but our immediate concern is chiefly with the second, namely, never to demand an exact finish, when it does not lead to a noble end. For observe, I have only dwelt upon the rudeness of Gothic, or any other kind of imperfectness, as admirable, where it was impossible to get design or thought without it. If you are to have the thought of a rough and untaught man, you must have it in a rough and untaught way; but from an educated man, who can without effort express his thoughts in an educated way, take the graceful expression, and be thankful. Only *get* the thought, and do not silence the peasant because he cannot speak good grammar, or until you have taught him his grammar. Grammar and refinement are good things, both, only be sure of the better thing first. And thus in art, delicate finish is desirable from the greatest masters, and is always given by them. In some places Michael Angelo, Leonardo, Phidias,

---

7. Although the Atlantic slave trade had been outlawed early in the 19th century, transatlantic trafficking in African slaves continued until slavery was made illegal everywhere in the Americas.

Perugino, Turner[8] all finished with the most exquisite care; and the finish they give always leads to the fuller accomplishment of their noble purposes. But lower men than these cannot finish, for it requires consummate knowledge to finish consummately, and then we must take their thoughts as they are able to give them. So the rule is simple: Always look for invention first, and after that, for such execution as will help the invention, and as the inventor is capable of without painful effort, and *no more*. Above all, demand no refinement of execution where there is no thought, for that is slaves' work, unredeemed. Rather choose rough work than smooth work, so only that the practical purpose be answered, and never imagine there is reason to be proud of anything that may be accomplished by patience and sandpaper.

I shall only give one example, which however will show the reader what I mean, from the manufacture already alluded to, that of glass. Our modern glass is exquisitely clear in its substance, true in its form, accurate in its cutting. We are proud of this. We ought to be ashamed of it. The old Venice glass was muddy, inaccurate in all its forms, and clumsily cut, if at all. And the old Venetian was justly proud of it. For there is this difference between the English and Venetian workman, that the former thinks only of accurately matching his patterns, and getting his curves perfectly true and his edges perfectly sharp, and becomes a mere machine for rounding curves and sharpening edges, while the old Venetian cared not a whit whether his edges were sharp or not, but he invented a new design for every glass that he made, and never molded a handle or a lip without a new fancy in it. And therefore, though some Venetian glass is ugly and clumsy enough, when made by clumsy and uninventive workmen, other Venetian glass is so lovely in its forms that no price is too great for it; and we never see the same form in it twice. Now you cannot have the finish and the varied form too. If the workman is thinking about his edges, he cannot be thinking of his design; if of his design, he cannot think of his edges. Choose whether you will pay for the lovely form or the perfect finish, and choose at the same moment whether you will make the worker a man or a grindstone.

Nay, but the reader interrupts me—"If the workman can design beautifully, I would not have him kept at the furnace. Let him be taken away and made a gentleman, and have a studio, and design his glass there, and I will have it blown and cut for him by common workmen, and so I will have my design and my finish too."

All ideas of this kind are founded upon two mistaken suppositions: the first, that one man's thoughts can be, or ought to be, executed by another man's hands; the second, that manual labor is a degradation, when it is governed by intellect.

On a large scale, and in work determinable by line and rule, it is indeed both possible and necessary that the thoughts of one man should be carried out by the labor of others; in this sense I have already defined the best architecture to be the expression of the mind of manhood by the hands of childhood. But on a smaller scale, and in a design which cannot be mathematically defined, one man's thoughts can never be expressed by another: and the dif-

---

8. All notable artists. Michelangelo (1475–1564), Italian sculptor, painter, and architect. Leonardo da Vinci (1452–1519), Italian painter, sculptor, and scientist. Phidias (born ca. 490 B.C.E.), an Athenian often called the greatest Greek sculptor. Perugino (Pietro di Cristoforo Vannucci, ca. 1450–1523). J. M. W. Turner (1775–1851), British painter.

ference between the spirit of touch of the man who is inventing, and of the man who is obeying directions, is often all the difference between a great and a common work of art. How wide the separation is between original and secondhand execution, I shall endeavor to show elsewhere; it is not so much to our purpose here as to mark the other and more fatal error of despising manual labor when governed by intellect; for it is no less fatal an error to despise it when thus regulated by intellect, than to value it for its own sake. We are always in these days endeavoring to separate the two; we want one man to be always thinking, and another to be always working, and we call one a gentleman, and the other an operative; whereas the workman ought often to be thinking, and the thinker often to be working, and both should be gentlemen, in the best sense. As it is, we make both ungentle, the one envying, the other despising, his brother; and the mass of society is made up of morbid thinkers, and miserable workers. Now it is only by labor that thought can be made healthy, and only by thought that labor can be made happy, and the two cannot be separated with impunity. It would be well if all of us were good handicraftsmen in some kind, and the dishonor of manual labor done away with altogether; so that though there should still be a trenchant distinction of race between nobles and commoners, there should not, among the latter, be a trenchant distinction of employment, as between idle and working men, or between men of liberal and illiberal professions. All professions should be liberal, and there should be less pride felt in peculiarity of employment, and more in excellence of achievement. And yet more, in each several[9] profession, no master should be too proud to do its hardest work. The painter should grind his own colours; the architect work in the mason's yard with his men; the master manufacturer be himself a more skillful operative than any man in his mills; and the distinction between one man and another be only in experience and skill, and the authority and wealth which these must naturally and justly obtain.

I should be led far from the matter in hand, if I were to pursue this interesting subject. Enough, I trust, has been said to show the reader that the rudeness or imperfection which at first rendered the term "Gothic" one of reproach is indeed, when rightly understood, one of the most noble characters of Christian architecture, and not only a noble but an *essential* one. It seems a fantastic paradox, but it is nevertheless a most important truth, that no architecture can be truly noble which is *not* imperfect. And this is easily demonstrable. For since the architect, whom we will suppose capable of doing all in perfection, cannot execute the whole with his own hands, he must either make slaves of his workmen in the old Greek, and present English fashion, and level his work to a slave's capacities, which is to degrade it; or else he must take his workmen as he finds them, and let them show their weaknesses together with their strength, which will involve the Gothic imperfection, but render the whole work as noble as the the intellect of the age can make it.

But the principle may be stated more broadly still. I have confined the illustration of it to architecture, but I must not leave it as if true of architecture only. Hitherto I have used the words imperfect and perfect merely to distinguish between work grossly unskillful, and work executed with average

9. Different.

precision and science; and I have been pleading that any degree of unskill-fulness should be admitted, so only that the laborer's mind had room for expression. But, accurately speaking, no good work whatever can be per-fect, and *the demand for perfection is always a sign of a misunderstanding of the ends of art*.

This for two reasons, both based on everlasting laws. The first, that no great man ever stops working till he has reached his point of failure; that is to say, his mind is always far in advance of his powers of execution, and the latter will now and then give way in trying to follow it; besides that he will always give to the inferior portions of his work only such inferior attention as they require; and according to his greatness he becomes so accustomed to the feeling of dissatisfaction with the best he can do, that in moments of lassitude or anger with himself he will not care though the beholder be dis-satisfied also. I believe there has only been one man who would not acknowl-edge this necessity, and strove always to reach perfection, Leonardo; the end of his vain effort being merely that he would take ten years to a picture, and leave it unfinished. And therefore, if we are to have great men working at all, or less men doing their best, the work will be imperfect, however beautiful. Of human work none but what is bad can be perfect, in its own bad way.[1]

The second reason is that imperfection is in some sort essential to all that we know of life. It is the sign of life in a mortal body, that is to say, of a state of progress and change. Nothing that lives is, or can be, rigidly per-fect; part of it is decaying, part nascent. The foxglove blossom—a third part bud, a third part past, a third part in full bloom—is a type of the life of this world. And in all things that live there are certain irregularities and defi-ciencies which are not only signs of life, but sources of beauty. No human face is exactly the same in its lines on each side, no leaf perfect in its lobes, no branch in its symmetry. All admit irregularity as they imply change; and to banish imperfection is to destroy expression, to check exertion, to para-lyze vitality. All things are literally better, lovelier, and more beloved for the imperfections which have been divinely appointed, that the law of human life may be Effort, and the law of human judgment, Mercy.

Accept this then for a universal law, that neither architecture nor any other noble work of man can be good unless it be imperfect; and let us be prepared for the otherwise strange fact, which we shall discern clearly as we approach the period of the Renaissance, that the first cause of the fall of the arts of Europe was a relentless requirement of perfection, incapable alike either of being silenced by veneration for greatness, or softened into forgiveness of simplicity.

Thus far then of the Rudeness or Savageness, which is the first mental element of Gothic architecture. It is an element in many other healthy archi-tectures also, as in Byzantine and Romanesque; but true Gothic cannot exist without it.

1851–53

1. The Elgin marbles are supposed by many per-sons to be "perfect." In the most important por-tions they indeed approach perfection, but only there. The draperies are unfinished, the hair and wool of the animals are unfinished, and the entire bas-reliefs of the frieze are roughly cut [Ruskin's note]. Ruskin is referring to the collection of stat-ues and friezes brought from Athens to England by Lord Elgin, works that were considered models of perfect realism.

GEORGE ELIOT
1819–1880

Like many English novelists (Charles Dickens being an exception) George Eliot came to novel writing relatively late in life. She was forty when her first novel, *Adam Bede* (1859), an immensely popular work, was published. The lives of her characters are, therefore, viewed from the vantage point of maturity and extensive experience; and this perspective is accentuated by her practice of setting her stories back in time to the period of her own childhood, or even earlier. In most of her novels, she evokes a preindustrial rural scene or the small-town life of the English Midlands, which she views with a combination of nostalgia and candid awareness of its limitations.

The place Eliot looks back on is usually the Warwickshire countryside. There, under her real name, Marian Evans, she spent her childhood at Arbury Farm, of which her father, Robert Evans, was supervisor and land agent. The time was the 1820s and 1830s (1819, the year of her birth, was an *annus mirabilis* for the nineteenth century, for in the same year were born John Ruskin, Herman Melville, Walt Whitman, and Queen Victoria). During these decades Evans read widely in and out of school and was also strongly affected by Evangelicism; she even advocated, at one point in her girlhood, giving up novelists such as Sir Walter Scott (who was later to influence her own novel writing) on the grounds that fiction was frivolous and time wasting. Her mother's death led to her leaving school at sixteen, and in the next four or five years she seems to have experienced bouts of depression and self-doubt. In a letter of 1871, looking back to the period, she likened her state of mind to that of Mary Wollstonecraft at the time of the earlier writer's attempted suicide: "Hopelessness has been to me, all through my life, but especially in the painful years of my youth, the chief source of wasted energy with all the consequent bitterness of regret. Remember, it has happened to many to be glad they did not commit suicide, though they once ran for the final leap, or as Mary Wollstonecraft did, wetted their garments well in the rain hoping to sink the better when they plunged."

At the age of twenty-one Evans moved with her father to the town of Coventry, and in this new setting her intellectual horizons were extensively widened. As the result of her association with a group of freethinking intellectuals, and her own studies of theology, she reluctantly decided that she could no longer believe in the Christian religion. Her decision created a painful break with her father, finally resolved when she agreed to observe the formality of attending church with him and he agreed, tacitly at least, that while there she could think what she liked.

These preoccupations with theological issues led to her first book, a translation in 1846 of *The Life of Jesus* by D. F. Strauss, one of the leading figures of the Higher Criticism in Germany. This criticism was the work of a group of scholars dedicated to testing the historical authenticity of biblical narratives in the light of modern methods of research. For the rest of her life, Evans continued to read extensively in English and continental philosophy; and when she moved to London in 1851, after her father's death, her impressive intellectual credentials led to her appointment as an assistant editor of the *Westminster Review,* a learned journal formerly edited by John Stuart Mill. In the years in which she served as editor, she wrote a number of essays, including "Margaret Fuller and Mary Wollstonecraft" and "Silly Novels by Lady Novelists," which she contributed to various periodicals in addition to the *Westminster Review.*

Her work at the *Review* brought her into contact with many important writers and thinkers. Among them was George Henry Lewes, a brilliant critic of literature and philosophy, with whom she fell in love. Lewes, a married man and father of three children, could not obtain a divorce. Evans therefore elected to live with him as a common-law wife, and what they called their "marriage" lasted happily until his death in 1878. In the last year of her life, she married an admirer and friend, J. W. Cross, who became her biographer.

Her earlier decision to live with Lewes was painfully made: "Light and easily broken ties are what I neither desire theoretically nor could live for practically. Women who are satisfied with such ties do *not* act as I have done—they obtain what they desire and are still invited to dinner." Mrs. Lewes, as she called herself, was not invited to dinner; instead, those who wanted to see her had themselves to seek her company at the house that she shared with Lewes, where she received visitors on Sunday afternoons. These Sunday afternoons became legendary occasions, over which she presided almost like a sibyl. However, her decision to live with Lewes cost her a number of social and family ties, including her relationship with her brother, Isaac, to whom she had been deeply attached since childhood. Isaac never spoke to her again after her elopement. It is reasonable to conjecture that this experience affects the stress, in all of her novels, on incidents involving choice. All of her characters are tested by situations in which they must choose, and the choices, as in *The Mill on the Floss* (1860), are often agonizingly painful.

Although she had occasionally tried her hand at fiction earlier in life, it was only after her relationship with Lewes became established that she turned her full attention to this form. *Scenes from Clerical Life* appeared in magazine installments in 1857 under the pen name that misled most of her readers (Dickens excepted) into believing the author to be a man—a "university man," it was commonly said, to Eliot's amusement and satisfaction. This work was followed by seven full-length novels in the 1860s and 1870s, most of which repeated the success of *Adam Bede* with the Victorian reading public and which, after a period of being out of favor in the early twentieth century, are now once more deeply admired by readers and critics. Virginia Woolf praised *Middlemarch* (1871–72) as "one of the few English novels written for grownup people," and later readers have found a similar maturity combined with a powerful creative energy in other novels by Eliot such as *The Mill on the Floss* and *Daniel Deronda* (1876).

When Eliot began writing fiction, she and Lewes were reading to each other the novels of Jane Austen. Eliot's fiction owes much to Austen's with its concern with provincial society, its satire of human motives, its focus on courtship. But Eliot brings to these subjects a philosophical and psychological depth very different in character from that of the novel of manners. Eliot's fiction typically combines expansive philosophic meditation with an acute dissection of her characters' motives and feelings.

In a famous passage from *Middlemarch,* Eliot compares herself with the great eighteenth-century novelist Henry Fielding:

> A great historian, as he insisted on calling himself, who had the happiness to be dead a hundred and twenty years ago, and so to take his place among the colossi whose huge legs our living pettiness is observed to walk under, glories in his copious remarks and digressions as the least imitable part of his work. . . . But Fielding lived when the days were longer. . . . We belated historians must not linger after his example; I at least have so much to do in unravelling certain human lots, and seeing how they were woven and interwoven, that all the light I can command must be concentrated on this particular web, and not dispersed over that tempting range of relevancies called the universe.

Despite her ironic disclaimer Eliot too prides herself on her remarks and digressions—as this passage, itself a digression, suggests. As a "belated historian," however, she focuses on the intersection of a few human lives at a particular time and place in her country's history. She frequently likened herself not only to a historian but to a scientist who, with a microscope, observes and analyzes the tangled web of character and circumstance that determines human history. As both comparisons imply, Eliot strives to present her fiction as a mirror that reflects without distortion our experience of life. But her insistence on art's transparency is often troubled both by her conscious-ness of its fictions and by her sense of the way in which the egoism we all share distorts our perceptions. Hence she portrays this egoism with a combination of acuity and compassion. It is this distinctive compounding of realism and sympathy that makes her, according to the French critic Ferdinand Brunetière, a better realist than her famous French contemporary Gustave Flaubert, author of *Madame Bovary* (1857). Often compared with Leo Tolstoy, she is, perhaps, the greatest English realist.

Eliot's definition of herself as a historian leads us to expect her novels to offer considerable insight into contemporary issues. The Woman Question, as her essay "Margaret Fuller and Mary Wollstonecraft" suggests, held particular interest for her. She typically chooses for her heroine a young woman, like Maggie Tulliver of *The Mill on the Floss* or Dorothea Brooke of *Middlemarch*, with a powerful imagination and a yearning to be more than her society allows her to be. The prelude to *Middle-march* speaks of the modern-day Saint Teresa, with the ardor and vision to found a religious order, caught at a historical moment that gives no outlet for her ambition. In her portrayal of the frustrations and yearnings of such a heroine, Eliot seems sympathetic to a feminist point of view. Yet her stress on the values of loyalty to one's past; of adherence to duty, despite personal desire; and of what William Wordsworth calls "little, nameless, unremembered acts of kindness and of love" suggests that her attitude toward the Woman Question is complex.

George Eliot wrote, "My function is that of the *aesthetic* not the doctrinal teacher." The largeness of vision through which Eliot enters into the consciousness of all her characters makes the perspective of her novels on many issues a complex one, for it is finally issues as they are refracted through the lens of human character that interest her.

Margaret Fuller and Mary Wollstonecraft[1]

The dearth of new books just now gives us time to recur to less recent ones which we have hitherto noticed but slightly; and among these we choose the late edition of Margaret Fuller's *Woman in the Nineteenth Century*, because we think it has been unduly thrust into the background by less comprehensive and candid productions on the same subject. Notwithstanding certain defects of taste and a sort of vague spiritualism and grandiloquence

1. Published in *The Leader* in 1855, this essay is a retrospective book review of two important femi-nist publications—*A Vindication of the Rights of Woman* (1792), by Mary Wollstonecraft (1759–1797), and *Woman in the Nineteenth Century* (1855; published originally as *The Great Lawsuit*, 1843) by Margaret Fuller (1810–1850), an Amer-ican essayist and editor whom Eliot warmly admired.

As Barbara Hardy notes, despite "her generous sympathy with Victorian feminism," George Eliot "played no active part in the movement." Eliot seems to have shared the view of women's relation to men expressed by the Prince in Alfred, Lord Tennyson's *The Princess* (1847), whose speeches

she cites in this essay. As she herself wrote in 1854 in another essay, "Women in France":

> Women became superior in France by being admitted to a common fund of ideas, to com-mon objects of interest with men; and this must ever be the essential condition at once of true womanly culture and of true social well-being. . . . Let the whole field of reality be laid open to woman as well as to man, and then that which is peculiar in the mental modifica-tion, instead of being, as it is now, a source of discord and repulsion between the sexes, will be found to be a necessary complement to the truth and beauty of life.

which belong to all but the very best American writers, the book is a valuable one; it has the enthusiasm of a noble and sympathetic nature, with the moderation and breadth and large allowance of a vigorous and cultivated understanding. There is no exaggeration of woman's moral excellence or intellectual capabilities; no injudicious insistence on her fitness for this or that function hitherto engrossed by men; but a calm plea for the removal of unjust laws and artificial restrictions, so that the possibilities of her nature may have room for full development, a wisely stated demand to disencumber her of the

> Parasitic forms
> That seem to keep her up, but drag her down—
> And leave her field to burgeon and to bloom
> From all within her, make herself her own
> To give or keep, to live and learn and be
> All that not harms distinctive womanhood.[2]

It is interesting to compare this essay of Margaret Fuller's published in its earliest form in 1843,[3] with a work on the position of woman, written between sixty and seventy years ago—we mean Mary Wollstonecraft's *Rights of Woman*. The latter work was not continued beyond the first volume; but so far as this carries the subject, the comparison, at least in relation to strong sense and loftiness of moral tone, is not at all disadvantageous to the woman of the last century. There is in some quarters a vague prejudice against the *Rights of Woman* as in some way or other a reprehensible book, but readers who go to it with this impression will be surprised to find it eminently serious, severely moral, and withal rather heavy—the true reason, perhaps, that no edition has been published since 1796, and that it is now rather scarce. There are several points of resemblance, as well as of striking difference, between the two books. A strong understanding is present in both; but Margaret Fuller's mind was like some regions of her own American continent, where you are constantly stepping from the sunny "clearings" into the mysterious twilight of the tangled forest—she often passes in one breath from forcible reasoning to dreamy vagueness; moreover, her unusually varied culture gives her great command of illustration. Mary Wollstonecraft, on the other hand, is nothing if not rational; she has no erudition, and her grave pages are lit up by no ray of fancy. In both writers we discern, under the brave bearing of a strong and truthful nature, the beating of a loving woman's heart, which teaches them not to undervalue the smallest offices of domestic care or kindliness. But Margaret Fuller, with all her passionate sensibility, is more of the literary woman, who would not have been satisfied without intellectual production; Mary Wollstonecraft, we imagine, wrote not at all for writing's sake, but from the pressure of other motives. So far as the difference of date allows, there is a striking coincidence in their trains of thought; indeed, every important idea in the *Rights of Woman,* except the combination of home education with a common day-school for boys and girls, reappears in Margaret Fuller's essay.

2. Tennyson's *The Princess* 7.253–58. As noted by Thomas Pinney, the quotation, slightly inaccurate, is from the unrevised 1847 text of the poem. See the passage containing these lines ["The woman's cause is man's"], p. 170.
3. I.e., the original version published in *The Dial;* it was revised and expanded in 1855.

One point on which they both write forcibly is the fact that, while men have a horror of such faculty or culture in the other sex as tends to place it on a level with their own, they are really in a state of subjection to ignorant and feeble-minded women. Margaret Fuller says:

> Wherever man is sufficiently raised above extreme poverty or brutal stupidity, to care for the comforts of the fireside, or the bloom and ornament of life, woman has always power enough, if she chooses to exert it, and is usually disposed to do so, in proportion to her ignorance and childish vanity. Unacquainted with the importance of life and its purposes, trained to a selfish coquetry and love of petty power, she does not look beyond the pleasure of making herself felt at the moment, and governments are shaken and commerce broken up to gratify the pique of a female favorite. The English shopkeeper's wife does not vote, but it is for her interest that the politician canvasses by the coarsest flattery.

Again:

> All wives, bad or good, loved or unloved, inevitably influence their husbands from the power their position not merely gives, but necessitates of coloring evidence and infusing feelings in hours when the— patient, shall I call him?—is off his guard.

Hear now what Mary Wollstonecraft says on the same subject:

> Women have been allowed to remain in ignorance and slavish dependence many, very many years, and still we hear of nothing but their fondness of pleasure and sway, their preference of rakes and soldiers, their childish attachment to toys, and the vanity that makes them value accomplishments more than virtues. History brings forward a fearful catalogue of the crimes which their cunning has produced, when the weak slaves have had sufficient address to overreach their masters. . . . When, therefore, I call women slaves, I mean in a political and civil sense; for indirectly they obtain too much power, and are debased by their exertions to obtain illicit sway. . . . The libertinism, and even the virtues of superior men, will always give women of some description great power over them; and these weak women, under the influence of childish passions and selfish vanity, *will throw a false light over the objects which the very men view with their eyes who ought to enlighten their judgment.* Men of fancy, and those sanguine characters who mostly hold the helm of human affairs in general, relax in the society of women; and surely I need not cite to the most superficial reader of history the numerous examples of vice and oppression which the private intrigues of female favorites have produced; not to dwell on the mischief that naturally arises from the blundering interposition of well-meaning folly. *For in the transactions of business it is much better to have to deal with a knave than a fool, because a knave adheres to some plan, and any plan of reason may be seen through sooner than a sudden flight of folly.* The power which vile and foolish women have had over wise men who possessed sensibility is notorious.

There is a notion commonly entertained among men that an instructed woman, capable of having opinions, is likely to prove an unpracticable yokefellow, always pulling one way when her husband wants to go the other, oracular in tone, and prone to give curtain lectures[4] on metaphysics. But surely, so far as obstinacy is concerned, your unreasoning animal is the most unmanageable of creatures, where you are not allowed to settle the question by a cudgel, a whip and bridle, or even a string to the leg. For our own parts, we see no consistent or commodious medium between the old plan of corporal discipline and that thorough education of women which will make them rational beings in the highest sense of the word. Wherever weakness is not harshly controlled it must *govern*, as you may see when a strong man holds a little child by the hand, how he is pulled hither and thither, and wearied in his walk by his submission to the whims and feeble movements of his companion. A really cultured woman, like a really cultured man, will be ready to yield in trifles. So far as we see, there is no indissoluble connection between infirmity of logic and infirmity of will, and a woman quite innocent of an opinion in philosophy, is as likely as not to have an indomitable opinion about the kitchen. As to airs of superiority, no woman ever had them in consequence of true culture, but only because her culture was shallow or unreal, only as a result of what Mrs. Malaprop well calls "the ineffectual qualities in a woman"[5]—mere acquisitions carried about, and not knowledge thoroughly assimilated so as to enter into the growth of the character.

To return to Margaret Fuller, some of the best things she says are on the folly of absolute definitions of woman's nature and absolute demarcations of woman's mission. "Nature," she says, "seems to delight in varying the arrangements, as if to show that she will be fettered by no rule; and we must admit the same varieties that she admits." Again: "If nature is never bound down, nor the voice of inspiration stifled, that is enough. We are pleased that women should write and speak, if they feel need of it, from having something to tell; but silence for ages would be no misfortune, if that silence be from divine command, and not from man's tradition." And here is a passage, the beginning of which has been often quoted:

> If you ask me what offices they [women] may fill, I reply—any. I do not care what case you put; let them be sea-captains if you will. I do not doubt there are women well fitted for such an office, and, if so, I should be as glad as to welcome the Maid of Saragossa, or the Maid of Missolonghi, or the Suliote heroine, or Emily Plater.[6] I think women need, especially at this juncture, a much greater range of occupation than they have, to rouse their latent powers. . . . In families that I know, some little girls like to saw wood, others to use carpenter's tools. Where these tastes are indulged, cheerfulness and good-humor are promoted. Where they are forbidden, because "such things are not proper for girls," they grow sul-

---

4. Douglas Jerrold (1803–1857) wrote comic sketches of a wife who delivers nightly lectures to her husband from behind their bed curtains, *Mrs. Caudle's Curtain Lectures* (1846).
5. See *The Rivals* (1775), 3.2 by Richard Brinsley Sheridan (1751–1816). In response to compliments about her "intellectual accomplishments," Mrs. Malaprop—famed for her mistaken use of words—exclaims: "Ah! few gentlemen, nowadays, know how to value the ineffectual qualities in a woman!"
6. A Polish patriot who became a captain in command of a company in the insurgent army fighting the Russians in 1831. "Maid of Saragossa": Maria Agustin, who fought against the French at the siege of Saragossa, in Spain, in 1808 (see Byron, *Childe Harold's Pilgrimage*, 1812, 1.54–56). "Maid of Missolonghi": an unidentified Greek, who must have made some heroic exploit during the Turkish sieges of that town in 1822 or 1826. "The Suliote heroine": probably Moscha, who led a band of three hundred women to rout the Turks during the siege of Souli, in Albania, in 1803.

len and mischievous. Fourier had observed these wants of women, as no one can fail to do who watches the desires of little girls, or knows the *ennui* that haunts grown women, except where they make to themselves a serene little world by art of some kind. He, therefore, in proposing a great variety of employments, in manufactures or the care of plants and animals, allows for one-third of women as likely to have a taste for masculine pursuits, one-third of men for feminine.[7] . . . I have no doubt, however, that a large proportion of women would give themselves to the same employments as now, because there are circumstances that must lead them. Mothers will delight to make the nest soft and warm. Nature would take care of that; no need to clip the wings of any bird that wants to soar and sing, or finds in itself the strength of pinion for a migratory flight unusual to its kind. The difference would be that *all* need not be constrained to employments for which *some* are unfit.

Apropos of the same subject, we find Mary Wollstonecraft offering a suggestion which the women of the United States have already begun to carry out. She says:

> Women, in particular, all want to be ladies, which is simply to have nothing to do, but listlessly to go they scarcely care where, for they cannot tell what. But what have women to do in society? I may be asked, but to loiter with easy grace; surely you would not condemn them all to suckle fools and chronicle small beer.[8] No. *Women might certainly study the art of healing, and be physicians as well as nurses. . . .* Business of various kinds they might likewise pursue, if they were educated in a more orderly manner. . . . Women would not then marry for a support, as men accept of places under government, and neglect the implied duties.

Men pay a heavy price for their reluctance to encourage self-help and independent resources in women. The precious meridian years of many a man of genius have to be spent in the toil of routine, that an "establishment" may be kept up for a woman who can understand none of his secret yearnings,[9] who is fit for nothing but to sit in her drawing-room like a doll-Madonna in her shrine. No matter. Anything is more endurable than to change our established formulae about women, or to run the risk of looking up to our wives instead of looking down on them. *Sit divus, dummodo non sit vivus* (let him be a god, provided he be not living),[1] said the Roman magnates of Romulus;[2] and so men say of women, let them be idols, useless absorbents of previous things, provided we are not obliged to admit them to be strictly fellow-beings, to be treated, one and all, with justice and sober reverence.

On one side we hear that woman's position can never be improved until women themselves are better; and, on the other, that women can never become better until their position is improved—until the laws are made more just, and a wider field opened to feminine activity. But we constantly

---

7. Charles Fourier (1772–1837), in his Utopian treatise *The New Industrial World* (1829–30), develops these theories in his discussion of "the Little Hordes."

8. Iago on the role of women; Shakespeare's *Othello* 2.1.162.

9. Cf. Eliot's fictional representation of such a situation in her account of Dr. Lydgate's married life in *Middlemarch* (1871–72).

1. Cf. *Historia Augusta* (ca. 4th century C.E.), *Life of Geta* 2, in which the same cynical comment is made on a proposal to have a man deified.

2. The legendary founder of Rome; after his death he was worshipped by the Romans as a god.

hear the same difficulty stated about the human race in general. There is a perpetual action and reaction between individuals and institutions; we must try and mend both by little and little—the only way in which human things can be mended. Unfortunately, many over-zealous champions of women assert their actual equality with men—nay, even their moral superiority to men—as a ground for their release from oppressive laws and restrictions. They lose strength immensely by this false position. If it were true, then there would be a case in which slavery and ignorance nourished virtue, and so far we should have an argument for the continuance of bondage. But we want freedom and culture for woman, because subjection and ignorance have debased her, and with her, Man; for—

> If she be small, slight-natured, miserable,
> How shall men grow?[3]

Both Margaret Fuller and Mary Wollstonecraft have too much sagacity to fall into this sentimental exaggeration. Their ardent hopes of what women may become do not prevent them from seeing and painting women as they are. On the relative moral excellence of men and women Mary Wollstonecraft speaks with the most decision:

> Women are supposed to possess more sensibility, and even humanity, than men, and their strong attachments and instantaneous emotions of compassion are given as proofs; but the clinging affection of ignorance has seldom anything noble in it, and may mostly be resolved into selfishness, as well as the affection of children and brutes. I have known many weak women whose sensibility was entirely engrossed by their husbands; and as for their humanity, it was very faint indeed, or rather it was only a transient emotion of compassion. Humanity does not consist "in a squeamish ear," says an eminent orator.[4] "It belongs to the mind as well as to the nerves." But this kind of exclusive affection, though it degrades the individual, should not be brought forward as a proof of the inferiority of the sex, because it is the natural consequence of confined views; for even women of superior sense, having their attention turned to little employments and private plans, rarely rise to heroism, unless when spurred on by love! and love, as an heroic passion, like genius, appears but once in an age. I therefore agree with the moralist who asserts "that women have seldom so much generosity as men"; and that their narrow affections, to which justice and humanity are often sacrificed, render the sex apparently inferior, especially as they are commonly inspired by men; but I contend that the heart would expand as the understanding gained strength, if women were not depressed[5] from their cradles.

We had marked several other passages of Margaret Fuller's for extract, but as we do not aim at an exhaustive treatment of our subject, and are only touching a few of its points, we have, perhaps, already claimed as much of the reader's attention as he will be willing to give to such desultory material.

1855

3. Tennyson's *The Princess* 7.249–50.
4. British statesman Charles James Fox (1749–1806). See Feu, *Memoirs of the Public Life of the Late Right Honourable Charles James Fox*, 1808.
5. Repressed, kept down.

From Silly Novels by Lady Novelists[1]

Silly Novels by Lady Novelists are a genus with many species, determined by the particular quality of silliness that predominates in them—the frothy, the prosy, the pious, or the pedantic. But it is a mixture of all these—a composite order of feminine fatuity, that produces the largest class of such novels, which we shall distinguish as the *mind-and-millinery* species. The heroine is usually an heiress, probably a peeress in her own right, with perhaps a vicious baronet, an amiable duke, and an irresistible younger son of a marquis as lovers in the foreground, a clergyman and a poet sighing for her in the middle distance, and a crowd of undefined adorers dimly indicated beyond. Her eyes and her wit are both dazzling; her nose and her morals are alike free from any tendency to irregularity; she has a superb *contralto* and a superb intellect; she is perfectly well-dressed and perfectly religious; she dances like a sylph, and reads the Bible in the original tongues. Or it may be that the heroine is not an heiress—that rank and wealth are the only things in which she is deficient; but she infallibly gets into high society, she has the triumph of refusing many matches and securing the best, and she wears some family jewels or other as a sort of crown of righteousness at the end. Rakish men either bite their lips in impotent confusion at her repartees, or are touched to penitence by her reproofs, which, on appropriate occasions, rise to a lofty strain of rhetoric; indeed, there is a general propensity in her to make speeches, and to rhapsodize at some length when she retires to her bedroom. In her recorded conversations she is amazingly eloquent, and in her unrecorded conversations, amazingly witty. She is understood to have a depth of insight that looks through and through the shallow theories of philosophers, and her superior instincts are a sort of dial by which men have only to set their clocks and watches, and all will go well. The men play a very subordinate part by her side. You are consoled now and then by a hint that they have affairs, which keeps you in mind that the working-day business of the world is somehow being carried on, but ostensibly the final cause of their existence is that they may accompany the heroine on her "starring" expedition through life. They see her at a ball, and are dazzled; at a flower-show, and they are fascinated; on a riding excursion, and they are witched[2] by her noble horsemanship; at church, and they are awed by the sweet solemnity of her demeanour. She is the ideal woman in feelings, faculties, and flounces. For all this, she as often as not marries the wrong person to begin with, and she suffers terribly from the plots and intrigues of the vicious baronet; but even death has a soft place in his heart for such a paragon, and remedies all mistakes for her just at the right moment. The vicious baronet is sure to be killed in a duel, and the tedious husband dies in his bed requesting his wife, as a particular favour to him, to marry the man she loves best, and having already dispatched a note to the lover informing him of the comfortable arrangement. Before matters arrive at this desirable issue our feelings are tried by seeing the noble, lovely, and gifted heroine pass through many *mauvais*[3] moments, but we have the

1. Published anonymously in the *Westminster Review*, this review essay, satirizing a number of contemporary novels, provides a good indication of Eliot's ideas about fiction at the time she was beginning her first story, "The Sad Fortunes of the Rev. Amos Barton."
2. Bewitched.
3. Bad (French).

satisfaction of knowing that her sorrows are wept into embroidered pocket-handkerchiefs, that her fainting form reclines on the very best upholstery, and that whatever vicissitudes she may undergo, from being dashed out of her carriage to having her head shaved in a fever, she comes out of them all with a complexion more blooming and locks more redundant[4] than ever.

We may remark, by the way, that we have been relieved from a serious scruple by discovering that silly novels by lady novelists rarely introduce us into any other than very lofty and fashionable society. We had imagined that destitute women turned novelists, as they turned governesses, because they had no other "lady-like" means of getting their bread. On this supposition, vacillating syntax and improbable incident had a certain pathos for us, like the extremely supererogatory pincushions and ill-devised nightcaps that are offered for sale by a blind man. We felt the commodity to be a nuisance, but we were glad to think that the money went to relieve the necessitous, and we pictured to ourselves lonely women struggling for a maintenance, or wives and daughters devoting themselves to the production of "copy" out of pure heroism,—perhaps to pay their husband's debts, or to purchase luxuries for a sick father. Under these impressions we shrank from criticising a lady's novel: her English might be faulty, but, we said to ourselves, her motives are irreproachable; her imagination may be uninventive, but her patience is untiring. Empty writing was excused by an empty stomach, and twaddle was consecrated by tears. But no! This theory of ours, like many other pretty theories, has had to give way before observation. Women's silly novels, we are now convinced, are written under totally different circumstances. The fair writers have evidently never talked to a tradesman except from a carriage window; they have no notion of the working-classes except as "dependents;" they think five hundred a-year[5] a miserable pittance; Belgravia[6] and "baronial halls" are their primary truths; and they have no idea of feeling interest in any man who is not at least a great landed proprietor, if not a prime minister. It is clear that they write in elegant boudoirs, with violet-colored ink and a ruby pen; that they must be entirely indifferent to publishers' accounts, and inexperienced in every form of poverty except poverty of brains. It is true that we are constantly struck with the want of verisimilitude in their representations of the high society in which they seem to live; but then they betray no closer acquaintance with any other form of life. If their peers and peeresses are improbable, their literary men, tradespeople, and cottagers are impossible; and their intellect seems to have the peculiar impartiality of reproducing both what they *have* seen and heard, and what they have *not* seen and heard, with equal unfaithfulness.

* * *

Writers of the mind-and-millinery school are remarkably unanimous in their choice of diction. In their novels, there is usually a lady or gentleman who is more or less of a upas tree:[7] the lover has a manly breast; minds are redolent of various things; hearts are hollow; events are utilized; friends are consigned

---

4. Abundant.
5. At this date an annual income of £500 would support a modest middle-class household with one or two servants.

6. A wealthy district of London.
7. A Javanese tree from which an arrow poison is derived; here a figurative cliché meaning "a poisonous influence."

to the tomb; infancy is an engaging period; the sun is a luminary that goes to his western couch, or gathers the rain-drops into his refulgent bosom; life is a melancholy boon; Albion and Scotia[8] are conversational epithets. There is a striking resemblance, too, in the character of their moral comments, such, for instance, as that "It is a fact, no less true than melancholy, that all people, more or less, richer or poorer, are swayed by bad example;" that "Books, however trivial, contain some subjects from which useful information may be drawn;" that "Vice can too often borrow the language of virtue;" that "Merit and nobility of nature must exist, to be accepted, for clamour and pretension cannot impose upon those too well read in human nature to be easily deceived;" and that, "In order to forgive, we must have been injured." There is, doubtless, a class of readers to whom these remarks appear peculiarly pointed and pungent; for we often find them doubly and trebly scored with the pencil, and delicate hands giving in their determined adhesion to these hardy novelties by a distinct *très vrai*,[9] emphasized by many notes of exclamation. The colloquial style of these novels is often marked by much ingenious inversion, and a careful avoidance of such cheap phraseology as can be heard every day. Angry young gentlemen exclaim—"'Tis ever thus, methinks;" and in the half-hour before dinner a young lady informs her next neighbour that the first day she read Shakspeare she "stole away into the park, and beneath the shadow of the greenwood tree, devoured with rapture the inspired page of the great magician." But the most remarkable efforts of the mind-and-millinery writers lie in their philosophic reflections. The authoress of "Laura Gay,"[1] for example, having married her hero and heroine, improves the event by observing that "if those sceptics, whose eyes have so long gazed on matter that they can no longer see aught else in man, could once enter with heart and soul into such bliss as this, they would come to say that the soul of man and the polypus[2] are not of common origin, or of the same texture." Lady novelists, it appears, can see something else besides matter; they are not limited to phenomena, but can relieve their eyesight by occasional glimpses of the *noumenon*,[3] and are, therefore, naturally better able than any one else to confound sceptics, even of that remarkable, but to us unknown school, which maintains that the soul of man is of the same texture as the polypus.

The most pitiable of all silly novels by lady novelists are what we may call the *oracular* species—novels intended to expound the writer's religious, philosophical, or moral theories. There seems to be a notion abroad among women, rather akin to the superstition that the speech and actions of idiots are inspired, and that the human being most entirely exhausted of common sense is the fittest vehicle of revelation. To judge from their writings, there are certain ladies who think that an amazing ignorance, both of science and of life, is the best possible qualification for forming an opinion on the knottiest moral and speculative questions. Apparently, their recipe for solving all such difficulties is something like this:—Take a woman's head, stuff it with a smattering of philosophy and literature chopped small, and with false notions of society baked hard, let it hang over a desk a few hours every day, and serve up hot in feeble English, when not required. You will rarely meet with a lady

8. Poetic clichés for England and Scotland, respectively.
9. Very true (French).
1. The 1856 novel Eliot has just satirized in the preceding section.
2. Polyp.
3. An object of purely rational, as opposed to sensual, perception (the latter being a *phenomenon*).

novelist of the oracular class who is diffident of her ability to decide on theological questions,—who has any suspicion that she is not capable of discriminating with the nicest accuracy between the good and evil in all church
parties,—who does not see precisely how it is that men have gone wrong
hitherto,—and pity philosophers in general that they have not had the opportunity of consulting her. Great writers, who have modestly contented themselves with putting their experience into fiction, and have thought it quite a
sufficient task to exhibit men and things as they are, she sighs over as deplorably deficient in the application of their powers. "They have solved no great
questions"—and she is ready to remedy their omission by setting before you a
complete theory of life and manual of divinity, in a love story, where ladies
and gentlemen of good family go through genteel vicissitudes, to the utter
confusion of Deists, Puseyites,[4] and ultra-Protestants, and to the perfect
establishment of that particular view of Christianity which either condenses
itself into a sentence of small caps, or explodes into a cluster of stars on the
three hundred and thirtieth page. It is true, the ladies and gentlemen will
probably seem to you remarkably little like any you have had the fortune or
misfortune to meet with, for, as a general rule, the ability of a lady novelist to
describe actual life and her fellow-men, is in inverse proportion to her confident eloquence about God and the other world, and the means by which she
usually chooses to conduct you to true ideas of the invisible is a totally false
picture of the visible.

* * *

The epithet "silly" may seem impertinent, applied to a novel which indicates
so much reading and intellectual activity as "The Enigma;"[5] but we use this
epithet advisedly. If, as the world has long agreed, a very great amount of
instruction will not make a wise man, still less will a very mediocre amount
of instruction make a wise woman. And the most mischievous form of feminine silliness is the literary form, because it tends to confirm the popular
prejudice against the more solid education of women. When men see girls
wasting their time in consultations about bonnets and ball dresses, and in gig-
gling or sentimental love-confidences, or middle-aged women mismanaging
their children, and solacing themselves with acrid gossip, they can hardly help
saying, "For Heaven's sake, let girls be better educated; let them have some
better objects of thought—some more solid occupations." But after a few
hours' conversation with an oracular literary woman, or a few hours' reading
of her books, they are likely enough to say, "After all, when a woman gets some
knowledge, see what use she makes of it! Her knowledge remains acquisition,
instead of passing into culture; instead of being subdued into modesty and
simplicity by a larger acquaintance with thought and fact, she has a feverish
consciousness of her attainments; she keeps a sort of mental pocket-mirror,
and is continually looking in it at her own 'intellectuality;' she spoils the taste
of one's muffin by questions of metaphysics; 'puts down' men at a dinner table
with her superior information; and seizes the opportunity of a *soirée* to cate-
chise us on the vital question of the relation between mind and matter. And

---

4. Protestants who believed in the importance of
liturgical sacraments (following Edward Pusey,
1800–1882). "Deists": Protestants who believed
in a personal God who created the universe but

who was completely beyond human experience.
5. The 1856 novel Eliot has just satirized in the
preceding section.

then, look at her writings! She mistakes vagueness for depth, bombast for eloquence, and affectation for originality; she struts on one page, rolls her eyes on another, grimaces in a third, and is hysterical in a fourth. She may have read many writings of great men, and a few writings of great women; but she is as unable to discern the difference between her own style and theirs as a Yorkshireman is to discern the difference between his own English and a Londoner's: rhodomontade[6] is the native accent of her intellect. No—the average nature of women is too shallow and feeble a soil to bear much tillage; it is only fit for the very lightest crops."

It is true that the men who come to such a decision on such very superficial and imperfect observation may not be among the wisest in the world; but we have not now to contest their opinion—we are only pointing out how it is unconsciously encouraged by many women who have volunteered themselves as representatives of the feminine intellect. We do not believe that a man was ever strengthened in such an opinion by associating with a woman of true culture, whose mind had absorbed her knowledge instead of being absorbed by it. A really cultured woman, like a really cultured man, is all the simpler and the less obtrusive for her knowledge; it has made her see herself and her opinions in something like just proportions; she does not make it a pedestal from which she flatters herself that she commands a complete view of men and things, but makes it a point of observation from which to form a right estimate of herself. She neither spouts poetry nor quotes Cicero[7] on slight provocation; not because she thinks that a sacrifice must be made to the prejudices of men, but because that mode of exhibiting her memory and Latinity does not present itself to her as edifying or graceful. She does not write books to confound philosophers, perhaps because she is able to write books that delight them. In conversation she is the least formidable of women, because she understands you, without wanting to make you aware that you *can't* understand her. She does not give you information, which is the raw material of culture,—she gives you sympathy, which is its subtlest essence.

A more numerous class of silly novels than the oracular, (which are generally inspired by some form of High Church, or transcendental Christianity,) is what we may call the *white neck-cloth* species, which represent the tone of thought and feeling in the Evangelical party. This species is a kind of genteel tract on a large scale, intended as a sort of medicinal sweetmeat for Low Church young ladies; an Evangelical substitute for the fashionable novel, as the May Meetings[8] are a substitute for the Opera. Even Quaker children, one would think, can hardly have been denied the indulgence of a doll; but it must be a doll dressed in a drab gown and a coal-scuttle bonnet—not a worldly doll, in gauze and spangles. And there are no young ladies, we imagine,—unless they belong to the Church of the United Brethren, in which people are married without any love-making[9]—who can dispense with love stories. Thus, for Evangelical young ladies there are Evangelical love stories, in which the vicissitudes of the tender passion are sanctified by saving views of Regeneration and the Atonement. These novels differ from

6. Inflated diction. It is assumed a Yorkshireman cannot discern the difference between his northern dialect and the speech of a Londoner.
7. Roman statesman and orator (106–43 B.C.E.),

and a staple of Latin instruction for centuries.
8. The Church of England's Missionary Society's annual spring meetings.
9. Courtship.

the oracular ones, as a Low Churchwoman often differs from a High Church-woman: they are a little less supercilious, and a great deal more ignorant, a little less correct in their syntax, and a great deal more vulgar.[1]

The Orlando[2] of Evangelical literature is the young curate, looked at from the point of view of the middle class, where cambric bands are under-stood to have as thrilling an effect on the hearts of young ladies as epau-lettes[3] have in the classes above and below it. In the ordinary type of these novels, the hero is almost sure to be a young curate, frowned upon, per-haps, by worldly mammas, but carrying captive the hearts of their daugh-ters, who can "never forget *that* sermon;" tender glances are seized from the pulpit stairs instead of the opera-box; *tête-à-têtes* are seasoned with quota-tions from Scripture, instead of quotations from the poets; and questions as to the state of the heroine's affections are mingled with anxieties as to the state of her soul. The young curate always has a background of well-dressed and wealthy, if not fashionable society;—for Evangelical silliness is as snob-bish as any other kind of silliness; and the Evangelical lady novelist, while she explains to you the type of the scapegoat on one page, is ambitious on another to represent the manners and conversation of aristocratic people. Her pictures of fashionable society are often curious studies considered as efforts of the Evangelical imagination; but in one particular the novels of the White Neck-cloth School are meritoriously realistic,—their favourite hero, the Evangelical young curate is always rather an insipid personage.

* * *

But, perhaps, the least readable of silly women's novels, are the *modern-antique* species, which unfold to us the domestic life of Jannes and Jambres, the private love affairs of Sennacherib, or the mental struggles and ultimate conversion of Demetrius the silversmith.[4] From most silly novels we can at least extract a laugh; but those of the modern antique school have a ponder-ous, a leaden kind of fatuity, under which we groan. What can be more demonstrative of the inability of literary women to measure their own powers, than their frequent assumption of a task which can only be justified by the rarest concurrence of acquirement with genius? The finest effort to reanimate the past is of course only approximative—is always more or less an infusion of the modern spirit into the ancient form,—

> Was ihr den Geist der Zeiten heisst,
> Das ist im Grund der Herren eigner Geist,
> In dem die Zeiten sich bespiegeln.[5]

Admitting that genius which has familiarized itself with all the relics of an ancient period can sometimes, by the force of its sympathetic divination, restore the missing notes in the "music of humanity," and reconstruct the

---

1. Common.
2. The romantic hero (in allusion to the hero of Shakespeare's *As You Like It*).
3. Attire characteristic of military men, as cam-bric bands (white neck-cloths) are of the clergy.
4. In Acts 19.24–27 the maker of statues of the Roman goddess Diana who denounces Paul for taking business away from him and his fellow craftsmen by converting people to Christianity.

Jannes and Jambres were Egyptian magicians who opposed Moses at Pharaoh's court (2 Timo-thy 3.8). Sennacherib was an Assyrian king who ruled from 705 to 681 B.C.E.
5. What they call the spirit of the age / is at the base the gentlemen's own spirit, / in which the ages are reflected (German; Goethe's *Faust I* [1808], *Nacht*, lines 577–79).

fragments into a whole which will really bring the remote past nearer to us, and interpret it to our duller apprehension,—this form of imaginative power must always be among the very rarest, because it demands as much accurate and minute knowledge as creative vigour. Yet we find ladies constantly choosing to make their mental mediocrity more conspicuous, by clothing it in a masquerade of ancient names; by putting their feeble sentimentality into the mouths of Roman vestals or Egyptian princesses, and attributing their rhetorical arguments to Jewish high-priests and Greek philosophers. * * *

"Be not a baker if your head be made of butter," says a homely proverb, which, being interpreted, may mean, let no woman rush into print who is not prepared for the consequences. We are aware that our remarks are in a very different tone from that of the reviewers who, with a perennial recurrence of precisely similar emotions, only paralleled, we imagine, in the experience of monthly nurses,[6] tell one lady novelist after another that they "hail" her productions "with delight." We are aware that the ladies at whom our criticism is pointed are accustomed to be told, in the choicest phraseology of puffery, that their pictures of life are brilliant, their characters well drawn, their style fascinating, and their sentiments lofty. But if they are inclined to resent our plainness of speech, we ask them to reflect for a moment on the chary praise, and often captious blame, which their panegyrists give to writers whose works are on the way to become classics. No sooner does a woman show that she has genius or effective talent, than she receives the tribute of being moderately praised and severely criticised. By a peculiar thermometric adjustment, when a woman's talent is at zero, journalistic approbation is at the boiling pitch; when she attains mediocrity, it is already at no more than summer heat; and if ever she reaches excellence, critical enthusiasm drops to the freezing point. Harriet Martineau, Currer Bell, and Mrs. Gaskell[7] have been treated as cavalierly as if they had been men. And every critic who forms a high estimate of the share women may ultimately take in literature, will, on principle, abstain from any exceptional indulgence towards the productions of literary women. For it must be plain to every one who looks impartially and extensively into feminine literature, that its greatest deficiencies are due hardly more to the want of intellectual power than to the want of those moral qualities that contribute to literary excellence—patient diligence, a sense of the responsibility involved in publication, and an appreciation of the sacredness of the writer's art. In the majority of women's books you see that kind of facility which springs from the absence of any high standard; that fertility in imbecile combination or feeble imitation which a little self-criticism would check and reduce to barrenness; just as with a total want of musical ear people will sing out of tune, while a degree more melodic sensibility would suffice to render them silent. The foolish vanity of wishing to appear in print, instead of being counterbalanced by any consciousness of the intellectual or moral derogation implied in futile authorship, seems to be encouraged by the extremely false impression that to write *at all* is a proof of superiority in a woman. On this ground, we believe that the average intellect of women

---

6. Women hired to look after mothers and babies in the first month after childbirth.
7. Eliot names three of the foremost British women writers of the 19th century. Martineau

(1802–1876), a prolific author in a range of nonfiction genres. Charlotte Brontë (1816–1855), novelist (first published under the pseudonym Bell). Elizabeth Gaskell (1810–1865), novelist.

is unfairly represented by the mass of feminine literature, and that while the few women who write well are very far above the ordinary intellectual level of their sex, the many women who write ill are very far below it. So that, after all, the severer critics are fulfilling a chivalrous duty in depriving the mere fact of feminine authorship of any false prestige which may give it a delusive attraction, and in recommending women of mediocre faculties—as at least a negative service they can render their sex—to abstain from writing.

The standing apology for women who become writers without any special qualification is, that society shuts them out from other spheres of occupation. Society is a very culpable entity, and has to answer for the manufacture of many unwholesome commodities, from bad pickles to bad poetry. But society, like "matter," and Her Majesty's Government, and other lofty abstractions, has its share of excessive blame as well as excessive praise. Where there is one woman who writes from necessity, we believe there are three women who write from vanity; and, besides, there is something so antiseptic in the mere healthy fact of working for one's bread, that the most trashy and rotten kind of feminine literature is not likely to have been produced under such circumstances. "In all labour there is profit;"[8] but ladies' silly novels, we imagine, are less the result of labour than of busy idleness.

Happily, we are not dependent on argument to prove that Fiction is a department of literature in which women can, after their kind, fully equal men. A cluster of great names, both living and dead, rush to our memories in evidence that women can produce novels not only fine, but among the very finest;—novels, too, that have a precious speciality, lying quite apart from masculine aptitudes and experience. No educational restrictions can shut women out from the materials of fiction, and there is no species of art which is so free from rigid requirements. Like crystalline masses, it may take any form, and yet be beautiful; we have only to pour in the right elements— genuine observation, humour, and passion. But it is precisely this absence of rigid requirement which constitutes the fatal seduction of novel-writing to incompetent women. Ladies are not wont to be very grossly deceived as to their power of playing on the piano; here certain positive difficulties of execution have to be conquered, and incompetence inevitably breaks down. Every art which has its absolute *technique* is, to a certain extent, guarded from the intrusions of mere left-handed imbecility. But in novel-writing there are no barriers for incapacity to stumble against, no external criteria to prevent a writer from mistaking foolish facility for mastery. And so we have again and again the old story of La Fontaine's ass, who puts his nose to the flute, and, finding that he elicits some sound, exclaims, "Moi, aussi, je joue de la flute;"[9]—a fable which we commend, at parting, to the consideration of any feminine reader who is in danger of adding to the number of "silly novels by lady novelists."

1856   1856

---

8. Proverbs 14.23.
9. I also play the flute (French). Jean de La Fontaine (1621–1695), French author of beast fables.

MATTHEW ARNOLD
1822–1888

How is a full and enjoyable life to be lived in a modern industrial society? This was the recurrent topic in the poetry and prose of Matthew Arnold. In his poetry the question itself is raised; in his prose some answers are attempted. "The misapprehensiveness [wrongheadedness] of his age is exactly what a poet is sent to remedy," wrote Robert Browning, and yet it is to Arnold's work, not Browning's, that the statement seems more applicable. In response to rapid and potentially dislocating social changes, Arnold strove to help his contemporaries achieve a richer intellectual and emotional existence.

Matthew Arnold was born in Laleham, a village in the valley of the Thames. At the age of six, Arnold was moved to Rugby School, where his father, Dr. Thomas Arnold, had become headmaster. As a clergyman Dr. Arnold was a leader of the liberal or Broad Church and hence one of the principal opponents of John Henry Newman. As a headmaster he became famous as an educational reformer, a teacher who instilled in his pupils an earnest preoccupation with moral and social issues and also an awareness of the connection between liberal studies and modern life. At Rugby his eldest son, Matthew, was directly exposed to the powerful force of the father's mind and character. The son's attitude toward this force was a mixture of attraction and repulsion. That he was permanently influenced by his father is evident in his poems and in his writings on religion, education, and politics; but like many sons of clergymen, he made a determined effort in his youth to be different. As a student at Oxford he behaved like a dandy. Elegantly and colorfully dressed, alternately languid or merry in manner, he refused to be serious and irritated more solemn undergraduate friends and acquaintances with his irreverent jokes. "His manner displeases, from its seeming foppery," wrote Charlotte Brontë after talking with the young man in later years. "The shade of Dr. Arnold," she added, "seemed to me to frown on his young representative." The son of Dr. Arnold thus appeared to have no connection with Rugby School's standards of earnestness. Even his studies did not seem to occupy him seriously. By a session of cramming, he managed to earn second-class honors in his final examinations, a near disaster that was redeemed by his election to a fellowship at Oriel College.

Arnold's biographers usually dismiss his youthful frivolity of spirit as only a temporary pose or mask, but it permanently colored his prose style, brightening his most serious criticism with geniality and wit. For most readers the jauntiness of his prose is a virtue, though others find it offensive. Anyone suspicious of urbanity and irony would applaud Walt Whitman's sour comment that Arnold is "one of the dudes [dandies, or shallow stylists] of literature." A more appropriate estimate of his manner is provided by Arnold's own description of the French writer Charles-Augustin Sainte-Beuve: "a critic of measure, not exuberant; of the centre, not provincial . . . with gay and amiable temper, his manner as good as his matter—the 'critique souriant' [smiling critic]."

Unlike authors such as Alfred, Lord Tennyson and Thomas Carlyle who committed themselves solely to their literary pursuits, Arnold confined his writing and reading to his spare time. In 1847 he took the post of private secretary to Lord Lansdowne; and in 1851, the year of his marriage, he became an inspector of schools, a demanding and time-consuming position that he held for thirty-five years. Although his work as an inspector may have reduced his output as a writer, it had several advantages. His extensive traveling in England took him to the homes of the more ardently Protestant middle classes, and when he criticized the dullness of middle-class life (as he often did), his scorn was based on intimate knowledge. His position also led to travel on the Continent to study the schools of Europe. As a critic of English education, he was thus able to make helpful comparisons and to draw on a stock of fresh ideas in the same way as in his literary criticism he used his familiarity with French, German, Italian, and classical literatures to talk knowledgeably about the distinctive qualities of English writers. Despite the monotony of much of his work as an inspector, Arnold became convinced of its importance. It contributed to what he regarded as his century's most important need: the development of a satisfactory national system of education.

In 1849 Arnold published *The Strayed Reveler*, his first volume of poetry. Eight years later, as a tribute to his poetic achievement, he was elected to the professorship of poetry at Oxford, a part-time position that he held for ten years. Later, like Charles Dickens and William Makepeace Thackeray before him, Arnold toured America to make money by lecturing. His lectures could leave audiences indifferent, but sometimes they were highly acclaimed: thus the *Washington Post* reported that, following a two-hour address in the U.S. capital, the African American leader Frederick Douglass "moved that a tremendous vote of thanks be tendered to the speaker." A further inducement for his two visits (in 1883 and 1886) was the opportunity of seeing his daughter Lucy, who had married an American. In 1888 Arnold died of a sudden heart attack.

Arnold's career as a writer can be roughly divided into four periods. In the 1850s most of his poems appeared; in the 1860s, literary criticism and social criticism; in the 1870s, his religious and educational writings; and in the 1880s, his second set of essays in literary criticism.

Today Arnold is perhaps better known as a writer of prose than as a poet, although individual poems such as "Dover Beach" (1867) continue to be widely popular. In his own era his decision to spend hardly any time composing poetry after 1860 was considered wrongheaded by some: "Tell Mat not to write any more of those prose things like *Literature and Dogma*," Tennyson wrote in a letter, wishing that Arnold would instead "give us something like his 'Thyrsis,' 'Scholar Gypsy,' or 'Forsaken Merman.'" Others have felt that he made the right move: Arnold's poetry has been criticized, in both the nineteenth and the twentieth centuries, on numerous grounds. Some have disliked its excessive reliance on italics instead of on meter to emphasize the meaning of a line, while others object to the prosy flatness of certain passages or, conversely, to overelaborated similes in others. Yet despite these cavils, many readers find much to cherish and admire. Given Arnold's sophistication as a writer, it is perhaps surprising that his evocations of nature function so memorably in his poetry: rather than simply providing a picturesque backdrop, the setting—seashore or river or mountaintop—draws the poem's meaning together. In this respect, as in many others, Arnold displays a debt to William Wordsworth, whose poetry he greatly admired; but he also draws on his own bond with particular landscapes, especially those associated with his youth and early adulthood. The stanzas of "The Scholar Gypsy" (1853), for instance—suffused in a deep familiarity with the changing patterns of the rural scene, from the "frail-leafed, white anemone" and "dark bluebells drenched with dews" of May to the "scarlet poppies" and "pale pink convolvulus" of August—record with sensuous care the distinct seasons of the English countryside and Arnold's nostalgic memories of the rambles of his Oxford days.

Arnold's own verdict on the qualities of his poetry is interesting. In an 1869 letter to his mother, he writes:

> My poems represent, on the whole, the main movement of mind of the last quarter of a century, and thus they will probably have their day as people become

conscious to themselves of what that movement of mind is, and interested in the literary productions which reflect it. It might be fairly urged that I have less poetical sentiment than Tennyson, and less intellectual vigour and abundance than Browning; yet, because I have perhaps more of a fusion of the two than either of them, and have more regularly applied that fusion to the main line of modern development, I am likely enough to have my turn, as they have had theirs.

The emphasis in the letter on "movement of mind" suggests that Arnold's poetry and prose should be studied together. Such an approach can be fruitful provided that it does not obscure the important difference between Arnold the poet and Arnold the critic. T. S. Eliot once said of his own writings that "in one's prose reflections one may be legitimately occupied with ideals, whereas in the writing of verse, one can deal only with actuality." Arnold's writings offer a nice verification of Eliot's seeming paradox. As a poet he usually records his own experiences, his own feelings of loneliness and isolation as a lover, his longing for a serenity that he cannot find, his melancholy sense of the passing of youth (more than for many men, Arnold's thirtieth birthday was an awe-inspiring landmark after which he felt, he said, "three parts iced over"). Above all he records his despair in a universe in which humanity's role seemed an incongruous as it was later to seem to Thomas Hardy. In a memorable passage of his "Stanzas from the Grande Chartreuse" (1855), he describes himself as "Wandering between two worlds, one dead, / The other powerless to be born." And addressing the representatives of a faith that seems to him dead, he cries: "Take me, cowled forms, and fence me round, / Till I possess my soul again." As a poet, then, like T. S. Eliot and W. H. Auden, Arnold provides a record of a troubled individual in a troubled society. This was "actuality" as he experienced it—an actuality, like Eliot's and Auden's, representative of his era. As a prose writer, a formulator of "ideals," he seeks a different role—to be what Auden calls the "healer" of a diseased society, or as he himself called Goethe, the "Physician of the iron age." And in this difference we have a clue to answering the question of why Arnold virtually abandoned the writing of poetry to move into criticism. One reason was his dissatisfaction with the kind of poetry he was writing.

In one of his fascinating letters to his friend Arthur Hugh Clough in the 1850s (letters that provide the best insight we have into Arnold's mind and tastes), this note of dissatisfaction is struck: "I am glad you like the *Gypsy Scholar*—but what does it *do* for you? Homer *animates*—Shakespeare *animates*—in its poor way I think *Sohrab and Rustum animates*—the *Gypsy Scholar* at best awakens a pleasing melancholy. But this is not what we want." It is evident that early in his career Arnold had evolved a theory of what poetry should do for its readers, a theory based, in part, on his impression of what classical poetry had achieved. To help make life bearable, poetry, in Arnold's view, must bring joy. As he says in the 1853 preface to his *Poems*, it must "inspirit and rejoice the reader"; it must "convey a charm, and infuse delight." Such a demand does not exclude tragic poetry but does exclude works "in which suffering finds no vent in action; in which a continual state of mental distress is prolonged." Of Charlotte Brontë's novel *Villette* (1853) he says witheringly: "The writer's mind contains nothing but hunger, rebellion, and rage . . . No fine writing can hide this thoroughly, and it will be fatal to her in the long run." Judged by such a standard, most nineteenth-century poems, including his own long poem *Empedocles on Etna* (1852), were unsatisfactory. And when Arnold tried to write poems that would meet his own requirements—*Sohrab and Rustum* (1853) or *Balder Dead* (1855)—he felt that something was lacking. By the late 1850s he thus found himself at a dead end. Turning aside to literary criticism enabled him partially to escape the dilemma. In his prose his melancholy and "morbid" personality was subordinated to the resolutely cheerful and purposeful character he had created for himself by an effort of will.

Arnold's two volumes of *Essays in Criticism* (1865, 1888) repeatedly show how authors as different as Marcus Aurelius, Leo Tolstoy, Homer, and Wordsworth provide the virtues he sought in his reading. Among these virtues was plainness of style.

Although he could on occasion recommend the richness of language of such poets as John Keats or Tennyson—their "natural magic," as he called it—Arnold usually preferred literature that was unadorned. And beyond stylistic excellences, the principal virtue he admired as a critic was the quality of "high seriousness." In a world in which the role of formal religion appeared to be shrinking, Arnold increasingly emphasized that the poet must be a serious thinker who could offer guidance to his readers. This belief perhaps caused him to undervalue other qualities in literature: in "The Study of Poetry" (1880), for instance, he displays little appreciation for Chaucer's humor and chooses instead to castigate him for his lack of high seriousness.

In "The Function of Criticism at the Present Time" (1864), Arnold makes clear that he regarded good literary criticism, like literature itself, as a potent force in producing what he conceived as a civilized society. From a close study of this essay one could forecast the third stage of his career: his excursion into the criticism of society that was to culminate in *Culture and Anarchy* (1869) and *Friendship's Garland* (1871).

Arnold's starting point as a critic of society is different from that of Carlyle and John Ruskin. The older prophets attacked the Victorian middle classes on the grounds of their materialism, their selfish indifference to the sufferings of the poor—their immorality, in effect. Arnold argued instead that the "Philistines," as he called them, were not so much wicked as ignorant, narrow-minded, and suffering from the dullness of their private lives. This novel analysis was reinforced by Arnold's conviction that the world of the future, both in England and in America, would be a middle-class world and therefore would be dominated by a class inadequately equipped either to lead or to enjoy civilized living.

To establish this point Arnold employed cajolery, satire, and even quotations from current newspapers with considerable effect. He also used memorable catch phrases (such as "sweetness and light") that sometimes pose an obstacle to understanding the complexities of his position. His view of civilization, for example, was pared down to a four-point formula of the four "powers": conduct, intellect and knowledge, beauty, and social life and manners. Applying this simple formula to a range of civilizations, Arnold had a scale by which to judge the virtues as well as the inadequacies of different countries. When he turned this instrument on his own country, he usually awarded the Victorian middle classes an A in the first category (conduct) but a failing grade in the other three categories. It is not surprising that he also had pronounced opinions on what he viewed as the distinct national characters of different peoples: a sample of this strain in Arnold's writing appears in the extract from his lectures *On the Study of Celtic Literature* (1867) on p. 1372.

Arnold's relentless exposure of middle-class narrow-mindedness in his own country eventually led him into the arena of religious controversy. As a critic of religious institutions he was arguing, in effect, that just as the middle classes did not know how to lead full lives, neither did they know how to read the Bible intelligently or attend church intelligently. Of the Christian religion he remarked that there are two things "that surely must be clear to anybody with eyes in his head. One is, that men cannot do without it; the other that they cannot do with it as it is." His three full-length studies of the Bible, including *Literature and Dogma* (1873), are thus best considered a postscript to his social criticism. The Bible, to Arnold, was a great work of literature like the *Odyssey*, and the Church of England was a great national institution like Parliament. Both Bible and Church must be preserved not because historical Christianity was credible but because both, when properly understood, were agents of what he called "culture"—they contributed to making humanity more civilized.

Culture is perhaps Arnold's most familiar catchword, although what he meant by it has sometimes been misunderstood. He used the term to capture the qualities of an open-minded intelligence (as described in "The Function of Criticism")—a refusal to take things on authority. In this respect Arnold appears close to T. H. Huxley and J. S. Mill. But the word also connotes a full awareness of humanity's past and a capacity to enjoy the best works of art, literature, history, and philosophy that have come down to us from that past. As a way of viewing life in all its aspects, including the social, political, and religious, culture represents for Arnold the most effective cure for the ills of a sick society. It is his principal prescription.

The attempt to define culture brings us to a final aspect of Arnold's career as a critic: his writings on education, in which he sought to make cultural values, as he said, "prevail." Most obviously these writings comprise his reply to Huxley (his admirably reasoned essay "Literature and Science," 1882) and his volumes of official reports written as an inspector of schools. Less obviously, they comprise all his prose. At their core is his belief that good education is *the* crucial need. Arnold was essentially a great teacher. He has the faults of a teacher—a tendency to repeat himself, to lean too hard on formulaic phrases—and he displays something of the lectern manner at times. He also has the great teacher's virtues, in particular the ability to skillfully convey to us the conviction on which all his arguments are based. This conviction is that the humanist tradition of which he is the expositor can enable the individual man or woman to live life more fully and to change the course of society. He believes that a democratic society can thrive only if its citizens become educated in what he saw as the great Western tradition, "the best that is known and thought." These values, which some readers find elitist, make Arnold both timely and controversial. Arnold fought for these values with the gloves on— kid gloves, his opponents used to say—and he provided a lively exhibition of footwork that is a pleasure to observe. Yet the gracefulness of the display should not obscure the fact that he lands hard blows squarely on his opponents.

Although his lifelong attacks on the inadequacies of Puritanism make Arnold one of the most anti-Victorian figures of his age, behind his attacks is a characteristically Victorian assumption: that the Puritan middle classes *can* be changed, that they are, as we would more clumsily say, educable. In 1852, writing to Clough on the subject of equality (a political objective in which he believed by conviction if not by instinct), Arnold observed: "I am more and more convinced that the world tends to become more comfortable for the mass, and more uncomfortable for those of any natural gift or distinction—and it is as well perhaps that it should be so—for hitherto the gifted have astonished and delighted the world, but not trained or inspired or in any real way changed it." Arnold's gifts as a poet and critic enabled him to do both: to delight the world and to change it.

Isolation. To Marguerite[1]

> We were apart; yet, day by day,
> I bade my heart more constant be.
> I bade it keep the world away,
> And grow a home for only thee;
> 5   Nor feared but thy love likewise grew,
> Like mine, each day, more tried, more true.
>
> The fault was grave! I might have known,
> What far too soon, alas! I learned—
> The heart can bind itself alone,

1. Addressed to a woman Arnold is reputed to have met in Switzerland in the 1840s. It has been commonly assumed that she was French or Swiss; but some recent biographies speculate she might have been Mary Claude, a woman Arnold knew in England at this same period who, though English, had connections with Germany and had translated German prose and verse.

10 And faith may oft be unreturned.
Self-swayed our feelings ebb and swell—
Thou lov'st no more—Farewell! Farewell!
Farewell!—and thou, thou lonely heart,[2]
Which never yet without remorse
15 Even for a moment didst depart
From thy remote and spherèd course
To haunt the place where passions reign—
Back to thy solitude again!

Back with the conscious thrill of shame
20 Which Luna felt, that summer night,
Flash through her pure immortal frame,
When she forsook the starry height
To hang over Endymion's sleep
Upon the pine-grown Latmian steep.[3]
25 Yet she, chaste queen, had never proved
How vain a thing is mortal love,
Wandering in Heaven, far removed.
But thou hast long had place to prove°   test
This truth—to prove, and make thine own:
30 "Thou hast been, shalt be, art, alone."

Or, if not quite alone, yet they
Which touch thee are unmating things—
Ocean and clouds and night and day;
Lorn autumns and triumphant springs;
35 And life, and others' joy and pain,
And love, if love, of happier men.

Of happier men—for they, at least,
Have *dreamed* two human hearts might blend
In one, and were through faith released
40 From isolation without end
Prolonged; nor knew, although not less
Alone than thou, their loneliness.

1849   1857

To Marguerite—Continued

Yes! in the sea of life enisled,°   *encircled*
With echoing straits between us thrown,
Dotting the shoreless watery wild,
We mortal millions live *alone*.
5 The islands feel the enclasping flow,
And then their endless bounds they know.

2. Presumably the speaker's heart, not Marguerite's.
3. Luna (or Diana), virgin goddess of the moon,
fell in love with Endymion, a handsome shepherd
whom she discovered asleep on Mount Latmos.

But when the moon their hollows lights,
And they are swept by balms of spring,
And in their glens, on starry nights,
10   The nightingales divinely sing;
And lovely notes, from shore to shore,
Across the sounds and channels pour—

Oh! then a longing like despair
Is to their farthest caverns sent;
15   For surely once, they feel, we were
Parts of a single continent!
Now round us spreads the watery plain—
Oh might our marges° meet again!   *margins, edges*

Who ordered that their longing's fire
20   Should be, as soon as kindled, cooled?
Who renders vain their deep desire?—
A God, a God their severance ruled!
And bade betwixt their shores to be
The unplumbed, salt, estranging sea.

1849   1852

The Buried Life

Light flows our war of mocking words, and yet,
Behold, with tears mine eyes are wet!
I feel a nameless sadness o'er me roll.
Yes, yes, we know that we can jest,
5   We know, we know that we can smile!
But there's a something in this breast,
To which thy light words bring no rest,
And thy gay smiles no anodyne.
Give me thy hand, and hush awhile,
10   And turn those limpid eyes on mine,
And let me read there, love! thy inmost soul.

Alas! is even love too weak
To unlock the heart, and let it speak?
Are even lovers powerless to reveal
15   To one another what indeed they feel?
I knew the mass of men concealed
Their thoughts, for fear that if revealed
They would by other men be met
With blank indifference, or with blame reproved;
20   I knew they lived and moved
Tricked° in disguises, alien to the rest   *dressed up*
Of men, and alien to themselves—and yet
The same heart beats in every human breast!

But we, my love!—doth a like spell benumb
25 Our hearts, our voices?—must we too be dumb?
Ah! well for us, if even we,
Even for a moment, can get free
Our heart, and have our lips unchained;
For that which seals them hath been deep-ordained!

30 Fate, which foresaw
How frivolous a baby man would be—
By what distractions he would be possessed,
How he would pour himself in every strife,
And well-nigh change his own identity—
35 That it might keep from his capricious play
His genuine self, and force him to obey
Even in his own despite his being's law,
Bade through the deep recesses of our breast
The unregarded river of our life
40 Pursue with indiscernible flow its way;
And that we should not see
The buried stream, and seem to be
Eddying at large in blind uncertainty,
Though driving on with it eternally.

45 But often, in the world's most crowded streets,[1]
But often, in the din of strife,
There rises an unspeakable desire
After the knowledge of our buried life;
A thirst to spend our fire and restless force
50 In tracking out our true, original course;
A longing to inquire
Into the mystery of this heart which beats
So wild, so deep in us—to know
Whence our lives come and where they go.
55 And many a man in his own breast then delves,
But deep enough, alas! none ever mines.
And we have been on many thousand lines,
And we have shown, on each, spirit and power;
But hardly have we, for one little hour,
60 Been on our own line, have we been ourselves—
Hardly had skill to utter one of all
The nameless feelings that course through our breast,
But they course on forever unexpressed.
And long we try in vain to speak and act
65 Our hidden self, and what we say and do
Is eloquent, is well—but 'tis not true!
And then we will no more be racked
With inward striving, and demand

---

1. This passage, like many others in Arnold's poetry, illustrates William Wordsworth's effect on his writings. In this instance cf. Wordsworth's "Tintern Abbey (1798), lines 25–27: "But oft, in lonely rooms, and 'mid the din / Of towns and cities, I have owed to them, / In hours of weariness, sensations sweet." Cf. also *The Prelude* (1850) 7.626: "How oft amid those overflowing streets."

Of all the thousand nothings of the hour
70 Their stupefying power;
Ah yes, and they benumb us at our call!
Yet still, from time to time, vague and forlorn,
From the soul's subterranean depth upborne
As from an infinitely distant land,
75 Come airs, and floating echoes, and convey
A melancholy into all our day.[2]

Only—but this is rare—
When a beloved hand is laid in ours,
When, jaded with the rush and glare
80 Of the interminable hours,
Our eyes can in another's eyes read clear,
When our world-deafened ear
Is by the tones of a loved voice caressed—
A bolt is shot back somewhere in our breast,
85 And a lost pulse of feeling stirs again.
The eye sinks inward, and the heart lies plain,
And what we mean, we say, and what we would, we know.
A man becomes aware of his life's flow,
And hears its winding murmur; and he sees
90 The meadows where it glides, the sun, the breeze.

And there arrives a lull in the hot race
Wherein he doth forever chase
That flying and elusive shadow, rest.
An air of coolness plays upon his face,
95 And an unwonted calm pervades his breast.
And then he thinks he knows
The hills where his life rose,
And the sea where it goes.

1852

Memorial Verses[1]

April 1850

Goethe in Weimar sleeps, and Greece,
Long since, saw Byron's struggle cease.
But one such death remained to come;
The last poetic voice is dumb—
5 We stand today by Wordsworth's tomb.

2. Cf. Wordworth's "Ode: Intimations of Immortality" (1807), lines 149–51: "Those shadowy recollections, / Which, be they what they may, / Are yet the fountain light of all our day."
1. This elegy was written shortly after Wordsworth had died in April 1850, at the age of eighty. Arnold had known the poet as a man and deeply admired his writings—as is evident not only in this poem but in his late essay "Wordsworth" (1888). Byron, who died in Greece in 1824, had affected Arnold profoundly in his youth, but later that strenuous "Titanic" (line 14) poetry seemed to him less satisfactory, its value limited by its lack of serenity. He gives his final verdict on Byron in his essay in Essays in Criticism: Second Series (1888). He regarded Goethe, who died in 1832, as a great philosophical poet and the most significant man of letters of the early 19th century.

When Byron's eyes were shut in death,
We bowed our head and held our breath.
He taught us little; but our soul
Had *felt* him like the thunder's roll.
10   With shivering heart the strife we saw
Of passion with eternal law;
And yet with reverential awe
We watched the fount of fiery life
Which served for that Titanic strife.
15   When Goethe's death was told, we said:
Sunk, then, is Europe's sagest head.
Physician of the iron age,
Goethe has done his pilgrimage.
He took the suffering human race,
20   He read each wound, each weakness clear;
And struck his finger on the place,
And said: *Thou ailest here, and here!*
He looked on Europe's dying hour
Of fitful dream and feverish power;
25   His eye plunged down the weltering strife,
The turmoil of expiring life—
He said: *The end is everywhere,*
Art still has truth, take refuge there!
And he was happy, if to know
30   Causes of things, and far below
His feet to see the lurid flow
Of terror, and insane distress,
And headlong fate, be happiness.

And Wordsworth!—Ah, pale ghosts, rejoice!
35   For never has such soothing voice
Been to your shadowy world conveyed,
Since erst,° at morn, some wandering shade   *formerly*
Heard the clear song of Orpheus[2] come
Through Hades, and the mournful gloom.
40   Wordsworth has gone from us—and ye,
Ah, may ye feel his voice as we!
He too upon a wintry clime
Had fallen—on this iron time
Of doubts, disputes, distractions, fears.
45   He found us when the age had bound
Our souls in its benumbing round;
He spoke, and loosed our heart in tears.
He laid us as we lay at birth
On the cool flowery lap of earth,
50   Smiles broke from us and we had ease;
The hills were round us, and the breeze
Went o'er the sunlit fields again;
Our foreheads felt the wind and rain.

---

2. By means of his beautiful music, the legendary Greek singer Orpheus won his way through Hades as he searched for his dead wife, Eurydice.

Our youth returned; for there was shed
55 On spirits that had long been dead,
Spirits dried up and closely furled,
The freshness of the early world.

Ah! since dark days still bring to light
Man's prudence and man's fiery might,
60 Time may restore us in his course
Goethe's sage mind and Byron's force;
But where will Europe's latter hour
Again find Wordsworth's healing power?
Others will teach us how to dare,
65 And against fear our breast to steel;
Others will strengthen us to bear—
But who, ah! who, will make us feel?
The cloud of mortal destiny,
Others will front it fearlessly—
70 But who, like him, will put it by?

Keep fresh the grass upon his grave
O Rotha,[3] with thy living wave!
Sing him thy best! for few or none
Hears thy voice right, now he is gone.

1850   1850

Lines Written in Kensington Gardens[1]

In this lone, open glade I lie,
Screened by deep boughs on either hand;
And at its end, to stay the eye,
Those black-crowned, red-boled pine trees stand!

5   Birds here make song, each bird has his,
Across the girdling city's hum.
How green under the boughs it is!
How thick the tremulous sheep-cries come![2]

Sometimes a child will cross the glade
10   To take his nurse his broken toy;
Sometimes a thrush flit overhead
Deep in her unknown day's employ.

Here at my feet what wonders pass,
What endless, active life is here!
15   What blowing daisies, fragrant grass!
An air-stirred forest, fresh and clear.

3. A river near Wordsworth's burial place.   2. Sheep sometimes grazed in London parks.
1. A park in the heart of London.

Scarce fresher is the mountain sod
Where the tired angler lies, stretched out,
And, eased of basket and of rod,
20   Counts his day's spoil, the spotted trout.

In the huge world, which roars hard° by,   *close*
Be others happy if they can!
But in my helpless cradle I
Was breathed on by the rural Pan.[3]

25   I, on men's impious uproar hurled,
Think often, as I hear them rave,
That peace has left the upper world
And now keeps only in the grave.

Yet here is peace forever new!
30   When I who watch them am away,
Still all things in this glade go through
The changes of their quiet day.

Then to their happy rest they pass!
The flowers upclose, the birds are fed,
35   The night comes down upon the grass,
The child sleeps warmly in his bed.

Calm soul of all things! make it mine
To feel, amid the city's jar,
That there abides a peace of thine,
40   Man did not make, and cannot mar.

The will to neither strive nor cry,
The power to feel with others give!
Calm, calm me more! nor let me die
Before I have begun to live.

                                       1852

The Scholar Gypsy

The story of a seventeenth-century student who left Oxford and joined a band of gypsies had made a strong impression on Arnold. In the poem he wistfully imagines that the spirit of this scholar is still to be encountered in the Cumner countryside near Oxford, having achieved immortality by a serene pursuit of the secret of human existence. Like Keats's nightingale, the scholar has escaped "the weariness, the fever, and the fret" of modern life.

At the outset the poet addresses a shepherd who has been helping him in his search for traces of the scholar. The shepherd is addressed as *you*. After line 61, with the shift to *thou* and *thy*, the person addressed is the scholar, and the poet thereafter sometimes uses the pronoun *we* to indicate he is speaking for all humanity of later generations.

---

3. In Greek mythology the god of woods and pastures.

About the setting Arnold wrote to his brother Tom on May 15, 1857: "You alone of my brothers are associated with that life at Oxford, the *freest* and most delightful part, perhaps, of my life, when with you and Clough and Walrond I shook off all the bonds and formalities of the place, and enjoyed the spring of life and that unforgotten Oxfordshire and Berkshire country. Do you remember a poem of mine called 'The Scholar Gipsy'? It was meant to fix the remembrance of those delightful wanderings of ours in the Cumner Hills."

The passage from Joseph Glanvill's *Vanity of Dogmatizing* (1661) that inspired the poem was included by Arnold as a note:

> There was very lately a lad in the University of Oxford, who was by his poverty forced to leave his studies there; and at last to join himself to a company of vagabond gypsies. Among these extravagant people, by the insinuating subtilty of his carriage, he quickly got so much of their love and esteem as that they discovered to him their mystery. After he had been a pretty while exercised in the trade, there chanced to ride by a couple of scholars, who had formerly been of his acquaintance. They quickly spied out their old friend among the gypsies; and he gave them an account of the necessity which drove him to that kind of life, and told them that the people he went with were not such imposters as they were taken for, but that they had a traditional kind of learning among them, and could do wonders by the power of imagination, their fancy binding that of others: that himself had learned much of their art, and when he had compassed the whole secret, he intended, he said, to leave their company, and give the world an account of what he had learned.

The Scholar Gypsy

<blockquote>

Go, for they call you, shepherd, from the hill;
  Go, shepherd, and untie the wattled cotes![1]
    No longer leave thy wistful flock unfed,
    Nor let thy bawling fellows rack their throats,
5   Nor the cropped herbage shoot another head.
      But when the fields are still,
    And the tired men and dogs all gone to rest,
      And only the white sheep are sometimes seen
      Cross and recross the strips of moon-blanched green,
10 Come, shepherd, and again begin the quest!

Here, where the reaper was at work of late—
  In this high field's dark corner, where he leaves
    His coat, his basket, and his earthen cruse,[2]
    And in the sun all morning binds the sheaves,
15   Then here, at noon, comes back his stores to use—
      Here will I sit and wait,
    While to my ear from uplands far away
      The bleating of the folded° flocks is borne,   *penned up*
      With distant cries of reapers in the corn°—   *grain or wheat*
20 All the live murmur of a summer's day.

</blockquote>

---

1. Sheepfolds woven from sticks.   2. Pot or jug for carrying his drink.

Screened is this nook o'er the high, half-reaped field,
And here till sundown, shepherd! will I be.
Through the thick corn the scarlet poppies peep,
And round green roots and yellowing stalks I see
25   Pale pink convolvulus in tendrils creep;
          And air-swept lindens yield
Their scent, and rustle down their perfumed showers
Of bloom on the bent grass where I am laid,
And bower me from the August sun with shade;
30   And the eye travels down to Oxford's towers.

And near me on the grass lies Glanvill's book—
Come, let me read the oft-read tale again!
The story of the Oxford scholar poor,
Of pregnant parts[3] and quick inventive brain,
35   Who, tired of knocking at preferment's door,
          One summer morn forsook
His friends, and went to learn the gypsy lore,
And roamed the world with that wild brotherhood,
And came, as most men deemed, to little good,
40   But came to Oxford and his friends no more.

But once, years after, in the country lanes,
Two scholars, whom at college erst° he knew,   *long ago*
          Met him, and of his way of life inquired;
Whereat he answered, that the gypsy crew,
45   His mates, had arts to rule as they desired
              The workings of men's brains,
And they can bind them to what thoughts they will.
"And I," he said, "the secret of their art,
When fully learned, will to the world impart;
50   But it needs heaven-sent moments for this skill."

This said, he left them, and returned no more.—
But rumors hung about the countryside,
          That the lost Scholar long was seen to stray,
Seen by rare glimpses, pensive and tongue-tied,
55   In hat of antique shape, and cloak of grey,
              The same the gypsies wore.
Shepherds had met him on the Hurst[4] in spring;
At some lone alehouse in the Berkshire moors,
On the warm ingle-bench,[5] the smock-frocked boors°   *rustics*
60   Had found him seated at their entering,

But, 'mid their drink and clatter, he would fly.
And I myself seem half to know thy looks,
          And put the shepherds, wanderer! on thy trace;
And boys who in lone wheatfields scare the rooks

3. Of rich conception, many ideas.
4. A hill near Oxford. All the place names in the
poem (except those in the final two stanzas) refer
to the countryside near Oxford.
5. Fireside bench.

65 I ask if thou hast passed their quiet place;
        Or in my boat I lie
    Moored to the cool bank in the summer heats,
        'Mid wide grass meadows which the sunshine fills,
        And watch the warm, green-muffled Cumner hills,
70 And wonder if thou haunt'st their shy retreats.

    For most, I know, thou lov'st retired ground!
        Thee at the ferry Oxford riders blithe,
        Returning home on summer nights, have met
    Crossing the stripling Thames at Bab-lock-hithe,[6]
75   Trailing in the cool stream thy fingers wet,
            As the punt's rope chops round;[7]
    And leaning backward in a pensive dream,
        And fostering in thy lap a heap of flowers
        Plucked in shy fields and distant Wychwood bowers,
80 And thine eyes resting on the moonlit stream.

    And then they land, and thou art seen no more!—
        Maidens, who from the distant hamlets come
        To dance around the Fyfield elm in May,
    Oft through the darkening fields have seen thee roam,
85   Or cross a stile into the public way.
            Oft thou hast given them store
    Of flowers—the frail-leafed, white anemone,
        Dark bluebells drenched with dews of summer eves,
        And purple orchises with spotted leaves—
90 But none hath words she can report of thee.

    And, above Godstow Bridge, when hay time's here
        In June, and many a scythe in sunshine flames,
        Men who through those wide fields of breezy grass
    Where black-winged swallows haunt the glittering Thames,
95   To bathe in the abandoned lasher[8] pass,
            Have often passed thee near
    Sitting upon the river bank o'ergrown;
        Marked thine outlandish garb, thy figure spare,
        Thy dark vague eyes, and soft abstracted air—
100 But, when they came from bathing, thou wast gone!

    At some lone homestead in the Cumner hills,
        Where at her open door the housewife darns,
        Thou hast been seen, or hanging on a gate
    To watch the threshers in the mossy barns.
105   Children, who early range these slopes and late
            For cresses from the rills,

6. Or Bablock Hythe (a *hithe* or *hythe* is a landing place on a river). "Stripling Thames": narrow upper reaches of the river before it broadens out to its full width.
7. The scholar's flat-bottomed boat ("punt") is tied up by a rope at the riverbank near the ferry crossing like the speaker's boat (in the previous stanza), which was "moored to the cool bank." The motion of the boat as it is stirred by the current of the river causes the chopping sound of the rope in the water.
8. Water that spills over a dam or weir.

Have known thee eying, all an April day,
   The springing pastures and the feeding kine;°   *cattle*
     And marked thee, when the stars come out and shine,
110 Through the long dewy grass move slow away.

In autumn, on the skirts of Bagley Wood—
   Where most the gypsies by the turf-edged way
     Pitch their smoked tents, and every bush you see
   With scarlet patches tagged and shreds of grey,
115   Above the forest ground called Thessaly—
      The blackbird, picking food,
   Sees thee, nor stops his meal, nor fears at all;
     So often has he known thee past him stray,
     Rapt, twirling in thy hand a withered spray,
120 And waiting for the spark from heaven to fall.

And once, in winter, on the causeway chill
   Where home through flooded fields foot-travelers go,
     Have I not passed thee on the wooden bridge,
   Wrapped in thy cloak and battling with the snow,
125   Thy face tow'rd Hinksey and its wintry ridge?
      And thou hast climbed the hill,
   And gained the white brow of the Cumner range;
     Turned once to watch, while thick the snowflakes fall,
     The line of festal light in Christ Church hall[9]—
130 Then sought thy straw in some sequestered grange.°   *farmhouse*

But what—I dream! Two hundred years are flown
   Since first thy story ran through Oxford halls,
     And the grave Glanvill did the tale inscribe
   That thou wert wandered from the studious walls
135   To learn strange arts, and join a gypsy tribe;
      And thou from earth art gone
   Long since, and in some quiet churchyard laid—
     Some country nook, where o'er thy unknown grave
     Tall grasses and white flowering nettles wave,
140 Under a dark, red-fruited yew tree's shade.

—No, no, thou hast not felt the lapse of hours!
   For what wears out the life of mortal men?
     'Tis that from change to change their being rolls;
   'Tis that repeated shocks, again, again,
145   Exhaust the energy of strongest souls
      And numb the elastic powers.
   Till having used our nerves with bliss and teen,°   *vexation*
     And tired upon a thousand schemes our wit,
     To the just-pausing Genius[1] we remit
150 Our worn-out life, and are—what we have been.

---

9. The dining hall of this Oxford college.
1. Perhaps the spirit of the universe, which
pauses briefly to receive back the life given to us.

(In Roman mythology a *genius* was an attendant
spirit.)

Thou hast not lived, why should'st thou perish, so?
Thou hadst *one* aim, *one* business, *one* desire;
    Else wert thou long since numbered with the dead!
    Else hadst thou spent, like other men, thy fire!
155   The generations of thy peers are fled,
            And we ourselves shall go;
    But thou possessest an immortal lot,
        And we imagine thee exempt from age
        And living as thou liv'st on Glanvill's page,
160   Because thou hadst—what we, alas! have not.

For early didst thou leave the world, with powers
Fresh, undiverted to the world without,
    Firm to their mark, not spent on other things;
Free from the sick fatigue, the languid doubt,
165   Which much to have tried, in much been baffled, brings.
            O life unlike to ours!
    Who fluctuate idly without term or scope,
        Of whom each strives, nor knows for what he strives,
        And each half[2] lives a hundred different lives;
170   Who wait like thee, but not, like thee, in hope.

Thou waitest for the spark from heaven! and we,
Light half-believers of our casual creeds,
    Who never deeply felt, nor clearly willed,
    Whose insight never has borne fruit in deeds,
175   Whose vague resolves never have been fulfilled;
            For whom each year we see
    Breeds new beginnings, disappointments new;
        Who hesitate and falter life away,
        And lose tomorrow the ground won today—
180   Ah! do not we, wanderer! await it too?

Yes, we await it!—but it still delays,
And then we suffer! and amongst us one,[3]
    Who most has suffered, takes dejectedly
    His seat upon the intellectual throne;
185   And all his store of sad experience he
            Lays bare of wretched days;
    Tells us his misery's birth and growth and signs,
        And how the dying spark of hope was fed,
        And how the breast was soothed, and how the head,
190   And all his hourly varied anodynes.

This for our wisest! and we others pine,
And wish the long unhappy dream would end,
    And waive all claim to bliss, and try to bear;
    With close-lipped patience for our only friend,

2. An adverb modifying "lives."
3. Probably Goethe, although possibly referring   to Tennyson, whose *In Memoriam* had appeared
    in 1850.

195   Sad patience, too near neighbor to despair—
          But none has hope like thine!
       Thou through the fields and through the woods dost stray,
          Roaming the countryside, a truant boy,
          Nursing thy project in unclouded joy,
200   And every doubt long blown by time away.

       O born in days when wits were fresh and clear,
          And life ran gaily as the sparkling Thames;
          Before this strange disease of modern life,
       With its sick hurry, its divided aims,
205   Its heads o'ertaxed, its palsied hearts, was rife—
          Fly hence, our contact fear!
       Still fly, plunge deeper in the bowering wood!
       Averse, as Dido did with gesture stern
       From her false friend's approach in Hades turn,[4]
210   Wave us away, and keep thy solitude!

       Still nursing the unconquerable hope,
       Still clutching the inviolable shade,
          With a free, onward impulse brushing through,
       By night, the silvered branches of the glade—
215   Far on the forest skirts, where none pursue.
          On some mild pastoral slope
       Emerge, and resting on the moonlit pales
          Freshen thy flowers as in former years
          With dew, or listen with enchanted ears,
220   From the dark dingles,° to the nightingales!   *small deep valleys*

       But fly our paths, our feverish contact fly!
       For strong the infection of our mental strife,
          Which, though it gives no bliss, yet spoils for rest;
       And we should win thee from thy own fair life,
225   Like us distracted, and like us unblest.
          Soon, soon thy cheer would die,
       Thy hopes grow timorous, and unfixed thy powers,
       And thy clear aims be cross and shifting made;
       And then thy glad perennial youth would fade,
230   Fade, and grow old at last, and die like ours.

       Then fly our greetings, fly our speech and smiles!
       —As some grave Tyrian trader, from the sea,
          Descried at sunrise an emerging prow
       Lifting the cool-haired creepers stealthily,
235   The fringes of a southward-facing brow
          Among the Aegean isles;
       And saw the merry Grecian coaster come,
          Freighted with amber grapes, and Chian wine,

---

4. Dido committed suicide after her lover, Aeneas, deserted her. When he later encountered her in Hades, she silently turned away from him (see Virgil's *Aeneid*, book 6).

Green, bursting figs, and tunnies° steeped in brine—   *tuna fish*
240   And knew the intruders on his ancient home,

The young lighthearted masters of the waves—
And snatched his rudder, and shook out more sail;
And day and night held on indignantly
O'er the blue Midland waters with the gale,
245   Betwixt the Syrtes[5] and soft Sicily,
To where the Atlantic raves
Outside the western straits; and unbent sails
There, where down cloudy cliffs, through sheets of foam,
Shy traffickers, the dark Iberians[6] come;
250   And on the beach undid his corded bales.[7]

[handwritten: images, sounds, often rhyming / not-rhyming]

1853

Dover Beach

[handwritten margin left: movement of the ocean waves is very central to the poem]

The sea is calm tonight. *A*
The tide is full, the moon lies fair *B*
Upon the straits—on the French coast the light *[handwritten: enjambment memups rhyme present]*
Gleams and is gone; the cliffs of England stand, *C*
5   Glimmering and vast, out in the tranquil bay. *D*
Come to the window, sweet is the night air! *B D*
Only, from the long line of spray *D*
Where the sea meets the moon-blanched land, *E*
Listen! you hear the grating roar *E*
Of pebbles which the waves draw back, and fling, *F*
10   At their return, up the high strand, *C*
Begin, and cease, and then again begin, *G*
With tremulous cadence slow, and bring *F*
The eternal note of sadness in. *G*

[handwritten: invitation to see something beautiful once there to hear the sorrow]

[handwritten right margin: starts w/ very peaceful, calm, imagery, transitions into sound imagery that is very melancholy evokes sorrow]

5. Shoals off the coast of North Africa.
6. Dark inhabitants of Spain and Portugal—perhaps associated with gypsies.
7. The elaborate simile of the final two stanzas has been variously interpreted. The trader from Tyre (a Phoenician city, on the coast of what is now Lebanon) is disconcerted to see a new business rival, "the merry Grecian coaster," emerging from one of his habitual trading ports in the Greek islands. Like the Scholar Gypsy, when similarly intruded on by hearty extroverts, he resolves to flee and seek a less competitive sphere of life.

The reference (line 249) to the Iberians as "*shy traffickers*" (traders) is explained by Kenneth Allott as having been derived from Herodotus's *History* (4.196). Herodotus describes a distinctive method of selling goods established by merchants from Carthage who used to sail through the Strait of Gibraltar to trade with the inhabitants of the coast of West Africa. The Carthaginians would leave bales of their merchandise on display along the beaches and, without having seen their prospective customers, would return to their ships. The shy natives would then come down from their inland hiding places and set gold beside the bales they wished to buy. When the natives withdrew in their turn, the Carthaginians would return to the beach and decide whether payments were adequate, a process repeated until agreement was reached. On the Atlantic coasts this method of bargaining persisted into the 19th century. As William Beloe, a translator of the ancient Greek historian, noted in 1844: "In this manner they transact their exchange without seeing one another, or without the least instance of dishonesty . . . on either side." For the solitary Tyrian trader such a procedure, with its avoidance of "contact" (line 221), would have been especially appropriate.

15   Sophocles long ago
      Heard it on the Aegean, and it brought
      Into his mind the turbid ebb and flow
      Of human misery;[8] we
      Find also in the sound a thought,
20   Hearing it by this distant northern sea.

      The Sea of Faith
      Was once, too, at the full, and round earth's shore
      Lay like the folds of a bright girdle furled.[9]
      But now I only hear
25   Its melancholy, long, withdrawing roar,
      Retreating, to the breath
      Of the night wind, down the vast edges drear
      And naked shingles[1] of the world.

      Ah, love, let us be true
30   To one another! for the world, which seems
      To lie before us like a land of dreams,
      So various, so beautiful, so new,
      Hath really neither joy, nor love, nor light,
      Nor certitude, nor peace, nor help for pain;
35   And we are here as on a darkling plain
      Swept with confused alarms of struggle and flight,
      Where ignorant armies[2] clash by night.

ca. 1851   1867

Stanzas from the Grande Chartreuse[1]

      Through Alpine meadows soft-suffused
      With rain, where thick the crocus blows,
      Past the dark forges long disused,
      The mule track from Saint Laurent goes.
5   The bridge is crossed, and slow we ride,
      Through forest, up the mountainside.

8. A reference to a chorus in *Antigone* that compares human sorrow to the sound of the waves moving the sand beneath them (lines 585–91).

9. This difficult line means, in general, that at high tide the sea envelops the land closely. Its forces are "gathered" up (to use William Wordsworth's term) like the "folds" of bright clothing ("girdle") that have been compressed ("furled"). At ebb tide, as the sea retreats, it is unfurled and spread out. It still surrounds the shoreline but not as an "enclasping flow" (as in "To Marguerite—Continued").

1. Beaches covered with pebbles.

2. Perhaps alluding to conflicts in Arnold's own time such as occurred during the revolutions of 1848 in Europe, or at the Siege of Rome by the French in 1849 (the poem's date of composition is unknown, although generally assumed to

be 1851). But the passage also refers back to another battle, one that occurred more than two thousand years earlier when an Athenian army was attempting an invasion of Sicily at nighttime. As this "night battle" was described by the ancient Greek historian Thucydides in his *History of the Peloponnesian War* (7.44), the invaders became confused by darkness and slaughtered many of their own men. Hence "ignorant armies."

1. A monastery situated high in the French Alps. It was established in 1084 by St. Bruno, founder of the Carthusians (line 30), whose austere regimen of solitary contemplation, fasting, and religious exercises (lines 37–44) had remained virtually unchanged for centuries. Arnold visited the site on September 7, 1851, accompanied by his bride. His account may be compared with that by William Wordsworth (*Prelude* [1850] 6.414–88), who had made a similar visit in 1790.

The autumnal evening darkens round,
The wind is up, and drives the rain;
While, hark! far down, with strangled sound
10 Doth the Dead Guier's[2] stream complain,
Where that wet smoke, among the woods,
Over his boiling cauldron broods.

Swift rush the spectral vapors white
Past limestone scars° with ragged pines,   *cliffs*
15 Showing—then blotting from our sight!—
Halt—through the cloud-drift something shines!
High in the valley, wet and drear,
The huts of Courrerie appear.

Strike leftward! cries our guide; and higher
20 Mounts up the stony forest way.
At last the encircling trees retire;
Look! through the showery twilight grey
What pointed roofs are these advance?—
A palace of the Kings of France?

25 Approach, for what we seek is here!
Alight, and sparely sup, and wait
For rest in this outbuilding near;
Then cross the sward and reach that gate.
Knock; pass the wicket!° Thou art come   *gate*
30 To the Carthusians' world-famed home.

The silent courts, where night and day
Into their stone-carved basins cold
The splashing icy fountains play—
The humid corridors behold!
35 Where, ghostlike in the deepening night,
Cowled forms brush by in gleaming white.

The chapel, where no organ's peal
Invests the stern and naked prayer—
With penitential cries they kneel
40 And wrestle; rising then, with bare
And white uplifted faces stand,
Passing the Host from hand to hand;[3]

Each takes, and then his visage wan
Is buried in his cowl once more.
45 The cells!—the suffering Son of Man
Upon the wall—the knee-worn floor—

2. The Guiers Mort River flows down from the monastery and joins the Guiers Vif in the valley below; in French, Mort and Vif mean "dead" and "alive," respectively. Wordsworth speaks of the two rivers as "the sister streams of Life and Death."
3. Arnold, during his short visit, may not actually have witnessed Mass in the monastery. During the service the consecrated wafer ("the Host") is not passed from the hand of the officiating priest to the hands of the communicant (as is the practice in Arnold's own Anglican Church) but is placed directly on the tongue of the communicant (who kneels rather than stands).

And where they sleep, that wooden bed,
Which shall their coffin be, when dead![4]

The library, where tract and tome
50   Not to feed priestly pride are there,
To hymn the conquering march of Rome,
Nor yet to amuse, as ours are!
They paint of souls the inner strife,
Their drops of blood, their death in life.

55   The garden, overgrown—yet mild,
See, fragrant herbs[5] are flowering there!
Strong children of the Alpine wild
Whose culture is the brethren's care;
Of human tasks their only one,
60   And cheerful works beneath the sun.

Those halls, too, destined to contain
Each its own pilgrim-host of old,
From England, Germany, or Spain—
All are before me! I behold
65   The House, the Brotherhood austere!
—And what am I, that I am here?

For rigorous teachers seized my youth,
And purged its faith, and trimmed its fire,
Showed me the high, white star of Truth,
70   There bade me gaze, and there aspire.
Even now their whispers pierce the gloom:
What dost thou in this living tomb?

Forgive me, masters of the mind![6]
At whose behest I long ago
75   So much unlearnt, so much resigned—
I come not here to be your foe!
I seek these anchorites, not in ruth,[7]
To curse and to deny your truth;

Not as their friend, or child, I speak!
80   But as, on some far northern strand,
Thinking of his own Gods, a Greek
In pity and mournful awe might stand
Before some fallen Runic stone[8]—
For both were faiths, and both are gone.

4. A Carthusian is buried on a wooden plank but does not sleep in a coffin.
5. From which the liqueur Chartreuse is manufactured. Sales of this liqueur provide the principal revenues for the monastery's upkeep.
6. Writers whose insistence on testing religious beliefs in the light of fact and reason persuaded Arnold that faith in Christianity (especially in the Roman Catholic or Anglo-Catholic forms) was no longer tenable in the modern world.
7. Remorse for having adopted the rationalist view of Christianity.
8. A monument inscribed in Teutonic letters (runes), emblematic of a Nordic religion that has become extinct. The relic reminds the Greek that his own religion is likewise dying and will soon be extinct (see Preface to *Poems* [1853], p. 440).

85   Wandering between two worlds, one dead,
     The other powerless to be born,
     With nowhere yet to rest my head,
     Like these, on earth I wait forlorn.
     Their faith, my tears, the world deride—
90   I come to shed them at their side.

     Oh, hide me in your gloom profound,
     Ye solemn seats of holy pain!
     Take me, cowled forms, and fence me round,
     Till I possess my soul again;
95   Till free my thoughts before me roll,
     Not chafed by hourly false control!

     For the world cries your faith is now
     But a dead time's exploded dream;
     My melancholy, sciolists[9] say,
100 Is a passed mode, an outworn theme—
     As if the world had ever had
     A faith, or sciolists been sad!

     Ah, if it *be* passed, take away,
     At least, the restlessness, the pain;
105 Be man henceforth no more a prey
     To these out-dated stings again!
     The nobleness of grief is gone—
     Ah, leave us not the fret alone!

     But—if you[1] cannot give us ease—
110 Last of the race of them who grieve
     Here leave us to die out with these
     Last of the people who believe!
     Silent, while years engrave the brow;
     Silent—the best are silent now.

115 Achilles[2] ponders in his tent,
     The kings of modern thought[3] are dumb;
     Silent they are, though not content,
     And wait to see the future come.
     They have the grief men had of yore,
120 But they contend and cry no more.

---

9. Superficial-minded persons who pretend to know the answers to all questions.
1. It is not clear whether the speaker has resumed addressing his "rigorous teachers" (line 67) or (as would seem more likely) a combination of the sciolists, who scorn the speaker's melancholy, and the worldly, who scorn the faith of the monks. See his address to the "sons of the world" (lines 161–68).
2. Until the death of Patroclus, he refused to participate in the Trojan War; hence he is similar to modern intellectual leaders who refuse to speak out about their frustrated sense of alienation.
3. Variously but never satisfactorily identified as John Henry Newman or Thomas Carlyle (the latter was said to have preached the gospel of silence in forty volumes). Another advocate of stoical silence was the French poet Alfred de Vigny (1797–1863).

Our fathers[4] watered with their tears
This sea of time whereon we sail,
Their voices were in all men's ears
Who passed within their puissant hail.
125   Still the same ocean round us raves,
But we stand mute, and watch the waves.

For what availed it, all the noise
And outcry of the former men?—
Say, have their sons achieved more joys,
130   Say, is life lighter now than then?
The sufferers died, they left their pain—
The pangs which tortured them remain.

What helps it now, that Byron bore,
With haughty scorn which mocked the smart,
135   Through Europe to the Aetolian shore[5]
The pageant of his bleeding heart?
That thousands counted every groan,
And Europe made his woe her own?

What boots° it, Shelley! that the breeze   *avails*
140   Carried thy lovely wail away,
Musical through Italian trees
Which fringe thy soft blue Spezzian bay?[6]
Inheritors of thy distress
Have restless hearts one throb the less?

145   Or are we easier, to have read,
O Obermann![7] the sad, stern page,
Which tells us how thou hidd'st thy head
From the fierce tempest of thine age
In the lone brakes° of Fontainebleau,   *thickets*
150   Or chalets near the Alpine snow?

Ye slumber in your silent grave!
The world, which for an idle day
Grace to your mood of sadness gave,
Long since hath flung her weeds° away.   *mourning clothes*
155   The eternal trifler[8] breaks your spell;
But we—we learnt your lore too well!

Years hence, perhaps, may dawn an age,
More fortunate, alas! than we,
Which without hardness will be sage,
160   And gay without frivolity.
Sons of the world, oh, speed those years;
But, while we wait, allow our tears!

---

4. Predecessors among the Romantic writers such as Byron.
5. Region in Greece where Byron died.
6. The Gulf of Spezia in Italy, where Percy Bysshe Shelley was drowned.
7. Melancholy hero of *Obermann* (1804), a novel by the French writer Étienne Sénancour (1770–1846).
8. The sciolist, as in line 99.

Allow them! We admire with awe
The exulting thunder of your race;
165   You give the universe your law,
You triumph over time and space!
Your pride of life, your tireless powers,
We laud them, but they are not ours.

We are like children reared in shade
170   Beneath some old-world abbey wall,
Forgotten in a forest glade,
And secret from the eyes of all.
Deep, deep the greenwood round them waves,
Their abbey, and its close° of graves!   *enclosure*

175   But, where the road runs near the stream,
Oft through the trees they catch a glance
Of passing troops in the sun's beam—
Pennon, and plume, and flashing lance!
Forth to the world those soldiers fare,
180   To life, to cities, and to war!

And through the wood, another way,
Faint bugle notes from far are borne,
Where hunters gather, staghounds bay,
Round some fair forest-lodge at morn.
185   Gay dames are there, in sylvan green;
Laughter and cries—those notes between!

The banners flashing through the trees
Make their blood dance and chain their eyes;
That bugle music on the breeze
190   Arrests them with a charmed surprise.
Banner by turns and bugle woo:
Ye shy recluses, follow too!

O children, what do ye reply?—
"Action and pleasure, will ye roam
195   Through these secluded dells to cry
And call us?—but too late ye come!
Too late for us your call ye blow,
Whose bent° was taken long ago.   *natural inclination*

"Long since we pace this shadowed nave;
200   We watch those yellow tapers shine,
Emblems of hope over the grave,
In the high altar's depth divine;
The organ carries to our ear
Its accents of another sphere.[9]

9. The organ music is from the abbey in the greenwood (line 174), as contrasted with the monastery on the mountaintop in which there is no organ (line 37).

205 "Fenced early in this cloistral round
Of reverie, of shade, of prayer,
How should we grow in other ground?
How can we flower in foreign air?
—Pass, banners, pass, and bugles, cease;
210 And leave our desert to its peace!"

1852(?)   1855

Preface to *Poems* (1853)

In two small volumes of poems, published anonymously, one in 1849, the other in 1852, many of the poems which compose the present volume have already appeared. The rest are now published for the first time.

I have, in the present collection, omitted the poem from which the volume published in 1852 took its title.[1] I have done so, not because the subject of it was a Sicilian Greek born between two and three thousand years ago, although many persons would think this a sufficient reason. Neither have I done so because I had, in my own opinion, failed in the delineation which I intended to effect. I intended to delineate the feelings of one of the last of the Greek religious philosophers, one of the family of Orpheus and Musaeus,[2] having survived his fellows, living on into a time when the habits of Greek thought and feeling had begun fast to change, character to dwindle, the influence of the Sophists[3] to prevail. Into the feelings of a man so situated there entered much that we are accustomed to consider as exclusively modern; how much, the fragments of Empedocles[4] himself which remain to us are sufficient at least to indicate. What those who are familiar only with the great monuments of early Greek genius suppose to be its exclusive characteristics, have disappeared; the calm, the cheerfulness, the disinterested objectivity have disappeared; the dialogue of the mind with itself has commenced; modern problems have presented themselves, we hear already the doubts, we witness the discouragement, of Hamlet and of Faust.[5]

The representation of such a man's feelings must be interesting, if consistently drawn. We all naturally take pleasure, says Aristotle, in any imitation

1. *Empedocles on Etna*, the long poem that supplied the title for Arnold's second collection of poems, portrays the disillusioned reflections of the Greek philosopher and scientist Empedocles and culminates in the speaker's suicide on Mount Etna in Sicily, in the 5th century B.C.E. Because of his dissatisfaction with what he calls the "morbid" tone of *Empedocles on Etna*, Arnold continued to exclude it from his volumes of poetry until 1867, when he reprinted it at the request, he said, "of a man of genius, whom it had the honour and good fortune to interest—Mr. Robert Browning." It should be noted that in the arguments developed in the preface against his own poem (and against 19th-century poetry in general), Arnold is exclusively concerned with narrative and dramatic poetry. The preface, as he remarked in 1854, "leaves . . . untouched the question, how far, and in what manner, the opinions there expressed respecting the choice of subjects apply to lyric poetry; that region of the poetical field which is chiefly cultivated at present."

2. Pupil of the poet and musician Orpheus. The latter was the legendary founder of the Orphic religion that flourished in 6th-century B.C.E. Greece and later declined.

3. Greek rhetoricians, often criticized because of their reputed emphasis on winning arguments rather than on truth or knowledge.

4. Empedocles' writings (medical and scientific treatises in verse) have survived only in fragments.

5. Johann Faustus (ca. 1480–ca. 1540), a German teacher and magician who became the subject of many stories and folktales, and later the hero of the plays by Christopher Marlowe (1604) and Goethe (1808–32).

or representation whatever;[6] this is the basis of our love of poetry; and we take pleasure in them, he adds, because all knowledge is naturally agreeable to us; not to the philosopher only, but to mankind at large. Every representation therefore which is consistently drawn may be supposed to be interesting, inasmuch as it gratifies this natural interest in knowledge of all kinds. What is *not* interesting is that which does not add to our knowledge of any kind; that which is vaguely conceived and loosely drawn; a representation which is general, indeterminate, and faint, instead of being particular, precise, and firm.

Any accurate representation may therefore be expected to be interesting; but, if the representation be a poetical one, more than this is demanded. It is demanded, not only that it shall interest, but also that it shall inspirit and rejoice the reader; that it shall convey a charm, and infuse delight. For the muses, as Hesiod says, were born that they might be "a forgetfulness of evils, and a truce from cares":[7] and it is not enough that the poet should add to the knowledge of men, it is required of him also that he should add to their happiness. "All art," says Schiller, "is dedicated to Joy, and there is no higher and no more serious problem, than how to make men happy. The right art is that alone, which creates the highest enjoyment."[8]

A poetical work, therefore, is not yet justified when it has been shown to be an accurate, and therefore interesting representation; it has to be shown also that it is a representation from which men can derive enjoyment. In presence of the most tragic circumstances, represented in a work of Art, the feeling of enjoyment, as is well known, may still subsist; the representation of the most utter calamity, of the liveliest anguish, is not sufficient to destroy it; the more tragic the situation, the deeper becomes the enjoyment; and the situation is more tragic in proportion as it becomes more terrible.

What then are the situations, from the representation of which, though accurate, no poetical enjoyment can be derived? They are those in which the suffering finds no vent in action; in which a continuous state of mental distress is prolonged, unrelieved by incident, hope, or resistance; in which there is everything to be endured, nothing to be done. In such situations there is inevitably something morbid, in the description of them something monotonous. When they occur in actual life, they are painful, not tragic; the representation of them in poetry is painful also.

To this class of situations, poetically faulty as it appears to me, that of Empedocles, as I have endeavored to represent him, belongs; and I have therefore excluded the poem from the present collection.

And why, it may be asked, have I entered into this explanation respecting a matter so unimportant as the admission or exclusion of the poem in question? I have done so, because I was anxious to avow that the sole reason for its exclusion was that which has been stated above; and that it has not been excluded in deference to the opinion which many critics of the present day appear to entertain against subjects chosen from distant times and countries: against the choice, in short, of any subjects but modern ones.

6. See Aristotle's *Poetics,* especially 1, 2, 4, 7, 14.
7. From *Theogony* 52–56, by the Greek poet Hesiod (ca. 700 B.C.E.).
8. J. C. F. von Schiller's "On the Use of the Cho-

rus in Tragedy," prefatory essay to *The Bride of Messina* (1803). Schiller (1759–1805), German poet, playwright, and critic; see *Friedrich Schiller's Works* (1903) 8.224.

"The poet," it is said, and by an intelligent critic, "the poet who would really fix the public attention must leave the exhausted past, and draw his subjects from matters of present import, and *therefore* both of interest and novelty."[9]

Now this view I believe to be completely false. It is worth examining, inasmuch as it is a fair sample of a class of critical dicta everywhere current at the present day, having a philosophical form and air, but no real basis in fact; and which are calculated to vitiate the judgment of readers of poetry, while they exert, so far as they are adopted, a misleading influence on the practice of those who write it.

What are the eternal objects of poetry, among all nations and at all times? They are actions; human actions; possessing an inherent interest in themselves, and which are to be communicated in an interesting manner by the art of the poet.[1] Vainly will the latter imagine that he has everything in his own power; that he can make an intrinsically inferior action equally delightful with a more excellent one by his treatment of it; he may indeed compel us to admire his skill, but his work will possess, within itself, an incurable defect.

The poet, then, has in the first place to select an excellent action; and what actions are the most excellent? Those, certainly, which most powerfully appeal to the great primary human affections: to those elementary feelings which subsist permanently in the race, and which are independent of time. These feelings are permanent and the same; that which interests them is permanent and the same also. The modernness or antiquity of an action, therefore, has nothing to do with its fitness for poetical representation; this depends upon its inherent qualities. To the elementary part of our nature, to our passions, that which is great and passionate is eternally interesting; and interesting solely in proportion to its greatness and to its passion. A great human action of a thousand years ago is more interesting to it than a smaller human action of today, even though upon the representation of this last the most consummate skill may have been expended, and though it has the advantage of appealing by its modern language, familiar manners, and contemporary allusions, to all our transient feelings and interests. These, however, have no right to demand of a poetical work that it shall satisfy them; their claims are to be directed elsewhere. Poetical works belong to the domain of our permanent passions; let them interest these, and the voice of all subordinate claims upon them is at once silenced.

Achilles, Prometheus, Clytemnestra, Dido—what modern poem presents personages as interesting, even to us moderns, as these personages of an "exhausted past"? We have the domestic epic dealing with the details of modern life which pass daily under our eyes;[2] we have poems representing modern personages in contact with the problems of modern life, moral, intellectual, and social; these works have been produced by poets the most distinguished of their nation and time; yet I fearlessly assert that *Hermann and Dorothea, Childe Harold, Jocelyn, The Excursion*,[3] leave the reader cold

9. In the *Spectator* of April 2nd, 1853. The words quoted were not used with reference to poems of mine [Arnold's note]. According to Arnold, the "intelligent critic" was R. S. Rintoul, editor of the *Spectator*.
1. Cf. Aristotle's *Poetics* 6.

2. Perhaps alluding to poems such as Tennyson's *The Princess* (1847) and Alexander Smith's *Life Drama* (1853) or to the modern novel.
3. Long poems by Goethe (1797), Byron (1818), Alphonse-Marie-Louis de Lamartine (1836), and William Wordsworth (1814), respectively.

in comparison with the effect produced upon him by the latter books of the *Iliad,* by the *Oresteia,* or by the episode of Dido.[4] And why is this? Simply because in the three last-named cases the action is greater, the personages nobler, the situations more intense: and this is the true basis of the interest in a poetical work, and this alone.

It may be urged, however, that past actions may be interesting in themselves, but that they are not to be adopted by the modern poet, because it is impossible for him to have them clearly present to his own mind, and he cannot therefore feel them deeply, nor represent them forcibly. But this is not necessarily the case. The externals of a past action, indeed, he cannot know with the precision of a contemporary; but his business is with its essentials. The outward man of Oedipus or of Macbeth, the houses in which they lived, the ceremonies of their courts, he cannot accurately figure to himself; but neither do they essentially concern him. His business is with their inward man; with their feelings and behavior in certain tragic situations, which engage their passions as men; these have in them nothing local and casual; they are as accessible to the modern poet as to a contemporary.

The date of an action, then, signifies nothing: the action itself, its selection and construction, this is what is all-important. This the Greeks understood far more clearly than we do. The radical difference between their poetical theory and ours consists, as it appears to me, in this: that, with them, the poetical character of the action in itself, and the conduct of it, was the first consideration; with us, attention is fixed mainly on the value of the separate thoughts and images which occur in the treatment of an action. They regarded the whole; we regard the parts. With them, the action predominated over the expression of it; with us, the expression predominates over the action. Not that they failed in expression, or were inattentive to it; on the contrary, they are the highest models of expression, the unapproached masters of the *grand style:* but their expression is so excellent because it is so admirably kept in its right degree of prominence; because it is so simple and so well subordinated; because it draws its force directly from the pregnancy of the matter which it conveys. For what reason was the Greek tragic poet confined to so limited a range of subjects? Because there are so few actions which unite in themselves, in the highest degree, the conditions of excellence: and it was not thought that on any but an excellent subject could an excellent poem be constructed. A few actions, therefore, eminently adapted for tragedy, maintained almost exclusive possession of the Greek tragic stage; their significance appeared inexhaustible; they were as permanent problems, perpetually offered to the genius of every fresh poet. This too is the reason of what appears to us moderns a certain baldness of expression in Greek tragedy; of the triviality with which we often reproach the remarks of the chorus, where it takes part in the dialogue: that the action itself, the situation of Orestes, or Merope, or Alcmaeon,[5] was to stand the central point of interest, unforgotten, absorbing, principal; that no accessories were for a moment to distract the spectator's attention from this; that the tone of the parts was to be perpetually

---

4. See Virgil's *Aeneid,* book 4. *Oresteia:* a trilogy of plays by Aeschylus that tells the story of Agamemnon's murder by his wife, Clytemnestra, and the vengeance taken by their son, Orestes.
5. The son of a legendary Greek hero, who, like

Orestes, avenged his father's death by killing his mother. He was the subject of several Greek plays now lost. Merope, queen of Messene in Greece, appears in plays by Euripides and in Arnold's own play *Merope* (1858).

kept down, in order not to impair the grandiose effect of the whole. The terrible[6] old mythic story on which the drama was founded stood, before he entered the theater, traced in its bare outlines upon the spectator's mind; it stood in his memory, as a group of statuary, faintly seen, at the end of a long and dark vista: then came the poet, embodying outlines, developing situations, not a word wasted, not a sentiment capriciously thrown in: stroke upon stroke, the drama proceeded: the light deepened upon the group; more and more it revealed itself to the riveted gaze of the spectator: until at last, when the final words were spoken, it stood before him in broad sunlight, a model of immortal beauty.

This was what a Greek critic demanded; this was what a Greek poet endeavored to effect. It signified nothing to what time an action belonged; we do not find that the *Persae* occupied a particularly high rank among the dramas of Aeschylus, because it represented a matter of contemporary interest:[7] this was not what a cultivated Athenian required, he required that the permanent elements of his nature should be moved; and dramas of which the action, though taken from a long-distant mythic time, yet was calculated to accomplish this in a higher degree than that of the *Persae,* stood higher in his estimation accordingly. The Greeks felt, no doubt, with their exquisite sagacity of taste, that an action of present times was too near them, too much mixed up with what was accidental and passing, to form a sufficiently grand, detached, and self-subsistent object for a tragic poem: such objects belonged to the domain of the comic poet, and of the lighter kinds of poetry. For the more serious kinds, for *pragmatic* poetry, to use an excellent expression of Polybius,[8] they were more difficult and severe in the range of subjects which they permitted. Their theory and practice alike, the admirable treatise of Aristotle, and the unrivaled works of their poets, exclaim with a thousand tongues—"All depends upon the subject; choose a fitting action, penetrate yourself with the feeling of its situations; this done, everything else will follow."

But for all kinds of poetry alike there was one point on which they were rigidly exacting; the adaptability of the subject to the kind of poetry selected, and the careful construction of the poem.

How different a way of thinking from this is ours! We can hardly at the present day understand what Menander[9] meant when he told a man who inquired as to the progress of his comedy that he had finished it, not having yet written a single line, because he had constructed the action of it in his mind. A modern critic would have assured him that the merit of his piece depended on the brilliant things which arose under his pen as he went along. We have poems which seem to exist merely for the sake of single lines and passages; not for the sake of producing any total impression. We have critics who seem to direct their attention merely to detached expressions, to the language about the action, not to the action itself, I verily think that the majority of them do not in their hearts believe that there is such a thing as a total impression to be derived from a poem at all, or to be demanded from a poet; they think the term a commonplace of metaphysical criticism. They will per-

6. Terrifying, awe-inspiring.
7. Aeschylus's *Persians* (472 B.C.E.) portrays the Greek victory over the Persian invaders, which had occurred only a few years before the play was produced.
8. Greek historian (ca. 200–ca. 118 B.C.E.).
9. Greek writer of comedies (ca. 342–ca. 292 B.C.E.).

mit the poet to select any action he pleases, and to suffer that action to go as it will, provided he gratifies them with occasional bursts of fine writing, and with a shower of isolated thoughts and images. That is, they permit him to leave their poetical sense ungratified, provided that he gratifies their rhetorical sense and their curiosity. Of his neglecting to gratify these, there is little danger. He needs rather to be warned against the danger of attempting to gratify these alone; he needs rather to be perpetually reminded to prefer his action to everything else; so to treat this, as to permit its inherent excellences to develop themselves, without interruption from the intrusion of his personal peculiarities; most fortunate, when he most entirely succeeds in effacing himself, and in enabling a noble action to subsist as it did in nature.

But the modern critic not only permits a false practice; he absolutely prescribes false aims.—"A true allegory of the state of one's own mind in a representative history," the poet is told, "is perhaps the highest thing that one can attempt in the way of poetry."[1] And accordingly he attempts it. An allegory of the state of one's own mind, the highest problem of an art which imitates actions! No assuredly, it is not, it never can be so: no great poetical work has ever been produced with such an aim. *Faust* itself, in which something of the kind is attempted, wonderful passages as it contains, and in spite of the unsurpassed beauty of the scenes which relate to Margaret, *Faust* itself, judged as a whole, and judged strictly as a poetical work, is defective: its illustrious author, the greatest poet of modern times, the greatest critic of all times, would have been the first to acknowledge it; he only defended his work, indeed, by asserting it to be "something incommensurable."[2]

The confusion of the present times is great, the multitude of voices counseling different things bewildering, the number of existing works capable of attracting a young writer's attention and of becoming his models, immense. What he wants is a hand to guide him through the confusion, a voice to prescribe to him the aim which he should keep in view, and to explain to him that the value of the literary works which offer themselves to his attention is relative to their power of helping him forward on his road towards this aim. Such a guide the English writer at the present day will nowhere find. Failing this, all that can be looked for, all indeed that can be desired is, that his attention should be fixed on excellent models; that he may reproduce, at any rate, something of their excellence, by penetrating himself with their works and by catching their spirit, if he cannot be taught to produce what is excellent independently.

Foremost among these models for the English writer stands Shakespeare: a name the greatest perhaps of all poetical names; a name never to be mentioned without reverence. I will venture, however, to express a doubt, whether the influence of his works, excellent and fruitful for the readers of poetry, for the great majority, has been of unmixed advantage to the writers of it. Shakespeare indeed chose excellent subjects; the world could afford no better than Macbeth, or Romeo and Juliet, or Othello: he had no theory respecting the necessity of choosing subjects of present import, or the paramount interest attaching to allegories of the state of one's own mind; like all great poets, he

1. *North British Review* 19 (August 1853): 180 (U.S. ed.). Arnold seems not to have noticed that Goethe (a critic he revered) had been cited earlier in the article as the authority for this critical generalization.

2. J. Eckermann's *Conversations with Goethe*, January 3, 1830.

knew well what constituted a poetical action; like them, wherever he found such an action, he took it; like them, too, he found his best in past times. But to these general characteristics of all great poets he added a special one of his own; a gift, namely, of happy, abundant, and ingenious expression, eminent and unrivaled: so eminent as irresistibly to strike the attention first in him, and even to throw into comparative shade his other excellences as a poet. Here has been the mischief. These other excellences were his fundamental excellences *as a poet;* what distinguishes the artist from the mere amateur, says Goethe, is *Architectonicè* in the highest sense;[3] that power of execution, which creates, forms, and constitutes: not the profoundness of single thoughts, not the richness of imagery, not the abundance of illustration. But these attractive accessories of a poetical work being more easily seized than the spirit of the whole, and these accessories being possessed by Shakespeare in an unequaled degree, a young writer having recourse to Shakespeare as his model runs great risk of being vanquished and absorbed by them, and, in consequence, of reproducing, according to the measure of his power, these, and these alone.[4] Of this preponderating quality of Shakespeare's genius, accordingly almost the whole of modern English poetry has, it appears to me, felt the influence. To the exclusive attention on the part of his imitators to this it is in a great degree owing, that of the majority of modern poetical works the details alone are valuable, the composition worthless. In reading them one is perpetually reminded of that terrible sentence on a modern French poet: *Il dit tout ce qu'il veut, mais malheureusement il n'a rien à dire.*[5]

Let me give an instance of what I mean. I will take it from the works of the very chief among those who seem to have been formed in the school of Shakespeare: of one whose exquisite genius and pathetic death render him forever interesting. I will take the poem of *Isabella, or the Pot of Basil,* by Keats. I choose this rather than the *Endymion,* because the latter work (which a modern critic has classed with the *Fairy Queen!*)[6] although undoubtedly there blows through it the breath of genius, is yet as a whole so utterly incoherent, as not strictly to merit the name of a poem at all. The poem of *Isabella,* then, is a perfect treasure house of graceful and felicitous words and images: almost in every stanza there occurs one of those vivid and picturesque turns of expression, by which the object is made to flash upon the eye of the mind, and which thrill the reader with a sudden delight. This one short poem contains, perhaps, a greater number of happy[7] single expressions which one could quote than all the extant tragedies of Sophocles. But the action, the story? The action in itself is an excellent one; but so feebly is it conceived by the poet, so loosely constructed, that the effect produced by it, in and for itself, is absolutely null. Let the reader, after he has finished the poem of

---

3. In the essay "Concerning the So-called Dilettantism" (1799) in his *Werke* (1833) 44.262–63.
4. Cf. Arnold's letter to Clough (October 28, 1852):

> More and more I feel that the difference between a mature and a youthful age of the world compels the poetry of the former to use great plainness of speech . . . and that Keats and Shelley were on a false track when they set themselves to reproduce the exuberance of expression, the charm, the richness of images, and the felicity, of the Elizabethan poets.

5. He says everything he wishes to, but unfortunately he has nothing to say (French). A comment about Théophile Gautier (1811–1872), whose emphasis on style was severely criticized by Arnold in his late essay "Wordsworth" (1888).
6. In the *North British Review* 19 (August 1853): 172–74, John Keats's *Endymion* (1818) is twice linked with Edmund Spenser's *Faerie Queene* (1590) as "leisurely compositions of the sweet sensuous order."
7. Well-judged, fitting.

Keats, turn to the same story in the *Decameron*:[8] he will then feel how pregnant and interesting the same action has become in the hands of a great artist, who above all things delineates his object; who subordinates expression to that which it is designed to express.

I have said that the imitators of Shakespeare, fixing their attention on his wonderful gift of expression, have directed their imitation to this, neglecting his other excellences. These excellences, the fundamental excellences of poetical art, Shakespeare no doubt possessed them—possessed many of them in a splendid degree; but it may perhaps be doubted whether even he himself did not sometimes give scope to his faculty of expression to the prejudice of a higher poetical duty. For we must never forget that Shakespeare is the great poet he is from his skill in discerning and firmly conceiving an excellent action, from his power of intensely feeling a situation, of intimately associating himself with a character; not from his gift of expression, which rather even leads him astray, degenerating sometimes into a fondness for curiosity of expression, into an irritability of fancy, which seems to make it impossible for him to say a thing plainly, even when the press of the action demands the very direct language, or its level character the very simplest. Mr. Hallam, than whom it is impossible to find a saner and more judicious critic, has had the courage (for at the present day it needs courage) to remark, how extremely and faultily difficult Shakespeare's language often is.[9] It is so: you may find main scenes in some of his greatest tragedies, *King Lear* for instance, where the language is so artificial, so curiously tortured, and so difficult, that every speech has to be read two or three times before its meaning can be comprehended. This overcuriousness of expression is indeed but the excessive employment of a wonderful gift—of the power of saying a thing in a happier way than any other man; nevertheless, it is carried so far that one understands what M. Guizot meant, when he said that Shakespeare appears in his language to have tried all styles except that of simplicity.[1] He has not the severe and scrupulous self-restraint of the ancients, partly no doubt, because he had a far less cultivated and exacting audience. He has indeed a far wider range than they had, a far richer fertility of thought; in this respect he rises above them. In his strong conception of his subject, in the genuine way in which he is penetrated with it, he resembles them, and is unlike the moderns. But in the accurate limitation of it, the conscientious rejection of superfluities, the simple and rigorous development of it from the first line of his work to the last, he falls below them, and comes nearer to the moderns. In his chief works, besides what he has of his own, he has the elementary soundness of the ancients; he has their important action and their large and broad manner; but he has not their purity of method. He is therefore a less safe model; for what he has of his own is personal, and inseparable from his own rich nature; it may be imitated and exaggerated, it cannot be learned or applied as an art. He is above all suggestive; more valuable, therefore, to young writers as men than as artists. But clearness of arrangement, rigor of development, simplicity of style—these may to a certain extent be learned; and these may, I am convinced, be learned best

8. By Boccaccio (1353): fourth day, fifth story.
9. *Introduction to the Literature of Europe* (1838–39), chap. 23, by the historian Henry Hallam (1779–1859).

1. F. P. G. Guizot (1787–1874), French historian, discusses Shakespeare's sonnets in his *Shakespeare et Son Temps* (1852) 114.

from the ancients, who although infinitely less suggestive than Shakespeare, are thus, to the artist, more instructive.

What, then, it will be asked, are the ancients to be our sole models? the ancients with their comparatively narrow range of experience, and their widely different circumstances? Not, certainly, that which is narrow in the ancients, nor that in which we can no longer sympathize. An action like the action of the *Antigone* of Sophocles, which turns upon the conflict between the heroine's duty to her brother's corpse and that to the laws of her country, is no longer one in which it is possible that we should feel a deep interest. I am speaking too, it will be remembered, not of the best sources of intellectual stimulus for the general reader, but of the best models of instruction for the individual writer. This last may certainly learn of the ancients, better than anywhere else, three things which it is vitally important for him to know: the all-importance of the choice of a subject; the necessity of accurate construction; and the subordinate character of expression. He will learn from them how unspeakably superior is the effect of the one moral impression left by a great action treated as a whole, to the effect produced by the most striking single thought or by the happiest image. As he penetrates into the spirit of the great classical works, as he becomes gradually aware of their intense significance, their noble simplicity, and their calm pathos, he will be convinced that it is this effect, unity and profoundness of moral impression, at which the ancient poets aimed; that it is this which constitutes the grandeur of their works, and which makes them immortal. He will desire to direct his own efforts towards producing the same effect. Above all, he will deliver himself from the jargon of modern criticism, and escape the danger of producing poetical works conceived in the spirit of the passing time, and which partake of its transitoriness.

The present age makes great claims upon us; we owe it service, it will not be satisfied without our admiration. I know not how it is, but their commerce with the ancients appears to me to produce, in those who constantly practice it, a steadying and composing effect upon their judgment, not of literary works only, but of men and events in general. They are like persons who have had a very weighty and impressive experience; they are more truly than others under the empire of facts, and more independent of the language current among those with whom they live. They wish neither to applaud nor to revile their age; they wish to know what it is, what it can give them, and whether this is what they want. What they want, they know very well; they want to educe and cultivate what is best and noblest in themselves; they know, too, that this is no easy task—χαλεπὸν, as Pittacus said, χαλεπὸν ἐσθλὸν ἔμμεναι²—and they ask themselves sincerely whether their age and its literature can assist them in the attempt. If they are endeavoring to practice any art, they remember the plain and simple proceedings of the old artists, who attained their grand results by penetrating themselves with some noble and significant action, not by inflating themselves with a belief in the pre-eminent importance and greatness of their own times. They do not talk of their mission, nor of interpreting their age, nor of the coming poet; all this, they know, is the mere delirium of vanity; their business is not to praise their age, but to afford to the men who live in it the highest pleasure which they are capable

---

2. It is hard to be good (Greek); an aphorism of the statesman and sage Pittacus (ca. 650–570 B.C.E.).

of feeling. If asked to afford this by means of subjects drawn from the age itself, they ask what special fitness the present age has for supplying them. They are told that it is an era of progress, an age commissioned to carry out the great ideas of industrial development and social amelioration. They reply that with all this they can do nothing; that the elements they need for the exercise of their art are great actions, calculated powerfully and delightfully to affect what is permanent in the human soul; that so far as the present age can supply such actions, they will gladly make use of them; but that an age wanting in moral grandeur can with difficulty supply such, and an age of spiritual discomfort with difficulty be powerfully and delightfully affected by them.

A host of voices will indignantly rejoin that the present age is inferior to the past neither in moral grandeur nor in spiritual health. He who possesses the discipline I speak of will content himself with remembering the judgments passed upon the present age, in this respect, by the two men, the one of strongest head, the other of widest culture, whom it has produced; by Goethe and by Niebuhr.[3] It will be sufficient for him that he knows the opinions held by these two great men respecting the present age and its literature; and that he feels assured in his own mind that their aims and demands upon life were such as he would wish, at any rate, his own to be; and their judgment as to what is impeding and disabling such as he may safely follow. He will not, however, maintain a hostile attitude towards the false pretensions of his age: he will content himself with not being overwhelmed by them. He will esteem himself fortunate if he can succeed in banishing from his mind all feelings of contradiction, and irritation, and impatience; in order to delight himself with the contemplation of some noble action of a heroic time, and to enable others, through his representation of it, to delight in it also.

I am far indeed from making any claim, for myself, that I possess this discipline; or for the following poems, that they breathe its spirit. But I say, that in the sincere endeavor to learn and practice, amid the bewildering confusion of our times, what is sound and true in poetical art, I seemed to myself to find the only sure guidance, the only solid footing, among the ancients. They, at any rate, knew what they wanted in art, and we do not. It is this uncertainty which is disheartening, and not hostile criticism. How often have I felt this when reading words of disparagement or of cavil: that it is the uncertainty as to what is really to be aimed at which makes our difficulty, not the dissatisfaction of the critic, who himself suffers from the same uncertainty. *Non me tua fervida terrent Dicta; . . . Dii me terrent, et Jupiter hostis.*[4]

Two kinds of *dilettanti*, says Goethe, there are in poetry: he who neglects the indispensable mechanical part, and thinks he has done enough if he shows spirituality and feeling; and he who seeks to arrive at poetry merely by mechanism, in which he can acquire an artisan's readiness, and is without soul and matter.[5] And he adds, that the first does most harm to art, and the last to himself. If we must be *dilettanti*; if it is impossible for us, under the circumstances amidst which we live, to think clearly, to feel nobly, and to delineate firmly; if we cannot attain to the mastery of the great artists; let

---

3. B. G. Niebuhr (1776–1831), German historian. Both writers felt that their own age had added little to the store of great literature.
4. The gods frighten me, and [having] Jupiter as an enemy (Latin); Virgil's *Aeneid* 12.894–95.

Turnus, a warrior abandoned by the gods, is replying to Aeneas, who has taunted him with being afraid.
5. See "Concerning the So-called Dilettantism" (1799) in his *Werke* (1833) 44.281.

us, at least, have so much respect for our art as to prefer it to ourselves. Let us not bewilder our successors; let us transmit to them the practice of poetry, with its boundaries and wholesome regulative laws, under which excellent works may again, perhaps, at some future time, be produced, not yet fallen into oblivion through our neglect, not yet condemned and canceled by the influence of their eternal enemy, caprice.

1853

From The Function of Criticism at the Present Time[1]

Many objections have been made to a proposition which, in some remarks of mine on translating Homer,[2] I ventured to put forth; a proposition about criticism, and its importance at the present day. I said: "Of the literature of France and Germany, as of the intellect of Europe in general, the main effort, for now many years, has been a critical effort; the endeavor, in all branches of knowledge, theology, philosophy, history, art, science, to see the object as in itself it really is." I added, that owing to the operation in English literature of certain causes, "almost the last thing for which one would come to English literature is just that very thing which now Europe most desires—criticism"; and that the power and value of English literature was thereby impaired. More than one rejoinder declared that the importance I here assigned to criticism was excessive, and asserted the inherent superiority of the creative effort of the human spirit over its critical effort. And the other day, having been led by a Mr. Shairp's excellent notice of Wordsworth[3] to turn again to his biography, I found, in the words of this great man, whom I, for one, must always listen to with the profoundest respect, a sentence passed on the critic's business, which seems to justify every possible disparagement of it. Wordsworth says in one of his letters:

> The writers in these publications (the Reviews), while they prosecute their inglorious employment, cannot be supposed to be in a state of mind very favorable for being affected by the finer influences of a thing so pure as genuine poetry.

And a trustworthy reporter[4] of his conversation quotes a more elaborate judgment to the same effect:

> Wordsworth holds the critical power very low, infinitely lower than the inventive; and he said today that if the quantity of time consumed in

---

1. This essay served as an introduction to *Essays in Criticism* (1865).
2. *On Translating Homer* (1861).
3. J. C. Shairp's essay "Wordsworth: The Man and the Poet" was published in 1864. Arnold comments in a footnote:

I cannot help thinking that a practice, common in England during the last century, and still followed in France, of printing a notice of this kind—a notice by a competent critic—to serve as an introduction to an eminent author's works, might be revived among us with advan-

tage. To introduce all succeeding editions of Wordsworth, Mr. Shairp's notice might, it seems to me, excellently serve; it is written from the point of view of an admirer, nay, of a disciple, and that is right; but then the disciple must be also, as in this case he is, a critic, a man of letters, not, as too often happens, some relation or friend with no qualification for his task except affection for his author.

4. Christopher Wordsworth, *Memoirs of William Wordsworth* (1851).

writing critiques on the works of others were given to original composition, of whatever kind it might be, it would be much better employed; it would make a man find out sooner his own level, and it would do infinitely less mischief. A false or malicious criticism may do much injury to the minds of others; a stupid invention, either in prose or verse, is quite harmless.

It is almost too much to expect of poor human nature, that a man capable of producing some effect in one line of literature, should, for the greater good of society, voluntarily doom himself to impotence and obscurity in another. Still less is this to be expected from men addicted to the composition of the "false or malicious criticism" of which Wordsworth speaks. However, everybody would admit that a false or malicious criticism had better never have been written. Everybody, too, would be willing to admit, as a general proposition, that the critical faculty is lower than the inventive. But is it true that criticism is really, in itself, a baneful and injurious employment; is it true that all time given to writing critiques on the works of others would be much better employed if it were given to original composition, of whatever kind this may be? Is it true that Johnson had better have gone on producing more *Irenes*[5] instead of writing his *Lives of the Poets;* nay, is it certain that Wordsworth himself was better employed in making his Ecclesiastical Sonnets than when he made his celebrated Preface[6] so full of criticism, and criticism of the works of others? Wordsworth was himself a great critic, and it is to be sincerely regretted that he has not left us more criticism; Goethe was one of the greatest of critics, and we may sincerely congratulate ourselves that he has left us so much criticism. Without wasting time over the exaggeration which Wordsworth's judgment on criticism clearly contains, or over an attempt to trace the causes—not difficult, I think, to be traced—which may have led Wordsworth to this exaggeration, a critic may with advantage seize an occasion for trying his own conscience, and for asking himself of what real service, at any given moment, the practice of criticism either is or may be made to his own mind and spirit, and to the minds and spirits of others.

The critical power is of lower rank than the creative. True; but in assenting to this proposition, one or two things are to be kept in mind. It is undeniable that the exercise of a creative power, that a free creative activity, is the highest function of man; it is proved to be so by man's finding in it his true happiness. But it is undeniable, also, that men may have the sense of exercising this free creative activity in other ways than in producing great works of literature or art; if it were not so, all but a very few men would be shut out from the true happiness of all men. They may have it in well-doing, they may have it in learning, they may have it even in criticizing. This is one thing to be kept in mind. Another is, that the exercise of the creative power in the production of great works of literature or art, however high this exercise of it may rank, is not at all epochs and under all conditions possible; and that therefore labor may be vainly spent in attempting it, which might with more fruit be used in preparing for it, in rendering it possible. This creative power works with elements, with materials; what if it has not those materials, those

---

5. *Irene* (1749) is a clumsy play by Samuel Johnson (1709–1784), whose *Lives of the Poets* (1779–81) is a major work of criticism.

6. To *Lyrical Ballads* (1800). "Ecclesiastical Sonnets": a sonnet sequence (1821–22) by Wordsworth, usually regarded as minor verse.

elements, ready for its use? In that case it must surely wait till they are ready. Now, in literature—I will limit myself to literature, for it is about literature that the question arises—the elements with which the creative power works are ideas; the best ideas on every matter which literature touches, current at the time. At any rate we may lay it down as certain that in modern literature no manifestation of the creative power not working with these can be very important or fruitful. And I say *current* at the time, not merely accessible at the time; for creative literary genius does not principally show itself in discovering new ideas, that is rather the business of the philosopher. The grand work of literary genius is a work of synthesis and exposition, not of analysis and discovery; its gift lies in the faculty of being happily inspired by a certain intellectual and spiritual atmosphere, by a certain order of ideas, when it finds itself in them; of dealing divinely with these ideas, presenting them in the most effective and attractive combinations—making beautiful works with them, in short. But it must have the atmosphere, it must find itself amidst the order of ideas, in order to work freely; and these it is not so easy to command. This is why great creative epochs in literature are so rare, this is why there is so much that is unsatisfactory in the productions of many men of real genius; because, for the creation of a masterwork of literature two powers must concur, the power of the man and the power of the moment, and the man is not enough without the moment; the creative power has, for its happy exercise, appointed elements, and those elements are not in its own control.

Nay, they are more within the control of the critical power. It is the business of the critical power, as I said in the words already quoted, "in all branches of knowledge, theology, philosophy, history, art, science, to see the object as in itself it really is." Thus it tends, at last, to make an intellectual situation of which the creative power can profitably avail itself. It tends to establish an order of ideas, if not absolutely true, yet true by comparison with that which it displaces; to make the best ideas prevail. Presently these new ideas reach society, the touch of truth is the touch of life, and there is a stir and growth everywhere; out of this stir and growth come the creative epochs of literature.

Or, to narrow our range, and quit these considerations of the general march of genius and of society—considerations which are apt to become too abstract and impalpable—everyone can see that a poet, for instance, ought to know life and the world before dealing with them in poetry; and life and the world being in modern times very complex things, the creation of a modern poet, to be worth much, implies a great critical effort behind it; else it must be a comparatively poor, barren, and short-lived affair. This is why Byron's poetry had so little endurance in it, and Goethe's so much; both Byron and Goethe had a great productive power, but Goethe's was nourished by a great critical effort providing the true materials for it, and Byron's was not; Goethe knew life and the world, the poet's necessary subjects, much more comprehensively and thoroughly than Byron. He knew a great deal more of them, and he knew them much more as they really are.

It has long seemed to me that the burst of creative activity in our literature, through the first quarter of this century, had about it in fact something premature; and that from this cause its productions are doomed, most of them, in spite of the sanguine hopes which accompanied and do still accompany them, to prove hardly more lasting than the productions of far less splendid epochs. And this prematureness comes from its having proceeded without having its proper data, without sufficient materials to work with. In other words, the English poetry of the first quarter of this century, with plenty of energy, plenty of creative force, did not know enough. This makes Byron so empty of matter, Shelley so incoherent, Wordsworth even, profound as he is, yet so wanting in completeness and variety. Wordsworth cared little for books, and disparaged Goethe. I admire Wordsworth, as he is, so much that I cannot wish him different; and it is vain, no doubt, to imagine such a man different from what he is, to suppose that he *could* have been different. But surely the one thing wanting to make Wordsworth an even greater poet than he is—his thought richer, and his influence of wider application—was that he should have read more books, among them, no doubt, those of that Goethe whom he disparaged without reading him.

But to speak of books and reading may easily lead to a misunderstanding here. It was not really books and reading that lacked to our poetry at this epoch: Shelley had plenty of reading, Coleridge had immense reading. Pindar and Sophocles[7]—as we all say so glibly, and often with so little discernment of the real import of what we are saying—had not many books; Shakespeare was no deep reader. True; but in the Greece of Pindar and Sophocles, in the England of Shakespeare, the poet lived in a current of ideas in the highest degree animating and nourishing to the creative power; society was, in the fullest measure, permeated by fresh thought, intelligent and alive. And this state of things is the true basis for the creative power's exercise, in this it finds its data, its materials, truly ready for its hand; all the books and reading in the world are only valuable as they are helps to this. Even when this does not actually exist, books and reading may enable a man to construct a kind of semblance of it in his own mind, a world of knowledge and intelligence in which he may live and work. This is by no means an equivalent to the artist for the nationally diffused life and thought of the epochs of Sophocles or Shakespeare; but, besides that it may be a means of preparation for such epochs, it does really constitute, if many share in it, a quickening and sustaining atmosphere of great value. Such an atmosphere the many-sided learning and the long and widely combined critical effort of Germany formed for Goethe, when he lived and worked. There was no national glow of life and thought there as in the Athens of Pericles or the England of Elizabeth.[8] That was the poet's weakness. But there was a sort of equivalent for it in the complete culture and unfettered thinking of a large body of Germans. That was his strength. In the England of the first quarter of this century there was neither a national glow of life and thought, such as we had in the age of Elizabeth, nor yet a culture and a force of learning and criticism such as were to be found in Germany. Therefore the creative power of poetry wanted, for success in the highest sense, materials and a basis; a thorough interpretation of the world was necessarily denied to it.

At first sight it seems strange that out of the immense stir of the French Revolution and its age should not have come a crop of works of genius equal

---

7. Greek tragedian (ca. 496–406 B.C.E.). Pindar (518–438 B.C.E.), Greek lyric poet.
8. Elizabeth I (1533–1603; reigned 1558–1603). Pericles (ca. 495–429 B.C.E.), the leading states-

man of Athens during the period of the city's most outstanding achievements in art, literature, and politics.

to that which came out of the stir of the great productive time of Greece, or out of that of the Renascence, with its powerful episode the Reformation. But the truth is that the stir of the French Revolution took a character which essentially distinguished it from such movements as these. These were, in the main, disinterestedly intellectual and spiritual movements; movements in which the human spirit looked for its satisfaction in itself and in the increased play of its own activity. The French Revolution took a political, practical character. The movement, which went on in France under the old *régime*, from 1700 to 1789, was far more really akin than that of the Revolution itself to the movement of the Renascence; the France of Voltaire and Rousseau[9] told far more powerfully upon the mind of Europe than the France of the Revolution. Goethe reproached this last expressly with having "thrown quiet culture back."[1] Nay, and the true key to how much in our Byron, even in our Wordsworth, is this!—that they had their source in a great movement of feeling, not in a great movement of mind. The French Revolution, however—that object of so much blind love and so much blind hatred—found undoubtedly its motive power in the intelligence of men, and not in their practical sense; this is what distinguishes it from the English Revolution of Charles the First's time.[2] This is what makes it a more spiritual event than our Revolution, an event of much more powerful and worldwide interest, though practically less successful; it appeals to an order of ideas which are universal, certain, permanent. 1789 asked of a thing, Is it rational? 1642 asked of a thing, Is it legal? or, when it went furthest, Is it according to conscience? This is the English fashion, a fashion to be treated, within its own sphere, with the highest respect; for its success, within its own sphere, has been prodigious. But what is law in one place is not law in another; what is law here today is not law even here tomorrow; and as for conscience, what is binding on one man's conscience is not binding on another's. The old woman who threw her stool at the head of the surpliced minister in St. Giles's Church at Edinburgh[3] obeyed an impulse to which millions of the human race may be permitted to remain strangers. But the prescriptions of reason are absolute, unchanging, of universal validity; *to count by tens is the easiest way of counting*—that is a proposition of which everyone, from here to the Antipodes, feels the force; at least I should say so if we did not live in a country where it is not impossible that any morning we may find a letter in the *Times* declaring that a decimal coinage is an absurdity.[4] That a whole nation should have been penetrated with an enthusiasm for pure reason, and with an ardent zeal for making its prescriptions triumph, is a very remarkable thing, when we consider how little of mind, or anything so worthy and quickening as mind, comes into the motives which alone, in general, impel great masses of men. In spite of the extravagant direction given to this enthusiasm, in spite

9. Jean-Jacques Rousseau (1712–1778), Swiss-born French philosopher and political theorist. Voltaire (1694–1778), pen name of the French writer François Marie Arouet.
1. See "Vier Jahreszeiten Herbst" (1796) in his *Werke* (1887) 1.354.
2. Disputes between Charles I (1600–1649; reigned 1625–49) and Parliament led in 1642 to civil war and ultimately to the king's beheading. (Eleven years later his son, Charles II, was recalled from exile and proclaimed king.)

3. In 1637 rioting broke out in Scotland against a new kind of church service that was prescribed by Charles I. The riot was started by an old woman hurling a stool at a clergyman, whom she accused of saying Mass.
4. In 1863 a proposal in Parliament to introduce the French decimal system for weights and measures had provoked articles in the London *Times* defending the English system (of ounces and pounds or inches and feet) as more practical. Decimal coinage was finally instituted in 1971.

of the crimes and follies in which it lost itself, the French Revolution derives from the force, truth, and universality of the ideas which it took for its law, and from the passion with which it could inspire a multitude for these ideas, a unique and still living power; it is—it will probably long remain—the greatest, the most animating event in history. And as no sincere passion for the things of the mind, even though it turn out in many respects an unfortunate passion, is ever quite thrown away and quite barren of good, France has reaped from hers one fruit—the natural and legitimate fruit though not precisely the grand fruit she expected: she is the country in Europe where *the people* is most alive.

But the mania for giving an immediate political and practical application to all these fine ideas of the reason was fatal. Here an Englishman is in his element: on this theme we can all go on for hours. And all we are in the habit of saying on it has undoubtedly a great deal of truth. Ideas cannot be too much prized in and for themselves, cannot be too much lived with; but to transport them abruptly into the world of politics and practice, violently to revolutionize this world to their bidding—that is quite another thing. There is the world of ideas and there is the world of practice; the French are often for suppressing the one and the English the other; but neither is to be suppressed. A member of the House of Commons said to me the other day: "That a thing is an anomaly, I consider to be no objection to it whatever." I venture to think he was wrong; that a thing is an anomaly *is* an objection to it, but absolutely and in the sphere of ideas: it is not necessarily, under such and such circumstances, or at such and such a moment, an objection to it in the sphere of politics and practice. Joubert[5] has said beautifully: *"C'est la force et le droit qui règlent toutes choses dans le monde; la force en attendant le droit."*—"Force and right are the governors of this world; force till right is ready." *Force till right is ready;* and till right is ready, force, the existing order of things, is justified, is the legitimate ruler. But right is something moral, and implies inward recognition, free assent of the will; we are not ready for right—*right,* so far as we are concerned, is *not ready*—until we have attained this sense of seeing it and willing it. The way in which for us it may change and transform force, the existing order of things, and become, in its turn, the legitimate ruler of the world, should depend on the way in which, when our time comes, we see it and will it. Therefore for other people enamored of their own newly discerned right, to attempt to impose it upon us as ours, and violently to substitute their right for our force, is an act of tyranny, and to be resisted. It sets at nought the second great half of our maxim, *force till right is ready.* This was the grand error of the French Revolution; and its movement of ideas, by quitting the intellectual sphere and rushing furiously into the political sphere, ran, indeed a prodigious and memorable course, but produced no such intellectual fruit as the movement of ideas of the Renascence, and created, in opposition to itself, what I may call an *epoch of concentration.* The great force of that epoch of concentration was England; and the great voice of that epoch of concentration was Burke.[6] It is the fashion to treat Burke's writings on the French Revolution

---

5. Joseph Joubert (1754–1824), French moralist about whom Arnold wrote in his *Essays in Criticism.*
6. Edmund Burke (1729–1797), prominent statesman and author of *Reflections on the French Revolution* (1790), which expressed the conservative opposition to revolutionary theories.

as superannuated and conquered by the event; as the eloquent but unphilo-
sophical tirades of bigotry and prejudice. I will not deny that they are often
disfigured by the violence and passion of the moment, and that in some
directions Burke's view was bounded, and his observation therefore at fault.
But on the whole, and for those who can make the needful corrections, what
distinguishes these writings is their profound, permanent, fruitful, philosophical truth, They contain the true philosophy of an epoch of concentration, dissipate the heavy atmosphere which its own nature is apt to engender
round it, and make its resistance rational instead of mechanical.

But Burke is so great because, almost alone in England, he brings thought
to bear upon politics, he saturates politics with thought. It is his accident[7]
that his ideas were at the service of an epoch of concentration, not of an
epoch of expansion; it is his characteristic that he so lived by ideas, and
had such a source of them welling up within him, that he could float even an
epoch of concentration and English Tory politics with them. It does not hurt
him that Dr. Price[8] and the Liberals were enraged with him; it does not even
hurt him that George the Third and the Tories were enchanted with him. His
greatness is that he lived in a world which neither English Liberalism nor
English Toryism is apt to enter—the world of ideas, not the world of catch-
words and party habits. So far is it from being really true of him that he "to
party gave up what was meant for mankind,"[9] that at the very end of his fierce
struggle with the French Revolution, after all his invectives against its false
pretensions, hollowness, and madness, with his sincere convictions of its
mischievousness, he can close a memorandum on the best means of combat-
ing it, some of the last pages he ever wrote[1]—the *Thoughts on French Affairs*,
in December 1791—with these striking words:

> The evil is stated, in my opinion, as it exists. The remedy must be where
> power, wisdom, and information, I hope, are more united with good
> intentions than they can be with me. I have done with this subject, I
> believe, forever. It has given me many anxious moments for the last two
> years. *If a great change is to be made in human affairs, the minds of men
> will be fitted to it; the general opinions and feelings will draw that way.
> Every fear, every hope will forward it; and then they who persist in oppos-
> ing this mighty current in human affairs, will appear rather to resist the
> decrees of Providence itself, than the mere designs of men. They will not
> be resolute and firm, but perverse and obstinate.*

That return of Burke upon himself has always seemed to me one of the
finest things in English literature, or indeed in any literature. That is what I
call living by ideas: when one side of a question has long had your earnest
support, when all your feelings are engaged, when you hear all round you no
language but one, when your party talks this language like a steam engine
and can imagine no other—still to be able to think, still to be irresistibly carried, if so it be, by the current of thought to the opposite side of the question,
and, like Balaam, to be unable to speak anything *but what the Lord has put in*

---

7. Fortune.
8. Richard Price (1723–1791), a prorevolution-
ary clergyman who was an opponent of Burke's.
9. From the poem "Retaliation" (1774) by Oliver
Goldsmith (1728–1774).

1. Arnold was mistaken; Burke continued to
write for another six years after 1791. According
to Arnold's editor, R. H. Super, the mistake was
caused by misunderstanding a passage in one of
Burke's letters.

your mouth.[2] I know nothing more striking, and I must add that I know nothing more un-English.

For the Englishman in general is like my friend the Member of Parliament, and believes, point-blank, that for a thing to be an anomaly is absolutely no objection to it whatever. He is like the Lord Auckland[3] of Burke's day, who, in a memorandum on the French Revolution, talks of certain "miscreants, assuming the name of philosophers, who have presumed themselves capable of establishing a new system of society." The Englishman has been called a political animal, and he values what is political and practical so much that ideas easily become objects of dislike in his eyes, and thinkers, "miscreants," because ideas and thinkers have rashly meddled with politics and practice. This would be all very well if the dislike and neglect confined themselves to ideas transported out of their own sphere, and meddling rashly with practice; but they are inevitably extended to ideas as such, and to the whole life of intelligence; practice is everything, a free play of the mind is nothing. The notion of the free play of the mind upon all subjects being a pleasure in itself, being an object of desire, being an essential provider of elements without which a nation's spirit, whatever compensations it may have for them, must, in the long run, die of inanition, hardly enters into an Englishman's thoughts. It is noticeable that the word *curiosity*, which in other languages is used in a good sense, to mean, as a high and fine quality of man's nature, just this disinterested love of a free play of the mind on all subjects, for its own sake—it is noticeable, I say, that this word has in our language no sense of the kind, no sense but a rather bad and disparaging one. But criticism, real criticism, is essentially the exercise of this very quality. It obeys an instinct prompting it to try to know the best that is known and thought in the world, irrespectively of practice, politics, and everything of the kind; and to value knowledge and thought as they approach this best, without the intrusion of any other considerations whatever. This is an instinct for which there is, I think, little original sympathy in the practical English nature, and what there was of it has undergone a long benumbing period of blight and suppression in the epoch of concentration which followed the French Revolution.

But epochs of concentration cannot well endure forever; epochs of expansion, in the due course of things, follow them. Such an epoch of expansion seems to be opening in this country. In the first place all danger of a hostile forcible pressure of foreign ideas upon our practice has long disappeared; like the traveler in the fable, therefore, we begin to wear our cloak a little more loosely.[4] Then, with a long peace, the ideas of Europe steal gradually and amicably in, and mingle, though in infinitesimally small quantities at a time, with our own notions. Then, too, in spite of all that is said about the absorbing and brutalizing influence of our passionate material progress, it seems to me indisputable that this progress is likely, though not certain, to lead in the end to an apparition of intellectual life; and that man, after he has made himself perfectly comfortable and has now to determine what to do with himself next, may begin to remember that he has a mind, and that

2. Balaam, a false and worldly prophet, pronounced a blessing on the Israelites instead of the curse he had intended (Numbers 22.38).
3. William Eden, first Baron Auckland (1744–1814), statesman and diplomat.

4. In Aesop's fable of the wind and the sun, the two compete to see who is more powerful. The sun wins by causing the traveler to take off his coat (the goal of both), whereas the wind can only make him hold it closely.

the mind may be made the source of great pleasure. I grant it is mainly the privilege of faith, at present, to discern this end to our railways, our business, and our fortune-making; but we shall see if, here as elsewhere, faith is not in the end the true prophet. Our ease, our traveling, and our unbounded liberty to hold just as hard and securely as we please to the practice to which our notions have given birth, all tend to beget an inclination to deal a little more freely with these notions themselves, to canvass them a little, to penetrate a little into their real nature. Flutterings of curiosity, in the foreign sense of the word, appear amongst us, and it is in these that criticism must look to find its account. Criticism first; a time of true creative activity, perhaps—which, as I have said, must inevitably be preceded amongst us by a time of criticism—hereafter, when criticism has done its work.

It is of the last importance that English criticism should clearly discern what rule for its course, in order to avail itself of the field now opening to it, and to produce fruit for the future, it ought to take. The rule may be summed up in one word—*disinterestedness*.[5] And how is criticism to show disinterestedness? By keeping aloof from what is called "the practical view of things"; by resolutely following the law of its own nature, which is to be a free play of the mind on all subjects which it touches. By steadily refusing to lend itself to any of those ulterior, political, practical considerations about ideas, which plenty of people will be sure to attach to them, which perhaps ought often to be attached to them, which in this country at any rate are certain to be attached to them quite sufficiently, but which criticism has really nothing to do with. Its business is, as I have said, simply to know the best that is known and thought in the world, and by in its turn making this known, to create a current of true and fresh ideas. Its business is to do this with inflexible honesty, with due ability; but its business is to do no more, and to leave alone all questions of practical consequences and applications, questions which will never fail to have due prominence given to them. Else criticism, besides being really false to its own nature, merely continues in the old rut which it has hitherto followed in this country, and will certainly miss the chance now given to it. For what is at present the bane of criticism in this country? It is that practical considerations cling to it and stifle it. It subserves interests not its own. Our organs of criticism are organs of men and parties having practical ends to serve, and with them those practical ends are the first thing and the play of mind the second; so much play of mind as is compatible with the prosecution of those practical ends is all that is wanted. An organ like the *Revue des Deux Mondes*,[6] having for its main function to understand and utter the best that is known and thought in the world, existing, it may be said, as just an organ for a free play of the mind, we have not. But we have the *Edinburgh Review*, existing as an organ of the old Whigs, and for as much play of mind as may suit its being that; we have the *Quarterly Review*, existing as an organ of the Tories, and for as much play of mind as may suit its being that; we have the *British Quarterly Review*, existing as an organ of the political Dissenters, and for as much play of mind as may suit its being that; we

5. This key word in Arnold's argument connotes independence and objectivity of mind. It means not having an interest, in the sense of an ax to grind. It does not mean lack of interest.
6. An international magazine of exceptionally high quality, founded in Paris in 1829.

have the *Times*, existing as an organ of the common, satisfied, well-to-do Englishman, and for as much play of mind as may suit its being that. And so on through all the various fractions, political and religious, of our society; every fraction has, as such, its organ of criticism, but the notion of combining all fractions in the common pleasure of a free disinterested play of mind meets with no favor. Directly this play of mind wants to have more scope, and to forget the pressure of practical considerations a little, it is checked, it is made to feel the chain. We saw this the other day in the extinction, so much to be regretted, of the *Home and Foreign Review*.[7] Perhaps in no organ of criticism in this country was there so much knowledge, so much play of mind; but these could not save it. The *Dublin Review* subordinates play of mind to the practical business of English and Irish Catholicism, and lives. It must needs be that men should act in sects and parties, that each of these sects and parties should have its organ, and should make this organ subserve the interests of its action; but it would be well, too, that there should be a criticism, not the minister of these interests, not their enemy, but absolutely and entirely independent of them. No other criticism will ever attain any real authority or make any real way towards its end—the creating a current of true and fresh ideas.

It is because criticism has so little kept in the pure intellectual sphere, has so little detached itself from practice, has been so directly polemical and controversial, that it has so ill accomplished, in this country, its best spiritual work, which is to keep man from a self-satisfaction which is retarding and vulgarizing, to lead him towards perfection, by making his mind dwell upon what is excellent in itself, and the absolute beauty and fitness of things. A polemical practical criticism makes men blind even to the ideal imperfection of their practice, makes them willingly assert its ideal perfection, in order the better to secure it against attack; and clearly this is narrowing and baneful for them. If they were reassured on the practical side, speculative considerations of ideal perfection they might be brought to entertain, and their spiritual horizon would thus gradually widen. Sir Charles Adderley[8] says to the Warwickshire farmers:

> Talk of the improvement of breed! Why, the race we ourselves represent, the men and women, the old Anglo-Saxon race, are the best breed in the whole world. . . . The absence of a too enervating climate, too unclouded skies, and a too luxurious nature, has produced so vigorous a race of people, and has rendered us so superior to all the world.

Mr. Roebuck says to the Sheffield cutlers:[9]

> I look around me and ask what is the state of England? Is not property safe? Is not every man able to say what he likes? Can you not walk from one end of England to the other in perfect security? I ask you whether, the world over or in past history, there is anything like it? Nothing. I pray that our unrivaled happiness may last.

7. A liberal Catholic periodical, founded in 1862, which ceased publication in 1864.
8. Conservative politician and wealthy landowner (1814–1905).

9. Makers of knives and forks. John Arthur Roebuck (1801–1879), radical politician and representative in Parliament for the industrial city of Sheffield, famous for its metalworking trades.

Now obviously there is a peril for poor human nature in words and thoughts of such exuberant self-satisfaction, until we find ourselves safe in the streets of the Celestial City.

> *Das wenige verschwindet leicht dem Blicke*
> *Der vorwärts sieht, wie viel noch übrig bleibt—*[1]

says Goethe; "the little that is done seems nothing when we look forward and see how much we have yet to do." Clearly this is a better line of reflection for weak humanity, so long as it remains on this earthly field of labor and trial.

But neither Sir Charles Adderley nor Mr. Roebuck is by nature inaccessible to considerations of this sort. They only lose sight of them owing to the controversial life we all lead, and the practical form which all speculation takes with us. They have in view opponents whose aim is not ideal, but practical; and in their zeal to uphold their own practice against these innovators, they go so far as even to attribute to this practice an ideal perfection. Somebody has been wanting to introduce a six-pound franchise, or to abolish church-rates,[2] or to collect agricultural statistics by force, or to diminish local self-government. How natural, in reply to such proposals, very likely improper or ill-timed, to go a little beyond the mark and to say stoutly, "Such a race of people as we stand, so superior to all the world! The old Anglo-Saxon race, the best breed in the whole world! I pray that our unrivaled happiness may last! I ask you whether, the world over or in past history, there is anything like it?" And so long as criticism answers this dithyramb by insisting that the old Anglo-Saxon race would be still more superior to all others if it had no church-rates, or that our unrivaled happiness would last yet longer with a six-pound franchise, so long will the strain, "The best breed in the whole world!" swell louder and louder, everything ideal and refining will be lost out of sight, and both the assailed and their critics will remain in a sphere, to say the truth, perfectly unvital, a sphere in which spiritual progression is impossible. But let criticism leave church-rates and the franchise alone, and in the most candid spirit, without a single lurking thought of practical innovation, confront with our dithyramb this paragraph on which I stumbled in a newspaper immediately after reading Mr. Roebuck:

> A shocking child murder has just been committed at Nottingham.[3] A girl named Wragg left the workhouse there on Saturday morning with her young illegitimate child. The child was soon afterwards found dead on Mapperly Hills, having been strangled. Wragg is in custody.

Nothing but that; but, in juxtaposition with the absolute eulogies of Sir Charles Adderley and Mr. Roebuck, how eloquent, how suggestive are those few lines! "Our old Anglo-Saxon breed, the best in the whole world!"—how much that is harsh and ill-favored there is in this best! *Wragg!* If we are to talk of ideal perfection, of "the best in the whole world," has anyone reflected what a touch of grossness in our race, what an original shortcoming in the more delicate spiritual perceptions, is shown by the natural growth amongst us of such hideous names—Higginbottom, Stiggins, Bugg! In Ionia and

---

1. Goethe's *Iphigenie auf Tauris* (1787) 1.2.91–92.
2. Taxes supporting the Church of England. "Six-pound franchise": a radical proposal to extend the right to vote to anyone owning land worth £6 annual rent.
3. It occurred on September 10, 1864.

Attica[4] they were luckier in this respect than "the best race in the world"; by the Ilissus[5] there was no Wragg, poor thing! And "our unrivaled happiness"— what an element of grimness, bareness, and hideousness mixes with it and blurs it; the workhouse, the dismal Mapperly Hills[6]—how dismal those who have seen them will remember—the gloom, the smoke, the cold, the strangled illegitimate child! "I ask you whether, the world over or in past history, there is anything like it?" Perhaps not, one is inclined to answer; but at any rate, in that case, the world is very much to be pitied. And the final touch— short, bleak and inhuman: *Wragg is in custody.* The sex lost in the confusion of our unrivaled happiness; or (shall I say?) the superfluous Christian name lopped off by the straightforward vigor of our old Anglo-Saxon breed! There is profit for the spirit in such contrasts as this; criticism serves the cause of perfection by establishing them. By eluding sterile conflict, by refusing to remain in the sphere where alone narrow and relative conceptions have any worth and validity, criticism may diminish its momentary importance, but only in this way has it a chance of gaining admittance for those wider and more perfect conceptions to which all its duty is really owed. Mr. Roebuck will have a poor opinion of an adversary who replies to his defiant songs of triumph only by murmuring under his breath, *Wragg is in custody*; but in no other way will these songs of triumph be induced gradually to moderate themselves, to get rid of what in them is excessive and offensive, and to fall into a softer and truer key.

It will be said that it is a very subtle and indirect action which I am thus prescribing for criticism, and that, by embracing in this manner the Indian[7] virtue of detachment and abandoning the sphere of practical life, it condemns itself to a slow and obscure work. Slow and obscure it may be, but it is the only proper work of criticism. The mass of mankind will never have any ardent zeal for seeing things as they are; very inadequate ideas will always satisfy them. On these inadequate ideas reposes, and must repose, the general practice of the world. That is as much as saying that whoever sets himself to see things as they are will find himself one of a very small circle; but it is only by this small circle resolutely doing its own work that adequate ideas will ever get current at all. The rush and roar of practical life will always have a dizzying and attracting effect upon the most collected spectator, and tend to draw him into its vortex; most of all will this be the case where that life is so powerful as it is in England. But it is only by remaining collected, and refusing to lend himself to the point of view of the practical man, that the critic can do the practical man any service, and it is only by the greatest sincerity in pursuing his own course, and by at last convincing even the practical man of his sincerity, that he can escape misunderstandings which perpetually threaten him.

For the practical man is not apt for fine distinctions, and yet in these distinctions truth and the highest culture greatly find their account. But it is not easy to lead a practical man—unless you reassure him as to your practical intentions, you have no chance of leading him—to see that a thing which

---

4. The district in Greece that includes Athens. Ionia is an area of the west coast of present-day Turkey where Homer was believed to have lived.
5. A stream south of Athens.

6. Adjacent to the coal-mining and industrial area of Nottingham (later associated with the writings of D. H. Lawrence).
7. I.e., Hindu.

he has always been used to look at from one side only, which he greatly values, and which, looked at from that side, quite deserves, perhaps, all the prizing and admiring which he bestows upon it—that this thing, looked at from another side, may appear much less beneficent and beautiful, and yet retain all its claims to our practical allegiance. Where shall we find language innocent enough, how shall we make the spotless purity of our intentions evident enough, to enable us to say to the political Englishman that the British Constitution itself, which, seen from the practical side, looks such a magnificent organ of progress and virtue, seen from the speculative side— with its compromises, its love of facts, its horror of theory, its studied avoidance of clear thoughts—that, seen from this side, our august Constitution sometimes looks—forgive me, shade of Lord Somers!—a colossal machine for the manufacture of Philistines?[8] How is Cobbett[9] to say this and not be misunderstood, blackened as he is with the smoke of a lifelong conflict in the field of political practice? how is Mr. Carlyle to say it and not be misunderstood, after his furious raid into this field with his *Latter-day Pamphlets*? how is Mr. Ruskin, after his pugnacious political economy?[1] I say, the critic must keep out of the region of immediate practice in the political, social, humanitarian sphere if he wants to make a beginning for that more free speculative treatment of things, which may perhaps one day make its benefits felt even in this sphere, but in a natural and thence irresistible manner.

* * *

If I have insisted so much on the course which criticism must take where politics and religion are concerned, it is because, where these burning matters are in question, it is most likely to go astray. I have wished, above all, to insist on the attitude which criticism should adopt towards things in general; on its right tone and temper of mind. But then comes another question as to the subject matter which literary criticism should most seek. Here, in general, its course is determined for it by the idea which is the law of its being; the idea of a disinterested endeavour to learn and propagate the best that is known and thought in the world, and thus to establish a current of fresh and true ideas. By the very nature of things, as England is not all the world, much of the best that is known and thought in the world cannot be of English growth, must be foreign; by the nature of things, again, it is just this that we are least likely to know, while English thought is streaming in upon us from all sides, and takes excellent care that we shall not be ignorant of its existence. The English critic of literature, therefore, must dwell much on foreign thought, and with particular heed on any part of it, which, while significant and fruitful in itself, is for any reason specially likely to escape him. Again, judging is often spoken of as the critic's one business, and so in some sense it is; but the judgment which almost insensibly forms itself in a fair and clear

---

8. The unenlightened middle classes, whose opposition to the defenders of culture is akin to that of the biblical tribe that fought against the people of Israel, "the children of light." Arnold's repeated use of this parallel has established the term in our language. John Somers (1651–1716), statesman responsible for formulating the Declaration of Rights.

9. William Cobbett (1762–1835), vehement reformer and champion of the poor and oppressed.
1. Reference to *Unto This Last* (1862), in which John Ruskin shifted from art criticism to an attack on traditional theories of economics. In *Latter-Day Pamphlets* (1850), Thomas Carlyle expressed bitter antidemocratic views.

mind, along with fresh knowledge, is the valuable one; and thus knowledge, and ever fresh knowledge, must be the critic's great concern for himself. And it is by communicating fresh knowledge, and letting his own judgment pass along with it—but insensibly, and in the second place, not the first, as a sort of companion and clue, not as an abstract lawgiver—that the critic will generally do most good to his readers. Sometimes, no doubt, for the sake of establishing an author's place in literature, and his relation to a central standard (and if this is not done, how are we to get at our *best in the world?*) criticism may have to deal with a subject matter so familiar that fresh knowledge is out of the question, and then it must be all judgment; an enunciation and detailed application of principles. Here the great safeguard is never to let oneself become abstract, always to retain an intimate and lively consciousness of the truth of what one is saying, and, the moment this fails us, to be sure that something is wrong. Still under all circumstances, this mere judgment and application of principles is, in itself, not the most satisfactory work to the critic; like mathematics, it is tautological, and cannot well give us, like fresh learning, the sense of creative activity.

But stop, some one will say; all this talk is of no practical use to us whatever; this criticism of yours is not what we have in our minds when we speak of criticism; when we speak of critics and criticism, we mean critics and criticism of the current English literature of the day; when you offer to tell criticism its function, it is to this criticism that we expect you to address yourself. I am sorry for it, for I am afraid I must disappoint these expectations. I am bound by my own definition of criticism: *a disinterested endeavour to learn and propagate the best that is known and thought in the world.* How much of current English literature comes into this "best that is known and thought in the world"? Not very much I fear; certainly less, at this moment, than of the current literature of France or Germany. Well, then, am I to alter my definition of criticism, in order to meet the requirements of a number of practicing English critics, who, after all, are free in their choice of a business? That would be making criticism lend itself just to one of those alien practical considerations, which, I have said, are so fatal to it. One may say, indeed, to those who have to deal with the mass—so much better disregarded—of current English literature, that they may at all events endeavour, in dealing with this, to try it, so far as they can, by the standard of the best that is known and thought in the world; one may say, that to get anywhere near this standard, every critic should try and possess one great literature, at least, besides his own; and the more unlike his own, the better. But, after all, the criticism I am really concerned with—the criticism which alone can much help us for the future, the criticism which, throughout Europe, is at the present day meant, when so much stress is laid on the importance of criticism and the critical spirit—is a criticism which regards Europe as being, for intellectual and spiritual purposes, one great confederation, bound to a joint action and working to a common result, and whose members have, for their proper outfit, a knowledge of Greek, Roman, and Eastern antiquity, and of one another. Special, local, and temporary advantages being put out of account, that modern nation will in the intellectual and spiritual sphere make most progress, which most thoroughly carries out this program. And what is that but saying that we too, all of us, as individuals, the more thoroughly we carry it out, shall make the more progress?

There is so much inviting us!—what are we to take? what will nourish us in growth towards perfection? That is the question which, with the immense field of life and of literature lying before him, the critic has to answer; for himself first, and afterwards for others. In this idea of the critic's business the essays brought together in the following pages have had their origin; in this idea, widely different as are their subjects, they have, perhaps, their unity.

I conclude with what I said at the beginning: to have the sense of creative activity is the great happiness and the great proof of being alive, and it is not denied to criticism to have it; but then criticism must be sincere, simple, flexible, ardent, ever widening its knowledge. Then it may have, in no contemptible measure, a joyful sense of creative activity; a sense which a man of insight and conscience will prefer to what he might derive from a poor, starved, fragmentary, inadequate creation. And at some epochs no other creation is possible.

Still, in full measure, the sense of creative activity belongs only to genuine creation; in literature we must never forget that. But what true man of letters ever can forget it? It is no such common matter for a gifted nature to come into possession of a current of true and living ideas, and to produce amidst the inspiration of them, that we are likely to underrate it. The epochs of Aeschylus[2] and Shakespeare make us feel their pre-eminence. In an epoch like those is, no doubt, the true life of literature; there is the promised land, towards which criticism can only beckon. That promised land it will not be ours to enter, and we shall die in the wilderness:[3] but to have desired to enter it, to have saluted it from afar, is already, perhaps, the best distinction among contemporaries; it will certainly be the best title to esteem with posterity.

1864, 1865

From Culture and Anarchy[1]

From *Chapter 1. Sweetness and Light*

The impulse of the English race towards moral development and self-conquest has nowhere so powerfully manifested itself as in Puritanism. Nowhere has Puritanism found so adequate an expression as in the reli-

---

2. Greek tragedian (525–456 B.C.E.).
3. An allusion to the fate of rebellious Israelites (Numbers 14.26–35).
1. Arnold began *Culture and Anarchy* in the context of the turbulent political debate that preceded the passage of the second Reform Bill in 1867. The political climate seemed to some to threaten anarchy, to which Arnold opposed culture. A characteristic quality of the cultured state of mind is summed up, for his purposes, in his formula "sweetness and light," a phrase suggesting reasonableness of temper and intellectual insight. Arnold derived the phrase from a fable contrasting the spider with the bee in Jonathan Swift's *The Battle of the Books* (1704). The spider (representing a narrow, self-centered, and uncultured mind) spins out of itself "nothing at all but

flybane and cobweb." The bee (representing a cultured mind that has drawn nourishment from the humanist tradition) ranges far and wide and makes in its hive honey and also wax out of which candles may be made. Therefore, the bee, Swift says, furnishes humankind "with the two noblest of things, which are sweetness and light."

The selections printed here illustrate aspects of Arnold's indictment of the middle classes for their lack of sweetness and light. The first and third expose the narrowness and dullness of middle-class Puritan religious institutions in both the 17th and 19th centuries. The second, "Doing As One Likes," shows the limitations of the middle-class political bias and the irresponsibility of laissez-faire economics. Here Arnold is most close to Thomas Carlyle and John Ruskin.

gious organization of the Independents.[2] The modern Independents have a newspaper, the *Nonconformist*, written with great sincerity and ability. The motto, the standard, the profession of faith which this organ of theirs carries aloft, is: "The Dissidence of Dissent and the Protestantism of the Protestant religion." There is sweetness and light, and an ideal of complete harmonious human perfection! One need not go to culture and poetry to find language to judge it. Religion, with its instinct for perfection, supplies language to judge it, language, too, which is in our mouths every day. "Finally, be of one mind, united in feeling," says St. Peter.[3] There is an ideal which judges the Puritan ideal: "The Dissidence of Dissent and the Protestantism of the Protestant religion!" And religious organizations like this are what people believe in, rest in, would give their lives for! Such, I say, is the wonderful virtue of even the beginnings of perfection, of having conquered even the plain faults of our animality, that the religious organization which has helped us to do it can seem to us something precious, salutary, and to be propagated, even when it wears such a brand of imperfection on its forehead as this. And men have got such a habit of giving to the language of religion a special application, of making it a mere jargon, that for the condemnation which religion itself passes on the shortcomings of their religious organizations they have no ear; they are sure to cheat themselves and to explain this condemnation away. They can only be reached by the criticism which culture, like poetry, speaking of language not to be sophisticated, and resolutely testing these organizations by the ideal of a human perfection complete on all sides, applies to them.

But men of culture and poetry, it will be said, are again and again failing, and failing conspicuously, in the necessary first stage to a harmonious perfection, in the subduing of the great obvious faults of our animality, which it is the glory of these religious organizations to have helped us to subdue. True, they do often so fail. They have often been without the virtues as well as the faults of the Puritan; it has been one of their dangers that they so felt the Puritan's faults that they too much neglected the practice of his virtues. I will not, however, exculpate them at the Puritan's expense. They have often failed in morality, and morality is indispensable. And they have been punished for their failure, as the Puritan has been rewarded for his performance. They have been punished wherein they erred; but their ideal of beauty, of sweetness and light, and a human nature complete on all its sides, remains the true ideal of perfection still; just as the Puritan's ideal of perfection remains narrow and inadequate, although for what he did well he has been richly rewarded. Notwithstanding the mighty results of the Pilgrim Fathers' voyage, they and their standard of perfection are rightly judged when we figure to ourselves Shakespeare or Virgil[4]—souls in whom sweetness and light, and all that in human nature is most humane, were eminent—accompanying them on their voyage, and think what intolerable company Shakespeare and Virgil would have found them! In the same way let us judge the religious organizations which we see all around us. Do not let us deny the good and

---

2. A 17th-century Puritan group (of which Oliver Cromwell was an adherent), allied with the Congregationalists.

3. Cf. 1 Peter 3.8.
4. Roman poet (70–19 B.C.E.).

the happiness which they have accomplished; but do not let us fail to see clearly that their idea of human perfection is narrow and inadequate, and that the Dissidence of Dissent and the Protestantism of the Protestant religion will never bring humanity to its true goal. As I said with regard to wealth: Let us look at the life of those who live in and for it—so I say with regard to the religious organizations. Look at the life imaged in such a newspaper as the *Nonconformist*—a life of jealousy of the Establishment,[5] disputes, tea-meetings, openings of chapels, sermons; and then think of it as an ideal of a human life completing itself on all sides, and aspiring with all its organs after sweetness, light, and perfection!

From *Chapter 2. Doing As One Likes*

* * *

When I began to speak of culture, I insisted on our bondage to machinery,[6] on our proneness to value machinery as an end in itself, without looking beyond it to the end for which alone, in truth, it is valuable. Freedom, I said, was one of those things which we thus worshiped in itself, without enough regarding the ends for which freedom is to be desired. In our common notions and talk about freedom, we eminently show our idolatry of machinery. Our prevalent notion is—and I quoted a number of instances to prove it—that it is a most happy and important thing for a man merely to be able to do as he likes. On what he is to do when he is thus free to do as he likes, we do not lay so much stress. Our familiar praise of the British Constitution under which we live, is that it is a system of checks—a system which stops and paralyzes any power in interfering with the free action of individuals. To this effect Mr. Bright,[7] who loves to walk in the old ways of the Constitution, said forcibly in one of his great speeches, what many other people are every day saying less forcibly, that the central idea of English life and politics is *the assertion of personal liberty*. Evidently this is so; but evidently, also, as feudalism, which with its ideas, and habits of subordination was for many centuries silently behind the British Constitution, dies out, and we are left with nothing but our system of checks, and our notion of its being the great right and happiness of an Englishman to do as far as possible what he likes, we are in danger of drifting towards anarchy. We have not the notion, so familiar on the Continent and to antiquity, of *the State*—the nation in its collective and corporate character, entrusted with stringent powers for the general advantage, and controlling individual wills in the name of an interest wider than that of individuals. We say, what is very true, that this notion is often made instrumental to tyranny; we say that a State is in reality made up of the individuals who compose it, and that every individual is the best judge of his own interests. Our leading class is an aristocracy, and no aristocracy likes the notion of a State-authority greater than itself, with a stringent administrative machinery superseding the decorative inutilities of lord-lieutenancy, deputy-

---

5. The Church of England or the Established Church.
6. Arnold uses this word to signify systems of operation and organization, not mechanized apparatus.
7. John Bright (1811–1889), self-made businessman who became a noted orator and politician.

lieutenancy, and the *posse comitatus*,[8] which are all in its own hands. Our middle class, the great representative of trade and Dissent, with its maxims of every man for himself in business, every man for himself in religion, dreads a powerful administration which might somehow interfere with it; and besides, it has its own decorative inutilities of vestrymanship[9] and guardianship, which are to this class what lord-lieutenancy and the county magistracy are to the aristocratic class, and a stringent administration might either take these functions out of its hands, or prevent its exercising them in its own comfortable, independent manner, as at present.

Then as to our working class. This class, pressed constantly by the hard daily compulsion of material wants, is naturally the very center and stronghold of our national idea, that it is man's ideal right and felicity to do as he likes. I think I have somewhere related how M. Michelet[1] said to me of the people of France, that it was "a nation of barbarians civilized by the conscription." He meant that through their military service the idea of public duty and of discipline was brought to the mind of these masses, in other respects so raw and uncultivated. Our masses are quite as raw and uncultivated as the French; and so far from their having the idea of public duty and of discipline, superior to the individual's self-will, brought to their mind by a universal obligation of military service, such as that of the conscription—so far from their having this, the very idea of a conscription is so at variance with our English notion of the prime right and blessedness of doing as one likes, that I remember the manager of the Clay Cross works in Derbyshire told me during the Crimean war,[2] when our want of soldiers was much felt and some people were talking of a conscription, that sooner than submit to a conscription the population of that district would flee to the mines, and lead a sort of Robin Hood life underground.

For a long time, as I have said, the strong feudal habits of subordination and deference continued to tell upon the working class. The modern spirit has now almost entirely dissolved those habits, and the anarchical tendency of our worship of freedom in and for itself, of our superstitious faith, as I say, in machinery, is becoming very manifest. More and more, because of this our blind faith in machinery, because of our want of light to enable us to look beyond machinery to the end for which machinery is valuable, this and that man, and this and that body of men, all over the country, are beginning to assert and put in practice an Englishman's right to do what he likes; his right to march where he likes, meet where he likes, enter where he likes, hoot as he likes, threaten as he likes, smash as he likes.[3] All this, I say, tends to anarchy; and though a number of excellent people, and particularly my friends of the Liberal or progressive party, as they call themselves, are kind enough to reassure us by saying that these are trifles, that a few transient outbreaks of rowdyism signify nothing, that our system of liberty is one which itself cures all the evils which it works, that the educated and intelligent classes stand in

8. Power of the county (Latin); a feudal method of enforcing law by local authorities instead of by agencies of the central government.
9. A vestryman is an appointed member on a local church council.
1. Jules Michelet (1798–1874), French historian.

2. A war (1854–56) in which Britain joined France, Sardinia, and Turkey in fighting against Russia in Ukraine.
3. A reference to the riots of 1866 in which a London mob demolished the iron railings enclosing Hyde Park.

overwhelming strength and majestic repose, ready, like our military force in riots, to act at a moment's notice—yet one finds that one's Liberal friends generally say this because they have such faith in themselves and their nostrums, when they shall return, as the public welfare requires, to place and power. But this faith of theirs one cannot exactly share, when one has so long had them and their nostrums at work, and see that they have not prevented our coming to our present embarrassed condition. And one finds, also, that the outbreaks of rowdyism tend to become less and less of trifles, to become more frequent rather than less frequent; and that meanwhile our educated and intelligent classes remain in their majestic repose, and somehow or other, whatever happens, their overwhelming strength, like our military force in riots, never does act.

How indeed, *should* their overwhelming strength act, when the man who gives an inflammatory lecture, or breaks down the park railings, or invades a Secretary of State's office, is only following an Englishman's impulse to do as he likes; and our own conscience tells us that we ourselves have always regarded this impulse as something primary and sacred? Mr. Murphy[4] lectures at Birmingham, and showers on the Catholic population of that town "words," says the Home Secretary, "only fit to be addressed to thieves or murderers." What then? Mr. Murphy has his own reasons of several kinds. He suspects the Roman Catholic Church of designs upon Mrs. Murphy; and he says if mayors and magistrates do not care for their wives and daughters, he does. But, above all, he is doing as he likes; or, in worthier language, asserting his personal liberty. "I will carry out my lectures if they walk over my body as a dead corpse, and I say to the Mayor of Birmingham that he is my servant while I am in Birmingham, and as my servant he must do his duty and protect me." Touching and beautiful words, which find a sympathetic chord in every British bosom! The moment it is plainly put before us that a man is asserting his personal liberty, we are half disarmed; because we are believers in freedom, and not in some dream of a right reason to which the assertion of our freedom is to be subordinated. Accordingly, the Secretary of State had to say that although the lecturer's language was "only fit to be addressed to thieves or murderers," yet, "I do not think he is to be deprived, I do not think that anything I have said could justify the inference that he is to be deprived, of the right of protection in a place built by him for the purpose of these lectures; because the language was not language which afforded grounds for a criminal prosecution." No, nor to be silenced by Mayor, or Home Secretary, or any administrative authority on earth, simply on their notion of what is discreet and reasonable! This is in perfect consonance with our public opinion, and with our national love for the assertion of personal liberty.

* * *

4. An orator whose inflammatory anti-Catholic public speech "The Errors of the Roman Church" led to rioting in Birmingham and other cities in 1867.

From *Chapter 5. Porro Unum Est Necessarium*[5]

* * *

Sweetness and light evidently have to do with the bent or side in humanity which we call Hellenic. Greek intelligence has obviously for its essence the instinct for what Plato[6] calls the true, firm, intelligible law of things; the law of light, of seeing things as they are. Even in the natural sciences, where the Greeks had not time and means adequately to apply this instinct, and where we have gone a great deal further than they did, it is this instinct which is the root of the whole matter and the ground of all our success; and this instinct the world has mainly learnt of the Greeks, inasmuch as they are humanity's most signal manifestation of it. Greek art, again, Greek beauty, have their root in the same impulse to see things as they really are, inasmuch as Greek art and beauty rest on fidelity to nature—the *best* nature—and on a delicate discrimination of what this best nature is. To say we work for sweetness and light, then, is only another way of saying that we work for Hellenism. But, oh! cry many people, sweetness and light are not enough; you must put strength or energy along with them, and make a kind of trinity of strength, sweetness and light, and then, perhaps, you may do some good. That is to say, we are to join Hebraism, strictness of the moral conscience, and manful walking by the best light we have, together with Hellenism, inculcate both, and rehearse[7] the praises of both.

Or, rather, we may praise both in conjunction, but we must be careful to praise Hebraism most. "Culture," says an acute, though somewhat rigid critic, Mr. Sidgwick,[8] "diffuses sweetness and light. I do not undervalue these blessings, but religion gives fire and strength, and the world wants[9] fire and strength even more than sweetness and light." By religion, let me explain, Mr. Sidgwick here means particularly that Puritanism on the insufficiency of which I have been commenting and to which he says I am unfair. Now, no doubt, it is possible to be a fanatical partisan of light and the instincts which push us to it, a fanatical enemy of strictness of moral conscience and the instincts which push us to it. A fanaticism of this sort deforms and vulgarizes the well-known work, in some respects so remarkable, of the late Mr. Buckle.[1] Such a fanaticism carries its own mark with it, in lacking sweetness; and its own penalty, in that, lacking sweetness, it comes in the end to lack light too. And the Greeks—the great exponents of humanity's bent for sweetness and light united, of its perception that the truth of things must be at the same time beauty—singularly escaped the fanaticism which we moderns, whether we Hellenize or whether we Hebraize, are so apt to show. They arrived—though failing, as has been said, to give adequate practical satisfaction to the claims of man's moral side—at the idea of a comprehensive adjustment of the claims of both the sides in man, the moral as well as the intellectual, of a full

---

5. But one thing is needful (Latin; Luke 10.42). This chapter develops a contrast established in chap. 4 between *Hebraism* (Puritan morality and energetic devotion to work) and *Hellenism* (cultivation of the aesthetic and intellectual understanding of life). The Puritan middle classes, according to Arnold, think that the "one thing needful" is the Hebraic form of virtue.

6. Greek philosopher (ca. 427–ca. 347 B.C.E.).
7. Repeat.
8. Henry Sidgwick (1838–1900), philosopher whose article on Arnold appeared in *Macmillan's Magazine* (Aug. 1867).
9. Lacks.
1. Henry Thomas Buckle (1821–1862), author of *A History of Civilization* (1857–61).

estimate of both, and of a reconciliation of both; an idea which is philosophi-
cally of the greatest value, and the best of lessons for us moderns. So we
ought to have no difficulty in conceding to Mr. Sidgwick that manful walking
by the best light one has—fire and strength as he calls it—has its high value
as well as culture, the endeavor to see things in their truth and beauty, the
pursuit of sweetness and light. But whether at this or that time, and to this
or that set of persons, one ought to insist most on the praises of fire and
strength, or on the praises of sweetness and light, must depend, one would
think, on the circumstances and needs of that particular time and those
particular persons. And all that we have been saying, and indeed any glance
at the world around us, shows that with us, with the most respectable and
strongest part of us, the ruling force is now, and long has been, a Puritan
force—the care for fire and strength, strictness of conscience, Hebraism,
rather than the care for sweetness and light, spontaneity of consciousness,
Hellenism.

Well, then, what is the good of our now rehearsing the praises of fire and
strength to ourselves, who dwell too exclusively on them already? When Mr.
Sidgwick says so broadly, that the world wants fire and strength even more
than sweetness and light, is he not carried away by a turn for broad generalization? does he not forget that the world is not all of one piece, and every
piece with the same needs at the same time? It may be true that the Roman
world at the beginning of our era, or Leo the Tenth's Court at the time of
the Reformation, or French society in the eighteenth century,[2] needed fire
and strength even more than sweetness and light. But can it be said that
the Barbarians who overran the empire needed fire and strength even more
than sweetness and light; or that the Puritans needed them more; or that
Mr. Murphy, the Birmingham lecturer, and the Rev. W. Cattle[3] and his
friends, need them more?

The Puritan's great danger is that he imagines himself in possession of a
rule telling him the *unum necessarium,* or one thing needful, and that he
then remains satisfied with a very crude conception of what this rule really
is and what it tells him, thinks he has now knowledge and henceforth needs
only to act, and, in this dangerous state of assurance and self-satisfaction,
proceeds to give full swing to a number of the instincts of his ordinary self.
Some of the instincts of his ordinary self he has, by the help of his rule of
life, conquered; but others which he has not conquered by this help he is so
far from perceiving to need subjugation, and to be instincts of an inferior
self, that he even fancies it to be his right and duty, in virtue of having conquered a limited part of himself, to give unchecked swing to the remainder.
He is, I say, a victim of Hebraism, of the tendency to cultivate strictness of
conscience rather than spontaneity of consciousness. And what he wants is
a larger conception of human nature, showing him the number of other
points at which his nature must come to its best, besides the points which
he himself knows and thinks of. There is no *unum necessarium,* or one thing
needful, which can free human nature from the obligation of trying to come
to its best at all these points. The real *unum necessarium* for us is to come to

---

2. Societies representing an excess of sophisticated worldliness as at the courts of a Roman
emperor such as Nero (54–68 C.E.) or of Pope Leo
X (1513–21) or Louis XV (1715–74), respectively.

3. A Nonconformist clergyman who was chair-
man of the anti-Catholic meeting addressed by
Murphy in 1867 (see chapter 2, "Doing As One
Likes," p. 466).

our best at all points. Instead of our "one thing needful," justifying in us vulgarity, hideousness, ignorance, violence—our vulgarity, hideousness, ignorance, violence, are really so many touchstones[4] which try our one thing needful, and which prove that in the state, at any rate, in which we ourselves have it, it is not all we want. And as the force which encourages us to stand staunch and fast by the rule and ground we have is Hebraism, so the force which encourages us to go back upon this rule, and to try the very ground on which we appear to stand, is Hellenism—a turn for giving our consciousness free play and enlarging its range. And what I say is, not that Hellenism is always for everybody more wanted than Hebraism, but that for the Rev. W. Cattle at this particular moment, and for the great majority of us his fellow countrymen, it is more wanted.

* * *

1868, 1869

From The Study of Poetry[1]

"The future of poetry is immense, because in poetry, where it is worthy of its high destinies, our race, as time goes on, will find an ever surer and surer stay. There is not a creed which is not shaken, not an accredited dogma which is not shown to be questionable, not a received tradition which does not threaten to dissolve. Our religion has materialized itself in the fact, in the supposed fact; it has attached its emotion to the fact, and now the fact is failing it. But for poetry the idea is everything; the rest is a world of illusion, of divine illusion. Poetry attaches its emotion to the idea; the idea *is* the fact. The strongest part of our religion today is its unconscious poetry."

Let me be permitted to quote these words of my own, as uttering the thought which should, in my opinion, go with us and govern us in all our study of poetry. In the present work[2] it is the course of one great contributory stream to the world-river of poetry that we are invited to follow. We are here invited to trace the stream of English poetry. But whether we set ourselves, as here, to follow only one of the several streams that make the mighty river of poetry, or whether we seek to know them all, our governing thought should be the same. We should conceive of poetry worthily, and more highly than it has been the custom to conceive of it. We should conceive of it as capable of

---

4. For the importance to Arnold of the concept of the touchstone—a succinct instance or standard by which to judge other materials—see also "The Study of Poetry" (next selection).
1. Aside from its vindication of the importance of literature, this essay is an interesting example of the variety of Arnold's reading. To know literature in only one language seemed to him not to know literature. His personal *Notebooks* show that throughout his active life he continued to read books in French, German, Italian, Latin, and Greek. His favorite authors in these languages are used by him as a means of testing English poetry. The testing is sometimes a severe one. Readers

may also protest that despite Arnold's wit, his essay is limited by an incomplete recognition of the values of comic literature, a shortcoming abundantly evident in the discussion of Chaucer. Nevertheless, whether we agree or disagree with some of Arnold's verdicts, we can be attracted by the combination of traditionalism and impressionism on which these verdicts are based, and we can enjoy the memorable phrasemaking in which the verdicts are expressed. "The Study of Poetry" has been extraordinarily potent in shaping literary tastes in England and in America.
2. An anthology of English poetry for which this essay served as the introduction.

higher uses, and called to higher destinies, than those which in general men have assigned to it hitherto. More and more mankind will discover that we have to turn to poetry to interpret life for us, to console us, to sustain us. Without poetry, our science will appear incomplete; and most of what now passes with us for religion and philosophy will be replaced by poetry. Science, I say, will appear incomplete without it. For finely and truly does Wordsworth call poetry "the impassioned expression which is in the countenance of all science";[3] and what is a countenance without its expression? Again, Wordsworth finely and truly calls poetry "the breath and finer spirit of all knowledge": our religion, parading evidences such as those on which the popular mind relies now; our philosophy, pluming itself on its reasonings about causation and finite and infinite being; what are they but the shadows and dreams and false shows of knowledge? The day will come when we shall wonder at ourselves for having trusted to them, for having taken them seriously; and the more we perceive their hollowness, the more we shall prize "the breath and finer spirit of knowledge" offered to us by poetry.

But if we conceive thus highly of the destinies of poetry, we must also set our standard for poetry high, since poetry, to be capable of fulfilling such high destinies, must be poetry of a high order of excellence. We must accustom ourselves to a high standard and to a strict judgment. * * *

The best poetry is what we want; the best poetry will be found to have a power of forming, sustaining, and delighting us, as nothing else can. A clearer, deeper sense of the best in poetry, and of the strength and joy to be drawn from it, is the most precious benefit which we can gather from a poetical collection such as the present. And yet in the very nature and conduct of such a collection there is inevitably something which tends to obscure in us the consciousness of what our benefit should be, and to distract us from the pursuit of it. We should therefore steadily set it before our minds at the outset, and should compel ourselves to revert constantly to the thought of it as we proceed.

Yes; constantly in reading poetry, a sense for the best, the really excellent, and of the strength and joy to be drawn from it, should be present in our minds and should govern our estimate of what we read. But this real estimate, the only true one, is liable to be superseded, if we are not watchful, by two other kinds of estimate, the historic estimate and the personal estimate, both of which are fallacious. A poet or a poem may count to us historically, they may count to us on grounds personal to ourselves, and they may count to us really. They may count to us historically. The course of development of a nation's language, thought, and poetry, is profoundly interesting; and by regarding a poet's work as a stage in this course of development we may easily bring ourselves to make it of more importance as poetry than in itself it really is, we may come to use a language of quite exaggerated praise in criticizing it; in short, to overrate it. So arises in our poetic judgments the fallacy caused by the estimate which we may call historic. Then, again, a poet or a poem may count to us on grounds personal to ourselves. Our personal affinities, likings, and circumstances, have great power to sway our estimate of this or that poet's work, and to make us attach more importance to it as poetry than in itself it really possesses, because to us it is, or has been, of

3. Preface to *Lyrical Ballads* (1800).

high importance. Here also we overrate the object of our interest, and apply to it a language of praise which is quite exaggerated. And thus we get the source of a second fallacy in our poetic judgments—the fallacy caused by an estimate which we may call personal.

* * *

The historic estimate is likely in especial to affect our judgment and our language when we are dealing with ancient poets; the personal estimate when we are dealing with poets our contemporaries, or at any rate modern. The exaggerations due to the historic estimate are not in themselves, perhaps, of very much gravity. Their report hardly enters the general ear; probably they do not always impose even on the literary men who adopt them. But they lead to a dangerous abuse of language. So we hear Caedmon,[4] amongst our own poets, compared to Milton. I have already noticed the enthusiasm of one accomplished French critic for "historic origins."[5] Another eminent French critic, M. Vitet, comments upon that famous document of the early poetry of his nation, the *Chanson de Roland*.[6] It is indeed a most interesting document. The *joculator* or *jongleur*[7] Taillefer, who was with William the Conqueror's army at Hastings,[8] marched before the Norman troops, so said the tradition, singing "of Charlemagne and of Roland and of Oliver, and of the vassals who died at Roncevaux"; and it is suggested that in the *Chanson de Roland* by one Turoldus or *Theŕoulde*, a poem preserved in a manuscript of the twelfth century in the Bodleian Library at Oxford, we have certainly the matter, perhaps even some of the words, of the chant which Taillefer sang. The poem has vigor and freshness; it is not without pathos. But M. Vitet is not satisfied with seeing in it a document of some poetic value, and of very high historic and linguistic value; he sees in it a grand and beautiful work, a monument of epic genius. In its general design he finds the grandiose conception, in its details he finds the constant union of simplicity with greatness, which are the marks, he truly says, of the genuine epic, and distinguish it from the artificial epic of literary ages. One thinks of Homer; this is the sort of praise which is given to Homer, and justly given. Higher praise there cannot well be, and it is the praise due to epic poetry of the highest order only, and to no other. Let us try, then, the *Chanson de Roland* at its best. Roland, mortally wounded, lays himself down under a pine tree, with his face turned towards Spain and the enemy—

> De plusurs choses à remembrer li prist,
> De tantes teres cume li bers cunquist,
> De dulce France, des humes de sun lign,
> De Carlemagne sun seignor ki l'nurrit.[9]

4. A 7th-century Old English poet.
5. Charles d'Héricault (1823–1899), a French critic cited earlier in a passage omitted here. Arnold had mildly reprimanded him for his "historical" bias in praising a 15th-century poet, Clément Marot, at the expense of classical 17th-century poets such as Racine.
6. An 11th-century epic poem in Old French that tells of the 8th-century wars of Charlemagne against the Moors in Spain and of the bravery of the French leaders Roland and Oliver. Ludovic

Vitet (1802–1873) wrote of it in his *Essais Historiques et Littéraires* (1862).
7. Jester or minstrel (French).
8. The battle in 1066 in which Harold II was killed and the English army defeated.
9. "Then began he to call many things to remembrance—all the lands which his valor conquered and pleasant France, and the men of his lineage, and Charlemagne his liege lord who nourished him." *Chanson de Roland* 3.939–42 [Arnold's note].

That is primitive work, I repeat, with an undeniable poetic quality of its own. It deserves such praise, and such praise is sufficient for it. But now turn to Homer—

> Ὣς φάτο τοὺς δ' ἤδη κάτεχεν φυσίζοος αἶα
> ἐν Λακεδαίμονι αὖθι, φίλῃ ἐν πατρίδι γαίῃ.[1]

We are here in another world, another order of poetry altogether; here is rightly due such supreme praise as that which M. Vitet gives to the *Chanson de Roland*. If our words are to have any meaning, if our judgments are to have any solidity, we must not heap that supreme praise upon poetry of an order immeasurably inferior.

Indeed there can be no more useful help for discovering what poetry belongs to the class of the truly excellent, and can therefore do us most good, than to have always in one's mind lines and expressions of the great masters, and to apply them as a touchstone to other poetry. Of course we are not to require this other poetry to resemble them; it may be very dissimilar. But if we have any tact we shall find them, when we have lodged them well in our minds, an infallible touchstone for detecting the presence or absence of high poetic quality, and also the degree of this quality, in all other poetry which we may place beside them. Short passages, even single lines, will serve our turn quite sufficiently. Take the two lines which I have just quoted from Homer, the poet's comment on Helen's mention of her brothers—or take his

> Ἀ δειλώ, τί σφῶϊ δόμεν Πηλῆϊ ἄνακτι
> θνητῷ; ὑμεῖς δ' ἐστὸν ἀγήρω τ' ἀθανάτω τε.
> ἦ ἵνα δυστήνοισι μεῖ ἀνδράσιν ἄλγε' ἔχητον;[2]

the address of Zeus to the horses of Peleus—or take finally his

> Καὶ σέ, γέρον, τὸ πρὶν μὲν ἀκούομεν ὄλβιον εἶναι.[3]

the words of Achilles to Priam, a suppliant before him. Take that incomparable line and a half of Dante, Ugolino's tremendous words—

> Io no piangeva; sì dentro impietrai.
> Piangevan elli[4] . . .

take the lovely words of Beatrice to Virgil—

> Io son fatta da Dio, sua mercè, tale,
> Che la vostra miseria non mi tange,
> Nè fiamma d'esto incendio non m'assale[5] . . .

take the simple, but perfect, single line—

> In la sua volontade è nostra pace.[6]

1. "So said she; they long since in Earth's soft arms were reposing, / There, in their own dear land, their fatherland, Lacedaemon." *Iliad* 3.243–44 (translated by Dr. Hawtrey) [Arnold's note].
2. "Ah, unhappy pair, why gave we you to King Peleus, to a mortal? but ye are without old age, and immortal. Was it that with men born to misery ye might have sorrow?" *Iliad* 17.443–45 [Arnold's note].
3. "Nay, and thou too, old man, in former days wast, as we hear, happy." *Iliad* 24.543 [Arnold's note]. Priam, king of Troy, has begged Achilles to return the body of his son Hector, whom the Greek warrior had killed.
4. "I wailed not, so of stone I grew within; *they* wailed." *Inferno* 33.49–50 [Arnold's note].
5. "Of such sort hath God, thanked be His mercy, made me, that your misery toucheth me not, neither doth the flame of this fire strike me." *Inferno* 2.91–93 [Arnold's note]. The Roman poet Virgil is Dante's guide.
6. "In His will is our peace." *Paradiso* 3.85 [Arnold's note].

Take of Shakespeare a line or two of Henry the Fourth's expostulation with sleep—

> Wilt thou upon the high and giddy mast
> Seal up the shipboy's eyes, and rock his brains
> In cradle of the rude imperious surge[7] . . .

and take, as well, Hamlet's dying request to Horatio—

> If thou didst ever hold me in thy heart,
> Absent thee from felicity awhile,
> And in this harsh world draw thy breath in pain,
> To tell my story[8] . . .

Take of Milton that Miltonic passage—

> Darkened so, yet shone
> Above them all the archangel; but his face
> Deep scars of thunder had intrenched, and care
> Sat on his faded cheek[9] . . .

add two such lines as—

> And courage never to submit or yield
> And what is else not to be overcome[1] . . .

and finish with the exquisite close to the loss of Proserpine, the loss

> . . . which cost Ceres all that pain
> To seek her through the world.[2]

These few lines, if we have tact and can use them, are enough even of themselves to keep clear and sound our judgments about poetry, to save us from fallacious estimates of it, to conduct us to a real estimate.

The specimens I have quoted differ widely from one another, but they have in common this: the possession of the very highest poetical quality. If we are thoroughly penetrated by their power, we shall find that we have acquired a sense enabling us, whatever poetry may be laid before us, to feel the degree in which a high poetical quality is present or wanting there. Critics give themselves great labour to draw out what in the abstract constitutes the characters of a high quality of poetry. It is much better simply to have recourse to concrete examples—to take specimens of poetry of the high, the very highest quality, and to say: The characters of a high quality of poetry are what is expressed *there*. They are far better recognized by being felt in the verse of the master, than by being perused in the prose of the critic. Nevertheless if we are urgently pressed to give some critical account of them, we may safely, perhaps, venture on laying down, not indeed how and why the characters arise, but where and in what they arise. They are in the matter and substance of the poetry, and they are in its manner and style. Both of these, the substance and matter on the one hand, the style and manner on the other, have a mark, an accent, of high beauty, worth, and power. But if

---

7. *2 Henry IV* 3.1.18–20.
8. *Hamlet* 5.2.288–91.
9. *Paradise Lost* 1.599–602.
1. *Paradise Lost* 1.108–9.

2. *Paradise Lost* 4.271–72. Ceres, the Roman goddess of grain, searched for her daughter Proserpina, not knowing that she had been abducted by Pluto, the god of the underworld.

we are asked to define this mark and accent in the abstract, our answer must be: No, for we should thereby be darkening the question, not clearing it. The mark and accent are as given by the substance and matter of that poetry, by the style and manner of that poetry, and of all other poetry which is akin to it in quality.

Only one thing we may add as to the substance and matter of poetry, guiding ourselves by Aristotle's profound observation that the superiority of poetry over history consists in its possessing a higher truth and a higher seriousness ($\phi\iota\lambda o\sigma o\phi\acute\omega\tau\epsilon\rho o\nu$ $\kappa\alpha\grave\iota$ $\sigma\pi o\upsilon\delta\alpha\iota\acute o\tau\epsilon\rho o\nu$).[3] Let us add, therefore, to what we have said, this: that the substance and matter of the best poetry acquire their special character from possessing, in an eminent degree, truth and seriousness. We may add yet further, what is in itself evident, that to the style and manner of the best poetry their special character, their accent, is given by their diction, and, even yet more, by their movement. And though we distinguish between the two characters, the two accents, of superiority, yet they are nevertheless vitally connected one with the other. The superior character of truth and seriousness, in the matter and substance of the best poetry, is inseparable from the superiority of diction and movement marking its style and manner. The two superiorities are closely related, and are in steadfast proportion one to the other. So far as high poetic truth and seriousness are wanting to a poet's matter and substance, so far also, we may be sure, will a high poetic stamp of diction and movement be wanting to his style and manner. In proportion as this high stamp of diction and movement, again, is absent from a poet's style and manner, we shall find, also, that high poetic truth and seriousness are absent from his substance and matter.

So stated, these are but dry generalities; their whole force lies in their application. And I could wish every student of poetry to make the application of them for himself. Made by himself, the application would impress itself upon his mind far more deeply than made by me. Neither will my limits allow me to make any full application of the generalities above propounded; but in the hope of bringing out, at any rate, some significance in them, and of establishing an important principle more firmly by their means, I will, in the space which remains to me, follow rapidly from the commencement the course of our English poetry with them in my view.

* * *

Chaucer's * * * poetical importance does not need the assistance of the historic estimate; it is real. He is a genuine source of joy and strength, which is flowing still for us and will flow always. He will be read, as time goes on, far more generally than he is read now. His language is a cause of difficulty for us; but so also, and I think in quite as great a degree, is the language of Burns.[4] In Chaucer's case, as in that of Burns, it is a difficulty to be unhesitatingly accepted and overcome.

If we ask ourselves wherein consists the immense superiority of Chaucer's poetry over the romance poetry—why it is that in passing from this to Chaucer we suddenly feel ourselves to be in another world, we shall find that his superiority is both in the substance of his poetry and in the style of

3. Aristotle's *Poetics* 9.
4. Robert Burns (1759–1796), whose language is difficult because he frequently uses Scottish dialect.

his poetry. His superiority in substance is given by his large, free, simple, clear yet kindly view of human life—so unlike the total want, in the romance poets, of all intelligent command of it. Chaucer has not their helplessness; he has gained the power to survey the world from a central, a truly human point of view. We have only to call to mind the Prologue to *The Canterbury Tales*. The right comment upon it is Dryden's: "It is sufficient to say, according to the proverb, that *here is God's plenty*." And again: "He is a perpetual fountain of good sense."[5] It is by a large, free, sound representation of things, that poetry, this high criticism of life, has truth of substance; and Chaucer's poetry has truth of substance.

Of his style and manner, if we think first of the romance poetry and then of Chaucer's divine liquidness of diction, his divine fluidity of movement, it is difficult to speak temperately. They are irresistible, and justify all the rapture with which his successors speak of his "gold dewdrops of speech."[6] Johnson misses the point entirely when he finds fault with Dryden for ascribing to Chaucer the first refinement of our numbers, and says that Gower[7] also can show smooth numbers and easy rhymes. The refinement of our numbers means something far more than this. A nation may have versifiers with smooth numbers and easy rhymes, and yet may have no real poetry at all. Chaucer is the father of our splendid English poetry; he is our "well of English undefiled,"[8] because by the lovely charm of his diction, the lovely charm of his movement, he makes an epoch and founds a tradition. In Spenser, Shakespeare, Milton, Keats, we can follow the tradition of the liquid diction, the fluid movement, of Chaucer; at one time it is his liquid diction of which in these poets we feel the virtue, and at another time it is his fluid movement. And the virtue is irresistible.

Bounded as is my space, I must yet find room for an example of Chaucer's virtue, as I have given examples to show the virtue of the great classics. I feel disposed to say that a single line is enough to show the charm of Chaucer's verse; that merely one line like this—

> O martyr souded[9] in virginitee!

has a virtue of manner and movement such as we shall not find in all the verse of romance poetry—but this is saying nothing. The virtue is such as we shall not find, perhaps, in all English poetry, outside the poets whom I have named as the special inheritors of Chaucer's tradition. A single line, however, is too little if we have not the strain of Chaucer's verse well in our memory; let us take a stanza. It is from *The Prioress's Tale*, the story of the Christian child murdered in a Jewry[1]—

> My throte is cut unto my nekke-bone
> Saidè this child, and as by way of kinde
> I should have deyd, yea, longè time agone;
> But Jesu Christ, as ye in bookès finde,

---

5. Both quotations are from John Dryden's (1631–1700) preface to his *Fables Ancient and Modern* (1700).
6. "The Life of Our Lady," a poem by John Lydgate (ca. 1370–ca.1451).
7. John Gower (ca. 1325–1408), friend of Chaucer and author of the *Confessio Amantis*, a long poem in octosyllabic couplets. Samuel Johnson

(1709–1784), critic, essayist, and poet.
8. Said of Chaucer by Edmund Spenser (1552–1599) in *The Faerie Queene* (1590) 4.2.32.
9. The French *soudé*: soldered, fixed fast [Arnold's note]. From *The Canterbury Tales, The Prioress's Tale* (line 127); Chaucer wrote "souded to" rather than "souded in."
1. Jewish ghetto.

> Will that his glory last and be in minde,
> And for the worship of his mother dere
> Yet may I sing *O Alma* loud and clere.

Wordsworth has modernized this Tale, and to feel how delicate and evanescent is the charm of verse, we have only to read Wordsworth's first three lines of this stanza after Chaucer's—

> My throat is cut unto the bone, I trow,
> Said this young child, and by the law of kind
> I should have died, yea, many hours ago.

The charm is departed. It is often said that the power of liquidness and fluidity in Chaucer's verse was dependent upon a free, a licentious dealing with language, such as is now impossible; upon a liberty, such as Burns too enjoyed, of making words like *neck, bird,* into a dissyllable by adding to them, and words like *cause, rhyme,* into a dissyllable by sounding the *e* mute. It is true that Chaucer's fluidity is conjoined with this liberty, and is admirably served by it; but we ought not to say that it was dependent upon it. It was dependent upon his talent. Other poets with a like liberty do not attain to the fluidity of Chaucer; Burns himself does not attain to it. Poets, again, who have a talent akin to Chaucer's, such as Shakespeare or Keats, have known how to attain to his fluidity without the like liberty.

And yet Chaucer is not one of the great classics. His poetry transcends and effaces, easily and without effort, all the romance poetry of Catholic Christendom; it transcends and effaces all the English poetry contemporary with it, it transcends and effaces all the English poetry subsequent to it down to the age of Elizabeth. Of such avail is poetic truth of substance, in its natural and necessary union with poetic truth of style. And yet, I say, Chaucer is not one of the great classics. He has not their accent. What is wanting to him is suggested by the mere mention of the name of the first great classic of Christendom, the immortal poet who died eighty years before Chaucer—Dante. The accent of such verse as

In la sua volontade è nostra pace[2] . . .

is altogether beyond Chaucer's reach; we praise him, but we feel that this accent is out of the question for him. It may be said that it was necessarily out of the reach of any poet in the England of that stage of growth. Possibly; but we are to adopt a real, not a historic, estimate of poetry. However we may account for its absence, something is wanting, then, to the poetry of Chaucer, which poetry must have before it can be placed in the glorious class of the best. And there is no doubt what that something is. It is the σπουδαιότης, the high and excellent seriousness, which Aristotle assigns as one of the grand virtues of poetry. The substance of Chaucer's poetry, his view of things and his criticism of life, has largeness, freedom, shrewdness, benignity; but it has not this high seriousness. Homer's criticism of life has it, Dante's has it, Shakespeare's has it. It is this chiefly which gives to our spirits what they can rest upon; and with the increasing demands of our modern ages upon poetry, this virtue of giving us what we can rest upon will be more and more highly esteemed. A voice from

2. See p. 474, n. 6.

the slums of Paris, fifty or sixty years after Chaucer, the voice of poor Villon out of his life of riot and crime, has at its happy moments (as, for instance, in the last stanza of *La Belle Heaulmière*)[3] more of this important poetic virtue of seriousness than all the productions of Chaucer. But its apparition[4] in Villon, and in men like Villon, is fitful; the greatness of the great poets, the power of their criticism of life, is that their virtue is sustained.

To our praise, therefore, of Chaucer as a poet there must be this limitation: he lacks the high seriousness of the great classics, and therewith an important part of their virtue. Still, the main fact for us to bear in mind about Chaucer is his sterling value according to that real estimate which we firmly adopt for all poets. He has poetic truth of substance, though he has not high poetic seriousness, and corresponding to his truth of substance he has an exquisite virtue of style and manner. With him is born our real poetry.

For my present purpose I need not dwell on our Elizabethan poetry, or on the continuation and close of this poetry in Milton. We all of us profess to be agreed in the estimate of this poetry; we all of us recognize it as great poetry, our greatest, and Shakespeare and Milton as our poetical classics. The real estimate, here, has universal currency. With the next age of our poetry divergency and difficulty begin. An historic estimate of that poetry has established itself; and the question is, whether it will be found to coincide with the real estimate.

The age of Dryden, together with our whole eighteenth century which followed it, sincerely believed itself to have produced poetical classics of its own, and even to have made advance, in poetry, beyond all its predecessors. Dryden regards as not seriously disputable the opinion "that the sweetness of English verse was never understood or practiced by our fathers."[5] Cowley[6] could see nothing at all in Chaucer's poetry. Dryden heartily admired it, and, as we have seen, praised its matter admirably; but of its exquisite manner and movement all he can find to say is that "there is the rude sweetness of a Scotch tune in it, which is natural and pleasing, though not perfect."[7] Addison,[8] wishing to praise Chaucer's numbers, compares them with Dryden's own. And all through the eighteenth century, and down even into our own times, the stereotyped phrase of approbation for good verse found in our early poetry has been, that it even approached the verse of Dryden, Addison, Pope, and Johnson.

Are Dryden and Pope poetical classics? Is the historic estimate, which represents them as such, and which has been so long established that it cannot easily give way, the real estimate? Wordsworth and Coleridge, as is well known, denied it; but the authority of Wordsworth and Coleridge does not weigh much with the young generation, and there are many signs to show that the eighteenth century and its judgments are coming into favor again. Are the favorite poets of the eighteenth century classics?

3. The name *Heaulmière* is said to be derived from a headdress (helm) worn as a mask by courtesans. In Villon's ballad a poor old creature of this class laments her days of youth and beauty. The last stanza of the ballad runs thus—*"Ainsi le bon temps regretons / Entrenous, pauvres vieilles sottes, / Assises bas, à croppetons, / Tout en ung tas comme pelottes; / A petit feu de chenevottes / Tost allumeé's, tost estaincles, / Et jadis fusmes si mignottes! / Ainsi en prend à maintz et maintes."* [It may be translated:] "Thus amongst ourselves we regret the good time, poor silly old things, low-seated on our heels, all in a heap like so many balls; by a little fire of hemp stalks, soon lighted, soon spent. And once we were such darlings! So fares it with many and many a one" [Arnold's note]. François Villon (1431–1484), French poet and vagabond.

4. Appearance.

5. *Essay on Dramatic Poesy* (1668).

6. Abraham Cowley (1618–1667), English poet.

7. Preface to his *Fables.*

8. Joseph Addison (1672–1719), essayist and poet.

It is impossible within my present limits to discuss the question fully. And what man of letters would not shrink from seeming to dispose dictatorially of the claims of two men who are, at any rate, such masters in letters as Dryden and Pope; two men of such admirable talent, both of them, and one of them, Dryden, a man, on all sides, of such energetic and genial power? And yet, if we are to gain the full benefit from poetry, we must have the real estimate of it. I cast about for some mode of arriving, in the present case, at such an estimate without offense. And perhaps the best way is to begin, as it is easy to begin, with cordial praise.

When we find Chapman,[9] the Elizabethan translator of Homer, expressing himself in his preface thus: "Though truth in her very nakedness sits in so deep a pit, that from Gades to Aurora and Ganges few eyes can sound her, I hope yet those few here will so discover and confirm that, the date being out of her darkness in this morning of our poet, he shall now gird his temples with the sun," we pronounce that such a prose is intolerable. When we find Milton writing: "And long it was not after, when I was confirmed in this opinion, that he, who would not be frustrate of his hope to write well hereafter in laudable things, ought himself to be a true poem"[1]—we pronounce that such a prose has its own grandeur, but that it is obsolete and inconvenient. But when we find Dryden telling us: "What Virgil wrote in the vigor of his age, in plenty and at ease, I have undertaken to translate in my declining years; struggling with wants, oppressed with sickness, curbed in my genius, liable to be misconstrued in all I write"[2]—then we exclaim that here at last we have the true English prose, a prose such as we would all gladly use if we only knew how. Yet Dryden was Milton's contemporary.

But after the Restoration the time had come when our nation felt the imperious need of a fit prose. So, too, the time had likewise come when our nation felt the imperious need of freeing itself from the absorbing preoccupation which religion in the Puritan age had exercised. It was impossible that this freedom should be brought about without some negative excess, without some neglect and impairment of the religious life of the soul; and the spiritual history of the eighteenth century shows us that the freedom was not achieved without them. Still, the freedom was achieved; the preoccupation, an undoubtedly baneful and retarding one if it had continued, was got rid of. And as with religion amongst us at that period, so it was also with letters. A fit prose was a necessity; but it was impossible that a fit prose should establish itself amongst us without some touch of frost to the imaginative life of the soul. The needful qualities for a fit prose are regularity, uniformity, precision, balance. The men of letters, whose destiny it may be to bring their nation to the attainment of a fit prose, must of necessity, whether they work in prose or in verse, give a predominating, an almost exclusive attention to the qualities of regularity, uniformity, precision, balance. But an almost exclusive attention to these qualities involves some repression and silencing of poetry.

We are to regard Dryden as the puissant and glorious founder, Pope as the splendid high priest, of our age of prose and reason, of our excellent and indispensable eighteenth century. For the purposes of their mission and des-

---

9. George Chapman (ca. 1559–1634), poet and dramatist; the quotation is from his translation (1598–1611) of the *Iliad*.

1. "Apology for Smectymnuus" (1642).
2. "Postscript to the Reader" (1698) in his translation of Virgil.

tiny their poetry, like their prose, is admirable. Do you ask me whether Dryden's verse, take it almost where you will, is not good?

> A milk-white Hind, immortal and unchanged,
> Fed on the lawns and in the forest ranged.[3]

I answer: Admirable for the purposes of the inaugurator of an age of prose and reason. Do you ask me whether Pope's verse, take it almost where you will, is not good?

> To Hounslow Heath I point, and Banstead Down;
> Thence comes your mutton, and these chicks my own.[4]

I answer: Admirable for the purposes of the high priest of an age of prose and reason. But do you ask me whether such verse proceeds from men with an adequate poetic criticism of life, from men whose criticism of life has a high seriousness, or even, without that high seriousness, has poetic largeness, freedom, insight, benignity? Do you ask me whether the application of ideas to life in the verse of these men, often a powerful application, no doubt, is a powerful *poetic* application? Do you ask me whether the poetry of these men has either the matter or the inseparable manner of such an adequate poetic criticism; whether it has the accent of

> Absent thee from felicity awhile . . .

or of

> And what is else not to be overcome . . .

or of

> O martyr souded in virginitee!

I answer: It has not and cannot have them; it is the poetry of the builders of an age of prose and reason. Though they may write in verse, though they may in a certain sense be masters of the art of versification, Dryden and Pope are not classics of our poetry, they are classics of our prose.

Gray[5] is our poetical classic of that literature and age; the position of Gray is singular, and demands a word of notice here. He has not the volume or the power of poets who, coming in times more favorable, have attained to an independent criticism of life. But he lived with the great poets, he lived, above all, with the Greeks, through perpetually studying and enjoying them; and he caught their poetic point of view for regarding life, caught their poetic manner. The point of view and the manner are not self-sprung in him, he caught them of others; and he had not the free and abundant use of them. But whereas Addison and Pope never had the use of them, Gray had the use of them at times. He is the scantiest and frailest of classics in our poetry, but he is a classic.[6]

* * *

3. *The Hind and the Panther* (1687) 1.1–2.
4. *Imitations of Horace* (1737), Satire 2.2.143–44.
5. Thomas Gray (1716–1771), British poet.
6. After Gray, the only other poet discussed by Arnold is Burns (not printed here). Arnold concludes that "Burns, like Chaucer, comes short of the high seriousness of the great classics."

At any rate the end to which the method and the estimate are designed to lead, and from leading to which, if they do lead to it, they get their whole value—the benefit of being able clearly to feel and deeply to enjoy the best, the truly classic, in poetry—is an end, let me say it once more at parting, of supreme importance. We are often told that an era is opening in which we are to see multitudes of a common sort of readers, and masses of a common sort of literature; that such readers do not want and could not relish any-thing better than such literature, and that to provide it is becoming a vast and profitable industry. Even if good literature entirely lost currency with the world, it would still be abundantly worth while to continue to enjoy it by oneself. But it never will lose currency with the world, in spite of momentary appearances; it never will lose supremacy. Currency and supremacy are insured to it, not indeed by the world's deliberate and conscious choice, but by something far deeper—by the instinct of self-preservation in humanity.

1880

Literature and Science[1]

Practical people talk with a smile of Plato and of his absolute ideas: and it is impossible to deny that Plato's ideas do often seem unpractical and unpracticable, and especially when one views them in connection with the life of a great work-a-day world like the United States. The necessary staple of the life of such a world Plato regards with disdain; handicraft and trade and the working professions he regards with disdain; but what becomes of the life of an industrial modern community if you take handicraft and trade and the working professions out of it? The base mechanic arts and handi-crafts, says Plato, bring about a natural weakness in the principle of excel-lence in a man, so that he cannot govern the ignoble growths in him, but nurses them, and cannot understand fostering any other. Those who exer-cise such arts and trades, as they have their bodies, he says, marred by their vulgar businesses, so they have their souls, too, bowed and broken by them. And if one of these uncomely people has a mind to seek self-culture and philosophy, Plato compares him to a bald little tinker, who has scraped together money, and has got his release from service, and has had a bath, and bought a new coat, and is rigged out like a bridegroom about to marry the daughter of his master who has fallen into poor and helpless estate.[2]

Nor do the working professions fare any better than trade at the hands of Plato. He draws for us an inimitable picture of the working lawyer, and of his life of bondage; he shows how this bondage from his youth up has stunted and warped him, and made him small and crooked of soul, encompassing him with difficulties which he is not man enough to rely on justice and truth as means to encounter, but has recourse, for help out of them, to

1. Delivered as a lecture during Arnold's tour of the United States in 1883 and published in *Discourses in America* (1885), this essay has become a classic contribution to a subject endlessly debated. Its main argument was summed up by Stuart P. Sherman: "If Arnold had said outright that the study of letters helps us to *bear* the grand results of science, he would not have been guilty of a superficial epigram; he would have spoken from the depths of his experience."
2. *Republic* 6.495.

falsehood and wrong. And so, says Plato, this poor creature is bent and broken, and grows up from boy to man without a particle of soundness in him, although exceedingly smart and clever in his own esteem.[3]

One cannot refuse to admire the artist who draws these pictures. But we say to ourselves that his ideas show the influence of a primitive and obsolete order of things, when the warrior caste and the priestly caste were alone in honor, and the humble work of the world was done by slaves. We have now changed all that; the modern majesty consists in work, as Emerson declares;[4] and in work, we may add, principally of such plain and dusty kind as the work of cultivators of the ground, handicraftsmen, men of trade and business, men of the working professions. Above all is this true in a great industrious community such as that of the United States.

Now education, many people go on to say, is still mainly governed by the ideas of men like Plato, who lived when the warrior caste and the priestly or philosophical class were alone in honor, and the really useful part of the community were slaves. It is an education fitted for persons of leisure in such a community. This education passed from Greece and Rome to the feudal communities of Europe, where also the warrior caste and the priestly caste were alone held in honor, and where the really useful and working part of the community, though not nominally slaves as in the pagan world, were practically not much better off than slaves, and not more seriously regarded. And how absurd it is, people end by saying, to inflict this education upon an industrious modern community, where very few indeed are persons of leisure, and the mass to be considered has not leisure, but is bound, for its own great good, and for the great good of the world at large, to plain labor and to industrial pursuits, and the education in question tends necessarily to make men dissatisfied with these pursuits and unfitted for them!

That is what is said. So far I must defend Plato, as to plead that his view of education and studies is in the general, as it seems to me, sound enough, and fitted for all sorts and conditions of men, whatever their pursuits may be. "An intelligent man," says Plato, "will prize those studies which result in his soul getting soberness, righteousness, and wisdom, and will less value the others."[5] I cannot consider *that* a bad description of the aim of education, and of the motives which should govern us in the choice of studies, whether we are preparing ourselves for a hereditary seat in the English House of Lords or for the pork trade in Chicago.

Still I admit that Plato's world was not ours, that his scorn of trade and handicraft is fantastic,[6] that he had no conception of a great industrial community such as that of the United States, and that such a community must and will shape its education to suit its own needs. If the usual education handed down to it from the past does not suit it, it will certainly before long drop this and try another. The usual education in the past has been mainly literary. The question is whether the studies which were long supposed to be the best for all of us are practically the best now; whether others are not better. The tyranny of the past, many think, weighs on us injuriously in the predominance given to letters in education. The question is raised whether,

3. *Republic* 3.405.
4. See "Literary Ethics," an address delivered at Dartmouth College in 1838 by Ralph Waldo
Emerson (1803–1882).
5. *Republic* 9.591.
6. Unconvincing, fanciful.

to meet the needs of our modern life, the predominance ought not now to pass from letters to science; and naturally the question is nowhere raised with more energy than here in the United States. The design of abasing what is called "mere literary instruction and education," and of exalting what is called "sound, extensive, and practical scientific knowledge," is, in this intensely modern world of the United States, even more perhaps than in Europe, a very popular design, and makes great and rapid progress.

I am going to ask whether the present movement for ousting letters from their old predominance in education, and for transferring the predominance in education to the natural sciences, whether this brisk and flourishing movement ought to prevail, and whether it is likely that in the end it really will prevail. An objection may be raised which I will anticipate. My own studies have been almost wholly in letters, and my visits to the field of the natural sciences have been very slight and inadequate, although those sciences have always strongly moved my curiosity. A man of letters, it will perhaps be said, is not competent to discuss the comparative merits of letters and natural science as means of education. To this objection I reply, first of all, that his incompetence, if he attempts the discussion but is really incompetent for it, will be abundantly visible; nobody will be taken in; he will have plenty of sharp observers and critics to save mankind from that danger. But the line I am going to follow is, as you will soon discover, so extremely simple, that perhaps it may be followed without failure even by one who for a more ambitious line of discussion would be quite incompetent.

Some of you may possibly remember a phrase of mine which has been the object of a good deal of comment; an observation to the effect that in our culture, the aim being *to know ourselves and the world,* we have, as the means to this end, *to know the best which has been thought and said in the world.*[7] A man of science, who is also an excellent writer and the very prince of debaters, Professor Huxley, in a discourse at the opening of Sir Josiah Mason's college at Birmingham,[8] laying hold of this phrase, expanded it by quoting some more words of mine, which are these: "The civilized world is to be regarded as now being, for intellectual and spiritual purposes, one great confederation, bound to a joint action and working to a common result; and whose members have for their proper outfit a knowledge of Greek, Roman, and Eastern antiquity, and of one another. Special local and temporary advantages being put out of account, that modern nation will in the intellectual and spiritual sphere make most progress, which most thoroughly carries out this program."

Now on my phrase, thus enlarged, Professor Huxley remarks that when I speak of the above-mentioned knowledge as enabling us to know ourselves and the world, I assert *literature* to contain the materials which suffice for thus making us know ourselves and the world. But it is not by any means clear, says he, that after having learnt all which ancient and modern literatures have to tell us, we have laid a sufficiently broad and deep foundation for that criticism of life, that knowledge of ourselves and the world, which constitutes culture. On the contrary, Professor Huxley declares that he finds himself "wholly unable to admit that either nations or individuals will

7. See "The Function of Criticism at the Present Time" (p. 450).
8. See "Science and Culture" (p. 497).

The Victorian Age
(1830–1901)

Slave Ship (Slavers Throwing Overboard the Dead and Dying—Typhoon Coming On),
J. M. W. Turner, 1840

The subject of Turner's painting—slaves thrown overboard, still in chains, as a storm
approaches—is the occasion for apocalyptic use of light and color. For several years John
Ruskin owned this painting, a gift from his father; but he later sold it, finding the subject "too
painful to live with." While many contemporaries criticized the painting for what they saw as
its extravagance, Ruskin praised it as Turner's noblest work, in a passage from *Modern
Painters* that is one of Ruskin's own finest passages of prose painting (p. 385).

Work, Ford Madox Brown, 1852,
1856–63

Brown's painting constructs a
comprehensive picture of Victorian
society through the relationships of
various classes of the population to
work. The excavators at the center
represent work in its essential,
physical form; the leisured gentry
on horseback at the top of the
painting have no need to work; the
ragged girl in the foreground cares
for her orphaned brothers and
sisters. Under the trees are
vagrants and distressed haymakers.
Thomas Carlyle and F. D. Maurice,
"brain workers" whose social ideas
influenced the painting, stand on
the right.

The Awakening Conscience, William Holman Hunt, 1853–54

As John Ruskin's letter to the *Times* (p. 512) points out, every detail of Hunt's painting of a fallen woman, hearing the voice of conscience while in the arms of her lover, has symbolic resonance—the soiled glove on the carpet, the bird that has escaped the cat, the songs on the piano ("Oft in the Stilly Night") and on the floor ("Tears, Idle Tears"), the window through which the woman gazes, reflected in the mirror behind the couple. Like Millais's *Ophelia,* the painting surrounds and interprets its subject with a crowded canvas of discrete, photographically rendered objects.

Soul's Beauty, Dante Gabriel Rossetti, 1864–70

Also titled *Sibylla Palmifera* (the palm-bearing sibyl), *Soul's Beauty* represents the unattainable ideal that inspires the artist. Painted as a companion to the sonnet of the same name, the picture strives to represent and evoke the erotic and aesthetic absorption the poem allegorizes. Rossetti devoted the last fifteen years of his painting career to these looming frontal portraits with richly decorated backgrounds, the details of which carry symbolic significance (in this painting, the arch of life, the cupid, the poppies, the skull, the butterflies).

Body's Beauty, Dante Gabriel Rossetti, 1864–73

Also titled *Lady Lilith* (after Adam's first wife, who ran away to become a witch), *Body's Beauty* represents sensual absorption. Paired with the sonnet of the same name, the painting associates the sexual allure of the woman at the center with the golden hair that represents her value, and her narcissistic contemplation of herself with the art that she embodies. Like the Lady of Shalott, Lady Lilith is a weaver but a deadly one—the poppies and roses surrounding her link death and sexuality.

The Beguiling of Merlin, Edward
Burne-Jones, 1870–74

Burne-Jones draws on a medieval
version of the Arthurian legend for
this painting, in which Merlin's pupil,
Nimuë (also called Nimiane, Vivian,
or Vivien), uses one of Merlin's own
spells to imprison him in a hawthorn
tree. The winding branches of the
tree, echoed in the Medusa-like
snakes of Nimuë's hair, create a flat
decorative surface. Although the
Nimuë of the story is a femme fatale
enchanting the helpless Merlin, her
posture and expression and the
similarity of the two faces make the
painting ambiguous.

The Passing of Arthur,
Julia Margaret Cameron, 1875

Using photography in the way that
earlier artists had used engravings to
illustrate literary texts, Cameron
produced a set of tableaux vivants for
Tennyson's *Idylls of the King,* posing
family and friends in costume, in a
combination of reality and fantasy
that recalls the Pre-Raphaelites. This
photograph illustrates lines 361–93
of *The Passing of Arthur* (pp. 242–43),
where the three queens attend the
dying king in the barge that takes
him to Avalon.

Nocturne in Black and Gold, the Falling Rocket, James A. M. Whistler, 1875

Whistler's impressionist painting of fireworks approaches the abstraction suggested in his title. He emphatically rejected the precise depiction of objects in earlier Victorian painting. When the critic John Ruskin saw the painting in Grosvenor Gallery, he wrote in *Fors Clavigera* that he "never expected to hear a coxcomb ask two hundred guineas for flinging a pot of paint in the public's face." Whistler sued Ruskin for libel and won; but he was awarded damages of only one farthing, and the trial left him financially ruined.

really advance, if their outfit draws nothing from the stores of physical science. An army without weapons of precision, and with no particular base of operations, might more hopefully enter upon a campaign on the Rhine, than a man, devoid of a knowledge of what physical science has done in the last century, upon a criticism of life."

This shows how needful it is for those who are to discuss any matter together, to have a common understanding as to the sense of the terms they employ—how needful, and how difficult. What Professor Huxley says, implies just the reproach which is so often brought against the study of belles-lettres, as they are called: that the study is an elegant one, but slight and ineffectual; a smattering of Greek and Latin and other ornamental things, of little use for anyone whose object is to get at truth, and to be a practical man. So, too, M. Renan[9] talks of the "superficial humanism" of a school course which treats us as if we were all going to be poets, writers, preachers, orators, and he opposes this humanism to positive science, or the critical search after truth. And there is always a tendency in those who are remonstrating against the predominance of letters in education, to understand by letters belles-lettres, and by belles-lettres a superficial humanism, the opposite of science or true knowledge.

But when we talk of knowing Greek and Roman antiquity, for instance, which is the knowledge people have called the humanities, I for my part mean a knowledge which is something more than a superficial humanism, mainly decorative. "I call all teaching *scientific*," says Wolf,[1] the critic of Homer, "which is systematically laid out and followed up to its original sources. For example: a knowledge of classical antiquity is scientific when the remains of classical antiquity are correctly studied in the original languages." There can be no doubt that Wolf is perfectly right; that all learning is scientific which is systematically laid out and followed up to its original sources, and that a genuine humanism is scientific.

When I speak of knowing Greek and Roman antiquity, therefore, as a help to knowing ourselves and the world, I mean more than a knowledge of so much vocabulary, so much grammar, so many portions of authors in the Greek and Latin languages, I mean knowing the Greeks and Romans, and their life and genius,[2] and what they were and did in the world; what we get from them, and what is its value. That, at least, is the ideal; and when we talk of endeavoring to know Greek and Roman antiquity, as a help to knowing ourselves and the world, we mean endeavoring so to know them as to satisfy this ideal, however much we may still fall short of it.

The same also as to knowing our own and other modern nations, with the like aim of getting to understand ourselves and the world. To know the best that has been thought and said by the modern nations, is to know, says Professor Huxley, "only what modern *literatures* have to tell us; it is the criticism of life contained in modern literature." And yet "the distinctive character of our times," he urges, "lies in the vast and constantly increasing part which is played by natural knowledge." And how, therefore, can a man, devoid of knowledge of what physical science has done in the last century, enter hopefully upon a criticism of modern life?

9. Ernest Renan (1823–1892), French religious philosopher and archaeologist.
1. Friedrich August Wolf (1759–1824), German scholar.
2. Characteristic spirit or excellence.

Let us, I say, be agreed about the meaning of the terms we are using. I talk of knowing the best which has been thought and uttered in the world; Professor Huxley says this means knowing *literature*. Literature is a large word; it may mean everything written with letters or printed in a book. Euclid's *Elements* and Newton's *Principia*[3] are thus literature. All knowledge that reaches us through books is literature. But by literature Professor Huxley means belles-lettres. He means to make me say, that knowing the best which has been thought and said by the modern nations is knowing their belles-lettres and no more. And this is no sufficient equipment, he argues, for a criticism of modern life. But as I do not mean, by knowing ancient Rome, knowing merely more or less of Latin belles-lettres, and taking no account of Rome's military, and political, and legal, and administrative work in the world; and as, by knowing ancient Greece, I understand knowing her as the giver of Greek art, and the guide to a free and right use of reason and to scientific method, and the founder of our mathematics and physics and astronomy and biology—I understand knowing her as all this, and not merely knowing certain Greek poems, and histories, and treatises, and speeches—so as to the knowledge of modern nations also. By knowing modern nations, I mean not merely knowing their belles-lettres, but knowing also what has been done by such men as Copernicus, Galileo, Newton, Darwin. "Our ancestors learned," says Professor Huxley, "that the earth is the center of the visible universe, and that man is the cynosure of things terrestrial; and more especially was it inculcated that the course of nature had no fixed order, but that it could be, and constantly was, altered." "But for us now," continues Professor Huxley, "the notions of the beginning and the end of the world entertained by our forefathers are no longer credible. It is very certain that the earth is not the chief body in the material universe, and that the world is not subordinated to man's use. It is even more certain that nature is the expression of a definite order, with which nothing interferes." "And yet," he cries, "the purely classical education advocated by the representatives of the humanists in our day gives no inkling of all this."

In due place and time I will just touch upon that vexed question of classical education; but at present the question is as to what is meant by knowing the best which modern nations have thought and said. It is not knowing their belles-lettres merely which is meant. To know Italian belles-lettres is not to know Italy, and to know English belles-lettres is not to know England. Into knowing Italy and England there comes a great deal more, Galileo and Newton amongst it. The reproach of being a superficial humanism, a tincture of belles-lettres, may attach rightly enough to some other disciplines; but to the particular discipline recommended when I proposed knowing the best that has been thought and said in the world, it does not apply. In that best I certainly include what in modern times has been thought and said by the great observers and knowers of nature.

There is, therefore, really no question between Professor Huxley and me as to whether knowing the great results of the modern scientific study of nature is not required as a part of our culture, as well as knowing the products of literature and art. But to follow the processes by which those results

3. A comprehensive treatise on mathematics (ca. 300 B.C.E.) and a foundational work of modern physics (*The Mathematical Principles of Natural Philosophy*, 1687), respectively.

are reached, ought, say the friends of physical science, to be made the staple of education for the bulk of mankind. And here there does arise a question between those whom Professor Huxley calls with playful sarcasm "the Levites of culture," and those whom the poor humanist is sometimes apt to regard as its Nebuchadnezzars.[4]

The great results of the scientific investigation of nature we are agreed upon knowing, but how much of our study are we bound to give to the processes by which those results are reached? The results have their visible bearing on human life. But all the processes, too, all the items of fact, by which those results are reached and established, are interesting. All knowledge is interesting to a wise man, and the knowledge of nature is interesting to all men. It is very interesting to know, that, from the albuminous white of the egg, the chick in the egg gets the materials for its flesh, bones, blood, and feathers; while, from the fatty yolk of the egg, it gets the heat and energy which enable it at length to break its shell and begin the world. It is less interesting, perhaps, but still it is interesting, to know that when a taper burns, the wax is converted into carbonic acid and water. Moreover, it is quite true that the habit of dealing with facts, which is given by the study of nature, is, as the friends of physical science praise it for being, an excellent discipline. The appeal, in the study of nature, is constantly to observation and experiment; not only is it said that the thing is so, but we can be made to see that it is so. Not only does a man tell us that when a taper burns the wax is converted into carbonic acid and water, as a man may tell us, if he likes, that Charon[5] is punting his ferry boat on the river Styx, or that Victor Hugo is a sublime poet, or Mr. Gladstone[6] the most admirable of statesmen; but we are made to see that the conversion into carbonic acid and water does actually happen. This reality of natural knowledge it is, which makes the friends of physical science contrast it, as a knowledge of things, with the humanist's knowledge, which is, say they, a knowledge of words. And hence Professor Huxley is moved to lay it down that, "for the purpose of attaining real culture, an exclusively scientific education is at least as effectual as an exclusively literary education." And a certain President of the Section for Mechanical Science in the British Association is, in Scripture phrase, "very bold,"[7] and declares that if a man, in his mental training, "has substituted literature and history for natural science, he has chosen the less useful alternative." But whether we go these lengths or not, we must all admit that in natural science the habit gained of dealing with facts is a most valuable discipline, and that everyone should have some experience of it.

More than this, however, is demanded by the reformers. It is proposed to make the training in natural science the main part of education, for the great majority of mankind at any rate. And here, I confess, I part company with the friends of physical science, with whom up to this point I have been agreeing. In differing from them, however, I wish to proceed with the utmost caution and diffidence. The smallness of my own acquaintance with

---

4. Huxley implies that the humanists are hidebound conservatives like the Levites, priests who were preoccupied with traditional ritual observances. Arnold implies that the scientists may be like Nebuchadnezzar, a Babylonian king who destroyed the temple of Jerusalem.
5. In Greek mythology the boatman who con-

ducted the souls of the dead across the river Styx.
6. William Ewart Gladstone (1809–1898), leader of the Liberal Party from 1868 to 1875 and from 1880 to 1894 and prime minister four times. Hugo (1802–1885), French poet and novelist.
7. Romans 10.20.

the disciplines of natural science is ever before my mind, and I am fearful of doing these disciplines an injustice. The ability and pugnacity of the partisans of natural science make them formidable persons to contradict. The tone of tentative inquiry, which befits a being of dim faculties and bounded knowledge, is the tone I would wish to take and not to depart from. At present it seems to me, that those who are for giving to natural knowledge, as they call it, the chief place in the education of the majority of mankind, leave one important thing out of their account: the constitution of human nature. But I put this forward on the strength of some facts not at all recondite, very far from it; facts capable of being stated in the simplest possible fashion, and to which, if I so state them, the man of science will, I am sure, be willing to allow their due weight.

Deny the facts altogether, I think, he hardly can. He can hardly deny, that when we set ourselves to enumerate the powers which go to the building up of human life, and say that they are the power of conduct, the power of intellect and knowledge, the power of beauty, and the power of social life and manners—he can hardly deny that this scheme, though drawn in rough and plain lines enough, and not pretending to scientific exactness, does yet give a fairly true representation of the matter. Human nature is built up by these powers; we have the need for them all. When we have rightly met and adjusted the claims of them all, we shall then be in a fair way for getting soberness and righteousness, with wisdom. This is evident enough, and the friends of physical science would admit it.

But perhaps they may not have sufficiently observed another thing: namely, that the several powers just mentioned are not isolated, but there is, in the generality of mankind, a perpetual tendency to relate them one to another in divers ways. With one such way of relating them I am particularly concerned now. Following our instinct for intellect and knowledge, we acquire pieces of knowledge; and presently, in the generality of men, there arises the desire to relate these pieces of knowledge to our sense for conduct, to our sense for beauty—and there is weariness and dissatisfaction if the desire is balked. Now in this desire lies, I think, the strength of that hold which letters have upon us.

All knowledge is, as I said just now, interesting; and even items of knowledge which from the nature of the case cannot well be related, but must stand isolated in our thoughts, have their interest. Even lists of exceptions have their interest. If we are studying Greek accents, it is interesting to know that *pais* and *pas,* and some other monosyllables of the same form of declension, do not take the circumflex upon the last syllable of the genitive plural, but vary, in this respect, from the common rule. If we are studying physiology, it is interesting to know that the pulmonary artery carries dark blood and the pulmonary vein carries bright blood, departing in this respect from the common rule for the division of labor between the veins and the arteries. But everyone knows how we seek naturally to combine the pieces of our knowledge together, to bring them under general rules, to relate them to principles; and how unsatisfactory and tiresome it would be to go on forever learning lists of exceptions, or accumulating items of fact which must stand isolated.

Well, that same need of relating our knowledge, which operates here within the sphere of our knowledge itself, we shall find operating, also, outside that sphere. We experience, as we go on learning and knowing—the vast majority of us experience—the need of relating what we have learnt and known to the sense which we have in us for conduct, to the sense which we have in us for beauty.

A certain Greek prophetess of Mantineia in Arcadia, Diotima by name, once explained to the philosopher Socrates that love, and impulse, and bent of all kinds, is, in fact, nothing else but the desire in men that good should forever be present to them. This desire for good, Diotima assured Socrates, is our fundamental desire, of which fundamental desire every impulse in us is only some one particular form.[8] And therefore this fundamental desire it is, I suppose—this desire in men that good should be forever present to them—which acts in us when we feel the impulse for relating our knowledge to our sense for conduct and to our sense for beauty. At any rate, with men in general the instinct exists. Such is human nature. And the instinct, it will be admitted, is innocent, and human nature is preserved by our following the lead of its innocent instincts. Therefore, in seeking to gratify this instinct in question, we are following the instinct of self-preservation in humanity.

But, no doubt, some kinds of knowledge cannot be made to directly serve the instinct in question, cannot be directly related to the sense for beauty, to the sense for conduct. These are instrument knowledges; they lead on to other knowledges, which can. A man who passes his life in instrument knowledges is a specialist. They may be invaluable as instruments to something beyond, for those who have the gift thus to employ them; and they may be disciplines in themselves wherein it is useful for everyone to have some schooling. But it is inconceivable that the generality of men should pass all their mental life with Greek accents or with formal logic. My friend Professor Sylvester, who is one of the first[9] mathematicians in the world, holds transcendental doctrines as to the virtue of mathematics, but those doctrines are not for common men. In the very Senate House and heart of our English Cambridge[1] I once ventured, though not without an apology for my profaneness, to hazard the opinion that for the majority of mankind a little of mathematics, even, goes a long way. Of course this is quite consistent with their being of immense importance as an instrument to something else; but it is the few who have the aptitude for thus using them, not the bulk of mankind.

The natural sciences do not, however, stand on the same footing with these instrument knowledges. Experience shows us that the generality of men will find more interest in learning that, when a taper burns, the wax is converted into carbonic acid and water, or in learning the explanation of the phenomenon of dew, or in learning how the circulation of the blood is carried on, than they find in learning that the genitive plural of *pais* and *pas* does not take the circumflex on the termination. And one piece of natural knowledge is added to another, and others are added to that, and at last we come to propositions so interesting as Mr. Darwin's famous proposition that "our ancestor was a hairy quadruped furnished with a tail and pointed ears, probably arboreal in his habits."[2] Or we come to propositions of such

8. Plato's *Symposium* 201–7.
9. Foremost. James J. Sylvester (1814–1897), professor of mathematics at Johns Hopkins University and at Oxford.
1. In its original form "Literature and Science"

had been delivered as a lecture at Cambridge University, where mathematics traditionally has been emphasized.
2. *The Descent of Man* (1871), chap. 21 (see, p. 615).

reach and magnitude as those which Professor Huxley delivers, when he says that the notions of our forefathers about the beginning and the end of the world were all wrong, and that nature is the expression of a definite order with which nothing interferes.

Interesting, indeed, these results of science are, important they are, and we should all of us be acquainted with them. But what I now wish you to mark is, that we are still, when they are propounded to us and we receive them, we are still in the sphere of intellect and knowledge. And for the generality of men there will be found, I say, to arise, when they have duly taken in the proposition that their ancestor was "a hairy quadruped furnished with a tail and pointed ears, probably arboreal in his habits," there will be found to arise an invincible desire to relate this proposition to the sense in us for conduct, and to the sense in us for beauty. But this the men of science will not do for us, and will hardly even profess to do. They will give us other pieces of knowledge, other facts, about other animals and their ancestors, or about plants, or about stones, or about stars; and they may finally bring us to those great "general conceptions of the universe, which are forced upon us all," says Professor Huxley, "by the progress of physical science." But still it will be *knowledge* only which they give us; knowledge not put for us into relation with our sense for conduct, our sense for beauty, and touched with emotion by being so put; not thus put for us, and therefore, to the majority of mankind, after a certain while, unsatisfying, wearying.

Not to the born naturalist, I admit. But what do we mean by a born naturalist? We mean a man in whom the zeal for observing nature is so uncommonly strong and eminent, that it marks him off from the bulk of mankind. Such a man will pass his life happily in collecting natural knowledge and reasoning upon it, and will ask for nothing, or hardly anything, more. I have heard it said that the sagacious and admirable naturalist whom we lost not very long ago, Mr. Darwin, once owned to a friend that for his part he did not experience the necessity for two things which most men find so necessary to them—religion and poetry; science and the domestic affections, he thought, were enough. To a born naturalist, I can well understand that this should seem so. So absorbing is his occupation with nature, so strong his love for his occupation, that he goes on acquiring natural knowledge and reasoning upon it, and has little time or inclination for thinking about getting it related to the desire in man for conduct, the desire in man for beauty. He relates it to them for himself as he goes along, so far as he feels the need; and he draws from the domestic affections all the additional solace necessary. But then Darwins are extremely rare. Another great and admirable master of natural knowledge, Faraday,[3] was a Sandemanian. That is to say, he related his knowledge to his instinct for conduct and to his instinct for beauty, by the aid of that respectable Scottish sectary, Robert Sandeman.[4] And so strong, in general, is the demand of religion and poetry to have their share in a man, to associate themselves with his knowing, and to relieve and rejoice it, that, probably, for one man amongst us with the disposition to do as Darwin did in this respect, there are at least fifty with the disposition to do as Faraday.

3. Michael Faraday (1791–1867), British chemist.
4. Founder of a Scottish sect bearing his name (1718–1771). "Sectary": zealous member of a sect.

Education lays hold upon us, in fact, by satisfying this demand. Professor Huxley holds up to scorn medieval education, with its neglect of the knowledge of nature, its poverty even of literary studies, its formal logic devoted to "showing how and why that which the Church said was true must be true." But the great medieval Universities were not brought into being, we may be sure, by the zeal for giving a jejune and contemptible education. Kings have been their nursing fathers, and queens have been their nursing mothers,[5] but not for this. The medieval Universities came into being, because the supposed knowledge, delivered by Scripture and the Church, so deeply engaged men's hearts, by so simply, easily, and powerfully relating itself to their desire for conduct, their desire for beauty. All other knowledge was dominated by this supposed knowledge and was subordinated to it, because of the surpassing strength of the hold which it gained upon the affections of men, by allying itself profoundly with their sense for conduct, their sense for beauty.

But now, says Professor Huxley, conceptions of the universe fatal to the notions held by our forefathers have been forced upon us by physical science. Grant to him that they are thus fatal, that the new conceptions must and will soon become current everywhere, and that everyone will finally perceive them to be fatal to the beliefs of our forefathers. The need of humane letters, as they are truly called, because they serve the paramount desire in men that good should be forever present to them—the need of humane letters, to establish a relation between the new conceptions, and our instinct for beauty, our instinct for conduct, is only the more visible. The Middle Age could do without humane letters, as it could do without the study of nature, because its supposed knowledge was made to engage its emotions so powerfully. Grant that the supposed knowledge disappears, its power of being made to engage the emotions will of course disappear along with it—but the emotions themselves, and their claim to be engaged and satisfied, will remain. Now if we find by experience that humane letters have an undeniable power of engaging the emotions, the importance of humane letters in a man's training becomes not less, but greater, in proportion to the success of modern science in extirpating what it calls "medieval thinking."

Have humane letters, then, have poetry and eloquence, the power here attributed to them of engaging the emotions, and do they exercise it? And if they have it and exercise it, *how* do they exercise it, so as to exert an influence upon man's sense for conduct, his sense for beauty? Finally, even if they both can and do exert an influence upon the senses in question, how are they to relate to them the results—the modern results—of natural science? All these questions may be asked. First, have poetry and eloquence the power of calling out the emotions? The appeal is to experience. Experience shows that for the vast majority of men, for mankind in general, they have the power. Next, do they exercise it? They do. But then, *how* do they exercise it so as to affect man's sense for conduct, his sense for beauty? And this is perhaps a case for applying the Preacher's words: "Though a man labour to seek it out, yet he shall not find it; yea, farther, though a wise man think to know it, yet shall he not be able to find it."[6] Why should it be one

---

5. Isaiah 49.23.
6. Ecclesiastes 8.17 [Arnold's note].

thing, in its effect upon the emotions, to say, "Patience is a virtue," and quite another thing, in its effect upon the emotions, to say with Homer,

$$τλητὸν\ γὰρ\ Μοῖραι\ θυμὸν\ θέσαν\ ἀνθρώποιοιν^7—$$

"for an enduring heart have the destinies appointed to the children of men"? Why should it be one thing, in its effect upon the emotions, to say with the philosopher Spinoza, *Felicitas in eo consistit quod homo suum esse conservare potest*—"Man's happiness consists in his being able to preserve his own essence,"[8] and quite another thing, in its effect upon the emotions, to say with the Gospel, "What is a man advantaged, if he gain the whole world, and lose himself, forfeit himself?"[9] How does this difference of effect arise? I cannot tell, and I am not much concerned to know; the important thing is that it does arise, and that we can profit by it. But how, finally, are poetry and eloquence to exercise the power of relating the modern results of natural science to man's instinct for conduct, his instinct for beauty? And here again I answer that I do not know *how* they will exercise it, but that they can and will exercise it I am sure. I do not mean that modern philosophical poets and modern philosophical moralists are to come and relate for us, in express terms, the results of modern scientific research to our instinct for conduct, our instinct for beauty. But I mean that we shall find, as a matter of experience, if we know the best that has been thought and uttered in the world, we shall find that the art and poetry and eloquence of men who lived, perhaps, long ago, who had the most limited natural knowledge, who had the most erroneous conceptions about many important matters, we shall find that this art, and poetry, and eloquence, have in fact not only the power of refreshing and delighting us, they have also the power—such is the strength and worth, in essentials, of their authors' criticism of life—they have a fortifying, and elevating, and quickening, and suggestive power, capable of wonderfully helping us to relate the results of modern science to our need for conduct, our need for beauty. Homer's conceptions of the physical universe were, I imagine, grotesque; but really, under the shock of hearing from modern science that "the world is not subordinated to man's use, and that man is not the cynosure of things terrestrial," I could, for my own part, desire no better comfort than Homer's line which I quoted just now,

$$τλητὸν\ γὰρ\ Μοῖραι\ θυμὸν\ θέσαν\ ἀνθρώποισιν—$$

"for an enduring heart have the destinies appointed to the children of men"!

And the more that men's minds are cleared, the more that the results of science are frankly accepted, the more that poetry and eloquence come to be received and studied as what in truth they really are—the criticism of life by gifted men, alive and active with extraordinary power at an unusual number of points—so much the more will the value of humane letters, and of art also, which is an utterance having a like kind of power with theirs, be felt and acknowledged, and their place in education be secured.

Let us therefore, all of us, avoid indeed as much as possible any invidious comparison between the merits of humane letters, as means of education, and the merits of the natural sciences. But when some President of a Sec-

7. *Iliad* 24.49 [Arnold's note].
8. *Ethics* (1677) 4.18.

9. Luke 9.25.

tion for Mechanical Science insists on making the comparison, and tells us that "he who in his training has substituted literature and history for natural science has chosen the less useful alternative," let us make answer to him that the student of humane letters only, will, at least, know also the great general conceptions brought in by modern physical science; for science, as Professor Huxley says, forces them upon us all. But the student of the natural sciences only, will, by our very hypothesis, know nothing of humane letters; not to mention that in setting himself to be perpetually accumulating natural knowledge, he sets himself to do what only specialists have in general the gift for doing genially. And so he will probably be unsatisfied, or at any rate incomplete, and even more incomplete than the student of humane letters only.

I once mentioned in a school report, how a young man in one of our English training colleges having to paraphrase the passage in *Macbeth* beginning,

> Can'st thou not minister to a mind diseased?[1]

turned this line into, "Can you not wait upon the lunatic?" And I remarked what a curious state of things it would be, if every pupil of our national schools knew, let us say, that the moon is two thousand one hundred and sixty miles in diameter, and thought at the same time that a good paraphrase for

> Can'st thou not minister to a mind diseased?

was, "Can you not wait upon the lunatic?" If one is driven to choose, I think I would rather have a young person ignorant about the moon's diameter, but aware that "Can you not wait upon the lunatic?" is bad, than a young person whose education had been such as to manage things the other way.

Or to go higher than the pupils of our national schools. I have in my mind's eye a member of our British Parliament who comes to travel here in America, who afterwards relates his travels, and who shows a really masterly knowledge of the geology of this great country and of its mining capabilities, but who ends by gravely suggesting that the United States should borrow a prince from our Royal Family, and should make him their king, and should create a House of Lords of great landed proprietors after the pattern of ours; and then America, he thinks, would have her future happily and perfectly secured. Surely, in this case, the President of the Section for Mechanical Science would himself hardly say that our member of Parliament, by concentrating himself upon geology and mineralogy, and so on, and not attending to literature and history, had "chosen the more useful alternative."

If then there is to be separation and option between humane letters on the one hand, and the natural sciences on the other, the great majority of mankind, all who have not exceptional and overpowering aptitudes for the study of nature, would do well, I cannot but think, to choose to be educated in humane letters rather than in the natural sciences. Letters will call out their being at more points, will make them live more.

I said that before I ended I would just touch on the question of classical education, and I will keep my word. Even if literature is to retain a large place in our education, yet Latin and Greek, say the friends of progress, will certainly have to go. Greek is the grand offender in the eyes of these gentlemen.

1. Shakespeare's *Macbeth* 5.3.42.

The attackers of the established course of study think that against Greek, at any rate, they have irresistible arguments. Literature may perhaps be needed in education, they say; but why on earth should it be Greek literature? Why not French or German? Nay, "has not an Englishman models in his own literature of every kind of excellence?"[2] As before, it is not on any weak pleadings of my own that I rely for convincing the gainsayers; it is on the constitution of human nature itself, and on the instinct of self-preservation in humanity. The instinct for beauty is set in human nature, as surely as the instinct for knowledge is set there, or the instinct for conduct. If the instinct for beauty is served by Greek literature and art as it is served by no other literature and art, we may trust to the instinct of self-preservation in humanity for keeping Greek as part of our culture. We may trust to it for even making the study of Greek more prevalent than it is now. Greek will come, I hope, some day to be studied more rationally than at present; but it will be increasingly studied as men increasingly feel the need in them for beauty, and how powerfully Greek art and Greek literature can serve this need. Women will again study Greek, as Lady Jane Grey[3] did; I believe that in that chain of forts, with which the fair host of the Amazons are now engirdling our English universities,[4] I find that here in America, in colleges like Smith College in Massachusetts, and Vassar College in the State of New York, and in the happy families of the mixed universities out West, they are studying it already.

Defuit una mihi symmetria prisca—"The antique symmetry was the one thing wanting to me," said Leonardo da Vinci; and he was an Italian. I will not presume to speak for the Americans, but I am sure that, in the Englishman, the want of this admirable symmetry of the Greeks is a thousand times more great and crying than in any Italian. The results of the want show themselves most glaringly, perhaps, in our architecture, but they show themselves, also, in all our art. *Fit details strictly combined, in view of a large general result nobly conceived;* that is just the beautiful *symmetria prisca* of the Greeks, and it is just where we English fail, where all our art fails. Striking ideas we have, and well-executed details we have; but that high symmetry which, with satisfying and delightful effect, combines them, we seldom or never have. The glorious beauty of the Acropolis at Athens did not come from single fine things stuck about on that hill, a statue here, a gateway there—no, it arose from all things being perfectly combined for a supreme total effect. What must not an Englishman feel about our deficiencies in this respect, as the sense for beauty, whereof this symmetry is an essential element, awakens and strengthens within him! what will not one day be his respect and desire for Greece and its *symmetria prisca,* when the scales drop from his eyes as he walks the London streets, and he sees such a lesson in meanness as the Strand, for instance, in its true deformity! But here we are coming to our friend Mr. Ruskin's province,[5] and I will not intrude upon it, for he is its very sufficient guardian.

And so we at last find, it seems, we find flowing in favor of the humanities the natural and necessary stream of things, which seemed against them

---

2. Cf. Huxley's "Science and Culture" (p. 497).
3. Reputed to be a learned scholar in Greek. Grey (1537–1554) was proclaimed queen of England in 1553 but was forced to abdicate the throne nine days later. She was executed by order of Queen Mary.
4. Colleges for women at Oxford and Cambridge.
5. In books such as *The Stones of Venice* (1851–53), John Ruskin had criticized the "meanness" of Victorian architecture.

when we started. The "hairy quadruped furnished with a tail and pointed ears, probably arboreal in his habits," this good fellow carried hidden in his nature, apparently, something destined to develop into a necessity for humane letters. Nay, more; we seem finally to be even led to the further conclusion that our hairy ancestor carried in his nature, also, a necessity for Greek.

And therefore, to say the truth, I cannot really think that humane letters are in much actual danger of being thrust out from their leading place in education, in spite of the array of authorities against them at this moment. So long as human nature is what it is, their attractions will remain irresistible. As with Greek, so with letters generally: they will some day come, we may hope, to be studied more rationally, but they will not lose their place. What will happen will rather be that there will be crowded into education other matters besides, far too many; there will be, perhaps, a period of unsettlement and confusion and false tendency; but letters will not in the end lose their leading place. If they lose it for a time, they will get it back again. We shall be brought back to them by our wants and aspirations. And a poor humanist may possess his soul in patience, neither strive nor cry,[6] admit the energy and brilliancy of the partisans of physical science, and their present favor with the public, to be far greater than his own, and still have a happy faith that the nature of things works silently on behalf of the studies which he loves, and that, while we shall all have to acquaint ourselves with the great results reached by modern science, and to give ourselves as much training in its disciplines as we can conveniently carry, yet the majority of men will always require humane letters; and so much the more, as they have the more and the greater results of science to relate to the need in man for conduct, and to the need in him for beauty.

1882, 1885

6. Matthew 12.19; "possess his soul in patience," Luke 21.19.

THOMAS HENRY HUXLEY
1825–1895

I n Victorian controversies over religion and education, one of the most distinctive participants was Thomas Henry Huxley, a scientist who wrote clear, readable, and very persuasive English prose. Huxley's literary skill was responsible for his being lured out of his laboratory onto the platforms of public debate where his role was to champion, as he said, "the application of scientific methods of investigation to all the problems of life."

Huxley, a schoolmaster's son, was born in a London suburb. Until beginning the study of medicine, at seventeen, he had had little formal education, but taught himself classical and modern languages and the rudiments of scientific theory. In 1846, after receiving his degree in medicine, he embarked on a long voyage to the South

Seas during which he studied the marine life of the tropical oceans and established a considerable reputation as a zoologist. Later he made investigations in geology and physiology, completing a total of 250 research papers during his lifetime. He also held teaching positions and served on public committees, but it was as a popularizer of science that he made his real mark. His popularizing was of two kinds. The first was to make the results of scientific investigations intelligible to a large audience. Such lectures as "On a Piece of Chalk" (not included here) are models of clear, vivid exposition that can be studied with profit by anyone interested in the art of teaching. His second kind of popularizing consisted of expounding the values of scientific education or of the application of scientific thinking to problems in religion. Here Huxley excels not so much as a teacher as a debater. In 1860 he demonstrated his argumentative skill when, as Darwin's defender or "bulldog," he demolished Bishop Wilberforce in a battle over *The Origin of Species* (an account of the confrontation, written by Huxley's son Leonard, appears in the "Evolution" cluster). In the 1870s, in such lectures as "Science and Culture" (1880), he engaged in more genial fencing with Matthew Arnold concerning the relative importance of the study of science or the humanities in education. And in the 1880s he debated with William Gladstone on the topic of interpreting the Bible. His essay "Agnosticism and Christianity" (1889) indicates his premises in this controversy.

Summing up his own career in his "Autobiography" (1890), Huxley noted that he had subordinated his ambition for scientific fame to other ends: "to the popularization of science; to the development and organization of scientific education; to the endless series of battles and skirmishes over evolution; and to untiring opposition to that ecclesiastical spirit, that clericalism, which . . . to whatever denomination it may belong, is the deadly enemy of science." In fighting these "battles" Huxley operated from different bases. Most of the time he wrote as a biologist engaged in assessing all assumptions by the tests of laboratory science. In this role he argued that humans are merely animals and that traditional religion is a tissue of superstitions and lies. For some recent critics Huxley comes close to setting up his own religion of sorts, so fervent and sweeping is his rhetoric in defense of scientific naturalism. Further, it has been argued that the emphasis he and other like-minded writers placed on the inevitability of English technological progress significantly affected Britain's expansionist imperial policies in the last quarter of the nineteenth century. Nevertheless, Huxley's vision was broader than that of most of his comrades in the science and religion debates. In fact, he often wrote as a humanist and even as a follower of Thomas Carlyle. As he stated in a letter: "*Sartor Resartus* led me to know that a deep sense of religion was compatible with the entire absence of theology." In this second role he argued that humans are a very special kind of animal whose great distinction is that they are endowed with a moral sense and with freedom of the will; creatures who are admirable not for following nature but for departing from nature. The humanistic streak muddies the seemingly clear current of Huxley's thinking yet makes him a more interesting figure than he might otherwise have been. It is noteworthy that in the writings of his grandsons—Julian Huxley, a biologist, and Aldous Huxley, a novelist—a similar division of mind can once more be detected.

Even in his dying, T. H. Huxley continued his role as controversialist. The words he asked to be engraved on his tomb are typical of his view of life and typical, also, in the effect they had on his contemporaries, some of whom found the epitaph to be shocking:

> Be not afraid, ye waiting hearts that weep
> For still he giveth His beloved sleep,
> And if an endless sleep He wills, so best.

From Science and Culture[1]

[THE VALUES OF EDUCATION IN THE SCIENCES]

From the time that the first suggestion to introduce physical science into ordinary education was timidly whispered, until now, the advocates of scientific education have met with opposition of two kinds. On the one hand, they have been pooh-poohed by the men of business who pride themselves on being the representatives of practicality; while, on the other hand, they have been excommunicated by the classical scholars, in their capacity of Levites in charge of the ark of culture[2] and monopolists of liberal education.

The practical men believed that the idol whom they worship—rule of thumb—has been the source of the past prosperity, and will suffice for the future welfare of the arts and manufactures. They are of opinion that science is speculative rubbish; that theory and practice have nothing to do with one another; and that the scientific habit of mind is an impediment, rather than an aid, in the conduct of ordinary affairs.

I have used the past tense in speaking of the practical men—for although they were very formidable thirty years ago, I am not sure that the pure species has not been extirpated. In fact, so far as mere argument goes, they have been subjected to such a *feu d'enfer*[3] that it is a miracle if any have escaped. But I have remarked that your typical practical man has an unexpected resemblance to one of Milton's angels. His spiritual wounds, such as are inflicted by logical weapons, may be as deep as a well and as wide as a church door,[4] but beyond shedding a few drops of ichor,[5] celestial or otherwise, he is no whit the worse. So, if any of these opponents be left, I will not waste time in vain repetition of the demonstrative evidence of the practical value of science; but knowing that a parable will sometimes penetrate where syllogisms fail to effect an entrance, I will offer a story for their consideration.

Once upon a time, a boy, with nothing to depend upon but his own vigorous nature, was thrown into the thick of the struggle for existence in the midst of a great manufacturing population. He seems to have had a hard fight, inasmuch as, by the time he was thirty years of age, his total disposable funds amounted to twenty pounds. Nevertheless, middle life found him giving proof of his comprehension of the practical problems he had been roughly called upon to solve, by a career of remarkable prosperity.

Finally, having reached old age with its well-earned surroundings of "honour, troops of friends,"[6] the hero of my story bethought himself of those who were making a like start in life, and how he could stretch out a helping hand to them.

After long and anxious reflection this successful practical man of business could devise nothing better than to provide them with the means of obtain-

---

1. This essay was first delivered as an address in 1880. The occasion had been the opening of a new Scientific College at Birmingham, which had been endowed by Sir Josiah Mason (1795–1881), a self-made businessman. For Matthew Arnold's reply to Huxley's argument, see his essay "Literature and Science" (p. 482).
2. In the Old Testament the whole tribe of Levi was entrusted with Israel's ritual observances (Numbers 3.1–13); in Joshua 3.6, priests carried the Ark of the Covenant.
3. Hellfire (French).
4. Shakespeare's *Romeo and Juliet* 3.1.92–93.
5. Ethereal fluid that supposedly flows through the veins of the gods. On angels' wounds see Milton's *Paradise Lost* 6.320–56.
6. Shakespeare's *Macbeth* 5.3.26.

ing "sound, extensive, and practical scientific knowledge." And he devoted a large part of his wealth and five years of incessant work to this end.

I need not point the moral of a tale which, as the solid and spacious fabric of the Scientific College assures us, is no fable, nor can anything which I could say intensify the force of this practical answer to practical objections.

We may take it for granted then, that, in the opinion of those best qualified to judge, the diffusion of thorough scientific education is an absolutely essential condition of industrial progress; and that the College which has been opened today will confer an inestimable boon upon those whose livelihood is to be gained by the practice of the arts and manufactures of the district.

The only question worth discussion is whether the conditions under which the work of the College is to be carried out are such as to give it the best possible chance of achieving permanent success.

Sir Josiah Mason, without doubt most wisely, has left very large freedom of action to the trustees, to whom he proposes ultimately to commit the administration of the College, so that they may be able to adjust its arrangements in accordance with the changing conditions of the future. But, with respect to three points, he has laid most explicit injunctions upon both administrators and teachers.

Party politics are forbidden to enter into the minds of either, so far as the work of the College is concerned; theology is as sternly banished from its precincts; and finally, it is especially declared that the College shall make no provision for "mere literary instruction and education."

It does not concern me at present to dwell upon the first two injunctions any longer than may be needful to express my full conviction of their wisdom. But the third prohibition brings us face to face with those other opponents of scientific education, who are by no means in the moribund condition of the practical man, but alive, alert, and formidable.

It is not impossible that we shall hear this express exclusion of "literary instruction and education" from a College which, nevertheless, professes to give a high and efficient education, sharply criticized. Certainly the time was that the Levites of culture would have sounded their trumpets against its walls as against an educational Jericho.[7]

How often have we not been told that the study of physical science is incompetent to confer culture; that it touches none of the higher problems of life; and, what is worse, that the continual devotion to scientific studies tends to generate a narrow and bigoted belief in the applicability of scientific methods to the search after truth of all kinds? How frequently one has reason to observe that no reply to a troublesome argument tells so well as calling its author a "mere scientific specialist." And, as I am afraid it is not permissible to speak of this form of opposition to scientific education in the past tense; may we not expect to be told that this, not only omission, but prohibition, of "mere literary instruction and education" is a patent example of scientific narrow-mindedness?

I am not acquainted with Sir Josiah Mason's reasons for the action which he has taken; but if, as I apprehend is the case, he refers to the ordinary

7. Seven priests blew their trumpets before the city walls of Jericho to bring the walls down (Joshua 6.6–20).

classical course of our schools and universities by the name of "mere literary instruction and education," I venture to offer sundry reasons of my own
in support of that action.

For I hold very strongly by two convictions: The first is that neither the
discipline nor the subject matter of classical education is of such direct value
to the student of physical science as to justify the expenditure of valuable
time upon either; and the second is that for the purpose of attaining real
culture, an exclusively scientific education is at least as effectual as an exclusively literary education.

I need hardly point out to you that these opinions, especially the latter, are
diametrically opposed to those of the great majority of educated Englishmen,
influenced as they are by school and university traditions. In their belief, culture is obtainable only by a liberal education; and a liberal education is synonymous, not merely with education and instruction in literature, but in one
particular form of literature, namely, that of Greek and Roman antiquity.
They hold that the man who has learned Latin and Greek, however little, is
educated; while he who is versed in other branches of knowledge, however
deeply, is a more or less respectable specialist, not admissible into the cultured caste. The stamp of the educated man, the University degree, is not
for him.

I am too well acquainted with the generous catholicity[8] of spirit, the true
sympathy with scientific thought, which pervades the writings of our chief
apostle of culture[9] to identify him with these opinions; and yet one may cull
from one and another of those epistles to the Philistines, which so much
delight all who do not answer to that name, sentences which lend them some
support.

Mr. Arnold tells us that the meaning of culture is "to know the best that
has been thought and said in the world." It is the criticism of life contained in
literature. That criticism regards "Europe as being, for intellectual and spiritual purposes, one great confederation, bound to a joint action and working
to a common result; and whose members have, for their common outfit, a
knowledge of Greek, Roman, and Eastern antiquity, and of one another. Special, local, and temporary advantages being put out of account, that modern
nation will in the intellectual and spiritual sphere make most progress, which
most thoroughly carries out this program. And what is that but saying that
we too, all of us, as individuals, the more thoroughly we carry it out, shall
make the more progress?"[1]

We have here to deal with two distinct propositions. The first, that a criticism of life is the essence of culture; the second, that literature contains the
materials which suffice for the construction of such criticism.

I think that we must all assent to the first proposition. For culture certainly means something quite different from learning or technical skill. It
implies the possession of an ideal, and the habit of critically estimating
the value of things by comparison with a theoretic standard. Perfect culture
should supply a complete theory of life, based upon a clear knowledge
alike of its possibilities and of its limitations.

8. Universality.
9. I.e., Matthew Arnold. For his discussion of the
Philistines, Arnold's name for the dull and narrow-
minded middle classes, see "Culture and Anarchy" (p. 464).
1. Arnold, "The Function of Criticism at the
Present Time" (p. 450).

But we may agree to all this, and yet strongly dissent from the assumption that literature alone is competent to supply this knowledge. After having learnt all that Greek, Roman, and Eastern antiquity have thought and said, and all that modern literature have to tell us, it is not self-evident that we have laid a sufficiently broad and deep foundation for that criticism of life which constitutes culture.

Indeed, to anyone acquainted with the scope of physical science, it is not at all evident. Considering progress only in the "intellectual and spiritual sphere," I find myself wholly unable to admit that either nations or individuals will really advance, if their common outfit draws nothing from the stores of physical science. I should say that an army, without weapons of precision and with no particular base of operations, might more hopefully enter upon a campaign on the Rhine than a man, devoid of a knowledge of what physical science has done in the last century, upon a criticism of life.

When a biologist meets with an anomaly, he instinctively turns to the study of development to clear it up. The rationale of contradictory opinions may with equal confidence be sought in history.

It is, happily, no new thing that Englishmen should employ their wealth in building and endowing institutions for educational purposes. But, five or six hundred years ago, deeds of foundation expressed or implied conditions as nearly as possible contrary to those which have been thought expedient by Sir Josiah Mason. That is to say, physical science was practically ignored, while a certain literary training was enjoined as a means to the acquirement of knowledge which was essentially theological.

The reason of this singular contradiction between the actions of men alike animated by a strong and disinterested desire to promote the welfare of their fellows, is easily discovered.

At that time, in fact, if anyone desired knowledge beyond such as could be obtained by his own observation, or by common conversation, his first necessity was to learn the Latin language, inasmuch as all the higher knowledge of the western world was contained in words written in that language. Hence, Latin grammar, with logic and rhetoric, studied through Latin, were the fundamentals of education. With respect to the substance of the knowledge imparted through this channel, the Jewish and Christian Scriptures, as interpreted and supplemented by the Romish Church,[2] were held to contain a complete and infallibly true body of information.

Theological dicta were, to the thinkers of those days, that which the axioms and definitions of Euclid[3] are to the geometers of these. The business of the philosophers of the Middle Ages was to deduce from the data furnished by the theologians, conclusions in accordance with ecclesiastical decrees. They were allowed the high privilege of showing, by logical process, how and why that which the Church said was true, must be true. And if their demonstrations fell short of or exceeded this limit, the Church was maternally ready to check their aberrations; if need were, by the help of the secular arm.

Between the two, our ancestors were furnished with a compact and complete criticism of life. They were told how the world began and how it would

2. I.e., Roman Catholic.
3. Greek mathematician (active ca. 300 B.C.E.).

His *Elements* remained a standard text of geometrical reasoning through the 19th century.

end; they learned that all material existence was but a base and insignificant blot upon the fair face of the spiritual world, and that nature was, to all intents and purposes, the playground of the devil; they learned that the earth is the center of the visible universe, and that man is the cynosure of things terrestrial, and more especially was it inculcated that the course of nature had no fixed order, but that it could be, and constantly was, altered by the agency of innumerable spiritual beings, good and bad, according as they were moved by the deeds and prayers of men. The sum and substance of the whole doctrine was to produce the conviction that the only thing really worth knowing in this world was how to secure that place in a better which, under certain conditions, the Church promised.

Our ancestors had a living belief in this theory of life, and acted upon it in their dealings with education, as in all other matters. Culture meant saintliness—after the fashion of the saints of those days; the education that led to it was, of necessity, theological; and the way to theology lay through Latin.

That the study of nature—further than was requisite for the satisfaction of everyday wants—should have any bearing on human life was far from the thoughts of men thus trained. Indeed, as nature had been cursed for man's sake, it was an obvious conclusion that those who meddled with nature were likely to come into pretty close contact with Satan. And, if any born scientific investigator followed his instincts, he might safely reckon upon earning the reputation, and probably upon suffering the fate, of a sorcerer.

Had the western world been left to itself in Chinese isolation, there is no saying how long this state of things might have endured. But, happily, it was not left to itself. Even earlier than the thirteenth century, the development of Moorish civilization in Spain and the great movement of the Crusades had introduced the leaven which, from that day to this, has never ceased to work. At first, through the intermediation of Arabic translations, afterwards by the study of the originals, the western nations of Europe became acquainted with the writings of the ancient philosophers and poets, and, in time, with the whole of the vast literature of antiquity.

Whatever there was of high intellectual aspiration or dominant capacity in Italy, France, Germany, and England, spent itself for centuries in taking possession of the rich inheritance left by the dead civilizations of Greece and Rome. Marvelously aided by the invention of printing,[4] classical learning spread and flourished. Those who possessed it prided themselves on having attained the highest culture then within the reach of mankind.

And justly. For, saving Dante on his solitary pinnacle, there was no figure in modern literature at the time of the Renaissance to compare with the men of antiquity; there was no art to compete with their sculpture; there was no physical science but that which Greece had created. Above all, there was no other example of perfect intellectual freedom—of the unhesitating acceptance of reason as the sole guide to truth and the supreme arbiter of conduct.

The new learning necessarily soon exerted a profound influence upon education. The language of the monks and schoolmen[5] seemed little better than gibberish to scholars fresh from Virgil and Cicero,[6] and the study of Latin

4. In the mid-15th century.
5. Exponents of the theology, philosophy, and logic of the medieval period in Europe.

6. The two Roman writers generally viewed as the masters of, respectively, Latin poetry and Latin prose.

was placed upon a new foundation. Moreover, Latin itself ceased to afford the sole key to knowledge. The student who sought the highest thought of antiquity found only a secondhand reflection of it in Roman literature, and turned his face to the full light of the Greeks. And after a battle, not altogether dissimilar to that which is at present being fought over the teaching of physical science, the study of Greek was recognized as an essential element of all higher education.

Then the Humanists, as they were called, won the day; and the great reform which they effected was of incalculable service to mankind. But the nemesis of all reformers is finality; and the reformers of education, like those of religion, fell into the profound, however common, error of mistaking the beginning for the end of the work of reformation.

The representatives of the Humanists, in the nineteenth century, take their stand upon classical education as the sole avenue to culture as firmly as if we were still in the age of Renaissance. Yet, surely, the present intellectual relations of the modern and the ancient worlds are profoundly different from those which obtained three centuries ago. Leaving aside the existence of a great and characteristically modern literature, of modern painting, and, especially, of modern music, there is one feature of the present state of the civilized world which separates it more widely from the Renaissance than the Renaissance was separated from the Middle Ages.

This distinctive character of our own times lies in the vast and constantly increasing part which is played by natural knowledge. Not only is our daily life shaped by it; not only does the prosperity of millions of men depend upon it, but our whole theory of life has long been influenced, consciously or unconsciously, by the general conceptions of the universe which have been forced upon us by physical science.

In fact, the most elementary acquaintance with the results of scientific investigation shows us that they offer a broad and striking contradiction to the opinion so implicitly credited and taught in the Middle Ages.

The notions of the beginning and the end of the world entertained by our forefathers are no longer credible. It is very certain that the earth is not the chief body in the material universe, and that the world is not subordinated to man's use. It is even more certain that nature is the expression of a definite order with which nothing interferes, and that the chief business of mankind is to learn that order and govern themselves accordingly. Moreover this scientific "criticism of life" presents itself to us with different credentials from any other. It appeals not to authority, nor to what anybody may have thought or said, but to nature. It admits that all our interpretations of natural fact are more or less imperfect and symbolic, and bids the learner seek for truth not among words but among things. It warns us that the assertion which outstrips evidence is not only a blunder but a crime.

The purely classical education advocated by the representatives of the Humanists in our day gives no inkling of all this. A man may be a better scholar than Erasmus,[7] and know no more of the chief causes of the present intellectual fermentation than Erasmus did. Scholarly and pious persons, worthy of all respect, favor us with allocutions upon the sadness of the antagonism of science to their medieval way of thinking, which betray an

---

7. Eminent Dutch humanist and scholar (1466–1536).

ignorance of the first principles of scientific investigation, an incapacity for understanding what a man of science means by veracity, and an unconscious-ness of the weight of established scientific truths, which is almost comical.

* * *

Thus I venture to think that the pretensions of our modern Humanists to the possession of the monopoly of culture and to the exclusive inheritance of the spirit of antiquity must be abated, if not abandoned. But I should be very sorry that anything I have said should be taken to imply a desire on my part to depreciate the value of classical education, as it might be and as it sometimes is. The native capacities of mankind vary no less than their oppor-tunities; and while culture is one, the road by which one man may best reach it is widely different from that which is most advantageous to another. Again, while scientific education is yet inchoate and tentative, classical edu-cation is thoroughly well organized upon the practical experience of genera-tions of teachers. So that, given ample time for learning and estimation for ordinary life, or for a literary career, I do not think that a young Englishman in search of culture can do better than follow the course usually marked out for him, supplementing its deficiencies by his own efforts.

But for those who mean to make science their serious occupation; or who intend to follow the profession of medicine; or who have to enter early upon the business of life; for all these, in my opinion, classical education is a mistake; and it is for this reason that I am glad to see "mere literary educa-tion and instruction" shut out from the curriculum of Sir Josiah Mason's College, seeing that its inclusion would probably lead to the introduction of the ordinary smattering of Latin and Greek.

Nevertheless, I am the last person to question the importance of genuine literary education, or to suppose that intellectual culture can be complete without it. An exclusively scientific training will bring about a mental twist as surely as an exclusively literary training. The value of the cargo does not compensate for a ship's being out of trim; and I should be very sorry to think that the Scientific College would turn out none but lopsided men.

There is no need, however, that such a catastrophe should happen. Instruc-tion in English, French, and German is provided, and thus the three great-est literatures of the modern world are made accessible to the student.

French and German, and especially the latter language, are absolutely indispensable to those who desire full knowledge in any department of sci-ence. But even supposing that the knowledge of these languages acquired is not more than sufficient for purely scientific purposes, every Englishman has, in his native tongue, an almost perfect instrument of literary expres-sion; and, in his own literature, models of every kind of literary excellence. If an Englishman cannot get literary culture out of his Bible, his Shakespeare, his Milton, neither, in my belief, will the profoundest study of Homer and Sophocles, Virgil and Horace, give it to him.

Thus, since the constitution of the College makes sufficient provision for literary as well as for scientific education, and since artistic instruction is also contemplated, it seems to me that a fairly complete culture is offered to all who are willing to take advantage of it.

1880, 1881

From Agnosticism and Christianity[1]

[AGNOSTICISM DEFINED]

Nemo ergo ex me scire quaerat, quod me nescire scio, nisi forte ut nescire discat.
—AUGUSTINUS, *De Civ. Dei*, XII.7.[2]

The present discussion has arisen out of the use, which has become general in the last few years, of the terms "Agnostic"[3] and "Agnosticism."

The people who call themselves "Agnostics" have been charged with doing so because they have not the courage to declare themselves "Infidels." It has been insinuated that they have adopted a new name in order to escape the unpleasantness which attaches to their proper denomination. To this wholly erroneous imputation I have replied by showing that the term "Agnostic" did, as a matter of fact, arise in a manner which negatives it; and my statement has not been, and cannot be, refuted. Moreover, speaking for myself, and without impugning the right of any other person to use the term in another sense, I further say that Agnosticism is not properly described as a "negative" creed, nor indeed as a creed of any kind, except in so far as it expresses absolute faith in the validity of a principle, which is as much ethical as intellectual. This principle may be stated in various ways, but they all amount to this: that it is wrong for a man to say that he is certain of the objective truth of any proposition unless he can produce evidence which logically justifies that certainty. This is what Agnosticism asserts; and, in my opinion, it is all that is essential to Agnosticism. That which Agnostics deny and repudiate, as immoral, is the contrary doctrine, that there are propositions which men ought to believe, without logically satisfactory evidence; and that reprobation ought to attach to the profession of disbelief in such inadequately supported propositions. The justification of the Agnostic principles lies in the success which follows upon its application, whether in the field of natural, or in that of civil, history; and in the fact that, so far as these topics are concerned, no sane man thinks of denying its validity.

Still speaking for myself, I add that though Agnosticism is not, and cannot be, a creed, except in so far as its general principle is concerned; yet that the application of that principle results in the denial of, or the suspension of judgment concerning, a number of propositions respecting which our contemporary ecclesiastical "gnostics" profess entire certainty. And, in so far as these eccelesiastical persons can be justified in their old-established custom (which many nowadays think more honored in the breach than the observance) of using opprobrious names to those who differ from them, I fully admit their right to call me and those who think with me "Infidels"; all I have ventured to urge is that they must not expect us to speak of ourselves by that title.

---

1. This essay appeared in a magazine in 1889 as a reply to critics who had argued that agnostics were simply infidels under a new name. It was later included in Huxley's volume *Essays on Some Controverted Questions* (1892).

2. No one, therefore, should seek to learn knowledge from me, for I know that I do not know—unless indeed he wishes to learn that he does not know (Latin); St. Augustine, *City of God* 12.7.
3. The term *agnostic* was coined by Huxley.

The extent of the region of the uncertain, the number of the problems the investigation of which ends in a verdict of not proven, will vary according to the knowledge and the intellectual habits of the individual Agnostic. I do not very much care to speak of anything as "unknowable." What I am sure about is that there are many topics about which I know nothing; and which, so far as I can see, are out of reach of my faculties. But whether these things are knowable by anyone else is exactly one of those matters which is beyond my knowledge, though I may have a tolerably strong opinion as to the probabilities of the case. Relatively to myself, I am quite sure that the region of uncertainty—the nebulous country in which words play the part of realities—is far more extensive than I could wish. Materialism and Idealism; Theism and Atheism; the doctrine of the soul and its mortality or immortality—appear in the history of philosophy like the shades of Scandinavian heroes, eternally slaying one another and eternally coming to life again in a metaphysical "Nifelheim."[4] It is getting on for twenty-five centuries, at least, since mankind began seriously to give their minds to these topics. Generation after generation, philosophy has been doomed to roll the stone uphill; and, just as all the world swore it was at the top, down it has rolled to the bottom again.[5] All this is written in innumerable books; and he who will toil through them will discover that the stone is just where it was when the work began. Hume saw this; Kant[6] saw it; since their time, more and more eyes have been cleansed of the films which prevented them from seeing it; until now the weight and number of those who refuse to be the prey of verbal mystifications has begun to tell in practical life.

It was inevitable that a conflict should arise between Agnosticism and Theology; or rather, I ought to say, between Agnosticism and Ecclesiasticism. For Theology, the science, is one thing; and Ecclesiasticism, the championship of a foregone conclusion[7] as to the truth of a particular form of Theology, is another. With scientific Theology, Agnosticism has no quarrel. On the contrary, the Agnostic, knowing too well the influence of prejudice and idiosyncrasy, even on those who desire most earnestly to be impartial, can wish for nothing more urgently than that the scientific theologian should not only be at perfect liberty to thresh out the matter in his own fashion; but that he should, if he can, find flaws in the Agnostic position; and, even if demonstration is not to be had, that he should put, in their full force, the grounds of the conclusions he thinks probable. The scientific theologian admits the Agnostic principle, however widely his results may differ from those reached by the majority of Agnostics.

But, as between Agnosticism and Ecclesiasticism, or, as our neighbors across the Channel call it, Clericalism, there can be neither peace nor truce. The Cleric asserts that it is morally wrong not to believe certain propositions, whatever the results of a strict scientific investigation of the evidence of these propositions. He tells us "that religious error is, in itself, of an immoral

4. In Norse mythology realms of cold and darkness.
5. Cf. the Greek story of Sisyphus, who was in Hades, condemned to keep rolling a stone uphill, which always rolled downhill again before it reached the summit.
6. Immanuel Kant (1724–1804), German philosopher who focused in large part on defining the limits of human knowledge. The writings of the Scottish empiricist David Hume (1711–1776) were a major influence on his work.
7. Let us maintain, before we have proved. This seeming paradox is the secret of happiness. (Dr. Newman, "Tract 85") [Huxley's note]. For John Henry Cardinal Newman, see p. 62.

nature."[8] He declares that he has prejudged certain conclusions, and looks upon those who show cause for arrest of judgment as emissaries of Satan. It necessarily follows that, for him, the attainment of faith, not the ascertainment of truth, is the highest aim of mental life. And, on careful analysis of the nature of this faith, it will too often be found to be, not the mystic process of unity with the Divine, understood by the religious enthusiast; but that which the candid simplicity of a Sunday scholar once defined it to be. "Faith," said this unconscious plagiarist of Tertullian,[9] "is the power of saying you believe things which are incredible."

Now I, and many other Agnostics, believe that faith, in this sense, is an abomination; and though we do not indulge in the luxury of self-righteousness so far as to call those who are not of our way of thinking hard names, we do feel that the disagreement between ourselves and those who hold this doctrine is even more moral than intellectual. It is desirable there should be an end of any mistakes on this topic. If our clerical opponents were clearly aware of the real state of the case, there would be an end of the curious delusion, which often appears between the lines of their writings, that those whom they are so fond of calling "Infidels" are people who not only ought to be, but in their hearts are, ashamed of themselves. It would be discourteous to do more than hint the antipodal opposition of this pleasant dream of theirs to facts.

The clerics and their lay allies commonly tell us that if we refuse to admit that there is good ground for expressing definite convictions about certain topics, the bonds of human society will dissolve and mankind lapse into savagery. There are several answers to this assertion. One is that the bonds of human society were formed without the aid of their theology; and, in the opinion of not a few competent judges, have been weakened rather than strengthened by a good deal of it. Greek science, Greek art, the ethics of old Israel, the social organization of old Rome, contrived to come into being, without the help of anyone who believed in a single distinctive article of the simplest of the Christian creeds. The science, the art, the jurisprudence, the chief political and social theories, of the modern world have grown out of those of Greece and Rome—not by favor of, but in the teeth of, the fundamental teachings of early Christianity, to which science, art, and any serious occupation with the things of this world, were alike despicable.

Again, all that is best in the ethics of the modern world, in so far as it has not grown out of Greek thought, or Barbarian manhood, is the direct development of the ethics of old Israel. There is no code of legislation, ancient or modern, at once so just and so merciful, so tender to the weak and poor, as the Jewish law; and, if the Gospels are to be trusted, Jesus of Nazareth himself declared that he taught nothing but that which lay implicitly, or explicitly, in the religious and ethical system of his people.

---

8. Dr. Newman, *Essay on Development* [Huxley's note]. See *An Essay on the Development of Christian Doctrine* (1845).
9. Early Christian author and theologian (ca. 155–ca. 222). Tertullian wrote of Christ's resurrection, "It is certain because it is impossible" (*De Carne Christi* 5).

And the scribe said unto him, Of a truth, Teacher, thou hast well said that he is one; and there is none other but he and to love him with all the heart, and with all the understanding, and with all the strength, and to love his neighbour as himself, is much more than all whole burnt offerings and sacrifices. (Mark xii.32–33)

Here is the briefest of summaries of the teaching of the prophets of Israel of the eighth century;[1] does the Teacher, whose doctrine is thus set forth in his presence, repudiate the exposition? Nay; we are told, on the contrary, that Jesus saw that he "answered discreetly," and replied, "Thou are not far from the kingdom of God."

So that I think that even if the creeds, from the so-called "Apostles'" to the so-called "Athanasian,"[2] were swept into oblivion; and even if the human race should arrive at the conclusion that, whether a bishop washes a cup or leaves it unwashed, is not a matter of the least consequence, it will get on very well. The causes which have led to the development of morality in mankind, which have guided or impelled us all the way from the savage to the civilized state, will not cease to operate because a number of ecclesiastical hypotheses turn out to be baseless. And, even if the absurd notion that morality is more the child of speculation than of practical necessity and inherited instinct, had any foundation; if all the world is going to thieve, murder, and otherwise misconduct itself as soon as it discovers that certain portions of ancient history are mythical; what is the relevance of such arguments to any one who holds by the Agnostic principle?

Surely, the attempt to cast out Beelzebub by the aid of Beelzebub[3] is a hopeful procedure as compared to that of preserving morality by the aid of immorality. For I suppose it is admitted that an Agnostic may be perfectly sincere, may be competent, and may have studied the question at issue with as much care as his clerical opponents. But, if the Agnostic really believes what he says, the "dreadful consequence" argufier (consistently, I admit, with his own principles) virtually asks him to abstain from telling the truth, or to say what he believes to be untrue, because of the supposed injurious consequences to morality. "Beloved brethren, that we may be spotlessly moral, before all things let us lie," is the sum total of many an exhortation addressed to the "Infidel." Now, as I have already pointed out, we cannot oblige our exhorters. We leave the practical application of the convenient doctrines of "Reserve" and "Non-natural interpretation" to those who invented them.[4]

I trust that I have now made amends for any ambiguity, or want of fullness, in my previous exposition of that which I hold to be the essence of the Agnostic doctrine. Henceforward, I might hope to hear no more of the assertion that we are necessarily Materialists, Idealists, Atheists, Theists, or any other ists, if experience had led me to think that the proved falsity of a statement was any guarantee against its repetition. And those who appreciate the nature of our position will see, at once, that when Ecclesiasticism declares that we ought to believe this, that, and the other, and are very wicked

1. See Deuteronomy 6.4–5; 1 Samuel 15.22.
2. Two important summaries of Christian doctrine. The Athanasian creed dates back to ca. 361; the Apostles' baptismal creed developed between the 2nd and 9th centuries.
3. Mark 3.22–27.

4. A way of maintaining assent to a Scriptural passage without accepting its literal or obvious sense; a device here stigmatized as intellectually dishonest. "Reserve": "an intentional suppression of truth in cases where it might lead to inconvenience" (OED).

if we don't, it is impossible for us to give any answer but this: We have not the slightest objection to believe anything you like, if you will give us good grounds for belief; but, if you cannot, we must respectfully refuse, even if that refusal should wreck morality and insure our own damnation several times over. We are quite content to leave that to the decision of the future. The course of the past has impressed us with the firm conviction that no good ever comes of falsehood, and we feel warranted in refusing even to experiment in that direction.

* * *

1889, 1892

Pre-Raphaelitism

In his autobiography, W. B. Yeats writes of his youth, "I was in all things Pre-Raphaelite." Yeats's statement suggests that Pre-Raphaelitism was not only a movement in nineteenth-century art, but also a cultural attitude—a complex of taste, style, and belief. The movement began among a set of young artists studying painting at the Royal Academy in the late 1840s. In revolt against the compositional principles of the academic art of their day, which derived from the work of the Italian Renaissance painter Raphael (1483–1520), they came together in 1848 to form a secret society they named the Pre-Raphaelite Brotherhood, signing their paintings with the mysterious initials "PRB." The leaders of the group were William Holman Hunt, John Everett Millais, and Dante Gabriel Rossetti, all young at the time—twenty-one, nineteen, and twenty. Although the bright colors, foreshortened perspective, and medieval subjects of some of their early paintings suggest medieval models, they embraced such models because of their commitment to a new ideal of naturalism. Art since Raphael, they felt, paid more attention to conventional formulas of picture making; to find a purer naturalism, the artist needed to go back to the art before Raphael. In their pursuit of realism their strongest influence was John Ruskin. Hunt had read *Modern Painters* in 1847, and introduced it to his fellow artists. The Pre-Raphaelites aspired to paint directly from nature, working in the open air, often making extraordinary efforts to achieve a photographic fidelity of detail. To depict the nighttime landscape accurately for his religious painting of Christ, *The Light of the World*, Hunt constructed a straw hut in a farm orchard, where he worked by the light of the full moon.

As soon as they began to exhibit their paintings in 1849, the Pre-Raphaelites provoked energetic debate. To expound their ideas about art and to publish writing by themselves and their friends, they founded *The Germ*, the first journal ever published by an artistic group. (It was in *The Germ* that Rossetti's poem "The Blessed Damozel" originally appeared.) The controversy about their work reached a peak in 1850, when John Everett Millais exhibited his painting *Christ in the House of His Parents*. Charles Dickens virulently attacked the painting in his journal, *Household Words*; the figures in the painting, he wrote, "might be undressed in any hospital where dirty drunkards, in a high state of varicose veins, are received." Ruskin came to the defense, both in letters to the *Times* and in a pamphlet, *Pre-Raphaelitism*. The argument was essentially about realism: should the artist represent sacred subjects with naturalistic models? The Pre-Raphaelites' rendition of detail was equally controversial; their canvases were crowded with objects, each weighted with symbolic meaning and painted with photographic accuracy.

By 1853, the Pre-Raphaelite Brotherhood had begun to disintegrate. "The P.R.B. is in its decadence," Christina Rossetti wrote in a whimsical sonnet. In 1853 Millais was elected to the Royal Academy against which he had rebelled; Hunt began a series of trips to the Holy Land to paint biblical scenes on location; and Rossetti, in his sister's words, shunned "the vulgar optic." However, other artists began to adopt their principles, and collectors started to acquire their work.

Meanwhile, Rossetti had turned to painting watercolors on medieval themes. His work attracted the admiration of two undergraduates at Oxford, Edward Burne-Jones and William Morris, who independently had developed an interest in all things medieval. Burne-Jones sought Rossetti out, and the three formed a partnership. In 1857 the three gained a commission to paint murals from the *Morte d'Arthur* in the Debating Society Hall of the Oxford Union. At Rossetti's urging, Morris and Burne-Jones rented a flat in Bloomsbury, which they began to decorate in medieval style, designing and making furniture, just as they imagined medieval artisans might do—a project that led Morris in 1861 to establish a firm to make handcrafted furniture, tapestries, wallpaper, fabric, and other decorative objects. Rossetti also encouraged Morris to write poetry, his sister Christina began to publish her work, and he himself started to publish again for the first time since the short-lived *Germ*. While painting the Oxford murals, Rossetti met Algernon Charles Swinburne, at the time an undergraduate, who started to move in Pre-Raphaelite circles. The association of Rossetti, Morris, and Burne-Jones thus became the nucleus of a second phase of Pre-Raphaelitism, one central to the emergence in the last third of the century of aestheticism in poetry and of the Arts and Crafts movement. The second phase of Pre-Raphaelite painting presents many contrasts to the first. In the 1860s Rossetti began to paint looming images of women incarnating various aspects of female beauty; Burne-Jones concentrated on legends and myths represented in a highly mannered, dreamy style.

Despite the stylistic contrasts between the two phases of Pre-Raphaelitism, they share a changed understanding of the artist in relationship to society. The artist defines himself as apart from society, self-consciously avant-garde, in rebellion against artistic and cultural conventions. This rebellion takes a number of overlapping, sometimes conflicting forms: naturalism, medievalism, aestheticism. Throughout the evolution of Pre-Raphaelitism, painting and poetry remain closely allied, and not merely because Rossetti was at once painter and poet. Both the original Pre-Raphaelite Brotherhood and the group that came together at Oxford in the late 1850s frequently chose literary subjects for their paintings; the poets among them wrote works that fused fantasy with a vivid sense of visual detail. Both groups were trying to explore the symbol, whether the plenitude of details weighted with meaning in Hunt's *The Awakening Conscience* or the looming female figures that Rossetti painted and described in his paired paintings and sonnets, *Soul's Beauty* and *Body's Beauty*. Pre-Raphaelitism has been a difficult term to define in the history of poetry and painting because it seems to encompass such conflicting elements—microscopic fidelity to detail, dreamlike reverie, prominence of pattern and design. Late in his life, Rossetti dismissed the seriousness of the Pre-Raphaelite Brotherhood, claiming that the banding together under that title was all a joke of a half-dozen boys. But he conceded that the movement was serious. In the course of its history, that movement came to define more than a style of painting; it was an attitude toward design that shaped the Arts and Crafts movement, an attitude toward symbol central to aestheticism and decadence, and a vision of the arts in relationship both to each other and to society that had a deep impact on writers like the young Yeats, developing their work in the final decade of the century.

Reproductions of *Christ in the House of His Parents*, *The Awakening Conscience*, *Soul's Beauty*, *Body's Beauty*, and other Pre-Raphaelite works appear in this volume's color insert; additional images are available in the NAEL Archive.

CHARLES DICKENS

Dickens (1812–1870) published the following article in *Household Words*, the weekly journal he edited.

From Old Lamps for New Ones

In the fifteenth century, a certain feeble lamp of art arose in the Italian town of Urbino. This poor light, Raphael Sanzio by name, better known to a few miserably mistaken wretches in these later days, as Raphael (another burned at the same time, called Titian),[1] was fed with a preposterous idea of Beauty—with a ridiculous power of etherealising, and exalting to the very Heaven of Heavens, what was most sublime and lovely in the expression of the human face divine on Earth—with the truly contemptible conceit of finding in poor humanity the fallen likeness of the angels of GOD, and raising it up again to their pure spiritual condition. This very fantastic whim effected a low revolution in Art, in this wise, that Beauty came to be regarded as one of its indispensable elements. In this very poor delusion, Artists have continued until this present nineteenth century, when it was reserved for some bold aspirants to "put it down."

The Pre-Raphael Brotherhood, Ladies and Gentlemen, is the dread Tribunal which is to set this matter right. Walk up, walk up; and here, conspicuous on the wall of the Royal Academy of Art in England, in the eighty-second year of their annual exhibition, you shall see what this new Holy Brotherhood, this terrible Police that is to disperse all Post-Raphael offenders, has "been and done!"

You come—in this Royal Academy Exhibition, which is familiar with the works of WILKIE, COLLINS, ETTY, EASTLAKE, LESLIE, MACLISE, TURNER, STANFIELD, LANDSEER, ROBERTS, DANBY, CRESWICK, LEE, WEBSTER, HERBERT, DYCE, COPE,[2] and others who would have been renowned as great masters in any age or country—you come, in this place, to the contemplation of a Holy Family.[3] You will have the goodness to discharge from your minds all Post-Raphael ideas, all religious aspirations, all elevating thoughts; all tender, awful, sorrowful, ennobling, sacred, graceful, or beautiful associations; and to prepare yourselves, as befits such a subject—Pre-Raphaelly considered—for the lowest depths of what is mean, odious, repulsive, and revolting.

You behold the interior of a carpenter's shop. In the foreground of that carpenter's shop is a hideous, wry-necked, blubbering, red-headed boy, in a bed-gown; who appears to have received a poke in the hand, from the stick

---

1. Raphael (1483–1520) and Titian (1490–1576), painters of the Italian Renaissance.
2. All 19th-century British painters exhibited at the Royal Academy.

3. See the color insert for a reproduction of this painting, *Christ in the House of His Parents*, by John Everett Millais.

of another boy with whom he has been playing in an adjacent gutter, and to be holding it up for the contemplation of a kneeling woman, so horrible in her ugliness, that (supposing it were possible for any human creature to exist for a moment with that dislocated throat) she would stand out from the rest of the company as a Monster, in the vilest cabaret in France, or the lowest gin-shop in England. Two almost naked carpenters, master and journeyman, worthy companions of this agreeable female, are working at their trade; a boy, with some small flavor of humanity in him, is entering with a vessel of water; and nobody is paying any attention to a snuffy old woman who seems to have mistaken that shop for the tobacconist's next door, and to be hopelessly waiting at the counter to be served with half an ounce of her favourite mixture. Wherever it is possible to express ugliness of feature, limb, or attitude, you have it expressed. Such men as the carpenters might be undressed in any hospital where dirty drunkards, in a high state of varicose veins, are received. Their very toes have walked out of Saint Giles's.[4]

This, in the nineteenth century, and in the eighty-second year of the annual exhibition of the National Academy of Art, is the Pre-Raphael representation to us, Ladies and Gentlemen, of the most solemn passage which our minds can ever approach. This, in the nineteenth century, and in the eighty-second year of the annual exhibition of the National Academy of Art, is what Pre-Raphael Art can do to render reverence and homage to the faith in which we live and die!

1850

4. A slum district in central London.

JOHN RUSKIN

This letter from Ruskin (1819–1900) appeared in the London *Times*.

["The Awakening Conscience"]

SIR,—Your kind insertion of my notes on Mr. Hunt's principal picture[1] encourages me to hope that you may yet allow me room in your columns for a few words respecting his second work in the Royal Academy, the "Awakening Conscience."[2] Not that this picture is obscure, or its story feebly told. I am at a loss to know how its meaning could be rendered more distinctly, but assuredly it is not understood. People gaze at it in a blank wonder, and leave it hopelessly; so that, though it is almost an insult to the painter to explain his thoughts in this instance, I cannot persuade myself to leave it

1. *The Light of the World,* a painting of the figure of Jesus.

2. See the color insert for a reproduction of this painting.

thus misunderstood. The poor girl has been sitting singing with her seducer; some chance words of the song, "Oft in the stilly night,"[3] have struck upon the numbed places of her heart; she has started up in agony; he, not seeing her face, goes on singing, striking the keys carelessly with his gloved hand.

I suppose that no one possessing the slightest knowledge of expression could remain untouched by the countenance of the lost girl, rent from its beauty into sudden horror; the lips half open, indistinct in their purple quivering; the teeth set hard; the eyes filled with the fearful light of futurity, and with tears of ancient days.[4] But I can easily understand that to many persons the careful rendering of the inferior details in this picture cannot but be at first offensive, as calling their attention away from the principal subject. It is true that detail of this kind has long been so carelessly rendered, that the perfect finishing of it becomes a matter of curiosity, and therefore an interruption to serious thought. But, without entering into the question of the general propriety of such treatment, I would only observe that, at least in this instance, it is based on a truer principle of the pathetic than any of the common artistical expedients of the schools. Nothing is more notable than the way in which even the most trivial objects force themselves upon the attention of a mind which has been fevered by violent and distressful excitement. They thrust themselves forward with a ghastly and unendurable distinctness, as if they would compel the sufferer to count, or measure, or learn them by heart. Even to the mere spectator a strange interest exalts the accessories of a scene in which he bears witness to human sorrow. There is not a single object in all that room—common, modern, vulgar (in the vulgar sense, as it may be), but it becomes tragical, if rightly read. That furniture so carefully painted, even to the last vein of the rosewood—is there nothing to be learnt from that terrible lustre of it, from its fatal newness; nothing there that has the old thoughts of home upon it, or that is ever to become a part of home? Those embossed books, vain and useless—they also new—marked with no happy wearing of beloved leaves; the torn and dying bird upon the floor; the gilded tapestry, with the fowls of the air feeding on the ripened corn; the picture above the fireplace, with its single drooping figure—the woman taken in adultery;[5] nay, the very hem of the poor girl's dress, at which the painter has laboured so closely, thread by thread, has story in it, if we think how soon its pure whiteness may be soiled with dust and rain, her outcast feet failing in the street; and the fair garden flowers, seen in that reflected sunshine of the mirror,—these also have their language—

> "Hope not to find delight in us, they say,
> For we are spotless, Jessy—we are pure."[6]

I surely need not go on. Examine the whole range of the walls of the Academy,—nay, examine those of all our public and private galleries,—and while pictures will be met with by the thousand which literally tempt to evil, by the thousand which are directed to the meanest trivialities of incident or emotion, by the thousand to the delicate fancies of inactive religion, there will

3. A song, with words by the Irish poet Thomas Moore (1779–1852), about the pull of childhood memories.
4. Hunt later softened the look on the girl's face in the original painting at the request of its buyer, who found he couldn't bear to look at it.
5. John, 8.3.
6. From "Elegy 26" by British poet William Shenstone (1714–1763).

not be found one powerful as this to meet full in the front the moral evil of the age in which it is painted; to waken into mercy the cruel thoughtlessness of youth, and subdue the severities of judgment into the sanctity of compassion.

I have the honour to be, Sir,

Your obedient servant,

THE AUTHOR OF "MODERN PAINTERS."

1854

JOHN RUSKIN

This selection is taken from the fourth of a series of lectures on architecture and painting that Ruskin delivered in Edinburgh, later published as a book.

From Pre-Raphaelitism

Pre-Raphaelitism has but one principle, that of absolute, uncompromising truth in all that it does, obtained by working everything, down to the most minute detail, from nature, and from nature only. Every Pre-Raphaelite landscape background is painted to the last touch, in the open air, from the thing itself. Every Pre-Raphaelite figure, however studied in expression, is a true portrait of some living person. Every minute accessory is painted in the same manner. And one of the chief reasons for the violent opposition with which the school has been attacked by other artists, is the enormous cost of care and labour which such a system demands from those who adopt it, in contradistinction to the present slovenly and imperfect style.

This is the main Pre-Raphaelite principle. But the battle which its supporters have to fight is a hard one; and for that battle they have been fitted by a very peculiar character.

You perceive that the principal resistance they have to make is to that spurious beauty, whose attractiveness had tempted men to forget, or to despise, the more noble quality of sincerity: and in order at once to put them beyond the power of temptation from this beauty, they are, as a body, characterised by a total absence of sensibility to the ordinary and popular forms of artistic gracefulness; while, to all that still lower kind of prettiness, which regulates the disposition of our scenes upon the stage, and which appears in our lower art, as in our annuals, our commonplace portraits, and statuary, the Pre-Raphaelites are not only dead, but they regard it with a contempt and aversion approaching to disgust. This character is absolutely necessary

1. Or, where imagination is necessarily trusted to, by always endeavouring to conceive a fact as it really was likely to have happened, rather than as it most prettily *might* have happened. The various members of the school are not all equally severe in carrying out its principles, some of them trusting their memory or fancy very far; only all agreeing in the effort to make their memories as to seem like portraiture, and their fancy as probably to seem like memory [Ruskin's note].

to them in the present time; but it, of course, occasionally renders their work comparatively unpleasing. As the school becomes less aggressive, and more authoritative—which it will do—they will enlist into their ranks men who will work, mainly, upon their principles, and yet embrace more of those characters which are generally attractive, and this great ground of offence will be removed.

Again: you observe that as landscape painters, their principles must, in great part, confine them to mere foreground work; and singularly enough, that they may not be tempted away from this work, they have been born with comparatively little enjoyment of those evanescent effects and distant sublimities which nothing but the memory can arrest, and nothing but a daring conventionalism portray. But for this work they are not now needed. Turner,[2] the first and greatest of the Pre-Raphaelites, has done it already; he, though his capacity embraced everything, and though he would sometimes, in his foregrounds, paint the spots upon a dead trout, and the dyes upon a butterfly's wing, yet for the most part delighted to begin at that very point where the other branches of Pre-Raphaelitism become powerless.

[Lastly. The habit of constantly carrying everything up to the utmost point of completion deadens the Pre-Raphaelites in general to the merits of men who, with an equal love of truth up to a certain point, yet express themselves habitually with speed and power, rather than with finish, and give abstracts of truth rather than total truth.] Probably to the end of time artists will more or less be divided into these classes, and it will be impossible to make men like Millais understand the merits of men like Tintoret,[3] but this is the more to be regretted because the Pre-Raphaelites have enormous powers of imagination, as well as of realisation, and do not yet themselves know of how much they would be capable, if they sometimes worked on a larger scale, and with a less laborious finish.

With all their faults, their pictures are, since Turner's death, the best—incomparably the best—on the walls of the Royal Academy; and such works as Mr. Hunt's[4] "Claudio and Isabella" have never been rivalled, in some respects never approached, at any other period of art.

This I believe to be a most candid statement of all their faults and all their deficiencies; not such, you perceive, as are likely to arrest their progress. The "magna est veritas"[5] was never more sure of accomplishment than by these men. Their adversaries have no chance with them. They will gradually unite their influence with whatever is true or powerful in the reactionary art of other countries; and on their works such a school will be founded as shall justify the third age of the world's civilisation, and render it as great in creation as it has been in discovery.

And now let me remind you but of one thing more. As you examine into the career of historical painting, you will be more and more struck with the

2. J. M. W. Turner (1775–1851), British landscape painter whom Ruskin praised as the model of truth to nature in art in *Modern Painters*. The atmospheric effects and evocation of light in Turner's painting seem to place him at a far distance from the Pre-Raphaelites, but Ruskin saw their work as expressing different aspects of naturalism. See Ruskin's description of Turner's *Slave Ship*, from *Modern Painters* p. 385 and the color insert for a reproduction of the painting.
3. Tintoretto (1518–1594), Italian Renaissance painter known for special lighting effects. John Everett Millais (1829–1896), one of the leading Pre-Raphaelites.
4. William Holman Hunt (1827–1910), a leading Pre-Raphaelite painter.
5. "Great is truth" (1 Esdras 4.41).

fact I have this evening stated to you,—that none was ever truly great but that which represented the living forms and daily deeds of the people among whom it arose—that all precious historical work records, not the past, but the present. Remember, therefore, that it is not so much in *buying* pictures, as in *being* pictures, that you can encourage a noble school. The best patronage of art is not that which seeks for the pleasures of sentiment in a vague ideality, not for beauty of form in a marble image; but that which educates your children into living heroes, and binds down the flights and the fondnesses of the heart into practical duty and faithful devotion.

1853   1859

WILLIAM MICHAEL ROSSETTI

R ossetti (1829–1919) published his brother Dante Gabriel's letters in 1895. This account of the aesthetic principles of Pre-Raphaelitism comes from the memoir he included in the first volume.

[The Pre-Raphaelite Manifesto]

Had the Præraphaelite Brotherhood any ulterior aim beyond that of producing good works of art? Yes, and No. Assuredly it had the aim of developing such *ideas* as are suited to the medium of fine art, and of bringing the arts of form into general unison with what is highest in other arts, especially poetry. Likewise the aim of showing by contrast how threadbare were the pretensions of most painters of the day, and how incapable they were of constituting or developing any sort of School of Art worthy of the name. In the person of two at least of its members, Hunt and Collinson,[1] it had also a definite relation to a Christian, and not a pagan or latitudinarian, line of thought. On the other hand, the notion that the Brotherhood, as such, had anything whatever to do with particular movements in the religious world—whether Roman Catholicism, Anglican Tractarianism,[2] or what not—is totally, and, to one who formed a link in its composition, even ludicrously, erroneous. To say that Præraphaelitism was part of "the ever-rising protest and rebellion of our century against artificial authority," as in the cases of "the French Revolution" and Wordsworth and Darwin, etc.,[3] is not indeed untrue, but is far too vague to account for anything. Again, the so-called German Præraphaelites—such as Schnorr, Overbeck, and Cornelius[4]—were in no repute with the young British artists. They did, however, admire very much certain designs by

1. William Holman Hunt (1827–1910) and James Collinson (1825–1881), both original members of the Pre-Raphaelite Brotherhood.
2. Mid-19th-century Anglican movement to bring church ritual closer to its Catholic roots.
3. Esther Wood's *Dante Gabriel Rossetti and the Pre-Raphaelite Movement* (1894), 9.
4. Julius Schnorr von Carolsfeld (1794–1872), Johann Friedrich Overbeck (1789–1869), and Peter von Cornelius (1783–1867), German Romantic artists called the Nazarenes with principles similar to those of the British Pre-Raphaelites.

Fuhrich[5] from the Legend of St. Genevieve. Neither was Ruskin their inciter, though it is true that Hunt had read and laid to heart in 1847 the first volume of *Modern Painters*, the only thing then current as Ruskin's work. I do not think any other P.R.B. (with the possible exception of Collinson) had, up to 1848 or later, read him at all. That the Præraphaelites valued moral and spiritual ideas as an important section of the ideas germane to fine art is most true, and not one of them was in the least inclined to do any work of a gross, lascivious, or sensual description; but neither did they limit the province of art to the spiritual or the moral. I will therefore take it upon me to say that the bond of union among the Members of the Brotherhood was really and simply this—1, To have genuine ideas to express; 2, to study Nature attentively, so as to know how to express them; 3, to sympathize with what is direct and serious and heartfelt in previous art, to the exclusion of what is conventional and self-parading and learned by rote; and 4, and most indispensable of all, to produce thoroughly good pictures and statues.

[handwritten annotation: Rossetti's ideas about what Præraph Præraph...s were doing 1895]

5. Joseph von Führich (1800–1876), a Nazarene painter.

DANTE GABRIEL ROSSETTI
1828–1882

Dante Gabriel Rossetti was the son of an Italian patriot and scholar whose political activities had led to his being exiled to England. The Rossetti household in London was one in which liberal politics and artistic topics were hotly debated; all four children—Maria Francesca, Dante Gabriel, William Michael, and Christina Georgina—wrote, drew, or engaged in scholarly pursuits from a young age. Displaying extraordinary early promise both as a painter and as a poet, Dante Gabriel luxuriated in colors and textures, and was especially drawn to feminine beauty. His view of life and art, derived in part from his close study of John Keats's poems and letters, anticipated by many years the aesthetic movement later to be represented by men such as Walter Pater, Oscar Wilde, and the painter James McNeill Whistler, who insisted that art must be exclusively concerned with the beautiful, not with the useful or didactic.

The beauty that Rossetti admired in the faces of women was of a distinctive kind. In at least two of his models he found what he sought. The first was his wife, Elizabeth Siddal, whose suicide in 1862 haunted him with a sense of guilt for the rest of his life. The other was Jane Morris, the wife of his friend William Morris. In Rossetti's paintings both of these models are shown with dreamy stares, as if they were breathless from visions of heaven; but counteracting this impression is an emphasis on parted lips and voluptuous curves suggesting a more earthly kind of ecstasy. Similar combinations of spirituality and physicality, or mind and body, are to be found in many of Rossetti's poems. For instance, the central figure of "The Blessed

Damozel" (1850), a poem begun when Rossetti was eighteen and was heavily influenced by the work of Dante Alighieri, leans on "the gold bar of heaven" and makes it "warm" with her bosom. In "Jenny" (1870), another work started in Rossetti's early adulthood, a male speaker muses about the life and thoughts of the young prostitute whose head rests upon his knee as she sleeps: his speculations thus replace, or stand in for, more overt sexual acts between them. And *The House of Life* (1870), his sonnet sequence, undertakes to explore the relationship of spirit to body in love. Some Victorian readers found little Dante-like spirituality in *The House of Life;* the critic Robert Buchanan, for example, saw only lewd sensuality, and his 1871 pamphlet, "The Fleshly School of Poetry," treated Rossetti's poetry to the most severe abuse. Buchanan's attack hurt the poet profoundly and contributed to the recurring bouts of nervous depression from which he suffered in the remaining years of his life.

Rossetti and his artist friends called women such as Jane Morris "stunners." The epithet can also be applied to Rossetti's poetry, especially his later writings. In his maturity he used stunning polysyllabic diction to convey opulence and density. Earlier poems such as "My Sister's Sleep" (1850) are usually much less elaborate in manner and reflect the original aesthetic values of the Pre-Raphaelite movement in which Rossetti played a central and founding role. Just as Rossetti grew away from the Pre-Raphaelite manner in his painting, he also adopted a richly ornate style in his poetry. In both the early and the late phases of his art, however, many have viewed him as essentially a poet in his painting and a painter in his poetry. "Colour and metre," he once said, "these are the true patents of nobility in painting and poetry, taking precedence of all intellectual claims."

The Blessed Damozel[1]

The blessed damozel leaned out
    From the gold bar of heaven;
Her eyes were deeper than the depth
    Of waters stilled at even;
5   She had three lilies in her hand,
    And the stars in her hair were seven.

Her robe, ungirt from clasp to hem,
    No wrought flowers did adorn,
But a white rose of Mary's gift,
10   For service meetly° worn;   *fittingly*
Her hair that lay along her back
    Was yellow like ripe corn.°   *grain*

Herseemed[2] she scarce had been a day
    One of God's choristers;

1. A poetic version of "damsel," signifying a young unmarried lady. Rossetti once explained that "Blessed Damozel" is related to Edgar Allan Poe's "The Raven" (1845), a poem he admired. "I saw that Poe had done the utmost it was possible to do with the grief of the lover on earth, and so I determined to reverse the conditions, and give utterance to the yearning of the loved one in heaven." The thoughts of the damozel's still-living lover appear in the poem in parentheses.
2. It seemed to her.

15 The wonder was not yet quite gone
        From that still look of hers;
    Albeit, to them she left, her day
        Had counted as ten years.

    (To one it is ten years of years.
20   . . . Yet now, and in this place,
    Surely she leaned o'er me—her hair
        Fell all about my face. . . .
    Nothing: the autumn-fall of leaves.
        The whole year sets apace.)

25 It was the rampart of God's house
        That she was standing on;
    By God built over the sheer depth
        The which is Space begun;
    So high, that looking downward thence
30   She scarce could see the sun.

    It lies in heaven, across the flood
        Of ether, as a bridge.
    Beneath the tides of day and night
        With flame and darkness ridge
35 The void, as low as where this earth
        Spins like a fretful midge.

    Around her, lovers, newly met
        'Mid deathless love's acclaims,
    Spoke evermore among themselves
40   Their heart-remembered names;
    And the souls mounting up to God
        Went by her like thin flames.

    And still she bowed herself and stooped
        Out of the circling charm;
45 Until her bosom must have made
        The bar she leaned on warm,
    And the lilies lay as if asleep
        Along her bended arm.

    From the fixed place of heaven she saw
50   Time like a pulse shake fierce
    Through all the worlds. Her gaze still strove
        Within the gulf to pierce
    Its path; and now she spoke as when
        The stars sang in their spheres.

55 The sun was gone now; the curled moon
        Was like a little feather
    Fluttering far down the gulf; and now
        She spoke through the still weather.

The Blessed Damozel
(1875–78; detail). In the second phase of his painting career, Rossetti turned from the religious and literary subjects of his early work (see, for instance, his illustration for "The Lady of Shalott," p. 151) to huge sensual portraits of women, often designed as companion pieces to his poems. For other examples of Rossetti's visual art, see the frontispiece he drew for his sister Christina's first volume of poems, p. 547, and his paintings in the color insert in this volume and in the NAEL Archive.

Her voice was like the voice the stars
60   Had when they sang together.[3]

(Ah, sweet! Even now, in that bird's song,
        Strove not her accents there,
Fain to be harkened? When those bells
        Possessed the midday air,
65   Strove not her steps to reach my side
        Down all the echoing stair?)

"I wish that he were come to me,
        For he will come," she said.
"Have I not prayed in heaven?—on earth,
70   Lord, Lord, has he not prayed?
Are not two prayers a perfect strength?
        And shall I feel afraid?

"When round his head the aureole° clings,   *halo*
        And he is clothed in white,
75   I'll take his hand and go with him
        To the deep wells of light;

3. Job 38.7.

As unto a stream we will step down,
    And bathe there in God's sight.

"We two will stand beside that shrine,
80   Occult,° withheld, untrod,   *hidden, mysterious*
Whose lamps are stirred continually
    With prayer sent up to God;
And see our old prayers, granted, melt
    Each like a little cloud.

85 "We two will lie i' the shadow of
    That living mystic tree[4]
Within whose secret growth the Dove[5]
    Is sometimes felt to be,
While every leaf that His plumes touch
90   Saith His Name audibly.

"And I myself will teach to him,
    I myself, lying so,
The songs I sing here; which his voice
    Shall pause in, hushed and slow,
95 And find some knowledge at each pause,
    Or some new thing to know."

(Alas! We two, we two, thou say'st!
    Yea, one wast thou with me
That once of old. But shall God lift
100   To endless unity
The soul whose likeness with thy soul
    Was but its love for thee?)

"We two," she said, "will seek the groves
    Where the lady Mary is,
105 With her five handmaidens, whose names
    Are five sweet symphonies,
Cecily, Gertrude, Magdalen,
    Margaret, and Rosalys.[6]

"Circlewise sit they, with bound locks
110   And foreheads garlanded;
Into the fine cloth white like flame
    Weaving the golden thread,
To fashion the birth-robes for them
    Who are just born, being dead.

115 "He shall fear, haply,° and be dumb;   *perhaps*
    Then will I lay my cheek
To his, and tell about our love,

4. The tree of life, as described in an apocalyptic vision in the Bible (Revelation 22.2).
5. A tangible manifestation of the Holy Spirit (Mark 1.10), frequent in Christian art.

6. Rossetti creates this list of Mary's handmaidens from various saints, historical figures, and allegorical characters.

Not once abashed or weak;
And the dear Mother will approve
120　　My pride, and let me speak.

"Herself shall bring us, hand in hand,
To Him round whom all souls
Kneel, the clear-ranged unnumbered heads
Bowed with their aureoles;
125　And angels meeting us shall sing
To their citherns and citoles.[7]

"There will I ask of Christ the Lord
Thus much for him and me—
Only to live as once on earth
130　With Love—only to be,
As then awhile, forever now,
Together, I and he."

She gazed and listened and then said,
Less sad of speech than mild—
135　"All this is when he comes." She ceased.
The light thrilled toward her, filled
With angels in strong, level flight.
Her eyes prayed, and she smiled.

(I saw her smile.) But soon their path
140　Was vague in distant spheres;
And then she cast her arms along
The golden barriers,
And laid her face between her hands,
And wept. (I heard her tears.)

1846　　　　　　　　　　　　　　　　　　　　　1850

My Sister's Sleep[1]

She fell asleep on Christmas Eve.
At length the long-ungranted shade
Of weary eyelids overweighed
The pain nought else might yet relieve.

5　Our mother, who had leaned all day
Over the bed from chime to chime,
Then raised herself for the first time,
And as she sat her down, did pray.

Her little worktable was spread
10　With work to finish. For° the glare　　　　　　*because of*

7. Guitarlike instruments.
1. The incident in this poem is imaginary, not autobiographical.

Made by her candle, she had care
To work some distance from the bed.

Without, there was a cold moon up,
   Of winter radiance sheer and thin;
15   The hollow halo it was in
Was like an icy crystal cup.

Through the small room, with subtle sound
   Of flame, by vents the fireshine drove
   And reddened. In its dim alcove
20 The mirror shed a clearness round.

I had been sitting up some nights,
   And my tired mind felt weak and blank;
   Like a sharp strengthening wine it drank
The stillness and the broken lights.

25 Twelve struck. That sound, by dwindling years
   Heard in each hour, crept off; and then
   The ruffled silence spread again,
Like water that a pebble stirs.

Our mother rose from where she sat;
30   Her needles, as she laid them down,
   Met lightly, and her silken gown
Settled—no other noise than that.

"Glory unto the Newly Born!"
   So, as said angels, she did say,
35   Because we were in Christmas Day,
Though it would still be long till morn.

Just then in the room over us
   There was a pushing back of chairs,
   As some who had sat unawares
40 So late, now heard the hour, and rose.

With anxious softly-stepping haste
   Our mother went where Margaret lay,
   Fearing the sounds o'erhead—should they
Have broken her long watched-for rest!

45 She stooped an instant, calm, and turned,
   But suddenly turned back again;
   And all her features seemed in pain
With woe, and her eyes gazed and yearned.

For my part, I but hid my face,
50   And held my breath, and spoke no word.
   There was none spoken; but I heard
The silence for a little space.

Our mother bowed herself and wept;
And both my arms fell, and I said,
55 "God knows I knew that she was dead."
And there, all white, my sister slept.

Then kneeling, upon Christmas morn
A little after twelve o'clock,
We said, ere the first quarter struck,
60 "Christ's blessing on the newly born!"

1847   1850

Jenny

Vengeance of Jenny's case! Fie on her! Never name her, child!
—(Mrs. Quickly.)[1]

Lazy laughing languid Jenny,
Fond of a kiss and fond of a guinea,[2]
Whose head upon my knee to-night
Rests for a while, as if grown light
5 With all our dances and the sound
To which the wild tunes spun you round:
Fair Jenny mine, the thoughtless queen
Of kisses which the blush between
Could hardly make much daintier;
10 Whose eyes are as blue skies, whose hair
Is countless gold incomparable:
Fresh flower, scarce touched with signs that tell
Of Love's exuberant hotbed:—Nay,
Poor flower left torn since yesterday
15 Until to-morrow leave you bare;
Poor handful of bright spring-water
Flung in the whirlpool's shrieking face;
Poor shameful Jenny, full of grace[3]
Thus with your head upon my knee;—
20 Whose person or whose purse may be
The lodestar° of your reverie?   *guiding star*

This room of yours, my Jenny, looks
A change from mine so full of books,
Whose serried[4] ranks hold fast, forsooth,
25 So many captive hours of youth,—
The hours they thieve from day and night
To make one's cherished work come right,

---

1. Shakespeare, *The Merry Wives of Windsor*
4.1.53–54. Mistress Quickly continues: "if she
be a whore."
2. English gold coin worth twenty-one shillings.

3. Allusion to the first line of the prayer to the
Virgin Mary: "Hail Mary, full of grace."
4. Pressed close together.

And leave it wrong for all their theft,
Even as to-night my work was left:
30 Until I vowed that since my brain
And eyes of dancing seemed so fain,°   *desirous*
My feet should have some dancing too:—
And thus it was I met with you.
Well, I suppose 'twas hard to part,
35 For here I am. And now, sweetheart,
You seem too tired to get to bed.

It was a careless life I led
When rooms like this were scarce so strange
Not long ago. What breeds the change,—
40 The many aims or the few years?
Because to-night it all appears
Something I do not know again.

The cloud's not danced out of my brain—
The cloud that made it turn and swim
45 While hour by hour the books grew dim.
Why, Jenny, as I watch you there,—
For all your wealth of loosened hair,
Your silk ungirdled and unlac'd
And warm sweets open to the waist.
50 All golden in the lamplight's gleam,—
You know not what a book you seem,
Half-read by lightning in a dream!
How should you know, my Jenny? Nay,
And I should be ashamed to say:—
55 Poor beauty, so well worth a kiss!
But while my thought runs on like this
With wasteful whims more than enough,
I wonder what you're thinking of.

If of myself you think at all,
60 What is the thought?—conjectural
On sorry matters best unsolved?—
Or inly° is each grace revolved   *inwardly*
To fit me with a lure?—or (sad
To think!) perhaps you're merely glad
65 That I'm not drunk or ruffianly
And let you rest upon my knee.

For sometimes, were the truth confess'd,
You're thankful for a little rest,—
Glad from the crush to rest within,
70 From the heart-sickness and the din
Where envy's voice at virtue's pitch
Mocks you because your gown is rich;
And from the pale girl's dumb rebuke,
Whose ill-clad grace and toil-worn look
75 Proclaim the strength that keeps her weak,

And other nights than yours bespeak;
And from the wise unchildish elf,
To schoolmate lesser than himself
Pointing you out, what thing you are:—
80   Yes, from the daily jeer and jar,
From shame and shame's outbraving too,
Is rest not sometimes sweet to you?—
But most from the hatefulness of man,
Who spares not to end what he began,
85   Whose acts are ill and his speech ill,
Who, having used you at his will,
Thrusts you aside, as when I dine
I serve° the dishes and the wine.   *treat*

Well, handsome Jenny mine, sit up:
90   I've filled our glasses, let us sup,
And do not let me think of you,
Lest shame of yours suffice for two.
What, still so tired? Well, well then, keep
Your head there, so you do not sleep;
95   But that the weariness may pass
And leave you merry, take this glass.
Ah! lazy lily hand, more bless'd
If ne'er in rings it had been dress'd
Nor ever by a glove conceal'd!

100   Behold the lilies of the field,
They toil not neither do they spin;
(So doth the ancient text[5] begin,—
Not of such rest as one of these
Can share.) Another rest and ease
105   Along each summer-sated path
From its new lord the garden hath,
Than that whose spring in blessings ran
Which praised the bounteous husbandman,°   *farmer*
Ere yet, in days of hankering breath,
110   The lilies sickened unto death.

What, Jenny, are your lilies dead?
Aye, and the snow-white leaves are spread
Like winter on the garden-bed.
But you had roses left in May,—
115   They were not gone too. Jenny, nay,
But must your roses die, and those
Their purfled[6] buds that should unclose?
Even so; the leaves are curled apart,
Still red as from the broken heart,
120   And here's the naked stem of thorns.

---

5. Matthew 6.28.   6. With a decorative edging.

Nay, nay, mere words. Here nothing warns
As yet of winter. Sickness here
Or want alone could waken fear,—
Nothing but passion wrings a tear.
125 Except when there may rise unsought
Haply at times a passing thought
Of the old days which seem to be
Much older than any history
That is written in any book;
130 When she would lie in fields and look
Along the ground through the blown grass
And wonder where the city was,
Far out of sight, whose broil and bale°   *turmoil and evil*
They told her then for a child's tale.

135   Jenny, you know the city now.
A child can tell the tale there, how
Some things which are not yet enroll'd
In market-lists are bought and sold
Even till the early Sunday light,
140 When Saturday night is market-night
Everywhere, be it dry or wet,
And market-night in the Haymarket.[7]
Our learned London children know,
Poor Jenny, all your pride and woe;
145 Have seen your lifted silken skirt
Advertise dainties through the dirt;
Have seen your coach-wheels splash rebuke
On virtue; and have learned your look
When, wealth and health slipped past, you stare
150 Along the streets alone, and there,
Round the long park, across the bridge,
The cold lamps at the pavement's edge
Wind on together and apart,
A fiery serpent for your heart.

155   Let the thoughts pass, an empty cloud I
Suppose I were to think aloud,—
What if to her all this were said?
Why, as a volume seldom read
Being opened halfway shuts again,
160 So might the pages of her brain
Be parted at such words, and thence
Close back upon the dusty sense.
For is there hue or shape defin'd
In Jenny's desecrated mind,
165 Where all contagious currents meet,
A Lethe[8] of the middle street?
Nay, it reflects not any face,

7. Street in London frequented by prostitutes.
8. The river of forgetfulness in the Greek underworld. Gutters in London often ran through the
middle of the street.

Nor sound is in its sluggish pace,
But as they coil those eddies° clot,   *small whirlpools*
170 And night and day remember not.

Why, Jenny, you're asleep at last!—
Asleep, poor Jenny, hard and fast,—
So young and soft and tired; so fair,
With chin thus nestled in your hair,
175 Mouth quiet, eyelids almost blue
As if some sky of dreams shone through!

Just as another woman sleeps!
Enough to throw one's thoughts in heaps
Of doubt and horror,—what to say
180 Or think,—this awful secret sway,
The potter's power over the clay!
Of the same lump (it has been said)
For honour and dishonour made,[9]
Two sister vessels. Here is one.

185 My cousin Nell is fond of fun,
And fond of dress, and change, and praise,
So mere a woman in her ways:
And if her sweet eyes rich in youth
Are like her lips that tell the truth,
190 My cousin Nell is fond of love.
And she's the girl I'm proudest of.
Who does not prize her, guard her well?
The love of change, in cousin Nell,
Shall find the best and hold it dear:
195 The unconquered mirth turn quieter
Not through her own, through others' woe:
The conscious pride of beauty glow
Beside another's pride in her,
One little part of all they share.
200 For Love himself shall ripen these
In a kind soil to just increase
Through years of fertilizing peace.

Of the same lump (as it is said)
For honour and dishonour made,
205 Two sister vessels. Here is one.

It makes a goblin[1] of the sun.

So pure,—so fall'n! How dare to think
Of the first common kindred link?
Yet, Jenny, till the world shall burn
210 It seems that all things take their turn;

---

9. Romans 9.21: "Hath not the potter power over   unto honour, and another unto dishonour?"
the clay, of the same lump to make one vessel   1. A gold coin (slang).

And who shall say but this fair tree
May need, in changes that may be,
Your children's children's charity?
Scorned then, no doubt, as you are scorn'd!
215 Shall no man hold his pride forewarn'd
Till in the end, the Day of Days,
At Judgment, one of his own race,
As frail and lost as you, shall rise,—
His daughter, with his mother's eyes?

220   How Jenny's clock ticks on the shelf!
Might not the dial scorn itself
That has such hours to register?
Yet as to me, even so to her
Are golden sun and silver moon,
225 In daily largesse of earth's boon,
Counted for life-coins to one tune.
And if, as blindfold fates are toss'd,
Through some one man this life be lost,
Shall soul not somehow pay for soul?

230   Fair shines the gilded aureole°   *halo*
In which our highest painters place
Some living woman's simple face.
And the stilled features thus descried
As Jenny's long throat droops aside,—
235 The shadows where the cheeks are thin,
And pure wide curve from ear to chin,—
With Raffael's, Leonardo's[2] hand
To show them to men's souls, might stand,
Whole ages long, the whole world through,
240 For preachings of what God can do.
What has man done here? How atone,
Great God, for this which man has done?
And for the body and soul which by
Man's pitiless doom must now comply
245 With lifelong hell, what lullaby
Of sweet forgetful second birth
Remains? All dark. No sign on earth
What measure of God's rest endows
The many mansions of his house.[3]

250   If but a woman's heart might see
Such erring heart unerringly
For once! But that can never be.

    Like a rose shut in a book
In which pure women may not look,
255 For its base pages claim control

---

2. The painters Raphael (Raffaello Sanzio, 1483–1520) and Leonardo da Vinci (1452–1519).

3. Cf. John 14.2: "In my Father's house are many mansions."

To crush the flower within the soul;
Where through each dead rose-leaf that clings,
Pale as transparent Psyche-wings,[4]
To the vile text, are traced such things
260　As might make lady's cheek indeed
More than a living rose to read;
So nought save foolish foulness may
Watch with hard eyes the sure decay:
And so the life-blood of this rose,
265　Puddled with shameful knowledge, flows
Through leaves no chaste hand may unclose;
Yet still it keeps such faded show
Of when 'twas gathered long ago,
That the crushed petals' lovely grain,
270　The sweetness of the sanguine° stain,　　　　　　　　　*bloodred*
Seen of a woman's eyes, must make
Her pitiful heart, so prone to ache,
Love roses better for its sake:—
Only that this can never be:—
275　Even so unto her sex is she.

　　Yet, Jenny, looking long at you,
The woman almost fades from view.
A cipher of man's changeless sum
Of lust, past, present, and to come,
280　Is left. A riddle that one shrinks
To challenge from the scornful sphinx.[5]

　　Like a toad within a stone
Seated while Time crumbles on;
Which sits there since the earth was curs'd
285　For Man's transgression at the first;
Which, living through all centuries,
Not once has seen the sun arise;
Whose life, to its cold circle charmed,
The earth's whole summers have not warmed;
290　Which always—whitherso the stone
Be flung—sits there, deaf, blind, alone;—
Aye, and shall not be driven out
Till that which shuts him round about
Break at the very Master's stroke,
295　And the dust thereof vanish as smoke,
And the seed of Man vanish as dust:—
Even so within this world is Lust.

　　Come, come, what use in thoughts like this?
Poor little Jenny, good to kiss,—

4. The soul, often symbolized by a butterfly that escaped the body after death. Also, in the well-known story told by Apuleius (*The Golden Ass*, 2nd century C.E.), Psyche was a maiden beloved by Cupid.

5. In Greek mythology a monster with a lion's body, bird's wings, and woman's face. The answer to her riddle—what walks on four legs in the morning, two at noon, and three in the evening?—is man, at different ages.

300   You'd not believe by what strange roads
      Thought travels, when your beauty goads
      A man to-night to think of toads!
      Jenny, wake up . . . Why, there's the dawn!

      And there's an early waggon drawn
305   To market, and some sheep that jog
      Bleating before a barking dog;
      And the old streets come peering through
      Another night that London knew;
      And all as ghostlike as the lamps.

310   So on the wings of day decamps
      My last night's frolic. Glooms begin
      To shiver off as lights creep in
      Past the gauze curtains half drawn-to,
      And the lamp's doubled shade grows blue,—
315   Your lamp, my Jenny, kept alight,
      Like a wise virgin's, all one night![6]
      And in the alcove coolly spread
      Glimmers with dawn your empty bed;
      And yonder your fair face I see
320   Reflected lying on my knee,
      Where teems with first foreshadowings
      Your pier-glass[7] scrawled with diamond rings:
      And on your bosom all night worn
      Yesterday's rose now droops forlorn,
325   But dies not yet this summer morn.

      And now without, as if some word
      Had called upon them that they heard,
      The London sparrows far and nigh
      Clamour together suddenly;
330   And Jenny's cage-bird grown awake
      Here in their song his part must take,
      Because here too the day doth break.

      And somehow in myself the dawn
      Among stirred clouds and veils withdrawn
335   Strikes greyly on her. Let her sleep.
      But will it wake her if I heap
      These cushions thus beneath her head
      Where my knee was? No,—there's your bed,
      My Jenny, while you dream. And there
340   I lay among your golden hair,
      Perhaps the subject of your dreams,
      These golden coins.
                  For still one deems

---

6. Cf. Matthew 25.1–13. In the parable of the wise and foolish virgins, the wise virgins took sufficient oil to keep their lamps burning all night.

7. A mirror. Lovers would scratch their names on it with the diamonds in their rings.

That Jenny's flattering sleep confers
New magic on the magic purse,—
345   Grim web, how clogged with shrivelled flies!
Between the threads fine fumes arise
And shape their pictures in the brain.
There roll no streets in glare and rain.
Nor flagrant man-swine whets his tusk;
350   But delicately sighs in musk
The homage of the dim boudoir;
Or like a palpitating star
Thrilled into song, the opera-night
Breathes faint in the quick pulse of light;
355   Or at the carriage-window shine
Rich wares for choice; or, free to dine,
Whirls through its hour of health (divine
For her) the concourse of the Park.
And though in the discounted dark
360   Her functions there and here are one,
Beneath the lamps and in the sun
There reigns at least the acknowledged belle
Apparelled beyond parallel.
Ah Jenny, yes, we know your dreams.

365   For even the Paphian[8] Venus seems
A goddess o'er the realms of love,
When silver-shrined in shadowy grove:
Aye, or let offerings nicely plac'd
But hide Priapus[9] to the waist,
370   And whoso looks on him shall see
An eligible deity.

Why, Jenny, waking here alone
May help you to remember one,
Though all the memory's long outworn
375   Of many a double-pillowed morn.
I think I see you when you wake,
And rub your eyes for me, and shake
My gold, in rising, from your hair,
A Danaë[1] for a moment there.

380   Jenny, my love rang true! for still
Love at first sight is vague, until
That tinkling makes him audible.

And must I mock you to the last,
Ashamed of my own shame,—aghast
385   Because some thoughts not born amiss
Rose at a poor fair face like this?

8. Of Paphos, a city on Cyprus that was the site
of a famous temple of Aphrodite (the Roman
Venus). Also, a term for prostitute.
9. A Greek fertility god, whose symbol was the
phallus.
1. In Greek mythology a maiden whom Zeus visited in the form of a shower of gold.

Well, of such thoughts so much I know:
In my life, as in hers, they show,
By a far gleam which I may near,
390   A dark path I can strive to clear.

Only one kiss. Good-bye, my dear.

1848   1870

From The House of Life

The Sonnet

A Sonnet is a moment's monument—
    Memorial from the Soul's eternity
    To one dead deathless hour. Look that it be,
Whether for lustral° rite or dire portent,   *purificatory*
5 Of its own arduous fullness reverent;
    Carve it in ivory or in ebony,
    As Day or Night may rule; and let Time see
Its flowering crest impearled and orient.

A Sonnet is a coin; its face reveals
10   The soul—its converse, to what Power 'tis due—
Whether for tribute to the august appeals
    Of Life, or dower in Love's high retinue,
It serve; or, 'mid the dark wharf's cavernous breath,
In Charon's[1] palm it pay the toll to Death.

Nuptial Sleep[2]

At length their long kiss severed, with sweet smart:°   *pain*
    And as the last slow sudden drops are shed
    From sparkling eaves when all the storm has fled,
So singly flagged the pulses of each heart.
5 Their bosoms sundered, with the opening start
    Of married flowers to either side outspread
    From the knit stem; yet still their mouths, burnt red,
Fawned on each other where they lay apart.

Sleep sank them lower than the tide of dreams,
10   And their dreams watched them sink, and slid away.
Slowly their souls swam up again, through gleams
    Of watered light and dull drowned waifs of day;
Till from some wonder of new woods and streams
    He woke, and wondered more: for there she lay.

1. In classical mythology the ferryman who, for a fee, rowed the souls of the dead across the river Styx.
2. In "The Fleshly School of Poetry" (1871), Robert Buchanan made this poem the focus of his attack on what he felt was Rossetti's lewd sensuality in the 1870 volume *Poems*. In 1881, when Rossetti published his next collection of poems, he omitted this sonnet from *The House of Life*.

19. Silent Noon

Your hands lie open in the long fresh grass—
    The finger-points look through like rosy blooms;
    Your eyes smile peace. The pasture gleams and glooms
'Neath billowing skies that scatter and amass.
5 All round our nest, far as the eye can pass,
    Are golden kingcup-fields with silver edge
    Where the cow-parsley skirts the hawthorn hedge.
'Tis visible silence, still as the hourglass.

Deep in the sun-searched growths the dragonfly
10 Hangs like a blue thread loosened from the sky—
    So this winged hour is dropped to us from above.
Oh! clasp we to our hearts, for deathless dower,
This close-companioned inarticulate hour
    When twofold silence was the song of love.

77. Soul's Beauty[3]

Under the arch of Life, where love and death,
    Terror and mystery, guard her shrine, I saw
    Beauty enthroned; and though her gaze struck awe,
I drew it in as simply as my breath.
5 Hers are the eyes which, over and beneath,
    The sky and sea bend on thee,—which can draw,
    By sea or sky or woman, to one law,
The allotted bondman° of her palm and wreath.   *slave*

This is that Lady Beauty, in whose praise
10 Thy voice and hand shake still,—long known to thee
      By flying hair and fluttering hem,—the beat
      Following her daily of thy heart and feet,
    How passionately and irretrievably,
In what fond flight, how many ways and days!

78. Body's Beauty

Of Adams's first wife, Lilith, it is told
    (The witch he loved before the gift of Eve,)
    That, ere the snake's, her sweet tongue could deceive,
And her enchanted hair was the first gold.
5 And still she sits, young while the earth is old,
    And subtly of herself contemplative,
    Draws men to watch the bright web she can weave,
Till heart and body and life are in its hold.

3. This sonnet and the next were not originally part of *The House of Life,* but were composed to accompany paintings with the same names as the sonnets' original titles (see the color insert). The original title of "Soul's Beauty" was "Sibylla Palmifera," or "palm-bearing sibyl." Sibyls are prophetesses; one of them, the Sibyl of Cumae, wrote her prophecies on palm leaves. The original title of "Body's Beauty" was "Lilith"; in Talmudic legend, Lilith, Adam's first wife, ran away from her husband and became a witch.

The rose and poppy are her flowers; for where
10   Is he not found, O Lilith, whom shed scent
And soft-shed kisses and soft sleep shall snare?
    Lo! as that youth's eyes burned at thine, so went
    Thy spell through him, and left his straight neck bent
And round his heart one strangling golden hair.

1848–80   1870, 1881

CHRISTINA ROSSETTI
1830–1894

Referring to the title of George Gissing's 1893 novel about women who choose not to marry, the critic Jerome McGann calls Christina Rossetti "one of nineteenth-century England's greatest 'Odd Women.'" Her life had little apparent incident. She was the youngest child in the Rossetti family. Her father was an exiled Italian patriot who wrote poetry and commentaries on Dante that tried to find evidence in his poems of mysterious ancient conspiracies; her mother was an Anglo-Italian who had worked as a governess. Their household was a lively gathering place for Italian exiles, full of conversation of politics and culture; and Christina, like her brothers Dante Gabriel and William Michael, was encouraged to develop an early love for art and literature and to draw and write poetry from a very early age. When she was an adolescent, her life changed dramatically: her father became a permanent invalid, the family's economic situation worsened, and her own health deteriorated. Subsequently she, her mother, and her sister became intensely involved with the Anglo-Catholic movement within the Church of England. For the rest of her life, Rossetti governed herself by strict religious principles, giving up theater, opera, and chess; on two occasions she canceled plans for marriage because of religious scruples, breaking her first engagement when her fiancé reverted to Roman Catholicism and ultimately refusing to marry a second suitor because he seemed insufficiently concerned with religion. She lived a quiet life, occupying herself with charitable work—including ten years of volunteer service at a penitentiary for fallen women—with caring for her family, and with writing poetry.

Rossetti's first volume of poetry, *Goblin Market and Other Poems* (1862), contains all the different poetic modes that mark her achievement—pure lyric, narrative fable, ballad, and the devotional verse to which she increasingly turned in her later years. The most remarkable poem in the book is the title piece, which early established its popularity as a seemingly simple moral fable for children. Later readers have likened it to S. T. Coleridge's *The Rime of the Ancient Mariner* (1798) and have detected in it a complex representation of the religious themes of temptation and sin, and of redemption by vicarious suffering; the fruit that tempts Laura, however, clearly is not from the tree of knowledge but from the orchard of sensual delights. In its deceptively simple style *Goblin Market,* like many of Rossetti's poems, demonstrates her affinity with the early aims of the Pre-Raphaelite group, though her work as a whole resists this classification. A consciousness of gender often leads her to criticize the conventional representation of women in Pre-Raphaelite art, as in her sonnet "In an Artist's Studio" (1896), and a stern religious vision controls the sensuous impulses typical of

Pre-Raphaelite poetry and painting. Virginia Woolf has described the distinctive combination of sensuousness and religious severity in Rossetti's work:

> Your poems are full of gold dust and "sweet geraniums' varied brightness"; your eye noted incessantly how rushes are "velvet headed," and lizards have a "strange metallic mail"—your eye, indeed, observed with a sensual pre-Raphaelite intensity that must have surprised Christina the Anglo-Catholic. But to her you owed perhaps the fixity and sadness of your muse. . . . No sooner have you feasted on beauty with your eyes than your mind tells you that beauty is vain and beauty passes. Death, oblivion, and rest lap round your songs with their dark wave.

William Michael Rossetti wrote of his sister, "She was replete with the spirit of self-postponement." Christina Rossetti was a poet who created, in Sandra M. Gilbert and Susan Gubar's phrase, "an aesthetics of renunciation." She writes a poetry of deferral, of deflection, of negation, whose very denials and constraints give her a powerful way to articulate a poetic self in critical relationship to the little that the world offers. Like Emily Dickinson, she often, as in "Winter: My Secret" (1862), uses a coy playfulness and sardonic wit to reduce the self but at the same time to preserve for it a secret inner space. And like Dickinson, she wrote many poems of an extraordinarily pure lyric beauty that made Virginia Woolf compare Rossetti's work to that of classical composers: "Your instinct was so sure, so direct, so intense that it produced poems that sing like music in one's ears—like a melody by Mozart or an air by Gluck."

Song

She sat and sang alway
    By the green margin of a stream,
Watching the fishes leap and play
    Beneath the glad sunbeam.

5 I sat and wept alway
    Beneath the moon's most shadowy beam,
Watching the blossoms of the May
    Weep leaves into the stream.

I wept for memory;
10   She sang for hope that is so fair:
My tears were swallowed by the sea;
    Her songs died on the air.

1848   1862

Song

When I am dead, my dearest,
    Sing no sad songs for me;
Plant thou no roses at my head,
    Nor shady cypress tree:[1]

1. The cypress tree is associated with mourning.

5   Be the green grass above me
       With showers and dewdrops wet;
    And if thou wilt, remember,
       And if thou wilt, forget.

    I shall not see the shadows,
10   I shall not feel the rain;
    I shall not hear the nightingale
       Sing on, as if in pain:
    And dreaming through the twilight
       That doth not rise nor set,
15   Haply° I may remember,   *perhaps*
       And haply may forget.

1848   1862

After Death

The curtains were half drawn, the floor was swept
    And strewn with rushes, rosemary and may[1]
    Lay thick upon the bed on which I lay,
Where thro' the lattice ivy-shadows crept.
5   He leaned above me, thinking that I slept
    And could not hear him; but I heard him say:
"Poor child, poor child": and as he turned away
Came a deep silence, and I knew he wept.
He did not touch the shroud, or raise the fold
10   That hid my face, or take my hand in his,
       Or ruffle the smooth pillows for my head:
    He did not love me living; but once dead
He pitied me; and very sweet it is
To know he still is warm tho' I am cold.

1849   1862

Dead before Death

Ah! changed and cold, how changed and very cold!
    With stiffened smiling lips and cold calm eyes:
    Changed, yet the same; much knowing, little wise;
This was the promise of the days of old!
5   Grown hard and stubborn in the ancient mould,
    Grown rigid in the sham of lifelong lies:
    We hoped for better things as years would rise,
But it is over as a tale once told.

1. Plants associated with death.

All fallen the blossom that no fruitage bore,
10   All lost the present and the future time,
All lost, all lost, the lapse that went before:
So lost till death shut-to the opened door,
     So lost from chime to everlasting chime,
So cold and lost for ever evermore.

1854   1862

Cobwebs

It is a land with neither night nor day,
     Nor heat nor cold, nor any wind, nor rain,
     Nor hills nor valleys; but one even plain
Stretches thro' long unbroken miles away:
5   While thro' the sluggish air a twilight grey
     Broodeth; no moons or seasons wax and wane,
     No ebb and flow are there along the main,°   ocean
No bud-time no leaf-falling, there for aye:°—   forever
No ripple on the sea, no shifting sand,
10   No beat of wings to stir the stagnant space,
No pulse of life thro' all the loveless land:
And loveless sea; no trace of days before,
     No guarded home, no toil-won resting place,
No future hope no fear for evermore.

1855   1896

A Triad

Three sang of love together: one with lips
     Crimson, with cheeks and bosom in a glow,
Flushed to the yellow hair and finger tips;
     And one there sang who soft and smooth as snow
5   Bloomed like a tinted hyacinth at a show;
And one was blue with famine after love,
     Who like a harpstring snapped rang harsh and low
The burden of what those were singing of.
One shamed herself in love; one temperately
10   Grew gross in soulless love, a sluggish wife;
One famished died for love. Thus two of three
     Took death for love and won him after strife;
One droned in sweetness like a fattened bee:
     All on the threshold, yet all short of life.

1856   1862

In an Artist's Studio[1]

One face looks out from all his canvases,
　　One selfsame figure sits or walks or leans;
　　We found her hidden just behind those screens,
That mirror gave back all her loveliness.
5　A queen in opal or in ruby dress,
　　A nameless girl in freshest summer-greens,
　　A saint, an angel;—every canvas means
The same one meaning, neither more nor less.
He feeds upon her face by day and night,
10　And she with true kind eyes looks back on him
Fair as the moon and joyful as the light:
　　Not wan with waiting, not with sorrow dim;
Not as she is, but was when hope shone bright;
　　Not as she is, but as she fills his dream.

1856   1896

A Birthday

My heart is like a singing bird
　　Whose nest is in a watered shoot;°   *slim branch*
My heart is like an apple tree
　　Whose boughs are bent with thickset fruit;
5　My heart is like a rainbow shell
　　That paddles in a halcyon° sea;   *tranquil*
My heart is gladder than all these
　　Because my love is come to me.

Raise me a dais of silk and down;
10　Hang it with vair° and purple dyes;   *squirrel fur*
Carve it in doves and pomegranates,
　　And peacocks with a hundred eyes;
Work it in gold and silver grapes,
　　In leaves and silver fleurs-de-lys;
15　Because the birthday of my life
　　Is come, my love is come to me.

1857   1862

---

1. According to Christina's brother William
Michael, this poem focuses on the work of their
older brother, Dante Gabriel: "The reference is
apparently to our brother's studio, and to his constantly repeated heads of the lady whom he afterwards married, Miss Siddal."

An Apple-Gathering

I plucked pink blossoms from mine apple tree
    And wore them all that evening in my hair:
Then in due season when I went to see
        I found no apples there.

5   With dangling basket all along the grass
    As I had come I went the selfsame track:
My neighbours mocked me while they saw me pass
        So empty-handed back.

Lilian and Lilias smiled in trudging by,
10   Their heaped-up basket teazed me like a jeer;
Sweet-voiced they sang beneath the sunset sky,
        Their mother's home was near.

Plump Gertrude passed me with her basket full,
    A stronger hand than hers helped it along;
15 A voice talked with her thro' the shadows cool
        More sweet to me than song.

Ah Willie, Willie, was my love less worth
    Than apples with their green leaves piled above?
I counted rosiest apples on the earth
20   Of far less worth than love.

So once it was with me you stooped to talk
    Laughing and listening in this very lane:
To think that by this way we used to walk
        We shall not walk again!

25 I let my neighbours pass me, ones and twos
    And groups; the latest said the night grew chill,
And hastened: but I loitered, while the dews
        Fell fast I loitered still.

1857   1862

[handwritten marginal note: about sex before marriage (?)]

Winter: My Secret

I tell my secret? No indeed, not I:
Perhaps some day, who knows?
But not today; it froze, and blows, and snows,
And you're too curious: fie!
5   You want to hear it? well:
Only, my secret's mine, and I won't tell.

Or, after all, perhaps there's none:
Suppose there is no secret after all,
But only just my fun.
10 Today's a nipping day, a biting day;
In which one wants a shawl,
A veil, a cloak, and other wraps:
I cannot ope to every one who taps,
And let the draughts come whistling thro' my hall;
15 Come bounding and surrounding me,
Come buffeting, astounding me,
Nipping and clipping thro' my wraps and all.
I wear my mask for warmth: who ever shows
His nose to Russian snows
20 To be pecked at by every wind that blows?
You would not peck? I thank you for good will,
Believe, but leave that truth untested still.

Spring's an expansive time: yet I don't trust
March with its peck of dust,
25 Nor April with its rainbow-crowned brief showers,
Nor even May, whose flowers
One frost may wither thro' the sunless hours.

Perhaps some languid summer day,
When drowsy birds sing less and less,
30 And golden fruit is ripening to excess,
If there's not too much sun nor too much cloud,
And the warm wind is neither still nor loud,
Perhaps my secret I may say,
Or you may guess.

1857   1862

Up-Hill

Does the road wind up-hill all the way?
    Yes, to the very end.
Will the day's journey take the whole long day?
    From morn to night, my friend.

5 But is there for the night a resting-place?
    A roof for when the slow dark hours begin.
May not the darkness hide it from my face?
    You cannot miss that inn.

Shall I meet other wayfarers at night?
10   Those who have gone before.
Then must I knock, or call when just in sight?
    They will not keep you standing at that door.

Shall I find comfort, travel-sore and weak?
 Of labour you shall find the sum.
15 Will there be beds for me and all who seek?
 Yea, beds for all who come.

1858   1862

Goblin Market

Morning and evening
Maids heard the goblins cry:
"Come buy our orchard fruits,
Come buy, come buy:
5 Apples and quinces,
Lemons and oranges,
Plump unpecked cherries,
Melons and raspberries,
Bloom-down-cheeked peaches,
10 Swart-headed mulberries,
Wild free-born cranberries,
Crab-apples, dewberries,
Pine-apples, blackberries,
Apricots, strawberries;—
15 All ripe together
In summer weather,—
Morns that pass by,
Fair eves that fly;
Come buy, come buy:
20 Our grapes fresh from the vine,
Pomegranates full and fine,
Dates and sharp bullaces,
Rare pears and greengages,
Damsons[1] and bilberries,
25 Taste them and try:
Currants and gooseberries,
Bright-fire-like barberries,
Figs to fill your mouth,
Citrons from the South,
30 Sweet to tongue and sound to eye;
Come buy, come buy."

Evening by evening
Among the brookside rushes,
Laura bowed her head to hear,
35 Lizzie veiled her blushes:
Crouching close together
In the cooling weather,
With clasping arms and cautioning lips,
With tingling cheeks and finger tips.
40 "Lie close," Laura said,

---

1. Bullaces, greengages, and damsons are varieties of plums.

Pricking up her golden head:
"We must not look at goblin men,
We must not buy their fruits:
Who knows upon what soil they fed
45 Their hungry thirsty roots?"
"Come buy," call the goblins
Hobbling down the glen.
"Oh," cried Lizzie, "Laura, Laura,
You should not peep at goblin men."
50 Lizzie covered up her eyes,
Covered close lest they should look;
Laura reared her glossy head,
And whispered like the restless brook:
"Look, Lizzie, look, Lizzie,
55 Down the glen tramp little men.
One hauls a basket,
One bears a plate,
One lugs a golden dish
Of many pounds weight.
60 How fair the vine must grow
Whose grapes are so luscious;
How warm the wind must blow
Thro' those fruit bushes."
"No," said Lizzie: "No, no, no;
65 Their offers should not charm us,
Their evil gifts would harm us."
She thrust a dimpled finger
In each ear, shut eyes and ran:
Curious Laura chose to linger
70 Wondering at each merchant man.
One had a cat's face,
One whisked a tail,
One tramped at a rat's pace,
One crawled like a snail,
75 One like a wombat prowled obtuse and furry,
One like a ratel[2] tumbled hurry skurry.
She heard a voice like voice of doves
Cooing all together:
They sounded kind and full of loves
80 In the pleasant weather.

Laura stretched her gleaming neck
Like a rush-imbedded swan,
Like a lily from the beck,°   *small brook*
Like a moonlit poplar branch,
85 Like a vessel at the launch
When its last restraint is gone.

Backwards up the mossy glen
Turned and trooped the goblin men,

2. South African mammal resembling a badger (pronounced *ray-tell*).

With their shrill repeated cry,
90 "Come buy, come buy."
When they reached where Laura was
They stood stock still upon the moss,
Leering at each other,
Brother with queer brother;
95 Signalling each other,
Brother with sly brother.
One set his basket down,
One reared° his plate;   *raised*
One began to weave a crown
100 Of tendrils, leaves and rough nuts brown
(Men sell not such in any town);
One heaved the golden weight
Of dish and fruit to offer her:
"Come buy, come buy," was still their cry.
105 Laura stared but did not stir,
Longed but had no money:
The whisk-tailed merchant bade her taste
In tones as smooth as honey,
The cat-faced purr'd,
110 The rat-paced spoke a word
Of welcome, and the snail-paced even was heard;
One parrot-voiced and jolly
Cried "Pretty Goblin" still° for "Pretty Polly;"—   *always*
One whistled like a bird.

115 But sweet-tooth Laura spoke in haste:
"Good folk, I have no coin;
To take were to purloin:
I have no copper in my purse,
I have no silver either,
120 And all my gold is on the furze[3]
That shakes in windy weather
Above the rusty heather."
"You have much gold upon your head,"
They answered all together:
125 "Buy from us with a golden curl."
She clipped a precious golden lock,
She dropped a tear more rare than pearl,
Then sucked their fruit globes fair or red:
Sweeter than honey from the rock.[4]
130 Stronger than man-rejoicing wine,[5]
Clearer than water flowed that juice;
She never tasted such before,
How should it cloy with length of use?
She sucked and sucked and sucked the more
135 Fruits which that unknown orchard bore;
She sucked until her lips were sore;
Then flung the emptied rinds away

3. Gorse; a wild shrub with thorns and small yel-   4. Psalms 81.16.
low flowers.   5. Psalms 104.15.

But gathered up one kernel-stone,
And knew not was it night or day
140   As she turned home alone.

Lizzie met her at the gate
Full of wise upbraidings:
"Dear, you should not stay so late,
Twilight is not good for maidens;
145   Should not loiter in the glen
In the haunts of goblin men.
Do you not remember Jeanie,
How she met them in the moonlight,
Took their gifts both choice and many,
150   Ate their fruits and wore their flowers
Plucked from bowers
Where summer ripens at all hours?
But ever in the noonlight
She pined and pined away;
155   Sought them by night and day,
Found them no more but dwindled and grew grey;
Then fell with the first snow,
While to this day no grass will grow
Where she lies low:
160   I planted daisies there a year ago
That never blow.°   *bloom*
You should not loiter so."
"Nay, hush," said Laura:
"Nay, hush, my sister:
165   I ate and ate my fill,
Yet my mouth waters still;
Tomorrow night I will
Buy more:" and kissed her:
"Have done with sorrow;
170   I'll bring you plums tomorrow
Fresh on their mother twigs,
Cherries worth getting;
You cannot think what figs
My teeth have met in,
175   What melons icy-cold
Piled on a dish of gold
Too huge for me to hold,
What peaches with a velvet nap,
Pellucid grapes without one seed:
180   Odorous indeed must be the mead
Whereon they grow, and pure the wave they drink
With lilies at the brink,
And sugar-sweet their sap."

Golden head by golden head,
185   Like two pigeons in one nest
Folded in each other's wings,
They lay down in their curtained bed:

Like two blossoms on one stem,
Like two flakes of new-fall'n snow,
190 Like two wands of ivory
Tipped with gold for awful° kings.   *awe-inspiring*
Moon and stars gazed in at them,
Wind sang to them lullaby,
Lumbering owls forbore to fly,
195 Not a bat flapped to and fro
Round their rest:
Cheek to cheek and breast to breast
Locked together in one nest.

Early in the morning
200 When the first cock crowed his warning,
Neat like bees, as sweet and busy,
Laura rose with Lizzie:
Fetched in honey, milked the cows,
Aired and set to rights the house,
205 Kneaded cakes of whitest wheat,
Cakes for dainty mouths to eat,
Next churned butter, whipped up cream,
Fed their poultry, sat and sewed;
Talked as modest maidens should:
210 Lizzie with an open heart,
Laura in an absent dream,
One content, one sick in part;
One warbling for the mere bright day's delight,
One longing for the night.

215 At length slow evening came:
They went with pitchers to the reedy brook;
Lizzie most placid in her look,
Laura most like a leaping flame.
They drew the gurgling water from its deep;
220 Lizzie plucked purple and rich golden flags,°   *irises*
Then turning homewards said: "The sunset flushes
Those furthest loftiest crags;
Come, Laura, not another maiden lags,
No wilful squirrel wags,
225 The beasts and birds are fast asleep."
But Laura loitered still among the rushes
And said the bank was steep.

And said the hour was early still,
The dew not fall'n, the wind not chill:
230 Listening ever, but not catching
The customary cry,
"Come buy, come buy,"
With its iterated jingle
Of sugar-baited words:
235 Not for all her watching
Once discerning even one goblin

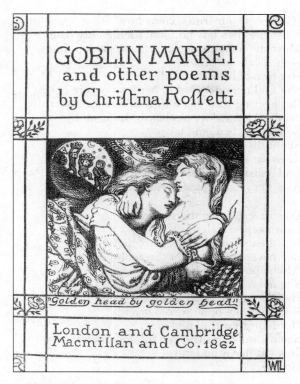

Goblin Market. This frontispiece is one of the two illustrations that Dante Gabriel Rossetti provided for his sister's first volume of poetry in 1862.

Racing, whisking, tumbling, hobbling;
Let alone the herds
That used to tramp along the glen,
240   In groups or single,
Of brisk fruit-merchant men.

Till Lizzie urged, "O Laura, come;
I hear the fruit-call but I dare not look:
You should not loiter longer at this brook:
245   Come with me home.
The stars rise, the moon bends her arc,
Each glowworm winks her spark,
Let us get home before the night grows dark:
For clouds may gather
250   Tho' this is summer weather,
Put out the lights and drench us thro';
Then if we lost our way what should we do?"

Laura turned cold as stone
To find her sister heard that cry alone,
255   That goblin cry,

"Come buy our fruits, come buy."
Must she then buy no more such dainty fruit?
Must she no more such succous° pasture find,   *juicy, succulent*
Gone deaf and blind?
260 Her tree of life drooped from the root:
She said not one word in her heart's sore ache;
But peering thro' the dimness, nought discerning,
Trudged home, her pitcher dripping all the way;
So crept to bed, and lay
265 Silent till Lizzie slept;
Then sat up in a passionate yearning,
And gnashed her teeth for baulked desire, and wept
As if her heart would break.

Day after day, night after night,
270 Laura kept watch in vain
In sullen silence of exceeding pain.
She never caught again the goblin cry:
"Come buy, come buy;"—
She never spied the goblin men
275 Hawking their fruits along the glen:
But when the noon waxed bright
Her hair grew thin and gray;
She dwindled, as the fair full moon doth turn
To swift decay and burn
280 Her fire away.

One day remembering her kernel-stone
She set it by a wall that faced the south;
Dewed it with tears, hoped for a root,
Watched for a waxing shoot,
285 But there came none;
It never saw the sun,
It never felt the trickling moisture run:
While with sunk eyes and faded mouth
She dreamed of melons, as a traveller sees
290 False waves in desert drouth
With shade of leaf-crowned trees,
And burns the thirstier in the sandful breeze.

She no more swept the house,
Tended the fowls or cows,
295 Fetched honey, kneaded cakes of wheat,
Brought water from the brook:
But sat down listless in the chimney-nook
And would not eat.

Tender Lizzie could not bear
300 To watch her sister's cankerous care
Yet not to share.
She night and morning
Caught the goblins' cry:

"Come buy our orchard fruits,
305 Come buy, come buy:"—
Beside the brook, along the glen,
She heard the tramp of goblin men,
The voice and stir
Poor Laura could not hear;
310 Longed to buy fruit to comfort her,
But feared to pay too dear.
She thought of Jeanie in her grave,
Who should have been a bride;
But who for joys brides hope to have
315 Fell sick and died
In her gay prime,
In earliest Winter time,
With the first glazing rime,
With the first snow-fall of crisp Winter time.

320 Till Laura dwindling
Seemed knocking at Death's door:
Then Lizzie weighed° no more   *evaluated, considered*
Better and worse;
But put a silver penny in her purse,
325 Kissed Laura, crossed the heath with clumps of furze
At twilight, halted by the brook:
And for the first time in her life
Began to listen and look.

Laughed every goblin
330 When they spied her peeping:
Came towards her hobbling,
Flying, running, leaping,
Puffing and blowing,
Chuckling, clapping, crowing,
335 Clucking and gobbling,
Mopping and mowing,[6]
Full of airs and graces,
Pulling wry faces,
Demure grimaces,
340 Cat-like and rat-like,
Ratel-and wombat-like,
Snail-paced in a hurry,
Parrot-voiced and whistler,
Helter skelter, hurry skurry,
345 Chattering like magpies,
Fluttering like pigeons,
Gliding like fishes,—
Hugged her and kissed her,
Squeezed and caressed her:
350 Stretched up their dishes,
Panniers, and plates:

6. Grimacing, making faces.

"Look at our apples
Russet and dun,
Bob at our cherries,
355   Bite at our peaches,
Citrons and dates,
Grapes for the asking,
Pears red with basking
Out in the sun,
360   Plums on their twigs;
Pluck them and suck them,
Pomegranates, figs."—

"Good folk," said Lizzie,
Mindful of Jeanie:
365   "Give me much and many:"—
Held out her apron,
Tossed them her penny.
"Nay, take a seat with us,
Honour and eat with us,"
370   They answered grinning:
"Our feast is but beginning.
Night yet is early,
Warm and dew-pearly,
Wakeful and starry:
375   Such fruits as these
No man can carry;
Half their bloom would fly,
Half their dew would dry,
Half their flavour would pass by.
380   Sit down and feast with us,
Be welcome guest with us,
Cheer you and rest with us."—
"Thank you," said Lizzie: "But one waits
At home alone for me:
385   So without further parleying,
If you will not sell me any
Of your fruits tho' much and many,
Give me back my silver penny
I tossed you for a fee."—

390   They began to scratch their pates,
No longer wagging, purring,
But visibly demurring,
Grunting and snarling.
One called her proud,
395   Cross-grained, uncivil;
Their tones waxed loud,
Their looks were evil.
Lashing their tails
They trod and hustled her,
400   Elbowed and jostled her,
Clawed with their nails,

Barking, mewing, hissing, mocking,
Tore her gown and soiled her stocking,
Twitched her hair out by the roots,
405 Stamped upon her tender feet,
Held her hands and squeezed their fruits
Against her mouth to make her eat.

White and golden Lizzie stood,
Like a lily in a flood,—
410 Like a rock of blue-veined stone
Lashed by tides obstreperously,—
Like a beacon left alone
In a hoary roaring sea,
Sending up a golden fire,—
415 Like a fruit-crowned orange-tree
White with blossoms honey-sweet
Sore beset by wasp and bee,—
Like a royal virgin town
Topped with gilded dome and spire
420 Close beleaguered by a fleet
Mad to tug her standard down.

correlation of being beautiful w/ being pure & virtuous, and strong against temptation

One may lead a horse to water,
Twenty cannot make him drink.
Tho' the goblins cuffed and caught her,
425 Coaxed and fought her,
Bullied and besought her,
Scratched her, pinched her black as ink,
Kicked and knocked her,
Mauled and mocked her,
430 Lizzie uttered not a word;
Would not open lip from lip
Lest they should cram a mouthful in:
But laughed in heart to feel the drip
Of juice that syruped all her face,
435 And lodged in dimples of her chin,
And streaked her neck which quaked like curd.
At last the evil people
Worn out by her resistance
Flung back her penny, kicked their fruit
440 Along whichever road they took,
Not leaving root or stone or shoot;
Some writhed into the ground,
Some dived into the brook
With ring and ripple,
445 Some scudded on the gale without a sound,
Some vanished in the distance.

In a smart, ache, tingle,
Lizzie went her way;
Knew not was it night or day;
450 Sprang up the bank, tore thro' the furze,

Threaded copse and dingle,
And heard her penny jingle
Bouncing in her purse,
Its bounce was music to her ear.
455 She ran and ran
As if she feared some goblin man
Dogged her with gibe or curse
Or something worse:
But not one goblin skurried after,
460 Nor was she pricked by fear;
The kind heart made her windy-paced
That urged her home quite out of breath with haste
And inward laughter.

She cried "Laura," up the garden,
465 "Did you miss me?
Come and kiss me.
Never mind my bruises,
Hug me, kiss me, suck my juices
Squeezed from goblin fruits for you,
470 Goblin pulp and goblin dew.
Eat me, drink me, love me;
Laura, make much of me:
For your sake I have braved the glen
And had to do with goblin merchant men."

475 Laura started from her chair,
Flung her arms up in the air,
Clutched her hair:
"Lizzie, Lizzie, have you tasted
For my sake the fruit forbidden?
480 Must your light like mine be hidden,
Your young life like mine be wasted,
Undone in mine undoing
And ruined in my ruin,
Thirsty, cankered, goblin-ridden?"—
485 She clung about her sister,
Kissed and kissed and kissed her:
Tears once again
Refreshed her shrunken eyes,
Dropping like rain
490 After long sultry drouth;
Shaking with aguish° fear, and pain,   *feverish*
She kissed and kissed her with a hungry mouth.

Her lips began to scorch,
That juice was wormwood to her tongue,
495 She loathed the feast:
Writhing as one possessed she leaped and sung,
Rent all her robe, and wrung
Her hands in lamentable haste,
And beat her breast.

500　Her locks streamed like the torch
　　Borne by a racer at full speed,
　　Or like the mane of horses in their flight,
　　Or like an eagle when she stems[7] the light
　　Straight toward the sun,
505　Or like a caged thing freed,
　　Or like a flying flag when armies run.

　　Swift fire spread thro' her veins, knocked at her heart,
　　Met the fire smouldering there
　　And overbore its lesser flame;
510　She gorged on bitterness without a name:
　　Ah! fool, to choose such part
　　Of soul-consuming care!
　　Sense failed in the mortal strife:
　　Like the watch-tower of a town
515　Which an earthquake shatters down,
　　Like a lightning-stricken mast,
　　Like a wind-uprooted tree
　　Spun about,
　　Like a foam-topped waterspout
520　Cast down headlong in the sea,
　　She fell at last;
　　Pleasure past and anguish past,
　　Is it death or is it life?

　　Life out of death.
525　That night long Lizzie watched by her,
　　Counted her pulse's flagging stir,
　　Felt for her breath,
　　Held water to her lips, and cooled her face
　　With tears and fanning leaves:
530　But when the first birds chirped about their eaves,
　　And early reapers plodded to the place
　　Of golden sheaves,
　　And dew-wet grass
　　Bowed in the morning winds so brisk to pass,
535　And new buds with new day
　　Opened of cup-like lilies on the stream,
　　Laura awoke as from a dream,
　　Laughed in the innocent old way,
　　Hugged Lizzie but not° twice or thrice;　　　　　　*not only*
540　Her gleaming locks showed not one thread of grey,
　　Her breath was sweet as May
　　And light danced in her eyes.

　　Days, weeks, months, years
　　Afterwards, when both were wives
545　With children of their own;
　　Their mother-hearts beset with fears,

7. Makes headway against.

Their lives bound up in tender lives;
Laura would call the little ones
And tell them of her early prime,
550 Those pleasant days long gone
Of not-returning time:
Would talk about the haunted glen,
The wicked, quaint° fruit-merchant men,   *strange*
Their fruits like honey to the throat
555 But poison in the blood;
(Men sell not such in any town:)
Would tell them how her sister stood
In deadly peril to do her good,
And win the fiery antidote:
560 Then joining hands to little hands
Would bid them cling together,
"For there is no friend like a sister
In calm or stormy weather;
To cheer one on the tedious way,
565 To fetch one if one goes astray,
To lift one if one totters down,
To strengthen whilst one stands."

1859   1862

"No, Thank You, John"

I never said I loved you, John:
    Why will you teaze me day by day,
And wax a weariness to think upon
    With always "do" and "pray"?

5   You know I never loved you, John;
    No fault of mine made me your toast:
Why will you haunt me with a face as wan
    As shows an hour-old ghost?

I dare say Meg or Moll would take
10   Pity upon you, if you'd ask:
And pray don't remain single for my sake
    Who can't perform that task.

I have no heart?—Perhaps I have not;
    But then you're mad to take offence
15 That I don't give you what I have not got:
    Use your own common sense.

Let bygones be bygones:
    Don't call me false, who owed not to be true:
I'd rather answer "No" to fifty Johns
20   Than answer "Yes" to you.

Let's mar our pleasant days no more,
    Song-birds of passage, days of youth:
Catch at today, forget the days before:
    I'll wink° at your untruth.   *close (both) eyes*

25   Let us strike hands as hearty friends;
    No more, no less; and friendship's good:
Only don't keep in view ulterior ends,
    And points not understood

In open treaty. Rise above
30   Quibbles and shuffling off and on:
Here's friendship for you if you like; but love,—
    No, thank you, John.

1860   1862

Promises Like Pie-Crust

Promise me no promises,
    So will I not promise you:
Keep we both our liberties,
    Never false and never true:
5   Let us hold the die uncast,
    Free to come as free to go:
For I cannot know your past,
    And of mine what can you know?

You, so warm, may once have been
10   Warmer towards another one:
I, so cold, may once have seen
    Sunlight, once have felt the sun:
Who shall show us if it was
    Thus indeed in time of old?
15   Fades the image from the glass,
    And the fortune is not told.

If you promised, you might grieve
    For lost liberty again:
If I promised, I believe
20   I should fret to break the chain.
Let us be the friends we were,
    Nothing more but nothing less:
Many thrive on frugal fare
    Who would perish of excess.

1861   1896

In Progress

Ten years ago it seemed impossible
   That she should ever grow so calm as this,
   With self-remembrance in her warmest kiss
And dim dried eyes like an exhausted well.
5   Slow-speaking when she has some fact to tell,
   Silent with long-unbroken silences,
   Centred in self yet not unpleased to please,
Gravely monotonous like a passing bell.[1]
Mindful of drudging daily common things,
10   Patient at pastime, patient at her work,
   Wearied perhaps but strenuous certainly.
   Sometimes I fancy we may one day see
Her head shoot forth seven stars from where they lurk
And her eyes lightnings and her shoulders wings.

1862   1896

A Life's Parallels

Never on this side of the grave again,
   On this side of the river,
On this side of the garner° of the grain,   *storehouse*
   Never,—

5   Ever while time flows on and on and on,
   That narrow noiseless river,
Ever while corn bows heavy-headed, wan,
   Ever,—

Never despairing, often fainting, rueing,
10   But looking back, ah never!
Faint yet pursuing, faint yet still pursuing
   Ever.

1881

From Later Life

17

Something this foggy day, a something which
   Is neither of this fog nor of today,
   Has set me dreaming of the winds that play
Past certain cliffs, along one certain beach,
5   And turn the topmost edge of waves to spray:

1. Bell rung during or after a person's death, a death bell.

Ah pleasant pebbly strand so far away,
   So out of reach while quite within my reach,
     As out of reach as India or Cathay!°   *China (poetic)*
I am sick of where I am and where I am not,
10   I am sick of foresight and of memory,
   I am sick of all I have and all I see,
     I am sick of self, and there is nothing new;
Oh weary impatient patience of my lot!—
     Thus with myself: how fares it, Friends, with you?

1881

Cardinal Newman[1]

In the grave, whither thou goest[2]

O weary Champion of the Cross, lie still:
   Sleep thou at length the all-embracing sleep:
   Long was thy sowing-day, rest now and reap:
Thy fast was long, feast now thy spirit's fill.
5   Yea, take thy fill of love, because thy will
   Chose love not in the shallows but the deep:
   Thy tides were springtides, set against the neap[3]
Of calmer souls: thy flood rebuked their rill.°   *small stream*
Now night has come to thee—please God, of rest:
10   So some time must it come to every man;
   To first and last, where many last are first.[4]
Now fixed and finished thine eternal plan,
   Thy best has done its best, thy worst its worst:
Thy best its best, Please God, thy best its best.

1890

Sleeping at Last

Sleeping at last, the trouble & tumult over,
   Sleeping at last, the struggle & horror past,
Cold & white out of sight of friend & of lover
   Sleeping at last.

5   No more a tired heart downcast or overcast,
No more pangs that wring or shifting fears that hover,
   Sleeping at last in a dreamless sleep locked fast.

---

1. Written on the occasion of the death of John
Henry Cardinal Newman (1801–1890).
2. Ecclesiastes 9.10.
3. Tides that do not rise to the high-water mark

of the spring tides.
4. Rossetti alludes to the parable of the vineyard, in which "the last shall be first." See Matthew 20.16, Luke 13.30.

Fast asleep. Singing birds in their leafy cover
    Cannot wake her, nor shake her the gusty blast.
10   Under the purple thyme and the purple clover
        Sleeping at last.

1896

WILLIAM MORRIS
1834–1896

I n his autobiography William Butler Yeats observes that if some angel offered him the choice, he would rather live William Morris's life than his own or any other man's. Morris's career was more multifaceted than that of any other Victorian writer. He was a poet, a writer of prose romances, a painter, a designer of furniture, a businessman, a printer, and a leader of the British socialist movement.

Born of wealthy parents and brought up in the Essex countryside, he went to Oxford with the intention of becoming a clergyman. However, art for him soon displaced religion. At Oxford he discovered the work of John Ruskin, which was, in his words, "a revelation." Later in life he wrote, "It was through him that I learned to give form to my discontent. . . . Apart from the desire to produce beautiful things, the leading passion of my life has been and is hatred of modern civilization." Morris's career in many ways realized Ruskin's views. In 1861 Morris and several friends founded a company to design and produce furniture, wallpaper, textiles, stained glass, tapestries, and carpets, objects still prized today as masterpieces of decorative art. Morris's aim was not only to make beautiful things but to restore creativity to modern manufacture, much as Ruskin had urged in "The Nature of Gothic," a chapter in *The Stones of Venice* (1851–53). The minor arts, he believed, were in a state of complete degradation; through his firm he wanted to restore beauty of design and individual craftsmanship.

In his design work Morris developed close ties with the Pre-Raphaelite Brotherhood; its cofounder Dante Gabriel Rossetti became a particular friend. In 1858 Morris published a remarkable book of poetry, *The Defence of Guenevere, and other Poems*, which some critics regard as the finest book of Pre-Raphaelite verse. Using medieval materials, the poems plunge the reader into the middle of dramatic situations with little sense of larger narrative context or even right and wrong, where little is clear but the vividness of the characters' perceptions. After *The Defence of Guenevere*, Morris turned from lyric to narrative, publishing *The Life and Death of Jason* (1867) and *The Earthly Paradise* (1868–70), a series of twenty-four classical and medieval tales. He then discovered the Icelandic sagas. He cotranslated the *Volsunga Saga* and wrote a poem based on it, *The Story of Sigurd the Volsung* (1876). In 1877 he founded the Society for the Protection of Ancient Buildings.

In the late 1870s, after Morris came to the conclusion that art could not have real life and growth under the commercialism of modern society, he turned to socialism. In 1883 he joined the Socialist Democratic Federation; the next year he led the secession of a large faction to found the Socialist League. He was at the center of socialist activity in England through the rest of the decade. At the famous debates held on Sunday evenings at Morris's house, political and literary figures regularly gathered, including Yeats and George Bernard Shaw. Morris lectured and wrote tirelessly for the cause, producing essays, columns, and a series of socialist literary works, including *A Dream of John Ball* (1887) and *News from Nowhere* (1890), a utopian vision of life under communism in twenty-first-century England.

In 1890 Morris's health failed and factionalism brought his leadership of the Socialist League to an end. In 1891 he cofounded the Kelmscott Press, the first fine art press in England, whose masterpiece was the Kelmscott Chaucer, an edition of *The Canterbury Tales* with illustrations by the Pre-Raphaelite painter Edward Burne Jones and designs by Morris himself.

In the obituary he published after Morris's death, Shaw wrote, "He was ultramodern—not merely up-to-date, but far ahead of it: his wall papers, his hangings, his tapestries, and his printed books have the twentieth century in every touch of them." Not only did Morris develop design principles that remained important in the twentieth century, but he also had a radical vision of the relationship of aesthetics to politics. He was, as Shaw said, "a complete artist."

The Defence of Guenevere

For this poem Morris created strikingly original adaptations of episodes from one of his favorite books, Thomas Malory's *Morte Darthur* (1470). In Malory's narrative, Arthur's kingdom is eventually destroyed by dissension among his followers; especially damaging to the king's reign are rumors of an adulterous relationship between Queen Guenevere and Arthur's chief knight, Launcelot. Morris's poem alludes to two occasions in Malory's work when Guenevere is discovered in apparently compromising circumstances that lead to public accusations of adultery. On the first occasion (described in lines 167–220), her accuser, Sir Mellyagraunce, is challenged by Launcelot to a trial of battle. After Mellyagraunce is slain, the queen's honor is temporarily restored, though in Morris's telling this earlier scandal is revived by Sir Gauwaine in his accusations against her. The second occasion, which occurs just before Morris's poem opens, is more seriously incriminating. Thirteen knights plot successfully to trap Launcelot when he is visiting the queen's chamber at night at her invitation (events described in lines 242–76). In his escape Launcelot kills all but one of the knights—an event that later leads to civil war. In Malory's version there is no formal trial of the queen after Launcelot's escape; she is simply told of her sentence—she will be burned at the stake—and is thereafter rescued by Launcelot, who takes her away to safety in his castle. In inventing his trial scene Morris probably drew from a different episode in Malory (book 18, chapter 3), which ends with Sir Gauwaine accusing Guenevere of murder and treason in the presence of many other knights.

According to Morris's daughter, this poem originally opened with a long introductory passage of description and background. Because Morris subsequently decided to omit it, we are plunged at once into a dramatic scene much like those that begin some of the poems of Robert Browning (the Victorian poet whom Morris most admired). Also reminiscent of Browning's work are the constant shifts in Guenevere's speech from an awareness of her present situation to the recollection of moments in her past, such as the spring day early in her marriage to Arthur when Launcelot first kissed her.

The year after Morris's poem appeared, four books of Tennyson's *Idylls of the King*, including one that focused on Guenevere, were published. It is interesting to compare the two portraits of the queen, especially their pictoral qualities, but Morris's powerful depiction of an eloquent Guenevere is very different from Tennyson's subdued representation of a guilt-ridden wife. Equally fascinating is a comparison of the two poems with Morris's painting *Queen Guenevere* (1858). Despite his copious production of visual artifacts, this is the only full-size oil painting Morris ever finished. His model for Guenevere, who stands pensively in front of a rumpled bed, was Jane Burden, who became his wife the following year.

The Defence of Guenevere

But, knowing now that they would have her speak,
She threw her wet hair backward from her brow,
Her hand close to her mouth touching her cheek,

As though she had had there a shameful blow,
5   And feeling it shameful to feel aught° but shame   *anything*
All through her heart, yet felt her cheek burned so,

She must a little touch it; like one lame
She walked away from Gauwaine, with her head
Still lifted up; and on her cheek of flame

10   The tears dried quick; she stopped at last and said:
"O knights and lords, it seems but little skill°   *use*
To talk of well-known things past now and dead.

"God wot° I ought to say, I have done ill,   *knows*
And pray you all forgiveness heartily!
15   Because you must be right, such great lords—still

"Listen, suppose your time were come to die,
And you were quite alone and very weak;
Yea, laid a dying while very mightily

"The wind was ruffling up the narrow streak
20   Of river through your broad lands running well:
Suppose a hush should come, then someone speak:

"'One of these cloths is heaven, and one is hell,
Now choose one cloth forever, which they be,
I will not tell you, you must somehow tell

25   "'Of your own strength and mightiness; here, see!'
Yea, yea, my lord, and you to ope your eyes,
At foot of your familiar bed to see

"A great God's angel standing, with such dyes,
Not known on earth, on his great wings, and hands,
30   Held out two ways, light from the inner skies

"Showing him well, and making his commands
Seem to be God's commands, moreover, too,
Holding within his hands the cloths on wands;

"And one of these strange choosing cloths was blue,
35   Wavy and long, and one cut short and red;
No man could tell the better of the two.

"After a shivering half hour you said,
'God help! heaven's color, the blue'; and he said, 'hell.'
Perhaps you then would roll upon your bed,

40 "And cry to all good men that loved you well,
'Ah Christ! if only I had known, known, known';
Launcelot went away, then I could tell,

"Like wisest man how all things would be, moan,
And roll and hurt myself, and long to die,
45 And yet fear much to die for what was sown.

"Nevertheless you, O Sir Gauwaine, lie,
Whatever may have happened through these years,
God knows I speak truth, saying that you lie."

Her voice was low at first, being full of tears,
50 But as it cleared, it grew full loud and shrill,
Growing a windy shriek in all men's ears,

A ringing in their startled brains, until
She said that Gauwaine lied, then her voice sunk,
And her great eyes began again to fill,

55 Though still she stood right up, and never shrunk,
But spoke on bravely, glorious lady fair!
Whatever tears her full lips may have drunk,

She stood, and seemed to think, and wrung her hair,
Spoke out at last with no more trace of shame,
60 With passionate twisting of her body there:

"It chanced upon a day that Launcelot came
To dwell at Arthur's court: at Christmas time
This happened; when the heralds sung his name,

"'Son of King Ban[1] of Benwick,' seemed to chime
65 Along with all the bells that rang that day,
O'er the white roofs, with little change of rhyme.

"Christmas and whitened winter passed away,
And over me the April sunshine came,
Made very awful with black hail-clouds, yea.

70 "And in Summer I grew white with flame,
And bowed my head down—Autumn, and the sick
Sure knowledge things would never be the same,

---

1. Launcelot's father, a king of Brittany.

"However often Spring might be most thick
Of blossoms and buds, smote on me, and I grew
75 Careless of most things, let the clock tick, tick,

"To my unhappy pulse, that beat right through
My eager body; while I laughed out loud,
And let my lips curl up at false or true,

"Seemed cold and shallow without any cloud.
80 Behold my judges, then the cloths were brought:
While I was dizzied thus, old thoughts would crowd,

"Belonging to the time ere I was bought
By Arthur's great name and his little love,
Must I give up forever then, I thought,

85 "That which I deemed would ever round me move
Glorifying all things; for a little word,[2]
Scarce ever meant at all, must I now prove

"Stone-cold for ever? Pray you, does the Lord
Will that all folks should be quite happy and good?
90 I love God now a little, if this cord[3]

"Were broken, once for all what striving could
Make me love anything in earth or heaven.
So day by day it grew, as if one should

"Slip slowly down some path worn smooth and even,
95 Down to a cool sea on a summer day;
Yet still in slipping there was some small leaven

"Of stretched hands catching small stones by the way,
Until one surely reached the sea at last,
And felt strange new joy as the worn head lay

100 "Back, with the hair like seaweed; yea all past
Sweat of the forehead, dryness of the lips,
Washed utterly out by the dear waves o'ercast,

"In the lone sea, far off from any ships!
Do I not know now of a day in Spring?
105 No minute of that wild day ever slips

"From out my memory; I hear thrushes sing,
And wheresoever I may be, straightway
Thoughts of it all come up with most fresh sting:

"I was half mad with beauty on that day,
110 And went without my ladies all alone,
In a quiet garden walled round every way;

---

2. Her marriage vow.   3. Her bond with Launcelot.

"I was right joyful of that wall of stone,
That shut the flowers and trees up with the sky,
And trebled all the beauty: to the bone,

115 "Yea right through to my heart, grown very shy
With weary thoughts, it pierced, and made me glad;
Exceedingly glad, and I knew verily,

"A little thing just then had° made me mad;   *would have*
I dared not think, as I was wont to do,
120 Sometimes, upon my beauty; if I had

"Held out my long hand up against the blue,
And, looking on the tenderly darkened fingers,
Thought that by rights one ought to see quite through,

"There, see you, where the soft still light yet lingers,
125 Round by the edges; what should I have done,
If this had joined with yellow spotted singers,

"And startling green drawn upward by the sun?
But shouting, loosed out, see now! all my hair,
And trancedly stood watching the west wind run

130 "With faintest half-heard breathing sound—why there
I lose my head e'en now in doing this;
But shortly listen—In that garden fair

"Came Launcelot walking; this is true, the kiss
Wherewith we kissed in meeting that spring day,
135 I scarce dare talk of the remembered bliss,

"When both our mouths went wandering in one way,
And aching sorely, met among the leaves;
Our hands being left behind strained far away.

"Never within a yard of my bright sleeves
140 Had Launcelot come before—and now, so nigh!
After that day why is it Guenevere grieves?

"Nevertheless you, O Sir Gauwaine, lie,
Whatever happened on through all those years,
God knows I speak truth, saying that you lie.

145 "Being such a lady could I weep these tears
If this were true? A great queen such as I
Having sinned this way, straight her conscience sears;

"And afterwards she liveth hatefully,
Slaying and poisoning, certes° never weeps—   *certainly*
150 Gauwaine, be friends now, speak me lovingly.

"Do I not see how God's dear pity creeps
All through your frame, and trembles in your mouth?
Remember in what grave your mother sleeps,

"Buried in some place far down in the south,
155   Men are forgetting as I speak to you;
By her head severed in that awful drouth

"Of pity that drew Agravaine's fell° blow,[4]   *cruel*
I pray your pity! let me not scream out
Forever after, when the shrill winds blow

160   "Through half your castle-locks! let me not shout
Forever after in the winter night
When you ride out alone! in battle rout

"Let not my rusting tears make your sword light!°   *weak*
Ah! God of mercy how he turns away!
165   So, ever must I dress me to the fight,

"So—let God's justice work! Gauwaine, I say,
See me hew down your proofs: yea all men know
Even as you said how Mellyagraunce one day,

"One bitter day in *la Fausse Garde*,[5] for so
170   All good knights held it after, saw—
Yea, sirs, by cursed unknightly outrage; though

"You, Gauwaine, held his word without a flaw,
This Mellyagraunce saw blood upon my bed[6]—
Whose blood then pray you? is there any law

175   "To make a queen say why some spots of red
Lie on her coverlet? or will you say,
'Your hands are white, lady, as when you wed,

"'Where did you bleed?' and must I stammer out—'Nay,
I blush indeed, fair lord, only to rend
180   My sleeve up to my shoulder, where there lay

"'A knife-point last night': so must I defend
The honor of the lady Guenevere?
Not so, fair lords, even if the world should end

---

4. In Morris's version Gauwaine's brother, Agravaine, beheads their mother, Morgan Le Fay, after she is accused of adultery. In Malory's narrative another brother, Gaheris, kills her (book 10, chap. 24).
5. The False Castle (French); a term expressing her contempt. Launcelot's castle is named the Joyous Garde.
6. In an earlier episode in Malory's narrative,

Guenevere and some of her young knights who have been wounded in a skirmish are confined for a night in a room in Mellyagraunce's castle. Discovering bloodstains on her bedclothes the following morning, Mellyagraunce accuses her of adulterous relations with one of the wounded knights. Actually her visiting bedfellow had been Launcelot, who had cut his hand on the window bars as he climbed into her room.

"This very day, and you were judges here
185   Instead of God. Did you see Mellyagraunce
When Launcelot stood by him? what white fear

"Curdled his blood, and how his teeth did dance,
His side sink in? as my knight cried and said,
'Slayer of unarmed men, here is a chance!

190   "'Setter of traps,[7] I pray you guard your head,
By God I am so glad to fight with you,
Stripper of ladies,[8] that my hand feels lead

"'For driving weight; hurrah now! draw and do,
For all my wounds are moving in my breast,
195   And I am getting mad with waiting so.'

"He struck his hands together o'er the beast,
Who fell down flat, and groveled at his feet,
And groaned at being slain so young—'at least.'

"My knight said, 'Rise you, sir, who are so fleet
200   At catching ladies, half-armed will I fight,
My left side all uncovered!' then I weet,°   *know*

"Up sprang Sir Mellyagraunce with great delight
Upon his knave's face; not until just then
Did I quite hate him, as I saw my knight

205   "Along the lists look to my stake and pen°   *prison*
With such a joyous smile, it made me sigh
From agony beneath my waist-chain,[9] when

"The fight began, and to me they drew nigh;
Ever Sir Launcelot kept him on the right,
210   And traversed warily, and ever high

"And fast leaped caitiff's° sword, until my knight   *coward's*
Sudden threw up his sword to his left hand,
Caught it, and swung it; that was all the fight.

"Except a spout of blood on the hot land;
215   For it was hottest summer; and I know
I wondered how the fire, while I should stand,

"And burn, against the heat, would quiver so,
Yards above my head; thus these matters went:
Which things were only warnings of the woe

7. Mellyagraunce tried to prevent Launcelot from coming to defend the queen's honor by making him fall through a trapdoor into a dungeon.
8. Mellyagraunce discovers the bloodstains on Guenevere's bedclothes by pulling open her bed-

curtains; he had intended to rape the queen.
9. She is chained to a stake, at which she will be burned if Launcelot fails to overcome her accuser.

220 "That fell on me. Yet Mellyagraunce was shent,°   *destroyed*
For Mellyagraunce had fought against the Lord;
Therefore, my lords, take heed lest you be blent°   *blinded*

"With all this wickedness; say no rash word
Against me, being so beautiful; my eyes,
225 Wept all away to gray, may bring some sword

"To drown you in your blood; see my breast rise,
Like waves of purple sea, as here I stand;
And how my arms are moved in wonderful wise,

"Yea also at my full heart's strong command,
230 See through my long throat how the words go up
In ripples to my mouth; how in my hand

"The shadow lies like wine within a cup
Of marvelously colored gold; yea now
This little wind is rising, look you up,

235 "And wonder how the light is falling so
Within my moving tresses: will you dare,
When you have looked a little on my brow,

"To say this thing is vile? or will you care
For any plausible lies of cunning woof,[1]
240 When you can see my face with no lie there

"Forever? am I not a gracious proof—
'But in your chamber Launcelot was found'—
Is there a good knight then would stand aloof,

"When a queen says with gentle queenly sound:
245 'O true as steel come now and talk with me,
I love to see your step upon the ground

"'Unwavering, also well I love to see
That gracious smile light up your face, and hear
Your wonderful words, that all mean verily

250 "'The thing they seem to mean: good friend, so dear
To me in everything, come here tonight,
Or else the hours will pass most dull and drear;

"'If you come not, I fear this time I might
Get thinking over much of times gone by,
255 When I was young, and green hope was in sight:

---

1. The threads woven across the threads stretched lengthwise on a loom (the warp). Guenevere imagines these lies as being woven on a loom.

"'For no man cares now to know why I sigh;
And no man comes to sing me pleasant songs,
Nor any brings me the sweet flowers that lie

"'So thick in the gardens; therefore one so longs
260 To see you, Launcelot; that we may be
Like children once again, free from all wrongs

"'Just for one night.' Did he not come to me?
What thing could keep true Launcelot away
If I said 'Come?' there was one less than three

265 "In my quiet room that night, and we were gay;
Till sudden I rose up, weak, pale, and sick,
Because a bawling broke our dream up, yea

"I looked at Launcelot's face and could not speak,
For he looked helpless too, for a little while;
270 Then I remember how I tried to shriek,

"And could not, but fell down; from tile to tile
The stones they threw up rattled o'er my head
And made me dizzier; till within a while

"My maids were all about me, and my head
275 On Launcelot's breast was being soothed away
From its white chattering, until Launcelot said—

"By God! I will not tell you more today,
Judge any way you will—what matters it?
You know quite well the story of that fray,

280 "How Launcelot stilled their bawling, the mad fit
That caught up Gauwaine—all, all, verily,
But just that which would save me; these things flit.

"Nevertheless you, O Sir Gauwaine, lie,
Whatever may have happened these long years,
285 God knows I speak truth, saying that you lie!

"All I have said is truth, by Christ's dear tears."
She would not speak another word, but stood.
Turned sideways; listening, like a man who hears

His brother's trumpet sounding through the wood
290 Of his foes' lances. She leaned eagerly,
And gave a slight spring sometimes, as she could

At last hear something really; joyfully
Her cheek grew crimson, as the headlong speed

Of the roan charger° drew all men to see,   *battle horse*
295 The knight who came was Launcelot at good need.

1858

How I Became a Socialist[1]

I am asked by the Editor to give some sort of a history of the above conversion, and I feel that it may be of some use to do so, if my readers will look upon me as a type of a certain group of people, but not so easy to do clearly, briefly and truly. Let me, however, try. But first, I will say what I mean by being a Socialist, since I am told that the word no longer expresses definitely and with certainty what it did ten years ago. Well, what I mean by Socialism is a condition of society in which there should be neither rich nor poor, neither master nor master's man, neither idle nor overworked, neither brain-sick brain workers, nor heart-sick hand workers, in a word, in which all men would be living in equality of condition, and would manage their affairs unwastefully, and with the full consciousness that harm to one would mean harm to all—the realization at last of the meaning of the word COMMONWEALTH.

Now this view of Socialism which I hold to-day, and hope to die holding, is what I began with; I had no transitional period, unless you may call such a brief period of political radicalism during which I saw my ideal clear enough, but had no hope of any realization of it. That came to an end some months before I joined the (then) Democratic Federation,[2] and the meaning of my joining that body was that I had conceived a hope of the realization of my ideal. If you ask me how much of a hope, or what I thought we Socialists then living and working would accomplish towards it, or when there would be effected any change in the face of society, I must say, I do not know. I can only say that I did not measure my hope, nor the joy that it brought me at the time. For the rest, when I took that step I was blankly ignorant of economics; I had never so much as opened Adam Smith, or heard of Ricardo, or of Karl Marx.[3] Oddly enough, I *had* read some of Mill,[4] to wit, those posthumous papers of his (published, was it in the *Westminster Review* or the *Fortnightly?*) in which he attacks Socialism in its Fourierist[5] guise. In those papers he put the arguments, as far as they go, clearly and honestly, and the result, so far as I was concerned, was to convince me that Socialism was a necessary change, and that it was possible to bring it about in our own days. Those papers put the finishing touch to my conversion to Socialism. Well, having joined a Socialist body (for the Federation soon became definitely Socialist), I put

1. Written for the socialist magazine *Justice* in 1894.
2. The first socialist organization in London, founded in 1881.
3. German political philosopher (1818–1883), who developed the concept of communism; his *Capital* (1867–94) is an analysis of capitalism. Smith (1723–1790), Scottish economist who argued that natural laws of production and exchange govern economies and produce wealth. Smith's work was an important justification of capitalism and laissez-faire (noninterventionist) economics. David Ricardo (1772–1823), English economist whose labor theory of value influenced Marx.
4. James Mill (1773–1836), philosopher, political economist, and historian, and the father of John Stuart Mill.
5. Characteristic of a political philosophy, developed by Charles Fourier (1772–1837), that advocated a social reorganization to equalize wealth.

some conscience into trying to learn the economical side of Socialism, and even tackled Marx, though I must confess that, whereas I thoroughly enjoyed the historical part of "Capital," I suffered agonies of confusion of the brain over reading the pure economics of that great work. Anyhow, I read what I could, and will hope that some information stuck to me from my reading; but more, I must think, from continuous conversation with such friends as Bax and Hyndman and Scheu,[6] and the brisk course of propaganda meetings which were going on at the time, and in which I took my share. Such finish to what of education in practical Socialism as I am capable of I received afterwards from some of my Anarchist friends, from whom I learned, quite against their intention, that Anarchism was impossible, much as I learned from Mill against *his* intention that Socialism was necessary.

But in this telling how I fell into *practical* Socialism I have begun, as I perceive, in the middle, for in my position of a well-to-do man, not suffering from the disabilities which oppress a working-man at every step, I feel that I might never have been drawn into the practical side of the question if an ideal had not forced me to seek towards it. For politics as politics, *i.e.*, not regarded as a necessary if cumbersome and disgustful means to an end, would never have attracted me, nor when I had become conscious of the wrongs of society as it now is, and the oppression of poor people, could I have ever believed in the possibility of a *partial* setting right of those wrongs. In other words, I could never have been such a fool as to believe in the happy and "respectable" poor.

If, therefore, my ideal forced me to look for practical Socialism, what was it that forced me to conceive of an ideal? Now, here comes in what I said (in this paper) of my being a type of a certain group of mind.

Before the uprising of *modern* Socialism almost all intelligent people either were, or professed themselves to be, quite contented with the civilization of this century. Again, almost all of these really were thus contented, and saw nothing to do but to perfect the said civilization by getting rid of a few ridiculous survivals of the barbarous ages. To be short, this was the *Whig*[7] frame of mind, natural to the modern prosperous middle-class men, who, in fact, as far as mechanical progress is concerned, have nothing to ask for, if only Socialism would leave them alone to enjoy their plentiful style.

But besides these contented ones there were others who were not really contented, but had a vague sentiment of repulsion to the triumph of civilization, but were coerced into silence by the measureless power of Whiggery. Lastly, there were a few who were in open rebellion against the said Whiggery—a few, say two, Carlyle and Ruskin. The latter, before my days

6. Ernest Belfort Bax (1854–1926), H. M. Hyndman (1842–1921), and Andreas Scheu (1844–1927), leaders in the early English socialist movement.
7. From the monarchical crisis of 1678–81 onward, the term *Whig* (from *whiggamore*, a Scottish name for a cattle driver) designated a member of one of the two major parliamentary alliances (the Tories being the opposing group). Originally an aristocratic faction interested in reducing the power of the Crown, the Whigs became progressively associated with reform, and thus formed important bonds with other groups and individuals, such as moneyed industrialists, champions of free trade, and religious dissenters. This Whig-Radical coalition was known colloquially as the Liberal Party from 1839 onward; it adopted the name officially when it assumed the form of a modern political party in the 1860s. The term *Whig* remained in informal use, often in connection with a self-congratulatory state of mind most famously promulgated by Thomas Babington Macaulay (1800–1859). His writings presented all English history as leading up to the parliamentary Reform Bill of 1832, and celebrated contemporary English life as the pinnacle of human achievement and civilization (see the first extract in "Industrialism: Progress or Decline?" on p. 628).

of practical Socialism, was my master towards the ideal aforesaid, and, looking backward, I cannot help saying, by the way, how deadly dull the world would have been twenty years ago but for Ruskin! It was through him that I learned to give form to my discontent, which I must say was not by any means vague. Apart from the desire to produce beautiful things, the leading passion of my life has been and is hatred of modern civilization. What shall I say of it now, when the words are put into my mouth, my hope of its destruction—what shall I say of its supplanting by Socialism?

What shall I say concerning its mastery of and its waste of mechanical power, its commonwealth so poor, its enemies of the commonwealth so rich, its stupendous organization—for the misery of life! Its contempt of simple pleasures which everyone could enjoy but for its folly? Its eyeless vulgarity which has destroyed art, the one certain solace of labour? All this I felt then as now, but I did not know why it was so. The hope of the past times was gone, the struggles of mankind for many ages had produced nothing but this sordid, aimless, ugly confusion; the immediate future seemed to me likely to intensify all the present evils by sweeping away the last survivals of the days before the dull squalor of civilization had settled down on the world. This was a bad lookout indeed, and, if I may mention myself as a personality and not as a mere type, especially so to a man of my disposition, careless of metaphysics and religion, as well as of scientific analysis, but with a deep love of the earth and the life on it, and a passion for the history of the past of mankind. Think of it! Was it all to end in a counting-house on the top of a cinder-heap, with Podsnap's[8] drawing-room in the offing, and a Whig committee dealing out champagne to the rich and margarine to the poor in such convenient proportions as would make all men contented together, though the pleasure of the eyes was gone from the world, and the place of Homer was to be taken by Huxley?[9] Yet, believe me, in my heart, when I really forced myself to look towards the future, that is what I saw in it, and, as far as I could tell, scarce anyone seemed to think it worth while to struggle against such a consummation of civilization. So there I was in for a fine pessimistic end of life, if it had not somehow dawned on me that amidst all this filth of civilization the seeds of a great chance, what we others call Social-Revolution, were beginning to germinate. The whole face of things was changed to me by that discovery, and all I had to do then in order to become a Socialist was to hook myself on to the practical movement, which, as before said, I have tried to do as well as I could.

To sum up, then, the study of history and the love and practice of art forced me into a hatred of the civilization which, if things were to stop as they are, would turn history into inconsequent nonsense, and make art a collection of the curiosities of the past which would have no serious relation to the life of the present.

But the consciousness of revolution stirring amidst our hateful modern society prevented me, luckier than many others of artistic perceptions, from crystallizing into a mere railer against "progress" on the one hand, and on the other from wasting time and energy in any of the numerous schemes by

8. Podsnap is a character in Charles Dickens's *Our Mutual Friend* (1865) who represents the epitome of pretentious middle-class respectability. "Counting-house": accountant's office.
9. T. H. Huxley (1825–1895), writer on science, education, and philosophy (see p. 495).

which the quasi-artistic of the middle classes hope to make art grow when it has no longer any root, and thus I became a practical Socialist.

A last word or two. Perhaps some of our friends will say, what have we to do with these matters of history and art? We want by means of Social-Democracy to win a decent livelihood, we want in some sort to live, and that at once. Surely any one who professes to think that the question of art and cultivation must go before that of the knife and fork (and there are some who do propose that) does not understand what art means, or how that its roots must have a soil of a thriving and unanxious life. Yet it must be remembered that civilization has reduced the workman to such a skinny and pitiful existence, that he scarcely knows how to frame a desire for any life much better than that which he now endures perforce. It is the province of art to set the true ideal of a full and reasonable life before him, a life to which the perception and creation of beauty, the enjoyment of real pleasure that is, shall be felt to be as necessary to man as his daily bread, and that no man, and no set of men, can be deprived of this except by mere opposition, which should be resisted to the utmost.

1894   1894

ALGERNON CHARLES SWINBURNE
1837–1909

I n a review of Charles Baudelaire's *Les Fleurs du Mal* (1857), Algernon Charles Swinburne remarks that "the mass of readers seem actually to think that a poem is the better for containing a moral lesson." He goes on to praise the courage and sense of a man who acts on the conviction "that the art of poetry has nothing to do with didactic matter at all." Certainly Swinburne's poems are not didactic in the sense of containing traditional moral values. As John Morley commented while reviewing Swinburne's first volume of poems, "He is so firmly and avowedly fixed in an attitude of revolt against the current notions of decency and dignity and social duty that to beg of him to be a little more decent, to fly a little less persistently and gleefully to the animal side of human nature, is simply to beg him to be something different from Mr. Swinburne." Swinburne set about shocking his elders by a variety of rebellious gestures. In religion he appeared to be a pagan; in politics, a liberal republican dedicated to the overthrow of established governments. On the subjects of love and sex, he was similarly unconventional. Frequently preoccupied with the pleasures of the lover who inflicts or accepts pain (particularly with the excitement of flagellation), Swinburne also often turns in his poetry to the theme of homoerotic desire, a taboo topic for his Victorian audience. As Arnold Bennett said of "Anactoria" (1866), a dramatic monologue in which the poet Sappho addresses a woman with whom she is madly in love, Swinburne played "a rare trick" on England by "enshrining in the topmost heights of its literature a lovely poem that cannot be discussed."

To a more limited extent, Swinburne also expressed his rebellion against established codes by his personal behavior. He came from a distinguished family and attended Eton and Oxford, but sought the company of the bohemians of Paris and of London, where he became temporarily associated with Dante Gabriel Rossetti and other Pre-Raphaelites. By 1879 his alcoholism had profoundly affected his frail physique, and he was obliged to put himself into the protective custody of a friend, Theodore Watts-Dunton, who took him to the countryside and kept him alive although sobered and tamed.

Swinburne continued to write voluminously and sometimes memorably, but his most fascinating poetry appeared in his early publications. He described his early play *Atalanta in Calydon* (1865) as "pure Greek," and his command of classical allusions here, as well as in other poems, is indeed impressive. Yet the kind of spirit that he found in Greek literature was not the traditional quality of classic serenity admired by Matthew Arnold. Like Percy Bysshe Shelley (the poet he most closely resembles), Swinburne loved Greece as a land of liberty in which men had expressed themselves with the fewest restraints. To call such an ardently romantic poet "classical" requires a series of qualifying clauses that makes the term meaningless.

In his play and in the volume that followed it, *Poems and Ballads* (1866), Swinburne demonstrated a metrical virtuosity that dazzled his early readers and is still dazzling. Those who demand that poetry should make sense, first and foremost, may find that much of his poetry is not to their taste. What he offers, instead, are heady rhythmical patterns in which words are relished as much for their sound as for their meaning.

> There lived a singer in France of old
> By the tideless dolorous midland sea.
> In a land of sand and ruin and gold
> Here shone one woman, and none but she.

These lines from "The Triumph of Time" (1866) have often been cited to illustrate Swinburne's qualities. Like some poems of the later French symbolists, such passages defy traditional kinds of critical analysis and oblige us to reconsider the variety of ways in which poetry may achieve its effects.

Another noteworthy aspect of these poems is their recurring preoccupation with death, as in the memorable re-creations of Proserpina's underworld garden, frozen in timelessness. And as the critic Jerome McGann notes: "No English poet has composed more elegies than Swinburne." The death of any prominent figure, such as Robert Browning, almost always prompted Swinburne to compose a poem for the occasion. "Ave atque Vale" (1868), his farewell to Baudelaire, is an especially moving tribute, and shows Swinburne focusing on a subject extremely close to his heart. For Swinburne the work of his beloved French poet possessed a "languid, lurid beauty"; to us the phrase may seem equally applicable to Swinburne's poetry.

Hymn to Proserpine

(*After the Proclamation in Rome of the Christian Faith*)

Vicisti, Galilaee[1]

I have lived long enough, having seen one thing, that love hath an end;
Goddess and maiden and queen, be near me now and befriend.
Thou art more than the day or the morrow, the seasons that laugh or that
    weep;

---

1. Thou hast conquered, O Galilean (Latin); words supposedly addressed to Jesus, who grew up in   Galilee, by the Roman emperor Julian the Apostate on his deathbed in 363. Julian had tried to

For these give joy and sorrow; but thou, Proserpina, sleep.
5   Sweet is the treading of wine, and sweet the feet of the dove;
But a goodlier gift is thine than foam of the grapes or love.
Yea, is not even Apollo,[2] with hair and harpstring of gold,
A bitter god to follow, a beautiful god to behold?
I am sick of singing; the bays[3] burn deep and chafe. I am fain°   *glad*
10   To rest a little from praise and grievous pleasure and pain.
For the gods we know not of, who give us our daily breath,
We know they are cruel as love or life, and lovely as death.

O gods dethroned and deceased, cast forth, wiped out in a day!
From your wrath is the world released, redeemed from your chains, men say.
15   New gods are crowned in the city; their flowers have broken your rods;
They are merciful, clothed with pity, the young compassionate gods.
But for me their new device is barren, the days are bare;
Things long past over suffice, and men forgotten that were.
Time and the gods are at strife; ye dwell in the midst thereof,
20   Draining a little life from the barren breasts of love.
I say to you, cease, take rest; yea, I say to you all, be at peace,
Till the bitter milk of her breast and the barren bosom shall cease.
Wilt thou yet take all, Galilean? But these thou shalt not take—
The laurel, the palms, and the paean, the breasts of the nymphs in the
     brake,°   *thicket*
25   Breasts more soft than a dove's, that tremble with tenderer breath;
And all the wings of the Loves, and all the joy before death;
All the feet of the hours that sound as a single lyre,
Dropped and deep in the flowers, with strings that flicker like fire.
More than these wilt thou give, things fairer than all these things?
30   Nay, for a little we live, and life hath mutable wings.
A little while and we die; shall life not thrive as it may?
For no man under the sky lives twice, outliving his day.
And grief is a grievous thing, and a man hath enough of his tears;
Why should he labor, and bring fresh grief to blacken his years?

35   Thou hast conquered, O pale Galilean; the world has grown gray from thy
     breath;
We have drunken of things Lethean,[4] and fed on the fullness of death.
Laurel is green for a season, and love is sweet for a day;
But love grows bitter with treason, and laurel outlives not May.
Sleep, shall we sleep after all? for the world is not sweet in the end;
40   For the old faiths loosen and fall, the new years ruin and rend.
Fate is a sea without shore, and the soul is a rock that abides;

revive paganism and to discourage Christianity, which, after a proclamation in 313, had been tolerated in Rome. His efforts were unsuccessful. The speaker of the poem, a Roman patrician and also a poet (line 9), is like Emperor Julian: he prefers the old order of pagan gods. His hymn is addressed to the goddess Proserpina (the Greek Persephone), who was carried off by Pluto (Hades) to be queen of the underworld. In this role she is addressed in the poem as goddess of death and of sleep. The speaker also associates her with the earth (line 93) because she was the daughter of Ceres (or Deme-ter), goddess of agriculture, whose Greek name means "Earth Mother." Swinburne may have derived some details here from the 4th-century Latin poet Claudian, whose long narrative *The Rape of Proserpina* provides helpful background for this hymn.
2. Classical god of poetry, and in art the ideal of young male beauty.
3. Laurel leaves of a poet's crown.
4. I.e., of Lethe (literally, "Forgetfulness"), a river in the underworld.

But her ears are vexed with the roar and her face with the foam of the
    tides.
O lips that the live blood faints in, the leavings of racks and rods!
O ghastly glories of saints, dead limbs of gibbeted gods!
45 Though all men abase them before you in spirit, and all knees bend,
I kneel not, neither adore you, but standing look to the end.

All delicate days and pleasant, all spirits and sorrows are cast
Far out with the foam of the present that sweeps to the surf of the past;
Where beyond the extreme sea wall, and between the remote sea gates,
50 Waste water washes, and tall ships founder, and deep death waits;
Where, mighty with deepening sides, clad about with the seas as with
    wings,
And impelled of invisible tides, and fulfilled of unspeakable things,
White-eyed and poisonous-finned, shark-toothed and serpentine-curled,
Rolls, under the whitening wind of the future, the wave of the world.
55 The depths stand naked in sunder behind it, the storms flee away;
In the hollow before it the thunder is taken and snared as a prey;
In its sides is the north wind bound; and its salt is of all men's tears,
With light of ruin, and sound of changes, and pulse of years;
With travail of day after day, and with trouble of hour upon hour.
60 And bitter as blood is the spray; and the crests are as fangs that devour;
And its vapor and storm of its steam as the sighing of spirits to be;
And its noise as the noise in a dream; and its depths as the roots of the
    sea;
And the height of its heads as the height of the utmost stars of the air;
And the ends of the earth at the might thereof tremble, and time is made
    bare.
65 Will ye bridle the deep sea with reins, will ye chasten the high sea with
    rods?[5]
Will ye take her to chain her with chains, who is older than all ye gods?
All ye as a wind shall go by, as a fire shall ye pass and be past;
Ye are gods, and behold, ye shall die, and the waves be upon you at last.
In the darkness of time, in the deeps of the years, in the changes of things,
70 Ye shall sleep as a slain man sleeps, and the world shall forget you or
    kings.
Though the feet of thine high priests tread where thy lords and our
    forefathers trod,
Though these that were gods are dead, and thou being dead art a god,
Though before thee the throned Cytherean[6] be fallen, and hidden her
    head,
Yet thy kingdom shall pass, Galilean, thy dead shall go down to thee dead.

75 Of the maiden thy mother men sing as a goddess with grace clad around;
Thou art throned where another was king; where another was queen she is
    crowned.
Yea, once we had sight of another; but now she is queen, say these.
Not as thine, not as thine was our mother, a blossom of flowering seas,

---

5. According to the ancient Greek historian
Herodotus, after storm waves destroyed his bridge
the enraged Xerxes, king of the Persians, ordered
that the Hellespont be whipped; see *History*

7.33–34.
6. Venus (or Aphrodite), who was born from the
waves near the island of Cythera.

Clothed round with the world's desire as with raiment, and fair as the
    foam.
80 And fleeter than kindled fire, and a goddess, and mother of Rome.[7]
For thine came pale and a maiden, and sister to sorrow; but ours,
Her deep hair heavily laden with odour and colour of flowers,
White rose of the rose-white water, a silver splendour, a flame,
Bent down unto us that besought her, and earth grew sweet with her
    name.
85 For thine came weeping, a slave among slaves, and rejected; but she
Came flushed from the full-flushed wave, and imperial, her foot on the sea.
And the wonderful waters knew her, the winds and the viewless ways,
And the roses grew rosier, and bluer the sea-blue stream of the bays.

Ye are fallen, our lords, by what token? we wist that ye should not fall.
90 Ye were all so fair that are broken; and one more fair than ye all.
But I turn to her° still, having seen she shall surely abide in   *Proserpina*
    the end.
Goddess and maiden and queen, be near me now and befriend.
O daughter of earth, of my mother, her crown and blossom of birth,
I am also, I also, thy brother; I go as I came unto earth.
95 In the night where thine eyes are as moons are in heaven, the night where
    thou art,
Where the silence is more than all tunes, where sleep overflows from the
    heart,
Where the poppies are sweet as the rose in our world, and the red rose is
    white,
And the wind falls faint as it blows with the fume of the flowers of the
    night,
And the murmur of spirits that sleep in the shadow of gods from afar
100 Grows dim in thine ears and deep as the deep dim soul of a star,
In the sweet low light of thy face, under heavens untrod by the sun,
Let my soul with their souls find place, and forget what is done and
    undone.
Thou art more than the gods who number the days of our temporal breath;
For these give labor and slumber; but thou, Proserpina, death.
105 Therefore now at thy feet I abide for a season in silence. I know
I shall die as my fathers died, and sleep as they sleep; even so.
For the glass° of the years is brittle wherein we gaze for a span.   *mirror*
A little soul for a little bears up this corpse which is man.
So long I endure, no longer; and laugh not again, neither weep.
110 For there is no god found stronger than death; and death is a sleep.

1866

<hr/>

7. Romans traced their legendary origins back to Aeneas, a Trojan prince who was the son of Aphrodite.

Hermaphroditus[1]

1

Lift up thy lips, turn round, look back for love,
    Blind love that comes by night and casts out rest
    Of all things tired thy lips look weariest,
Save the long smile that they are wearied of.
5   Ah sweet, albeit no love be sweet enough,
    Choose of two loves and cleave unto the best;
    Two loves at either blossom of thy breast
Strive until one be under and one above.
    Their breath is fire upon the amorous air,
10 Fire in thine eyes and where thy lips suspire:°   *breathe out*
And whosoever hath seen thee, being so fair,
    Two things turn all his life and blood to fire;
A strong desire begot on great despair,
    A great despair cast out by strong desire.

2

15 Where between sleep and life some brief space is,
    With love like gold bound round about the head,
    Sex to sweet sex with lips and limbs is wed,
Turning the fruitful feud of hers and his
    To the waste wedlock of a sterile kiss;
20   Yet from them something like as fire is shed
    That shall not be assuaged till death be dead,
Though neither life nor sleep can find out this.
Love made himself of flesh that perisheth
    A pleasure-house for all the loves his kin;
25 But on the one side sat a man like death,
    And on the other a woman sat like sin.
So with veiled eyes and sobs between his breath
    Love turned himself and would not enter in.

3

Love, is it love or sleep or shadow or light
30   That lies between thine eyelids and thine eyes?
    Like a flower laid upon a flower it lies,
Or like the night's dew laid upon the night.
Love stands upon thy left hand and thy right,
    Yet by no sunset and by no moonrise
35   Shall make thee man and ease a woman's sighs,
Or make thee woman for a man's delight.
To what strange end hath some strange god made fair
    The double blossom of two fruitless flowers?
Hid love in all the folds of all thy hair,
40   Fed thee on summers, watered thee with showers,

---

1. Son of Hermes and Aphrodite. One day as he bathed in a spring, Salmacis, the nymph of the spring, fell in love with him. When he rejected her, she clung to him, praying that their bodies never be separated. The gods answered her prayer, making their bodies one. The statue in the Louvre that inspired this poem, a Roman copy of a Greek original, shows the god lying on his side, with the breasts of a woman and the genitals of a man.

Given all the gold that all the seasons wear
    To thee that art a thing of barren hours?

4

Yea, love, I see; it is not love but fear.
    Nay, sweet, it is not fear but love, I know;
45   Or wherefore should thy body's blossom blow
So sweetly, or thine eyelids leave so clear
Thy gracious eyes that never made a tear—
    Though for their love our tears like blood should flow,
    Though love and life and death should come and go,
50   So dreadful, so desirable, so dear?
Yea, sweet, I know; I saw in what swift wise°   *how swiftly*
    Beneath the woman's and the water's kiss
Thy moist limbs melted into Salmacis,
And the large light turned tender in thine eyes,
55   And all thy boy's breath softened into sighs;
    But Love being blind,[2] how should he know of this?

Au Musée du Louvre, *Mars* 1863.[3]

1863   1866

Ave atque Vale[1]

In Memory of Charles Baudelaire

Nous devrions pourtant lui porter quelques fleurs;
Les morts, les pauvres morts, ont de grandes douleurs,
Et quand Octobre souffle, émondeur des vieux arbres,
Son vent mélancolique à l'entour de leurs marbres,
Certe, ils doivent trouver les vivants bien ingrats.
            —"Les Fleurs du Mal."[2]

1

Shall I strew on thee rose or rue or laurel,[3]
    Brother, on this that was the veil[4] of thee?

2. Love, personified in classical mythology as Eros or Cupid, is often represented as blindfolded or blind.

3. At the Museum of the Louvre, March 1863 (French).

1. Hail and farewell (Latin); from an elegy by Catullus occasioned by a visit to the grave of his brother, to whom he brought gifts, a situation closely echoed in Swinburne's final stanza. Swinburne's elegy also begins with a visit to the grave of a man whom the poet regards as a brother but had never met. Charles Baudelaire (1821–1867) had impressed Swinburne as one of the "most perfect poets of the century." In 1861, in an essay on the 2nd edition of Baudelaire's collection *Les Fleurs du Mal* (*Flowers of Evil*, 1857), Swinburne had commented on the French poet's preoccupation with "sad and strange things"—"the sharp and cruel enjoyments of pain, the acrid relish of suffering felt or inflicted"; "it has the languid, lurid beauty of close and threatening weather—a heavy, heated temperature, with dangerous hothouse scents in it." These qualities are also celebrated in the elegy, into which are woven many allusions to Baudelaire's poems, especially "Litanies de Satan," which Swinburne regarded as the keynote poem of *Les Fleurs du Mal.*

2. From "La Servante au Grand Coeur" ("The Great-hearted Servant"): We must nevertheless bring some flowers to her [or him]. / The dead, the poor dead, have great sadnesses, / And when October, the pruner of old trees, blows, / Its melancholy wind in the vicinity of their marble tombs, / Then indeed they must find the living highly ungrateful (French).

3. Respectively, symbols of love, mourning, and poetic fame.

4. I.e., the body as a veil for the soul.

Or quiet sea-flower molded by the sea,
Or simplest growth of meadow-sweet or sorrel,
5   Such as the summer-sleepy Dryads° weave,   *wood nymphs*
Waked up by snow-soft sudden rains at eve?
Or wilt thou rather, as on earth before,
    Half-faded fiery blossoms, pale with heat
    And full of bitter summer, but more sweet
10 To thee than gleanings of a northern shore
      Trod by no tropic feet?[5]

2

For always thee the fervid languid glories
    Allured of heavier suns in mightier skies;
Thine ears knew all the wandering watery sighs
15 Where the sea sobs round Lesbian promontories,
    The barren kiss of piteous wave to wave
    That knows not where is that Leucadian grave[6]
Which hides too deep the supreme head of song.
    Ah, salt and sterile as her kisses were,
20   The wild sea winds her and the green gulfs bear
Hither and thither, and vex and work her wrong,
    Blind gods that cannot spare.

3

Thou sawest, in thine old singing season, brother,
    Secrets and sorrows unbeheld of us:
25   Fierce loves, and lovely leaf-buds poisonous,
Bare to thy subtler eye, but for none other
    Blowing by night in some unbreathed-in clime;
    The hidden harvest of luxurious time,
Sin without shape, and pleasure without speech;
30   And where strange dreams in a tumultuous sleep
    Make the shut eyes of stricken spirits weep;
And with each face thou sawest the shadow on each,
    Seeing as men sow men reap.[7]

4

O sleepless heart and sombre soul unsleeping,
35   That were athirst for sleep and no more life
    And no more love, for peace and no more strife!
Now the dim gods of death have in their keeping
    Spirit and body and all the springs of song,
    Is it well now where love can do no wrong,
40   Where stingless pleasure has no foam or fang
    Behind the unopening closure of her lips?

5. A voyage to the tropics in Baudelaire's youth made a lasting impact on his poetry.
6. According to legend, the poet Sappho, who was born on the island of Lesbos, killed herself by leaping from the rock of Leucas into the Ionian Sea. In this section Swinburne makes allusions to Baudelaire's "Lesbos."
7. Cf. Galatians 6.7: "Whatsoever a man soweth, that shall he also reap."

Is it not well where soul from body slips
   And flesh from bone divides without a pang
      As dew from flower-bell drips?

5

45 It is enough; the end and the beginning
      Are one thing to thee, who art past the end.
      O hand unclasped of unbeholden friend,
   For thee no fruits to pluck, no palms for winning,
      No triumph and no labour and no lust,
50   Only dead yew-leaves and a little dust.
   O quiet eyes wherein the light saith naught,
      Whereto the day is dumb, nor any night
      With obscure finger silences your sight,
   Nor in your speech the sudden soul speaks thought,
55   Sleep, and have sleep for light.

6

Now all strange hours and all strange loves are over,
      Dreams and desires and sombre songs and sweet,
      Hast thou found place at the great knees and feet
   Of some pale Titan-woman like a lover,
60   Such as thy vision here solicited,[8]
      Under the shadow of her fair vast head,
   The deep division of prodigious breasts,
      The solemn slope of mighty limbs asleep,
      The weight of awful tresses that still keep
65 The savor and shade of old-world pine forests
      Where the wet hill-winds weep?

7

Hast thou found any likeness for thy vision?
      O gardener of strange flowers, what bud, what bloom,
      Hast thou found sown, what gathered in the gloom?
70 What of despair, of rapture, of derision,
      What of life is there, what of ill or good?
      Are the fruits grey like dust or bright like blood?
   Does the dim ground grow any seed of ours,
      The faint fields quicken any terrene° root,   *earthly*
75   In low lands where the sun and moon are mute
   And all the stars keep silence? Are there flowers
      At all, or any fruit?

8

Alas, but though my flying song flies after,
      O sweet strange elder singer, thy more fleet

---

8. An allusion to Baudelaire's "La Géante" ("The Giantess").

80   Singing, and footprints of thy fleeter feet,
Some dim derision of mysterious laughter
    From the blind tongueless warders of the dead,
    Some gainless glimpse of Proserpine's[9] veiled head,
Some little sound of unregarded tears
85   Wept by effaced unprofitable eyes,
    And from pale mouths some cadence of dead sighs—
These only, these the hearkening spirit hears,
    Sees only such things rise.

9

Thou art far too far for wings of words to follow,
90   Far too far off for thought or any prayer.
    What ails us with thee, who are wind and air?
What ails us gazing where all seen is hollow?
    Yet with some fancy, yet with some desire,
    Dreams pursue death as winds a flying fire,
95   Our dreams pursue our dead and do not find.
    Still, and more swift than they, the thin flame flies,
    The low light fails us in elusive skies,
Still the foiled earnest ear is deaf, and blind
    Are still the eluded eyes.

10

100 Not thee, O never thee, in all time's changes,
    Not thee, but this the sound of thy sad soul,
    The shadow of thy swift spirit, this shut scroll
I lay my hand on, and not death estranges
    My spirit from communion of thy song—
105   These memories and these melodies that throng
Veiled porches of a Muse funereal[1]—
    These I salute, these touch, these clasp and fold
    As though a hand were in my hand to hold,
Or through mine ears a mourning musical[2]
110   Of many mourners rolled.

11

I among these, I also, in such station
    As when the pyre was charred, and piled the sods,
    And offering to the dead made, and their gods,
The old mourners had, standing to make libation,
115   I stand, and to the gods and to the dead
    Do reverence without prayer or praise, and shed
Offering to these unknown, the gods of gloom,
    And what of honey and spice my seedlands bear,
    And what I may of fruits in this chilled air,

---

9. Queen of the underworld.
1. According to Jerome McGann, Swinburne associates Baudelaire's distinctive kind of poetry with a tenth muse, one who inspires songs of lamentation ("funereal").
2. I.e., a musical mourning.

120 And lay, Orestes-like, across the tomb
  A curl of severed hair.[3]

12

 But by no hand nor any treason stricken,
  Not like the low-lying head of Him, the King,
  The flame that made of Troy a ruinous thing,
125 Thou liest, and on this dust no tears could quicken
  There fall no tears like theirs[4] that all men hear
  Fall tear by sweet imperishable tear
 Down the opening leaves of holy poets' pages.
  Thee not Orestes, not Electra mourns;
130 But bending us-ward with memorial urns
 The most high Muses that fulfill all ages
  Weep, and our God's heart yearns.

13

 For, sparing of his sacred strength, not often
  Among us darkling here the lord of light[5]
135 Makes manifest his music and his might
  In hearts that open and in lips that soften
  With the soft flame and heat of songs that shine.
  Thy lips indeed he touched with bitter wine,
 And nourished them indeed with bitter bread;
140 Yet surely from his hand thy soul's food came;
 The fire that scarred thy spirit at his flame
 Was lighted, and thine hungering heart he fed
  Who feeds our hearts with fame.

14

 Therefore he too now at thy soul's sunsetting,
145 God of all suns and songs he too bends down
  To mix his laurel with thy cypress[6] crown.
 And save thy dust from blame and from forgetting,
  Therefore he too, seeing all thou wert and art,
  Compassionate, with sad and sacred heart,
150 Mourns thee of many his children the last dead,
  And hallows with strange tears and alien sighs
  Thine unmelodious mouth and sunless eyes,
 And over thine irrevocable head
  Sheds light from the under skies.[7]

3. For lines 120–29, see *The Libation Bearers*, the second play in Aeschylus's *Oresteia* trilogy. King Agamemnon, after returning home victorious from Troy, is brutally killed by his wife, Clytemnestra. His son, Orestes, places two locks of his hair on Agamemnon's grave in tribute; they are discovered soon thereafter by his sister Electra, who visits her father's grave to offer mourning libations.
4. Referring to the muses and holy poets, not to Orestes and Electra [noted by Jerome McGann].
5. Apollo, god of light and poetry.
6. Associated with mourning. "Laurel": the crown of Apollo, a wreath honoring poets.
7. I.e., flickering light of the underworld.

15

155 And one weeps with him in the ways Lethean,[8]
    And stains with tears her changing bosom chill;
    That obscure Venus of the hollow hill,
That thing transformed which was the Cytherean,
    With lips that lost their Grecian laugh divine
160   Long since, and face no more called Erycine;[9]
A ghost, a bitter and luxurious god.
    Thee also with fair flesh and singing spell
    Did she, a sad and second prey,[1] compel
Into the footless places once more trod,
165   And shadows hot from hell.

16

And now no sacred staff shall break in blossom,[2]
    No choral salutation lure to light
    A spirit sick with perfume and sweet night
And love's tired eyes and hands and barren bosom.
170   There is no help for these things; none to mend
    And none to mar; not all our songs, O friend,
Will make death clear or make life durable.
    Howbeit with rose and ivy and wild vine
    And with wild notes about this dust of thine
175 At least I fill the place where white dreams dwell[3]
    And wreathe an unseen shrine.

17

Sleep; and if life was bitter to thee, pardon,
    If sweet, give thanks; thou hast no more to live;
    And to give thanks is good, and to forgive.
180 Out of the mystic and the mournful garden
    Where all day through thine hands in barren braid
    Wove the sick flowers of secrecy and shade,
Green buds of sorrow and sin, and remnants grey,
    Sweet-smelling, pale with poison, sanguine-hearted,
185   Passions that sprang from sleep and thoughts that started,
Shall death not bring us all as thee one day
    Among the days departed?

---

8. Of Lethe, the river of forgetfulness in Hades.
9. The Venus of medieval legends held her court inside a mountain in Germany (the Hörselberg). This later Venus is a transformed version of the joyous foam-born goddess associated with the island of Cythera and also worshipped in Sicily at a shrine on Mount Eryx (hence "Erycine"). The Roman poet Horace described her as "blithe goddess of Eryx, about whom hover mirth and desire" (*Odes* 1.2.33–34).
1. The first "prey" of Venus had been Tannhäuser, whom she had lured into the "footless places" of her cave. Baudelaire is her "second prey." Swinburne, after reading Baudelaire's 1861 pamphlet on Wagner's *Tannhäuser* (1845), described this Venus as "the queen of evil, the lady of lust."
2. Such a miraculous event occurred when Tannhäuser made a pilgrimage to Rome to seek absolution for having lived in sin with Venus. Previously the pope had denied absolution until the day his staff should bloom.
3. Presumably the abode of the ghosts of the dead.

18

For thee, O now a silent soul, my brother,
   Take at my hands this garland, and farewell.
190   Thin is the leaf, and chill the wintry smell,
And chill the solemn earth, a fatal mother,
   With sadder than the Niobean womb,[4]
   And in the hollow of her breasts a tomb.
Content thee, howsoe'er, whose days are done;
195   There lies not any troublous thing before,
   Nor sight nor sound to war against thee more,
For whom all winds are quiet as the sun,
   All waters as the shore.

1866–67   1868

4. After Niobe boasted of having more children than the goddess Leto, the goddess's children—Apollo and Diana (Artemis)—killed them all.

WALTER PATER
1839–1894

*S*tudies in the History of the Renaissance, a collection of essays published in 1873, was the first of several volumes that established Walter Pater as one of the most influential writers of the late Victorian period. His flair for critical writing may have first been sparked when he was an undergraduate at Oxford (1858–62), where he heard and enjoyed the lectures of Matthew Arnold, who was then professor of poetry. After graduation Pater remained at Oxford, a shy bachelor who spent his life teaching classics (for the story of his earlier years see "The Child in the House" [1895], an autobiographical sketch that provides a helpful introduction to all of his writings). In view of his quiet disposition Pater was surprised and even alarmed by the impact made by his books on young readers of the 1870s and 1880s. Some of his younger followers such as Oscar Wilde and George Moore may have misread him. As T. S. Eliot wrote somewhat primly, "[Pater's] view of art, as expressed in *The Renaissance,* impressed itself upon a number of writers in the nineties, and propagated some confusion between life and art which is not wholly irresponsible for some untidy lives." It can be demonstrated that Pater's writings (especially his historical novel *Marius the Epicurean,* 1885) have much in common with the works of his earnest-minded mid-Victorian predecessors, but his disciples overlooked these similarities. To them his work seemed strikingly different and, in its quiet way, more subversive than the head-on attacks against traditional Victorianism made by Algernon Charles Swinburne or Samuel Butler. Instead of recommending a continuation of the painful quest for Truth that had dominated Oxford in the days of John Henry Newman, Pater assured his readers that the quest was pointless. Truth, he said, is relative. And instead of echoing Thomas Carlyle's call to duty and social responsibilities, Pater reminded his readers that life passes quickly and that our only responsibility is to enjoy fully "this short day of frost and sun"—to relish its sensations, especially those sensations provoked by works of art.

This epicurean gospel was conveyed in a highly wrought prose style that baffles anyone who likes to read quickly. Pater believed that prose was as difficult an art as poetry, and he expected his own elaborate sentences to be savored. Like Gustave Flaubert (1821–1880), the French novelist whom he admired, Pater painstakingly revised his sentences with special attention to their rhythms, seeking always the right word, *le mot juste*, as Flaubert called it. For many years Pater's day would begin with his making a careful study of a dictionary. What Pater said of Dante is an apt description of his own polished style: "He is one of those artists whose general effect largely depends on vocabulary, on the minute particles of which his work is wrought, on the colour and outline of single words and phrases." An additional characteristic of his highly wrought style is its relative absence of humor. Pater was valued among his friends for his flashes of wit and for his lively and irreverent conversation, but in his writings such traits are suppressed. As Michael Levey observed in *The Case of Walter Pater* (1978), "Even for irony the mood of his writing is almost too intense."

In addition to being a key figure in the transition from mid-Victorianism to the "decadence" of the 1890s, Pater commands our attention as the writer of exemplary impressionistic criticism. In each of his essays he seeks to communicate what he called the "special unique impression of pleasure" made on him by the works of some artist or writer. His range of subjects included the dialogues of Plato, the paintings of Leonardo da Vinci, the plays of Shakespeare, and the writings of the French Romantic school of the nineteenth century. Of particular value to students of English literature are his discriminating studies of William Wordsworth, Samuel Taylor Coleridge, Charles Lamb, and Sir Thomas Browne in his volume of *Appreciations* (1889) and his essay on the poetry of William Morris titled "Aesthetic Poetry" (1868). These and other essays by Pater were praised by Oscar Wilde in a review in 1890 as "absolutely modern, in the true meaning of the term modernity. For he to whom the present is the only thing that is present, knows nothing of the age in which he lives. . . . The true critic is he who bears within himself the dreams and ideas and feelings of myriad generations, and to whom no form of thought is alien, no emotional impulse obscure."

The final sentences of his *Appreciations* volume are a revealing indication of Pater's critical position. After having attempted to show the differences between the classical and romantic schools of art, he concludes that most great artists combine the qualities of both. "To discriminate schools, of art, of literature," he writes, "is, of course, part of the obvious business of literary criticism: but, in the work of literary production, it is easy to be overmuch occupied concerning them. For, in truth, the legitimate contention is, not of one age or school of literary art against another, but of all successive schools alike, against the stupidity which is dead to the substance, and the vulgarity which is dead to form."

From Studies in the History of the Renaissance

Preface

Many attempts have been made by writers on art and poetry to define beauty in the abstract, to express it in the most general terms, to find some universal formula for it. The value of these attempts has most often been in the suggestive and penetrating things said by the way. Such discussions help us very little to enjoy what has been well done in art or poetry, to discriminate between what is more and what is less excellent in them, or to use words like beauty, excellence, art, poetry, with a more precise meaning than they would otherwise have. Beauty, like all other qualities presented to human experience, is relative; and the definition of it becomes unmeaning and useless in proportion to its abstractness. To define beauty, not in the most abstract but in the most concrete terms possible, to find not its universal formula, but the formula which expresses most adequately this or that special manifestation of it, is the aim of the true student of aesthetics.

"To see the object as in itself it really is,"[1] has been justly said to be the aim of all true criticism whatever; and in aesthetic criticism the first step towards seeing one's object as it really is, is to know one's own impression as it really is, to discriminate it, to realize it distinctly. The objects with which aesthetic criticism deals—music, poetry, artistic and accomplished forms of human life—are indeed receptacles of so many powers or forces: they possess, like the products of nature, so many virtues or qualities. What is this song or picture, this engaging personality presented in life or in a book, to *me*? What effect does it really produce on me? Does it give me pleasure? and if so, what sort or degree of pleasure? How is my nature modified by its presence, and under its influence? The answers to these questions are the original facts with which the aesthetic critic has to do; and, as in the study of light, of morals, of number, one must realize such primary data for one's self, or not at all. And he who experiences these impressions strongly, and drives directly at the discrimination and analysis of them, has no need to trouble himself with the abstract question what beauty is in itself, or what its exact relation to truth or experience—metaphysical questions, as unprofitable as metaphysical questions elsewhere. He may pass them all by as being, answerable or not, of no interest to him.

The aesthetic critic, then, regards all the objects with which he has to do, all works of art, and the fairer forms of nature and human life, as powers or forces producing pleasurable sensations, each of a more or less peculiar or unique kind. This influence he feels, and wishes to explain, by analyzing and reducing it to its elements. To him, the picture, the landscape, the engaging personality in life or in a book, "La Gioconda," the hills of Carrara, Pico of Mirandola,[2] are valuable for their virtues, as we say, in speaking of a herb, a wine, a gem; for the property each has of affecting one with a special, a unique, impression of pleasure. Our education becomes complete in proportion as our susceptibility to these impressions increases in depth and variety. And the function of the aesthetic critic is to distinguish, to analyze, and separate from its adjuncts, the virtue by which a picture, a landscape, a fair personality in life or in a book, produces this special impression of beauty or pleasure, to indicate what the source of that impression is, and under what conditions it is experienced. His end is reached when he has disengaged that virtue, and noted it, as a chemist notes some natural element, for himself and others; and the rule for those who would reach this end is

1. Matthew Arnold, "The Function of Criticism at the Present Time" (1864; p. 450)
2. Pico della Mirandola (1463–1494), Italian philosopher and classical scholar, subject of an essay by Pater that was included in *Studies in the His-* *tory of the Renaissance*. "La Gioconda": another name for Leonardo da Vinci's painting the *Mona Lisa* (1503–6; see p. 588). "The hills of Carrara": marble quarries in Italy, particularly associated with Michelangelo (1475–1564).

stated with great exactness in the words of a recent critic of Sainte-Beuve: *De se borner à connaître de près les belles choses, et à s'en nourrir en exquis amateurs, en humanistes accomplis.*[3]

What is important, then, is not that the critic should possess a correct abstract definition of beauty for the intellect, but a certain kind of temperament, the power of being deeply moved by the presence of beautiful objects. He will remember always that beauty exists in many forms. To him all periods, types, schools of taste, are in themselves equal. In all ages there have been some excellent workmen, and some excellent work done. The question he asks is always: In whom did the stir, the genius, the sentiment of the period find itself? where was the receptacle of its refinement, its elevation, its taste? "The ages are all equal," says William Blake, "but genius is always above its age."[4]

Often it will require great nicety to disengage this virtue from the commoner elements with which it may be found in combination. Few artists, not Goethe or Byron even, work quite cleanly, casting off all debris, and leaving us only what the heat of their imagination has wholly fused and transformed. Take, for instance, the writings of Wordsworth. The heat of his genius, entering into the substance of his work, has crystallized a part, but only a part, of it; and in that great mass of verse there is much which might well be forgotten. But scattered up and down it, sometimes fusing and transforming entire compositions, like the stanzas on *Resolution and Independence,* or the *Ode on the Recollections of Childhood,*[5] sometimes, as if at random, depositing a fine crystal here or there, in a matter it does not wholly search through and transmute, we trace the action of his unique, incommunicable faculty, that strange, mystical sense of a life in natural things, and of man's life as a part of nature, drawing strength and color and character from local influences, from the hills and streams, and from natural sights and sounds. Well! that is the *virtue,* the active principle in Wordsworth's poetry; and then the function of the critic of Wordsworth is to follow up that active principle, to disengage it, to mark the degree in which it penetrates his verse.

The subjects of the following studies are taken from the history of the *Renaissance,* and touch what I think the chief points in that complex, many-sided movement. I have explained in the first of them what I understand by the word, giving it a much wider scope than was intended by those who originally used it to denote that revival of classical antiquity in the fifteenth century which was only one of many results of a general excitement and enlightening of the human mind, but of which the great aim and achievements of what, as Christian art, is often falsely opposed to the Renaissance, were another result. This outbreak of the human spirit may be traced far into the Middle Age itself, with its motives already clearly pronounced, the care for physical beauty, the worship of the body, the breaking down of those limits which the religious system of the Middle Age imposed on the heart and the imagination. I have taken as an example of this movement, this ear-

3. To confine themselves to knowing beautiful things intimately, and to sustain themselves by these, as sensitive amateurs and accomplished humanists do (French). In 1980 the editor Donald J. Hill discovered that this quotation is *by* the French man of letters Charles-Augustin Sainte-Beuve (1804–1869) rather than about him; therefore, Hill conjectures that "a recent critic" ought to be "a recent critique."

4. From Blake's annotations to *The Works of Sir Joshua Reynolds* (1778). The "genius" was the German artist Albrecht Dürer (1471–1528).

5. Wordsworth's ode is actually titled "Intimations of Immortality from Recollections of Early Childhood"; both poems were published in 1807.

lier Renaissance within the Middle Age itself, and as an expression of its qualities, two little compositions in early French; not because they constitute the best possible expression of them, but because they help the unity of my series, inasmuch as the Renaissance ends also in France, in French poetry, in a phase of which the writings of Joachim du Bellay[6] are in many ways the most perfect illustration. The Renaissance, in truth, put forth in France an aftermath, a wonderful later growth, the products of which have to the full that subtle and delicate sweetness which belongs to a refined and comely decadence, just as its earliest phases have the freshness which belongs to all periods of growth in art, the charm of *ascêsis*,[7] of the austere and serious girding of the loins in youth.

But it is in Italy, in the fifteenth century, that the interest of the Renaissance mainly lies—in that solemn fifteenth century which can hardly be studied too much, not merely for its positive results in the things of the intellect and the imagination, its concrete works of art, its special and prominent personalities, with their profound aesthetic charm, but for its general spirit and character, for the ethical qualities of which it is a consummate type.

The various forms of intellectual activity which together make up the culture of an age, move for the most part from different starting points, and by unconnected roads. As products of the same generation they partake indeed of a common character, and unconsciously illustrate each other; but of the producers themselves, each group is solitary, gaining what advantage or disadvantage there may be in intellectual isolation. Art and poetry, philosophy and the religious life, and that other life of refined pleasure and action in the conspicuous places of the world, are each of them confined to its own circle of ideas, and those who prosecute either of them are generally little curious of the thoughts of others. There come, however, from time to time, eras of more favorable conditions, in which the thoughts of men draw nearer together than is their wont, and the many interests of the intellectual world combine in one complete type of general culture. The fifteenth century in Italy is one of these happier eras, and what is sometimes said of the age of Pericles is true of that of Lorenzo:[8] it is an age productive in personalities, many-sided, centralized, complete. Here, artists and philosophers and those whom the action of the world has elevated and made keen, do not live in isolation, but breathe a common air, and catch light and heat from each other's thoughts. There is a spirit of general elevation and enlightenment in which all alike communicate. The unity of this spirit gives unity to all the various products of the Renaissance; and it is to this intimate alliance with mind, this participation in the best thoughts which that age produced, that the art of Italy in the fifteenth century owes much of its grave dignity and influence.

I have added an essay on Winckelmann,[9] as not incongruous with the studies which precede it, because Winckelmann, coming in the eighteenth century, really belongs in spirit to an earlier age. By his enthusiasm for the things of the intellect and the imagination for their own sake, by his Hellenism, his

---

6. French poet and critic (ca. 1522–1560), subject of another essay in *Studies of the History of the Renaissance*.
7. Asceticism (Greek).
8. Lorenzo de Medici (1449–1492, also known as Lorenzo the Magnificent), ruler of Florence and patron of the arts. Pericles (ca. 495–429 B.C.E.), a statesman who led Athens during its period of greatest political and cultural dominance.
9. Johann Joachim Winckelmann (1717–1768), German classicist.

lifelong struggle to attain to the Greek spirit, he is in sympathy with the humanists of a previous century. He is the last fruit of the Renaissance, and explains in a striking way its motive and tendencies.

["LA GIOCONDA"][1]

"La Gioconda" is, in the truest sense, Leonardo's masterpiece, the revealing instance of his mode of thought and work. In suggestiveness, only the "Melancholia" of Dürer is comparable to it; and no crude symbolism disturbs the effect of its subdued and graceful mystery. We all know the face and hands of the figure, set in its marble chair, in that circle of fantastic rocks, as in some faint light under sea. Perhaps of all ancient pictures time has chilled it least. As often happens with works in which invention seems to reach its limit, there is an element in it given to, not invented by, the master. In that inestimable folio of drawings, once in the possession of Vasari, were certain designs by Verrocchio,[2] faces of such impressive beauty that Leonardo in his boyhood copied them many times. It is hard not to connect with these designs of the elder, by-past master, as with its germinal principle, the unfathomable smile, always with a touch of something sinister in it, which plays over all Leonardo's work. Besides, the picture is a portrait. From childhood we see this image defining itself on the fabric of his dreams, and but for express historical testimony, we might fancy that this was but his ideal lady, embodied and beheld at last. What was the relationship of a living Florentine to this creature of his thought? By what strange affinities had the dream and the person grown up thus apart, and yet so closely together? Present from the first incorporeally in Leonardo's brain, dimly traced in the designs of Verrocchio, she is found present at last in Il Giocondo's house. That there is much of mere portraiture in the picture is attested by the legend that by artificial means, the presence of mimes[3] and flute-players, that subtle expression was protracted on the face. Again, was it in four years and by renewed labor never really completed, or in four months and as by stroke of magic, that the image was projected?

The presence that rose thus so strangely beside the waters, is expressive of what in the ways of a thousand years men had come to desire. Hers is the head upon which all "the ends of the world are come,"[4] and the eyelids are a little weary. It is a beauty wrought out from within upon the flesh, the deposit, little cell by cell, of strange thoughts and fantastic reveries and exquisite passions. Set it for a moment beside one of those white Greek goddesses or beautiful women of antiquity, and how would they be troubled by this beauty, into which the soul with all its maladies has passed! All the thoughts and experience of the world have etched and molded there, in that which they have of power to refine and make expressive the outward form, the animalism of Greece, the lust of Rome, the mysticism of the Middle Age

---

1. Or *Mona Lisa*, the famous painting by Leonardo da Vinci (1452–1519) that now hangs in the Louvre in Paris. The sitter for the portrait may have been Lisa, the third wife of the Florentine Francesco del Giocondo (to whom Pater refers as "Il Giocondo")—hence her title, La Gioconda. *Mona* (more correctly *Monna*) *Lisa* means "Madonna Lisa" or "My Lady Lisa." This selection

is drawn from the essay on Leonardo.
2. Andrea del Verrocchio (1435–1488), Florentine painter and sculptor. Giorgio Vasari (1511–1574), author of *Lives of the Most Excellent Italian Painters* (1550).
3. Mimics or clowns.
4. 1 Corinthians 10.11.

with its spiritual ambition and imaginative loves, the return of the Pagan world, the sins of the Borgias.[5] She is older than the rocks among which she sits; like the vampire, she has been dead many times, and learned the secrets of the grave; and has been a diver in deep seas, and keeps their fallen day about her; and trafficked for strange webs with Eastern merchants, and, as Leda, was the mother of Helen of Troy,[6] and, as Saint Anne, the mother of Mary; and all this has been to her but as the sound of lyres and flutes, and lives only in the delicacy with which it has molded the changing lineaments, and tinged the eyelids and the hands. The fancy of a perpetual life, sweeping together ten thousand experiences, is an old one; and modern philosophy has conceived the idea of humanity as wrought upon by, and summing up in itself, all modes of thought and life. Certainly Lady Lisa might stand as the embodiment of the old fancy, the symbol of the modern idea.

Conclusion[7]

Λέγει που Ἡράκλειτος ὅτι πάντα χωρεῖ καὶ οὐδὲν μένει[8]

To regard all things and principles of things as inconstant modes or fashions has more and more become the tendency of modern thought. Let us begin with that which is without—our physical life. Fix upon it in one of its more exquisite intervals, the moment, for instance, of delicious recoil from the flood of water in summer heat. What is the whole physical life in that moment but a combination of natural elements to which science gives their names? But those elements, phosphorus and lime and delicate fibers, are present not in the human body alone: we detect them in places most remote from it. Our physical life is a perpetual motion of them—the passage of the blood, the waste and repairing of the lenses of the eye, the modification of the tissues of the brain under every ray of light and sound—processes which science reduces to simpler and more elementary forces. Like the elements of which we are composed, the action of these forces extends beyond us: it rusts iron and ripens corn.[9] Far out on every side of us those elements are broadcast, driven in many currents; and birth and gesture and death and the springing of violets from the grave are but a few out of ten thousand resultant combinations. That clear, perpetual outline of face and limb is but an image of ours, under which we group them—a design in a web, the actual threads of which pass out beyond it. This at least of flamelike our life has, that it is but the concurrence, renewed from moment to moment, of forces parting sooner or later on their ways.

Or, if we begin with the inward world of thought and feeling, the whirlpool is still more rapid, the flame more eager and devouring. There it is no longer the gradual darkening of the eye, the gradual fading of colour from the wall— movements of the shore-side, where the water flows down indeed, though in

---

5. A powerful Italian family during the Renaissance, notorious for scandalous conduct.
6. Helen's father was Zeus (who approached Leda in the form of a swan).
7. This brief "Conclusion" was omitted in the second edition of this book, as I conceived it might possibly mislead some of those young men into whose hands it might fall. On the whole, I have thought it best to reprint it here, with some

slight changes which bring it closer to my original meaning. I have dealt more fully in *Marius the Epicurean* with the thoughts suggested by it [Pater's note to the 3rd edition, 1888].
8. Heraclitus says, "All things give way; nothing remaineth" [Pater's translation]. The Greek philosopher was active ca. 500 B.C.E.
9. Grain.

apparent rest—but the race of the midstream, a drift of momentary acts of sight and passion and thought. At first sight experience seems to bury us under a flood of external objects, pressing upon us with a sharp and importunate reality, calling us out of ourselves in a thousand forms of action. But when reflection begins to play upon those objects they are dissipated under its influence; the cohesive force seems suspended like some trick of magic; each object is loosed into a group of impressions—colour, odour, texture—in the mind of the observer. And if we continue to dwell in thought on this world, not of objects in the solidity with which language invests them, but of impressions, unstable, flickering, inconsistent, which burn and are extinguished with our consciousness of them, it contracts still further: the whole scope of observation is dwarfed into the narrow chamber of the individual mind. Experience, already reduced to a group of impressions, is ringed round for each one of us by that thick wall of personality through which no real voice has ever pierced on its way to us, or from us to that which we can only conjecture to be without. Every one of those impressions is the impression of the individual in his isolation, each mind keeping as a solitary prisoner its own dream of a world. Analysis goes a step farther still, and assures us that those impressions of the individual mind to which, for each one of us, experience dwindles down, are in perpetual flight; that each of them is limited by time, and that as time is infinitely divisible, each of them is infinitely divisible also; all that is actual in it being a single moment, gone while we try to apprehend it, of which it may ever be more truly said that it has ceased to be than that it is. To such a tremulous wisp constantly reforming itself on the stream, to a single sharp impression, with a sense in it, a relic more or less fleeting, of such moments gone by, what is real in our life fines itself down. It is with this movement, with the passage and dissolution of impressions, images, sensations, that analysis leaves off—that continual vanishing away, that strange, perpetual weaving and unweaving of ourselves.

Philosophiren, says Novalis, *ist dephlegmatisiren, vivificiren.*[1] The service of philosophy, of speculative culture, towards the human spirit is to rouse, to startle it to a life of constant and eager observation. Every moment some form grows perfect in hand or face; some tone on the hills or the sea is choicer than the rest; some mood of passion or insight or intellectual excitement is irresistibly real and attractive to us—for that moment only. Not the fruit of experience, but experience itself, is the end. A counted number of pulses only is given to us of a variegated, dramatic life. How may we see in them all that is to be seen in them by the finest senses? How shall we pass most swiftly from point to point, and be present always at the focus where the greatest number of vital forces unite in their purest energy?

To burn always with this hard, gemlike flame, to maintain this ecstasy, is success in life. In a sense it might even be said that our failure is to form habits: for, after all, habit is relative to a stereotyped world, and meantime it is only the roughness of the eye that makes any two persons, things, situations, seem alike. While all melts under our feet, We may well grasp at any exquisite passion, or any contribution to knowledge that seems by a lifted

---

1. To philosophize is to cast off inertia, to make oneself alive (German). "Novalis" was the pseudonym of Friedrich von Hardenberg (1772–1801), German Romantic writer.

horizon to set the spirit free for a moment, or any stirring of the senses, strange dyes, strange colours, and curious odours, or work of the artist's hands, or the face of one's friend. Not to discriminate every moment some passionate attitude in those about us, and in the very brilliancy of their gifts some tragic dividing of forces on their ways, is, on this short day of frost and sun, to sleep before evening. With this sense of the splendour of our experience and of its awful[2] brevity, gathering all we are into one desperate effort to see and touch, we shall hardly have time to make theories about the things we see and touch. What we have to do is to be forever curiously testing new opinions and courting new impressions, never acquiescing in a facile orthodoxy of Comte, or of Hegel,[3] or of our own. Philosophical theories or ideas, as points of view, instruments of criticism, may help us to gather up what might otherwise pass unregarded by us. "Philosophy is the microscope of thought."[4] The theory or idea or system which requires of us the sacrifice of any part of this experience, in consideration of some interest into which we cannot enter, or some abstract theory we have not identified with ourselves, or of what is only conventional, has no real claim upon us.

One of the most beautiful passages of Rousseau[5] is that in the sixth book of the *Confessions,* where he describes the awakening in him of the literary sense. An undefinable taint of death had clung always about him, and now in early manhood he believed himself smitten by mortal disease. He asked himself how he might make as much as possible of the interval that remained; and he was not biased by anything in his previous life when he decided that it must be by intellectual excitement, which he found just then in the clear, fresh writings of Voltaire.[6] Well! we are all *condamnés* as Victor Hugo[7] says: we are all under sentence of death but with a sort of indefinite reprieve—*les hommes sont tous condamnés à mort avec des sursis indéfinis*: we have an interval, and then our place knows us no more. Some spend this interval in listlessness, some in high passions, the wisest, at least among "the children of this world,"[8] in art and song. For our one chance lies in expanding that interval, in getting as many pulsations as possible into the given time. Great passions may give us this quickened sense of life, ecstasy and sorrow of love, the various forms of enthusiastic activity, disinterested or otherwise, which come naturally to many of us. Only be sure it is passion—that it does yield you this fruit of a quickened, multiplied consciousness. Of such wisdom, the poetic passion, the desire of beauty, the love of art for its own sake, has most. For art comes to you proposing frankly to give nothing but the highest quality to your moments as they pass, and simply for those moments' sake.

1868   1873

---

2. Awe-inspiring.
3. Georg W. F. Hegel (1770–1831), German idealistic philosopher. Auguste Comte (1798–1857), French founder of positivism.
4. The quotation is taken from the novel *Les Misérables* (1862) by the French writer Victor Hugo (1802–1885).
5. Jean-Jacques Rousseau (1712–1778), Swiss-

born French political theorist and philosopher; his *Confessions* were published in 1781 and 1788.
6. The pen name of the French author and philosopher François-Marie Arouet (1694–1778).
7. The quotation is taken from his work *Le Dernier Jour d'un Condamné* (*The Last Day of a Condemned Man,* 1832).
8. Luke 16.8.

GERARD MANLEY HOPKINS
1844–1889

I t has been said that the most important date in Gerard Manley Hopkins's career was 1918, twenty-nine years after his death, for it was then that the first publication of his poems made them accessible to the world of readers. During his lifetime these remarkable poems, most of them celebrating the wonders of God's creation, had been known only to a small circle of friends, including his literary executor, the poet Robert Bridges, who waited until 1918 before releasing them to a publisher. Partly because his work was first made public in a twentieth-century volume, but especially because of his striking experiments in meter and diction, Hopkins was widely hailed as a pioneering figure of "modern" literature, miraculously unconnected with his fellow Victorian poets (who during the 1920s and 1930s were largely out of fashion among critical readers). And this way of classifying and evaluating his writings has long persisted. In 1936 a substantial selection of his poems led off *The Faber Book of Modern Verse,* one of the most influential anthologies of the century, featuring poets such as W. H. Auden, Dylan Thomas, and T. S. Eliot (the only one whose selections occupy more pages than those allotted to Hopkins). And the first four editions of *The Norton Anthology of English Literature* (1962–79) grouped Hopkins with these twentieth-century poets. To reclassify him is not to repudiate his earlier reputation as a modern but rather to suggest that his work can be better understood and appreciated if it is restored to the Victorian world out of which it developed.

Hopkins was born near London into a large and cultivated family in comfortable circumstances. After a brilliant career at Highgate School, he entered Oxford in 1863, where he was exposed to a variety of Victorian ways of thinking, both secular and religious. Among the influential leaders at Oxford was Matthew Arnold, professor of poetry; but more important for Hopkins was his tutor, Walter Pater, an aesthetician whose emphasis on the intense apprehension of sensuous beauty struck a responsive chord in Hopkins. At Oxford he was also exposed to the Broad Church theology of one of the tutors at his college (Balliol), Benjamin Jowett. But Hopkins became increasingly attracted first to the High Church movement represented at Oxford by Edward Pusey, and then to Roman Catholicism. Profoundly influenced by John Henry Newman's conversion to Rome and by subsequent conversations with Newman, Hopkins entered the Roman Catholic Church in 1866. The estrangement from his family that resulted from his conversion was very painful for him; his parents' letters to him were so "terrible" (he reported to Newman) that he could not bear to "read them twice." And this alienation was heightened by his decision not only to become a Roman Catholic but to become a priest and, in particular, a Jesuit priest, for many Victorian Protestants regarded the Jesuit order with a special distrust. For the rest of his life, Hopkins served as a priest and teacher in various places, among them Oxford, Liverpool, and Lancashire. In 1884 he was appointed professor of classics at University College in Dublin.

At school and at Oxford in the early 1860s, Hopkins had written poems in the vein of John Keats. He burned most of these early writings after his conversion (although drafts survive), for he believed that his vocation must require renouncing such personal satisfactions as the writing of poems. Only after his superiors in the church encouraged him to do so did he resume writing poetry. Yet during the seven years of silence, as his letters show, he had been thinking about experimenting with what he called a "new rhythm." The result, in 1876, was his rhapsodic lyric-narrative, "The Wreck of the Deutschland," a long ode about the wreck of a ship in which five Franciscan nuns were drowned. The style of the poem was so distinctive that the editor of the Jesuit magazine to which he had submitted it "dared not print it," as Hopkins reported. During the remaining fourteen years of his life, Hopkins wrote poems but seldom submitted them for publication, partly because he was convinced that poetic fame was incompatible with his religious vocation but also because of a fear that readers would be discouraged by the eccentricity of his work.

Hopkins's sense of his own uniqueness is in accord with the larger philosophy that informs his poetry. Drawing on the theology of Duns Scotus, a medieval philosopher, he felt that everything in the universe was characterized by what he called *inscape,* the distinctive design that constitutes individual identity. This identity is not static but dynamic. Each being in the universe "selves," that is, enacts its identity. And the human being, the most highly selved, the most individually distinctive being in the universe, recognizes the inscape of other beings in an act that Hopkins calls *instress,* the apprehension of an object in an intense thrust of energy toward it that enables one to realize its specific distinctiveness. Ultimately, the instress of inscape leads one to Christ, for the individual identity of any object is the stamp of divine creation on it. In the act of instress, therefore, the human being becomes a celebrant of the divine, at once recognizing God's creation and enacting his or her own God-given identity within it.

Poetry for Hopkins enacts this celebration. It is instress, and it realizes the inscape of its subject in its own distinctive design. Hopkins wrote, "But as air, melody, is what strikes me most of all in music and design in painting, so design, pattern or what I am in the habit of calling 'inscape' is what I above all aim at in poetry." To create inscape, Hopkins seeks to give each poem a unique design that captures the initial inspiration when he is "caught" by his subject. Many of the characteristics of Hopkins's style—his disruption of conventional syntax, his coining and compounding of words, his use of ellipsis and repetition—can be understood as ways of representing the stress and action of the brain in moments of inspiration. He creates compounds to represent the unique interlocking of the characteristics of an object—"piece-bright," "dapple-dawn-drawn," "blue-bleak." He omits syntactical connections to fuse qualities more intensely—"the dearest freshness deep down things." He creates puns to suggest how God's creation rhymes and chimes in a divine patterning. He violates conventional syntactic order to represent the shape of mental experience. In the act of imaginative apprehension, a language particular to the moment generates itself.

Hopkins also uses a new rhythm to give each poem its distinctive design. In the new metric system he created, which he called *sprung rhythm,* lines have a given number of stresses, but the number and placement of unstressed syllables is highly variable. Hopkins rarely marks all the intended stresses, only those that readers might not anticipate. To indicate stressed syllables, Hopkins often uses both the stress (´) and the "great stress" (῀). A curved line marks an "outride"—one or more syllables added to a foot but not counted in the scansion of the line; they indicate a stronger stress on the preceding syllable and a short pause after the outride. Here, for example, is the scansion for the first three lines of "The Windhover":

> I caúght this mórning mórning's mínion, kíng-
> dom of dáylight's daúphin, dapple-dawn-drawn Fálcon, in his ríding
> Of the rólling level underneáth him steady aír, and stríding

Hopkins argued that sprung rhythm was the natural rhythm of common speech and written prose, as well as of music. He found a model for it in Old English poetry and in nursery rhymes, but he claimed that it had not been used in English poetry since the Elizabethan age.

The density and difficulty that result from Hopkins's unconventional rhythm and syntax make his poetry seem modern, but his concern with the imagination's shaping of the natural world puts him very much in the Romantic tradition; and his creation of a rough and difficult style, designed to capture the mind's own motion, resembles the style of Robert Browning. "A horrible thing has happened to me," Hopkins wrote in 1864, "I have begun to *doubt* Tennyson." He criticizes Tennyson for using the grand style as a smooth and habitual poetic speech. Like Algernon Charles Swinburne, Walter Pater, and Henry James as well as Browning, Hopkins displays a new mannerism, characteristic of the latter part of the nineteenth century, which paradoxically combines an elaborate aestheticism with a more complex representation of consciousness.

In Hopkins's early poetry his singular apprehension of the beauty of individual objects always brings him to an ecstatic illumination of the presence of God. But in his late poems, the so-called terrible sonnets, his distinctive individuality comes to isolate him from the God who made him thus. Hopkins wrote, "To me there is no resemblance: searching nature, I taste *self* but at one tankard, that of my own being." In the terrible sonnets Hopkins confronts the solipsism to which his own stress on individuality seems to lead him. Like the mad speakers of so many Victorian dramatic monologues, he cannot escape a world solely of his own imagining. Yet even these poems of despair, which simultaneously echo the bleaker side of the Romantic tradition and anticipate more modern attitudes, reflect a traditional religious vision: the dark night of the soul as described by the Spanish mystic Saint John of the Cross.

In his introduction to *The Oxford Book of Modern Verse,* Yeats calls Hopkins's poetry "a last development of poetical diction." Yeats's remark indicates the anomaly that Hopkins's work poses. Perhaps it is only appropriate for a writer who stressed the uniqueness of inscape to strike us with the individuality of his achievement.

God's Grandeur

The world is charged with the grandeur of God.
    It will flame out, like shining from shook foil;[1]
    It gathers to a greatness, like the ooze of oil
Crushed.[2] Why do men then now not reck his rod?
5 Generations have trod, have trod, have trod;
    And all is seared with trade; bleared, smeared with toil;
    And wears man's smudge and shares man's smell: the soil
Is bare now, nor can foot feel, being shod.

And for° all this, nature is never spent;   *despite*
10   There lives the dearest freshness deep down things;
And though the last lights off the black West went
    Oh, morning, at the brown brink eastward, springs—
Because the Holy Ghost over the bent
    World broods with warm breast and with ah! bright wings.

1877   1918

1. Hopkins explained this image in a letter: "I mean foil in its sense of leaf or tinsel. . . . Shaken goldfoil gives off broad glares like sheet lightning and also, and this is true of nothing else, owing to its zigzag dints and creasings and network of small many cornered facets, a sort of fork lightning too."
2. I.e., from the crushing of olives.

The Starlight Night

Look at the stars! look, look up at the skies!
  O look at all the fire-folk sitting in the air!
  The bright boroughs, the circle-citadels there!
Down in dim woods the diamond delves!° the elves'-eyes!   *quarries*
5   The grey lawns cold where gold, where quickgold;[1] lies!
  Wind-beat whitebeam! airy abeles° set on a flare!   *white poplars*
  Flake-doves sent floating forth at a farmyard scare!—
Ah well! it is all a purchase, all is a prize.

Buy then! bid then!—What?—Prayer, patience, alms, vows.
10   Look, look: a May-mess,[2] like on orchard boughs!
  Look! March-bloom, like on mealed-with-yellow sallows![3]
These are indeed the barn; withindoors house
The shocks. This piece-bright paling[4] shuts the spouse
  Christ home, Christ and his mother and all his hallows.°   *saints*

1877   1918

As Kingfishers[1] Catch Fire

As kingfishers catch fire, dragonflies draw flame;
  As tumbled over rim in roundy wells
  Stones ring; like each tucked° string tells, each hung bell's   *plucked*
Bow swung finds tongue to fling out broad its name;
5 Each mortal thing does one thing and the same:
  Deals out that being indoors° each one dwells;   *within*
  Selves[2]—goes itself; *myself* it speaks and spells,
Crying *What I do is me: for that I came.*

I say more: the just man justices;[3]
10   Keeps gráce: thát keeps all his goings graces;
Acts in God's eye what in God's eye he is—
  Chríst. For Christ plays in ten thousand places,
Lovely in limbs, and lovely in eyes not his
  To the Father through the features of men's faces.

1877   1918

---

1. Coined by analogy with quicksilver. The starlight night resembles the lawns below it, where the dew, reflecting the starlight, looks like gold.
2. A profusion of growing things such as May blossoms.
3. Willows, here with yellow spots like meal.

4. This word choice connects the upright siding of the barn's walls to the planks (or "pales") of a fence. "Shocks": sheaves of grain.
1. Small, brightly colored birds.
2. Fulfills its individuality.
3. Acts in a just manner.

Spring

Nothing is so beautiful as Spring—
   When weeds, in wheels, shoot long and lovely and lush;
   Thrush's eggs look little low heavens, and thrush
Through the echoing timber does so rinse and wring
5   The ear, it strikes like lightnings to hear him sing;
   The glassy peartree leaves and blooms, they brush
   The descending blue; that blue is all in a rush
With richness; the racing lambs too have fair their fling.

What is all this juice and all this joy?
10   A strain of the earth's sweet being in the beginning
In Eden garden.—Have, get, before it cloy,
   Before it cloud, Christ, lord, and sour with sinning,
Innocent mind and Mayday in girl and boy,
   Most, O maid's child,[1] thy choice and worthy the winning.

1877   1918

The Windhover[1]

To Christ our Lord

I caught this morning morning's minion,° king-   *darling*
   dom of daylight's dauphin,[2] dapple-dawn-drawn Falcon, in his riding
   Of the rolling level underneath him steady air, and striding
High there, how he rung upon the rein[3] of a wimpling° wing   *rippling*
5 In his ecstasy! then off, off forth on swing,
   As a skate's heel sweeps smooth on a bow-bend: the hurl and gliding
   Rebuffed the big wind. My heart in hiding
Stirred for a bird,—the achieve of, the mastery of the thing!

Brute beauty and valour and act, oh, air, pride, plume, here
10   Buckle![4] AND the fire that breaks from thee then, a billion
Times told lovelier, more dangerous, O my chevalier!°   *knight*

No wonder of it: shéer plód makes plough down sillion[5]
Shine, and blue-bleak embers, ah my dear,
   Fall, gall[6] themselves, and gash gold-vermilion.

1877   1918

---

1. Jesus, son of the Virgin Mary.
1. Kestrel, a small falcon noted for hovering in the air.
2. A prince who is heir to the French throne.
3. Circled at the end of a rein.
4. The verb can be read as imperative or indica-
tive. All three meanings are relevant: to prepare for action, to fasten together, to collapse.
5. The ridge between two furrows of a plowed field.
6. Break the surface of.

Pied[1] Beauty

Glory be to God for dappled things—
    For skies of couple-colour as a brinded[2] cow;
      For rose-moles all in stipple upon trout that swim;
Fresh-firecoal chestnut-falls,[3] finches' wings;
5   Landscape plotted and pieced—fold, fallow, and plough;[4]
      And áll trádes, their gear and tackle and trim.°   *equipment*

All things counter,° original, spare,° strange;   *contrary / rare*
    Whatever is fickle, freckled (who knows how?)
    With swift, slow; sweet, sour; adazzle, dim;
10 He fathers-forth whose beauty is past change:
               Praise him.

1877   1918

Hurrahing in Harvest

Summer ends now; now, barbarous in beauty, the stooks[1] rise
Around; up above, what wind-walks! what lovely behaviour
Of silk-sack clouds! has wilder, wilful-wavier
Meal-drift moulded ever and melted across skies?

5 I walk, I lift up, I lift up heart, eyes,
    Down all that glory in the heavens to glean our Saviour;
And, éyes, heárt, what looks, what lips yet gave you a
Rapturous love's greeting of realer, of rounder replies?

And the azurous hung hills are his world-wielding shoulder
10 Majestic—as a stallion stalwart, very-violet-sweet!—
These things, these things were here and but the beholder
Wanting; which two when they once meet,
The heart rears wings bold and bolder
And hurls for him, O half hurls earth for him off under his feet.

1877   1918

1. Of two or more colors in blotches, variegated.
2. Brownish orange in color with streaks of gray.
3. I.e., freshly fallen chestnuts, bright as coals.
4. Divided into fields used as pastures ("fold"), lying fallow, or plowed for cultivation. The landscape thus appears like patches of different colors.
1. Sheaves of grain.

Binsey Poplars

felled 1879

My aspens dear, whose airy cages quelled,
Quelled or quenched in leaves the leaping sun,
All felled, felled, are all felled;
  Of a fresh and following folded rank
5   Not spared, not one
        That dandled a sandalled
      Shadow that swam or sank
On meadow and river and wind-wandering
    weed-winding bank.

10 O if we but knew what we do
      When we delve° or hew—   *dig*
    Hack and rack° the growing green!   *torture*
      Since country is so tender
    To touch, her being só slender,
15   That, like this sleek and seeing ball°   *the eye*
    But a prick will make no eye at all,
    Where we, even where we mean
      To mend her we end her,
      When we hew or delve:
20 After-comers cannot guess the beauty been.
      Ten or twelve, only ten or twelve
    Strokes of havoc únselve°   *rob of self*
      The sweet especial scene,
      Rural scene, a rural scene,
25   Sweet especial rural scene.

1879   1918

Duns Scotus's Oxford[1]

Towery city and branchy between towers;
Cuckoo-echoing, bell-swarmèd, lark-charmèd, rook-racked, river-rounded;
The dapple-eared lily below thee; that country and town did
Once encounter in, here coped and poisèd powers;

5 Thou hast a base and brickish skirt there, sours
That neighbour-nature thy grey beauty is grounded
Best in;[2] graceless growth, thou hast confounded
Rural rural keeping—folk, flocks, and flowers.

---

1. Duns Scotus, the medieval theologian, lectured at Oxford about 1301. His idea that individuality is the final perfection of any creature influenced Hopkins's conception of inscape. When Hopkins came on two of Scotus's commentaries in 1872, he wrote that he was immediately "flush with a new stroke of enthusiasm . . . when I took in any inscape of the sky or sea I thought of Scotus."

2. Hopkins contrasts the "here" of the "grey beauty" of the medieval city of Oxford, where country and town are both protected ("coped," as

Yet ah! this air I gather and I release
10 He lived on; these weeds and waters, these walls are what
He haunted who of all men most sways my spirits to peace;

Of realty° the rarest-veinèd unraveller; a not   *reality*
Rivalled insight, be rival Italy or Greece;
Who fired France for Mary without spot.[3]

1879   1918

Felix Randal

Felix Randal the farrier,° O is he dead then? my duty   *blacksmith*
   all ended,
Who have watched his mould of man, big-boned and hardy-handsome
Pining, pining, till time when reason rambled in it and some
Fatal four disorders, fleshed there, all contended?

5 Sickness broke him. Impatient, he cursed at first, but mended
Being anointed[1] and all; though a heavenlier heart began some
Months earlier, since I had our sweet reprieve and ransom[2]
Tendered to him. Ah well, God rest him all road ever[3] he offended!
This seeing the sick endears them to us, us too it endears.
10 My tongue had taught thee comfort, touch had quenched thy tears,
Thy tears that touched my heart, child, Felix, poor Felix Randal;
How far from then forethought of, all thy more boisterous years,
When thou at the random[4] grim forge, powerful amidst peers,
Didst fettle° for the great grey drayhorse his bright and   *prepare*
   battering sandal!

1880   1918

Spring and Fall:[1]

to a young child

Márgarét, áre you gríeving
Over Goldengrove unleaving?
Leáves, líke the things of man, you
With your fresh thoughts care for, can you?
5 Áh! ás the heart grows older

---

within a priest's cloak) and in equilibrium ("poisèd powers"), with the "there" of its new surburban "brickish skirt" (housing developments and industrial complexes that were built around the perimeter of the city in the 19th century).
3. In Paris, Scotus was influential in defending the doctrine of the Immaculate Conception—i.e., that Mary's mother, St. Anne, conceived her daughter without sin.
1. In Extreme Unction (the sacrament for the dying.)

2. Holy Communion preceded by confession and absolution.
3. In whatever way.
4. Built with stones of irregular size and shape.
1. This deceptively simple poem is deeply informed by Christian theology: according to Catholic doctrine, the fall of Adam and Eve brought into the world both mortality and the legacy of Original Sin for all human beings ("the blight man was born for").

It will come to such sights colder
By and by, nor spare a sigh
Though worlds of wanwood leafmeal[2] lie;
And yet you *will* weep and know why.
10 Now no matter, child, the name:
Sórrow's spríngs áre the same.
Nor mouth had, no nor mind, expressed
What heart heard of, ghost° guessed: spirit
It ís the blight man was born for,
15 It is Margaret you mourn for.

1880   1918

[Carrion Comfort][1]

Not, I'll not, carrion comfort, Despair, not feast on thee,[2]
Not untwist—slack they may be—these last strands of man
In me ór, most weary, cry *I can no more*. I can;
Can something, hope, wish day come, not choose not to be.

5 But ah, but O thou terrible, why wouldst thou rude on me
Thy wring-world right foot rock?[3] lay a lionlimb against me?
      scan
With darksome devouring eyes my bruisèd bones? and fan,
O in turns of tempest, me heaped there; me frantic to avoid
      thee and flee?

Why? That my chaff might fly; my grain lie,[4] sheer and clear.
10 Nay in all that toil, that coil,° since (seems) I kissed the rod,   tumult
Hand rather,[5] my heart lo! lapped strength, stole joy, would
      laugh, chéer.
Cheer whom though? The Hero whose heaven-handling
      flung me, fóot tród
Me? or me that fought him? O which one? is it each one?
      That night, that year
Of now done darkness I wretch lay wrestling with (my God!)
      my God.

1885   1918

<hr>

2. Coined by analogy with piecemeal. "Wanwood": pale or dim; the forest may be pale because
of light-colored autumn leaves or dim because
light is filtered through the leaves.
1. This title was supplied by Hopkins's literary
executor, the poet Robert Bridges (1844–1930).
The poem is one of the "terrible sonnets," as are
the three following poems.
2. The satisfaction of giving in to despair as a
kind of "comfort" is implicitly likened to a vulture's satisfaction in feasting on dead flesh.
3. I.e., why would you roughly rock me with your
world-wringing right foot?
4. Metaphors of winnowing, or removing the
empty husks ("chaff") that are blown away from
the valuable grain that remains, appear frequently in the Bible to represent the separation of
virtue from wickedness. See, e.g., Psalms 1.4,
Luke 3.16–17.
5. I.e., the hand that wields the rod.

No worst, there is none

No worst, there is none. Pitched past pitch of grief,
More pangs will, schooled at forepangs, wilder wring.
Comforter, where, where is your comforting?
Mary, mother of us, where is your relief?

5　My cries heave, herds-long;[1] huddle in a main, a chief-
woe, world-sorrow; on an age-old anvil wince and sing—
Then lull, then leave off. Fury had shrieked "No ling-
ering! Let me be fell:° force[2] I must be brief."　　　　*fierce, cruel*
O the mind, mind has mountains; cliffs of fall
10　Frightful, sheer, no-man-fathomed. Hold them cheap
May who ne'er hung there. Nor does long our small
Durance° deal with that steep or deep. Here! creep,　　*endurance*
Wretch, under a comfort serves in a whirlwind: all
Life death does end and each day dies with sleep.

1885　　　　　　　　　　　　　　　　　　　　　　　　　　　　1918

I wake and feel the fell of dark, not day

I wake and feel the fell° of dark, not day.　　　　　　*cruelty*
What hours, O what black hoürs we have spent
This night! what sights you, heart, saw; ways you went!
And more must, in yet longer light's delay.

5　With witness I speak this. But where I say
Hours I mean years, mean life. And my lament
Is cries countless, cries like dead letters[1] sent
To dearest him that lives alas! away.

I am gall, I am heartburn. God's most deep decree
10　Bitter would have me taste: my taste was me;
Bones built in me, flesh filled, blood brimmed the curse.

Selfyeast of spirit a dull dough sours. I see
The lost are like this, and their scourge to be
As I am mine, their sweating selves; but worse.

1885　　　　　　　　　　　　　　　　　　　　　　　　　　　　1918

1. Like the succession of cries made by cattle that
have been following one another in a long line.
2. Necessarily, inevitably.

1. Letters undelivered or returned to the sender
by the post office.

That Nature Is a Heraclitean Fire[1] and of the Comfort of the Resurrection

Cloud-puffball, torn tufts, tossed pillows | flaunt forth, then chevy°   *race*
    on an air-
built thoroughfare: heaven-roysterers,° in gay-gangs | they   *swaggerers*
    throng; they glitter in marches.
Down roughcast, down dazzling whitewash, | wherever an elm arches.
Shivelights and shadowtackle[2] in long | lashes lace, lance, and pair.
5 Delightfully the bright wind boisterous | ropes, wrestles, beats earth bare
Of yestertempest's creases; in pool and rut peel parches[3]
Squandering ooze to squeezed | dough, crust, dust; stanches, starches
Squadroned masks and manmarks[4] | treadmire toil there
Footfretted in it. Million-fuelèd, | nature's bonfire burns on.
10 But quench her bonniest, dearest | to her, her clearest-selvèd° *most individual*
          spark
Man, how fast his firedint | his mark on mind, is gone!
Both are in an unfathomable, all is in an enormous dark
Drowned. O pity and indig | nation! Manshape, that shone
Sheer off, disseveral,° a star, | death blots black out; nor mark   *separate*
15   Is any of him at all so stark
But vastness blurs and time | beats level. Enough! the Resurrection,
A heart's-clarion! Away grief's gasping, | joyless days, dejection.
          Across my foundering deck shone
A beacon, an eternal beam. | Flesh fade, and mortal trash
20 Fall to the residuary worm; | world's wildfire, leave but ash:
          In a flash, at a trumpet crash,
I am all at once what Christ is, | since he was what I am, and
This Jack, joke, poor potsherd, | patch, matchwood,[5] immortal diamond,
          Is immortal diamond.

1888   1918

Thou art indeed just, Lord

*Justus quidem tu es, Domine, si disputem tecum; verumtamen justa
loquar ad te: Quare via impiorum prosperatur? &c.[1]*

Thou art indeed just, Lord, if I contend
With thee; but, sir, so what I plead is just.
Why do sinners' ways prosper? and why must
Disappointment all I endeavour end?

---

1. The Greek philosopher Heraclitus (flourished ca. 500 B.C.E.) taught that all things are in flux and that they ultimately return to the basic principle of fire.
2. Branches imagined as the shadows of a ship's rigging. "Shivelights": strips of light.
3. Ruts described as peeled places. "Parches" is a verb whose subject is *wind*.

4. The marks that people have made on the earth by walking ("footfretted") on it.
5. Kindling. "Jack": ordinary man.
1. "Righteous art thou, O Lord, when I plead with thee: yet let me talk with thee of thy judgments: Wherefore doth the way of the wicked prosper?" (Jeremiah 12.1). The Latin was Hopkins's title.

5   Wert thou my enemy, O thou my friend,
How wouldst thou worse, I wonder, than thou dost
Defeat, thwart me? Oh, the sots and thralls of lust
Do in spare hours more thrive than I that spend,

    Sir, life upon thy cause. See, banks and brakes°   *thickets*
10   Now, leavèd how thick! lacèd they are again
With fretty chervil,[2] look, and fresh wind shakes

    Them; birds build—but not I build; no, but strain,
Time's eunuch, and not breed one work that wakes.
Mine, O thou lord of life, send my roots rain.

1889   1918

From Journal[1]

May 3 [1866]. Cold. Morning raw and wet, afternoon fine. Walked then with Addis, crossing Bablock Hythe, round by Skinner's Weir[2] through many fields into the Witney road. Sky sleepy blue without liquidity. From Cumnor Hill saw St. Philip's and the other spires through blue haze rising pale in a pink light. On further side of the Witney road hills, just fleeced with grain or other green growth, by their dips and waves foreshortened here and there and so differenced in brightness and opacity the green on them, with delicate effect. On left, brow of the near hill glistening with very bright newly turned sods and a scarf of vivid green slanting away beyond the skyline, against which the clouds shewed the slightest tinge of rose or purple. Copses in grey-red or grey-yellow—the tinges immediately forerunning the opening of full leaf. Meadows skirting Seven-bridge road voluptuous green. Some oaks are out in small leaf. Ashes not out, only tufted with their fringy blooms. Hedges springing richly. Elms in small leaf, with more or less opacity. White poplars most beautiful in small grey crisp spray-like leaf. Cowslips capriciously colouring meadows in creamy drifts. Bluebells, purple orchis. Over the green water of the river passing the slums of the town and under its bridges swallows shooting, blue and purple above and shewing their amber-tinged breasts reflected in the water, their flight unsteady with wagging wings and leaning first to one side then the other. Peewits flying. Towards sunset the sky partly swept, as often, with moist white cloud, tailing off across which are morsels of grey-black woolly clouds. Sun seemed to make a bright liquid hole in this, its texture had an upward northerly sweep or drift from the W, marked softly in grey. Dog violets. Eastward after sunset range of clouds rising in bulky heads moulded softly in tufts or bunches of snow—so it looks—

2. A kind of herb, related to parsley.

1. With the exception of one year, Hopkins kept a journal from May 1866 to Feb. 1875. Its most interesting entries are minutely observed descriptions of natural phenomena, which reveal the character of his imagination. The brackets and abbreviations are Hopkins's.

2. Dam. William E. Addis (1844–1917), friend of Hopkins at Oxford; like him he became a Catholic convert and priest. The places mentioned are around Oxford. Compare Matthew Arnold's evocation of this same landscape in "The Scholar Gypsy" (p. 427).

and membered somewhat elaborately, rose-coloured. Notice often imperfect fairy rings. Apple and other fruit trees blossomed beautifully.

* * *

Feb.—1870. One day in the Long Retreat (which ended on Xmas Day) they were reading in the refectory Sister Emmerich's account[3] of the Agony in the Garden[4] and I suddenly began to cry and sob and could not stop. I put it down for this reason, that if I had been asked a minute beforehand I should have said that nothing of the sort was going to happen and even when it did I stood in a manner wondering at myself not seeing in my reason the traces of an adequate cause for such strong emotion—the traces of it I say because of course the cause in itself is adequate for the sorrow of a lifetime. I remember much the same thing on Maundy Thursday when the presanctified Host[5] was carried to the sacristy. But neither the weight nor the stress of sorrow, that is to say of the thing which should cause sorrow, by themselves move us or bring the tears as a sharp knife does not cut for being pressed as long as it is pressed without any shaking of the hand but there is always one touch, something striking sideways and unlooked for, which in both cases undoes resistance and pierces, and this may be so delicate that the pathos seems to have gone directly to the body and cleared the understanding in its passage. On the other hand the pathetic touch by itself, as in dramatic pathos, will only draw slight tears if its matter is not important or not of import to us, the strong emotion coming from a force which was gathered before it was discharged: in this way a knife may pierce the flesh which it had happened only to graze and only grazing will go no deeper.

* * *

May 18 [1870].—Great brilliancy and projection: the eye seemed to fall perpendicular from level to level along our trees, the nearer and further Park; all things hitting the sense with double but direct instress. * * *

This was later. One day when the bluebells were in bloom I wrote the following. I do not think I have ever seen anything more beautiful than the bluebell I have been looking at. I know the beauty of our Lord by it. It[s inscape] is [mixed of] strength and grace, like an ash [tree]. The head is strongly drawn over [backwards] and arched down like a cutwater[6] [drawing itself back from the line of the keel.] The lines of the bells strike and overlie this, rayed but not symmetrically, some lie parallel. They look steely against [the] paper, the shades lying between the bells and behind the cockled petal-ends and nursing up the precision of their distinctness, the petal-ends themselves being delicately lit. Then there is the straightness of the trumpets in the bells softened by the slight entasis[7] and [by] the square splay of the mouth. One bell, the lowest, some way detached and carried on a longer footstalk, touched out with the tips of the petals on oval / not like the rest in a plane perpendicular of the axis of the bell but a little atilt, and so with [the] square-in-rounding turns of the petals.

3. *The Dolorous Passion of Our Lord Jesus Christ; from the Meditations of Anne Catherine Emmerich,* an Augustinian nun (1774–1824).
4. Luke 22.39–44.
5. The bread wafer sanctified for Holy Commu-

nion. "Maundy Thursday": the Thursday before Easter, day of the Last Supper.
6. The forward edge of a ship's prow.
7. Outward curvature.

* * *

Aug. 10 [1872].—I was looking at high waves. The breakers always are parallel to the coast and shape themselves to it except where the curve is sharp however the wind blows. They are rolled out by the shallowing shore just as a piece of putty between the palms whatever its shape runs into a long roll. The slant ruck[8] or crease one sees in them shows the way of the wind. The regularity of the barrels surprised and charmed the eye; the edge behind the comb or crest was as smooth and bright as glass. It may be noticed to be green behind and silver white in front: the silver marks where the air begins, the pure white is foam, the green / solid water. Then looked at to the right or left they are scrolled over like mouldboards[9] or feathers or jibsails seen by the edge. It is pretty to see the hollow of the barrel disappearing as the white combs on each side run along the wave gaining ground till the two meet at a pitch and crush and overlap each other.

About all the turns of the scaping from the break and flooding of wave to its run out again I have not yet satisfied myself. The shores are swimming and the eyes have before them a region of milky surf but it is hard for them to unpack the huddling and gnarls of the water and law out the shapes and the sequence of the running: I catch however the looped or forked wisp made by every big pebble the backwater runs over—if it were clear and smooth there would be a network from their overlapping, such as can in fact be seen on smooth sand after the tide is out—; then I saw it run browner, the foam dwindling and twitched into long chains of suds, while the strength of the back-draught shrugged the stones together and clocked them one against another.

1959

---

8. Fold or crease.   9. Curved iron plates attached to plowshares.

Victorian Issues

EVOLUTION

One of the most dramatic controversies in the Victorian age concerned theories of evolution. This controversy exploded into prominence in 1859 when Charles Darwin's *Origin of Species* was published, but it had been rumbling for many years previously. Sir Charles Lyell's *Principles of Geology* (1830) and Robert Chambers's popular book *Vestiges of Creation* (1843–46) had already raised issues that Tennyson aired in his *In Memoriam A. H. H.* (1850). It was Darwin, however, with his monumental marshaling of evidence to establish his theory of natural selection, who finally brought the topic fully into the open, and the public, as well as the experts, took sides.

The opposition aroused by Darwin's treatise came from two different quarters. The first consisted of some of his fellow scientists, who affirmed that his theory was unsound. The second consisted of religious leaders who attacked his theory because it seemed to contradict a literal interpretation of the Bible. Sometimes the two kinds of opposition combined forces, as in 1860 when his scientific opponents selected Bishop Wilberforce to be their spokesman in spearheading their attack on *The Origin of Species*. In replying to such attacks, Darwin had the good fortune to be supported by two of the ablest popularizers of science in his day, T. H. Huxley and John Tyndall. Moreover, although shy by temperament, Darwin was himself (as Tyndall affirms and the selections printed here will illustrate) an exceptionally effective expositor of his own theories.

Darwin rightly saw himself as a scientist and for the most part restricted his attention to observations about the natural world; the applications of his concept of "the survival of the fittest" to activities within and between human societies and cultures, which came to be known in the late nineteenth century as "Social Darwinism," were primarily conducted by other writers, most notably Herbert Spencer. Nevertheless, the shock that Darwin felt as a young man when he first saw the "savages" of South America's Tierra del Fuego (described in the extract provided from *The Descent of Man,* 1871) stayed with him all his life, and was probably one of the factors that caused him to speculate about social behaviors and systems in evolutionary terms.

It is instructive to compare the selections here with Tennyson's *In Memoriam,* Robert Browning's "Caliban upon Setebos" (1864), and the extracts from the writings of Huxley.

CHARLES DARWIN

Charles Darwin (1809–1882) developed an interest in geology and biology at Cambridge, where he was studying to become a clergyman. Aided by a private income, he resolved to devote the rest of his life to scientific research. The observations he made during a long voyage to the South Seas on the HMS *Beagle* (on which he served as a naturalist) led Darwin to construct hypotheses about evolution. In 1858, more than twenty years after his return to England from his voyage, he ven-

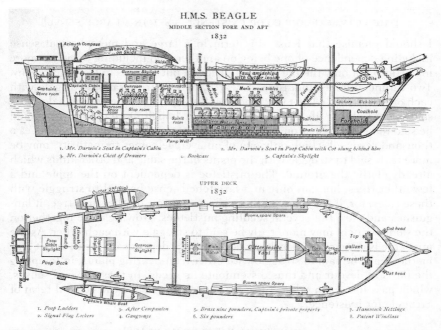

The Beagle. These diagrams appeared in Darwin's *Journal of Researches into the Natural History and Geology of the Countries Visited During the Voyage Round the World of HMS Beagle* (1890).

tured to submit a paper developing his theory of the origin of species. A year later, when his theory appeared in book form, as *The Origin of Species*, Darwin emerged as a famous and controversial figure.

From The Origin of Species

From *Chapter 3. Struggle for Existence*

We will now discuss in a little more detail the struggle for existence. Nothing is easier than to admit in words the truth of the universal struggle for life, or more difficult—at least I have found it so—than constantly to bear this conclusion in mind. Yet unless it be thoroughly engrained in the mind, the whole economy of nature, with every fact on distribution, rarity, abundance, extinction, and variation, will be dimly seen or quite misunderstood. We behold the face of nature bright with gladness, we often see superabundance of food; we do not see or we forget, that the birds which are idly singing round us mostly live on insects or seeds, and are thus constantly destroying life; or we forget how largely these songsters, or their eggs, or their nestlings, are destroyed by birds and beasts of prey; we do not always bear in mind, that, though food may be now superabundant, it is not so at all seasons of each recurring year.

[THE TERM, STRUGGLE FOR EXISTENCE, USED IN A LARGE SENSE]

I should premise that I use this term in a large and metaphorical sense including dependence of one being on another, and including (which is more important) not only the life of the individual, but success in leaving progeny. Two canine animals, in a time of dearth, may be truly said to struggle with each other which shall get food and live. But a plant on the edge of a desert is said to struggle for life against the drought, though more properly it should be said to be dependent on the moisture. A plant which annually produces a thousand seeds, of which only one of an average comes to maturity, may be more truly said to struggle with the plants of the same and other kinds which already clothe the ground. The mistletoe is dependent on the apple and a few other trees, but can only in a farfetched sense be said to struggle with these trees, for, if too many of these parasites grow on the same tree, it languishes and dies. But several seedling mistletoes, growing close together on the same branch, may more truly be said to struggle with each other. As the mistletoe is disseminated by birds, its existence depends on them; and it may methodically be said to struggle with other fruit-bearing plants, in tempting the birds to devour and thus disseminate its seeds. In these several senses, which pass into each other, I use for convenience' sake the general term of Struggle for Existence.

[GEOMETRICAL RATIO OF INCREASE]

A struggle for existence inevitably follows from the high rate at which all organic beings tend to increase. Every being, which during its natural lifetime produces several eggs or seeds, must suffer destruction during some period of its life, and during some season or occasional year, otherwise, on the principle of geometrical increase, its numbers would quickly become so inordinately great that no country could support the product. Hence, as more individuals are produced than can possibly survive, there must in every case be a struggle for existence, either one individual with another of the same species, or with the individuals of distinct species, or with the physical conditions of life. It is the doctrine of Malthus[1] applied with manifold force to the whole animal and vegetable kingdoms; for in this case there can be no artificial increase of food, and no prudential restraint from marriage. Although some species may be now increasing, more or less rapidly, in numbers, all cannot do so, for the world would not hold them.

There is no exception to the rule that every organic being naturally increases at so high a rate, that, if not destroyed, the earth would soon be covered by the progeny of a single pair. Even slow-breeding man has doubled in twenty-five years, and at this rate, in less than a thousand years, there would literally not be standing-room for his progeny. Linnæus[2] has calculated that if an annual plant produced only two seeds—and there is no plant so unproductive as this—and their seedlings next year produced two, and so on, then in twenty years there should be a million plants. The elephant is

1. Thomas Robert Malthus (1766–1834), British social theorist who argued that the population, increasing geometrically, would grow beyond the means of subsistence, which increased arithmetically, without the necessary natural checks of poverty, disease, and starvation.
2. Carl Linnaeus (1707–1778), Swedish naturalist who developed the binomial system—genus plus species name—for naming plants and animals (e.g., *Viola tricolor*, see p. 609).

reckoned the slowest breeder of all known animals, and I have taken some pains to estimate its probable minimum rate of natural increase; it will be safest to assume that it begins breeding when thirty years old, and goes on breeding till ninety years old, bringing forth six young in the interval, and surviving till one hundred years old; if this be so, after a period of from 740 to 750 years there would be nearly nineteen million elephants alive, descended from the first pair.

* * *

[COMPLEX RELATIONS OF ALL ANIMALS AND PLANTS TO EACH OTHER IN THE STRUGGLE FOR EXISTENCE]

Many cases are on record showing how complex and unexpected are the checks and relations between organic beings, which have to struggle together in the same country.

* * *

Nearly all our orchidaceous plants absolutely require the visits of insects to remove their pollen-masses and thus to fertilise them. I find from experiments that humble-bees[3] are almost indispensable to the fertilisation of the heartsease (Viola tricolor), for other bees do not visit this flower. I have also found that the visits of bees are necessary for the fertilisation of some kinds of clover; for instance, 20 heads of Dutch clover (Trifolium repens) yielded 2,290 seeds, but 20 other heads protected from bees produced not one. Again, 100 heads of red clover (T. pratense) produced 2,700 seeds, but the same number of protected heads produced not a single seed. Humble-bees alone visit red clover, as other bees cannot reach the nectar. It has been suggested that moths may fertilise the clovers; but I doubt whether they could do so in the case of the red clover, from their weight not being sufficient to depress the wing petals. Hence we may infer as highly probable that, if the whole genus of humble-bees became extinct or very rare in England, the heartsease and red clover would become very rare, or wholly disappear. The number of humble-bees in any district depends in a great measure upon the number of field-mice, which destroy their combs and nests; and Col. Newman,[4] who has long attended to the habits of humble-bees, believes that "more than two-thirds of them are thus destroyed all over England." Now the number of mice is largely dependent, as every one knows, on the number of cats; and Col. Newman says, "Near villages and small towns I have found the nests of humble-bees more numerous than elsewhere, which I attribute to the number of cats that destroy the mice." Hence it is quite credible that the presence of a feline animal in large numbers in a district might determine, through the intervention first of mice and then of bees, the frequency of certain flowers in that district!

In the case of every species, many different checks, acting at different periods of life, and during different seasons or years, probably come into play; some one check or some few being generally the most potent; but all will concur in determining the average number or even the existence of the

3. Bumblebees.
4. Henry Wenman Newman (1788–1865), Brit- ish army officer who succeeded to his father's estates in 1829.

species. In some cases it can be shown that widely-different checks act on the same species in different districts. When we look at the plants and bushes clothing an entangled bank, we are tempted to attribute their proportional numbers and kinds to what we call chance. But how false a view is this! Every one has heard that when an American forest is cut down a very different vegetation springs up; but it has been observed that ancient Indian ruins in the Southern United States, which must formerly have been cleared of trees, now display the same beautiful diversity and proportion of kinds as in the surrounding virgin forest. What a struggle must have gone on during long centuries between the several kinds of trees each annually scattering its seeds by the thousand; what war between insect and insect—between insects, snails, and other animals with birds and beasts of prey—all striving to increase, all feeding on each other, or on the trees, their seeds and seedlings, or on the other plants which first clothed the ground and thus checked

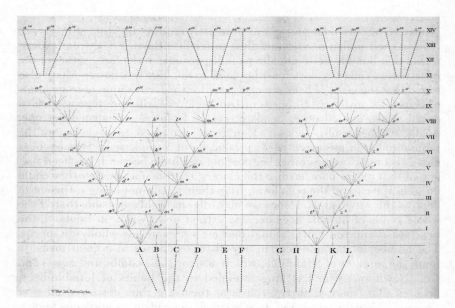

Evolutionary Descent in Species. Darwin included this diagram in chapter 4 to "aid us in understanding this rather perplexing subject." "A to L represent the species of a genus large in its own country. . . . The little fan of diverging dotted lines of unequal lengths proceeding from (A), may represent its varying offspring. The variations are supposed to be extremely slight, but of the most diversified nature; they are not supposed all to appear simultaneously, but often after long intervals of time; nor are they all supposed to endure for equal periods. Only those variations which are in some way profitable will be preserved or naturally selected. And here the importance of the principle of benefit being derived from divergence of character comes in; for this will generally lead to the most different or divergent variations (represented by the outer dotted lines) being preserved and accumulated by natural selection. When a dotted line reaches one of the horizontal lines, and is there marked by a small numbered letter, a sufficient amount of variation is supposed to have been accumulated to have formed a fairly well-marked variety, such as would be thought worthy of record in a systematic work." The full explanation of the diagram runs to more than nine pages.

the growth of the trees! Throw up a handful of feathers, and all fall to the ground according to definite laws; but how simple is the problem where each shall fall compared to that of the action and reaction of the innumerable plants and animals which have determined, in the course of centuries, the proportional numbers and kinds of trees now growing on the old Indian ruins!

From *Chapter 15. Recapitulation and Conclusion*

I see no good reason why the views given in this volume should shock the religious feelings of any one. It is satisfactory, as showing how transient such impressions are, to remember that the greatest discovery ever made by man, namely, the law of the attraction of gravity, was also attacked by Leibnitz,[5] "as subversive of natural, and inferentially of revealed, religion." A celebrated author and divine has written to me that "he has gradually learnt to see that it is just as noble a conception of the Deity to believe that He created a few original forms capable of self-development into other and needful forms, as to believe that He required a fresh act of creation to supply the voids caused by the action of His laws."

Why, it may be asked, until recently did nearly all the most eminent living naturalists and geologists disbelieve in the mutability of species? It cannot be asserted that organic beings in a state of nature are subject to no variation; it cannot be proved that the amount of variation in the course of long ages is a limited quality; no clear distinction has been, or can be, drawn between species and well-marked varieties. It cannot be maintained that species when intercrossed are invariably sterile, and varieties invariably fertile; or that sterility is a special endowment and sign of creation. The belief that species were immutable productions was almost unavoidable as long as the history of the world was thought to be of short duration;[6] and now that we have acquired some idea of the lapse of time, we are too apt to assume, without proof, that the geological record is so perfect that it would have afforded us plain evidence of the mutation of species, if they had undergone mutation.

But the chief cause of our natural unwillingness to admit that one species has given birth to clear and distinct species, is that we are always slow in admitting great changes of which we do not see the steps. The difficulty is the same as that felt by so many geologists, when Lyell[7] first insisted that long lines of inland cliffs had been formed, and great valleys excavated, by the agencies which we see still at work. The mind cannot possibly grasp the full meaning of the term of even a million years; it cannot add up and perceive the full effects of many slight variations, accumulated during an almost infinite number of generations.

Although I am fully convinced of the truth of the views given in this volume under the form of an abstract, I by no means expect to convince

5. Gottfried Wilhelm Leibniz (1646–1716), German philosopher and mathematician; he was a contemporary of Isaac Newton, who set forth the law of universal gravitation.
6. Calculations based on the genealogies within the Bible put the age of the world at no more than six thousand years.

7. Charles Lyell (1797–1875), geologist whose book *Principles of Geology* (1830–33) was important in dissociating geological theory from the Bible and in establishing nature as the record of the earth's history, which he saw as a process of lengthy and gradual change rather than swift catastrophic events.

experienced naturalists whose minds are stocked with a multitude of facts all viewed, during a long course of years, from a point of view directly opposite to mine. It is so easy to hide our ignorance under such expressions as the "plan of creation," "unity of design," &c., and to think that we give an explanation when we only re-state a fact. Any one whose disposition leads him to attach more weight to unexplained difficulties than to the explanation of a certain number of facts will certainly reject the theory. A few naturalists, endowed with much flexibility of mind, and who have already begun to doubt the immutability of species, may be influenced by this volume; but I look with confidence to the future,—to young and rising naturalists, who will be able to view both sides of the question with impartiality.[8] Whoever is led to believe that species are mutable will do good service by conscientiously expressing his conviction; for thus only can the load of prejudice by which this subject is overwhelmed be removed.

* * *

It may be asked how far I extend the doctrine of the modification of species. The question is difficult to answer, because the more distinct the forms are which we consider, by so much the arguments in favour of community of descent become fewer in number and less in force. But some arguments of the greatest weight extend very far. All the members of whole classes are connected together by a chain of affinities, and all can be classed on the same principle, in groups subordinate to groups. Fossil remains sometimes tend to fill up very wide intervals between existing orders.

Organs in a rudimentary condition plainly show that an early progenitor had the organ in a fully developed condition; and this in some cases implies an enormous amount of modification in the descendants. Throughout whole classes various structures are formed on the same pattern, and at a very early age the embryos closely resemble each other. Therefore I cannot doubt that the theory of descent with modification embraces all the members of the same great class or kingdom. I believe that animals are descended from at most only four or five progenitors, and plants from an equal or lesser number.

Analogy would lead me one step farther, namely, to the belief that all animals and plants are descended from some one prototype. But analogy may be a deceitful guide. Nevertheless all living things have much in common, in their chemical composition, their cellular structure, their laws of growth, and their liability to injurious influences. We see this even in so trifling a fact as that the same poison often similarly affects plants and animals; or that the poison secreted by the gall-fly produces monstrous growths on the wild rose or oak-tree. With all organic beings excepting perhaps some of the very lowest, sexual production seems to be essentially similar. With all, as far as is at present known the germinal vesicle is the same; so that all organisms start from a common origin. If we look even to the two main divisions—namely, to the animal and vegetable kingdoms—certain low forms are so far

8. Despite the initial theological resistance to Darwin's theory, his ideas were swiftly accepted by his fellow scientists, and intellectual elites, even in the Church, soon followed suit. It would take much longer for the larger public to come around, although Darwin's burial in Westminster Abbey—a great civic honor—suggests he had won over many of his fellow citizens.

intermediate in character that naturalists have disputed to which kingdom they should be referred. As Professor Asa Gray[9] has remarked, "the spores and other reproductive bodies of many of the lower algae may claim to have first a characteristically animal, and then an unequivocally vegetable existence." Therefore, on the principle of natural selection with divergence of character, it does not seem incredible that, from such low and intermediate form, both animals and plants may have been developed; and, if we admit this, we must likewise admit that all the organic beings which have ever lived on this earth may be descended from some one primordial form.

* * *

When we feel assured that all the individuals of the same species, and all the closely allied species of most genera, have within a not very remote period descended from one parent, and have migrated from some one birthplace; and when we better know the many means of migration, then, by the light which geology now throws, and will continue to throw, on former changes of climate and of the level of the land, we shall surely be enabled to trace in an admirable manner the former migrations of the inhabitants of the whole world. Even at present, by comparing the differences between the inhabitants of the sea on the opposite sides of a continent, and the nature of the various inhabitants on that continent, in relation to their apparent means of immigration, some light can be thrown on ancient geography.

The noble science of Geology loses glory from the extreme imperfection of the record.[1] The crust of the earth with its imbedded remains must not be looked at as a well-filled museum, but as a poor collection made at hazard and at rare intervals. The accumulation of each great fossiliferous formation will be recognised as having depended on an unusual concurrence of favourable circumstances, and the blank intervals between the successive stages as having been of vast duration. But we shall be able to gauge with some security the duration of these intervals by a comparison of the preceding and succeeding organic forms. We must be cautious in attempting to correlate as strictly contemporaneous two formations, which do not include many identical species, by the general succession of the forms of life. As species are produced and exterminated by slowly acting and still existing causes, and not by miraculous acts of creation; and as the most important of all causes of organic change is one which is almost independent of altered and perhaps suddenly altered physical conditions, namely, the mutual relation of organism to organism,—the improvement of one organism entailing the improvement or the extermination of others; it follows, that the amount of organic change in the fossils of consecutive formations probably serves as a fair measure of the relative though not actual lapse of time. A number of species, however, keeping in a body might remain for a long period unchanged, whilst within the same period several of these species by migrating into new countries and coming into competition with foreign associates, might become

9. American botanist (1810–1888).
1. Geology had captured the early Victorian imagination, largely thanks to the radical theories of Charles Lyell and to mounting interest in dinosaurs (a term coined in 1842 by the pioneering comparative anatomist Sir Richard Owen, who

was the first to classify "dinosauria" as a suborder of large extinct reptiles). Perhaps Darwin here forecasts one reason popular interest would shift in the later part of the century; after his *Origin* was published, biology, not geology, became the focal point of public debate.

modified; so that we must not overrate the accuracy of organic change as a measure of time.

In the future I see open fields for far more important researches. Psychology will be securely based on the foundation already well laid by Mr. Herbert Spencer,[2] that of the necessary acquirement of each mental power and capacity by gradation. Much light will be thrown on the origin of man and his history.

Authors of the highest eminence seem to be fully satisfied with the view that each species has been independently created. To my mind it accords better with what we know of the laws impressed on matter by the Creator, that the production and extinction of the past and present inhabitants of the world should have been due to secondary causes, like those determining the birth and death of the individual. When I view all beings not as special creations, but as the lineal descendants of some few beings which lived long before the first bed of the Cambrian system was deposited,[3] they seem to me to become ennobled. Judging from the past, we may safely infer that not one living species will transmit its unaltered likeness to a distant futurity. And of the species now living very few will transmit progeny of any kind to a far distant futurity; for the manner in which all organic beings are grouped, shows that the greater number of species in each genus, and all the species in many genera, have left no descendants, but have become utterly extinct. We can so far take a prophetic glance into futurity as to foretell that it will be the common and widely-spread species, belonging to the larger and dominant groups within each class, which will ultimately prevail and procreate new and dominant species. As all the living forms of life are the lineal descendants of those which lived long before the Cambrian epoch, we may feel certain that the ordinary succession by generation has never once been broken, and that no cataclysm has desolated the whole world. Hence we may look with some confidence to a secure future of great length. And as natural selection works solely by and for the good of each being, all corporeal and mental endowments will tend to progress towards perfection.

It is interesting to contemplate a tangled bank, clothed with many plants of many kinds, with birds singing on the bushes, with various insects flitting about, and with worms crawling through the damp earth, and to reflect that these elaborately constructed forms, so different from each other, and dependent upon each other in so complex a manner, have all been produced by laws acting around us. These laws, taken in the largest sense, being Growth with Reproduction; Inheritance which is almost implied by reproduction; Variability from the indirect and direct action of the conditions of life, and from use and disuse: a Ratio of Increase so high as to lead to a Struggle for Life, and as a consequence to Natural Selection, entailing Divergence of Character and the Extinction of less-improved forms. Thus, from the war of nature, from famine and death, the most exalted object which we are capable of conceiving, namely, the production of the higher animals, directly follows. There is grandeur in this view of life, with its several powers, having been originally breathed by the Creator into a few forms or into one; and that,

---

2. British social theorist (1820–1903), who developed the concept of Social Darwinism.
3. I.e., before the earliest geological period of the Paleozoic (now dated at more than 540 million years ago).

whilst this planet has gone cycling on according to the fixed law of gravity, from so simple a beginning endless forms most beautiful and most wonderful have been, and are being evolved.

1859

CHARLES DARWIN

After he published *The Origin of Species,* Darwin wrote several treatises, some of which develop and clarify the theory of natural selection. One of these works, *The Descent of Man* (1871), was especially provocative in its stress on the similarities between humans and animals and in its naturalistic explanations of the beautiful colorings of birds, insects, and flowers.

From The Descent of Man

[NATURAL SELECTION AND SEXUAL SELECTION][1]

A brief summary will here be sufficient to recall to the reader's mind the more salient points in this work. Many of the views which have been advanced are highly speculative, and some no doubt will prove erroneous; but I have in every case given the reasons which have led me to one view rather than to another. It seemed worth while to try how far the principle of evolution would throw light on some of the more complex problems in the natural history of man. False facts are highly injurious to the progress of science, for they often long endure; but false views, if supported by some evidence, do little harm, as everyone takes a salutary pleasure in proving their falseness; and when this is done, one path towards error is closed and the road to truth is often at the same time opened.

The main conclusion arrived at in this work, and now held by many naturalists who are well competent to form a sound judgment, is that man is descended from some less highly organized form. The grounds upon which this conclusion rests will never be shaken, for the close similarity between man and the lower animals in embryonic development, as well as in innumerable points of structure and constitution, both of high and of the most trifling importance—the rudiments which he retains, and the abnormal reversions to which he is occasionally liable—are facts which cannot be disputed. They have long been known, but until recently they told us nothing with respect to the origin of man. Now when viewed by the light of our knowledge of the whole organic world, their meaning is unmistakable. The great principle of evolution stands up clear and firm, when these groups of facts are considered in connection with others, such as the mutual affinities of the members of the same group, their geographical distribution in past and present times, and their geological succession. It is incredible that all these

1. From chap. 21.

facts should speak falsely. He who is not content to look, like a savage, at the phenomena of nature as disconnected cannot any longer believe that man is the work of a separate act of creation. He will be forced to admit that the close resemblance of the embryo of man to that, for instance, of a dog—the construction of his skull, limbs, and whole frame, independently of the uses to which the parts may be put, on the same plan with that of other mammals— the occasional reappearance of various structures, for instance of several distinct muscles, which man does not normally possess, but which are common to the Quadrumana[2]—and a crowd of analogous facts—all point in the plainest manner to the conclusion that man is the codescendant with other mammals of a common progenitor.

* * *

By considering the embryological structure of man—the homologies which he presents with the lower animals, the rudiments which he retains, and the reversions to which he is liable—we can partly recall in imagination the former condition of our early progenitors; and can approximately place them in their proper position in the zoological series. We thus learn that man is descended from a hairy quadruped, furnished with a tail and pointed ears, probably arboreal in its habits, and an inhabitant of the Old World. This creature, if its whole structure had been examined by a naturalist, would have been classed amongst the Quadrumana, as surely as would the common and still more ancient progenitor of the Old and New World monkeys. The Quadrumana and all the higher mammals are probably derived from an ancient marsupial animal, and this through a long line of diversified forms, either from some reptile-like or some amphibianlike creature, and this again from some fishlike animal. In the dim obscurity of the past we can see that the early progenitor of all the Vertebrata must have been an aquatic animal, provided with branchiae,[3] with the two sexes united in the same individual, and with the most important organs of the body (such as the brain and heart) imperfectly developed. This animal seems to have been more like the larvae of our existing marine ascidians[4] than any other known form.

* * *

Sexual selection has been treated at great length in these volumes; for, as I have attempted to show, it has played an important part in the history of the organic world.

* * *

The belief in the power of sexual selection rests chiefly on the following considerations. The characters which we have the best reason for supposing to have been thus acquired are confined to one sex; and this alone renders it probable that they are in some way connected with the act of reproduction. These characters in innumerable instances are fully developed only at maturity; and often during only a part of the year, which is always the breeding

2. Animals, such as monkeys, whose hind feet and forefeet can be used as hands—hence "four-handed."
3. Gills.

4. Part of a group of marine animals called tunicata, or popularly "sea squirts," sometimes assumed to be ancestors of the vertebrate animals.

season. The males (passing over a few exceptional cases) are the most active in courtship; they are the best armed, and are rendered the most attractive in various ways. It is to be especially observed that the males display their attractions with elaborate care in the presence of the females; and that they rarely or never display them excepting during the season of love. It is incredible that all this display should be purposeless. Lastly we have distinct evidence with some quadrupeds and birds that the individuals of the one sex are capable of feeling a strong antipathy or preference for certain individuals of the opposite sex.

Bearing these facts in mind, and not forgetting the marked results of man's unconscious selection, it seems to me almost certain that if the individuals of one sex were during a long series of generations to prefer pairing with certain individuals of the other sex, characterized in some peculiar manner, the offspring would slowly but surely become modified in this same manner. I have not attempted to conceal that, excepting when the males are more numerous than the females, or when polygamy prevails, it is doubtful how the more attractive males succeed in leaving a larger number of offspring to inherit their superiority in ornaments or other charms than the less attractive males; but I have shown that this would probably follow from the females—especially the more vigorous females which would be the first to breed, preferring not only the more attractive but at the same time the more vigorous and victorious males.

Although we have some positive evidence that birds appreciate bright and beautiful objects, as with the bowerbirds of Australia, and although they certainly appreciate the power of song, yet I fully admit that it is an astonishing fact that the females of many birds and some mammals should be endowed with sufficient taste for what has apparently been effected through sexual selection; and this is even more astonishing in the case of reptiles, fish, and insects. But we really know very little about the minds of the lower animals. It cannot be supposed that male birds of paradise or peacocks, for instance, should take so much pains in erecting, spreading, and vibrating their beautiful plumes before the females for no purpose. We should remember the fact given on excellent authority in a former chapter, namely that several peahens, when debarred from an admired male, remained widows during a whole season rather than pair with another bird.

Nevertheless I know of no fact in natural history more wonderful than that the female argus pheasant should be able to appreciate the exquisite shading of the ball-and-socket ornaments and the elegant patterns on the wing feathers of the male. He who thinks that the male was created as he now exists must admit that the great plumes, which prevent the wings from being used for flight, and which, as well as the primary feathers, are displayed in a manner quite peculiar to this one species during the act of courtship, and at no other time, were given to him as an ornament. If so, he must likewise admit that the female was created and endowed with the capacity of appreciating such ornaments. I differ only in the conviction that the male argus pheasant acquired his beauty gradually, through the females having preferred during many generations the more highly ornamented males; the aesthetic capacity of the females having been advanced through exercise or habit in the same manner as our own taste is gradually improved. In the male, through the fortunate chance of a few feathers not having been modified, we can distinctly see how simple spots with a little fulvous[5] shading on one side might have been developed by small and graduated steps into the wonderful ball-and-socket ornaments; and it is probable that they were actually thus developed.

* * *

He who admits the principle of sexual selection will be led to the remarkable conclusion that the cerebral system not only regulates most of the existing functions of the body, but has indirectly influenced the progressive development of various bodily structures and of certain mental qualities. Courage, pugnacity, perseverance, strength and size of body, weapons of all kinds, musical organs, both vocal and instrumental, bright colours, stripes and marks, and ornamental appendages have all been indirectly gained by the one sex or the other, through the influence of love and jealousy, through the appreciation of the beautiful in sound, color or form, and through the exertion of a choice; and these powers of the mind manifestly depend on the development of the cerebral system.

* * *

The main conclusion arrived at in this work, namely that man is descended from some lowly-organized form, will, I regret to think, be highly distasteful to many persons. But there can hardly be a doubt that we are descended from barbarians. The astonishment which I felt on first seeing a party of Fuegians[6] on a wild and broken shore will never be forgotten by me, for the reflection at once rushed into my mind—such were our ancestors. These men were absolutely naked and bedaubed with paint, their long hair was tangled, their mouths frothed with excitement, and their expression was wild, startled, and distrustful. They possessed hardly any arts,[7] and like wild animals lived on what they could catch; they had no government, and were merciless to everyone not of their own small tribe. He who has seen a savage in his native land will not feel much shame, if forced to acknowledge that the blood of some more humble creature flows in his veins. For my own part I would as soon be descended from that heroic little monkey, who braved his dreaded enemy in order to save the life of his keeper; or from that old baboon, who, descending from the mountains, carried away in triumph his young comrade from a crowd of astonished dogs[8]—as from a savage who delights to torture his enemies, offers up bloody sacrifices, practices infanticide without remorse, treats his wives like slaves, knows no decency, and is haunted by the grossest superstitions.

Man may be excused for feeling some pride at having risen, though not through his own exertions, to the very summit of the organic scale; and the fact of his having thus risen, instead of having been aboriginally placed there, may give him hopes for a still higher destiny in the distant future. But we are not here concerned with hopes or fears, only with the truth as far as our reason allows us to discover it. I have given the evidence to the best of my ability; and we must acknowledge, as it seems to me, that man with all his noble qualities, with sympathy which feels for the most debased, with

5. Dull yellow.
6. Natives inhabiting the islands off the southern tip of South America, Tierra del Fuego, which Darwin had visited in 1832. See his *Voyage of the*

Beagle (1839), chap. 10.
7. Crafts and skills.
8. Incidents described in chap. 4 to demonstrate that animals may be endowed with a moral sense.

benevolence which extends not only to other men but to the humblest living creature, with his godlike intellect which has penetrated into the movements and constitution of the solar system—with all these exalted powers— Man still bears in his bodily frame the indelible stamp of his lowly origin.

1871

LEONARD HUXLEY

At meetings of the British Association for the Advancement of Science, the reading of a paper is followed by a discussion. In 1860, at Oxford, this discussion developed into a debate between Thomas Henry Huxley (1825–1895), a defender of Charles Darwin's theories, and Bishop Samuel Wilberforce (1805–1873). Although he had studied mathematics as an undergraduate, Wilberforce could hardly lay claim to be a scientist. He was willing, nevertheless, to speak on behalf of those scientists who disagreed with *The Origin of Species* (1859), and he reportedly came to the meeting ready to "smash Darwin." The bishop's principal qualifications for this role were his great powers as a smoothly persuasive orator (he was commonly known by his detractors as "Soapy Sam"), but he met more than his match in Huxley.

Because no complete transcript of this celebrated debate was made at the time, Huxley's son Leonard (1860–1933), in writing his father's biography, had to reconstruct the scene by combining quotations from reports made by magazine writers and other witnesses. The account given here is from chapter 14.

From The Life and Letters of Thomas Henry Huxley

[THE HUXLEY-WILBERFORCE DEBATE AT OXFORD]

The famous Oxford Meeting of 1860 was of no small importance in Huxley's career. It was not merely that he helped to save a great cause from being stifled under misrepresentation and ridicule—that he helped to extort for it a fair hearing; it was now that he first made himself known in popular estimation as a dangerous adversary in debate—a personal force in the world of science which could not be neglected. From this moment he entered the front fighting line in the most exposed quarter of the field. * * *

It was the merest chance, as I have already said, that Huxley attended the meeting of the section that morning. Dr. Draper[1] of New York was to read a paper on the *Intellectual Development of Europe considered with reference to the views of Mr. Darwin.* "I can still hear," writes one who was present, "the American accents of Dr. Draper's opening address when he asked 'Air we a fortuitous concourse of atoms?'" However, it was not to hear him, but the eloquence of the Bishop, that the members of the Association crowded in such numbers into the Lecture Room of the Museum, that this, the appointed meeting place of the section, had to be abandoned for the long west room,

---

1. John W. Draper (1811–1882), British-born chemist, photographer, and historian who was a professor at the University of the City of New York.

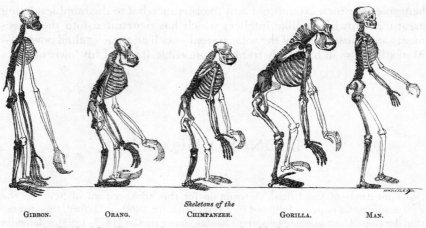

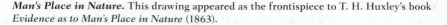

GIBBON.   ORANG.   *Skeletons of the*
CHIMPANZEE.   GORILLA.   MAN.

Photographically reduced from Diagrams of the natural size (except that of the Gibbon ,which was twice as large as nature), drawn by Mr. Waterhouse Hawkins from specimens in the Museum of the Royal College of Surgeons.

Man's Place in Nature. This drawing appeared as the frontispiece to T. H. Huxley's book *Evidence as to Man's Place in Nature* (1863).

since cut in two by a partition for the purposes of the library. It was not term time, nor were the general public admitted; nevertheless the room was crowded to suffocation long before the protagonists appeared on the scene, 700 persons or more managing to find places. The very windows by which the room was lighted down the length of its west side were packed with ladies, whose white handkerchiefs, waving and fluttering in the air at the end of the Bishop's speech, were an unforgettable factor in the acclamation of the crowd.

On the east side between the two doors was the platform. Professor Henslow, the President of the section, took his seat in the center; upon his right was the Bishop, and beyond him again Dr. Draper; on his extreme left was Mr. Dingle, a clergyman from Lanchester, near Durham, with Sir J. Hooker and Sir J. Lubbock in front of him, and nearer the center, Professor Beale of King's College, London, and Huxley.[2]

The clergy, who shouted lustily for the Bishop, were massed in the middle of the room; behind them in the northwest corner a knot of undergraduates (one of these was T. H. Green,[3] who listened but took no part in the cheering) had gathered together beside Professor Brodie,[4] ready to lift their voices, poor minority though they were, for the opposite party. Close to them stood one of the few men among the audience already in Holy orders, who joined in—and indeed led—the cheers for the Darwinians.

So "Dr. Draper droned out his paper, turning first to the right hand and then to the left, of course bringing in a reference to the *Origin of Species* which set the ball rolling."

2. Except for the clergyman Dingle, all those named are scientists of some repute. John Stevens Henslow (1796–1861), professor of botany at Cambridge. Sir Joseph Dalton Hooker (1817–1911), botanist (and Henslow's son-in-law). Sir John Lubbock (1834–1913), banker, statesman, naturalist, and Darwin's neighbor. Lionel Smith Beale (1828–1905), professor of medicine.
3. Later a prominent British philosopher (1836–1882).
4. Sir Benjamin Brodie (1783–1862), physiologist and surgeon.

An hour or more that paper lasted, and then discussion began. The President "wisely announced *in limine*[5] that none who had not valid arguments to bring forward on one side or the other would be allowed to address the meeting; a caution that proved necessary, for no fewer than four combatants had their utterances burked[6] by him, because of their indulgence in vague declamation."

First spoke (writes Professor Farrar[7]) a layman from Brompton, who gave his name as being one of the Committee of the (newly formed) Economic section of the Association. He, in a stentorian voice, let off his theological venom. Then jumped up Richard Greswell[8] with a thin voice, saying much the same, but speaking as a scholar; but we did not merely want any theological discussion, so we shouted them down. Then a Mr. Dingle got up and tried to show that Darwin would have done much better if he had taken him into consultation. He used the blackboard and began a mathematical demonstration on the question—"Let this point A be man, and let that point B be the mawnkey." He got no further; he was shouted down with cries of "mawnkey." None of these had spoken more than three minutes. It was when these were shouted down that Henslow said he must demand that the discussion should rest on *scientific* grounds only.

Then there were calls for the Bishop, but he rose and said he understood his friend Professor Beale had something to say first. Beale, who was an excellent histologist,[9] spoke to the effect that the new theory ought to meet with fair discussion, but added, with great modesty, that he himself had not sufficient knowledge to discuss the subject adequately. Then the Bishop spoke the speech that you know, and the question about his mother being an ape, or his grandmother.

From the scientific point of view, the speech was of small value. It was evident from his mode of handling the subject that he had been "crammed up to the throat," and knew nothing at first hand; he used no argument beyond those to be found in his *Quarterly* article, which appeared a few days later, and is now admitted to have been inspired by Owen.[1] "He ridiculed Darwin badly and Huxley savagely; but," confesses one of his strongest opponents, "all in such dulcet tones, so persuasive a manner, and in such well turned periods, that I who had been inclined to blame the President for allowing a discussion that could serve no scientific purpose, now forgave him from the bottom of my heart."

The Bishop spoke thus "for full half an hour with inimitable spirit, emptiness and unfairness." "In a light, scoffing tone, florid and fluent, he assured us there was nothing in the idea of evolution; rock pigeons were what rock pigeons had always been. Then, turning to his antagonist with a smiling insolence, he begged to know, was it through his grandfather or his grandmother that he claimed his descent from a monkey?"

This was the fatal mistake of his speech. Huxley instantly grasped the tactical advantage which the descent to personalities gave him. He turned to Sir

5. As a starting point (Latin).
6. Suppressed, hushed.
7. Adam Storey Farrar (1826–1905), canon of Durham and professor of divinity at Durham University.
8. A clergyman who was a tutor of Worcester College, Oxford.

9. A biologist specializing in the study of the minute structure of the tissues of plants and animals.
1. Sir Richard Owen (1804–1892), a leading zoologist and paleontologist who was opposed to Darwin's theories. Wilberforce's review of Darwin's *The Origin of Species* (1859) appeared in the July 1860 issue of the *Quarterly Review*.

Benjamin Brodie, who was sitting beside him, and emphatically striking his hand upon his knee, exclaimed, "The Lord hath delivered him into mine hands."[2] The bearing of the exclamation did not dawn upon Sir Benjamin until after Huxley had completed his "forcible and eloquent" answer to the scientific part of the Bishop's argument, and proceeded to make his famous retort.

> On this (continues the writer in *Macmillan's Magazine*) Mr. Huxley slowly and deliberately arose. A slight tall figure, stern and pale, very quiet and very grave, he stood before us and spoke those tremendous words—words which no one seems sure of now, nor, I think, could remember just after they were spoken, for their meaning took away our breath, though it left us in no doubt as to what it was. He was not ashamed to have a monkey for his ancestor; but he would be ashamed to be connected with a man who used great gifts to obscure the truth. No one doubted his meaning, and the effect was tremendous. One lady fainted and had to be carried out; I, for one, jumped out of my seat.

The fullest and probably most accurate account of these concluding words is the following, from a letter of the late John Richard Green, then an undergraduate, to his friend, afterwards Professor Boyd Dawkins:[3]

> I asserted—and I repeat—that a man has no reason to be ashamed of having an ape for his grandfather. If there were an ancestor whom I should feel shame in recalling it would rather be a man—a man of restless and versatile intellect—who, not content with an equivocal success in his own sphere of activity, plunges into scientific questions with which he has no real acquaintance, only to obscure them by an aimless rhetoric, and distract the attention of his hearers from the real point at issue by eloquent digressions and skilled appeals to religious prejudice.

The result of this encounter, though a check to the other side, cannot, of course, be represented as an immediate and complete triumph for evolutionary doctrine. This was precluded by the character and temper of the audience, most of whom were less capable of being convinced by the arguments than shocked by the boldness of the retort, although, being gentlefolk, as Professor Farrar remarks, they were disposed to admit on reflection that the Bishop had erred on the score of taste and good manners. Nevertheless, it was a noticeable feature of the occasion, Sir M. Foster[4] tells me, that when Huxley rose he was received coldly, just a cheer of encouragement from his friends, the audience as a whole not joining in it. But as he made his points the applause grew and widened, until, when he sat down, the cheering was not very much less than that given to the Bishop. To that extent he carried an unwilling audience with him by the force of his speech. The debate on the ape question, however, was continued elsewhere during the next two years, and the evidence was completed by the unanswerable demonstrations of Sir W. H. Flower[5] at the Cambridge meeting of the Association in 1862.

---

2. Cf. 2 Samuel 5.19 (where the Lord promises to deliver the Philistines into David's hands).
3. William Boyd Dawkins (1838–1929), British geologist and archaeologist. Green (1837–1883), British historian.
4. Sir Michael Foster (1836–1907), British physiologist and educator.
5. Sir William Henry Flower (1831–1899), British zoologist.

THE DESCENT OF MAN.

Figurative Party. "So long as *I* am a Man, Sorr, what does it matther to me whether me *Great-Grandfather* was an Anthropoid Ape or not, Sorr!"

Literal Party. "Haw! Wather disagweeable for your *Gwate Gwand-mother,* wasn't it!"

The Descent of Man. This cartoon by George du Maurier (1834–1896) appeared in the popular satirical magazine *Punch* in 1873. The phonetic rendering of the speech of the "Figurative Party" (sitting on the table) marks him as Irish; that of the "Literal Party" (and his clothing), a member of the upper classes.

The importance of the Oxford meeting lay in the open resistance that was made to authority, at a moment when even a drawn battle was hardly less effectual than acknowledged victory. Instead of being crushed under ridicule, the new theories secured a hearing, all the wider, indeed, for the startling nature of their defense.

1901

SIR EDMUND GOSSE

Philip Henry Gosse (1810–1888) was a zoologist of some repute and also an ardent adherent of a strict Protestant sect, the Plymouth Brethren. In an attempt to reconcile his scientific knowledge with his fundamentalist religious position, Gosse published in 1857 a work called *Omphalos,* the Greek word for "navel." The term is of central significance in the book's primary assertion that the earth carries the marks of a past that did not actually happen: just as Adam and Eve were created with navels even though they had not been born to a mother, Gosse argues, so had God created the world with what appear to be millions of years' worth of accumulated rock strata. The book pleased no one. Gosse's agonized experience is described by his son, the literary critic Sir Edmund Gosse (1849–1928), in an autobiography published in 1907. This selection is from chapter 5.

From Father and Son

So, through my Father's brain, in that year of scientific crisis, 1857, there rushed two kinds of thought, each absorbing, each convincing, yet totally irreconcilable. There is a peculiar agony in the paradox that truth has two forms, each of them indisputable, yet each antagonistic to the other. It was this discovery, that there were two theories of physical life, each of which was true, but the truth of each incompatible with the truth of the other, which shook the spirit of my Father with perturbation. It was not, really, a paradox, it was a fallacy, if he could only have known it, but he allowed the turbid volume of superstition to drown the delicate stream of reason. He took one step in the service of truth, and then he drew back in an agony, and accepted the servitude of error.

This was the great moment in the history of thought when the theory of the mutability of species was preparing to throw a flood of light upon all departments of human speculation and action. It was becoming necessary to stand emphatically in one army or the other. Lyell[1] was surrounding himself with disciples, who were making strides in the direction of discovery. Darwin had long been collecting facts with regard to the variation of animals and plants. Hooker and Wallace, Asa Gray and even Agassiz,[2] each in his own sphere, were coming closer and closer to a perception of that secret which was first to reveal itself clearly to the patient and humble genius of Darwin. In the year before, in 1856, Darwin, under pressure from Lyell, had begun that modest statement of the new revelation, that "abstract of an essay," which developed so mightily into *The Origin of Species*. Wollaston's *Variation of Species*[3] had just appeared, and had been a nine days' wonder in the wilderness.

On the other side, the reactionaries, although never dreaming of the fate which hung over them, had not been idle. In 1857 the astounding question had for the first time been propounded with contumely,[4] "What, then, did we come from orangoutang?" The famous *Vestiges of Creation*[5] had been supplying a sugar-and-water panacea for those who could not escape from the

1. Sir Charles Lyell (1797–1875), British geologist.
2. Noted scientists. Sir Joseph Dalton Hooker (1817–1911), British botanist and explorer. Alfred Russel Wallace (1823–1913), British naturalist. Asa Gray (1810–1888), American botanist. Louis Agassiz (1807–1873), Swiss geologist and comparative anatomist.
3. *On the Variation of Species, with Especial Ref-*

erence to Insecta (1856), by the British entomologist Thomas V. Wollaston (1822–1878).
4. Insolent or insulting language or treatment.
5. This popular work of 1843–46 by Robert Chambers claimed to be "the first attempt to connect the natural sciences into a history of creation"; it asserted that all parts of nature were evolving onward and upward toward a greater state of perfection under God's direction.

trend of evidence, and who yet clung to revelation. Owen[6] was encouraging reaction by resisting, with all the strength of his prestige, the theory of the mutability of species.

In this period of intellectual ferment, as when a great political revolution is being planned, many possible adherents were confidentially tested with hints and encouraged to reveal their bias in a whisper. It was the notion of Lyell, himself a great mover of men, that, before the doctrine of natural selection was given to a world which would be sure to lift up at it a howl of execration, a certain bodyguard of sound and experienced naturalists, expert in the description of species, should be privately made aware of its tenor. Among those who were thus initiated, or approached with a view towards possible illumination, was my Father. He was spoken to by Hooker, and later on by Darwin, after meetings of the Royal Society[7] in the summer of 1857.

My Father's attitude towards the theory of natural selection was critical in his career, and oddly enough, it exercised an immense influence on my own experience as a child. Let it be admitted at once, mournful as the admission is, that every instinct in his intelligence went out at first to greet the new light. It had hardly done so, when a recollection of the opening chapter of Genesis checked it at the outset. He consulted with Carpenter,[8] a great investigator, but one who was fully as incapable as himself of remodeling his ideas with regard to the old, accepted hypotheses. They both determined, on various grounds, to have nothing to do with the terrible theory, but to hold steadily to the law of the fixity of species.* * *

My Father had never admired Sir Charles Lyell. I think that the famous Lord Chancellor manner of the geologist intimidated him, and we undervalue the intelligence of those whose conversation puts us at a disadvantage. For Darwin and Hooker, on the other hand, he had a profound esteem, and I know not whether this had anything to do with the fact that he chose, for his impetuous experiment in reaction, the field of geology, rather than that of zoology or botany. Lyell had been threatening to publish a book on the geological history of Man, which was to be a bombshell flung into the camp of the catastrophists. My Father, after long reflection, prepared a theory of his own, which, as he fondly hoped, would take the wind out of Lyell's sails, and justify geology to godly readers of Genesis. It was, very briefly, that there had been no gradual modification of the surface of the earth, or slow development of organic forms, but that when the catastrophic act of creation took place, the world presented, instantly, the structural appearance of a planet on which life had long existed.

The theory, coarsely enough, and to my Father's great indignation, was defined by a hasty press as being this—that God hid the fossils in the rocks in order to tempt geologists into infidelity. In truth, it was the logical and inevitable conclusion of accepting, literally, the doctrine of a sudden act of creation; it emphasized the fact that any breach in the circular course of nature could be conceived only on the supposition that the object created bore false witness to past processes, which had never taken place.

6. Sir Richard Owen (1804–1892), a leading British zoologist and paleontologist who was opposed to Darwin's theories.
7. The Royal Society of London for the Promotion of Natural Knowledge; founded in 1660, it was an important meeting place for independent scientists.
8. William B. Carpenter (1813–1885), British naturalist.

Never was a book cast upon the waters with greater anticipations of success than was this curious, this obstinate, this fanatical volume. My Father lived in a fever of suspense, waiting for the tremendous issue. This *Omphalos* of his, he thought, was to bring all the turmoil of scientific speculation to a close, fling geology into the arms of Scripture, and make the lion eat grass with the lamb.[9] It was not surprising, he admitted, that there had been experienced an ever-increasing discord between the facts which geology brings to light and the direct statements of the early chapters of Genesis. Nobody was to blame for that. My Father, and my Father alone, possessed the secret of the enigma; he alone held the key which could smoothly open the lock of geological mystery. He offered it, with a glowing gesture, to atheists and Christians alike. This was to be the universal panacea; this the system of intellectual therapeutics which could not but heal all the maladies of the age. But, alas! atheists and Christians alike looked at it, and laughed, and threw it away.

In the course of that dismal winter, as the post began to bring in private letters, few and chilly, and public reviews, many and scornful, my Father looked in vain for the approval of the churches, and in vain for the acquiescence of the scientific societies, and in vain for the gratitude of those "thousands of thinking persons," which he had rashly assured himself of receiving. As his reconciliation of Scripture statements and geological deductions was welcomed nowhere; as Darwin continued silent, and the youthful Huxley was scornful, and even Charles Kingsley,[1] from whom my Father had expected the most instant appreciation, wrote that he could not "give up the painful and slow conclusion of five and twenty years' study of geology, and believe that God has written on the rocks one enormous and superfluous lie"—as all this happened or failed to happen, a gloom, cold and dismal, descended upon our morning teacups.* * *

1907

9. Allusion to the biblical prophecy of a new world order in which "the wolf also shall dwell with the lamb . . . and the lion shall eat straw like the ox" (Isaiah 11.6–7).
1. Clergyman and novelist (1819–1875).

INDUSTRIALISM: PROGRESS OR DECLINE?

In 1835 the French statesman and author Alexis de Tocqueville wrote of Manchester: "From this foul drain, the greatest stream of human industry flows out to fertilize the whole world. From this filthy sewer pure gold flows. Here humanity attains its most complete development and its most brutish, here civilization works its miracles and civilized man is turned almost into a savage." De Tocqueville's graphic sense of the wealth and the wretchedness that the Industrial Revolution had created epitomized contemporary responses to the way in which manufacturing had transformed nineteenth-century England. Victorians debated whether the machine age was a blessing or a curse, whether the economic system was making humanity happier or more miserable. Did the Industrial Revolution represent progress, and how, in fact, was progress to be defined?

The Industrial Revolution was the result of a complex set of causes, none of which, by itself, could have given rise to the phenomenon: the crucial technological innovations would have meant little without notable population growth, an increase in agricultural efficiency that released much of the workforce from field labor, and key economic changes, such as greater mobility of capital. Transformations in the production of textiles led to the first and most dramatic break with age-old practices. First powered by hand, or sometimes by water, machinery to speed up spinning and weaving processes was developed in England in the eighteenth century; by the 1780s manufacturers were installing steam engines, newly improved by James Watt, in large buildings called mills or factories. Mill towns, producing cotton or woollen cloth for the world's markets, grew quickly in northern England; the population of the city of Manchester, for example, increased tenfold in the years between 1760 and 1830. The development of the railways in the 1830s initiated a new phase in the industrial age, marked by an enormous expansion in the production of iron and coal. By the beginning of the Victorian period, the Industrial Revolution had already created profound economic and social changes. Hundreds of thousands of workers had migrated to the industrial towns, where they lived in horribly crowded, unsanitary housing and labored very long hours—fourteen a day or more—at very low wages. Employers often preferred to hire women and children, who worked for even less money than men.

Moved by the terrible suffering of the workers, which was intensified by a severe depression in the early 1840s, writers and legislators drew increasingly urgent attention to the condition of the working class. A number of parliamentary committees and commissions in the 1830s and 1840s introduced testimony about working conditions in mines and factories that led to the beginning of government regulation and inspection, particularly of the working conditions of women and children. Other eyewitness accounts created a growing consciousness of the plight of the workers. In *The Condition of the Working Class* (1845), Friedrich Engels described the conclusions he drew in the twenty months he spent observing industrial conditions in Manchester. In a series of interviews written for the *Morning Chronicle* (1849–52), later published as *London Labour and the London Poor* (1861–62), the journalist Henry Mayhew created a portrait of working London by collecting scores of interviews with workers. Novels portraying the painful consequences of industrialism, such as Elizabeth Gaskell's *Mary Barton* (1848) and *North and South* (1855) and Charles Dickens's *Hard Times* (1854), began to appear.

The terrible living and working conditions of industrial laborers led a number of writers to see the Industrial Revolution as an appalling retrogression. Thomas Carlyle and John Ruskin both lamented the changed conditions of labor, the loss of craftsmanship and individual creativity, and the disappearance of what Karl Marx called the "feudal, patriarchal, idyllic relations" between employer and employee that they believed had existed in earlier economies. They criticized industrial manufacture not only for the misery of the conditions it created but also for its regimentation of minds and hearts as well as bodies and resources. In works such as *Past and Present* (1843) and *Unto This Last* (1860), Carlyle and Ruskin advocated a nostalgic and conservative ideal, in which employers and workers returned to a medieval relationship to craft and to authority and responsibility. Other writers drew more radical conclusions. William Morris's perception of the workers' plight led him to socialism, though a socialism with a medieval ideal; and Marx, in collaboration with Engels, based *The Communist Manifesto* of 1848 in part on Engels's observation of Manchester in *The Condition of the Working Class*. The outrage expressed by these authors is very different from the satisfaction evident in the writings of the historian Thomas Babington Macaulay, who congratulated England on the progress that industrialism had enabled.

It is instructive to compare the selections in this section with Carlyle's chapter "Captains of Industry" from *Past and Present*; Elizabeth Barrett Browning's poem about child labor, "The Cry of the Children" (1843); Ruskin's arguments about manufacture in *The Stones of Venice* (1851–53); and William Morris's explanation in "How I Became a Socialist" (1894).

For additional texts and images concerning industrialism, see the NAEL Archive.

THOMAS BABINGTON MACAULAY

I n a book titled *Colloquies on the Progress and Prospects of Society* (1829), the poet Robert Southey (1774–1843) had sought to expose the evils of industrialism and to assert the superiority of the traditional feudal and agricultural way of life of England's past. His romantic conservatism provoked Macaulay (1800–1859) to review the book in a long and characteristic essay, published in the *Edinburgh Review* (1830). As in his popular *History of England* (1849–61), Macaulay seeks here to demolish his opponent with a bombardment of facts and figures, demonstrating that industrialism and middle-class government have resulted in progress and increased comforts for humankind.

From A Review of Southey's *Colloquies*

[EVIDENCE OF PROGRESS]

* * * Perhaps we could not select a better instance of the spirit which pervades the whole book than the passages in which Mr. Southey gives his opinion of the manufacturing system. There is nothing which he hates so bitterly. It is, according to him, a system more tyrannical than that of the feudal ages, a system of actual servitude, a system which destroys the bodies and degrades the minds of those who are engaged in it. He expresses a hope that the competition of other nations may drive us out of the field; that our foreign trade may decline; and that we may thus enjoy a restoration of national sanity and strength. But he seems to think that the extermination of the whole manufacturing population would be a blessing, if the evil could be removed in no other way.

Mr. Southey does not bring forward a single fact in support of these views; and, as it seems to us, there are facts which lead to a very different conclusion. In the first place, the poor rate[1] is very decidedly lower in the manufacturing than in the agricultural districts. If Mr. Southey will look over the Parliamentary returns on this subject, he will find that the amount of parochial relief required by the laborers in the different counties of England is almost exactly in inverse proportion to the degree in which the manufacturing system has been introduced into those counties. The returns for the years ending in March, 1825, and in March, 1828, are now before us. In the former year we find the poor rate highest in Sussex,[2] about twenty shillings to every inhabitant. Then come Buckinghamshire, Essex, Suffolk, Bedfordshire, Huntingdonshire, Kent, and Norfolk. In all these the rate is above fifteen shillings a head. We will not go through the whole. Even in Westmoreland and the North Riding of Yorkshire, the rate is at more than eight shillings. In Cumberland and Monmouthshire, the most fortunate of all the agricultural

---

1. Taxes on property, to provide food and lodging for the unemployed or unemployable. The amount or rate of such taxes varied from district to district in England, depending on local conditions of unemployment.
2. A predominantly agricultural district.

districts, it is at six shillings. But in the West Riding of Yorkshire,[3] it is as low as five shillings: and when we come to Lancashire, we find it at four shillings, one-fifth of what it is in Sussex. The returns of the year ending in March, 1828, are a little, and but a little, more unfavourable to the manufacturing districts. Lancashire, even in that season of distress, required a smaller poor rate than any other district, and little more than one-fourth of the poor rate raised in Sussex. Cumberland alone, of the agricultural districts, was as well off as the West Riding of Yorkshire. These facts seem to indicate that the manufacturer[4] is both in a more comfortable and in a less dependent situation than the agricultural laborer.

As to the effect of the manufacturing system on the bodily health, we must beg leave to estimate it by a standard far too low and vulgar for a mind so imaginative as that of Mr. Southey, the proportion of births and deaths. We know that, during the growth of this atrocious system, this new misery, to use the phrases of Mr. Southey, this new enormity, this birth of a portentous age, this pest which no man can approve whose heart is not seared or whose understanding has not been darkened, there has been a great diminution of mortality, and that this diminution has been greater in the manufacturing towns than anywhere else. The mortality still is, as it always was, greater in towns than in the country. But the difference has diminished in an extraordinary degree. There is the best reason to believe that the annual mortality of Manchester, about the middle of the last century, was one in twenty-eight. It is now reckoned at one in forty-five. In Glasgow and Leeds a similar improvement has taken place. Nay, the rate of mortality in those three great capitals of the manufacturing districts is now considerably less than it was, fifty years ago, over England and Wales, taken together, open country and all. We might with some plausibility maintain that the people live longer because they are better fed, better lodged, better clothed, and better attended in sickness, and that these improvements are owing to that increase of national wealth which the manufacturing system has produced.

Much more might be said on this subject. But to what end? It is not from bills of mortality and statistical tables that Mr. Southey has learned his political creed. He cannot stoop to study the history of the system which he abuses, to strike the balance between the good and evil which it has produced, to compare district with district, or generation with generation. We will give his own reason for his opinion, the only reason which he gives for it, in his own words:

> We remained a while in silence looking upon the assemblage of dwellings below. Here, and in the adjoining hamlet of Millbeck, the effects of manufacturer and of agriculture may be seen and compared. The old cottages are such as the poet and the painter equally delight in beholding. Substantially built of the native stone without mortar, dirtied with no white lime, and their long low roofs covered with slate, if they had been raised by the magic of some indigenous Amphion's music,[5] the materials could not have adjusted themselves more beautifully in accord with the surrounding scene; and time has still further harmonized them with weather stains, lichens, and moss, short grasses, and short fern,

3. A manufacturing district.
4. I.e., factory worker.
5. According to Greek mythology, Amphion's

magical skill as a harp player caused the walls of Thebes to be erected without human aid.

and stoneplants of various kinds. The ornamented chimneys, round or square, less adorned than those which, like little turrets, crest the houses of the Portuguese peasantry, and yet not less happily suited to their place; the hedge of clipped box beneath the windows, the rose bushes beside the door, the little patch of flower ground, with its tall hollyhocks in front; the garden beside, the beehives, and the orchard with its bank of daffodils and snowdrops, the earliest and the profusest in these parts, indicate in the owners some portion of ease and leisure, some regard to neatness and comfort, some sense of natural, and innocent, and healthful enjoyment. The new cottages of the manufacturers are upon the manufacturing pattern—naked, and in a row.

"How is it," said I, "that everything which is connected with manufactures presents such features of unqualified deformity? From the largest of Mammon's temples down to the poorest hovel in which his helotry[6] are stalled, these edifices have all one character. Time will not mellow them; nature will neither clothe nor conceal them; and they will remain always as offensive to the eye as to the mind."

Here is wisdom. Here are the principles on which nations are to be governed. Rosebushes and poor rates, rather than steam engines and independence. Mortality and cottages with weather stains, rather than health and long life with edifices which time cannot mellow. We are told that our age has invented atrocities beyond the imagination of our fathers; that society has been brought into a state compared with which extermination would be a blessing; and all because the dwellings of cotton-spinners are naked and rectangular. Mr. Southey has found out a way, he tells us, in which the effects of manufactures and agriculture may be compared. And what is this way? To stand on a hill, to look at a cottage and a factory, and to see which is the prettier. Does Mr. Southey think that the body of the English peasantry live, or ever lived, in substantial or ornamented cottages, with boxhedges, flower gardens, beehives, and orchards? If not, what is his parallel worth? We despise those mock philosophers,[7] who think that they serve the cause of science by depreciating literature and the fine arts. But if anything could excuse their narrowness of mind, it would be such a book as this. It is not strange that, when one enthusiast makes the picturesque the test of political good, another should feel inclined to proscribe altogether the pleasures of taste and imagination.

* * *

It is not strange that, differing so widely from Mr. Southey as to the past progress of society, we should differ from him also as to its probable destiny. He thinks, that to all outward appearance, the country is hastening to destruction; but he relies firmly on the goodness of God. We do not see either the piety or the rationality of thus confidently expecting that the Supreme Being will interfere to disturb the common succession of causes and effects. We, too, rely on his goodness, on his goodness as manifested, not in extraor-

6. I.e., slaves (helots were a class of serfs in ancient Sparta). "Mammon": the devil of covetousness.
7. Presumably such Utilitarian philosophers as Jeremy Bentham (1748–1832), who had equated poetry with pushpin, an idle pastime. It should be noted, however, that although Macaulay often attacked the Utilitarians for their narrow preoccupation with theory, his own position had much in common with theirs.

dinary interpositions, but in those general laws which it has pleased him to establish in the physical and in the moral world. We rely on the natural tendency of the human intellect to truth, and on the natural tendency of society to improvement. We know no well-authenticated instance of a people which has decidedly retrograded in civilization and prosperity, except from the influence of violent and terrible calamities, such as those which laid the Roman Empire in ruins, or those which, about the beginning of the sixteenth century, desolated Italy.[8] We know of no country which, at the end of fifty years of peace and tolerably good government, has been less prosperous than at the beginning of that period. The political importance of a state may decline, as the balance of power is disturbed by the introduction of new forces. Thus the influence of Holland and of Spain is much diminished. But are Holland and Spain poorer than formerly? We doubt it. Other countries have outrun them. But we suspect that they have been positively, though not relatively, advancing. We suspect that Holland is richer than when she sent her navies up the Thames,[9] that Spain is richer than when a French king was brought captive to the footstool of Charles the Fifth.[1]

History is full of the signs of this natural progress of society. We see in almost every part of the annals of mankind how the industry of individuals, struggling up against wars, taxes, famines, conflagrations, mischievous prohibitions, and more mischievous protections, creates faster than governments can squander, and repairs whatever invaders can destroy. We see the wealth of nations increasing, and all the arts of life approaching nearer and nearer to perfection, in spite of the grossest corruption and the wildest profusion on the part of rulers.

The present moment is one of great distress. But how small will that distress appear when we think over the history of the last forty years; a war,[2] compared with which all other wars sink into insignificance; taxation, such as the most heavily taxed people of former times could not have conceived; a debt larger than all the public debts that ever existed in the world added together; the food of the people studiously rendered dear;[3] the currency imprudently debased, and imprudently restored. Yet is the country poorer than in 1790? We firmly believe that, in spite of all the misgovernment of her rulers, she has been almost constantly becoming richer and richer. Now and then there has been a stoppage, now and then a short retrogression; but as to the general tendency there can be no doubt. A single breaker may recede; but the tide is evidently coming in.

If we were to prophesy that in the year 1930 a population of fifty millions, better fed, clad, and lodged than the English of our time, will cover these islands, that Sussex and Huntingdonshire will be wealthier than the wealthiest parts of the West Riding of Yorkshire now are, that cultivation, rich as

8. These "calamities" were invasions by outside powers: in 410 the Visigoths sacked Rome, and the French and Spanish fought for control of the Italian states in the early 16th century.
9. In 1667 a Dutch fleet displayed its power by sailing up the river Thames without being challenged by the English navy.
1. Charles V, Holy Roman emperor (and king of Spain as Charles I), captured the king of France, Francis I, in the battle of Pavia (1525).

2. The wars against France and Napoleon, extending, with some interruptions, from 1792 to 1815. During the war years England lost one in six men of fighting age and had to endure the pressure of Napoleon's trade boycotts. Historian Derek Beales claims that the resulting economic disruption was comparable to that experienced in World War I.
3. Expensive.

that of a flower garden, will be carried up to the very tops of Ben Nevis and Helvellyn,[4] that machines constructed on principles yet undiscovered will be in every house, that there will be no highways but railroads, no traveling but by steam, that our debt, vast as it seems to us, will appear to our great-grandchildren a trifling encumbrance, which might easily be paid off in a year or two, many people would think us insane. We prophesy nothing; but this we say: If any person had told the Parliament which met in perplexity and terror after the crash in 1720[5] that in 1830 the wealth of England would surpass all their wildest dreams, that the annual revenue would equal the principal of that debt which they considered as an intolerable burden, that for one man of ten thousand pounds then living there would be five men of fifty thousand pounds, that London would be twice as large and twice as populous, and that nevertheless the rate of mortality would have diminished to one-half of what it then was, that the post office would bring more into the exchequer than the excise and customs had brought in together under Charles the Second, that stage coaches would run from London to York in twenty-four hours, that men would be in the habit of sailing without wind, and would be beginning to ride without horses, our ancestors would have given as much credit to the prediction as they gave to *Gulliver's Travels*.[6] Yet the prediction would have been true; and they would have perceived that it was not altogether absurd, if they had considered that the country was then raising every year a sum which would have purchased the fee-simple of the revenue of the Plantagenets,[7] ten times what supported the Government of Elizabeth, three times what, in the time of Cromwell,[8] had been thought intolerably oppressive. To almost all men the state of things under which they have been used to live seems to be the necessary state of things. We have heard it said that five per cent is the natural interest of money, that twelve is the natural number of a jury, that forty shillings is the natural qualification of a county voter. Hence it is that, though in every age everybody knows that up to his own time progressive improvement has been taking place, nobody seems to reckon on any improvement during the next generation. We cannot absolutely prove that those are in error who tell us that society has reached a turning point, that we have seen our best days. But so said all who came before us, and with just as much apparent reason. "A million a year will beggar us," said the patriots of 1640. "Two millions a year will grind the country to powder," was the cry in 1660. "Six millions a year, and a debt of fifty millions!" exclaimed Swift, "the high allies have been the ruin of us." "A hundred and forty millions of debt!" said Junius;[9] "well may we say that we owe Lord Chatham more than we shall ever pay, if we owe him such a load as this." "Two hundred and forty millions of debt!" cried all the statesmen of 1783 in chorus; "what abilities, or what economy on the part of a minister, can save a country so burdened?" We know that if, since 1783, no fresh

4. Mountains in Scotland and in the English Lake District, respectively.
5. The first great stock market crash, commonly known as the South Sea Bubble.
6. The 1726 novel by the Irish churchman, satirist, and poet Jonathan Swift (1667–1745). Charles II reigned from 1660 to 1685.
7. The Plantagenet family provided the monarchs of England from 1145 to 1485. "Fee-simple": absolute ownership of their estates.

8. Oliver Cromwell effectively ruled England from the beheading of Charles I in 1651 until his own death in 1658. Elizabeth I reigned from 1558 to 1603.
9. Pseudonym of a political commentator whose letters (1769–72) usually praised William Pitt, earl of Chatham (1708–1778). Pitt, as leader of the war against France, which gained Canada for England, could have been blamed for running his country into debt.

debt had been incurred, the increased resources of the country would have enabled us to defray that debt at which Pitt, Fox, and Burke[1] stood aghast, nay, to defray it over and over again, and that with much lighter taxation than what we have actually borne. On what principle is it that, when we see nothing but improvement behind us, we are to expect nothing but deterioration before us?

It is not by the intermeddling of Mr. Southey's idol, the omniscient and omnipotent State, but by the prudence and energy of the people, that England has hitherto been carried forward in civilization; and it is to the same prudence and the same energy that we now look with comfort and good hope. Our rulers will best promote the improvement of the nation by strictly confining themselves to their own legitimate duties, by leaving capital to find its most lucrative course, commodities their fair price, industry and intelligence their natural reward, idleness and folly their natural punishment, by maintaining peace, by defending property, by diminishing the price of law, and by observing strict economy in every department of the State. Let the Government do this: the People will assuredly do the rest.

1830

1. Noted statesmen and members of Parliament in Great Britain. William Pitt the Younger (1759–1806). Charles James Fox (1749–1806). Edmund Burke (1729–1797).

THE CHILDREN'S EMPLOYMENT COMMISSION

Although official attempts to regulate child labor began in 1788, when Parliament passed the Chimney Sweepers Act, the more general problem was not addressed until well into the nineteenth century. Government investigations (Select Committees and Royal Commissions) took place in 1816 and the early 1830s and led to numerous legislative measures, but most of their provisions were meaningless because they were not enforced. The Factories Regulation Act of 1833 marks the first significant point of successful intervention: the act both established a minimum age for all workers in textile mills (nine years old) and set limits to the hours that children in different age groups and women could work in a week. More broadly, a Royal Commission was convened in 1842–43 to examine "the mines and collieries of the United Kingdom and all trades and manufactures whatever in which children work together in numbers." The reports of the commission, from which the following excerpt and two illustrations (on p. 634) are taken, caused dismay and disbelief when they were made generally available; Elizabeth Barrett Browning's poem "The Cry of the Children" (1843) was one of the many public responses to the scandal. In the legislation that followed, girls and women were banned from mine work; although the authors of the bill had also hoped to prohibit the employment of boys under thirteen years of age, parliamentary debate knocked the age down to ten.

The first illustration shows a hurrier, a worker who dragged a loaded corve, or wagon; these weighed between two hundred and five hundred pounds and were attached to the hurrier by a chain. The passageways in the mine (or pit) were sometimes only sixteen inches high. The second illustration presents a thruster, who

"Hurrier." An illustration of a "hurrier" in a Yorkshire coalmine, from the 1842–43 Children's Employment Commission report.

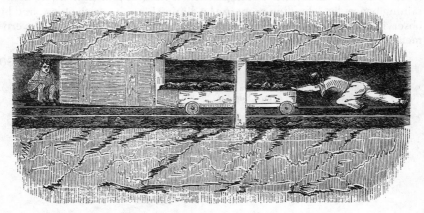

"Trapper" and "Thruster." An illustration of a "trapper" and a "thruster" in a Lancashire coalmine, from the 1842–43 Children's Employment Commission report.

pushed a corve. The child on the left is a trapper: the youngest workers of all, these five- or six-year-olds sat alone in darkness to open and close the doors that controlled the mine's ventilation system. The extract comes from the evidence collected by Commissioner S. S. Scriven, who visited the mines in the West Riding of Yorkshire in the company of a local doctor and lawyer, and interviewed the child laborers there.

From First Report of the Commissioners, Mines

[CHILD MINE-WORKER IN YORKSHIRE]
Margaret Gomley, Living at Lindley Moor, aged 9. May 7

They call me Peggy for my nick-name down here, but my right name is Margaret; I am about nine years, or going nine; I have been at work in the pit thrusting corves above a year; come in the morning sometimes at seven o'clock, sometimes half-past seven, and I go sometimes home at six o'clock, sometimes at seven when I do over-work. I get my breakfast of porridge before

I come, and bring a piece of muffin, which I eat on coming to pit; I get my dinner at 12 o'clock, which is a dry muffin, and sometimes butter on, but have no time allowed to stop to eat it, I eat it while I am thrusting the load; I get no tea, but get some supper when I get home, and then go to bed when I have washed me; and am very tired. I worked in pit last winter; I don't know at what hour I went down, as we have no clock, but it was day-light; it was six o'clock when we came up, but not always. They flog us down in the pit, sometimes with their hand upon my bottom, which hurts me very much; Thomas Copeland flogs me more than once in a day, which makes me cry. There are two other girls working with me, and there was four, but one left because she had the bellyache; I am poorly myself sometimes with bellyache, and sometimes headache. I had rather lake than go into the pit; I get 5*d.* a-day, but I had rather set cards[1] for 5*d.* a-day than go into the pit. The men often swear at me; many times they say Damn thee, and other times God damn thee (and such like), Peggy.

[Commissioner Scriven's commentary]

I descended this pit accompanied by one of the banksmen,[2] and, on alighting at the bottom, found the entrance to the mainway 2 feet 10 inches, and, which extended 500 yards. The bottom was deep in mire, and, as I had no corves low enough to convey me to the workings, waited some time under the dripping shaft the arrival of the hurriers, as I had reason to suspect there were some very young children labouring there. At length three girls arrived, with as many boys. It was impossible in the dark to distinguish the sexes. They were all naked excepting their shifts or shirts. Having placed one into the corve, I gave the signal, and ascended. On alighting on the pit's bank I discovered that it was a girl. I could not have believed that I should have found human nature so degraded. There is nothing that I can conceive amidst all the misery and wretchedness in the worst of factories equal to this. Mr. Holroyd, solicitor, and Mr. Brook, surgeon, practising in Stainland, were present, who confessed that, although living within a few miles, they could not have believed that such a system of unchristian cruelty could have existed.

1842–43

---

1. I.e., work in a textile factory, where workers programmed looms to weave patterns with a series of punched cards. "Lake": play truant, or hookey (Yorkshire dialect). "5*d.*": five pence (*d.* abbreviates *denarius*, "penny" in Latin).
2. Colliery supervisors who worked above ground.

FRIEDRICH ENGELS

These eyewitness accounts from *The Condition of the Working Class* (1845) describe conditions of 1844, when Engels (1820–1895), the son of a successful German industrialist, had been living in England, chiefly in Manchester. The book was translated from the German into English in 1885, and first published in Britain in 1891; this translation is by W. O. Henderson and W. H. Chaloner (1958). The first two paragraphs are the conclusion of chapter 2, *The Industrial Proletariat*; the balance is from chapter 3.

From The Great Towns

Industry and commerce attain their highest stage of development in the big towns, so that it is here that the effects of industrialization on the wage earners can be most clearly seen. It is in these big towns that the concentration of property has reached its highest point. Here the manners and customs of the good old days have been most effectively destroyed. Here the very name of "Merry England" has long since been forgotten, because the inhabitants of the great manufacturing centers have never even heard from their grandparents what life was like in those days. In these towns there are only rich and poor, because the lower middle classes are fast disappearing. At one time this section of the middle classes was the most stable social group, but now it has become the least stable. It is represented in the big factory towns today partly by a few survivors from a bygone age and partly by a group of people who are anxious to get rich as quickly as possible. Of these shady speculators and dubious traders one becomes rich while ninety-nine go bankrupt. Indeed, for more than half of those who have failed, bankruptcy has become a habit.

The vast majority of the inhabitants of these towns are the workers. We propose to discuss their condition and to discover how they have been influenced by life and work in the great factory towns.

* * *

London is unique, because it is a city in which one can roam for hours without leaving the built-up area and without seeing the slightest sign of the approach of open country. This enormous agglomeration of population on a single spot has multiplied a hundred-fold the economic strength of the two and a half million inhabitants concentrated there. This great population has made London the commercial capital of the world and has created the gigantic docks in which are assembled the thousands of ships which always cover the River Thames. I know nothing more imposing than the view one obtains of the river when sailing from the sea up to London Bridge. Especially above Woolwich the houses and docks are packed tightly together on both banks of the river. The further one goes up the river the thicker becomes the concentration of ships lying at anchor, so that eventually only a narrow shipping lane is left free in midstream. Here hundreds of steamships dart rapidly to and fro. All this is so magnificent and impressive that one is lost in admiration. The traveler has good reason to marvel at England's greatness even before he steps on English soil.

It is only later that the traveler appreciates the human suffering which has made all this possible. He can only realize the price that has been paid for all this magnificence after he has tramped the pavements of the main streets of London for some days and has tired himself out by jostling his way through the crowds and dodging the endless stream of coaches and carts which fills the streets. It is only when he has visited the slums of this great city that it dawns upon him that the inhabitants of modern London have had to sacrifice so much that is best in human nature in order to create those wonders of civilization with which their city teems. The vast majority of Londoners have had to let so many of their potential creative faculties lie dormant, stunted and unused in order that a small, closely-knit group of their fellow citizens could develop to the full the qualities with which nature has endowed them. The restless and noisy activity of the crowded streets is highly distasteful, and it is surely abhorrent to human nature itself. Hundreds of thousands of men and women drawn from all classes and ranks of society pack the streets of London. Are they not all human beings with the same innate characteristics and potentialities? Are they not all equally interested in the pursuit of happiness? And do they not all aim at happiness by following similar methods? Yet they rush past each other as if they had nothing in common. They are tacitly agreed on one thing only—that everyone should keep to the right of the pavement so as not to collide with the stream of people moving in the opposite direction. No one even thinks of sparing a glance for his neighbor in the streets. The more that Londoners are packed into a tiny space, the more repulsive and disgraceful becomes the brutal indifference with which they ignore their neighbors and selfishly concentrate upon their private affairs. We know well enough that this isolation of the individual— this narrow-minded egotism—is everywhere the fundamental principle of modern society. But nowhere is this selfish egotism so blatantly evident as in the frantic bustle of the great city. The disintegration of society into individuals, each guided by his private principles and each pursuing his own aims has been pushed to its furthest limits in London. Here indeed human society has been split into its component atoms.

From this it follows that the social conflict—the war of all against all—is fought in the open. * * * Here men regard their fellows not as human beings, but as pawns in the struggle for existence. Everyone exploits his neighbor with the result that the stronger tramples the weaker under foot. The strongest of all, a tiny group of capitalists, monopolize everything, while the weakest, who are in the vast majority, succumb to the most abject poverty.

What is true of London is true also of all the great towns, such as Manchester, Birmingham, and Leeds. Everywhere one finds on the one hand the most barbarous indifference and selfish egotism and on the other the most distressing scenes of misery and poverty. Signs of social conflict are to be found everywhere. Everyone turns his house into a fortress to defend himself—under the protection of the law—from the depredations of his neighbors. Class warfare is so open and shameless that it has to be seen to be believed. The observer of such an appalling state of affairs must shudder at the consequences of such feverish activity and can only marvel that so crazy a social and economic structure should survive at all.

* * *

Every great town has one or more slum areas into which the working classes are packed. Sometimes, of course, poverty is to be found hidden away in alleys close to the stately homes of the wealthy. Generally, however, the workers are segregated in separate districts where they struggle through life as best they can out of sight of the more fortunate classes of society. The slums of the English towns have much in common—the worst houses in a town being found in the worst districts. They are generally unplanned wildernesses of one- or two-storied terrace houses[1] built of brick. Wherever possible these have cellars which are also used as dwellings. These little houses of three or four rooms and a kitchen are called cottages, and throughout England, except for some parts of London, are where the working classes normally live. These streets themselves are usually unpaved and full of holes. They are filthy and strewn with animal and vegetable refuse. Since they have neither gutters nor drains the refuse accumulates in stagnant, stinking puddles. Ventilation in the slums is inadequate owing to the hopelessly unplanned nature of these areas. A great many people live huddled together in a very small area, and so it is easy to imagine the nature of the air in these workers' quarters. However, in fine weather the streets are used for the drying of washing, and clothes lines are stretched across the streets from house to house and wet garments are hung out on them.

We propose to describe some of these slums in detail.

* * *

If we cross Blackstone Edge on foot or take the train we reach Manchester, the regional capital of South Lancashire, and enter the classic home of English industry. This is the masterpiece of the Industrial Revolution and at the same time the mainspring of all the workers' movements. Once more we are in a beautiful hilly countryside. The land slopes gently down toward the Irish Sea, intersected by the charming green valleys of the Ribble, the Irwell, the Mersey, and their tributaries. A hundred years ago this region was to a great extent thinly populated marshland. Now it is covered with towns and villages and is the most densely populated part of England. In Lancashire—particularly in Manchester—is to be found not only the origin but the heart of the industry of the United Kingdom. Manchester Exchange is the thermometer which records all the fluctuations of industrial and commercial activity. The evolution of the modern system of manufacture has reached its climax in Manchester. It was in the South Lancashire cotton industry that Water and steam power first replaced hand machines. It was here that such machines as the power-loom and the self-acting mule[2] replaced the old hand-loom and spinning wheel. It is here that the division of labor has been pushed to its furthest limits. These three factors are the essence of modern industry. In all three of them the cotton industry was the pioneer and remains ahead in all branches of industry. In the circumstances it is to be expected that it is in this region that the inevitable consequences of industrialization in so far as they affect the working classes are most strikingly evident. Nowhere else can the life and conditions of the industrial proletariat be studied in all their aspects as in South Lancashire. Here can be seen most clearly the degradation into which the worker sinks owing to the introduction of steam power, machinery, and the division of labor. Here, too, can be seen most the strenuous efforts of the proletariat to raise themselves from their degraded situation. I propose to examine conditions in Manchester in greater detail for two reasons. In the first place, Manchester is the classic

1. Row houses.
2. A machine that automatically winds spun yarn directly onto spindles.

type of modern industrial town. Secondly, I know Manchester as well as I know my native town and I know more about it than most of its inhabitants.

*   *   *   *claiming authority*

Owing to the curious lay-out of the town it is quite possible for someone to live for years in Manchester and to travel daily to and from his work without ever seeing a working-class quarter or coming into contact with an artisan. He who visits Manchester simply on business or for pleasure need never see the slums, mainly because the working-class districts and the middle-class districts are quite distinct. This division is due partly to deliberate policy and partly to instinctive and tacit agreement between the two social groups. In those areas where the two social groups happen to come into contact with each other the middle classes sanctimoniously ignore the existence of their less fortunate neighbors. In the center of Manchester there is a fairly large commercial district, which is about half a mile long and half a mile broad. This district is almost entirely given over to offices and warehouses. Nearly the whole of this district has no permanent residents and is deserted at night, when only policemen patrol its dark, narrow thoroughfares with their bull's-eye lanterns.[3] This district is intersected by certain main streets which carry an enormous volume of traffic. The lower floors of the buildings are occupied by shops of dazzling splendor. A few of the upper stories on these premises are used as dwellings and the streets present a relatively busy appearance until late in the evening. Around this commercial quarter there is a belt of built-up areas on the average one and a half miles in width, which is occupied entirely by working-class dwellings. This area of workers' houses includes all Manchester proper, except the center, all Salford and Hulme, an important part of Pendleton and Chorlton, two-thirds of Ardwick, and certain small areas of Cheetham Hill and Broughton. Beyond this belt of working-class houses or dwellings lie the districts inhabited by the middle classes and the upper classes. The former are to be found in regularly laid out streets near the working-class districts—in Chorlton and in the remoter parts of Cheetham Hill. The villas of the upper classes are surrounded by gardens and lie in the higher and remoter parts of Chorlton and Ardwick or on the breezy heights of Cheetham Hill, Broughton, and Pendleton. The upper class enjoy healthy country air and live in luxurious and comfortable dwellings which are linked to the center of Manchester by omnibuses which run every fifteen or thirty minutes. To such an extent has the convenience of the rich been considered in the planning of Manchester that these plutocrats can travel from their houses to their places of business in the center of the town by the shortest routes, which run entirely through working-class districts, without even realizing how close they are to the misery and filth which lie on both sides of the road.

*   *   *

I will now give a description of the working-class districts of Manchester. The first of them is the Old Town, which lies between the northern limit of the commercial quarter and the River Irk. Here even the better streets, such as Todd Street, Long Millgate, Withy Grove, and Shudehill are narrow

---

3. Lanterns that have a hemispherical lens.

and tortuous. The houses are dirty, old, and tumble-down. The sidestreets have been built in a disgraceful fashion. If one enters the district near the "Old Church" and goes down Long Millgate, one sees immediately on the right hand side a row of antiquated houses where not a single front wall is standing upright. This is a remnant of the old Manchester of the days before the town became industrialized. The original inhabitants and their children have left for better houses in other districts, while the houses in Long Millgate, which no longer satisfied them, were left to a tribe of workers containing a strong Irish element. Here one is really and truly in a district which is quite obviously given over entirely to the working classes, because even the shopkeepers and the publicans of Long Millgate make no effort to give their establishments a semblance of cleanliness. The condition of this street may be deplorable, but it is by no means as bad as the alleys and courts which lie behind it, and which can be approached only by covered passages so narrow that two people cannot pass. Anyone who has never visited these courts and alleys can have no idea of the fantastic[4] way in which the houses have been packed together in disorderly confusion in impudent defiance of all reasonable principles of town planning. And the fault lies not merely in the survival of old property from earlier periods in Manchester's history. Only in quite modern times has the policy of cramming as many houses as possible on to such space as was not utilized in earlier periods reached its climax. The result is that today not an inch of space remains between the houses and any further building is now physically impossible. To prove my point I reproduce a small section of a plan of Manchester.[5] It is by no means the worst slum in Manchester and it does not cover one-tenth of the area of Manchester.

This sketch will be sufficient to illustrate the crazy[6] layout of the whole district lying near the River Irk. There is a very sharp drop of some 15 to 30 feet down to the south bank of the Irk at this point. As many as three rows of houses have generally been squeezed onto this precipitous slope. The lowest row of houses stands directly on the bank of the river while the front walls of the highest row stand on the crest of the ridge in Long Millgate. Moreover, factory buildings are also to be found on the banks of the river. In short the layout of the upper part of Long Millgate at the top of the rise is just as disorderly and congested as the lower part of the street. To the right and left a number of covered passages from Long Millgate give access to several courts. On reaching them one meets with a degree of dirt and revolting filth the like of which is not to be found elsewhere. The worst courts are those leading down to the Irk, which contain unquestionably the most dreadful dwellings I have ever seen. In one of these courts, just at the entrance where the covered passage ends, there is a privy without a door. This privy is so dirty that the inhabitants of the court can only enter or leave the court if they are prepared to wade through puddles of stale urine and excrement. Anyone who wishes to confirm this description should go to the first court on the bank of the Irk above Ducie Bridge. Several tanneries are situated on the bank of the river and they fill the neighborhood with the stench of animal putrefaction. The only way of getting to the courts below Ducie Bridge is by going down flights of narrow dirty steps and one

4. Confused, haphazard.
5. Not reprinted here.

6. Unsound, flawed.

can only reach the houses by treading over heaps of dirt and filth. The first court below Ducie Bridge is called Allen's Court. At the time of the cholera [1832] this court was in such a disgraceful state that the sanitary inspectors [of the local Board of Health] evacuated the inhabitants. The court was then swept and fumigated with chlorine. In his pamphlet[7] Dr. Kay gives a horrifying description of conditions in this court at that time. Since Kay wrote this pamphlet, this court appears to have been at any rate partly demolished and rebuilt. If one looks down the river from Ducie Bridge one does at least see several ruined walls and high piles of rubble, side by side with some recently built houses. The view from this bridge, which is mercifully concealed by a high parapet from all but the tallest mortals, is quite characteristic of the whole district. At the bottom the Irk flows, or rather, stagnates. It is a narrow, coal-black, stinking river full of filth and rubbish which it deposits on the more low-lying right bank. In dry weather this bank presents the spectacle of a series of the most revolting blackish-green puddles of slime from the depths of which bubbles of miasmatic gases constantly rise and create a stench which is unbearable even to those standing on the bridge forty or fifty feet above the level of the water. Moreover, the flow of the river is continually interrupted by numerous high weirs, behind which large quantities of slime and refuse collect and putrefy. Above Ducie Bridge there are some tall tannery buildings, and further up there are dye-works, bone mills, and gasworks. All the filth, both liquid and solid, discharged by these works finds its way into the River Irk, which also receives the contents of the adjacent sewers and privies. The nature of the filth deposited by this river may well be imagined. If one looks at the heaps of garbage below Ducie Bridge one can gauge the extent to which accumulated dirt, filth, and decay permeate the courts on the steep left bank of the river. The houses are packed very closely together and since the bank of the river is very steep it is possible to see a part of every house. All of them have been blackened by soot, all of them are crumbling with age and all have broken window panes and window frames. In the background there are old factory buildings which look like barracks. On the opposite, low-lying bank of the river, one sees a long row of houses and factories. The second house is a roofless ruin, filled with refuse, and the third is built in such a low situation that the ground floor is uninhabitable and has neither doors nor windows. In the background one sees the paupers' cemetery, and the stations of the railways to Liverpool and Leeds. Behind these buildings is situated the workhouse, Manchester's "Poor Law Bastille."[8] The workhouse is built on a hill and from behind its high walls and battlements seems to threaten the whole adjacent working-class quarter like a fortress.

Above Ducie Bridge the left bank of the Irk becomes flatter and the right bank of the Irk becomes steeper and so the condition of the houses on both sides of the river becomes worse rather than better. Turning left from the main street which is still Long Millgate, the visitor can easily lose his way. He wanders aimlessly from one court to another. He turns one corner after another through innumerable narrow dirty alleyways and passages, and in

---

7. *The Moral and Physical Conditions of the Working Classes Employed in the Cotton Manufacture in Manchester* (1832), by the British doctor and public health and education reformer James Phillips Kay-Shuttleworth (1804–1877).

8. The workhouses established by the Poor Laws of the 1830s, because of the strict regimens enforced on inmates, were commonly likened to prisons such as the Bastille in Paris.

only a few minutes he has lost all sense of direction and does not know which way to turn. The area is full of ruined or half-ruined buildings. Some of them are actually uninhabited and that means a great deal in this quarter of the town. In the houses one seldom sees a wooden or a stone floor, while the doors and windows are nearly always broken and badly fitting. And as for the dirt! Everywhere one sees heaps of refuse, garbage, and filth. There are stagnant pools instead of gutters and the stench alone is so overpowering that no human being, even partially civilized, would find it bearable to live in such a district.[9] The recently constructed extension of the Leeds railway which crosses the Irk at this point has swept away some of these courts and alleys, but it has thrown open to public gaze some of the others. So it comes about that there is to be found immediately under the railway bridge a court which is even filthier and more revolting than all the others. This is simply because it was formerly so hidden and secluded that it could only be reached with considerable difficulty, [but is now exposed to the human eye]. I thought I knew this district well, but even I would never have found it had not the railway viaduct made a breach in the slums at this point. One walks along a very rough path on the river bank, in between clothes-posts and washing lines to reach a chaotic group of little, one-storied, one-roomed cabins. Most of them have earth floors, and working, living, and sleeping all take place in the one room. In such a hole, barely six feet long and five feet wide, I saw two beds—and what beds and bedding!—which filled the room, except for the fireplace and the doorstep. Several of these huts, as far as I could see, were completely empty, although the door was open and the inhabitants were leaning against the door posts. In front of the doors filth and garbage abounded. I could not see the pavement, but from time to time, I felt it was there because my feet scraped it. This whole collection of cattle sheds for human beings was surrounded on two sides by houses and a factory and on a third side by the river. [It was possible to get to this slum by only two routes]. One was the narrow path along the river bank, while the other was a narrow gateway which led to another human rabbit warren which was nearly as badly built and was nearly in such a bad condition as the one I have just described.

Enough of this! All along the Irk slums of this type abound. There is an unplanned and chaotic conglomeration of houses, most of which are more or less unhabitable. The dirtiness of the interiors of these premises is fully in keeping with the filth that surrounds them. How can people dwelling in such places keep clean! There are not even adequate facilities for satisfying the most natural daily needs. There are so few privies that they are either

[margin handwritten note: inspiring empathy]

---

9. Cf. another account of Manchester slums of the same decade in Elizabeth Gaskell's novel *Mary Barton* (1848), chap. 6:

Women from their doors tossed household slops of *every* description into the gutter; they ran into the next pool, which overflowed and stagnated. Heaps of ashes were stepping-stones, on which the passer-by, who cared in the least for cleanliness, took care not to put his foot. Our friends [two factory workers] were not dainty, but even they picked their way, till they got to some steps leading down . . . into the cellar in which a family of human beings lived. . . .

After the account I have given of the state of the street, no one can be surprised that on going into the cellar inhabited by Davenport, the smell was so foetid as almost to knock the two men down. Quickly recovering themselves, as those inured to such things do, they began to penetrate the thick darkness of the place, and to see three or four children rolling on the damp, nay wet brick floor, through which the stagnant, filthy moisture of the street oozed up; the fireplace was empty and black; the wife sat on her husband's lair [couch], and cried in the dank loneliness.

filled up everyday or are too far away for those who need to use them. How can these people wash when all that is available is the dirty water of the Irk? Pumps and piped water are to be found only in the better-class districts of the town. Indeed no one can blame these helots[1] of modern civilization if their homes are no cleaner than the occasional pigsties which are a feature of these slums. There are actually some property owners who are not ashamed to let[2] dwellings such as those which are to be found below Scotland Bridge. Here on the quayside a mere six feet from the water's edge is to be found a row of six or seven cellars, the bottoms of which are at least two feet beneath the low-water level of the Irk. [What can one say of the owner of] the corner house—situated on the opposite bank of the river above Scotland Bridge—who actually lets the upper floor although the premises downstairs are quite uninhabitable and no attempt has been made to board up the gaps left by the disappearance of doors and windows? This sort of thing is by no means uncommon in this part of Manchester, where, owing to the lack of conveniences, such deserted ground floors are often used by the whole neighborhood as privies.

1845

1. I.e., slaves (helots were a class of serfs in ancient Sparta).   2. Rent.

CHARLES KINGSLEY

The following selection is from chapter 8 of *Alton Locke*, a novel by Kingsley (1819–1875). Under the influence of Thomas Carlyle's writings and also as a result of his own observations, Kingsley, a clergyman, became deeply concerned with the sufferings of the working classes. The speaker here, a young tailor, is accompanied by an elderly Scottish bookseller, Sandy Mackaye.

From Alton Locke

[A LONDON SLUM]

It was a foul, chilly, foggy Saturday night. From the butchers' and greengrocers' shops the gaslights flared and flickered, wild and ghastly, over haggard groups of slipshod dirty women, bargaining for scraps of stale meat and frostbitten vegetables, wrangling about short weight and bad quality. Fish stalls and fruit stalls lined the edge of the greasy pavement, sending up odours as foul as the language of sellers and buyers. Blood and sewer water crawled from under doors and out of spouts, and reeked down the gutters among offal, animal and vegetable, in every stage of putrefaction. Foul vapours rose from cow sheds and slaughterhouses, and the doorways of undrained alleys, where the inhabitants carried the filth out on their shoes from the backyard into

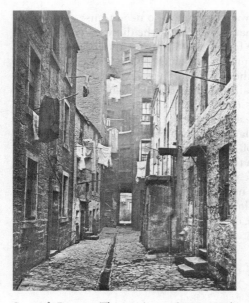

Scottish Poverty. Thomas Annan (1829–1887) was one of the first photographers to record the housing conditions of the poor. This image of Scottish poverty in the late 1860s ("Close, No. 75 High Street") appeared in his book *The Old Closes and Streets of Glasgow* (1877).

the court, and from the court up into the main street; while above, hanging like cliffs over the streets—those narrow, brawling torrents of filth, and poverty, and sin—the houses with their teeming load of life were piled up into the dingy, choking night. A ghastly, deafening, sickening sight it was. Go, scented Belgravian![1] and see what London is! and then go to the library which God has given thee—one often fears in vain—and see what science says this London might be!

* * *

We went on through a back street or two, and then into a huge, miserable house, which, a hundred years ago, perhaps, had witnessed the luxury, and rung to the laughter of some one great fashionable family, alone there in their glory. Now every room of it held its family, or its group of families—a phalanstery[2] of all the fiends—its grand staircase, with the carved balustrades rotting and crumbling away piecemeal, converted into a common sewer for all its inmates. Up stair after stair we went, while wails of children, and curses of men, steamed out upon the hot stifling rush of air from every doorway, till, at the topmost story, we knocked at a garret door. We entered. Bare it was of furniture, comfortless, and freezing cold; but, with the exception of the plaster dropping from the roof, and the broken windows, patched with rags and paper, there was a scrupulous neatness about the whole, which contrasted strangely with the filth and slovenliness outside. There was no bed in the room—no table. On a broken chair by the chimney sat a miserable old woman, fancying that she was warming her hands over embers which had long been cold, shaking her head, and muttering to herself, with palsied lips, about the guardians[3] and the workhouse; while upon a few rags on the floor lay a girl, ugly, smallpox-marked, hollow-eyed, emaciated, her only bedclothes the skirt of a large handsome new riding habit, at which two other girls, wan and tawdry, were astitching busily, as they sat right and left of her on the floor. The old woman took no notice of us as we entered; but one of the girls looked up, and, with a

1. Inhabitant of Belgravia, a wealthy residential district of London.
2. A kind of model cooperative community proposed by the French socialist Charles Fourier
(1772–1837).
3. Members of the local Board of Guardians, the body that supervised the workhouse.

pleased gesture of recognition, put her finger up to her lips, and whispered, "Ellen's asleep."

"I'm not asleep, dears," answered a faint unearthly voice; "I was only praying. Is that Mr. Mackaye?"

"Aye, my lassies; but ha' ye gotten na fire the nicht?"

"No," said one of them, bitterly, "we've earned no fire tonight, by fair trade or foul either."

1850

CHARLES DICKENS

The following selection is from chapter 5 of *Hard Times*, a novel by Dickens (1812–1870). The picture of Coketown was based on his impressions of the raw industrial towns of central and northern England such as Manchester and, in particular, Preston, a cotton-manufacturing center in Lancashire.

From Hard Times

[COKETOWN]

It was a town of red brick, or of brick that would have been red if the smoke and ashes had allowed it; but as matters stood it was a town of unnatural red and black like the painted face of a savage. It was a town of machinery and tall chimneys, out of which interminable serpents of smoke trailed themselves forever and ever, and never got uncoiled. It had a black canal in it, and a river that ran purple with ill-smelling dye, and vast piles of buildings full of windows where there was a rattling and a trembling all day long, and where the piston of the steam engine worked monotonously up and down like the head of an elephant in a state of melancholy madness. It contained several large streets all very like one another, and many small streets still more like one another, inhabited by people equally like one another, who all went in and out at the same hours, with the same sound upon the same pavements, to do the same work, and to whom every day was the same as yesterday and tomorrow, and every year the counterpart of the last and the next.

These attributes of Coketown were in the main inseparable from the work by which it was sustained; against them were to be set off, comforts of life which found their way all over the world, and elegancies of life which made, we will not ask how much of the fine lady, who could scarcely bear to hear the place mentioned. The rest of its features were voluntary, and they were these.

You saw nothing in Coketown but what was severely workful. If the members of a religious persuasion built a chapel there—as the members of eighteen religious persuasions had done—they made it a pious warehouse of red brick, with sometimes (but this is only in highly ornamented examples) a bell in a birdcage on the top of it. The solitary exception was the New Church; a stuccoed edifice with a square steeple over the door terminating in four short pinnacles like florid wooden legs. All the public inscriptions in the town were painted alike, in severe characters of black and white. The jail might have been the infirmary, the infirmary might have been the jail, the town hall might have been either, or both, or anything else, for anything that appeared to the contrary in the graces of their construction. Fact, fact, fact, everywhere in the material aspect of the town; fact, fact, fact, everywhere in the immaterial. The M'Choakumchild school was all fact, and the school of design was all fact, and the relations between master and man were all fact, and everything was fact between the lying-in hospital[1] and the cemetery, and what you couldn't state in figures, or show to be purchasable in the cheapest market and salable in the dearest, was not, and never should be, world without end, Amen.

1854

1. Maternity hospital.

ANONYMOUS

I n 1965 A. L. Lloyd, a collector of British folk songs, heard "Poverty Knock" from a weaver who had learned it sixty years earlier. The song dates from before that.

Poverty Knock[1]

REFRAIN[2]

Poverty, poverty knock!
Me loom is a-sayin' all day.
Poverty, poverty knock!
Gaffer's° too skinny° to pay.   *The foreman's / stingy*
Poverty, poverty knock!
Keepin' one eye on the clock.
Ah know ah can guttle°   *eat*
When ah hear me shuttle
Go: Poverty, poverty knock!

Up every mornin' at five.
Ah wonder that we keep alive.
Tired an' yawnin' on the cold mornin',
It's back to the dreary old drive.

1. The sound of a 19th-century loom.   2. Repeated after each stanza.

⁵ Oh dear, we're goin' to be late.
Gaffer is stood at the gate.
We're out o' pocket, our wages they're docket°   *docked*
We'll 'a' to buy grub on the slate.³

An' when our wages they'll bring,
¹⁰ We're often short of a string.⁴
While we are fratchin' wi' gaffer for snatchin',⁵
We know to his brass° he will cling.   *money*

We've got to wet our own yarn
By dippin' it into the tarn.°   *pool*
¹⁵ It's wet an' soggy an' makes us feel groggy,
An' there's mice in that dirty old barn.

Oh dear, me poor 'ead it sings.
Ah should have woven three strings,
But threads are breakin' and my back is achin'.
²⁰ Oh dear, ah wish ah had wings.

Sometimes a shuttle flies out,
Gives some poor woman a clout.
Ther she lies bleedin', but nobody's 'eedin'.
Who's goin' t'carry her out?

²⁵ Tuner⁶ should tackle me loom.
'E'd rather sit on his bum.
'E's far too busy a-courtin' our Lizzie,
An' ah cannot get 'im to come.

Lizzie is so easy led.
³⁰ Ah think that 'e teks her to bed.
She allus was skinny, now look at her pinny.°   *pinafore*
It's just about time they was wed.

1967

3. On credit, as recorded on a piece of slate.
4. Not paid for all our work. "String": a piece of cloth.
5. Cheating. "Fratchin'": quarreling.
6. The man who maintains the loom.

HENRY MAYHEW

I n 1849 Mayhew (1812–1887) was asked by the *Morning Chronicle* to be the metropolitan correspondent for its series "Labour and the Poor." His interviews with workers and street folk, later published as a book, convey a vivid sense of the lives of London's poor.

From London Labour and the London Poor

[BOY INMATE OF THE CASUAL WARDS[1]]

I am now seventeen. My father was a cotton-spinner in Manchester, but has been dead ten years; and soon after that my mother went into the workhouse, leaving me with an aunt; and I had to work in a cotton factory. As young as I was, I earned 2s. 2d.[2] a-week at first. I can read well, and write a little. I worked at the factory two years, and was then earning 7s. a-week. I then ran away, for I had always a roving mind; but I should have stayed if my master hadn't knocked me about so. I thought I should make my fortune in London— I'd heard it was such a grand place. I had read in novels and romances,— halfpenny and penny books,—about such things, but I've met with nothing of the kind. I started without money, and begged my way from Manchester to London, saying I was going up to look for work. I wanted to see the place more than anything else. I suffered very much on the road, having to be out all night often; and the nights were cold, though it was summer. When I got to London all my hopes were blighted. I could get no further. I never tried for work in London, for I believe there are no cotton factories in it; besides, I wanted to see life. I begged, and slept in the unions.[3] I got acquainted with plenty of boys like myself. We met at the casual wards, both in London and the country. I have now been five years at this life. We were merry enough in the wards, we boys, singing and telling stories.

* * *

I live a roving life, at first, being my own master. I was fond of going to plays, and such-like, when I got money; but now I'm getting tired of it, and wish for something else. I have tried for work at cotton factories in Lancashire and Yorkshire, but never could get any. I'm sure I could settle now. I couldn't have done that two years ago, the roving spirit was so strong upon me and the company I kept got a strong hold on me. Two winters back, there was a regular gang of us boys in London. After sleeping at a union, we would fix where to meet at night to get into another union to sleep. There were thirty of us that way, all boys; besides forty young men, and thirty young women. Sometimes we walked the streets all night. We didn't rob, at least I never saw any robbing. We had pleasure in chaffing[4] the policemen, and some of us got taken up. I always escaped. We got broken up in time,—some's dead, some's gone to sea, some into the country, some home, and some lagged.[5] Among them were many young lads very expert in reading, writing, and arithmetic. One young man—he was only twenty-five—could speak several languages: he had been to sea. He was then begging, though a strong young man. I suppose he liked that life: some soon got tired of it.

I often have suffered from cold and hunger. I never made more than 3d. a-day in money, take the year round, by begging; some make more than

---

1. Short-term poor shelters.
2. Two shillings, two pence (s. for *solidus* and d. for *denarius*, Latin for "shilling" and "penny," respectively).
3. Shelters for the poor maintained by two or

more parishes.
4. Making fun of.
5. Were transported to one of Britain's penal colonies or were arrested (slang).

London. "Over the city by the railway" was one of the 180 drawings by French artist Gustave Doré (1832–1883) that appeared in his book *London: A Pilgrimage* (1872).

6*d*. . . . but then, I've had meat and bread given besides. I say nothing when I beg, but that I am a poor boy out of work and starving. I never stole anything in my life. I've often been asked to do so by my mates. I never would. The young women steal the most. I know, least, I did know, two that kept young men, their partners, going about the country with them, chiefly by their stealing. Some do so by their prostitution. Those go as partners are all prostitutes. There is a great deal of sickness among the young men and women, but I never was ill these last seven years. Fevers, colds, and venereal diseases, are very common.

1851

ANNIE BESANT

I n 1873 Besant (1847–1933) left the Church and her marriage to an Anglican clergyman to become active in feminist and socialist causes. When she heard about the high dividends and low wages at the match factory of Bryant and May, she wrote a series of articles, including this one published in the magazine *Link*, that led to a public boycott and a strike of fourteen hundred match workers.

The "White Slavery" of London Match Workers

Bryant and May, now a limited liability company, paid last year a dividend of 23 per cent to its shareholders; two years ago it paid a dividend of 25 per cent, and the original £5 shares were then quoted for sale at £18 7s. 6d.[1] The highest dividend paid has been 38 per cent.

Let us see how the money is made with which these monstrous dividends are paid.* * *

The hour for commencing work is 6.30 in summer and 8 in winter; work concludes at 6 P.M. Half-an-hour is allowed for breakfast and an hour for dinner. This long day of work is performed by young girls, who have to stand the whole of the time. A typical case is that of a girl of 16, a piece-worker; she earns 4s. a week, and lives with a sister, employed by the same firm, who "earns good money, as much as 8s. or 9s. per week." Out of the earnings 2s. is paid for the rent of one room; the child lives on only bread-and-butter and tea, alike for breakfast and dinner, but related with dancing eyes that once a month she went to a meal where "you get coffee, and bread and butter, and jam, and marmalade, and lots of it." . . . The splendid salary of 4s. is subject to deductions in the shape of fines; if the feet are dirty, or the ground under the bench is left untidy, a fine of 3d. is inflicted; for putting "burnts"— matches that have caught fire during the work—on the bench 1s. has been forfeited, and one unhappy girl was once fined 2s. 6d. for some unknown crime. If a girl leaves four or five matches on her bench when she goes for a fresh "frame" she is fined 3d., and in some departments a fine of 3d. is inflicted for talking. If a girl is late she is shut out for "half the day," that is for

Strikers. Bryant and May match factory workers on strike.

the morning six hours, and 5d. is deducted out of her day's 8d. One girl was fined 1s. for letting the web twist around a machine in the endeavour to save her fingers from being cut, and was sharply told to take care of the machine, "never mind your fingers." Another, who carried out the instructions and lost a finger thereby, was left unsupported while she was helpless. The wage covers the duty of submitting to an occasional blow from a foreman; one, who appears to be a gentleman of variable temper, "clouts" them "when he is mad."

One department of the work consists in taking matches out of a frame and putting them into boxes; about three frames can be

1. Eighteen pounds, seven shillings, six pence (s. for *solidus* and d. for *denarius*, Latin for "shilling" and "penny," respectively).

done in an hour, and $\frac{1}{2}d$ is paid for each frame emptied; only one frame is given out at a time, and the girls have to run downstairs and upstairs each time to fetch the frame, thus much increasing their fatigue. One of the delights of the frame work is the accidental firing of the matches: when this happens the worker loses the work, and if the frame is injured she is fined or "sacked." 5s. a week had been earned at this by one girl I talked to.

The "fillers" get $\frac{3}{4}d$. a gross for filling boxes; at "boxing," *i.e.* wrapping papers round the boxes, they can earn from 4s. 6d. to 5s. a week. A very rapid "filler" has been known to earn once "as much as 9s." in a week, and 6s. a week "sometimes." The making of boxes is not done in the factory; for these $2\frac{1}{4}d$. a gross is paid to people who work in their own homes, and "find your own paste." Daywork is a little better paid than piecework, and is done chiefly by married women, who earn as much sometimes as 10s. a week, the piecework falling to the girls. Four women day workers, spoken of with reverent awe, earn—13s. a week.

A very bitter memory survives in the factory. Mr. Theodore Bryant, to show his admiration of Mr. Gladstone[2] and the greatness of his own public spirit, bethought him to erect a statue to that eminent statesman. In order that his workgirls might have the privilege of contributing, he stopped 1s. each out of their wages, and further deprived them of half-a-day's work by closing the factory, "giving them a holiday." ("We don't want no holidays," said one of the girls pathetically, for—needless to say—the poorer employees of such a firm lose their wages when a holiday is "given.") So furious were the girls at this cruel plundering, that many went to the unveiling of the statue with stones and bricks in their pockets, and I was conscious of a wish that some of those bricks had made an impression on Mr. Bryant's conscience. Later on they surrounded the statue—"we paid for it" they cried savagely—shouting and yelling, and a gruesome story is told that some cut their arms and let their blood trickle on the marble paid for, in very truth, by their blood. . . .

Such is a bald account of one form of white slavery as it exists in London. With chattel slaves Mr. Bryant could not have made his huge fortune, for he could not have fed, clothed, and housed them for 4s. a week each, and they would have had a definite money value which would have served as a protection. But who cares for the fate of these white wage slaves? Born in slums, driven to work while still children, undersized because underfed, oppressed because helpless, flung aside as soon as worked out, who cares if they die or go on the streets,[3] provided only that the Bryant and May shareholders get their 23 per cent, and Mr. Theodore Bryant can erect statues and buy parks? Oh if we had but a people's Dante, to make a special circle in the Inferno for those who live on this misery,[4] and suck wealth out of the starvation of helpless girls.

Failing a poet to hold up their conduct to the execration of posterity, enshrined in deathless verse, let us strive to touch their consciences, *i.e.* their pockets, and let us at least avoid being "partakers of their sins," by abstaining from using their commodities.

1888

2. William Ewart Gladstone (1809–1898), leader of the Liberal Party from 1868 to 1875 and from 1880 to 1894 and prime minister four times.
3. Become prostitutes.
4. In his *Inferno* the Italian poet Dante Alighieri (1265–1321) describes hell as divided into different levels, or circles, for different kinds of sinners, with each sin carrying its own specific punishments.

ADA NIELD CHEW

B orn on a farm in North Staffordshire, Chew (1870–1945) left school at the age of eleven to help her mother with taking care of house and family. In her early twenties she worked as a tailor in a factory in Crewe. She wrote a series of letters to the *Crewe Chronicle* about working conditions in the factory. When her identity was discovered, an uproar ensued, and she was fired. She became active in politics and continued to write for political causes.

A Living Wage for Factory Girls at Crewe, 5 May 1894

Sir,

—Will you grant me space in your sensible and widely read paper to complain of a great grievance of the class—that of tailoresses in some of the Crewe factories—to which I belong? I have hoped against hope that some influential man (or woman) would take up our cause and put us in the right way to remedy—for of course there is a remedy—for the evils we are suffering from. But although one cannot open a newspaper without seeing what all sorts and conditions of men are constantly agitating for and slowly but surely obtaining—as in the miners' eight hour bill[1]—only very vague mention is ever made of the under-paid, over-worked "Factory Girl." And I have come to the conclusion, sir, that as long as we are silent ourselves and apparently content with our lot, so long shall we be left in the enjoyment [?] of that lot.

The rates paid for the work done by us are so fearfully low as to be totally inadequate to—I had almost said keep body and soul together. Well, sir, it is a fact which I could prove, if necessary, that we are compelled, not by our employers, but by stern necessity, in order to keep ourselves in independence, which self-respecting girls even in our class of life like to do, to work so many hours—I would rather not say how many—that life loses its savour, and our toil, which in moderation and at a fair rate of remuneration would be pleasurable, becomes drudgery of the most wearisome kind.

To take what may be considered a good week's wage the work has to be so close and unremitting that we cannot be said to "live"—we merely exist. We eat, we sleep, we work, endlessly, ceaselessly work, from Monday morning till Saturday night, without remission. Cultivation of the mind? How is it possible? Reading? Those of us who are determined to live like human beings and require food for mind as well as body are obliged to take time which is necessary for sleep to gratify this desire. As for recreation and enjoying the beauties of nature, the seasons come and go, and we have barely time to notice whether it is spring or summer.

1. Bill limiting miners' work shifts to eight hours.

Certainly we have Sundays: but Sunday is to many of us, after our week of slavery, a day of exhaustion. It has frequently been so in my case, and I am not delicate. This, you will understand, sir, is when work is plentiful. Of course we have slack times, of which the present is one (otherwise I should not have time to write to you). It may be said that we should utilise these slack times for recruiting our bodies and cultivating our minds. Many of us do so, as far as is possible in the anxious state we are necessarily in, knowing that we are not earning our "keep," for it is not possible, absolutely not possible, for the average ordinary "hand" to earn enough in busy seasons, even with the overtime I have mentioned, to make up for slack ones.

"A living wage!" Ours is a lingering, dying wage. Who reaps the benefit of our toil? I read sometimes of a different state of things in other factories, and if in others, why not those in Crewe? I have just read the report of the Royal Commission on Labour. Very good, but while Royal Commissions are enquiring and reporting and making suggestions, some of the workers are being hurried to their graves.

I am afraid I am trespassing a great deal on your space, sir, but my subject has such serious interest for me—I sometimes wax very warm as I sit stitching and thinking over our wrongs—that they, and the knowledge that your columns are always open to the needy, however humble, must be my excuse.

I am, sir, yours sincerely,
A CREWE FACTORY GIRL
Crewe, 1 May 1894

Editor's note: Our correspondent writes a most intelligent letter; and if she is a specimen of the factory girl, then Crewe factory proprietors should be proud of their "hands." We shall be glad to hear further from our correspondent as to the wages paid, the numbers of hours worked, and the conditions of their employment. *Crewe Chronicle*, 5 May 1894

1894

THE "WOMAN QUESTION":
THE VICTORIAN DEBATE ABOUT GENDER

"The greatest social difficulty in England today is the relationship between men and women. The principal difference between ourselves and our ancestors is that they took society as they found it while we are self-conscious and perplexed. The institution of marriage might almost seem just now to be upon trial." This assertion by Justin M'Carthy, appearing in an essay on novels in the *Westminster Review* (July 1864), could be further extended, for on trial throughout the Victorian period was not only the institution of marriage but the family itself and, most particularly, the traditional roles of women as wives, mothers, and daughters. The "Woman Question," as it was called, engaged many Victorians, both male and female.

As indicated in our introduction to the Victorian age, the Woman Question encompassed not one question but many. The mixed opinions of Queen Victoria illustrate some of its different aspects. Believing in education for her sex, she gave support and encouragement to the founding of a college for women in 1847. On the other hand, she opposed the concept of votes for women, which she described in a letter as "this mad folly." Equally thought-provoking are her comments on women and marriage. Happily married herself until the death of Prince Albert in 1861, Victoria was nevertheless aware of some of the sacrifices marriage imposed on women. Writing in 1858 to her recently married daughter, she remarked: "There is great happiness . . . in devoting oneself to another who is worthy of one's affection; still, men are very selfish and the woman's devotion is always one of submission which makes our poor sex so very unenviable. This you will feel hereafter—I know; though it cannot be otherwise as God has willed it so."

Many of the queen's female subjects shared her assumptions that woman's role was to be accepted as divinely willed—as illustrated in the selections from Sarah Ellis's popular work of 1839, *The Women of England*, a manual of inspirational advice now usually classified with more practical books like Mrs. Beeton's *Book of Household Management* (1861) as "domestic conduct literature." The required "submission" of which the queen wrote was justified in many quarters on the grounds of the supposed intellectual inferiority of women. As popularly accepted lore expressed it: "Average Weight of Man's Brain 3½ lbs; Woman's 2 lbs, 11 ozs." In the minds of many, then, the possessors of the "shallower brain" (to borrow a phrase from the speaker of Tennyson's "Locksley Hall," 1842), naturally deserved a dependent role. In reminding wives of their range of duties, another nineteenth-century conduct book available in many editions, *The Female Instructor*, recommended that a wife always wear her wedding ring so that whenever she felt "ruffled," she might "cast [her] eyes upon it, and call to mind who gave it to [her]." In this climate it would follow that a woman who tried to cultivate her intellect beyond drawing-room accomplishments was violating the order of Nature and of religious tradition. Woman was to be valued, instead, for other qualities considered especially characteristic of her sex: tenderness of understanding, unworldliness and innocence, domestic affection, and, in various degrees, submissiveness.

By virtue of these qualities, woman became an object to be worshiped—an "angel in the house," as Coventry Patmore described her in the title of his popular poem (1854–62). In a similar vein John Ruskin insisted in his highly influential and much-reprinted essay "Of Queens' Gardens" (1865) that men and women "are in nothing alike, and the happiness and perfection of both depends on each asking and receiving from the other what the other can only give": the powers of "a true wife," he felt, made the home "a sacred place." A number of feminists as well as more traditional thinkers held this ideal view of woman's character, but, as George Eliot argues in her essay on Mary Wollstonecraft (see p. 401), the exalted pedestal on which women were placed was one of the principal obstacles to their achieving any alteration in status. That woman's position in society and in marriage was taken as a natural, and thus inevitable, state also stood in the way of change. Echoing the arguments of Wollstonecraft and John Stuart Mill, the feminist writer Mona Caird contended in 1888 that the institution of marriage was socially constructed and had a specific history: far from being a relationship ordained by God, marriage was an association that could and ought to be reinvented to promote freedom and equality for both partners.

Caird recognizes that the type of marriage she envisions is a distant ideal: to move toward it, she calls for a "gradual alteration of opinion which will rebuild [established institutions] from the very foundation." Earlier in the century those established institutions appear to have left some women, married and unmarried alike, dissatisfied and unfulfilled. It is commonly said that boredom was a particular problem for Victorian women, but generalizations about underoccupied females in this era need to be severely qualified. In the mid-Victorian period, one-quarter of England's female population had jobs, most of them onerous and low paying. At the same time other women earned their livings by working as prostitutes (the existence of this "Great

Social Evil," as the Victorians regarded it, being one indication that the "angel in the house" was not always able to exert her moralizing influence on her mate or her male children). While the millions of women employed as domestics, seamstresses, factory workers, farm laborers, or prostitutes had many problems, excessive leisure was not chief among them. To be bored was the privilege of wives and daughters in upper- and middle-class homes, establishments in which feminine idleness was treasured as a status symbol. Among this small and influential segment of the population, as the novelist Dinah Maria Mulock emphasizes, comfortably well-off wives and daughters found that there was "nothing to do," because in such households the servants ran everything, even taking over the principal role in rearing children. Freed from demanding domestic duties, such women could not then devote their unoccupied time to other labors, for there were few sanctioned opportunities for interesting and challenging work, and little support or encouragement for serious study or artistic endeavor. If family finances failed and they were called on "to do" something, women from these classes faced considerable difficulties: their severely limited choice of respectable paid occupations meant that many sought employment as governesses. Frequently taken up as a topic in novels of the period, the complex and compromised social position of the governess is, for instance, a notable feature of Charlotte Brontë's *Jane Eyre* (1847). Brontë's character, however, does not limit her criticism to her own impoverished plight when she expresses her frustration with the social attitudes that governed the behavior of women of her class more broadly:

> Women are supposed to be very calm generally: but women feel just as men feel; they need exercise for their faculties and a field for their efforts as much as their brothers do; they suffer from too rigid a restraint, too absolute a stagnation, precisely as men would suffer; and it is narrow-minded in their more privileged fellow-creatures to say that they ought to confine themselves to making puddings and knitting stockings, to playing on the piano and embroidering bags. It is thoughtless to condemn them, or laugh at them, if they seek to do more or learn more than custom has pronounced necessary for their sex.

George Meredith, in his *Essay on Comedy* (1873), develops the same argument; the test of a civilization, he writes, is whether men "consent to talk on equal terms with their women, and to listen to them." Yet at least two reviewers of *Jane Eyre*, both women, regarded such proposals as tantamount to sedition. Margaret Oliphant called the novel "A wild declaration of the 'Rights of Women' in a new aspect," and Elizabeth Rigby attacked its "pervading tone of ungodly discontent."

In some households such discontent, whether godly or ungodly, led to a daughter's open rebellion. One remarkable rebel was Florence Nightingale, who found family life in the 1850s intolerably pointless and, despite parental opposition, cut loose from home to carve out a career for herself in nursing and in hospital administration.

As chronicled by Sir Walter Besant, similar drives for independence produced extraordinary changes for women during the late Victorian period, making a wide variety of professional opportunities available to them. The era also witnessed the arrival of the much-debated phenomenon of the "New Woman": frequently satirized as simply a bicycle-riding, cigarette-smoking, mannish creature, this confident and assertive figure burst onto the scene in the 1890s, often becoming the focus of attention in articles, stories, and plays (the character of Vivie in George Bernard Shaw's *Mrs. Warren's Profession* [1898] is a good example of the type), and, indeed, the author of literary works herself. Women of course had begun to be published before Victoria's reign, and many women became successful novelists. And yet embarking on such a career was never an easy choice. The selections from Harriet Martineau's autobiography included here suggest some of the obstacles, internal and external, against which the aspiring woman writer struggled. Inevitably, some female writers were hacks, and they provide George Eliot with easy targets for ridicule in her essay "Silly

Novels by Lady Novelists" (1856). Nonetheless, women emerge as major novelists during the period, as illustrated in the careers of the Brontë sisters and Eliot herself.

It is instructive to compare the texts collected below with Eliot's judicious essay on the Woman Question, inspired by her rereading of Mary Wollstonecraft—and with her fiction. For these issues engaged Eliot's attention in her novels as well, as is demonstrated in her highly complex portrait of Maggie Tulliver, the bookish early-Victorian heroine of *The Mill on the Floss* (1860). To be sure, not all her female characters are frustrated and discontented; as a realist Eliot recognized that many upper- and middle-class women apparently found their leisurely lives fully enjoyable. In *Middlemarch* (1871–72), for example, Celia Brooke Chetham rejoices in her comfortable life as wife and mother on a country estate. Yet to her sister Dorothea (whom Celia regards with affectionate indulgence as an eccentric misfit), the traditional womanly lot in life is as painfully frustrating as Florence Nightingale had found it. It was on behalf of such women as Dorothea that John Stuart Mill developed his argument in *The Subjection of Women* (1869), a classic essay that should be read in conjunction with the selections in this section. Also revealing in this context are some of the extracts above from Tennyson's 1847 poem *The Princess* ("The woman's cause is man's") and from Elizabeth Barrett Browning's *Aurora Leigh* (1857), a novel in verse that portrays the life of a woman poet (book 1 describes how the typical girl's education constricts a woman's mind, and book 2 features Aurora's defense of her vocation as a poet). Frances Power Cobbe's 1862 paper "The Education of Women, and How It Would Be Affected by University Examinations," excerpted in "Beacons of the Future?", provides a further useful perspective.

For additional texts on Victorian debates about gender, see the NAEL Archive.

SARAH STICKNEY ELLIS

I n 1837 the essayist Sarah Stickney (1812?–1872) married William Ellis, a missionary, and began to work with him for the temperance movement and other evangelical causes. Ellis's 1839 book on women's education and domestic roles became a best seller, going through sixteen editions in two years. In the 1840s she founded a girls' school that put into practice her belief that feminine education should cultivate what she called "the heart" rather than the intellectual faculties of her pupils.

From The Women of England: Their Social Duties and Domestic Habits

[DISINTERESTED KINDNESS]

To men belongs the potent—(I had almost said the *omnipotent*) consideration of worldly aggrandizement; and it is constantly misleading their steps, closing their ears against the voice of conscience, and beguiling them with the promise of peace, where peace was never found.

* * *

How often has man returned to his home with a mind confused by the many voices, which in the mart, the exchange, or the public assembly, have addressed themselves to his inborn selfishness, or his worldly pride; and while his integ-

Home Comforts. The original caption to this frontispiece to *The Women of England* runs
as follows: "It is the home comforts and fireside virtues."

rity was shaken, and his resolution gave way beneath the pressure of apparent
necessity, or the insidious pretenses of expediency, he has stood corrected
before the clear eye of woman, as it looked directly to the naked truth, and
detected the lurking evil of the specious act he was about to commit. Nay, so
potent may have become this secret influence, that he may have borne it
about with him like a kind of second conscience, for mental reference, and
spiritual counsel, in moments of trial; and when the snares of the world were
around him, and temptations from within and without have bribed over the
witness in his own bosom, he has thought of the humble monitress[1] who sat
alone, guarding the fireside comforts of his distant home; and the remembrance of her character, clothed in moral beauty, has scattered the clouds
before his mental vision, and sent him back to that beloved home, a wiser and
a better man.

The women of England, possessing the grand privilege of being better
instructed than those of any other country, in the minutiae of domestic comfort, have obtained a degree of importance in society far beyond what their
unobtrusive virtues would appear to claim. The long-established customs of
their country have placed in their hands the high and holy duty of cherishing
and protecting the minor morals of life, from whence springs all that is elevated in purpose, and glorious in action. The sphere of their direct personal
influence is central, and consequently small; but its extreme operations are
as widely extended as the range of human feeling. They may be less striking

1. Female adviser or mentor.

in society than some of the women of other countries, and may feel themselves, on brilliant and stirring occasions, as simple, rude, and unsophisticated in the popular science of excitement; but as far as the noble daring of Britain has sent forth her adventurous sons, and that is to every point of danger on the habitable globe, they have borne along with them a generosity, a disinterestedness, and a moral courage, derived in no small measure from the female influence of their native country.

It is a fact well worthy of our serious attention, and one which bears immediately upon the subject under consideration, that the present state of our national affairs is such as to indicate that the influence of woman in counteracting the growing evils of society is about to be more needed than ever.

* * *

In order to ascertain what kind of education is most effective in making woman what she ought to be, the best method is to inquire into the character, station, and peculiar duties of woman throughout the largest portion of her earthly career; and then ask, for what she is most valued, admired, and beloved?

In answer to this, I have little hesitation in saying—for her disinterested[2] kindness. Look at all the heroines, whether of romance or reality—at all the female characters that are held up to universal admiration—at all who have gone down to honored graves, amongst the tears and lamentations of their survivors. Have these been the learned, the accomplished women; the women who could solve problems, and elucidate systems of philosophy? No: or if they have, they have also been women who were dignified with the majesty of moral greatness.

* * *

Let us single out from any particular seminary[3] a child who has been there from the years of ten to fifteen, and reckon, if it can be reckoned, the pains that have been spent in making that child proficient in Latin. Have the same pains been spent in making her disinterestedly kind? And yet what man is there in existence who would not rather his wife should be free from selfishness, than be able to read Virgil without the use of a dictionary?

* * *

I still cling fondly to the hope that some system of female instruction will be discovered, by which the young women of England may be sent from school to the homes of their parents, habituated to be on the watch for every opportunity of doing good to others; making it the first and the last inquiry of every day, "What can I do to make my parents, my brothers, or my sisters, more happy? I am but a feeble instrument in the hands of Providence, but as He will give me strength, I hope to pursue the plan to which I have been accustomed, of seeking my own happiness only in the happiness of others."

1839

---

2. I.e., independent, impartial.
3. School (in the early 19th century, often specifically a private school for girls).

COVENTRY PATMORE

Originally published between 1854 and 1862, *The Angel in the House*, a long poem about courtship and marriage by Coventry Patmore (1823–1896), became a best seller in the United States and later in Britain. Dedicated to the author's first wife, Emily Augusta Andrews, the poem celebrates their fifteen years of married life. (She died in 1862, and Patmore, who lived another three decades, remarried twice.) The poem, popular among Patmore's contemporaries (including Gerard Manley Hopkins and John Ruskin), fell out of favor in later years. Feminist critics such as Virginia Woolf criticized *The Angel in the House* both for the sentimentality of its ideal of woman and for the oppressive effect of this ideal on women's lives. Since Woolf, the phrase "the angel in the house" has often been used to encapsulate a patronizing Victorian attitude toward women, for which the poem is cited as prime evidence.

From The Angel in the House

The Paragon

When I behold the skies aloft
    Passing the pageantry of dreams,
The cloud whose bosom, cygnet-soft,
    A couch for nuptial Juno[1] seems,
5 The ocean broad, the mountains bright,
    The shadowy vales with feeding herds,
I from my lyre the music smite,
    Nor want for justly matching words.
All forces of the sea and air,
10   All interests of hill and plain,
I so can sing, in seasons fair,
    That who hath felt may feel again.
Elated oft by such free songs,
    I think with utterance free to raise
15 That hymn for which the whole world longs,
    A worthy hymn in woman's praise;
A hymn bright-noted like a bird's,
    Arousing these song-sleepy times
With rhapsodies of perfect words,
20   Ruled by returning kiss of rhymes.
But when I look on her and hope
    To tell with joy what I admire,
My thoughts lie cramp'd in narrow scope,
    Or in the feeble birth expire;
25 No mystery of well-woven speech,
    No simplest phrase of tenderest fall,
No liken'd excellence can reach

1. In Roman mythology the wife of the chief god (Jupiter) and a goddess presiding especially over the married life of women.

Her, the most excellent of all,
The best half of creation's best,
30   Its heart to feel, its eye to see,
The crown and complex of the rest,
   Its aim and its epitome.
Nay, might I utter my conceit,°   *fancy, idea*
   'Twere after all a vulgar song,
35   For she's so simply, subtly sweet,
   My deepest rapture does her wrong.
Yet is it now my chosen task
   To sing her worth as Maid and Wife;
Nor happier post than this I ask,
40   To live her laureate[2] all my life.
On wings of love uplifted free,
   And by her gentleness made great,
I'll teach how noble man should be
   To match with such a lovely mate;
45   And then in her may move the more
   The woman's wish to be desired,
(By praise increased,) till both shall soar,
   With blissful emulations fired.
And, as geranium, pink,° or rose   *type of flower*
50   Is thrice itself through power of art,
So may my happy skill disclose
   New fairness even in her fair heart;
Until that churl shall nowhere be
   Who bends not, awed, before the throne
55   Of her affecting majesty,
   So meek, so far unlike our own;
Until (for who may hope too much
   From her who wields the powers of love?)
Our lifted lives at last shall touch
60   That happy goal to which they move;
Until we find, as darkness rolls
   Away, and evil mists dissolve,
The nuptial contrasts are the poles
   On which the heavenly spheres revolve.

1854–62

2. I.e., to be the one who celebrates her in poetry.

JOHN RUSKIN

Ruskin (1819–1900) began his career writing about art but eventually became one of England's fiercest social critics. In 1864 he delivered two lectures in the industrial city of Manchester—the first, "Of Kings' Treasuries," supporting the development of public libraries in the name of "noble education" and the second, "Of

Queens' Gardens," on the special powers and duties of women. Published together the following year as *Sesame and Lilies*, the essays were considered ideal reading matter for middle-class young women and enjoyed exceptional sales for the remainder of the nineteenth century. In recent years "Of Queens' Gardens," with its assertions about the distinct differences between men and women, and their respective roles in the two separate spheres of public and private life, has become a classic text for the examination of Victorian ideology.

From Of Queens' Gardens

Now their separate characters are briefly these. The man's power is active, progressive, defensive. He is eminently the doer, the creator, the discoverer, the defender. His intellect is for speculation and invention; his energy for adventure, for war, and for conquest, wherever war is just, wherever conquest necessary. But the woman's power is for rule, not for battle,—and her intellect is not for invention or creation, but for sweet ordering, arrangement, and decision. She sees the qualities of things, their claims, and their places. Her great function is Praise; she enters into no contest, but infallibly adjudges the crown of contest. By her office, and place, she is protected from all danger and temptation, The man, in his rough work in open world, must encounter all peril and trial;—to him, therefore, must be the failure, the offence, the inevitable error: often he must be wounded, or subdued; often misled; and *always* hardened. But he guards the woman from all this; within his house, as ruled by her, unless she herself has sought it, need enter no danger, no temptation, no cause of error or offence. This is the true nature of home—it is the place of Peace; the shelter, not only from all injury, but from all terror, doubt, and division. In so far as it is not this, it is not home; so far as the anxieties of the outer life penetrate into it, and the inconsistently-minded, unknown, unloved, or hostile society of the outer world is allowed by either husband or wife to cross the threshold, it ceases to be home; it is then only a part of that outer world which you have roofed over, and lighted fire in. But so far as it is a sacred place, a vestal temple, a temple of the hearth watched over by Household Gods, before whose faces none may come but those whom they can receive with love,—so far as it is this, and roof and fire are types only of a nobler shade and light,—shade as of the rock in a weary land, and light as of the Pharos[1] in the stormy sea;—so far it vindicates the name, and fulfils the praise, of Home.

And wherever a true wife comes, this home is always round her. The stars only may be over her head; the glowworm in the night-cold grass may be the only fire at her foot; but home is yet wherever she is; and for a noble woman it stretches far round her, better than ceiled with cedar, or painted with vermilion,[2] shedding its quiet light far, for those who else were homeless.

This, then, I believe to be,—will you not admit it to be?—the woman's true place and power. But do not you see that, to fulfil this, she must—as far as

---

1. A lighthouse that was one of the Seven Wonders of the Ancient World (its island is now part of the city of Alexandria). The phrase "rock in a weary land" alludes to Isaiah 32.2.
2. Cf. Jeremiah 22.14. "Ceiled": roofed over.

one can use such terms of a human creature—be incapable of error? So far as she rules, all must be right, or nothing is. She must be enduringly, incorruptibly good; instinctively, infallibly wise—wise, not for self-development, but for self-renunciation: wise, not that she may set herself above her husband, but that she may never fail from his side: wise, not with the narrowness of insolent and loveless pride, but with the passionate gentleness of an infinitely variable, because infinitely applicable, modesty of service—the true changefulness of woman. In that great sense—"La donna è mobile," not "Qual piúm' al vento";[3] no, nor yet "Variable as the shade, by the light quivering aspen made";[4] but variable as the *light*, manifold in fair and serene division, that it may take the colour of all that it falls upon, and exalt it.

* * *

1864   1865

3. "Women are as fickle as feathers in the wind," the first two lines of the famous aria by the wom-

anizing Duke in Giuseppe Verdi's *Rigoletto* (1851).
4. Sir Walter Scott, *Marmion* (1808) 6.30.

HARRIET MARTINEAU

Martineau (1802–1876), who grew up in the town of Norwich, suffered a painfully unhappy childhood and adolescence both because of recurring illnesses and because of the strict and narrow lifestyle of her middle-class Unitarian family. A prolific author, she produced many kinds of books—history, political and economic theory, travel narratives, fiction, translation. She was best known for her collection of instructive stories, *Illustrations of Political Economy* (1832–34); but she also dealt with a wide variety of other issues, such as slavery in the United States (she was an early supporter of the abolitionists). Her *Autobiography*, written in 1855, was published in 1877. In the first selection she is eighteen years old.

From Autobiography

When I was young, it was not thought proper for young ladies to study very conspicuously; and especially with pen in hand. Young ladies (at least in provincial towns) were expected to sit down in the parlour to sew,—during which reading aloud was permitted,—or to practice their music; but so as to be fit to receive callers, without any signs of bluestockingism[1] which could be reported abroad. Jane Austen herself, the Queen of novelists, the immortal creator of Anne Elliott, Mr. Knightley,[2] and a score or two more of unrivalled intimate friends of the whole public, was compelled by the

1. Female intellectualism or literary activity (from the so-called bluestocking clubs of the 18th century—informal gatherings of women with literary interests and select men of letters; as the derisive name implies, some of the men attending

habitually wore unconventional blue worsted rather than silk stockings).
2. Major characters from, respectively, the novels *Persuasion* (1817) and *Emma* (1815) by Austen (1775–1817).

feelings of her family to cover up her manuscripts with a large piece of muslin work, kept on the table for the purpose, whenever any genteel people came in. So it was with other young ladies, for some time after Jane Austen was in her grave; and thus my first studies in philosophy were carried on with great care and reserve. I was at the work table regularly after breakfast,—making my own clothes, or the shirts of the household, or about some fancy work: I went out walking with the rest,—before dinner in winter, and after tea in summer: and if ever I shut myself into my own room for an hour of solitude, I knew it was at the risk of being sent for to join the sewing-circle, or to read aloud,—I being the reader, on account of my growing deafness.[3] But I won time for what my heart was set upon, nevertheless,—either in the early morning, or late at night. I had a strange passion for translating, in those days; and a good preparation it proved for the subsequent work of my life. Now, it was meeting James at seven in the morning to read Lowth's Prelections[4] in the Latin, after having been busy since five about something else, in my own room. Now it was translating Tacitus,[5] in order to try what was the utmost compression of style that I could attain.—About this I may mention an incident while it occurs. We had all grown up with a great reverence for Mrs. Barbauld[6] (which she fully deserved from much wiser people than ourselves) and, reflectively, for Dr. Aikin,[7] her brother,—also able in his way, and far more industrious, but without her genius. Among a multitude of other labours, Dr. Aikin had translated the Agricola[8] of Tacitus. I went into such an enthusiasm over the original, and especially over the celebrated concluding passage, that I thought I would translate it, and correct it by Dr. Aikin's, which I could procure from our public library. I did it, and found my own translation unquestionably the best of the two. I had spent an infinity of pains over it,—word by word; and I am confident I was not wrong in my judgment. I stood pained and mortified before my desk, I remember, thinking how strange and small a matter was human achievement, if Dr. Aikin's fame was to be taken as a testimony of literary desert. I had beaten him whom I had taken for my master. I need not point out that, in the first place, Dr. Aikin's fame did not hang on this particular work; nor that, in the second place, I had exaggerated his fame by our sectarian estimate of him.[9] I give the incident as a curious little piece of personal experience, and one which helped to make me like literary labour more for its own sake, and less for its rewards, than I might otherwise have done.—Well: to return to my translating propensities. Our cousin J. M. L., then studying for his profession in Norwich, used to read Italian with Rachel[1] and me,—also before breakfast. We made some considerable progress, through the usual course of prose authors and poets; and out of this grew a fit which Rachel and I at one time took, in concert with our companions and neighbours, the C.'s, to translate

3. Martineau's hearing problems worsened in adolescence, and she became almost entirely deaf.
4. *Praelectiones de Sacra Poesi Herbraeorum* (*Lectures on Hebrew Poetry*, 1753–70), by Robert Lowth (1710–1787), an English bishop and scholar. James was James Martineau (1805–1900), Harriet's younger brother, who later became a renowned Unitarian preacher and moral philosopher.
5. Roman historian (ca. 55–ca. 120), whose writings offer a model of concise prose.

6. Anna Laetitia Barbauld (1743–1825), poet and writer of prose for children.
7. John Aikin (1747–1822), English physician, author, and biographer; he collaborated with his sister in some publications.
8. A biography of Julius Agricola (40–93 C.E.), Tacitus's father-in-law and a Roman senator and general. Aikin's translation, which went into several editions, was first published in 1774.
9. Aikin, like Martineau, was a Unitarian.
1. Martineau's younger sister.

Petrarch.[2] Nothing could be better as an exercise in composition than translating Petrarch's sonnets into English of the same limits. It was putting ourselves under compulsion to do with the Italian what I had set myself
voluntarily to do with the Latin author. I believe we really succeeded pretty
well; and I am sure that all these exercises were a singularly apt preparation
for my after work. At the same time, I went on studying Blair's Rhetoric[3] (for
want of a better guide) and inclining mightily to every kind of book or process which could improve my literary skill,—really as if I had foreseen how
I was to spend my life.

* * *

At this time,—(I think it must have been in 1821,) was my first appearance
in print. * * * My brother James, then my idolized companion, discovered
how wretched I was when he left me for his college, after the vacation; and
he told me that I must not permit myself to be so miserable. He advised me
to take refuge, on each occasion, in a new pursuit; and on that particular
occasion, in an attempt at authorship. I said, as usual, that I would if he
would: to which he answered that it would never do for him, a young student,
to rush into print before the eyes of his tutors; but he desired me to write
something that was in my head, and try my chance with it in the "Monthly
Repository,"—the poor little Unitarian periodical in which I have mentioned
that Talfourd[4] tried his young powers. What James desired, I always did, as
of course; and after he had left me to my widowhood soon after six o'clock,
one bright September morning, I was at my desk before seven, beginning a
letter to the Editor of the "Monthly Repository,"—that editor being the formidable prime minister of his sect,—Rev. Robert Aspland.[5] I suppose I must
tell what that first paper was, though I had much rather not; for I am so
heartily ashamed of the whole business as never to have looked at the article
since the first flutter of it went off. It was on Female Writers on Practical
Divinity. I wrote away, in my abominable scrawl of those days, on foolscap
paper,[6] feeling mightily like a fool all the time. I told no one, and carried my
expensive packet to the post-office myself, to pay the postage. I took the letter V for my signature,—I cannot at all remember why. The time was very
near the end of the month: I had no definite expectation that I should ever
hear any thing of my paper; and certainly did not suppose it could be in the
forthcoming number. That number was sent in before service-time on a
Sunday morning. My heart may have been beating when I laid hands on it;
but it thumped prodigiously when I saw my article there, and, in the Notices
to Correspondents, a request to hear more from V. of Norwich. There is
certainly something entirely peculiar in the sensation of seeing oneself in
print for the first time:—the lines burn themselves in upon the brain in a
way of which black ink is incapable, in any other mode. So I felt that day,
when I went about with my secret.—I have said what my eldest brother was
to us,—in what reverence we held him. He was just married, and he and his
bride asked me to return from chapel with them to tea. After tea he said,

---

2. Italian poet (Francesco Petrarca, 1304–1374).
3. *Lectures on Rhetoric and Belles Lettres* (1784),
by Hugh Blair (1718–1800), a Scottish divine and
professor of rhetoric, which expressed 18th-
century ideals of prose style.

4. Sir Thomas Noon Talfourd (1795–1854),
English lawyer and author.
5. A Unitarian divine (1782–1845).
6. A thirteen-by-sixteen-inch sheet of paper.

"Come now, we have had plenty of talk; I will read you something;" and he held out his hand for the new "Repository." After glancing at it, he exclaimed, "They have got a new hand here. Listen." After a paragraph, he repeated, "Ah! this is a new hand; they have had nothing so good as this for a long while." (It would be impossible to convey to any who do not know the "Monthly Repository" of that day, how very small a compliment this was.) I was silent, of course. At the end of the first column, he exclaimed about the style, looking at me in some wonder at my being as still as a mouse. Next (and well I remember his tone, and thrill to it still) his words were—"What a fine sentence that is! Why, do you not think so?" I mumbled out, sillily enough, that it did not seem any thing particular. "Then," said he, "you were not listening. I will read it again. There now!" As he still got nothing out of me, he turned round upon me, as we sat side by side on the sofa, with "Harriet, what is the matter with you? I never knew you so slow to praise any thing before." I replied, in utter confusion,—"I never could baffle any body. The truth is, that paper is mine." He made no reply; read on in silence, and spoke no more till I was on my feet to come away. He then laid his hand on my shoulder, and said gravely (calling me 'dear' for the first time) "Now, dear, leave it to other women to make shirts and darn stockings; and do you devote yourself to this." I went home in a sort of dream, so that the squares of the pavement seemed to float before my eyes. That evening made me an authoress.

* * *

While I was at Newcastle [1829], a change, which turned out a very happy one, was made in our domestic arrangements. * * * I call it a misfortune, because in common parlance it would be so treated; but I believe that my mother and all her other daughters would have joined heartily, if asked, in my conviction that it was one of the best things that ever happened to us. My mother and her daughters lost, at a stroke, nearly all they had in the world by the failure of the house,—the old manufactory,—in which their money was placed. We never recovered more than the merest pittance; and at the time, I, for one, was left destitute;—that is to say, with precisely one shilling in my purse. The effect upon me of this new "calamity," as people called it, was like that of a blister upon a dull, weary pain, or series of pains. I rather enjoyed it, even at the time; for there was scope for action; whereas, in the long, dreary series of preceding trials, there was nothing possible but endurance. In a very short time, my two sisters at home and I began to feel the blessing of a wholly new freedom. I, who had been obliged to write before breakfast, or in some private way, had henceforth liberty to do my own work in my own way; for we had lost our gentility. Many and many a time since have we said that, but for that loss of money, we might have lived on in the ordinary provincial method of ladies with small means, sewing, and economizing, and growing narrower every year; whereas, by being thrown, while it was yet time, on our own resources, we have worked hard and usefully, won friends, reputation and independence, seen the world abundantly, abroad and at home, and, in short, have truly lived instead of vegetated.

1855   1877

ANONYMOUS

I n early February 1858 a letter appeared in the London *Times* above the signature "One More Unfortunate." This individual, who claimed to be a prostitute, described her respectable upbringing and her experience as a governess, lamented her disgrace, and called on men to be more compassionate in their reform efforts. Responding in part to this piece, another letter, also apparently from a prostitute and titled "The Great Social Evil," was then published on February 24, 1858. Although it is impossible to establish definitively whether the letter writers were genuinely who they said they were, the story of how the second correspondent came to be a prostitute, which appears in the following extract, would have seemed extremely plausible to contemporary readers. This selection can profitably be compared with other representations and considerations of prostitutes and "fallen women" in this volume, such as those that appear in Dante Gabriel Rossetti's poem "Jenny" (1870) and his painting *Found* (1855); William Holman Hunt's painting *The Awakening Conscience* (1853–54) and John Ruskin's contemporaneous discussion of it; and George Bernard Shaw's 1898 play *Mrs Warren's Profession*.

The Great Social Evil

To the Editor of the Times

Sir,—another "Unfortunate," but of a class entirely different from the one who has already instructed the public in your columns, presumes to address you.

I am a stranger to all the fine sentiments which still linger in the bosom of your correspondent. I have none of those youthful recollections which, contrasting her early days with her present life, aggravate the misery of the latter. My parents did not give me any education; they did not instil into my mind virtuous precepts nor set me a good example. All my experiences in early life were gleaned among associates who knew nothing of the laws of God but by dim tradition and faint report, and whose chiefest triumphs of wisdom consisted in picking their way through the paths of destitution in which they were cast by cunning evasion or in open defiance of the laws of man.

* * *

Let me tell you something of my parents. My father's most profitable occupation was brickmaking. When not employed at this he did anything he could get to do. My mother worked with him in the brickfield, and so did I and a progeny of brothers and sisters; for, somehow or other, although my parents occupied a very unimportant space in the world, it pleased God to make them fruitful. We all slept in the same room. There were few privacies, few family secrets in our house.

* * *

I was a very pretty child, and had a sweet voice; of course I used to sing. Most London boys and girls of the lower classes sing. "My face is my for-

Found, Dante Gabriel Rossetti. The artist began this painting in oils in 1854, but it was still unfinished at the time of his death in 1882.

tune, kind Sir, she said" was the ditty on which I bestowed most pains, and my father and mother would wink knowingly as I sang it. The latter would also tell me how pretty she was when young, and how she sang, and what a fool she had been, and how well she might have done had she been wise.

Frequently we had quite a stir in our colony.[1] Some young lady who had quitted the paternal restraints, or perhaps, been started off, none knew whither or how, to seek her fortune, would reappear among us with a profusion of ribands, fine clothes, and lots of cash. Visiting the neighbours, treating indiscriminately, was the order of the day on such occasions, without any more definite information of the means by which the dazzling transformation had been effected than could be conveyed by knowing winks and the words "luck" and "friends." Then she would disappear and leave us in our dirt, penury, and obscurity. You cannot conceive, Sir, how our young ambition was stirred by these visitations.

Now commences an important era in my life. I was a fine, robust, healthy girl, 13 years of age. I had larked with the boys of my own age. I had huddled with them, boys and girls together, all night long in our common haunts. I had seen much and heard abundantly of the mysteries of the sexes. To me such things had been matters of common sight and common talk. For some time I had trembled and coquetted on the verge of a strong curiosity, and a natural desire, and without a particle of affection, scarce a partiality, I lost what? not my virtue, for I never had any. That which is commonly, but untruly called virtue, I gave away.

You reverend Mr. Philanthropist—what call you virtue? Is it not the principle, the essence, which keeps watch and ward over the conduct, over the substance, the materiality? No such principle ever kept watch and ward over me, and I repeat that I never lost that which I never had—my virtue.

According to my own ideas at the time I only extended my rightful enjoyments. Opportunity was not long wanting to put my newly-acquired knowledge to profitable use. In the commencement of my fifteenth year one of our beribanded visitors took me off, and introduced me to the great world, and thus commenced my career as what you better classes call a prostitute. I cannot say that I felt any other shame than the bashfulness of a noviciate

1. I.e., neighborhood, group of streets.

introduced to strange society. Remarkable for good looks, and no less so for good temper, I gained money, dressed gaily, and soon agreeably astonished my parents and old neighbours by making a descent upon them.

Passing over the vicissitudes of my course, alternating between reckless gaiety and extreme destitution, I improved myself greatly; and at the age of 18 was living partly under the protection of one who thought he discovered that I had talent, and some good qualities as well as beauty, who treated me more kindly and considerately than I had ever before been treated, and thus drew from me something like a feeling of regard, but not sufficiently strong to lift me to that sense of my position which the so-called virtuous and respectable members of society seem to entertain. Under the protection of this gentleman, and encouraged by him, I commenced the work of my education; that portion of education which is comprised in some knowledge of my own language and the ordinary accomplishments of my sex;—moral science, as I believe it is called, has always been an enigma to me, and is so to this day.

* * *

Now, what if I am a prostitute, what business has society to abuse me? Have I received any favours at the hands of society? If I am a hideous cancer in society, are not the causes of the disease to be sought in the rottenness of the carcass? Am I not its legitimate child; no bastard, Sir? Why does my unnatural parent repudiate me, and what has society ever done for me, that I should do anything for it, and what have I ever done against society that it should drive me into a corner and crush me to the earth? I have neither stolen (at least not since I was a child), nor murdered, nor defrauded. I earn my money and pay my way, and try to do good with it, according to my ideas of good. I do not get drunk, nor fight, nor create uproar in the streets or out of them. I do not use bad language. I do not offend the public eye by open indecencies. I go to the Opera, I go to Almack's,[2] I go to the theatres, I go to quiet, well-conducted casinos, I go to all places of public amusement, behaving myself with as much propriety as society can exact. I pay business visits to my tradespeople, the most fashionable of the West-end.[3] My milliners, my silk-mercers,[4] my bootmaker know, all of them, who I am and how I live, and they solicit my patronage as earnestly and cringingly as if I were Madam, the lady of the right rev. patron of the Society for the Suppression of Vice.[5] They find my money as good and my pay better (for we are robbed on every hand) than that of Madam, my Lady; and, if all the circumstances and conditions of our lives had been reversed, would Madam, my Lady, have done better or been better than I?

I speak for others as well as for myself, for the very great majority, nearly all of the real undisguised prostitutes in London, spring from my class, and are made by and under pretty much such conditions of life as I have narrated, and particularly by untutored and unrestrained intercourse of the sexes in early life. We come from the dregs of society, as our so-called betters term it. What business has society to have dregs—such dregs as we? You railers of the Society for the Suppression of Vice, you the pious, the moral, the respectable, as you call yourselves, who stand on your smooth and pleas-

---

2. Assembly rooms, the scene of social functions.
3. The affluent area of central London and location of fashionable shops and theaters.

4. Dealers in textiles.
5. A society founded in 1802.

ant side of the great gulf you have dug and keep between yourselves and the dregs, why don't you bridge it over, or fill it up, and by some humane and generous process absorb us into your leavened mass, until we become interpenetrated with goodness like yourselves? Why stand on your eminence shouting that we should be ashamed of ourselves? What have we to be ashamed of, we who do not know what shame is—the shame you mean? I conduct myself prudently, and defy you and your policemen too. Why stand you there mouthing with sleek face about morality? What is morality? Will you make us responsible for what we never knew? Teach us what is right and tutor us in good before you punish us for doing wrong. We who are the real prostitutes of the true natural growth of society, and no impostors, will not be judged by "One more Unfortunate," nor measured by any standard of her setting up. She is a mere chance intruder in our ranks, and has no business there.

* * *

Hurling big figures at us, it is said that there are 80,000 of us in London alone—which is a monstrous falsehood—and of this 80,000, poor hardworking sewing girls, sewing women, are numbered in by thousands and called indiscriminately prostitutes; writing, preaching, speechifying, that they have lost their virtue too.

It is a cruel calumny to call them in mass prostitutes; and, as for their virtue, they lose it as one loses his watch who is robbed by the highway thief. Their virtue is the watch, and society is the thief. These poor women toiling on starvation wages, while penury, misery, and famine clutch them by the throat and say, "Render up your body or die."

* * *

Admire this magnificent shop in this fashionable street; its front, fittings, and decorations cost not less than a thousand pounds. The respectable master of the establishment keeps his carriage, and lives in his countryhouse. He has daughters too; his patronesses are fine ladies, the choicest impersonations of society. Do they think, as they admire the taste and elegance of that tradesman's show, of the poor creatures who wrought it, and of what they were paid for it? Do they reflect on the weary toiling fingers, on the eyes dim with watching, on the bowels yearning with hunger, on the bended frames, on the broken constitutions, on poor human nature driven to its coldest corner and reduced to its narrowest means in the production of these luxuries and adornments? This is an old story! Would it not be truer and more charitable to call these poor souls "victims?"—some gentler, some more humane name than prostitute—to soften by some Christian expression, if you cannot better the un-Christian system, the opprobrium of a fate to which society has itself driven them by the direst straits? What business has society to point its finger in scorn, and to raise its voice in reprobation of them? Are they not its children, born of its cold indifference, of its callous selfishness, of its cruel pride?

Sir, I have trespassed on your patience beyond limit, and yet much remains to be said, which I leave for further communication if you think proper to insert this. The difficulty of dealing with the evil is not so great as society considers it. Setting aside "the sin," we are not so bad as we are thought to be. The difficulty is for society to set itself, with the necessary earnestness, self-humiliation, and self-denial to the work. But of this hereafter. To deprive us of proper and harmless amusements, to subject us in mass to the pressure of force—of force wielded, for the most part, by ignorant, and often by brutal men—is only to add the cruelty of active persecution to the cruelty of the passive indifference which made us as we are.

I remain your humble servant,
ANOTHER UNFORTUNATE

1858

DINAH MARIA MULOCK

I n 1857 Mulock (1826–1887) published her best-known novel, the Victorian best seller *John Halifax, Gentleman*. This work was followed the year after by *A Woman's Thoughts on Women* and subsequently by other, sometimes more overtly feminist, novels. In 1864 she married George Craik, a partner in the publishing firm Macmillan; her works often appear under the name Dinah Maria Craik.

From A Woman's Thoughts about Women

[SOMETHING TO DO]

Man and woman were made for, and not like one another. Only one "right" we have to assert in common with mankind—and that is as much in our hands as theirs—the right of having something to do.

* * *

But how few parents ever consider this! Tom, Dick, and Harry, aforesaid, leave school and plunge into life; "the girls" likewise finish their education, come home, and stay at home. That is enough. Nobody thinks it needful to waste a care upon them. Bless them, pretty dears, how sweet they are! papa's nosegay[1] of beauty to adorn his drawing-room. He delights to give them all they can desire—clothes, amusements, society; he and mamma together take every domestic care off their hands; they have abundance of time and nothing to occupy it; plenty of money, and little use for it; pleasure without end, but not one definite object of interest or employment; flattery and flummery[2] enough, but no solid food whatever to satisfy mind or heart—if they happen to possess either—at the very emptiest and most craving season[3] of both. They have literally nothing whatever to do.

* * *

And so their whole energies are devoted to the massacre of old Time. They prick him to death with crochet and embroidery needles; strum him deaf

---

1. Posy, small bouquet of flowers.
2. Nonsense (literally, a sweet and insubstantial dessert).
3. Seasoning, salt and pepper.

with piano and harp playing—*not* music; cut him up with morning visitors, or leave his carcass in ten-minute parcels at every "friend's" house they can think of. Finally, they dance him defunct at all sort of unnatural hours; and then, rejoicing in the excellent excuse, smother him in sleep for a third of the following day. Thus he dies, a slow, inoffensive, perfectly natural death; and they will never recognize his murder till, on the confines of this world, or from the unknown shores of the next, the question meets them: "What have you done with Time?"—Time, the only mortal gift bestowed equally on every living soul, and excepting the soul, the only mortal loss which is totally irretrievable.

* * *

But "what am I to do with my life?" as once asked me one girl out of the numbers who begin to feel aware that, whether marrying or not, each possesses an individual life, to spend, to use, or to lose. And herein lies the momentous question.

* * *

A definite answer to this question is simply impossible. Generally—and this is the best and safest guide—she will find her work lying very near at hand: some desultory tastes to condense into regular studies, some faulty household quietly to remodel, some child to teach, or parent to watch over. All these being needless or unattainable, she may extend her service out of the home into the world, which perhaps never at any time so much needed the help of us women. And hardly one of its charities and duties can be done so thoroughly as by a wise and tender woman's hand.

* * *

These are they who are little spoken of in the world at large. * * * They have made for themselves a place in the world: the harsh, practical, yet not ill-meaning world, where all find their level soon or late, and where a frivolous young maid sunk into a helpless old one, can no more expect to keep her pristine position than a last year's leaf to flutter upon a spring bough. But an old maid who deserves well of this same world, by her ceaseless work therein, having won her position, keeps it to the end.

Not an ill position either, or unkindly; often higher and more honourable than that of many a mother of ten sons. In households, where "Auntie" is the universal referee, nurse, playmate, comforter, and counselor: in society, where "that nice Miss So-and-so,"

Tea. A middle-class British Victorian family takes tea.

though neither clever, handsome, nor young, is yet such a person as can neither be omitted nor overlooked: in charitable works, where she is "such a practical body—always knows exactly what to do, and how to do it": or perhaps, in her own house, solitary indeed, as every single woman's home must be, yet neither dull nor unhappy in itself, and the nucleus of cheerfulness and happiness to many another home besides.

* * *

Published or unpublished, this woman's life is a goodly chronicle, the title page of which you may read in her quiet countenance; her manner, settled, cheerful, and at ease; her unfailing interest in all things and all people. You will rarely find she thinks much about herself; she has never had time for it. And this her life-chronicle, which, out of its very fullness, has taught her that the more one does, the more one finds to do—she will never flourish in your face, or the face of Heaven, as something uncommonly virtuous and extraordinary. She knows that, after all, she has simply done what it was her duty to do.

But—and when her place is vacant on earth, this will be said of her assuredly, both here and Otherwhere—"*She hath done what she could.*"

1858

FLORENCE NIGHTINGALE

I n 1854 Nightingale (1820–1910) became famous for organizing a contingent of nurses to care for sick and wounded soldiers during the Crimean War, an event that provided an outlet for her passionate desire to change the world of hospital treatment. But Nightingale achieved her dream of an active and productive life only after many years of waiting; at the age of thirty-two she was still living at home, unmarried (having declined several proposals). Some members of her well-to-do family, in particular her mother, strongly opposed her nursing ambitions and pressured her to remain at home. In 1852, so bored with family and social life that she thought of suicide, she began writing *Cassandra,* which she called her "family manuscript"; it records her frustrations before she escaped into a professional world where there was "something to do." In 1859 she revised the manuscript, and a few copies were privately printed that year, but it was not published until 1928. The title refers to the Trojan princess whose true prophecies went unheeded by those around her because she was judged insane.

From Cassandra

[NOTHING TO DO]

Why have women passion, intellect, moral activity—these three—and a place in society where no one of the three can be exercised? Men say that God punishes for complaining. No, but men are angry with misery. They are irritated with women for not being happy. They take it as a personal offense. To God alone may women complain without insulting Him!

* * *

Is discontent a privilege?

Yes, it is a privilege for you to suffer for your race—a privilege not reserved to the Redeemer, and the martyrs alone, but one enjoyed by numbers in every age.

The commonplace life of thousands; and in that is its only interest—its only merit as a history; viz., that it *is* the type of common sufferings—the story of one who has not the courage to resist nor to submit to the civilization of her time—is this.

Poetry and imagination begin life. A child will fall on its knees on the gravel walk at the sight of a pink hawthorn in full flower, when it is by itself, to praise God for it.

Then comes intellect. It wishes to satisfy the wants which intellect creates for it. But there is a physical, not moral, impossibility of supplying the wants of the intellect in the state of civilization at which we have arrived. The stimulus, the training, the time, are all three wanting to us; or, in other words, the means and inducements are not there.

Look at the poor lives we lead. It is a wonder that we are so good as we are, not that we are so bad. In looking round we are struck with the power of the organizations[1] we see, not with their want of power. Now and then, it is true, we are conscious that *there* is an inferior organization, but, in general, just the contrary. Mrs A. has the imagination, the poetry of a Murillo,[2] and has sufficient power of execution to show that she might have had a great deal more. Why is she not a Murillo? From a material difficulty, not a mental one. If she has a knife and fork in her hands for three hours of the day, she cannot have a pencil or brush. Dinner is the great sacred ceremony of this day, the great sacrament. To be absent from dinner is equivalent to being ill. Nothing else will excuse us from it. Bodily incapacity is the only apology valid. If she has a pen and ink in her hands during other three hours, writing answers for the penny post,[3] again, she cannot have her pencil, and so *ad infinitum* through life. People have no type before them in their lives, neither fathers nor mothers, nor the children themselves. They look at things in detail. They say, "It is very desirable that A., my daughter, should go to such a party, should know such a lady, should sit by such a person." It is true. But what standard have they before them of the nature and destination of man? The very words are rejected as pedantic. But might they not, at least, have a type in their minds that such an one might be a discoverer through her intellect, such another through her art, a third through her moral power?

Women often try one branch of intellect after another in their youth, e.g., mathematics. But that, least of all, is compatible with the life of "society." It is impossible to follow up anything systematically. Women often long to enter some man's profession where they would find direction, competition

---

1. Beings, organisms.
2. Bartolomé Murillo (1617–1682), Spanish painter.
3. Replying (to social correspondence and invi-

tations) in letters, which would then be mailed; a uniform rate of a penny for each letter was instituted in 1840.

(or rather opportunity of measuring the intellect with others) and, above all, time.

In those wise institutions, mixed as they are with many follies, which will last as long as the human race lasts, because they are adapted to the wants of the human race; those institutions which we call monasteries, and which, embracing much that is contrary to the laws of nature, are yet better adapted to the union of the life of action and that of thought than any other mode of life with which we are acquainted; in many such, four and a half hours, at least, are daily set aside for thought, rules are given for thought, training and opportunity afforded. Among us there is *no* time appointed for this purpose, and the difficulty is that, in our social life, we must be always doubtful whether we ought not to be with somebody else or be doing something else.

Are men better off than women in this?

If one calls upon a friend in London and sees her son in the drawing room, it strikes one as odd to find a young man sitting idle in his mother's drawing room in the morning. For men, who are seen much in those haunts, there is no end of the epithets we have: "knights of the carpet," "drawing-room heroes," "ladies' men." But suppose we were to see a number of men in the morning sitting round a table in the drawing-room, looking at prints, doing worsted work,[4] and reading little books, how we should laugh! A member of the House of Commons was once known to do worsted work. Of another man was said, "His only fault is that he is too good; he drives out with his mother every day in the carriage, and if he is asked anywhere he answers that he must dine with his mother, but, if she can spare him, he will come in to tea, and he does not come."

Now, why is it more ridiculous for a man than for a woman to do worsted work and drive out every day in the carriage? Why should we laugh if we were to see a parcel of men sitting round a drawing room table in the morning, and think it all right if they were women?

Is man's time more valuable than woman's? or is the difference between man and woman this, that woman has confessedly nothing to do?

Women are never supposed to have any occupation of sufficient importance *not* to be interrupted, except "suckling their fools";[5] and women themselves have accepted this, have written books to support it, and have trained themselves so as to consider whatever they do as *not* of such value to the world or to others, but that they can throw it up at the first "claim of social life." They have accustomed themselves to consider intellectual occupation as a merely selfish amusement, which it is their "duty" to give up for every trifler more selfish than themselves.

* * *

Women have no means given them, whereby they *can* resist the "claims of social life." They are taught from their infancy upwards that it is a wrong, ill-tempered, and a misunderstanding of "woman's mission" (with a great M) if they do not allow themselves *willingly* to be interrupted at all hours. If a woman has once put in a claim to be treated as a man by some work of

4. Embroidery or other needlework with fine woollen yarn.
5. See Iago's cynical comments on the role of

women in Shakespeare's *Othello* 2.1.162: "To suckle fools, and chronicle small beer." "Small beer" colloquially means "unimportant matters."

science or art or literature, which she can *show* as the "fruit of her leisure," then she will be considered justified in *having* leisure (hardly, perhaps, even then). But if not, not. If she has nothing to show, she must resign herself to her fate.

"I like riding about this beautiful place, why don't you? I like walking about the garden, why don't you?" is the common expostulation—as if we were children, whose spirits rise during a fortnight's holiday, who think that they will last forever—and look neither backwards nor forwards.

Society triumphs over many. They wish to regenerate the world with their institutions, with their moral philosophy, with their love. Then they sink to living from breakfast till dinner, from dinner till tea, with a little worsted work, and to looking forward to nothing but bed.

When shall we see a life full of steady enthusiasm, walking straight to its aim, flying home, as that bird is now, against the wind—with the calmness and the confidence of one who knows the laws of God and can apply them?

* * *

When shall we see a woman making a *study* of what she does? Married women cannot; for a man would think, if his wife undertook any great work with the intention of carrying it out—of making anything but a sham of it—that she would "suckle his fools and chronicle his small beer" less well for it—that he would not have so good a dinner—that she would destroy, as it is called, his domestic life.

The intercourse of[6] man and woman—how frivolous, how unworthy it is! Can we call *that* the true vocation of woman—her high career? Look round at the marriages which you know. The true marriage—that noble union, by which a man and woman become together the one perfect being—probably does not exist at present upon earth.

It is not surprising that husbands and wives seem so little part of one another. It is surprising that there is so much love as there is. For there is no food for it. What does it live upon—what nourishes it? Husbands and wives never seem to have anything to say to one another. What do they talk about? Not about any great religious, social, political questions or feelings. They talk about who shall come to dinner, who is to live in this lodge and who in that, about the improvement of the place, or when they shall go to London. If there are children, they form a common subject of some nourishment. But, even then, the case is oftenest thus—the husband is to think of how they are to get on in life; the wife of bringing them up at home.

But any real communion between husband and wife—any descending into the depths of their being, and drawing out thence what they find and comparing it—do we ever dream of such a thing? Yes, we may dream of it during the season of "passion," but we shall not find it afterwards. We even expect it to go off, and lay our account that it will. If the husband has, by chance, gone into the depths of *his* being, and found there anything unorthodox, he, oftenest, conceals it carefully from his wife—he is afraid of "unsettling her opinions."

* * *

6. Social communication between.

For a woman is "by birth a Tory"[7]—has often been said—by education a "Tory," we mean.

Women dream till they have no longer the strength to dream; those dreams against which they so struggle, so honestly, vigorously, and conscientiously, and so in vain, yet which are their life, without which they could not have lived; those dreams go at last. All their plans and visions seem vanished, and they know not where; gone, and they cannot recall them. They do not even remember them. And they are left without the food of reality or of hope.

Later in life, they neither desire nor dream, neither of activity, nor of love, nor of intellect. The last often survives the longest. They wish, if their experiences would benefit anybody, to give them to someone. But they never find an hour free in which to collect their thoughts, and so discouragement becomes ever deeper and deeper, and they less and less capable of undertaking anything.

It seems as if the female spirit of the world were mourning everlastingly over blessings, not *lost*, but which she has never had, and which, in her discouragement she feels that she never will have, they are so far off.

The more complete a woman's organization, the more she will feel it, till at last there shall arise a woman, who will resume, in her own soul, all the sufferings of her race, and that woman will be the Saviour of her race.

1852–59   1928

7. Nickname for a member or supporter of the British Conservative Party, which generally sought to preserve the established religious and political order.

MONA CAIRD

In several novels and many essays, the feminist writer Mona Caird (1854–1932) explored the position of women in Victorian society. *The Daughters of Danaus* (1894) features a heroine whose desire to pursue a musical career conflicts with her family ties and responsibilities. Caird's article "Marriage," which appeared in the *Westminster Review* in 1888, inspired a heated exchange in the journals of the 1890s. Her essays on the subject of marriage were later collected and published as *The Morality of Marriage, and Other Essays on the Status and Destiny of Woman* (1897).

From Marriage

We come then to the conclusion that the present form of marriage—exactly in proportion to its conformity with orthodox ideas—is a vexatious failure. If certain people have made it a success by ignoring those orthodox ideas, such instances afford no argument in favour of the institution as it stands. We are also led to conclude that modern "Respectability" draws its life-blood from the degradation of womanhood in marriage and in prostitution. But what is to be done to remedy these manifold evils? how is marriage to be rescued from a mercenary society, torn from the arms of "Respectability," and established on a footing which will make it no longer an insult to human dignity?

First of all we must set up an ideal, undismayed by what will seem its Utopian impossibility. Every good thing that we enjoy to-day was once the dream of a "crazy enthusiast" mad enough to believe in the power of ideas and in the power of man to have things as he wills. The ideal marriage then, despite all dangers and difficulties, should be *free*. So long as love and trust and friendship remain, no bonds are necessary to bind two people together; life apart will be empty and colourless; but whenever these cease the tie becomes false and iniquitous, and no one ought to have power to enforce it. The matter is one in which any interposition, whether of law or of society, is an impertinence. Even the idea of "duty" ought to be excluded from the most perfect marriage, because the intense attraction of one being for another, the intense desire for one another's happiness, would make interchanges of whatever kind the outcome of a feeling far more passionate than that of duty. It need scarcely be said that there must be a full understanding and acknowledgment of the obvious right of the woman to *possess herself* body and soul, to give or withhold herself body and soul exactly as she wills. The moral right here is so palpable, and its denial implies ideas so low and offensive to human dignity, that no fear of consequences ought to deter us from making this liberty an element of our ideal, in fact its fundamental principle. Without it, no ideal could hold up its head. Moreover, "consequences" in the long run are never beneficent, where obvious moral rights are disregarded. The idea of a perfectly free marriage would imply the possibility of any form of contract being entered into between the two persons, the State and society standing aside, and recognizing the entirely private character of the transaction.

The economical independence of woman is the first condition of free marriage. She ought not to be tempted to marry, or to remain married, for the sake of bread and butter. But the condition is a very hard one to secure. Our present competitive system, with the daily increasing ferocity of the struggle for existence, is fast reducing itself to an absurdity, woman's labour helping to make the struggle only the fiercer. The problem now offered to the mind and conscience of humanity is to readjust its industrial organization in such a way as to gradually reduce this absurd and useless competition within reasonable limits, and to bring about in its place some form of cooperation, in which no man's interest will depend on the misfortune of his neighbour, but rather on his neighbour's happiness and welfare. It is idle to say that this cannot be done; the state of society shows quite clearly that it *must* be done sooner or later; otherwise some violent catastrophe will put an end to a condition of things which is hurrying towards impossibility. Under improved economical conditions the difficult problem of securing the real independence of women, and thence of the readjustment of their position in relation to men and to society would find easy solution.

When girls and boys are educated together, when the unwholesome atmosphere of social life becomes fresher and nobler, when the pressure of existence slackens (as it will and *must* do), and when the whole nature has thus a chance to expand, such additions to the scope and interest of life will cease to be thought marvellous or "unnatural." "Human nature" has more variety of powers and is more responsive to conditions than we imagine. It is hard to believe in things for which we feel no capacity in ourselves, but fortunately such things exist in spite of our placid unconsciousness. Give room for the development of individuality, and individuality develops, to the amazement of spectators! Give freedom in marriage, and each pair will enter upon their union after their own particular fashion, creating a refreshing diversity in modes of life, and consequently of character. Infinitely preferable will this be to our own gloomy uniformity, the offspring of our passion to be in all things exactly like our neighbours.

The proposed freedom in marriage would of course have to go hand-in-hand with the co-education of the sexes. It is our present absurd interference with the natural civilizing influences of one sex upon the other, that creates half the dangers and difficulties of our social life, and gives colour to the fears of those who would hedge round marriage with a thousand restraints or so-called safeguards, ruinous to happiness, and certainly not productive of a satisfactory social condition. Already the good results of this method of co-education have been proved by experiment in America, but we ought to go farther in this direction than our go-ahead cousins have yet gone. Meeting freely in their working-hours as well as at times of recreation, men and women would have opportunity for forming reasonable judgments of character, for making friendships irrespective of sex, and for giving and receiving that inspiring influence which apparently can only be given by one sex to the other.[1] There would also be a chance of forming genuine attachments founded on friendship; marriage would cease to be the haphazard thing it is now; girls would no longer fancy themselves in love with a man because they had met none other on terms equally intimate, and they would not be tempted to marry for the sake of freedom and a place in life, for existence would be free and full from the beginning.

The general rise in health, physical and moral, following the improvement in birth, surroundings, and training, would rapidly tell upon the whole state of society. Any one who has observed carefully knows how grateful a response the human organism gives to improved conditions, if only these remain constant. We should have to deal with healthier, better equipped, more reasonable men and women, possessing well-developed minds, and hearts kindly disposed towards their fellow-creatures. Are such people more likely to enter into a union frivolously and ignorantly than are the average men and women of today? Surely not. If the number of divorces did not actually decrease there would be the certainty that no couple remained united against their will, and that no lives were sacrificed to a mere convention. With the social changes which would go hand in hand with changes in the status of marriage, would come inevitably many fresh forms of human power, and thus all sorts of new and stimulating influences would be brought to bear upon

---

1. Mr. Henry Stanton, in his work on *The Woman Question in Europe*, speaks of the main idea conveyed in Legouvé's *Histoire des Femmes* as follows:—"Equality in difference is its key-note. The question is not to make woman a man, but to complete man by woman" [Caird's note]. Caird is probably imperfectly recalling the name of Theodore Stanton (1851–1925), the editor of *The Woman Question in Europe: A Series of Original Essays* (1884). *Histoire Morale des Femmes (Moral History of Women)*, by Ernest Legouvé (1807–1903), was published in Paris in 1849.

society. No man has a right to consider himself educated until he has been under the influence of cultivated women, and the same may be said of women as regards men.[2] Development involves an increase of complexity. It is so in all forms of existence, vegetable and animal; it is so in human life. It will be found that men and women as they increase in complexity can enter into a numberless variety of relationships, abandoning no good gift that they now possess, but adding to their powers indefinitely, and thence to their emotions and experiences. The action of the man's nature upon the woman's and of the woman's upon the man's, is now only known in a few instances; there is a whole world yet to explore in this direction, and it is more than probable that the future holds a discovery in the domain of spirit as great as that of Columbus in the domain of matter.

With regard to the dangers attending these readjustments, there is no doubt much to be said. The evils that hedge around marriage are linked with other evils, so that movement is difficult and perilous indeed. Nevertheless, we have to remember that we now live in the midst of dangers, and that human happiness is cruelly murdered by our systems of legalized injustice. By sitting still circumspectly and treating our social system as if it were a card-house which would tumble down at a breath, we merely wait to see it fall from its own internal rottenness, and *then* we shall have dangers to encounter indeed! The time has come, not for violent overturning of established institutions before people admit that they are evil, but for a gradual alteration of opinion which will rebuild them from the very foundation. The method of the most enlightened reformer is to crowd out old evil by new good, and to seek to sow the seed of the nobler future where alone it can take root and grow to its full height: in the souls of men and women. Far-seeing we ought to be, but we know in our hearts right well that fear will never lead us to the height of our ever-growing possibility. Evolution has ceased to be a power driving us like dead leaves on a gale; thanks to science, we are no longer entirely blind, and we aspire to direct that mighty force for the good of humanity. We see a limitless field of possibility opening out before us; the adventurous spirit in us might leap up at the wonderful romance of life! We recognize that no power, however trivial, fails to count in the general sum of things which moves this way or that—towards heaven or hell, according to the preponderating motives of individual units. We shall begin, slowly but surely, to see the folly of permitting the forces of one sex to pull against and neutralize the workings of the other, to the confusion of our efforts and the checking of our progress. We shall see, in the relations of men and women to one another, the source of all good or of all evil, precisely as those relations are true and noble and equal, or false and low and unjust. With this belief we shall seek to move opinion in all the directions that may bring us to this "consummation devoutly to be wished,"[3] and we look forward steadily, hoping and working for the day when men and women shall be comrades and fellow-workers as well as lovers and husbands and wives, when the rich and many-sided happiness which they have the power to bestow one on

---

2. Mrs. Cady Stanton believes that there is a sex in mind, and that men can only be inspired to their highest achievements by women, while women are stimulated to their utmost only by men [Caird's note]. Elizabeth Cady Stanton (1815–1902), prominent American women's suffragist.

3. Cf. Shakespeare's *Hamlet* 3.1.65–66.

another shall no longer be enjoyed in tantalizing snatches, but shall gladden and give new life to all humanity. That will be the day prophesied by Lewis Morris[4] in *The New Order*—

"When man and woman in an equal union
Shall merge, and marriage be a true communion."

1888

4. Welsh poet (1833–1907).

WALTER BESANT

B esant (1836–1901) was a literary critic, historian, and novelist. His history *The Queen's Reign* (1897) celebrated the improvements that he felt he had witnessed during his lifetime.

From The Queen's Reign

[THE TRANSFORMATION OF WOMEN'S STATUS BETWEEN 1837 AND 1897]

Let me present to you, first, an early Victorian girl, born about the Waterloo year;[1] next, her granddaughter, born about 1875. * * *

The young lady of 1837 * * * cannot reason on any subject whatever because of her ignorance—as she herself would say, because she is a woman. In her presence, and indeed in the presence of ladies generally, men talk trivialities. * * * It has often been charged against Thackeray[2] that his good women were insipid. Thackeray, like most artists, could only draw the women of his own time, and at that time they were undoubtedly insipid. Men, I suppose, liked them so. To be childishly ignorant; to carry shrinking modesty so far as to find the point of a shoe projecting beyond the folds of a frock indelicate; to confess that serious subjects were beyond a woman's grasp; never even to pretend to form an independent judgment; to know nothing of Art, History, Science, Literature, Politics, Sociology, Manners—men liked these things; women yielded to please the men; her very ignorance formed a subject of laudable pride with the Englishwoman of the Forties. * * * There was something Oriental in the seclusion of women in the home, and their exclusion from active and practical life.

* * *

Let us turn to the Englishwoman—the young Englishwoman—of 1897. She is educated. Whatever things are taught to the young man are taught to the

1. I.e., 1815, the year Napoleon Bonaparte was defeated by British and Prussian forces at the Battle of Waterloo.
2. William Makepeace Thackeray (1811–1863),

British novelist. The character of Amelia Sedley, in his novel *Vanity Fair* (1848), is cited by Besant as typical of the "insipid" women of the 1840s.

young woman. If she wants to explore the wickedness of the world she can do so, for it is all in the books. The secrets of Nature are not closed to her; she can learn the structure of the body if she wishes. At school, at college, she studies just as the young man studies, but harder and with greater concentration. * * * She has invaded the professions. She cannot become a priest, because the Oriental prejudice against women still prevails, so that women in High Church places are not allowed to sing in the choir, or to play the organ, not to speak of preaching. * * * In the same way she cannot enter the Law. Some day she will get over this restriction, but not yet. For a long time she was kept out of medicine. That restriction is now removed; she can, and she does, practice as a physician or a surgeon, generally

A "New Woman." This illustration from American fashion magazine *Harper's Bazar* ("*Bazaar*" from 1930 onward) features two of the three most common elements that appeared in representations of the "New Woman": bicycles, pantaloons, and cigarettes.

the former.[3] I believe that she has shown in this profession, as in her university studies, she can stand, *inter pares*,[4] among her equals and her peers, not her superiors. There is no branch of literature in which women have not distinguished themselves. * * * In music they compose, but not greatly; they play and sing divinely. The acting of the best among them is equal to that of any living man. They have become journalists, in some cases of remarkable ability; in fact, there are thousands of women who now make their livelihood by writing in all its branches. As for the less common professions—the accountants, architects, actuaries, agents—they are rapidly being taken over by women.

It is no longer a question of necessity; women do not ask themselves whether they must earn their own bread, or live a life of dependence. Necessity or no necessity they demand work, with independence and personal liberty. Whether they will take upon them the duties and responsibilities of marriage, they postpone for further consideration. I believe that, although in the first eager running there are many who profess to despise marriage, the voice of nature and the instinctive yearning for love will prevail.

3. The first woman to have her name placed on the British Medical Register was Elizabeth Blackwell (who earned her degree in the United States), in 1859; it took another two decades for women to gain the right to study and take the required examinations in medicine in Great Britain.
4. Among equals (Latin).

Personal independence: that is the keynote of the situation. Mothers no longer attempt the old control over their daughters: they would find it impossible. The girls go off by themselves on their bicycles;[5] they go about as they please; they neither compromise themselves nor get talked about. For the first time in man's history it is regarded as a right and proper thing to trust a girl as a boy insists upon being trusted. Out of this personal freedom will come, I daresay, a change in the old feelings of young man to maiden. He will not see in her a frail, tender plant which must be protected from cold winds; she can protect herself perfectly well. He will not see in her any longer a creature of sweet emotions and pure aspirations, coupled with a complete ignorance of the world, because she already knows all that she wants to know. Nor will he see in her a companion whose mind is a blank, and whose conversation is insipid, because she already knows as much as he knows himself. Nor, again, will he see in her a housewife whose whole time will be occupied in superintending servants or in making, brewing, confecting things with her own hand.

1897

5. Modern bicycles (with wheels of equal size and pneumatic tires) began to be manufactured in the late 1880s and became extremely popular in Europe and the United States.

EMPIRE AND NATIONAL IDENTITY

By the end of the nineteenth century, nearly a quarter of the earth's land surface was part of the British Empire, and more than four hundred million people were governed (however nominally) from Great Britain. Queen Victoria's far-flung empire was a truly heterogeneous entity, controlled by heterogeneous practices. It included Crown Colonies such as Jamaica, ruled from Britain, and protectorates such as Uganda, which had relinquished only partial sovereignty to Britain. Ireland was a kind of internal colony whose demands for home rule were alternately entertained and discounted. India had started the century under the control of a private entity, the East India Company, but was ruled directly from Britain after the 1857 Indian Mutiny (the first war of Indian independence), and Victoria was crowned empress of India in 1877. Canada, with its substantial European population, had been virtually self-governing from the middle of the nineteenth century onward and was increasingly considered a near-equal partner in the imperial project; Australia enjoyed a parallel status, despite its inauspicious earlier history as the site of British penal colonies. By contrast, colonies and protectorates with large indigenous populations, such as Sierra Leone, or with large transplanted populations of ex-slaves and non-European laborers, such as Trinidad, would not gain autonomy until the twentieth century.

The scope of imperial enterprise at the close of the Victorian era is especially astounding given Britain's catastrophic loss of its American colonies (historians generally view the American Revolution of 1776 as marking the end of the first British Empire). But although empire was never a central preoccupation of the government during the first half of the nineteenth century, the second empire had continued to grow; Britain seized a number of new territories, greatly expanded its colonies in Australia and Canada (which saw large-scale British emigration), and steadily pushed its way across the Indian subcontinent. A far more rapid expansion took place between 1870 and 1900, three decades that witnessed "the new imperialism"—

a significantly different British mode of empire building that would continue until World War I (1914–18). Britain's rivalry with its European neighbors was an instrumental factor: the balance of power in Europe had shifted in the wake of the Franco-Prussian War (1870–71), leading to competition for new territories. Particularly fierce was "the scramble for Africa," as the brutal partitioning of that continent was called. Expansion did not go unchallenged—the British fought both with indigenous peoples and with other European powers or settlers in numerous conflicts—but it progressed at an astonishing pace nonetheless.

To summarize Britain's attitude toward its imperial activities over the centuries is no easy task. The historian Sir John Seeley famously remarked in *The Expansion of England* (1883) that "we seem, as it were, to have conquered and peopled half the world in a fit of absence of mind," but many would now counter that economic motives were always present and that Britain was driven to claim territories outside its national borders primarily by the urge to obtain raw materials such as sugar, spices, tea, tin, and rubber; to procure markets for its own goods; and to secure trade routes. From this perspective Britain's enhanced national pride in its expanding physical size, and thus ever-increasing political and military clout, was an important side effect of commercial growth but did not instigate its exploits overseas. To look at the British Empire in this way is to see it at its most naked and to confront head-on the desire for financial profit that occasioned the physical violence and cultural devastation that so often accompanied its arrival in, and occupation of, another land. As Marlow comments in Joseph Conrad's *Heart of Darkness* (1902), "The conquest of the earth, which mostly means the taking it away from those who have a different complexion or slightly flatter noses than ourselves, is not a pretty thing when you look into it too much." But Conrad's storyteller cannot leave it at that, adding, "What redeems it is the idea only." As we try to understand, if not redeem, the British Empire, we must investigate some of the principal ideas that collected around this huge and diverse phenomenon, and that underwent significant shifts over the decades of Victoria's reign.

Joseph Chamberlain asserts in "The True Conception of Empire" (1897) that the balance sheet dictated what early-nineteenth-century Britons thought about their relationship with the colonies: having in the previous century "appeared rather in the light of a grasping and absentee landlord desiring to take from his tenants the utmost rents he could exact," Britain, shaken by its American losses, worried that some of its overseas enterprises would prove a financial drain. Yet India was another story, and by 1800 the importance to British prosperity of the trading opportunities in that continent was already viewed as axiomatic. In managing its businesses, however, the East India Company grew progressively more entangled with issues of Indian administration and politics; in its turn the British government became increasingly concerned with overseeing, and ultimately taking over, these functions. From this state of affairs a notion of trusteeship began to emerge—a belief that Britain had the responsibility to provide good government for the Indian people. Underlying this conviction was the assumption that Britain would thereby bestow the benefits of its culturally and morally superior civilization upon a lesser people (Thomas Babington Macaulay's confident pronouncements in his 1835 "Minute on Indian Education" evince this sentiment with particular succinctness). Evangelical Christianity played a contributory role as well, and not just through the missionaries who worked in India beginning in the early nineteenth century. More broadly, for the majority of Britons who believed that Protestantism was the one true faith, and that it was their religious duty to bring the potential for salvation to as many souls as possible, the imposition of British rule was divinely sanctioned. But there was still no widespread popular or governmental enthusiasm for the idea of imperialism as Britain's special destiny, and various factors, not least England's long and troubled relationship with Ireland, ensured that many viewed the project of colonial rule with

Victoria Presenting a Bible. *The Secret of England's Greatness (Queen Victoria Presenting a Bible in the Audience Chamber at Windsor)*, Thomas Jones Barker, ca. 1863.

suspicion throughout the middle years of the century. With the rise of the new imperialism, however, preexisting ideas about Britain's superiority, now bolstered by supposedly "scientific" theories supporting the notion of its evolutionary advancement, were channeled into a romantic vision of the British Empire as a tremendous force for the good not only of the residents of Great Britain or those overseas of traditionally "British" descent but of the whole world. In the last three decades of Victoria's rule (and well into the twentieth century), a large proportion of British people took pride simultaneously in the global supremacy of their empire and in what they perceived to be their generous and selfless willingness to pick up the thankless, but necessary, task of imperial rule ("the white man's burden," as Rudyard Kipling would call it in another context). Only if we appreciate just how genuinely many Britons believed that they and their country were performing a noble duty can we begin to make sense of the feelings of outraged surprise and betrayal (often accompanied by virulent racism and vicious reprisals) that erupted when subjugated peoples periodically rose up against British control.

The British Empire had an incalculable physical and psychological impact on the individuals and cultures it colonized, but it also significantly changed the colonizers themselves, both at home and abroad. The need to concentrate on the imperial mission affected in theoretical and practical ways the consolidation of a specifically *British* identity: the conflicted relations and characteristic differences between people from the various parts of the British Isles (politically dominant England and long-conquered Wales, Scotland, and Ireland) appeared less significant when set against the much more obvious inequities of power and greater cultural, racial, religious, and linguistic differences across the globe. A number of similar processes worked to solidify nationhood more generally. For instance, members of the working class in

Great Britain only rarely connected their subordination to the English ruling class with that suffered by colonized peoples: they were much more likely to understand their identity through those "ties of kindred, of religion, of history, and of language," as Chamberlain puts it, that bound them to other historically British citizens, however privileged. Intensified competition with the empire-building powers of continental Europe after the Franco-Prussian War also played an important role, as did the mounting stridency of other nationalist movements abroad. In the last quarter of the century, the patriotic fervor celebrating the achievements of the British nation as a whole increased dramatically—a phenomenon undoubtedly assisted by the growth both in the size of the reading public (literacy was practically universal in Britain by 1900, thanks to the progressive extension of elementary education) and in the number of flag-waving newspapers, periodicals, and books available for it to consume.

The citizens of Great Britain were thus welded into a more cohesive whole. But few of them were ready to accept the peoples of the colonies (and especially indigenous nonwhite populations) as truly "British," despite the inclusive rhetoric of empire (the "one imperial whole" that Alfred, Lord Tennyson salutes in his poem on the opening of the Indian and Colonial Exhibition of 1886). Of course, there were exceptions: recounting his experiences on a visit to Britain for that same exhibition, the Indian T. N. Mukharji remembers that on one occasion in London, "somebody called me a foreigner. 'He is no foreigner!' cried several voices, 'He is a British subject as you and I.'" To J. A. Hobson, the author of the influential *Imperialism: A Study* (1902), the importance of this casual affirmation of shared subjecthood was negligible, given that "not five per cent of the population of our Empire are possessed of any appreciable portion of the political and civil liberties which are the basis of British civilisation." Writing after Britain's imperial confidence had been severely damaged by the unanticipated length and difficulty of the Anglo-Boer War of 1899–1902 in South Africa, Hobson in his meticulous analysis aimed not only to cast serious doubt on imperialism's putative financial benefit to Britain but also to demonstrate the overall falsity of the empire's claim to support the extension of self-government in its territories. In exposing the repeated misrepresentations and self-serving justifications at the heart of the British Empire, Hobson joined voices with others around the globe, such as the West Indian intellectual J. J. Thomas, and entered a tradition of anti-imperial critique that was to grow exponentially in the twentieth century.

Selections elsewhere in the volume are also markedly concerned with Britain's relationship with other parts of the world, and its understanding of its own identity. Numerous texts testify to the Victorians' fascination with what they saw as both the exotic appeal and the mysterious threat of distant cultures; for instance, Tennyson's poem "Locksley Hall" (1842) reflects on "yonder shining Orient," while the sense of menace in Conan Doyle's story "The Speckled Band" (1892) is intimately connected to its villain's Indian connections. Matthew Arnold's prose writings frequently address the issue of national character; John Henry Newman sets forth an ideal of English manliness in his "definition of a gentleman" in Discourse 8 of *The Idea of a University* (1852). The versions of this ideal from the apex of Great Britain's period of national pride that appear in this section's poems by W. E. Henley and Henry Newbolt may profitably be compared to another highly popular work, Kipling's "If—" (1910); Kipling's other poems and his novella *The Man Who Would Be King* (1888) are also essential reading for those interested in the intensification of imperial enthusiasm at the end of Victoria's reign. At the same time we should heed the warning of the postcolonial critic Gayatri Spivak against limiting any investigation of empire and national identity only to those writings that seem overtly concerned with the topic. "It should not be possible to read nineteenth-century British literature," she insists at the beginning of an analysis of Charlotte Brontë's *Jane Eyre* (1847), "without remembering that imperialism, understood as England's social mission, was a crucial part of the cultural representation of England to the English." In other words, images, explanations, and justifications of this massive enterprise were continually created and reflected through-out the pages of a wide range of Victorian texts.

For additional texts on the subject of empire, see the NAEL Archive.

THOMAS BABINGTON MACAULAY

The historian, essayist, and parliamentarian Macaulay (1800–1859) served as a member of the supreme council of the East India Company from 1834 to 1838, and in that capacity he oversaw major educational and legal reforms. His "Minute," or official memorandum, was written to rebut those council members who believed that Indian students should continue to be educated in Sanskrit and Persian as well as in English; Macaulay's party carried the argument.

From Minute on Indian Education

We now come to the gist of the matter. We have a fund to be employed as Government shall direct for the intellectual improvement of the people of this country. The simple question is, what is the most useful way of employing it?

All parties seem to be agreed on one point, that the dialects commonly spoken among the natives of this part of India contain neither literary or sci-entific information, and are, moreover, so poor and rude that, until they are enriched from some other quarter, it will not be easy to translate any valuable work into them. It seems to be admitted on all sides that the intellectual improvement of those classes of the people who have the means of pursuing higher studies can at present be effected only by means of some language not vernacular amongst them.

What, then, shall that language be? One half of the Committee main-tain that it should be the English. The other half strongly recommend the Arabic[1] and Sanscrit. The whole question seems to me to be, which lan-guage is the best worth knowing?

I have no knowledge of either Sanscrit or Arabic.—But I have done what I could to form a correct estimate of their value. I have read translations of the most celebrated Arabic and Sanscrit works. I have conversed both here and at home with men distinguished by their proficiency in the Eastern tongues. I am quite ready to take the Oriental learning at the valuation of the Orientalists themselves. I have never found one among them who could deny that a single shelf of a good European library was worth the whole native lit-erature of India and Arabia. The intrinsic superiority of the Western litera-ture is, indeed, fully admitted by those members of the Committee who support the Oriental plan of education.

---

1. Actually Persian, the language (written in Arabic script) of the Mogul dynasty that had ruled much of India since the 16th century.

It will hardly be disputed, I suppose, that the department of literature in which the Eastern writers stand highest is poetry. And I certainly never met with any Orientalist who ventured to maintain that the Arabic and Sanscrit poetry could be compared to that of the great European nations. But, when we pass from works of imagination to works in which facts are recorded and general principles investigated, the superiority of the Europeans becomes absolutely immeasurable. It is, I believe, no exaggeration to say, that all the historical information which has been collected from all the books written in the Sanscrit language is less valuable than what may be found in the most paltry abridgments used at preparatory schools in England. In every branch of physical or moral philosophy the relative position of the two nations is nearly the same.

How, then, stands the case? We have to educate a people who cannot at present be educated by means of their mother-tongue. We must teach them some foreign language. The claims of our own language it is hardly necessarily to recapitulate. It stands pre-eminent even among the languages of the West. It abounds with works of imagination not inferior to the noblest which Greece has bequeathed to us; with models of every species of eloquence; with historical compositions, which, considered merely as narratives, have seldom been surpassed, and which, considered as vehicles of ethical and political instruction, have never been equalled; with just and lively representations of human life and human nature; with the most profound speculations on metaphysics, morals, government, jurisprudence, and trade; with full and correct information respecting every experimental science which tends to preserve the health, to increase the comfort, or to expand the intellect of man. Whoever knows that language, has ready access to all the vast intellectual wealth, which all the wisest nations of the earth have created and hoarded in the course of ninety generations. It may safely be said that the literature now extant in that language is of far greater value than all the literature which three hundred years ago was extant in all the languages of the world spoken together. Nor is this all. In India, English is the language spoken by the ruling class. It is spoken by the higher class of natives at the seats of Government. It is likely to become the language of commerce throughout the seas of the East. It is the language of two great European communities which are rising, the one in the south of Africa, the other in Australasia; communities which are every year becoming more important, and more closely connected with our Indian empire. Whether we look at the intrinsic value of our literature or at the particular situation of this country, we shall see the strongest reason to think that, of all foreign tongues, the English tongue is that which would be the most useful to our native subjects.

* * *

It is said that the Sanscrit and Arabic are the languages in which the sacred books of a hundred millions of people are written, and that they are, on that account, entitled to peculiar[2] encouragement. Assuredly it is the duty of the British Government in India to be not only tolerant, but neutral on all religious questions. But to encourage the study of a literature admitted to be

2. Special.

of small intrinsic value only because that literature inculcates the most serious errors on the most important subjects, is a course hardly reconcilable
with reason, with morality, or even with that very neutrality which ought, as
we all agree, to be sacredly preserved. It is confessed that a language is barren of useful knowledge. We are told to teach it because it is fruitful of monstrous superstitions. We are to teach false history, false astronomy, false
medicine, because we find them in company with a false religion.

* * *

In one point I fully agree with the gentlemen to whose general views I am
opposed. I feel, with them, that it is impossible for us, with our limited
means, to attempt to educate the body of the people. We must at present do
our best to form a class who may be interpreters between us and the millions
whom we govern; a class of persons, Indian in blood and colour, but English
in taste, in opinions, in morals, and in intellect. To that class we may leave it
to refine the vernacular dialects of the country, to enrich those dialects with
terms of science borrowed from the Western nomenclature, and to render
them by degrees fit vehicles for conveying knowledge to the great mass of
the population.

* * *

1835   1835

WILLIAM HOWARD RUSSELL

One of the first war correspondents, the Irish-born Russell (1820–1907) became
famous for his dispatches to the London *Times* during the Crimean War
(1854–56) and later reported on the American Civil War (1861–65). After the outbreak of the Indian Mutiny (1857–59), a rebellion of native troops and peasantry,
later referred to in India as the First War of Indian Independence, Russell traveled to
northern India to report on the revolt's suppression by British troops. More sympathetic toward the Indians than most Victorians, Russell debunked many of the most
shocking rumors about the rape, torture, and killing of British people and criticized
the cruelty of indiscriminate British reprisals. In the following excerpts he reflects on
the fate of the British community at Cawnpore, which surrendered to the Indian
rebels and was subsequently massacred.

From My Diary in India, In the Year 1858–9

[CAWNPORE]

February 12th.—* * * The scenes where great crimes have been perpetrated
ever possess an interest, which I would not undertake to stigmatise as morbid; and surely among the sites rendered infamous for all time, Cawnpore
will be pre-eminent as the magnitude of the atrocities with which it is con-

nected. But, though pre-eminent among crimes, the massacre of Cawnpore is by no means singular or unprecedented in any of the circumstances which mark turpitude and profundity of guilt. We who suffered from it think that there never was such wickedness in the world, and the incessant efforts of a gang of forgers and utterers of lies have surrounded it with horrors needlessly invented in the hope of adding to the indignation and burning desire for vengeance which the naked facts aroused. Helpless garrisons, surrendering under capitulation, have been massacred ere now; men, women, and children have been ruthlessly butchered by the enemies of their race ere now; risings, such as that of the people of Pontus under Mithridates, of the Irish Roman Catholics against the Protestant settlers in 1641, of the actors in the Sicilian vespers, of the assassins who smote and spared none on the eve of St. Bartholomew,[1] have taken place before, and have been over and over again attended by inhuman cruelty, violation, and torture. The history of mediaeval Europe affords many instances of crimes as great as those of Cawnpore; the history of civilized nations could afford some parallel to them even in modern times. In fact, the peculiar[2] aggravation of the Cawnpore massacres was this, that the deed was done by a subject race—by black men who dared to shed the blood of their masters and mistresses, and to butcher poor helpless ladies and children, who were the women and offspring of the dominant and conquering people. Here we had not only a servile war and a sort of Jacquerie[3] combined, but we had a war of religion, a war of race, a war of revenge, mingled together in a contest in which the insurgents were also actuated by some national promptings to shake off the yoke of a stranger, and to reestablish the full power of native chiefs, and the full sway of native religions. There is a kind of God's revenge against murder in the unsuccessful issue of all enterprises commenced in massacre, and carried on by cruelty and bloodshed. Whatever the causes of the mutiny and the revolt, it is clear enough that one of the modes by which the leaders, as if by common instinct, determined to effect their end was, the destruction of every white man, woman, or child who fell into their hands—a design which the kindliness of the people, or motives of policy, frustrated on many remarkable occasions. It must be remembered that the punishments of the Hindoo are cruel, and whether he be mild or not, he certainly is not, any more than the Mussulman,[4] distinguished for clemency towards his enemies. But philosophize and theorize as we may, Cawnpore will be a name ever heard by English ears with horror long after the present generation has passed away.

* * *

February 13th.—* * * The difficulty, in my mind, was to believe that it [Cawnpore] could ever have been defended at all. Make every allowance for

---

1. All incidents in which culturally or religiously distinct minorities were attacked by members of a dominant population. Mithradates VI, the ruler of Pontus, a kingdom of northeast Asia Minor, led his armies to massacre Roman and Italian residents in Asia in 88 B.C.E. In 1641 in Ulster, a county in northern Ireland, dispossessed native Irish Catholics rose up against English and Scottish Protestant settlers. Sicilians rebelled in 1282 against Charles I, the French-born king of Naples (son of Louis VIII and brother of Louis IX of

France). In 1572, on the evening before the feast day of St. Bartholomew (August 24), some Catholic nobles in the French royal court began a massacre of Huguenots (French Protestants), giving new impetus to a lengthy religious civil war.
2. Particular.
3. Peasant rebellion. The term derives from the 1358 uprising of peasants, known derisively as "Jacques," against nobles in northern France.
4. Muslim.

Cawnpore. A contemporary engraving, entitled "Massacre at Cawnpore."

the effects of weather, for circumstances, it is still the most wretched defensive position that could be imagined. Honour to those who defended it! Pity for their fate! Above all, pity for the lot of those whom the strong arms and brave hearts failed to save from the unknown dangers of that foul treachery! It was a horrible spot! Inside the shattered rooms, which had been the scene of such devotion and suffering, are heaps of rubbish and filth. The intrenchment is used as a *cloaca maxima*[5] by the natives, camp-followers, coolies, and others who bivouac in the sandy plains around it. The smells are revolting. Rows of gorged vultures sit with outspread wings on the mouldering parapets, or perch in clusters on the two or three leafless trees at the angle of the works by which we enter. I shot one with my revolver; and as the revolting creature disgorged its meal, twisting its bare black snake-like neck to and fro, I made a vow I would never incur the risk of beholding such a disgusting sight again.

* * *

February 14th.—* * * All the country about Cawnpore is covered with the finest powdered dust, two or three inches deep, which rises into the air on the smallest provocation. It is composed of sand, pulverized earth, and the brick powder and mortar of the dilapidated houses; whatever, in fact, can turn into dust. As the natives shuffle along, their pointed slippers fling up suffocating clouds of this unpleasant compound, and when these slippers are multiplied by thousands, the air is filled with a floating stratum of it, fifteen or eighteen feet high, and extending over the whole of the station. Even in the old days, when the roads were watered, the sta-

5. Largest sewer (Latin), after the main sewer draining northeast Rome (which even in the classical period was covered).

tion of Cawnpore had a bad notoriety for dust. What an earthquake to shake to pieces, what a volcano to smother with lava and ashes, has this mutiny been! Not alone cities, but confidence and trust have gone, never more to be restored!

Among those heaps of dust and ashes, those arid mounds of brick, those new-made trenches, I try in vain to realize what was once this station of Cawnpore. The solemn etiquette, the visits to the Brigadier and the General *en grande tenue*,[6] the invitations to dinner, the white kid-gloves, the balls, the liveries, the affectation of the *plus haut des hauts tons*,[7] the millinery anxieties of the ladies, the ices, and champagne, and supper, the golden-robed Nana Sahib,[8] moving about amid haughty stares and ill-concealed dislike. "What the deuce does the General ask that nigger here for?" The little and big flirtations, the drives on the road—a dull, ceremonious pleasure—the faded fun of the private theatricals, the exotic absurdities of the masonic revels, the marryings and givings in marriage, the little bills done by the rich bunneahs,[9] the small and great pecuniary relations between the station and the bazaar, the sense of security—and then on all this exaggerated relief of an English garrison-town and watering-place, the deep gloom of apprehension—at first "a shave of old Smith's,"[1] then a well-authenticated report, then a certainty of disaffection—rolling like thunder-clouds, and darkening the glassy surface of the gay society till it burst on it in stormy and cruel reality. But I cannot.

"Ah! you should have seen Cawnpore in its palmy days, when there were two cavalry regiments here, a lot of artillery, and three regiments of infantry in the cantonments.[2] Chock full of pretty women! The private theatricals every week; balls, and picnics, and dinners every evening. By Jove! it's too horrible to look at it now!" And so, indeed, it was. But one is tempted to ask if there is not some lesson and some warning given to our race in reference to India by the tremendous catastrophe of Cawnpore? I am deeply impressed by the difficulty of ruling India, as it is now governed by force, exercised by a few who are obliged to employ natives as the instruments of coercion. That force is the base of our rule I have no doubt; for I see nothing else but force employed in our relations with the governed. The efforts to improve the condition of the people are made by bodies or individuals who have no connection with the Government. The action of the Government in matters of improvement is only excited by considerations of revenue. Does it—as the great instructor of the people, the exponent of our superior morality and civilization—does it observe treaties, keep faith, pursue a fixed and equitable policy, and follow the precepts of Christianity in its conduct towards states and peoples? Are not our courts of law condemned by ourselves? Are not our police admitted to be a curse and a blight upon the country? In effect, the grave, unhappy doubt which settles on my mind is, whether India is the better for our rule, so far as regards the social condition of the great mass of the

6. In full military dress (French).
7. The highest of high fashions (French).
8. A dispossessed Hindu ruler who took at least nominal charge of the rebel forces at Cawnpore and who was seen by many British as the master-mind behind the massacres.
9. The receipts written up by wealthy merchants.

1. An unconfirmed report (military slang) of an incident from Lieutenant Colonel George Acklom Smith at his post at Fatehgarh, sixty miles from Cawnpore.
2. Permanent military stations in British India. "Palmy": prosperous.

people. We have put down widow-burning,[3] we have sought to check infanticide; but I have travelled hundreds of miles through a country peopled with beggars and covered with wigwam villages.

1858–59   1860

3. Suttee, the custom of a Hindu widow willingly immolating herself on her husband's funeral pyre; it was outlawed by the British in 1829.

ANONYMOUS

In 1845 potato blight severely damaged the crop in Ireland. Its return over the next several years caused widespread famine and disease, killing 1.5 million people and leading another million to emigrate. The British government's wholly inadequate response to the famine, which included exporting grain from Ireland while Irish people starved, contributed to the long-standing bitterness against British rule. Some came together in 1858 to advocate the use of force to liberate Ireland; taking their name from a group of legendary Irish warriors, they called themselves the Fenians, or Irish Republican Brotherhood, forerunners of the Irish Republican Army. Often thwarted by British infiltration of their ranks, the Fenians organized a rebellion in March 1867 that the British easily quelled. *The Nation*, a newspaper established in 1842 to promote Irish self-government, published the following statement around the time of that uprising.

[Proclamation of an Irish Republic]

The Irish People to the World

We have suffered centuries of outrage, enforced poverty, and bitter misery. Our rights and liberties have been trampled on by an alien aristocracy, who, treating us as foes, usurped our lands, and drew away from our unfortunate country all material riches. The real owners of the soil were removed to make room for cattle, and driven across the ocean to seek the means of living, and the political rights denied to them at home, while our men of thought and action were condemned to loss of life and liberty. But we never lost the memory and hope of a national existence. We appealed in vain to the reason and sense of justice of the dominant powers.

Our mildest remonstrances were met with sneers and contempt. Our appeals to arms were always unsuccessful.

To-day, having no honourable alternative left, we again appeal to force as our last resource. We accept the conditions of appeal, manfully deeming it better to die in the struggle for freedom than to continue an existence of utter serfdom.

All men are born with equal rights, and in associating to protect one another and share public burthens, justice demands that such associations should rest upon a basis which maintains equality instead of destroying it.

We therefore declare that, unable longer to endure the curse of Monarchical Government, we aim at founding a Republic based on universal suffrage, which shall secure to all the intrinsic value of their labour.

The soil of Ireland, at present in the possession of an oligarchy, belongs to us, the Irish people, and to us it must be restored.

We declare, also, in favour of absolute liberty of conscience, and the complete separation of Church and State.

We appeal to the Highest Tribunal for evidence of the justness of our cause. History bears testimony to the intensity of our sufferings, and we declare, in the face of our brethren, that we intend no war against the people of England—our war is against the aristocratic locusts, whether English or Irish, who have eaten the verdure of our fields—against the aristocratic leeches who drain alike our fields and theirs.

Republicans of the entire world, our cause is your cause. Our enemy is your enemy. Let your hearts be with us. As for you, workmen of England, it is not only your hearts we wish, but your arms. Remember the starvation and degradation brought to your firesides by the oppression of labour. Remember the past, look well to the future, and avenge yourselves by giving liberty to your children in the coming struggle for human liberty.

Herewith we proclaim the Irish Republic,
    THE PROVISIONAL GOVERNMENT.

1867

MATTHEW ARNOLD

The following selection comes from a series of lectures on Celtic literature delivered by Arnold (1822–1888) in his capacity as professor of poetry at Oxford University. From the eighteenth century onward, the word *Celtic* had been used as a descriptor of the family of languages that included Welsh, Cornish, Irish, and Gaelic. In a slippage from language to ethnicity or "race" that was common in the nineteenth and twentieth centuries, the term *Celt* was frequently applied to anyone who spoke (or was descended from those who spoke) a Celtic language. The following exposition on the distinctive features of "the Celt" connects to Arnold's broader interest in national identities. As the critic Lionel Trilling remarked in his 1949 study, "Arnold was at pains to show that the English are an amalgam of several 'bloods'—German, Norman, Celtic"; each of these distinctive "bloods," or races, in Arnold's opinion, required the balance of the others to constitute a truly successful national character. At the end of his lectures, Arnold called on Oxford to create a professorship of Celtic "to send . . . a message of peace to Ireland."

From On the Study of Celtic Literature

And as in material civilisation he has been ineffectual, so has the Celt been ineffectual in politics. This colossal, impetuous, adventurous wanderer, the Titan of the early world, who in primitive times fills so large a place on earth's scene, dwindles and dwindles as history goes on, and at last is shrunk to what we now see him. For ages and ages the world has been constantly slipping, ever more and more, out of the Celt's grasp. "They went forth to the war," Ossian says most truly, *"but they always fell."*[1]

And yet, if one sets about constituting an ideal genius, what a great deal of the Celt does one find oneself drawn to put into it! Of an ideal genius one does not want the elements, any of them, to be in a state of weakness; on the contrary, one wants all of them to be in the highest state of power; but with a law of measure, of harmony, presiding over the whole. So the sensibility[2] of the Celt, if everything else were not sacrificed to it, is a beautiful and admirable force. For sensibility, the power of quick and strong perception and emotion, is one of the very prime constituents of genius, perhaps its most positive constituent; it is to the soul what good senses are to the body, the grand natural condition of successful activity. Sensibility gives genius its materials; one cannot have too much of it, if one can but keep its master and not be its slave. Do not let us wish that the Celt had had less sensibility, but that he had been more master of it. Even as it is, if his sensibility has been a source of weakness to him, it has been a source of power too, and a source of happiness. Some people have found in the Celtic nature and its sensibility the main root out of which chivalry and romance and the glorification of a feminine ideal spring; this is a great question, with which I cannot deal here. Let me notice in passing, however, that there is, in truth, a Celtic air about the extravagance of chivalry, its reaction against the despotism of fact, its straining human nature further than it will stand. But putting all this question of chivalry and its origin on one side, no doubt the sensibility of the Celtic nature, its nervous exaltation, have something feminine in them, and the Celt is thus peculiarly[3] disposed to feel the spell of the feminine idiosyncrasy; he has an affinity to it; he is not far from its secret. Again, his sensibility gives him a peculiarly near and intimate feeling of nature and the life of nature; here, too, he seems in a special way attracted by the secret before him, the secret of natural beauty and natural magic, and to be close to it, to half-divine it. In the productions of the Celtic genius, nothing, perhaps, is so interesting as the evidences of this power: I shall have occasion to give specimens of them by-and-by. The same sensibility made the Celts full of reverence and enthusiasm for genius, learning, and the things of the mind; *to be a bard, freed a man,*—that is a characteristic stroke of this generous and ennobling ardour of theirs, which no race has ever shown more strongly. Even the extravagance and exaggeration of the sentimental Celtic nature has often something romantic and attractive about it, something which has a sort of smack of misdirected good. The Celt, undisciplinable, anarchical, and turbulent by nature, but out of affection and admiration giving himself body and soul to some leader, that is not a promising political temperament, it is just the opposite of the Anglo-Saxon temperament, disciplinable and steadily obedient within certain limits, but retaining an inalienable part of freedom and self-dependence; but it is a temperament for which one has a

---

1. A quotation from the poem "Cath-Loda," one of the works that the Scottish poet James Macpherson (1736–1796) claimed to have translated from the Gaelic writings of Ossian, a 3rd-century poet-warrior figure in traditional Irish folklore. A committee of scholars appointed in 1797 determined that the prose poems were largely composed by Macpherson.
2. Susceptibility to emotional influence.
3. Especially.

kind of sympathy notwithstanding. And very often, for the gay defiant reaction against fact of the lively Celtic nature one has more than sympathy; one feels, in spite of the extravagance, in spite of good sense disapproving, magnetised and exhilarated by it. The Gauls[4] had a rule inflicting a fine on every warrior who, when he appeared on parade, was found to stick out too much in front,—to be corpulent, in short. Such a rule is surely the maddest article of war ever framed, and to people to whom nature has assigned a large volume of intestines, must appear, no doubt, horrible; but yet has it not an audacious, sparkling, immaterial manner with it, which lifts one out of routine, and sets one's spirits in a glow?

All tendencies of human nature are in themselves vital and profitable; when they are blamed, they are only to be blamed relatively, not absolutely. This holds true of the Saxon's phlegm as well as of the Celt's sentiment. Out of the steady humdrum habit of the creeping Saxon, as the Celt calls him,— out of his way of going near the ground,—has come, no doubt, Philistinism,[5] that plant of essentially Germanic growth, flourishing with its genuine marks only in the German fatherland, Great Britain and her colonies, and the United States of America; but what a soul of goodness there is in Philistinism itself! and this soul of goodness I, who am often supposed to be Philistinism's mortal enemy merely because I do not wish it to have things all its own way, cherish as much as anybody. This steady-going habit leads at last, as I have said, up to science, up to the comprehension and interpretation of the world. With us in Great Britain, it is true, it does not seem to lead so far as that; it is in Germany, where the habit is more unmixed, that it can lead to science. Here with us it seems at a certain point to meet with a conflicting force, which checks it and prevents its pushing on to science; but before reaching this point what conquests has it not won! and all the more, perhaps, for stopping short at this point, for spending its exertions within a bounded field, the field of plain sense, of direct practical utility. How it has augmented the comforts and conveniences of life for us! Doors that open, windows that shut, locks that turn, razors that shave, coats that wear, watches that go, and a thousand more such good things, are the invention of the Philistines.

* * *

1867

4. The name given by the Romans to a Celtic people living in modern-day France.
5. A label Arnold repeatedly used for the attitude of the unenlightened middle classes of his time, in whose opposition to the defenders of culture he sees a resemblance to the biblical tribe who fought against the people of Israel, "the children of light."

JAMES ANTHONY FROUDE

The historian Froude (1818–1894) came to fame as the author of a twelve-volume *History of England* (1856–70) and the biography of his mentor, Thomas Carlyle (1882–1884). Inspired by his visits to South Africa to explore other parts of the empire, he toured British possessions in the Caribbean in the winter of 1886–87 and there gathered information for *The English in the West Indies* (1888), in which he expressed his belief that the colonies populated by nonwhite people were not suited to self-rule. In the following selection he focuses on his travels in Trinidad, a Caribbean island that passed from Spanish to British control near the end of the eighteenth century.

From The English in the West Indies

Trinidad is not one of our oldest possessions, but we had held it long enough for the old planter civilisation to take root and grow, and our road led us through jungles of flowering shrubs which were running wild over what had been once cultivated estates. Stranger still (for one associates colonial life instinctively with what is new and modern), we came at one place on an avenue of vast trees, at the end of which stood the ruins of a mansion of some great man of the departed order. Great man he must have been, for there was a gateway half crumbled away on which were his crest and shield in stone, with supporters on either side, like the Baron of Bradwardine's Bears;[1] fallen now like them, but unlike them never, I fear, to be set up again. The Anglo-West Indians, like the English gentry in Ireland, were a fine race of men in their day, and perhaps the improving them off the earth has been a less beneficial process in either case than we are in the habit of supposing.

Entering among the hills we came on their successors. In Trinidad there are 18,000 freeholders, most of them negroes and representatives of the old slaves. Their cabins are spread along the road on either side, overhung with bread-fruit trees, tamarinds, calabash trees, out of which they make their cups and water jugs. The luscious granadilla climbs among the branches; plantains throw their cool shade over the doors; oranges and limes and citrons perfume the air, and droop their boughs under the weight of their golden burdens. There were yams in the gardens and cows in the paddocks, and cocoa bushes loaded with purple or yellow pods. Children played about in swarms, in happy idleness and abundance, with schools, too, at intervals, and an occasional Catholic chapel, for the old religion prevails in Trinidad, never having been disturbed. What form could human life assume more charming than that which we were now looking on? Once more, the earth does not contain any peasantry so well off, so well cared for, so happy, so sleek and contented as the sons and daughters of the emancipated slaves in the English West Indian Islands. Sugar may fail the planter, but cocoa, which each peasant can grow with small effort for himself, does not fail and will not. He may 'better his condition,' if he has any such ambition, without stirring beyond his own ground, and so far, perhaps, his ambition may extend, if it is not turned off upon politics. Even the necessary evils of the tropics are not many or serious. His skin is proof against mosquitoes. There are snakes in Trinidad as there were snakes in Eden. 'Plenty snakes,' said one of them who was at work in his garden, 'plenty snakes, but no bitee.' As to costume, he would prefer the costume of innocence if he was allowed. Clothes in such a climate are super-

---

1. A reference to Sir Walter Scott's *Waverley* (1814). The baron's battlements are adorned with carved stone bears that are torn down during the novel and restored to their original position by its end.

fluous for warmth, and to the minds of the negroes, unconscious as they are of shame, superfluous for decency.

* * *

We made several similar small expeditions into the settled parts of the neighbourhood, seeing always (whatever else we saw) the boundless happiness of the black race. Under the rule of England in these islands the two million of these poor brothers-in-law of ours are the most perfectly contented specimens of the human race to be found upon the planet. Even Schopenhauer,[2] could he have known them, would have admitted that there were some of us who were not hopelessly wretched. If happiness be the satisfaction of every conscious desire, theirs is a condition which admits of no improvement: were they independent, they might quarrel among themselves, and the weaker become the bondmen[3] of the stronger; under the beneficent despotism of the English Government, which knows no difference of colour and permits no oppression, they can sleep, lounge, and laugh away their lives as they please, fearing no danger. If they want money, work and wages are waiting for them. No one can say what may be before them hereafter. The powers which envy human beings too perfect felicity may find ways one day of disturbing the West Indian negro; but so long as the English rule continues, he may be assured of the same tranquil existence.

As life goes he has been a lucky mortal. He was taken away from Dahomey and Ashantee[4]—to be a slave indeed, but a slave to a less cruel master than he would have found at home. He had a bad time of it occasionally, and the plantation whip and the branding irons are not all dreams, yet his owner cared for him at least as much as he cared for his cows and his horses. Kind usage to animals is more economical than barbarity, and Englishmen in the West Indies were rarely inhuman. Lord Rodney[5] says:

'I have been often in all the West India Islands, and I have often made my observations on the treatment of the negro slaves, and can aver that I never knew the least cruelty inflicted on them, but that in general they lived better than the honest day-labouring man in England, without doing a fourth part of his work in a day, and I am fully convinced that the negroes in our islands are better provided for and live better than when in Guinea.'[6]

Rodney, it is true, was a man of facts and was defective in sentiment. Let us suppose him wrong, let us believe the worst horrors of the slave trade or slave usage as fluent tongue of missionary or demagogue has described them, yet nevertheless, when we consider what the lot of common humanity has been and is, we shall be dishonest if we deny that the balance has been more than redressed; and the negroes who were taken away out of Africa, as compared with those who were left at home, were as the 'elect to salvation,'[7] who after a brief purgatory are secured an eternity of blessedness. The one

2. Arthur Schopenhauer (1788–1860), German philosopher who emphasized the tragedy of life.
3. I.e., bondsmen, slaves.
4. Also Asante, Ashanti (now part of Ghana), like Dahomey an area of western Africa that prospered in the 18th and 19th centuries and engaged in the slave trade.
5. George Brydges Rodney (1719–1792), British admiral who commanded several naval campaigns against Britain's rival colonial powers in the West Indies.
6. Region of western Africa involved in the slave trade until the middle of the 19th century (the transatlantic slave trade had been outlawed by Britain and the United States in 1807 and 1808, respectively).
7. In Calvinist Protestantism, the "elect" are those people chosen by God to be saved from eternal damnation.

condition is the maintenance of the authority of the English crown. The whites of the islands cannot equitably rule them. They have not shaken off the old traditions. If, for the sake of theory or to shirk responsibility, we force them to govern themselves, the state of Hayti[8] stands as a ghastly example of the condition into which they will then inevitably fall. If we persist, we shall be sinning against light—the clearest light that was ever given in such affairs. The most hardened believers in the regenerating effects of political liberty cannot be completely blind to the ruin which the infliction of it would necessarily bring upon the race for whose interests they pretend particularly to care.

* * *

1886–87   1888

8. Haiti, which gained its independence following a slave revolt that began in 1791. Through much of the 19th century, it experienced rapid and sometimes violent changes of leadership.

JOHN JACOB THOMAS

Thomas (ca. 1840–1889), a descendant of slaves, was born into poverty on the Caribbean island of Trinidad. Primarily a self-educated intellectual, he became a linguist, folklorist, teacher, civil servant, editor, and author. His *Froudacity* (1889) is a spirited book-length rebuttal of James Anthony Froude's *English in the West Indies* (1888), challenging its assumptions about the inferiority of nonwhite people and exposing its mistakes and its misrepresentations of his native land.

From Froudacity

From *Social Revolution*

Never was the Knight of La Mancha[1] more convinced of his imaginary mission to redress the wrongs of the world than Mr. James Anthony Froude seems to be of his ability to alter the course of events, especially those bearing on the destinies of the Negro in the British West Indies. The doctrinaire style of his utterances, his sublime indifference as to what Negro opinion and feelings may be, on account of his revelations, are uniquely charming. In that portion of his book headed "Social Revolution" our author, with that mixture of frankness and cynicism which is so dear to the soul of the British *esprit fort*[2] of today, has challenged a comparison between British Colonial policy on the one hand, and the Colonial policy of France and Spain on the other. This he does with an evident recklessness that his approval of Spain and France involves a definite condemnation of his own country. However, let us hear him:—

1. Don Quixote, the title character of Miguel de Cervantes' novel (1605, 1615); the name became synonymous with foolish, self-deluded idealism.
2. Freethinker (French).

"The English West Indies, like other parts of the world, are going through a silent revolution. Elsewhere the revolution, as we hope, is a transition state, a new birth; a passing away of what is old and worn out, that a fresh and healthier order may rise in its place. In the West Indies the most sanguine of mortals will find it difficult to entertain any such *hope at all*."

As Mr. Froude is speaking dogmatically here of *his*, or rather *our*, West Indies, let us hear him as he proceeds:—

"We have been a ruling power there for two hundred and fifty years; the *whites whom we planted as our representatives* are drifting into ruin, and they regard England and England's policy as the principal cause of it. The *blacks whom, in a fit of virtuous benevolence*, we emancipated, do not feel *particularly obliged to us*. They think, if they think at all, that they were ill-treated originally, and have received no more than was due to them."

Thus far. Now, as to "the *whites* whom we planted as our *representatives*," and who, Mr. Froude avers, are drifting into ruin, we confess to a total ignorance of their whereabouts in these islands in this jubilee year of Negro Emancipation.[3] Of the *representatives* of Britain immediately before and after Emancipation we happen to know something, which, on the testimony of Englishmen, Mr. Froude will be made quite welcome to before our task is ended. With respect to Mr. Froude's statement as to the ingratitude of the emancipated Blacks, if it is aimed at the slaves who were actually set free, it is utterly untrue; for no class of persons, in their humble and artless way, are more attached to the Queen's majesty, whom they regard as incarnating in her gracious person the benevolence which Mr. Froude so jauntily scoffs at. But if our censor's remark under this head is intended for the present generation of Blacks, it is a pure and simple absurdity. What are *we* Negroes of the present day to be grateful for to the US, personified by Mr. Froude and the Colonial Office exportations? We really believe, from what we know of Englishmen, that very few indeed would regard Mr. Froude's reproach otherwise than as a palpable adding of insult to injury. Obliged to "us," indeed! Why, Mr. Froude, who speaks of us as dogs and horses, suggests that the same kindliness of treatment that secures the attachment of those noble brutes would have the same result in our case. With the same consistency that marks his utterances throughout his book, he tells his readers "that there is no original or congenital difference between the capacity of the White and the Negro races." He adds, too, significantly: "With the *same chances* and with the same *treatment*, I believe that distinguished men would be produced *equally* from *both* races." After this truthful testimony, which Pelion upon Ossa[4] of evidence has confirmed, does Mr. Froude, in the fatuity of his skin-pride, believe that educated men, worthy of the name, would be otherwise than resentful, if not disgusted, at being shunted out of bread in their own native land, which their parents' labours and taxes have made desirable, in order to afford room to blockheads, vulgarians, or worse, imported from beyond the seas? Does Mr. Froude's scorn of the Negroes' skin extend,

3. The fifty-year anniversary of the freeing of slaves in the British West Indies. Slavery was abolished in British colonial possessions in 1833, but ex-slaves working on plantations were apprenticed to their former owners until 1838.

4. I.e., mountains. The proverbial phrase "to heap Ossa upon Pelion" derives from Greek mythology and the unsuccessful attempt of the giants to scale Olympus and threaten the gods by stacking one mountain on top of the other.

inconsistently on his part, to their intelligence and feelings also? And if so, what has the Negro to care—if let alone and not wantonly thwarted in his aspirations? It sounds queer, not to say unnatural and scandalous, that Englishmen should in these days of light be the champions of injustice towards their fellow-subjects, not for any intellectual or moral disqualification, but on the simple account of the darker skin of those who are to be assailed and thwarted in their life's career and aspirations. Really, are we to be grateful that the colour difference should be made the basis and justification of the dastardly denials of justice, social, intellectual, and moral, which have characterized the *régime* of those who Mr. Froude boasts were left to be the representatives of Britain's morality and fair play?

* * *

1889

ALFRED, LORD TENNYSON

In his capacity as poet laureate, Tennyson (1809–1892) was invited by Albert Edward, the Prince of Wales and Queen Victoria's eldest son, to write a poem for the opening of the Indian and Colonial Exhibition of 1886. It was one of numerous elaborately staged and popular events—hosted by London after the success of the Great Exhibition in 1851—that made a spectacle of colonial products, crafts, and peoples for the British public. Tennyson's verses were set to music by Sir Arthur Sullivan (1842–1900) and sung at the inaugural ceremony at the Albert Hall in the presence of the queen.

Opening of the Indian and Colonial Exhibition by the Queen

Written at the Request of the Prince of Wales

I

Welcome, welcome with one voice!
In your welfare we rejoice,
Sons and brothers that have sent,
From isle and cape and continent,
5   Produce of your field and flood,
Mount and mine, and primal wood;
Works of subtle brain and hand,
And splendours of the morning land,°   *the East*
Gifts from every British zone;
10   Britons, hold your own![1]

---

1. A phrase reminiscent of Tennyson's earlier "Britons, Guard Your Own" (1852), a poem that supported the formation of a militia against the threat of French forces.

II

May we find, as ages run,
The mother featured in the son;
And may yours for ever be
That old strength and constancy
15 Which has made your fathers great
In our ancient island State,
And wherever her flag fly,
Glorying between sea and sky,
Makes the might of Britain known;
20   Britons, hold your own!

III

Britain fought her sons of yore—
Britain fail'd; and never more,
Careless of our growing kin,
Shall we sin our fathers' sin,
25 Men that in a narrower day—
Unprophetic rulers they—
Drove from out the mother's nest
That young eagle of the West°   *United States*
To forage for herself alone;
30   Britons, hold your own!

IV

Sharers of our glorious past,
Brothers, must we part at last?
Shall we not thro' good and ill
Cleave to one another still?
35 Britain's myriad voices call,
'Sons, be welded each and all,
Into one imperial whole,
One with Britain, heart and soul!
One life, one flag, one fleet, one Throne!'
40   Britons, hold your own!

1886

T. N. MUKHARJI

Trailokya Nath Mukharji, a government official and Brahman (a member of the highest Hindu caste), traveled to England with the Indian delegation for the Indian and Colonial Exhibition of 1886. On his return home his impressions of the trip were serialized in a weekly Indian newspaper, and then reprinted in a book published in London and Calcutta. In the following selection Mukharji describes his experiences with, and observations of, the British.

From A Visit to Europe

[THE INDIAN AND COLONIAL EXHIBITION]

Another place of considerable interest to the natives of England was the Indian Bazar where Hindu and Muhammadan artisans carried on their avocations, to witness which men, women and children flocked from all parts of the kingdom. A dense crowd always stood there, looking at our men as they wove the gold brocade, sang the patterns of the carpet[1] and printed the calico with the hand. They were as much astonished to see the Indians produce works of art with the aid of rude apparatus they themselves had discarded long ago, as a Hindu would be to see a chimpanzee officiating as a priest in a funeral ceremony and reading out Sanskrit texts from a palm leaf book spread before him. We were very interesting beings no doubt, so were the Zulus before us, and so is the Sioux chief at the present time (1887). Human nature everywhere thirsts for novelty, and measures out its favours in proportion to the rarity and oddity of a thing. It was from the ladies that we received the largest amount of patronage. We were pierced through and through by stares from eyes of all colours—green, gray, blue and black—and every movement and act of ours, walking, sitting, eating, reading, received its full share of "O, I, never!" The number of wives we left behind at home was also a constant theme of speculation among them, and shrewd guesses were sometimes made on this point, 250 being a favourite number. You could tell any amount of stories on this subject without exciting the slightest suspicion. Once, one of our number told a pretty waitress—"I am awfully pleased with you, and I want to marry you. Will you accept the fortieth wifeship in my household which became vacant just before I left my country?" She asked—"How many wives have you altogether?" "Two hundred and fifty, the usual number," was the ready answer. "What became of your wife, number 40?" "I killed her, because one morning she could not cook my porridge well." The poor girl was horrified, and exclaimed—"O you monster, O you wretch!" Then she narrated the sad fate of a friend of hers. She was a sweet little child, when an African student studying in Edinburgh came and wooed her. They got married in England and fondly loved each other. Everything went well as long as the pair lived in England, but after a short time he took his fair wife to his desert home in Liberia. Not a single white man or woman could she see there, and she felt very lonely. But the sight of her mother-in-law, who dressed in feathers and skins came dancing into the house half-tipsy, was more than she could bear. She pined for a short time and died.

Of course, every nation in the world considers other nations as savages or at least much inferior to itself. It was so from the beginning and it will be so as long as human nature will retain its present character. We did not therefore wonder that the common people should take us for barbarians, awkward as we were in every respect. They have very strict notions of dress,

---

1. When carpets are produced on handlooms, overseers sometimes sing out the number and color of each thread needed for the pattern; the weavers then repeat back the instructions in a chorus.

The Indian and Colonial Exhibition. This depiction of the Gawlior Gateway, entrance to the Indian Palace at the Indian and Colonial Exhibition, appeared in the *Illustrated London News* in July 1886.

manners and the general bearing of a man, any deviation from which is seriously noticed. Utmost indulgence was however shewn to us everywhere. Her Majesty was graciously pleased to lay aside the usual rules, and this favour was shewn us wherever we went. Gentlemen and ladies of high education and culture, however, honoured us as the representatives of the most ancient nation now existing on the face of the earth. They would frequently ask us home, get up private parties and arrange for all sorts of amusements. In other houses we grew more intimate and formed part of the family party. To these we were always welcome, and could go and come whenever we liked. We got some friends among them, and these gentlemen would often come and fetch us home if we absented ourselves for more than the ordinary length of time. I fondly remember the happy days I passed with them, and feel thankful for the kindness they shewed me during my sojourn in their country.

In public matters non-official gentlemen were also very partial to us. "We want to hear the turbanned gentleman" was the wish often and often expressed. But we ceased not to be a prodigious wonder to strangers and to the common people. Would they discuss us so freely if they knew that we understood their language? It was very amusing to hear what they said about us. Often when fatigued with work, or when cares and anxieties cast a gloom upon our mind, we found such talks about us more refreshing than a glass of port wine. I wish I had the ability to do justice to the discussing power of these ladies and gentlemen exercised in their kind notice of us, for in that case I could produce one of the most interesting books ever published. Or if I had known that I would be required to write an account of my visit to Europe, I would have taken notes of at least some of the remarkable hits on truth unconsciously made by ignorant people from the country, which are applicable to all nations and which set one to philosophise on the material difference that exists between our own estimate of ourselves and the estimate which others form of us.

If we were interesting beings in the eyes of the Londoners, who had oftener opportunities of seeing their fellow subjects from the far East, how much more would we be so to the simple villagers who came by thousands to see the wonders of the Exhibition. Their conduct towards us was always kind and respectful. They liked to talk to us, and whenever convenient we tried to satisfy their curiosity. Men, women and children, whose relations are in India serving as soldiers or in any other capacity, would come through the crowd, all panting, to shake hands with us and ask about their friends. Many queer incidents happened in this way. "Do you know Jim,—James Robinson you know of —— Regiment?" asked a fat elderly woman, who one day came bustling through the crowd and took me by storm, without any of those preliminary manœuvres usually adopted to open a conversation with a stranger. I expressed my regret in not having the honour of Jim's acquaintance. The good old lady then explained to me that she was Jim's aunt, and gave me a long history of her nephew, and the circumstances which led to his enlistment as a soldier. If the truant nephew lost the golden opportunity of sending through us his dutiful message to his aunt, she on her part was not wanting in her affectionate remembrances of him. Among other things, most of which I did not understand, for she did not speak the English we ordinarily hear nor was her language quite coherent at the time, she begged me to carry to Jim the important intelligence that Mrs. Jones' fat pig obtained a prize at the Smithfield Agricultural Show.[2] I shewed my alacrity to carry the message right off to Jim in the wilds of Upper Burma by immediately taking leave of the lady, who joined her friends and explained to them that I was a bosom friend of her nephew.

Once, I was sitting in one of the swellish[3] restaurants at the Exhibition, glancing over a newspaper which I had no time to read in the morning. At a neighbouring table sat a respectable-looking family group evidently from the country, from which furtive glances were occasionally thrown in my direction. I thought I might do worse than having a little fun, if any could be made out of the notice that was being taken of me. I seemed to be suddenly aware that I was being looked at, which immediately scared away half a dozen eyes from my table. It took fully five minutes' deep undivided attention to my paper again to reassure and tempt out those eyes from the plates where they took refuge, and the glances from them, which at first flashed and flickered like lightning, became steadier the more my mind seemed to get absorbed in the subject I was reading. The closer inspection to which I submitted ended in my favour. Perhaps, no symptom being visible in my external appearance of the cannibalistic tendencies of my heart, or owing probably to the notion that I must have by that time got over my partiality for

2. Britain's most important agricultural event, held annually in London since 1799.   3. Stylish.

human flesh, or knowing at least that the place was safe enough against any treacherous spring which I might take into my head to make upon them, or owing to whatever other cause, the party gradually grew bolder, began to talk in whispers and actually tried to attract my attention towards them. The latter duty ultimately devolved upon the beauty of the party, a pretty girl of about seventeen. Of course it was not intended for my ears, but somehow I heard her say—"Oh, how I wish to speak to him?" Could I withstand such an appeal? I rose and approaching the little Curiosity asked—"Did you speak to me, young lady?" She blushed and hung down her head. Her papa came to the rescue. "My daughter, Sir, is delighted with the magnificent things brought from your country to this Exhibition. She saw some writing in your language on a few plates and shields, and is anxious to know its meaning. We did not know whom to ask, when we saw you. Will you take a seat here, and do me the honour to take a glass of something with me? What will it be? Sparkling moselle?[4] I find is good here; or shall it be champagne or anything stronger?" He said. The preferred glass was declined with thanks, but I took a chair and explained the meaning of some of the verses damascened on the Koftgari ware.[5] The young lady soon got over her bashfulness, and talked with a vivacity which I did not expect from her. She was delighted with everything I said, expressed her astonishment at my knowledge of English, and complimented me for the performance of the band brought from *my country, viz.*, the West Indian band composed of Negroes and Mulattos, which compliment made me wince a little, but nevertheless I went on chattering for a quarter of an hour and furnishing her with sufficient means to annihilate her friend Minnie, Jane or Lizzy or whoever she might be, and to brag among her less fortunate relations for six months to come of her having actually seen and talked to a genuine "Blackie."

* * *

1887   1889

4. A white wine.
5. Steel merchandise of Indian manufacture with an inlaid pattern in gold.

WILLIAM ERNEST HENLEY

Editor of many periodicals, Henley (1849–1903) was a powerful figure in literary circles in the 1880s and 1890s, and published a highly influential anthology in 1892; subtitled "A Book of Verse for Boys," *Lyra Heroica* (Latin for *The Heroic Lyre,* or harp) was intended for use in schools and is filled with poetic accounts of selfless and noble deeds that often involve dying for one's country in battle. Many of Henley's own poems are similarly patriotic; others relate to his experiences fighting tuberculosis of the bone, a devastating and painful illness that resulted in the amputation of one of his legs. "Invictus" was composed while Henley was a patient at Edinburgh Royal Infirmary under the care of Sir Joseph Lister (1827–1912), pioneer of antiseptic surgery, who managed to save his other leg.

Invictus[1]

Out of the night that covers me,
　Black as the Pit from pole to pole,
I thank whatever gods may be
　For my unconquerable soul.

5　In the fell° clutch of circumstance　　　　　　　　　*cruel*
　I have not winced nor cried aloud.
Under the bludgeonings of chance
　My head is bloody, but unbowed.

Beyond this place of wrath and tears
10　Looms but the Horror of the shade,
And yet the menace of the years
　Finds, and shall find, me unafraid.

It matters not how strait° the gate,　　　　　　　　　*narrow*
　How charged with punishments the scroll,
15　I am the master of my fate;
　I am the captain of my soul.

1875　　　　　　　　　　　　　　　　　　　　　　　　　1888

1. Unconquered (Latin). Sir Arthur Quiller Couch (1863–1944) added this title when he included the poem in the *Oxford Book of English Verse 1250–1900* (1900).

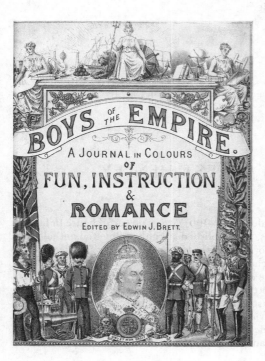

Boys of the Empire. Edwin J. Brett published numerous popular weekly magazines for boys from 1866 onward; this cover dates from 1882.

SIR HENRY JOHN NEWBOLT

A practicing lawyer until 1899, Newbolt (1862–1938) composed novels, history books, and a play over the course of his writing career, but his literary reputation was secured by the stirring patriotic poems, often in ballad form and on naval themes, that he published in such volumes as *Admirals All* (1897), *The Island Race* (1898), and *Songs of the Sea* (1904). Newbolt was knighted in 1915; in 1921 he chaired a governmental investigation of the teaching of English in the schools of England and Wales.

Vitaï Lampada[1]

There's a breathless hush in the Close[2] to-night—
    Ten to make and the match to win—
A bumping pitch and a blinding light,
    An hour to play and the last man in.
5   And it's not for the sake of a ribboned coat,
    Or the selfish hope of a season's fame,
But his Captain's hand on his shoulder smote
    "Play up! play up! and play the game!"

The sand of the desert is sodden red,—
10   Red with the wreck of a square[3] that broke;—
The Gatling's[4] jammed and the colonel dead
    And the regiment blind with dust and smoke.
The river of death has brimmed his banks,
    And England's far, and Honour a name,
15   But the voice of a schoolboy rallies the ranks,
    "Play up! play up! and play the game!"

This is the word that year by year
    While in her place the School is set
Every one of her sons must hear,
20   And none that hears it dare forget.
This they all with a joyful mind
    Bear through life like a torch in flame,
And falling fling to the host behind—
    "Play up! play up! and play the game!"

1897

1. The torch of life (Latin); see *De Rerum Natura* (*On the Nature of the Universe*) II. 79, by the Roman poet and philosopher Lucretius (ca. 99–ca. 55 B.C.E.). The words are taken from a description of a relay race in which a flaming torch is passed from runner to runner.
2. The name of the cricket ground at Clifton College, an elite boarding school for boys founded in Bristol in 1862. Newbolt won a scholarship to Clifton from his local grammar school and became head boy there in 1881.
3. A combat formation taken by an infantry unit when threatened with cavalry attack.
4. Forerunner of the modern machine gun, the Gatling gun was invented in the United States in 1861.

JOSEPH CHAMBERLAIN

Chamberlain (1836–1914) was a manufacturer who made his fortune at the age of thirty-eight; he spent the rest of his life in politics, generally allying himself with radical causes. An enthusiastic promoter of imperial expansion and consolidation, he was appointed colonial secretary in 1895. The following selection is taken from a speech Chamberlain delivered in 1897 at the Royal Colonial Institute's annual dinner; published later that year in his *Foreign and Colonial Speeches*, the text records the frequent "cheers" and "laughter" and expressions of agreement ("hear, hear") that greeted his performance.

From The True Conception of Empire

It seems to me that there are three distinct stages in our Imperial history. We began to be, and we ultimately became, a great Imperial Power in the eighteenth century, but, during the greater part of that time, the colonies were regarded, not only by us, but by every European Power that possessed them, as possessions valuable in proportion to the pecuniary advantage which they brought to the mother country which, under that order of ideas, was not truly a mother at all, but appeared rather in the light of a grasping and absentee landlord desiring to take from his tenants the utmost rents he could exact. The colonies were valued and maintained because it was thought that they would be a source of profit—of direct profit—to the mother country.

That was the first stage, and when we were rudely awakened by the War of Independence in America from this dream, that the colonies could be held for our profit alone, the second chapter was entered upon, and public opinion seems then to have drifted to the opposite extreme; and, because the colonies were no longer a source of revenue, it seems to have been believed and argued by many people that their separation from us was only a matter of time, and that that separation should be desired and encouraged lest haply they might prove an encumbrance and a source of weakness.

It was while those views were still entertained, while the little England-ers[1]—(laughter)—were in their full career, that this Institute was founded to protest against doctrines so injurious to our interests—(cheers)—and so derogatory to our honour; and I rejoice that what was then, as it were, "a voice crying in the wilderness"[2] is now the expressed and determined will of the overwhelming majority of the British people. (Loud cheers.) Partly by the efforts of this Institute and similar organisations, partly by the writings of such men as Froude and Seeley[3]—(hear, hear)—but mainly by the

1. Critics of imperial expansion who advocated sharply limiting the scope and responsibilities of the British Empire.
2. Allusion to the Gospels, especially Matthew 3.3; the phrase is usually interpreted as referring to John the Baptist's prophecies of the coming of Jesus.

3. Sir John Robert Seeley (1834–1895), English historian, essayist, and author of *The Expansion of England* (1883), which portrays the growth of the British Empire as a natural process. James Anthony Froude (1818–1894), English author and historian (see p. 695).

instinctive good sense and patriotism of the people at large, we have now reached the third stage in our history, and the true conception of our Empire. (Cheers.)

What is that conception? As regards the self-governing colonies[4] we no longer talk of them as dependencies. The sense of possession has given place to the sentiment of kinship. We think and speak of them as part of ourselves—(cheers)—as part of the British Empire, united to us, although they may be dispersed throughout the world, by ties of kindred, of religion, of history, and of language, and joined to us by the seas that formerly seemed to divide us. (Cheers.)

But the British Empire is not confined to the self-governing colonies and the United Kingdom. It includes a much greater area, a much more numerous population in tropical climes, where no considerable European settlement is possible, and where the native population must always vastly outnumber the white inhabitants; and in these cases also the same change has come over the Imperial idea. Here also the sense of possession has given place to a different sentiment—the sense of obligation. We feel now that our rule over these territories can only be justified if we can show that it adds to the happiness and prosperity of the people—(cheers)—and I maintain that our rule does, and has, brought security and peace and comparative prosperity to countries that never knew these blessings before. (Cheers.)

In carrying out this work of civilisation we are fulfilling what I believe to be our national mission, and we are finding scope for the exercise of those faculties and qualities which have made of us a great governing race. (Cheers.) I do not say that our success has been perfect in every case, I do not say that all our methods have been beyond reproach; but I do say that in almost every instance in which the rule of the Queen has been established and the great *Pax Britannica*[5] has been enforced, there has come with it greater security to life and property, and a material improvement in the condition of the bulk of the population. (Cheers.) No doubt, in the first instance, when these conquests have been made, there has been bloodshed, there has been loss of life among the native populations, loss of still more precious lives among those who have been sent out to bring these countries into some kind of disciplined order, but it must be remembered that that is the condition of the mission we have to fulfil.

＊　＊　＊

You cannot have omelettes without breaking eggs; you cannot destroy the practices of barbarism, of slavery, of superstition, which for centuries have desolated the interior of Africa, without the use of force; but if you will fairly contrast the gain to humanity with the price which we are bound to pay for it, I think you may well rejoice in the result of such expeditions as those which have recently been conducted with such signal success—

4. Canada, New Zealand, Australia, and South Africa.
5. British peace (Latin), which the British Empire supposedly imposed on its colonial possessions (by analogy with the *pax Romana* of the Roman Empire).

(cheers)—in Nyassaland, Ashanti, Benin, and Nupé[6]—expeditions which may have, and indeed have, cost valuable lives, but as to which we may rest assured that for one life lost a hundred will be gained, and the cause of civilisation and the prosperity of the people will in the long run be eminently advanced. (Cheers.) But no doubt such a state of things, such a mission as I have described, involve heavy responsibility. In the wide dominions of the Queen the doors of the temple of Janus[7] are never closed—(hear, hear)—and it is a gigantic task that we have undertaken when we have determined to wield the sceptre of empire. Great is the task, great is the responsibility, but great is the honour—

THE RHODES COLOSSUS
STRIDING FROM CAPE TOWN TO CAIRO.

Cecil Rhodes. "The Rhodes Colossus, Striding from Cape Town to Cairo" (1892), by Edward Linley Sambourne (1844–1910).

(cheers); and I am convinced that the conscience and the spirit of the country will rise to the height of its obligations, and that we shall have the strength to fulfil the mission which our history and our national character have imposed upon us. (Cheers.)

* * *

1897   1897

---

6. All areas of British exploration on the African continent during the last decades of the 19th century. Nyassaland (or Nyasaland), a region of southeastern Africa that constitutes modern-day Malawï. Ashanti (also Asante, Ashantee), a western African state located in the territory of present-day Ghana. Benin, a state in western Africa later incorporated into Nigeria. Nupé, an area of western Africa that is now part of Nigeria.
7. Twin-faced Roman god of doorways. The doors to his temple near the Roman Forum were kept open during wartime and closed during times of peace.

J. A. HOBSON

John Atkinson Hobson (1858–1940), the distinguished Liberal economist and author, first taught classics and then worked as a lecturer in English literature and economics for the Oxford University Extension Delegacy and for the London Society for the Extension of University Teaching, before becoming a freelance writer. His many books include *Problems of Poverty* (1891), *The Evolution of Modern Capitalism* (1894), *The Problem of the Unemployed* (1896), and *John Ruskin, Social Reformer* (1898).

From Imperialism: A Study

[THE POLITICAL SIGNIFICANCE OF IMPERIALISM]

The curious ignorance which prevails regarding the political character and tendencies of Imperialism cannot be better illustrated than by the following passage from a learned work upon "The History of Colonisation":[1] "The extent of British dominion may perhaps be better imagined than described, when the fact is appreciated that, of the entire land surface of the globe, approximately one-fifth is actually or theoretically under that flag, while more than one-sixth of all the human beings living in this planet reside under one or the other type of English colonisation. The names by which authority is exerted are numerous, and processes are distinct, but the goals to which this manifold mechanism is working are very similar. According to the climate, the natural conditions and the inhabitants of the regions affected, procedure and practice differ. The means are adapted to the situation; there is not any irrevocable, immutable line of policy: from time to time, from decade to decade, English statesmen have applied different treatments to the same territory. Only one fixed rule of action seems to exist; it is to promote the interests of the colony to the utmost, to develop its scheme of government as rapidly as possible, and eventually to elevate it from the position of inferiority to that of association. Under the charm of this beneficent spirit the chief colonial establishments of Great Britain have already achieved substantial freedom, without dissolving nominal ties; the other subordinate possessions are aspiring to it, while, on the other hand, this privilege of local independence has enabled England to assimilate with ease many feudatory States[2] into the body politic of her system." Here then is the theory that Britons are a race endowed, like the Romans, with a genius for government, that our colonial and imperial policy is animated by a resolve to spread throughout the world the arts of free self-government which we enjoy at home,[3] and that in truth we are accomplishing this work.

---

1. H. C. Morris, *The History of Colonization* (1900), vol. 2, p. 80 [Hobson's note]. The work's full title is *The History of Colonization from the Earliest Times to the Present Day.*
2. Feudally subject states.

3. "The British Empire is a galaxy of free States," said Sir W. Laurier in a speech, 8 July 1902 [Hobson's note]. Sir Wilfrid Laurier (1841–1919), Canadian political leader.

Now, without discussing here the excellencies or the defects of the British theory and practice of representative self-government, to assert that our "fixed rule of action" has been to educate our dependencies in this theory and practice is quite the largest misstatement of the facts of our colonial and imperial policy that is possible. Upon the vast majority of the populations throughout our Empire we have bestowed no real powers of self-government, nor have we any serious intention of doing so, or any serious belief that it is possible for us to do so.

Of the three hundred and sixty-seven millions of British subjects outside these isles, not more than ten millions, or one in thirty-seven, have any real self-government for purposes of legislation and administration.

Political freedom, and civil freedom, so far as it rests upon the other, are simply non-existent for the over-whelming majority of British subjects. In the self-governing colonies of Australasia and North America alone is responsible representative government a reality, and even there considerable populations of outlanders,[4] as in West Australia, or servile labour, as in Queensland, temper the genuineness of democracy. In Cape Colony and Natal recent events[5] testify how feebly the forms and even the spirit of the free British institutions have taken root in States where the great majority of the population were always excluded from political rights. The franchise and the rights it carries will remain virtually a white monopoly in so-called self-governing colonies, where the coloured population is to the white as four to one and ten to one respectively.

In certain of our older Crown colonies there exists a representative element in the government. While the administration is entirely vested in a governor appointed by the Crown, assisted by a council nominated by him, the colonists elect a portion of the legislative assembly. The following colonies belong to this order: Jamaica, Barbados, Trinidad, Bahamas, British Guiana, Windward Islands, Bermudas, Malta, Mauritius, Ceylon.

The representative element differs considerably in size and influence in these colonies, but nowhere does it outnumber the non-elected element. It thus becomes an advisory rather than a really legislative factor. Not merely is the elected always dominated in numbers by the non-elected element, but in all cases the veto of the Colonial Office is freely exercised upon measures passed by the assemblies. To this it should be added that in nearly all cases a fairly high property qualification is attached to the franchise, precluding the coloured people from exercising an elective power proportionate to their numbers and their stake in the country.

The entire population of these modified Crown colonies amounted to 5,700,000 in 1898.[6]

The overwhelming majority of the subjects of the British Empire are under Crown colony government, or under protectorates. In neither case do they enjoy any of the important political rights of British citizens: in neither case are they being trained in the arts of free British institutions. In the Crown colony the population exercises no political privileges. The governor, appointed

4. Foreigners denied full citizenship.
5. The Anglo-Boer War of 1899–1902, fought between the British and the Dutch Afrikaners, or Boers, who had settled in regions of South Africa. Cape Colony and Natal, former British colonies now part of modern-day South Africa, were sites of long-standing friction between the British and the Boers.
6. In all essential features, India and Egypt are to be classed as Crown colonies [Hobson's note].

by the Colonial Office, is absolute, alike for legislation and administration; he is aided by a council of local residents usually chosen by himself or by home authority, but its function is merely advisory, and its advice can be and frequently is ignored. In the vast protectorates we have assumed in Africa and Asia there is no tincture of British representative government; the British factor consists in arbitrary acts of irregular interference with native government. Exceptions to this exist in the case of districts assigned to Chartered Companies, where business men, animated avowedly by business ends, are permitted to exercise arbitrary powers of government over native populations under the imperfect check of some British Imperial Commissioner.

Again, in certain native and feudatory States of India our Empire is virtually confined to government of foreign relations, military protection, and a veto upon grave internal disorder, the real administration of the countries being left in the hands of native princes or headmen. However excellent this arrangement may be, it lends little support to the general theory of the British Empire as an educator of free political institutions.

Where British government is real, it does not carry freedom or self-government; where it does carry a certain amount of freedom and self-government, it is not real. Not five per cent of the population of our Empire are possessed of any appreciable portion of the political and civil liberties which are the basis of British civilisation. Outside the ten millions of British subjects in Canada, Australia, and New Zealand, no considerable body is endowed with full self-government in the more vital matters, or is being "elevated from the position of inferiority to that of association."

This is the most important of all facts for students of the present and probable future of the British Empire. We have taken upon ourselves in these little islands the responsibility of governing huge aggregations of lower races in all parts of the world by methods which are antithetic to the methods of government which we most value for ourselves.

1902

"Beacons of the Future"? Education in Victorian Britain

"It's a very cheery thing to come into London by any of these lines which run high, and allow you to look down upon the houses like this."

I thought he was joking, for the view was sordid enough, but he soon explained himself.

"Look at those big, isolated clumps of building rising up above the slates, like brick islands in a lead-coloured sea."

"The board-schools."

"Light-houses, my boy! Beacons of the future! Capsules with hundreds of bright little seeds in each, out of which will spring the wise, better England of the future."

This exchange between Sherlock Holmes and his friend and chronicler Dr. Watson occurs in "The Adventure of the Naval Treaty," a story published in 1893. The words that Sir Arthur Conan Doyle puts into his detective's mouth are strikingly positive. When Holmes points to examples of public elementary schools from his train window, he registers a confident satisfaction that his country has acted well in the past and that it will improve still further in the future. The buildings are the result of measures put in place to deliver education to the children of the poor; England will eventually reap the benefits of their nurtured talents and thus become a brighter place.

In some respects the congratulatory tone of Holmes's remarks is appropriate. The expansion of many different types of education is one of the truly remarkable features of the Victorian era. These transformations were driven largely by the changes associated with the Industrial Revolution—growth in population, migration to the cities, democratization, and an increasing need for educated professionals, particularly in the sciences and engineering. And in quantitative terms the biggest single development did indeed occur within the systems of elementary education that the detective commends so glowingly here. In 1851, the average continuous period spent at school by a working-class child was only two years, with fully one third of the children in England and Wales receiving no education at all; by 1900 nearly 90 percent of the child population went to school for seven to eight years. Yet in other respects the achievement is less estimable. Although Britain was the world's richest and most developed country in the nineteenth century, basic education did not reach many of the nation's children until the relatively late date of 1870; the process of making schooling compulsory and free for all took even longer. Furthermore, had Holmes entered a classroom in one of those "brick islands," he would have discovered an educational environment quite dissimilar to those experienced in their early days by males of his and Watson's class. Finally, access to continued education was extremely restricted throughout the Victorian era and beyond, with few opportunities for children of the majority working classes to ascend to secondary, let alone university level, studies.

Gaining an understanding of the major developments in elementary, secondary, and higher educational provision enlightens the study of Victorian literature in numerous ways. The spread of education changed the demographics of authorship and the nature of the reading public; this development was met by a correspondent explosion within the publishing industry, which over the course of the century produced for its new and diverse readerships a progressively varied array of newspapers, periodicals, magazines, pamphlets, and books. Major debates about the purpose and character of education at all levels engaged the leading intellectuals of the time: who should be educated and how, what should be the relationship of professional to liberal arts education, and what should be the relative importance given to the study of the sciences versus the study of the classics. Yet education was not just a topic for theoretical discussion in the writings of the day; rather, it was a pressing concern within a huge number of works in verse and prose, intimately connected to their investigations of both the potential for personal and social development, and the deleterious effects of existing inequities of educational provision and opportunity.

To begin with elementary education: two main factors conspired to hamper the establishment of a national, state-supported system. In the first place, the infighting of the various religious denominations made British Parliament loath to involve itself in what was a highly contentious issue; while most agreed that the children of the poor should receive a Christian education, members of different churches were bitterly opposed to the prospect of another sect's tenets being propagated in the classroom. In the second place, there were few supporters for the idea that a common education should be given to all; instead, for much of the nineteenth century, and in some quarters even longer, a significant proportion of the upper, middle, and even working classes believed that it was fitting for the different orders of society to receive different types of instruction. As a result, Victorian education manifests marked class stratification. Widely held views about the different intellectual abilities and appropriate destinies of males and females also had their effects, creating the broadest disparity between the kinds of schooling deemed suitable for boys and girls of the upper and middle classes; certain types of sex discrimination operated in the education of working-class children too. Examining basic educational provisions across the long stretch of the Victorian period is then a complex affair; the instruction any given individual received depended on his or her class and sex and on the date and location of that education.

Throughout the nineteenth century, boys and girls at relatively well-to-do levels of society usually received the rudiments of education at home from parents, governesses, or tutors, but their experiences tended to diverge sharply thereafter. Many sons of the nation's elite proceeded, frequently via preparatory schools, to one of a select group of institutions such as Eton, Westminster, Winchester, Harrow, Rugby, Charterhouse, or Shrewsbury—private, fee-paying schools, some in existence since the fourteenth and fifteenth centuries, which in this period came to be known, confusingly enough, as "the public schools." Although a good number of these seats of learning had been originally established to educate local or needy children, their patronage by wealthy and aristocratic families had, by the beginning of the Victorian era, transformed them into exclusive boarding institutions for a geographically diverse selection of boys from rich and powerful homes. By all accounts, however, they offered an indifferent and often brutal education and were badly in need of reform; the zealous attempts of Thomas Arnold, headmaster of Rugby School from 1828 to 1841, to infuse his pupils with what he saw as sound Christian values represent the best known of these improving efforts, enshrined as they are within the highly popular *Tom Brown's School Days*, a novel published in 1857 by Thomas Hughes.

Dr. Arnold declared that he was concerned to foster in his charges "first, religious and moral principle, secondly, gentlemanly conduct, thirdly, intellectual ability"; readers of Hughes's novel might be forgiven for concluding that book learning actually ran a poor fourth to sporting excellence. Academic study in these elite establishments was almost exclusively focused on the classics; much of the school day was spent translating or paraphrasing literature in Greek and Latin. This also constituted the staple diet in the country's longstanding network of around 830 grammar schools—day schools for advanced pupils (generally aged from ten or eleven years up) "in which the learned languages are grammatically taught," as Johnson's *Dictionary* put it. Although, like the public schools with which they shared a common heritage, most of them held in their histories some connection with the provision of free education for at least a proportion of their pupils, grammar schools in this period were generally perceived as institutions for the education of the sons of the middle classes, and they frequently charged fees. Those that did not, a government inquiry concluded in 1868, were in a dire state (coming after the Newcastle Commission [1858–61] into the provision of "sound and cheap elementary instruction," and the Clarendon Commission [1861–64], which examined the nine most prestigious public schools, this inquiry, the Taunton Commission of 1864–68, represented the final section of a tripartite, class-stratified, investigation of the schools of England and Wales, an investigation that led to a number of parliamentary acts for reform).

Various other limitations in the grammar school system had long been apparent, especially their uneven and inadequate distribution across the country. Dissatisfaction with both this and their exclusively classical curriculum in certain portions of the professional middle classes had brought additional and alternative forms of schooling into being from the last quarter of the eighteenth century onward. At that time both new establishments, such as Warrington Academy for the sons of Dissenters, and newly configured grammar schools had begun to complement the ancient languages with living tongues or substitute them entirely. Further curricular innovation was a hallmark of the Victorian era; especially in the industrial cities increasing pressure for scientific and technical education led to the foundation of new grammars like the Mathematical and Commercial School in Leeds (later "Leeds Modern Grammar") in 1845.

While their brothers studied in the public schools, the grammar schools, or one of a growing number of privately run institutions, girls in middle- and upper-class families were much more likely to continue their lessons at home throughout their teenaged years. Private schools for girls—both boarding and day—also existed, but only in rare instances did the curriculum contain the classics or come close to anything like academic rigor. Responding in part to the Taunton Commission's identification of a "general deficiency" in the provision of secondary schooling for middle- and upper-class girls, a National Union for Improvement of the Education of Women of All Classes (later the "Women's Education Union") was founded in 1871, which proceeded to establish the Girls' Public Day School Company with the aim of providing an alliance of academic high schools; thirty-seven institutions were in operation by 1905. There were also some places for girls in both single-sex and coeducational grammar schools, but the network of geographic coverage here was even more inadequate than that which existed for boys.

The story of British education for the majority juvenile population, the children of the less-privileged classes, properly begins with the Sunday School movement of the 1780s; during the week small informal common day schools, often run by old women and thus also known as "dame schools," had for many years provided for a modest fee what was in effect a form of child minding with a modicum of teaching thrown in (Charles Dickens, whose novels depict and satirize numerous forms of educational institution, presents in *Great Expectations* [1860–61] what seems an amusingly accurate picture of one such establishment in the mid-1810s). Thanks in large part to evangelical fervor, however, the first half of the nineteenth century witnessed the creation of new institutions that transformed the educational landscape. By 1850, the largest number of children at school attended voluntary institutions set up by the National Society, an educational charity formed by the Church of England in 1811; additional schools were run by the British and Foreign School Society (an ostensibly nonsectarian, but functionally nonconformist, entity) and other religious groups, most notably the Wesleyans and Roman Catholics. As a result of these endeavors, the proportion of the nation's sons and daughters who received some education in day schools jumped from around 30 percent in 1818 to 60 percent in 1851; over two million children were at school by mid-century.

The charitable bodies running the schools were able to cope with their burgeoning populations largely because of the methods developed by two individuals, Andrew Bell and Joseph Lancaster. Both men, associated with the National Society and the B. F. S. S., respectively, pioneered the use of monitors; in addition, Bell promoted the teaching manual and Lancaster the reading card. By delegating work to unpaid recruits from the cohort of older pupils, only one teacher, in theory, was required to control an entire school, however large. In time, though, concerns about the instruction dispensed in these establishments and the need for a national education policy became the subject of mounting debate. From 1833 onward, after Parliament voted to supply a grant to support the religious societies' school-building programs, the government grew progressively more involved in popular education, establishing a Committee of Council on Education to oversee the institution of a new teacher-training program with pupil-teacher apprenticeships and colleges for certification, a system of grants, and inspections of all schools in receipt of official funds. After the Newcastle Commission delivered its findings in 1861, and amid increasing clamor for greater value for public monies, these measures culminated in the 1861–62 Revised Code of elementary education. This established a simplified set of "Standards" in reading, writing, and arithmetic and a new system of "payment by results"; a school's annual financial grant depended on how many pupils could demonstrate to a visiting inspector that they had reached the approved level for their year in the core subjects. After the Elementary Education Act of 1870 (often called "Forster's Act," in reference to the Liberal Party's vice president, W. E. Forster, who sponsored it through Parliament) made it possible for locally created school boards to set up schools in districts where the network of institutions, church-supported or otherwise, was inadequate, progressively larger numbers of the new "Board Schools" (Sherlock Holmes's "lighthouses") joined the existing elementaries to make the Standards part of the lives of millions of children. Although over the next forty-four years the code was "infinitely revised" (to quote the sardonic observation of Matthew Arnold, to date the most celebrated member of Her Majesty's Inspectorate of Schools), its pared-down curriculum, and more especially the teaching methods used to deliver it, were thought by many to be responsible for creating a joylessly inflexible and at times unduly punitive regimen within the classrooms of the poor. Whether these schools functioned as "Beacons of the future!" remains an open question.

Higher education also underwent dramatic changes in this period. While a number of seats of advanced learning had been founded in Scotland and Ireland over the course of the sixteenth, seventeenth, and eighteenth centuries, in 1800 there were just two universities in England—Oxford and Cambridge—both restricted to members of the Church of England and socially elite in their character. By 1900, several new kinds of institutions were in existence—more than a dozen new university colleges, most in cities in the midlands and the north; technical institutes, offering education in science and engineering; mechanics' institutes, offering adult education to men of the working class; and women's colleges, including women's colleges at both Oxford and Cambridge.

England's first new university since the medieval period was established in the nation's capital. Originally two colleges—University College London, founded in 1826 under the name London University, to provide university education for students not members of the Church of England, and King's College London, founded by King George in 1829 as an Anglican alternative to London University—the University of London was chartered in 1836 as a federation of the two with the power to grant degrees. New university colleges were soon founded in other cities, often by wealthy merchants or industrialists; the most illustrious of these was Owens College Manchester, founded in 1851 with a bequest from John Owens, a wealthy textile merchant. These new colleges often gave more emphasis in their curriculum to the sciences and to modern languages, and they frequently federated with local medical colleges, which had responsibility for training doctors. Until the 1880s, all university degrees for work in these colleges were granted by the University of London, but in the last decades of the nineteenth century, they began to achieve independent university status.

During the same decades when the university system was expanding, a new kind of institution developed—mechanics institutes, designed to provide lectures, classes, and lending libraries for members of the working class. By mid-century, there were over seven hundred such institutes in England, Scotland, and Ireland. Some were short lived, some still exist today, and others developed into technical institutes or university colleges. There were many debates about the institutes: whether they should provide artisans knowledge of the scientific principles underlying their craft or give working-class men basic education and general culture, whether working men could afford the membership fee or had the time and energy to attend classes, whether politics was an appropriate subject of study, and whether women should have the right to attend. A project similar in its inspiration was the establishment by the Christian Socialists in 1854 in London of the Working Men's College, designed to provide a liberal education to skilled workers. Early supporters included Charles Kingsley, John Stuart Mill, Dante Gabriel Rossetti, and John Ruskin.

As higher education expanded, there was fierce debate about women's access to it. In 1848, Frederick Denison Maurice founded Queen's College, London, largely to improve the education of governesses and certify their proficiency. More like a secondary school than a college in the modern sense, it was followed by others like it, which seemed insufficient to feminists, who believed that women should have the right to earn university degrees. At Cambridge, Girton College was founded in 1869, Newnham, in 1871; in 1879 two women's colleges were founded at Oxford. In the 1870s both the University of London, often acting for its northern colleges, and universities in Scotland began to give women degrees. Although they had women's colleges, Oxford did not finally award women degrees until 1920, Cambridge not until 1948.

As the structure of higher education changed, Victorian intellectuals gave extensive thought to the nature and purposes of the university. Perhaps the most important book written about university education in the nineteenth century, John Henry Newman's *The Idea of a University* (1852), was originally a set of lectures, given in Dublin, designed to set out the principles of the Roman Catholic university that the church had asked him to establish there. John Stuart Mill used the occasion of his election as rector of St. Andrews University in Scotland to deliver an address about his views of higher education; Thomas Henry Huxley similarly used the occasion of the opening of a new scientific college in Birmingham to deliver a manifesto about the place of science in university education, *Science and Culture*, to which Matthew Arnold responded in *Literature and Science*. (Arnold's essay and selections from Huxley and Newman are included in the anthology.) These works were not only important in their own day; their arguments shape much of the debate about the mission of colleges and universities today.

It is instructive to compare the texts included in this section with those already mentioned in this introduction and numerous other selections from the anthology. The excerpt from John Stuart Mill's *Autobiography* shows the writer reflecting on some of the problematic effects of the high-powered education he had received from his father, the leading Utilitarian philosopher James Mill; Elizabeth Barrett Browning provides an amusing if disturbing description of the scattershot nature of a well-to-do young lady's home-based tuition in Book 1 of *Aurora Leigh*; the anthology's two plays, Oscar Wilde's *The Importance of Being Earnest* and George Bernard Shaw's *Mrs Warren's Profession* also offer some interesting perspectives on female education. A further rewarding read is *The Princess*, Tennyson's long poem about its heroine Ida's establishment of a women-only university. But nineteenth-century writing in general has a vast amount to offer the student interested in the educational practices, attitudes, and experiences of the period. Children's literature is an obvious destination, while large numbers of Victorian autobiographies and novels offer rich hunting grounds; of especial value here are the era's *Bildungsromanen* (the German term for novels that trace the intellectual and emotional formation of individual figures), in which the question of education is of fundamental importance.

CHARLES DICKENS

Of the fourteen novels Dickens (1812–1870) completed, only one, his eleventh, is an "Industrial novel," a work dealing with the new modes of existence that had come into being in the northern manufacturing cities. *Hard Times* sets its action in the fictional "Coketown," a "severely workful" place in which every part of life is regimented and mechanistic. With its rigid adherence to all things factual, Mr. M'Choakumchild's school embodies the governing beliefs of Coketown; as such, it represents Dickens's attack on what he saw as the excessively rationalistic doctrines of Utilitarian philosophy and the undue influence he felt they were exerting on the country's burgeoning systems of public education. While the picture of school life the first two chapters present is hardly a realistic vision of actual classroom experience of the time, Dickens nevertheless had done his homework to ensure the accuracy of certain details; his summary of the contents of M'Choakumchild's education, for example, is closely based on the Committee of Council on Education's 1854 series of questions for the examination of trainee teachers.

From Hard Times

Chapter 1. The One Thing Needful[1]

"Now, what I want is, Facts. Teach these boys and girls nothing but Facts. Facts alone are wanted in life. Plant nothing else, and root out every thing else. You can only form the minds of reasoning animals upon Facts: nothing else will ever be of any service to them. This is the principle on which I bring up my own children, and this is the principle on which I bring up these children. Stick to Facts, sir!"

The scene was a plain, bare, monotonous vault of a school-room, and the speaker's square forefinger emphasized his observations by underscoring every sentence with a line on the schoolmaster's sleeve. The emphasis was helped by the speaker's square wall of a forehead, which had his eyebrows for its base, while his eyes found commodious cellarage in two dark caves, overshadowed by the wall. The emphasis was helped by the speaker's mouth, which was wide, thin, and hard set. The emphasis was helped by the speaker's voice, which was inflexible, dry, and dictatorial. The emphasis was helped by the speaker's hair, which bristled on the skirts of his bald head, a plantation of firs to keep the wind from its shining surface, all covered with knobs, like the crust of a plum pie, as if the head had scarcely warehouse-room for the hard facts stored inside. The speaker's obstinate carriage, square coat, square legs, square shoulders—nay, his very neck-cloth, trained to take him by the throat with an unaccommodating grasp, like a stubborn fact, as it was—all helped the emphasis.

"In this life, we want nothing but Facts, sir; nothing but Facts!"

The speaker, and the schoolmaster, and the third grown person present, all backed a little, and swept with their eyes the inclined plane of little vessels then and there arranged in order, ready to have imperial[2] gallons of facts poured into them until they were full to the brim.

Chapter 2. Murdering the Innocents[3]

Thomas Gradgrind, sir. A man of realities. A man of facts and calculations. A man who proceeds upon the principle that two and two are four, and nothing over, and who is not to be talked into allowing for any thing over.

1. Luke 10.42; these are Christ's words to Martha, when he says that her sister made the right decision to listen to wise advice rather than attend to household matters.

2. The official system of nonmetric weights and measures used in Great Britain at that time.
3. I.e., the slaughter of children ordered by King Herod; see Matthew 2.16.

Thomas Gradgrind, sir—peremptorily Thomas—Thomas Gradgrind. With a rule and a pair of scales, and the multiplication table always in his pocket, sir, ready to weigh and measure any parcel of human nature, and tell you exactly what it comes to. It is a mere question of figures, a case of simple arithmetic. You might hope to get some other nonsensical belief into the head of George Gradgrind, or Augustus Gradgrind, or John Gradgrind, or Joseph Gradgrind (all supposititious, non-existent persons), but into the head of Thomas Gradgrind—no, sir!

In such terms Mr. Gradgrind always mentally introduced himself, whether to his private circle of acquaintance, or to the public in general. In such terms, no doubt, substituting the words "boys and girls," for "sir," Thomas Gradgrind now presented Thomas Gradgrind to the little pitchers before him, who were to be filled so full of facts.

Indeed, as he eagerly sparkled at them from the cellarage before mentioned, he seemed a kind of cannon loaded to the muzzle with facts, and prepared to blow them clean out of the regions of childhood at one discharge. He seemed a galvanizing apparatus,[4] too, charged with a grim mechanical substitute for the tender young imaginations that were to be stormed away.

"Girl number twenty," said Mr. Gradgrind, squarely pointing with his square forefinger, "I don't know that girl. Who is that girl?"

"Sissy Jupe, sir," explained number twenty, blushing, standing up, and courtesying.

"Sissy is not a name," said Mr. Gradgrind. "Don't call yourself Sissy. Call yourself Cecilia."

"It's father as calls me Sissy, sir," returned the young girl in a trembling voice, and with another courtesy.

"Then he has no business to do it," said Mr. Gradgrind. "Tell him he mustn't. Cecilia Jupe. Let me see. What is your father?"

"He belongs to the horse-riding,[5] if you please, sir."

Mr. Gradgrind frowned, and waved off the objectionable calling with his hand.

"We don't want to know any thing about that, here. You mustn't tell us about that, here. Your father breaks horses, don't he?"

"If you please, sir, when they can get any to break, they do break horses in the ring, sir."

"You mustn't tell us about the ring, here. Very well, then. Describe your father as a horsebreaker. He doctors sick horses, I dare say?"

"Oh yes, sir."

"Very well, then. He is a veterinary surgeon, a farrier and horsebreaker. Give me your definition of a horse."

(Sissy Jupe thrown into the greatest alarm by this demand).

"Girl number twenty unable to define a horse!" said Mr. Gradgrind, for the general behoof of all the little pitchers. "Girl number twenty possessed of no facts, in reference to one of the commonest of animals! Some boy's definition of a horse. Bitzer, yours."

---

4. Scientific equipment named after the Italian scientist Luigi Galvani (1737–1798), who discovered how to stimulate animal tissue with electrical current.

5. Here, synonym for the circus, in which Sissy Jupe's father is a clown.

The square finger, moving here and there, lighted suddenly on Bitzer, perhaps because he chanced to sit in the same ray of sunlight which, darting in at one of the bare windows of the intensely whitewashed room, irradiated Sissy. For the boys and girls sat on the face of the inclined plane in two compact bodies, divided up the centre by a narrow interval; and Sissy, being at the corner of a row on the sunny side, came in for the beginning of a sunbeam, of which Bitzer, being at the corner of a row on the other side, a few rows in advance, caught the end. But, whereas the girl was so dark-eyed and dark-haired, that she seemed to receive a deeper and more lustrous colour from the sun when it shone upon her, the boy was so light-eyed and light-haired that the self-same rays appeared to draw out of him what little colour he ever possessed. His cold eyes would hardly have been eyes, but for the short ends of lashes which, by bringing them into immediate contrast with something paler than themselves, expressed their form. His short-cropped hair might have been a mere continuation of the sandy freckles on his forehead and face. His skin was so unwholesomely deficient in the natural tinge, that he looked as though, if he were cut, he would bleed white.

"Bitzer," said Thomas Gradgrind. "Your definition of a horse."

"Quadruped. Graminivorous. Forty teeth, namely twenty-four grinders, four eye-teeth, and twelve incisive. Sheds coat in the spring; in marshy countries, sheds hoofs, too. Hoofs hard, but requiring to be shod with iron. Age known by marks in mouth."[6] Thus (and much more) Bitzer.

"Now girl number twenty," said Mr. Gradgrind. "You know what a horse is."

She courtesied again, and would have blushed deeper, if she could have blushed deeper than she had blushed all this time. Bitzer, after rapidly blinking at Thomas Gradgrind with both eyes at once, and so catching the light upon his quivering ends of lashes that they looked like the antennæ of busy insects, put his knuckles to his freckled forehead, and sat down again.

The third gentleman now stepped forth. A mighty man at cutting and drying, he was; a government officer; in his way (and in most other people's too), a professed pugilist; always in training, always with a system to force down the general throat like a bolus,[7] always to be heard of at the bar of his little Public-office, ready to fight all England. To continue in fistic phraseology, he had a genius for coming up to the scratch, wherever and whatever it was, and proving himself an ugly customer. He would go in and damage any subject whatever with his right, follow up with his left, stop, exchange, counter, bore his opponent (he always fought All England) to the ropes, and fall upon him neatly.[8] He was certain to knock the wind out of common-sense, and render that unlucky adversary deaf to the call of time. And he

6. Dickens here satirizes the form (and complex Latinate vocabulary) of the object lesson, a method of instruction originally developed by the Swiss educationalist Johann Pestalozzi (1746–1827), which was popularized in Britain by its inclusion in the curriculum of the influential Battersea teacher training college opened by the central figure in English public education during the mid-19th century, James Kay-Shuttleworth (1804–1877).

7. A large pill. The concerns of the government officer, the "third gentleman" here, make it likely that Dickens is satirizing the agenda of the new Department of Practical Art (established in 1852) and the recent introduction of drawing into the elementary curriculum.

8. The phrases in these three sentences stem from the sport of prizefighting, or bare-knuckle boxing. "All England": the national boxing competition.

had it in charge from high authority to bring about the great public-office Millennium,[9] when Commissioners should reign upon earth.

"Very well," said this gentleman, briskly smiling, and folding his arms. "That's a horse. Now, let me ask you, girls and boys, Would you paper a room with representations of horses?"

After a pause, one half the children cried in chorus, "Yes, sir!" Upon which the other half, seeing in the gentleman's face that Yes was wrong, cried out in chorus, "No, sir!"—as the custom is, in these examinations.

"Of course, No. Why wouldn't you?"

A pause. One corpulent slow boy, with a wheezy manner of breathing, ventured the answer, Because he wouldn't paper a room at all, but would paint it.

"You *must* paper it," said the gentleman, rather warmly.

"You must paper it," said Thomas Gradgrind, "whether you like it or not. Don't tell *us* you wouldn't paper it. What do you mean, boy?"

"I'll explain to you, then," said the gentleman, after another and a dismal pause, "why you wouldn't paper a room with representations of horses. Do you ever see horses walking up and down the sides of rooms in reality—in fact? Do you?"

"Yes, sir!" from one half. "No, sir!" from the other.

"Of course, no," said the gentleman, with an indignant look at the wrong half. "Why, then, you are not to see any where, what you don't see in fact; you are not to have any where, what you don't have in fact. What is called Taste, is only another name for Fact."

Thomas Gradgrind nodded his approbation.

"This is a new principle, a discovery, a great discovery," said the gentleman. "Now, I'll try you again. Suppose you were going to carpet a room. Would you use a carpet having a representation of flowers upon it?"

There being a general conviction by this time that "No, sir!" was always the right answer to this gentleman, the chorus of No was very strong. Only a few feeble stragglers said Yes; among them Sissy Jupe.

"Girl number twenty," said the gentleman, smiling in the calm strength of knowledge.

Sissy blushed, and stood up.

"So you would carpet your room—or your husband's room, if you were a grown woman, and had a husband—with representations of flowers, would you?" said the gentleman. "Why would you?"

"If you please, sir, I am very fond of flowers," returned the girl.

"And is that why you would put tables and chairs upon them, and have people walking over them with heavy boots?"

"It wouldn't hurt them, sir. They wouldn't crush and wither, if you please, sir. They would be the pictures of what was very pretty and pleasant, and I would fancy—"

"Ay, ay, ay! But you mustn't fancy," cried the gentleman, quite elated by coming so happily to his point. "That's it! You are never to fancy."

"You are not, Mary Jupe," Thomas Gradgrind solemnly repeated, "to do any thing of that kind."

---

9. The coming thousand-year reign of Christ, prophesied in Revelation 20.1–5; figuratively, then, a wonderful period in the future.

"Fact, fact, fact!" said the gentleman. And "Fact, fact, fact!" repeated Thomas Gradgrind.

"You are to be in all things regulated and governed," said the gentleman, "by fact. We hope to have, before long, a board of fact, composed of commissioners of fact, who will force the people to be a people of fact, and of nothing but fact. You must discard the word Fancy altogether. You have nothing to do with it. You are not to have, in any object of use or ornament, what would be a contradiction in fact. You don't walk upon flowers in fact; you can not be allowed to walk upon flowers in carpets. You don't find that foreign birds and butterflies come and perch upon your crockery; you can not be permitted to paint foreign birds and butterflies upon your crockery. You never meet with quadrupeds going up and down walls; you must not have quadrupeds represented upon walls. You must use," said the gentleman, "for all these purposes, combinations and modifications (in primary colors) of mathematical figures which are susceptible of proof and demonstration. This is the new discovery. This is fact. This is taste."

The girl courtesied, and sat down. She was very young, and she looked as if she were frightened by the matter of fact prospect the world afforded.

"Now, if Mr. M'Choakumchild," said the gentleman, "will proceed to give his first lesson here, Mr. Gradgrind, I shall be happy, at your request, to observe his mode of procedure."

Mr. Gradgrind was much obliged. "Mr. M'Choakumchild, we only wait for you."

So, Mr. M'Choakumchild began in his best manner. He and some one hundred and forty other school-masters, had been lately turned at the same time, in the same factory, on the same principles, like so many pianoforte legs. He had been put through an immense variety of paces, and had answered volumes of head-breaking questions. Orthography, etymology, syntax, and prosody, biography, astronomy, geography, and general cosmography, the sciences of compound proportion, algebra, land surveying and leveling, vocal music, and drawing from models, were all at the ends of his ten chilled fingers. He had worked his stony way into Her Majesty's most Honourable Privy Council's Schedule B, and had taken the bloom of the higher branches of mathematics and physical science, French, German, Latin, and Greek. He knew all about all the Water Sheds of all the world (whatever they are), and all the histories of all the peoples, and all the names of all the rivers and mountains, and all the productions, manners, and customs of all the countries, and all their boundaries and bearings on the two-and-thirty points of the compass.[1] Ah, rather overdone, M'Choakumchild. If he had only learnt a little less, how infinitely better he might have taught much more!

He went to work in this preparatory lesson, not unlike Morgiana in the Forty Thieves: looking into all the vessels ranged before him, one after another, to see what they contained.[2] Say, good M'Choakumchild. When

1. This paragraph accurately abstracts details from the two-year program of required studies ("Schedule B") that was drawn up in 1854 for the country's thirty-four teacher-training colleges by the government's Committee of Council on Education ("Her Majesty's most Honorable Privy Council").

2. In the tale of "Ali Baba and the Forty Thieves" in the *Arabian Nights*, the slave girl (Morgiana) killed the thieves when she poured boiling oil into the jars in which they were hiding.

from thy boiling store, thou shalt fill each jar brim full by-and-by, dost thou think that thou wilt always kill outright the robber Fancy lurking within— or sometimes only maim him and distort him!

1854

LEWIS CARROLL

The following selection is from *Alice's Adventures in Wonderland,* a book for children by Charles Lutwidge Dodgson (1832–1898), who was a clergyman and lecturer in mathematics at Oxford University. This work and its successor, *Through the Looking Glass* (1871), originated in stories told to the young daughters of Dean Liddell, who was the principal of Christ Church, the Oxford college where Dodgson lived. While both books are famous for the succession of extraordinary encounters and events their heroine experiences in Wonderland and the Looking Glass world, they also provide a wealth of information about the forms and contents of a well-to-do little girl's education at the midpoint of the Victorian era.

From Alice's Adventures in Wonderland

From *Chapter 2*

Alice took up the fan and gloves, and, as the hall was very hot, she kept fanning herself all the time she went on talking: "Dear, dear! How queer everything is to-day! And yesterday things went on just as usual. I wonder if I've been changed in the night? Let me think: was I the same when I got up this morning? I almost think I can remember feeling a little different. But if I'm not the same, the next question is, Who in the world am I? Ah, *that's* the great puzzle!" And she began thinking over all the children she knew, that were of the same age as herself, to see if she could have been changed for any of them.

"I'm sure I'm not Ada," she said, "for her hair goes in such long ringlets, and mine doesn't go in ringlets at all; and I'm sure I can't be Mabel, for I know all sorts of things, and she, oh! She knows such a very little! Besides, *she's* she, and *I'm* I, and—oh dear, how puzzling it all is! I'll try if I know all the things I used to know. Let me see: four times fives is twelve, and four times six is thirteen, and four times seven is—oh dear! I shall never get to twenty at that rate! However, the Multiplication Table doesn't signify: let's try Geography. London is the capital of Paris, and Paris is the capital of Rome, and Rome—no, *that's* all wrong, I'm certain! I must have been changed for Mabel! I'll try and say '*How doth the little—*'"[1] and she crossed

1. Alice here begins to recite "Against Idleness and Mischief" ("How doth the little busy bee . . ."), one of the most famous poems in the *Divine Songs* (1715), a collection of religious and moral verses composed expressly for children to memorize by pedagogue and hymn-writer Isaac Watts (1674–1748).

her hands on her lap, as if she were saying lessons, and began to repeat it, but her voice sounded hoarse and strange, and the words did not come the same as they used to do:—

> *"How doth the little crocodile*
> *Improve his shining tail,*
> *And pour the waters of the Nile*
> *On every golden scale!*
> *How cheerfully he seems to grin,*
> *How neatly spreads his claws,*
> *And welcomes little fishes in*
> *With gently smiling jaws!"*

"I'm sure those are not the right words," said poor Alice, and her eyes filled with tears again as she went on, "I must be Mabel after all, and I shall have to go and live in that poky little house, and have next to no toys to play with, and oh! ever so many lessons to learn! No, I've made up my mind about it: if I'm Mabel, I'll stay down here! It'll be no use their putting their heads down and saying, 'Come up again, dear!' I shall only look up and say, 'Who am I, then? Tell me that first, and then, if I like being that person, I'll come up: if not, I'll stay down here till I'm some-body else'—but, oh dear!" cried Alice with a sudden burst of tears, "I do wish they *would* put their heads down! I am so *very* tired of being all alone here!"

From *Chapter 9*

"When we were little," the Mock Turtle went on at last, more calmly, though still sobbing a little now and then, "we went to school in the sea. The mas-ter was an old Turtle—we used to call him Tortoise—"

"Why did you call him Tortoise, if he wasn't one?" Alice asked.

"We called him Tortoise because he taught us," said the Mock Turtle angrily; "really you are very dull!"

"You ought to be ashamed of yourself for asking such a simple question," added the Gryphon; and then they both sat silent and looked at poor Alice, who felt ready to sink into the earth. At last the Gryphon said to the Mock Turtle, "Drive on, old fellow! Don't be all day about it!" and he went on in these words.

"Yes, we went to school in the sea, though you mayn't believe it—"

"I never said I didn't!" interrupted Alice.

"You did," said the Mock Turtle.

"Hold your tongue!" added the Gryphon, before Alice could speak again. The Mock Turtle went on.

"We had the best of educations—in fact, we went to school every day—"

"*I've* been to a day-school too," said Alice; "you needn't be so proud as all that."

"With extras?" asked the Mock Turtle a little anxiously.

"Yes," said Alice, "we learned French and music."

"And washing?" said the Mock Turtle.

"Certainly not!" said Alice indignantly.

"Ah! Then yours wasn't a really good school," said the Mock Turtle in a tone of great relief. "Now at *ours* they had at the end of the bill, 'French, music, *and washing*—extra.'"[2]

"You couldn't have wanted it much," said Alice; "living at the bottom of the sea."

"I couldn't afford to learn it," said the Mock Turtle with a sigh. "I only took the regular course."

"What was that?" enquired Alice.

"Reeling and Writhing, of course, to begin with," the Mock Turtle replied: "and then the different branches of Arithmetic—Ambition, Distraction, Uglification, and Derision."

"I never heard of 'Uglification.'" Alice ventured to say. "What is it?"

The Gryphon lifted up both its paws in surprise. "Never heard of uglifying!" it exclaimed. "You know what to beautify is, I suppose?"

"Yes," said Alice, doubtfully: "it means—to—make—anything—prettier."

"Well then," the Gryphon went on, "if you don't know what to uglify is, you *are* a simpleton."

Alice did not feel encouraged to ask any more questions about it, so she turned to the Mock Turtle, and said, "What else had you to learn?"

"Well, there was Mystery," the Mock Turtle replied, counting off the subjects on his flappers,—"Mystery, ancient and modern, with Seaography: then Drawling—the Drawling-master was an old conger-eel, that used to come once a week: *he* taught us Drawling, Stretching, and Fainting in Coils."[3]

"What was *that* like?" said Alice.

"Well, I can't show it you, myself," the Mock Turtle said: "I'm too stiff. And the Gryphon never learnt it."

"Hadn't time," said the Gryphon: "I went to the Classical master, though. He was an old crab, *he* was."

"I never went to him," the Mock Turtle said with a sigh: "he taught Laughing and Grief, they used to say."

"So he did, so he did," said the Gryphon, sighing in his turn, and both creatures hid their faces in their paws.

"And how many hours a day did you do lessons?" said Alice, in a hurry to change the subject.

"Ten hours the first day," said the Mock Turtle: "nine the next, and so on."

"What a curious plan!" exclaimed Alice.

"That's the reason they're called lessons," the Gryphon remarked: "because they lessen from day to day."

This was quite a new idea to Alice, and she thought it over a little before she made her next remark. "Then the eleventh day must have been a holiday?"

"Of course it was," said the Mock Turtle.

"And how did you manage on the twelfth?" Alice went on eagerly.

"That's enough about lessons," the Gryphon interrupted in a very decided tone: "tell her something about the games now."

1865

2. The joke here depends on the Mock Turtle's confounding "extras," in the sense of additional educational subjects, with the "extras" added onto the bill for regular tuition.
3. I.e., drawing, sketching, and painting in oils.

THOMAS HUGHES

I n addition to his literary labors, Hughes (1822–1896) also worked as a lawyer, a Liberal Party member of Parliament, and an avid social reformer. *Tom Brown's School Days* was by far and away his most successful publication; inspired by the feeling that "good might be done by a real novel for boys—not didactic . . . but distinctly aiming at being interesting," he had written it when his oldest son, Maurice, was eight and about to leave home for boarding school. The novel was semi-autobiographical, drawing heavily on Hughes's own experience as a pupil in the 1830s at Rugby, one of the country's elite public schools. Hughes's time at the school coincided with that of Thomas Arnold (1795–1842), Rugby's most charismatic headmaster (and father of Matthew Arnold, 1822–1888), who sought to eradicate the traditional lawlessness and brutality of upper-class male education by infusing it with Christian values and moral purpose. Although he does not appear in the following extracts, Arnold ("the Doctor") is one of the central presences in *Tom Brown's School Days* (as is Flashman, the hated bully of the school).

From Tom Brown's School Days

From *Part One, Chapter 8*

In no place in the world has individual character more weight than at a public school. Remember this, I beseech you, all you boys who are getting into the upper forms.[1] Now is the time in all your lives, probably, when you may have more wide influence for good or evil on the society you live in than you ever can have again. Quit[2] yourselves like men, then; speak up, and strike out if necessary, for whatsoever is true, and manly, and lovely, and of good report; never try to be popular, but only to do your duty and help others to do theirs, and you may leave the tone of feeling in the school higher than you found it, and so be doing good, which no living soul can measure, to generations of your countrymen yet unborn. For boys follow one another in herds like sheep, for good or evil; they hate thinking, and have rarely any settled principles. Every school, indeed, has its own traditionary standard of right and wrong, which cannot be transgressed with impunity, marking certain things as low and blackguard, and certain others as lawful and right. This standard is ever varying, though it changes only slowly, and little by little; and, subject only to such standard, it is the leading boys for the time being who give the tone to all the rest, and make the School either a noble institution for the training of Christian Englishmen, or a place where a young boy will get more evil than he would if he were turned out to make his way in London streets, or anything between these two extremes.

---

1. I.e., higher grades or classes for older boys.   2. Acquit, behave.

From *Part Two, Chapter* 5

It was drawing toward the close of Arthur's first half-year, and the May evenings were lengthening out. Locking-up[3] was not till eight o'clock, and everybody was beginning to talk about what he would do in the holidays. The shell,[4] in which form all our *dramatis personæ* now are, were reading among other things the last book of Homer's *Iliad*, and had worked through it as far as the speeches of the women over Hector's body. It is a whole school day, and four or five of the School-house boys (among whom are Arthur, Tom, and East) are preparing third lesson together. They have finished the regulation forty lines, and are for the most part getting very tired, notwithstanding the exquisite pathos of Helen's lamentation. And now several long, four-syllabled words come together, and the boy with the dictionary strikes work.

"I am not going to look out any more words," says he; "we've done the quantity. Ten to one we sha'n't get so far. Let's go out into the close."

"Come along, boys," cries East, always ready to leave the grind, as he called it; "our old coach is laid up, you know, and we shall have one of the new masters, who's sure to go slow and let us down easy."

So an adjournment to the close was carried *nem. con.*,[5] little Arthur not daring to uplift his voice; but, being deeply interested in what they were reading, stayed quietly behind and learned on for his own pleasure.

As East had said, the regular master of the form was unwell, and they were to be heard by one of the new masters, quite a young man, who had only just left the university. Certainly, it would be hard lines if, by dawdling as much as possible in coming in and taking their places, entering into long-winded explanations of what was the usual course of the regular master of the form, and others of the stock contrivances of boys for wasting time in school, they could not spin out the lesson so that he should not work them though more than the forty lines; as to which quantity there was a perpetual fight going on between the master and his form, the latter insisting, and enforcing by passive resistance, that it was the prescribed quantity of Homer for a shell lesson, the former that there was no fixed quantity, but that they must always be ready to go on to fifty or sixty lines if there were time within the hour. However, notwithstanding all their efforts, the new master got on horribly quick; he seemed to have the bad taste to be really interested in the lesson, and to be trying to work them up into something like appreciation of it, giving them good, spirited English words instead of the wretched, bald stuff into which they rendered poor old Homer; and construing over each piece himself to them, after each boy, to show them how it should be done.

Now the clock strikes the three-quarters; there is only a quarter of an hour more; but the forty lines are all but done. So the boys, one after another, who are called up, stick more and more, and make balder and ever more bald[6] work of it. The poor young master is pretty nearly beat by this

---

3. I.e., the time when boys had to be in their studies to work on their lessons.
4. The lower fourth form, or class (a meaning specific only to the public schools). The boys in this class are between thirteen and fifteen years of age.
5. Short for "nemine contradicente," without objection (Latin).
6. I.e., more and more inadequate.

time, and feels ready to knock his head against the wall, or his fingers against somebody else's head. So he gives up altogether the lower and middle parts of the form, and looks round in despair at the boys on the top bench,[7] to see if there is one out of whom he can strike a spark or two, and who will be too chivalrous to murder the most beautiful utterances of the most beautiful woman of the old world. His eye rests on Arthur, and he calls him up to finish construing Helen's speech. Whereupon all the other boys draw long breaths and begin to stare about and take it easy. They are all safe; Arthur is the head of the form, and sure to be able to construe, and that will tide on safely till the hour strikes.

Arthur proceeds to read out the passage in Greek before construing it, as the custom is. Tom, who isn't paying much attention, is suddenly caught by the falter in his voice as he reads the two lines—

Ἀλλὰ σὺ τόν γ᾽ ἐπέεσσι παραιφάμενος καγέρυκες,
Σὸς τ᾽ ἀγανοφροσύνῃ καὰ σοῖς ἀγανοῖς ἐπέεσσιν.[8]

He looks up at Arthur. "Why, bless us," thinks he, "what can be the matter with the young un? He's never going to get floored. He's sure to have learned to the end." Next moment he is reassured by the spirited tone in which Arthur begins construing, and betakes himself to drawing dogs' heads in his notebook, while the master, evidently enjoying the change, turns his back on the middle bench and stands before Arthur, beating a sort of time with his hand and foot, and saying, "Yes, yes," "very well," as Arthur goes on.

But as he nears the fatal two lines Tom catches that falter and again looks up. He sees that there is something the matter—Arthur can hardly get on at all. What can it be?

Suddenly at this point Arthur breaks down altogether and fairly bursts out crying, and dashes the cuff of his jacket across his eyes, blushing up to the roots of his hair and feeling as if he should like to go down suddenly through the floor. The whole form are taken aback; most of them stare stupidly at him, while those who are gifted with presence of mind find their places and look steadily at their books, in hopes of not catching the master's eye and getting called up in Arthur's place.

The master looks puzzled for a moment, and then seeing, as the fact is, that the boy is really affected to tears by the most touching thing in Homer, perhaps in all profane poetry put together, steps up to him and lays his hand kindly on his shoulder, saying, "Never mind, my little man, you've construed very well. Stop a minute, there's no hurry."

Now, as luck would have it, there sat next above Tom that day, in the middle bench of the form, a big boy, by name Williams, generally supposed to be the cock of the shell,[9] therefore of all the school below the fifths. The small boys, who are great speculators on the prowess of their elders, used to hold forth to one another about Williams's great strength, and to discuss whether East or Brown would take a licking from him. He was called Slogger[1] Williams, from the force with which it was supposed he could hit. In the

---

7. In this setting, a pupil's physical position in the classroom was directly related to his academic standing in that class; the best students, then, sat on the bench at the very front of the room.
8. "But you calmed them down every time and

stopped them out of the gentleness of your heart, with your gentle words" (Greek). From *Iliad* 24.771–72, trans. E. V. Rieu.
9. I.e., toughest boy in the class.
1. I.e., slugger; a hard hitter.

main, he was a rough, good-natured fellow enough, but very much alive to his own dignity. He reckoned himself the king of the form, and kept up his position with a strong hand, especially in the matter of forcing boys not to construe more than the legitimate forty lines. He had already grunted and grumbled to himself when Arthur went on reading beyond the forty lines. But now that he had broken down just in the middle of all the long words, the Slogger's wrath was fairly roused.

"Sneaking little brute," muttered he, regardless of prudence, "clapping on the waterworks just in the hardest place; see if I don't punch his head after fourth lesson."

"Whose?" said Tom, to whom the remark seemed to be addressed.

"Why, that little sneak Arthur's," replied Williams.

"No, you sha'n't," said Tom.

"Hullo!" exclaimed Williams, looking at Tom with great surprise for a moment, and then giving him a sudden dig in the ribs with his elbow, which sent Tom's books flying on the floor and called the attention of the master, who turned suddenly round and, seeing the state of things, said:

"Williams, go down three places, and then go on."

The Slogger found his legs very slowly, and proceeded to go below Tom and two other boys with great disgust, and then, turning round and facing the master, said, "I haven't learned any more, sir; our lesson is only forty lines."

"Is that so?" said the master, appealing generally to the top bench. No answer.

"Who is the head boy of the form?" said he, waxing wroth.

"Arthur, sir," answered three or four boys, indicating our friend.

"Oh, your name's Arthur. Well, now, what is the length of your regular lesson?"

Arthur hesitated a moment, and then said, "We call it only forty lines, sir."

"How do you mean, you call it?"

"Well, sir, Mr. Graham says we ain't to stop there when there's time to construe more."

"I understand," said the master. "Williams, go down three more places, and write me out the lesson in Greek and English. And now, Arthur, finish construing."

"Oh! would I be in Arthur's shoes after fourth lesson?" said the little boys to one another; but Arthur finished Helen's speech without any further catastrophe, and the clock struck four, which ended third lesson.

Another hour was occupied in preparing and saying fourth lesson, during which Williams was bottling up his wrath; and when five struck, and the lessons for the day were over, he prepared to take summary vengeance on the innocent cause of his misfortune.

Tom was detained in school a few minutes after the rest, and, on coming out into the quadrangle, the first thing he saw was a small ring of boys applauding Williams, who was holding Arthur by the collar.

"There, you young sneak," said he, giving Arthur a cuff on the head with his other hand, "what made you say that—"

"Hullo!" said Tom, shouldering into the crowd; "you drop that, Williams; you sha'n't touch him."

"Who'll stop me?" said the Slogger, raising his hand again.

"I," said Tom; and, suiting the action to the word, struck the arm which held Arthur's arm so sharply that the Slogger dropped it with a start and turned the full current of his wrath on Tom.

"Will you fight?"

"Yes, of course."

"Huzza! there's going to be a fight between Slogger Williams and Tom Brown!"

1857

THE EDUCATION DEPARTMENT OF THE COMMITTEE OF COUNCIL

Following the Newcastle Commission of 1858–61, an investigation into the provision of "sound and cheap elementary instruction," the government instituted the Revised Code for all schools in receipt of public monies in 1861–62. The code established a series of graded Standards, with a certain level of competence expected after each year's instruction; it also ushered in the "payment by results" system whereby schools were subject to monetary penalties if their pupils did not individually satisfy inspectors that they could meet the prescribed targets. The schoolwide syllabus for the three Rs ("reading, 'riting, and 'rithmetic"), the most important elements of the curriculum, is set out in the following table, which is taken from the New Code of 1879. (By this date numerous revisions had been made to the Revised Code, relaxing, for instance, its original rigidity by allowing schools to enter whole classes of older children for grant-awarding examinations in such subjects as history, geography, and grammar.) Standards corresponded roughly to age, with six-year-olds expected to reach Standard I, and eleven-year-olds Standard VI; at that time, however, children were able to leave school at age ten.

From The New Code of 1879

	Standard I.	Standard II.	Standard III.	Standard IV.	Standard V.	Standard VI.
Reading	To read a short paragraph from a book, not confined to words of one syllable.	To read with intelligence a short paragraph from an elementary reading book.	To read with intelligence a short paragraph from a more advanced reading book.	To read with intelligence a few lines of prose or poetry selected by the inspector.	Improved reading.	Reading with fluency and expression.

(continued)

(*continued*)

	Standard I.	Standard II.	Standard III.	Standard IV.	Standard V.	Standard VI.
Writing	Copy in manuscript character a line of print, on slates or in copy books, at choice of managers; and write from dictation a few common words.	A sentence from the same book, slowly read once, and then dictated. Copy books (large or half-text) to be shown.	A sentence slowly dictated once from the same book. Copy books to be shown (small hand, capital letters and figures).	Eight lines slowly dictated once from a reading book. Copy books to be shown (improved small hand).	Writing from memory the substance of a short story read out twice; spelling, grammar, and handwriting to be considered.	A short theme or letter, the composition, spelling, grammar, and handwriting to be considered.
Arithmetic[1]	Notation and numeration up to 1,000. Simple addition and subtraction of numbers of not more than four figures, and the multiplication table, to 6 times 12.	Notation and numeration up to 100,000. The four simple rules to short division (inclusive).	Notation and numeration up to 1,000,000. Long division and compound addition and subtraction (money).	Compound rules (money) and reduction (common weights and measures).	Practice, bills of parcels, and simple proportion.	Proportion, vulgar and decimal fractions.

1. The work of girls will be judged more leniently than that of boys; and the Inspector may examine scholars in the work of any Standard lower than that in which they are presented [Education Department's note].

FLORA THOMPSON

The following selection is from *Lark Rise*, the first of three autobiographical novels by Thompson (1876–1947), which were subsequently published in one volume as *Lark Rise to Candleford* (1945). Thompson, the child of a stonemason and a nursemaid, grew up in a rural district of Oxfordshire, where she attended the local Church of England elementary school in Cottisford; she then worked in various post offices in southern England before marrying in 1903 and beginning her literary career. Thompson's detailed and precise portrayal of the isolated communities in which she spent her childhood and adolescence has made *Lark Rise to Candleford* one of Britain's best-loved memoirs of country life. Here "Fordlow school" stands in for Cottisford National School; "Laura," for Flora herself; and "Edmund," for Flora's favorite brother, Edwin, who was later killed in World War I.

From Lark Rise

From *Chapter 11. School*

The schoolmistress in charge of the Fordlow school at the beginning of the 'eighties had held that position for fifteen years and seemed to her pupils as much a fixture as the school building; but for most of that time she had been engaged to the squire's head gardener and her long reign was drawing to a close.[1]

She was, at that time, about forty, and was a small, neat little body with a pale, slightly pock-marked face, snaky black curls hanging down to her shoulders, and eyebrows arched into a perpetual inquiry. She wore in school stiffly starched, holland[2] aprons with bibs, one embroidered with red one week, and one with blue the next, and was seldom seen without a posy of flowers pinned on her breast and another tucked into her hair.

Every morning, when school had assembled, and Governess, with her starched apron and bobbing curls appeared in the doorway, there was a great rustling and scraping of curtseying and pulling of forelocks.[3] 'Good morning, children,' 'Good morning, ma'am,' were the formal, old-fashioned greetings. Then, under her determined fingers the harmonium wheezed out 'Once in Royal', or 'We are but little children weak', prayers followed, and the day's work began.

Reading, writing, and arithmetic were the principle subjects, with a Scripture lesson every morning, and needlework every afternoon for the girls. There was no assistant mistress; Governess taught all the classes simultaneously, assisted only by two monitors—ex-scholars, aged about twelve, who were paid a shilling a week each for their services.

Every morning at ten o'clock the Rector arrived to take the older children for Scripture. He was a parson of the old school; a commanding figure, tall and stout, with white hair, ruddy cheeks and an aristocratically beaked nose, and he was as far as possible removed by birth, education, and worldly circumstances from the lambs of his flock. He spoke to them from a great height, physical, mental, and spiritual. 'To order myself lowly and reverently before my betters' was the clause he underlined in the Church Catechism, for had he not been divinely appointed pastor and master to those little rustics and was it not one of his chief duties to teach them to realize this? As a man, he was kindly disposed—a giver of blankets and coals at Christmas, and of soup and milk puddings to the sick.

His lesson consisted of Bible reading, turn and turn about round the class, of reciting from memory the names of the kings of Israel and repeating the Church Catechism. After that, he would deliver a little lecture on morals and behaviour. The children must not lie or steal or be discontented or envious. God had placed them just where they were in the social order and given them their own especial work to do; to envy others or to try to change their own lot in life was a sin of which he hoped they would never be guilty. From his lips the children heard nothing of that God who is Truth and Beauty and Love; but they learned for him and repeated to him long passages from the Authorized Version, thus laying up treasure for themselves;[4] so the lessons, in spite of much aridity, were valuable.

Scripture over and the Rector bowed and curtsied out of the door, ordinary lessons began. Arithmetic was considered the most important of the subjects taught, and those who were good at figures ranked high in their

1. Women teachers for National Schools at the time did not have to resign after marriage, but some chose to do so.
2. A kind of smooth, hard-wearing linen.
3. Tugging a lock of hair at the front of one's

head was a traditional gesture of deference to a superior.
4. Cf. Matthew 6.19. "Authorized Version": the 1611 translation of the Bible used by the Church of England, also known as the King James Bible.

classes. It was very simple arithmetic, extending only to the first four rules, with the money sums, known as 'bills of parcels', for the most advanced pupils.

The writing lesson consisted of the copying of copperplate maxims: 'A fool and his money are soon parted'; 'Waste not, want not'; 'Count ten before you speak', and so on. Once a week composition would be set, usually in the form of writing a letter describing some recent event. This was regarded chiefly as a spelling test.

History was not taught formally; but history readers were in use containing such picturesque stories as those of King Alfred and the cakes, King Canute commanding the waves, the loss of the White Ship, and Raleigh spreading his cloak for Queen Elizabeth.[5]

There were no geography readers, and, excepting what could be gleaned from the descriptions of different parts of the world in the ordinary readers, no geography was taught. But, for some reason or other, on the walls of the schoolroom were hung splendid maps: The World, Europe, North America, South America, England, Ireland, and Scotland. During long waits in class for her turn to read, or to have her copy or sewing examined, Laura would gaze on these maps until the shapes of the countries with their islands and inlets became photographed on her brain. Baffin Bay and the land around the poles were especially fascinating to her.

Once a day, at whatever hour the poor, overworked mistress could find time, a class would be called out to toe the chalked semicircle on the floor for a reading lesson. This lesson, which should have been pleasant, for the reading matter was good, was tedious in the extreme. Many of the children read so slowly and haltingly that Laura, who was impatient by nature, longed to take hold of their words and drag them out of their mouths, and it often seemed to her that her own turn to read would never come. As often as she could do so without being detected, she would turn over and peep between the pages of her own *Royal Reader*,[6] and, studiously holding the book to her nose, pretend to be following the lesson while she was pages ahead.

There was plenty there to enthral any child: 'The Skater Chased by Wolves'; 'The Siege of Torquilstone', from *Ivanhoe*;[7] Fenimore Cooper's *Prairie on Fire*; and Washington Irving's *Capture of Wild Horses*.

Then there were fascinating descriptions of such far-apart places as Greenland and the Amazon; of the Pacific Ocean with its fairy islands and coral reefs; the snows of Hudson Bay Territory and the sterile heights of the Andes. Best of all she loved the description of the Himalayas, which began: 'Northward of the great plain of India, and along its whole extent, towers

5. Four of the most popular stories of British history, frequently recounted in books for children. The legend of Alfred (king of Wessex from 871 to 899) letting a peasant woman's cakes burn because he was preoccupied with the problems of his kingdom originated in 12th-century chronicles. The story of Canute (Cnut, the Viking ruler who was king of England from 1016 to 1035) demonstrating the limit of earthly power through his inability to stop the tide coming in also originated in the 12th century. Henry I (king of England from 1100 to 1135) lost his son and heir, William, in a shipwreck in 1120. The story of the courtly act that Sir Walter Raleigh (1552–1618) performed for Elizabeth I (queen of England from 1558 to 1603) is most likely apocryphal.

6. One of a popular graded series of reading books, first published by Thomas Nelson and Sons just after the 1870 Elementary Education Act.

7. A novel (1819) by Sir Walter Scott (1771–1832). "The Skater Chased by Wolves" is an account by a Mr. Whitehead of his escape from wolves.

the sublime mountain region of the Himalayas, ascending gradually until it terminates in a long range of summits wrapped in perpetual snow.'

Interspersed between the prose readings were poems: 'The Slave's Dream'; 'Young Lochinvar'; 'The Parting of Douglas and Marmion', Tennyson's 'Brook' and 'Ring out, Wild Bells'; Byron's 'Shipwreck'; Hogg's 'Skylark', and many more. 'Lochiel's Warning'[8] was a favourite with Edmund, who often, in bed at night, might be heard declaiming: 'Lochiel! Lochiel! beware of the day! while Laura, at any time, with or without encouragement, was ready to 'look back into other years' with Henry Glassford Bell, and recite his scenes from the life of Mary Queen of Scots, reserving her most impressive tone for the concluding couplet:

> Lapped by a dog. Go think of it in silence and alone,
> Then weigh against a grain of sand the glories of a throne.[9]

But long before their schooldays were over they knew every piece in the books by heart and it was one of their greatest pleasures in life to recite them to each other. By that time Edmund had appropriated Scott and could repeat hundreds of lines, always showing a preference for scenes of single combat between warrior chiefs. The selection in the *Royal Readers*, then, was an education in itself for those who took to it kindly; but the majority of the children would have none of it; saying that the prose was 'dry old stuff' and that they hated 'portry'.

Those children who read fluently, and there were several of them in every class, read in a monotonous sing-song, without expression, and apparently without interest. Yet there were very few really stupid children in the school, as is proved by the success of many of them in after life, and though few were interested in their lessons, they nearly all showed an intelligent interest in other things—the boys in field work and crops and cattle and agricultural machinery; the girls in dress, other people's love affairs and domestic details.

It is easy to imagine the education authorities of that day, when drawing up the scheme for that simple but sound education, saying, 'Once teach them to read and they will hold the key to all knowledge.' But the scheme did not work out. If the children, by the time they left school, could read well enough to read the newspaper and perhaps an occasional book for amusement, and write well enough to write their own letters, they had no wish to go farther. Their interest was not in books, but in life, and especially the life that lay immediately about them. At school they worked unwillingly, upon compulsion, and the life of the schoolmistress was a hard one.

As Miss Holmes went from class to class, she carried the cane and laid it upon the desk before her; not necessarily for use, but as a reminder, for some of the bigger boys were very unruly. She punished by a smart stroke on each hand. 'Put out your hand,' she would say, and some boys would openly spit on each hand before proffering it. Others murmured and muttered before and after a caning and threatened to 'tell me feyther';[1] but she remained calm and cool, and after the punishment had been inflicted there was a marked improvement—for a time.

---

8. By Thomas Campbell (1777–1844). "The Slave's Dream" is by Henry Wadsworth Longfellow (1807–1882). "Young Lochinvar" and "The Parting of Douglas and Marmion" are by Scott.

9. Like many of the other poems mentioned here, "Mary Queen of Scots" by Bell (1803–1874) appeared in book 5 of the Royal Reader series.
1. Father (dialect).

It must be remembered that in those days a boy of eleven was nearing the end of his school life. Soon he would be at work; already he felt himself nearly a man and too old for petticoat government.[2] Moreover, those were country boys, wild and rough, and many of them as tall as she was. Those who had failed to pass Standard IV and so could not leave school until they were eleven, looked upon that last year as a punishment inflicted upon them by the school authorities and behaved accordingly.[3] In this they were encouraged by their parents, for a certain section of these resented their boys being kept at school when they might be earning. 'What do our young Alf want wi' a lot o' book-larnin?' they would say. 'He can read and write and add up as much money as he's ever likely to get. What more do he want?' Then a neighbour of more advanced views would tell them: 'A good education's everything in these days. You can't get on in the world if you ain't had one,' for they read their newspapers and new ideas were percolating, though slowly. It was only the second generation to be forcibly fed with the fruit of the tree of knowledge: what wonder if it did not always agree with it.

Meanwhile, Miss Holmes carried her cane about with her. A poor method of enforcing discipline, according to modern educational ideas; but it served. It may be that she and her like all over the country at that time were breaking up the ground that other, later comers to the field, with a knowledge of child psychology and with tradition and experiment behind them, might sow the good seed.

She seldom used the cane on the girls and still more seldom on the infants. Standing in a corner with their hands on their heads was their punishment. She gave little treats and encouragements, too, and, although the children called her 'Susie' behind her back, they really liked and respected her. Many times there came a knock at the door and a smartly dressed girl on holidays, or a tall young soldier on leave, in his scarlet tunic and pillbox cap, looked in 'to see Governess'.

1939

2. I.e., too old to be ruled by a woman.
3. Attendance at age ten had been made compulsory in England and Wales in 1880 and was raised to eleven in 1893. In the interim period, pupils aged ten were able to leave school if they passed the Standard specified for their particular district.

FREDERICK DENISON MAURICE

Frederick Denison Maurice (1805–1872) was a prominent clergyman, theologian, professor, and writer. In 1848 he founded Queen's College in London, the first girls' school granted a royal charter and, at about the same time, helped start the Christian socialist movement. His theological views were often controversial with more conservative Christians. In 1853 he was dismissed from his professorships at King's College, London, for arguing that there was no basis in scripture for the belief that sinners would suffer for eternity in hell. He then founded the

Working Men's College, designed to provide lectures and classes for working-class men; it opened its doors in 1854 to 140 students; it still exists today to provide "a liberal education for workers." In the set of lectures, *Learning and Working*, from which two selections are reprinted here, Maurice sets out his ideas about adult education.

From Learning and Working

From *Lecture V. The Studies in a Working College*

What, therefore, I gather from the willingness they have shown to receive musical instruction,[1] is (1) That all other instruction should speak to them as this does, less as distinguished by particular occupations, than as sharers of a common humanity, and as capable of entering into the feeling of it, in spite of their different pursuits, or by means of them. (2) That it being regarded as the great end of studies to raise and cultivate that which is human, the arbitrary division of them into useful and entertaining should be discarded as illogical and embarrassing. (3) That they should have a considerable number of studies presented to them, out of which they may choose the one or two which have most attractions for them. (4) That though they never should be invited to devote more time to any studies than is compatible with their ordinary occupations, they should be led to perceive that there is a relation between all studies; that the boundary lines between them are often artificial and imaginary; that when they are most real, and when it is most needful to distinguish between their objects and their spheres, they again blend together when they are contemplated in reference to our lives and duties.

I could not even venture to speak of a course of studies for a College of Working Men, without making these preliminary remarks. For you will be ready to exclaim—'Course of studies! what a wild dream is this! Here are ignorant, untrained men, with an hour or two which they can with great difficulty snatch out of a day of extreme toil, and you fancy that you can give them a regular systematic indoctrination in a dozen or fifteen subjects, to understand any one of which would require all the wits of ordinary people of our class, who have had a preparatory discipline of many years.' I am guilty of no such monstrous extravagances. I am going to speak of various branches of knowledge, between which I feel there is a close inward connexion. I wish the working man to understand that there is this connexion. But I would have him understand it, not by plunging into all these studies together, or even into one after another, but by learning under a teacher who feels the connexion himself; who is in friendly and continual intercourse with other teachers, each trying to initiate his pupils into the subject with which he is most familiar. I allow for the short time, the very short time, which the working man is able to give to any subject. I do not anticipate the day, which, nevertheless, I trust our children will see, if we

---

1. Maurice is referring to a successful program, described in the previous lecture, that John Pyke Hullah (1812–1884) developed to teach music in Mechanics' Institutes.

do not, when Mr. Wilson's principle[2] will be carried out to its full extent, when the Factory shall become the College, when Working and Learning shall be regarded as inseparable. I take things as I find them. The hard won evening hours are all I ask for. I do not wish the married man—I do not expect the bachelor—to give up half or a third of these to the college. What I think he may do, if there is a subject which has already some hold upon him, of which he wishes for any reason to take hold of, is to come for an hour or hour and a half, when that subject is taught, week after week. He can, if he likes and if he lives, spread his lessons over a much wider tract of years than the ordinary student in a University; since he is not preparing for work, but in the midst of work. The Degree need not terminate his career, as it does that of the other; he may, therefore, make some amends for a little time at first, by the greater time afterwards. But he may make much better amends than this, if he is really awake and interested in that which he is about. He may speak of it at home with his wife and children; he may think of it, and even, as the mathematical students I alluded to are in the habit of doing, read about it, when his work is merely mechanical.[3] And then when he feels that his mind is freer and more orderly for this part of learning, and if he has seen something on the right or left of it which is needed to bring out the full sense of it, he may betake himself to that, or he may work with dogged pertinacity in his own original mine, till he has brought out some of its deeper and more hidden treasures.

From *Lecture VI. The Teachers in a Working College*

The words University and College point to a corporate life, not to a hard indoctrination. I doubt whether any teaching of our manual workers is possible, unless we can convert these words into realities.

It is a conviction of this kind which has led a few friends of mine to propose a College for Working Men in the northern part of London. They answer with tolerable exactness to the description I have given of the persons from whom it is reasonable to demand such an effort. They are all at work themselves, in occupations which they believe to be vocations, and which they do not hold it would be right to forsake under any plea of benevolence to their fellow-creatures. They do not, therefore, aim at forming a guild or order of Teachers. They are already admitted into their different guilds as members of the Inns of Court, or the Colleges of Surgeons or Physicians, as Artists, as Ministers of the Gospel, as Tradesmen, as Operatives.[4] What they believe is best for themselves—best for the special fraternity to which they belong, in respect of the work which it is pledged to do, as well as of the science which it is pledged to advance—is that they should keep up an intercourse with men of different callings, and should do what in them lies, that those who are engaged merely in manual labour should

---

2. In a previous lecture Maurice had described an experiment in which candle manufacturer James P. Wilson provided education and recreation for the children who worked in his factory.
3. In an earlier lecture Maurice had spoken about factory workers who study mathematics amid the noise of the mills.
4. Skilled workers. "Inns of Court": professional associations of lawyers.

feel that also to be a high calling. They may differ among themselves about some of the ways in which this end should be accomplished; they are perfectly agreed that one of the ways, and the most effectual, is to strive, that the manual worker may have a share in all the best treasures with which God has been pleased to endow them. They do not think they have any business to consider how few of these treasures they may possess in comparison with many of their contemporaries; by all means, let those who have more give more; all they have to do is to ask how they make what they have most useful, and how they may increase it by communicating it. Their design is far from ambitious. It is not to found a College for the workers of England, or of London. It is simply to make an experiment, necessarily on a very small scale, in the neighbourhood which is nearest to the places in which most of them are busy during the day. If Working and Learning are to be combined, learning must come to the door of the workshop and factory, till the better day when it shall be allowed to enter into them. The north of London is not a region for great manufactories; but it is a region where there are handicraftsmen of all sorts and descriptions; it affords a fair enough opportunity for a trial though I am far from saying that in Birmingham or Manchester, or other parts of the Metropolis, it may not be made with greater advantages.

* * *

We propose to commence our undertaking next November. I do not mean that we shall form our College then—that is formed already. The Teachers are the members of a Society, into which any persons above sixteen years of age, who can read and write, and know the first four rules of arithmetic, are eligible to enter. We divide our College year into Terms; we even call our adoption of pupils into the College, Matriculation. These phrases indicate what we are aiming at. We wish to do what our fathers did when they provided Colleges for England,[5] as it was in those days. I say for *England;* I will not make the antithesis sharper by saying *for the upper and middle classes.* For that was not their intention at all. They educated Englishmen, to whatever class they might belong. They matriculated them into societies regularly organized, that they might know they were connected with that which is permanent, not merely with that which is artificial and transitory; with what is human and divine, not merely with producing and exchanging. This testimony is more necessary for London in the nineteenth century, than for Oxford and Cambridge in the fourteenth. If we can help to bear it, and so to associate together different periods in our country's history, as well as different portions of our population, we may endure a heavier penalty than that of being called pedantical.

The method of our teaching must, of course, be affected by the character of the different subjects; still the general principle of it has been agreed upon; I may say, it has in a measure been acted on. I alluded in my last Lecture to an experiment in Theological instruction which had satisfied me that the consideration of the most difficult questions was favourable to

---

5. Oxford and Cambridge.

earnestness and reverence. With that experiment our College may be said to have originated. A Scripture class has been held on Sunday evenings. A book of the Bible is read through. The Teacher endeavours to unfold the sense of it passage by passage. It becomes the subject of conversation. The pupils, state their perplexities with freedom. He points out what seems to him the solution of them. It would be ridiculous to say that this plan excludes Dogmatism. The Teacher, of course, expresses his own convictions. He does not dream of suppressing them because they may not be those of his auditors. But as he believes that his pupils cannot receive his meaning, however they might receive his words and repeat them, if they are merely dead listeners, he rejoices much when they prove to him practically, even by putting him to a severe probation, that they are not so. Though the same course cannot be followed in all cases, we have at least determined that we will be Tutors rather than Professors, that we will give Lessons not Lectures, and that one half of the lessons shall be catechetical,[6] and shall refer to the subject that had been treated of when the class last met. As we may not always be able to set our pupils tasks and exercises in the interval between the Lectures, this plan may in some degree supply the place of them, and may assist their memories.

I need not give you a list of the subjects we mean to introduce into our Course. I sketched a general outline of them in the last Lecture; a special programme will be published at the beginning of each term. Politics and Public Health will be the innovations.[7] History and Geography will be made to illustrate each other. Shakspeare's plays will be preferred to Hume[8] when we are illustrating the records of our own country; Drawing will be treated with the honour which belongs to it as a most living and practical discipline for the eye and the hand, the head and the heart. If we should not find that Vocal Music is already taught in our immediate neighbourhood, as well and cheaply as it can be taught, we shall claim for it a conspicuous place in our Course. We shall try to give the study of Words as much pre-eminence and dignity in this College as it has had in any, though we shall teach English words and English Grammar before we venture upon any modern or classical language. The teachers in the different branches of pure Mathematics, and of Natural Philosophy, will be in continual communication with each other. To secure a gradation of studies such as they could wish, will of course be difficult. Still we have proofs enough of the ardour of working people in these pursuits, to believe that it will not be impossible. Our teachers will endeavour as far as they can to avoid technicalities and long words. But they will avoid just as earnestly a superficial and frivolous way of treating the great facts and laws of the universe, as if they were condescending to the capacities of men immeasurably below them, instead of laboring, with the consciousness of their own ignorance, to raise men a little more ignorant into some apprehension of the meaning of the world in which God has placed them, and of the relation in which they themselves stand to it.

---

6. Taught through the technique of questions and answers.

7. Many felt that politics should not be taught in classes designed for working men because the subject might provoke social unrest.

8. David Hume (1711–1776), Scottish philosopher.

As our great object is in all ways to show our respect for the working people, not to insult them, we have no notion of offering them this education gratuitously. They are to pay for it. The fees will be arranged according to the scale which is adopted in the principal Mechanics' Institutes of London. They will not cover the expenses of the College. We want a Library; and though the original teachers will receive nothing, they fully hope to raise up teachers among the working men themselves, who ought to be properly remunerated. This is one of the chief objects which they set before themselves, though they never desire to see the time arrive when the instructors shall be exclusively, or even chiefly, from this class. They hope and trust that professional men of all kinds, that men of letters, that students fresh from the Universities, that statesmen and divines, will always be found to take part in this education, will always feel that by doing so they are fulfilling their proper tasks, and educating themselves.

1855

FRANCES POWER COBBE

Frances Power Cobbe (1822–1904) was a writer, reformer, and activist. She was born in Dublin on her family's estate; her father's death in 1857 freed her to leave home and pursue her own interests and ambitions. Cobbe traveled to Italy, worked with reformer Mary Carpenter on the education of poor children, and was deeply involved in feminist causes, including university education for women, their entry into the professions, women's suffrage, and women's legal protection in marriage. She wrote on theological issues and was one of the leaders of the antivivisection movement, founding two organizations to campaign against animal experimentation. The occasion of the paper reprinted here, which was presented to the Social Science Association in London in 1862, was the debate about admitting women as candidates for degrees at the University of London, a change not achieved until 1878.

The Education of Women, and How It Would Be Affected by University Examinations

The subject of the Education of Women of the higher classes is one which has undergone singular fluctuations in public opinion. There have been times when England and Italy boasted of the literary attainments of a Lady Jane Grey and a Vittoria Colonna,[1] and there have been times when the

---

1. Italian noblewoman and poet (1490–1547). Lady Jane Grey (1537–1554), eldest granddaughter of Mary Tudor, very briefly queen of England and reputedly one of the most learned women of her day.

Chinese proverb seemed in force, and it was assumed that "the glory of a man is knowledge, but the glory of a woman is to renounce knowledge." For the last half-century, however, the tide seems to have set pretty steadily in the direction of feminine erudition. Our grandmothers understood spelling and writing, Blair's Sermons and long whist.[2] Our mothers to these attainments added French and the pianoforte, and those items (always unimportant in a woman's education), history and geography. In our own youth we acquired, in a certain shadowy way peculiar to the boarding-schools of that remote period, three or four languages and three or four instruments, the use of the globes and of the dumb-bells, moral philosophy and Poonah-painting.[3] How profound and accurate was this marvelous education (usually completed at the mature age of sixteen) it is needless to remark. A new generation has appeared, and he who will peruse the splendid curriculum of one of the Ladies' Colleges, of Bedford Square, or Harley Street,[4] for instance, will perceive that becoming an accomplished young lady is a much more serious affair now than it was in "the merry times when we were young."

The question has now arisen, This wider and deeper education, how far is it to go? Have we reached its reasonable limit, or shall we see it carried much farther? If it be found desirable to push it into higher branches of study and greater perfection of acquirements, how will this best be accomplished? In particular, the grave query has lately been mooted,[5] "Will those University examinations and academical honours, which have long been reckoned all-powerful in advancing the education of men, be found equally efficacious in aiding that of women? Ought they to be opened to female competition, and a Free Trade in knowledge established between the sexes? Or, on the contrary, does there appear just cause why this door, at all events, should for ever be closed to the possible progress of women?

Before offering a few suggestions on this subject, I crave permission to make some general observations on the present condition of young women of the higher classes, and their special wants at this moment. A knowledge of these wants has alone induced me to obey the request to give such little aid as may be in my power to their efforts after a better state of things. Few indeed can be unaware that they are passing through a transition period of no small difficulty, and that there is urgent need for revision of many of the old social regulations regarding them. No class has felt more than they the rise in the atmosphere of modern thoughts; and where their mothers lived healthily enough in closed chambers, they are stifling. New windows must be opened to the light, new air of heaven admitted, and then we shall see bloom in women's cheeks, and light in their eyes, such as they have never worn before.

The miseries of the poor are doubtless greatest of all, but there are other miseries beside theirs which it behoves us also to consider. The wretchedness of an empty brain is perhaps as hard to bear as that of an empty purse, and a heart without hope as cheerless as a fireless grate.[6] As society is now

---

2. A card game. "Blair's Sermons": a popular collection of sermons by Sir Hugh Blair, a Scottish clergyman (1727–1800).
3. A style of flower and bird painting popular in the 19th century.
4. Queen's College in Harley Street and the

Ladies College in Bedford Square were both established in the late 1840s to provide instruction to women (but not degrees).
5. Put forward.
6. A grated fireplace.

constituted, no inconsiderable portion of women's lives are aimless and profitless. There are Eugénie Grandets by hundreds in all our towns, and Marianas in Moated Granges in the country, whose existence is no better than that of "the weed on Lethe's banks,"[7] and yet who were given by Providence powers whereby they might have become sources of happiness to all around them. For (let us hope it will some time or other be recognized) there *are* purposes in the order of Providence for the lives of single women and childless wives, and they too are meant to have their share of human happiness. Most people prefer to ignore their existence as a class to be contemplated in the education of women, but it is as vain to do so as it is cruel. All of us know enough of those hapless households where the wife, having no children and few home duties, undergoes the most deplorable depreciation of character for want of employment of heart and mind; and her nature, if originally weak and small, shrivels up in petty vanities and contentions; and if strong and high, falls too often blasted by the thunderstorms of passion accumulated in the moveless and unwholesome atmosphere. All of us know those other households, none less hapless, where grown-up daughters, unneeded by their parents, are kept from all usefulness or freedom of action, frittering away the prime of their days in the busy idleness of trivial accomplishments; till, when all energy to begin a new course is gone, the parents die at last, and each one sinks into the typical "Old Maid," dividing her life henceforth in her small lodgings, between "*la médisance, le jeu, et la devotion.*"[8]

All this is pitiful enough. We may laugh at it; but it is not the less a miserable destiny, and one, moreover, which it is often almost impossible for a young woman to shake off. If she be a Roman Catholic, she may leave her home and go into a nunnery in all honour and credit; but the exchange is perhaps no great gain. If she be a Protestant, friends, parents, neighbours, and all her little world cry out lustily if she think of leaving her father's roof for any end, however good or noble, save only that one sacred vocation of matrimony, for which she may lawfully leave a blind father and dying mother, and go to India with Ensign Anybody. These curiosities of public opinion need surely to be set right. Let me plead with those men and women whose lives are rich and full, whose every hour has its duty or its pleasure, who can say,

> "How beautiful it is to be alive!
> To wake each morn as if the Maker's grace
> Did us afresh from nothingness derive,"[9]

to think of these poor, narrow, withered existences, and not say, "How can we keep women just what we would like—images set up in a niche?" but, "What can we do to give to a vast number of our fellow-creatures all the joys of a useful and honourable life?" Again, there are numbers of young women who are free, so far as the wishes of their parents go, to devote

---

7. Perhaps a reference to *Hamlet* 1.5.32–33: "And duller shouldst thou be than the fat weed / That roots itself in ease on Lethe wharf." Eugénie Grandet was the heroine of the novel of the same name by Honoré de Balzac (1799–1850); she lived a lonely, barren life. Mariana was the central figure in Tennyson's "Mariana"; she was abandoned in a moated grange.
8. Gossip, diversion, and religious observance (French).
9. Henry Septimus Sutton (1825–1901), *Rose's Diary*, 21.1–3.

themselves to practical usefulness. But the employment of women of the upper classes is one of the most difficult of achievements. At nearly every door they knock in vain; and, what is worse, they are sometimes told they are unfit for work (even for philanthropic work), *because* they are not soundly educated, or possessed of steady business habits. Yet when they seek to obtain such education, here again they meet the bolted door!

It is needless to go on farther. Enough has been said, I trust, to show that young women (both those possessed of the means of independent mainte- nance, and those desiring to support themselves by intelligent labour) are sadly in need of some further improvements in their condition. Among the ways in which it may be possible to effect such improvements, a high educa- tion manifestly stands foremost—a great good in itself, and needful for nearly all further steps of advance. On this subject also I must say a few words, and notably, to refute some popular misconceptions regarding it.

The idea that there is a natural incompatibility between classical studies and feminine duties, and that a highly-educated lady is necessarily a bad wife and mother, is indeed an idea venerable from its antiquity and wide dif- fusion. "I would rather make women good wives than teach them Latin," is a favourite species of apothegm,[1] whose parallel, however (for all the sense it possesses), might be found in saying, "I would rather make women good wives than make them eat their breakfasts!" Storing the mind with declen- sions, or the mouth with tea and toast, are neither of them, in the nature of things, antithetic to becoming a careful housewife and an affectionate com- panion. As Sydney Smith[2] remarked, "A woman's love for her offspring hardly depends on her ignorance of Greek, nor need we apprehend that she will forsake an infant for a quadratic equation." *A priori*, the thing is not probable, and actually we see that a very different doctrine holds good. Few of us, I think, would fail to cite in their own circles the best cultivated women as precisely those whose homes are the happiest, who exercise therein that spirit of order and love of beauty, and, above all, that sense of the sacredness of even the smallest duties, which comes of true culture of mind. These pri- vate examples of moral excellence in studious women we cannot often quote on such occasions as the present. I may be permitted, however, to name two of them who have become household words among us all, and both of whom it has been my rare fortune to know very intimately. They are examples respectively of the two great lines in which a woman's virtue may be best displayed: the home duties of the wife and mother, and the out-of-door duties of the philanthropist.

The woman whose home was the happiest I ever saw, whose aged hus- band (as I have many times heard him) "rose up and called her blessed"[3] above all, and whose children are among the most devoted, was the same woman who in her youth outstripped nearly all the men of her time in the paths of science, and who in her beloved and honoured age is still studying reverently the wonders of God's Creation,—that woman is Mary Somerville.[4]

---

1. Maxim.
2. English writer and clergyman (1771–1845).
3. Proverbs 21.38.

4. Scottish scientist and mathematician (1780–1872).

And the woman whose philanthropy has been the most perfect, who has done more than any beside to save the criminal and vagrant children of our land, and whose whole time and heart are given to their instruction, that woman is the same who taught Homer and Virgil as assistant in her father's school at eighteen,—that woman is Mary Carpenter.[5]

We now proceed a step farther in our argument. After the examples cited, it may perhaps be assumed as proved that a high education does not in itself unfit women from performing either domestic or philanthropic duties; but that, on the contrary, it is a thing to be desired on every account. Our next position obviously is this: If a high education is to be desired for women, ought it not to be sought for them in those same University studies and honours which have so long proved efficacious in the case of men? Here another objection straightway rises up against us: "A *high* education (it is said) may be desirable for women, but not a *University* education; for that would be to assimilate the training of the two sexes, and any step in such a direction must be fatal, as tending to obliterate the natural differences between them."

A most weighty objection indeed would this be, were it founded on fact.

No *man* can possibly less desire any obliteration of the mental characteristics of the two sexes, than does every woman who has an intelligent care for the welfare of her own. But is such erasure indeed *possible*? Is it not clear enough that the Creator has endowed men and women with different constitutions of mind as of body? and need we be under the slightest apprehension that any kind of education whatever will efface those differences? Education is, after all, only what its etymology implies—the educing, the drawing out, of the powers of the individual. If we, then, draw out a *woman's* powers to the very uttermost, we shall only educe her *womanliness*. We cannot give her a man's powers any more than we can give a man a woman's brilliancy of intuition, or any other gift. We can only educe her God-given *woman's* nature, and so make her a more perfect woman. These differences will, I affirm, come out in every line of woman's expanding powers—in study, quite as much as in all beside. If a woman apply herself to Art, it will be a fresh type of beauty she will reveal. If she devote herself to philanthropic labours, she will not work like a man, from *without*—by outward legislation, but as a woman, from *within*—by the influence of one heart on another. Not by force of will, not by despotic volition does a woman ever do any good. She has abandoned somewhat of her womanhood when she exerts such powers. Even in teaching a class of little children, she rules not by authority, but by winning each little heart to voluntary submission. And in every other work it is the same. Her true victory must ever be an inward one,—a greater and more perfect victory, therefore, than was ever gained by conqueror's sword. And in matters of study it will be the same. Woman learns differently from man; and when she is able to teach, she teaches differently and with different lessons. If ever the day arrives when women shall be able to deal worthily with the subjects of our highest interests, we shall all be the better, I believe, for completing man's ideal of religion and morals

5. English social and educational reformer (1807–1877).

by that of woman, and learning to add to his Law of Justice her Law of Love, and to his faith in God's fatherly care, her faith in His motherly tenderness,— that blessed lesson forgotten too long: that "as a woman hath compassion on the son of her womb, even so the Lord hath pity on us all"![6]

* * *

If these views be true, it follows that the highest education we can give will never efface, in the slightest degree, the natural characteristics of a woman's mind. Another argument, however, is here urged against us. It is said, "Let it be granted that you will not make women *masculine* by teaching them Greek and Euclid; yet, it may still appear that Greek and Euclid are very inappropriate studies for women—useless in themselves, if not detrimental in the way supposed. A woman's mind has natural *affinities* to the lighter studies, and *repulsions* to the heavier ones. Let us have an entirely different course of studies, suited to the feminine soul, and then, perhaps, the form of a University education may be beneficial."

* * *

Now to bring woman's education out of the stage of imperfection in which it stops, it seems evident that some test and standard of perfection is needful. And this test to be sought and applied must be made a goal to which women will strive as ensuring some sort of prize. Scholarships and similar rewards are already used with much benefit at Bedford and other Ladies' Colleges. But the prize which naturally belongs to perfection of attainment is simply its *recognition*,—such public and secure recognition of it as shall make it available for all subsequent purposes. Herein will women find (as men have long found) the sufficient stimulus to strain up to that point, without which, in fact, education must ever be most incomplete. What the education of Oxford and Cambridge would be were there no such things as "Little-go" and "Great-go,"[7] no examinations or strivings for degrees, women's education has hitherto been—nay, it has been worse, for it has been stopped at an age earlier than the collegiate education of men begins, and all the best years of study have been lost to her. We would now alter these things. We would obtain for women the right to such academical honours as would afford a sufficient motive and stimulus for thorough, accurate, and sustained study by young women past mere girlhood, and able to acquire the higher branches of knowledge. This *general* and great benefit would be the first object—the raising for *all* women the standard of education. But, beside this general utility, we believe that great special use would accrue to certain classes of women (and through them to the community) from thus opening to them the benefit of University education.

First, as regards those intending to be governesses. Here will be first provided an exceedingly high standard, held out with due encouragements for those who seek the chief places in the profession. An entirely new class of instructresses will, we believe, be thence created. Secondly, mothers, whether themselves well taught or ignorant, will know on what they depend

---

6. Cf. Isaiah 49.15: "Can a woman forget her sucking child, that she should not have compassion on the son of her womb? yea, they may forget, yet will I not forget thee."
7. Examination held in the second year and final examination before the degree.

when they engage such governesses; and not, as now, find themselves constantly deceived by shallow pretence, and references to ill-judging employers. Thirdly, and above all, a few dozen *accurately* trained governesses would, I am convinced, do much to revolutionize the present state of female education in the country, by giving to their pupils the same habits of solid and accurate study they have themselves acquired. The slovenly lessons, the half-corrected exercises, will then, we hope, be at an end; and the young lady's schoolroom become a mental gymnasium, where health and soundness of mind will be gained for life, instead of what it now is too often—a place where ineradicable habits are acquired of mental scrambling and shuffling, of shallowness and false show. And again, these certificates will be of importance as preliminary steps to the introduction of women into the medical profession. On this great subject I have no space worthily to speak, and can therefore only refer to it as one of the improvements most to be desired. Such little experience as I have myself had of such matters has lain among a class the most piteous assuredly in the community—the sufferers from incurable disease. I can only record my conviction that a large number of women among them would have been saved from agonizing deaths had they been able in the first stages of their disorder to obtain the advice of female doctors. There are other employments beside those of governesses and physicians—clerkships, secretaryships, and the like, to which the admission of women will be universally facilitated by the proposed degrees. These matters are, however, sufficiently obvious to require no discussion.

I hope I have now in some measure demonstrated—first, that some improvement is needed in the condition of young women, and that a better education is one of the stages of such improvement. Secondly, that a high education does not make women *less* able and willing to perform their natural duties, but better and more intelligently able and willing to do so. Thirdly, that to assimilate the *forms* of a woman's education to that of a man by means of examinations and academical honours, and also the *substance* of it by means of classical and mathematical studies, will in nowise tend to efface the natural differences of their minds, which depend not on any accidental circumstances, to be regulated by education, but on innate characteristics given by the Creator. Fourthly, that there are many positive benefits, general and particular, to be expected from such Examinations and Honours, such classical and mathematical studies being opened to women.

* * *

In conclusion, I would venture to make one appeal: do not let us in this, or any other matter connected with women's claims, allow ourselves to be drawn aside by those prejudices which on both sides distract us. To a woman of refined feeling, that popular Ogress, the Strong-minded Female, is so distasteful, that she is inclined rather to leave her whole sex to mental starvation than contribute to the sustenance of one specimen of the genus. To a man with a spark of fun in his composition, the temptation to perpetrate jokes about Mistresses of Arts and Spinsters of Arts is perfectly irresistible. But, after all, refined women will best prevent the growth of strong-mindedness, in its obnoxious sense, by bringing their own good taste to help their sisters, whom the harsh struggles of life under a woman's disadvantages have perhaps somewhat hardened and embittered. And men who laugh at the absurdities (incident, alas! in some mysterious way to all the doings of women), will also in graver moments feel that there is another side to the subject, not a ludicrous one; and that the answer of the poor frogs to the boys in the fable might often be made by human sufferers: "throwing stones may be fun to you, but it is death to us."[8] To aid a woman in distress was deemed in the old days of chivalry the chiefest honour of the bravest knight; it is assuredly no less an honour now for wise and generous men to aid the whole sex to a better and nobler life, and to the developing more perfectly, because more fully and freely, that Womanhood which God has also made in His own image—a divine and holy thing.

1862

8. Aesop's "The Boys and the Frogs."

JOHN STUART MILL

I n 1865 John Stuart Mill (1806–1873) was chosen to be the rector of the University of St. Andrews, Scotland's oldest university (it had been founded in 1410). The Universities Act of 1858 had changed the nature of the position. No longer necessarily an internal appointment, the rector was elected to a three-year term by the students; his principal duty was to preside over meetings of the University Court, the university's main governing body. In his inaugural address celebrating his election, from which a selection is given here (the entire speech took three hours to deliver), Mill focuses on the major issues in the national debate about university education at the time—the relationship of professional and liberal education and the relative importance of the study of the classics and the study of science. Several essays in this volume address these topics: John Henry Cardinal, Newman's *The Idea of a University,* Thomas Henry Huxley's *Science and Culture,* and Matthew Arnold's *Literature and Science.*

From Inaugural Address Delivered to the University of St. Andrews

The proper function of an University in national education is tolerably well understood. At least there is a tolerably general agreement about what an University is not. It is not a place of professional education. Universities are not intended to teach the knowledge required to fit men for some special mode of gaining their livelihood. Their object is not to make skilful lawyers, or physicians, or engineers, but capable and cultivated human beings. It is very right that there should be public facilities for the study of professions. It is well that there should be Schools of Law, and of Medicine, and it would be well if there were schools of engineering, and the industrial arts. The countries which have such institutions are greatly the better for them; and there is something to be said for having them in the same localities, and under the same general superintendence, as the establishments devoted to education properly so called. But these things are no part of what every generation owes to the next, as that on which its civilization and worth will principally depend. They are needed only by a comparatively few, who are under the strongest private inducements to acquire them by their own efforts; and even those few do not require them until after their education, in the ordinary sense, has been complete. Whether those whose speciality they are, will learn them as a branch of intelligence or as a mere trade, and whether, having learnt them, they will make a wise and conscientious use of them or the reverse, depends less on the manner in which they are taught their profession, than upon what sort of minds they bring to it—what kind of intelligence, and of conscience, the general system of education has developed in them. Men are men before they are lawyers, or physicians, or merchants, or manufacturers; and if you make them capable and sensible men, they will make themselves capable and sensible lawyers or physicians. What professional men should carry away with them from an University, is not professional knowledge, but that which should direct the use of their professional knowledge, and bring the light of general culture to illuminate the technicalities of a special pursuit. Men may be competent lawyers without general education, but it depends on general education to make them philosophic lawyers—who demand, and are capable of apprehending, principles, instead of merely cramming their memory with details. And so of all other useful pursuits, mechanical included. Education makes a man a more intelligent shoemaker, if that be his occupation, but not by teaching him how to make shoes; it does so by the mental exercise it gives, and the habits it impresses.

This, then, is what a mathematician would call the higher limit of University education: its province ends where education, ceasing to be general, branches off into departments adapted to the individual's destination in life. The lower limit is more difficult to define. An University is not concerned with elementary instruction: the pupil is supposed to have acquired that before coming here. But where does elementary instruction end, and the higher studies begin? Some have given a very wide extension to the idea of elementary instruction. According to them, it is not the office of an University to give instruction in single branches of knowledge from the commencement. What the pupil should be taught here (they think), is to methodize his knowledge: to look at every separate part of it in its relation to the other parts, and to the whole; combining the partial glimpses which he has obtained of the field of human knowledge at different points, into a general map, if I may so speak, of the entire region; observing how all knowledge is connected, how we ascend to one branch by means of another, how the higher modifies the lower, and the lower helps us to understand the higher; how every existing reality is a compound of many properties, of which each science or distinct mode of study reveals but a small part, but the whole of which must be included to enable us to know it truly as a fact in Nature, and not as a mere abstraction.

This last stage of general education, destined to give the pupil a comprehensive and connected view of the things which he has already learnt separately, includes a philosophic study of the Methods of the sciences; the modes in which the human intellect proceeds from the known to the unknown. We must be taught to generalize our conception of the resources which the human mind possesses for the exploration of nature; to understand how man discovers the real facts of the world, and by what tests he can judge whether he has really found them. And doubtless this is the crown and consummation of a liberal education: but before we restrict an University to this highest department of instruction—before we confine it to teaching, not knowledge, but the philosophy of knowledge—we must be assured that the knowledge itself has been acquired elsewhere. Those who take this view of the function of an University are not wrong in thinking that the schools, as distinguished from the universities, ought to be adequate to teaching every branch of general instruction required by youth, so far as it can be studied apart from the rest. But where are such schools to be found? Since science assumed its modern character, nowhere: and in these islands even less than elsewhere. This ancient kingdom, thanks to its great religious reformers, had the inestimable advantage, denied to its southern sister, of excellent parish schools, which gave, really and not in pretence, a considerable amount of valuable literary instruction to the bulk of the population, two centuries earlier than in any other country. But schools of a still higher description have been, even in Scotland, so few and inadequate, that the Universities have had to perform largely the functions which ought to be performed by schools; receiving students at an early age, and undertaking not only the work for which the schools should have prepared them, but much of the preparation, itself. Every Scottish University is not an University only, but a High School, to supply the deficiency of other schools. And if the English Universities do not do the same, it is not because the same need does not exist, but because it is disregarded. Youths come to the Scottish Universities ignorant, and are there taught. The majority of those who come to the English Universities come still more ignorant, and ignorant they go away.

In point of fact, therefore, the office of a Scottish University comprises the whole of a liberal education, from the foundations upwards. And the scheme of your Universities has, almost from the beginning, really aimed at including the whole, both in depth and in breadth. You have not, as the English Universities so long did, confined all the stress of your teaching, all your real effort to teach, within the limits of two subjects, the classical languages and mathematics. You did not wait till the last few years to establish a Natural Science and a Moral Science Tripos.[1] Instruction in both those departments was organized long ago: and your teachers of those subjects have not been nominal professors, who did not lecture: some of the greatest names in physical and in moral science have taught in your Universities, and by their teaching contributed to form some of the most distinguished intellects of the last and present centuries. To comment upon the course of education at the Scottish Universities is to pass in review every essential

1. An honors examination for the bachelor's degree in a particular area of study.

department of general culture. The best use, then, which I am able to make of the present occasion, is to offer a few remarks on each of those departments, considered in its relation to human cultivation at large: adverting to the nature of the claims which each has to a place in liberal education; in what special manner they each conduce to the improvement of the individual mind and the benefit of the race; and how they all conspire to the common end, the strengthening, exalting, purifying, and beautifying of our common nature, and the fitting out of mankind with the necessary mental implements for the work they have to perform through life.

Let me first say a few words on the great controversy of the present day with regard to the higher education, the difference which most broadly divides educational reformers and conservatives; the vexed question between the ancient languages and the modern, sciences and arts; whether general education should be classical—let me use a wider expression, and say literary—or scientific. A dispute as endlessly, and often as fruitlessly agitated as that old controversy which it resembles, made memorable by the names of Swift and Sir William Temple in England and Fontenelle[2] in France—the contest for superiority between the ancients and the moderns. This question, whether we should be taught the classics or the sciences, seems to me, I confess, very like a dispute whether painters should cultivate drawing or colouring, or, to use a more homely illustration, whether a tailor should make coats or trousers. I can only reply by the question, why not both? Can anything deserve the name of a good education which does not include literature and science too? If there were no more to be said than that scientific education teaches us to think, and literary education to express our thoughts, do we not require both? and is not any one a poor, maimed, lopsided fragment of humanity who is deficient in either? We are not obliged to ask ourselves whether it is more important to know the languages or the sciences. Short as life is, and shorter still as we make it by the time we waste on things which are neither business, nor meditation, nor pleasure, we are not so badly off that our scholars need be ignorant of the laws and properties of the world they live in, or our scientific men destitute of poetic feeling and artistic cultivation. I am amazed at the limited conception which many educational reformers have formed to themselves of a human being's power of acquisition. The study of science, they truly say, is indispensable: our present education neglects it: there is truth in this too, though it is not all truth: and they think it impossible to find room for the studies which they desire to encourage, but by turning out, at least from general education, those which are now chiefly cultivated. How absurd, they say, that the whole of boyhood should be taken up in acquiring an imperfect knowledge of two dead languages. Absurd indeed: but is the human mind's capacity to learn, measured by that of Eton and Westminster[3] to teach? I should prefer to see these reformers pointing their attacks against the shameful inefficiency of the schools, public and private, which pretend to teach these two languages and do not. I should like to hear them denounce

2. Jonathan Swift (1667–1745), William Temple (1628–1699), and Bernard le Bovier de Fontenelle (1657–1757) all wrote works on the 17th- and 18th-century controversy about whether modern works surpass the classics.
3. Elite English secondary schools (two of the renowned "public schools").

the wretched methods of teaching, and the criminal idleness and supineness, which waste the entire boyhood of the pupils without really giving to most of them more than a smattering, if even that, of the only kind of knowledge which is even pretended to be cared for. Let us try what conscientious and intelligent teaching can do, before we presume to decide what cannot be done.

1867

THOMAS HARDY

Greeted by harsh criticism in the press and even a book burning (by the Bishop of Wakefield), *Jude the Obscure* was the last novel that Thomas Hardy (1840–1928) wrote. Its reception, Hardy later said, cured him of further interest in novel writing. It tells the story of a poor young man, Jude Fawley, who yearns to go to university and become a scholar. Studying Greek and Latin on his own, he manages to get to Christminster (modeled on Oxford) by finding work as a stonemason. The controversy that greeted Hardy's novel stemmed from its candid treatment of sex and its criticism of the institution of marriage, portrayed through Jude's relationships with his wife, Arabella, and his cousin, Sue Bridehead, whom he loves. The selection here depicts Jude's first view of Christminster.

From Jude the Obscure

Not a soul was visible on the hedgeless highway, or on either side of it, and the white road seemed to ascend and diminish till it joined the sky. At the very top it was crossed at right angles by a green "ridgeway"—the Ickneild Street[1] and original Roman road through the district. This ancient track ran east and west for many miles, and down almost to within living memory had been used for driving flocks and herds to fairs and markets. But it was now neglected and overgrown.

The boy had never before strayed so far north as this from the nestling hamlet in which he had been deposited by the carrier from a railway station southward,[2] one dark evening some few months earlier, and till now he had had no suspicion that such a wide, flat, low-lying country lay so near at hand, under the very verge of his upland world. The whole northern semicircle between east and west, to a distance of forty or fifty miles, spread itself before him; a bluer, moister atmosphere, evidently, than that he breathed up here.

Not far from the road stood a weather-beaten old barn of reddish-grey brick and tile. It was known as the Brown House by the people of the locality. He was about to pass it when he perceived a ladder against the eaves;

1. Ancient road crossing England.
2. Jude is an orphan, recently sent to live with his great-aunt after the death of his parents.

and the reflection that the higher he got, the further he could see, led Jude to stand and regard it. On the slope of the roof two men were repairing the tiling. He turned into the ridgeway and drew towards the barn.

When he had wistfully watched the workmen for some time he took courage, and ascended the ladder till he stood beside them.

"Well, my lad, and what may you want up here?"

"I wanted to know where the city of Christminster is, if you please."

"Christminster is out across there, by that clump. You can see it—at least you can on a clear day. Ah, no, you can't now."

The other tiler, glad of any kind of diversion from the monotony of his labour, had also turned to look towards the quarter designated. "You can't often see it in weather like this," he said. "The time I've noticed it is when the sun is going down in a blaze of flame, and it looks like—I don't know what."

"The heavenly Jerusalem,"[3] suggested the serious urchin.

"Ay—though I should never ha' thought of it myself. . . . But I can't see no Christminster to-day."

The boy strained his eyes also; yet neither could he see the far-off city. He descended from the barn, and abandoning Christminster with the versatility of his age he walked along the ridge-track, looking for any natural objects of interest that might lie in the banks thereabout. When he repassed the barn to go back to Marygreen he observed that the ladder was still in its place, but that the men had finished their day's work and gone away.

It was waning towards evening; there was still a faint mist, but it had cleared a little except in the damper tracts of subjacent country and along the river-courses. He thought again of Christminster, and wished, since he had come two or three miles from his aunt's house on purpose, that he could have seen for once this attractive city of which he had been told. But even if he waited here it was hardly likely that the air would clear before night. Yet he was loth to leave the spot, for the northern expanse became lost to view on retreating towards the village only a few hundred yards.

He ascended the ladder to have one more look at the point the men had designated, and perched himself on the highest rung, overlying the tiles. He might not be able to come so far as this for many days. Perhaps if he prayed, the wish to see Christminster might be forwarded. People said that, if you prayed, things sometimes came to you, even though they sometimes did not. He had read in a tract that a man who had begun to build a church, and had no money to finish it, knelt down and prayed, and the money came in by the next post. Another man tried the same experiment, and the money did not come; but he found afterwards that the breeches he knelt in were made by a wicked Jew. This was not discouraging, and turning on the ladder Jude knelt on the third rung, where, resting against those above it, he prayed that the mist might rise.

He then seated himself again, and waited. In the course of ten or fifteen minutes the thinning mist dissolved altogether from the northern horizon, as it had already done elsewhere, and about a quarter of an hour before the time of sunset the westward clouds parted, the sun's position being partially

3. The dwelling place in heaven of the saints.

uncovered, and the beams streaming out in visible lines between two bars of slaty cloud. The boy immediately looked back in the old direction.

Some way within the limits of the stretch of landscape, points of light like the topaz gleamed. The air increased in transparency with the lapse of minutes, till the topaz points showed themselves to be the vanes, windows, wet roof slates, and other shining spots upon the spires, domes, freestone-work, and varied outlines that were faintly revealed. It was Christminster, unquestionably; either directly seen, or miraged in the peculiar atmosphere.

The spectator gazed on and on till the windows and vanes lost their shine, going out almost suddenly like extinguished candles. The vague city became veiled in mist. Turning to the west, he saw that the sun had disappeared. The foreground of the scene had grown funereally dark, and near objects put on the hues and shapes of chimaeras.

He anxiously descended the ladder, and started homewards at a run, try-ing not to think of giants, Herne the Hunter, Apollyon lying in wait for Christian, or of the captain[4] with the bleeding hole in his forehead and the corpses round him that remutinied every night on board the bewitched ship. He knew that he had grown out of belief in these horrors, yet he was glad when he saw the church tower and the lights in the cottage windows, even though this was not the home of his birth, and his great-aunt did not care much about him.

Inside and round about that old woman's "shop" window, with its twenty-four little panes set in lead-work, the glass of some of them oxidized with age, so that you could hardly see the poor penny articles exhibited within, and forming part of a stock which a strong man could have carried, Jude had his outer being for some long tideless time. But his dreams were as gigantic as his surroundings were small.

Through the solid barrier of cold cretaceous upland to the northward he was always beholding a gorgeous city—the fancied place he had likened to the new Jerusalem, though there was perhaps more of the painter's imagi-nation and less of the diamond merchant's in his dreams thereof than in those the Apocalyptic writer.[5] And the city acquired a tangibility, a perma-nence, a hold on his life, mainly from the one nucleus of fact that the man for whose knowledge and purposes he had so much reverence was actually living there; not only so but living among the more thoughtful and mentally shining ones therein.[6]

In sad wet seasons, though he knew it must rain at Christminster too, he could hardly believe that it rained so drearily there. Whenever he could get away from the confines of the hamlet for an hour or two, which was not often, he would steal off to the Brown House on the hill and strain his eyes persistently; sometimes to be rewarded by the sight of a dome or spire, at other times by a little smoke, which in his estimate had some of the mysti-cism of incense.

Then the day came when it suddenly occurred to him that if he ascended to the point of view after dark, or possibly went a mile or two further, he

---

4. A figure in a German ghost story. Herne the Hunter is a legendary wild ghost hunter on horseback. Christian is the pilgrim in John Bun-yan's *The Pilgrim's Progress* (1678), who meets the archdevil Apollyon in the Valley of Humiliation.

5. John describes the new Jerusalem in Revela-tion 21.2.
6. The schoolmaster in Jude's village, Mr. Phillotson, had just left to try to get a degree at Christminster.

would see the night lights of the city. It would be necessary to come back alone, but even that consideration did not deter him, for he could throw a little manliness into his mood, no doubt.

The project was duly executed. It was not late when he arrived at the place of outlook, only just after dusk, but a black north-east sky, accompanied by a wind from the same quarter, made the occasion dark enough. He was rewarded; but what he saw was not the lamps in rows, as he had half expected. No individual light was visible, only a halo or glow-fog overarching the place against the black heavens behind it, making the light and the city seem distant but a mile or so.

He set himself to wonder on the exact point in the glow where the schoolmaster might be—he who never communicated with anybody at Marygreen now; who was as if dead to them here. In the glow he seemed to see Phillotson promenading at ease, like one of the forms in Nebuchadnezzar's furnace.[7]

He had heard that breezes travelled at the rate of ten miles an hour, and the fact now came into his mind. He parted his lips as he faced the north-east, and drew in the wind as if it were a sweet liquor.

"You," he said, addressing the breeze caressingly "were in Christminster city between one and two hours ago, floating along the streets, pulling round the weather-cocks, touching Mr. Phillotson's face, being breathed by him; and now you are here, breathed by me—you, the very same."

Suddenly there came along this wind something towards him—a message from the place—from some soul residing there, it seemed. Surely it was the sound of bells, the voice of the city, faint and musical, calling to him, "We are happy here!"

He had become entirely lost to his bodily situation during this mental leap, and only got back to it by a rough recalling. A few yards below the brow of the hill on which he paused a team of horses made its appearance, having reached the place by dint of half an hour's serpentine progress from the bottom of the immense declivity. They had a load of coals behind them—a fuel that could only be got into the upland by this particular route. They were accompanied by a carter, a second man, and a boy, who now kicked a large stone behind one of the wheels, and allowed the panting animals to have a long rest, while those in charge took a flagon off the load and indulged in a drink round.

They were elderly men, and had genial voices. Jude addressed them, inquiring if they had come from Christminster.

"Heaven forbid, with this load!" said they.

"The place I mean is that one yonder." He was getting so romantically attached to Christminster that, like a young lover alluding to his mistress, he felt bashful at mentioning its name again. He pointed to the light in the sky—hardly perceptible to their older eyes.

"Yes. There do seem a spot a bit brighter in the nor'-east than elsewhere, though I shouldn't ha' noticed it myself, and no doubt it med be Christminster."

Here a little book of tales which Jude had tucked up under his arm, having brought them to read on his way hither before it grew dark, slipped and

7. Refusing to worship King Nebuchadnezzar's golden idol, Shadrach, Meshach, and Abednego were cast into a fiery furnace where they were miraculously unharmed (Daniel 3.24–25).

fell into the road. The carter eyed him while he picked it up and straightened the leaves.

"Ah, young man," he observed, "you'd have to get your head screwed on t'other way before you could read what they read there."

"Why?" asked the boy.

"Oh, they never look at anything that folks like we can understand," the carter continued, by way of passing the time. "On'y foreign tongues used in the days of the Tower of Babel,[8] when no two families spoke alike. They read that sort of thing as fast as a night-hawk will whir. 'Tis all learning there—nothing but learning, except religion. And that's learning too, for I never could understand it. Yes, 'tis a serious-minded place. Not but there's wenches in the streets o' nights. . . . You know, I suppose, that they raise pa'sons[9] there like radishes in a bed? And though it do take—how many years, Bob?—five years to turn a larruping hobble-de-hoy[1] chap into a solemn preaching man with no corrupt passions, they'll do it, if it can be done, and polish un off like the workmen they be, and turn un out wi' a long face, and a long black coat and waistcoat, and a religious collar and hat, same as they used to wear in the Scriptures, so that his own mother wouldn't know un sometimes. . . . There, 'tis their business, like anybody else's."

"But how should you know."

"Now don't you interrupt, my boy. Never interrupt your senyers.[2] Move the fore hoss aside, Bobby; here's som'at coming. . . . You must mind that I be a-talking of the college life. 'Em lives on a lofty level; there's no gainsaying it, though I myself med not think much of 'em. As we be here in our bodies on this high ground, so be they in their minds—noble-minded men enough, no doubt—some on 'em—able to earn hundreds by thinking out loud. And some on 'em be strong young fellows that can earn a'most as much in silver cups. As for music, there's beautiful music everywhere in Christminster. You med be religious, or you med not, but you can't help striking in your homely note with the rest. And there's a street in the place—the main street—that ha'n't another like it in the world. I should think I did know a little about Christminster!"

By this time the horses had recovered breath and bent to their collars again. Jude, throwing a last adoring look at the distant halo, turned and walked beside his remarkably well-informed friend, who had no objection to telling him as they moved on more yet of the city—its towers and halls and churches. The waggon turned into a cross-road, whereupon Jude thanked the carter warmly for his information, and said he only wished he could talk half as well about Christminster as he.

"Well, 'tis oonly what has come in my way," said the carter unboastfully. "I've never been there, no more than you; but I've picked up the knowledge here and there, and you be welcome to it. A-getting about the world as I do, and mixing with all classes of society, one can't help hearing of things. A friend o' mine, that used to clane[3] the boots at the Crozier Hotel in Christminster when he was in his prime, why, I knowed un as well as my own brother in his later years."

---

8. Tower in Genesis built by men to reach the heavens. In punishment for their presumption, God made the men speak different languages unintelligible to each other (Genesis 11).

9. Parsons.
1. Slouching, awkward, and gawky.
2. Seniors.
3. Clean.

Jude continued his walk homeward alone, pondering so deeply that he forgot to feel timid. He suddenly grew older. It had been the yearning of his heart to find something to anchor on, to cling to—for some place which he could call admirable. Should he find that place in this city if he could get there? Would it be a spot in which, without fear of farmers, or hindrance, or ridicule, he could watch and wait, and set himself to some mighty undertaking like the men of old of whom he had heard? As the halo had been to his eyes when gazing at it a quarter of an hour earlier, so was the spot mentally to him as he pursued his dark way.

"It is a city of light," he said to himself.

"The tree of knowledge grows there,"[4] he added a few steps further on.

"It is a place that teachers of men spring from and go to."

"It is what you may call a castle, manned by scholarship and religion."

After this figure he was silent a long while, till he added:

"It would just suit me."

1895

4. The tree of knowledge of good and evil from the garden of Eden (Genesis 2.9).

Late Victorians

The state of mind prevailing during the final decades of the nineteenth century was characterized previously (in the introduction to the Victorian age) as typical neither of the earlier Victorians nor of the twentieth century. As a result of their between-centuries role, writers of the 1880s and 1890s are sometimes styled "Late Victorians"—a perfectly legitimate label, chronologically speaking—and sometimes (more ambiguously) "the first of the 'moderns.'" In this anthology, we retain as Late Victorians those writers who made their chief contribution before 1900. And we reserve for the twentieth century a number of writers already on the scene in the last two decades of Victoria's reign whose work achieved particular prominence in the twentieth century: these are William Butler Yeats, Joseph Conrad, A. E. Housman, and Thomas Hardy. The treatment of Hardy's writings exemplifies this principle. He was born fifteen to twenty years before most of the writers of the 1880s and 1890s, and his last two great novels, *Tess of the D'Urbervilles* and *Jude the Obscure*, were published in 1891 and 1896 respectively. But because it was only after 1900 that Hardy made his name as a poet, we include him in the twentieth century, even though many of the attitudes toward life and literature in his poetry are recognizably Victorian and his writings can be considered as having contributed, in part, to the overall accomplishments of Victorian literature. To be sure, the same generalizations might be made about Gerard Manley Hopkins, whom we include in the Victorian section because he wrote during the Victorian period—even though his work was not published until 1918, when it had a great effect on modernist poets and critics. That such placements can be problematic is a striking reminder that literary history, like all history, resists being divided into the time categories we set up for convenient reference.

The writers most closely identified with the fin de siècle (the French for, literally, "end of the century"), a phrase often used in connection with this period, were proponents of "art for art's sake": they believed that art should be restricted to celebrating beauty in a highly polished style, unconcerned with controversial issues such as politics. These tenets are perhaps most frequently associated with Oscar Wilde, but the "aesthetes," as these artists and writers were called, included painters such as James McNeill Whistler, critics such as Arthur Symons, and the young Yeats. In 1936, when Yeats in old age was compiling an anthology of "modern verse," he looked back, as he often did, to the group of poets of the 1890s to which he had once been attached. They styled themselves the Rhymers' Club, and they met at a restaurant in London to read their poems aloud to each other. Yeats recalled that an admiration for the writings of Walter Pater was a badge of membership. Indeed, the first "poem" in his anthology is a passage of Pater's prose that Yeats prints as verse—the passage about the *Mona Lisa* in *Studies in the History of the Renaissance* (1873) that begins "She is older than the rocks among which she sits."

The Rhymers' Club poets liked to think of themselves as anti-Victorians, and they had some cause to do so—they consciously revolted against the moral earnestness of early Victorian prophets such as Thomas Carlyle and against a large set of middle-class opinions that they enjoyed mocking. Even Matthew Arnold, although appreciated for his ridicule of middle-class Philistines, was suspect in the eyes of the aesthetes because he had attacked, in his essay on William Wordsworth, the French poet Théophile Gautier, whom they viewed as a chief progenitor of the aesthetic movement. What Alfred, Lord Tennyson called in 1873 "poisonous honey stolen from France" was, in the 1890s, favored fare. Yet the credo of art for art's sake also had roots in the writings of earlier nineteenth-century British writers. The poets of the aesthetic movement were in a sense the last heirs of the Romantics; the appeal to sensation in their imagery goes back through Dante Gabriel Rossetti and Tennyson to John Keats. They developed this sensationalism much more histrionically than did their predecessors, however, seeking compensation for the drabness of ordinary life in melancholy suggestiveness, antibourgeois outrageousness, heady ritualism, world weariness, or mere emotional debauchery—qualities that led some critics to denounce the fin de siècle as a time of decadence and degeneration. But the importance of this era of English literary history does not lie in its writers' sensationalism and desire to shock. Their strongly held belief in the independence of art, their view that a work of art has its own unique kind of value—that, in T. S. Eliot's phrase, poetry must be judged "as poetry and not another thing"—is what most strongly influenced later generations. Not only did the aesthetic movement nurse the young Yeats and provide him with his lifelong belief in poetry as poetry rather than as a means to some moral or other end; it also provided some of the principal schools of twentieth-century criticism with their basic assumptions. "Art for art's sake" was in the 1890s a provocative slogan; in the modern period many leading critics (usually associated with the tenets of New Criticism in North America, and Practical Criticism in Great Britain) were largely concerned with demonstrating the uniqueness of the literary use of language. They sought to train readers to see works of literary art as possessing a special kind of form, a special kind of meaning, and hence a special kind of value. In this regard the later critics were the heirs of the nineties, however much they modified or enriched the legacy. It was the poets of the fin de siècle, too, who first absorbed the influence of the French *symboliste* poets, an influence that became pervasive in the twentieth century and is especially strong (in different ways) in the poetry of Yeats and Eliot.

Though this era is characterized as "decadent," the poetry of the period was more various than that label suggests. Much as Wilde and Aubrey Beardsley expanded the range of male literary identity through their dandyism and effeminacy, women writers of the aesthetic movement such as the pseudonymous Michael Field (Katharine Harris Bradley and her niece Edith Emma Cooper) and Mary Elizabeth Coleridge made equally untraditional claims for women's experience, as Field translated and elaborated on Sappho's poems and Coleridge took on the witch's voice. There were also poets, such as William Ernest Henley, Henry Newbolt, and Rudyard Kipling, whose tone was strenuously masculine. Their celebrated and widely memorized poems "Invictus" and "Vitaï Lampada" (which appear on pp. 706 and 707, respectively), and "If—" set forth uncompromising codes of elite male honor and conduct, and have thus been seen as key utterances of the fervent imperial and martial spirit that was another important characteristic of the era. In other respects Kipling's poetry, in particular, shares a commitment to realism that links him to naturalist novelists of the period such as George Gissing and George Moore; certainly his distinctive re-creation of the lives of common soldiers in the British army overseas brought new voices into literature in English and thereby extended its demographic reach.

Realism of another brand is evident in the tightly crafted dramas of the playwright George Bernard Shaw. Works such as *Mrs Warren's Profession* (1898) reveal that some late-century artists wanted to engage with the pressing social, moral, and political issues of the day, and strove to challenge their audiences with thorny problems. Readers were unsettled, too, by one of the best-selling novellas of the period, *The Strange Case of Dr. Jekyll and Mr. Hyde* (1886). Although this horror story owes its allegiance to Gothicism rather than realism, many critics suggest that Robert Louis Stevenson's tale of a man split between his respectable public identity and an amoral secret self captures key anxieties of the fin de siècle. Within Wilde's oeuvre this theme is most closely embodied in the novel *The Picture of Dorian Gray* (1891), but it also has an important place, in a very different mode, within *The Importance of Being Earnest* (performed 1895). In this light, bright, and sparkling drama, the concept of the

Salome. Oscar Wilde asked Aubrey Beardsley (1872–1898) to
illustrate the English translation of his play *Salome* (1894; the
original version of the play [1891] was in French); this image is
titled *Climax*.

double life is central to the two principal male characters, who have both invented
fictitious characters (Algernon's Bunbury and Jack's brother Ernest) that enable
them to indulge their desires. Two male characters are also at the heart of one of the
most popular literary creations of the last decades of the nineteenth century, the
Sherlock Holmes stories (the first, "A Study in Scarlet," was published in 1887). Bringing together an ultra-rationalistic detective and his faithfully stolid sidekick (and
chronicler) Dr. Watson, Sir Arthur Conan Doyle provided yet another variation on
the theme of a complementary relationship. Dark secrets too were of obvious structural importance to these serial fictions; although Holmes's brilliance could be relied
on to shed light on each case's mystery, the puzzle of his own character and incompletely known history was another story altogether, and one that continues to capture readers' imaginations to this day.

   In its variety of literary expressions, the fin de siècle manifests something akin to
a split personality. Sometimes that division appears within the work of a single writer.
Kipling has often been seen primarily as the spokesman of the British Empire, the
poet who coined the phrase "the white man's burden" to describe the northern races'

necessary shouldering of the heavy weight of imperial rule. Yet Kipling also created the short story "The Man Who Would Be King" (1888), a highly ambivalent allegory of empire, and wrote "Recessional" for Queen Victoria's Diamond Jubilee in 1897. Instead of offering a complacent celebration of her sixty-year reign, this hymn delivers a haunting elegy: by placing the achievements of his country and his century in the vaster perspectives of human history, Kipling makes us fully aware of their fragility.

MICHAEL FIELD
Katharine Bradley (1846–1914)
Edith Cooper (1862–1913)

Michael Field was the pseudonym adopted by Katharine Bradley and her niece Edith Cooper; together they published twenty-seven verse plays and eight volumes of poems. When Robert Browning wrote to Michael Field to praise a volume of plays, Cooper responded by comparing her collaborative relationship with Bradley to that of two famous Jacobean playwrights: "My Aunt and I work together after the fashion of Beaumont and Fletcher. She is my senior, by but fifteen years. She has lived with me, taught me, encouraged me and joined me to her poetic life." When Browning let slip the secret of their authorship, Bradley begged him to maintain the disguise. The revelation of their secret, she pleaded, "would indeed be utter ruin to us," adding, "We have many things to say that the world will not tolerate from a woman's lips."

Katharine Harris Bradley lost her father, a tobacco manufacturer, when she was two and her mother when she was twenty-two. After her mother's death Bradley attended Newnham College, the newly established women's college at Cambridge, and the Collège de France in Paris. On her return home she joined John Ruskin's Guild of Saint George, a small utopian society. When Bradley wrote to Ruskin telling him that she had lost God and found a Skye terrier, he angrily ended their friendship. Shortly thereafter she began attending classes at Bristol University with her niece, Edith Emma Cooper, whom she had adopted and raised after Edith's mother became ill. The two became lovers and began a life of writing and traveling together. Their first joint volume of poetry, *Long Ago* (1889), was inspired by Henry Wharton's 1885 edition of the writings of the ancient Greek poet Sappho, the first English translation to represent the object of Sappho's love poems as a woman. The preface to *Long Ago* explains their attempt to create poems elaborating on Sappho's fragments: "Devoutly as the fiery-bosomed Greek turned in her anguish to Aphrodite to accomplish her heart's desires, I have turned to the one woman who has dared to speak unfalteringly of the fearful mastery of love."

Bradley and Cooper knew most of the literary figures of the 1890s, including Walter Pater, Oscar Wilde, and William Butler Yeats, although their relationship to the decadent movement was complex. The eroticism of their early poetry, with its frank expression of love between women, seems consistent with the spirit of the decade, but Bradley and Cooper sharply criticized the work of the artist Aubrey Beardsley for its depravity and withdrew one of their poems from publication in *The Yellow Book* to protest its style (Beardsley was the journal's art editor). In 1906 they converted to Roman Catholicism when their beloved chow dog died, thus reversing the substitution of dog for God that Bradley had flippantly described to Ruskin three decades earlier. In 1911 Cooper was diagnosed with cancer. Suffering too from cancer, which she kept a secret from Cooper to spare her pain, Bradley survived her niece by only eight months.

[Maids, not to you my mind doth change]

Ταῖς κάλαις ὔμμιν [το] νόημα τῶμον οὐ διάμειπτον.[1]

Maids, not to you my mind doth change;
Men I defy, allure, estrange,
Prostrate, make bond or free:
Soft as the stream beneath the plane°   *tree*
5 To you I sing my love's refrain;
Between us is no thought of pain,
   Peril, satiety.

Soon doth a lover's patience tire,
But ye to manifold desire
10 Can yield response, ye know
When for long, museful days I pine,
The presage at my heart divine;
To you I never breathe a sign
Of inward want or woe.

15 When injuries my spirit bruise,
Allaying virtue ye infuse
With unobtrusive skill:
And if care frets ye come to me
As fresh as nymph from stream or tree,
20 And with your soft vitality
   My weary bosom fill.

1889

[A girl]

A girl,
Her soul a deep-wave pearl
Dim, lucent of all lovely mysteries;
A face flowered for heart's ease,
5 A brow's grace soft as seas
Seen through faint forest-trees:
A mouth, the lips apart,
Like aspen-leaflets trembling in the breeze
From her tempestuous heart.
10 Such: and our souls so knit,
I leave a page half-writ—

1. A fragment from the works of the Greek poet Sappho (born ca. 612 B.C.E.); the epigraph is translated in the first line of the poem.

The work begun
Will be to heaven's conception done,
If she come to it.

1893

Unbosoming

The love that breeds
In my heart for thee!
As the iris is full, brimful of seeds,
And all that it flowered for among the reeds
5   Is packed in a thousand vermilion-beads
That push, and riot, and squeeze, and clip,°   *clutch*
Till they burst the sides of the silver scrip,°   *purse*
And at last we see
What the bloom, with its tremulous, bowery fold
10   Of zephyr-petal at heart did hold:
So my breast is rent
With the burthen and strain of its great content;
For the summer of fragrance and sighs is dead,
The harvest-secret is burning red,
15   And I would give thee, after my kind,
The final issues of heart and mind.

1893

[It was deep April, and the morn]

It was deep April, and the morn
   Shakspere was born;[1]
The world was on us, pressing sore;
My Love and I took hands and swore,
5   Against the world, to be
Poets and lovers evermore,
To laugh and dream on Lethe's[2] shore,
To sing to Charon[3] in his boat,
Heartening the timid souls afloat;
10   Of judgment never to take heed,
But to those fast-locked souls to speed,
Who never from Apollo[4] fled,
Who spent no hour among the dead;
       Continually
15   With them to dwell,
Indifferent to heaven and hell.

1893

---

1. Shakespeare's birthday is traditionally ascribed to the date April 23, 1564.
2. The river of forgetfulness in the underworld (a reference, like those that follow, to classical mythology).
3. The ferryman who rows the dead across the river Styx to the underworld.
4. God of poetry and of the sun.

To Christina Rossetti

Lady, we would behold thee moving bright
As Beatrice or Matilda[1] mid the trees,
Alas! thy moan was as a moan for ease
And passage through cool shadows to the night:
5   Fleeing from love, hadst thou not poet's right
To slip into the universe? The seas
Are fathomless to rivers drowned in these,
And sorrow is secure in leafy light.
Ah, had this secret touched thee, in a tomb
10 Thou hadst not buried thy enchanting self,
As happy Syrinx[2] murmuring with the wind,
Or Daphne,[3] thrilled through all her mystic bloom,
From safe recess as genius[4] or as elf,
Thou hadst breathed joy in earth and in thy kind.

1896

Nests in Elms

The rooks are cawing up and down the trees!
Among their nests they caw. O sound I treasure,
Ripe as old music is, the summer's measure,
Sleep at her gossip, sylvan mysteries,
5   With prate and clamour to give zest of these—
In rune I trace the ancient law of pleasure,
Of love, of all the busy-ness of leisure,
With dream on dream of never-thwarted ease.
O homely birds, whose cry is harbinger
10 Of nothing sad, who know not anything
Of sea-birds' loneliness, of Procne's[1] strife,
Rock round me when I die! So sweet it were
To die by open doors, with you on wing
Humming the deep security of life.

1908

---

1. An idealized virgin in Dante's *Purgatorio*
(28.30), who explains to the poet that he is in
the Garden of Eden. Beatrice, Dante's idealized
beloved, appears to the poet in the Earthly Paradise at the top of the mountain of Purgatory.
2. A nymph who, when pursued by Pan, prayed to
the river nymphs to save her; she was transformed
into reeds, from which Pan made his flute (in
Greek, *syrinx* literally means "Panpipe").
3. A nymph who, to escape Apollo's pursuit, was
transformed into a laurel tree (the literal mean-

ing of *daphnē* in Greek).
4. The spirit of a place.
1. In Greek mythology Procne's husband, King
Tereus, raped her sister, Philomela. Tereus then
ripped out Philomela's tongue to keep her from
revealing the crime, but she wove the story into a
tapestry. In revenge Procne killed their son and
served him to Tereus in a stew. When the sisters
fled Tereus, all three were changed into birds:
Tereus, into a hoopoe; Procne, a nightingale; and
Philomela, a swallow.

Eros[1]

O Eros of the mountains, of the earth,
One thing I know of thee that thou art old,
Far, sovereign, lonesome tyrant of the dearth
Of chaos, ruler of the primal cold!
5   None gave thee nurture: chaos' icy rings
Pressed on thy plenitude. O fostering power,
Thine the first voice, first warmth, first golden wings,
First blowing zephyr, earliest opened flower,
Thine the first smile of Time: thou hast no mate,
10 Thou art alone forever, giving all:
After thine image, Love, thou did'st create
Man to be poor, man to be prodigal;
And thus, O awful° god, he is endued   *awe-inspiring*
With the raw hungers of thy solitude.

1908

1. Love (Greek); in Greek mythology the god of love.

ROBERT LOUIS STEVENSON
1850–1894

Robert Louis (originally Lewis) Balfour Stevenson was born in Edinburgh on November 13, 1850, the only child of Margaret Balfour and Thomas Stevenson, a well-known marine engineer and designer of lighthouses. His family was part of the respectable Scottish middle classes, a membership that would both benefit Stevenson—although there were difficult stretches in his relationship with his father, he generally did not have to worry about money—and leave him with a restlessness for adventure and excitement. Driven at the same time by a quest for a climate that would ease his chronically diseased lungs, Stevenson traveled more broadly than any other prominent Victorian writer. And yet it could be argued that although he was constantly on the move in far-flung lands, Stevenson returned again and again in his creative fiction, explicitly or implicitly, to the tensions of his own personal and national heritage—to the pronounced conflicts of his upbringing and of Scotland's somber, religiously oppressive society.

An awkward sensitive boy, Stevenson was subjected to the disciplinary strictures of his stern Presbyterian father and to the more affectionate, although also deeply devout, care of his mother and his nurse. Plagued by night terrors and bouts of sickness, the young Stevenson seemed "in body . . . assuredly badly set up," as a schoolmate said in later years; "his limbs were long, lean, and spidery, and his chest flat, so as almost to suggest some malnutrition." This constitutional weakness was to afflict Stevenson throughout his life, and he enjoyed only short periods of reasonable health. As a student at Edinburgh University, Stevenson soon began to avoid the engineering classes that would have enabled him to follow in his father's footsteps, and embarked instead on a course of reading—"an extensive and highly rational system of truancy," as he called it—to learn how to become a writer. In time, as a compromise to placate his father, he switched to the study of law; although he never practiced as a lawyer, he did pass the Scottish bar examination in 1875. But Stevenson's interests clearly lay elsewhere; in this period he began reading scandalous French poetry and hanging around brothels, where the prostitutes nicknamed him "Velvet Jacket." His appearance and wit attracted attention: describing their first encounter in 1873, Stevenson's friend the folklorist and writer Andrew Lang later recalled that he "wore a wide blue cloak, with a grace that hovered between that of an Italian poet and an early pirate. It was impossible not to discover, in a short conversation, that he was very clever."

At the age of twenty-two, Stevenson further distanced himself from his father by confessing that he had turned both socialist and agnostic; he subsequently began to spend increasingly longer periods in France, partly because of respiratory troubles but also to be in the company of painters and writers. Back in Britain he developed important and useful friendships with artistic and literary figures, including Sidney Colvin, a professor of art, and the poet and editor W. E. Henley; with their support Stevenson started to publish essays and books of travel writing. As if to complete his breach with bourgeois Scottish respectability, Stevenson then fell in love with Fanny Osbourne, an American woman ten years his senior, who was estranged from her husband but not yet divorced.

In 1879 Stevenson's global wanderings began in earnest, starting with a trip to California to marry the newly divorced Fanny. Despite constant travel and recurrent illness, Stevenson found the time and energy to write. *Treasure Island*, begun as an amusement for his stepson, was his first popular success: serialized in 1881 and published in book form in 1883, the story of the cabin boy Jim Hawkins's adventures includes a covert portrait of Stevenson's one-legged friend Henley in the figure of the pirate Long John Silver. Soon thereafter he published another children's classic: *A Child's Garden of Verses* (1885), a collection of poems dedicated to his former nurse. In the years to come, Stevenson worked in numerous genres, including short fiction, swashbuckling romances, historical adventures (*Kidnapped*, 1886, a story set in Scotland just after the Jacobite rebellion of 1745, and its sequel, *Catriona*, 1893), and more gothic undertakings, such as the bleak and brooding novel *The Master of Ballantrae* (1889).

The work that first established Stevenson's critical reputation, however, was a horror story that prefigured *The Master of Ballantrae*'s fascination with the darker side of human nature and reflected his long-standing interest in the idea of a double life: *The Strange Case of Dr. Jekyll and Mr. Hyde*, written in 1885 and published the following year. The novella rapidly became a best seller in both Britain and America, and like Mary Shelley's *Frankenstein* of 1818 (to which *Jekyll and Hyde* pays homage at various moments) and Bram Stoker's *Dracula* (1897), the story has enjoyed a continuous and lively presence in popular culture up to the present day. Yet our familiarity with the outline of the tale may not prepare us for the psychological and ethical complexity of the original. Certainly the novelist's friends found *Jekyll and Hyde* genuinely unnerving: the writer and historian J. A. Symonds wrote to Stevenson that the story "has left such a deeply painful impression on my heart that I do not know how I am ever to turn to it again," while Lang commented that "we would welcome a spectre, a ghoul, or even a vampire, rather than meet Mr. Edward Hyde." For some, many aspects of the novella have seemed markedly Scottish in flavor: the novelist G. K. Chesterton insisted that its London is really Edinburgh, its Englishmen actually Scotsmen—"No modern English lawyer," he protested of the character Mr. Utterson, "ever read a book of dry divinity in the evening, merely because it was Sunday." Nevertheless, the distinctive tone and theme of *Jekyll and Hyde* have led many critics to characterize it—often together with another work that shares its preoccupation with the divided self, Oscar Wilde's *Picture of Dorian Gray* (1891)—as an expression of quintessentially fin de siècle anxieties.

From 1888 onward the Stevensons embarked on a series of journeys in the South Seas, once again in the hope that the climate would benefit the writer's health. They eventually settled in Samoa, where Stevenson became a favorite with the locals (who called him Tusitala, or "teller of tales") before he died of a cerebral hemorrhage in 1894. At the time of his death, Stevenson was only forty-four years old and still furiously at work, this time on a historical novel titled *Weir of Hermiston*.

The Strange Case of Dr. Jekyll and Mr. Hyde

Story of the Door

Mr. Utterson the lawyer was a man of a rugged countenance, that was never lighted by a smile; cold, scanty and embarrassed in discourse; backward in sentiment; lean, long, dusty, dreary and yet somehow lovable. At friendly meetings, and when the wine was to his taste, something eminently human beaconed from his eye; something indeed which never found its way into his talk, but which spoke not only in these silent symbols of the after-dinner face, but more often and loudly in the acts of his life. He was austere with himself; drank gin when he was alone, to mortify a taste for vintages; and though he enjoyed the theatre, had not crossed the doors of one for twenty years. But he had an approved[1] tolerance for others; sometimes wondering, almost with envy, at the high pressure of spirits involved in their misdeeds; and in any extremity inclined to help rather than to reprove. "I incline to Cain's heresy,"[2] he used to say quaintly: "I let my brother go to the devil in his own way." In this character, it was frequently his fortune to be the last reputable acquaintance and the last good influence in the lives of down-going men. And to such as these, so long as they came about his chambers, he never marked a shade of change in his demeanour.

No doubt the feat was easy to Mr. Utterson; for he was undemonstrative at the best, and even his friendship seemed to be founded in a similar catholicity[3] of good-nature. It is the mark of a modest man to accept his friendly circle ready-made from the hands of opportunity; and that was the lawyer's way. His friends were those of his own blood or those whom he had known the longest; his affections, like ivy, were the growth of time, they implied no aptness in the object. Hence, no doubt, the bond that united him to Mr. Richard Enfield, his distant kinsman, the well-known man about town. It was a nut to crack for many, what these two could see in each other, or what subject they could find in common. It was reported by those who encountered them in their Sunday walks, that they said nothing, looked singularly dull, and would hail with obvious relief the appearance of a friend. For

1. Proved.
2. Refusal of responsibility for one's fellow human beings. After Cain kills his brother, Abel, and God

asks where Abel is, Cain responds, "Am I my brother's keeper?" (Genesis 4.9).
3. Universality.

all that, the two men put the greatest store by these excursions, counted them the chief jewel of each week, and not only set aside occasions of pleasure, but even resisted the calls of business, that they might enjoy them uninterrupted.

It chanced on one of these rambles that their way led them down a by-street in a busy quarter of London. The street was small and what is called quiet, but it drove a thriving trade on the week-days. The inhabitants were all doing well, it seemed, and all emulously hoping to do better still, and laying out the surplus of their gains in coquetry;[4] so that the shop fronts stood along that thoroughfare with an air of invitation, like rows of smiling saleswomen. Even on Sunday, when it veiled its more florid charms and lay comparatively empty of passage, the street shone out in contrast to its dingy neighbourhood, like a fire in a forest; and with its freshly painted shutters, well-polished brasses, and general cleanliness and gaiety of note, instantly caught and pleased the eye of the passenger.[5]

Two doors from one corner, on the left hand going east, the line was broken by the entry of a court; and just at that point, a certain sinister block of building thrust forward its gable on the street. It was two storeys high; showed no window, nothing but a door on the lower storey and a blind forehead of discoloured wall on the upper; and bore in every feature, the marks of prolonged and sordid negligence. The door, which was equipped with neither bell nor knocker, was blistered and distained.[6] Tramps slouched into the recess and struck matches on the panels; children kept shop upon the steps; the schoolboy had tried his knife on the mouldings; and for close on a generation, no one had appeared to drive away these random visitors or to repair their ravages.

Mr. Enfield and the lawyer were on the other side of the by-street; but when they came abreast of the entry, the former lifted up his cane and pointed.

"Did you ever remark that door?" he asked; and when his companion had replied in the affirmative, "It is connected in my mind," added he, "with a very odd story."

"Indeed?" said Mr. Utterson, with a slight change of voice, "and what was that?"

"Well, it was this way," returned Mr. Enfield: "I was coming home from some place at the end of the world, about three o'clock of a black winter morning, and my way lay through a part of town where there was literally nothing to be seen but lamps. Street after street, and all the folks asleep—street after street, all lighted up as if for a procession and all as empty as a church—till at last I got into that state of mind when a man listens and listens and begins to long for the sight of a policeman. All at once, I saw two figures: one little man who was stumping along eastward at a good walk, and the other a girl of maybe eight or ten who was running as hard as she was able down a cross street. Well, sir, the two ran into one another naturally enough at the corner; and then came the horrible part of the thing; for the man trampled calmly over the child's body and left her screaming on the ground. It sounds nothing to hear, but it was hellish to see. It wasn't like a

4. Attractive display.
5. Passerby.
6. Discolored.

man; it was like some damned Juggernaut.[7] I gave a view halloa,[8] took to my heels, collared my gentleman, and brought him back to where there was already quite a group about the screaming child. He was perfectly cool and made no resistance, but gave me one look, so ugly that it brought out the sweat on me like running. The people who had turned out were the girl's own family; and pretty soon, the doctor, for whom she had been sent, put in his appearance. Well, the child was not much the worse, more frightened, according to the Sawbones;[9] and there you might have supposed would be an end to it. But there was one curious circumstance. I had taken a loathing to my gentleman at first sight. So had the child's family, which was only natural. But the doctor's case was what struck me. He was the usual cut and dry apothecary, of no particular age and colour, with a strong Edinburgh accent, and about as emotional as a bagpipe. Well, sir, he was like the rest of us; every time he looked at my prisoner, I saw that Sawbones turn sick and white with the desire to kill him. I knew what was in his mind, just as he knew what was in mine; and killing being out of the question, we did the next best. We told the man we could and would make such a scandal out of this, as should make his name stink from one end of London to the other. If he had any friends or any credit,[1] we undertook that he should lose them. And all the time, as we were pitching it in red hot, we were keeping the women off him as best we could, for they were as wild as harpies.[2] I never saw a circle of such hateful faces; and there was the man in the middle, with a kind of black, sneering coolness—frightened too, I could see that—but carrying it off, sir, really like Satan. 'If you choose to make capital out of this accident,' said he, 'I am naturally helpless. No gentleman but wishes to avoid a scene,' says he. 'Name your figure.' Well, we screwed him up to a hundred pounds for the child's family; he would have clearly liked to stick out; but there was something about the lot of us that meant mischief, and at last he struck.[3] The next thing was to get the money; and where do you think he carried us but to that place with the door?—whipped out a key, went in, and presently came back with the matter of ten pounds in gold and a cheque for the balance on Coutts's,[4] drawn payable to bearer and signed with a name that I can't mention, though it's one of the points of my story, but it was a name at least very well known and often printed. The figure was stiff; but the signature was good for more than that, if it was only genuine. I took the liberty of pointing out to my gentleman that the whole business looked apocryphal, and that a man does not, in real life, walk into a cellar door at four in the morning and come out of it with another man's cheque for close upon a hundred pounds. But he was quite easy and sneering. 'Set your mind at rest,' says he, 'I will stay with you till the banks open and cash the cheque myself.' So we all set off, the doctor, and the child's father, and our friend and myself, and passed the rest of the night in my chambers; and next day, when we had breakfasted, went in a body to the bank. I gave in the check

---

7. A relentless destructive force. From Jagannath, a Hindu deity considered a form of Vishnu or his avatar Krishna. Pilgrims travel to an annual festival to watch a huge statue of the god dragged on a cart through Puri, a city in the Indian state of Odisha; 19th-century reports, furnished by European travelers, of worshippers throwing themselves under the wheels to be crushed were most

likely apocryphal.
8. Shout.
9. Doctor (slang).
1. Good name.
2. In classical mythology monsters with women's faces and bodies and birds' wings and claws.
3. Gave in.
4. A prestigious London bank.

myself, and said I had every reason to believe it was a forgery. Not a bit of it. The cheque was genuine."

"Tut-tut," said Mr. Utterson.

"I see you feel as I do," said Mr. Enfield. "Yes, it's a bad story. For my man was a fellow that nobody could have to do with, a really damnable man; and the person that drew the cheque is the very pink of the proprieties, celebrated too, and (what makes it worse) one of your fellows who do what they call good. Black mail, I suppose; an honest man paying through the nose for some of the capers of his youth. Black Mail House is what I call that place with the door, in consequence. Though even that, you know, is far from explaining all," he added, and with the words fell into a vein of musing.

From this he was recalled by Mr. Utterson asking rather suddenly: "And you don't know if the drawer of the cheque lives there?"

"A likely place, isn't it?" returned Mr. Enfield. "But I happen to have noticed his address; he lives in some square or other."

"And you never asked about the—place with the door?" said Mr. Utterson.

"No, sir: I had a delicacy," was the reply. "I feel very strongly about putting questions; it partakes too much of the style of the day of judgment. You start a question, and it's like starting a stone. You sit quietly on the top of a hill; and away the stone goes, starting others; and presently some bland old bird (the last you would have thought of) is knocked on the head in his own back garden and the family have to change their name. No, sir, I make it a rule of mine: the more it looks like Queer Street,[5] the less I ask."

"A very good rule, too," said the lawyer.

"But I have studied the place for myself," continued Mr. Enfield. "It seems scarcely a house. There is no other door, and nobody goes in or out of that one but, once in a great while, the gentleman of my adventure. There are three windows looking on the court on the first floor;[6] none below; the windows are always shut but they're clean. And then there is a chimney which is generally smoking; so somebody must live there. And yet it's not so sure; for the buildings are so packed together about that court, that it's hard to say where one ends and another begins."

The pair walked on again for a while in silence; and then "Enfield," said Mr. Utterson, "that's a good rule of yours."

"Yes, I think it is," returned Enfield.

"But for all that," continued the lawyer, "there's one point I want to ask: I want to ask the name of that man who walked over the child."

"Well," said Mr. Enfield, "I can't see what harm it would do. It was a man of the name of Hyde."

"H'm," said Mr. Utterson. "What sort of a man is he to see?"

"He is not easy to describe. There is something wrong with his appearance; something displeasing, something downright detestable. I never saw a man I so disliked, and yet I scarce know why. He must be deformed somewhere; he gives a strong feeling of deformity, although I couldn't specify the point. He's an extraordinary looking man, and yet I really can name nothing out of the way. No, sir; I can make no hand of it; I can't describe him. And it's not want of memory; for I declare I can see him this moment."

---

5. I.e., looks like someone is in trouble or a bad fix (slang).

6. I.e., the first floor above the ground floor (what Americans call the second floor).

Mr. Utterson again walked some way in silence and obviously under a weight of consideration. "You are sure he used a key?" he inquired at last.

"My dear sir . . ." began Enfield, surprised out of himself.

"Yes, I know," said Utterson; "I know it must seem strange. The fact is, if I do not ask you the name of the other party, it is because I know it already. You see, Richard, your tale has gone home. If you have been inexact in any point, you had better correct it."

"I think you might have warned me," returned the other with a touch of sullenness. "But I have been pedantically exact, as you call it. The fellow had a key; and what's more, he has it still. I saw him use it, not a week ago."

Mr. Utterson sighed deeply but said never a word; and the young man presently resumed. "Here is another lesson to say nothing," said he. "I am ashamed of my long tongue. Let us make a bargain never to refer to this again."

"With all my heart," said the lawyer. "I shake hands on that, Richard."

Search for Mr. Hyde

That evening Mr. Utterson came home to his bachelor house in sombre spirits and sat down to dinner without relish. It was his custom of a Sunday, when this meal was over, to sit close by the fire, a volume of some dry divinity[7] on his reading desk, until the clock of the neighbouring church rang out the hour of twelve, when he would go soberly and gratefully to bed. On this night, however, as soon as the cloth was taken away, he took up a candle and went into his business room. There he opened his safe, took from the most private part of it a document endorsed on the envelope as Dr. Jekyll's Will, and sat down with a clouded brow to study its contents. The will was holograph,[8] for Mr. Utterson, though he took charge of it now that it was made, had refused to lend the least assistance in the making of it; it provided not only that, in case of the decease of Henry Jekyll, M.D., D.C.L., LL.D., F.R.S.,[9] etc., all his possessions were to pass into the hands of his "friend and benefactor Edward Hyde," but that in case of Dr. Jekyll's "disappearance or unexplained absence for any period exceeding three calendar months," the said Edward Hyde should step into the said Henry Jekyll's shoes without further delay and free from any burthen or obligation, beyond the payment of a few small sums to the members of the doctor's household. This document had long been the lawyer's eyesore. It offended him both as a lawyer and as a lover of the sane and customary sides of life, to whom the fanciful was the immodest. And hitherto it was his ignorance of Mr. Hyde that had swelled his indignation; now, by a sudden turn, it was his knowledge. It was already bad enough when the name was but a name of which he could learn no more. It was worse when it began to be clothed upon with detestable attributes; and out of the shifting, insubstantial mists that had so long baffled his eye, there leaped up the sudden, definite presentment[1] of a fiend.

"I thought it was madness," he said, as he replaced the obnoxious paper in the safe, "and now I begin to fear it is disgrace."

7. Theology.
8. In the author's handwriting.
9. Doctor of Medicine, Doctor of Civil Law, Doctor of Laws, and Fellow of the Royal Society, respectively.
1. Image.

With that he blew out his candle, put on a greatcoat, and set forth in the direction of Cavendish Square, that citadel of medicine,[2] where his friend, the great Dr. Lanyon, had his house and received his crowding patients. "If anyone knows, it will be Lanyon," he had thought.

The solemn butler knew and welcomed him; he was subjected to no stage of delay, but ushered direct from the door to the dining-room where Dr. Lanyon sat alone over his wine. This was a hearty, healthy, dapper, red-faced gentleman, with a shock of hair prematurely white, and a boisterous and decided manner. At sight of Mr. Utterson, he sprang up from his chair and welcomed him with both hands. The geniality, as was the way of the man, was somewhat theatrical to the eye; but it reposed on genuine feeling. For these two were old friends, old mates both at school and college, both thorough respecters of themselves and of each other, and, what does not always follow, men who thoroughly enjoyed each other's company.

After a little rambling talk, the lawyer led up to the subject which so disagreeably preoccupied his mind.

"I suppose, Lanyon," said he, "you and I must be the two oldest friends that Henry Jekyll has?"

"I wish the friends were younger," chuckled Dr. Lanyon. "But I suppose we are. And what of that? I see little of him now."

"Indeed?" said Utterson. "I thought you had a bond of common interest."

"We had," was the reply. "But it is more than ten years since Henry Jekyll became too fanciful for me. He began to go wrong, wrong in mind; and though of course I continue to take an interest in him for old sake's sake, as they say, I see and I have seen devilish little of the man. Such unscientific balderdash," added the doctor, flushing suddenly purple, "would have estranged Damon and Pythias."[3]

This little spirit of temper was somewhat of a relief to Mr. Utterson. "They have only differed on some point of science," he thought; and being a man of no scientific passions (except in the matter of conveyancing,[4]) he even added: "It is nothing worse than that!" He gave his friend a few seconds to recover his composure, and then approached the question he had come to put. "Did you ever come across a protégé of his—one Hyde?" he asked.

"Hyde?" repeated Lanyon. "No. Never heard of him. Since my time."

That was the amount of information that the lawyer carried back with him to the great, dark bed on which he tossed to and fro, until the small hours of the morning began to grow large. It was a night of little ease to his toiling mind, toiling in mere[5] darkness and besieged by questions.

Six o'clock struck on the bells of the church that was so conveniently near to Mr. Utterson's dwelling, and still he was digging at the problem. Hitherto it had touched him on the intellectual side alone; but now his imagination also was engaged, or rather enslaved; and as he lay and tossed in the gross darkness of the night and the curtained room, Mr. Enfield's tale went by before his mind in a scroll of lighted pictures. He would be aware of the great field of lamps of a nocturnal city; then of the figure of a man walking swiftly; then of a child running from the doctor's; and then these met, and

2. A once-aristocratic neighborhood where fashionable doctors had their offices. "Greatcoat": long, heavy overcoat.
3. Two inseparable youths in Greek legend whose willingness to die for each other symbolizes true friendship.
4. Legal transfer of property by writing deeds.
5. Pure.

that human Juggernaut trod the child down and passed on regardless of her screams. Or else he would see a room in a rich house, where his friend lay asleep, dreaming and smiling at his dreams; and then the door of that room would be opened, the curtains of the bed plucked apart, and the sleeper recalled,[6] and lo! there would stand by his side a figure to whom power was given, and even at that dead hour, he must rise and do its bidding. The figure in these two phases haunted the lawyer all night; and if at any time he dozed over, it was but to see it glide more stealthily through sleeping houses, or move the more swiftly and still the more swiftly, even to dizziness, through wider labyrinths of lamp-lighted city, and at every street corner crush a child and leave her screaming. And still the figure had no face by which he might know it; even in his dreams, it had no face, or one that baffled him and melted before his eyes; and thus it was that there sprang up and grew apace in the lawyer's mind a singularly strong, almost an inordinate, curiosity to behold the features of the real Mr. Hyde. If he could but once set eyes on him, he thought the mystery would lighten and perhaps roll altogether away, as was the habit of mysterious things when well examined. He might see a reason for his friend's strange preference or bondage (call it which you please) and even for the startling clause of the will. At least it would be a face worth seeing: the face of a man who was without bowels of mercy:[7] a face which had but to show itself to raise up, in the mind of the unimpressionable Enfield, a spirit of enduring hatred.

From that time forward, Mr. Utterson began to haunt the door in the bystreet of shops. In the morning before office hours, at noon when business was plenty, and time scarce, at night under the face of the fogged city moon, by all lights and at all hours of solitude or concourse, the lawyer was to be found on his chosen post.

"If he be Mr. Hyde," he had thought, "I shall be Mr. Seek."

And at last his patience was rewarded. It was a fine dry night; frost in the air; the streets as clean as a ballroom floor; the lamps, unshaken by any wind, drawing a regular pattern of light and shadow. By ten o'clock, when the shops were closed, the by-street was very solitary and, in spite of the low growl of London from all round, very silent. Small sounds carried far; domestic sounds out of the houses were clearly audible on either side of the roadway; and the rumour[8] of the approach of any passenger preceded him by a long time. Mr. Utterson had been some minutes at his post, when he was aware of an odd, light footstep drawing near. In the course of his nightly patrols, he had long grown accustomed to the quaint effect with which the footfalls of a single person, while he is still a great way off, suddenly spring out distinct from the vast hum and clatter of the city. Yet his attention had never before been so sharply and decisively arrested; and it was with a strong, superstitious prevision of success that he withdrew into the entry of the court.

The steps drew swiftly nearer, and swelled out suddenly louder as they turned the end of the street. The lawyer, looking forth from the entry, could soon see what manner of man he had to deal with. He was small and very plainly dressed, and the look of him, even at that distance, went somehow strongly against the watcher's inclination. But he made straight for the door,

6. Revived, awakened.   8. Noise.
7. Compassion.

crossing the roadway to save time; and as he came, he drew a key from his pocket like one approaching home.

Mr. Utterson stepped out and touched him on the shoulder as he passed. "Mr. Hyde, I think?"

Mr. Hyde shrank back with a hissing intake of the breath. But his fear was only momentary; and though he did not look the lawyer in the face, he answered coolly enough: "That is my name. What do you want?"

"I see you are going in," returned the lawyer. "I am an old friend of Dr. Jekyll's—Mr. Utterson of Gaunt Street—you must have heard my name; and meeting you so conveniently, I thought you might admit me."

"You will not find Dr. Jekyll; he is from home," replied Mr. Hyde, blowing in the key. And then suddenly, but still without looking up, "How did you know me?" he asked.

"On your side," said Mr. Utterson, "will you do me a favour?"

"With pleasure," replied the other. "What shall it be?"

"Will you let me see your face?" asked the lawyer.

Mr. Hyde appeared to hesitate, and then, as if upon some sudden reflection, fronted about with an air of defiance; and the pair stared at each other pretty fixedly for a few seconds. "Now I shall know you again," said Mr. Utterson. "It may be useful."

"Yes," returned Mr. Hyde, "it is as well we have met; and à propos, you should have my address." And he gave a number of a street in Soho.[9]

"Good God!" thought Mr. Utterson, "can he, too, have been thinking of the will?" But he kept his feelings to himself and only grunted in acknowledgment of the address.

"And now," said the other, "how did you know me?"

"By description," was the reply.

"Whose description?"

"We have common friends," said Mr. Utterson.

"Common friends?" echoed Mr. Hyde, a little hoarsely. "Who are they?"

"Jekyll, for instance," said the lawyer.

"He never told you," cried Mr. Hyde, with a flush of anger. "I did not think you would have lied."

"Come," said Mr. Utterson, "that is not fitting language."

The other snarled aloud into a savage laugh; and the next moment, with extraordinary quickness, he had unlocked the door and disappeared into the house.

The lawyer stood awhile when Mr. Hyde had left him, the picture of disquietude. Then he began slowly to mount the street, pausing every step or two and putting his hand to his brow like a man in mental perplexity. The problem he was thus debating as he walked, was one of a class that is rarely solved. Mr. Hyde was pale and dwarfish, he gave an impression of deformity without any nameable malformation, he had a displeasing smile, he had borne himself to the lawyer with a sort of murderous mixture of timidity and boldness, and he spoke with a husky, whispering and somewhat broken voice; all these were points against him, but not all of these together could explain the hitherto unknown disgust, loathing and fear with which Mr. Utterson regarded him. "There must be something else," said the perplexed gentleman.

---

9. Seedy district in central London. "À propos": by the way (French).

"There *is* something more, if I could find a name for it. God bless me, the man seems hardly human! Something troglodytic,[1] shall we say? or can it be the old story of Dr. Fell?[2] or is it the mere radiance of a foul soul that thus transpires through, and transfigures, its clay continent?[3] The last, I think; for, O my poor old Harry Jekyll, if ever I read Satan's signature upon a face, it is on that of your new friend."

Round the corner from the by-street, there was a square of ancient, handsome houses, now for the most part decayed from their high estate and let in flats and chambers to all sorts and conditions of men: map-engravers, architects, shady lawyers and the agents of obscure enterprises. One house, however, second from the corner, was still occupied entire; and at the door of this, which wore a great air of wealth and comfort, though it was now plunged in darkness except for the fanlight, Mr. Utterson stopped and knocked. A well-dressed, elderly servant opened the door.

"Is Dr. Jekyll at home, Poole?" asked the lawyer.

"I will see, Mr. Utterson," said Poole, admitting the visitor, as he spoke, into a large, low-roofed, comfortable hall, paved with flags,[4] warmed (after the fashion of a country house) by a bright, open fire, and furnished with costly cabinets of oak. "Will you wait here by the fire, sir? or shall I give you a light in the dining-room?"

"Here, thank you," said the lawyer, and he drew near and leaned on the tall fender.[5] This hall, in which he was now left alone, was a pet fancy of his friend the doctor's; and Utterson himself was wont to speak of it as the pleasantest room in London. But to-night there was a shudder in his blood; the face of Hyde sat heavy on his memory; he felt (what was rare with him) a nausea and distaste of life; and in the gloom of his spirits, he seemed to read a menace in the flickering of the firelight on the polished cabinets and the uneasy starting of the shadow on the roof. He was ashamed of his relief, when Poole presently returned to announce that Dr. Jekyll was gone out.

"I saw Mr. Hyde go in by the old dissecting-room door, Poole," he said. "Is that right, when Dr. Jekyll is from home?"

"Quite right, Mr. Utterson, sir," replied the servant. "Mr. Hyde has a key."

"Your master seems to repose a great deal of trust in that young man, Poole," resumed the other musingly.

"Yes, sir, he do indeed," said Poole. "We have all orders to obey him."

"I do not think I ever met Mr. Hyde?" asked Utterson.

"O, dear no, sir. He never *dines* here," replied the butler. "Indeed we see very little of him on this side of the house; he mostly comes and goes by the laboratory."

"Well, good-night, Poole."

"Good-night, Mr. Utterson."

And the lawyer set out homeward with a very heavy heart. "Poor Harry Jekyll," he thought, "my mind misgives me he is in deep waters! He was wild when he was young; a long while ago to be sure; but in the law of God, there is no statute of limitations. Ay, it must be that; the ghost of some old sin, the

---

1. Like a prehistoric cave dweller or apelike.
2. A figure from the nursery rhyme "I do not like thee Dr. Fell; / The reason why I cannot tell."
3. Container.
4. Flagstones, large stone slabs.
5. Metal frame in front of a fireplace.

cancer of some concealed disgrace: punishment coming, *pede claudo*,[6] years after memory has forgotten and self-love condoned the fault." And the lawyer, scared by the thought, brooded awhile on his own past, groping in all the corners of memory, lest by chance some Jack-in-the-Box of an old iniquity should leap to light there. His past was fairly blameless; few men could read the rolls of their life with less apprehension; yet he was humbled to the dust by the many ill things he had done, and raised up again into a sober and fearful gratitude by the many that he had come so near to doing, yet avoided. And then by a return on his former subject, he conceived a spark of hope. "This Master Hyde, if he were studied," thought he, "must have secrets of his own; black secrets, by the look of him; secrets compared to which poor Jekyll's worst would be like sunshine. Things cannot continue as they are. It turns me cold to think of this creature stealing like a thief to Harry's bedside; poor Harry, what a wakening! And the danger of it; for if this Hyde suspects the existence of the will, he may grow impatient to inherit. Ay, I must put my shoulder to the wheel—if Jekyll will but let me," he added, "if Jekyll will only let me." For once more he saw before his mind's eye, as clear as a transparency, the strange clauses of the will.

Dr. Jekyll Was Quite at Ease

A fortnight later, by excellent good fortune, the doctor gave one of his pleasant dinners to some five or six old cronies, all intelligent, reputable men and all judges of good wine; and Mr. Utterson so contrived that he remained behind after the others had departed. This was no new arrangement, but a thing that had befallen many scores of times. Where Utterson was liked, he was liked well. Hosts loved to detain the dry lawyer, when the light-hearted and the loose-tongued had already their foot on the threshold; they liked to sit awhile in his unobtrusive company, practising for solitude, sobering their minds in the man's rich silence after the expense and strain of gaiety. To this rule, Dr. Jekyll was no exception; and as he now sat on the opposite side of the fire—a large, well-made, smooth-faced man of fifty, with something of a slyish cast perhaps, but every mark of capacity and kindness—you could see by his looks that he cherished for Mr. Utterson a sincere and warm affection.

"I have been wanting to speak to you, Jekyll," began the latter. "You know that will of yours?"

A close observer might have gathered that the topic was distasteful; but the doctor carried it off gaily. "My poor Utterson," said he, "you are unfortunate in such a client. I never saw a man so distressed as you were by my will; unless it were that hide-bound pedant, Lanyon, at what he called my scientific heresies. O, I know he's a good fellow—you needn't frown—an excellent fellow, and I always mean to see more of him; but a hide-bound pedant for all that; an ignorant, blatant pedant. I was never more disappointed in any man than Lanyon."

"You know I never approved of it," pursued Utterson, ruthlessly disregarding the fresh topic.

"My will? Yes, certainly, I know that," said the doctor, a trifle sharply. "You have told me so."

6. With lame foot (Latin). From the Roman poet Horace's *Odes* 3.2.32: "Rarely has Vengeance with her lame foot abandoned the wicked man with a head start on her."

"Well, I tell you so again," continued the lawyer. "I have been learning something of young Hyde."

The large handsome face of Dr. Jekyll grew pale to the very lips, and there came a blackness about his eyes. "I do not care to hear more," said he. "This is a matter I thought we had agreed to drop."

"What I heard was abominable," said Utterson.

"It can make no change. You do not understand my position," returned the doctor, with a certain incoherency of manner. "I am painfully situated, Utterson; my position is a very strange—a very strange one. It is one of those affairs that cannot be mended by talking."

"Jekyll," said Utterson, "you know me: I am a man to be trusted. Make a clean breast of this in confidence; and I make no doubt I can get you out of it."

"My good Utterson," said the doctor, "this is very good of you, this is downright good of you, and I cannot find words to thank you in. I believe you fully; I would trust you before any man alive, ay, before myself, if I could make the choice; but indeed it isn't what you fancy; it is not so bad as that; and just to put your good heart at rest, I will tell you one thing: the moment I choose, I can be rid of Mr. Hyde. I give you my hand upon that; and I thank you again and again; and I will just add one little word, Utterson, that I'm sure you'll take in good part: this is a private matter, and I beg of you to let it sleep."

Utterson reflected a little, looking in the fire.

"I have no doubt you are perfectly right," he said at last, getting to his feet.

"Well, but since we have touched upon this business, and for the last time I hope," continued the doctor, "there is one point I should like you to understand. I have really a very great interest in poor Hyde. I know you have seen him; he told me so; and I fear he was rude. But I do sincerely take a great, a very great interest in that young man; and if I am taken away, Utterson, I wish you to promise me that you will bear with him and get his rights for him. I think you would, if you knew all; and it would be a weight off my mind if you would promise."

"I can't pretend that I shall ever like him," said the lawyer.

"I don't ask that," pleaded Jekyll, laying his hand upon the other's arm; "I only ask for justice; I only ask you to help him for my sake, when I am no longer here."

Utterson heaved an irrepressible sigh. "Well," said he, "I promise."

The Carew Murder Case

Nearly a year later, in the month of October, 18—, London was startled by a crime of singular ferocity and rendered all the more notable by the high position of the victim. The details were few and startling. A maid servant living alone in a house not far from the river, had gone upstairs to bed about eleven. Although a fog rolled over the city in the small hours, the early part of the night was cloudless, and the lane, which the maid's window overlooked, was brilliantly lit by the full moon. It seems she was romantically given, for she sat down upon her box,[7] which stood immediately under the window, and

7. Servants, and other members of the poorer classes, typically stored their few items of clothing in a wooden box.

fell into a dream of musing. Never (she used to say, with streaming tears, when she narrated that experience), never had she felt more at peace with all men or thought more kindly of the world. And as she so sat she became aware of an aged and beautiful gentleman with white hair, drawing near along the lane; and advancing to meet him, another and very small gentleman, to whom at first she paid less attention. When they had come within speech (which was just under the maid's eyes) the older man bowed and accosted the other with a very pretty manner of politeness. It did not seem as if the subject of his address were of great importance; indeed, from his pointing, it sometimes appeared as if he were only inquiring his way; but the moon shone on his face as he spoke, and the girl was pleased to watch it, it seemed to breathe such an innocent and old-world kindness of disposition, yet with something high too, as of a well-founded self-content. Presently her eye wandered to the other, and she was surprised to recognise in him a certain Mr. Hyde, who had once visited her master and for whom she had conceived a dislike. He had in his hand a heavy cane, with which he was trifling; but he answered never a word, and seemed to listen with an ill-contained impatience. And then all of a sudden he broke out in a great flame of anger, stamping with his foot, brandishing the cane, and carrying on (as the maid described it) like a madman. The old gentleman took a step back, with the air of one very much surprised and a trifle hurt; and at that Mr. Hyde broke out of all bounds and clubbed him to the earth. And next moment, with ape-like fury, he was trampling his victim under foot and hailing down a storm of blows, under which the bones were audibly shattered and the body jumped upon the roadway. At the horror of these sights and sounds, the maid fainted.

It was two o'clock when she came to herself and called for the police. The murderer was gone long ago; but there lay his victim in the middle of the lane, incredibly mangled. The stick with which the deed had been done, although it was of some rare and very tough and heavy wood, had broken in the middle under the stress of this insensate cruelty; and one splintered half had rolled in the neighbouring gutter—the other, without doubt, had been carried away by the murderer. A purse and a gold watch were found upon the victim; but no cards or papers, except a sealed and stamped envelope, which he had been probably carrying to the post,[8] and which bore the name and address of Mr. Utterson.

This was brought to the lawyer the next morning, before he was out of bed; and he had no sooner seen it and been told the circumstances, than he shot out a solemn lip. "I shall say nothing till I have seen the body," said he; "this may be very serious. Have the kindness to wait while I dress." And with the same grave countenance he hurried through his breakfast and drove to the police station, whither the body had been carried. As soon as he came into the cell, he nodded.

"Yes," said he, "I recognise him. I am sorry to say that this is Sir Danvers Carew."

"Good God, sir," exclaimed the officer, "is it possible?" And the next moment his eye lighted up with professional ambition. "This will make a deal of noise," he said. "And perhaps you can help us to the man." And he briefly narrated what the maid had seen, and showed the broken stick.

8. I.e., postal letter box.

Mr. Utterson had already quailed at the name of Hyde; but when the stick was laid before him, he could doubt no longer; broken and battered as it was, he recognised it for one that he had himself presented many years before to Henry Jekyll.

"Is this Mr. Hyde a person of small stature?" he inquired.

"Particularly small and particularly wicked-looking, is what the maid calls him," said the officer.

Mr. Utterson reflected; and then, raising his head, "If you will come with me in my cab," he said, "I think I can take you to his house."

It was by this time about nine in the morning, and the first fog of the season. A great chocolate-coloured pall lowered[9] over heaven, but the wind was continually charging and routing these embattled vapours; so that as the cab crawled from street to street, Mr. Utterson beheld a marvellous number of degrees and hues of twilight; for here it would be dark like the back-end of evening; and there would be a glow of a rich, lurid brown, like the light of some strange conflagration; and here, for a moment, the fog would be quite broken up, and a haggard shaft of daylight would glance in between the swirling wreaths. The dismal quarter of Soho seen under these changing glimpses, with its muddy ways, and slatternly passengers, and its lamps, which had never been extinguished or had been kindled afresh to combat this mournful reinvasion of darkness, seemed, in the lawyer's eyes, like a district of some city in a nightmare. The thoughts of his mind, besides, were of the gloomiest dye; and when he glanced at the companion of his drive, he was conscious of some touch of that terror of the law and the law's officers, which may at times assail the most honest.

As the cab drew up before the address indicated, the fog lifted a little and showed him a dingy street, a gin palace, a low French eating house, a shop for the retail of penny numbers[1] and twopenny salads, many ragged children huddled in the doorways, and many women of many different nationalities passing out, key in hand, to have a morning glass; and the next moment the fog settled down again upon that part, as brown as umber, and cut him off from his blackguardly surroundings. This was the home of Henry Jekyll's favourite; of a man who was heir to quarter of a million sterling.[2]

An ivory-faced and silvery-haired old woman opened the door. She had an evil face, smoothed by hypocrisy; but her manners were excellent. Yes, she said, this was Mr. Hyde's, but he was not at home; he had been in that night very late, but had gone away again in less than an hour; there was nothing strange in that; his habits were very irregular, and he was often absent; for instance, it was nearly two months since she had seen him till yesterday.

"Very well, then, we wish to see his rooms," said the lawyer; and when the woman began to declare it was impossible, "I had better tell you who this person is," he added. "This is Inspector Newcomen of Scotland Yard."

A flash of odious joy appeared upon the woman's face. "Ah!" said she, "he is in trouble! What has he done?"

Mr. Utterson and the inspector exchanged glances. "He don't seem a very popular character," observed the latter. "And now, my good woman, just let me and this gentleman have a look about us."

---

9. Was gloomy and threatening.
1. Cheap serial installments of popular fiction.

"Gin palace": cheap bar.
2. I.e., pounds sterling.

In the whole extent of the house, which but for the old woman remained otherwise empty, Mr. Hyde had only used a couple of rooms; but these were furnished with luxury and good taste. A closet was filled with wine; the plate was of silver, the napery[3] elegant; a good picture hung upon the walls, a gift (as Utterson supposed) from Henry Jekyll, who was much of a connoisseur; and the carpets were of many piles and agreeable in colour. At this moment, however, the rooms bore every mark of having been recently and hurriedly ransacked; clothes lay about the floor, with their pockets inside out; lock-fast drawers stood open; and on the hearth there lay a pile of gray ashes, as though many papers had been burned. From these embers the inspector disinterred the butt end of a green cheque book, which had resisted the action of the fire; the other half of the stick was found behind the door; and as this clinched his suspicions, the officer declared himself delighted. A visit to the bank, where several thousand pounds were found to be lying to the murderer's credit, completed his gratification.

"You may depend upon it, sir," he told Mr. Utterson: "I have him in my hand. He must have lost his head, or he never would have left the stick or, above all, burned the cheque book. Why, money's life to the man. We have nothing to do but wait for him at the bank, and get out the handbills."

This last, however, was not so easy of accomplishment; for Mr. Hyde had numbered few familiars—even the master of the servant maid had only seen him twice; his family could nowhere be traced; he had never been photographed; and the few who could describe him differed widely, as common observers will. Only on one point, were they agreed; and that was the haunting sense of unexpressed deformity with which the fugitive impressed his beholders.

Incident of the Letter

It was late in the afternoon, when Mr. Utterson found his way to Dr. Jekyll's door, where he was at once admitted by Poole, and carried down by the kitchen offices and across a yard which had once been a garden, to the building which was indifferently[4] known as the laboratory or the dissecting rooms. The doctor had bought the house from the heirs of a celebrated surgeon; and his own tastes being rather chemical than anatomical, had changed the destination[5] of the block at the bottom of the garden. It was the first time that the lawyer had been received in that part of his friend's quarters; and he eyed the dingy, windowless structure with curiosity, and gazed round with a distasteful sense of strangeness as he crossed the theatre,[6] once crowded with eager students and now lying gaunt and silent, the tables laden with chemical apparatus, the floor strewn with crates and littered with packing straw, and the light falling dimly through the foggy cupola. At the further end, a flight of stairs mounted to a door covered with red baize; and through this, Mr. Utterson was at last received into the doctor's cabinet.[7] It was a large room, fitted round with glass presses, furnished, among other things, with a

---

3. Table linen.
4. Without distinction.
5. Purpose.
6. Room with tiers of rising seats surrounding a

central platform, used for lectures and medical demonstrations.
7. Small private room. "Baize": coarse woolen material.

cheval-glass[8] and a business table, and looking out upon the court by three dusty windows barred with iron. A fire burned in the grate; a lamp was set lighted on the chimney shelf, for even in the houses the fog began to lie thickly; and there, close up to the warmth, sat Dr. Jekyll, looking deadly sick. He did not rise to meet his visitor, but held out a cold hand and bade him welcome in a changed voice.

"And now," said Mr. Utterson, as soon as Poole had left them, "you have heard the news?"

The doctor shuddered. "They were crying it in the square," he said. "I heard them in my dining-room."

"One word," said the lawyer. "Carew was my client, but so are you, and I want to know what I am doing. You have not been mad enough to hide this fellow?"

"Utterson, I swear to God," cried the doctor, "I swear to God I will never set eyes on him again. I bind my honour to you that I am done with him in this world. It is all at an end. And indeed he does not want my help; you do not know him as I do; he is safe, he is quite safe; mark my words, he will never more be heard of."

The lawyer listened gloomily; he did not like his friend's feverish manner. "You seem pretty sure of him," said he; "and for your sake, I hope you may be right. If it came to a trial, your name might appear."

"I am quite sure of him," replied Jekyll; "I have grounds for certainty that I cannot share with anyone. But there is one thing on which you may advise me. I have—I have received a letter; and I am at a loss whether I should show it to the police. I should like to leave it in your hands, Utterson; you would judge wisely, I am sure; I have so great a trust in you."

"You fear, I suppose, that it might lead to his detection?" asked the lawyer.

"No," said the other. "I cannot say that I care what becomes of Hyde; I am quite done with him. I was thinking of my own character, which this hateful business has rather exposed."

Utterson ruminated awhile; he was surprised at his friend's selfishness, and yet relieved by it. "Well," said he, at last, "let me see the letter."

The letter was written in an odd, upright hand and signed "Edward Hyde": and it signified, briefly enough, that the writer's benefactor, Dr. Jekyll, whom he had long so unworthily repaid for a thousand generosities, need labour under no alarm for his safety, as he had means of escape on which he placed a sure dependence. The lawyer liked this letter well enough; it put a better colour on the intimacy than he had looked for; and he blamed himself for some of his past suspicions.

"Have you the envelope?" he asked.

"I burned it," replied Jekyll, "before I thought what I was about. But it bore no postmark. The note was handed in."

"Shall I keep this and sleep upon it?" asked Utterson.

"I wish you to judge for me entirely," was the reply. "I have lost confidence in myself."

"Well, I shall consider," returned the lawyer. "And now one word more: it was Hyde who dictated the terms in your will about that disappearance?"

---

8. Large freestanding mirror, hinged on a frame. "Presses": cupboards with glass doors.

The doctor seemed seized with a qualm of faintness; he shut his mouth tight and nodded.

"I knew it," said Utterson. "He meant to murder you. You have had a fine escape."

"I have had what is far more to the purpose," returned the doctor solemnly: "I have had a lesson—O God, Utterson, what a lesson I have had!" And he covered his face for a moment with his hands.

On his way out, the lawyer stopped and had a word or two with Poole. "By the bye," said he, "there was a letter handed in to-day: what was the messenger like?" But Poole was positive nothing had come except by post; "and only circulars by that," he added.

This news sent off the visitor with his fears renewed. Plainly the letter had come by the laboratory door; possibly, indeed, it had been written in the cabinet; and if that were so, it must be differently judged, and handled with the more caution. The newsboys, as he went, were crying themselves hoarse along the footways: "Special edition. Shocking murder of an M.P."[9] That was the funeral oration of one friend and client; and he could not help a certain apprehension lest the good name of another should be sucked down in the eddy of the scandal. It was, at least, a ticklish decision that he had to make; and self-reliant as he was by habit, he began to cherish a longing for advice. It was not to be had directly; but perhaps, he thought, it might be fished for.

Presently after, he sat on one side of his own hearth, with Mr. Guest, his head clerk, upon the other, and midway between, at a nicely calculated distance from the fire, a bottle of a particular old wine that had long dwelt unsunned in the foundations of his house. The fog still slept on the wing above the drowned city, where the lamps glimmered like carbuncles;[1] and through the muffle and smother of these fallen clouds, the procession of the town's life was still rolling in through the great arteries with a sound as of a mighty wind. But the room was gay with firelight. In the bottle the acids were long ago resolved; the imperial dye[2] had softened with time, as the colour grows richer in stained windows; and the glow of hot autumn afternoons on hillside vineyards, was ready to be set free and to disperse the fogs of London. Insensibly the lawyer melted. There was no man from whom he kept fewer secrets than Mr. Guest; and he was not always sure that he kept as many as he meant. Guest had often been on business to the doctor's; he knew Poole; he could scarce have failed to hear of Mr. Hyde's familiarity about the house; he might draw conclusions: was it not as well, then, that he should see a letter which put that mystery to rights? and above all since Guest, being a great student and critic of handwriting, would consider the step natural and obliging? The clerk, besides, was a man of counsel; he would scarce read so strange a document without dropping a remark; and by that remark Mr. Utterson might shape his future course.

"This is a sad business about Sir Danvers," he said.

"Yes, sir, indeed. It has elicited a great deal of public feeling," returned Guest. "The man, of course, was mad."

9. Member of Parliament.
1. Precious fiery-red stones.

2. Purple.

"I should like to hear your views on that," replied Utterson. "I have a document here in his handwriting; it is between ourselves, for I scarce know what to do about it; it is an ugly business at the best. But there it is; quite in your way: a murderer's autograph."

Guest's eyes brightened, and he sat down at once and studied it with passion. "No, sir," he said: "not mad; but it is an odd hand."

"And by all accounts a very odd writer," added the lawyer.

Just then the servant entered with a note.

"Is that from Dr. Jekyll, sir?" inquired the clerk. "I thought I knew the writing. Anything private, Mr. Utterson?"

"Only an invitation to dinner. Why? Do you want to see it?"

"One moment. I thank you, sir;" and the clerk laid the two sheets of paper alongside and sedulously compared their contents. "Thank you, sir," he said at last, returning both; "it's a very interesting autograph."

There was a pause, during which Mr. Utterson struggled with himself. "Why did you compare them, Guest?" he inquired suddenly.

"Well, sir," returned the clerk, "there's a rather singular resemblance; the two hands are in many points identical: only differently sloped."

"Rather quaint,"[3] said Utterson.

"It is, as you say, rather quaint," returned Guest.

"I wouldn't speak of this note, you know," said the master.

"No, sir," said the clerk. "I understand."

But no sooner was Mr. Utterson alone that night than he locked the note into his safe, where it reposed from that time forward. "What!" he thought. "Henry Jekyll forge for a murderer!" And his blood ran cold in his veins.

Remarkable Incident of Dr. Lanyon

Time ran on; thousands of pounds were offered in reward, for the death of Sir Danvers was resented as a public injury; but Mr. Hyde had disappeared out of the ken of the police as though he had never existed. Much of his past was unearthed, indeed, and all disreputable: tales came out of the man's cruelty, at once so callous and violent; of his vile life, of his strange associates, of the hatred that seemed to have surrounded his career; but of his present whereabouts, not a whisper. From the time he had left the house in Soho on the morning of the murder, he was simply blotted out; and gradually, as time drew on, Mr. Utterson began to recover from the hotness of his alarm, and to grow more at quiet with himself. The death of Sir Danvers was, to his way of thinking, more than paid for by the disappearance of Mr. Hyde. Now that that evil influence had been withdrawn, a new life began for Dr. Jekyll. He came out of his seclusion, renewed relations with his friends, became once more their familiar guest and entertainer; and whilst he had always been known for charities, he was now no less distinguished for religion. He was busy, he was much in the open air, he did good; his face seemed to open and brighten, as if with an inward consciousness of service; and for more than two months, the doctor was at peace.

On the 8th of January Utterson had dined at the doctor's with a small party; Lanyon had been there; and the face of the host had looked from one

3. Odd, unusual.

to the other as in the old days when the trio were inseparable friends. On the 12th, and again on the 14th, the door was shut against the lawyer. "The doctor was confined to the house," Poole said, "and saw no one." On the 15th, he tried again, and was again refused; and having now been used for the last two months to see his friend almost daily, he found this return of solitude to weigh upon his spirits. The fifth night he had in Guest to dine with him; and the sixth he betook himself to Dr. Lanyon's.

There at least he was not denied admittance; but when he came in, he was shocked at the change which had taken place in the doctor's appearance. He had his death-warrant written legibly upon his face. The rosy man had grown pale; his flesh had fallen away; he was visibly balder and older; and yet it was not so much these tokens of a swift physical decay that arrested the lawyer's notice, as a look in the eye and quality of manner that seemed to testify to some deep-seated terror of the mind. It was unlikely that the doctor should fear death; and yet that was what Utterson was tempted to suspect. "Yes," he thought; "he is a doctor, he must know his own state and that his days are counted; and the knowledge is more than he can bear." And yet when Utterson remarked on his ill-looks, it was with an air of great firmness that Lanyon declared himself a doomed man.

"I have had a shock," he said, "and I shall never recover. It is a question of weeks. Well, life has been pleasant; I liked it; yes, sir, I used to like it. I sometimes think if we knew all, we should be more glad to get away."

"Jekyll is ill, too," observed Utterson. "Have you seen him?"

But Lanyon's face changed, and he held up a trembling hand. "I wish to see or hear no more of Dr. Jekyll," he said in a loud, unsteady voice. "I am quite done with that person; and I beg that you will spare me any allusion to one whom I regard as dead."

"Tut-tut," said Mr. Utterson; and then after a considerable pause, "Can't I do anything?" he inquired. "We are three very old friends, Lanyon; we shall not live to make others."

"Nothing can be done," returned Lanyon; "ask himself."

"He will not see me," said the lawyer.

"I am not surprised at that," was the reply. "Some day, Utterson, after I am dead, you may perhaps come to learn the right and wrong of this. I cannot tell you. And in the meantime, if you can sit and talk with me of other things, for God's sake, stay and do so; but if you cannot keep clear of this accursed topic, then, in God's name, go, for I cannot bear it."

As soon as he got home, Utterson sat down and wrote to Jekyll, complaining of his exclusion from the house, and asking the cause of this unhappy break with Lanyon; and the next day brought him a long answer, often very pathetically worded, and sometimes darkly mysterious in drift. The quarrel with Lanyon was incurable. "I do not blame our old friend," Jekyll wrote, "but I share his view that we must never meet. I mean from henceforth to lead a life of extreme seclusion; you must not be surprised, nor must you doubt my friendship, if my door is often shut even to you. You must suffer me to go my own dark way. I have brought on myself a punishment and a danger that I cannot name. If I am the chief of sinners, I am the chief of sufferers also. I could not think that this earth contained a place for sufferings and terrors so unmanning; and you can do but one thing, Utterson, to lighten this destiny, and that is to respect my silence." Utterson was amazed; the dark influence of Hyde had been withdrawn, the doctor had returned to his old tasks and amities; a week ago, the prospect had smiled with every promise of a cheerful and an honoured age; and now in a moment, friendship, and peace of mind, and the whole tenor of his life were wrecked. So great and unprepared a change pointed to madness; but in view of Lanyon's manner and words, there must lie for it some deeper ground.

A week afterwards Dr. Lanyon took to his bed, and in something less than a fortnight he was dead. The night after the funeral, at which he had been sadly affected, Utterson locked the door of his business room, and sitting there by the light of a melancholy candle, drew out and set before him an envelope addressed by the hand and sealed with the seal of his dead friend. "PRIVATE: for the hands of G. J. Utterson ALONE, and in case of his predecease *to be destroyed unread*," so it was emphatically superscribed; and the lawyer dreaded to behold the contents. "I have buried one friend today," he thought: "what if this should cost me another?" And then he condemned the fear as a disloyalty, and broke the seal. Within there was another enclosure, likewise sealed, and marked upon the cover as "not to be opened till the death or disappearance of Dr. Henry Jekyll." Utterson could not trust his eyes. Yes, it was disappearance; here again, as in the mad will which he had long ago restored to its author, here again were the idea of a disappearance and the name of Henry Jekyll bracketted. But in the will, that idea had sprung from the sinister suggestion of the man Hyde; it was set there with a purpose all too plain and horrible. Written by the hand of Lanyon, what should it mean? A great curiosity came on the trustee, to disregard the prohibition and dive at once to the bottom of these mysteries; but professional honour and faith to his dead friend were stringent obligations; and the packet slept in the inmost corner of his private safe.

It is one thing to mortify curiosity, another to conquer it; and it may be doubted if, from that day forth, Utterson desired the society of his surviving friend with the same eagerness. He thought of him kindly; but his thoughts were disquieted and fearful. He went to call indeed; but he was perhaps relieved to be denied admittance; perhaps, in his heart, he preferred to speak with Poole upon the doorstep and surrounded by the air and sounds of the open city, rather than to be admitted into that house of voluntary bondage, and to sit and speak with its inscrutable recluse. Poole had, indeed, no very pleasant news to communicate. The doctor, it appeared, now more than ever confined himself to the cabinet over the laboratory, where he would sometimes even sleep; he was out of spirits, he had grown very silent, he did not read; it seemed as if he had something on his mind. Utterson became so used to the unvarying character of these reports, that he fell off little by little in the frequency of his visits.

Incident at the Window

It chanced on Sunday, when Mr. Utterson was on his usual walk with Mr. Enfield, that their way lay once again through the by-street; and that when they came in front of the door, both stopped to gaze on it.

"Well," said Enfield, "that story's at an end at least. We shall never see more of Mr. Hyde."

"I hope not," said Utterson. "Did I ever tell you that I once saw him, and shared your feeling of repulsion?"

"It was impossible to do the one without the other," returned Enfield. "And by the way, what an ass you must have thought me, not to know that this was a back way to Dr. Jekyll's! It was partly your own fault that I found it out, even when I did."

"So you found it out, did you?" said Utterson. "But if that be so, we may step into the court and take a look at the windows. To tell you the truth, I am uneasy about poor Jekyll; and even outside, I feel as if the presence of a friend might do him good."

The court was very cool and a little damp, and full of premature twilight, although the sky, high up overhead, was still bright with sunset. The middle one of the three windows was half way open; and sitting close beside it, taking the air with an infinite sadness of mien, like some disconsolate prisoner, Utterson saw Dr. Jekyll.

"What! Jekyll!" he cried. "I trust you are better."

"I am very low, Utterson," replied the doctor, drearily, "very low. It will not last long, thank God."

"You stay too much indoors," said the lawyer. "You should be out, whipping up the circulation like Mr. Enfield and me. (This is my cousin—Mr. Enfield—Dr. Jekyll.) Come now; get your hat and take a quick turn with us."

"You are very good," sighed the other. "I should like to very much; but no, no, no, it is quite impossible; I dare not. But indeed, Utterson, I am very glad to see you; this is really a great pleasure; I would ask you and Mr. Enfield up, but the place is really not fit."

"Why then," said the lawyer, good-naturedly, "the best thing we can do is to stay down here and speak with you from where we are."

"That is just what I was about to venture to propose," returned the doctor with a smile. But the words were hardly uttered, before the smile was struck out of his face and succeeded by an expression of such abject terror and despair, as froze the very blood of the two gentlemen below. They saw it but for a glimpse, for the window was instantly thrust down; but that glimpse had been sufficient, and they turned and left the court without a word. In silence, too, they traversed the by-street; and it was not until they had come into a neighbouring thoroughfare, where even upon a Sunday there were still some stirrings of life, that Mr. Utterson at last turned and looked at his companion. They were both pale; and there was an answering horror in their eyes.

"God forgive us, God forgive us," said Mr. Utterson.

But Mr. Enfield only nodded his head very seriously, and walked on once more in silence.

The Last Night

Mr. Utterson was sitting by his fireside one evening after dinner, when he was surprised to receive a visit from Poole.

"Bless me, Poole, what brings you here?" he cried; and then taking a second look at him, "What ails you?" he added; "is the doctor ill?"

"Mr. Utterson," said the man, "there is something wrong."

"Take a seat, and here is a glass of wine for you," said the lawyer. "Now, take your time, and tell me plainly what you want."

"You know the doctor's ways, sir," replied Poole, "and how he shuts himself up. Well, he's shut up again in the cabinet; and I don't like it, sir—I wish I may die if I like it. Mr. Utterson, sir, I'm afraid."

"Now, my good man," said the lawyer, "be explicit. What are you afraid of?"

"I've been afraid for about a week," returned Poole, doggedly disregarding the question, "and I can bear it no more."

The man's appearance amply bore out his words; his manner was altered for the worse; and except for the moment when he had first announced his terror, he had not once looked the lawyer in the face. Even now, he sat with the glass of wine untasted on his knee, and his eyes directed to a corner of the floor. "I can bear it no more," he repeated.

"Come," said the lawyer, "I see you have some good reason, Poole; I see there is something seriously amiss. Try to tell me what it is."

"I think there's been foul play," said Poole, hoarsely.

"Foul play!" cried the lawyer, a good deal frightened and rather inclined to be irritated in consequence. "What foul play? What does the man mean?"

"I daren't say, sir," was the answer; "but will you come along with me and see for yourself?"

Mr. Utterson's only answer was to rise and get his hat and great coat; but he observed with wonder the greatness of the relief that appeared upon the butler's face, and perhaps with no less, that the wine was still untasted when he set it down to follow.

It was a wild, cold, seasonable night of March, with a pale moon, lying on her back as though the wind had tilted her, and a flying wrack of the most diaphanous and lawny[4] texture. The wind made talking difficult, and flecked the blood into the face. It seemed to have swept the streets unusually bare of passengers, besides; for Mr. Utterson thought he had never seen that part of London so deserted. He could have wished it otherwise; never in his life had he been conscious of so sharp a wish to see and touch his fellow-creatures; for struggle as he might, there was born in upon his mind a crushing anticipation of calamity. The square, when they got there, was all full of wind and dust, and the thin trees in the garden were lashing themselves along the railing. Poole, who had kept all the way a pace or two ahead, now pulled up in the middle of the pavement, and in spite of the biting weather, took off his hat and mopped his brow with a red pocket-handkerchief. But for all the hurry of his coming, these were not the dews of exertion that he wiped away, but the moisture of some strangling anguish; for his face was white and his voice, when he spoke, harsh and broken.

"Well, sir," he said, "here we are, and God grant there be nothing wrong."

"Amen, Poole," said the lawyer.

Thereupon the servant knocked in a very guarded manner; the door was opened on the chain; and a voice asked from within, "Is that you, Poole?"

"It's all right," said Poole. "Open the door."

The hall, when they entered it, was brightly lighted up; the fire was built high; and about the hearth the whole of the servants, men and women, stood huddled together like a flock of sheep. At the sight of Mr. Utterson, the housemaid broke into hysterical whimpering; and the cook, crying out "Bless God! it's Mr. Utterson," ran forward as if to take him in her arms.

---

4. Of fine linen. "Wrack": i.e., rack, a mass of high clouds driven by the wind.

"What, what? Are you all here?" said the lawyer peevishly. "Very irregular, very unseemly; your master would be far from pleased."

"They're all afraid," said Poole.

Blank silence followed, no one protesting; only the maid lifted up her voice and now wept loudly.

"Hold your tongue!" Poole said to her, with a ferocity of accent that testified to his own jangled nerves; and indeed, when the girl had so suddenly raised the note of her lamentation, they had all started and turned towards the inner door with faces of dreadful expectation. "And now," continued the butler, addressing the knife-boy, "reach me a candle, and we'll get this through hands[5] at once." And then he begged Mr. Utterson to follow him, and led the way to the back garden.

"Now, sir," said he, "you come as gently as you can. I want you to hear, and I don't want you to be heard. And see here, sir, if by any chance he was to ask you in, don't go."

Mr. Utterson's nerves, at this unlooked-for termination, gave a jerk that nearly threw him from his balance; but he recollected his courage and followed the butler into the laboratory building and through the surgical theatre, with its lumber[6] of crates and bottles, to the foot of the stair. Here Poole motioned him to stand on one side and listen; while he himself, setting down the candle and making a great and obvious call on his resolution, mounted the steps and knocked with a somewhat uncertain hand on the red baize of the cabinet door.

"Mr. Utterson, sir, asking to see you," he called; and even as he did so, once more violently signed to the lawyer to give ear.

A voice answered from within: "Tell him I cannot see anyone," it said complainingly.

"Thank you, sir," said Poole, with a note of something like triumph in his voice; and taking up his candle, he led Mr. Utterson back across the yard and into the great kitchen, where the fire was out and the beetles were leaping on the floor.

"Sir," he said, looking Mr. Utterson in the eyes, "was that my master's voice?"

"It seems much changed," replied the lawyer, very pale, but giving look for look.

"Changed? Well, yes, I think so," said the butler. "Have I been twenty years in this man's house, to be deceived about his voice? No, sir; master's made away with; he was made away with, eight days ago, when we heard him cry out upon the name of God; and *who's* in there instead of him, and *why* it stays there, is a thing that cries to Heaven, Mr. Utterson!"

"This is a very strange tale, Poole; this is rather a wild tale, my man," said Mr. Utterson, biting his finger. "Suppose it were as you suppose, supposing Dr. Jekyll to have been—well, murdered, what could induce the murderer to stay? That won't hold water; it doesn't commend itself to reason."

"Well, Mr. Utterson, you are a hard man to satisfy, but I'll do it yet," said Poole. "All this last week (you must know) him, or it, or whatever it is that lives in that cabinet, has been crying night and day for some sort of medicine and cannot get it to his mind. It was sometimes his way—the master's, that is—to write his orders on a sheet of paper and throw it on the stair. We've had

---

5. We'll deal with this.   6. Random accumulation of disused objects.

nothing else this week back; nothing but papers, and a closed door, and the very meals left there to be smuggled in when nobody was looking. Well, sir, every day, ay, and twice and thrice in the same day, there have been orders and complaints, and I have been sent flying to all the wholesale chemists in town. Every time I brought the stuff back, there would be another paper telling me to return it, because it was not pure, and another order to a different firm. This drug is wanted bitter bad, sir, whatever for."

"Have you any of these papers?" asked Mr. Utterson.

Poole felt in his pocket and handed out a crumpled note, which the lawyer, bending nearer to the candle, carefully examined. Its contents ran thus: "Dr. Jekyll presents his compliments to Messrs. Maw. He assures them that their last sample is impure and quite useless for his present purpose. In the year 18—, Dr. J. purchased a somewhat large quantity from Messrs. M. He now begs them to search with the most sedulous care, and should any of the same quality be left, to forward it to him at once. Expense is no consideration. The importance of this to Dr. J. can hardly be exaggerated." So far the letter had run composedly enough, but here with a sudden splutter of the pen, the writer's emotion had broken loose. "For God's sake," he had added, "find me some of the old."

"This is a strange note," said Mr. Utterson; and then sharply, "How do you come to have it open?"

"The man at Maw's was main angry, sir, and he threw it back to me like so much dirt," returned Poole.

"This is unquestionably the doctor's hand, do you know?" resumed the lawyer.

"I thought it looked like it," said the servant rather sulkily; and then, with another voice, "But what matters hand of write?" he said. "I've seen him!"

"Seen him?" repeated Mr. Utterson. "Well?"

"That's it!" said Poole. "It was this way. I came suddenly into the theatre from the garden. It seems he had slipped out to look for this drug or whatever it is; for the cabinet door was open, and there he was at the far end of the room digging among the crates. He looked up when I came in, gave a kind of cry, and whipped upstairs into the cabinet. It was but for one minute that I saw him, but the hair stood upon my head like quills. Sir, if that was my master, why had he a mask upon his face? If it was my master, why did he cry out like a rat, and run from me? I have served him long enough. And then . . ." The man paused and passed his hand over his face.

"These are all very strange circumstances," said Mr. Utterson, "but I think I begin to see daylight. Your master, Poole, is plainly seized with one of those maladies that both torture and deform the sufferer; hence, for aught I know, the alteration of his voice; hence the mask and the avoidance of his friends; hence his eagerness to find this drug, by means of which the poor soul retains some hope of ultimate recovery—God grant that he be not deceived! There is my explanation; it is sad enough, Poole, ay, and appalling to consider; but it is plain and natural, hangs well together, and delivers us from all exorbitant alarms."

"Sir," said the butler, turning to a sort of mottled pallor, "that thing was not my master, and there's the truth. My master"—here he looked round him and began to whisper—"is a tall, fine build of a man, and this was more of a dwarf." Utterson attempted to protest. "O, sir," cried Poole, "do you think

I do not know my master after twenty years? Do you think I do not know where his head comes to in the cabinet door, where I saw him every morning of my life? No, sir, that thing in the mask was never Dr. Jekyll—God knows what it was, but it was never Dr. Jekyll; and it is the belief of my heart that there was murder done."

"Poole," replied the lawyer, "if you say that, it will become my duty to make certain. Much as I desire to spare your master's feelings, much as I am puzzled by this note which seems to prove him to be still alive, I shall consider it my duty to break in that door."

"Ah, Mr. Utterson, that's talking!" cried the butler.

"And now comes the second question," resumed Utterson: "Who is going to do it?"

"Why, you and me," was the undaunted reply.

"That's very well said," returned the lawyer; "and whatever comes of it, I shall make it my business to see you are no loser."

"There is an axe in the theatre," continued Poole; "and you might take the kitchen poker for yourself."

The lawyer took that rude but weighty instrument into his hand, and balanced it. "Do you know, Poole," he said, looking up, "that you and I are about to place ourselves in a position of some peril?"

"You may say so, sir, indeed," returned the butler.

"It is well, then, that we should be frank," said the other. "We both think more than we have said; let us make a clean breast. This masked figure that you saw, did you recognise it?"

"Well, sir, it went so quick, and the creature was so doubled up, that I could hardly swear to that," was the answer. "But if you mean, was it Mr. Hyde?—why, yes, I think it was! You see, it was much of the same bigness; and it had the same quick, light way with it; and then who else could have got in by the laboratory door? You have not forgot, sir, that at the time of the murder he had still the key with him? But that's not all. I don't know, Mr. Utterson, if ever you met this Mr. Hyde?"

"Yes," said the lawyer, "I once spoke with him."

"Then you must know as well as the rest of us that there was something queer about that gentleman—something that gave a man a turn—I don't know rightly how to say it, sir, beyond this: that you felt it in your marrow kind of cold and thin."

"I own I felt something of what you describe," said Mr. Utterson.

"Quite so, sir," returned Poole. "Well, when that masked thing like a monkey jumped from among the chemicals and whipped into the cabinet, it went down my spine like ice. O, I know it's not evidence, Mr. Utterson; I'm book-learned enough for that; but a man has his feelings, and I give you my bible-word it was Mr. Hyde!"

"Ay, ay," said the lawyer. "My fears incline to the same point. Evil, I fear, founded—evil was sure to come—of that connection. Ay, truly, I believe you; I believe poor Harry is killed; and I believe his murderer (for what purpose, God alone can tell) is still lurking in his victim's room. Well, let our name be vengeance. Call Bradshaw."

The footman came at the summons, very white and nervous.

"Pull yourself together, Bradshaw," said the lawyer. "This suspense, I know, is telling upon all of you; but it is now our intention to make an end of it.

Poole, here, and I are going to force our way into the cabinet. If all is well, my shoulders are broad enough to bear the blame. Meanwhile, lest anything should really be amiss, or any malefactor seek to escape by the back, you and the boy must go round the corner with a pair of good sticks and take your post at the laboratory door. We give you ten minutes, to get to your stations."

As Bradshaw left, the lawyer looked at his watch. "And now, Poole, let us get to ours," he said; and taking the poker under his arm, led the way into the yard. The scud[7] had banked over the moon, and it was now quite dark. The wind, which only broke in puffs and draughts into that deep well of building, tossed the light of the candle to and fro about their steps, until they came into the shelter of the theatre, where they sat down silently to wait. London hummed solemnly all around; but nearer at hand, the stillness was only broken by the sounds of a footfall moving to and fro along the cabinet floor.

"So it will walk all day, sir," whispered Poole; "ay, and the better part of the night. Only when a new sample comes from the chemist, there's a bit of a break. Ah, it's an ill-conscience that's such an enemy to rest! Ah, sir, there's blood foully shed in every step of it! But hark again, a little closer—put your heart in your ears, Mr. Utterson, and tell me, is that the doctor's foot?"

The steps fell lightly and oddly, with a certain swing, for all they went so slowly; it was different indeed from the heavy creaking tread of Henry Jekyll. Utterson sighed. "Is there never anything else?" he asked.

Poole nodded. "Once," he said. "Once I heard it weeping!"

"Weeping? how that?" said the lawyer, conscious of a sudden chill of horror.

"Weeping like a woman or a lost soul," said the butler. "I came away with that upon my heart, that I could have wept too."

But now the ten minutes drew to an end. Poole disinterred the axe from under a stack of packing straw; the candle was set upon the nearest table to light them to the attack; and they drew near with bated breath to where that patient foot was still going up and down, up and down, in the quiet of the night.

"Jekyll," cried Utterson, with a loud voice, "I demand to see you." He paused a moment, but there came no reply. "I give you fair warning, our suspicions are aroused, and I must and shall see you," he resumed; "if not by fair means, then by foul—if not of your consent, then by brute force!"

"Utterson," said the voice, "for God's sake, have mercy!"

"Ah, that's not Jekyll's voice—it's Hyde's!" cried Utterson. "Down with the door, Poole!"

Poole swung the axe over his shoulder; the blow shook the building, and the red baize door leaped against the lock and hinges. A dismal screech, as of mere animal terror, rang from the cabinet. Up went the axe again, and again the panels crashed and the frame bounded; four times the blow fell; but the wood was tough and the fittings were of excellent workmanship; and it was not until the fifth, that the lock burst in sunder and the wreck of the door fell inwards on the carpet.

The besiegers, appalled by their own riot and the stillness that had succeeded, stood back a little and peered in. There lay the cabinet before their eyes in the quiet lamplight, a good fire glowing and chattering on the hearth, the kettle singing its thin strain, a drawer or two open, papers neatly set

7. Loose clouds driven rapidly before the wind.

forth on the business table, and nearer the fire, the things laid out for tea: the quietest room, you would have said, and, but for the glazed presses full of chemicals, the most commonplace that night in London.

Right in the midst there lay the body of a man sorely contorted and still twitching. They drew near on tip-toe, turned it on its back and beheld the face of Edward Hyde. He was dressed in clothes far too large for him, clothes of the doctor's bigness; the cords of his face still moved with a semblance of life, but life was quite gone: and by the crushed phial in the hand and the strong smell of kernels[8] that hung upon the air, Utterson knew that he was looking on the body of a self-destroyer.

"We have come too late," he said sternly, "whether to save or punish. Hyde is gone to his account; and it only remains for us to find the body of your master."

The far greater proportion of the building was occupied by the theatre, which filled almost the whole ground story and was lighted from above, and by the cabinet, which formed an upper story at one end and looked upon the court. A corridor joined the theatre to the door on the by-street; and with this the cabinet communicated separately by a second flight of stairs. There were besides a few dark closets and a spacious cellar. All these they now thoroughly examined. Each closet needed but a glance, for all were empty, and all, by the dust that fell from their doors, had stood long unopened. The cellar, indeed, was filled with crazy lumber,[9] mostly dating from the times of the surgeon who was Jekyll's predecessor; but even as they opened the door they were advertised of the uselessness of further search, by the fall of a perfect mat of cobweb which had for years sealed up the entrance. Nowhere was there any trace of Henry Jekyll, dead or alive.

Poole stamped on the flags of the corridor. "He must be buried here," he said, hearkening to the sound.

"Or he may have fled," said Utterson, and he turned to examine the door in the by-street. It was locked; and lying near by on the flags, they found the key, already stained with rust.

"This does not look like use," observed the lawyer.

"Use!" echoed Poole. "Do you not see, sir, it is broken? much as if a man had stamped on it."

"Ay," continued Utterson, "and the fractures, too, are rusty." The two men looked at each other with a scare. "This is beyond me, Poole," said the lawyer. "Let us go back to the cabinet."

They mounted the stair in silence, and still with an occasional awestruck glance at the dead body, proceeded more thoroughly to examine the contents of the cabinet. At one table, there were traces of chemical work, various measured heaps of some white salt being laid on glass saucers, as though for an experiment in which the unhappy man had been prevented.

"That is the same drug that I was always bringing him," said Poole; and even as he spoke, the kettle with a startling noise boiled over.

This brought them to the fireside, where the easy-chair was drawn cosily up, and the tea things stood ready to the sitter's elbow, the very sugar in the cup. There were several books on a shelf; one lay beside the tea things open,

8. I.e., pits: cyanide smells of bitter almond or of peach pits.   9. See p. 788, n. 6.

and Utterson was amazed to find it a copy of a pious work, for which Jekyll had several times expressed a great esteem, annotated, in his own hand, with startling blasphemies.

Next, in the course of their review of the chamber, the searchers came to the cheval glass, into whose depths they looked with an involuntary horror. But it was so turned as to show them nothing but the rosy glow playing on the roof, the fire sparkling in a hundred repetitions along the glazed front of the presses, and their own pale and fearful countenances stooping to look in.

"This glass have seen some strange things, sir," whispered Poole.

"And surely none stranger than itself," echoed the lawyer in the same tones. "For what did Jekyll"—he caught himself up at the word with a start, and then conquering the weakness—"what could Jekyll want with it?" he said.

"You may say that!" said Poole.

Next they turned to the business table. On the desk, among the neat array of papers, a large envelope was uppermost, and bore, in the doctor's hand, the name of Mr. Utterson. The lawyer unsealed it, and several enclosures fell to the floor. The first was a will, drawn in the same eccentric terms as the one which he had returned six months before, to serve as a testament in case of death and as a deed of gift in case of disappearance; but in place of the name of Edward Hyde, the lawyer, with indescribable amazement, read the name of Gabriel John Utterson. He looked at Poole, and then back at the paper, and last of all at the dead malefactor stretched upon the carpet.

"My head goes round," he said. "He has been all these days in possession; he had no cause to like me; he must have raged to see himself displaced; and he has not destroyed this document."

He caught up the next paper; it was a brief note in the doctor's hand and dated at the top. "O Poole!" the lawyer cried, "he was alive and here this day. He cannot have been disposed of in so short a space; he must be still alive, he must have fled! And then, why fled? and how? and in that case, can we venture to declare this suicide? O, we must be careful. I foresee that we may yet involve your master in some dire catastrophe."

"Why don't you read it, sir?" asked Poole.

"Because I fear," replied the lawyer solemnly. "God grant I have no cause for it!" And with that he brought the paper to his eyes and read as follows:

"My DEAR UTTERSON,—When this shall fall into your hands, I shall have disappeared, under what circumstances I have not the penetration to foresee, but my instinct and all the circumstances of my nameless situation tell me that the end is sure and must be early. Go then, and first read the narrative which Lanyon warned me he was to place in your hands; and if you care to hear more, turn to the confession of

"Your unworthy and unhappy friend,
"HENRY JEKYLL."

"There was a third enclosure?" asked Utterson.

"Here, sir," said Poole, and gave into his hands a considerable packet sealed in several places.

The lawyer put it in his pocket. "I would say nothing of this paper. If your master has fled or is dead, we may at least save his credit. It is now ten; I must go home and read these documents in quiet; but I shall be back before midnight, when we shall send for the police."

They went out, locking the door of the theatre behind them; and Utterson, once more leaving the servants gathered about the fire in the hall, trudged back to his office to read the two narratives in which this mystery was now to be explained.

Dr. Lanyon's Narrative

On the ninth of January, now four days ago, I received by the evening delivery a registered envelope, addressed in the hand of my colleague and old school-companion, Henry Jekyll. I was a good deal surprised by this; for we were by no means in the habit of correspondence; I had seen the man, dined with him, indeed, the night before; and I could imagine nothing in our intercourse that should justify formality of registration. The contents increased my wonder; for this is how the letter ran:

"10th December,[1] 18—

"DEAR LANYON,—You are one of my oldest friends; and although we may have differed at times on scientific questions, I cannot remember, at least on my side, any break in our affection. There was never a day when, if you had said to me, 'Jekyll, my life, my honour, my reason, depend upon you,' I would not have sacrificed my left hand to help you. Lanyon, my life, my honour, my reason, are all at your mercy; if you fail me tonight I am lost. You might suppose, after this preface, that I am going to ask you for something dishonourable to grant. Judge for yourself.

"I want you to postpone all other engagements for to-night—ay, even if you were summoned to the bedside of an emperor; to take a cab, unless your carriage should be actually at the door; and with this letter in your hand for consultation, to drive straight to my house. Poole, my butler, has his orders; you will find him waiting your arrival with a locksmith. The door of my cabinet is then to be forced: and you are to go in alone; to open the glazed press (letter E) on the left hand, breaking the lock if it be shut; and to draw out, *with all its contents as they stand*, the fourth drawer from the top or (which is the same thing) the third from the bottom. In my extreme distress of mind, I have a morbid fear of misdirecting you; but even if I am in error, you may know the right drawer by its contents: some powders, a phial and a paper book. This drawer I beg of you to carry back with you to Cavendish Square exactly as it stands.

"That is the first part of the service: now for the second. You should be back, if you set out at once on the receipt of this, long before midnight; but I will leave you that amount of margin, not only in the fear of one of those obstacles that can neither be prevented nor foreseen, but

---

1. Stevenson's own error; the first sentence of *Dr. Lanyon's Narrative* makes it clear that the letter should be dated "9th January." Literary critic Richard Dury attributes the slip to the following circumstances: Stevenson had originally wanted to publish his story in time for the Christmas market and align Lanyon's witnessing of Hyde's transformation with December, a time for mysterious events. Later he forgot to change this detail.

because an hour when your servants are in bed is to be preferred for what will then remain to do. At midnight, then, I have to ask you to be alone in your consulting room, to admit with your own hand into the house a man who will present himself in my name, and to place in his hands the drawer that you will have brought with you from my cabinet. Then you will have played your part and earned my gratitude completely. Five minutes afterwards, if you insist upon an explanation, you will have understood that these arrangements are of capital importance; and that by the neglect of one of them, fantastic as they must appear, you might have charged your conscience with my death or the shipwreck of my reason.

"Confident as I am that you will not trifle with this appeal, my heart sinks and my hand trembles at the bare thought of such a possibility. Think of me at this hour, in a strange place, labouring under a blackness of distress that no fancy can exaggerate, and yet well aware that, if you will but punctually serve me, my troubles will roll away like a story that is told. Serve me, my dear Lanyon, and save

"Your friend,
H. J."

"P. S.—I had already sealed this up when a fresh terror struck upon my soul. It is possible that the post-office may fail me, and this letter not come into your hands until to-morrow morning. In that case, dear Lanyon, do my errand when it shall be most convenient for you in the course of the day; and once more expect my messenger at midnight. It may then already be too late; and if that night passes without event, you will know that you have seen the last of Henry Jekyll."

Upon the reading of this letter, I made sure my colleague was insane; but till that was proved beyond the possibility of doubt, I felt bound to do as he requested. The less I understood of this farrago[2] the less I was in a position to judge of its importance; and an appeal so worded could not be set aside without a grave responsibility. I rose accordingly from table, got into a hansom, and drove straight to Jekyll's house. The butler was awaiting my arrival; he had received by the same post as mine a registered letter of instruction, and had sent at once for a locksmith and a carpenter. The tradesmen came while we were yet speaking; and we moved in a body to old Dr. Denman's surgical theatre, from which (as you are doubtless aware) Jekyll's private cabinet is most conveniently entered. The door was very strong, the lock excellent; the carpenter avowed he would have great trouble and have to do much damage, if force were to be used; and the locksmith was near despair. But this last was a handy fellow, and after two hours' work, the door stood open. The press marked E was unlocked; and I took out the drawer, had it filled up with straw and tied in a sheet, and returned with it to Cavendish Square.

Here I proceeded to examine its contents. The powders were neatly enough made up, but not with the nicety of the dispensing chemist; so that it was plain they were of Jekyll's private manufacture: and when I opened one of the wrappers I found what seemed to me a simple crystalline salt of a white

2. Mixture.

colour. The phial, to which I next turned my attention, might have been about half full of a blood-red liquor, which was highly pungent to the sense of smell and seemed to me to contain phosphorus and some volatile ether. At the other ingredients I could make no guess. The book was an ordinary version book[3] and contained little but a series of dates. These covered a period of many years, but I observed that the entries ceased nearly a year ago and quite abruptly. Here and there a brief remark was appended to a date, usually no more than a single word: "double" occurring perhaps six times in a total of several hundred entries; and once very early in the list and followed by several marks of exclamation, "total failure!!!" All this, though it whetted my curiosity, told me little that was definite. Here were a phial of some tincture, a paper of some salt, and the record of a series of experiments that had led (like too many of Jekyll's investigations) to no end of practical usefulness. How could the presence of these articles in my house affect either the honour, the sanity, or the life of my flighty colleague? If his messenger could go to one place, why could he not go to another? And even granting some impediment, why was this gentleman to be received by me in secret? The more I reflected the more convinced I grew that I was dealing with a case of cerebral disease; and though I dismissed my servants to bed, I loaded an old revolver, that I might be found in some posture of self-defence.

Twelve o'clock had scarce rung out over London, ere the knocker sounded very gently on the door. I went myself at the summons, and found a small man crouching against the pillars of the portico.

"Are you come from Dr. Jekyll?" I asked.

He told me "yes" by a constrained gesture; and when I had bidden him enter, he did not obey me without a searching backward glance into the darkness of the square. There was a policeman not far off, advancing with his bull's eye[4] open; and at the sight, I thought my visitor started and made greater haste.

These particulars struck me, I confess, disagreeably; and as I followed him into the bright light of the consulting room, I kept my hand ready on my weapon. Here, at last, I had a chance of clearly seeing him. I had never set eyes on him before, so much was certain. He was small, as I have said; I was struck besides with the shocking expression of his face, with his remarkable combination of great muscular activity and great apparent debility of constitution, and—last but not least—with the odd, subjective disturbance caused by his neighbourhood. This bore some resemblance to incipient rigour,[5] and was accompanied by a marked sinking of the pulse. At the time, I set it down to some idiosyncratic, personal distaste, and merely wondered at the acuteness of the symptoms; but I have since had reason to believe the cause to lie much deeper in the nature of man, and to turn on some nobler hinge than the principle of hatred.

This person (who had thus, from the first moment of his entrance, struck in me what I can only describe as a disgustful curiosity) was dressed in a fashion that would have made an ordinary person laughable; his clothes, that is to say, although they were of rich and sober fabric, were enormously too large for him in every measurement—the trousers hanging on his legs and rolled up to keep them from the ground, the waist of the coat below his haunches, and the collar sprawling wide upon his shoulders. Strange to relate, this ludicrous accoutrement was far from moving me to laughter. Rather, as there was something abnormal and misbegotten in the very essence of the creature that now faced me—something seizing,[6] surprising and revolting—this fresh disparity seemed but to fit in with and to reinforce it; so that to my interest in the man's nature and character, there was added a curiosity as to his origin, his life, his fortune and status in the world.

These observations, though they have taken so great a space to be set down in, were yet the work of a few seconds. My visitor was, indeed, on fire with sombre excitement.

"Have you got it?" he cried. "Have you got it?" And so lively was his impatience that he even laid his hand upon my arm and sought to shake me.

I put him back, conscious at his touch of a certain icy pang along my blood. "Come, sir," said I. "You forget that I have not yet the pleasure of your acquaintance. Be seated, if you please." And I showed him an example, and sat down myself in my customary seat and with as fair an imitation of my ordinary manner to a patient, as the lateness of the hour, the nature of my preoccupations, and the horror I had of my visitor, would suffer me to muster.

"I beg your pardon, Dr. Lanyon," he replied civilly enough. "What you say is very well founded; and my impatience has shown its heels to my politeness. I come here at the instance[7] of your colleague, Dr. Henry Jekyll, on a piece of business of some moment; and I understood . . ." He paused and put his hand to his throat, and I could see, in spite of his collected manner, that he was wrestling against the approaches of the hysteria—"I understood, a drawer . . ."

But here I took pity on my visitor's suspense, and some perhaps on my own growing curiosity.

"There it is, sir," said I, pointing to the drawer, where it lay on the floor behind a table and still covered with the sheet.

He sprang to it, and then paused, and laid his hand upon his heart: I could hear his teeth grate with the convulsive action of his jaws; and his face was so ghastly to see that I grew alarmed both for his life and reason.

"Compose yourself," said I.

He turned a dreadful smile to me, and as if with the decision of despair, plucked away the sheet. At sight of the contents, he uttered one loud sob of such immense relief that I sat petrified. And the next moment, in a voice that was already fairly well under control, "Have you a graduated[8] glass?" he asked.

I rose from my place with something of an effort and gave him what he asked.

He thanked me with a smiling nod, measured out a few minims[9] of the red tincture and added one of the powders. The mixture, which was at first of a reddish hue, began, in proportion as the crystals melted, to brighten in colour, to effervesce audibly, and to throw off small fumes of vapour.

6. Powerfully impressive.
7. Request.
8. Marked with lines to indicate quantities.

9. Drops (a minim is a liquid measure equal to 1/480th of an ounce).

Suddenly and at the same moment, the ebullition[1] ceased and the compound changed to a dark purple, which faded again more slowly to a watery green. My visitor, who had watched these metamorphoses with a keen eye, smiled, set down the glass upon the table, and then turned and looked upon me with an air of scrutiny.

"And now," said he, "to settle what remains. Will you be wise? will you be guided? will you suffer me to take this glass in my hand and to go forth from your house without further parley? or has the greed of curiosity too much command of you? Think before you answer, for it shall be done as you decide. As you decide, you shall be left as you were before, and neither richer nor wiser, unless the sense of service rendered to a man in mortal distress may be counted as a kind of riches of the soul. Or, if you shall so prefer to choose, a new province of knowledge and new avenues to fame and power shall be laid open to you, here, in this room, upon the instant; and your sight shall be blasted by a prodigy to stagger the unbelief of Satan."

"Sir," said I, affecting a coolness that I was far from truly possessing, "you speak enigmas, and you will perhaps not wonder that I hear you with no very strong impression of belief. But I have gone too far in the way of inexplicable services to pause before I see the end."

"It is well," replied my visitor. "Lanyon, you remember your vows: what follows is under the seal of our profession. And now, you who have so long been bound to the most narrow and material views, you who have denied the virtue of transcendental medicine, you who have derided your superiors—behold!"

He put the glass to his lips and drank at one gulp. A cry followed; he reeled, staggered, clutched at the table and held on, staring with injected[2] eyes, gasping with open mouth; and as I looked there came, I thought, a change—he seemed to swell—his face became suddenly black and the features seemed to melt and alter—and the next moment, I had sprung to my feet and leaped back against the wall, my arm raised to shield me from that prodigy, my mind submerged in terror.

"O God!" I screamed, and "O God!" again and again; for there before my eyes—pale and shaken, and half fainting, and groping before him with his hands, like a man restored from death—there stood Henry Jekyll!

What he told me in the next hour, I cannot bring my mind to set on paper. I saw what I saw, I heard what I heard, and my soul sickened at it; and yet now when that sight has faded from my eyes, I ask myself if I believe it, and I cannot answer. My life is shaken to its roots; sleep has left me; the deadliest terror sits by me at all hours of the day and night; I feel that my days are numbered, and that I must die; and yet I shall die incredulous. As for the moral turpitude that man unveiled to me, even with tears of penitence, I cannot, even in memory, dwell on it without a start of horror. I will say but one thing, Utterson, and that (if you can bring your mind to credit it) will be more than enough. The creature who crept into my house that night was, on Jekyll's own confession, known by the name of Hyde and hunted for in every corner of the land as the murderer of Carew.

HASTIE LANYON.

---

1. Bubbling.   2. Swollen.

Henry Jekyll's Full Statement of the Case

I was born in the year 18— to a large fortune, endowed besides with excellent parts,[3] inclined by nature to industry, fond of the respect of the wise and good among my fellow-men, and thus, as might have been supposed, with every guarantee of an honourable and distinguished future. And indeed the worst of my faults was a certain impatient gaiety of disposition, such as has made the happiness of many, but such as I found it hard to reconcile with my imperious desire to carry my head high, and wear a more than commonly grave countenance before the public. Hence it came about that I concealed my pleasures; and that when I reached years of reflection, and began to look round me and take stock of my progress and position in the world, I stood already committed to a profound duplicity of life. Many a man would have even blazoned such irregularities as I was guilty of; but from the high views that I had set before me, I regarded and hid them with an almost morbid sense of shame. It was thus rather the exacting nature of my aspirations than any particular degradation in my faults, that made me what I was, and, with even a deeper trench than in the majority of men, severed in me those provinces of good and ill which divide and compound man's dual nature. In this case, I was driven to reflect deeply and inveterately on that hard law of life, which lies at the root of religion and is one of the most plentiful springs of distress. Though so profound a double-dealer, I was in no sense a hypocrite; both sides of me were in dead earnest; I was no more myself when I laid aside restraint and plunged in shame, than when I laboured, in the eye of day, at the furtherance of knowledge or the relief of sorrow and suffering. And it chanced that the direction of my scientific studies, which led wholly towards the mystic and the transcendental, reacted and shed a strong light on this consciousness of the perennial war among my members. With every day, and from both sides of my intelligence, the moral and the intellectual, I thus drew steadily nearer to that truth, by whose partial discovery I have been doomed to such a dreadful shipwreck: that man is not truly one, but truly two. I say two, because the state of my own knowledge does not pass beyond that point. Others will follow, others will outstrip me on the same lines; and I hazard the guess that man will be ultimately known for a mere polity of multifarious, incongruous and independent denizens. I for my part, from the nature of my life, advanced infallibly in one direction and in one direction only. It was on the moral side, and in my own person, that I learned to recognise the thorough and primitive duality of man; I saw that, of the two natures that contended in the field of my consciousness, even if I could rightly be said to be either, it was only because I was radically both; and from an early date, even before the course of my scientific discoveries had begun to suggest the most naked possibility of such a miracle, I had learned to dwell with pleasure, as a beloved day-dream, on the thought of the separation of these elements. If each, I told myself, could but be housed in separate identities, life would be relieved of all that was unbearable; the unjust might go his way, delivered from the aspirations and remorse of his more upright twin; and the just could walk steadfastly and securely on his upward path, doing the good things in which he found his pleasure, and

3. Abilities.

no longer exposed to disgrace and penitence by the hands of this extraneous evil. It was the curse of mankind that these incongruous faggots[4] were thus bound together—that in the agonised womb of consciousness, these polar twins should be continuously struggling. How, then, were they dissociated?

I was so far in my reflections when, as I have said, a side light began to shine upon the subject from the laboratory table. I began to perceive more deeply than it has ever yet been stated, the trembling immateriality, the mist-like transience, of this seemingly so solid body in which we walk attired. Certain agents I found to have the power to shake and to pluck back that fleshly vestment, even as a wind might toss the curtains of a pavilion. For two good reasons, I will not enter deeply into this scientific branch of my confession. First, because I have been made to learn that the doom and burthen of our life is bound forever on man's shoulders, and when the attempt is made to cast it off, it but returns upon us with more unfamiliar and more awful pressure. Second, because, as my narrative will make, alas! too evident, my discoveries were incomplete. Enough, then, that I not only recognised my natural body for the mere aura and effulgence of certain of the powers that made up my spirit, but managed to compound a drug by which these powers should be dethroned from their supremacy, and a second form and countenance substituted, none the less natural to me because they were the expression, and bore the stamp, of lower elements in my soul.

I hesitated long before I put this theory to the test of practice. I knew well that I risked death; for any drug that so potently controlled and shook the very fortress of identity, might by the least scruple[5] of an overdose or at the least inopportunity in the moment of exhibition, utterly blot out that immaterial tabernacle which I looked to it to change. But the temptation of a discovery so singular and profound, at last overcame the suggestions of alarm. I had long since prepared my tincture; I purchased at once, from a firm of wholesale chemists, a large quantity of a particular salt which I knew, from my experiments, to be the last ingredient required; and late one accursed night, I compounded the elements, watched them boil and smoke together in the glass, and when the ebullition had subsided, with a strong glow of courage, drank off the potion.

The most racking pangs succeeded: a grinding in the bones, deadly nausea, and a horror of the spirit that cannot be exceeded at the hour of birth or death. Then these agonies began swiftly to subside, and I came to myself as if out of a great sickness. There was something strange in my sensations, something indescribably new and, from its very novelty, incredibly sweet. I felt younger, lighter, happier in body; within I was conscious of a heady recklessness, a current of disordered sensual images running like a mill race[6] in my fancy, a solution of the bonds of obligation, an unknown but not an innocent freedom of the soul. I knew myself, at the first breath of this new life, to be more wicked, tenfold more wicked, sold a slave to my original evil; and the thought, in that moment, braced and delighted me like wine. I stretched out my hands, exulting in the freshness of these sensations; and in the act, I was suddenly aware that I had lost in stature.

4. Bundles of sticks used for fuel.
5. A minute amount (literally, an apothecaries'
weight equal to about 1.3 grams).
6. Water current that drives a mill wheel.

There was no mirror, at that date, in my room; that which stands beside me as I write, was brought there later on and for the very purpose of these transformations. The night, however, was far gone into the morning—the morning, black as it was, was nearly ripe for the conception of the day—the inmates of my house were locked in the most rigorous hours of slumber; and I determined, flushed as I was with hope and triumph, to venture in my new shape as far as to my bedroom. I crossed the yard, wherein the constellations looked down upon me, I could have thought, with wonder, the first creature of that sort that their unsleeping vigilance had yet disclosed to them; I stole through the corridors, a stranger in my own house; and coming to my room, I saw for the first time the appearance of Edward Hyde.

I must here speak by theory alone, saying not that which I know, but that which I suppose to be most probable. The evil side of my nature, to which I had now transferred the stamping efficacy, was less robust and less developed than the good which I had just deposed. Again, in the course of my life, which had been, after all, nine-tenths a life of effort, virtue and control, it had been much less exercised and much less exhausted. And hence, as I think, it came about that Edward Hyde was so much smaller, slighter and younger than Henry Jekyll. Even as good shone upon the countenance of the one, evil was written broadly and plainly on the face of the other. Evil besides (which I must still believe to be the lethal side of man) had left on that body an imprint of deformity and decay. And yet when I looked upon that ugly idol in the glass, I was conscious of no repugnance, rather of a leap of welcome. This, too, was myself. It seemed natural and human. In my eyes it bore a livelier image of the spirit, it seemed more express and single, than the imperfect and divided countenance I had been hitherto accustomed to call mine. And in so far I was doubtless right. I have observed that when I wore the semblance of Edward Hyde, none could come near to me at first without a visible misgiving of the flesh. This, as I take it, was because all human beings, as we meet them, are commingled out of good and evil: and Edward Hyde, alone in the ranks of mankind, was pure evil.

I lingered but a moment at the mirror: the second and conclusive experiment had yet to be attempted; it yet remained to be seen if I had lost my identity beyond redemption and must flee before daylight from a house that was no longer mine; and hurrying back to my cabinet, I once more prepared and drank the cup, once more suffered the pangs of dissolution, and came to myself once more with the character, the stature and the face of Henry Jekyll.

That night I had come to the fatal cross roads. Had I approached my discovery in a more noble spirit, had I risked the experiment while under the empire of generous or pious aspirations, all must have been otherwise, and from these agonies of death and birth, I had come forth an angel instead of a fiend. The drug had no discriminating action; it was neither diabolical nor divine; it but shook the doors of the prison-house of my disposition; and like the captives of Philippi, that which stood within ran forth.[7] At that time my virtue slumbered; my evil, kept awake by ambition, was alert and swift to seize the occasion; and the thing that was projected was Edward Hyde.

7. Cf. Acts 16.26, when the apostle Paul and his friend Silas were imprisoned at Philippi, a city in eastern Macedonia, an earthquake freed all the prisoners (none of whom fled).

Hence, although I had now two characters as well as two appearances, one was wholly evil, and the other was still the old Henry Jekyll, that incongruous compound of whose reformation and improvement I had already learned to despair. The movement was thus wholly towards the worse.

Even at that time, I had not yet conquered my aversion to the dryness of a life of study. I would still be merrily disposed at times; and as my pleasures were (to say the least) undignified, and I was not only well known and highly considered, but growing towards the elderly man, this incoherency of my life was daily growing more unwelcome. It was on this side that my new power tempted me until I fell in slavery. I had but to drink the cup, to doff at once the body of the noted professor, and to assume, like a thick cloak, that of Edward Hyde. I smiled at the notion; it seemed to me at the time to be humorous; and I made my preparations with the most studious care. I took and furnished that house in Soho, to which Hyde was tracked by the police; and engaged as housekeeper a creature whom I well knew to be silent and unscrupulous. On the other side, I announced to my servants that a Mr. Hyde (whom I described) was to have full liberty and power about my house in the square; and to parry mishaps, I even called and made myself a familiar object, in my second character. I next drew up that will to which you so much objected; so that if anything befell me in the person of Dr. Jekyll, I could enter on that of Edward Hyde without pecuniary loss. And thus fortified, as I supposed, on every side, I began to profit by the strange immunities of my position.

Men have before hired bravos[8] to transact their crimes, while their own person and reputation sat under shelter. I was the first that ever did so for his pleasures. I was the first that could thus plod in the public eye with a load of genial respectability, and in a moment, like a schoolboy, strip off these lendings[9] and spring headlong into the sea of liberty. But for me, in my impenetrable mantle, the safety was complete. Think of it—I did not even exist! Let me but escape into my laboratory door, give me but a second or two to mix and swallow the draught that I had always standing ready; and whatever he had done, Edward Hyde would pass away like the stain of breath upon a mirror; and there in his stead, quietly at home, trimming the midnight lamp in his study, a man who could afford to laugh at suspicion, would be Henry Jekyll.

The pleasures which I made haste to seek in my disguise were, as I have said, undignified; I would scarce use a harder term. But in the hands of Edward Hyde, they soon began to turn towards the monstrous. When I would come back from these excursions, I was often plunged into a kind of wonder at my vicarious depravity. This familiar[1] that I called out of my own soul, and sent forth alone to do his good pleasure, was a being inherently malign and villainous; his every act and thought centered on self; drinking pleasure with bestial avidity from any degree of torture to another; relentless like a man of stone. Henry Jekyll stood at times aghast before the acts of Edward Hyde; but the situation was apart from ordinary laws, and insidiously relaxed the grasp of conscience. It was Hyde, after all, and Hyde alone, that

8. Thugs.
9. Borrowed clothing; a reference to King Lear's cry on the heath, "Off, off you lendings!" (Shake-

speare, *King Lear* 3.4.97).
1. Spirit or demon.

was guilty. Jekyll was no worse; he woke again to his good qualities seemingly unimpaired; he would even make haste, where it was possible, to undo the evil done by Hyde. And thus his conscience slumbered.

Into the details of the infamy at which I thus connived (for even now I can scarce grant that I committed it) I have no design of entering; I mean but to point out the warnings and the successive steps with which my chastisement approached. I met with one accident which, as it brought on no consequence, I shall no more than mention. An act of cruelty to a child aroused against me the anger of a passer-by, whom I recognised the other day in the person of your kinsman; the doctor and the child's family joined him; there were moments when I feared for my life; and at last, in order to pacify their too just resentment, Edward Hyde had to bring them to the door, and pay them in a cheque drawn in the name of Henry Jekyll. But this danger was easily eliminated from the future, by opening an account at another bank in the name of Edward Hyde himself; and when, by sloping my own hand backward, I had supplied my double with a signature, I thought I sat beyond the reach of fate.

Some two months before the murder of Sir Danvers, I had been out for one of my adventures, had returned at a late hour, and woke the next day in bed with somewhat odd sensations. It was in vain I looked about me; in vain I saw the decent furniture and tall proportions of my room in the square; in vain that I recognised the pattern of the bed curtains and the design of the mahogany frame; something still kept insisting that I was not where I was, that I had not wakened where I seemed to be, but in the little room in Soho where I was accustomed to sleep in the body of Edward Hyde. I smiled to myself, and, in my psychological way began lazily to inquire into the elements of this illusion, occasionally, even as I did so, dropping back into a comfortable morning doze. I was still so engaged when, in one of my more wakeful moments, my eyes fell upon my hand. Now the hand of Henry Jekyll (as you have often remarked) was professional in shape and size: it was large, firm, white and comely. But the hand which I now saw, clearly enough, in the yellow light of a mid-London morning, lying half shut on the bed clothes, was lean, corded, knuckly, of a dusky pallor and thickly shaded with a swart[2] growth of hair. It was the hand of Edward Hyde.

I must have stared upon it for near half a minute, sunk as I was in the mere stupidity of wonder, before terror woke up in my breast as sudden and startling as the crash of cymbals; and bounding from my bed, I rushed to the mirror. At the sight that met my eyes, my blood was changed into something exquisitely thin and icy. Yes, I had gone to bed Henry Jekyll, I had awakened Edward Hyde. How was this to be explained? I asked myself; and then, with another bound of terror—how was it to be remedied? It was well on in the morning; the servants were up; all my drugs were in the cabinet—a long journey down two pair of stairs, through the back passage, across the open court and through the anatomical theatre, from where I was then standing horror-struck. It might indeed be possible to cover my face; but of what use was that, when I was unable to conceal the alteration in my stature? And then with an overpowering sweetness of relief, it came back upon my mind that the servants were already used to the coming and

2. Dark.

going of my second self. I had soon dressed, as well as I was able, in clothes of my own size: had soon passed through the house, where Bradshaw stared and drew back at seeing Mr. Hyde at such an hour and in such a strange array; and ten minutes later, Dr. Jekyll had returned to his own shape and was sitting down, with a darkened brow, to make a feint of breakfasting.

Small indeed was my appetite. This inexplicable incident, this reversal of my previous experience, seemed, like the Babylonian finger on the wall,[3] to be spelling out the letters of my judgment; and I began to reflect more seriously than ever before on the issues and possibilities of my double existence. That part of me which I had the power of projecting, had lately been much exercised and nourished; it had seemed to me of late as though the body of Edward Hyde had grown in stature, as though (when I wore that form) I were conscious of a more generous tide of blood; and I began to spy a danger that, if this were much prolonged, the balance of my nature might be permanently overthrown, the power of voluntary change be forfeited, and the character of Edward Hyde become irrevocably mine. The power of the drug had not been always equally displayed. Once, very early in my career, it had totally failed me; since then I had been obliged on more than one occasion to double, and once, with infinite risk of death, to treble the amount; and these rare uncertainties had cast hitherto the sole shadow on my contentment. Now, however, and in the light of that morning's accident, I was led to remark that whereas, in the beginning, the difficulty had been to throw off the body of Jekyll, it had of late gradually but decidedly transferred itself to the other side. All things therefore seemed to point to this: that I was slowly losing hold of my original and better self, and becoming slowly incorporated with my second and worse.

Between these two, I now felt I had to choose. My two natures had memory in common, but all other faculties were most unequally shared between them. Jekyll (who was composite) now with the most sensitive apprehensions, now with a greedy gusto, projected and shared in the pleasures and adventures of Hyde; but Hyde was indifferent to Jekyll, or but remembered him as the mountain bandit remembers the cavern in which he conceals himself from pursuit. Jekyll had more than a father's interest; Hyde had more than a son's indifference. To cast in my lot with Jekyll, was to die to those appetites which I had long secretly indulged and had of late begun to pamper. To cast it in with Hyde, was to die to a thousand interests and aspirations, and to become, at a blow and forever, despised and friendless. The bargain might appear unequal; but there was still another consideration in the scales; for while Jekyll would suffer smartingly in the fires of abstinence, Hyde would be not even conscious of all that he had lost. Strange as my circumstances were, the terms of this debate are as old and commonplace as man; much the same inducements and alarms cast the die for any tempted and trembling sinner; and it fell out with me, as it falls with so vast a majority of my fellows, that I chose the better part and was found wanting in the strength to keep to it.

Yes, I preferred the elderly and discontented doctor, surrounded by friends and cherishing honest hopes; and bade a resolute farewell to the liberty, the

---

3. In Daniel 5.5–31; the writing foretold the overthrow of Belshazzar, the Babylonian king, because of his transgressions against the Lord.

comparative youth, the light step, leaping impulses and secret pleasures, that I had enjoyed in the disguise of Hyde. I made this choice perhaps with some unconscious reservation, for I neither gave up the house in Soho, nor destroyed the clothes of Edward Hyde, which still lay ready in my cabinet. For two months, however, I was true to my determination; for two months I led a life of such severity as I had never before attained to, and enjoyed the compensations of an approving conscience. But time began at last to obliterate the freshness of my alarm; the praises of conscience began to grow into a thing of course; I began to be tortured with throes and longings, as of Hyde struggling after freedom; and at last, in an hour of moral weakness, I once again compounded and swallowed the transforming draught.

I do not suppose that, when a drunkard reasons with himself upon his vice, he is once out of five hundred times affected by the dangers that he runs through his brutish, physical insensibility; neither had I, long as I had considered my position, made enough allowance for the complete moral insensibility and insensate readiness to evil, which were the leading characters of Edward Hyde. Yet it was by these that I was punished. My devil had been long caged, he came out roaring. I was conscious, even when I took the draught, of a more unbridled, a more furious propensity to ill. It must have been this, I suppose, that stirred in my soul that tempest of impatience with which I listened to the civilities of my unhappy victim; I declare, at least, before God, no man morally sane could have been guilty of that crime upon so pitiful a provocation; and that I struck in no more reasonable spirit than that in which a sick child may break a plaything. But I had voluntarily stripped myself of all those balancing instincts by which even the worst of us continues to walk with some degree of steadiness among temptations; and in my case, to be tempted, however slightly, was to fall.

Instantly the spirit of hell awoke in me and raged. With a transport of glee, I mauled the unresisting body, tasting delight from every blow; and it was not till weariness had begun to succeed, that I was suddenly, in the top fit of my delirium, struck through the heart by a cold thrill of terror. A mist dispersed; I saw my life to be forfeit; and fled from the scene of these excesses, at once glorifying and trembling, my lust of evil gratified and stimulated, my love of life screwed to the topmost peg.[4] I ran to the house in Soho, and (to make assurance doubly sure) destroyed my papers; thence I set out through the lamplit streets, in the same divided ecstasy of mind, gloating on my crime, light-headedly devising others in the future, and yet still hastening and still hearkening in my wake for the steps of the avenger. Hyde had a song upon his lips as he compounded the draught, and as he drank it, pledged[5] the dead man. The pangs of transformation had not done tearing him, before Henry Jekyll, with streaming tears of gratitude and remorse, had fallen upon his knees and lifted his clasped hands to God. The veil of self-indulgence was rent from head to foot.[6] I saw my life as a whole: I followed it up from the days of childhood, when I had walked with my father's hand, and through the self-denying toils of my professional life, to arrive again and again, with the same sense of unreality, at the damned horrors of the evening. I could have screamed aloud; I sought with tears and prayers to smother down the

4. Strained to the highest point.
5. Drank a toast to.

6. See Matthew 27.51: "the veil of the temple was rent in twain, from the top to the bottom."

crowd of hideous images and sounds with which my memory swarmed against me; and still, between the petitions, the ugly face of my iniquity stared into my soul. As the acuteness of this remorse began to die away, it was succeeded by a sense of joy. The problem of my conduct was solved. Hyde was thenceforth impossible; whether I would or not, I was now confined to the better part of my existence; and O, how I rejoiced to think it! with what willing humility, I embraced anew the restrictions of natural life! with what sincere renunciation, I locked the door by which I had so often gone and come, and ground the key under my heel!

The next day, came the news that the murder had been overlooked,[7] that the guilt of Hyde was patent to the world, and that the victim was a man high in public estimation. It was not only a crime, it had been a tragic folly. I think I was glad to know it; I think I was glad to have my better impulses thus buttressed and guarded by the terrors of the scaffold. Jekyll was now my city of refuge; let but Hyde peep out an instant, and the hands of all men would be raised to take and slay him.

I resolved in my future conduct to redeem the past; and I can say with honesty that my resolve was fruitful of some good. You know yourself how earnestly in the last months of last year, I laboured to relieve suffering; you know that much was done for others, and that the days passed quietly, almost happily for myself. Nor can I truly say that I wearied of this beneficent and innocent life; I think instead that I daily enjoyed it more completely; but I was still cursed with my duality of purpose; and as the first edge of my penitence wore off, the lower side of me, so long indulged, so recently chained down, began to growl for license. Not that I dreamed of resuscitating Hyde; the bare idea of that would startle me to frenzy: no, it was in my own person, that I was once more tempted to trifle with my conscience; and it was as an ordinary secret sinner, that I at last fell before the assaults of temptation.

There comes an end to all things; the most capacious measure is filled at last; and this brief condescension to my evil finally destroyed the balance of my soul. And yet I was not alarmed; the fall seemed natural, like a return to the old days before I had made my discovery. It was a fine, clear, January day, wet under foot where the frost had melted, but cloudless overhead; and the Regent's Park[8] was full of winter chirrupings and sweet with spring odours. I sat in the sun on a bench; the animal within me licking the chops of memory; the spiritual side a little drowsed, promising subsequent penitence, but not yet moved to begin. After all, I reflected, I was like my neighbours; and then I smiled, comparing myself with other men, comparing my active goodwill with the lazy cruelty of their neglect. And at the very moment of that vain-glorious thought, a qualm came over me, a horrid nausea and the most deadly shuddering. These passed away, and left me faint; and then as in its turn the faintness subsided, I began to be aware of a change in the temper of my thoughts, a greater boldness, a contempt of danger, a solution of the bonds of obligation. I looked down; my clothes hung formlessly on my shrunken limbs; the hand that lay on my knee was corded and hairy. I was once more Edward Hyde. A moment before I had been safe of all men's respect, wealthy, beloved—the cloth laying for me in the dining-room at home; and now I was

---

7. Seen from above.　　　　　　　　8. A large park in northwest London.

the common quarry of mankind, hunted, houseless, a known murderer, thrall to the gallows.

My reason wavered, but it did not fail me utterly. I have more than once observed that, in my second character, my faculties seemed sharpened to a point and my spirits more tensely elastic; thus it came about that, where Jekyll perhaps might have succumbed, Hyde rose to the importance of the moment. My drugs were in one of the presses of my cabinet; how was I to reach them? That was the problem that (crushing my temples in my hands) I set myself to solve. The laboratory door I had closed. If I sought to enter by the house, my own servants would consign me to the gallows. I saw I must employ another hand, and thought of Lanyon. How was he to be reached? how persuaded? Supposing that I escaped capture in the streets, how was I to make my way into his presence? and how should I, an unknown and displeasing visitor, prevail on the famous physician to rifle the study of his colleague, Dr. Jekyll? Then I remembered that of my original character, one part remained to me: I could write my own hand; and once I had conceived that kindling spark, the way that I must follow became lighted up from end to end.

Thereupon, I arranged my clothes as best I could, and summoning a passing hansom, drove to an hotel in Portland Street, the name of which I chanced to remember. At my appearance (which was indeed comical enough, however tragic a fate these garments covered) the driver could not conceal his mirth. I gnashed my teeth upon him with a gust of devilish fury; and the smile withered from his face—happily for him—yet more happily for myself, for in another instant I had certainly dragged him from his perch. At the inn, as I entered, I looked about me with so black a countenance as made the attendants tremble; not a look did they exchange in my presence; but obsequiously took my orders, led me to a private room, and brought me wherewithal to write. Hyde in danger of his life was a creature new to me; shaken with inordinate anger, strung to the pitch of murder, lusting to inflict pain. Yet the creature was astute; mastered his fury with a great effort of the will; composed his two important letters, one to Lanyon and one to Poole; and that he might receive actual evidence of their being posted, sent them out with directions that they should be registered.

Thenceforward, he sat all day over the fire in the private room, gnawing his nails; there he dined, sitting alone with his fears, the waiter visibly quailing before his eye; and thence, when the night was fully come, he set forth in the corner of a closed cab, and was driven to and fro about the streets of the city. He, I say—I cannot say, I. That child of Hell had nothing human; nothing lived in him but fear and hatred. And when at last, thinking the driver had begun to grow suspicious, he discharged the cab and ventured on foot, attired in his misfitting clothes, an object marked out for observation, into the midst of the nocturnal passengers, these two base passions raged within him like a tempest. He walked fast, hunted by his fears, chattering to himself, skulking through the less frequented thoroughfares, counting the minutes that still divided him from midnight. Once a woman spoke to him, offering, I think, a box of lights.[9] He smote her in the face, and she fled.

9. Matches.

When I came to myself at Lanyon's, the horror of my old friend perhaps affected me somewhat: I do not know; it was at least but a drop in the sea to the abhorrence with which I looked back upon these hours. A change had come over me. It was no longer the fear of the gallows, it was the horror of being Hyde that racked me. I received Lanyon's condemnation partly in a dream; it was partly in a dream that I came home to my own house and got into bed. I slept after the prostration of the day, with a stringent and profound slumber which not even the nightmares that wrung me could avail to break. I awoke in the morning shaken, weakened, but refreshed. I still hated and feared the thought of the brute that slept within me, and I had not of course forgotten the appalling dangers of the day before; but I was once more at home, in my own house and close to my drugs; and gratitude for my escape shone so strong in my soul that it almost rivalled the brightness of hope.

I was stepping leisurely across the court after breakfast, drinking the chill of the air with pleasure, when I was seized again with those indescribable sensations that heralded the change; and I had but the time to gain the shelter of my cabinet, before I was once again raging and freezing with the passions of Hyde. It took on this occasion a double dose to recall me to myself; and alas! six hours after, as I sat looking sadly in the fire, the pangs returned, and the drug had to be re-administered. In short, from that day forth it seemed only by a great effort as of gymnastics, and only under the immediate stimulation of the drug, that I was able to wear the countenance of Jekyll. At all hours of the day and night, I would be taken with the premonitory shudder; above all, if I slept, or even dozed for a moment in my chair, it was always as Hyde that I awakened. Under the strain of this continually impending doom and by the sleeplessness to which I now condemned myself, ay, even beyond what I had thought possible to man, I became, in my own person, a creature eaten up and emptied by fever, languidly weak both in body and mind, and solely occupied by one thought: the horror of my other self. But when I slept, or when the virtue of the medicine wore off, I would leap almost without transition (for the pangs of transformation grew daily less marked) into the possession of a fancy brimming with images of terror, a soul boiling with causeless hatreds, and a body that seemed not strong enough to contain the raging energies of life. The powers of Hyde seemed to have grown with the sickliness of Jekyll. And certainly the hate that now divided them was equal on each side. With Jekyll, it was a thing of vital instinct. He had now seen the full deformity of that creature that shared with him some of the phenomena of consciousness, and was co-heir with him to death: and beyond these links of community, which in themselves made the most poignant part of his distress, he thought of Hyde, for all his energy of life, as of something not only hellish but inorganic. This was the shocking thing; that the slime of the pit seemed to utter cries and voices; that the amorphous dust gesticulated and sinned; that what was dead, and had no shape, should usurp the offices of life. And this again, that that insurgent horror was knit to him closer than a wife, closer than an eye; lay caged in his flesh, where he heard it mutter and felt it struggle to be born; and at every hour of weakness, and in the confidence of slumber, prevailed against him, and deposed him out of life. The hatred of Hyde for Jekyll, was of a different order. His terror of the gallows drove him continually to commit temporary suicide, and return to his subordinate station of a part instead of a person; but he loathed the necessity, he loathed the despondency into which Jekyll was now fallen, and he resented the dislike with which he was himself regarded. Hence the apelike tricks that he would play me, scrawling in my own hand blasphemies on the pages of my books, burning the letters and destroying the portrait of my father; and indeed, had it not been for his fear of death, he would long ago have ruined himself in order to involve me in the ruin. But his love of life is wonderful; I go further: I, who sicken and freeze at the mere thought of him, when I recall the abjection and passion of this attachment, and when I know how he fears my power to cut him off by suicide, I find it in my heart to pity him.

It is useless, and the time awfully fails me, to prolong this description; no one has ever suffered such torments, let that suffice; and yet even to these, habit brought—no, not alleviation—but a certain callousness of soul, a certain acquiescence of despair; and my punishment might have gone on for years, but for the last calamity which has now fallen, and which has finally severed me from my own face and nature. My provision of the salt, which had never been renewed since the date of the first experiment, began to run low. I sent out for a fresh supply, and mixed the draught; the ebullition followed, and the first change of colour, not the second; I drank it and it was without efficiency. You will learn from Poole how I have had London ransacked; it was in vain; and I am now persuaded that my first supply was impure, and that it was that unknown impurity which lent efficacy to the draught.

About a week has passed, and I am now finishing this statement under the influence of the last of the old powders. This, then, is the last time, short of a miracle, that Henry Jekyll can think his own thoughts or see his own face (now how sadly altered!) in the glass. Nor must I delay too long to bring my writing to an end; for if my narrative has hitherto escaped destruction, it has been by a combination of great prudence and great good luck. Should the throes of change take me in the act of writing it, Hyde will tear it in pieces; but if some time shall have elapsed after I have laid it by, his wonderful selfishness and circumscription to the moment will probably save it once again from the action of his apelike spite. And indeed the doom that is closing on us both, has already changed and crushed him. Half an hour from now, when I shall again and forever reindue[1] that hated personality, I know how I shall sit shuddering and weeping in my chair, or continue, with the most strained and fearstruck ecstasy of listening, to pace up and down this room (my last earthly refuge) and give ear to every sound of menace. Will Hyde die upon the scaffold? or will he find courage to release himself at the last moment? God knows; I am careless;[2] this is my true hour of death, and what is to follow concerns another than myself. Here then, as I lay down the pen and proceed to seal up my confession, I bring the life of that unhappy Henry Jekyll to an end.

1885   1886

---

1. Put on again.   2. Indifferent.

OSCAR WILDE
1854–1900

I n Oscar Wilde's comedy *The Importance of Being Earnest* (1895) Jack Worthing claims to have received a telegram about the death of his (imaginary) rakish brother Ernest in a Paris hotel. Five years later Wilde died in a hotel in Paris, where he was living in exile. The coincidence seems a curious paradigm of Wilde's career, for the connections between his life and his art were unusually close. Indeed, in his last years he told André Gide that he seemed to have put his genius into his life and only his talent into his writings.

His father, Sir William, was a distinguished surgeon in Dublin, where Wilde was born and grew up. After studying classics at Trinity College, Dublin, he won a scholarship to Oxford and there established a brilliant academic record. At Oxford he came under the influence of the aesthetic theories of John Ruskin (who was at the time professor of fine arts) and, more important, of Walter Pater. With characteristic hyperbole Wilde affirmed of Pater's *Studies in the History of the Renaissance* (1873): "It is my golden book; I never travel anywhere without it. But it is the very flower of decadence; the last trumpet should have sounded the moment it was written."

After graduating in 1878, Wilde moved to London, where his fellow Irishmen George Bernard Shaw and William Butler Yeats were also to settle. Here Wilde quickly established himself both as a writer and as a spokesperson for the school of "art for art's sake." In Wilde's view this school included not only French poets and critics but also a line of English poets going back through Dante Gabriel Rossetti and the Pre-Raphaelites to John Keats. In 1882 he visited America for a long (and successful) lecture tour, during which he startled audiences by airing the gospel of the "aesthetic movement." In one of these lectures, he asserted that "to disagree with three fourths of all England on all points of view is one of the first elements of sanity."

For his role as a spokesperson for aestheticism, Wilde had many gifts. From all accounts he was a dazzling conversationalist. Yeats reported, after first listening to him: "I never before heard a man talking with perfect sentences, as if he had written them all overnight with labour and yet all spontaneous." Wilde delighted his listeners not only by his polished wordplay but also by uttering opinions that were both outrageous and incongruous—for example, his solemn affirmation that Queen Victoria was one of the three women he most admired and whom he would have married "with pleasure" (the other two were the actress Sarah Bernhardt and Lillie Langtry, reputedly a mistress of Victoria's son Edward, Prince of Wales).

In addition to his mastery of witty conversation, Wilde had the gifts of an actor who delights in gaining attention. Pater had been a very shy and reticent man, but there was nothing reticent about his disciple, who had early discovered that a flamboyant style of dress was one of the most effective means of gaining attention. Like the dandies of the earlier decades of the nineteenth century (including Benjamin Disraeli and Charles Dickens), Wilde favored colorful costumes in marked contrast to the sober black suits of the late-Victorian middle classes. A green carnation in his buttonhole and velvet knee breeches became for Wilde badges of his youthful iconoclasm; and even when he approached middle age, he continued to emphasize the gap between generations. In a letter written when he was forty-two years old, he remarks: "The opinions of the old on matters of Art are, of course, of no value whatever."

Wilde's campaign quickly gained an amused response from middle-class quarters. In 1881 W. S. Gilbert and Sir Arthur Sullivan staged their comic opera *Patience,* which mocked the affectations of the aesthetes in the character of Bunthorne, especially in his song "If You're Anxious for to Shine in the High Aesthetic Line."

Wilde's successes for seventeen years in England and America were, of course, not limited to his self-advertising stunts as a dandy. In his writings he excelled in a variety of genres: as a critic of literature and of society (*The Decay of Lying*, 1889, and *The Soul of Man under Socialism*, 1891) and also as a novelist, poet, and dramatist. Much of his prose, including *The Critic as Artist* (1890), develops Pater's aestheticism, particularly its sense of the superiority of art to life and its lack of obligation to any standards of mimesis. His novel *The Picture of Dorian Gray*, which created a sensation when it was published in 1891, takes a somewhat different perspective. The novel is a strikingly ingenious story of a handsome young man and his selfish pursuit of sensual pleasures. Until the end of the book he remains fresh and healthy in appearance while his portrait mysteriously changes into a horrible image of his corrupted soul. Although the preface to the novel (reprinted here) emphasizes that art and morality are totally separate, in the novel, at least in its later chapters, Wilde seems to be portraying the evils of self-regarding hedonism.

As a poet Wilde felt overshadowed by the Victorian predecessors whom he admired—Robert Browning, D. G. Rossetti, and Algernon Charles Swinburne—and had trouble finding his own voice. Many of the poems in his first volume (1881) are highly derivative, but pieces such as "Impression du Matin" (1885) and "The Harlot's House" (1881) offer a distinctive perspective on city streets that seems to anticipate early poems by T. S. Eliot. His most outstanding success, however, was as a writer of comedies; staged in London and New York from 1892 through 1895, these included *Lady Windermere's Fan, A Woman of No Importance, An Ideal Husband*, and *The Importance of Being Earnest*.

In the spring of 1895 this triumphant success suddenly crumbled when Wilde was arrested and sentenced to prison, with hard labor, for two years. Although Wilde was married and the father of two children, he did not hide his relationships with men, and in fact ended up shaping, to his personal cost, a long-standing public image of "the homosexual." When he began a romance (in 1891) with the handsome young poet Lord Alfred Douglas, he set in motion the events that brought about his ruin. In 1895 Lord Alfred's father, the marquess of Queensberry, accused Wilde of homosexuality; Wilde recklessly sued for libel, lost the case, and was thereupon arrested and convicted for what had only recently come onto the statute books as a serious offense. (A late addition to the Criminal Law Amendment Act of 1885, known as the Labouchère Amendment after the member of Parliament who had proposed it, effectively criminalized all forms of sexual relations between men.) The revulsion of feeling against him in Britain and America was violent, and the aesthetic movement suffered a severe setback not only with the public but among writers as well.

His two years in jail led Wilde to write two sober and emotionally high-pitched works, his poem *The Ballad of Reading Gaol* (1898) and his prose confession *De Profundis* (1905). After leaving prison, Wilde, a ruined man, emigrated to France, where he lived out the last three years of his life under an assumed name. Before his departure from England he had been divorced and declared a bankrupt, and in France he had to rely on friends for financial support. Wilde is buried in Paris in the Père Lachaise cemetery.

Impression du Matin[1]

The Thames nocturne of blue and gold[2]
    Changed to a harmony in grey;
    A barge with ochre-colored hay
Dropped from the wharf:[3] and chill and cold

5   The yellow fog came creeping down
    The bridges, till the houses' walls
    Seemed changed to shadows, and St. Paul's
Loomed like a bubble o'er the town.[4]

Then suddenly arose the clang
10   Of waking life; the streets were stirred
    With country wagons; and a bird
Flew to the glistening roofs and sang.

But one pale woman all alone,
    The daylight kissing her wan hair,
15   Loitered beneath the gas lamps' flare,
With lips of flame and heart of stone.

1881

The Harlot's House

We caught the tread of dancing feet,
We loitered down the moonlit street,
And stopped beneath the Harlot's house.

Inside, above the din and fray,
5   We heard the loud musicians play
The "Treues Liebes Herz" of Strauss.[1]

Like strange mechanical grotesques,
Making fantastic arabesques,
The shadows raced across the blind.

10   We watched the ghostly dancers spin
To sound of horn and violin,
Like black leaves wheeling in the wind.

---

1. Impression of the morning (French).
2. Cf. the "Nocturnes" (paintings of nighttime scenes) by James McNeill Whistler in the 1870s. *Nocturne in Blue and Gold: Old Battersea Bridge* was one of this series; it was painted by 1875 but given its present title in 1892. In the next line Wilde may be referring to an earlier painting by Whistler, *Harmony in Gray and Green: Miss Cic-*

ely Alexander (1872–74).
3. I.e., left the wharf and went down river with the ebb tide.
4. I.e., the large dome of St. Paul's Cathedral in London.
1. *Heart of True Love*, a waltz by the Austrian composer and "Waltz King" Johann Strauss (1825–1899).

Like wire-pulled automatons,
Slim silhouetted skeletons
15 Went sidling through the slow quadrille,[2]

Then took each other by the hand,
And danced a stately saraband;[3]
Their laughter echoed thin and shrill.

Sometimes a clockwork puppet pressed
20 A phantom lover to her breast,
Sometimes they seemed to try to sing,

Sometimes a horrible marionette
Came out, and smoked its cigarette
Upon the steps like a live thing.[4]

25 Then turning to my love I said,
"The dead are dancing with the dead,
The dust is whirling with the dust."

But she, she heard the violin,
And left my side, and entered in;
30 Love passed into the house of Lust.

Then suddenly the tune went false,
The dancers wearied of the waltz,
The shadows ceased to wheel and whirl,

And down the long and silent street,
35 The dawn, with silver-sandaled feet,
Crept like a frightened girl.

1885, 1908

From The Critic as Artist[1]

[CRITICISM ITSELF AN ART]

ERNEST   Gilbert, you sound too harsh a note. Let us go back to the more gracious fields of literature. What was it you said? That it was more difficult to talk about a thing than to do it?

GILBERT [*After a pause.*]   Yes: I believe I ventured upon that simple truth. Surely you see now that I am right? When man acts he is a puppet.

---

2. An intricate dance involving four couples facing each other in a square.
3. A slow and stately dance, originating in Spain.
4. In an illustration for the poem by Althea Gyles (approved by Wilde), the marionette is pictured as a man in evening dress.
1. In "the library of a house in Piccadilly," Gilbert and Ernest, two sophisticated young men, are talking about the use and function of criticism.

Earlier in the dialogue Ernest had complained that criticism is officious and useless: "Why should the artist be troubled by the shrill clamour of criticism? Why should those who cannot create take upon themselves to estimate the value of creative work?" Gilbert, in his reply, argues that criticism is creative in its own right. He digresses to compare the life of action unfavorably with the life of art: actions are dangerous and their results

When he describes he is a poet. The whole secret lies in that. It was easy enough on the sandy plains by windy Ilion[2] to send the notched arrow from the painted bow, or to hurl against the shield of hide and flamelike brass the long ash-handled spear. It was easy for the adulterous queen to spread the Tyrian carpets for her lord,[3] and then, as he lay couched in the marble bath, to throw over his head the purple net, and call to her smooth-faced lover to stab through the meshes at the heart that should have broken at Aulis.[4] For Antigone[5] even, with Death waiting for her as her bridegroom, it was easy to pass through the tainted air at noon, and climb the hill, and strew with kindly earth the wretched naked corse that had no tomb. But what of those who wrote about these things? What of those who gave them reality, and made them live forever? Are they not greater than the men and women they sing of? "Hector that sweet knight is dead."[6] And Lucian[7] tells us how in the dim underworld Menippus saw the bleaching skull of Helen, and marveled that it was for so grim a favour that all those horned ships were launched, those beautiful mailed men laid low, those towered cities brought to dust. Yet, every day the swanlike daughter of Leda comes out on the battlements, and looks down at the tide of war. The greybeards wonder at her loveliness, and she stands by the side of the king.[8] In his chamber of stained ivory lies her leman.[9] He is polishing his dainty armour, and combing the scarlet plume. With squire and page, her husband passes from tent to tent. She can see his bright hair, and hears, or fancies that she hears, that clear cold voice. In the courtyard below, the son of Priam is buckling on his brazen cuirass. The white arms of Andromache[1] are around his neck. He sets his helmet on the ground, lest their babe should be frightened. Behind the embroidered curtains of his pavilion sits Achilles,[2] in perfumed raiment, while in harness of gilt and silver the friend of his soul[3] arrays himself to go forth to fight. From a curiously carven chest that his mother Thetis had brought to his shipside, the Lord of the Myrmidons[4] takes out that mystic chalice that the lip of man had never touched, and cleanses it with brimstone, and with fresh water cools it, and, having washed his hands, fills with black wine its burnished hollow, and spills the thick

---

unpredictable; "if we lived long enough to see the results of our actions it may be that those who call themselves good would be sickened by a dull remorse, and those whom the world calls evil stirred by a noble joy." The excerpt printed here begins immediately after this digression.

2. Troy. Gilbert is referring to Homer's *Iliad*.

3. Agamemnon, king of Mycenae. Aeschylus's tragedy of that name tells how his wife, Clytemnestra ("the adulterous queen"), and his cousin Aegisthus ("her smooth-faced lover") conspired to murder him. He hubristically walked on carpets dyed purple, a color derived from shellfish off Tyre (a city located in what is today Lebanon).

4. Where Agamemnon sacrificed his daughter Iphigenia (so that the Greek fleet could sail for Troy), thus incurring Clytemnestra's wrath.

5. Antigone defied Creon, king of Thebes, by sprinkling earth on the body of her brother whose burial Creon had forbidden, and was punished by death; see Sophocles' play *Antigone*

(ca. 441 B.C.E.).

6. Cf. Shakespeare's *Love's Labour's Lost* 5.2.647: "The sweet war-man [Hector] is dead and rotten."

7. Greek satirist (b. ca. 120 C.E.), one of whose main influences was Menippus (early 3rd century B.C.E.), a Greek philosopher who was the first to express his views in a seriocomic style. The reference is to Lucian's *Dialogues of the Dead*.

8. Priam. Homer in *Iliad* 3.156–58 describes the old men of Troy admiring the beauty of Helen, daughter of Leda and of Zeus (who came to Leda in the form of a swan).

9. Lover (i.e., Paris).

1. Wife of Hector, one of the sons of Priam and the finest Trojan warrior.

2. Son of Peleus and of the sea nymph Thetis; Achilles was the greatest Greek warrior fighting in the Trojan War. The scene set here is a tissue of recollections from the *Iliad*.

3. I.e., Patroclus.

4. Warriors who accompanied Achilles to Troy.

grape-blood upon the ground in honor of Him whom at Dodona[5] bare-footed prophets worshipped, and prays to Him, and knows not that he prays in vain, and that by the hands of two knights from Troy, Panthous' son, Euphorbus, whose love-locks were looped with gold, and the Pria-mid,[6] the lion-hearted, Patroclus, the comrade of comrades, must meet his doom. Phantoms, are they? Heroes of mist and mountain? Shadows in a song? No: they are real. Action! What is action? It dies at the moment of its energy. It is a base concession to fact. The world is made by the singer for the dreamer.

ERNEST   While you talk it seems to me to be so.

GILBERT   It is so in truth. On the mouldering citadel of Troy lies the liz-ard like a thing of green bronze. The owl has built her nest in the palace of Priam. Over the empty plain wander shepherd and goatherd with their flocks, and where, on the wine-surfaced, oily sea, οἶνοψ πόντος,[7] as Homer calls it, copper-prowed and streaked with vermilion, the great galleys of the Danaoi[8] came in their gleaming crescent, the lonely tunny-fisher[9] sits in his little boat and watches the bobbing corks of his net. Yet, every morning the doors of the city are thrown open, and on foot, or in horse-drawn chariot, the warriors go forth to battle, and mock their enemies from behind their iron masks. All day long the fight rages, and when night comes the torches gleam by the tents, and the cresset[1] burns in the hall. Those who live in marble or on painted panel know of life but a single exquisite instant, eternal indeed in its beauty, but limited to one note of passion or one mood of calm. Those whom the poet makes live have their myriad emotions of joy and terror, of courage and despair, of pleasure and of suffering. The seasons come and go in glad or sad-dening pageant, and with winged or leaden feet the years pass by before them. They have their youth and their manhood, they are children, and they grow old. It is always dawn for St. Helena, as Veronese saw her at the window.[2] Through the still morning air the angels bring her the sym-bol of God's pain.[3] The cool breezes of the morning lift the gilt threads from her brow. On that little hill by the city of Florence, where the lovers of Giorgione[4] are lying, it is always the solstice of noon, made so lan-guorous by summer suns that hardly can the slim naked girl dip into the marble tank the round bubble of clear glass, and the long fingers of the lute player rest idly upon the chords. It is twilight always for the danc-ing nymphs whom Corot[5] set free among the silver poplars of France. In eternal twilight they move, those frail diaphanous figures, whose trem-ulous white feet seem not to touch the dew-drenched grass they tread on. But those who walk in epos,[6] drama, or romance, see through the labouring months the young moons wax and wane, and watch the night from evening unto morning star, and from sunrise unto sunsetting can

5. Seat of a very ancient oracle of Zeus.
6. The son of Priam, i.e., Hector. With Euphor-bus's help he killed Patroclus, and in turn he was slain by Achilles.
7. Wine-dark sea (Greek).
8. Greeks.
9. Tuna fishers.
1. Metal basket holding fuel burned for illumi-nation, often hung from the ceiling.
2. One of the best-known works of the Italian

painter Paolo Veronese (Paolo Caliari, 1528–1588) is *Helena's Vision*.
3. I.e., the cross.
4. Italian painter (ca. 1477–1511), the most bril-liant colorist of his time. The painting is *The Concert*.
5. Jean-Baptiste-Camille Corot (1796–1875), French painter best known for his shimmering trees.
6. Epic poetry.

note the shifting day with all its gold and shadow. For them, as for us, the flowers bloom and wither, and the Earth, that Green-tressed Goddess as Coleridge calls her,[7] alters her raiment for their pleasure. The statue is concentrated to one moment of perfection. The image stained upon the canvas possesses no spiritual element of growth or change. If they know nothing of death, it is because they know little of life, for the secrets of life and death belong to those, and those only, whom the sequence of time affects, and who possess not merely the present but the future, and can rise or fall from a past of glory or of shame. Movement, that problem of the visible arts, can be truly realized by Literature alone. It is Literature that shows us the body in its swiftness and the soul in its unrest.

ERNEST Yes; I see now what you mean. But, surely, the higher you place the creative artist, the lower must the critic rank.

GILBERT Why so?

ERNEST Because the best that he can give us will be but an echo of rich music, a dim shadow of clear-outlined form. It may, indeed, be that life is chaos, as you tell me that it is; that its martyrdoms are mean and its heroisms ignoble; and that it is the function of Literature to create, from the rough material of actual existence, a new world that will be more marvellous, more enduring, and more true than the world that common eyes look upon, and through which common natures seek to realize their perfection. But surely, if this new world has been made by the spirit and touch of a great artist, it will be a thing so complete and perfect that there will be nothing left for the critic to do. I quite understand now, and indeed admit most readily, that it is far more difficult to talk about a thing than to do it. But it seems to me that this sound and sensible maxim, which is really extremely soothing to one's feelings, and should be adopted as its motto by every Academy of Literature all over the world, applies only to the relations that exist between Art and Life, and not to any relations that there may be between Art and Criticism.

GILBERT But, surely, Criticism is itself an art. And just as artistic creation implies the working of the critical faculty, and, indeed, without it cannot be said to exist at all, so Criticism is really creative in the highest sense of the word. Criticism is, in fact, both creative and independent.

ERNEST Independent?

GILBERT Yes; independent. Criticism is no more to be judged by any low standard of imitation or resemblance than is the work of poet or sculptor. The critic occupies the same relation to the work of art that he criticizes as the artist does to the visible world of form and colour, or the unseen world of passion and of thought. He does not even require for the perfection of his art the finest materials. Anything will serve his purpose. And just as out of the sordid and sentimental amours of the silly wife of a small country doctor in the squalid village of Yonville-l'Abbaye, near Rouen, Gustave Flaubert[8] was able to create a classic, and make a masterpiece of style, so, from subjects of little or of no importance, such as the pictures in this year's Royal Academy,[9] or in any year's Royal

---

7. Cf. S. T. Coleridge's "Hymn to the Earth" (1834), line 10, where Earth is called "Green-haired Goddess."
8. French novelist (1821–1880); the reference is to his novel *Madame Bovary* (1857).
9. The Royal Academy of Arts, founded in 1768, holds an annual summer exhibition of new work.

Academy for that matter, Mr. Lewis Morris's poems, M. Ohnet's novels, or the plays of Mr. Henry Arthur Jones,[1] the true critic can, if it be his pleasure so to direct or waste his faculty of contemplation, produce work that will be flawless in beauty and instinct with intellectual subtlety. Why not? Dullness is always an irresistible temptation for brilliancy, and stupidity is the permanent *Bestia Trionfans*[2] that calls wisdom from its cave. To an artist so creative as the critic, what does subject matter signify? No more and no less than it does to the novelist and the painter. Like them, he can find his motives everywhere. Treatment is the test. There is nothing that has not in it suggestion or challenge.

ERNEST   But is Criticism really a creative art?

GILBERT   Why should it not be? It works with materials, and puts them into a form that is at once new and delightful. What more can one say of poetry? Indeed, I would call criticism a creation within a creation. For just as the great artists, from Homer and Aeschylus, down to Shakespeare and Keats, did not go directly to life for their subject matter, but sought for it in myth, and legend, and ancient tale, so the critic deals with materials that others have, as it were, purified for him, and to which imaginative form and colour have been already added. Nay, more, I would say that the highest Criticism, being the purest form of personal impression, is in its way more creative than creation, as it has least reference to any standard external to itself, and is, in fact, its own reason for existing, and, as the Greeks would put it, in itself, and to itself, an end. Certainly, it is never trammeled by any shackles of verisimilitude. No ignoble considerations of probability, that cowardly concession to the tedious repetitions of domestic or public life, affect it ever. One may appeal from fiction unto fact. But from the soul there is no appeal.

ERNEST   From the soul?

GILBERT   Yes, from the soul. That is what the highest criticism really is, the record of one's own soul. It is more fascinating than history, as it is concerned simply with oneself. It is more delightful than philosophy, as its subject is concrete and not abstract, real and not vague. It is the only civilized form of autobiography, as it deals not with the events, but with the thoughts of one's life, not with life's physical accidents of deed or circumstance, but with the spiritual moods and imaginative passions of the mind. I am always amused by the silly vanity of those writers and artists of our day who seem to imagine that the primary function of the critic is to chatter about their second-rate work. The best that one can say of most modern creative art is that it is just a little less vulgar than reality, and so the critic, with his fine sense of distinction and sure instinct of delicate refinement, will prefer to look into the silver mirror or through the woven veil, and will turn his eyes away from the chaos and clamour of actual existence, though the mirror be tarnished and the veil be torn. His sole

---

1. Wilde is mischievously suggesting his low opinion of the contemporary writers just named. Morris (1833–1907) was a popular Welsh poet and essayist often ridiculed by the critics. Georges Ohnet (1848–1918) was a French novelist and dramatist. Jones (1851–1929) was one of the leading English playwrights of his time.

2. Triumphant beast (Wilde's mixture of Italian and Latin); a reference to *Spaccio della Bestia Trionfante* (*Expulsion of the Triumphant Beast*, 1584), a philosophical allegory by the Italian philosopher Giordano Bruno.

aim is to chronicle his own impressions. It is for him that pictures are painted, books written, and marble hewn into form.

ERNEST   I seem to have heard another theory of Criticism.

GILBERT   Yes: it has been said by one whose gracious memory we all revere,[3] and the music of whose pipe once lured Proserpina from her Sicilian fields, and made those white feet stir, and not in vain, the Cumnor cowslips, that the proper aim of Criticism is to see the object as in itself it really is. But this is a very serious error, and takes no cognizance of Criticism's most perfect form, which is in its essence purely subjective, and seeks to reveal its own secret and not the secret of another. For the highest Criticism deals with art not as expressive but as impressive purely.

ERNEST   But is that really so?

GILBERT   Of course it is. Who cares whether Mr. Ruskin's views on Turner[4] are sound or not? What does it matter? That mighty and majestic prose of his, so fervid and so fiery-colored in its noble eloquence, so rich in its elaborate symphonic music, so sure and certain, at its best, in subtle choice of word and epithet, is at least as great a work of art as any of those wonderful sunsets that bleach or rot on their corrupted canvases in England's Gallery; greater indeed, one is apt to think at times, not merely because its equal beauty is more enduring, but on account of the fuller variety of its appeal, soul speaking to soul in those long-cadenced lines, not through form and colour alone, though through these, indeed, completely and without loss, but with intellectual and emotional utterance, with lofty passion and with loftier thought, with imaginative insight, and with poetic aim; greater, I always think, even as Literature is the greater art. Who, again, cares whether Mr. Pater has put into the portrait of Mona Lisa[5] something that Leonardo never dreamed of? The painter may have been merely the slave of an archaic smile, as some have fancied, but whenever I pass into the cool galleries of the Palace of the Louvre, and stand before that strange figure "set in its marble chair in that cirque of fantastic rocks, as in some faint light under sea," I murmur to myself, "She is older than the rocks among which she sits; like the vampire, she has been dead many times, and learned the secrets of the grave; and has been a diver in deep seas, and keeps their fallen day about her: and trafficked for strange webs with Eastern merchants; and, as Leda, was the mother of Helen of Troy, and, as St. Anne, the mother of Mary; and all this has been to her but as the sound of lyres and flutes, and lives only in the delicacy with which it has moulded the changing lineaments, and tinged the eyelids and the hands." And I say to my friend, "The presence that thus so strangely rose beside the waters is expressive of what in the ways of a thousand years man had come to desire"; and he answers me, "Hers is the head upon which all 'the ends of the world are come,' and the eyelids are a little weary."

3. I.e., Matthew Arnold, whose poem "Thyrsis" (1866; lines 91–100) evokes the legend of Proserpina, a goddess associated with the pastoral landscapes of Sicily. Arnold believed that it would be "in vain" to summon Proserpina to visit the Cumnor hills landscape (near Oxford), but Wilde's speaker here flatters Arnold that the summons was so beautiful that it was "not in vain." For the prose passage about the "aim of Criticism," see Arnold's "The Function of Criticism at the Present Time" (1864; p. 450).

4. For John Ruskin's defense of the paintings of J. M. W. Turner, see Modern Painters (1843), especially his praise of Turner's The Slave Ship (p. 450).

5. All remaining references in this paragraph and the first in the next are to Walter Pater's Studies in the History of the Renaissance (p. 584).

And so the picture becomes more wonderful to us than it really is, and reveals to us a secret of which, in truth, it knows nothing, and the music of the mystical prose is as sweet in our ears as was that flute-player's music that lent to the lips of La Gioconda[6] those subtle and poisonous curves. Do you ask me what Leonardo would have said had any one told him of this picture that "all the thoughts and experience of the world had etched and moulded therein that which they had of power to refine and make expressive the outward form, the animalism of Greece, the lust of Rome, the reverie of the Middle Age with its spiritual ambition and imaginative loves, the return of the Pagan world, the sins of the Borgias?" He would probably have answered that he had contemplated none of these things, but had concerned himself simply with certain arrangements of lines and masses, and with new and curious colour-harmonies of blue and green. And it is for this very reason that the criticism which I have quoted is criticism of the highest kind. It treats the work of art simply as a starting point for a new creation. It does not confine itself—let us at least suppose so for the moment—to discovering the real intention of the artist and accepting that as final. And in this it is right, for the meaning of any beautiful created thing is, at least, as much in the soul of him who looks at it, as it was in his soul who wrought it. Nay, it is rather the beholder who lends to the beautiful thing its myriad meanings, and makes it marvelous for us, and sets it in some new relation to the age, so that it becomes a vital portion of our lives, and symbol of what we pray for, or perhaps of what, having prayed for, we fear that we may receive. The longer I study, Ernest, the more clearly I see that the beauty of the visible arts is, as the beauty of music, impressive[7] primarily, and that it may be marred, and indeed often is so, by any excess of intellectual intention on the part of the artist. For when the work is finished it has, as it were, an independent life of its own, and may deliver a message far other than that which was put into its lips to say. Sometimes, when I listen to the overture to *Tannhäuser*,[8] I seem indeed to see that comely knight treading delicately on the flower-strewn grass, and to hear the voice of Venus calling to him from the caverned hill. But at other times it speaks to me of a thousand different things, of myself, it may be, and my own life, or of the lives of others whom one has loved and grown weary of loving, or of the passions that man has known, or of the passions that man has not known, and so has sought for. Tonight it may fill one with that ΕΡΩΣ ΤΩΝ ΑΔΥΝΑΤΩΝ, that *amour de l'impossible*,[9] which falls like a madness on many who think they live securely and out of reach of harm, so that they sicken suddenly with the poison of unlimited desire, and, in the infinite pursuit of what they may not obtain, grow faint and swoon or stumble. Tomorrow, like the music of which Aristotle and Plato tell us, the noble Dorian music of the Greek,[1] it may perform the office of a physician, and give us an anodyne against pain, and heal the spirit that is

---

6. I.e., the *Mona Lisa* (the portrait was of the wife of Francesco del Gioconda—hence "La Gioconda").
7. I.e., designed to create an impression of the senses.
8. The 1845 opera by Richard Wagner, based on the legend of a 14th-century German poet who

fell under the spell of Venus and lived with her in a mountain, Hörselberg.
9. Love of the impossible, in Greek (in capital letters, perhaps to give the effect of an inscription) and in French.
1. Both Plato (*Republic* 3) and Aristotle (*Politics* 8) praise the educational appropriateness of the

wounded, and "bring the soul into harmony with all right things." And what is true about music is true about all the arts. Beauty has as many meanings as man has moods. Beauty is the symbol of symbols. Beauty reveals everything, because it expresses nothing. When it shows us itself, it shows us the whole fiery-coloured world.

ERNEST   But is such work as you have talked about really criticism?

GILBERT   It is the highest Criticism, for it criticizes not merely the individual work of art, but Beauty itself, and fills with wonder a form which the artist may have left void, or not understood, or understood incompletely.

ERNEST   The highest Criticism, then, is more creative than creation, and the primary aim of the critic is to see the object as in itself it really is not; that is your theory, I believe?

GILBERT   Yes, that is my theory. To the critic the work of art is simply a suggestion for a new work of his own, that need not necessarily bear any obvious resemblance to the thing it criticizes. The one characteristic of a beautiful form is that one can put into it whatever one wishes, and see in it whatever one chooses to see; and the Beauty, that gives to creation its universal and aesthetic element, makes the critic a creator in his turn, and whispers of a thousand different things which were not present in the mind of him who carved the statue or painted the panel or graved the gem.

It is sometimes said by those who understand neither the nature of the highest Criticism nor the charm of the highest Art, that the pictures that the critic loves most to write about are those that belong to the anecdotage of painting, and that deal with scenes taken out of literature or history. But this is not so. Indeed, pictures of this kind are far too intelligible. As a class, they rank with illustrations, and even considered from this point of view are failures, as they do not stir the imagination, but set definite bounds to it. For the domain of the painter is, as I suggested before, widely different from that of the poet. To the latter belongs life in its full and absolute entirety; not merely the beauty that men look at, but the beauty that men listen to also; not merely the momentary grace of form or the transient gladness of colour, but the whole sphere of feeling, the perfect cycle of thought. The painter is so far limited that it is only through the mask of the body that he can show us the mystery of the soul; only through conventional images that he can handle ideas; only through its physical equivalents that he can deal with psychology. And how inadequately does he do it then, asking us to accept the torn turban of the Moor for the noble rage of Othello, or a dotard in a storm for the wild madness of Lear! Yet it seems as if nothing could stop him. Most of our elderly English painters spend their wicked and wasted lives in poaching upon the domain of the poets, marring their motives by clumsy treatment, and striving to render, by visible form or colour, the marvel of what is invisible, the splendour of what is not seen. Their pictures are, as a natural consequence, insufferably tedious. They have degraded the invisible arts into the obvious arts, and the one thing not worth looking at is the obvious. I do not say that poet and painter may not treat of the same subject. They have always done so, and will always do

---

Dorian mode (Aristotle calls it especially steady and manly), as opposed to eastern music; the

Dorians were a people of ancient Greece, the last of the northern invaders (ca. 1100–950 B.C.E.).

so. But while the poet can be pictorial or not, as he chooses, the painter must be pictorial always. For a painter is limited, not to what he sees in nature, but to what upon canvas may be seen.

And so, my dear Ernest, pictures of this kind will not really fascinate the critic. He will turn from them to such works as make him brood and dream and fancy, to works that possess the subtle quality of suggestion, and seem to tell one that even from them there is an escape into a wider world. It is sometimes said that the tragedy of an artist's life is that he cannot realize his ideal. But the true tragedy that dogs the steps of most artists is that they realize their ideal too absolutely. For, when the ideal is realized, it is robbed of its wonder and its mystery, and becomes simply a new starting point for an ideal that is other than itself. This is the reason why music is the perfect type of art. Music can never reveal its ultimate secret. This, also, is the explanation of the value of limitations in art. The sculptor gladly surrenders imitative colour, and the painter the actual dimensions of form, because by such renunciations they are able to avoid too definite a presentation of the Real, which would be mere imitation, and too definite a realization of the Ideal, which would be too purely intellectual. It is through its very incompleteness that Art becomes complete in beauty, and so addresses itself, not to the faculty of recognition nor to the faculty of reason, but to the aesthetic sense alone, which, while accepting both reason and recognition as stages of apprehension, subordinates them both to a pure synthetic impression of the work of art as a whole, and, taking whatever alien emotional elements the work may possess, uses their very complexity as a means by which a richer unity may be added to the ultimate impression itself. You see, then, how it is that the aesthetic critic rejects these obvious modes of art that have but one message to deliver, and having delivered it become dumb and sterile, and seeks rather for such modes as suggest reverie and mood, and by their imaginative beauty make all interpretations true, and no interpretation final. Some resemblance, no doubt, the creative work of the critic will have to the work that has stirred him to creation, but it will be such resemblance as exists, not between Nature and the mirror that the painter of landscape or figure may be supposed to hold up to her, but between Nature and the work of the decorative artist. Just as on the flowerless carpets of Persia, tulip and rose blossom indeed and are lovely to look on, though they are not reproduced in visible shape or line; just as the pearl and purple of the sea shell is echoed in the church of St. Mark at Venice; just as the vaulted ceiling of the wondrous chapel at Ravenna is made gorgeous by the gold and green and sapphire of the peacock's tail, though the birds of Juno[2] fly not across it; so the critic reproduces the work that he criticizes in a mode that is never imitative, and part of whose charm may really consist in the rejection of resemblance, and shows us in this way not merely the meaning but also the mystery of Beauty, and, by transforming each art into literature, solves once for all the problem of Art's unity.

---

2. Peacocks, associated in classical mythology with the goddess Juno (in Greek, Hera) because she is said to have set in the bird's tail the eyes of hundred-eyed Argus, who died in her service.

But I see it is time for supper. After we have discussed some Chambertin and a few ortolans,[3] we will pass on to the question of the critic considered in the light of the interpreter.

ERNEST   Ah! you admit, then, that the critic may occasionally be allowed to see the object as in itself it really is.

GILBERT   I am not quite sure. Perhaps I may admit it after supper. There is a subtle influence in supper.

1890, 1891

Preface to *The Picture of Dorian Gray*

The artist is the creator of beautiful things.

To reveal art and conceal the artist is art's aim.

The critic is he who can translate into another manner or a new material his impression of beautiful things.

The highest, as the lowest, form of criticism is a mode of autobiography.

Those who find ugly meanings in beautiful things are corrupt without being charming. This is a fault.

Those who find beautiful meanings in beautiful things are the cultivated. For these there is hope.

They are the elect to whom beautiful things mean only Beauty.

There is no such thing as a moral or an immoral book.

Books are well written, or badly written. That is all.

The nineteenth-century dislike of Realism is the rage of Caliban[1] seeing his own face in a glass.

The nineteenth-century dislike of Romanticism is the rage of Caliban not seeing his own face in a glass.

The moral life of man forms part of the subject matter of the artist, but the morality of art consists in the perfect use of an imperfect medium. No artist desires to prove anything. Even things that are true can be proved.

No artist has ethical sympathies. An ethical sympathy in an artist is an unpardonable mannerism of style.

No artist is ever morbid. The artist can express everything.

Thought and language are to the artist instruments of an art.

Vice and Virtue are to the artist materials for an art.

From the point of view of form, the type of all the arts is the art of the musician.

From the point of view of feeling, the actor's craft is the type.

All art is at once surface and symbol.

Those who go beneath the surface do so at their peril.

Those who read the symbol do so at their peril.

It is the spectator, and not life, that art really mirrors.

---

3. Small birds esteemed by epicures for their delicate flavor. "Chambertin": one of the finest wines of Burgundy.

1. The character in Shakespeare's *The Tempest* who is half-human, half-monster.

Diversity of opinion about a work of art shows that the work is new, complex, and vital.

When critics disagree the artist is in accord with himself. We can forgive a man for making a useful thing as long as he does not admire it. The only excuse for making a useless thing is that one admires it intensely.

All art is quite useless.

1891

The Importance of Being Earnest

Of the four stage comedies by Wilde, his last, *The Importance of Being Earnest*, is generally regarded as his masterpiece. It was first staged in February 1895 and was an immediate hit. Only one critic failed to find it delightful; curiously, this was Wilde's fellow playwright from Ireland, George Bernard Shaw, who, though amused, found Wilde's wit "hateful" and "sinister," and thought the play exhibited "real degeneracy." Despite Shaw's complaints, the first London production ran for eighty-six performances; but when Wilde was sentenced to prison, production ceased for several years. Shortly before his death it was revived in London and New York, and it has subsequently become a classic.

In its original version the play was in four acts. At the request of the stage producer, Wilde reduced it to three acts—the version almost always used in performances and the version reprinted here. A few of the notes in the text cite passages from the four-act version.

The play was first published in 1899. Earlier, in an interview, Wilde had described his overall aim in writing it: "It has as its philosophy . . . that we should treat all the trivial things of life seriously, and all the serious things of life with sincere and studied triviality." Just before his death he remarked that although he was pleased with the "bright and happy" tone and temper of his play, he wished it might have had a "higher seriousness of intent." Later critics have found this seriousness of intent in the play's deconstruction of Victorian moral and social values. Like another Victorian masterpiece of the absurd, *Alice's Adventures in Wonderland* (1865), *The Importance of Being Earnest* empties manners and morals of their underlying sense to create a nominalist world where earnest is not a quality of character but a name, where words, to paraphrase Humpty Dumpty in *Through the Looking-Glass* (1871), mean what you choose them to mean, neither more nor less.

The literary ancestry of Wilde's play has been variously identified. In its witty word-play and worldly attitudes it has been likened to comedies of the Restoration period such as William Congreve's *Love for Love* (1695). In its genial and lighthearted tone, it has some affinities with the festive comedies of Shakespeare, such as *Twelfth Night* (ca. 1601), and with Oliver Goldsmith's *She Stoops to Conquer* (1773). A more immediate predecessor was *Engaged* (1877), a comic play by W. S. Gilbert that anticipated some of the burlesque effects exploited by Wilde, such as the inviolable imperturbability of the speakers and the interrupting of sentimental scenes by the consumption of food. Gilbert's advice to the actors who were putting on his *Engaged* is worth citing as a clue to how *The Importance of Being Earnest* may be most effectively imagined as a stage representation:

> It is absolutely essential to the success of this piece that it should be played with the most perfect earnestness and gravity throughout. . . . Directly the actors show that they are conscious of the absurdity of their utterances the piece begins to drag.

The Importance of Being Earnest

First Act

SCENE—*Morning room in* ALGERNON'*s flat in Half-Moon Street.*[1]

The room is luxuriously and artistically furnished. The sound of a piano is heard in the adjoining room.

> [LANE *is arranging afternoon tea on the table, and after the music has ceased,* ALGERNON *enters.*]

ALGERNON   Did you hear what I was playing, Lane?

LANE   I didn't think it polite to listen, sir.

ALGERNON   I'm sorry for that, for your sake. I don't play accurately—anyone can play accurately—but I play with wonderful expression. As far as the piano is concerned, sentiment is my forte. I keep science for Life.

LANE   Yes, sir.

ALGERNON   And, speaking of the science of Life, have you got the cucumber sandwiches cut for Lady Bracknell?[2]

LANE   Yes, sir. [*Hands them on a salver.*]

ALGERNON [*Inspects them, takes two, and sits down on the sofa.*]   Oh! . . . by the way, Lane, I see from your book[3] that on Thursday night, when Lord Shoreham and Mr. Worthing were dining with me, eight bottles of champagne are entered as having been consumed.

LANE   Yes, sir; eight bottles and a pint.

ALGERNON   Why is it that at a bachelor's establishment the servants invariably drink the champagne? I ask merely for information.

LANE   I attribute it to the superior quality of the wine, sir. I have often observed that in married households the champagne is rarely of a first-rate brand.

ALGERNON   Good Heavens! Is marriage so demoralizing as that?

LANE   I believe it *is* a very pleasant state, sir. I have had very little experience of it myself up to the present. I have only been married once. That was in consequence of a misunderstanding between myself and a young person.

ALGERNON [*Languidly.*]   I don't know that I am much interested in your family life, Lane.

LANE   No, sir; it is not a very interesting subject. I never think of it myself.

ALGERNON   Very natural, I am sure. That will do, Lane, thank you.

LANE   Thank you, sir.   [LANE *goes out.*]

ALGERNON   Lane's views on marriage seem somewhat lax. Really, if the lower orders don't set us a good example, what on earth is the use of them? They seem, as a class, to have absolutely no sense of moral responsibility.

> [*Enter* LANE.]

LANE   Mr. Ernest Worthing.

> [*Enter* JACK.]   [LANE *goes out.*]

---

1. A highly fashionable location (at the time of the play) in the West End of London.
2. Bracknell is the name of a place in Berkshire where the mother of Lord Alfred Douglas had her summer home, which Wilde had visited.
3. Cellar book, in which records were kept of wines.

ALGERNON   How are you, my dear Ernest? What brings you up to town?

JACK   Oh, pleasure, pleasure! What else should bring one anywhere? Eating as usual, I see, Algy!

ALGERNON [*Stiffly.*]   I believe it is customary in good society to take some slight refreshment at five o'clock. Where have you been since last Thursday?

JACK [*Sitting down on the sofa.*]   In the country.

ALGERNON   What on earth do you do there?

JACK [*Pulling off his gloves.*]   When one is in town one amuses oneself. When one is in the country one amuses other people. It is excessively boring.

ALGERNON   And who are the people you amuse?

JACK [*Airily.*]   Oh, neighbours, neighbours.

ALGERNON   Got nice neighbours in your part of Shropshire?

JACK   Perfectly horrid! Never speak to one of them.

ALGERNON How immensely you must amuse them! [*Goes over and takes sandwich.*]   By the way, Shropshire is your county, is it not?

JACK   Eh? Shropshire?[4] Yes, of course. Hallo! Why all these cups? Why cucumber sandwiches? Why such reckless extravagance in one so young? Who is coming to tea?

ALGERNON   Oh! merely Aunt Augusta and Gwendolen.

JACK   How perfectly delightful!

ALGERNON   Yes, that is all very well; but I am afraid Aunt Augusta won't quite approve of your being here.

JACK   May I ask why?

ALGERNON   My dear fellow, the way you flirt with Gwendolen is perfectly disgraceful. It is almost as bad as the way Gwendolen flirts with you.

JACK   I am in love with Gwendolen. I have come up to town expressly to propose to her.

ALGERNON   I thought you had come up for pleasure? . . . I call that business.

JACK   How utterly unromantic you are!

ALGERNON   I really don't see anything romantic in proposing. It is very romantic to be in love. But there is nothing romantic about a definite proposal. Why, one may be accepted. One usually is, I believe. Then the excitement is all over. The very essence of romance is uncertainty. If ever I get married, I'll certainly try to forget the fact.

JACK   I have no doubt about that, dear Algy. The Divorce Court was specially invented for people whose memories are so curiously constituted.

ALGERNON   Oh! there is no use speculating on that subject. Divorces are made in Heaven—[JACK *puts out his hand to take a sandwich.* ALGERNON *at once interferes.*] Please don't touch the cucumber sandwiches. They are ordered specially for Aunt Augusta. [*Takes one and eats it.*]

JACK   Well, you have been eating them all the time.

---

4. As we learn later, the estate is in Hertfordshire, a long distance from Shropshire. In the four-act version of the play, when this discrepancy is pointed out by Algernon, Jack replies: "My dear fellow! Surely you don't expect me to be accurate about geography? No gentleman is accurate about geography. Why, I got a prize for geography when I was at school. I can't be expected to know anything about it now."

ALGERNON   That is quite a different matter. She is my aunt. [*Takes plate from below.*] Have some bread and butter. The bread and butter is for Gwendolen. Gwendolen is devoted to bread and butter.

JACK [*Advancing to table and helping himself.*]   And very good bread and butter it is too.

ALGERNON   Well, my dear fellow, you need not eat as if you were going to eat it all. You behave as if you were married to her already. You are not married to her already, and I don't think you ever will be.

JACK   Why on earth do you say that?

ALGERNON   Well, in the first place, girls never marry the men they flirt with. Girls don't think it right.

JACK   Oh, that is nonsense!

ALGERNON   It isn't. It is a great truth. It accounts for the extraordinary number of bachelors that one sees all over the place. In the second place, I don't give my consent.

JACK   Your consent!

ALGERNON   My dear fellow, Gwendolen is my first cousin. And before I allow you to marry her, you will have to clear up the whole question of Cecily. [*Rings bell.*]

JACK   Cecily! What on earth do you mean? What do you mean, Algy, by Cecily? I don't know anyone of the name of Cecily.
    [*Enter* LANE.]

ALGERNON   Bring me that cigarette case Mr. Worthing left in the smoking-room the last time he dined here.

LANE   Yes, sir.   [LANE *goes out.*]

JACK   Do you mean to say you have had my cigarette case all this time? I wish to goodness you had let me know. I have been writing frantic letters to Scotland Yard[5] about it. I was very nearly offering a large reward.

ALGERNON   Well, I wish you would offer one. I happen to be more than usually hard up.[6]

JACK   There is no good offering a large reward now that the thing is found.
    [*Enter* LANE *with the cigarette case on a salver.* ALGERNON *takes it at once.* LANE *goes out.*]

ALGERNON   I think that is rather mean of you, Ernest, I must say. [*Opens case and examines it.*] However, it makes no matter, for, now that I look at the inscription inside, I find that the thing isn't yours after all.

JACK   Of course it's mine. [*Moving to him.*] You have seen me with it a hundred times, and you have no right whatsoever to read what is written inside. It is a very ungentlemanly thing to read a private cigarette case.

ALGERNON   Oh! it is absurd to have a hard-and-fast rule about what one should read and what one shouldn't. More than half of modern culture depends on what one shouldn't read.

JACK   I am quite aware of the fact, and I don't propose to discuss modern culture. It isn't the sort of thing one should talk of in private. I simply want my cigarette case back.

ALGERNON   Yes; but this isn't your cigarette case. This cigarette case is a present from someone of the name of Cecily, and you said you didn't know anyone of that name.

---

5. Police headquarters in London.   6. Short of money.

JACK   Well, if you want to know, Cecily happens to be my aunt.

ALGERNON   Your aunt!

JACK   Yes. Charming old lady she is, too. Lives at Tunbridge Wells.[7] Just give it back to me, Algy.

ALGERNON   [*Retreating to back of sofa.*]   But why does she call herself little Cecily if she is your aunt and lives at Tunbridge Wells? [*Reading.*] "From little Cecily with her fondest love."

JACK   [*Moving to sofa and kneeling upon it.*]   My dear fellow, what on earth is there in that? Some aunts are tall, some aunts are not tall. That is a matter that surely an aunt may be allowed to decide for herself. You seem to think that every aunt should be exactly like your aunt! That is absurd! For Heaven's sake give me back my cigarette case. [*Follows Algy round the room.*]

ALGERNON   Yes. But why does your aunt call you her uncle? "From little Cecily, with her fondest love to her dear Uncle Jack." There is no objection, I admit, to an aunt being a small aunt, but why an aunt, no matter what her size may be, should call her own nephew her uncle, I can't quite make out. Besides, your name isn't Jack at all; it is Ernest.

JACK   It isn't Ernest; it's Jack.

ALGERNON   You have always told me it was Ernest. I have introduced you to everyone as Ernest. You answer to the name of Ernest. You look as if your name was Ernest. You are the most earnest looking person I ever saw in my life. It is perfectly absurd your saying that your name isn't Ernest. It's on your cards. Here is one of them. [*Taking it from case.*] "Mr. Ernest Worthing, B. 4, The Albany."[8] I'll keep this as a proof that your name is Ernest if ever you attempt to deny it to me, or to Gwendolen, or to anyone else. [*Puts the card in his pocket.*]

JACK   Well, my name is Ernest in town and Jack in the country, and the cigarette case was given to me in the country.

ALGERNON   Yes, but that does not account for the fact that your small Aunt Cecily, who lives at Tunbridge Wells, calls you her dear uncle. Come, old boy, you had much better have the thing out at once.

JACK   My dear Algy, you talk exactly as if you were a dentist. It is very vulgar to talk like a dentist when one isn't a dentist. It produces a false impression.

ALGERNON   Well, that is exactly what dentists always do. Now, go on! Tell me the whole thing. I may mention that I have always suspected you of being a confirmed and secret Bunburyist; and I am quite sure of it now.

JACK   Bunburyist? What on earth do you mean by a Bunburyist?

ALGERNON   I'll reveal to you the meaning of that incomparable expression as soon as you are kind enough to inform me why you are Ernest in town and Jack in the country.

JACK   Well, produce my cigarette case first.

ALGERNON   Here it is. [*Hands cigarette case.*] Now produce your explanation, and pray make it improbable. [*Sits on sofa.*]

JACK   My dear fellow, there is nothing improbable about my explanation at all. In fact it's perfectly ordinary. Old Mr. Thomas Cardew, who adopted

7. A fashionable resort town south of London.
8. A former residence of the duke of Albany (brother of George IV) near Piccadilly that had been converted to elegant apartments.

me when I was a little boy, made me in his will guardian to his grand-daughter, Miss Cecily Cardew. Cecily, who addresses me as her uncle from motives of respect that you could not possibly appreciate, lives at my place in the country under the charge of her admirable governess, Miss Prism.

ALGERNON   Where is that place in the country, by the way?

JACK   That is nothing to you, dear boy. You are not going to be invited. . . . I may tell you candidly that the place is not in Shropshire.

ALGERNON   I suspected that, my dear fellow! I have Bunburyed all over Shropshire on two separate occasions. Now, go on. Why are you Ernest in town and Jack in the country?

JACK   My dear Algy, I don't know whether you will be able to understand my real motives. You are hardly serious enough. When one is placed in the position of guardian, one has to adopt a very high moral tone on all subjects. It's one's duty to do so. And as a high moral tone can hardly be said to conduce very much to either one's health or one's happiness, in order to get up to town I have always pretended to have a younger brother of the name of Ernest, who lives in the Albany, and gets into the most dreadful scrapes. That, my dear Algy, is the whole truth pure and simple.

ALGERNON   The truth is rarely pure and never simple. Modern life would be very tedious if it were either, and modern literature a complete impossibility!

JACK   That wouldn't be at all a bad thing.

ALGERNON   Literary criticism is not your forte, my dear fellow. Don't try it. You should leave that to people who haven't been at a University. They do it so well in the daily papers. What you really are is a Bunburyist. I was quite right in saying you were a Bunburyist. You are one of the most advanced Bunburyists I know.

JACK   What on earth do you mean?

ALGERNON   You have invented a very useful young brother called Ernest, in order that you may be able to come up to town as often as you like. I have invented an invaluable permanent invalid called Bunbury, in order that I may be able to go down into the country whenever I choose. Bunbury is perfectly invaluable. If it wasn't for Bunbury's extraordinary bad health, for instance, I wouldn't be able to dine with you at Willis's tonight, for I have been really engaged[9] to Aunt Augusta for more than a week.

JACK   I haven't asked you to dine with me anywhere tonight.

ALGERNON   I know. You are absurdly careless about sending out invitations. It is very foolish of you. Nothing annoys people so much as not receiving invitations.

JACK   You had much better dine with your Aunt Augusta.

ALGERNON   I haven't the smallest intention of doing anything of the kind. To begin with, I dined there on Monday, and once a week is quite enough to dine with one's own relations. In the second place, whenever I do dine there I am always treated as a member of the family, and sent down with[1] either no woman at all, or two. In the third place, I know perfectly well whom she will place me next to, tonight. She will place

---

9. I.e., committed to attend her dinner party. "Willis's": a first-class restaurant in the vicinity of St. James's Street, in the center of London.
1. I.e., required to escort, as a dinner partner.

me next Mary Farquhar, who always flirts with her own husband across the dinner table. That is not very pleasant. Indeed, it is not even decent . . . and that sort of thing is enormously on the increase. The amount of women in London who flirt with their own husbands is perfectly scandalous. It looks so bad. It is simply washing one's clean linen in public. Besides, now that I know you to be a confirmed Bunburyist, I naturally want to talk to you about Bunburying. I want to tell you the rules.

JACK   I'm not a Bunburyist at all. If Gwendolen accepts me, I am going to kill my brother, indeed I think I'll kill him in any case. Cecily is a little too much interested in him. It is rather a bore. So I am going to get rid of Ernest. And I strongly advise you to do the same with Mr. . . . with your invalid friend who has the absurd name.

ALGERNON   Nothing will induce me to part with Bunbury, and if you ever get married, which seems to me extremely problematic, you will be very glad to know Bunbury. A man who marries without knowing Bunbury has a very tedious time of it.

JACK   That is nonsense. If I marry a charming girl like Gwendolen, and she is the only girl I ever saw in my life that I would marry, I certainly won't want to know Bunbury.

ALGERNON   Then your wife will. You don't seem to realize, that in married life three is company and two is none.

JACK [*Sententiously.*]   That, my dear young friend, is the theory that the corrupt French Drama has been propounding for the last fifty years.[2]

ALGERNON   Yes; and that the happy English home has proved in half the time.

JACK   For heaven's sake, don't try to be cynical. It's perfectly easy to be cynical.

ALGERNON   My dear fellow, it isn't easy to be anything nowadays. There's such a lot of beastly competition about. [*The sound of an electric bell is heard.*] Ah! that must be Aunt Augusta. Only relatives, or creditors, ever ring in that Wagnerian manner.[3] Now, if I get her out of the way for ten minutes, so that you can have an opportunity for proposing to Gwendolen, may I dine with you tonight at Willis's?

JACK   I suppose so, if you want to.

ALGERNON   Yes, but you must be serious about it. I hate people who are not serious about meals. It is so shallow of them.

[*Enter* LANE.]

LANE   Lady Bracknell and Miss Fairfax.

[ALGERNON *goes forward to meet them. Enter* LADY BRACKNELL *and* GWENDOLEN.]

LADY BRACKNELL   Good afternoon, dear Algernon, I hope you are behaving very well.

ALGERNON   I'm feeling very well, Aunt Augusta.

LADY BRACKNELL   That's not quite the same thing. In fact the two things rarely go together. [*Sees* JACK *and bows to him with icy coldness.*]

---

2. Almost all the plays by the leading French playwrights of the second half of the 19th century (Alexandre Dumas *fils*, Émile Augier, and Victorien Sardou) focus on marital infidelity. As Brander Matthews, an American critic, noted in 1882, "the trio—husband, wife, and lover" had become "almost universal" in the French theater.
3. Insistently loud, like some of the music in the large-scale operas of Richard Wagner (1813–1883).

ALGERNON [*To* GWENDOLEN.]   Dear me, you are smart![4]

GWENDOLEN   I am always smart! Aren't I, Mr. Worthing?

JACK   You're quite perfect, Miss Fairfax.

GWENDOLEN   Oh! I hope I am not that. It would leave no room for developments, and I intend to develop in many directions. [GWENDOLEN *and* JACK *sit down together in the corner.*]

LADY BRACKNELL   I'm sorry if we are a little late, Algernon, but I was obliged to call on dear Lady Harbury. I hadn't been there since her poor husband's death. I never saw a woman so altered; she looks quite twenty years younger. And now I'll have a cup of tea, and one of those nice cucumber sandwiches you promised me.

ALGERNON   Certainly, Aunt Augusta. [*Goes over to tea-table.*]

LADY BRACKNELL   Won't you come and sit here, Gwendolen?

GWENDOLEN   Thanks, mamma,[5] I'm quite comfortable where I am.

ALGERNON [*Picking up empty plate in horror.*]   Good heavens! Lane! Why are there no cucumber sandwiches? I ordered them specially.

LANE [*Gravely.*]   There were no cucumbers in the market this morning, sir. I went down twice.

ALGERNON   No cucumbers!

LANE   No, sir. Not even for ready money.[6]

ALGERNON   That will do, Lane, thank you.

LANE   Thank you, sir.

ALGERNON   I am greatly distressed, Aunt Augusta, about there being no cucumbers, not even for ready money.

LADY BRACKNELL   It really makes no matter, Algernon. I had some crumpets[7] with Lady Harbury, who seems to me to be living entirely for pleasure now.

ALGERNON   I hear her hair has turned quite gold from grief.

LADY BRACKNELL   It certainly has changed its colour. From what cause I, of course, cannot say. [ALGERNON *crosses and hands tea.*] Thank you. I've quite a treat for you tonight, Algernon. I am going to send you down with Mary Farquhar. She is such a nice woman, and so attentive to her husband. It's delightful to watch them.

ALGERNON   I am afraid, Aunt Augusta, I shall have to give up the pleasure of dining with you tonight after all.

LADY BRACKNELL [*Frowning.*]   I hope not, Algernon. It would put my table completely out. Your uncle would have to dine upstairs.[8] Fortunately he is accustomed to that.

ALGERNON   It is a great bore, and, I need hardly say, a terrible disappointment to me, but the fact is I have just had a telegram to say that my poor friend Bunbury is very ill again. [*Exchanges glances with* JACK.] They seem to think I should be with him.

LADY BRACKNELL   It is very strange. This Mr. Bunbury seems to suffer from curiously bad health.

ALGERNON   Yes; poor Bunbury is a dreadful invalid.

---

4. Elegantly fashionable.
5. Pronounced with the accent on the second syllable.
6. Immediate payment in cash (rather than on credit).
7. Round griddle breads, served toasted.
8. Because otherwise she would have more women than men at the table.

LADY BRACKNELL Well, I must say, Algernon, that I think it is high time that Mr. Bunbury made up his mind whether he was going to live or to die. This shilly-shallying with the question is absurd. Nor do I in any way approve of the modern sympathy with invalids. I consider it morbid. Illness of any kind is hardly a thing to be encouraged in others. Health is the primary duty of life. I am always telling that to your poor uncle, but he never seems to take much notice . . . as far as any improvement in his ailments goes. I should be obliged if you would ask Mr. Bunbury, from me, to be kind enough not to have a relapse on Saturday, for I rely on you to arrange my music for me. It is my last reception, and one wants something that will encourage conversation, particularly at the end of the season[9] when everyone has practically said whatever they had to say, which, in most cases, was probably not much.

ALGERNON I'll speak to Bunbury, Aunt Augusta, if he is still conscious, and I think I can promise you he'll be all right by Saturday. Of course the music is a great difficulty. You see, if one plays good music, people don't listen, and if one plays bad music, people don't talk. But I'll run over the program I've drawn out, if you will kindly come into the next room for a moment.

LADY BRACKNELL Thank you, Algernon. It is very thoughtful of you. [*Rising, and following* ALGERNON.] I'm sure the program will be delightful, after a few expurgations. French songs I cannot possibly allow. People always seem to think that they are improper, and either look shocked, which is vulgar, or laugh, which is worse. But German sounds a thoroughly respectable language, and indeed, I believe is so. Gwendolen, you will accompany me.

GWENDOLEN Certainly, mamma.

[LADY BRACKNELL *and* ALGERNON *go into the music room,* GWENDOLEN *remains behind.*]

JACK Charming day it has been, Miss Fairfax.

GWENDOLEN Pray don't talk to me about the weather, Mr. Worthing. Whenever people talk to me about the weather, I always feel quite certain that they mean something else. And that makes me so nervous.

JACK I do mean something else.

GWENDOLEN I thought so. In fact, I am never wrong.

JACK And I would like to be allowed to take advantage of Lady Bracknell's temporary absence . . .

GWENDOLEN I would certainly advise you to do so. Mamma has a way of coming back suddenly into a room that I have often had to speak to her about.

JACK [*Nervously.*] Miss Fairfax, ever since I met you I have admired you more than any girl . . . I have ever met since . . . I met you.

GWENDOLEN Yes, I am quite aware of the fact. And I often wish that in public, at any rate, you had been more demonstrative. For me you have always had an irresistible fascination. Even before I met you I was far from indifferent to you. [JACK *looks at her in amazement.*] We live, as I hope you know, Mr. Worthing, in an age of ideals. The fact is constantly

---

9. The social season, extending from May through July, when people of fashion came into London from their country estates for entertainments and parties.

mentioned in the more expensive monthly magazines, and has reached the provincial pulpits, I am told: and my ideal has always been to love someone of the name of Ernest. There is something in that name that inspires absolute confidence. The moment Algernon first mentioned to me that he had a friend called Ernest, I knew I was destined to love you.

JACK You really love me, Gwendolen?

GWENDOLEN Passionately!

JACK Darling! You don't know how happy you've made me.

GWENDOLEN My own Ernest!

JACK But you don't really mean to say that you couldn't love me if my name wasn't Ernest?

GWENDOLEN But your name is Ernest.

JACK Yes, I know it is. But supposing it was something else? Do you mean to say you couldn't love me then?

GWENDOLEN [*Glibly.*] Ah! that is clearly a metaphysical speculation, and like most metaphysical speculations has very little reference at all to the actual facts of real life, as we know them.

JACK Personally, darling, to speak quite candidly, I don't much care about the name of Ernest . . . I don't think the name suits me at all.

GWENDOLEN It suits you perfectly. It is a divine name. It has a music of its own. It produces vibrations.

JACK Well, really, Gwendolen, I must say that I think there are lots of other much nicer names. I think Jack, for instance, a charming name.

GWENDOLEN Jack? . . . No, there is very little music in the name Jack, if any at all, indeed. It does not thrill. It produces absolutely no vibrations. . . . I have known several Jacks, and they all, without exception, were more than usually plain. Besides, Jack is a notorious domesticity for John! And I pity any woman who is married to a man called John. She would probably never be allowed to know the entrancing pleasure of a single moment's solitude. The only really safe name is Ernest.

JACK Gwendolen, I must get christened at once—I mean we must get married at once. There is no time to be lost.

GWENDOLEN Married, Mr. Worthing?

JACK [*Astounded.*] Well . . . surely. You know that I love you, and you led me to believe, Miss Fairfax, that you were not absolutely indifferent to me.

GWENDOLEN I adore you. But you haven't proposed to me yet. Nothing has been said at all about marriage. The subject has not even been touched on.

JACK Well . . . may I propose to you now?

GWENDOLEN I think it would be an admirable opportunity. And to spare you any possible disappointment, Mr. Worthing, I think it only fair to tell you quite frankly beforehand that I am fully determined to accept you.

JACK Gwendolen!

GWENDOLEN Yes, Mr. Worthing, what have you got to say to me?

JACK You know what I have got to say to you.

GWENDOLEN Yes, but you don't say it.

JACK Gwendolen, will you marry me? [*Goes on his knees.*]

GWENDOLEN Of course I will, darling. How long you have been about it! I am afraid you have had very little experience in how to propose.

JACK   My own one, I have never loved anyone in the world but you.

GWENDOLEN   Yes, but men often propose for practice. I know my brother Gerald does. All my girlfriends tell me so. What wonderfully blue eyes you have, Ernest! They are quite, quite blue. I hope you will always look at me just like that, especially when there are other people present.

   [*Enter* LADY BRACKNELL.]

LADY BRACKNELL   Mr. Worthing! Rise, sir, from this semi-recumbent posture. It is most indecorous.

GWENDOLEN   Mamma! [*He tries to rise; she restrains him.*] I must beg you to retire. This is no place for you. Besides, Mr. Worthing has not quite finished yet.

LADY BRACKNELL   Finished what, may I ask?

GWENDOLEN   I am engaged to Mr. Worthing, mamma.

   [*They rise together.*]

LADY BRACKNELL   Pardon me, you are not engaged to anyone. When you do become engaged to someone, I, or your father, should his health permit him, will inform you of the fact. An engagement should come on a young girl as a surprise, pleasant or unpleasant, as the case may be. It is hardly a matter that she could be allowed to arrange for herself. . . . And now I have a few questions to put to you, Mr. Worthing. While I am making these inquiries, you, Gwendolen, will wait for me below in the carriage.

GWENDOLEN [*Reproachfully.*]   Mamma!

LADY BRACKNELL   In the carriage, Gwendolen! [GWENDOLEN *goes to the door. She and* JACK *blow kisses to each other behind* LADY BRACKNELL's *back.* LADY BRACKNELL *looks vaguely about as if she could not understand what the noise was. Finally turns round.*] Gwendolen, the carriage!

GWENDOLEN   Yes, mamma. [*Goes out, looking back at* JACK.]

LADY BRACKNELL [*Sitting down.*]   You can take a seat, Mr. Worthing.

   [*Looks in her pocket for notebook and pencil.*]

JACK   Thank you, Lady Bracknell, I prefer standing.

LADY BRACKNELL [*Pencil and notebook in hand.*]   I feel bound to tell you that you are not down on my list of eligible young men, although I have the same list as the dear Duchess of Bolton has. We work together, in fact. However, I am quite ready to enter your name, should your answers be what a really affectionate mother requires. Do you smoke?

JACK   Well, yes, I must admit I smoke.

LADY BRACKNELL   I am glad to hear it. A man should always have an occupation of some kind. There are far too many idle men in London as it is. How old are you?

JACK   Twenty-nine.

LADY BRACKNELL   A very good age to be married at. I have always been of opinion that a man who desires to get married should know either everything or nothing. Which do you know?

JACK [*After some hesitation.*]   I know nothing, Lady Bracknell.

LADY BRACKNELL   I am pleased to hear it. I do not approve of anything that tampers with natural ignorance. Ignorance is like a delicate exotic fruit; touch it and the bloom is gone. The whole theory of modern education is radically unsound. Fortunately in England, at any rate, education produces no effect whatsoever. If it did, it would prove a serious danger to the upper classes, and probably lead to acts of violence in Grosvenor Square.[1] What is your income?

JACK   Between seven and eight thousand a year.

LADY BRACKNELL [*Makes a note in her book.*]   In land, or in investments?

JACK   In investments, chiefly.

LADY BRACKNELL   That is satisfactory. What between the duties expected of one during one's lifetime, and the duties exacted from one after one's death,[2] land has ceased to be either a profit or a pleasure. It gives one position, and prevents one from keeping it up. That's all that can be said about land.

JACK   I have a country house with some land, of course, attached to it, about fifteen hundred acres, I believe; but I don't depend on that for my real income. In fact, as far as I can make out, the poachers are the only people who make anything out of it.

LADY BRACKNELL   A country house! How many bedrooms? Well, that point can be cleared up afterwards. You have a town house, I hope? A girl with a simple, unspoiled nature, like Gwendolen, could hardly be expected to reside in the country.

JACK   Well, I own a house in Belgrave Square,[3] but it is let by the year to Lady Bloxham. Of course, I can get it back whenever I like, at six months' notice.

LADY BRACKNELL   Lady Bloxham? I don't know her.

JACK   Oh, she goes about very little. She is a lady considerably advanced in years.

LADY BRACKNELL   Ah, nowadays that is no guarantee of respectability of character. What number in Belgrave Square?

JACK   149.

LADY BRACKNELL [*Shaking her head.*]   The unfashionable side. I thought there was something. However, that could easily be altered.

JACK   Do you mean the fashion, or the side?

LADY BRACKNELL [*Sternly.*]   Both, if necessary, I presume. What are your politics?

JACK   Well, I am afraid I really have none. I am a Liberal Unionist.[4]

LADY BRACKNELL   Oh, they count as Tories. They dine with us. Or come in the evening, at any rate. Now to minor matters. Are your parents living?

JACK   I have lost both my parents.

LADY BRACKNELL   Both? To lose one parent may be regarded as a misfortune—to lose *both* seems like carelessness. Who was your father? He was evidently a man of some wealth. Was he born in what the Radical papers call the purple of commerce, or did he rise from the ranks of aristocracy?

JACK   I am afraid I really don't know. The fact is, Lady Bracknell, I said I had lost my parents. It would be nearer the truth to say that my parents seem to have lost me. . . . I don't actually know who I am by birth. I was . . . well, I was found.

---

1. A fashionable residential area in the West End of London.
2. The wordplay is on "death duties"—i.e., inheritance taxes.
3. Another fashionable residential area in the

West End.
4. A splinter group of members of the Liberal Party who in 1886, led by Joseph Chamberlain, joined forces with the Conservative Party (the "Tories") in opposing home rule for Ireland.

LADY BRACKNELL Found!

JACK The late Mr. Thomas Cardew, an old gentleman of a very charitable and kindly disposition, found me, and gave me the name of Worthing, because he happened to have a first-class ticket for Worthing in his pocket at the time. Worthing is a place in Sussex. It is a seaside resort.

LADY BRACKNELL Where did the charitable gentleman who had a first-class ticket for this seaside resort find you?

JACK [*Gravely.*] In a handbag.

LADY BRACKNELL A handbag?

JACK [*Very seriously.*] Yes, Lady Bracknell. I was in a handbag—a somewhat large, black leather handbag, with handles to it—an ordinary handbag, in fact.

LADY BRACKNELL In what locality did this Mr. James, or Thomas, Cardew come across this ordinary handbag?

JACK In the cloak room at Victoria Station. It was given to him in mistake for his own.[5]

LADY BRACKNELL The cloak room at Victoria Station?

JACK Yes. The Brighton line.

LADY BRACKNELL The line is immaterial. Mr. Worthing, I confess I feel somewhat bewildered by what you have just told me. To be born, or at any rate, bred in a handbag, whether it had handles or not, seems to me to display a contempt for the ordinary decencies of family life that reminds one of the worst excesses of the French Revolution. And I presume you know what that unfortunate movement led to? As for the particular locality in which the handbag was found, a cloak room at a railway station might serve to conceal a social indiscretion—has probably, indeed, been used for that purpose before now—but it could hardly be regarded as an assured basis for a recognized position in good society.

JACK May I ask you then what you would advise me to do? I need hardly say I would do anything in the world to ensure Gwendolen's happiness.

LADY BRACKNELL I would strongly advise you, Mr. Worthing, to try and acquire some relations as soon as possible, and to make a definite effort to produce at any rate one parent, of either sex, before the season is quite over.[6]

JACK Well, I don't see how I could possibly manage to do that. I can produce the handbag at any moment, it is in my dressing room at home. I really think that should satisfy you, Lady Bracknell.

LADY BRACKNELL Me, sir! What has it to do with me? You can hardly imagine that I and Lord Bracknell would dream of allowing our only daughter—a girl brought up with the utmost care—to marry into a cloak room, and form an alliance with a parcel? Good morning, Mr. Worthing!

[LADY BRACKNELL *sweeps out in majestic indignation.*]

---

5. In the four-act version of the play, Jack explains further what happened to Mr. Cardew: "He did not discover the error till he arrived at his own house. All subsequent efforts to ascertain who I was were unavailing."

6. In the four-act version of the play, Jack later comments to Algernon about Lady Bracknell's demands about locating parents: "After all what does it matter whether a man has ever had a father and mother or not? Mothers, of course, are all right. They pay a chap's bills and don't bother him. But fathers bother a chap and never pay his bills. I don't know a single chap at the club who speaks to his father." And Algernon remarks: "Yes. Fathers are certainly not popular just at present. . . . They are like these chaps, the minor poets. They are never quoted."

JACK Good morning! [ALGERNON, *from the other room, strikes up the Wedding March.* JACK *looks perfectly furious, and goes to the door.*] For goodness' sake don't play that ghastly tune, Algy! How idiotic you are!
[*The music stops, and* ALGERNON *enters cheerily.*]

ALGERNON Didn't it go off all right, old boy? You don't mean to say Gwendolen refused you? I know it is a way she has. She is always refusing people. I think it is most ill-natured of her.

JACK Oh, Gwendolen is as right as a trivet.[7] As far as she is concerned, we are engaged. Her mother is perfectly unbearable. Never met such a Gorgon[8] . . . I don't really know what a Gorgon is like, but I am quite sure that Lady Bracknell is one. In any case, she is a monster, without being a myth, which is rather unfair . . . I beg your pardon, Algy, I suppose I shouldn't talk about your own aunt in that way before you.

ALGERNON My dear boy, I love hearing my relations abused. It is the only thing that makes me put up with them at all. Relations are simply a tedious pack of people who haven't got the remotest knowledge of how to live, nor the smallest instinct about when to die.

JACK Oh, that is nonsense!

ALGERNON It isn't!

JACK Well, I won't argue about the matter. You always want to argue about things.

ALGERNON That is exactly what things were originally made for.

JACK Upon my word, if I thought that, I'd shoot myself . . . [*A pause.*] You don't think there is any chance of Gwendolen becoming like her mother in about a hundred and fifty years, do you, Algy?

ALGERNON All women become like their mothers. That is their tragedy. No man does. That's his.

JACK Is that clever?

ALGERNON It is perfectly phrased! and quite as true as any observation in civilized life should be.

JACK I am sick to death of cleverness. Everybody is clever nowadays. You can't go anywhere without meeting clever people. The thing has become an absolute public nuisance. I wish to goodness we had a few fools left.

ALGERNON We have.

JACK I should extremely like to meet them. What do they talk about?

ALGERNON The fools? Oh! about the clever people, of course.

JACK What fools!

ALGERNON By the way, did you tell Gwendolen the truth about your being Ernest in town, and Jack in the country?

JACK [*In a very patronizing manner.*] My dear fellow, the truth isn't quite the sort of thing one tells to a nice sweet refined girl. What extraordinary ideas you have about the way to behave to a woman!

ALGERNON The only way to behave to a woman is to make love to[9] her, if she is pretty, and to someone else if she is plain.

JACK Oh, that is nonsense.

ALGERNON What about your brother? What about the profligate Ernest?

---

7. Proverbial expression meaning reliably steady, like a tripod ("trivet") used to support pots over a fire.
8. In classical mythology a snake-haired female monster; at the sight of her, other creatures turned to stone.
9. Woo, court.

JACK   Oh, before the end of the week I shall have got rid of him. I'll say he died in Paris of apoplexy. Lots of people die of apoplexy, quite suddenly, don't they?

ALGERNON   Yes, but it's hereditary, my dear fellow. It's a sort of thing that runs in families. You had much better say a severe chill.

JACK   You are sure a severe chill isn't hereditary, or anything of that kind?

ALGERNON   Of course it isn't!

JACK   Very well, then. My poor brother Ernest is carried off suddenly in Paris, by a severe chill. That gets rid of him.[1]

ALGERNON   But I thought you said that . . . Miss Cardew was a little too much interested in your poor brother Ernest? Won't she feel his loss a good deal?

JACK   Oh, that is all right. Cecily is not a silly romantic girl, I am glad to say. She has got a capital appetite, goes on long walks, and pays no attention at all to her lessons.

ALGERNON   I would rather like to see Cecily.

JACK   I will take very good care you never do. She is excessively pretty, and she is only just eighteen.

ALGERNON   Have you told Gwendolen yet that you have an excessively pretty ward who is only just eighteen?

JACK   Oh! one doesn't blurt these things out to people. Cecily and Gwendolen are perfectly certain to be extremely great friends. I'll bet you anything you like that half an hour after they have met, they will be calling each other sister.

ALGERNON   Women only do that when they have called each other a lot of other things first. Now, my dear boy, if we want to get a good table at Willis's, we really must go and dress. Do you know it is nearly seven?

JACK [*Irritably.*]   Oh! it always is nearly seven.

ALGERNON   Well, I'm hungry.

JACK   I never knew you when you weren't. . . .

ALGERNON   What shall we do after dinner? Go to the theatre?

JACK   Oh no! I loathe listening.

ALGERNON   Well, let us go to the club?

JACK   Oh, no! I hate talking.

ALGERNON   Well, we might trot around to the Empire[2] at ten?

JACK   Oh no! I can't bear looking at things. It is so silly.

ALGERNON   Well, what shall we do?

JACK   Nothing!

ALGERNON   It is awfully hard work doing nothing. However, I don't mind hard work where there is no definite object of any kind.

   [*Enter* LANE.]

LANE   Miss Fairfax.

   [*Enter* GWENDOLEN. LANE *goes out.*]

ALGERNON   Gwendolen, upon my word!

GWENDOLEN   Algy, kindly turn your back. I have something very particular to say to Mr. Worthing.

1. In the four-act version of the play, Jack explains further: "I'll wear mourning for him, of course; that would be only decent. I don't at all mind wearing mourning. I think that all black, with a good pearl pin, rather smart. Then I'll go down home and break the news to my household."

2. A music hall in Leicester Square that featured light entertainment.

ALGERNON   Really, Gwendolen, I don't think I can allow this at all.

GWENDOLEN   Algy, you always adopt a strictly immoral attitude towards life. You are not quite old enough to do that. [ALGERNON *retires to the fireplace.*]

JACK   My own darling!

GWENDOLEN   Ernest, we may never be married. From the expression on mamma's face I fear we never shall. Few parents nowadays pay any regard to what their children say to them. The old-fashioned respect for the young is fast dying out. Whatever influence I ever had over mamma, I lost at the age of three. But although she may prevent us from becoming man and wife, and I may marry someone else, and marry often, nothing that she can possibly do can alter my eternal devotion to you.

JACK   Dear Gwendolen!

GWENDOLEN   The story of your romantic origin, as related to me by mamma, with unpleasing comments, has naturally stirred the deeper fibres of my nature. Your Christian name has an irresistible fascination. The simplicity of your character makes you exquisitely incomprehensible to me. Your town address at the Albany I have. What is your address in the country?

JACK   The Manor House, Woolton, Hertfordshire.

   [ALGERNON, *who has been carefully listening, smiles to himself, and writes the address on his shirt-cuff.*[3] *Then picks up the Railway Guide.*]

GWENDOLEN   There is a good postal service, I suppose? It may be necessary to do something desperate. That of course will require serious consideration. I will communicate with you daily.

JACK   My own one!

GWENDOLEN   How long do you remain in town?

JACK   Till Monday.

GWENDOLEN   Good! Algy, you may turn round now.

ALGERNON   Thanks, I've turned round already.

GWENDOLEN   You may also ring the bell.

JACK   You will let me see you to your carriage, my own darling?

GWENDOLEN   Certainly.

JACK [*To* LANE, *who now enters.*]   I will see Miss Fairfax out.

LANE   Yes, sir. [JACK *and* GWENDOLEN *go off.*]

   [LANE *presents several letters on a salver to* ALGERNON. *It is to be surmised that they are bills, as* ALGERNON *after looking at the envelopes, tears them up.*]

ALGERNON   A glass of sherry, Lane.

LANE   Yes, sir.

ALGERNON   Tomorrow, Lane, I'm going Bunburying.

LANE   Yes, sir.

ALGERNON   I shall probably not be back till Monday. You can put up my dress clothes, my smoking jacket,[4] and all the Bunbury suits . . .

LANE   Yes, sir. [*Handing sherry.*]

ALGERNON   I hope tomorrow will be a fine day, Lane.

---

3. Because shirt cuffs were heavily starched they provided a good surface on which to make notes.
4. Coat worn when gentlemen assembled in a room designated for smoking. The object was to avoid contaminating their regular clothing with the smell of cigars or pipes, which was considered offensive to ladies. "Put up": pack up.

LANE   It never is, sir.

ALGERNON   Lane, you're a perfect pessimist.

LANE   I do my best to give satisfaction, sir.

[*Enter* JACK. LANE *goes off.*]

JACK   There's a sensible, intellectual girl! the only girl I ever cared for in my life. [ALGERNON *is laughing immoderately.*] What on earth are you so amused at?

ALGERNON   Oh, I'm a little anxious about poor Bunbury, that is all.

JACK   If you don't take care, your friend Bunbury will get you into a serious scrape some day.

ALGERNON   I love scrapes. They are the only things that are never serious.

JACK   Oh, that's nonsense, Algy. You never talk anything but nonsense.

ALGERNON   Nobody ever does.

[JACK *looks indignantly at him, and leaves the room.* ALGERNON *lights a cigarette, reads his shirt-cuff, and smiles.*]

ACT-DROP[5]

Second Act

SCENE—*Garden at the Manor House. A flight of grey stone steps leads up to the house. The garden, an old-fashioned one, full of roses. Time of year, July. Basket chairs, and a table covered with books, are set under a large yew tree.*

[MISS PRISM[6] *discovered seated at the table.* CECILY *is at the back watering flowers.*]

MISS PRISM [*Calling.*]   Cecily, Cecily! Surely such a utilitarian occupation as the watering of flowers is rather Moulton's duty than yours? Especially at a moment when intellectual pleasures await you. Your German grammar is on the table. Pray open it at page fifteen. We will repeat yesterday's lesson.

CECILY [*Coming over very slowly.*]   But I don't like German. It isn't at all a becoming language. I know perfectly well that I look quite plain after my German lesson.

MISS PRISM   Child, you know how anxious your guardian is that you should improve yourself in every way. He laid particular stress on your German, as he was leaving for town yesterday. Indeed, he always lays stress on your German when he is leaving for town.

CECILY   Dear Uncle Jack is so very serious! Sometime he is so serious that I think he cannot be quite well.

MISS PRISM [*Drawing herself up.*]   Your guardian enjoys the best of health, and his gravity of demeanour is especially to be commended in one so comparatively young as he is. I know no one who has a higher sense of duty and responsibility.

CECILY   I suppose that is why he often looks a little bored when we three are together.

5. A special curtain lowered during theatrical performances to denote intervals between acts or scenes.
6. The name recalls Charles Dickens's *Little Dor-* *rit* (1855–57), in which Mrs. General, a prim and proper teacher of manners for young ladies, trains them to repeat "prunes and prism" aloud because this exercise "gives a pretty form to the lips."

MISS PRISM   Cecily! I am surprised at you. Mr. Worthing has many troubles in his life. Idle merriment and triviality would be out of place in his conversation. You must remember his constant anxiety about that unfortunate young man his brother.

CECILY   I wish Uncle Jack would allow that unfortunate young man, his brother, to come down here sometimes. We might have a good influence over him, Miss Prism. I am sure you certainly would. You know German, and geology, and things of that kind influence a man very much. [CECILY *begins to write in her diary.*]

MISS PRISM [*Shaking her head.*]   I do not think that even I could produce any effect on a character that according to his own brother's admission is irretrievably weak and vacillating. Indeed I am not sure that I would desire to reclaim him. I am not in favor of this modern mania for turning bad people into good people at a moment's notice. As a man sows so let him reap.[7] You must put away your diary, Cecily. I really don't see why you should keep a diary at all.

CECILY   I keep a diary in order to enter the wonderful secrets of my life. If I didn't write them down I should probably forget all about them.

MISS PRISM   Memory, my dear Cecily, is the diary that we all carry about with us.

CECILY   Yes, but it usually chronicles the things that have never happened, and couldn't possibly have happened. I believe that Memory is responsible for nearly all the three-volume novels that Mudie[8] sends us.

MISS PRISM   Do not speak slightingly of the three-volume novel, Cecily. I wrote one myself in earlier days.

CECILY   Did you really, Miss Prism? How wonderfully clever you are! I hope it did not end happily? I don't like novels that end happily. They depress me so much.

MISS PRISM   The good ended happily, and the bad unhappily. That is what Fiction means.

CECILY   I suppose so. But it seems very unfair. And was your novel ever published?

MISS PRISM   Alas! no. The manuscript unfortunately was abandoned. I use the word in the sense of lost or mislaid. To your work, child, these speculations are profitless.

CECILY [*Smiling.*]   But I see dear Dr. Chasuble[9] coming up through the garden.

MISS PRISM [*Rising and advancing.*]   Dr. Chasuble! This is indeed a pleasure.

[*Enter* CANON CHASUBLE.]

CHASUBLE   And how are we this morning? Miss Prism, you are, I trust, well?

CECILY   Miss Prism has just been complaining of a slight headache. I think it would do her so much good to have a short stroll with you in the Park, Dr. Chasuble.

MISS PRISM   Cecily, I have not mentioned anything about a headache.

---

7. Cf. Galatians 6.7: "whatsoever a man soweth, that shall he also reap."
8. Mudie's Circulating Library, which lent copies of new three-volume novels (usually sentimental tales) to subscribers for a moderate fee. Mudie's power in controlling the book market, especially for novels, was on the wane by 1895.
9. A chasuble is an ornate garment worn by a priest.

CECILY   No, dear Miss Prism, I know that, but I felt instinctively that you had a headache. Indeed I was thinking about that, and not about my German lesson, when the Rector came in.

CHASUBLE   I hope, Cecily, you are not inattentive.

CECILY   Oh, I am afraid I am.

CHASUBLE   That is strange. Were I fortunate enough to be Miss Prism's pupil, I would hang upon her lips. [MISS PRISM *glares*.] I spoke metaphorically.—My metaphor was drawn from bees. Ahem! Mr. Worthing, I suppose, has not returned from town yet?

MISS PRISM   We do not expect him till Monday afternoon.

CHASUBLE   Ah yes, he usually likes to spend his Sunday in London. He is not one of those whose sole aim is enjoyment, as, by all accounts, that unfortunate young man his brother seems to be. But I must not disturb Egeria[1] and her pupil any longer.

MISS PRISM   Egeria? My name is Laetitia, Doctor.

CHASUBLE [*Bowing*.]   A classical allusion merely, drawn from the Pagan authors. I shall see you both no doubt at Evensong?[2]

MISS PRISM   I think, dear Doctor, I will have a stroll with you. I find I have a headache after all, and a walk might do it good.

CHASUBLE   With pleasure, Miss Prism, with pleasure. We might go as far as the schools and back.

MISS PRISM   That would be delightful. Cecily, you will read your Political Economy[3] in my absence. The chapter on the Fall of the Rupee[4] you may omit. It is somewhat too sensational. Even these metallic problems have their melodramatic side. [*Goes down the garden with* DR. CHASUBLE.]

CECILY [*Picks up books and throws them back on table*.]   Horrid Political Economy! Horrid Geography! Horrid, horrid German!
    [*Enter* MERRIMAN *with a card on a salver*.]

MERRIMAN   Mr. Ernest Worthing has just driven over from the station. He has brought his luggage with him.

CECILY [*Takes the card and reads it*.]   "Mr. Ernest Worthing, B. 4, The Albany, W." Uncle Jack's brother! Did you tell him Mr. Worthing was in town?

MERRIMAN   Yes, Miss. He seemed very much disappointed. I mentioned that you and Miss Prism were in the garden. He said he was anxious to speak to you privately for a moment.

CECILY.   Ask Mr. Ernest Worthing to come here. I suppose you had better talk to the housekeeper about a room for him.

MERRIMAN   Yes, Miss.   [MERRIMAN *goes off*.]

CECILY   I have never met any really wicked person before. I feel rather frightened. I am so afraid he will look just like everyone else. [*Enter* ALGERNON, *very gay and debonair*.] He does!

ALGERNON [*Raising his hat*.]   You are my little cousin Cecily, I'm sure.

CECILY   You are under some strange mistake. I am not little. In fact, I believe I am more than usually tall for my age. [ALGERNON *is rather*

---

1. In Roman legend a nymph who gave counsel to the second king of Rome. Her name was therefore also used as an epithet for a woman who provides guidance.
2. Evening church services.

3. I.e., book about economics.
4. The basic unit of currency in India. British civil servants who worked in India were paid in rupees and would suffer from its fall in value.

taken aback.] But I am your cousin Cecily. You, I see from your card, are Uncle Jack's brother, my cousin Ernest, my wicked cousin Ernest.

ALGERNON   Oh! I am not really wicked at all, cousin Cecily. You mustn't think that I am wicked.

CECILY   If you are not, then you have certainly been deceiving us all in a very inexcusable manner. I hope you have not been leading a double life, pretending to be wicked and being really good all the time. That would be hypocrisy.

ALGERNON [*Looks at her in amazement*]   Oh! Of course I have been rather reckless.

CECILY   I am glad to hear it.

ALGERNON   In fact, now you mention the subject, I have been very bad in my own small way.

CECILY   I don't think you should be so proud of that, though I am sure it must have been very pleasant.

ALGERNON   It is much pleasanter being here with you.

CECILY   I can't understand how you are here at all. Uncle Jack won't be back till Monday afternoon.

ALGERNON   That is a great disappointment. I am obliged to go up by the first train on Monday morning. I have a business appointment that I am anxious . . . to miss.

CECILY   Couldn't you miss it anywhere but in London?

ALGERNON   No: the appointment is in London.

CECILY   Well, I know, of course, how important it is not to keep a business engagement, if one wants to retain any sense of the beauty of life, but still I think you had better wait till Uncle Jack arrives. I know he wants to speak to you about your emigrating.

ALGERNON   About my what?

CECILY   Your emigrating. He has gone up to buy your outfit.

ALGERNON   I certainly wouldn't let Jack buy my outfit. He has no taste in neckties at all.

CECILY   I don't think you will require neckties. Uncle Jack is sending you to Australia.[5]

ALGERNON   Australia? I'd sooner die.

CECILY   Well, he said at dinner on Wednesday night, that you would have to choose between this world, the next world, and Australia.

ALGERNON   Oh, well! The accounts I have received of Australia and the next world are not particularly encouraging. This world is good enough for me, cousin Cecily.

CECILY   Yes, but are you good enough for it?

ALGERNON   I'm afraid I'm not that. That is why I want you to reform me. You might make that your mission, if you don't mind, cousin Cecily.

CECILY   I'm afraid I've no time, this afternoon.

ALGERNON   Well, would you mind my reforming myself this afternoon?

CECILY   It is rather Quixotic of you. But I think you should try.

ALGERNON   I will. I feel better already.

---

5. The British had originally viewed Australia as a place to which they banished their criminals. By this time, however, it was perceived in some quarters as a place, like Canada, to which families might send harmless but useless members, who would be paid an allowance to remain abroad.

CECILY   You are looking a little worse.

ALGERNON   That is because I am hungry.

CECILY   How thoughtless of me. I should have remembered that when one is going to lead an entirely new life, one requires regular and wholesome meals. Won't you come in?

ALGERNON   Thank you. Might I have a buttonhole[6] first? I never have any appetite unless I have a buttonhole first.

CECILY   A Maréchal Niel?[7] [*Picks up scissors.*]

ALGERNON   No, I'd sooner have a pink rose.

CECILY   Why? [*Cuts a flower.*]

ALGERNON   Because you are like a pink rose, cousin Cecily.

CECILY   I don't think it can be right for you to talk to me like that. Miss Prism never says such things to me.

ALGERNON   Then Miss Prism is a shortsighted old lady. [CECILY *puts the rose in his buttonhole.*] You are the prettiest girl I ever saw.

CECILY   Miss Prism says that all good looks are a snare.

ALGERNON   They are a snare that every sensible man would like to be caught in.

CECILY   Oh! I don't think I would care to catch a sensible man. I shouldn't know what to talk to him about.

[*They pass into the house.* MISS PRISM *and* DR. CHASUBLE *return.*]

MISS PRISM   You are too much alone, dear Dr. Chasuble. You should get married. A misanthrope I can understand—a womanthrope, never!

CHASUBLE   [*With a scholar's shudder.*][8]   Believe me, I do not deserve so neologistic a phrase. The precept as well as the practice of the Primitive Church[9] was distinctly against matrimony.

MISS PRISM   [*Sententiously.*]   That is obviously the reason why the Primitive Church has not lasted up to the present day. And you do not seem to realize, dear Doctor, that by persistently remaining single, a man converts himself into a permanent public temptation. Men should be more careful; this very celibacy leads weaker vessels astray.

CHASUBLE   But is a man not equally attractive when married?

MISS PRISM   No married man is ever attractive except to his wife.

CHASUBLE   And often, I've been told, not even to her.

MISS PRISM   That depends on the intellectual sympathies of the woman. Maturity can always be depended on. Ripeness can be trusted. Young women are green. [DR. CHASUBLE *starts.*] I spoke horticulturally. My metaphor was drawn from fruits. But where is Cecily?

CHASUBLE   Perhaps she followed us to the schools.

[*Enter* JACK *slowly from the back of the garden. He is dressed in the deepest mourning, with crape hat-band and black gloves.*]

MISS PRISM   Mr. Worthing!

CHASUBLE   Mr. Worthing?

MISS PRISM   This is indeed a surprise. We did not look for you till Monday afternoon.

---

6. I.e., a flower to wear in the buttonhole of his coat lapel.
7. A chrome-yellow variety of rose named after Adolphe Niel (1802–1869), one of the generals of Napoleon III.
8. He shudders because instead of using the cor-

rect word for woman hater, *misogynist,* she has coined her own term, one that is etymologically nonsensical.
9. The early Christian Church, of the 1st to 4th centuries.

JACK [*Shakes* MISS PRISM's *hand in a tragic manner.*] I have returned sooner than I expected. Dr. Chasuble, I hope you are well?

CHASUBLE Dear Mr. Worthing, I trust this garb of woe does not betoken some terrible calamity?

JACK My brother.

MISS PRISM More shameful debts and extravagance?

CHASUBLE Still leading his life of pleasure?

JACK [*Shaking his head.*] Dead!

CHASUBLE Your brother Ernest dead?

JACK Quite dead.

MISS PRISM What a lesson for him! I trust he will profit by it.

CHASUBLE Mr. Worthing, I offer you my sincere condolence. You have at least the consolation of knowing that you were always the most generous and forgiving of brothers.

JACK Poor Ernest! He had many faults, but it is a sad, sad blow.

CHASUBLE Very sad indeed. Were you with him at the end?

JACK No. He died abroad; in Paris, in fact. I had a telegram last night from the manager of the Grand Hotel.

CHASUBLE Was the cause of death mentioned?

JACK A severe chill, it seems.

MISS PRISM As a man sows, so shall he reap.

CHASUBLE [*Raising his hand.*] Charity, dear Miss Prism, charity! None of us are perfect. I myself am peculiarly susceptible to drafts. Will the interment take place here?

JACK No. He seemed to have expressed a desire to be buried in Paris.

CHASUBLE In Paris! [*Shakes his head.*] I fear that hardly points to any very serious state of mind at the last. You would no doubt wish me to make some slight allusion to this tragic domestic affliction next Sunday. [JACK *presses his hand convulsively.*] My sermon on the meaning of the manna in the wilderness can be adapted to almost any occasion, joyful, or, as in the present case, distressing. [*All sigh.*] I have preached it at harvest celebrations, christenings, confirmations, on days of humiliation and festal days. The last time I delivered it was in the Cathedral, as a charity sermon on behalf of the Society for the Prevention of Discontent among the Upper Orders. The Bishop, who was present, was much struck by some of the analogies I drew.

JACK Ah! That reminds me, you mentioned christenings, I think, Dr. Chasuble? I suppose you know how to christen all right? [DR. CHASUBLE *looks astounded.*] I mean, of course, you are continually christening, aren't you?

MISS PRISM It is, I regret to say, one of the Rector's most constant duties in this parish. I have often spoken to the poorer classes on the subject. But they don't seem to know what thrift is.

CHASUBLE But is there any particular infant in whom you are interested, Mr. Worthing? Your brother was, I believe, unmarried, was he not?

JACK Oh yes.

MISS PRISM [*Bitterly.*] People who live entirely for pleasure usually are.

JACK But it is not for any child, dear Doctor. I am very fond of children. No! the fact is, I would like to be christened myself, this afternoon, if you have nothing better to do.

CHASUBLE But surely, Mr. Worthing, you have been christened already?

JACK   I don't remember anything about it.

CHASUBLE   But have you any grave doubts on the subject?

JACK   I certainly intend to have. Of course I don't know if the thing would bother you in any way, or if you think I am a little too old now.

CHASUBLE   Not at all. The sprinkling, and, indeed, the immersion of adults is a perfectly canonical practice.

JACK   Immersion!

CHASUBLE   You need have no apprehensions. Sprinkling is all that is necessary, or indeed I think advisable. Our weather is so changeable. At what hour would you wish the ceremony performed?

JACK   Oh, I might trot round about five if that would suit you.

CHASUBLE   Perfectly, perfectly! In fact I have two similar ceremonies to perform at that time. A case of twins that occurred recently in one of the outlying cottages on your own estate. Poor Jenkins the carter, a most hardworking man.

JACK   Oh! I don't see much fun in being christened along with other babies. It would be childish. Would half-past five do?

CHASUBLE   Admirably! Admirably! [*Takes out watch.*] And now, dear Mr. Worthing, I will not intrude any longer into a house of sorrow. I would merely beg you not to be too much bowed down by grief. What seem to us bitter trials are often blessings in disguise.

MISS PRISM   This seems to me a blessing of an extremely obvious kind.

[*Enter* CECILY *from the house.*]

CECILY   Uncle Jack! Oh, I am pleased to see you back. But what horrid clothes you have got on! Do go and change them.

MISS PRISM   Cecily!

CHASUBLE   My child! my child! [CECILY *goes towards* JACK; *he kisses her brow in a melancholy manner.*]

CECILY   What is the matter, Uncle Jack? Do look happy! You look as if you had toothache, and I have got such a surprise for you. Who do you think is in the dining room? Your brother!

JACK   Who?

CECILY   Your brother Ernest. He arrived about half an hour ago.

JACK   What nonsense! I haven't got a brother!

CECILY   Oh, don't say that. However badly he may have behaved to you in the past he is still your brother. You couldn't be so heartless as to disown him. I'll tell him to come out. And you will shake hands with him, won't you, Uncle Jack? [*Runs back into the house.*]

CHASUBLE   These are very joyful tidings.

MISS PRISM   After we had all been resigned to his loss, his sudden return seems to me peculiarly distressing.

JACK   My brother is in the dining room? I don't know what it all means. I think it is perfectly absurd.

[*Enter* ALGERNON *and* CECILY *hand in hand. They come slowly up to* JACK.]

JACK   Good heavens! [*Motions* ALGERNON *away.*]

ALGERNON   Brother John, I have come down from town to tell you that I am very sorry for all the trouble I have given you, and that I intend to lead a better life in the future. [JACK *glares at him and does not take his hand.*]

CECILY   Uncle Jack, you are not going to refuse your own brother's hand?

JACK   Nothing will induce me to take his hand. I think his coming down here disgraceful. He knows perfectly well why.

CECILY   Uncle Jack, do be nice. There is some good in everyone. Ernest has just been telling me about his poor invalid friend Mr. Bunbury whom he goes to visit so often. And surely there must be much good in one who is kind to an invalid, and leaves the pleasures of London to sit by a bed of pain.

JACK   Oh! he has been talking about Bunbury, has he?

CECILY   Yes, he has told me all about poor Mr. Bunbury, and his terrible state of health.

JACK   Bunbury! Well, I won't have him talk to you about Bunbury or about anything else. It is enough to drive one perfectly frantic.

ALGERNON   Of course I admit that the faults were all on my side. But I must say that I think that Brother John's coldness to me is peculiarly painful. I expected a more enthusiastic welcome, especially considering it is the first time I have come here.

CECILY   Uncle Jack, if you don't shake hands with Ernest, I will never forgive you.

JACK   Never forgive me?

CECILY   Never, never, never!

JACK   Well, this is the last time I shall ever do it. [*Shakes hands with* ALGERNON *and glares.*]

CHASUBLE   It's pleasant, is it not, to see so perfect a reconciliation? I think we might leave the two brothers together.

MISS PRISM   Cecily, you will come with us.

CECILY   Certainly, Miss Prism. My little task of reconciliation is over.

CHASUBLE   You have done a beautiful action today, dear child.

MISS PRISM   We must not be premature in our judgments.

CECILY   I feel very happy. [*They all go off.*]

JACK   You young scoundrel, Algy, you must get out of this place as soon as possible. I don't allow any Bunburying here.

[*Enter* MERRIMAN.]

MERRIMAN   I have put Mr. Ernest's things in the room next to yours, sir. I suppose that is all right?

JACK   What?

MERRIMAN   Mr. Ernest's luggage, sir. I have unpacked it and put it in the room next to your own.

JACK   His luggage?

MERRIMAN   Yes, sir. Three portmanteaus, a dressing case, two hat-boxes, and a large luncheon basket.[1]

ALGERNON   I am afraid I can't stay more than a week this time.

JACK   Merriman, order the dogcart[2] at once. Mr. Ernest has been suddenly called back to town.

---

1. According to *Cassell's Domestic Dictionary* (1877–79), "a convenient little receptacle in which gentlemen who are going out shooting for the day, or artists who wish to sketch, can carry their luncheon with them." "Portmanteaus": large leather suitcases. A "dressing case" (also according to *Cassell's*) was "ordinarily made of rosewood, mahogany or coromandel wood." It was supposed to include "scent bottles, jars for pomade and tooth-powders, hair brushes and combs, shaving, nail and tooth brushes, razors and strop, nail scissors, button-hook, tweezer, nail file and penknife" [noted by Russell Jackson].

2. A horse-drawn cart with seats, originally designed to carry hunters and their hunting dogs.

MERRIMAN   Yes, sir.   [*Goes back into the house.*]

ALGERNON   What a fearful liar you are, Jack. I have not been called back to town at all.

JACK   Yes, you have.

ALGERNON   I haven't heard anyone call me.

JACK   Your duty as a gentleman calls you back.

ALGERNON   My duty as a gentleman has never interfered with my pleasures in the smallest degree.

JACK   I can quite understand that.

ALGERNON   Well, Cecily is a darling.

JACK   You are not to talk of Miss Cardew like that. I don't like it.

ALGERNON   Well, I don't like your clothes. You look perfectly ridiculous in them. Why on earth don't you go up and change? It is perfectly childish to be in deep mourning for a man who is actually staying for a whole week with you in your house as a guest. I call it grotesque.

JACK   You are certainly not staying with me for a whole week as a guest or anything else. You have got to leave . . . by the four-five train.

ALGERNON   I certainly won't leave you so long as you are in mourning. It would be most unfriendly. If I were in mourning you would stay with me, I suppose. I should think it very unkind if you didn't.

JACK   Well, will you go if I change my clothes?

ALGERNON   Yes, if you are not too long. I never saw anybody take so long to dress, and with such little result.

JACK   Well, at any rate, that is better than being always overdressed as you are.

ALGERNON   If I am occasionally a little overdressed, I make up for it by being always immensely overeducated.

JACK   Your vanity is ridiculous, your conduct an outrage, and your presence in my garden utterly absurd. However, you have got to catch the four-five, and I hope you will have a pleasant journey back to town. This Bunburying, as you call it, has not been a great success for you. [*Goes into the house.*]

ALGERNON   I think it has been a great success. I'm in love with Cecily, and that is everything.

> [*Enter* CECILY *at the back of the garden. She picks up the can and begins to water the flowers.*]

But I must see her before I go, and make arrangements for another Bunbury. Ah, there she is.

CECILY   Oh, I merely came back to water the roses. I thought you were with Uncle Jack.

ALGERNON   He's gone to order the dogcart for me.

CECILY   Oh, is he going to take you for a nice drive?

ALGERNON   He's going to send me away.

CECILY   Then have we got to part?

ALGERNON   I am afraid so. It's very painful parting.

CECILY   It is always painful to part from people whom one has known for a very brief space of time. The absence of old friends one can endure with equanimity. But even a momentary separation from anyone to whom one has just been introduced is almost unbearable.

ALGERNON   Thank you.

[*Enter* MERRIMAN.]

MERRIMAN   The dogcart is at the door, sir. [ALGERNON *looks appealingly at* CECILY.]

CECILY   It can wait, Merriman . . . for . . . five minutes.

MERRIMAN   Yes, Miss.   [*Exit* MERRIMAN.]

ALGERNON   I hope, Cecily, I shall not offend you if I state quite frankly and openly that you seem to me to be in every way the visible personification of absolute perfection.

CECILY   I think your frankness does you great credit, Ernest. If you will allow me I will copy your remarks into my diary. [*Goes over to table and begins writing in diary.*]

ALGERNON   Do you really keep a diary? I'd give anything to look at it. May I?

CECILY   Oh no. [*Puts her hand over it.*] You see, it is simply a very young girl's record of her own thoughts and impressions, and consequently meant for publication. When it appears in volume form I hope you will order a copy. But pray, Ernest, don't stop. I delight in taking down from dictation. I have reached "absolute perfection." You can go on. I am quite ready for more.

ALGERNON [*Somewhat taken aback.*]   Ahem! Ahem!

CECILY   Oh, don't cough, Ernest. When one is dictating one should speak fluently and not cough. Besides, I don't know how to spell a cough. [*Writes as* ALGERNON *speaks.*]

ALGERNON [*Speaking very rapidly.*]   Cecily, ever since I first looked upon your wonderful and incomparable beauty, I have dared to love you wildly, passionately, devotedly, hopelessly.

CECILY   I don't think that you should tell me that you love me wildly, passionately, devotedly, hopelessly. Hopelessly doesn't seem to make much sense, does it?

ALGERNON   Cecily!

[*Enter* MERRIMAN.]

MERRIMAN   The dogcart is waiting, sir.

ALGERNON   Tell it to come round next week, at the same hour.

MERRIMAN [*Looks at* CECILY, *who makes no sign.*]   Yes, sir.

[MERRIMAN *retires.*]

CECILY   Uncle Jack would be very much annoyed if he knew you were staying on till next week, at the same hour.

ALGERNON   Oh, I don't care about Jack. I don't care for anybody in the whole world but you. I love you, Cecily. You will marry me, won't you?

CECILY   You silly boy! Of course. Why, we have been engaged for the last three months.

ALGERNON   For the last three months?

CECILY   Yes, it will be exactly three months on Thursday.

ALGERNON   But how did we become engaged?

CECILY   Well, ever since dear Uncle Jack first confessed to us that he had a younger brother who was very wicked and bad, you of course have formed the chief topic of conversation between myself and Miss Prism. And of course a man who is much talked about is always very attractive. One feels there must be something in him after all. I daresay it was foolish of me, but I fell in love with you, Ernest.

ALGERNON   Darling! And when was the engagement actually settled?

CECILY   On the 14th of February last. Worn out by your entire ignorance of my existence, I determined to end the matter one way or the other, and after a long struggle with myself I accepted you under this dear old tree here. The next day I bought this little ring in your name, and this is the little bangle with the true lovers' knot I promised you always to wear.

ALGERNON   Did I give you this? It's very pretty, isn't it?

CECILY   Yes, you've wonderfully good taste, Ernest. It's the excuse I've always given for your leading such a bad life. And this is the box in which I keep all your dear letters. [*Kneels at table, opens box, and produces letters tied up with blue ribbon.*]

ALGERNON   My letters! But my own sweet Cecily, I have never written you any letters.

CECILY   You need hardly remind me of that, Ernest. I remember only too well that I was forced to write your letters for you. I always wrote three times a week, and sometimes oftener.

ALGERNON   Oh, do let me read them, Cecily?

CECILY   Oh, I couldn't possibly. They would make you far too conceited. [*Replaces box.*] The three you wrote me after I had broken off the engagement are so beautiful, and so badly spelled, that even now I can hardly read them without crying a little.

ALGERNON   But was our engagement ever broken off?

CECILY   Of course it was. On the 22nd of last March. You can see the entry if you like. [*Shows diary.*] "Today I broke off my engagement with Ernest. I feel it is better to do so. The weather still continues charming."

ALGERNON   But why on earth did you break it off? What had I done? I had done nothing at all. Cecily, I am very much hurt indeed to hear you broke it off. Particularly when the weather was so charming.

CECILY   It would hardly have been a really serious engagement if it hadn't been broken off at least once. But I forgave you before the week was out.

ALGERNON [*Crossing to her, and kneeling.*]   What a perfect angel you are, Cecily.

CECILY   You dear romantic boy. [*He kisses her, she puts her fingers through his hair.*] I hope your hair curls naturally, does it?

ALGERNON   Yes, darling, with a little help from others.

CECILY   I am so glad.

ALGERNON   You'll never break off our engagement again, Cecily?

CECILY   I don't think I could break it off now that I have actually met you. Besides, of course, there is the question of your name.

ALGERNON   Yes, of course. [*Nervously.*]

CECILY   You must not laugh at me, darling, but it had always been a girlish dream of mine to love someone whose name was Ernest. [ALGERNON *rises,* CECILY *also.*] There is something in that name that seems to inspire absolute confidence. I pity any poor married woman whose husband is not called Ernest.

ALGERNON   But, my dear child, do you mean to say you could not love me if I had some other name?

CECILY   But what name?

ALGERNON   Oh, any name you like—Algernon—for instance . . .

CECILY   But I don't like the name of Algernon.

ALGERNON   Well, my own dear, sweet, loving little darling, I really can't see why you should object to the name of Algernon. It is not at all a bad name. In fact, it is rather an aristocratic name. Half of the chaps who get into the Bankruptcy Court are called Algernon. But seriously, Cecily . . . [*Moving to her.*] . . . if my name was Algy, couldn't you love me?

CECILY [*Rising.*]   I might respect you, Ernest, I might admire your character, but I fear that I should not be able to give you my undivided attention.

ALGERNON   Ahem! Cecily! [*Picking up hat.*] Your Rector here is, I suppose, thoroughly experienced in the practice of all the rites and ceremonials of the Church?

CECILY   Oh, yes. Dr. Chasuble is a most learned man. He has never written a single book, so you can imagine how much he knows.

ALGERNON   I must see him at once on a most important christening—I mean on most important business.

CECILY   Oh!

ALGERNON   I shan't be away more than half an hour.

CECILY   Considering that we have been engaged since February the 14th, and that I only met you today for the first time, I think it is rather hard that you should leave me for so long a period as half an hour. Couldn't you make it twenty minutes?

ALGERNON   I'll be back in no time. [*Kisses her and rushes down the garden.*]

CECILY   What an impetuous boy he is! I like his hair so much. I must enter his proposal in my diary.
        [*Enter* MERRIMAN.]

MERRIMAN   A Miss Fairfax has just called to see Mr. Worthing. On very important business, Miss Fairfax states.

CECILY   Isn't Mr. Worthing in his library?

MERRIMAN   Mr. Worthing went over in the direction of the Rectory some time ago.

CECILY   Pray ask the lady to come out here; Mr. Worthing is sure to be back soon. And you can bring tea.

MERRIMAN   Yes, Miss.   [*Goes out.*]

CECILY   Miss Fairfax! I suppose one of the many good elderly women who are associated with Uncle Jack in some of his philanthropic work in London. I don't quite like women who are interested in philanthropic work. I think it is so forward of them.
        [*Enter* MERRIMAN.]

MERRIMAN   Miss Fairfax.
        [*Enter* GWENDOLEN.]   [*Exit* MERRIMAN.]

CECILY [*Advancing to meet her.*]   Pray let me introduce myself to you. My name is Cecily Cardew.

GWENDOLEN   Cecily Cardew? [*Moving to her and shaking hands.*] What a very sweet name! Something tells me that we are going to be great friends. I like you already more than I can say. My first impressions of people are never wrong.

CECILY   How nice of you to like me so much after we have known each other such a comparatively short time. Pray sit down.

GWENDOLEN [*Still standing up.*]   I may call you Cecily, may I not?

CECILY   With pleasure!

GWENDOLEN   And you will always call me Gwendolen, won't you?

CECILY   If you wish.

GWENDOLEN   Then that is all quite settled, is it not?

CECILY   I hope so. [*A pause. They both sit down together.*]

GWENDOLEN   Perhaps this might be a favourable opportunity for my mentioning who I am. My father is Lord Bracknell. You have never heard of papa, I suppose?

CECILY   I don't think so.

GWENDOLEN   Outside the family circle, papa, I am glad to say, is entirely unknown. I think that is quite as it should be. The home seems to me to be the proper sphere for the man. And certainly once a man begins to neglect his domestic duties he becomes painfully effeminate, does he not? And I don't like that. It makes men so very attractive. Cecily, mamma, whose views on education are remarkably strict, has brought me up to be extremely shortsighted; it is part of her system; so do you mind my looking at you through my glasses?

CECILY   Oh! not at all, Gwendolen. I am very fond of being looked at.

GWENDOLEN   [*After examining* CECILY *carefully through a lorgnette.*]   You are here on a short visit, I suppose.

CECILY   Oh no! I live here.

GWENDOLEN   [*Severely.*]   Really? Your mother, no doubt, or some female relative of advanced years, resides here also?

CECILY   Oh no! I have no mother, nor, in fact, any relations.

GWENDOLEN   Indeed?

CECILY   My dear guardian, with the assistance of Miss Prism, has the arduous task of looking after me.

GWENDOLEN   Your guardian?

CECILY   Yes, I am Mr. Worthing's ward.

GWENDOLEN   Oh! It is strange he never mentioned to me that he had a ward. How secretive of him! He grows more interesting hourly. I am not sure, however, that the news inspires me with feelings of unmixed delight. [*Rising and going to her.*] I am very fond of you, Cecily; I have liked you ever since I met you! But I am bound to state that now that I know that you are Mr. Worthing's ward, I cannot help expressing a wish you were—well just a little older than you seem to be—and not quite so very alluring in appearance. In fact, if I may speak candidly——

CECILY   Pray do! I think that whenever one has anything unpleasant to say, one should always be quite candid.

GWENDOLEN   Well, to speak with perfect candour, Cecily, I wish that you were fully forty-two, and more than usually plain for your age. Ernest has a strong upright nature. He is the very soul of truth and honour. Disloyalty would be as impossible to him as deception. But even men of the noblest possible moral character are extremely susceptible to the influence of the physical charms of others. Modern, no less than Ancient History, supplies us with many most painful examples of what I refer to. If it were not so, indeed, History would be quite unreadable.

CECILY   I beg your pardon, Gwendolen, did you say Ernest?

GWENDOLEN   Yes.

CECILY   Oh, but it is not Mr. Ernest Worthing who is my guardian. It is his brother—his elder brother.

GWENDOLEN [*Sitting down again.*]   Ernest never mentioned to me that he had a brother.

CECILY   I am sorry to say they have not been on good terms for a long time.

GWENDOLEN   Ah! that accounts for it. And now that I think of it I have never heard any man mention his brother. The subject seems distasteful to most men. Cecily, you have lifted a load from my mind. I was growing almost anxious. It would have been terrible if any cloud had come across a friendship like ours, would it not? Of course you are quite, quite sure that it is not Mr. Ernest Worthing who is your guardian?

CECILY   Quite sure. [*A pause.*] In fact, I am going to be his.

GWENDOLEN [*Inquiringly.*]   I beg your pardon?

CECILY [*Rather shy and confidingly.*]   Dearest Gwendolen, there is no reason why I should make a secret of it to you. Our little county newspaper is sure to chronicle the fact next week. Mr. Ernest Worthing and I are engaged to be married.

GWENDOLEN [*Quite politely, rising.*]   My darling Cecily, I think there must be some slight error. Mr. Ernest Worthing is engaged to me. The announcement will appear in the *Morning Post*[3] on Saturday at the latest.

CECILY [*Very politely, rising.*]   I am afraid you must be under some misconception. Ernest proposed to me exactly ten minutes ago. [*Shows diary.*]

GWENDOLEN [*Examines diary through her lorgnette carefully.*]   It is certainly very curious, for he asked me to be his wife yesterday afternoon at 5:30. If you would care to verify the incident, pray do so. [*Produces diary of her own.*] I never travel without my diary. One should always have something sensational to read in the train. I am so sorry, dear Cecily, if it is any disappointment to you, but I am afraid *I* have the prior claim.

CECILY   It would distress me more than I can tell you, dear Gwendolen, if it caused you any mental or physical anguish, but I feel bound to point out that since Ernest proposed to you he clearly has changed his mind.

GWENDOLEN [*Meditatively.*]   If the poor fellow has been entrapped into any foolish promise I shall consider it my duty to rescue him at once, and with a firm hand.

CECILY [*Thoughtfully and sadly.*]   Whatever unfortunate entanglement my dear boy may have got into, I will never reproach him with it after we are married.

GWENDOLEN   Do you allude to me, Miss Cardew, as an entanglement? You are presumptuous. On an occasion of this kind it becomes more than a moral duty to speak one's mind. It becomes a pleasure.

CECILY   Do you suggest, Miss Fairfax, that I entrapped Ernest into an engagement? How dare you? This is no time for wearing the shallow mask of manners. When I see a spade I call it a spade.

GWENDOLEN [*Satirically.*]   I am glad to say that I have never seen a spade. It is obvious that our social spheres have been widely different.

[*Enter* MERRIMAN, *followed by the footman. He carries a salver, tablecloth, and plate stand.* CECILY *is about to retort. The presence of the servants exercises a restraining influence, under which both girls chafe.*]

MERRIMAN   Shall I lay tea here as usual, Miss?

---

3. A popular journal featuring society gossip and also announcements of engagements and marriages.

CECILY [*Sternly, in a calm voice.*]   Yes, as usual.

[MERRIMAN *begins to clear table and lay cloth. A long pause.* CECILY *and* GWENDOLEN *glare at each other.*]

GWENDOLEN   Are there many interesting walks in the vicinity, Miss Cardew?

CECILY   Oh! yes! a great many. From the top of one of the hills quite close one can see five counties.

GWENDOLEN   Five counties! I don't think I should like that. I hate crowds.

CECILY [*Sweetly.*]   I suppose that is why you live in town?

[GWENDOLEN *bites her lip, and beats her foot nervously with her parasol.*]

GWENDOLEN [*Looking round.*]   Quite a well-kept garden this is, Miss Cardew.

CECILY   So glad you like it, Miss Fairfax.

GWENDOLEN   I had no idea there were any flowers in the country.

CECILY   Oh, flowers are as common here, Miss Fairfax, as people are in London.

GWENDOLEN   Personally I cannot understand how anybody manages to exist in the country, if anybody who is anybody does. The country always bores me to death.

CECILY   Ah! This is what the newspapers call agricultural depression, is it not? I believe the aristocracy are suffering very much from it just at present.[4] It is almost an epidemic amongst them, I have been told. May I offer you some tea, Miss Fairfax?

GWENDOLEN [*With elaborate politeness.*]   Thank you. [*Aside.*] Detestable girl! But I require tea!

CECILY [*Sweetly.*]   Sugar?

GWENDOLEN [*Superciliously.*]   No, thank you. Sugar is not fashionable any more, [CECILY *looks angrily at her, takes up the tongs and puts four lumps of sugar into the cup.*]

CECILY [*Severely.*]   Cake or bread and butter?

GWENDOLEN [*In a bored manner.*]   Bread and butter, please. Cake is rarely seen at the best houses nowadays.

CECILY [*Cuts a very large slice of cake, and puts it on the tray.*]   Hand that to Miss Fairfax.

[MERRIMAN *does so, and goes out with footman.* GWENDOLEN *drinks the tea and makes a grimace. Puts down cup at once, reaches out her hand to the bread and butter, looks at it, and finds it is cake. Rises in indignation.*]

GWENDOLEN   You have filled my tea with lumps of sugar, and though I asked most distinctly for bread and butter, you have given me cake. I am known for the gentleness of my disposition, and the extraordinary sweetness of my nature, but I warn you, Miss Cardew, you may go too far.

CECILY [*Rising.*]   To save my poor, innocent, trusting boy from the machinations of any other girl there are no lengths to which I would not go.

GWENDOLEN   From the moment I saw you I distrusted you. I felt that you were false and deceitful. I am never deceived in such matters. My first impressions of people are invariably right.

---

4. From the 1870s on, landowners (including aristocrats) had been suffering severe losses because of adverse economic conditions.

CECILY   It seems to me, Miss Fairfax, that I am trespassing on your valuable time. No doubt you have many other calls of a similar character to
make in the neighborhood.
    [*Enter* JACK.]

GWENDOLEN [*Catching sight of him.*]   Ernest! My own Ernest!

JACK   Gwendolen! Darling! [*Offers to kiss her.*]

GWENDOLEN [*Drawing back.*]   A moment! May I ask if you are engaged to
be married to this young lady? [*Points to* CECILY.]

JACK [*Laughing.*]   To dear little Cecily! Of course not! What could have
put such an idea into your pretty little head?

GWENDOLEN   Thank you. You may! [*Offers her cheek.*]

CECILY [*Very sweetly.*]   I knew there must be some misunderstanding,
Miss Fairfax. The gentleman whose arm is at present round your waist
is my dear guardian, Mr. John Worthing.

GWENDOLEN   I beg your pardon?

CECILY   This is Uncle Jack.

GWENDOLEN [*Receding.*]   Jack! Oh!
    [*Enter* ALGERNON.]

CECILY   Here is Ernest.

ALGERNON [*Goes straight over to* CECILY *without noticing anyone else.*]   My
own love! [*Offers to kiss her.*]

CECILY [*Drawing back.*]   A moment, Ernest! May I ask you—are you
engaged to be married to this young lady?

ALGERNON [*Looking round.*]   To what young lady? Good heavens!
Gwendolen!

CECILY   Yes! to good heavens, Gwendolen, I mean to Gwendolen.

ALGERNON [*Laughing.*]   Of course not! What could have put such an idea
into your pretty little head?

CECILY   Thank you. [*Presenting her cheek to be kissed.*] You may. [ALGER-
NON *kisses her.*]

GWENDOLEN   I felt there was some slight error, Miss Cardew. The gentleman who is now embracing you is my cousin, Mr. Algernon Moncrieff.

CECILY. [*Breaking away from* ALGERNON,]   Algernon Moncrieff! Oh! [*The
two girls move towards each other and put their arms round each other's
waists as if for protection.*]

CECILY   Are you called Algernon?

ALGERNON   I cannot deny it.

CECILY   Oh!

GWENDOLEN   Is your name really John?

JACK [*Standing rather proudly.*]   I could deny it if I liked, I could deny
anything if I liked. But my name certainly is John. It has been John for
years.

CECILY [*To* GWENDOLEN.]   A gross deception has been practiced on both
of us.

GWENDOLEN   My poor wounded Cecily!

CECILY   My sweet wronged Gwendolen!

GWENDOLEN [*Slowly and seriously.*]   You will call me sister, will you not?
[*They embrace.* JACK *and* ALGERNON *groan and walk up and down.*]

CECILY [*Rather brightly.*]   There is just one question I would like to be
allowed to ask my guardian.

GWENDOLEN   An admirable idea! Mr. Worthing, there is just one question I would like to be permitted to put to you. Where is your brother Ernest? We are both engaged to be married to your brother Ernest, so it is a matter of some importance to us to know where your brother Ernest is at present.

JACK [*Slowly and hesitatingly.*]   Gwendolen—Cecily—it is very painful for me to be forced to speak the truth. It is the first time in my life that I have ever been reduced to such a painful position, and I am really quite inexperienced in doing anything of the kind. However I will tell you quite frankly that I have no brother Ernest. I have no brother at all. I never had a brother in my life, and I certainly have not the smallest intention of ever having one in the future.

CECILY [*Surprised.*]   No brother at all?

JACK [*Cheerily.*]   None!

GWENDOLEN [*Severely.*]   Had you never a brother of any kind?

JACK [*Pleasantly.*]   Never. Not even of any kind.

GWENDOLEN   I am afraid it is quite clear, Cecily, that neither of us is engaged to be married to anyone.

CECILY   It is not a very pleasant position for a young girl suddenly to find herself in. Is it?

GWENDOLEN   Let us go into the house. They will hardly venture to come after us there.

CECILY   No, men are so cowardly, aren't they?

    [*They retire into the house with scornful looks.*]

JACK   This ghastly state of things is what you call Bunburying, I suppose?

ALGERNON   Yes, and a perfectly wonderful Bunbury it is. The most wonderful Bunbury I have ever had in my life.

JACK   Well, you've no right whatsoever to Bunbury here.

ALGERNON   That is absurd. One has a right to Bunbury anywhere one chooses. Every serious Bunburyist knows that.

JACK   Serious Bunburyist! Good heavens!

ALGERNON   Well, one must be serious about something, if one wants to have any amusement in life. I happen to be serious about Bunburying. What on earth you are serious about I haven't got the remotest idea. About everything, I should fancy. You have such an absolutely trivial nature.

JACK   Well, the only small satisfaction I have in the whole of this wretched business is that your friend Bunbury is quite exploded. You won't be able to run down to the country quite so often as you used to do, dear Algy. And a very good thing too.

ALGERNON   Your brother is a little off-colour, isn't he, dear Jack? You won't be able to disappear to London quite so frequently as your wicked custom was. And not a bad thing either.

JACK   As for your conduct towards Miss Cardew, I must say that your taking in a sweet, simple, innocent girl like that is quite inexcusable. To say nothing of the fact that she is my ward.

ALGERNON   I can see no possible defence at all for your deceiving a brilliant, clever, thoroughly experienced young lady like Miss Fairfax. To say nothing of the fact that she is my cousin.

JACK   I wanted to be engaged to Gwendolen, that is all. I love her.

ALGERNON   Well, I simply wanted to be engaged to Cecily. I adore her.

JACK   There is certainly no chance of your marrying Miss Cardew.

ALGERNON   I don't think there is much likelihood, Jack, of you and Miss Fairfax being united.

JACK   Well, that is no business of yours.

ALGERNON   If it was my business, I wouldn't talk about it. [*Begins to eat muffins.*] It is very vulgar to talk about one's business. Only people like stockbrokers do that, and then merely at dinner parties.

JACK   How can you sit there, calmly eating muffins when we are in this horrible trouble, I can't make out. You seem to me to be perfectly heartless.

ALGERNON   Well, I can't eat muffins in an agitated manner. The butter would probably get on my cuffs. One should always eat muffins quite calmly. It is the only way to eat them.

JACK   I say it's perfectly heartless your eating muffins at all, under the circumstances.

ALGERNON   When I am in trouble, eating is the only thing that consoles me. Indeed, when I am in really great trouble, as anyone who knows me intimately will tell you, I refuse everything except food and drink. At the present moment I am eating muffins because I am unhappy. Besides, I am particularly fond of muffins. [*Rising.*]

JACK [*Rising.*]   Well, that is no reason why you should eat them all in that greedy way. [*Takes muffins from* ALGERNON.]

ALGERNON [*Offering tea cake.*]   I wish you would have tea cake instead. I don't like tea cake.

JACK   Good heavens! I suppose a man may eat his own muffins in his own garden.

ALGERNON   But you have just said it was perfectly heartless to eat muffins.

JACK   I said it was perfectly heartless of you, under the circumstances. That is a very different thing.

ALGERNON   That may be. But the muffins are the same. [*He seizes the muffin dish from* JACK.]

JACK   Algy, I wish to goodness you would go.

ALGERNON   You can't possibly ask me to go without having some dinner. It's absurd. I never go without my dinner. No one ever does, except vegetarians and people like that. Besides I have just made arrangements with Dr. Chasuble to be christened at a quarter to six under the name of Ernest.

JACK   My dear fellow, the sooner you give up that nonsense the better. I made arrangements this morning with Dr. Chasuble to be christened myself at 5:30, and I naturally will take the name of Ernest. Gwendolen would wish it. We can't both be christened Ernest. It's absurd. Besides, I have a perfect right to be christened if I like. There is no evidence at all that I ever have been christened by anybody. I should think it extremely probable I never was, and so does Dr. Chasuble. It is entirely different in your case. You have been christened already.

ALGERNON   Yes, but I have not been christened for years.

JACK   Yes, but you have been christened. That is the important thing.

ALGERNON   Quite so. So I know my constitution can stand it. If you are not quite sure about your ever having been christened, I must say I think it rather dangerous your venturing on it now. It might make you very unwell. You can hardly have forgotten that someone very closely connected with you was very nearly carried off this week in Paris by a severe chill.

JACK   Yes, but you said yourself that a severe chill was not hereditary.

ALGERNON   It usen't to be, I know—but I daresay it is now. Science is always making wonderful improvements in things.

JACK [*Picking up the muffin dish.*]   Oh, that is nonsense; you are always talking nonsense.

ALGERNON   Jack, you are at the muffins again! I wish you wouldn't. There are only two left. [*Takes them.*] I told you I was particularly fond of muffins.

JACK   But I hate tea cake.

ALGERNON   Why on earth then do you allow tea cake to be served up for your guests? What ideas you have of hospitality!

JACK   Algernon! I have already told you to go. I don't want you here. Why don't you go!

ALGERNON   I haven't quite finished my tea yet! and there is still one muffin left. [*Jack groans, and sinks into a chair.* ALGERNON *still continues eating.*]

ACT-DROP

Third Act

SCENE—*Morning room*[5] *at the Manor House.*

[GWENDOLEN *and* CECILY *are at the window, looking out into the garden.*]

GWENDOLEN   The fact that they did not follow us at once into the house, as anyone else would have done, seems to me to show that they have some sense of shame left.

CECILY   They have been eating muffins. That looks like repentance.

GWENDOLEN [*After a pause.*]   They don't seem to notice us at all. Couldn't you cough?

CECILY   But I haven't got a cough.

GWENDOLEN   They're looking at us. What effrontery!

CECILY   They're approaching. That's very forward of them.

GWENDOLEN   Let us preserve a dignified silence.

CECILY   Certainly. It's the only thing to do now.

[*Enter* JACK *followed by* ALGERNON. *They whistle some dreadful popular air from a British Opera.*[6]]

GWENDOLEN   This dignified silence seems to produce an unpleasant effect.

CECILY   A most distasteful one.

GWENDOLEN   But we will not be the first to speak.

CECILY   Certainly not.

GWENDOLEN   Mr. Worthing, I have something very particular to ask you. Much depends on your reply.

5. A relatively informally furnished room for receiving visitors making morning calls (usually close friends of the host or hostess). Afternoon visitors, on the other hand, would be received in the drawing room, a much more formal and elegant setting.

6. Probably a reference to one of the operas of W. S. Gilbert and Sir Arthur Sullivan.

CECILY   Gwendolen, your common sense is invaluable. Mr. Moncrieff, kindly answer me the following question. Why did you pretend to be my guardian's brother?

ALGERNON   In order that I might have an opportunity of meeting you.

CECILY   [*To* GWENDOLEN.]   That certainly seems a satisfactory explanation, does it not?

GWENDOLEN   Yes, dear, if you can believe him.

CECILY   I don't. But that does not affect the wonderful beauty of his answer.

GWENDOLEN   True. In matters of grave importance, style, not sincerity is the vital thing. Mr. Worthing, what explanation can you offer to me for pretending to have a brother? Was it in order that you might have an opportunity of coming up to town to see me as often as possible?

JACK   Can you doubt it, Miss Fairfax?

GWENDOLEN   I have the gravest doubts upon the subject. But I intend to crush them. This is not the moment for German scepticism.[7] [*Moving to* CECILY.] Their explanations appear to be quite satisfactory, especially Mr. Worthing's. That seems to me to have the stamp of truth upon it.

CECILY   I am more than content with what Mr. Moncrieff said. His voice alone inspires one with absolute credulity.

GWENDOLEN   Then you think we should forgive them?

CECILY   Yes. I mean no.

GWENDOLEN   True! I had forgotten. There are principles at stake that one cannot surrender. Which of us should tell them? The task is not a pleasant one.

CECILY   Could we not both speak at the same time?

GWENDOLEN   An excellent idea! I nearly always speak at the same time as other people. Will you take the time from me?

CECILY   Certainly. [GWENDOLEN *beats time with uplifted finger.*]

GWENDOLEN AND CECILY [*Speaking together.*]   Your Christian names are still an insuperable barrier. That is all!

JACK AND ALGERNON [*Speaking together.*]   Our Christian names! Is that all? But we are going to be christened this afternoon.

GWENDOLEN [*To* JACK.]   For my sake you are prepared to do this terrible thing?

JACK   I am.

CECILY [*To* ALGERNON.]   To please me you are ready to face this fearful ordeal?

ALGERNON   I am!

GWENDOLEN   How absurd to talk of the equality of the sexes! Where questions of self-sacrifice are concerned, men are infinitely beyond us.

JACK   We are. [*Clasps hands with* ALGERNON.]

CECILY   They have moments of physical courage of which we women know absolutely nothing.

GWENDOLEN [*To* JACK.]   Darling!

ALGERNON [*To* CECILY.]   Darling. [*They fall into each other's arms.*]

---

7. Many 19th-century German scholars (e.g., D. F. Strauss) were notorious among the British for being skeptical in their analyses of religious texts.

[*Enter* MERRIMAN. *When he enters he coughs loudly, seeing the situation.*]

MERRIMAN Ahem! Ahem! Lady Bracknell!

JACK Good heavens!

[*Enter* LADY BRACKNELL. *The couples separate in alarm. Exit* MERRIMAN.]

LADY BRACKNELL Gwendolen! What does this mean?

GWENDOLEN Merely that I am engaged to be married to Mr. Worthing, mamma.

LADY BRACKNELL Come here. Sit down. Sit down immediately. Hesitation of any kind is a sign of mental decay in the young, of physical weakness in the old. [*Turns to* JACK.] Apprised, sir, of my daughter's sudden flight by her trusty maid, whose confidence I purchased by means of a small coin, I followed her at once by a luggage train.[8] Her unhappy father is, I am glad to say, under the impression that she is attending a more than usually lengthy lecture by the University Extension Scheme on the Influence of a Permanent Income on Thought. I do not propose to undeceive him. Indeed I have never undeceived him on any question. I would consider it wrong. But of course, you will clearly understand that all communication between yourself and my daughter must cease immediately from this moment. On this point, as indeed on all points, I am firm.

JACK I am engaged to be married to Gwendolen, Lady Bracknell!

LADY BRACKNELL You are nothing of the kind, sir. And now, as regards Algernon! . . . Algernon!

ALGERNON Yes, Aunt Augusta.

LADY BRACKNELL May I ask if it is in this house that your invalid friend Mr. Bunbury resides?

ALGERNON [*Stammering.*] Oh! No! Bunbury doesn't live here. Bunbury is somewhere else at present. In fact, Bunbury is dead.

LADY BRACKNELL Dead! When did Mr. Bunbury die? His death must have been extremely sudden.

ALGERNON [*Airily.*] Oh! I killed Bunbury this afternoon. I mean poor Bunbury died this afternoon.

LADY BRACKNELL What did he die of?

ALGERNON Bunbury? Oh, he was quite exploded.

LADY BRACKNELL Exploded! Was he the victim of a revolutionary outrage? I was not aware that Mr. Bunbury was interested in social legislation. If so, he is well punished for his morbidity.

ALGERNON My dear Aunt Augusta, I mean he was found out! The doctors found out that Bunbury could not live, that is what I mean—so Bunbury died.

LADY BRACKNELL He seems to have had great confidence in the opinion of his physicians. I am glad, however, that he made up his mind at the last to some definite course of action, and acted under proper medical advice. And now that we have finally got rid of this Mr. Bunbury, may I ask, Mr. Worthing, who is that young person whose hand my nephew Algernon is now holding in what seems to me a peculiarly unnecessary manner?

8. Freight train.

JACK   That lady is Miss Cecily Cardew, my ward.

[LADY BRACKNELL *bows coldly to* CECILY.]

ALGERNON   I am engaged to be married to Cecily, Aunt Augusta.

LADY BRACKNELL   I beg your pardon?

CECILY   Mr. Moncrieff and I are engaged to be married, Lady Bracknell.

LADY BRACKNELL [*With a shiver, crossing to the sofa and sitting down.*]   I do not know whether there is anything peculiarly exciting in the air of this particular part of Hertfordshire, but the number of engagements that go on seems to me considerably above the proper average that statistics have laid down for our guidance. I think some preliminary inquiry on my part would not be out of place. Mr. Worthing, is Miss Cardew at all connected with any of the larger railway stations in London? I merely desire information. Until yesterday I had no idea that there were any families or persons whose origin was a Terminus.⁹ [JACK *looks perfectly furious, but restrains himself.*]

JACK [*In a clear, cold voice.*]   Miss Cardew is the granddaughter of the late Mr. Thomas Cardew of 149, Belgrave Square, S.W.; Gervase Park, Dorking, Surrey; and the Sporran, Fifeshire, N.B.¹

LADY BRACKNELL   That sounds not unsatisfactory. Three addresses always inspire confidence, even in tradesmen. But what proof have I of their authenticity?

JACK   I have carefully preserved the Court Guides² of the period. They are open to your inspection, Lady Bracknell.

LADY BRACKNELL [*Grimly.*]   I have known strange errors in that publication.

JACK   Miss Cardew's family solicitors are Messrs. Markby, Markby, and Markby.

LADY BRACKNELL   Markby, Markby, and Markby? A firm of the very highest position in their profession. Indeed I am told that one of the Mr. Markbys is occasionally to be seen at dinner parties. So far I am satisfied.

JACK [*Very irritably.*]   How extremely kind of you, Lady Bracknell! I have also in my possession, you will be pleased to hear, certificates of Miss Cardew's birth, baptism, whooping cough, registration, vaccination, confirmation, and the measles; both the German and the English variety.

LADY BRACKNELL   Ah! A life crowded with incident, I see; though perhaps somewhat too exciting for a young girl. I am not myself in favor of premature experiences. [*Rises, looks at her watch.*] Gwendolen! the time approaches for our departure. We have not a moment to lose. As a matter of form, Mr. Worthing, I had better ask you if Miss Cardew has any little fortune?

JACK   Oh! about a hundred and thirty thousand pounds in the Funds.³ That is all. Good-bye, Lady Bracknell. So pleased to have seen you.

LADY BRACKNELL [*Sitting down again.*]   A moment, Mr. Worthing. A hundred and thirty thousand pounds! And in the Funds! Miss Cardew seems to me a most attractive young lady, now that I look at her. Few girls of the present day have any really solid qualities, any of the qualities that

9. Station at the end of a railway line.
1. Presumably north Britain, i.e., Scotland.

2. Directories commonly used in the era.
3. Interest-bearing government bonds.

last, and improve with time. We live, I regret to say, in an age of surfaces. [*To* CECILY.] Come over here, dear, [CECILY *goes across.*] Pretty child! your dress is sadly simple, and your hair seems almost as Nature might have left it. But we can soon alter all that. A thoroughly experienced French maid produces a really marvellous result in a very brief space of time. I remember recommending one to young Lady Lancing, and after three months her own husband did not know her.

JACK [*Aside.*] And after six months nobody knew her.[4]

LADY BRACKNELL [*Glares at* JACK *for a few moments. Then bends, with a practiced smile, to* CECILY.] Kindly turn round, sweet child. [CECILY *turns completely round.*] No, the side view is what I want, [CECILY *presents her profile.*] Yes, quite as I expected. There are distinct social possibilities in your profile. The two weak points in our age are its want of principle and its want of profile. The chin a little higher, dear. Style largely depends on the way the chin is worn. They are worn very high, just at present. Algernon!

ALGERNON Yes, Aunt Augusta!

LADY BRACKNELL There are distinct social possibilities in Miss Cardew's profile.

ALGERNON Cecily is the sweetest, dearest, prettiest girl in the whole world. And I don't care twopence about social possibilities.

LADY BRACKNELL Never speak disrespectfully of Society, Algernon. Only people who can't get into it do that. [*To* CECILY.] Dear child, of course you know that Algernon has nothing but his debts to depend upon. But I do not approve of mercenary marriages. When I married Lord Bracknell I had no fortune of any kind. But I never dreamed for a moment of allowing that to stand in my way. Well, I suppose I must give my consent.

ALGERNON Thank you, Aunt Augusta.

LADY BRACKNELL Cecily, you may kiss me!

CECILY [*Kisses her.*] Thank you, Lady Bracknell.

LADY BRACKNELL You may also address me as Aunt Augusta for the future.

CECILY Thank you, Aunt Augusta.

LADY BRACKNELL The marriage, I think, had better take place quite soon.

ALGERNON Thank you, Aunt Augusta.

CECILY Thank you, Aunt Augusta.

LADY BRACKNELL To speak frankly, I am not in favour of long engagements. They give people the opportunity of finding out each other's character before marriage, which I think is never advisable.

JACK I beg your pardon for interrupting you, Lady Bracknell, but this engagement is quite out of the question. I am Miss Cardew's guardian, and she cannot marry without my consent until she comes of age. That consent I absolutely decline to give.

LADY BRACKNELL Upon what grounds may I ask? Algernon is an extremely, I may almost say an ostentatiously, eligible young man. He has nothing, but he looks everything. What more can one desire?

JACK It pains me very much to have to speak frankly to you, Lady Bracknell, about your nephew, but the fact is that I do not approve at all of his

4. I.e., she became socially unacceptable because of her scandalous behavior.

moral character. I suspect him of being untruthful. [ALGERNON *and* CECILY *look at him in indignant amazement.*]

LADY BRACKNELL Untruthful! My nephew Algernon? Impossible! He is an Oxonian.[5]

JACK I fear there can be no possible doubt about the matter. This afternoon, during my temporary absence in London on an important question of romance, he obtained admission to my house by means of the false pretence of being my brother. Under an assumed name he drank, I've just been informed by my butler, an entire pint bottle of my Perrier-Jouet, Brut, '89;[6] a wine I was specially reserving for myself. Continuing his disgraceful deception, he succeeded in the course of the afternoon in alienating the affections of my only ward. He subsequently stayed to tea, and devoured every single muffin. And what makes his conduct all the more heartless is, that he was perfectly well aware from the first that I have no brother, that I never had a brother, and that I don't intend to have a brother, not even of any kind. I distinctly told him so myself yesterday afternoon.

LADY BRACKNELL Ahem! Mr. Worthing, after careful consideration I have decided entirely to overlook my nephew's conduct to you.

JACK That is very generous of you, Lady Bracknell. My own decision, however, is unalterable. I decline to give my consent.

LADY BRACKNELL [*To* CECILY.] Come here, sweet child, [CECILY *goes over.*] How old are you, dear?

CECILY Well, I am really only eighteen, but I always admit to twenty when I go to evening parties.

LADY BRACKNELL You are perfectly right in making some slight alteration. Indeed, no woman should ever be quite accurate about her age. It looks so calculating. . . . [*In a meditative manner.*] Eighteen, but admitting to twenty at evening parties. Well, it will not be very long before you are of age and free from the restraints of tutelage. So I don't think your guardian's consent is, after all, a matter of any importance.

JACK Pray excuse me, Lady Bracknell, for interrupting you again, but it is only fair to tell you that according to the terms of her grandfather's will Miss Cardew does not come legally of age till she is thirty-five.

LADY BRACKNELL That does not seem to me to be a grave objection. Thirty-five is a very attractive age. London society is full of women of the very highest birth who have, of their own free choice, remained thirty-five for years. Lady Dumbleton is an instance in point. To my own knowledge she has been thirty-five ever since she arrived at the age of forty, which was many years ago now. I see no reason why our dear Cecily should not be even still more attractive at the age you mention than she is at present. There will be a large accumulation of property.

CECILY Algy, could you wait for me till I was thirty-five?

ALGERNON Of course I could, Cecily. You know I could.

CECILY Yes, I felt it instinctively, but I couldn't wait all that time. I hate waiting even five minutes for anybody. It always makes me rather cross.

---

5. I.e., he had been a student at Oxford (in medieval Latin, *Oxonia*).

6. An outstanding brand and year of dry champagne.

I am not punctual myself, I know, but I do like punctuality in others, and waiting, even to be married, is quite out of the question.

ALGERNON Then what is to be done, Cecily?

CECILY I don't know, Mr. Moncrieff.

LADY BRACKNELL My dear Mr. Worthing, as Miss Cardew states positively that she cannot wait till she is thirty-five—a remark which I am bound to say seems to me to show a somewhat impatient nature—I would beg of you to reconsider your decision.

JACK But my dear Lady Bracknell, the matter is entirely in your own hands. The moment you consent to my marriage with Gwendolen, I will most gladly allow your nephew to form an alliance with my ward.

LADY BRACKNELL [*Rising and drawing herself up.*] You must be quite aware that what you propose is out of the question.

JACK Then a passionate celibacy is all that any of us can look forward to.

LADY BRACKNELL This is not the destiny I propose for Gwendolen. Algernon, of course, can choose for himself. [*Pulls out her watch.*] Come, dear; [GWENDOLEN *rises.*] we have already missed five, if not six, trains. To miss any more might expose us to comment on the platform.
          [*Enter* DR. CHASUBLE.]

CHASUBLE Everything is quite ready for the christenings.

LADY BRACKNELL The christenings, sir! Is not that somewhat premature!

CHASUBLE [*Looking rather puzzled, and pointing to* JACK *and* ALGERNON.] Both these gentlemen have expressed a desire for immediate baptism.

LADY BRACKNELL At their age? The idea is grotesque and irreligious! Algernon, I forbid you to be baptized. I will not hear of such excesses. Lord Bracknell would be highly displeased if he learned that that was the way in which you wasted your time and money.

CHASUBLE Am I to understand then that there are to be no christenings at all this afternoon?

JACK I don't think that, as things are now, it would be of much practical value to either of us, Dr. Chasuble.

CHASUBLE I am grieved to hear such sentiments from you, Mr. Worthing. They savour of the heretical views of the Anabaptists,[7] views that I have completely refuted in four of my unpublished sermons. However, as your present mood seems to be one peculiarly secular, I will return to the church at once. Indeed, I have just been informed by the pew-opener[8] that for the last hour and a half Miss Prism has been waiting for me in the vestry.

LADY BRACKNELL [*Starting.*] Miss Prism! Did I hear you mention a Miss Prism?

CHASUBLE Yes, Lady Bracknell. I am on my way to join her.

LADY BRACKNELL Pray allow me to detain you for a moment. This matter may prove to be one of vital importance to Lord Bracknell and myself. Is this Miss Prism a female of repellent aspect, remotely connected with education?

---

7. A radical Protestant sect of the 17th century, whose repudiation of infant baptism was regarded as heretical by Anglicans.

8. A person employed at church services to usher worshippers to their pews and open the doors for them.

CHASUBLE [*Somewhat indignantly.*]   She is the most cultivated of ladies, and the very picture of respectability.

LADY BRACKNELL   It is obviously the same person. May I ask what position she holds in your household?

CHASUBLE [*Severely.*]   I am a celibate, madam.

JACK [*Interposing.*]   Miss Prism, Lady Bracknell, has been for the last three years Miss Cardew's esteemed governess and valued companion.

LADY BRACKNELL   In spite of what I hear of her, I must see her at once. Let her be sent for.

CHASUBLE [*Looking off.*]   She approaches; she is nigh.

[*Enter* MISS PRISM *hurriedly.*]

MISS PRISM   I was told you expected me in the vestry, dear Canon. I have been waiting for you there for an hour and three quarters. [*Catches sight of* LADY BRACKNELL *who has fixed her with a stony glare.* MISS PRISM *grows pale and quails. She looks anxiously round as if desirous to escape.*]

LADY BRACKNELL [*In a severe, judicial voice.*]   Prism! [MISS PRISM *bows her head in shame.*] Come here, Prism! [MISS PRISM *approaches in a humble manner.*] Prism! Where is that baby? [*General consternation. THE* CANON *starts back in horror.* ALGERNON *and* JACK *pretend to be anxious to shield* CECILY *and* GWENDOLEN *from hearing the details of a terrible public scandal.*] Twenty-eight years ago, Prism, you left Lord Bracknell's house, Number 104, Upper Grosvenor Street, in charge of a perambulator that contained a baby, of the male sex. You never returned. A few weeks later, through the elaborate investigations of the Metropolitan police, the perambulator was discovered at midnight, standing by itself in a remote corner of Bayswater.[9] It contained the manuscript of a three-volume novel of more than usually revolting sentimentality, [MISS PRISM *starts in involuntary indignation.*] But the baby was not there! [*Everyone looks at* MISS PRISM.] Prism! Where is that baby? [*A pause.*]

MISS PRISM   Lady Bracknell, I admit with shame that I do not know. I only wish I did. The plain facts of the case are these. On the morning of the day you mention, a day that is forever branded on my memory, I prepared as usual to take the baby out in its perambulator. I had also with me a somewhat old, but capacious handbag, in which I had intended to place the manuscript of a work of fiction that I had written during my few unoccupied hours. In a moment of mental abstraction, for which I never can forgive myself, I deposited the manuscript in the bassinette, and placed the baby in the handbag.

JACK [*Who has been listening attentively.*]   But where did you deposit the handbag?

MISS PRISM   Do not ask me, Mr. Worthing.

JACK   Miss Prism, this is a matter of no small importance to me. I insist on knowing where you deposited the handbag that contained that infant.

MISS PRISM   I left it in the cloak room of one of the larger railway stations in London.

JACK   What railway station?

MISS PRISM [*Quite crushed.*]   Victoria. The Brighton line. [*Sinks into a chair.*]

---

9. A once fashionable locality in the West End near Kensington Gardens.

JACK   I must retire to my room for a moment. Gwendolen, wait here for me.

GWENDOLEN   If you are not too long, I will wait here for you all my life.

[*Exit* JACK *in great excitement.*]

CHASUBLE   What do you think this means, Lady Bracknell?

LADY BRACKNELL   I dare not even suspect, Dr. Chasuble. I need hardly tell you that in families of high position strange coincidences are not supposed to occur. They are hardly considered the thing.

[*Noises heard overhead as if someone was throwing trunks about. Every-one looks up.*]

CECILY   Uncle Jack seems strangely agitated.

CHASUBLE   Your guardian has a very emotional nature.

LADY BRACKNELL   This noise is extremely unpleasant. It sounds as if he was having an argument. I dislike arguments of any kind. They are always vulgar, and often convincing.

CHASUBLE [*Looking up.*]   It has stopped now. [*The noise is redoubled.*]

LADY BRACKNELL   I wish he would arrive at some conclusion.

GWENDOLEN   This suspense is terrible. I hope it will last.

[*Enter* JACK *with a handbag of black leather in his hand.*]

JACK [*Rushing over to* MISS PRISM.]   Is this the handbag, Miss Prism? Examine it carefully before you speak. The happiness of more than one life depends on your answer.

MISS PRISM [*Calmly.*]   It seems to be mine. Yes, here is the injury it received through the upsetting of a Gower Street omnibus in younger and happier days. Here is the stain on the lining caused by the explosion of a temperance beverage,[1] an incident that occurred at Leamington. And here, on the lock, are my initials. I had forgotten that in an extravagant mood I had had them placed there. The bag is undoubtedly mine. I am delighted to have it so unexpectedly restored to me. It has been a great inconvenience being without it all these years.

JACK [*In a pathetic voice.*]   Miss Prism, more is restored to you than this handbag. I was the baby you placed in it.

MISS PRISM [*Amazed.*]   You!

JACK [*Embracing her.*]   Yes . . . mother!

MISS PRISM [*Recoiling in indignant astonishment*]   Mr. Worthing! I am unmarried!

JACK   Unmarried! I do not deny that is a serious blow. But after all, who has the right to cast a stone[2] against one who has suffered? Cannot repentance wipe out an act of folly? Why should there be one law for men, and another for women? Mother, I forgive you. [*Tries to embrace her again.*]

MISS PRISM [*Still more indignant.*]   Mr. Worthing, there is some error. [*Pointing to* LADY BRACKNELL.] There is the lady who can tell you who you really are.

JACK [*After a pause.*]   Lady Bracknell, I hate to seem inquisitive, but would you kindly inform me who I am?

LADY BRACKNELL   I am afraid that the news I have to give you will not altogether please you. You are the son of my poor sister, Mrs. Moncrieff, and consequently Algernon's elder brother.

---

1. A nonalcoholic drink.
2. When the scribes and Pharisees brought to Jesus an adulterous woman with the reminder that the law of Moses required her to be stoned, he answered: "He that is without sin among you, let him first cast a stone at her" (John 8.7).

JACK   Algy's elder brother! Then I have a brother after all. I knew I had a brother! I always said I had a brother! Cecily—how could you have ever doubted that I had a brother? [*Seizes hold of* ALGERNON.] Dr. Chasuble, my unfortunate brother. Miss Prism, my unfortunate brother. Gwendolen, my unfortunate brother. Algy, you young scoundrel, you will have to treat me with more respect in the future. You have never behaved to me like a brother in all your life.

ALGERNON   Well, not till today, old boy, I admit. I did my best, however, though I was out of practice. [*Shakes hands.*]

GWENDOLEN [*To* JACK.]   My own! But what own are you? What is your Christian name, now that you have become someone else?

JACK   Good heavens! . . . I had quite forgotten that point. Your decision on the subject of my name is irrevocable, I suppose?

GWENDOLEN   I never change, except in my affections.

CECILY   What a noble nature you have, Gwendolen!

JACK   Then the question had better be cleared up at once. Aunt Augusta, a moment. At the time when Miss Prism left me in the handbag, had I been christened already?

LADY BRACKNELL   Every luxury that money could buy, including christening, had been lavished on you by your fond and doting parents.

JACK   Then I was christened! That is settled. Now, what name was I given? Let me know the worst.

LADY BRACKNELL   Being the eldest son you were naturally christened after your father.

JACK [*Irritably.*]   Yes, but what was my father's Christian name?

LADY BRACKNELL [*Meditatively.*]   I cannot at the present moment recall what the General's Christian name was. But I have no doubt he had one. He was eccentric, I admit. But only in later years. And that was the result of the Indian climate, and marriage, and indigestion, and other things of that kind.

JACK   Algy! Can't you recollect what our father's Christian name was?

ALGERNON   My dear boy, we were never even on speaking terms. He died before I was a year old.

JACK   His name would appear in the Army Lists of the period, I suppose, Aunt Augusta?

LADY BRACKNELL   The General was essentially a man of peace, except in his domestic life. But I have no doubt his name would appear in any military directory.

JACK   The Army Lists of the last forty years are here. These delightful records should have been my constant study. [*Rushes to bookcase and tears the books out.*] M. Generals . . . Mallam, Maxbohm,[3] Magley, what ghastly names they have—Markby, Migsby, Mobbs, Moncrieff! Lieutenant 1840, Captain, Lieutenant Colonel, Colonel, General 1869, Christian names, Ernest John. [*Puts book very quietly down and speaks quite calmly.*] I always told you, Gwendolen, my name was Ernest, didn't I? Well it is Ernest after all. I mean it naturally is Ernest.

LADY BRACKNELL   Yes, I remember now that the General was called Ernest. I knew I had some particular reason for disliking the name.

---

3. A play on the name of Max Beerbohm (1872–1956), English essayist, caricaturist, and parodist.

GWENDOLEN   Ernest! My own Ernest! I felt from the first that you could have no other name!

JACK   Gwendolen, it is a terrible thing for a man to find out suddenly that all his life he has been speaking nothing but the truth. Can you forgive me?

GWENDOLEN   I can. For I feel that you are sure to change.

JACK   My own one!

CHASUBLE   [*To* MISS PRISM.]   Laetitia! [*Embraces her.*]

MISS PRISM [*Enthusiastically.*]   Frederick! At last!

ALGERNON   Cecily! [*Embraces her.*] At last!

JACK   Gwendolen! [*Embraces her.*] At last!

LADY BRACKNELL   My nephew, you seem to be displaying signs of triviality.

JACK   On the contrary, Aunt Augusta, I've now realized for the first time in my life the vital Importance of Being Earnest.

CURTAIN

performed 1895   1899

From De Profundis[1]

And the end of it all is that I have got to forgive you. I must do so. I don't write this letter to put bitterness into your heart, but to pluck it out of mine. For my own sake I must forgive you. One cannot always keep an adder in one's breast to feed on one, nor rise up every night to sow thorns in the garden of one's soul. It will not be difficult at all for me to do so, if you help me a little. Whatever you did to me in old days I always readily forgave. It did you no good then. Only one whose life is without stain of any kind can forgive sins. But now when I sit in humiliation and disgrace it is different. My forgiveness should mean a great deal to you now. Some day you will realise it. Whether you do so early or late, soon or not at all, my way is clear before me. I cannot allow you to go through life bearing in your heart the burden of having ruined a man like me. The thought might make you callously indifferent, or morbidly sad. I must take the burden from you and put it on my own shoulders.

I must say to myself that neither you nor your father, multiplied a thousand times over, could possibly have ruined a man like me: that I ruined myself: and that nobody, great or small, can be ruined except by his own hand. I am quite ready to do so. I am trying to do so, though you may not think it at the present moment. If I have brought this pitiless indictment against you, think

1. Out of the depths (Latin); Psalms 130.1: "Out of the depths have I cried unto thee, O Lord." While in prison in Reading Gaol, Wilde was allowed a pen and paper only to write letters. Given one sheet of paper at a time, which was taken away after it was filled, Wilde wrote this work as a letter to Lord Alfred Douglas, whose nickname was Bosie. Wilde titled it *Epistola: In Carcere et Vinculis* (*Letter: In Prison and in Chains*). He was given the manuscript on his release and turned it over to a friend, Robert Ross, who gave it its current title and published it in an abridged version in 1905, after Wilde's death. After Douglas's death in 1945, a fuller text was published by Wilde's son, Vyvyan Holland; but only in 1962, when scholars could consult the original manuscript, did a complete version appear.

what an indictment I bring without pity against myself. Terrible as what you did to me was, what I did to myself was far more terrible still.

I was a man who stood in symbolic relations to the art and culture of my age. I had realised this for myself at the very dawn of my manhood, and had forced my age to realise it afterwards. Few men hold such a position in their own lifetime and have it so acknowledged. It is usually discerned, if discerned at all, by the historian, or the critic, long after both the man and his age have passed away. With me it was different. I felt it myself, and made others feel it. Byron[2] was a symbolic figure, but his relations were to the passion of his age and its weariness of passion. Mine were to something more noble, more permanent, of more vital issue, of larger scope.

The gods had given me almost everything. I had genius, a distinguished name, high social position, brilliancy, intellectual daring: I made art a philosophy, and philosophy an art: I altered the minds of men and the colours of things: there was nothing I said or did that did not make people wonder: I took the drama, the most objective form known to art, and made it as personal a mode of expression as the lyric or the sonnet, at the same time that I widened its range and enriched its characterization: drama, novel, poem in rhyme, poem in prose, subtle or fantastic dialogue, whatever I touched I made beautiful in a new mode of beauty: to truth itself I gave what is false no less than what is true as its rightful province, and showed that the false and the true are merely forms of intellectual existence. I treated Art as the supreme reality, and life as a mere mode of fiction: I awoke the imagination of my century so that it created myth and legend around me: I summed up all systems in a phrase, and all existence in an epigram.

Along with these things, I had things that were different. I let myself be lured into long spells of senseless and sensual ease. I amused myself with being a *flâneur*,[3] a dandy, a man of fashion. I surrounded myself with the smaller natures and the meaner[4] minds. I became the spendthrift of my own genius, and to waste an eternal youth gave me a curious joy. Tired of being on the heights I deliberately went to the depths in the search for new sensations. What the paradox was to me in the sphere of thought, perversity became to me in the sphere of passion. Desire, at the end, was a malady, or a madness, or both. I grew careless of the lives of others. I took pleasure where it pleased me and passed on. I forgot that every little action of the common day makes or unmakes character, and that therefore what one has done in the secret chamber one has some day to cry aloud on the housetops. I ceased to be Lord over myself. I was no longer the Captain of my Soul,[5] and did not know it. I allowed you to dominate me, and your father to frighten me. I ended in horrible disgrace. There is only one thing for me now, absolute Humility: just as there is only one thing for you, absolute Humility also. You had better come down into the dust and learn it beside me.

I have lain in prison for nearly two years. Out of my nature has come wild despair; an abandonment to grief that was piteous even to look at: terrible and impotent rage: bitterness and scorn: anguish that wept aloud: misery that could find no voice: sorrow that was dumb. I have passed through every

---

2. George Gordon, Lord Byron (1788–1824), Romantic poet.
3. Idle stroller (French).
4. More shallow or more trivial.
5. See W. E. Henley's "Invictus" (1888), line 16.

possible mood of suffering. Better than Wordsworth himself I know what Wordsworth meant when he said:

> Suffering is permanent, obscure, and dark
> And has the nature of Infinity.[6]

But while there were times when I rejoiced in the idea that my sufferings were to be endless, I could not bear them to be without meaning. Now I find hidden away in my nature something that tells me that nothing in the whole world is meaningless, and suffering least of all. That something hidden away in my nature, like a treasure in a field, is Humility.

It is the last thing left in me, and the best: the ultimate discovery at which I have arrived: the starting-point for a fresh development. It has come to me right out of myself, so I know that it has come at the proper time. It could not have come before, nor later. Had anyone told me of it, I would have rejected it. Had it been brought to me, I would have refused it. As I found it, I want to keep it. I must do so. It is the one thing that has in it the elements of life, of a new life, a *Vita Nuova*[7] for me.

* * *

Morality does not help me. I am a born antinomian.[8] I am one of those who are made for exceptions, not for laws. But while I see that there is nothing wrong in what one does, I see that there is something wrong in what one becomes. It is well to have learned that.

Religion does not help me. The faith that others give to what is unseen, I give to what one can touch, and look at. My Gods dwell in temples made with hands, and within the circle of actual experience is my creed made perfect and complete: too complete it may be, for like many or all of those who have placed their Heaven in this earth, I have found in it not merely the beauty of Heaven, but the horror of Hell also. When I think about Religion at all, I feel as if I would like to found an order for those who cannot believe: the Confraternity of the Fatherless one might call it, where on an altar, on which no taper burned, a priest, in whose heart peace had no dwelling, might celebrate with unblessed bread and a chalice empty of wine. Everything to be true must become a religion. And agnosticism should have its ritual no less than faith. It has sown its martyrs, it should reap its saints, and praise God daily for having hidden Himself from man. But whether it be faith or agnosticism, it must be nothing external to me. Its symbols must be of my own creating. Only that is spiritual which makes its own form. If I may not find its secret within myself, I shall never find it. If I have not got it already, it will never come to me.

Reason does not help me. It tells me that the laws under which I am convicted are wrong and unjust laws, and the system under which I have suffered a wrong and unjust system. But, somehow, I have got to make both of these things just and right to me. And exactly as in Art one is only concerned with what a particular thing is at a particular moment to oneself, so it is also in the ethical evolution of one's character. I have got to make everything that

6. From *The Borderers* (written 1796–97), lines 1543–44.
7. New life (Italian); here Dante's earliest work (1292–94) about his love for Beatrice.
8. Rejecter of moral law.

has happened to me good for me. The plank-bed, the loathsome food, the hard ropes shredded into oakum till one's fingertips grow dull with pain, the menial offices[9] with which each day begins and finishes, the harsh orders that routine seems to necessitate, the dreadful dress that makes sorrow grotesque to look at, the silence, the solitude, the shame—each and all of these things I have to transform into a spiritual experience. There is not a single degradation of the body which I must not try and make into a spiritualizing of the soul.

I want to get to the point when I shall be able to say, quite simply and without affectation, that the two great turning-points of my life were when my father sent me to Oxford, and when society sent me to prison. I will not say that it is the best thing that could have happened to me, for that phrase would savour of too great bitterness towards myself. I would sooner say, or hear it said of me, that I was so typical a child of my age that in my perversity,[1] and for that perversity's sake, I turned the good things of my life to evil, and the evil things of my life to good. What is said, however, by myself or by others matters little. The important thing, the thing that lies before me, the thing that I have to do, or be for the brief remainder of my days one maimed, marred, and incomplete, is to absorb into my nature all that has been done to me, to make it part of me, to accept it without complaint, fear, or reluctance. The supreme vice is shallowness. Whatever is realized is right.

1897   1962

---

9. Duties. "Oakum": loose fiber from old hemp ropes, which prisoners were often made to shred.

1. I.e., obstinate desire to behave unconventionally.

GEORGE BERNARD SHAW
1856–1950

W inston Churchill described George Bernard Shaw as a "bright, nimble, fierce, and comprehending being, Jack Frost dancing bespangled in the sunshine." Born and raised in the Victorian period, this extraordinary character was an important and engaged public intellectual. His experience encompassed the momentous historical changes of the last half of the nineteenth century and the first half of the twentieth, and he made it his business to pronounce on them all in the witty epigrammatic style that characterizes his plays.

Like Oscar Wilde, the other playwright whose work changed the course of British drama, Shaw was an Irishman. Born in Dublin, he was, in his own words, "the fruit of an unsuitable marriage between two quite amiable people who finally separated in the friendliest fashion." His mother, an aspiring singer, went to London to pursue her musical career; Shaw followed five years later, in 1876, quitting the job he had held since the age of fifteen at a land agent's office. He intended to become a novelist. He spent much of his time in the Reading Room of the British Museum, where a young journalist named William Archer introduced himself because he was so intrigued by the combination of things Shaw was studying—Karl Marx's *Das Kapital* (vol. 1, 1867) and the score of Richard Wagner's opera *Tristan and Isolde* (1859).

These two works indicate the main involvements of Shaw's life in London. *Das Kapital* convinced him that socialism was the answer to society's problems. With the socialist economists Sidney and Beatrice Webb, Shaw joined the Fabian Society, a socialist organization that had committed itself to gradual reform rather than revolution. Shaw quickly became a leader in the group and its principal spokesperson. His pronouncements and tracts had a wit absent from most political writing. In *Fabian Tract No. 2* (1884), for example, he argued that nineteenth-century capitalism had divided society "into hostile classes, with large appetites and no dinners at one extreme and large dinners and no appetites at the other." Though painfully shy, he disciplined himself to become an accomplished public speaker. Accepting fees from no one, he spoke everywhere, stipulating only that he could speak on whatever subject he liked.

Meanwhile, his acquaintance with William Archer led him to journalism. He worked first as an art critic, then as a music critic, championing Wagner's operas and introducing a new standard of wit and judgment to music reviewing, writing for example of a hapless soprano who "fell fearlessly on Mozart and was defeated with heavy loss to the hearers," of a corps de ballet that "wandered about in the prompt corner as if some vivisector had removed from their heads that portion of the brain which enables us to find our way out the door," and of Schubert's "Death and the Maiden" quartet, which makes one "reconciled to Death and indifferent to the Maiden." Shaw then turned to drama criticism, where he later described his work as "a siege laid to the theatre of the XIXth Century by an author who had to cut his own way into it at the point of the pen, and throw some of its defenders into the moat." Just as he had championed Wagner's music, he now championed the plays of the Norwegian dramatist, Henrik Ibsen. In 1891 he published *The Quintessence of Ibsenism*, in which, in setting out the reasons for his admiration of Ibsen, he defined the kind of drama he wanted to write.

In the first ten years of his life in London, Shaw had written five unsuccessful novels. When he turned to drama in the 1890s, he found his medium. Shaw's first play, *Widowers' Houses* (1892), dealt with the problem of slum landlords. Though it ran for only two performances, Shaw's career as a dramatist was launched. In the course of his career he wrote more than fifty plays. Among the most famous are *Mrs Warren's Profession* (1893), *Arms and the Man* (1894), *Candida* (1894), *The Devil's Disciple* (1896), *Caesar and Cleopatra* (1898), *Man and Superman* (1903), *Major Barbara* (1905), *Androcles and the Lion* (1912), *Pygmalion* (1912; later the basis of the musical *My Fair Lady*), *Heartbreak House* (1919), *Back to Methuselah* (1920), and *Saint Joan* (1923). (Because the production and publication history of Shaw's plays is so complex, this list gives the date of composition for each.) Shaw at first had difficulty getting his plays performed. Therefore, in 1898 he decided to publish them in book form as *Plays Pleasant and Unpleasant*, for which he wrote a didactic preface—the first of many that he provided for his plays. Then, in 1904, the producer and Shakespearean scholar Harley Granville-Barker put on *Candida* at the Royal Court Theatre, which he was managing. The play was a success, and Shaw went on to work with Barker in creating the Royal Court's long-standing reputation as the center for avant-garde drama in London.

In *The Quintessence of Ibsenism*, Shaw defines the elements of the kind of theater he aspired to create:

> first, the introduction of the discussion and its development until it so overspreads and interpenetrates the action that it finally assimilates it, making play and discussion practically identical; and second, as a consequence of making the spectators themselves the persons of the drama, and the incidents of their own lives its incidents, the disuse of the old stage tricks by which audiences had to be induced to take an interest in unreal people and improbable circumstances.

Instead of these "tricks," Shaw wished to pioneer "a forensic technique of recrimination, disillusion, and penetration through ideals to the truth, with a free use of all the rhetorical and lyrical arts of the orator, the preacher, the pleader, and the rhapsodist." He created a drama of ideas, in which his characters strenuously argue points of view that justify their social positions—whether that of the prostitute in *Mrs Warren's Profession* or of the munitions manufacturer in *Major Barbara*. His object is to attack the complacencies and conventional moralism of his audience. By the rhetorical brilliance of his dialogue and by surprising reversals of plot conventions, Shaw manipulates his audience into a position of uncomfortable sympathy with points of view and characters that violate traditional assumptions.

By the end of the first decade of the twentieth century, as a result of the success of his plays at the Royal Court Theatre, Shaw had become a literary celebrity. Like Oscar Wilde, he had worked to develop a public persona, but with a substantial difference in aim. Whereas Wilde used his public image to define an aesthetic point of view, Shaw used his public personality—iconoclastic, clownish, argumentative—to advocate social ideas. He was radical in many respects. He was a vegetarian, a nonsmoker, and a nondrinker. He was courageous enough to be a pacifist in World War I. He championed the reform of English spelling and punctuation. He believed in women's rights and the abolition of private property. He also believed in the Life Force and progressive evolution, driven by the power of the human will, a point of view that led him to sympathize with Mussolini and other dictators before World War II. Shaw's insistent rationality made some of his contemporaries view him as bloodless. After seeing *Arms and the Man*, William Butler Yeats described a nightmare in which he was haunted by a sewing machine "that clicked and shone, but the incredible thing was that the machine smiled, smiled perpetually." However, Yeats goes on to say, "Yet I delighted in Shaw the formidable man. He could hit my enemies and the enemies of all I loved, as I could never hit, as no living author that was dear to me could ever hit."

Shaw wrote *Mrs Warren's Profession* in 1893; though it was published in *Plays Pleasant and Unpleasant* in 1898, its public performance was long prohibited by British censors. In 1902 the Stage Society, technically a private club and so not under the jurisdiction of the censors, gave performances for its own members. The play was produced in New York in 1905; but it was closed down by the police, and the producer and his company were arrested. They were eventually acquitted, and the play was allowed to continue. No legal public performance took place in England until 1926, the year after Shaw won the Nobel Prize.

Shaw's preface to the play attacks the confusions and contradictions involved in the censorship of plays and contains an eloquent plea for the recognition of the seriousness and morality of *Mrs Warren's Profession*. The play was written, he tells us, "to draw attention to the truth that prostitution is caused, not by female depravity and male licentiousness, but simply by underpaying, undervaluing, and overworking women so shamefully that the poorest of them are forced to resort to prostitution to keep body and soul together." He argues that Mrs. Warren's defense of herself in the play is "valid and unanswerable." (It is interesting to compare Mrs. Warren's defense with that of the correspondent to the London *Times* who, claiming to be a prostitute, wrote "The Great Social Evil" [p. 666].) Shaw's discussion of Mrs. Warren's self-justification continues:

> But it is no defence at all of the vice which she organizes. It is no defence of an immoral life to say that the alternative offered by society collectively to poor women is a miserable life, starved, overworked, fetid, ailing, ugly. Though it is quite natural and *right* for Mrs Warren to choose what is, according to her lights, the least immoral alternative, it is none the less infamous of society to offer such alternatives. For the alternatives offered are not morality and immorality but two sorts of immorality. The man who cannot see that starvation,

overwork, dirt, and disease are as anti-social as prostitution—that they are the vices and crimes of a nation, and not merely its misfortunes—is (to put it as politely as possible) a hopelessly Private Person.

This is Shaw's way of saying that such a man is a hopeless idiot; the word *idiot* comes from the Greek *idiōtēs*, "a private person," as distinct from one interested in public affairs.

Shaw's belief in spelling reform led him to introduce simplifications in his own texts that he insisted on his publishers using. These simplifications (omission of the apostrophe in a number of contractions, and the use of widely spaced letters rather than italics to indicate emphasis, for example) are retained in the selection reprinted here.

Mrs Warren's Profession

Act 1

Summer afternoon in a cottage garden on the eastern slope of a hill a little south of Haslemere in Surrey.[1] Looking up the hill, the cottage is seen in the left hand corner of the garden, with its thatched roof and porch, and a large latticed window to the left of the porch. A paling[2] completely shuts in the garden, except for a gate on the right. The common[3] rises uphill beyond the paling to the sky line. Some folded canvas garden chairs are leaning against the side bench in the porch. A lady's bicycle is propped against the wall, under the window. A little to the right of the porch a hammock is slung from two posts. A big canvas umbrella, stuck in the ground, keeps the sun off the hammock, in which a young lady lies reading and making notes, her head towards the cottage and her feet towards the gate. In front of the hammock, and within reach of her hand, is a common kitchen chair, with a pile of serious-looking books and a supply of writing paper on it.

A gentleman walking on the common comes into sight from behind the cottage. He is hardly past middle age, with something of the artist about him, unconventionally but carefully dressed, and clean-shaven except for a moustache, with an eager susceptible face and very amiable and considerate manners. He has silky black hair, with waves of grey and white in it. His eyebrows are white, his moustache black. He seems not certain of his way. He looks over the paling; takes stock of the place; and sees the young lady.

THE GENTLEMAN [*Taking off his hat.*]   I beg your pardon. Can you direct me to Hindhead View—Mrs Alison's?
THE YOUNG LADY [*Glancing up from her book.*]   This is Mrs Alison's. [*She resumes her work.*]
THE GENTLEMAN   Indeed! Perhaps—may I ask are you Miss Vivie Warren?
THE YOUNG LADY [*Sharply, as she turns on her elbow to get a good look at him.*]   Yes.
THE GENTLEMAN [*Daunted and conciliatory.*]   I'm afraid I appear intrusive. My name is Praed. [VIVIE *at once throws her books upon the chair, and gets out of the hammock.*]   Oh, pray dont let me disturb you.

1. County southeast of London.
2. Picket fence.

3. Area of open land for public use.

VIVIE [*Striding to the gate and opening it for him.*]   Come in, Mr Praed. [*He comes in.*] Glad to see you. [*She proffers her hand and takes his with a resolute and hearty grip. She is an attractive specimen of the sensible, able, highly-educated young middle-class Englishwoman. Age 22. Prompt, strong, confident, self-possessed. Plain business-like dress, but not dowdy. She wears a chatelaine*[4] *at her belt, with a fountain pen and a paper knife among its pendants.*]

PRAED   Very kind of you indeed, Miss Warren. [*She shuts the gate with a vigorous slam. He passes in to the middle of the garden, exercising his fingers, which are slightly numbed by her greeting.*] Has your mother arrived?

VIVIE [*Quickly, evidently scenting aggression.*]   Is she coming?

PRAED [*Surprised.*]   Didnt you expect us?

VIVIE   No.

PRAED   Now, goodness me, I hope Ive not mistaken the day. That would be just like me, you know. Your mother arranged that she was to come down from London and that I was to come over from Horsham to be introduced to you.

VIVIE [*Not at all pleased.*]   Did she? Hm! My mother has rather a trick of taking me by surprise—to see how I behave myself when she's away, I suppose. I fancy I shall take my mother very much by surprise one of these days, if she makes arrangements that concern me without consulting me beforehand. She hasnt come.

PRAED [*Embarrassed.*]   I'm really very sorry.

VIVIE [*Throwing off her displeasure.*]   It's not your fault, Mr Praed, is it? And I'm very glad youve come. You are the only one of my mother's friends I have ever asked her to bring to see me.

PRAED [*Relieved and delighted.*]   Oh, now this is really very good of you, Miss Warren!

VIVIE   Will you come indoors; or would you rather sit out here and talk?

PRAED   It will be nicer out here, dont you think?

VIVIE   Then I'll go and get you a chair. [*She goes to the porch for a garden chair.*]

PRAED [*Following her.*]   Oh, pray, pray! Allow me. [*He lays hands on the chair.*]

VIVIE [*Letting him take it.*]   Take care of your fingers: theyre rather dodgy things, those chairs. [*She goes across to the chair with the books on it; pitches them into the hammock; and brings the chair forward with one swing.*]

PRAED [*Who has just unfolded his chair.*]   Oh, now d o let me take that hard chair. I like hard chairs.

VIVIE   So do I. Sit down, Mr Praed. [*This invitation she gives with genial peremptoriness, his anxiety to please her clearly striking her as a sign of weakness of character on his part. But he does not immediately obey.*]

PRAED   By the way, though, hadnt we better go to the station to meet your mother?

VIVIE [*Coolly.*]   Why? She knows the way.

---

4. A decorative clasp or hook on a girdle or belt, to which a number of short chains are attached bearing household implements or ornaments.

PRAED [*Disconcerted.*]   Er—I suppose she does. [*He sits down.*]

VIVIE   Do you know, you are just like what I expected. I hope you are disposed to be friends with me.

PRAED [*Again beaming.*]   Thank you, my d e a r Miss Warren: thank you. Dear me! I'm glad your mother hasnt spoilt you!

VIVIE   How?

PRAED   Well, in making you too conventional. You know, my dear Miss Warren, I am a born anarchist. I hate authority. It spoils the relations between parent and child: even between mother and daughter. Now I was always afraid that your mother would strain her authority to make you very conventional. It's such a relief to find that she hasnt.

VIVIE   Oh! have I been behaving unconventionally?

PRAED   Oh no; oh dear no. At least not conventionally unconventionally, you understand. [*She nods and sits down. He goes on, with a cordial outburst.*] But it was so charming of you to say that you were disposed to be friends with me! You modern young ladies are splendid: perfectly splendid!

VIVIE [*Dubiously.*]   Eh? [*Watching him with dawning disappointment as to the quality of his brains and character.*]

PRAED   When I was your age, young men and women were afraid of each other: there was no good fellowship. Nothing real. Only gallantry copied out of novels, and as vulgar and affected as it could be. Maidenly reserve! gentlemanly chivalry! always saying no when you meant yes! simple purgatory for shy and sincere souls.

VIVIE   Yes, I imagine there must have been a frightful waste of time. Especially women's time.

PRAED   Oh, waste of life, waste of everything. But things are improving. Do you know, I have been in a positive state of excitement about meeting you ever since your magnificent achievements at Cambridge: a thing unheard of in my day. It was perfectly splendid, you tieing with the third wrangler.[5] Just the right place, you know. The first wrangler is always a dreamy, morbid fellow, in whom the thing is pushed to the length of a disease.

VIVIE   It doesnt pay. I wouldnt do it again for the same money.

PRAED [*Aghast.*]   The same money!

VIVIE   I did it for £50.

PRAED   Fifty pounds!

VIVIE   Yes. Fifty pounds. Perhaps you dont know how it was. Mrs. Latham, my tutor at Newnham,[6] told my mother that I could distinguish myself in the mathematical tripos if I went in for it in earnest. The papers were full just then of Phillipa Summers beating the senior wrangler.[7] You remember about it, of course.

PRAED   [*Shakes his head energetically.*]!!!

---

5. A term unique to Cambridge, denoting distinction in the final honors examination (known as the tripos) leading to a B.A. in mathematics. The person who achieved the top mark was the senior wrangler, followed by the junior wrangler and then the third wrangler.

6. Women's college at Cambridge University.
7. In 1890 Phillipa Fawcett was placed above the senior wrangler (although women began taking examinations in 1882, they were not admitted to the university until 1921 and gained full status only in 1947).

VIVIE   Well anyhow she did; and nothing would please my mother but that I should do the same thing. I said flatly it was not worth my while to face the grind since I was not going in for teaching; but I offered to try for fourth wrangler, or thereabouts, for £50. She closed with me at that, after a little grumbling; and I was better than my bargain. But I wouldn't do it again for that. Two hundred pounds would have been nearer the mark.

PRAED   [*Much damped.*]   Lord bless me! Thats a very practical way of looking at it.

VIVIE   Did you expect to find me an unpractical person?

PRAED   But surely it's practical to consider not only the work these honors cost, but also the culture they bring.

VIVIE   Culture! My dear Mr Praed: do you know what the mathematical tripos means? It means grind, grind, grind for six to eight hours a day at mathematics, and nothing but mathematics. I'm supposed to know something about science; but I know nothing except the mathematics it involves. I can make calculations for engineers, electricians, insurance companies, and so on; but I know next to nothing about engineering or electricity or insurance. I dont even know arithmetic well. Outside mathematics, lawn-tennis, eating, sleeping, cycling, and walking, I'm a more ignorant barbarian than any woman could possibly be who hadnt gone in for the tripos.

PRAED   [*Revolted.*]   What a monstrous, wicked, rascally system! I knew it! I felt at once that it meant destroying all that makes womanhood beautiful.

VIVIE   I dont object to it on that score in the least. I shall turn it to very good account, I assure you.

PRAED   Pooh! In what way?

VIVIE   I shall set up in chambers in the City, and work at actuarial calculations and conveyancing. Under cover of that I shall do some law, with one eye on the Stock Exchange all the time. Ive come down here by myself to read law: not for a holiday, as my mother imagines. I hate holidays.

PRAED   You make my blood run cold. Are you to have no romance, no beauty in your life?

VIVIE   I don't care for either, I assure you.

PRAED   You cant mean that.

VIVIE   Oh yes I do. I like working and getting paid for it. When I'm tired of working, I like a comfortable chair, a cigar, a little whisky, and a novel with a good detective story in it.

PRAED   [*Rising in a frenzy of repudiation.*]   I dont believe it. I am an artist; and I cant believe it: I refuse to believe it. It's only that you havnt discovered yet what a wonderful world art can open up to you.

VIVIE   Yes I have. Last May I spent six weeks in London with Honoria Fraser. Mamma thought we were doing a round of sightseeing together; but I was really at Honoria's chambers in Chancery Lane[8] every day, working away at actuarial calculations for her, and helping her as well as a greenhorn could. In the evenings we smoked and talked, and never dreamt of going out except for exercise. And I never enjoyed myself

---

8. I.e., office in the legal quarter of London.

more in my life. I cleared all my expenses, and got initiated into the business without a fee into the bargain.

PRAED   But bless my heart and soul, Miss Warren, do you call that discovering art?

VIVIE   Wait a bit. That wasnt the beginning. I went up to town on an invitation from some artistic people in Fitzjohn's Avenue:[9] one of the girls was a Newnham chum. They took me to the National Gallery[1]—

PRAED   [Approving.]   Ah!! [He sits down, much relieved.]

VIVIE   [Continuing.]—to the Opera—

PRAED   [Still more pleased.]   Good!

VIVIE   —and to a concert where the band played all the evening: Beethoven and Wagner and so on. I wouldnt go through that experience again for anything you could offer me. I held out for civility's sake until the third day; and then I said, plump out,[2] that I couldnt stand any more of it, and went off to Chancery Lane. Now you know the sort of perfectly splendid modern young lady I am. How do you think I shall get on with my mother?

PRAED   [Startled.]   Well, I hope—er—

VIVIE   It's not so much what you hope as what you believe, that I want to know.

PRAED   Well, frankly, I am afraid your mother will be a little disappointed. Not from any shortcoming on your part, you know: I dont mean that. But you are so different from her ideal.

VIVIE   Her what?!

PRAED   Her ideal.

VIVIE   Do you mean her ideal of me?

PRAED   Yes.

VIVIE   What on earth is it like?

PRAED   Well, you must have observed, Miss Warren, that people who are dissatisfied with their own bringing-up generally think that the world would be all right if everybody were to be brought up quite differently. Now your mother's life has been—er—I suppose you know—

VIVIE   Dont suppose anything, Mr Praed. I hardly know my mother. Since I was a child I have lived in England, at school or college, or with people paid to take charge of me. I have been boarded out all my life. My mother has lived in Brussels or Vienna and never let me go to her. I only see her when she visits England for a few days. I dont complain: it's been very pleasant; for people have been very good to me; and there has always been plenty of money to make things smooth. But dont imagine I know anything about my mother. I know far less than you do.

PRAED   [Very ill at ease.]   In that case—[He stops, quite at a loss. Then, with a forced attempt at gaiety] But what nonsense we are talking! Of course you and your mother will get on capitally. [He rises, and looks abroad at the view.] What a charming little place you have here!

VIVIE   [Unmoved.]   Rather a violent change of subject, Mr Praed. Why wont my mother's life bear being talked about?

---

9. A road in Hampstead (northwest London).
1. In Trafalgar Square; it contains one of the finest collections of western European paintings in the world.
2. Straight out, without hesitation.

PRAED   Oh, you really mustnt say that. Isnt it natural that I should have a certain delicacy in talking to my old friend's daughter about her behind her back? You and she will have plenty of opportunity of talking about it when she comes.

VIVIE   No: she wont talk about it either. [*Rising.*] However, I daresay you have good reasons for telling me nothing. Only, mind this, Mr Praed. I expect there will be a battle royal[3] when my mother hears of my Chancery Lane project.

PRAED   [*Ruefully.*]   I'm afraid there will.

VIVIE   Well, I shall win, because I want nothing but my fare to London to start there to-morrow earning my own living by devilling[4] for Honoria. Besides, I have no mysteries to keep up; and it seems she has. I shall use that advantage over her if necessary.

PRAED   [*Greatly shocked.*]   Oh no! No, pray. Youd not do such a thing.

VIVIE   Then tell me why not.

PRAED   I really cannot. I appeal to your good feeling. [*She smiles at his sentimentality.*] Besides you may be too bold. Your mother is not to be trifled with when she's angry.

VIVIE   You cant frighten me, Mr Praed. In that month at Chancery Lane I had opportunities of taking the measure of one or two women very like my mother. You may back me to win. But if I hit harder in my ignorance than I need, remember that it is you who refuse to enlighten me. Now, let us drop the subject. [*She takes her chair and replaces it near the hammock with the same vigorous swing as before.*]

PRAED   [*Taking a desperate resolution.*]   One word, Miss Warren. I had better tell you. It's very difficult; but—

[MRS WARREN *and* SIR GEORGE CROFTS *arrive at the gate,* MRS WARREN *is between 40 and 50, formerly pretty, showily dressed in a brilliant hat and a gay blouse fitting tightly over her bust and flanked by fashionable sleeves. Rather spoilt and domineering, and decidedly vulgar, but, on the whole, a genial and fairly presentable old blackguard[5] of a woman.*

CROFTS *is a tall powerfully-built man of about 50, fashionably dressed in the style of a young man. Nasal voice, reedier than might be expected from his strong frame. Clean-shaven bulldog jaws, large flat ears, and thick neck: gentlemanly combination of the most brutal types of city man, sporting man, and man about town.*]

VIVIE   Here they are. [*Coming to them as they enter the garden.*] How do, mater?[6] Mr Praed's been here this half hour waiting for you.

MRS WARREN   Well, if youve been waiting, Praddy, it's your own fault: I thought youd have the gumption[7] to know I was coming by the 3.10 train. Vivie: put your hat on, dear: youll get sunburnt. Oh, I forgot to introduce you. Sir George Crofts: my little Vivie.

[CROFTS *advances to* VIVIE *with his most courtly manner. She nods, but makes no motion to shake hands.*]

CROFTS   May I shake hands with a young lady whom I have known by reputation very long as the daughter of one of my oldest friends?

---

3. A fierce fight.
4. Acting as assistant to a barrister (trial lawyer) as a way of gaining legal experience.

5. Rogue.
6. Mother (Latin).
7. Here common sense.

VIVIE [*Who has been looking him up and down sharply.*] If you like. [*She takes his tenderly proffered hand and gives it a squeeze that makes him open his eyes; then turns away, and says to her mother*] Will you come in, or shall I get a couple more chairs? [*She goes into the porch for the chairs.*]

MRS WARREN Well George, what do you think of her?

CROFTS [*Ruefully.*] She has a powerful fist. Did you shake hands with her, Praed?

PRAED Yes: it will pass off presently.

CROFTS I hope so. [VIVIE *reappears with two more chairs. He hurries to her assistance.*] Allow me.

MRS WARREN [*Patronizingly.*] Let Sir George help you with the chairs, dear.

VIVIE [*Pitching them into his arms.*] Here you are. [*She dusts her hands and turns to* MRS WARREN.] Youd like some tea, wouldnt you?

MRS WARREN [*Sitting in* PRAED's *chair and fanning herself*] I'm dying for a drop to drink.

VIVIE I'll see about it. [*She goes into the cottage.*]

> [SIR GEORGE *has by this time managed to unfold a chair and plant it beside* MRS WARREN, *on her left. He throws the other on the grass and sits down, looking dejected and rather foolish, with the handle of his stick in his mouth.* PRAED, *still very uneasy, fidgets about the garden on their right.*]

MRS WARREN [*To* PRAED, *looking at* CROFTS.] Just look at him, Praddy: he looks cheerful, dont he? He's been worrying my life out these three years to have that little girl of mine shewn to him; and now that Ive done it, he's quite out of countenance. [*Briskly.*] Come! sit up, George; and take your stick out of your mouth, [CROFTS *sulkily obeys.*]

PRAED I think, you know—if you dont mind my saying so—that we had better get out of the habit of thinking of her as a little girl. You see she has really distinguished herself; and I'm not sure, from what I have seen of her, that she is not older than any of us.

MRS WARREN [*Greatly amused.*] Only listen to him, George! Older than any of us! Well, she has been stuffing you nicely with her importance.

PRAED But young people are particularly sensitive about being treated in that way.

MRS WARREN Yes; and young people have to get all that nonsense taken out of them, and a good deal more besides. Dont you interfere, Praddy: I know how to treat my own child as well as you do. [PRAED, *with a grave shake of his head, walks up the garden with his hands behind his back,* MRS WARREN *pretends to laugh, but looks after him with perceptible concern. Then she whispers to* CROFTS] Whats the matter with him? What does he take it like that for?

CROFTS [*Morosely.*] Youre afraid of Praed.

MRS WARREN What! Me! Afraid of dear old Praddy! Why, a fly wouldnt be afraid of him.

CROFTS Youre afraid of him.

MRS WARREN [*Angry.*] I'll trouble you to mind your own business, and not try any of your sulks on me. I'm not afraid of you, anyhow. If you cant make yourself agreeable, youd better go home. [*She gets up, and turning her back on him, finds herself face to face with* PRAED.] Come,

Praddy, I know it was only your tender-heartedness. Youre afraid I'll bully her.

PRAED   My dear Kitty: you think I'm offended. Dont imagine that: pray dont. But you know I often notice things that escape you; and though you never take my advice, you sometimes admit afterwards that you ought to have taken it.

MRS WARREN   Well, what do you notice now?

PRAED   Only that Vivie is a grown woman. Pray, Kitty, treat her with every respect.

MRS WARREN [*With genuine amazement.*]   Respect! Treat my own daughter with respect! What next, pray!

VIVIE [*Appearing at the cottage door and calling to* MRS WARREN.]   Mother: will you come to my room before tea?

MRS WARREN   Yes, dearie. [*She laughs indulgently at* PRAED'S *gravity, and pats him on the cheek as she passes him on her way to the porch.*] Dont be cross, Praddy. [*She follows* VIVIE *into the cottage.*]

CROFTS [*Furtively.*]   I say, Praed.

PRAED   Yes.

CROFTS   I want to ask you a rather particular question.

PRAED   Certainly. [*He takes* MRS WARREN'S *chair and sits close to* CROFTS.]

CROFTS   Thats right: they might hear us from the window. Look here: did Kitty ever tell you who that girl's father is?

PRAED   Never.

CROFTS   Have you any suspicion of who it might be?

PRAED   None.

CROFTS [*Not believing him.*]   I know, of course, that you perhaps might feel bound not to tell if she had said anything to you. But it's very awkward to be uncertain about it now that we shall be meeting the girl every day. We dont exactly know how we ought to feel towards her.

PRAED   What difference can that make? We take her on her own merits. What does it matter who her father was?

CROFTS [*Suspiciously.*]   Then you know who he was?

PRAED [*With a touch of temper.*]   I said no just now. Did you not hear me?

CROFTS   Look here, Praed. I ask you as a particular favor. If you do know [*Movement of protest from* PRAED.]—I only say, if you know you might at least set my mind at rest about her. The fact is, I feel attracted.

PRAED [*Sternly.*]   What do you mean?

CROFTS   Oh, dont be alarmed: it's quite an innocent feeling. Thats what puzzles me about it. Why, for all I know, *I* might be her father.

PRAED   You! Impossible!

CROFTS [*Catching him up cunningly.*]   You know for certain that I'm not?

PRAED   I know nothing about it, I tell you, any more than you. But really, Crofts—oh no, it's out of the question. Theres not the least resemblance.

CROFTS   As to that, theres no resemblance between her and her mother that I can see. I suppose she's not your daughter, is she?

PRAED [*Rising indignantly.*]   Really, Crofts—!

CROFTS   No offence, Praed. Quite allowable as between two men of the world.

PRAED [*Recovering himself with an effort and speaking gently and gravely.*] Now listen to me, my dear Crofts. [*He sits down again.*] I have nothing to do with that side of Mrs Warren's life, and never had. She has never spoken to me about it; and of course I have never spoken to her about it. Your delicacy[8] will tell you that a handsome woman needs some friends who are not—well, not on that footing with her. The effect of her own beauty would become a torment to her if she could not escape from it occasionally. You are probably on much more confidential terms with Kitty than I am. Surely you can ask her the question yourself.

CROFTS I have asked her, often enough. But she's so determined to keep the child all to herself that she would deny that it ever had a father if she could. [*Rising.*] I'm thoroughly uncomfortable about it, Praed.

PRAED [*Rising also.*] Well, as you are, at all events, old enough to be her dont mind agreeing that we both regard Miss Vivie in a parental way, as a young girl whom we are bound to protect and help. What do you say?

CROFTS [*Aggressively.*] I'm no older than you, if you come to that.

PRAED Yes you are, my dear fellow: you were born old. I was born a boy: Ive never been able to feel the assurance of a grown-up man in my life. [*He folds his chair and carries it to the porch.*]

MRS WARREN [*Calling from within the cottage.*] Prad-dee! George! Tea-ea-ea-ea!

CROFTS [*Hastily.*] She's calling us. [*He hurries in.*]
  [PRAED *shakes his head bodingly, and is following* CROFTS *when he is hailed by a young gentleman who has just appeared on the common, and is making for the gate. He is pleasant, pretty, smartly dressed, cleverly good-for-nothing, not long turned 20, with a charming voice and agreeably disrespectful manners. He carries a light sporting magazine rifle.*]

THE YOUNG GENTLEMAN Hallo! Praed!

PRAED Why, Frank Gardner! [FRANK *comes in and shakes hands cordially.*] What on earth are you doing here?

FRANK Staying with my father.

PRAED The Roman father?[9]

FRANK He's rector here. I'm living with my people this autumn for the sake of economy. Things came to a crisis in July: the Roman father had to pay my debts. He's stony broke in consequence; and so am I. What are you up to in these parts? Do you know the people here?

PRAED Yes: I'm spending the day with a Miss Warren.

FRANK [*Enthusiastically.*] What! Do you know Vivie? Isnt she a jolly girl? I'm teaching her to shoot with this. [*Putting down the rifle.*] I'm so glad she knows you: youre just the sort of fellow she ought to know. [*He smiles, and raises the charming voice almost to a singing tone as he exclaims*] It's ever so jolly to find you here, Praed.

PRAED I'm an old friend of her mother. Mrs Warren brought me over to make her daughter's acquaintance.

FRANK The mother! Is she here?

PRAED Yes: inside, at tea.

MRS WARREN [*Calling from within.*] Prad-dee-ee-ee-eee! The tea-cake'll be cold.

PRAED [*Calling.*] Yes, Mrs Warren. In a moment. Ive just met a friend here.

---

8. Sensitivity, tact.
9. I.e., a father with a Roman (strong) sense of duty, not a Roman Catholic priest. We learn in the next line that Frank's father is a clergyman in the Church of England.

MRS WARREN   A what?

PRAED [*Louder.*]   A friend.

MRS WARREN   Bring him in.

PRAED   All right, [*to* FRANK] Will you accept the invitation?

FRANK [*Incredulous, but immensely amused.*]   Is that Vivie's mother?

PRAED   Yes.

FRANK   By jove! What a lark! Do you think she'll like me?

PRAED   Ive no doubt youll make yourself popular, as usual. Come in and try.

> [*Moving towards the house.*]

FRANK   Stop a bit. [*Seriously.*] I want to take you into my confidence.

PRAED   Pray dont. It's only some fresh folly, like the barmaid at Redhill.[1]

FRANK   It's ever so much more serious than that. You say youve only just met Vivie for the first time?

PRAED   Yes.

FRANK [*Rhapsodically.*]   Then you can have no idea what a girl she is. Such character! Such sense! And her cleverness! Oh, my eye, Praed, but I can tell you she is clever! And—need I add?—she loves me.

CROFTS [*Putting his head out of the window.*]   I say, Praed: what are you about? Do come along. [*He disappears.*]

FRANK   Hallo! Sort of chap that would take a prize at a dog show, aint he? Who's he?

PRAED   Sir George Crofts, an old friend of Mrs Warren's. I think we had better come in.

> [*On their way to the porch they are interrupted by a call from the gate. Turning, they see an elderly clergyman looking over it.*]

THE CLERGYMAN [*Calling.*]   Frank!

FRANK   Hallo! [*To* PRAED.] The Roman father. [*To the clergyman.*] Yes, gov'nor:[2] all right: presently. [*To* PRAED.] Look here, Praed: youd better go in to tea. I'll join you directly.

PRAED   Very good. [*He goes into the cottage.*]

> [*The clergyman remains outside the gate, with his hands on the top of it. The* REV. SAMUEL GARDNER, *a beneficed clergyman[3] of the Established Church, is over 50. Externally he is pretentious, booming, noisy, important. Really he is that obsolescent social phenomenon the fool of the family dumped on the Church by his father, the patron, clamorously asserting himself as father and clergyman without being able to command respect in either capacity.*]

REV. SAMUEL   Well, sir. Who are your friends here, if I may ask?

FRANK   Oh, it's all right, gov'nor! Come in.

REV. SAMUEL   No sir; not until I know whose garden I am entering.

FRANK   It's all right. It's Miss Warren's.

REV. SAMUEL   I have not seen her at church since she came.

FRANK   Of course not: she's a third wrangler. Ever so intellectual. Took a higher degree than you did; so why should she go to hear you preach?

REV. SAMUEL   Dont be disrespectful, sir.

---

1. A nearby town.
2. I.e., governor, a common nickname given to a father or other male authority figure.
3. I.e., the recipient of an endowed Church office from which he receives income. Such positions were generally controlled by major landowners.

FRANK   Oh, it dont matter: nobody hears us. Come in. [*He opens the gate, unceremoniously pulling his father with it into the garden.*] I want to introduce you to her. Do you remember the advice you gave me last July, gov'nor?

REV. SAMUEL [*Severely.*]   Yes, I advised you to conquer your idleness and flippancy, and to work your way into an honorable profession and live on it and not upon me.

FRANK   No; thats what you thought of afterwards. What you actually said was that since I had neither brains nor money, I'd better turn my good looks to account by marrying somebody with both. Well, look here. Miss Warren has brains: you cant deny that.

REV. SAMUEL   Brains are not everything.

FRANK   No, of course not: theres the money—

REV. SAMUEL [*Interrupting him austerely.*]   I was not thinking of money, sir. I was speaking of higher things. Social position, for instance.

FRANK   I dont care a rap about that.

REV. SAMUEL   But I do, sir.

FRANK   Well, nobody wants you to marry her. Anyhow, she has what amounts to a high Cambridge degree; and she seems to have as much money as she wants.

REV. SAMUEL [*Sinking into a feeble vein of humor.*]   I greatly doubt whether she has as much money as you will want.

FRANK   Oh, come; I havnt been so very extravagant. I live ever so quietly; I dont drink; I dont bet much; and I never go regularly on the razzle-dazzle[4] as you did when you were my age.

REV. SAMUEL [*Booming hollowly.*]   Silence, sir.

FRANK   Well, you told me yourself, when I was making ever such an ass of myself about the barmaid at Redhill, that you once offered a woman £50 for the letters you wrote to her when—

REV. SAMUEL [*Terrified.*]   Sh-sh-sh, Frank, for heaven's sake! [*He looks round apprehensively. Seeing no one within earshot he plucks up courage to boom again, but more subduedly.*] You are taking an ungentlemanly advantage of what I confided to you for your own good, to save you from an error you would have repented all your life long. Take warning by your father's follies, sir; and dont make them an excuse for your own.

FRANK   Did you ever hear the story of the Duke of Wellington[5] and his letters?

REV. SAMUEL   No, sir; and I dont want to hear it.

FRANK   The old Iron Duke didnt throw away £50: not he. He just wrote: "Dear Jenny: publish and be damned! Yours affectionately, Wellington." Thats what you should have done.

REV. SAMUEL [*Piteously.*]   Frank, my boy: when I wrote those letters I put myself into that woman's power. When I told you about them I put myself, to some extent, I am sorry to say, in your power. She refused my money with these words, which I shall never forget. "Knowledge is power" she said; "and I never sell power." Thats more than twenty years ago; and

---

4. I.e., out on the town.
5. Arthur Wellesley (1769–1852), military hero and statesmen.

she has never made use of her power or caused me a moment's uneasiness. You are behaving worse to me than she did, Frank.

FRANK   Oh yes I dare say! Did you ever preach at her the way you preach at me every day?

REV. SAMUEL [*Wounded almost to tears.*]   I leave you sir. You are incorrigible. [*He turns towards the gate.*]

FRANK [*Utterly unmoved.*]   Tell them I shant be home to tea, will you, gov'nor, like a good fellow? [*He moves towards the cottage door and is met by* PRAED *and* VIVIE *coming out.*]

VIVIE. [*To* FRANK.]   Is that your father, Frank? I do so want to meet him.

FRANK   Certainly. [*Calling after his father.*] Gov'nor. Youre wanted. [*The parson turns at the gate, fumbling nervously at his hat.* PRAED *crosses the garden to the opposite side, beaming in anticipation of civilities.*] My father: Miss Warren.

VIVIE   [*Going to the clergyman and shaking his hand.*]   Very glad to see you here, Mr Gardner. [*Calling to the cottage.*] Mother: come along: youre wanted.

> [MRS WARREN *appears on the threshold, and is immediately transfixed recognizing the clergyman.*]

VIVIE [*Continuing.*]   Let me introduce—

MRS WARREN [*Swooping on the* REVEREND SAMUEL.]   Why, it's Sam Gardner, gone into the Church! Well, I never! Dont you know us, Sam? This is George Crofts, as large as life and twice as natural. Dont you remember me?

REV. SAMUEL [*Very red.*]   I really—er—

MRS WARREN   Of course you do. Why, I have a whole album of your letters still: I came across them only the other day.

REV. SAMUEL [*Miserably confused.*]   Miss Vavasour, I believe.

MRS WARREN [*Correcting him quickly in a loud whisper.*]   Tch! Nonsense! Mrs Warren: dont you see my daughter there?

Act 2

Inside the cottage after nightfall. Looking eastward from within instead of westward from without, the latticed window, with its curtains drawn, is now seen in the middle of the front wall of the cottage, with the porch door to the left of it. In the left-hand side wall is the door leading to the kitchen. Farther back against the same wall is a dresser with a candle and matches on it, and FRANK'S *rifle standing beside them, with the barrel resting in the plate-rack. In the centre a table stands with a lighted lamp on it.* VIVIE'S *books and writing materials are on a table to the right of the window, against the wall. The fireplace is on the right, with a settle:*[6] *there is no fire. Two of the chairs are set right and left of the table. The cottage door opens, shewing a fine starlit night without; and* MRS WARREN, *her shoulders wrapped in a shawl borrowed from* VIVIE, *enters, followed by* FRANK, *who throws his cap on the window seat. She has had enough of walking, and gives a gasp of relief as she unpins her hat; takes it off; sticks the pin through the crown; and puts it on the table.*

---

6. A high-backed wooden bench.

MRS WARREN   O Lord! I dont know which is the worst of the country, the walking or the sitting at home with nothing to do. I could do with a whisky and soda now very well, if only they had such a thing in this place.

FRANK   Perhaps Vivie's got some.

MRS WARREN   Nonsense! What would a young girl like her be doing with such things! Never mind: it dont matter. I wonder how she passes her time here! I'd a good deal rather be in Vienna.

FRANK   Let me take you there. [*He helps her to take off her shawl, gallantly giving her shoulders a very perceptible squeeze as he does so.*]

MRS WARREN   Ah! would you? I'm beginning to think youre a chip of the old block.

FRANK   Like the gov'nor, eh? [*He hangs the shawl on the nearest chair, and sits down.*]

MRS WARREN   Never you mind. What do you know about such things? Youre only a boy. [*She goes to the hearth, to be farther from temptation.*]

FRANK   Do come to Vienna with me? It'd be ever such larks.

MRS WARREN   No, thank you. Vienna is no place for you—at least not until youre a little older. [*She nods at him to emphasize this piece of advice. He makes a mock-piteous face, belied by his laughing eyes. She looks at him; then comes back to him.*] Now, look here, little boy [*taking his face in her hands and turning it up to her*]; I know you through and through by your likeness to your father, better than you know yourself. Dont you go taking any silly ideas into your head about me. Do you hear?

FRANK [*Gallantly wooing her with his voice.*]   Cant help it, my dear Mrs Warren: it runs in the family.
> [*She pretends to box his ears; then looks at the pretty laughing upturned face for a moment, tempted. At last she kisses him, and immediately turns away, out of patience with herself.*]

MRS WARREN   There! I shouldnt have done that. I am wicked. Never you mind, my dear: it's only a motherly kiss. Go and make love to[7] Vivie.

FRANK   So I have.

MRS WARREN [*Turning on him with a sharp note of alarm in her voice.*] What!

FRANK   Vivie and I are ever such chums.

MRS WARREN   What do you mean? Now see here: I wont have any young scamp tampering with my little girl. Do you hear? I wont have it.

FRANK [*Quite unabashed.*]   My dear Mrs Warren: dont you be alarmed. My intentions are honorable: ever so honorable; and your little girl is jolly well able to take care of herself. She dont need looking after half so much as her mother. She aint so handsome, you know.

MRS WARREN [*Taken aback by his assurance.*]   Well, you have got a nice healthy two inches thick of cheek all over you.[8] I dont know where you got it. Not from your father, anyhow.

CROFTS [*In the garden.*]   The gipsies, I suppose?

REV. SAMUEL [*Replying.*]   The broomsquires[9] are far worse.

MRS WARREN [*To FRANK.*]   S-sh! Remember! youve had your warning.

---

7. Woo, court.
8. I.e., you are very cheeky (presumptuous).
9. Minor country landowners.

[CROFTS *and the* REVEREND SAMUEL *come in from the garden, the clergyman continuing his conversation as he enters.*]

REV. SAMUEL   The perjury at the Winchester assizes[1] is deplorable.

MRS WARREN   Well? What became of you two? And wheres Praddy and Vivie?

CROFTS [*Putting his hat on the settle and his stick in the chimney corner.*] They went up the hill. We went to the village. I wanted a drink. [*He sits down on the settle, putting his legs up along the seat.*]

MRS WARREN   Well, she oughtnt to go off like that without telling me. [*To* FRANK.] Get your father a chair, Frank: where are your manners? [FRANK *springs up and gracefully offers his father his chair; and then takes another from the wall and sits down at the table, in the middle, with his father on his right and* MRS WARREN *on his left.*] George: where are you going to stay tonight? You cant stay here. And whats Praddy going to do?

CROFTS   Gardner'll put me up.

MRS WARREN   Oh no doubt youve taken care of yourself! But what about Praddy?

CROFTS   Dont know. I suppose he can sleep at the inn.

MRS WARREN   Havnt you room for him, Sam?

REV. SAMUEL   Well—er—you see, as rector here, I am not free to do as I like. Er—what is Mr Praed's social position?

MRS. WARREN   Oh, he's all right: he's an architect. What an old stick-in-the-mud you are, Sam!

FRANK   Yes, it's all right, gov'nor. He built that place down in Wales for the Duke. Caernarvon Castle[2] they call it. You must have heard of it. [*He winks with lightning smartness at* MRS WARREN, *and regards his father blandly.*]

REV. SAMUEL   Oh, in that case, of course we shall only be too happy. I suppose he knows the Duke personally.

FRANK   Oh, ever so intimately! We can stick him in Georgina's old room.

MRS WARREN   Well, thats settled. Now if those two would only come in and let us have supper. Theyve no right to stay out after dark like this.

CROFTS [*Aggressively.*]   What harm are they doing you?

MRS WARREN   Well, harm or not, I dont like it.

FRANK   Better not wait for them, Mrs Warren. Praed will stay out as long as possible. He has never known before what it is to stray over the heath on a summer night with my Vivie.

CROFTS [*Sitting up in some consternation.*]   I say, you know! Come!

REV. SAMUEL [*Rising, startled out of his professional manner into real force and sincerity.*]   Frank, once for all, it's out of the question. Mrs Warren will tell you that it's not to be thought of.

CROFTS   Of course not.

FRANK [*With enchanting placidity.*]   Is that so, Mrs Warren?

MRS WARREN [*Reflectively.*]   Well, Sam, I dont know. If the girl wants to get married, no good can come of keeping her unmarried.

REV. SAMUEL [*Astounded.*]   But married to him!—your daughter to my son! Only think: it's impossible.

---

1. Law courts.
2. Frank here plays on his father's ignorance and

snobbery: the castle was built in the 13th century.

CROFTS   Of course it's impossible. Dont be a fool, Kitty.

MRS WARREN [*Nettled.*]   Why not? Isnt my daughter good enough for your son?

REV. SAMUEL   But surely, my dear Mrs Warren, you know the reasons—

MRS WARREN [*Defiantly.*]   I know no reasons. If you know any, you can tell them to the lad, or to the girl, or to your congregation, if you like.

REV. SAMUEL [*Collapsing helplessly into his chair.*]   You know very well that I couldnt tell anyone the reasons. But my boy will believe me when I tell him there are reasons.

FRANK   Quite right, Dad: he will. But has your boy's conduct ever been influenced by your reasons?

CROFTS   You cant marry her: and thats all about it. [*He gets up and stands on the hearth, with his back to the fireplace, frowning determinedly.*]

MRS WARREN [*Turning on him sharply.*]   What have you got to do with it, pray?

FRANK [*With his prettiest lyrical cadence.*]   Precisely what I was going to ask, myself, in my own graceful fashion.

CROFTS [*To MRS WARREN.*]   I suppose you dont want to marry the girl to a man younger than herself and without either a profession or twopence to keep her on. Ask Sam, if you dont believe me. [*To the parson.*] How much more money are you going to give him?

REV. SAMUEL   Not another penny. He has had his patrimony; and he spent the last of it in July, [MRS WARREN'*s face falls.*]

CROFTS [*Watching her.*]   There! I told you. [*He resumes his place on the settle up his legs on the seat again, as if the matter were finally disposed of.*]

FRANK [*Plaintively.*]   This is ever so mercenary. Do you suppose Miss Warren's going to marry for money? If we love one another—

MRS WARREN   Thank you. Your love's a pretty cheap commodity, my lad. If you have no means of keeping a wife, that settles it: you cant have Vivie.

FRANK [*Much amused.*]   What do you say, gov'nor, eh?

REV. SAMUEL   I agree with Mrs Warren.

FRANK   And good old Crofts has already expressed his opinion.

CROFTS [*Turning angrily on his elbow.*]   Look here: I want none of your cheek.

FRANK [*Pointedly.*]   I'm ever so sorry to surprise you, Crofts, but you allowed yourself the liberty of speaking to me like a father a moment ago. One father is enough, thank you.

CROFTS [*Contemptuously.*]   Yah! [*He turns away again.*]

FRANK [*Rising.*]   Mrs Warren: I cannot give my Vivie up, even for your sake.

MRS WARREN [*Muttering.*]   Young scamp!

FRANK [*Continuing.*]   And as you no doubt intend to hold out other prospects to her, I shall lose no time in placing my case before her. [*They stare at him; and he begins to declaim gracefully.*]

> He either fears his fate too much,
> Or his deserts are small,
> That dares not put it to the touch
> To gain or lose it all.[3]

3. From the poem "My Dear and Only Love," by the Marquess of Montrose (1612–1650).

[*The cottage door opens whilst he is reciting; and* VIVIE *and* PRAED *come in. He breaks off.* PRAED *puts his hat on the dresser. There is an immediate improvement in the company's behavior,* CROFTS *takes down his legs from the settle and pulls himself together as* PRAED *joins him at the fireplace,* MRS WARREN *loses her ease of manner and takes refuge in querulousness.*]

MRS WARREN   Wherever have you been, Vivie?

VIVIE [*Taking off her hat and throwing it carelessly on the table.*]   On the hill.

MRS WARREN   Well, you shouldnt go off like that without letting me know. How could I tell what had become of you? And night coming on too!

VIVIE [*Going to the door of the kitchen and opening it, ignoring her mother.*] Now, about supper? [*All rise except* MRS WARREN.] We shall be rather crowded in here, I'm afraid.

MRS WARREN   Did you hear what I said, Vivie?

VIVIE [*Quietly.*]   Yes, mother. [*Reverting to the supper difficulty.*] How many are we? [*Counting.*] One, two, three, four, five, six. Well, two will have to wait until the rest are done: Mrs Alison has only plates and knives for four.

PRAED   Oh, it doesnt matter about me. I—

VIVIE   You have had a long walk and are hungry, Mr Praed: you shall have your supper at once. I can wait myself. I want one person to wait with me. Frank: are you hungry?

FRANK   Not the least in the world. Completely off my peck,[4] in fact.

MRS WARREN [*To* CROFTS.]   Neither are you, George. You can wait.

CROFTS   Oh, hang it. Ive eaten nothing since tea-time. Cant Sam do it?

FRANK   Would you starve my poor father?

REV. SAMUEL [*Testily.*]   Allow me to speak for myself, sir. I am perfectly willing to wait.

VIVIE [*Decisively.*]   Theres no need. Only two are wanted. [*She opens the door of the kitchen.*] Will you take my mother in, Mr Gardner. [*The parson takes* MRS WARREN; *and they pass into the kitchen.* PRAED *and* CROFTS *follow. All except* PRAED *clearly disapprove of the arrangement, but do not know how to resist it.* VIVIE *stands at the door looking in at them.*] Can you squeeze past to that corner, Mr Praed: it's rather a tight fit. Take care of your coat against the white-wash: thats right. Now, are you all comfortable?

PRAED [*Within.*]   Quite, thank you.

MRS WARREN [*Within.*]   Leave the door open, dearie. [VIVIE *frowns; but* FRANK *checks her with a gesture, and steals to the cottage door, which he softly sets wide open.*] Oh Lor, what a draught! Youd better shut it, dear.
    [VIVIE *shuts it with a slam, and then, noting with disgust that her mother's hat and shawl are lying about, takes them tidily to the window seat, whilst* FRANK *noiselessly shuts the cottage door.*]

FRANK [*Exulting.*]   Aha! Got rid of em. Well, Vivvums: what do you think of my governor?

VIVIE [*Preoccupied and serious.*]   Ive hardly spoken to him. He doesnt strike me as being a particularly able person.

---

4. Food (slang).

FRANK   Well, you know, the old man is not altogether such a fool as he looks. You see, he was shoved into the Church rather; and in trying to live up to it he makes a much bigger ass of himself than he really is. I dont dislike him as much as you might expect. He means well. How do you think youll get on with him?

VIVIE [*Rather grimly.*]   I dont think my future life will be much concerned with him, or with any of that old circle of my mother's, except perhaps Praed. [*She sits down on the settle.*] What do you think of my mother?

FRANK   Really and truly?

VIVIE   Yes, really and truly.

FRANK   Well, she's ever so jolly. But she's rather a caution, isn't she? And Crofts! Oh my eye, Crofts! [*He sits beside her.*]

VIVIE   What a lot, Frank!

FRANK   What a crew!

VIVIE [*With intense contempt for them.*]   If I thought that *I* was like that— that I was going to be a waster, shifting along from one meal to another with no purpose, and no character, and no grit in me, I'd open an artery and bleed to death without one moment's hesitation.

FRANK   Oh no, you wouldnt. Why should they take any grind when they can afford not to? I wish I had their luck. No: what I object to is their form. It isnt the thing: it's slovenly, ever so slovenly.

VIVIE   Do you think your form will be any better when youre as old as Crofts, if you dont work?

FRANK   Of course I do. Ever so much better. Vivvums mustnt lecture: her little boy's incorrigible. [*He attempts to take her face caressingly in his hands.*]

VIVIE [*Striking his hands down sharply.*]   Off with you: Vivvums is not in a humor for petting her little boy this evening. [*She rises and comes forward to the other side of the room.*]

FRANK [*Following her.*]   How unkind!

VIVIE [*Stamping at him.*]   Be serious. I'm serious.

FRANK   Good. Let us talk learnedly. Miss Warren: do you know that all the most advanced thinkers are agreed that half the diseases of modern civilization are due to starvation of the affections in the young. Now, I—

VIVIE [*Cutting him short.*]   You are very tiresome. [*She opens the inner door.*] Have you room for Frank there? He's complaining of starvation.

MRS WARREN [*Within.*]   Of course there is. [*Clatter of knives and glasses as she moves the things on the table.*] Here! theres room now beside me. Come along, Mr Frank.

FRANK   Her little boy will be ever so even with his Vivvums for this. [*He passes into the kitchen.*]

MRS WARREN [*Within.*]   Here, Vivie: come on you too, child. You must be famished. [*She enters, followed by* CROFTS, *who holds the door open for* VIVIE *with marked deference. She goes out without looking at him; and he shuts the door after her.*] Why, George, you cant be done: youve eaten nothing. Is there anything wrong with you?

CROFTS   Oh, all I wanted was a drink. [*He thrusts his hands in his pockets, and begins prowling about the room, restless and sulky.*]

MRS WARREN Well, I like enough to eat. But a little of that cold beef and cheese and lettuce goes a long way. [*With a sigh of only half repletion she sits down lazily on the settle.*]

CROFTS What do you go encouraging that young pup for?

MRS WARREN [*On the alert at once.*] Now see here, George: what are you up to about that girl? Ive been watching your way of looking at her. Remember: I know you and what your looks mean.

CROFTS Theres no harm in looking at her, is there?

MRS WARREN I'd put you out and pack you back to London pretty soon if I saw any of your nonsense. My girl's little finger is more to me than your whole body and soul. [CROFTS *receives this with a sneering grin.* MRS WARREN, *flushing a little at her failure to impose on him in the character of a theatrically devoted mother, adds in a lower key*] Make your mind easy: the young pup has no more chance than you have.

CROFTS Maynt a man take an interest in a girl?

MRS WARREN Not a man like you.

CROFTS How old is she?

MRS WARREN Never you mind how old she is.

CROFTS Why do you make such a secret of it?

MRS WARREN Because I choose.

CROFTS Well, I'm not fifty yet; and my property is as good as ever it was—

MRS WARREN [*Interrupting him.*] Yes; because youre as stingy as youre vicious.

CROFTS [*Continuing.*] And a baronet isnt to be picked up every day. No other man in my position would put up with you for a mother-in-law. Why shouldnt she marry me?

MRS WARREN You!

CROFTS We three could live together quite comfortably. I'd die before her and leave her a bouncing widow with plenty of money. Why not? It's been growing in my mind all the time Ive been walking with that fool inside there.

MRS WARREN [*Revolted.*] Yes; it's the sort of thing that would grow in your mind.

> [*He halts in his prowling; and the two look at one another, she stead-fastly, with a sort of awe behind her contemptuous disgust: he stealthily, with a carnal gleam in his eye and a loose grin.*]

CROFTS [*Suddenly becoming anxious and urgent as he sees no sign of sympathy in her.*] Look here, Kitty: youre a sensible woman: you neednt put on any moral airs. I'll ask no more questions; and you need answer none. I'll settle the whole property on her; and if you want a cheque for yourself on the wedding day, you can name any figure you like—in reason.

MRS WARREN So it's come to that with you, George, like all the other wornout old creatures!

CROFTS [*Savagely.*] Damn you!

> [*Before she can retort the door of the kitchen is opened; and the voices of the others are heard returning.* CROFTS, *unable to recover his presence of mind, hurries out of the cottage. The clergyman appears at the kitchen door.*]

REV. SAMUEL [*Looking around.*] Where is Sir George?

MRS WARREN   Gone out to have a pipe. [*The clergyman takes his hat from the table, and joins* MRS WARREN *at the fireside. Meanwhile* VIVIE *comes in, followed by* FRANK, *who collapses into the nearest chair with an air of extreme exhaustion.* MRS WARREN *looks round at* VIVIE *and says, with her affectation of maternal patronage even more forced than usual*] Well, dearie: have you had a good supper?

VIVIE   You know what Mrs Alison's suppers are. [*She turns to* FRANK *and pets him.*] Poor Frank! was all the beef gone? did it get nothing but bread and cheese and ginger beer? [*Seriously, as if she had done quite enough trifling for one evening.*] Her butter is really awful. I must get some down from the stores.

FRANK   Do, in heaven's name!

> [VIVIE *goes to the writing-table and makes a memorandum to order the butter.* PRAED *comes in from the kitchen, putting up his handkerchief, which he has been using as a napkin.*]

REV. SAMUEL   Frank, my boy: it is time for us to be thinking of home. Your mother does not know yet that we have visitors.

PRAED   I'm afraid we're giving trouble.

FRANK [*Rising.*]   Not the least in the world; my mother will be delighted to see you. She's a genuinely intellectual artistic woman; and she sees nobody here from one year's end to another except the gov'nor; so you can imagine how jolly dull it pans out for her. [*To his father.*] Youre not intellectual or artistic are you, pater?[5] So take Praed home at once; and I'll stay here and entertain Mrs Warren. Youll pick up Crofts in the garden. He'll be excellent company for the bull-pup.

PRAED [*Taking his hat from the dresser, and coming close to* FRANK.]   Come with us, Frank. Mrs Warren has not seen Miss Vivie for a long time; and we have prevented them from having a moment together yet.

FRANK [*Quite softened, and looking at* PRAED *with romantic admiration.*] Of course. I forgot. Ever so thanks for reminding me. Perfect gentleman, Praddy. Always were. My ideal through life. [*He rises to go, but pauses a moment between the two older men, and puts his hand on* PRAED's *shoulder.*] Ah, if you had only been my father instead of this unworthy old man! [*He puts his other hand on his father's shoulder.*]

REV. SAMUEL [*Blustering.*]   Silence, sir, silence; you are profane.

MRS WARREN [*Laughing heartily.*]   You should keep him in better order, Sam. Goodnight. Here: take George his hat and stick with my compliments.

REV. SAMUEL [*Taking them.*]   Goodnight. [*They shake hands. As he passes* VIVIE *he shakes hands with her also and bids her goodnight. Then, in booming command, to* FRANK.]   Come along, sir, at once. [*He goes out.*]

MRS WARREN   Byebye, Praddy.

PRAED   Byebye, Kitty.

> [*They shake hands affectionately and go out together, she accompanying him to the garden gate.*]

FRANK [*To* VIVIE.]   Kissums?

VIVIE [*Fiercely.*]   No. I hate you. [*She takes a couple of books and some paper from the writing-table, and sits down with them at the middle table, at the end next the fireplace.*]

---

5. Father (Latin).

FRANK [*Grimacing.*]   Sorry. [*He goes for his cap and rifle,* MRS WARREN *returns. He takes her hand.*] Goodnight, dear Mrs Warren. [*He kisses her hand. She snatches it away, her lips tightening, and looks more than half disposed to box his ears. He laughs mischievously and runs off, clapping-to the door behind him.*]

MRS WARREN [*Resigning herself to an evening of boredom now that the men are gone.*]   Did you ever in your life hear anyone rattle on so? Isnt he a tease? [*She sits at the table.*] Now that I think of it, dearie, dont you go on encouraging him. I'm sure he's a regular good-for-nothing.

VIVIE [*Rising to fetch more books.*]   I'm afraid so. Poor Frank! I shall have to get rid of him; but I shall feel sorry for him, though he's not worth it. That man Crofts does not seem to me to be good for much either: is he? [*She throws the books on the table rather roughly.*]

MRS WARREN [*Galled by* VIVIE's *indifference.*]   What do you know of men, child, to talk that way about them? Youll have to make up your mind to see a good deal of Sir George Crofts, as he's a friend of mine.

VIVIE [*Quite unmoved.*]   Why? [*She sits down and opens a book.*] Do you expect that we shall be much together? You and I, I mean?

MRS WARREN [*Staring at her.*]   Of course: until youre married. Youre not going back to college again.

VIVIE   Do you think my way of life would suit you? I doubt it.

MRS WARREN   Your way of life! What do you mean?

VIVIE [*Cutting a page of her book with the paper knife on her chatelaine.*] Has it really never occurred to you, mother, that I have a way of life like other people?

MRS WARREN   What nonsense is this youre trying to talk? Do you want to shew your independence, now that youre a great little person at school? Dont be a fool, child.

VIVIE [*Indulgently.*]   Thats all you have to say on the subject, is it, mother?

MRS WARREN [*Puzzled, then angry.*]   Dont you keep on asking me questions like that. [*Violently.*] Hold your tongue. [VIVIE *works on, losing no time, and saying nothing.*] You and your way of life, indeed! What next? [*She looks at* VIVIE *again. No reply.*] Your way of life will be what I please, so it will. [*Another pause.*] Ive been noticing these airs in you ever since you got that tripos or whatever you call it. If you think I'm going to put up with them youre mistaken; and the sooner you find it out, the better. [*Muttering.*] All I have to say on the subject, indeed! [*Again raising her voice angrily.*] Do you know who youre speaking to, Miss?

VIVIE [*Looking across at her without raising her head from her book.*]   No. Who are you? What are you?

MRS WARREN [*Rising breathless.*]   You young imp!

VIVIE   Everybody knows my reputation, my social standing, and the profession I intend to pursue. I know nothing about you. What is that way of life which you invite me to share with you and Sir George Crofts, pray?

MRS WARREN   Take care. I shall do something I'll be sorry for after, and you too.

VIVIE [*Putting aside her books with cool decision.*]   Well, let us drop the subject until you are better able to face it. [*Looking critically at her mother.*] You want some good walks and a little lawn tennis to set you up. You are shockingly out of condition: you were not able to manage twenty yards uphill today without stopping to pant; and your wrists are mere rolls of fat. Look at mine. [*She holds out her wrists.*]

MRS WARREN [*After looking at her helplessly, begins to whimper.*]   Vivie—

VIVIE [*Springing up sharply.*]   Now pray dont begin to cry. Anything but that. I really cannot stand whimpering. I will go out of the room if you do.

MRS WARREN [*Piteously.*]   Oh, my darling, how can you be so hard on me? Have I no rights over you as your mother?

VIVIE   Are you my mother?

MRS WARREN [*Appalled.*]   Am I your mother! Oh, Vivie!

VIVIE   Then where are our relatives? my father? our family friends? You claim the rights of a mother: the right to call me fool and child; to speak to me as no woman in authority over me at college dare speak to me; to dictate my way of life; and to force on me the acquaintance of a brute whom anyone can see to be the most vicious sort of London man about town. Before I give myself the trouble to resist such claims, I may as well find out whether they have any real existence.

MRS WARREN [*Distracted, throwing herself on her knees.*]   Oh no, no. Stop, stop. I am your mother: I swear it. Oh, you cant mean to turn on me—my own child! It's not natural. You believe me, dont you? Say you believe me.

VIVIE   Who was my father?

MRS WARREN   You dont know what youre asking. I cant tell you.

VIVIE [*Determinedly.*]   Oh yes you can, if you like. I have a right to know; and you know very well that I have that right. You can refuse to tell me, if you please; but if you do, you will see the last of me tomorrow morning.

MRS WARREN   Oh, it's too horrible to hear you talk like that. You wouldnt— you couldnt leave me.

VIVIE [*Ruthlessly.*]   Yes, without a moment's hesitation, if you trifle with me about this. [*Shivering with disgust.*] How can I feel sure that I may not have the contaminated blood of that brutal waster in my veins?

MRS WARREN   No, no. On my oath it's not he, nor any of the rest that you have ever met. I'm certain of that, at least.

[VIVIE's *eyes fasten sternly on her mother as the significance of this flashes on her.*]

VIVIE [*Slowly.*]   You are certain of that, at least. Ah! You mean that that is all you are certain of. [*Thoughtfully.*] I see. [MRS WARREN *buries her face in her hands.*] Dont do that, mother: you know you dont feel it a bit. [MRS WARREN *takes down her hands and looks up deplorably at* VIVIE, *who takes out her watch and says*] Well, that is enough for tonight. At what hour would you like breakfast? Is half-past eight too early for you?

MRS WARREN [*Wildly.*]   My God, what sort of woman are you?

VIVIE [*Coolly.*]   The sort the world is mostly made of, I should hope. Otherwise I dont understand how it gets its business done. Come [*taking her mother by the wrist, and pulling her up pretty resolutely*]: pull yourself together. Thats right.

MRS WARREN [*Querulously.*]   Youre very rough with me, Vivie.

VIVIE   Nonsense. What about bed? It's past ten.

MRS WARREN [*Passionately.*]   Whats the use of my going to bed? Do you think I could sleep?

VIVIE   Why not? I shall.

MRS WARREN   You! youve no heart. [*She suddenly breaks out vehemently in her natural tongue—the dialect of a woman of the people—with all her affectations of maternal authority and conventional manners gone, and an overwhelming inspiration of true conviction and scorn in her.*] Oh, I wont bear it: I wont put up with the injustice of it. What right have you to set yourself up above me like this? You boast of what you are to me—to me, who gave you the chance of being what you are. What chance had I! Shame on you for a bad daughter and a stuck-up prude!

VIVIE [*Sitting down with a shrug, no longer confident; for her replies, which have sounded sensible and strong to her so far, now begin to ring rather woodenly and even priggishly against the new tone of her mother.*]   Dont think for a moment I set myself above you in any way. You attacked me with the conventional authority of a mother: I defended myself with the conventional superiority of a respectable woman. Frankly, I am not going to stand any of your nonsense; and when you drop it I shall not expect you to stand any of mine. I shall always respect your right to your own opinions and your own way of life.

MRS WARREN   My own opinions and my own way of life! Listen to her talking! Do you think I was brought up like you? able to pick and choose my own way of life? Do you think I did what I did because I liked it, or thought it right, or wouldnt rather have gone to college and been a lady if I'd had the chance?

VIVIE   Everybody has some choice, mother. The poorest girl alive may not be able to choose between being Queen of England or Principal of Newn- ham; but she can choose between ragpicking and flower-selling, accord- ing to her taste. People are always blaming their circumstances for what they are. I dont believe in circumstances. The people who get on in this world are the people who get up and look for the circumstances they want, and, if they cant find them, make them.

MRS WARREN   Oh, it's easy to talk, very easy, isnt it? Here! would you like to know what my circumstances were?

VIVIE   Yes: you had better tell me. Wont you sit down?

MRS WARREN   Oh, I'll sit down: dont you be afraid. [*She plants her chair farther forward with brazen energy, and sits down.* VIVIE *is impressed in spite of herself.*] D'you know what your gran'mother was?

VIVIE   No.

MRS WARREN   No you dont. I do. She called herself a widow and had a fried-fish shop down by the Mint,[6] and kept herself and four daughters out of it. Two of us were sisters: that was me and Liz; and we were both good-looking and well made. I suppose our father was a well-fed man: mother pretended he was a gentleman; but I dont know. The other two were only half sisters: undersized, ugly, starved looking, hard working, honest poor creatures: Liz and I would have half-murdered them if mother hadnt half-murdered us to keep our hands off them. They were the respectable ones. Well, what did they get by their respectability? I'll tell you. One of them worked in a whitelead[7] factory twelve hours a day

6. The Royal Mint (where coins were produced) was close to the Tower in the east of London, at this time a poor area of the city.
7. A pigment used in paints.

for nine shillings a week until she died of lead poisoning. She only expected to get her hands a little paralyzed; but she died. The other was always held up to us as a model because she married a Government laborer in the Deptford victualling yard, and kept his room and the three children neat and tidy on eighteen shillings a week—until he took to drink. That was worth being respectable for, wasnt it?

VIVIE [*Now thoughtfully attentive.*]   Did you and your sister think so?

MRS WARREN   Liz didnt, I can tell you: she had more spirit. We both went to a church school—that was part of the ladylike airs we gave ourselves to be superior to the children that knew nothing and went nowhere—and we stayed there until Liz went out one night and never came back. I know the school-mistress thought I'd soon follow her example; for the clergy-man was always warning me that Lizzie'd end by jumping off Waterloo Bridge.[8] Poor fool: that was all he knew about it! But I was more afraid of the whitelead factory than I was of the river; and so would you have been in my place. That clergyman got me a situation as a scullery maid in a temperance restaurant where they sent out for anything you liked. Then I was waitress; and then I went to the bar at Waterloo station: fourteen hours a day serving drinks and washing glasses for four shillings a week and my board. That was considered a great promotion for me. Well, one cold, wretched night, when I was so tired I could hardly keep myself awake, who should come up for a half of Scotch but Lizzie, in a long fur cloak, elegant and comfortable, with a lot of sovereigns[9] in her purse.

VIVIE [*Grimly.*]   My aunt Lizzie!

MRS WARREN.   Yes; and a very good aunt to have, too. She's living down at Winchester now, close to the cathedral, one of the most respectable ladies there. Chaperones girls at the county ball, if you please. No river for Liz, thank you! You remind me of Liz a little: she was a first-rate business woman—saved money from the beginning—never let herself look too like what she was—never lost her head or threw away a chance. When she saw I'd grown up good-looking she said to me across the bar "What are you doing there, you little fool? wearing out your health and your appearance for other people's profit!" Liz was saving money then to take a house for herself in Brussels; and she thought we two could save faster than one. So she lent me some money and gave me a start; and I saved steadily and first paid her back, and then went into business with her as her partner. Why shouldnt I have done it? The house in Brussels was real high class: a much better place for a woman to be in than the factory where Anne Jane got poisoned. None of our girls were ever treated as I was treated in the scullery of that temperance place, or at the Waterloo bar, or at home. Would you have had me stay in them and become a worn out old drudge before I was forty?

VIVIE [*Intensely interested by this time.*]   No; but why did you choose that business? Saving money and good management will succeed in any business.

---

8. I.e., become a prostitute, and then throw her-self into the river Thames (traditionally pre-sented as the fate of fallen women).

9. Gold coins, each worth one pound. "A half": a half gill (two fluid ounces).

MRS WARREN Yes, saving money. But where can a woman get the money to save in any other business? Could you save out of four shillings a week and keep yourself dressed as well? Not you. Of course, if youre a plain woman and cant earn anything more; or if you have a turn for music, or the stage, or newspaper writing; thats different. But neither Liz nor I had any turn for such things: all we had was our appearance and our turn for pleasing men. Do you think we were such fools as to let other people trade in our good looks by employing us as shopgirls, or barmaids, or waitresses, when we could trade in them ourselves and get all the profits instead of starvation wages? Not likely.

VIVIE You were certainly quite justified—from the business point of view.

MRS WARREN Yes; or any other point of view. What is any respectable girl brought up to do but to catch some rich man's fancy and get the benefit of his money by marrying him?—as if a marriage ceremony could make any difference in the right or wrong of the thing! Oh! the hypocrisy of the world makes me sick! Liz and I had to work and save and calculate just like other people; elseways we should be as poor as any good-for-nothing drunken waster of a woman that thinks her luck will last for ever. [*With great energy.*] I despise such people: theyve no character; and if theres a thing I hate in a woman, it's want of character.

VIVIE Come now, mother: frankly! Isnt it part of what you call character in a woman that she should greatly dislike such a way of making money?

MRS WARREN Why, of course. Everybody dislikes having to work and make money; but they have to do it all the same. I'm sure Ive often pitied a poor girl; tired out and in low spirits, having to try to please some man that she doesnt care two straws for—some half-drunken fool that thinks he's making himself agreeable when he's teasing and worrying and disgusting a woman so that hardly any money could pay her for putting up with it. But she has to bear with disagreeables and take the rough with the smooth, just like a nurse in a hospital or anyone else. It's not work that any woman would do for pleasure, goodness knows; though to hear the pious people talk you would suppose it was a bed of roses.

VIVIE Still, you consider it worth while. It pays.

MRS WARREN Of course it's worth while to a poor girl, if she can resist temptation and is good-looking and well conducted and sensible. It's far better than any other employment open to her. I always thought that oughtnt to be. It cant be right, Vivie, that there shouldnt be better opportunities for women. I stick to that: it's wrong. But it's so, right or wrong; and a girl must make the best of it. But of course it's not worth while for a lady. If you took to it youd be a fool; but I should have been a fool if I'd taken to anything else.

VIVIE [*More and more deeply moved.*] Mother; suppose we were both as poor as you were in those wretched old days, are you quite sure that you wouldnt advise me to try the Waterloo bar, or marry a laborer, or even go into the factory?

MRS WARREN [*Indignantly.*] Of course not. What sort of mother do you take me for! How could you keep your self-respect in such starvation and slavery? And whats a woman worth? whats life worth? without self-respect! Why am I independent and able to give my daughter a first-rate education, when other women that had just as good opportunities are in the gutter? Because I always knew how to respect myself and control myself. Why is Liz looked up to in a cathedral town? The same reason. Where would we be now if we'd minded the clergyman's foolishness? Scrubbing floors for one and sixpence[1] a day and nothing to look forward to but the workhouse infirmary. Dont you be led astray by people who dont know the world, my girl. The only way for a woman to provide for herself decently is for her to be good to some man that can afford to be good to her. If she's in his own station of life, let her make him marry her; but if she's far beneath him she cant expect it: why should she? it wouldn't be for her own happiness. Ask any lady in London society that has daughters; and she'll tell you the same, except that I tell you straight and she'll tell you crooked. Thats all the difference.

VIVIE [*Fascinated, gazing at her.*]   My dear mother; you are a wonderful woman: you are stronger than all England. And are you really and truly not one wee bit doubtful—or—or—ashamed?

MRS WARREN   Well, of course, dearie, it's only good manners to be ashamed of it; it's expected from a woman. Women have to pretend to feel a great deal that they dont feel. Liz used to be angry with me for plumping out the truth about it. She used to say that when every woman could learn enough from what was going on in the world before her eyes, there was no need to talk about it to her. But then Liz was such a perfect lady! She had the true instinct of it; while I was always a bit of a vulgarian. I used to be so pleased when you sent me your photos to see that you were growing up like Liz: youve just her ladylike, determined way. But I cant stand saying one thing when everyone knows I mean another. Whats the use in such hypocrisy? If people arrange the world that way for women, theres no good pretending it's arranged the other way. No: I never was a bit ashamed really. I consider I had a right to be proud of how we managed everything so respectably, and never had a word against us, and how the girls were so well taken care of. Some of them did very well: one of them married an ambassador. But of course now I darent talk about such things: whatever would they think of us! [*She yawns.*] Oh dear! I do believe I'm getting sleepy after all. [*She stretches herself lazily, thoroughly relieved by her explosion, and placidly ready for her night's rest.*]

VIVIE   I believe it is I who will not be able to sleep now. [*She goes to the dresser and lights the candle. Then she extinguishes the lamp, darkening the room a good deal.*] Better let in some fresh air before locking up. [*She opens the cottage door, and finds that it is broad moonlight.*] What a beautiful night! Look! [*She draws aside the curtains of the window. The landscape is seen bathed in the radiance of the harvest moon rising over Blackdown.[2]*]

MRS WARREN [*With a perfunctory glance at the scene.*]   Yes, dear; but take care you dont catch your death of cold from the night air.

VIVIE [*Contemptuously.*]   Nonsense.

MRS WARREN [*Querulously.*]   Oh yes: everything I say is nonsense, according to you.

---

1. I.e., one and a half shillings.   2. A hill near Haslemere.

VIVIE [*Turning to her quickly.*]   No: really that is not so, mother. You have got completely the better of me tonight, though I intended it to be the other way. Let us be good friends now.

MRS WARREN [*Shaking her head a little ruefully.*]   So it has been the other way. But I suppose I must give in to it. I always got the worst of it from Liz; and now I suppose it'll be the same with you.

VIVIE   Well, never mind. Come: goodnight, dear old mother. [*She takes her mother in her arms.*]

MRS WARREN [*Fondly.*]   I brought you up well, didnt I, dearie?

VIVIE   You did.

MRS WARREN   And youll be good to your poor old mother for it, wont you?

VIVIE   I will, dear. [*Kissing her.*] Goodnight.

MRS WARREN [*With unction.*]   Blessings on my own dearie darling! a mother's blessing!

> [*She embraces her daughter protectingly, instinctively looking upward for divine sanction.*]

Act 3

In the Rectory garden next morning, with the sun shining from a cloudless sky. The garden wall has a five-barred wooden gate, wide enough to admit a carriage, in the middle. Beside the gate hangs a bell on a coiled spring, communicating with a pull outside. The carriage drive comes down the middle of the garden and then swerves to its left, where it ends in a little gravelled circus[3] opposite the Rectory porch. Beyond the gate is seen the dusty high road, parallel with the wall, bounded on the farther side by a strip of turf and an unfenced pine wood. On the lawn, between the house and the drive, is a clipped yew tree, with a garden bench in its shade. On the opposite side the garden is shut in by a box hedge; and there is a sundial on the turf, with an iron chair near it. A little path leads off through the box hedge, behind the sundial.

FRANK seated on the chair near the sundial, on which he has placed the morning papers, is reading The Standard. *His father comes from the house, red-eyed and shivery, and meets FRANK's eye with misgiving.*

FRANK [*Looking at his watch.*]   Half-past eleven. Nice hour for a rector to come down to breakfast!

REV. SAMUEL   Dont mock, Frank: dont mock. I am a little—er—[*Shivering.*]—

FRANK   Off color?

REV. SAMUEL [*Repudiating the expression.*]   No, sir: unwell this morning. Wheres your mother?

FRANK   Dont be alarmed: she's not here. Gone to town by the 11.13 with Bessie. She left several messages for you. Do you feel equal to receiving them now, or shall I wait til youve breakfasted?

REV. SAMUEL   I have breakfasted, sir. I am surprised at your mother going to town when we have people staying with us. Theyll think it very strange.

FRANK   Possibly she has considered that. At all events, if Crofts is going to stay here, and you are going to sit up every night with him until four, recalling the incidents of your fiery youth, it is clearly my mother's duty,

---

3. A round open space.

as a prudent housekeeper, to go up to the stores and order a barrel of whisky and few hundred siphons.

REV. SAMUEL   I did not observe that Sir George drank excessively.

FRANK   You were not in a condition to, gov'nor.

REV. SAMUEL   Do you mean to say that I—?

FRANK [*Calmly.*]   I never saw a beneficed clergyman less sober. The anecdotes you told about your past career were so awful that I really dont think Praed would have passed the night under your roof if it hadnt been for the way my mother and he took to one another.

REV. SAMUEL   Nonsense, sir. I am Sir George Crofts' host. I must talk to him about something; and he has only one subject. Where is Mr Praed now?

FRANK   He is driving my mother and Bessie to the station.

REV. SAMUEL   Is Crofts up yet?

FRANK   Oh, long ago. He hasnt turned a hair: he's in much better practice than you. Has kept it up ever since, probably. He's taken himself off somewhere to smoke.

> [FRANK *resumes his paper. The parson turns disconsolately towards the gate; then comes back irresolutely.*]

REV. SAMUEL   Er—Frank.

FRANK   Yes.

REV. SAMUEL   Do you think the Warrens will expect to be asked here after yesterday afternoon?

FRANK   Theyve been asked already.

REV. SAMUEL [*Appalled.*]   What!!!

FRANK   Crofts informed us at breakfast that you told him to bring Mrs Warren and Vivie over here today, and to invite them to make this house their home. My mother then found she must go to town by the 11.13 train.

REV. SAMUEL [*With despairing vehemence.*]   I never gave any such invitation. I never thought of such a thing.

FRANK [*Compassionately.*]   How do you know, gov'nor, what you said and thought last night?

PRAED [*Coming in through the hedge.*]   Good morning.

REV. SAMUEL   Good morning. I must apologize for not having met you at breakfast. I have a touch of—of—

FRANK   Clergyman's sore throat, Praed. Fortunately not chronic.

PRAED [*Changing the subject.*]   Well, I must say your house is in a charming spot here. Really most charming.

REV. SAMUEL   Yes: it is indeed. Frank will take you for a walk, Mr Praed, if you like. I'll ask you to excuse me: I must take the opportunity to write my sermon while Mrs Gardner is away and you are all amusing yourselves. You wont mind, will you?

PRAED   Certainly not. Dont stand on the slightest ceremony with me.

REV. SAMUEL   Thank you. I'll—er—er—[*He stammers his way to the porch and vanishes into the house.*]

PRAED   Curious thing it must be writing a sermon every week.

FRANK   Ever so curious, if he did it. He buys em. He's gone for some soda water.

PRAED   My dear boy: I wish you would be more respectful to your father. You know you can be so nice when you like.

FRANK   My dear Praddy: you forget that I have to live with the governor. When two people live together—it doesnt matter whether theyre father and son or husband and wife or brother and sister—they cant keep up the polite humbug thats so easy for ten minutes on an afternoon call. Now the governor, who unites to many admirable domestic qualities the irres-oluteness of a sheep and the pompousness and aggressiveness of a jackass—

PRAED   No, pray, pray, my dear Frank, remember! He is your father.

FRANK   I give him due credit for that. [*Rising and flinging down his paper.*] But just imagine his telling Crofts to bring the Warrens over here! He must have been ever so drunk. You know, my dear Praddy, my mother wouldnt stand Mrs Warren for a moment. Vivie mustnt come here until she's gone back to town.

PRAED   But your mother doesnt know anything about Mrs Warren, does she? [*He picks up the paper and sits down to read it.*]

FRANK   I don't know. Her journey to town looks as if she did. Not that my mother would mind in the ordinary way: she has stuck like a brick to lots of women who had got into trouble. But they were all nice women. Thats what makes the real difference. Mrs Warren, no doubt, has her merits; but she's ever so rowdy; and my mother simply wouldnt put up with her. So—hallo! [*This exclamation is provoked by the reappearance of the clergyman, who comes out of the house in haste and dismay.*]

REV. SAMUEL   Frank: Mrs Warren and her daughter are coming across the heath with Crofts: I saw them from the study windows. What am I to say about your mother?

FRANK   Stick on your hat and go out and say how delighted you are to see them; and that Frank's in the garden; and that mother and Bessie have been called to the bedside of a sick relative, and were ever so sorry they couldnt stop; and that you hope Mrs Warren slept well; and—and—say any blessed thing except the truth, and leave the rest to Providence.

REV. SAMUEL   But how are we to get rid of them afterwards?

FRANK   Theres no time to think of that now. Here! [*He bounds into the house.*]

REV. SAMUEL   He's so impetuous. I dont know what to do with him, Mr Praed.

FRANK   [*Returning with a clerical felt hat, which he claps on his father's head.*] Now: off with you. [*Rushing him through the gate.*] Praed and I'll wait here, to give the thing an unpremeditated air. [*The clergyman, dazed but obedient, hurries off.*]

FRANK   We must get the old girl back to town somehow, Praed. Come! Honestly, dear Praddy, do you like seeing them together?

PRAED   Oh, why not?

FRANK   [*His teeth on edge.*]   Dont it make your flesh creep ever so little? that wicked old devil, up to every villainy under the sun, I'll swear, and Vivie—ugh!

PRAED   Hush, pray. Theyre coming.

> [*The clergyman and* CROFTS *are seen coming along the road, followed by* MRS WARREN *and* VIVIE *walking affectionately together.*]

FRANK   Look: she actually has her arm round the old woman's waist. It's her right arm: she began it. She's gone sentimental, by God! Ugh! ugh! Now do you feel the creeps? [*The clergyman opens the gate; and* MRS

WARREN *and* VIVIE *pass him and stand in the middle of the garden looking at the house.* FRANK, *in an ecstasy of dissimulation, turns gaily to* MRS WARREN, *exclaiming*] Ever so delighted to see you, Mrs Warren. This quiet old rectory garden becomes you perfectly.

MRS WARREN Well, I never! Did you hear that, George? He says I look well in a quiet old rectory garden.

REV. SAMUEL [*Still holding the gate for* CROFTS, *who loafs through it, heavily bored.*] You look well everywhere, Mrs Warren.

FRANK Bravo, gov'nor! Now look here: lets have a treat before lunch. First lets see the church. Everyone has to do that. It's a regular old thirteenth century church, you know: the gov'nor's ever so fond of it, because he got up a restoration fund and had it completely rebuilt six years ago. Praed will be able to shew its points.

PRAED [*Rising.*] Certainly, if the restoration has left any to shew.

REV. SAMUEL [*Mooning hospitably at them.*] I shall be pleased, I'm sure, if Sir George and Mrs Warren really care about it.

MRS WARREN Oh, come along and get it over.

CROFTS [*Turning back towards the gate.*] Ive no objection.

REV. SAMUEL Not that way. We go through the fields, if you dont mind. Round here. [*He leads the way by the little path through the box hedge.*]

CROFTS Oh, all right. [*He goes with the parson.*]

[PRAED *follows with* MRS WARREN. VIVIE *does not stir: she watches them until they have gone, with all the lines of purpose in her face marking it strongly.*]

FRANK Aint you coming?

VIVIE No. I want to give you a warning, Frank. You were making fun of my mother just now when you said that about the rectory garden. That is barred in future. Please treat my mother with as much respect as you treat your own.

FRANK My dear Viv: she wouldnt appreciate it: the two cases require different treatment. But what on earth has happened to you? Last night we were perfectly agreed as to your mother and her set. This morning I find you attitudinizing sentimentally with your arm round your parent's waist.

VIVIE [*Flushing.*] Attitudinizing!

FRANK That was how it struck me. First time I ever saw you do a second-rate thing.

VIVIE [*Controlling herself.*] Yes, Frank: there has been a change; but I dont think it a change for the worse. Yesterday I was a little prig.

FRANK And today?

VIVIE [*Wincing; then looking at him steadily.*] Today I know my mother better than you do.

FRANK Heaven forbid!

VIVIE What do you mean?

FRANK Viv: theres a freemasonry[4] among thoroughly immoral people that you know nothing of. Youve too much character. Thats the bond between your mother and me: thats why I know her better than youll ever know her.

VIVIE You are wrong: you know nothing about her. If you knew the circumstances against which my mother had to struggle—

---

4. A secret understanding.

FRANK [*Adroitly finishing the sentence for her.*]   I should know why she is what she is, shouldnt I? What difference would that make? Circumstances or no circumstances, Viv, you wont be able to stand your mother.

VIVIE [*Very angrily.*]   Why not?

FRANK   Because she's an old wretch, Viv. If you ever put your arm round her waist in my presence again, I'll shoot myself there and then as a protest against an exhibition which revolts me.

VIVIE   Must I choose between dropping your acquaintance and dropping my mother's?

FRANK [*Gracefully.*]   That would put the old lady at ever such a disadvantage. No, Viv: your infatuated little boy will have to stick to you in any case. But he's all the more anxious that you shouldnt make mistakes. It's no use, Viv: your mother's impossible. She may be a good sort; but she's a bad lot, a very bad lot.

VIVIE [*Hotly.*]   Frank—! [*He stands his ground. She turns away and sits down on the bench under the yew tree, struggling to recover her self-command. Then she says*] Is she to be deserted by all the world because she's what you call a bad lot? Has she no right to live?

FRANK   No fear of that, Viv: she wont ever be deserted. [*He sits on the bench beside her.*]

VIVIE   But I am to desert her, I suppose.

FRANK [*Babyishly, lulling her and making love to her with his voice.*] Mustnt go live with her. Little family group of mother and daughter wouldnt be a success. Spoil our little group.

VIVIE [*Falling under the spell.*]   What little group?

FRANK   The babes in the wood:[5] Vivie and little Frank. [*He nestles against her like a weary child.*] Lets go and get covered up with leaves.

VIVIE [*Rhythmically, rocking him like a nurse.*]   Fast asleep, hand in hand, under the trees.

FRANK   The wise little girl with her silly little boy.

VIVIE   The dear little boy with his dowdy little girl.

FRANK   Ever so peaceful, and relieved from the imbecility of the little boy's father and the questionableness of the little girl's—

VIVIE [*Smothering the word against her breast.*]   Sh-sh-sh-sh! little girl wants to forget all about her mother. [*They are silent for some moments, rocking one another. Then* VIVIE *wakes up with a shock, exclaiming*] What a pair of fools we are! Come: sit up. Gracious! your hair. [*She smoothes it.*] I wonder do all grown up people play in that childish way when nobody is looking. I never did it when I was a child.

FRANK   Neither did I. You are my first playmate. [*He catches her hand to kiss it, but checks himself to look round first. Very unexpectedly, he sees* CROFTS *emerging from the box hedge.*] Oh damn!

VIVIE   Why damn, dear?

FRANK [*Whispering.*]   Sh! Here's this brute Crofts. [*He sits farther away from her with an unconcerned air.*]

CROFTS.   Could I have a few words with you, Miss Vivie?

---

5. Frank refers to the story of a brother and sister who are abandoned by their cruel uncle in the woods, then covered with leaves by the birds. Based on an incident in 16th-century Norfolk, the tale was first popularized as a ballad, and then in nursery stories and pantomimes.

VIVIE Certainly.

CROFTS [*To* FRANK.] Youll excuse me, Gardner. Theyre waiting for you in the church, if you don't mind.

FRANK [*Rising.*] Anything to oblige you, Crofts—except church. If you should happen to want me, Vivvums, ring the gate bell. [*He goes into the house with unruffled suavity.*]

CROFTS [*Watching him with a crafty air as he disappears, and speaking to* VIVIE *with an assumption of being on privileged terms with her.*] Pleasant young fellow that, Miss Vivie. Pity he has no money, isnt it?

VIVIE Do you think so?

CROFTS Well, whats he to do? No profession. No property. Whats he good for?

VIVIE I realize his disadvantages, Sir George.

CROFTS [*A little taken aback at being so precisely interpreted.*] Oh, it's not that. But while we're in this world we're in it; and money's money. [*Vivie does not answer.*] Nice day, isnt it?

VIVIE [*With scarcely veiled contempt for this effort at conversation.*] Very.

CROFTS [*With brutal good humor, as if he liked her pluck.*] Well, thats not what I came to say. [*Sitting down beside her.*] Now listen, Miss Vivie. I'm quite aware that I'm not a young lady's man.

VIVIE Indeed, Sir George?

CROFTS No; and to tell you the honest truth I dont want to be either. But when I say a thing I mean it; when I feel a sentiment I feel it in earnest; and what I value I pay hard money for. Thats the sort of man I am.

VIVIE It does you great credit, I'm sure.

CROFTS Oh, I dont mean to praise myself. I have my faults, Heaven knows: no man is more sensible of that than I am. I know I'm not perfect: thats one of the disadvantages of being a middle-aged man; for I'm not a young man, and I know it. But my code is a simple one, and, I think, a good one. Honor between man and man; fidelity between man and woman; and no cant about this religion or that religion, but an honest belief that things are making for good on the whole.

VIVIE [*With biting irony.*] "A power, not ourselves, that makes for righteousness," eh?[6]

CROFTS [*Taking her seriously.*] Oh certainly. Not ourselves, of course. You understand what I mean. Well, now as to practical matters. You may have an idea that Ive flung my money about; but I havnt: I'm richer today than when I first came into the property. Ive used my knowledge of the world to invest my money in ways that other men have overlooked; and whatever else I may be, I'm a safe man from the money point of view.

VIVIE It's very kind of you to tell me all this.

CROFTS Oh well, come, Miss Vivie: you neednt pretend you dont see what I'm driving at. I want to settle down with a Lady Crofts. I suppose you think me very blunt, eh?

VIVIE Not at all: I am much obliged to you for being so definite and businesslike. I quite appreciate the offer: the money, the position, Lady Crofts, and so on. But I think I will say no, if you dont mind. I'd rather not.

6. Vivie refers to Matthew Arnold's much-quoted words: "an abstract, an eternal power, or only a stream of tendency, not ourselves, and making for righteousness" (*Literature and Dogma* [1873], chap. 1).

[*She rises, and strolls across to the sundial to get out of his immediate neighborhood.*]

CROFTS [*Not at all discouraged, and taking advantage of the additional room left him on the seat to spread himself comfortably, as if a few preliminary refusals were part of the inevitable routine of courtship.*] I'm in no hurry. It was only just to let you know in case young Gardner should try to trap you. Leave the question open.

VIVIE [*Sharply.*] My no is final. I wont go back from it.

[CROFTS *is not impressed. He grins; leans forward with his elbows on his knees to prod with his stick at some unfortunate insect in the grass; and looks cunningly at her. She turns away impatiently.*]

CROFTS I'm a good deal older than you. Twenty-five years; quarter of a century. I shant live for ever; and I'll take care that you shall be well off when I'm gone.

VIVIE I am proof against even that inducement, Sir George. Dont you think youd better take your answer? There is not the slightest chance of my altering it.

CROFTS [*Rising after a final slash at a daisy, and coming nearer to her.*] Well, no matter. I could tell you some things that would change your mind fast enough; but I wont, because I'd rather win you by honest affection. I was a good friend to your mother: ask her whether I wasnt. She'd never have made the money that paid for your education if it hadnt been for my advice and help, not to mention the money I advanced her. There are not many men would have stood by her as I have. I put not less than £40,000 into it, from first to last.

VIVIE [*Staring at him.*] Do you mean to say you were my mother's business partner?

CROFTS Yes. Now just think of all the trouble and the explanations it would save if we were to keep the whole thing in the family, so to speak. Ask your mother whether she'd like to have to explain all her affairs to a perfect stranger.

VIVIE I see no difficulty, since I understand that the business is wound up, and the money invested.

CROFTS [*Stopping short, amazed.*] Wound up! Wind up a business thats paying 35 per cent in the worst years! Not likely. Who told you that?

VIVIE [*Her color quite gone.*] Do you mean that it is still—? [*She stops abruptly, and puts her hand on the sundial to support herself. Then she gets quickly to the iron chair and sits down.*] What business are you talking about?

CROFTS Well, the fact is it's not what would be considered exactly a high-class business in my set—the county set, you know—our set it will be if you think better of my offer. Not that theres any mystery about it: dont think that. Of course you know by your mother's being in it that it's perfectly straight and honest. Ive known her for many years; and I can say of her that she'd cut off her hands sooner than touch anything that was not what it ought to be. I'll tell you all about it if you like. I dont know whether youve found in travelling how hard it is to find a really comfortable private hotel.

VIVIE [*Sickened, averting her face.*] Yes: go on.

CROFTS   Well, thats all it is. Your mother has a genius for managing such things. We've got two in Brussels, one in Ostend, one in Vienna, and two in Budapest. Of course there are others besides ourselves in it; but we hold most of the capital; and your mother's indispensable as managing director. Youve noticed, I daresay, that she travels a good deal. But you see you cant mention such things in society. Once let out the word hotel and everybody says you keep a public-house.[7] You wouldnt like people to say that of your mother, would you? Thats why we're so reserved about it. By the way, youll keep it to yourself, wont you? Since it's been a secret so long, it had better remain so.

VIVIE   And this is the business you invite me to join you in?

CROFTS   Oh, no. My wife shant be troubled with business. Youll not be in it more than youve always been.

VIVIE   *I* always been! What do you mean?

CROFTS   Only that youve always lived on it. It paid for your education and the dress you have on your back. Dont turn up your nose at business, Miss Vivie: where would your Newnhams and Girtons[8] be without it?

VIVIE [*Rising, almost beside herself.*]   Take care. I know what this business is.

CROFTS [*Staring, with a suppressed oath.*]   Who told you?

VIVIE   Your partner. My mother.

CROFTS [*Black with rage.*]   The old—

VIVIE   Just so.
    [*He swallows the epithet and stands for a moment swearing and raging foully to himself. But he knows that his cue is to be sympathetic. He takes refuge in generous indignation.*]

CROFTS   She ought to have had more consideration for you. I'd never have told you.

VIVIE   I think you would probably have told me when we were married; it would have been a convenient weapon to break me in with.

CROFTS [*Quite sincerely.*]   I never intended that. On my word as a gentleman I didnt.
    [VIVIE *wonders at him. Her sense of the irony of his protest cools and braces her. She replies with contemptuous self-possession.*]

VIVIE   It does not matter. I suppose you understand that when we leave here today our acquaintance ceases.

CROFTS   Why? Is it for helping your mother?

VIVIE   My mother was a very poor woman who had no reasonable choice but to do as she did. You were a rich gentleman; and you did the same for the sake of 35 per cent. You are a pretty common sort of scoundrel, I think. That is my opinion of you.

CROFTS [*After a stare: not at all displeased, and much more at ease on these frank terms than on their former ceremonious ones.*]   Ha! ha! ha! ha! Go it, little missie, go it: it doesnt hurt me and it amuses you. Why the devil shouldnt I invest my money that way? I take the interest on my capital like other people: I hope you dont think I dirty my own hands with the work. Come! you wouldnt refuse the acquaintance of my mother's cousin the Duke of Belgravia because some of the rents he gets are earned in queer ways. You wouldnt cut[9] the Archbishop of Canterbury, I suppose,

7. I.e., a bar.
8. Girton, like Newnham, is a women's college   at Cambridge University.
9. Break off acquaintance with.

because the Ecclesiastical Commissioners have a few publicans and sinners among their tenants. Do you remember your Crofts scholarship at Newnham? Well, that was founded by my brother the M.P.[1] He gets his 22 per cent out of a factory with 600 girls in it, and not one of them getting wages enough to live on. How d'ye suppose they manage when they have no family to fall back on? Ask your mother. And do you expect me to turn my back on 35 per cent when all the rest are pocketing what they can, like sensible men? No such fool! If youre going to pick and choose your acquaintances on moral principles, youd better clear out of this country, unless you want to cut yourself out of all decent society.

VIVIE [*Conscience stricken.*] You might go on to point out that I myself never asked where the money I spent came from. I believe I am just as bad as you.

CROFTS [*Greatly reassured.*] Of course you are; and a very good thing too! What harm does it do after all? [*Rallying her jocularly.*] So you dont think me such a scoundrel now you come to think it over. Eh?

VIVIE I have shared profits with you; and I admitted you just now to the familiarity of knowing what I think of you.

CROFTS [*With serious friendliness.*] To be sure you did. You wont find me a bad sort: I dont go in for being superfine intellectually; but Ive plenty of honest human feeling; and the old Crofts breed comes out in a sort of instinctive hatred of anything low, in which I'm sure youll sympathize with me. Believe me, Miss Vivie, the world isnt such a bad place as the croakers[2] make out. As long as you dont fly openly in the face of society, society doesnt ask any inconvenient questions; and it makes precious short work of the cads who do. There are no secrets better kept than the secrets everybody guesses. In the class of people I can introduce you to, no lady or gentleman would so far forget themselves as to discuss my business affairs or your mother's. No man can offer you a safer position.

VIVIE [*Studying him curiously.*] I suppose you really think youre getting on famously with me.

CROFTS Well, I hope I may flatter myself that you think better of me than you did at first.

VIVIE [*Quietly.*] I hardly find you worth thinking about at all now. When I think of the society that tolerates you, and the laws that protect you! when I think of how helpless nine out of ten young girls would be in the hands of you and my mother! the unmentionable woman and her capitalist bully—

CROFTS [*Livid.*] Damn you!

VIVIE You need not. I feel among the damned already.

[*She raises the latch of the gate to open it and go out. He follows her and puts his hand heavily on the top bar to prevent its opening.*]

CROFTS [*Panting with fury.*] Do you think I'll put up with this from you, you young devil?

VIVIE [*Unmoved.*] Be quiet. Some one will answer the bell. [*Without flinching a step she strikes the bell with the back of her hand. It clangs harshly; and he starts back involuntarily. Almost immediately* FRANK *appears at the porch with his rifle.*]

1. Member of Parliament. 2. Those that prophesy doom.

FRANK [*With cheerful politeness.*]   Will you have the rifle, Viv; or shall I operate?

VIVIE   Frank: have you been listening?

FRANK [*Coming down into the garden.*]   Only for the bell, I assure you; so that you shouldn't have to wait. I think I shewed great insight into your character, Crofts.

CROFTS   For two pins I'd take that gun from you and break it across your head.

FRANK [*Stalking him cautiously.*]   Pray dont. I'm ever so careless in handling firearms. Sure to be a fatal accident, with a reprimand from the coroner's jury for my negligence.

VIVIE   Put the rifle away, Frank: it's quite unnecessary.

FRANK   Quite right, Viv. Much more sportsmanlike to catch him in a trap. [CROFTS, *understanding the insult, makes a threatening movement.*] *Crofts: there are fifteen cartridges in the magazine here; and I am a dead shot at the present distance and at an object of your size.*

CROFTS   Oh, you neednt be afraid. I'm not going to touch you.

FRANK   Ever so magnanimous of you under the circumstances! Thank you!

CROFTS   I'll tell you this before I go. It may interest you, since youre so fond of one another. Allow me, Mister Frank, to introduce you to your half-sister, the eldest daughter of the Reverend Samuel Gardner. Miss Vivie: your halfbrother. Good morning. [*He goes out through the gate and along the road.*]

FRANK [*After a pause of stupefaction, raising the rifle.*]   Youll testify before the coroner that it's an accident, Viv. [*He takes aim at the retreating figure of* CROFTS. VIVIE *seizes the muzzle and pulls it round against her breast.*]

VIVIE   Fire now. You may.

FRANK [*Dropping his end of the rifle hastily.*]   Stop! take care. [*She lets go. It falls on the turf.*] Oh, youve given your little boy such a turn. Suppose it had gone off! ugh! [*He sinks on the garden seat, overcome.*]

VIVIE   Suppose it had: do you think it would not have been a relief to have some sharp physical pain tearing through me?

FRANK [*Coaxingly.*]   Take it ever so easy, dear Viv. Remember; even if the rifle scared that fellow into telling the truth for the first time in his life, that only makes us the babes in the wood in earnest. [*He holds out his arms to her.*] Come and be covered up with leaves again.

VIVIE [*With a cry of disgust.*]   Ah, not that, not that. You make all my flesh creep.

FRANK   Why, whats the matter?

VIVIE   Goodbye. [*She makes for the gate.*]

FRANK [*Jumping up.*]   Hallo! Stop! Viv! Viv! [*She turns in the gateway.*] Where are you going to? Where shall we find you?

VIVIE   At Honoria Fraser's chambers, 67 Chancery Lane, for the rest of my life. [*She goes off quickly in the opposite direction to that taken by* CROFTS.]

FRANK   But I say—wait—dash it! [*He runs after her.*]

Act 4

HONORIA FRASER's *chambers in Chancery Lane. An office at the top of New Stone Buildings, with a plate-glass window, distempered walls, electric light, and a patent stove. Saturday afternoon. The chimneys of Lincoln's Inn[3] and the western sky beyond are seen through the window. There is a double writing table in the middle of the room, with a cigar box, ash pans, and a portable electric reading lamp almost snowed up in heaps of papers and books. This table has knee holes and chairs right and left and is very untidy. The clerk's desk, closed and tidy, with its high stool, is against the wall, near a door communicating with the inner rooms. In the opposite wall is the door leading to the public corridor. Its upper panel is of opaque glass, lettered in black on the outside,* FRASER AND WARREN. *A baize screen hides the corner between this door and the window.*

FRANK, *in a fashionable light-colored coaching suit, with his stick, gloves, and white hat in his hands, is pacing up and down the office. Somebody tries the door with a key.*

FRANK [*Calling.*]   Come in. It's not locked.
　　　[VIVIE *comes in, in her hat and jacket. She stops and stares at him.*]
VIVIE [*Sternly.*]   What are you doing here?
FRANK   Waiting to see you. Ive been here for hours. Is this the way you attend to your business? [*He puts his hat and stick on the table, and perches himself with a vault on the clerk's stool, looking at her with every appearance of being in a specially restless, teasing flippant mood.*]
VIVIE   Ive been away exactly twenty minutes for a cup of tea. [*She takes off her hat and jacket and hangs them up behind the screen.*] How did you get in?
FRANK   The staff had not left when I arrived. He's gone to play cricket on Primrose Hill.[4] Why dont you employ a woman, and give your sex a chance?
VIVIE   What have you come for?
FRANK [*Springing off the stool and coming close to her.*]   Viv: lets go and enjoy the Saturday half-holiday somewhere, like the staff. What do you say to Richmond,[5] and then a music hall, and a jolly supper?
VIVIE   Cant afford it. I shall put in another six hours work before I go to bed.
FRANK   Cant afford it, cant we? Aha! Look here. [*He takes out a handful of sovereigns and makes them chink.*] Gold, Viv: gold!
VIVIE   Where did you get it?
FRANK   Gambling, Viv: gambling. Poker.
VIVIE   Pah! It's meaner[6] than stealing it. No: I'm not coming. [*She sits down to work at the table, with her back to the glass door, and begins turning over the papers.*]
FRANK [*Remonstrating piteously.*]   But, my dear Viv, I want to talk to you ever so seriously.
VIVIE   Very well: sit down in Honoria's chair and talk here. I like ten minutes chat after tea. [*He murmurs.*] No use groaning: I'm inexorable. [*He takes the opposite seat disconsolately.*] Pass that cigar box, will you?

---

3. One of the four legal societies in London collectively known as the Inns of Court, which alone have the right to admit candidates to the English bar, thereby allowing them to practice law.
4. A park in northwest London.

5. A residential suburb in southwest London; there were beautiful views from Richmond Hill, but Frank might be proposing a riverside walk.
6. Lower, more degenerate.

FRANK [*Pushing the cigar box across.*] Nasty womanly habit. Nice men dont do it any longer.

VIVIE Yes: they object to the smell in the office; and weve had to take to cigarets. See! [*She opens the box and takes out a cigaret, which she lights. She offers him one; but he shakes his head with a wry face. She settles herself comfortably in her chair, smoking.*] Go ahead.

FRANK Well, I want to know what youve done—what arrangements youve made.

VIVIE Everything was settled twenty minutes after I arrived here. Honoria has found the business too much for her this year; and she was on the point of sending for me and proposing a partnership when I walked in and told her I hadnt a farthing[7] in the world. So I installed myself and packed her off for a fortnight's holiday. What happened at Haslemere when I left?

FRANK Nothing at all. I said youd gone to town on particular business.

VIVIE Well?

FRANK Well, either they were too flabbergasted to say anything, or else Crofts had prepared your mother. Anyhow, she didnt say anything; and Crofts didnt say anything; and Praddy only stared. After tea they got up and went; and Ive not seen them since.

VIVIE [*Nodding placidly with one eye on a wreath of smoke.*] Thats all right.

FRANK [*Looking round disparagingly.*] Do you intend to stick in this confounded place?

VIVIE [*Blowing the wreath decisively away, and sitting straight up.*] Yes. These two days have given me back all my strength and self-possession. I will never take a holiday again as long as I live.

FRANK [*With a very wry face.*] Mps! You look quite happy. And as hard as nails.

VIVIE [*Grimly.*] Well for me that I am!

FRANK [*Rising.*] Look here, Viv: we must have an explanation. We parted the other day under a complete misunderstanding. [*He sits on the table, close to her.*]

VIVIE [*Putting away the cigaret.*] Well: clear it up.

FRANK You remember what Crofts said?

VIVIE Yes.

FRANK That revelation was supposed to bring about a complete change in the nature of our feeling for one another. It placed us on the footing of brother and sister.

VIVIE Yes.

FRANK Have you ever had a brother?

VIVIE No.

FRANK Then you dont know what being brother and sister feels like? Now I have lots of sisters; and the fraternal feeling is quite familiar to me. I assure you my feeling for you is not the least in the world like it. The girls will go their way; I will go mine; and we shant care if we never see one another again. Thats brother and sister. But as to you, I cant be easy if I have to pass a week without seeing you. Thats not brother and

---

7. A quarter of a penny.

sister. It's exactly what I felt an hour before Crofts made his revelation. In short, dear Viv, it's love's young dream.

VIVIE [*Bitingly.*]   The same feeling, Frank, that brought your father to my mother's feet. Is that it?

FRANK [*So revolted that he slips off the table for a moment.*]   I very strongly object, Viv, to have my feelings compared to any which the Reverend Samuel is capable of harboring; and I object still more to a comparison of you to your mother. [*Resuming his perch.*] Besides, I dont believe the story. I have taxed my father with it, and obtained from him what I consider tantamount to a denial.

VIVIE   What did he say?

FRANK   He said he was sure there must be some mistake.

VIVIE   Do you believe him?

FRANK   I am prepared to take his word as against Crofts'.

VIVIE   Does it make any difference? I mean in your imagination or conscience; for of course it makes no real difference.

FRANK [*Shaking his head.*]   None whatever to me.

VIVIE   Nor to me.

FRANK [*Staring.*]   But this is ever so surprising! [*He goes back to his chair.*] I thought our whole relations were altered in your imagination and conscience, as you put it, the moment those words were out of the brute's muzzle.

VIVIE   No: it was not that. I didnt believe him. I only wish I could.

FRANK   Eh?

VIVIE   I think brother and sister would be a very suitable relation for us.

FRANK   You really mean that?

VIVIE   Yes. It's the only relation I care for, even if we could afford any other. I mean that.

FRANK [*Raising his eyebrows like one on whom a new light has dawned, and rising with quite an effusion of chivalrous sentiment.*]   My dear Viv: why didnt you say so before? I am ever so sorry for persecuting you. I understand, of course.

VIVIE [*Puzzled.*]   Understand what?

FRANK   Oh, I'm not a fool in the ordinary sense: only in the Scriptural sense of doing all the things the wise man declared to be folly, after trying them himself on the most extensive scale.[8] I see I am no longer Vivvum's little boy. Dont be alarmed: I shall never call you Vivvums again—at least unless you get tired of your new little boy, whoever he may be.

VIVIE   My new little boy!

FRANK [*With conviction.*]   Must be a new little boy. Always happens that way. No other way, in fact.

VIVIE   None that you know of, fortunately for you.
   [*Someone knocks at the door.*]

FRANK   My curse upon yon caller, whoe'er he be!

VIVIE   It's Praed. He's going to Italy and wants to say goodbye. I asked him to call this afternoon. Go and let him in.

---

8. Cf. Ecclesiastes 2.13: "Then I saw that wisdom excelleth folly."

FRANK   We can continue our conversation after his departure for Italy. I'll stay him out. [*He goes to the door and opens it.*] How are you, Praddy? Delighted to see you. Come in.

[PRAED, *dressed for travelling, comes in, in high spirits.*]

PRAED   How do you do, Miss Warren? [*She presses his hand cordially, though a certain sentimentality in his high spirits jars on her.*] I start in an hour from Holborn Viaduct.[9] I wish I could persuade you to try Italy.

VIVIE   What for?

PRAED   Why, to saturate yourself with beauty and romance, of course.

[VIVIE, *with a shudder, turns her chair to the table, as if the work waiting for her were a support to her.* PRAED *sits opposite to her.* FRANK *places a chair near* VIVIE, *and drops lazily and carelessly into it, talking at her over his shoulder.*]

FRANK   No use, Praddy. Viv is a little Philistine.[1] She is indifferent to my romance, and insensible to my beauty.

VIVIE   Mr Praed: once for all, there is no beauty and no romance in life for me. Life is what it is; and I am prepared to take it as it is.

PRAED [*Enthusiastically.*]   You will not say that if you come with me to Verona and on to Venice. You will cry with delight at living in such a beautiful world.

FRANK   This is most eloquent, Praddy. Keep it up.

PRAED   Oh, I assure you *I* have cried—I shall cry again, I hope—at fifty! At your age, Miss Warren, you would not need to go so far as Verona. Your spirits would absolutely fly up at the mere sight of Ostend. You would be charmed with the gaiety, the vivacity, the happy air of Brussels.

VIVIE [*Springing up with an exclamation of loathing.*]   Agh!

PRAED [*Rising.*]   Whats the matter?

FRANK [*Rising.*]   Hallo, Viv!

VIVIE [*To* PRAED, *with deep reproach.*]   Can you find no better example of your beauty and romance than Brussels to talk to me about?

PRAED [*Puzzled.*]   Of course it's very different from Verona. I dont suggest for a moment that—

VIVIE [*Bitterly.*]   Probably the beauty and romance come to much the same in both places.

PRAED [*Completely sobered and much concerned.*]   My dear Miss Warren: I—[*Looking inquiringly at* FRANK.] Is anything the matter?

FRANK   She thinks your enthusiasm frivolous, Praddy. She's had ever such a serious call.

VIVIE [*Sharply.*]   Hold your tongue, Frank. Dont be silly.

FRANK [*Sitting down.*]   Do you call this good manners, Praed?

PRAED [*Anxious and considerate.*]   Shall I take him away, Miss Warren? I feel sure we have disturbed you at your work.

VIVIE   Sit down: I'm not ready to go back to work yet. [PRAED *sits.*] You both think I have an attack of nerves. Not a bit of it. But there are two subjects I want dropped, if you dont mind. One of them [*To* FRANK.] is love's young dream in any shape or form: the other [*To* PRAED.] is the

9. A railway station in the City of London.
1. Matthew Arnold's term for a member of the dull and unenlightened middle classes; in his view their opposition to the defenders of culture makes them akin to the biblical tribe that fought against the people of Israel, "the people of light."

romance and beauty of life, especially Ostend and the gaiety of Brussels. You are welcome to any illusions you may have left on these subjects: I have none. If we three are to remain friends, I must be treated as a woman of business, permanently single [*To* FRANK.] and permanently unromantic. [*To* PRAED.]

FRANK   I also shall remain permanently single until you change your mind. Praddy: change the subject. Be eloquent about something else.

PRAED [*Diffidently.*]   I'm afraid theres nothing else in the world that I can talk about. The Gospel of Art is the only one I can preach. I know Miss Warren is a great devotee of the Gospel of Getting On; but we cant discuss that without hurting your feelings, Frank, since you are determined not to get on.

FRANK   Oh, dont mind my feelings. Give me some improving advice by all means: it does me ever so much good. Have another try to make a successful man of me, Viv. Come; lets have it all: energy, thrift, foresight, self-respect, character. Dont you hate people who have no character, Viv?

VIVIE [*Wincing.*]   Oh, stop, stop: let us have no more of that horrible cant. Mr Praed: if there are really only those two gospels in the world, we had better all kill ourselves; for the same taint is in both, through and through.

FRANK [*Looking critically at her.*]   There is a touch of poetry about you today, Viv, which has hitherto been lacking.

PRAED [*Remonstrating.*]   My dear Frank: arnt you a little unsympathetic?

VIVIE [*Merciless to herself.*]   No: it's good for me. It keeps me from being sentimental.

FRANK [*Bantering her.*]   Checks your strong natural propensity that way, dont it?

VIVIE [*Almost hysterically.*]   Oh yes; go on: dont spare me. I was sentimental for one moment in my life—beautifully sentimental—by moonlight; and now—

FRANK [*Quickly.*]   I say, Viv: take care. Dont give yourself away.

VIVIE   Oh, do you think Mr Praed does not know all about my mother? [*Turning on* PRAED.] You had better have told me that morning, Mr Praed. You are very old fashioned in your delicacies, after all.

PRAED   Surely it is you who are a little old fashioned in your prejudices, Miss Warren, I feel bound to tell you, speaking as an artist, and believing that the most intimate human relationships are far beyond and above the scope of the law, that though I know that your mother is an unmarried woman, I do not respect her the less on that account. I respect her more.

FRANK [*Airily.*]   Hear! Hear!

VIVIE [*Staring at him.*]   Is that all you know?

PRAED   Certainly that is all.

VIVIE   Then you neither of you know anything. Your guesses are innocence itself compared to the truth.

PRAED [*Rising, startled and indignant, and preserving his politeness with an effort.*]   I hope not. [*More emphatically.*] I hope not, Miss Warren.

FRANK [*Whistles.*]   Whew!

VIVIE   You are not making it easy for me to tell you, Mr Praed.

PRAED [*His chivalry drooping before their conviction.*]   If there is anything worse—that is, anything else—are you sure you are right to tell us, Miss Warren?

VIVIE   I am sure that if I had the courage I should spend the rest of my life in telling everybody—stamping and branding it into them until they all felt their part in its abomination as I feel mine. There is nothing I despise more than the wicked convention that protects these things by forbidding a woman to mention them. And yet I cant tell you. The two infamous words that describe what my mother is are ringing in my ears and struggling on my tongue; but I cant utter them: the shame of them is too horrible for me. [*She buries her face in her hands. The two men, astonished, stare at one another and then at her. She raises her head again desperately and snatches a sheet of paper and a pen.*] Here: let me draft you a prospectus.

FRANK   Oh, she's mad. Do you hear, Viv? mad. Come! pull yourself together.

VIVIE   You shall see. [*She writes.*] "Paid up capital: not less than £40,000 standing in the name of Sir George Crofts, Baronet, the chief shareholder. Premises at Brussels, Ostend, Vienna and Budapest. Managing director: Mrs Warren"; and now dont let us forget her qualifications: the two words. [*She writes the words and pushes the paper to them.*] There! Oh no: dont read it: dont! [*She snatches it back and tears it to pieces; then seizes her head in her hands and hides her face on the table.*]

> [FRANK, *who has watched the writing over his shoulder, and opened his eyes very widely at it, takes a card from his pocket; scribbles the two words on it; and silently hands it to* PRAED, *who reads it with amazement, and hides it hastily in his pocket.*]

FRANK [*Whispering tenderly.*]   Viv, dear: thats all right. I read what you wrote: so did Praddy. We understand. And we remain, as this leaves us at present, yours ever so devotedly.

PRAED   We do indeed, Miss Warren. I declare you are the most splendidly courageous woman I ever met.

> [*This sentimental compliment braces* VIVIE. *She throws it away from her with an impatient shake, and forces herself to stand up, though not without some support from the table.*]

FRANK   Dont stir, Viv, if you dont want to. Take it easy.

VIVIE   Thank you. You can always depend on me for two things: not to cry and not to faint. [*She moves a few steps towards the door of the inner room, and stops close to* PRAED *to say.*] I shall need much more courage than that when I tell my mother that we have come to the parting of the ways. Now I must go into the next room for a moment to make myself neat again, if you dont mind.

PRAED   Shall we go away?

VIVIE   No; I shall be back presently. Only for a moment. [*She goes into the other room,* PRAED *opening the door for her.*]

PRAED   What an amazing revelation! I'm extremely disappointed in Crofts: I am indeed.

FRANK   I'm not in the least. I feel he's perfectly accounted for at last. But what a facer[2] for me, Praddy! I cant marry her now.

---

2. A blow; an unpleasant surprise.

PRAED [*Sternly.*] Frank! [*The two look at one another,* FRANK *unruffled,* PRAED *deeply indignant.*] Let me tell you, Gardner, that if you desert her now you will behave very despicably.

FRANK Good old Praddy! Ever chivalrous! But you mistake: it's not the moral aspect of the case: it's the money aspect. I really cant bring myself to touch the old woman's money now.

PRAED And was that what you were going to marry on?

FRANK What else? *I* havnt any money, nor the smallest turn for making it. If I married Viv now she would have to support me; and I should cost her more than I am worth.

PRAED But surely a clever bright fellow like you can make something by your own brains.

FRANK Oh yes, a little. [*He takes out his money again.*] I made all that yesterday in an hour and a half. But I made it in a highly speculative business. No, dear Praddy: even if Bessie and Georgina marry millionaires and the governor dies after cutting them off with a shilling, I shall have only four hundred a year. And he wont die until he's three score and ten: he hasnt originality enough. I shall be on short allowance for the next twenty years. No short allowance for Viv, if I can help it. I withdraw gracefully and leave the field to the gilded youth of England. So thats settled. I shant worry her about it: I'll just send her a little note after we're gone. She'll understand.

PRAED [*Grasping his hand.*] Good fellow, Frank! I heartily beg your pardon. But must you never see her again?

FRANK Never see her again! Hang it all, be reasonable. I shall come along as often as possible, and be her brother. I cannot understand the absurd consequences you romantic people expect from the most ordinary transactions. [*A knock at the door.*] I wonder who this is. Would you mind opening the door? If it's a client it will look more respectable than if I appeared.

PRAED Certainly. [*He goes to the door and opens it.* FRANK *sits down in* VIVIE'*s chair to scribble a note.*] My dear Kitty: come in: come in.

[MRS WARREN *comes in, looking apprehensively round for* VIVIE. *She has done her best to make herself matronly and dignified. The brilliant hat is replaced by a sober bonnet, and the gay blouse covered by a costly black silk mantle. She is pitiably anxious and ill at ease: evidently panicstricken.*]

MRS WARREN [*To* FRANK.] What! Youre here, are you?

FRANK [*Turning in his chair from his writing, but not rising.*] Here, and charmed to see you. You come like a breath of spring.

MRS WARREN Oh, get out with your nonsense. [*In a low voice.*] Wheres Vivie?

[FRANK *points expressively to the door of the inner room, but says nothing.*]

MRS WARREN [*Sitting down suddenly and almost beginning to cry.*] Praddy: wont she see me, dont you think?

PRAED My dear Kitty: dont distress yourself. Why should she not?

MRS WARREN Oh, you never can see why not: youre too innocent. Mr Frank: did she say anything to you?

FRANK [*Folding his note.*] She must see you, if [*very expressively*] you wait til she comes in.

MRS WARREN [*Frightened.*]   Why shouldnt I wait?

> [FRANK *looks quizzically at her; puts his note carefully on the inkbottle, so that* VIVIE *cannot fail to find it when next she dips her pen; then rises and devotes his attention entirely to her.*]

FRANK   My dear Mrs Warren: suppose you were a sparrow—ever so tiny and pretty a sparrow hopping in the roadway—and you saw a steam roller coming in your direction, would you wait for it?

MRS WARREN   Oh, dont bother me with your sparrows. What did she run away from Haslemere like that for?

FRANK   I'm afraid she'll tell you if you rashly await her return.

MRS WARREN   Do you want me to go away?

FRANK   No: I always want you to stay. But I advise you to go away.

MRS WARREN   What! and never see her again!

FRANK   Precisely.

MRS WARREN [*Crying again.*]   Praddy: dont let him be cruel to me. [*She hastily checks her tears and wipes her eyes.*] She'll be so angry if she sees Ive been crying.

FRANK [*With a touch of real compassion in his airy tenderness.*]   You know that Praddy is the soul of kindness, Mrs Warren. Praddy: what do you say? Go or stay?

PRAED [*To* MRS WARREN.]   I really should be very sorry to cause you unnecessary pain; but I think perhaps you had better not wait. The fact is—[VIVIE *is heard at the inner door.*]

FRANK   Sh! Too late. She's coming.

MRS WARREN   Dont tell her I was crying, [VIVIE *comes in. She stops gravely on seeing* MRS WARREN, *who greets her with hysterical cheerfulness.*] Well, dearie. So here you are at last.

VIVIE   I am glad you have come: I want to speak to you. You said you were going, Frank, I think.

FRANK   Yes. Will you come with me, Mrs Warren? What do you say to a trip to Richmond, and the theatre in the evening? There is safety in Richmond. No steam roller there.

VIVIE   Nonsense, Frank. My mother will stay here.

MRS WARREN [*Scared.*]   I dont know: perhaps I'd better go. We're disturbing you at your work.

VIVIE [*With quiet decision.*]   Mr. Praed: please take Frank away. Sit down, mother, [MRS WARREN *obeys helplessly.*]

PRAED   Come, Frank. Goodbye, Miss Vivie.

VIVIE [*Shaking hands.*]   Goodbye. A pleasant trip.

PRAED   Thank you: thank you. I hope so.

FRANK [*To* MRS WARREN.]   Goodbye: youd ever so much better have taken my advice. [*He shakes hands with her. Then airily to* VIVIE] Byebye, Viv.

VIVIE   Goodbye. [*He goes out gaily without shaking hands with her.*]

PRAED [*Sadly.*]   Goodbye, Kitty.

MRS WARREN [*Sniveling.*]   —oobye!

> [PRAED *goes,* VIVIE, *composed and extremely grave, sits down in Honoria's chair, and waits for her mother to speak,* MRS WARREN, *dreading a pause, loses no time in beginning.*]

MRS WARREN   Well, Vivie, what did you go away like that for without saying a word to me? How could you do such a thing! And what have you done to poor George? I wanted him to come with me; but he shuffled out of it. I could see that he was quite afraid of you. Only fancy: he wanted me not to come. As if [*Trembling.*] I should be afraid of you, dearie, [VIVIE's *gravity deepens.*] But of course I told him it was all settled and comfortable between us, and that we were on the best of terms. [*She breaks down.*] Vivie: whats the meaning of this? [*She produces a commercial envelope, and fumbles at the enclosure with trembling fingers.*] I got it from the bank this morning.

VIVIE   It is my month's allowance. They sent it to me as usual the other day. I simply sent it back to be placed to your credit, and asked them to send you the lodgment receipt.[3] In future I shall support myself.

MRS WARREN [*Not daring to understand.*]   Wasnt it enough? Why didnt you tell me? [*With a cunning gleam in her eye.*] I'll double it: I was intending to double it. Only let me know how much you want.

VIVIE   You know very well that that has nothing to do with it. From this time I go my own way in my own business and among my own friends. And you will go yours. [*She rises.*] Goodbye.

MRS WARREN [*Rising, appalled.*]   Goodbye?

VIVIE   Yes: Goodbye. Come: dont let us make a useless scene: you understand perfectly well. Sir George Crofts has told me the whole business.

MRS WARREN [*Angrily.*]   Silly old—[*She swallows an epithet, and turns white at the narrowness of her escape from uttering it.*]

VIVIE   Just so.

MRS WARREN   He ought to have his tongue cut out. But I thought it was ended: you said you didnt mind.

VIVIE [*Steadfastly.*]   Excuse me: I d o mind.

MRS WARREN   But I explained—

VIVIE   You explained how it came about. You did not tell me that it is still going on. [*She sits.*]

> [MRS WARREN, *silenced for a moment, looks forlornly at* VIVIE, *who waits, secretly hoping that the combat is over. But the cunning expression comes back into* MRS WARREN's *face; and she bends across the table, sly and urgent, half whispering.*]

MRS WARREN   Vivie: do you know how rich I am?

VIVIE   I have no doubt you are very rich.

MRS WARREN   But you dont know all that that means: youre too young. It means a new dress every day; it means theatres and balls every night; it means having the pick of all the gentlemen in Europe at your feet; it means a lovely house and plenty of servants; it means the choicest of eating and drinking; it means everything you like, everything you want, everything you can think of. And what are you here? A mere drudge, toiling and moiling[4] early and late for your bare living and two cheap dresses a year. Think over it. [*Soothingly.*] Youre shocked, I know. I can enter into your feelings; and I think they do you credit; but trust me, nobody will blame you: you may take my word for that. I know what young girls are; and I know youll think better of it when youve turned it over in your mind.

---

3. Deposit slip.   4. Drudging.

VIVIE   So thats how it's done, is it? You must have said all that to many a woman, mother, to have it so pat.

MRS WARREN [*Passionately.*]   What harm am I asking you to do? [VIVIE *turns away contemptuously,* MRS WARREN *continues desperately.*] Vivie: listen to me: you dont understand: youve been taught wrong on purpose: you dont know what the world is really like.

VIVIE [*Arrested.*]   Taught wrong on purpose! What do you mean?

MRS WARREN   I mean that youre throwing away all your chances for nothing. You think that people are what they pretend to be: that the way you were taught at school and college to think right and proper is the way things really are. But it's not: it's all only a pretence, to keep the cowardly slavish common run of people quiet. Do you want to find that out, like other women, at forty, when youve thrown yourself away and lost your chances; or wont you take it in good time now from your own mother, that loves you and swears to you that it's truth: gospel truth? [*Urgently*] Vivie: the big people, the clever people, the managing people, all know it. They do as I do, and think what I think. I know plenty of them. I know them to speak to, to introduce you to, to make friends of for you. I dont mean anything wrong; thats what you dont understand: your head is full of ignorant ideas about me. What do the people that taught you know about life or about people like me? When did they ever meet me, or speak to me, or let anyone tell them about me? the fools! Would they ever have done anything for you if I hadnt paid them? Havnt I told you that I want you to be respectable? Havnt I brought you up to be respectable? And how can you keep it up without my money and my influence and Lizzie's friends? Cant you see that youre cutting your own throat as well as breaking my heart in turning your back on me?

VIVIE   I recognize the Crofts philosophy of life, mother. I heard it all from him that day at the Gardners'.

MRS WARREN   You think I want to force that played-out old sot on you! I dont, Vivie: on my oath I dont.

VIVIE   It would not matter if you did: you would not succeed, [MRS WARREN *winces, deeply hurt by the implied indifference towards her affectionate intention.* VIVIE, *neither understanding this nor concerning herself about it, goes on calmly.*]   Mother: you dont at all know the sort of person I am. I dont object to Crofts more than to any other coarsely built man of his class. To tell you the truth, I rather admire him for being strong-minded enough to enjoy himself in his own way and make plenty of money instead of living the usual shooting, hunting, dining-out, tailoring, loafing life of his set merely because all the rest do it. And I'm perfectly aware that if I'd been in the same circumstances as my aunt Liz, I'd have done exactly what she did. I dont think I'm more prejudiced or straitlaced than you: I think I'm less. I'm certain I'm less sentimental. I know very well that fashionable morality is all a pretence, and that if I took your money and devoted the rest of my life to spending it fashionably, I might be as worthless and vicious as the silliest woman could possibly want to be without having a word said to me about it. But I dont want to be worthless. I shouldnt enjoy trotting about the park to advertize my dressmaker and carriage builder, or being bored at the opera to shew off a shopwindowful of diamonds.

MRS WARREN [*Bewildered.*]   But—

VIVIE   Wait a moment: Ive not done. Tell me why you continue your business now that you are independent of it. Your sister, you told me, has left all that behind her. Why dont you do the same?

MRS WARREN   Oh, it's all very easy for Liz: she likes good society, and has the air of being a lady. Imagine me in a cathedral town! Why, the very rooks in the trees would find me out even if I could stand the dulness of it. I must have work and excitement, or I should go melancholy mad. And what else is there for me to do? The life suits me: I'm fit for it and not for anything else. If I didnt do it somebody else would; so I dont do any real harm by it. And then it brings in money; and I like making money. No; it's no use: I cant give it up—not for anybody. But what need you know about it? I'll never mention it. I'll keep Crofts away. I'll not trouble you much: you see I have to be constantly running about from one place to another. Youll be quit of me altogether when I die.

VIVIE   No: I am my mother's daughter. I am like you: I must have work, and must make more money than I spend. But my work is not your work, and my way not your way. We must part. It will not make much difference to us: instead of meeting one another for perhaps a few months in twenty years we shall never meet: thats all.

MRS WARREN [*Her voice stifled in tears.*]   Vivie: I meant to have been more with you: I did indeed.

VIVIE   It's no use, mother: I am not to be changed by a few cheap tears and entreaties any more than you are, I daresay.

MRS WARREN [*Wildly.*]   Oh, you call a mother's tears cheap.

VIVIE   They cost you nothing; and you ask me to give you the peace and quietness of my whole life in exchange for them. What use would my company be to you if you could get it? What have we two in common that could make either of us happy together?

MRS WARREN [*Lapsing recklessly into her dialect.*]   We're mother and daughter. I want my daughter. Ive a right to you. Who is to care for me when I'm old? Plenty of girls have taken to me like daughters and cried at leaving me; but I let them all go because I had you to look forward to. I kept myself lonely for you. Youve no right to turn on me now and refuse to do your duty as a daughter.

VIVIE [*Jarred and antagonized by the echo of the slums in her mother's voice.*]   My duty as a daughter! I thought we should come to that presently. Now once for all, mother, you want a daughter and Frank wants a wife. I dont want a mother; and I dont want a husband. I have spared neither Frank nor myself in sending him about his business. Do you think I will spare you?

MRS WARREN [*Violently.*]   Oh, I know the sort you are: no mercy for yourself or anyone else. *I* know. My experience has done that for me anyhow: I can tell the pious, canting, hard, selfish woman when I meet her. Well, keep yourself to yourself: I dont want you. But listen to this. Do you know what I would do with you if you were a baby again? aye, as sure as there's a Heaven above us.

VIVIE   Strangle me, perhaps.

MRS WARREN   No: I'd bring you up to be a real daughter to me, and not what you are now, with your pride and your prejudices and the college education you stole from me: yes, stole: deny it if you can: what was it but stealing? I'd bring you up in my own house, I would.

VIVIE [*Quietly.*]   In one of your own houses.

MRS WARREN [*Screaming.*]   Listen to her! listen to how she spits on her mother's grey hairs! Oh, may you live to have your own daughter tear and trample on you as you have trampled on me. And you will: you will. No woman ever had luck with a mother's curse on her.

VIVIE   I wish you wouldnt rant, mother. It only hardens me. Come: I suppose I am the only young woman you ever had in your power that you did good to. Dont spoil it all now.

MRS WARREN   Yes, Heaven forgive me, it's true; and you are the only one that ever turned on me. Oh, the injustice of it! the injustice! the injustice! I always wanted to be a good woman. I tried honest work; and I was slave-driven until I cursed the day I ever heard of honest work. I was a good mother; and because I made my daughter a good woman she turns me out as if I was a leper. Oh, if I only had my life to live over again! I'd talk to that lying clergyman in the school. From this time forth, so help me Heaven in my last hour, I'll do wrong and nothing but wrong. And I'll prosper on it.

VIVIE   Yes: it's better to choose your line and go through with it. If I had been you, mother, I might have done as you did; but I should not have lived one life and believed in another. You are a conventional woman at heart. That is why I am bidding you goodbye now. I am right, am I not?

MRS WARREN [*Taken aback.*]   Right to throw away all my money?

VIVIE   No: right to get rid of you? I should be a fool not to! Isnt that so?

MRS WARREN [*Sulkily.*]   Oh well, yes, if you come to that, I suppose you are. But Lord help the world if everybody took to doing the right thing! And now I'd better go than stay where I'm not wanted. [*She turns to the door.*]

VIVIE [*Kindly.*]   Wont you shake hands?

MRS WARREN [*After looking at her fiercely for a moment with a savage impulse to strike her.*]   No, thank you. Goodbye.

VIVIE [*Matter-of-factly.*]   Goodbye. [MRS WARREN *goes out, slamming the door behind her. The strain on* VIVIE's *face relaxes; her grave expression breaks up into one of joyous content; her breath goes out in a half sob, half laugh of intense relief. She goes buoyantly to her place at the writing-table; pushes the electric lamp out of the way; pulls over a great sheaf of papers; and is in the act of dipping her pen in the ink when she finds* FRANK's *note. She opens it unconcernedly and reads it quickly, giving a little laugh at some quaint turn of expression in it.*] And goodbye, Frank. [*She tears the note up and tosses the pieces into the wastepaper basket without a second thought. Then she goes at her work with a plunge, and soon becomes absorbed in its figures.*]

1893   1898

SIR ARTHUR CONAN DOYLE

1859–1930

O ne of ten children, Arthur Conan Doyle was born in Edinburgh on May 22, 1859, to parents of Irish descent. His father, Charles Altamont Doyle, worked as a civil servant but wished to be an artist; subject to depression and alcoholism for many years, he was eventually committed to an asylum in the 1880s. Despite the family's difficult circumstances, Conan Doyle's mother, Mary Foley, supported her son's passionate interest in reading and managed to send him at the age of nine to the preparatory school for the Roman Catholic Stonyhurst College, Britain's foremost Jesuit school. By the time Conan Doyle left Stonyhurst at the age of sixteen, however, he had rejected Christianity and become an agnostic.

From 1876 Conan Doyle studied medicine at the University of Edinburgh, where one of his teachers was Joseph Bell, a professor of clinical surgery. As Conan Doyle readily acknowledged in later years, Sherlock Holmes was modeled in part on Bell, who was remarkably skilled at deducing from minute physical details both his patients' ailments and their past histories and occupations. During this period Conan Doyle's medical training ran hand in hand with early forays into literary composition; he published his first story in *Chambers's Edinburgh Journal* at the age of twenty. After serving as ship's doctor on a voyage to West Africa, Conan Doyle established a medical practice in Southsea on the south coast of England in 1882. Here, with much time on his hands thanks to a dearth of patients, he began writing the detective stories that would make him famous. Sherlock Holmes's debut occurred in the novella *A Study in Scarlet*, which appeared in *Beeton's Christmas Annual* in 1887 and carried illustrations by Conan Doyle's father. After the publication of a second Holmes novella, *The Sign of Four*, a series of short stories titled "The Adventures of Sherlock Holmes" ran in *The Strand Magazine* from July 1891.

Published in the February issue of 1892 with illustrations by Sidney Paget, "The Adventure of the Speckled Band" was the eighth of the series. While the menace of the story is supplied by the violent and sinister Dr. Roylott and his web of exotic connections, the central puzzle is presented in its title: "The speckled band!" were the dying words of Roylott's stepdaughter Julia Stoner, the sister of Holmes's client, but to what had she been referring? During its composition Doyle referred to the story as a "thriller"; in later years, when asked which of his tales was his favorite, he chose this one. Many fans have agreed; readers' polls over the years have frequently rated "The Speckled Band" the best Holmes story of all. Certainly it is viewed as a paradigmatic example of a "locked room" mystery, a subdivision of the detective story genre in which a murder takes place in a closed space with either no, or a very limited set of, suspects.

Despite the enormous success of the series, Conan Doyle resented the fact that it drew his time and energies away from writing what he considered to be more serious work, such as historical fiction. He decided to kill Sherlock off because, as he explained to his mother in 1891, the detective took his mind "from better things"; at the same time Conan Doyle lamented that "it means I must bury my pocketbook with him." "The Final Problem," a story published in 1893, appeared to present readers with the fatal plunge of both their hero and his evil adversary Professor Moriarty over the Reichenbach Falls in Switzerland; Watson tracks their two sets of footprints heading to the cliff above the waterfall and discovers evidence of a violent struggle, but can find no signs of any return. Fans were outraged—"You brute" began one letter to the author—and after pressure from his publishers, Conan Doyle caved, producing first *The Hound of the Baskervilles* in 1901, which he cannily set before Holmes's death, and then later "resurrecting" his detective in 1903 in "The Empty House." In this story Watson learns the "truth" of that apparent Swiss death: Holmes had in fact hidden on a ledge within the cliff to escape the vengeance of Moriarty's henchman. Eventually the Sherlock Holmes canon encompassed fifty-six stories and four novellas. Of Conan Doyle's other writings only the Professor Challenger series (which includes *The Lost World* of 1912) enjoyed any real success; none of his historical novels ever captured the public's imagination like the two famous residents of 221b Baker Street.

Conan Doyle married in 1885; his wife, Louisa "Touie" Hawkins, died from tuberculosis in 1906. During her illness he developed an allegedly platonic relationship with Jean Leckie, whom he married in 1907; Conan Doyle had two children with his first wife and three with his second. Following the death of Touie, and the deaths of his son, brother, two brothers-in-law, and two nephews in and after World War I, Conan Doyle found considerable comfort in Christian Spiritualism, an occult religion that believed that contact could be made with the dead. The author's interest in the paranormal also manifested itself in other ways; it led, for instance, to his advocating in 1920 for the authenticity of a series of photographs of girls and fairies (the "Cottingley Fairies" were exposed as a hoax decades later) and dominated many of his later, nonfiction, writings. In earlier years Conan Doyle had participated in some of his country's important political and legal debates. His pamphlets on the Anglo-Boer War of 1899–1902 justified British military actions and led to his being knighted in 1902. Furthermore, his involvement in the George Edalji case—a miscarriage of justice in which a half-Indian man was wrongfully convicted of a crime—played an influential part in the establishment of the Court of Criminal Appeal in 1907. Conan Doyle died on July 7, 1930, and is buried in Hampshire.

The Speckled Band

In glancing over my notes of the seventy odd cases in which I have during the last eight years studied the methods of my friend Sherlock Holmes, I find many tragic, some comic, a large number merely strange, but none commonplace; for, working as he did rather for the love of his art than for the acquirement of wealth, he refused to associate himself with any investigation which did not tend towards the unusual, and even the fantastic.[1] Of all these varied cases, however, I cannot recall any which presented more singular features than that which was associated with the well-known Surrey family of the Roylotts of Stoke Moran.[2] The events in question occurred in the early days of my association with Holmes, when we were sharing rooms as bachelors, in Baker-street.[3] It is possible that I might have placed them upon record before, but a promise of secrecy was made at the time, from which I have only been freed during the last month by the untimely death of the lady to whom the pledge was given. It is perhaps as well that the facts should now come to light, for I have reasons to know there are widespread rumours as to the death of Dr. Grimesby Roylott which tend to make the matter even more terrible than the truth.

It was early in April, in the year '83, that I woke one morning to find Sherlock Holmes standing, fully dressed, by the side of my bed. He was a

1. So extreme as to challenge belief; incredible.
2. A fictitious location. Surrey is a county southeast of London.
3. Street in central London.

late riser as a rule, and, as the clock on the mantel-piece showed me that it was only a quarter past seven, I blinked up at him in some surprise, and perhaps just a little resentment, for I was myself regular in my habits.

"Very sorry to knock you up,[4] Watson," said he, "but it's the common lot this morning. Mrs. Hudson has been knocked up, she retorted upon me, and I on you."

"What is it, then? A fire?"

"No, a client. It seems that a young lady has arrived in a considerable state of excitement, who insists upon seeing me. She is waiting now in the sitting-room. Now, when young ladies wander about the Metropolis at this hour of the morning, and knock sleepy people up out of their beds, I presume that it is something very pressing which they have to communicate. Should it prove to be an interesting case, you would, I am sure, wish to follow it from the outset. I thought at any rate that I should call you, and give you the chance."

"My dear fellow, I would not miss it for anything."

I had no keener pleasure than in following Holmes in his professional investigations, and in admiring the rapid deductions, as swift as intuitions, and yet always founded on a logical basis, with which he unravelled the problems which were submitted to him. I rapidly threw on my clothes, and was ready in a few minutes to accompany my friend down to the sitting-room. A lady dressed in black and heavily veiled, who had been sitting in the window, rose as we entered.

"Good morning, madam," said Holmes, cheerily. "My name is Sherlock Holmes. This is my intimate friend and associate, Dr. Watson, before whom you can speak as freely as before myself. Ha, I am glad to see that Mrs. Hudson has had the good sense to light the fire. Pray draw up to it, and I shall order you a cup of hot coffee, for I observe that you are shivering."

"It is not cold which makes me shiver," said the woman in a low voice, changing her seat as requested.

"What then?"

"It is fear, Mr. Holmes. It is terror." She raised her veil as she spoke, and we could see that she was indeed in a pitiable state of agitation, her face all drawn and grey, with restless, frightened eyes, like those of some hunted animal. Her features and figure were those of a woman of thirty, but her hair was shot with premature grey, and her expression was weary and haggard. Sherlock Holmes ran her over with one of his quick, all-comprehensive glances.

"You must not fear," said he, soothingly, bending forward and patting her forearm. "We shall soon set matters right, I have no doubt. You have come in by train this morning, I see."

"You know me, then?"

"No, but I observe the second half of a return ticket in the palm of your left glove. You must have started early, and yet you had a good drive in a dog-cart,[5] along heavy roads, before you reached the station."

The lady gave a violent start, and stared in bewilderment at my companion.

"There is no mystery, my dear madam," said he, smiling. "The left arm of your jacket is spattered with mud in no less than seven places. The marks

4. I.e., wake you up by knocking.
5. A horse-drawn cart with seats, originally designed to carry hunters and their hunting dogs.

are perfectly fresh. There is no vehicle save a dog-cart which throws up mud in that way, and then only when you sit on the left-hand side of the driver."

"Whatever your reasons[6] may be, you are perfectly correct," said she. "I started from home before six, reached Leatherhead at twenty past, and came in by the first train to Waterloo.[7] Sir, I can stand this strain no longer, I shall go mad if it continues. I have no one to turn to—none, save only one, who cares for me, and he, poor fellow, can be of little aid. I have heard of you, Mr. Holmes; I have heard of you from Mrs. Farintosh, whom you helped in the hour of her sore need. It was from her that I had your address. Oh, sir, do you not think you could help me too, and at least throw a little light through the dense darkness which surrounds me? At present it is out of my power to reward you for your services, but in a month or two I shall be married, with the control of my own income, and then at least you shall not find me ungrateful."

Holmes turned to his desk, and unlocking it, drew out a small case-book which he consulted.

"Farintosh," said he. "Ah, yes, I recall the case; it was concerned with an opal tiara. I think it was before your time, Watson. I can only say, madam, that I shall be happy to devote the same care to your case as I did to that of your friend. As to reward, my profession is its reward; but you are at liberty to defray whatever expenses I may be put to, at the time which suits you best. And now I beg that you will lay before us everything that may help us in forming an opinion upon the matter."

"Alas!" replied our visitor. "The very horror of my situation lies in the fact that my fears are so vague, and my suspicions depend so entirely upon small points, which might seem trivial to another, that even he to whom of all others I have a right to look for help and advice looks upon all that I tell him about it as the fancies of a nervous woman. He does not say so, but I can read it from his soothing answers and averted eyes. But I have heard, Mr. Holmes, that you can see deeply into the manifold wickedness of the human heart. You may advise me how to walk amid the dangers which encompass me."

"I am all attention, madam."

"My name is Helen Stoner, and I am living with my stepfather, who is the last survivor of one of the oldest Saxon families in England, the Roylotts of Stoke Moran, on the western border of Surrey."

Holmes nodded his head. "The name is familiar to me," said he.

"The family was at one time among the richest in England, and the estate extended over the borders into Berkshire in the north, and Hampshire in the west. In the last century, however, four successive heirs were of a dissolute and wasteful disposition, and the family ruin was eventually completed by a gambler, in the days of the Regency.[8] Nothing was left save a few acres of ground, and the two-hundred-year-old house, which is itself crushed under a heavy mortgage. The last squire dragged out his existence there, living the horrible life of an aristocratic pauper; but his only son, my stepfather, seeing that he must adapt himself to the new conditions, obtained an advance from a relative, which enabled him to take a medical

---

6. Reasoning.
7. London railway station. Leatherhead is a town in Surrey.

8. From 1811 to 1820, the period when the son of George III functioned as ruler (Prince Regent) because of his father's insanity.

degree, and went out to Calcutta,[9] where, by his professional skill and his force of character, he established a large practice. In a fit of anger, however, caused by some robberies which had been perpetrated in the house, he beat his native butler to death, and narrowly escaped a capital sentence. As it was, he suffered a long term of imprisonment, and afterwards returned to England a morose and disappointed man.

"When Dr. Roylott was in India he married my mother, Mrs. Stoner, the young widow of Major-General Stoner, of the Bengal Artillery. My sister Julia and I were twins, and we were only two years old at the time of my mother's re-marriage. She had a considerable sum of money, not less than a thousand a year, and this she bequeathed to Dr. Roylott entirely whilst we resided with him, with a provision that a certain annual sum should be allowed to each of us in the event of our marriage. Shortly after our return to England my mother died—she was killed eight years ago in a railway accident near Crewe.[1] Dr. Roylott then abandoned his attempts to establish himself in practice in London, and took us to live with him in the old ancestral house at Stoke Moran. The money which my mother had left was enough for all our wants, and there seemed no obstacle to our happiness.

"But a terrible change came over our stepfather about this time. Instead of making friends and exchanging visits with our neighbours, who had at first been overjoyed to see a Roylott of Stoke Moran back in the old family seat, he shut himself up in his house, and seldom came out save to indulge in ferocious quarrels with whoever might cross his path. Violence of temper approaching to mania has been hereditary in the men of the family, and in my stepfather's case it had, I believe, been intensified by his long residence in the tropics. A series of disgraceful brawls took place, two of which ended in the police-court, until at last he became the terror of the village, and the folks would fly at his approach, for he is a man of immense strength, and absolutely uncontrollable in his anger.

"Last week he hurled the local blacksmith over a parapet[2] into a stream, and it was only by paying over all the money that I could gather together that I was able to avert another public exposure. He had no friends at all save the wandering gipsies, and he would give these vagabonds leave to encamp upon the few acres of bramble-covered land which represent the family estate, and would accept in return the hospitality of their tents, wandering away with them sometimes for weeks on end. He has a passion also for Indian animals, which are sent over to him by a correspondent, and he has at this moment a cheetah and a baboon, which wander freely over his grounds, and are feared by the villagers almost as much as their master.

"You can imagine from what I say that my poor sister Julia and I had no great pleasure in our lives. No servant would stay with us, and for a long time we did all the work of the house. She was but thirty at the time of her death, and yet her hair had already begun to whiten, even as mine has."

"Your sister is dead, then?"

"She died just two years ago, and it is of her death that I wish to speak to you. You can understand that, living the life which I have described, we were little likely to see any one of our own age and position. We had, however, an

9. Major city (now Kolkata) in eastern India.   2. Low wall.
1. Town in northwest England.

aunt, my mother's maiden sister, Miss Honoria Westphail, who lives near Harrow,[3] and we were occasionally allowed to pay short visits at this lady's house. Julia went there at Christmas two years ago, and met there a half-pay Major of Marines,[4] to whom she became engaged. My stepfather learned of the engagement when my sister returned, and offered no objection to the marriage; but within a fortnight of the day which had been fixed for the wedding, the terrible event occurred which has deprived me of my only companion."

Sherlock Holmes had been leaning back in his chair with his eyes closed, and his head sunk in a cushion, but he half opened his lids now, and glanced across at his visitor.

"Pray be precise as to details," said he.

"It is easy for me to be so, for every event of that dreadful time is seared into my memory. The manor house is, as I have already said, very old, and only one wing is now inhabited. The bedrooms in this wing are on the ground floor, the sitting-rooms being in the central block of the buildings. Of these bedrooms the first is Dr. Roylott's, the second my sister's, and the third my own. There is no communication between them, but they all open out into the same corridor. Do I make myself plain?"

"Perfectly so."

"The windows of the three rooms open out upon the lawn. That fatal night Dr. Roylott had gone to his room early, though we knew that he had not retired to rest, for my sister was troubled by the smell of the strong Indian cigars which it was his custom to smoke. She left her room, therefore, and came into mine, where she sat for some time, chatting about her approaching wedding. At eleven o'clock she rose to leave me, but she paused at the door and looked back.

"'Tell me, Helen,' said she, 'have you ever heard any one whistle in the dead of the night?'

"'Never,' said I.

"'I suppose that you could not possibly whistle yourself in your sleep?'

"'Certainly not. But why?'

"'Because during the last few nights I have always, about three in the morning, heard a low clear whistle. I am a light sleeper, and it has awakened me. I cannot tell where it came from—perhaps from the next room, perhaps from the lawn. I thought that I would just ask you whether you had heard it.'

"'No, I have not. It must be those wretched gipsies in the plantation.'

"'Very likely. And yet if it were on the lawn I wonder that you did not hear it also.'

"'Ah, but I sleep more heavily than you.'

"'Well, it is of no great consequence at any rate,' she smiled back at me, closed my door, and a few moments later I heard her key turn in the lock."

"Indeed," said Holmes. "Was it your custom always to lock yourselves in at night?"

"Always."

"And why?"

"I think that I mentioned to you that the Doctor kept a cheetah and a baboon. We had no feeling of security unless our doors were locked."

3. Small town ten miles northwest of London.
4. Officer in the British military receiving reduced pay because not on active service.

"Quite so. Pray proceed with your statement."

"I could not sleep that night. A vague feeling of impending misfortune impressed me. My sister and I, you will recollect, were twins, and you know how subtle are the links which bind two souls which are so closely allied. It was a wild night. The wind was howling outside, and the rain was beating and splashing against the windows. Suddenly, amidst all the hubbub of the gale, there burst forth the wild scream of a terrified woman. I knew that it was my sister's voice. I sprang from my bed, wrapped a shawl round me, and rushed into the corridor. As I opened my door I seemed to hear a low whistle, such as my sister described, and a few moments later a clanging sound, as if a mass of metal had fallen. As I ran down the passage my sister's door was unlocked, and revolved slowly upon its hinges. I stared at it horror-stricken, not knowing what was about to issue from it. By the light of the corridor lamp I saw my sister appear at the opening, her face blanched with terror, her hands groping for help, her whole figure swaying to and fro like that of a drunkard. I ran to her and threw my arms round her, but at that moment her knees seemed to give way and she fell to the ground. She writhed as one who is in terrible pain, and her limbs were dreadfully convulsed. At first I thought that she had not recognised me, but as I bent over her she suddenly shrieked out in a voice which I shall never forget, 'Oh, my God! Helen! It was the band! The speckled band!' There was something else which she would fain have said, and she stabbed with her finger into the air in the direction of the Doctor's room, but a fresh convulsion seized her and choked her words. I rushed out, calling loudly for my stepfather, and I met him hastening from his room in his dressing-gown. When he reached my sister's side she was unconscious, and though he poured brandy down her throat, and sent for medical aid from the village, all efforts were in vain, for she slowly sank and died without having recovered her consciousness. Such was the dreadful end of my beloved sister."

"One moment," said Holmes; "are you sure about this whistle and metallic sound? Could you swear to it?"

"That was what the county coroner asked me at the inquiry. It is my strong impression that I heard it, and yet among the crash of the gale, and the creaking of an old house, I may possibly have been deceived."

"Was your sister dressed?"

"No, she was in her nightdress. In her right hand was found the charred stump of a match, and in her left a matchbox."

"Showing that she had struck a light and looked about her when the alarm took place. That is important. And what conclusions did the coroner come to?"

"He investigated the case with great care, for Dr. Roylott's conduct had long been notorious in the county, but he was unable to find any satisfactory cause of death. My evidence showed that the door had been fastened upon the inner side, and the windows were blocked by old-fashioned shutters with broad iron bars, which were secured every night. The walls were carefully sounded, and were shown to be quite solid all round, and the flooring was also thoroughly examined, with the same result. The chimney is wide, but is barred up by four large staples. It is certain, therefore, that my sister was quite alone when she met her end. Besides, there were no marks of any violence upon her."

"How about poison?"

"The doctors examined her for it, but without success."

"What do you think that this unfortunate lady died of, then?"

"It is my belief that she died of pure fear and nervous shock, though what it was which frightened her I cannot imagine."

"Were there gipsies in the plantation at the time?"

"Yes, there are nearly always some there."

"Ah, and what did you gather from this allusion to a band—a speckled band?"

"Sometimes I have thought that it was merely the wild talk of delirium, sometimes that it may have referred to some band of people, perhaps to these very gipsies in the plantation. I do not know whether the spotted handkerchiefs which so many of them wear over their heads might have suggested the strange adjective which she used."

Holmes shook his head like a man who is far from being satisfied.

"These are very deep waters," said he; "pray go on with your narrative."

"Two years have passed since then, and my life has been until lately lonelier than ever. A month ago, however, a dear friend, whom I have known for many years, has done me the honour to ask my hand in marriage. His name is Armitage—Percy Armitage—the second son of Mr. Armitage, of Crane Water, near Reading.[5] My stepfather has offered no opposition to the match, and we are to be married in the course of the spring. Two days ago some repairs were started in the west wing of the building, and my bedroom wall has been pierced, so that I have had to move into the chamber in which my sister died, and to sleep in the very bed in which she slept. Imagine, then, my thrill of terror when last night, as I lay awake, thinking over her terrible fate, I suddenly heard in the silence of the night the low whistle which had been the herald of her own death. I sprang up and lit the lamp, but nothing was to be seen in the room. I was too shaken to go to bed again, however, so I dressed, and as soon as it was daylight I slipped down, got a dog-cart at the 'Crown' inn, which is opposite, and drove to Leatherhead, from whence I have come on this morning with the one object of seeing you and asking your advice."

"You have done wisely," said my friend. "But have you told me all?"

"Yes, all."

"Miss Roylott, you have not. You are screening your stepfather."

"Why, what do you mean?"

For answer Holmes pushed back the frill of black lace which fringed the hand that lay upon our visitor's knee. Five little livid spots, the marks of four fingers and a thumb, were printed upon the white wrist.

"You have been cruelly used," said Holmes.

The lady coloured deeply, and covered over her injured wrist. "He is a hard man," she said, "and perhaps he hardly knows his own strength."

There was a long silence, during which Holmes leaned his chin upon his hands and stared into the crackling fire.

"This is very deep business," he said at last. "There are a thousand details which I should desire to know before I decide upon our course of action. Yet we have not a moment to lose. If we were to come to Stoke

5. Large town west of London.

Moran to-day, would it be possible for us to see over these rooms without the knowledge of your stepfather?"

"As it happens, he spoke of coming into town to-day upon some most important business. It is probable that he will be away all day, and that there would be nothing to disturb you. We have a housekeeper now, but she is old and foolish, and I could easily get her out of the way."

"Excellent. You are not averse to this trip, Watson?"

"By no means."

"Then we shall both come. What are you going to do yourself?"

"I have one or two things which I would wish to do now that I am in town. But I shall return by the twelve o'clock train, so as to be there in time for your coming."

"And you may expect us early in the afternoon. I have myself some small business matters to attend to. Will you not wait and breakfast?"

"No, I must go. My heart is lightened already since I have confided my trouble to you. I shall look forward to seeing you again this afternoon." She dropped her thick black veil over her face, and glided from the room.

"And what do you think of it all, Watson?" asked Sherlock Holmes, leaning back in his chair.

"It seems to me to be a most dark and sinister business."

"Dark enough, and sinister enough."

"Yet if the lady is correct in saying that the flooring and walls are sound, and that the door, window, and chimney are impassable, then her sister must have been undoubtedly alone when she met her mysterious end."

"What becomes, then, of these nocturnal whistles, and what of the very peculiar words of the dying woman?"

"I cannot think."

"When you combine the ideas of whistles at night, the presence of a band of gipsies who are on intimate terms with this old doctor, the fact that we have every reason to believe that the doctor has an interest in preventing his stepdaughter's marriage, the dying allusion to a band, and finally, the fact that Miss Helen Stoner heard a metallic clang, which might have been caused by one of those metal bars which secured the shutters falling back into their place, I think that there is good ground to think that the mystery may be cleared along those lines."

"But what, then, did the gipsies do?"

"I cannot imagine."

"I see many objections to any such theory."

"And so do I. It is precisely for that reason that we are going to Stoke Moran this day. I want to see whether the objections are fatal, or if they may be explained away. But what, in the name of the devil!"

The ejaculation had been drawn from my companion by the fact that our door had been suddenly dashed open, and that a huge man framed himself in the aperture. His costume was a peculiar mixture of the professional and of the agricultural, having a black top hat, a long frock coat, and a pair of high gaiters,[6] with a hunting-crop swinging in his hand. So tall was he that his hat actually brushed the cross bar of the doorway, and his breadth seemed to span it across from side to side. A large face, seared with a thou-

---

6. Cloth or leather leggings.

sand wrinkles, burned yellow with the sun, and marked with every evil passion, was turned from one to the other of us, while his deep-set, bile-shot eyes, and his high thin fleshless nose, gave him somewhat the resemblance to a fierce old bird of prey.

"Which of you is Holmes?" asked this apparition.

"My name, sir, but you have the advantage of me," said my companion, quietly.

"I am Dr. Grimesby Roylott, of Stoke Moran."

"Indeed, Doctor," said Holmes, blandly. "Pray take a seat."

"I will do nothing of the kind. My stepdaughter has been here. I have traced her. What has she been saying to you?"

"It is a little cold for the time of the year," said Holmes.

"What has she been saying to you?" screamed the old man furiously.

"But I have heard that the crocuses promise well," continued my companion imperturbably.

"Ha! You put me off, do you?" said our new visitor, taking a step forward, and shaking his hunting-crop. "I know you, you scoundrel! I have heard of you before. You are Holmes the meddler."

My friend smiled.

"Holmes the busybody!"

His smile broadened.

"Holmes the Scotland-yard Jack-in-office."[7]

Holmes chuckled heartily. "Your conversation is most entertaining," said he. "When you go out close the door, for there is a decided draught."

"I will go when I have had my say. Don't you dare to meddle with my affairs. I know that Miss Stoner has been here—I traced her! I am a dangerous man to fall foul of! See here." He stepped swiftly forward, seized the poker, and bent it into a curve with his huge brown hands.

"See that you keep yourself out of my grip," he snarled, and hurling the twisted poker into the fireplace, he strode out of the room.

"He seems a very amiable person," said Holmes, laughing. "I am not quite so bulky, but if he had remained I might have shown him that my grip was not much more feeble than his own." As he spoke he picked up the steel poker, and with a sudden effort straightened it out again.

"Fancy his having the insolence to confound me with the official detective force! This incident gives zest to our investigation, however, and I only trust that our little friend will not suffer from her imprudence in allowing this brute to trace her. And now, Watson, we shall order breakfast, and afterwards I shall walk down to Doctors' Commons,[8] where I hope to get some data which may help us in this matter."

It was nearly one o'clock when Sherlock Holmes returned from his excursion. He held in his hand a sheet of blue paper, scrawled over with notes and figures.

"I have seen the will of the deceased wife," said he. "To determine its exact meaning I have been obliged to work out the present prices of the investments

7. Self-important official. Scotland Yard is the police headquarters in London.
8. Informal name of London civil-law establishment located near St. Paul's Cathedral that had in earlier times handled the registration of marriage licences, wills, and other legal documents. Copies of wills were at this time held at Somerset House on the Strand.

with which it is concerned. The total income, which at the time of the wife's death was little short of £1,100, is now through the fall in agricultural prices not more than £750. Each daughter can claim an income of £250, in case of marriage. It is evident, therefore, that if both girls had married this beauty would have had a mere pittance, while even one of them would cripple him to a very serious extent. My morning's work has not been wasted, since it has proved that he has the very strongest motives for standing in the way of anything of the sort. And now, Watson, this is too serious for dawdling, especially as the old man is aware that we are interesting ourselves in his affairs, so if you are ready we shall call a cab and drive to Waterloo. I should be very much obliged if you would slip your revolver into your pocket. An Eley's No. 2[9] is an excellent argument with gentlemen who can twist steel pokers into knots. That and a tooth-brush are, I think, all that we need."

At Waterloo we were fortunate in catching a train for Leatherhead, where we hired a trap[1] at the station inn, and drove for four or five miles through the lovely Surrey lanes. It was a perfect day, with a bright sun and a few fleecy clouds in the heavens. The trees and wayside hedges were just throwing out their first green shoots, and the air was full of the pleasant smell of the moist earth. To me at least there was a strange contrast between the sweet promise of the spring and this sinister quest upon which we were engaged. My companion sat in front of the trap, his arms folded, his hat pulled down over his eyes, and his chin sunk upon his breast, buried in the deepest thought. Suddenly, however, he started, tapped me on the shoulder, and pointed over the meadows.

"Look there!" said he.

A heavily-timbered park stretched up in a gentle slope, thickening into a grove at the highest point. From amidst the branches there jutted out the grey gables and high roof-tree[2] of a very old mansion.

"Stoke Moran?" said he.

"Yes, sir, that be the house of Dr. Grimesby Roylott," remarked the driver.

"There is some building going on there," said Holmes; "that is where we are going."

"There's the village," said the driver, pointing to a cluster of roofs some distance to the left; "but if you want to get to the house, you'll find it shorter to get over this stile,[3] and so by the footpath over the fields. There it is, where the lady is walking."

"And the lady, I fancy, is Miss Stoner," observed Holmes, shading his eyes. "Yes, I think we had better do as you suggest."

We got off, paid our fare, and the trap rattled back on its way to Leatherhead.

"I thought it as well," said Holmes, as we climbed the stile, "that this fellow should think we had come here as architects, or on some definite business. It may stop his gossip. Good afternoon, Miss Stoner. You see that we have been as good as our word."

Our client of the morning had hurried forward to meet us with a face which spoke her joy. "I have been waiting so eagerly for you," she cried,

9. A small powerful revolver (Conan Doyle most likely meant the Webley No. 2, a pistol that fired cartridges manufactured by Eley).
1. A small two-wheeled carriage.

2. Horizontal beam in a roof that supports the upper ends of the rafters.
3. A step or set of steps for climbing over a fence or wall.

shaking hands with us warmly. "All has turned out splendidly. Dr. Roylott has gone to town, and it is unlikely that he will be back before evening."

"We have had the pleasure of making the doctor's acquaintance," said Holmes, and in a few words he sketched out what had occurred. Miss Stoner turned white to the lips as she listened.

"Good heavens!" she cried, "he has followed me, then."

"So it appears."

"He is so cunning that I never know when I am safe from him. What will he say when he returns?"

"He must guard himself, for he may find that there is some one more cunning than himself upon his track. You must lock yourself up from him to-night. If he is violent, we shall take you away to your aunt's at Harrow. Now, we must make the best use of our time, so kindly take us at once to the rooms which we are to examine."

The building was of grey, lichen-blotched stone, with a high central portion, and two curving wings, like the claws of a crab, thrown out on each side. In one of these wings the windows were broken, and blocked with wooden boards, while the roof was partly caved in, a picture of ruin. The central portion was in little better repair, but the right-hand block was comparatively modern, and the blinds in the windows, with the blue smoke curling up from the chimneys, showed that this was where the family resided. Some scaffolding had been erected against the end wall, and the stonework had been broken into, but there were no signs of any workmen at the moment of our visit. Holmes walked slowly up and down the ill-trimmed lawn, and examined with deep attention the outsides of the windows.

"This, I take it, belongs to the room in which you used to sleep, the centre one to your sister's, and the one next to the main building to Dr. Roylott's chamber?"

"Exactly so. But I am now sleeping in the middle one."

"Pending the alterations, as I understand. By the way, there does not seem to be any very pressing need for repairs at that end wall."

"There were none. I believe that it was an excuse to move me from my room."

"Ah! that is suggestive. Now, on the other side of this narrow wing runs the corridor from which these three rooms open. There are windows in it, of course?"

"Yes, but very small ones. Too narrow for any one to pass through."

"As you both locked your doors at night your rooms were unapproachable from that side. Now, would you have the kindness to go into your room, and to bar your shutters."

Miss Stoner did so, and Holmes, after a careful examination through the open window, endeavoured in every way to force the shutter open, but without success. There was no slit through which a knife could be passed to raise the bar. Then with his lens[4] he tested the hinges, but they were of solid iron, built firmly into the massive masonry. "Hum!" said he, scratching his chin in some perplexity, "my theory certainly presents some difficulties. No one could pass these shutters if they were bolted. Well, we shall see if the inside throws any light upon the matter."

4. Magnifying glass.

A small side-door led into the whitewashed corridor from which the three bedrooms opened. Holmes refused to examine the third chamber, so we passed at once to the second, that in which Miss Stoner was now sleeping, and in which her sister, had met her fate. It was a homely[5] little room, with a low ceiling and a gaping fireplace, after the fashion of old country houses. A brown chest of drawers stood in one corner, a narrow white-counterpaned bed in another, and a dressing-table on the left-hand side of the window. These articles, with two small wickerwork chairs, made up all the furniture in the room, save for a square of Wilton carpet[6] in the centre. The boards round and the panelling of the walls were brown, worm-eaten oak, so old and discoloured that it may have dated from the original building of the house. Holmes drew one of the chairs into a corner and sat silent, while his eyes travelled round and round and up and down, taking in every detail of the apartment.

"Where does that bell communicate with?" he asked at last, pointing to a thick bell-rope which hung down beside the bed, the tassel actually lying upon the pillow.

"It goes to the housekeeper's room."

"It looks newer than the other things?"

"Yes, it was only put there a couple of years ago."

"Your sister asked for it, I suppose?"

"No, I never heard of her using it. We used always to get what we wanted for ourselves."

"Indeed, it seemed unnecessary to put so nice a bell-pull there. You will excuse me for a few minutes while I satisfy myself as to this floor." He threw himself down upon his face with his lens in his hand, and crawled swiftly backwards and forwards, examining minutely the cracks between the boards. Then he did the same with the woodwork with which the chamber was panelled. Finally he walked over to the bed and spent some time in staring at it, and in running his eye up and down the wall. Finally he took the bell-rope in his hand and gave it a brisk tug.

"Why, it's a dummy," said he.

"Won't it ring?"

"No, it is not even attached to a wire. This is very interesting. You can see now that it is fastened to a hook just above where the little opening of the ventilator is."

"How very absurd! I never noticed that before."

"Very strange!" muttered Holmes, pulling at the rope. "There are one or two very singular points about this room. For example, what a fool a builder must be to open a ventilator into another room, when, with the same trouble, he might have communicated with the outside air!"

"That is also quite modern," said the lady.

"Done about the same time as the bell-rope," remarked Holmes.

"Yes, there were several little changes carried out about that time."

"They seem to have been of a most interesting character—dummy bell-ropes, and ventilators which do not ventilate. With your permission, Miss Stoner, we shall now carry our researches into the inner apartment."

Dr. Grimesby Roylott's chamber was larger than that of his stepdaughter, but was as plainly furnished. A camp bed, a small wooden shelf full of

5. Simple, cozy.   6. A good-quality, cut-pile carpet.

books, mostly of a technical character, an armchair beside the bed, a plain wooden chair against the wall, a round table, and a large iron safe were the principal things which met the eye. Holmes walked slowly round and examined each and all of them with the keenest interest.

"What's in here?" he asked, tapping the safe.

"My stepfather's business papers."

"Oh! you have seen inside, then?"

"Only once, some years ago. I remember that it was full of papers."

"There isn't a cat in it, for example?"

"No. What a strange idea!"

"Well, look at this!" He took up a small saucer of milk which stood on the top of it.

"No; we don't keep a cat. But there is a cheetah and a baboon."

"Ah, yes, of course! Well, a cheetah is just a big cat, and yet a saucer of milk does not go very far in satisfying its wants, I daresay. There is one point which I should wish to determine." He squatted down in front of the wooden chair, and examined the seat of it with the greatest attention.

"Thank you. That is quite settled," said he, rising and putting his lens in his pocket. "Hullo! here is something interesting!"

The object which had caught his eye was a small dog lash[7] hung on one corner of the bed. The lash, however, was curled upon itself, and tied so as to make a loop of whipcord.

"What do you make of that, Watson?"

"It's a common enough lash. But I don't know why it should be tied."

"That is not quite so common, is it? Ah, me! it's a wicked world, and when a clever man turns his brains to crime it is the worst of all. I think that I have seen enough now, Miss Stoner, and, with your permission, we shall walk out upon the lawn."

I had never seen my friend's face so grim, or his brow so dark, as it was when we turned from the scene of this investigation. We had walked several times up and down the lawn, neither Miss Stoner nor myself liking to break in upon his thoughts before he roused himself from his reverie.

"It is very essential, Miss Stoner," said he, "that you should absolutely follow my advice in every respect."

"I shall most certainly do so."

"The matter is too serious for any hesitation. Your life may depend upon your compliance."

"I assure you that I am in your hands."

"In the first place, both my friend and I must spend the night in your room."

Both Miss Stoner and I gazed at him in astonishment.

"Yes, it must be so. Let me explain. I believe that that is the village inn over there?"

"Yes, that is the 'Crown.'"

"Very good. Your windows would be visible from there?"

"Certainly."

"You must confine yourself to your room, on pretence of a headache, when your stepfather comes back. Then when you hear him retire for the

7. Whip.

night, you must open the shutters of your window, undo the hasp, put your lamp there as a signal to us, and then withdraw with everything which you are likely to want into the room which you used to occupy. I have no doubt that, in spite of the repairs, you could manage there for one night."

"Oh, yes, easily."

"The rest you will leave in our hands."

"But what will you do?"

"We shall spend the night in your room, and we shall investigate the cause of this noise which has disturbed you."

"I believe, Mr. Holmes, that you have already made up your mind," said Miss Stoner, laying her hand upon my companion's sleeve.

"Perhaps I have."

"Then for pity's sake tell me what was the cause of my sister's death."

"I should prefer to have clearer proofs before I speak."

"You can at least tell me whether my own thought is correct, and if she died from some sudden fright."

"No, I do not think so. I think that there was probably some more tangible cause. And now, Miss Stoner, we must leave you, for if Dr. Roylott returned and saw us, our journey would be in vain. Good-bye, and be brave, for if you will do what I have told you, you may rest assured that we shall soon drive away the dangers that threaten you."

Sherlock Holmes and I had no difficulty in engaging a bedroom and sitting-room at the 'Crown' Inn. They were on the upper floor, and from our window we could command a view of the avenue gate, and of the inhabited wing of Stoke Moran Manor House. At dusk we saw Dr. Grimesby Roylott drive past, his huge form looming up beside the little figure of the lad who drove him. The boy had some slight difficulty in undoing the heavy iron gates, and we heard the hoarse roar of the Doctor's voice, and saw the fury with which he shook his clenched fists at him. The trap drove on, and a few minutes later we saw a sudden light spring up among the trees as the lamp was lit in one of the sitting-rooms.

"Do you know, Watson," said Holmes, as we sat together in the gathering darkness, "I have really some scruples as to taking you to-night. There is a distinct element of danger."

"Can I be of assistance?"

"Your presence might be invaluable."

"Then I shall certainly come."

"It is very kind of you."

"You speak of danger. You have evidently seen more in these rooms than was visible to me."

"No, but I fancy that I may have deduced a little more. I imagine that you saw all that I did."

"I saw nothing remarkable save the bell rope, and what purpose that could answer I confess is more than I can imagine."

"You saw the ventilator, too?"

"Yes, but I do not think that it is such a very unusual thing to have a small opening between two rooms. It was so small that a rat could hardly pass through."

"I knew that we should find a ventilator before ever we came to Stoke Moran."

"My dear Holmes!"

"Oh, yes, I did. You remember in her statement she said that her sister could smell Dr. Roylott's cigar. Now, of course that suggests at once that there must be a communication between the two rooms. It could only be a small one, or it would have been remarked upon at the Coroner's inquiry. I deduced a ventilator."

"But what harm can there be in that?"

"Well, there is at least a curious coincidence of dates. A ventilator is made, a cord is hung, and a lady who sleeps in the bed dies. Does not that strike you?"

"I cannot as yet see any connection."

"Did you observe anything very peculiar about that bed?"

"No."

"It was clamped to the floor. Did you ever see a bed fastened like that before?"

"I cannot say that I have."

"The lady could not move her bed. It must always be in the same relative position to the ventilator and to the rope—for so we may call it, since it was clearly never meant for a bell-pull."

"Holmes," I cried, "I seem to see dimly what you are hinting at. We are only just in time to prevent some subtle and horrible crime."

"Subtle enough, and horrible enough. When a doctor does go wrong, he is the first of criminals. He has nerve and he has knowledge. Palmer and Pritchard were among the heads of their profession.[8] This man strikes even deeper, but I think, Watson, that we shall be able to strike deeper still. But we shall have horrors enough before the night is over; for goodness' sake let us have a quiet pipe, and turn our minds for a few hours to something more cheerful."

About nine o'clock the light among the trees was extinguished, and all was dark in the direction of the Manor House. Two hours passed slowly away, and then, suddenly, just at the stroke of eleven, a single bright light shone out right in front of us.

"That is our signal," said Holmes, springing to his feet; "it comes from the middle window."

As we passed out he exchanged a few words with the landlord, explaining that we were going on a late visit to an acquaintance, and that it was possible that we might spend the night there. A moment later we were out on the dark road, a chill wind blowing in our faces, and one yellow light twinkling in front of us through the gloom to guide us on our sombre errand.

There was little difficulty in entering the grounds, for unrepaired breaches gaped in the old park wall. Making our way among the trees, we reached the lawn, crossed it, and were about to enter through the window, when out from a clump of laurel bushes there darted what seemed to be a hideous and distorted child, who threw itself on the grass with writhing limbs, and then ran swiftly across the lawn into the darkness.

"My God!" I whispered; "did you see it?"

8. William Palmer (the "Rugeley Poisoner") was executed in 1856 for the murder of an acquaintance; Edward William Pritchard was hanged in 1865 for poisoning his wife and mother-in-law. Both men were doctors but hardly "heads of their profession."

Holmes was for the moment as startled as I. His hand closed like a vice upon my wrist in his agitation. Then he broke into a low laugh, and put his lips to my ear.

"It is a nice household," he murmured. "That is the baboon."

I had forgotten the strange pets which the Doctor affected. There was a cheetah, too; perhaps we might find it upon our shoulders at any moment. I confess that I felt easier in my mind when, after following Holmes' example and slipping off my shoes, I found myself inside the bedroom. My companion noiselessly closed the shutters, moved the lamp on to the table, and cast his eyes round the room. All was as we had seen it in the day-time. Then creeping up to me and making a trumpet of his hand, he whispered into my ear again so gently that it was all that I could do to distinguish the words—

"The least sound would be fatal to our plans."

I nodded to show that I had heard.

"We must sit without a light. He would see it through the ventilator."

I nodded again.

"Do not go asleep; your very life may depend upon it. Have your pistol ready in case we should need it. I will sit on the side of the bed, and you in that chair."

I took out my revolver and laid it on the corner of the table.

Holmes had brought up a long thin cane, and this he placed upon the bed beside him. By it he laid the box of matches and the stump of a candle. Then he turned down the lamp, and we were left in darkness.

How shall I ever forget that dreadful vigil? I could not hear a sound, not even the drawing of a breath, and yet I knew that my companion sat open-eyed, within a few feet of me, in the same state of nervous tension in which I was myself. The shutters cut off the least ray of light, and we waited in absolute darkness. From outside came the occasional cry of a night bird, and once at our very window a long drawn, cat-like whine, which told us that the cheetah was indeed at liberty. Far away we could hear the deep tones of the parish clock, which boomed out every quarter of an hour. How long they seemed, those quarters! Twelve struck, and one, and two, and three, and still we sat waiting silently for whatever might befall.

Suddenly there was the momentary gleam of a light up in the direction of the ventilator, which vanished immediately, but was succeeded by a strong smell of burning oil and heated metal. Some one in the next room had lit a dark lantern.[9] I heard a gentle sound of movement, and then all was silent once more, though the smell grew stronger. For half an hour I sat with straining ears. Then suddenly another sound became audible—a very gentle, soothing sound, like that of a small jet of steam escaping continually from a kettle. The instant that we heard it, Holmes sprang from the bed, struck a match, and lashed furiously with his cane at the bell-pull.

"You see it, Watson?" he yelled. "You see it?"

But I saw nothing. At the moment when Holmes struck the light I heard a low, clear whistle, but the sudden glare flashing into my weary eyes made it impossible for me to tell what it was at which my friend lashed so savagely. I could, however, see that his face was deadly pale, and filled with horror and loathing.

9. A lantern with a sliding shutter or panel to dim or hide its light.

He had ceased to strike, and was gazing up at the ventilator, when suddenly there broke from the silence of the night the most horrible cry to which I have ever listened. It swelled up louder and louder, a hoarse yell of pain and fear and anger all mingled in the one dreadful shriek. They say that away down in the village, and even in the distant parsonage, that cry raised the sleepers from their beds. It struck cold to our hearts, and I stood gazing at Holmes, and he at me, until the last echoes of it had died away into the silence from which it rose.

"What can it mean?" I gasped.

"It means that it is all over," Holmes answered. "And perhaps, after all, it is for the best. Take your pistol, and we shall enter Dr. Roylott's room."

With a grave face he lit the lamp, and led the way down the corridor. Twice he struck at the chamber door without any reply from within. Then he turned the handle and entered, I at his heels, with the cocked pistol in my hand.

It was a singular sight which met our eyes. On the table stood a dark lantern with the shutter half open, throwing a brilliant beam of light upon the iron safe, the door of which was ajar. Beside this table, on the wooden chair, sat Dr. Grimesby Roylott, clad in a long grey dressing-gown, his bare ankles protruding beneath, and his feet thrust into red heelless Turkish slippers. Across his lap lay the short stock with the long lash which we had noticed during the day. His chin was cocked upwards, and his eyes were fixed in a dreadful rigid stare at the corner of the ceiling. Round his brow he had a peculiar yellow band, with brownish speckles, which seemed to be bound tightly round his head. As we entered he made neither sound nor motion.

"The band! the speckled band!" whispered Holmes.

I took a step forward. In an instant his strange headgear began to move, and there reared itself from among his hair the squat diamond-shaped head and puffed neck of a loathsome serpent.

"It is a swamp adder!"[1] cried Holmes—"the deadliest snake in India. He has died within ten seconds of being bitten. Violence does, in truth, recoil upon the violent, and the schemer falls into the pit which he digs for another.[2] Let us thrust this creature back into its den, and we can then remove Miss Stoner to some place of shelter, and let the county police know what has happened."

As he spoke he drew the dog whip swiftly from the dead man's lap, and throwing the noose round the reptile's neck, he drew it from its horrid perch, and, carrying it at arm's length threw it into the iron safe, which he closed upon it.

Such are the true facts of the death of Dr. Grimesby Roylott, of Stoke Moran. It is not necessary that I should prolong a narrative which has already run to too great a length, by telling how we broke the sad news to the terrified girl, how we conveyed her by the morning train to the care of her good aunt at Harrow, of how the slow process of official inquiry came to the conclusion that the Doctor met his fate while indiscreetly playing with a dangerous pet. The little which I had yet to learn of the case was told me by Sherlock Holmes as we travelled back next day.

---

1. An invented name for an imaginary reptile; there is no snake that completely fits the description given here.

2. Cf. Ecclesiastes 10.8: "He that diggeth a pit shall fall into it." The verse continues "and whoso breaketh an hedge, a serpent shall bite him."

"I had," said he, "come to an entirely erroneous conclusion, which shows, my dear Watson, how dangerous it always is to reason from insufficient data. The presence of the gipsies, and the use of the word 'band,' which was used by the poor girl, no doubt, to explain the appearance which she had caught a hurried glimpse of by the light of her match, were sufficient to put me upon an entirely wrong scent. I can only claim the merit that I instantly reconsidered my position when, however, it became clear to me that whatever danger threatened an occupant of the room could not come either from the window or the door. My attention was speedily drawn, as I have already remarked to you, to this ventilator, and to the bell rope which hung down to the bed. The discovery that this was a dummy, and that the bed was clamped to the floor, instantly gave rise to the suspicion that the rope was there as a bridge for something passing through the hole, and coming to the bed. The idea of a snake instantly occurred to me, and when I coupled it with my knowledge that the Doctor was furnished with a supply of creatures from India, I felt that I was probably on the right track. The idea of using a form of poison which could not possibly be discovered by any chemical test was just such a one as would occur to a clever and ruthless man who had had an Eastern training. The rapidity with which such a poison would take effect would also, from his point of view, be an advantage. It would be a sharp-eyed coroner indeed who could distinguish the two little dark punctures which would show where the poison fangs had done their work. Then I thought of the whistle. Of course, he must recall the snake before the morning light revealed it to the victim. He had trained it, probably by the use of the milk which we saw, to return to him when summoned.[3] He would put it through this ventilator at the hour that he thought best, with the certainty that it would crawl down the rope, and land on the bed. It might or might not bite the occupant, perhaps she might escape every night for a week, but sooner or later she must fall a victim.

"I had come to these conclusions before ever I had entered his room. An inspection of his chair showed me that he had been in the habit of standing on it, which, of course, would be necessary in order that he should reach the ventilator. The sight of the safe, the saucer of milk, and the loop of whipcord were enough to finally dispel any doubts which may have remained. The metallic clang heard by Miss Stoner was obviously caused by her father hastily closing the door of his safe upon its terrible occupant. Having once made up my mind, you know the steps which I took in order to put the matter to the proof. I heard the creature hiss, as I have no doubt that you did also, and I instantly lit the light and attacked it."

"With the result of driving it through the ventilator."

"And also with the result of causing it to turn upon its master at the other side. Some of the blows of my cane came home, and roused its snakish temper, so that it flew upon the first person it saw. In this way I am no doubt indirectly responsible for Dr. Grimesby Roylott's death, and I cannot say that it is likely to weigh very heavily upon my conscience."

1892

---

3. Objections have been made to this solution on the grounds that snakes are deaf, cannot climb up ropes, and do not (usually) drink milk.

MARY ELIZABETH COLERIDGE
1861–1907

The great-great-niece of Samuel Taylor Coleridge, Mary Elizabeth Coleridge, once wrote: "I have no fairy god-mother, but lay claim to a fairy great-great uncle, which is perhaps the reason that I am condemned to wander restlessly around the Gates of Fairyland, although I have never yet passed them." Born in London to a literary and musical family that regularly entertained guests such as Alfred, Lord Tennyson and Robert Browning, Coleridge lived her whole life at home with her parents and one sister. She was unusually well educated, under the supervision of a tutor, William Cory, a scholar and poet, who had been forced by scandal to leave his teaching position at Eton. Coleridge thus received an education usually reserved for boys. She knew six languages, including Greek, and studied philosophy. In the 1890s she began giving lessons in English literature to working girls; in 1895 she started to teach at the Working Woman's College, an activity she continued for the rest of her life. She died suddenly of appendicitis at the age of forty-six.

Coleridge's tutor, Cory, encouraged her to write poetry and short stories. When Henry Newbolt, a poet and family friend, joined her reading group (then composed of five women), the Quintette, he urged her to publish her first two novels. She later published three more, in addition to a number of stories and essays. Although she wrote poetry continuously, she published little of it during her life. When a manuscript of her poems was given to Robert Bridges, a family friend who was also close to Gerard Manley Hopkins and was responsible for the posthumous publication of Hopkins's poetry, Bridges recognized her talent. He made suggestions for revisions and encouraged her to publish a volume. She allowed two small volumes to be privately printed in the 1890s, under the pseudonym *Anodos*, or "The Wanderer"; most of her poetry was published after her death.

Although Coleridge did not participate in the feminist debates of her time, her poems contain a subversive sense of anarchic female energy. She believed women had a spiritual identity distinct from men's; she wrote, "I don't think we are separate only in body and in mind, I think we are separate in soul too." Some of her poems rewrite earlier texts. Sandra Gilbert and Susan Gubar have speculated that "The Other Side of a Mirror" (1896) portrays the mad Bertha Mason from Charlotte Brontë's *Jane Eyre* (1847); Angela Leighton and Margaret Reynolds have argued that "The Witch" (1907) reimagines Samuel Taylor Coleridge's visionary poem *Christabel* (1816). Both of these poems demonstrate another characteristic of her writing—presentation of a luminous narrative fragment with little sense of surrounding context. The effect, in the words of Newbolt, her friend, is one of "very deep shadows filled with strange shapes."

The Other Side of a Mirror

I sat before my glass one day,
  And conjured up a vision bare,
Unlike the aspects glad and gay,
  That erst° were found reflected there—   *formerly*

5   The vision of a woman, wild
      With more than womanly despair.

Her hair stood back on either side
    A face bereft of loveliness.
It had no envy now to hide
10   What once no man on earth could guess.
It formed the thorny aureole°   *halo*
    Of hard unsanctified distress.

Her lips were open—not a sound
    Came through the parted lines of red.
15   Whate'er it was, the hideous wound
    In silence and in secret bled.
No sigh relieved her speechless woe,
    She had no voice to speak her dread.

And in her lurid eyes there shone
20   The dying flame of life's desire,
Made mad because its hope was gone,
    And kindled at the leaping fire
Of jealousy, and fierce revenge,
    And strength that could not change nor tire.

25   Shade of a shadow in the glass,
    O set the crystal surface free!
Pass—as the fairer visions pass—
    Nor ever more return, to be
The ghost of a distracted hour,
30   That heard me whisper, "I am she!"

1882   1896

The Witch

I have walked a great while over the snow,
    And I am not tall nor strong.
My clothes are wet, and my teeth are set,
    And the way was hard and long.
5   I have wandered over the fruitful earth,
    But I never came here before.
Oh, lift me over the threshold, and let me in at the door!

The cutting wind is a cruel foe.
    I dare not stand in the blast.
10   My hands are stone, and my voice a groan,
    And the worst of death is past.
I am but a little maiden still,
    My little white feet are sore.
Oh, lift me over the threshold, and let me in at the door!

15 Her voice was the voice that women have,
    Who plead for their heart's desire.
    She came—she came—and the quivering flame
    Sank and died in the fire.
    It never was lit again on my hearth
20 Since I hurried across the floor,
    To lift her over the threshold, and let her in at the door.

1892   1907

RUDYARD KIPLING
1865–1936

Like many children born to upper- or middle-class Britons living in India in the Victorian era, Rudyard Kipling was sent to Great Britain at the age of six to begin his education. For the next six years in England, he was desperately unhappy; his parents had chosen to board him in a rigidly Calvinistic foster home, and he was treated with considerable cruelty. His parents finally removed him when he was twelve and sent him to a private school, where his experience was far better. His views in later life were deeply affected by the English schoolboy code of honor and duty, especially when it involved loyalty to a group or team. At seventeen he rejoined his parents in India, where his father taught sculpture at the Bombay School of Art. By the time he returned to England seven years later, the poems and stories he had written while working as a newspaper reporter in India had brought him early fame. In 1892 he married an American woman; they lived in Brattleboro, Vermont, until a fierce quarrel with his brother-in-law drove him back to England in 1896. Kipling settled on a country estate and purchased, at the turn of the century, an expensive early-model automobile. He seems to have been the first English author to own an automobile—an appropriate distinction, because he was intrigued by all kinds of machinery and feats of engineering. In this keen interest, as in many tastes, he differed markedly from his contemporaries in the 1890s, the aesthetes. Kipling was also the first English author to receive the Nobel Prize for Literature (1907).

In the final decades of the nineteenth century, India was the most important colony of Britain's empire—the "Jewel in the Crown," as Prime Minister Benjamin Disraeli had dubbed it. The English were consequently curious about the world of India, a world that Kipling's stories and poems helped them envision. Indeed, Leonard Woolf, Virginia Woolf's husband, wrote of his own experience in India in the early years of the twentieth century: "I could never make up my mind whether Kipling had moulded his characters accurately in the image of Anglo-Indian society or whether we were moulding our characters accurately in the image of a Kipling story." During his seven years in India in the 1880s, Kipling gained a rich experience of colonial life, which he presented in his stories and poems. His first volume of stories, *Plain Tales from the Hills* (1888), explores some of the psychological and moral problems of the Anglo-Indians and their relationship with the people they had colonized. In his two volumes of the *Jungle Book* (1894, 1895) he draws on the Indian scene to create a world of jungle animals. Capable, on occasion, of constructing offensive stereotypes, Kipling at other times demonstrates a remarkably detailed and intelligent interest in Indian culture, as in his complex novel *Kim* (1901): amid a welter of representations of different modes of existence, the contemplative and religious way of life of the Indian *lama*, or monk, is treated with no less respect and sympathy than the active and worldly way of life of the Victorian English governing classes.

In his poems Kipling also draws on the Indian scene, most commonly as it is viewed through the eyes of the men sent out from England to garrison the country and fight off invaders on the northwest frontiers. Kipling is usually thought of as the poet of British imperialism, as indeed he often was; but these poems about ordinary British soldiers in India contain little by way of flag-waving celebrations of the triumph of empire. The soldier who speaks in "The Widow at Windsor" (1892) is simply bewildered by the events in which he has taken part. As one of the soldiers of the queen (one of "Missis Victorier's sons"), he has done his duty, but he does not see the empire as a divine design to which he has contributed. Kipling develops a new subject in the working-class imperial soldier (a subject, we should note, who frequently gives voice to deeply racist attitudes), and thus a new way to portray modern social experience.

The common man's perspective, expressed in the accent of the London cockney, was one of the qualities that gained Kipling an immediate audience for his *Barrack-Room Ballads* (1890, 1892). For many years Kipling was extremely popular. What attracted his vast audience was not just the novelty of his subjects but also his mastery of swinging verse rhythms. To some degree Kipling's literary ancestry helps explain his success. In part he learned his craft as a poet from traditional sources. His own family had connections with the Pre-Raphaelites, and he was considerably influenced by such immediate literary predecessors as Robert Browning and Algernon Charles Swinburne. But two of the forces strongly influencing his style and rhythms were not traditional. One of these was the Protestant hymn. Both his parents were children of Methodist clergymen, and chapel singing, as well as preaching, affected him profoundly. "Three generations of Wesleyan ministers . . . lie behind me," he noted; the family tradition can be heard in such secular sermons as "If—" (1910) and the elegiac hymn "Recessional" (1897). The second influence came from what seems an antithetical secular quarter: the songs of the music hall. As a teenager in London, Kipling had enjoyed music hall entertainments, which were to reach their peak of popularity in the 1890s. Like Tennyson, Kipling knew how to make poems that call to be set to music, verses such as "Mandalay" (1890) or "Gentlemen-Rankers" (1892), with its memorable refrain: "We're poor little lambs who've lost our way, / Baa! Baa! Baa!" Much of Kipling's poetry is best appreciated with the melodies and ambience of the music hall in mind.

In recent years Kipling's stories have received more attention than his poems. By portraying the British community in India and its relationship with the people it ruled, Kipling created a rich and various fictional world that reflects on England's imperialism as lived by the officers of the empire in all their peculiar social relationships. "The Man Who Would Be King" (1888) presents an intriguing approach to the topic. The narrator, a newspaper editor, tells us of his dealings with a couple of "Loafers." Peachey Carnehan and Daniel Dravot have no official positions in India but are quick to exploit any opportunities their European status may afford them; this pair of rogues heads out to the mountainous region of Kafiristan, intent on establishing their own dynasty. An action-packed tale of adventure in faraway places with strange-sounding names, the story also invites us to think critically about the general project of empire—about the assumptions it holds, the methods it employs, and the human cost of its endeavors.

After leaving India, Kipling gradually turned to English subjects in his fiction, but the cataclysm of World War I did much to diminish his output. As chair of the Imperial War Graves Commission, he played a difficult and important public role, responsible for (among other things) choosing the words to be inscribed on countless monuments and memorials across the globe. Kipling's task was all the more poignant because the body of his only son, who had died in the battle of Loos (1915), was never found. A deeply melancholy autobiography, *Something of Myself*, was published in 1937, the year after Kipling's death.

The Man Who Would Be King[1]

"Brother to a Prince and fellow to a beggar if he be found worthy."[2]

The law, as quoted, lays down a fair conduct of life, and one not easy to follow. I have been fellow to a beggar again and again under circumstances which prevented either of us finding out whether the other was worthy. I have still to be brother to a Prince, though I once came near to kinship with what might have been a veritable King and was promised the reversion of[3] a Kingdom—army, law-courts, revenue and policy all complete. But, to-day, I greatly fear that my King is dead, and if I want a crown I must go and hunt it for myself.

The beginning of everything was in a railway train upon the road to Mhow from Ajmir.[4] There had been a Deficit in the Budget, which necessitated traveling, not Second-class, which is only half as dear as First-class, but by Intermediate, which is very awful indeed. There are no cushions in the Intermediate class, and the population are either Intermediate, which is Eurasian, or native, which for a long night journey is nasty, or Loafer,[5] which is amusing though intoxicated. Intermediates do not patronize refreshment-rooms. They carry their food in bundles and pots, and buy sweets from the native sweetmeat-sellers, and drink the roadside water. That is why in the hot weather Intermediates are taken out of the carriages dead, and in all weathers are most properly looked down upon.

My particular Intermediate happened to be empty till I reached Nasirabad, when a huge gentleman in shirt-sleeves entered, and, following the custom of Intermediates, passed the time of day. He was a wanderer and a vagabond like myself, but with an educated taste for whiskey. He told tales of things he had seen and done, of out-of-the-way corners of the Empire into which he had penetrated, and of adventures in which he risked his life for a few days' food. "If India was filled with men like you and me, not knowing more than the crows where they'd get their next day's rations, it isn't seventy millions of revenue the land would be paying—it's seven hundred millions," said he; and as I looked at his mouth and chin I was disposed to agree with him. We talked politics—the politics of Loaferdom that sees things from the underside where the lath and plaster is not smoothed

---

1. Kipling based his story on the true-life exploits of an American adventurer, Josiah Harlan, who awarded himself the title of prince after occupying a region in the Hindu Kush in the late 1830s.
2. Meant to suggest the principles of Freemasonry, a secret fraternal society that developed from the masons' guild in medieval Britain. By Victorian times it had grown to a prominent

organization, whose members were bound to help each other in times of distress. Kipling was a member.
3. Right to inherit.
4. These, and the other places mentioned at the beginning of the story, are in northern India.
5. A European in India with no official attachment or position.

off[6]—and we talked postal arrangements because my friend wanted to send a telegram back from the next station to Ajmir, which is the turning-off place from the Bombay to the Mhow line as you travel westward. My friend had no money beyond eight annas which he wanted[7] for dinner, and I had no money at all, owing to the hitch in the Budget before mentioned. Further, I was going into a wilderness where, though I should resume touch with the Treasury, there were no telegraph offices. I was, therefore, unable to help him in any way.

"We might threaten a Station-master, and make him send a wire on tick,"[8] said my friend, "but that'd mean inquiries for you and for me, and I've got my hands full these days. Did you say you are traveling back along this line within any days?"

"Within ten," I said.

"Can't you make it eight?" said he. "Mine is rather urgent business."

"I can send your telegram within ten days if that will serve you," I said.

"I couldn't trust the wire to fetch him now I think of it. It's this way. He leaves Delhi on the 23d for Bombay. That means he'll be running through Ajmir about the night of the 23d."

"But I'm going into the Indian Desert," I explained.

"Well *and* good," said he. "You'll be changing at Marwar Junction to get into Jodhpore territory—you must do that—and he'll be coming through Marwar Junction in the early morning of the 24th by the Bombay Mail. Can you be at Marwar Junction on that time? 'Twon't be inconveniencing you because I know that there's precious few pickings to be got out of these Central India States—even though you pretend to be correspondent of the *Backwoodsman*."[9]

"Have you ever tried that trick?" I asked.

"Again and again, but the Residents[1] find you out, and then you get escorted to the Border before you've time to get your knife into them. But about my friend here. I *must* give him a word o' mouth to tell him what's come to me or else he won't know where to go. I would take it more than kind of you if you was to come out of Central India in time to catch him at Marwar Junction, and say to him:—'He has gone South for the week.' He'll know what that means. He's a big man with a red beard, and a great swell[2] he is. You'll find him sleeping like a gentleman with all his luggage round him in a Second-class compartment. But don't you be afraid. Slip down the window, and say:—'He has gone South for the week,' and he'll tumble.[3] It's only cutting your time of stay in those parts by two days. I ask you as a stranger—going to the West,"[4] he said, with emphasis.

"Where have *you* come from?" said I.

"From the East," said he, "and I am hoping that you will give him the message on the Square[5]—for the sake of my Mother as well as your own."

6. I.e., the unfinished side of a wall.
7. Needed. "Annas": there are sixteen annas in a rupee, the basic monetary unit of India.
8. On credit.
9. This fictitious newspaper appears to be based on the Allahabad *Pioneer*, for which Kipling worked as a roving correspondent. The Central India States were quasi-independent "Native States," as they were also known, presided over by Indian royalty.
1. British political officers appointed to oversee affairs at the courts of Indian rulers.
2. Fashionable fellow.
3. Catch on, understand.
4. This phrase and the following one are from the code of the Freemasons.
5. Honestly.

Englishmen are not usually softened by appeals to the memory of their mothers, but for certain reasons, which will be fully apparent, I saw fit to agree.

"It's more than a little matter," said he, "and that's why I ask you to do it—and now I know that I can depend on you doing it. A Second-class carriage at Marwar Junction, and a red-haired man asleep in it. You'll be sure to remember. I get out at the next station, and I must hold on there till he comes or sends me what I want."

"I'll give the message if I catch him," I said, "and for the sake of your Mother as well as mine I'll give you a word of advice. Don't try to run the Central India States just now as the correspondent of the *Backwoodsman*. There's a real one knocking about here, and it might lead to trouble."

"Thank you," said he, simply, "and when will the swine be gone? I can't starve because he's ruining my work. I wanted to get hold of the Degumber Rajah down here about his father's widow, and give him a jump."

"What did he do to his father's widow, then?"

"Filled her up with red pepper and slippered her to death as she hung from a beam. I found that out myself, and I'm the only man that would dare going into the State to get hush-money for it. They'll try to poison me, same as they did in Chortumna when I went on the loot there. But you'll give the man at Marwar Junction my message?"

He got out at a little roadside station, and I reflected. I had heard, more than once, of men personating correspondents of newspapers and bleeding small Native States with threats of exposure, but I had never met any of the caste before. They lead a hard life, and generally die with great suddenness. The Native States have a wholesome horror of English newspapers, which may throw light on their peculiar methods of government, and do their best to choke correspondents with champagne, or drive them out of their mind with four-in-hand barouches.[6] They do not understand that nobody cares a straw for the internal administration of Native States so long as oppression and crime are kept within decent limits, and the ruler is not drugged, drunk, or diseased from one end of the year to the other. Native States were created by Providence in order to supply picturesque scenery, tigers, and tall-writing.[7] They are the dark places of the earth, full of unimaginable cruelty, touching the Railway and the Telegraph on one side, and, on the other, the days of Harun-al-Raschid.[8] When I left the train I did business with divers Kings, and in eight days passed through many changes of life. Sometimes I wore dress-clothes and consorted with Princes and Politicals,[9] drinking from crystal and eating from silver. Sometimes I lay out upon the ground and devoured what I could get, from a plate made of a flapjack, and drank the running water, and slept under the same rug as my servant. It was all in the day's work.

Then I headed for the Great Indian Desert upon the proper date, as I had promised, and the night Mail set me down at Marwar Junction, where a funny little, happy-go-lucky, native-managed railway runs to Jodhpore. The Bombay Mail from Delhi makes a short halt at Marwar. She arrived as I got in, and I had just time to hurry to her platform and go down the carriages.

6. Fashionable four-wheeled carriages.
7. Tall tales.
8. The caliph of Baghdad (763–809), who fig-

ures in many tales of the *Arabian Nights*.
9. I.e., Residents.

There was only one Second-class on the train. I slipped the window, and looked down upon a flaming red beard, half covered by a railway rug. That was my man, fast asleep, and I dug him gently in the ribs. He woke with a grunt, and I saw his face in the light of the lamps. It was a great and shining face.

"Tickets again?" said he.

"No," said I. "I am to tell you that he is gone South for the week. He is gone South for the week!"

The train had begun to move out. The red man rubbed his eyes. "He has gone South for the week," he repeated. "Now that's just like his impidence. Did he say that I was to give you anything?—'Cause I won't."

"He didn't," I said, and dropped away, and watched the red lights die out in the dark. It was horribly cold, because the wind was blowing off the sands. I climbed into my own train—not an Intermediate Carriage this time—and went to sleep.

If the man with the beard had given me a rupee I should have kept it as a memento of a rather curious affair. But the consciousness of having done my duty was my only reward.

Later on I reflected that two gentlemen like my friends could not do any good if they foregathered and personated correspondents of newspapers, and might, if they "stuck up"[1] one of the little rat-trap states of Central India or Southern Rajputana, get themselves into serious difficulties. I therefore took some trouble to describe them as accurately as I could remember to people who would be interested in deporting them; and succeeded, so I was later informed, in having them headed back from Degumber borders.

Then I became respectable, and returned to an Office where there were no Kings and no incidents except the daily manufacture of a newspaper. A newspaper office seems to attract every conceivable sort of person, to the prejudice of discipline. Zenana-mission ladies[2] arrive, and beg that the Editor will instantly abandon all his duties to describe a Christian prize-giving in a back-slum of a perfectly inaccessible village; Colonels who have been overpassed for commands sit down and sketch the outline of a series of ten, twelve, or twenty-four leading articles on Seniority *versus* Selection; missionaries wish to know why they have not been permitted to escape from their regular vehicles of abuse and swear at a brother missionary under special patronage of the editorial We; stranded theatrical companies troop up to explain that they cannot pay for their advertisements, but on their return from New Zealand or Tahiti will do so with interest; inventors of patent punkah[3]-pulling machines, carriage couplings and unbreakable swords and axle-trees call with specifications in their pockets and hours at their disposal; tea-companies enter and elaborate their prospectuses with the office pens; secretaries of ball-committees clamour to have the glories of their last dance more fully expounded; strange ladies rustle in and say:—"I want a hundred lady's cards printed *at once*, please," which is manifestly part of an Editor's duty; and every dissolute ruffian that ever tramped the Grand Trunk Road[4] makes it his business to ask for employment as a proof-reader. And, all

---

1. Fraudulently extorted money from. "Foregathered": met.
2. Female missionaries doing work among Indian women, who were customarily confined

to a part of the house called the *Zenana*.
3. Large swinging fan, usually worked by hand.
4. Major road connecting Calcutta and Delhi.

the time, the telephone-bell is ringing madly, and Kings are being killed on the Continent, and Empires are saying—"You're another," and Mister Gladstone is calling down brimstone upon the British Dominions,[5] and the little black copy-boys are whining, *"kaapi chay-ha-yeh"* (copy wanted) like tired bees, and most of the paper is as blank as Modred's shield.[6]

But that is the amusing part of the year. There are other six months wherein none ever come to call, and the thermometer walks inch by inch up to the top of the glass, and the office is darkened to just above reading-light, and the press machines are red-hot of touch, and nobody writes anything but accounts of amusements in the Hill-stations[7] or obituary notices. Then the telephone becomes a tinkling terror, because it tells you of the sudden deaths of men and women that you knew intimately, and the prickly-heat covers you as with a garment, and you sit down and write:—"A slight increase of sickness is reported from the Khuda Janta Khan[8] District. The outbreak is purely sporadic in its nature, and, thanks to the energetic efforts of the District authorities, is now almost at an end. It is, however, with deep regret we record the death, etc."

Then the sickness really breaks out, and the less recording and reporting the better for the peace of the subscribers. But the Empires and the Kings continue to divert themselves as selfishly as before, and the Foreman thinks that a daily paper really ought to come out once in twenty-four hours, and all the people at the Hill-stations in the middle of their amusements say:— "Good gracious! Why can't the paper be sparkling? I'm sure there's plenty going on up here."

That is the dark half of the moon, and, as the advertisements say, "must be experienced to be appreciated."

It was in that season, and a remarkably evil season, that the paper began running the last issue of the week on Saturday night, which is to say, Sunday morning, after the custom of a London paper. This was a great convenience, for immediately after the paper was put to bed,[9] the dawn would lower the thermometer from 96° to almost 84° for half an hour, and in that chill—you have no idea how cold is 84° on the grass until you begin to pray for it—a very tired man could set off to sleep ere the heat roused him.

One Saturday night it was my pleasant duty to put the paper to bed alone. A King or courtier or a courtesan or a community was going to die or get a new Constitution, or do something that was important on the other side of the world, and the paper was to be held open till the latest possible minute in order to catch the telegram. It was a pitchy black night, as stifling as a June night can be, and the *loo*, the red-hot wind from the westward, was booming among the tinder-dry trees and pretending that the rain was on its heels. Now and again a spot of almost boiling water would fall on the dust with the flop of a frog, but all our weary world knew that was only pretence. It was a shade cooler in the press-room than the office, so I sat there, while

5. Places under British control. William Ewart Gladstone (1809–1898), leader of the Liberal Party from 1868 to 1875 and 1880 to 1894, and four times prime minister; he strongly opposed overseas expansion. "Brimstone": i.e., fire and brimstone, the supposed torments of hell.
6. In British legend the shield of King Arthur's traitorous nephew was blank because he had done no deeds of valor.
7. Official outposts in the northern hills, to which many British people in India would retire during the hottest months.
8. "God Knows Town"; i.e., Nowheresville.
9. The final preparations were made for printing the newspaper.

the type clicked and clicked and the night-jars hooted at the windows, and the all but naked compositors wiped the sweat from their foreheads and called for water. The thing that was keeping us back, whatever it was, would not come off, though the *loo* dropped and the last type was set, and the whole round earth stood still in the choking heat, with its finger on its lip, to wait the event. I drowsed, and wondered whether the telegraph was a blessing, and whether this dying man, or struggling people, was aware of the inconvenience the delay was causing. There was no special reason beyond the heat and worry to make tension, but, as the clock hands crept up to three o'clock and the machines spun their fly-wheels two and three times to see that all was in order, before I said the word that would set them off, I could have shrieked aloud.

Then the roar and rattle of the wheels shivered the quiet into little bits. I rose to go away, but two men in white clothes stood in front of me. The first one said:—"It's him!" The second said:—"So it is!" And they both laughed almost as loudly as the machinery roared, and mopped their foreheads. "We see there was a light burning across the road and we were sleeping in that ditch there for coolness, and I said to my friend here, 'The office is open. Let's come along and speak to him as turned us back from the Degumber State,'" said the smaller of the two. He was the man I had met in the Mhow train, and his fellow was the red-bearded man of Marwar Junction. There was no mistaking the eyebrows of the one or the beard of the other.

I was not pleased, because I wished to go to sleep, not to squabble with loafers. "What do you want?" I asked.

"Half an hour's talk with you cool and comfortable, in the office," said the red-bearded man. "We'd *like* some drink—the Contrack doesn't begin yet, Peachey, so you needn't look—but what we really want is advice. We don't want money. We ask you as a favour, because you did us a bad turn about Degumber."

I led from the press-room to the stifling office with the maps on the walls, and the red-haired man rubbed his hands. "That's something like," said he. "This was the proper shop to come to. Now, Sir, let me introduce to you Brother[1] Peachey Carnehan, that's him, and Brother Daniel Dravot, that is *me*, and the less said about our professions the better, for we have been most things in our time. Soldier, sailor, compositor, photographer, proof-reader, street-preacher, and correspondents of the *Backwoodsman* when we thought the paper wanted one. Carnehan is sober, and so am I. Look at us first and see that's sure. It will save you cutting into my talk. We'll take one of your cigars apiece, and you shall see us light."

I watched the test. The men were absolutely sober, so I gave them each a tepid peg.[2]

"Well *and* good," said Carnehan of the eyebrows, wiping the froth from his moustache. "Let me talk now, Dan. We have been all over India, mostly on foot. We have been boiler-fitters, engine-drivers, petty contractors, and all that, and we have decided that India isn't big enough for such as us."

They certainly were too big for the office. Dravot's beard seemed to fill half the room and Carnehan's shoulders the other half, as they sat on the big

---

1. A title meant to recall the Freemason connection.
2. A drink.

table. Carnehan continued: "The country isn't half worked out because they that governs it won't let you touch it. They spend all their blessed time in governing it, and you can't lift a spade, nor chip a rock, nor look for oil, nor anything like that without all the Government saying—'Leave it alone and let us govern.' Therefore, such as it is, we will let it alone, and go away to some other place where a man isn't crowded and can come to his own. We are not little men, and there is nothing that we are afraid of except Drink, and we have signed a Contrack on that. *Therefore*, we are going away to be Kings."

"Kings in our own right," muttered Dravot.

"Yes, of course," I said. "You've been tramping in the sun, and it's a very warm night, and hadn't you better sleep over the notion? Come to-morrow."

"Neither drunk nor sunstruck," said Dravot. "We have slept over the notion half a year, and require to see Books and Atlases, and we have decided that there is only one place now in the world that two strong men can Sar-a-*whack*.[3] They call it Kafiristan.[4] By my reckoning it's the top right-hand corner of Afghanistan, not more than three hundred miles from Pesha-wur.[5] They have two and thirty heathen idols there, and we'll be the thirty-third. It's a mountainous country, and the women of those parts are very beautiful."

"But that is provided against in the Contrack," said Carnehan. "Neither Women nor Liquor, Daniel."

"And that's all we know, except that no one has gone there, and they fight, and in any place where they fight, a man who knows how to drill men can always be a King. We shall go to those parts and say to any King we find—'D'you want to vanquish your foes?' and we will show him how to drill men; for that we know better than anything else. Then we will subvert that King and seize his Throne and establish a Dy-nasty."

"You'll be cut to pieces before you're fifty miles across the Border," I said. "You have to travel through Afghanistan to get to that country. It's one mass of mountains and peaks and glaciers, and no Englishman has been through it. The people are utter brutes, and even if you reached them you couldn't do anything."

"That's more like," said Carnehan: "If you could think us a little more mad we would be more pleased. We have come to you to know about this country, to read a book about it, and to be shown maps. We want you to tell us that we are fools and to show us your books." He turned to the bookcases.

"Are you at all in earnest?" I said.

"A little," said Dravot, sweetly. "As big a map as you have got, even if it's all blank where Kafiristan is, and any books you've got. We can read, though we aren't very educated."

I uncased the big thirty-two-miles-to-the-inch map of India, and two smaller Frontier maps, hauled down volume INF-KAN of the *Encyclopaedia Britannica*, and the men consulted them.

"See here!" said Dravot, his thumb on the map. "Up to Jagdallak, Peachey and me know the road. We was there with Roberts's Army.[6] We'll have to

---

3. A reference to Sir James Brooke (1803–1868), "the White Rajah of Sarawak," who, in return for helping the rajah of Sarawak, in Borneo, put down a rebellion, succeeded him after his death, and established a dynasty.
4. A real place, in the Hindu Kush.

5. Peshawar, a large city in present-day Pakistan.
6. In the Second Afghan War (1878–80), a force under the command of General Frederick Roberts made a three-hundred-mile forced march through the area.

turn off to the right at Jagdallak through Laghmann territory. Then we get among the hills—fourteen thousand feet—fifteen thousand—it will be cold work there, but it don't look very far on the map."

I handed him Wood on the *Sources of the Oxus.*[7] Carnehan was deep in the *Encyclopaedia.*

"They're a mixed lot," said Dravot, reflectively; "and it won't help us to know the names of their tribes. The more tribes the more they'll fight, and the better for us. From Jagdallak to Ashang. H'mm!"

"But all the information about the country is as sketchy and inaccurate as can be," I protested. "No one knows anything about it really. Here's the file of the *United Services' Institute.* Read what Bellew says."

"Blow Bellew!" said Carnehan. "Dan, they're an all-fired lot of heathens, but this book here says they think they're related to us English."

I smoked while the men pored over Raverty, Wood, the maps, and the *Encyclopaedia.*

"There is no use your waiting," said Dravot, politely. "It's about four o'clock now. We'll go before six o'clock if you want to sleep, and we won't steal any of the papers. Don't you sit up. We're two harmless lunatics and if you come, to-morrow evening, down to the Serai[8] we'll say good-bye to you."

"You *are* two fools," I answered. "You'll be turned back at the Frontier or cut up the minute you set foot in Afghanistan. Do you want any money or a recommendation downcountry? I can help you to the chance of work next week."

"Next week we shall be hard at work ourselves, thank you," said Dravot. "It isn't so easy being a King as it looks. When we've got our Kingdom in going order we'll let you know, and you can come up and help us to govern it."

"Would two lunatics make a Contrack like that?" said Carnehan, with subdued pride, showing me a greasy half-sheet of note-paper on which was written the following. I copied it, then and there, as a curiosity:

This Contract between me and you persuing witnesseth in the name of God—Amen and so forth.

(One)   That me and you will settle this matter together: i.e., to be Kings of Kafiristan.

(Two)   That you and me will not, while this matter is being settled, look at any Liquor, nor any Woman, black, white or brown, so as to get mixed up with one or the other harmful.

(Three)   That we conduct ourselves with dignity and discretion and if one of us gets into trouble the other will stay by him.

Signed by you and me this day.
Peachey Taliaferro Carnehan.
Daniel Dravot.
Both Gentlemen at Large.

"There was no need for the last article," said Carnehan, blushing modestly; "but it looks regular. Now you know the sort of men that loafers are—we *are* loafers, Dan, until we get out of India—and *do* you think that

7. A river whose sources are in the area.
8. Place or building for the accommodation of travelers and their pack animals.

we would sign a Contrack like that unless we was in earnest? We have kept away from the two things that make life worth having."

"You won't enjoy your lives much longer if you are going to try this idiotic adventure. Don't set the office on fire," I said, "and go away before nine o'clock."

I left them still poring over the maps and making notes on the back of the "Contrack." "Be sure to come down to the Serai to-morrow," were their parting words.

The Kumharsen Serai is the great foursquare sink of humanity where the strings of camels and horses from the North load and unload. All the nationalities of Central Asia may be found there, and most of the folk of India proper. Balkh and Bokhara there meet Bengal and Bombay, and try to draw eye-teeth. You can buy ponies, turquoises, Persian pussy-cats, saddle-bags, fat-tailed sheep and musk in the Kumharsen Serai, and get many strange things for nothing. In the afternoon I went down there to see whether my friends intended to keep their word or were lying about drunk.

A priest attired in fragments of ribbons and rags stalked up to me, gravely twisting a child's paper whirligig.[9] Behind was his servant bending under the load of a crate of mud toys. The two were loading up two camels, and the inhabitants of the Serai watched them with shrieks of laughter.

"The priest is mad," said a horse-dealer to me. "He is going up to Kabul to sell toys to the Amir.[1] He will either be raised to honor or have his head cut off. He came in here this morning and has been behaving madly ever since."

"The witless are under the protection of God," stammered a flat-cheeked Usbeg[2] in broken Hindi. "They foretell future events."

"Would they could have foretold that my caravan would have been cut up by the Shinwaris almost within shadow of the Pass!"[3] grunted the Eusufzai agent of a Rajputana trading-house whose goods had been feloniously diverted into the hands of other robbers just across the Border, and whose misfortunes were the laughing-stock of the bazar. "Ohé, priest, whence come you and whither do you go?"

"From Roum[4] have I come," shouted the priest, waving his whirligig; "from Roum, blown by the breath of a hundred devils across the sea! O thieves, robbers, liars, the blessing of Pir Khan on pigs, dogs, and perjurers! Who will take the Protected of God to the North to sell charms that are never still to the Amir? The camels shall not gall,[5] the sons shall not fall sick, and the wives shall remain faithful while they are away, of the men who give me place in their caravan. Who will assist me to slipper the King of the Roos[6] with a golden slipper with a silver heel? The protection of Pir Khan be upon his labors!" He spread out the skirts of his gaberdine and pirouetted between the lines of tethered horses.

"There starts a caravan from Peshawur to Kabul in twenty days, *Huzrut*,"[7] said the Eusufzai trader. "My camels go therewith. Do thou also go and bring us good-luck."

---

9. Pinwheel.
1. The ruler of Afghanistan, based in the city of Kabul.
2. Person from Uzbekistan.
3. The Khyber or Khaiber Pass, running thirty-three miles through the mountains. Then on the northwest frontier of British India, it now links Afghanistan and Pakistan.
4. Turkey.
5. Become sore.
6. Czar of Russia.
7. Presence (an honorary form of address).

"I will go even now!" shouted the priest. "I will depart upon my winged camels, and be at Peshawur in a day! Ho! Hazar[8] Mir Khan," he yelled to his servant, "drive out the camels, but let me first mount my own."

He leaped on the back of his beast as it knelt, and, turning round to me, cried:—"Come thou also, Sahib, a little along the road, and I will sell thee a charm—an amulet that shall make thee King of Kafiristan."

Then the light broke upon me, and I followed the two camels out of the Serai till we reached open road and the priest halted.

"What d' you think o' that?" said he in English. "Carnehan can't talk their patter, so I've made him my servant. He makes a handsome servant. 'Tisn't for nothing that I've been knocking about the country for fourteen years. Didn't I do that talk neat? We'll hitch on to a caravan at Peshawur till we get to Jagdallak, and then we'll see if we can get donkeys for our camels, and strike into Kafiristan. Whirligigs for the Amir, O Lor! Put your hand under the camel-bags and tell me what you feel."

I felt the butt of a Martini,[9] and another and another.

"Twenty of 'em," said Dravot, placidly. "Twenty of 'em, and ammunition to correspond, under the whirligigs and the mud dolls."

"Heaven help you if you are caught with those things!" I said. "A Martini is worth her weight in silver among the Pathans."[1]

"Fifteen hundred rupees of capital—every rupee we could beg, borrow, or steal—are invested on these two camels," said Dravot. "We won't get caught. We're going through the Khaiber with a regular caravan. Who'd touch a poor mad priest?"

"Have you got everything you want?" I asked, overcome with astonishment.

"Not yet, but we shall soon. Give us a memento of your kindness, *Brother*. You did me a service yesterday, and that time in Marwar. Half my Kingdom shall you have, as the saying is." I slipped a small charm compass from my watch-chain and handed it up to the priest.

"Good-bye," said Dravot, giving me hand cautiously. "It's the last time we'll shake hands with an Englishman these many days. Shake hands with him, Carnehan," he cried, as the second camel passed me.

Carnehan leaned down and shook hands. Then the camels passed away along the dusty road, and I was left alone to wonder. My eye could detect no failure in the disguises. The scene in Serai attested that they were complete to the native mind. There was just the chance, therefore, that Carnehan and Dravot would be able to wander through Afghanistan without detection. But, beyond, they would find death, certain and awful death.

Ten days later a native friend of mine, giving me the news of the day from Peshawur, wound up his letter with:—"There has been much laughter here on account of a certain mad priest who is going in his estimation to sell petty gauds and insignificant trinkets which he ascribes as great charms to H. H.[2] the Amir of Bokhara. He passed through Peshawur and associated himself to the Second Summer caravan that goes to Kabul. The merchants are pleased, because through superstition they imagine that such mad fellows bring good-fortune."

---

8. Get ready.
9. Rifle issued to British infantry.

1. The principal tribe in Afghanistan.
2. His Highness.

The two, then, were beyond the Border. I would have prayed for them, but, that night, a real King died in Europe, and demanded an obituary notice.

The wheel of the world swings through the same phases again and again. Summer passed and winter thereafter, and came and passed again. The daily paper continued and I with it, and upon the third summer there fell a hot night, a night-issue, and a strained waiting for something to be telegraphed from the other side of the world, exactly as had happened before. A few great men had died in the past two years, the machines worked with more clatter, and some of the trees in the Office garden were a few feet taller. But that was all the difference.

I passed over to the press-room, and went through just such a scene as I have already described. The nervous tension was stronger than it had been two years before, and I felt the heat more acutely. At three o'clock I cried, "Print off," and turned to go, when there crept to my chair what was left of a man. He was bent into a circle, his head was sunk between his shoulders, and he moved his feet one over the other like a bear. I could hardly see whether he walked or crawled—this rag-wrapped, whining cripple who addressed me by name, crying that he was come back. "Can you give me a drink?" he whimpered. "For the Lord's sake, give me a drink!"

I went back to the office, the man following with groans of pain, and I turned up the lamp.

"Don't you know me?" he gasped, dropping into a chair, and he turned his drawn face, surmounted by a shock of grey hair, to the light.

I looked at him intently. Once before had I seen eyebrows that met over the nose in an inch-broad black band, but for the life of me I could not tell where.

"I don't know you," I said, handing him the whiskey. "What can I do for you?"

He took a gulp of the spirit raw, and shivered in spite of the suffocating heat.

"I've come back," he repeated; "and I was the King of Kafiristan—me and Dravot—crowned Kings we was! In this office we settled it—you setting there and giving us the books. I am Peachey—Peachey Taliaferro Carnehan, and you've been setting here ever since—O Lord!"

I was more than a little astonished, and expressed my feelings accordingly.

"It's true," said Carnehan, with a dry cackle, nursing his feet, which were wrapped in rags. "True as gospel. Kings we were, with crowns upon our heads—me and Dravot—poor Dan—oh, poor, poor Dan, that would never take advice, not though I begged of him!"

"Take the whiskey," I said, "and take your own time. Tell me all you can recollect of everything from beginning to end. You got across the border on your camels, Dravot dressed as a mad priest and you his servant. Do you remember that?"

"I ain't mad—yet, but I shall be that way soon. Of course I remember. Keep looking at me, or maybe my words will go all to pieces. Keep looking at me in my eyes and don't say anything."

I leaned forward and looked into his face as steadily as I could. He dropped one hand upon the table and I grasped it by the wrist. It was twisted like a bird's claw, and upon the back was a ragged, red, diamond-shaped scar.

"No, don't look there. Look at *me*," said Carnehan.

"That comes afterward, but for the Lord's sake don't distrack me. We left with that caravan, me and Dravot playing all sorts of antics to amuse the people we were with. Dravot used to make us laugh in the evenings when all the people was cooking their dinners—cooking their dinners, and . . . what did they do then? They lit little fires with sparks that went into Dravot's beard, and we all laughed—fit to die. Little red fires they was, going into Dravot's big red beard—so funny." His eyes left mine and he smiled foolishly.

"You went as far as Jagdallak with that caravan," I said, at a venture, "after you had lit those fires. To Jagdallak, where you turned off to try to get into Kafiristan."

"No, we didn't neither. What are you talking about? We turned off before Jagdallak, because we heard the roads was good. But they wasn't good enough for our two camels—mine and Dravot's. When we left the caravan, Dravot took off all his clothes and mine too, and said we would be heathen, because the Kafirs[3] didn't allow Mohammedans to talk to them. So we dressed betwixt and between, and such a sight as Daniel Dravot I never saw yet nor expect to see again. He burned half his beard, and slung a sheep-skin over his shoulder, and shaved his head into patterns. He shaved mine, too, and made me wear outrageous things to look like a heathen. That was in a most mountaineous country, and our camels couldn't go along any more because of the mountains. They were tall and black, and coming home I saw them fight like wild goats—there are lots of goats in Kafiristan. And these mountains, they never keep still, no more than goats. Always fighting they are, and don't let you sleep at night."

"Take some more whiskey," I said, very slowly. "What did you and Daniel Dravot do when the camels could go no further because of the rough roads that led into Kafiristan?"

"What did which do? There was a party called Peachey Taliaferro Carnehan that was with Dravot. Shall I tell you about him? He died out there in the cold. Slap from the bridge fell old Peachey, turning and twisting in the air like a penny whirligig that you can sell to the Amir—No; they was two for three ha'pence, those whirligigs, or I am much mistaken and woful sore. And then these camels were no use, and Peachey said to Dravot—'For the Lord's sake, let's get out of this before our heads are chopped off,' and with that they killed the camels all among the mountains, not having anything in particular to eat, but first they took off the boxes with the guns and the ammunition, till two men came along driving four mules. Dravot up and dances in front of them, singing,—'Sell me four mules.' Says the first man,—'If you are rich enough to buy, you are rich enough to rob;' but before ever he could put his hand to his knife, Dravot breaks his neck over his knee, and the other party runs away. So Carnehan loaded the mules with the rifles that was taken off the camels, and together we starts forward into those bitter cold mountaineous parts, and never a road broader than the back of your hand."

He paused for a moment, while I asked him if he could remember the nature of the country through which he had journeyed.

---

3. Non-Muslims.

"I am telling you as straight as I can, but my head isn't as good as it might be. They drove nails through it to make me hear better how Dravot died. The country was mountaineous and the mules were most contrary, and the inhabitants was dispersed and solitary. They went up and up, and down and down, and that other party, Carnehan, was imploring of Dravot not to sing and whistle so loud, for fear of bringing down the tremenjus avalanches. But Dravot says that if a King couldn't sing it wasn't worth being King, and whacked the mules over the rump, and never took no heed for ten cold days. We came to a big level valley all among the mountains, and the mules were near dead, so we killed them, not having anything in special for them or us to eat. We sat upon the boxes, and played odd and even[4] with the cartridges that was jolted out.

"Then ten men with bows and arrows ran down that valley, chasing twenty men with bows and arrows, and the row was tremenjus. They was fair men—fairer than you or me—with yellow hair and remarkable well built.[5] Says Dravot, unpacking the guns—'This is the beginning of the business. We'll fight for the ten men,' and with that he fires two rifles at the twenty men, and drops one of them at two hundred yards from the rock where we was sitting. The other men began to run, but Carnehan and Dravot sits on the boxes picking them off at all ranges, up and down the valley. Then we goes up to the ten men that had run across the snow too, and they fires a footy[6] little arrow at us. Dravot he shoots above their heads and they all falls down flat. Then he walks over and kicks them, and then he lifts them up and shakes hands all round to make them friendly like. He calls them and gives them the boxes to carry, and waves his hand for all the world as though he was King already. They takes the boxes and him across the valley and up the hill into a pine wood on the top, where there was half a dozen big stone idols. Dravot he goes to the biggest—a fellow they call Imbra—and lays a rifle and a cartridge at his feet, rubbing his nose respectful with his own nose, patting him on the head, and saluting in front of it. He turns round to the men and nods his head, and says,—'That's all right. I'm in the know too, and all these old jim-jams[7] are my friends.' Then he opens his mouth and points down it, and when the first man brings him food, he says—'No;' and when the second man brings him food, he says—'No;' but when one of the old priests and the boss of the village brings him food, he says—'Yes;' very haughty, and eats it slow. That was how we came to our first village, without any trouble, just as though we had tumbled from the skies. But we tumbled from one of those damned rope-bridges, you see, and you couldn't expect a man to laugh much after that."

"Take some more whiskey and go on," I said. "That was the first village you came into. How did you get to be King?"

"I wasn't King," said Carnehan. "Dravot he was the King, and a handsome man he looked with the gold crown on his head and all. Him and the other party stayed in that village, and every morning Dravot sat by the side of old Imbra, and the people came and worshipped. That was Dravot's order. Then a lot of men came into the valley, and Carnehan and Dravot picks them off

4. A game in which a player guesses the number of objects that another player is holding.
5. There was a legend that Alexander the Great had left a Greek colony in the area in the 4th century B.C.E.
6. Paltry, insignificant.
7. Knickknacks.

with the rifles before they knew where they was, and runs down into the valley and up again the other side, and finds another village, same as the first one, and the people all falls down flat on their faces, and Dravot says,— 'Now what is the trouble between you two villages?' and the people points to a woman, as fair as you or me, that was carried off, and Dravot takes her back to the first village and counts up the dead—eight there was. For each dead man Dravot pours a little milk on the ground and waves his arms like a whirligig and 'That's all right,' says he. Then he and Carnehan takes the big boss of each village by the arm and walks them down into the valley, and shows them how to scratch a line with a spear right down the valley, and gives each a sod of turf from both sides o' the line. Then all the people comes down and shouts like the devil and all, and Dravot says,—'Go and dig the land, and be fruitful and multiply,'[8] which they did, though they didn't understand. Then we asks the names of things in their lingo—bread and water and fire and idols and such, and Dravot leads the priest of each village up to the idol, and says he must sit there and judge the people, and if anything goes wrong he is to be shot.

"Next week they was all turning up the land in the valley as quiet as bees and much prettier, and the priests heard all the complaints and told Dravot in dumb show what it was about. 'That's just the beginning,' says Dravot. 'They think we're Gods.' He and Carnehan picks out twenty good men and shows them how to click off a rifle, and form fours, and advance in line, and they was very pleased to do so, and clever to see the hang of it. Then he takes out his pipe and his baccy-pouch and leaves one at one village and one at the other, and off we two goes to see what was to be done in the next valley. That was all rock, and there was a little village there, and Carnehan says,—'Send 'em to the old valley to plant,' and takes 'em there and gives 'em some land that wasn't took before. They were a poor lot, and we blooded 'em with a kid[9] before letting 'em into the new Kingdom. That was to impress the people, and then they settled down quiet, and Carnehan went back to Dravot, who had got into another valley, all snow and ice and most mountaineous. There was no people there, and the Army got afraid, so Dravot shoots one of them, and goes on till he finds some people in a village, and the Army explains that unless the people wants to be killed they had better not shoot their little matchlocks;[1] for they had matchlocks. We makes friends with the priest and I stays there alone with two of the Army, teaching the men how to drill, and a thundering big Chief comes across the snow with kettle-drums and horns twanging, because he heard there was a new God kicking about. Carnehan sights for the brown[2] of the men half a mile across the snow and wings one of them. Then he sends a message to the Chief that, unless he wished to be killed, he must come and shake hands with me and leave his arms behind. The Chief comes alone first, and Carnehan shakes hands with him and whirls his arms about, same as Dravot used, and very much surprised that Chief was, and strokes my eyebrows. Then Carnehan goes alone to the Chief, and asks him in dumb show if he had an enemy he hated. 'I have,' says the Chief. So Carnehan weeds out the pick of his men, and sets the two of the

---

8. God's command to Adam and Eve (Genesis 1.28).
9. I.e., a kid goat, a fake religious ritual.
1. Primitive muskets.

2. A hunting term, meaning to fire into the middle of a group of game birds rather than aiming at a particular one.

Army to show them drill, and at the end of two weeks the men can manoeuvre about as well as Volunteers. So he marches with the Chief to a great big plain on the top of a mountain, and the Chief's men rushes into a village and takes it; we three Martinis firing into the brown of the enemy. So we took that village too, and I gives the Chief a rag from my coat and says, 'Occupy till I come;'[3] which was scriptural. By way of a reminder, when me and the Army was eighteen hundred yards away, I drops a bullet near him standing on the snow, and all the people falls flat on their faces. Then I sends a letter to Dravot, wherever he be by land or by sea."

At the risk of throwing the creature out of train I interrupted,—"How could you write a letter up yonder?"

"The letter?—Oh!—The letter! Keep looking at me between the eyes, please. It was a string-talk letter, that we'd learned the way of it from a blind beggar in the Punjab."

I remember that there had once come to the office a blind man with a knotted twig and a piece of string which he wound round the twig according to some cipher of his own. He could, after the lapse of days or hours, repeat the sentence which he had reeled up. He had reduced the alphabet to eleven primitive sounds; and tried to teach me his method, but failed.

"I sent that letter to Dravot," said Carnehan; "and told him to come back because this Kingdom was growing too big for me to handle, and then I struck for the first valley, to see how the priests were working. They called the village we took along with the Chief, Bashkai, and the first village we took, Er-Heb. The priests at Er-Heb was doing all right, but they had a lot of pending cases about land to show me, and some men from another village had been firing arrows at night. I went out and looked for that village and fired four rounds at it from a thousand yards. That used all the cartridges I cared to spend, and I waited for Dravot, who had been away two or three months, and I kept my people quiet.

"One morning I heard the devil's own noise of drums and horns, and Dan Dravot marches down the hill with his Army and a tail of hundreds of men, and, which was the most amazing—a great gold crown on his head. 'My Gord, Carnehan,' says Daniel, 'this is a tremenjus business, and we've got the whole country as far as it's worth having. I am the son of Alexander by Queen Semiramis,[4] and you're my younger brother and a God too! It's the biggest thing we've ever seen. I've been marching and fighting for six weeks with the Army, and every footy[5] little village for fifty miles has come in rejoiceful; and more than that, I've got the key of the whole show, as you'll see, and I've got a crown for you! I told 'em to make two of 'em at a place called Shu, where the gold lies in the rock like suet in mutton. Gold I've seen, and turquoise I've kicked out of the cliffs, and there's garnets in the sands of the river, and here's a chunk of amber that a man brought me. Call up all the priests and, here, take your crown.'

"One of the men opens a black hair bag and I slips the crown on. It was too small and too heavy, but I wore it for the glory. Hammered gold it was— five pound weight, like a hoop of a barrel.

---

3. In Jesus's parable of the talents, a nobleman gives each of his servants a coin to invest with those instructions (Luke 19.13).

4. Legendary Assyrian queen.
5. Worthless.

"'Peachey,' says Dravot, 'we don't want to fight no more. The Craft's[6] the trick, so help me!' and he brings forward that same Chief that I left at Bashkai—Billy Fish we called him afterward, because he was so like Billy Fish that drove the big tank-engine at Mach on the Bolan[7] in the old days. 'Shake hands with him,' says Dravot, and I shook hands and nearly dropped, for Billy Fish gave me the Grip.[8] I said nothing, but tried him with the Fellow Craft Grip. He answers, all right, and I tried the Master's Grip, but that was a slip. 'A Fellow Craft he is!' I says to Dan. 'Does he know the word?' 'He does,' says Dan, 'and all the priests know. It's a miracle! The Chiefs and the priests can work a Fellow Craft Lodge in a way that's very like ours, and they've cut the marks on the rocks, but they don't know the Third Degree, and they've come to find out. It's Gord's Truth. I've known these long years that the Afghans knew up to the Fellow Craft Degree, but this is a miracle. A God and a Grand-Master of the Craft am I, and a Lodge in the Third Degree I will open, and we'll raise the head priests and the Chiefs of the villages.'

"'It's against all the law,' I says, 'holding a Lodge without warrant from any one; and we never held office in any Lodge.'

"'It's a master-stroke of policy,' says Dravot. 'It means running the country as easy as a four-wheeled bogy[9] on a down grade. We can't stop to inquire now, or they'll turn against us. I've forty Chiefs at my heel, and passed and raised according to their merit they shall be. Billet these men on the villages and see that we run up a Lodge of some kind. The temple of Imbra will do for the Lodge-room. The women must make aprons as you show them. I'll hold a levee[1] of Chiefs to-night and Lodge to-morrow.'

"I was fair run off my legs, but I wasn't such a fool as not to see what a pull this Craft business gave us. I showed the priests' families how to make aprons of the degrees, but for Dravot's apron the blue border and marks was made of turquoise lumps on white hide, not cloth. We took a great square stone in the temple for the Master's chair, and little stones for the officers' chairs, and painted the black pavement with white squares, and did what we could to make things regular.

"At the levee which was held that night on the hillside with big bonfires, Dravot gives out that him and me were Gods and sons of Alexander, and Past Grand-Masters in the Craft, and was come to make Kafiristan a country where every man should eat in peace and drink in quiet, and specially obey us. Then the Chiefs come round to shake hands, and they was so hairy and white and fair it was just shaking hands with old friends. We gave them names according as they was like men we had known in India—Billy Fish, Holly Wilworth, Pikky Kergan that was Bazar-master when I was at Mhow, and so on and so on.

"*The* most amazing miracle was at Lodge next night. One of the old priests was watching us continuous, and I felt uneasy, for I knew we'd have to fudge the Ritual, and I didn't know what the men knew. The old priest was a stranger come in from beyond the village of Bashkai. The minute Dravot puts on the Master's apron that the girls had made for him, the priest fetches a whoop and a howl, and tries to overturn the stone that Dravot was sitting on. 'It's all up

6. Freemasonry.
7. The Bolan Pass, which was brought under British control in 1879 during the Second Afghan War.
8. Freemason handshake.
9. Railway truck.
1. Gathering.

now,' I says. 'That comes of meddling with the Craft without warrant!' Dravot
never winked an eye, not when ten priests took and tilted over the Grand-
Master's chair—which was to say the stone of Imbra. The priest begins rubbing the bottom end of it to clear away the black dirt, and presently he shows
all the other priests the Master's Mark, same as was on Dravot's apron, cut
into the stone. Not even the priests of the temple of Imbra knew it was there.
The old chap falls flat on his face at Dravot's feet and kisses 'em. 'Luck again,'
says Dravot, across the Lodge to me, 'they say it's the missing Mark that no
one could understand the why of. We're more than safe now.' Then he bangs
the butt of his gun for a gavel and says:—'By virtue of the authority vested in
me by my own right hand and the help of Peachey, I declare myself Grand-
Master of all Freemasonry in Kafiristan in this the Mother Lodge o' the country, and King of Kafiristan equally with Peachey!' At that he puts on his crown
and I puts on mine—I was doing Senior Warden—and we opens the Lodge in
most ample form. It was a amazing miracle! The priests moved in Lodge
through the first two degrees almost without telling, as if the memory was
coming back to them. After that, Peachey and Dravot raised such as was
worthy—high priests and Chiefs of far-off villages. Billy Fish was the first, and
I can tell you we scared the soul out of him. It was not in any way according to
Ritual, but it served our turn. We didn't raise more than ten of the biggest
men, because we didn't want to make the Degree common. And they was
clamoring to be raised.

"'In another six months,' says Dravot, 'we'll hold another Communication[2] and see how you are working.' Then he asks them about their villages,
and learns that they was fighting one against the other and were fair sick
and tired of it. And when they wasn't doing that they was fighting with the
Mohammedans. 'You can fight those when they come into our country,' says
Dravot. 'Tell off[3] every tenth man of your tribes for a Frontier guard, and
send two hundred at a time to this valley to be drilled. Nobody is going to
be shot or speared any more so long as he does well, and I know that you
won't cheat me because you're white people—sons of Alexander—and not
like common, black Mohammedans. You are *my* people and by God,' says
he, running off into English at the end—'I'll make a damned fine Nation of
you, or I'll die in the making!'

"I can't tell all we did for the next six months because Dravot did a lot I
couldn't see the hang off, and he learned their lingo in a way I never could.
My work was to help the people plough, and now and again go out with
some of the Army and see what the other villages were doing, and make 'em
throw rope-bridges across the ravines which cut up the country horrid.
Dravot was very kind to me, but when he walked up and down in the pine
wood pulling that bloody red beard of his with both fists I knew he was
thinking plans I could not advise him about, and I just waited for orders.

"But Dravot never showed me disrespect before the people. They were
afraid of me and the Army, but they loved Dan. He was the best of friends
with the priests and the Chiefs; but any one could come across the hills with
a complaint and Dravot would hear him out fair, and call four priests
together and say what was to be done. He used to call in Billy Fish from

2. In Freemasonry an official Lodge meeting, in which all members have a part.
3. Count off.

Bashkai, and Pikky Kergan from Shu, and an old Chief we called Kafuze-lum—it was like enough to his real name—and hold councils with 'em when there was any fighting to be done in small villages. That was his Council of War, and the four priests of Bashkai, Shu, Khawak, and Madora was his Privy Council. Between the lot of 'em they sent me, with forty men and twenty rifles, and sixty men carrying turquoises, into the Ghorband country to buy those hand-made Martini rifles, that come out of the Amir's work-shops at Kabul, from one of the Amir's Herati regiments that would have sold the very teeth out of their mouths for turquoises.

"I stayed in Ghorband a month, and gave the Governor there the pick of my baskets for hush-money, and bribed the Colonel of the regiment some more, and, between the two and the tribes-people, we got more than a hun-dred handmade Martinis, a hundred good Kohat Jezails[4] that'll throw to six hundred yards, and forty man-loads of very bad ammunition for the rifles. I came back with what I had, and distributed 'em among the men that the Chiefs sent to me to drill. Dravot was too busy to attend to those things, but the old Army that we first made helped me, and we turned out five hundred men that could drill, and two hundred that knew how to hold arms pretty straight. Even those cork-screwed, hand-made guns was a miracle to them. Dravot talked big about powder-shops and factories, walking up and down in the pine wood when the winter was coming on.

"'I won't make a Nation,' says he. 'I'll make an Empire! These men aren't niggers; they're English! Look at their eyes—look at their mouths. Look at the way they stand up. They sit, on chairs in their own houses. They're the Lost Tribes,[5] or something like it, and they've grown to be English. I'll take a census in the spring if the priests don't get frightened. There must be a fair two million of 'em in these hills. The villages are full o' little children. Two million people—two hundred and fifty thousand fighting men—and all English! They only want the rifles and a little drilling. Two hundred and fifty thousand men, ready to cut in on Russia's right flank when she tries for India! Peachey, man,' he says, chewing his beard in great hunks, 'we shall be Emperors—Emperors of the Earth! Rajah Brooke will be a suckling[6] to us. I'll treat with the Viceroy[7] on equal terms. I'll ask him to send me twelve picked English—twelve that I know of—to help us govern a bit. There's Mackray, Sergeant-pensioner at Segowli—many's the good dinner he's given me, and his wife a pair of trousers. There's Donldn, the Warder of Tounghoo Jail; there's hundreds that I could lay my hand on if I was in India. The Viceroy shall do it for me. I'll send a man through in the spring for those men, and I'll write for a dispensation from the Grand-Lodge for what I've done as Grand-Master. That—and all the Sniders[8] that'll be thrown out when the native troops in India take up the Martini. They'll be worn smooth, but they'll do for fighting in these hills. Twelve English, a hundred thousand Sniders run through the Amir's country in driblets—I'd be content with twenty thousand in one year—and we'd be an Empire. When everything was shipshape, I'd hand over the crown—this crown I'm wearing now—to Queen Victoria on my knees, and she'd say: "Rise up, Sir

4. Afghan muskets.
5. Of the twelve original Hebrew tribes men-tioned in the Bible, ten were lost by assimilating with neighboring peoples.

6. Infant.
7. Head of the British administration in India. Rajah Brooke: see p. 949, n. 3.
8. Older rifles being replaced by Martinis.

Daniel Dravot." Oh, it's big! It's big, I tell you! But there's so much to be done in every place—Bashkai, Khawak, Shu, and everywhere else.'

"'What is it?' I says. There are no more men coming in to be drilled this autumn. Look at those fat, black clouds. They're bringing the snow.'

"'It isn't that,' says Daniel, putting his hand very hard on my shoulder; 'and I don't wish to say anything that's against you, for no other living man would have followed me and made me what I am as you have done. You're a first-class Commander-in-Chief, and the people know you; but—it's a big country, and somehow you can't help me, Peachey, in the way I want to be helped.'

"'Go to your blasted priests, then!' I said, and I was sorry when I made that remark, but it did hurt me sore to find Daniel talking so superior when I'd drilled all the men, and done all he told me.

"'Don't let's quarrel, Peachey,' says Daniel, without cursing. 'You're a King, too, and the half of this Kingdom is yours; but can't you see, Peachey, we want cleverer men than us now—three or four of 'em, that we can scatter about for our Deputies. It's a hugeous great State, and I can't always tell the right thing to do, and I haven't time for all I want to do, and here's the winter coming on and all.' He put half his beard into his mouth, and it was as red as the gold of his crown.

"'I'm sorry, Daniel,' says I. 'I've done all I could. I've drilled the men and shown the people how to stack their oats better; and I've brought in those tinware rifles from Ghorband—but I know what you're driving at. I take it Kings always feel oppressed that way.'

"'There's another thing too,' says Dravot, walking up and down. 'The winter's coming and these people won't be giving much trouble and if they do we can't move about. I want a wife.'

"'For Gord's sake leave the women alone!' I says. 'We've both got all the work we can, though I *am* a fool. Remember the Contrack, and keep clear o' women.'

"'The Contrack only lasted till such time as we was Kings; and Kings we have been these months past,' says Dravot, weighing his crown in his hand. 'You go get a wife too, Peachey—a nice, strappin', plump girl that'll keep you warm in the winter. They're prettier than English girls, and we can take the pick of 'em. Boil 'em once or twice in hot water, and they'll come as fair as chicken and ham.'

"'Don't tempt me!' I says. 'I will not have any dealings with a woman not till we are a dam' side more settled than we are now. I've been doing the work o' two men, and you've been doing the work o' three. Let's lie off a bit, and see if we can get some better tobacco from Afghan country and run in some good liquor; but no women.'

"'Who's talking o' *women*?' says Dravot. 'I said *wife*—a Queen to breed a King's son for the King. A Queen out of the strongest tribe, that'll make them your blood-brothers, and that'll lie by your side and tell you all the people thinks about you and their own affairs. That's what I want.'

"'Do you remember that Bengali woman I kept at Mogul Serai when I was a plate-layer?'[9] says I. 'A fat lot o' good she was to me. She taught me the lingo and one or two other things; but what happened? She ran away with the Station-master's servant and half my month's pay. Then she turned up at

9. Layer of railway track.

Dadur Junction in tow of a half-caste, and had the impidence to say I was her husband—all among the drivers in the running-shed!'

"'We've done with that,' says Dravot. 'These women are whiter than you or me, and a Queen I will have for the winter months.'

"'For the last time o' asking, Dan, do *not*,' I says. 'It'll only bring us harm. The Bible says that Kings ain't to waste their strength on women,[1] 'specially when they've got a new raw Kingdom to work over.'

"'For the last time of answering, I will,' said Dravot, and he went away through the pine-trees looking like a big red devil. The low sun hit his crown and beard on one side and the two blazed like hot coals.

"But getting a wife was not as easy as Dan thought. He put it before the Council, and there was no answer till Billy Fish said that he'd better ask the girls. Dravot damned them all round. 'What's wrong with me?' he shouts, standing by the idol Imbra. 'Am I a dog or am I not enough of a man for your wenches? Haven't I put the shadow of my hand over this country? Who stopped the last Afghan raid?' It was me really, but Dravot was too angry to remember. 'Who brought your guns? Who repaired the bridges? Who's the Grand-Master of the sign cut in the stone?' and he thumped his hand on the block that he used to sit on in Lodge, and at Council, which opened like Lodge always. Billy Fish said nothing, and no more did the others. 'Keep your hair on, Dan,' said I; 'and ask the girls. That's how it's done at Home, and these people are quite English.'

"'The marriage of the King is a matter of State,' says Dan, in a white-hot rage, for he could feel, I hope, that he was going against his better mind. He walked out of the Council-room, and the others sat still, looking at the ground.

"'Billy Fish,' says I to the Chief of Bashkai, 'what's the difficulty here? A straight answer to a true friend.' 'You know,' says Billy Fish. 'How should a man tell you who know everything? How can daughters of men marry Gods or Devils? It's not proper.'

"I remembered something like that in the Bible;[2] but if, after seeing us as long as they had, they still believed we were Gods, it wasn't for me to undeceive them.

"'A God can do anything,' says I. 'If the King is fond of a girl he'll not let her die.' 'She'll have to,' said Billy Fish. 'There are all sorts of Gods and Devils in these mountains, and now and again a girl marries one of them and isn't seen any more. Besides, you two know the Mark cut in the stone. Only the Gods know that. We thought you were men till you showed the sign of the Master.'

"I wished then that we had explained about the loss of the genuine secrets of a Master-Mason at the first go-off; but I said nothing. All that night there was a blowing of horns in a little dark temple half-way down the hill, and I heard a girl crying fit to die. One of the priests told us that she was being prepared to marry the King.

"'I'll have no nonsense of that kind,' says Dan. 'I don't want to interfere with your customs, but I'll take my own wife.' 'The girl's a little bit afraid,'

---

1. "Give not thy strength unto women, nor thy ways to that which destroyeth kings" (Proverbs 31.3).

2. "That the sons of God saw the daughters of men that they were fair; and they took them wives of all which they chose" (Genesis 6.2).

says the priest. 'She thinks she's going to die, and they are a-heartening of her up down in the temple.'

"'Hearten her very tender, then,' says Dravot, 'or I'll hearten you with the butt of a gun so that you'll never want to be heartened again.' He licked his lips, did Dan, and stayed up walking about more than half the night, thinking of the wife that he was going to get in the morning. I wasn't any means comfortable, for I knew that dealings with a woman in foreign parts, though you was a crowned King twenty times over, could not but be risky. I got up very early in the morning while Dravot was asleep, and I saw the priests talking together in whispers, and the Chiefs talking together too, and they looked at me out of the corners of their eyes.

"'What is up, Fish?' I says to the Bashkai man, who was wrapped up in his furs and looking splendid to behold.

"'I can't rightly say,' says he; 'but if you can induce the King to drop all this nonsense about marriage, you'll be doing him and me and yourself a great service.'

"'That I do believe,' says I. 'But sure, you know, Billy, as well as me, having fought against and for us, that the King and me are nothing more than two of the finest men that God Almighty ever made. Nothing more, I do assure you.'

"'That may be,' says Billy Fish, 'and yet I should be sorry if it was.' He sinks his head upon his great fur cloak for a minute and thinks. 'King,' says he, 'be you man or God or Devil, I'll stick by you to-day. I have twenty of my men with me, and they will follow me. We'll go to Bashkai until the storm blows over.'

"A little snow had fallen in the night, and everything was white except the greasy fat clouds that blew down and down from the north. Dravot came out with his crown on his head, swinging his arms and stamping his feet, and looking more pleased than Punch.[3]

"'For the last time, drop it, Dan,' says I, in a whisper. 'Billy Fish here says that there will be a row.'

"'A row among my people!' says Dravot. 'Not much. Peachey, you're a fool not to get a wife too. Where's the girl?' says he, with a voice as loud as the braying of a jackass. 'Call up all the Chiefs and priests, and let the Emperor see if his wife suits him.'

"There was no need to call any one. They were all there leaning on their guns and spears round the clearing in the centre of the pine wood. A deputation of priests went down to the little temple to bring up the girl, and the horns blew up fit to wake the dead. Billy Fish saunters round and gets as close to Daniel as he could, and behind him stood his twenty men with matchlocks. Not a man of them under six feet. I was next to Dravot, and behind me was twenty men of the regular Army. Up comes the girl, and a strapping wench she was, covered with silver and turquoises, but white as death, and looking back every minute at the priests.

"'She'll do,' said Dan, looking her over. 'What's to be afraid of, lass? Come and kiss me.' He puts his arm round her. She shuts his eyes, gives a bit of a squeak, and down goes her face in the side of Dan's flaming red beard.

---

3. Common expression: the character in the Punch-and-Judy puppet show has a fixed grin and is delighted with his evil deeds.

"'The slut's bitten me!' says he, clapping his hand to his neck, and, sure enough, his hand was red with blood. Billy Fish and two of his matchlock-men catches hold of Dan by the shoulders and drags him into the Bashkai lot, while the priests howl in their lingo,—'Neither God nor Devil, but a man!' I was all taken aback, for a priest cut at me in front, and the Army behind began firing into the Bashkai men.

"'God A-mighty!' says Dan. 'What is the meaning o' this?'

"'Come back! Come away!' says Billy Fish. 'Ruin and Mutiny is the matter. We'll break for Bashkai if we can.'

"I tried to give some sort of orders to my men—the men o' the regular Army—but it was no use, so I fired into the brown of 'em with an English Martini and drilled three beggars in a line. The valley was full of shouting, howling creatures, and every soul was shrieking, 'Not a God nor a Devil, but only a man!' The Bashkai troops stuck to Billy Fish all they were worth, but their matchlocks wasn't half as good as the Kabul breech-loaders, and four of them dropped. Dan was bellowing like a bull, for he was very wrathy; and Billy Fish had a hard job to prevent him running out at the crowd.

"'We can't stand,' says Billy Fish. 'Make a run for it down the valley! The whole place is against us.' The matchlock-men ran, and we went down the valley in spite of Dravot's protestations. He was swearing horribly and crying out that he was a King. The priests rolled great stones on us, and the regular Army fired hard, and there wasn't more than six men, not counting Dan, Billy Fish, and Me, that came down to the bottom of the valley alive.

"Then they stopped firing and the horns in the temple blew again. 'Come away—for Gord's sake come away!' says Billy Fish. 'They'll send runners out to all the villages before ever we get to Bashkai. I can protect you there, but I can't do anything now.'

"My own notion is that Dan began to go mad in his head from that hour. He stared up and down like a stuck pig. Then he was all for walking back alone and killing the priests with his bare hands; which he could have done. 'An Emperor am I,' says Daniel, 'and next year I shall be a Knight of the Queen.'

"'All right, Dan,' says I; 'but come along now while there's time.'

"'It's your fault,' says he, 'for not looking after your Army better. There was mutiny in the midst and you didn't know—you damned engine-driving, plate-laying, missionary's-pass-hunting hound!' He sat upon a rock and called me every foul name he could lay tongue to. I was too heart-sick to care, though it was all his foolishness that brought the smash.

"'I'm sorry, Dan,' says I, 'but there's no accounting for natives. This business is our Fifty-Seven.[4] Maybe we'll make something out of it yet, when we've got to Bashkai.'

"'Let's get to Bashkai, then,' says Dan, 'and, by God, when I come back here again I'll sweep the valley so there isn't a bug in a blanket left!'

"We walked all that day, and all that night Dan was stumping up and down on the snow, chewing his beard and muttering to himself.

"'There's no hope o' getting clear,' said Billy Fish. 'The priests will have sent runners to the villages to say that you are only men. Why didn't you stick

---

4. The year 1857 saw the beginning of a two-year rebellion of Indian troops of the British East India Company and peasantry against the British; known at the time as the "Indian Mutiny," this is now referred to as the First War of Indian Independence.

on as Gods till things was more settled? I'm a dead man,' says Billy Fish, and
he throws himself down on the snow and begins to pray to his Gods.

"Next morning we was in a cruel bad country—all up and down, no level
ground at all, and no food either. The six Bashkai men looked at Billy Fish
hungry-wise as if they wanted to ask something, but they said never a word.
At noon we came to the top of a flat mountain all covered with snow, and
when we climbed up into it, behold, there was an Army in position waiting
in the middle!

"'The runners have been very quick,' says Billy Fish, with a little bit of a
laugh. 'They are waiting for us.'

"Three or four men began to fire from the enemy's side, and a chance
shot took Daniel in the calf of the leg. That brought him to his senses. He
looks across the snow at the Army, and sees the rifles that we had brought
into the country.

"'We're done for,' says he. 'They are Englishmen, these people,—and it's
my blasted nonsense that has brought you to this. Get back, Billy Fish, and
take your men away; you've done what you could, and now cut for it. Carnehan,' says he, 'shake hands with me and go along with Billy. Maybe they
won't kill you. I'll go and meet 'em alone. It's me that did it. Me, the King!'

"'Go!' says I. 'Go to Hell, Dan. I'm with you here. Billy Fish, you clear
out, and we two will meet those folk.'

"'I'm a Chief,' says Billy Fish, quite quiet. 'I stay with you. My men can go.'

"The Bashkai fellows didn't wait for a second word, but ran off, and Dan
and me and Billy Fish walked across to where the drums were drumming
and the horns were horning. It was cold—awful cold. I've got that cold in
the back of my head now. There's a lump of it there."

The punkah-coolies[5] had gone to sleep. Two kerosene lamps were blazing
in the office, and the perspiration poured down my face and splashed on
the blotter as I leaned forward. Carnehan was shivering, and I feared that
his mind might go. I wiped my face, took a fresh grip of the piteously mangled hands, and said: "What happened after that?"

The momentary shift of my eyes had broken the clear current.

"What was you pleased to say?" whined Carnehan. "They took them without
any sound. Not a little whisper all along the snow, not though the King knocked
down the first man that set hand on him—not though old Peachey fired his last
cartridge into the brown of 'em. Not a single solitary sound did those swines
make. They just closed up tight, and I tell you their furs stunk. There was a
man called Billy Fish, a good friend of us all, and they cut his throat, Sir, then
and there, like a pig; and the King kicks up the bloody snow and says:—'We've
had a dashed fine run for our money. What's coming next?' But Peachey,
Peachey Taliaferro, I tell you, Sir, in confidence as betwixt two friends, he lost
his head, Sir. No, he didn't neither. The King lost his head, so he did, all along
o' one of those cunning rope-bridges. Kindly let me have the paper-cutter, Sir.
It tilted this way. They marched him a mile across that snow to a rope-bridge
over a ravine with a river at the bottom. You may have seen such. They prodded him behind like an ox. 'Damn your eyes!' says the King. 'D'you suppose I
can't die like a gentleman?' He turns to Peachey—Peachey that was crying
like a child. 'I've brought you to this, Peachey,' says he. 'Brought you out of

---

5. Servants who operate punkahs, or fans.

your happy life to be killed in Kafiristan, where you was late Commander-in-Chief of the Emperor's forces. Say you forgive me, Peachey.' 'I do,' says Peachey. 'Fully and freely do I forgive you, Dan.' 'Shake hands, Peachey,' says he. 'I'm going now.' Out he goes, looking neither right nor left, and when he was plumb in the middle of those dizzy dancing ropes, 'Cut, you beggars,' he shouts; and they cut, and old Dan fell, turning round and round and round twenty thousand miles, for he took half an hour to fall till he struck the water, and I could see his body caught on a rock with the gold crown close beside.

"But do you know what they did to Peachey between two pine trees? They crucified him, Sir, as Peachey's hand will show. They used wooden pegs for his hands and his feet; and he didn't die. He hung there and screamed, and they took him down next day, and said it was a miracle that he wasn't dead. They took him down—poor old Peachey that hadn't done them any harm—that hadn't done them any . . ."

He rocked to and fro and wept bitterly, wiping his eyes with the back of his scarred hands and moaning like a child for some ten minutes.

"They was cruel enough to feed him up in the temple, because they said he was more of a God than old Daniel that was a man. Then they turned him out on the snow, and told him to go home, and Peachey came home in about a year, begging along the roads quite safe; for Daniel Dravot he walked before and said:—'Come along, Peachey. It's a big thing we're doing.' The mountains they danced at night, and the mountains they tried to fall on Peachey's head, but Dan he held up his hand, and Peachey came along bent double. He never let go of Dan's hand, and he never let go of Dan's head. They gave it to him as a present in the temple, to remind him not to come again, and though the crown was pure gold, and Peachey was starving, never would Peachey sell the same. You knew Dravot, Sir! You knew Right Worshipful Brother Dravot! Look at him now!"

He fumbled in the mass of rags round his bent waist; brought out a black horsehair bag embroidered with silver thread; and shook therefrom on to my table—the dried, withered head of Daniel Dravot! The morning sun that had long been paling the lamps struck the red beard and blind, sunken eyes; struck, too, a heavy circlet of gold studded with raw turquoises, that Carnehan placed tenderly on the battered temples.

"You behold now," said Carnehan, "the Emperor in his habit as he lived[6]—the King of Kafiristan with his crown upon his head. Poor old Daniel that was a monarch once!"

I shuddered, for, in spite of defacements manifold, I recognized the head of the man of Marwar Junction. Carnehan rose to go. I attempted to stop him. He was not fit to walk abroad. "Let me take away the whiskey, and give me a little money," he gasped. "I was a King once. I'll go to the Deputy Commissioner and ask to set in the Poorhouse till I get my health. No, thank you, I can't wait till you get a carriage for me. I've urgent private affairs—in the south—at Marwar."

He shambled out of the office and departed in the direction of the Deputy Commissioner's house. That day at noon I had occasion to go down the blinding hot Mall, and I saw a crooked man crawling along the white dust

6. Allusion to Hamlet's description of his father's ghost: "My father, in his habit as he lived" (Shakespeare, *Hamlet* 3.4.126).

of the roadside, his hat in his hand, quavering dolorously after the fashion of street-singers at Home. There was not a soul in sight, and he was out of all possible earshot of the houses. And he sang through his nose, turning his head from right to left:

> "The Son of Man goes forth to war,
>   A golden crown to gain;
> His blood-red banner streams afar—
>   Who follows in his train?"[7]

I waited to hear no more, but put the poor wretch into my carriage and drove him off to the nearest missionary for eventual transfer to the Asylum. He repeated the hymn twice while he was with me, whom he did not in the least recognize, and I left him singing it to the missionary.

Two days later I inquired after his welfare of the Superintendent of the Asylum.

"He was admitted suffering from sunstroke. He died early yesterday morning," said the Superintendent. "Is it true that he was half an hour bareheaded in the sun at midday?"

"Yes," said I, "but do you happen to know if he had anything upon him by any chance when he died?"

"Not to my knowledge," said the Superintendent.

And there the matter rests.

1888

Danny Deever

"What are the bugles blowin' for?" said Files-on-Parade.[1]
"To turn you out, to turn you out," the Colour-Sergeant[2] said.
"What makes you look so white, so white?" said Files-on-Parade.
"I'm dreadin' what I've got to watch," the Colour-Sergeant said.
5   For they're hangin' Danny Deever, you can hear the Dead March play,
    The regiment's in 'ollow square[3]—they're hangin' him today;
    They've taken of his buttons off an' cut his stripes[4] away,
    An they're hangin' Danny Deever in the mornin'.

"What makes the rear rank breathe so 'ard?" said Files-on-Parade.
10 "It's bitter cold, it's bitter cold," the Colour-Sergeant said.
"What makes that front-rank man fall down?" said Files-on-Parade.
"A touch o' sun, a touch o' sun," the Colour-Sergeant said.
    They are hangin' Danny Deever, they are marchin' of 'im round,
    They 'ave 'alted Danny Deever by 'is coffin on the ground;
15   An' 'e'll swing in 'arf a minute for a sneakin' shootin' hound—
    O they're hangin' Danny Deever in the mornin'!

7. A well-known hymn, by Reginald Heber (1783–1826), corrected in later editions to the actual words of the first line: "The Son of God goes forth to war."
1. Army private. "Files" here should be spoken as two syllables (*fy-ulls*).
2. High-ranking noncommissioned officer.

3. Ceremonial formation in which the troops line four sides of a parade square, facing inward. "'Ollow": hollow. London Cockney speech often drops the *h* from words that start with this letter.
4. Chevrons denoting rank, worn by corporals and sergeants on the sleeves of their tunics.

"'Is cot was right-'and cot to mine," said Files-on-Parade.
"'E's sleepin' out an' far tonight," the Colour-Sergeant said.
"I've drunk 'is beer a score o' times," said Files-on-Parade.
20 "'E's drinkin bitter beer[5] alone," the Colour-Sergeant said.
  They are hangin' Danny Deever, you must mark 'im to 'is place,
  For 'e shot a comrade sleepin'—you must look 'im in the face;
  Nine 'undred of 'is county[6] an' the Regiment's disgrace,
  While they're hangin' Danny Deever in the mornin'.

25 "What's that so black agin the sun?" said Files-on-Parade.
  "It's Danny fightin' 'ard for life," the Colour-Sergeant said.
  "What's that that whimpers over'ead?" said Files-on-Parade.
  "It's Danny's soul that's passin' now," the Colour-Sergeant said.
  For they're done with Danny Deever, you can 'ear the quickstep play,
30 The regiment's in column, an' they're marchin' us away;
  Ho! the young recruits are shakin', an' they'll want their beer today,
  After hangin' Danny Deever in the mornin'.

                                                              1890

The Widow at Windsor

  'Ave you 'eard o' the Widow at Windsor
    With a hairy[1] gold crown on 'er 'ead?
  She 'as ships on the foam—she 'as millions at 'ome,
    An' she pays us poor beggars in red.[2]
5   (Ow, poor beggars in red!)
  There's 'er nick[3] on the cavalry 'orses,
    There's 'er mark[4] on the medical stores—
  An' 'er troopers° you'll find with a fair wind be'ind   *troopships*
    That takes us to various wars.
10   (Poor beggars!—barbarious wars!)
      Then 'ere's to the Widow at Windsor,
        An' 'ere's to the stores an' the guns,
      The men an' the 'orses what makes up the forces
        O' Missis Victorier's sons.
15   (Poor beggars! Victorier's sons!)

  Walk wide o' the Widow at Windsor,
    For 'alf o' Creation she owns:
  We 'ave bought 'er the same with the sword an' the flame,
    An' we've salted it down with our bones.
20   (Poor beggars!—it's blue with our bones!)

---

5. Or simply "bitter," a favorite variety of beer drunk in English pubs. The word *bitter* thus becomes a grim pun.
6. English regiments often bear the name of a particular county from which most of its members have been recruited (e.g., the Lancashire Fusiliers).
1. Airy, lofty. London Cockney speech often drops the *h* from words that start with this letter and sometimes adds an *h* to the beginning of words that start with a vowel.
2. British military uniforms were bright red.
3. A nick on one of their hoofs identified army horses as property of the Crown.
4. The queen's mark: "V.R.I." (*Victoria Regina et Imperatrix*, "Victoria Queen and Empress").

Hands off o' the sons o' the widow,
   Hands off o' the goods in 'er shop,
For the kings must come down an' the emperors frown
   When the Widow at Windsor says "Stop!"
25   (Poor beggars!—we're sent to say "Stop!")
    Then 'ere's to the Lodge o' the Widow,
      From the Pole to the Tropics it runs—
    To the Lodge that we tile with the rank an' the file,
      An' open in form with the guns.[5]
30   (Poor beggars!—it's always they guns!)

We 'ave 'eard o' the Widow at Windsor,
   It's safest to leave 'er alone:
For 'er sentries we stand by the sea an' the land
   Wherever the bugles are blown.[6]
35   (Poor beggars!—an' don't we get blown!)
Take 'old o' the Wings o' the Mornin',[7]
   An' flop round the earth till you're dead;
But you won't get away from the tune that they play
   To the bloomin' old rag° over'ead.   *i.e., the flag*
40   (Poor beggars!—it's 'ot over'ead!)
    Then 'ere's to the sons o' the Widow,
      Wherever, 'owever they roam.
   'Ere's all they desire, an' if they require
     A speedy return to their 'ome.
45   (Poor beggars!—they'll never see 'ome!)

                                            1892

Recessional[1]

1897

God of our fathers, known of old—
   Lord of our far-flung battle-line—
Beneath whose awful Hand we hold
   Dominion over palm and pine—
5 Lord God of Hosts, be with us yet
   Lest we forget—lest we forget!

---

5. Here, as in "The Man Who Would Be King," Kipling employs terms and concepts from Freemasonry (see p. 943, n. 2). Victoria's "Lodge" (her Masonic branch, or district) traverses the globe ("From the Pole to the Tropics"); the soldiers patrol its perimeters (to "tile" is to guard the door of a Masonic lodge), and gunfire stands in for the Masons' formal opening ceremonies.
6. Allusion to "Pro Rege Nostro" (1892), a poem by W. E. Henley (1849–1903).
7. Psalms 139.9.
1. A hymn sung as the clergy and choir leave a church in procession at the end of a service. Kipling's hymn was written on the occasion of the Jubilee celebrations honoring the sixtieth anniversary of Queen Victoria's reign, celebrations that had prompted a good deal of boasting in the press about the greatness of her empire. "Recessional" was first published in the London *Times*, and Kipling refused to accept any payment for its publication, then or later. After World War I the poem's refrain—"Lest we forget"—gained additional poignancy: it was employed as an epitaph on countless war memorials.

The tumult and the shouting dies—
The Captains and the Kings depart—
Still stands Thine ancient Sacrifice,
10 An humble and a contrite heart.[2]
Lord God of Hosts, be with us yet,
Lest we forget—lest we forget!

Far-called, our navies melt away—
 On dune and headland sinks the fire[3]—
15 Lo, all our pomp of yesterday
 Is one with Nineveh and Tyre![4]
Judge of the Nations, spare us yet,
Lest we forget—lest we forget!

If, drunk with sight of power, we loose
20 Wild tongues that have not Thee in awe—
Such boasting as the Gentiles use
 Or lesser breeds without the Law[5]—
Lord God of Hosts, be with us yet,
Lest we forget—lest we forget!

25 For heathen heart that puts her trust
 In reeking tube° and iron shard[6]—   *cannon, rifle*
All valiant dust that builds on dust,
  And guarding calls not Thee to guard—
For frantic boast and foolish word,
30 Thy mercy on Thy People, Lord!

1897   1897, 1899

The White Man's Burden[1]

Take up the White Man's burden—
 Send forth the best ye breed—
Go bind your sons to exile
 To serve your captives' need;
5 To wait in heavy harness,
 On fluttered folk and wild—
Your new-caught, sullen peoples,
 Half-devil and half-child.

---

2. Cf. Psalms 51.17: "The sacrifices of God are a broken spirit: a broken and a contrite heart, O God, thou wilt not despise."
3. Bonfires were lit on high ground all over Britain on the night of the Jubilee.
4. Once capitals of great empires. The ruins of Nineveh, in Assyria, were discovered buried in desert sands by British archaeologists in the 1850s. Tyre, in Phoenicia, had dwindled into a small Lebanese town.
5. Cf. Romans 2.14: "For when the Gentiles, which have not the law, do by nature the things contained in the law, these, having not the law,

are a law unto themselves."
6. Cf. Psalms 20.7: "Some trust in chariots, and some in horses, but we will remember the name of the Lord our God."
1. This poem was conceived for Queen Victoria's Jubilee in 1897, but Kipling abandoned it in favor of "Recessional." He returned to the poem when disagreements between Spain and the United States over Spanish colonial rule in Cuba and elsewhere sparked the Spanish-American War in 1898. In its revised form the poem reacts to resistance in the Philippines to the United States' assumption of colonial power.

Take up the White Man's burden—
10   In patience to abide,
To veil the threat of terror
    And check the show of pride;
By open speech and simple,
    An hundred times made plain,
15 To seek another's profit,
    And work another's gain.

Take up the White Man's burden—
    The savage wars of peace—
Fill full the mouth of Famine
20   And bid the sickness cease;
And when your goal is nearest
    The end for others sought,
Watch Sloth and heathen Folly
    Bring all your hope to nought.

25 Take up the White Man's burden—
    No tawdry rule of kings,
But toil of serf and sweeper[2]—
    The tale of common things.
The ports ye shall not enter,
30   The roads ye shall not tread,
Go make them with your living,
    And mark them with your dead.

Take up the White Man's burden—
    And reap his old reward:
35 The blame of those ye better,
    The hate of those ye guard—
The cry of hosts ye humour
    (Ah, slowly!) toward the light:—
'Why brought ye us from bondage,
40   Our loved Egyptian night?'[3]

Take up the White Man's burden—
    Ye dare not stoop to less—
Nor call too loud on Freedom
    To cloak your weariness;
45 By all ye cry or whisper,
    By all ye leave or do,
The silent, sullen peoples
    Shall weigh your Gods and you.

Take up the White Man's burden—
50 Have done with childish days—

2. Street sweeper, who in India would belong to the lowest caste.
3. Cf. Exodus 16.2–3. When the Israelites were hungry in the wilderness, they criticized Moses and Aaron for taking them from what they saw as the relative comfort of Egyptian slavery.

The lightly proffered laurel,[4]
   The easy, ungrudged praise.
Comes now, to search your manhood
   Through all the thankless years,
55 Cold, edged with dear-bought wisdom,
   The judgment of your peers!

                                     1899

If—

If you can keep your head when all about you
   Are losing theirs and blaming it on you;
If you can trust yourself when all men doubt you,
   But make allowance for their doubting too;
5 If you can wait and not be tired by waiting,
   Or being lied about, don't deal in lies,
Or being hated don't give way to hating,
   And yet don't look too good, nor talk too wise:

If you can dream—and not make dreams your master;
10 If you can think—and not make thoughts your aim,
If you can meet with Triumph and Disaster
   And treat those two impostors just the same;
If you can bear to hear the truth you've spoken
   Twisted by knaves to make a trap for fools,
15 Or watch the things you gave your life to, broken,
   And stoop and build 'em up with worn-out tools:

If you can make one heap of all your winnings
   And risk it on one turn of pitch-and-toss,[1]
And lose, and start again at your beginnings
20 And never breathe a word about your loss;
If you can force your heart and nerve and sinew
   To serve your turn long after they are gone,
And so hold on when there is nothing in you
   Except the Will which says to them: 'Hold on!'

25 If you can talk with crowds and keep your virtue,
   Or walk with Kings—nor° lose the common touch,   *and not*
If neither foes nor loving friends can hurt you,
   If all men count with you, but none too much;
If you can fill the unforgiving minute
30 With sixty seconds' worth of distance run,
Yours is the Earth and everything that's in it,
   And—which is more—you'll be a Man, my son!

                                     1910

---

4. A symbol of military distinction in the triumphs celebrated by victorious Roman generals (later, Roman emperors wore a laurel crown as part of their official regalia).

1. A game, played with coins, that combines skill (tossing a coin as close as possible to a fixed mark) and luck (flipping coins and keeping those that come up heads).

ERNEST DOWSON
1867–1900

Ernest Christopher Dowson spent much of his childhood traveling with his father on the Continent, mostly in France. His education was thus irregular and informal, but he acquired a thorough knowledge of French and of his favorite French writers—Gustave Flaubert, Honoré de Balzac, and Paul Verlaine—and a good knowledge of Latin poetry, especially Catullus, Propertius, and Horace. Dowson went to Oxford in 1886, but he did not take to regular academic instruction and left after a year. Though nominally assisting his father to manage a dock in the London district of Limehouse, Dowson spent most of his time writing poetry, stories, and essays and talking with Lionel Johnson, W. B. Yeats, and other members of the Rhymers' Club, in which he played a prominent part. Between 1890 and 1894 Dowson, though leading the irregular life of so many of the 1890s poets, produced his best work, and his volume *Verses* came out in 1896. Late nights and excessive drinking impaired a constitution already threatened by tuberculosis. He moved to France in 1894, making a living by translating from the French for an English publisher though his health was steadily worsening. After his return to England, he was discovered near death by a friend, who took the poet to his home and nursed Dowson until he died six weeks later.

Dowson was a member of what Yeats called "the tragic generation" of poets in the 1890s who seemed to be driven by their own restless energies to dissipation and premature death. As a poet he was considerably influenced by Algernon Charles Swinburne (whose feverish emotional tone he often captures very skillfully). Dowson experimented with a variety of meters, and in "Cynara" (1891) he used the twelve-syllable alexandrine as the normal line of a six-line stanza in a manner more common in French than in English poetry. He was also especially interested in the work of the French symbolist poets and in their theories of verbal suggestiveness and of poetry as incantation: he believed (as he once wrote in a letter) that a finer poetry could sometimes be achieved by "mere sound and music, with just a suggestion of sense."

Cynara

Non sum qualis eram bonae sub regno Cynarae.[1]

Last night, ah, yesternight, betwixt her lips and mine
There fell thy shadow, Cynara! thy breath was shed
Upon my soul between the kisses and the wine;
And I was desolate and sick of an old passion,

---

1. I am not as I was under the reign of the good Cynara (Latin; Horace, *Odes* 4.1.3–4). In this poem the poet pleads with Venus to stop tormenting him with love, because he is growing old and is no longer what he was when under the sway of Cynara (*Sin-ah-rah*), the girl he used to love. Of Dowson's "Cynara" W. B. Yeats later wrote: "Dowson, who seemed to drink so little and had so much dignity and reserve, was breaking his heart for the daughter of the keeper of an Italian eating house, in dissipation and drink." Dowson's "Cynara" was, in fact, a Polish girl by the name of Adelaide Foltinowicz; he fell in love with her when she was eleven and he was twenty-two years of age.

5   Yea, I was desolate and bowed my head:
I have been faithful to thee, Cynara! in my fashion.

All night upon mine heart I felt her warm heart beat,
Night-long within mine arms in love and sleep she lay;
Surely the kisses of her bought red mouth were sweet;
10 But I was desolate and sick of an old passion,
    When I awoke and found the dawn was grey:
I have been faithful to thee, Cynara! in my fashion.

I have forgot much, Cynara! gone with the wind,
Flung roses, roses riotously with the throng,
15 Dancing, to put thy pale, lost lilies out of mind;
But I was desolate and sick of an old passion,
    Yea, all the time, because the dance was long:
I have been faithful to thee, Cynara! in my fashion.

I cried for madder music and for stronger wine,
20 But when the feast is finished and the lamps expire,
Then falls thy shadow, Cynara! the night is thine;
And I am desolate and sick of an old passion,
    Yea, hungry for the lips of my desire:
I have been faithful to thee, Cynara! in my fashion.

1891, 1896

They Are Not Long

Vitae summa brevis spem nos vetat incohare longam.[1]

They are not long, the weeping and the laughter,
    Love and desire and hate:
I think they have no portion in us after
    We pass the gate.

5 They are not long, the days of wine and roses:
    Out of a misty dream
Our path emerges for a while, then closes
    Within a dream.

1896

---

1. The shortness of life prevents us from entertaining far-off hopes (Latin; Horace, *Odes* 1.4.15).

APPENDIXES

General Bibliography

This bibliography consists of a list of suggested general readings on English literature. Bibliographies for the authors in *The Norton Anthology of English Literature* are available online in the NAEL Archive (digital.wwnorton.com/englishlit10abc and digital.wwnorton.com/englishlit10def).

Suggested General Readings

Histories of England and of English Literature

Even the most distinguished of the comprehensive general histories written in past generations have come to seem outmoded. Innovative research in social, cultural, and political history has made it difficult to write a single coherent account of England from the Middle Ages to the present, let alone to accommodate in a unified narrative the complex histories of Scotland, Ireland, Wales, and the other nations where writing in English has flourished. Readers who wish to explore the historical matrix out of which the works of literature collected in this anthology emerged are advised to consult the studies of particular periods listed in the appropriate sections of this bibliography. The multivolume *Oxford History of England* and *New Oxford History of England* are useful, as are the three-volume *Peoples of the British Isles: A New History*, ed. Stanford Lehmberg, 1992; the nine-volume *Cambridge Cultural History of Britain*, ed. Boris Ford, 1992; the three-volume *Cambridge Social History of Britain, 1750–1950*, ed. F. M. L. Thompson, 1992; and the multivolume *Penguin History of Britain*, gen. ed. David Cannadine, 1996–. For Britain's imperial history, readers can consult the five-volume *Oxford History of the British Empire*, ed. Roger Louis, 1998–99, as well as *Gender and Empire*, ed. Philippa Levine, 2004. Given the cultural centrality of London, readers may find particular interest in *The London Encyclopaedia*, ed. Ben Weinreb et al., 3rd ed., 2008; Roy Porter, *London: A Social History*, 1994; and Jerry White, *London in the Nineteenth Century: "A Human Awful Wonder of God,"* 2007, and *London in the Twentieth Century: A City and Its People*, 2001.

Similar observations may be made about literary history. In the light of such initiatives as women's studies, new historicism, and postcolonialism, the range of authors deemed significant has expanded, along with the geographical and conceptual boundaries of literature in English. Attempts to capture in a unified account the great sweep of literature from *Beowulf* to the early twenty-first century have largely given way to studies of individual genres, carefully delimited time periods, and specific authors. For these more focused accounts, see the listings by period. Among the large-scale literary surveys, *The Cambridge Guide to Literature in English*, 3rd ed., 2006, is useful, as is the nine-volume *Penguin History of Literature*, 1993–94. *The Feminist Companion to Literature in English*, ed. Virginia Blain, Isobel Grundy, and Patricia Clements, 1990, is an important resource, and the editorial materials in *The Norton Anthology of Literature by Women*, 3rd ed., 2007, eds. Sandra M. Gilbert and Susan Gubar, constitute a concise history and set of biographies of women authors since the Middle Ages. *Annals of English Literature, 1475–1950*, rev. 1961, lists important publications year by year, together with the significant literary events for each year. Six volumes have been published in the *Oxford English Literary History*, gen. ed. Jonathan Bate, 2002–: Laura Ashe, *1000–1350: Conquest and Transformation*;

James Simpson, *1350–1547: Reform and Cultural Revolution*; Philip Davis, *1830–1880: The Victorians*; Chris Baldick, *1830–1880: The Modern Movement*; Randall Stevenson, *1960–2000: The Last of England?*; and Bruce King, *1948–2000: The Internationalization of English Literature*. See also *The Cambridge History of Medieval English Literature*, ed. David Wallace, 1999; *The Cambridge History of Early Medieval English Literature*, ed. Clare E. Lees, 2012; *The Cambridge History of Early Modern English Literature*, ed. David Loewenstein and Janel Mueller, 2003; *The Cambridge History of English Literature, 1660–1780*, ed. John Richetti, 2005; *The Cambridge History of English Romantic Literature*, ed. James Chandler, 2009; *The Cambridge History of Victorian Literature*, ed. Kate Flint, 2012; and *The Cambridge History of Twentieth-Century English Literature*, ed. Laura Marcus and Peter Nicholls, 2005.

Helpful treatments and surveys of English meter, rhyme, and stanza forms are Paul Fussell Jr., *Poetic Meter and Poetic Form*, rev. 1979; Donald Wesling, *The Chances of Rhyme: Device and Modernity*, 1980; Charles O. Hartman, *Free Verse: An Essay in Prosody*, 1983; John Hollander, *Rhyme's Reason: A Guide to English Verse*, rev. 1989; Derek Attridge, *Poetic Rhythm: An Introduction*, 1995; Robert Pinsky, *The Sounds of Poetry: A Brief Guide*, 1998; Mark Strand and Eavan Boland, eds., *The Making of a Poem: A Norton Anthology of Poetic Forms*, 2000; Helen Vendler, *Poems, Poets, Poetry*, 3rd ed., 2010; Virginia Jackson and Yopie Prins, eds., *The Lyric Theory Reader*, 2013; and Jonathan Culler, *Theory of the Lyric*, 2015.

On the development and functioning of the novel as a form, see Ian Watt, *The Rise of the Novel*, 1957; Gérard Genette, *Narrative Discourse: An Essay in Method*, 1980; *Theory of the Novel: A Historical Approach*, ed. Michael McKeon, 2000; McKeon, *The Origins of the English Novel, 1600–1740*, 15th anniversary ed., 2002; and *The Novel*, ed. Franco Moretti, 2 vols., 2006–07. *The Cambridge History of the English Novel*, eds. Robert L. Caserio and Clement Hawes, 2012; *A Companion to the English Novel*, eds. Stephen Arata et al., 2015; eight volumes have been published from *The Oxford History of the Novel in English*, 2011–16. On women novelists and readers, see Nancy Armstrong, *Desire and Domestic Fiction: A Political History of the Novel*, 1987; and Catherine Gallagher, *Nobody's Story: The Vanishing Acts of Women Writers in the Marketplace, 1670–1820*, 1994.

On the history of playhouse design, see Richard Leacroft, *The Development of the English Playhouse: An Illustrated Survey of Theatre Building in England from Medieval to Modern Times*, 1988. For a survey of the plays that have appeared on these and other stages, see Allardyce Nicoll, *British Drama*, rev. 1962; the eight-volume *Revels History of Drama in English*, gen. eds. Clifford Leech and T. W. Craik, 1975–83; and Alfred Harbage, *Annals of English Drama, 975–1700*, 3rd ed., 1989, rev. S. Schoenbaum and Sylvia Wagonheim; and the three volumes of *The Cambridge History of British Theatre*, eds. Jane Milling, Peter Thomson, and Joseph Donohue, 2004.

On some of the key intellectual currents that are at once reflected in and shaped by literature and contemporary literary criticism, Arthur O. Lovejoy's classic studies *The Great Chain of Being*, 1936, and *Essays in the History of Ideas*, 1948, remain valuable, along with such works as Georg Simmel, *The Philosophy of Money*, 1907; Lovejoy and George Boas, *Primitivism and Related Ideas in Antiquity*, 1935; Norbert Elias, *The Civilizing Process*, orig. pub. 1939, English trans. 1969; Simone de Beauvoir, *The Second Sex*, 1949; Frantz Fanon, *Black Skin, White Masks*, 1952, new trans. 2008; Ernst Cassirer, *The Philosophy of Symbolic Forms*, 4 vols., 1953–96; Ernst Kantorowicz, *The King's Two Bodies: A Study in Medieval Political Theology*, 1957, new ed. 1997; Hannah Arendt, *The Human Condition*, 1958; Richard Popkin, *The History of Skepticism from Erasmus to Descartes*, 1960; M. H. Abrams, *Natural Supernaturalism: Tradition and Revolution in Romantic Literature*, 1971; Michel Foucault, *Madness and Civilization: A History of Insanity in the Age of Reason*, Eng.

trans. 1965, and *The Order of Things: An Archaeology of the Human Sciences*, Eng. trans. 1970; Gaston Bachelard, *The Poetics of Space*, Eng. trans. 1969; Martin Jay, *The Dialectical Imagination: A History of the Frankfurt School and the Institute of Social Research, 1923–1950*, 1973, new ed. 1996; Hayden White, *Metahistory*, 1973; Roland Barthes, *The Pleasure of the Text*, Eng. trans. 1975; Jacques Derrida, *Of Grammatology*, Eng. trans. 1976, and *Dissemination*, Eng. trans. 1981; Richard Rorty, *Philosophy and the Mirror of Nature*, 1979; Gilles Deleuze and Félix Guattari, *A Thousand Plateaus*, 1980; Raymond Williams, *Keywords: A Vocabulary of Culture and Society*, rev. 1983; Pierre Bourdieu, *Distinction: A Social Critique of the Judgment of Taste*, Eng. trans. 1984; Michel de Certeau, *The Practice of Everyday Life*, Eng. trans. 1984; Hans Blumenberg, *The Legitimacy of the Modern Age*, Eng. trans. 1985; Jürgen Habermas, *The Philosophical Discourse of Modernity*, Eng. trans, 1987; Slavoj Žižek, *The Sublime Object of Ideology*, 1989; Homi Bhabha, *The Location of Culture*, 1994; Judith Butler, *The Psychic Life of Power: Theories in Subjection*, 1997; and Sigmund Freud, *Writings on Art and Literature*, ed. Neil Hertz, 1997.

Reference Works

The single most important tool for the study of literature in English is the *Oxford English Dictionary*, 2nd ed. 1989, 3rd ed. in process. The most current edition is available online to subscribers. The *OED* is written on historical principles: that is, it attempts not only to describe current word use but also to record the history and development of the language from its origins before the Norman conquest to the present. It thus provides, for familiar as well as archaic and obscure words, the widest possible range of meanings and uses, organized chronologically and illustrated with quotations. The *OED* can be searched as a conventional dictionary arranged a–z and also by subject, usage, region, origin, and timeline (the first appearance of a word). Beyond the *OED* there are many other valuable dictionaries, such as *The American Heritage Dictionary* (5th ed., 2016), *The Oxford Dictionary of Abbreviations*, *The Concise Oxford Dictionary of English Etymology*, *The Oxford Dictionary of English Grammar*, *A New Dictionary of Eponyms*, *The Oxford Essential Dictionary of Foreign Terms in English*, *The Oxford Dictionary of Idioms*, *The Concise Oxford Dictionary of Linguistics*, *The Oxford Guide to World English*, and *The Concise Oxford Dictionary of Proverbs*. Other valuable reference works include *The Cambridge Encyclopedia of the English Language*, 2nd ed., ed. David Crystal, 2003; *The Concise Oxford Companion to the English Language*; *Pocket Fowler's Modern English Usage*; and the numerous guides to specialized vocabularies, slang, regional dialects, and the like.

There is a steady flow of new editions of most major and many minor writers in English, along with a ceaseless outpouring of critical appraisals and scholarship. James L. Harner's *Literary Research Guide: An Annotated List of Reference Sources in English Literary Studies* (6th ed., 2009; online ed. available to subscribers at www.mlalrg.org/public) offers thorough, evaluative annotations of a wide range of sources. For the historical record of scholarship and critical discussion, *The New Cambridge Bibliography of English Literature*, ed. George Watson, 5 vols. (1969–77) and *The Cambridge Bibliography of English Literature*, 3rd ed., 5 vols. (1941–2000) are useful. The *MLA International Bibliography* (also online) is a key resource for following critical discussion of literatures in English. Ranging from 1926 to the present; it includes journal articles, essays, chapters from collections, books, and dissertations, and covers folklore, linguistics, and film. The *Annual Bibliography of English Language and Literature (ABELL)*, compiled by the Modern Humanities Research Association, lists monographs, periodical articles, critical editions of literary works, book reviews, and collections of essays published anywhere in the world; unpublished doctoral dissertations are covered for the period 1920–99 (available online to subscribers and as part of Literature Online, http://literature. proquest.com/marketing/index.jsp).

For compact biographies of English authors, see the multivolume *Oxford Dictionary of National Biography* (*DNB*), ed. H. C. G. Matthew and Brian Harrison, 2004; since 2004 the *DNB* has been extended online with three annual updates. Handy reference books of authors, works, and various literary terms and allusions include many volumes in the *Cambridge Companion* and *Oxford Companion* series (e.g., *The Cambridge Companion to Narrative*, ed David Herman, 2007; *The Oxford Companion to English Literature*, ed. Dinah Birch, rev. 2016; *The Cambridge Companion to Allegory*, ed. Rita Copeland and Peter Struck, 2010; etc.). Likewise, *The Princeton Encyclopedia of Poetry and Poetics*, ed. Roland Greene and others, 4th ed., is available online to subscribers in ProQuest Ebook Central. Handbooks that define and illustrate literary concepts and terms are *The Penguin Dictionary of Literary Terms and Literary Theory*, ed. J. A. Cuddon and M. A. R. Habib, 5th ed., 2015; William Harmon, *A Handbook to Literature*, 12th ed., 2011; *Critical Terms for Literary Study*, ed. Frank Lentricchia and Thomas McLaughlin, rev. 1995; and M. H. Abrams and Geoffrey Harpham, *A Glossary of Literary Terms*, 11th ed., 2014. Also useful are Richard Lanham, *A Handlist of Rhetorical Terms*, 2nd ed., 2012; Arthur Quinn, *Figures of Speech: 60 Ways to Turn a Phrase*, 1995; and the *Barnhart Concise Dictionary of Etymology*, ed. Robert K. Barnhart, 1995; and George Kennedy, *A New History of Classical Rhetoric*, 2009.

On the Greek and Roman backgrounds, see *The Cambridge History of Classical Literature* (vol. 1: *Greek Literature*, 1982; vol. 2: *Latin Literature*, 1989), both available online; *The Oxford Companion to Classical Literature*, ed. M. C. Howatson, 3rd ed., 2011; Gian Biagio Conte, *Latin Literature: A History*, 1994; *The Oxford Classical Dictionary*, 4th ed., 2012; Richard Rutherford, *Classical Literature: A Concise History*, 2005; and Mark P. O. Morford, Robert J. Lenardon, and Michael Sham, *Classical Mythology*, 10th ed., 2013. The Loeb Classical Library of Greek and Roman texts is now available online to subscribers at www.loebclassics.com.

Digital resources in the humanities have vastly proliferated since the previous edition of *The Norton Anthology of English Literature* and are continuing to grow rapidly. The NAEL Archive (accessed at digital.wwnorton.com/englishlit10abc and digital .wwnorton.com/englishlit10def) is the gateway to an extensive array of annotated texts, images, and other materials especially gathered for the readers of this anthology. Among other useful electronic resources for the study of English literature are enormous digital archives, available to subscribers: Early English Books Online (EEBO), http://eebo.chadwyck.com/home; Literature Online, http://literature.proquest.com/ marketing/index.jsp; and Eighteenth Century Collections Online (ECCO), www.gale .com/primary-sources/eighteenth-century-collections-online. There are also numerous free sites of variable quality. Many of the best of these are period or author specific and hence are listed in the period/author bibiliographies in the NAEL Archive. Among the general sites, one of the most useful and wide-ranging is Voice of the Shuttle (http://vos.ucsb.edu), which includes in its aggregation links to Bartleby.com and Project Gutenberg.

Literary Criticism and Theory

Nine volumes of the *Cambridge History of Literary Criticism* have been published, 1989– : *Classical Criticism*, ed. George A. Kennedy; *The Middle Ages*, ed. Alastair Minnis and Ian Johnson; *The Renaissance*, ed. Glyn P. Norton; *The Eighteenth Century*, ed. H. B. Nisbet and Claude Rawson; *Romanticism*, ed. Marshall Brown; *The Nineteenth Century ca. 1830–1914,* ed. M. A. R. Habib; *Modernism and the New Criticism*, ed. A. Walton Litz, Louis Menand, and Lawrence Rainey; *From Formalism to Poststructuralism*, ed. Raman Selden; and *Twentieth-Century Historical, Philosoph-*

ical, and Psychological Perspectives, ed. Christa Knellwolf and Christopher Norris. See also M. H. Abrams, *The Mirror and the Lamp: Romantic Theory and the Critical Tradition*, 1953; William K. Wimsatt and Cleanth Brooks, *Literary Criticism: A Short History*, 1957; René Wellek, *A History of Modern Criticism: 1750–1950*, 9 vols., 1955–93; Frank Lentricchia, *After the New Criticism*, 1980; and J. Hillis Miller, *On Literature*, 2002. Raman Selden, Peter Widdowson, and Peter Brooker have written *A Reader's Guide to Contemporary Literary Theory*, 5th ed., 2015. Other useful resources include *The Johns Hopkins Guide to Literary Theory and Criticism*, 2nd ed., 2004; *Literary Theory, an Anthology*, eds. Julie Rivkin and Michael Ryan, 1998; and *The Norton Anthology of Theory and Criticism*, 3rd ed., gen. ed. Vincent Leitch, 2018.

Modern approaches to English literature and literary theory were shaped by certain landmark works: William Empson, *Seven Types of Ambiguity*, 1930, 3rd ed. 1953, *Some Versions of Pastoral*, 1935, and *The Structure of Complex Words*, 1951; F. R. Leavis, *Revaluation*, 1936, and *The Great Tradition*, 1948; Lionel Trilling, *The Liberal Imagination*, 1950; T. S. Eliot, *Selected Essays*, 3rd ed. 1951, and *On Poetry and Poets*, 1957; Erich Auerbach, *Mimesis: The Representation of Reality in Western Literature*, 1953; William K. Wimsatt, *The Verbal Icon*, 1954; Northrop Frye, *Anatomy of Criticism*, 1957; Wayne C. Booth, *The Rhetoric of Fiction*, 1961, rev. ed. 1983; and W. J. Bate, *The Burden of the Past and the English Poet*, 1970. René Wellek and Austin Warren, *Theory of Literature*, rev. 1970, is a useful introduction to the variety of scholarly and critical approaches to literature up to the time of its publication. Jonathan Culler's *Literary Theory: A Very Short Introduction*, 1997, discusses recurrent issues and debates.

Beginning in the late 1960s, there was a significant intensification of interest in literary theory as a specific field. Certain forms of literary study had already been influenced by the work of the Russian linguist Roman Jakobson and the Russian formalist Viktor Shklovsky and, still more, by conceptions that derived or claimed to derive from Marx and Engels, but the full impact of these theories was not felt until what became known as the "theory revolution" of the 1970s and '80s. For Marxist literary criticism, see Georg Lukács, *Theory of the Novel*, 1920, trans. 1971; *The Historical Novel*, 1937, trans. 1983; and *Studies in European Realism*, trans. 1964; Walter Benjamin's essays from the 1920s and '30s represented in *Illuminations*, trans. 1986, and *Reflections*, trans. 1986; Mikhail Bakhtin's essays from the 1930s represented in *The Dialogic Imagination*, trans. 1981, and *Rabelais and His World*, 1941, trans. 1968; *Selections from the Prison Notebooks of Antonio Gramsci*, ed. and trans. Quintin Hoare and Geoffrey Smith, 1971; Raymond Williams, *Marxism and Literature*, 1977; Tony Bennett, *Formalism and Marxism*, 1979; Fredric Jameson, *The Political Unconscious: Narrative as a Socially Symbolic Act*, 1981; and Terry Eagleton, *Literary Theory: An Introduction*, 3rd ed., 2008, and *The Ideology of the Aesthetic*, 1990.

Structural linguistics and anthropology gave rise to a flowering of structuralist literary criticism; convenient introductions include Robert Scholes, *Structuralism in Literature: An Introduction*, 1974, and Jonathan Culler, *Structuralist Poetics*, 1975. Poststructuralist challenges to this approach are epitomized in such influential works as Jacques Derrida, *Writing and Difference*, 1967, trans. 1978, and Paul de Man, *Blindness and Insight: Essays in the Rhetoric of Contemporary Criticism*, 1971, 2nd ed., 1983. Poststructuralism is discussed in Jonathan Culler, *On Deconstruction*, 1982; Slavoj Žižek, *The Sublime Object of Ideology*, 1989; Fredric Jameson, *Postmodernism; or the Cultural Logic of Late Capitalism*, 1991; John McGowan, *Postmodernism and Its Critics*, 1991; and *Beyond Structuralism*, ed. Wendell Harris, 1996. A figure who greatly influenced both structuralism and poststructuralism is Roland Barthes, in *Mythologies*, trans. 1972, and *S/Z*, trans. 1974. Among other influential contributions to literary theory are the psychoanalytic approach in Harold Bloom, *The Anxiety of*

Influence, 1973; and the reader-response approach in Stanley Fish, *Is There a Text in This Class?: The Authority of Interpretive Communities*, 1980. For a retrospect on the theory decades, see Terry Eagleton, *After Theory*, 2003.

Influenced by these theoretical currents but not restricted to them, modern feminist literary criticism was fashioned by such works as Patricia Meyer Spacks, *The Female Imagination*, 1975; Ellen Moers, *Literary Women*, 1976; Elaine Showalter, *A Literature of Their Own*, 1977; and Sandra Gilbert and Susan Gubar, *The Madwoman in the Attic*, 1979. Subsequent studies include Jane Gallop, *The Daughter's Seduction: Feminism and Psychoanalysis*, 1982; Luce Irigaray, *This Sex Which Is Not One*, trans. 1985; Gayatri Chakravorty Spivak, *In Other Worlds: Essays in Cultural Politics*, 1987; Sandra Gilbert and Susan Gubar, *No Man's Land: The Place of the Woman Writer in the Twentieth Century*, 3 vols., 1988–94; Barbara Johnson, *A World of Difference*, 1989; Judith Butler, *Gender Trouble*, 1990; and the critical views sampled in Elaine Showalter, *The New Feminist Criticism*, 1985; *The Hélène Cixous Reader*, ed. Susan Sellers, 1994; *Feminist Literary Theory: A Reader*, ed. Mary Eagleton, 3rd ed., 2010; and *Feminisms: An Anthology of Literary Theory and Criticism*, eds. Robyn R. Warhol and Diane Price Herndl, 2nd ed., 1997; *The Cambridge Companion to Feminist Literary Theory*, ed. Ellen Rooney, 2006; *Feminist Literary Theory and Criticism*, ed. Sandra Gilbert and Susan Gubar, 2007; and *Feminist Literary Theory: A Reader*, ed. Mary Eagleton, 3rd ed., 2011.

Just as feminist critics used poststructuralist and psychoanalytic methods to place literature in conversation with gender theory, a new school emerged placing literature in conversation with critical race theory. Comprehensive introductions include *Critical Race Theory: The Key Writings That Formed the Movement*, eds. Kimberlé Crenshaw et al.; *The Routledge Companion to Race and Ethnicity*, ed. Stephen Caliendo and Charlton McIlwain, 2010; and *Critical Race Theory: An Introduction*, ed. Richard Delgado and Jean Stefancic, 3rd ed., 2017. For an important precursor in cultural studies, see Stuart Hall et al., *Policing the Crisis*, 1978. Seminal works include Henry Louis Gates, Jr., *The Signifying Monkey: A Theory of African-American Literature*, 1988; Patricia Williams, *The Alchemy of Race and Rights*, 1991; Toni Morrison, *Playing the Dark: Whiteness and the Literary Imagination*, 1992; Cornel West, *Race Matters*, 2001; and Gene Andrew Jarrett, *Representing the Race: A New Political History of African American Literature*, 2011. Helpful anthologies and collections of essays have emerged in recent decades, such as *The Oxford Companion to African American Literature*, eds., William L. Andrews, Frances Smith Foster, and Trudier Harris, 1997; also their *Concise Companion*, 2001; *The Cambridge Companion to Jewish American Literature*, eds. Hana Wirth-Nesher and Michael P. Kramer, 2003; *The Routledge Companion to Anglophone Caribbean Literature*, eds. Michael A. Bucknor and Alison Donnell, 2011; *The Routledge Companion to Latino/a Literature*, eds. Suzanne Bost and Frances R. Aparicio, 2013; *A Companion to African American Literature*, ed. Gene Andrew Jarrett, 2013; *The Routledge Companion to Asian American and Pacific Islander Literature*, ed. Rachel Lee, 2014; *The Cambridge Companion to Asian American Literature*, eds. Crystal Parikh and Daniel Y. Kim, 2015; and *The Cambridge Companion to British Black and Asian Literature (1945–2010)*, ed. Deirdre Osborne, 2016.

Gay literature and queer studies are represented in *Inside/Out: Lesbian Theories, Gay Theories*, ed. Diana Fuss, 1991; *The Lesbian and Gay Studies Reader*, eds. Henry Abelove, Michele Barale, and David Halperin, 1993; *The Columbia Anthology of Gay Literature: Readings from Western Antiquity to the Present Day*, ed. Byrne R. S. Fone, 1998; and by such books as Eve Sedgwick, *Between Men: English Literature and Male Homosocial Desire*, 1985, and *Epistemology of the Closet*, 1990; Diana Fuss, *Essentially Speaking: Feminism, Nature, and Difference*, 1989; Terry Castle, *The Apparitional Lesbian: Female Homosexuality and Modern Culture*, 1993; Leo Bersani, *Homos*, 1995; Gregory Woods, *A History of Gay Literature: The Male Tradition*,

1998; David Halperin, *How to Do the History of Homosexuality*, 2002; Judith Halberstam, *In a Queer Time and Place: Transgender Bodies, Subcultural Lives*, 2005; Heather Love, *Feeling Backward: Loss and the Politics of Queer History*, 2009; *The Cambridge History of Gay and Lesbian Literature*, eds. E. L. McCallum and Mikko Tuhkanen, 2014; and *The Cambridge Companion to Lesbian Literature*, ed. Jodie Medd, 2015.

New historicism is represented in Stephen Greenblatt, *Learning to Curse*, 1990; in the essays collected in *The New Historicism Reader*, ed. Harold Veeser, 1993; in *New Historical Literary Study: Essays on Reproducing Texts, Representing History*, eds. Jeffrey N. Cox and Larry J. Reynolds, 1993; and in Catherine Gallagher and Stephen Greenblatt, *Practicing New Historicism*, 2000. The related social and historical dimension of texts is discussed in Jerome McGann, *Critique of Modern Textual Criticism*, 1983; and *Scholarly Editing: A Guide to Research*, ed. D. C. Greetham, 1995. Characteristic of new historicism is an expansion of the field of literary interpretation still further in cultural studies; for a broad sampling of the range of interests, see Lawrence Grossberg, Cary Nelson, and Paula Treichler, eds., *Cultural Studies*, 1992; *The Cultural Studies Reader*, ed. Simon During, 3rd ed., 2007; and *A Cultural Studies Reader: History, Theory, Practice*, eds. Jessica Munns and Gita Rajan, 1996.

This expansion of the field is similarly reflected in postcolonial studies: see Frantz Fanon, *Black Skin, White Masks*, 1952, new trans. 2008, and *The Wretched of the Earth*, 1961, new trans. 2004; Edward Said, *Orientalism*, 1978, and *Culture and Imperialism*, 1993; *The Post-Colonial Studies Reader*, 2nd ed., 2006; and such influential books as Homi Bhabha, ed., *Nation and Narration*, 1990, and *The Location of Culture*, 1994; Robert J. C. Young, *Postcolonialism: An Historical Introduction*, 2001; Bill Ashcroft, Gareth Griffiths, and Helen Tiffin, *The Empire Writes Back: Theory and Practice in Post-Colonial Literatures*, 2nd ed. 2002; Elleke Boehmer, *Colonial and Postcolonial Literature*, 2nd ed. 2005; and *The Cambridge History of Postcolonial Literature*, ed. Ato Quayson, 2011; *The Cambridge Companion to the Postcolonial Novel*, ed. Ato Quayson, 2015; and *The Cambridge Companion to Postcolonial Poetry*, ed. Jahan Ramazani, 2017.

In the wake of the theory revolution, critics have focused on a wide array of topics, which can only be briefly surveyed here. One current of work, focusing on the history of emotion, is represented in Brian Massumi, *Parables for the Virtual*, 2002; Sianne Ngai, *Ugly Feelings*, 2005; *The Affect Theory Reader*, eds. Melissa Gregg and Gregory J. Seigworth, 2010; and Judith Butler, *Senses of the Subject*, 2015. A somewhat related current, examining the special role of traumatic memory in literature, is exemplified in Cathy Caruth, *Trauma: Explorations in Memory*, 1995; and Dominic LaCapra, *Writing History, Writing Trauma*, 2000. Work on the literary implications of cognitive science may be glimpsed in *Introduction to Cognitive Cultural Studies*, ed. Lisa Zunshine, 2010. Interest in quantitative approaches to literature was sparked by Franco Moretti, *Graphs, Maps, Trees: Abstract Models for Literary History*, 2005. For the growing field of digital humanities, see also Moretti, *Distant Reading*, 2013; *Defining Digital Humanities: A Reader*, eds. Melissa Terras, Julianne Nyhan, and Edward Vanhoutte, 2014; and *A New Companion to Digital Humanities*, eds. Susan Schreibman, Ray Siemens, and John Unsworth, 2nd ed., 2016. There has also been a flourishing of ecocriticism, or studies of literature and the environment, including *The Ecocriticism Reader: Landmarks in Literary Ecology*, eds. Cheryll Glotfelty and Harold Fromm, 1996; *Writing the Environment*, eds. Richard Kerridge and Neil Sammells, 1998; Jonathan Bate, *The Song of the Earth*, 2002; Lawrence Buell, *The Future of Environmental Criticism: Environmental Crisis and Literary Imagination*, 2005; Timothy Morton, *Ecology Without Nature*, 2009; and *The Oxford Handbook of Ecocriticism*, ed. Greg Garrard, 2014. Related are the emerging fields of animal studies and posthumanism, where key works include

Bruno Latour, *We Have Never Been Modern*, 1993; Steve Baker, *Postmodern Animal*, 2000; Jacques Derrida, *The Animal That Therefore I Am*, trans. 2008; Cary Wolfe, *Animal Rites: American Culture, the Discourse of Species, and Posthumanist Theory*, 2003, and *What is Posthumanism?* 2009; Kari Weil, *Thinking Animals: Why Animal Studies Now?* 2012; and Aaron Gross and Anne Vallely, eds. *Animals and the Human Imagination: A Companion to Animal Studies*, 2012; and *Critical Animal Studies: Thinking the Unthinkable*, ed. John Sorenson, 2014. The relationship between literature and law is central to such works as *Interpreting Law and Literature: A Hermeneutic Reader*, eds. Sanford Levinson and Steven Mailloux, 1988; *Law's Stories: Narrative and Rhetoric in the Law*, eds. Peter Brooks and Paul Gerwertz, 1998; and *Literature and Legal Problem Solving: Law and Literature as Ethical Discourse*, Paul J. Heald, 1998. Ethical questions in literature have been usefully explored by, among others, Geoffrey Galt Harpham in *Getting It Right: Language, Literature, and Ethics*, 1997, and Derek Attridge in *The Singularity of Literature*, 2004. Finally, approaches to literature, such as formalism and literary biography, that seemed superseded in the theoretical ferment of the late twentieth century, have had a powerful resurgence. A renewed interest in form is evident in Susan Stewart, *Poetry and the Fate of the Senses*, 2002; *Reading for Form*, eds. Susan J. Wolfson and Marshall Brown, 2007; and Caroline Levine, *Forms: Whole, Rhythm, Hierarchy, Network*, 2015. Interest in the history of the book was spearheaded by D. F. McKenzie's *Bibliography and the Sociology of Texts*, 1986; Jerome McGann's *The Textual Condition*, 1991; and Roger Chartier's *The Order of Books: Readers, Authors, and Libraries in Europe Between the Fourteenth and Eighteenth Centuries*, 1994. See also *The Cambridge History of the Book in Britain*, 7 vols., 1998–2017; and *The Practice and Representation of Reading in England*, eds. James Raven, Helen Small, and Naomi Tadmor, 2007; *The Book History Reader*, eds. David Finkelstein and Alistair McCleery, 2nd ed., 2006; and *The Cambridge Companion to the History of the Book*, ed. Leslie Howsam, 2014.

Anthologies representing a range of recent approaches include *Modern Criticism and Theory*, ed. David Lodge, 1988; *Contemporary Literary Criticism*, ed. Robert Con Davis and Ronald Schlieffer, 4th ed., 1998; and *The Norton Anthology of Theory and Criticism*, gen. ed. Vincent Leitch, 3rd ed., 2018.

Literary Terminology*

Using simple technical terms can sharpen our understanding and streamline our discussion of literary works. Some terms, such as the ones in section A, help us address the internal style, structure, form, and kind of works. Other terms, such as those in section B, provide insight into the material forms in which literary works have been produced.

In analyzing what they called "rhetoric," ancient Greek and Roman writers determined the elements of what we call "style" and "structure." Our literary terms are derived, via medieval and Renaissance intermediaries, from the Greek and Latin sources. In the definitions that follow, the etymology, or root, of the word is given when it helps illuminate the word's current usage.

Most of the examples are drawn from texts in this anthology.

Words **boldfaced** within definitions are themselves defined in this appendix. Some terms are defined within definitions; such words are *italicized*.

A. Terms of Style, Structure, Form, and Kind

accent (synonym "stress"): a term of **rhythm**. The special force devoted to the voicing of one syllable in a word over others. In the noun "accent," for example, the accent, or stress, is on the first syllable.

act: the major subdivision of a play, usually divided into **scenes.**

aesthetics (from Greek, "to feel, apprehend by the senses"): the philosophy of artistic meaning as a distinct mode of apprehending untranslatable truth, defined as an alternative to rational enquiry, which is purely abstract. Developed in the late eighteenth century by the German philosopher Immanuel Kant especially.

Alexandrine: a term of **meter.** In French verse a line of twelve syllables, and, by analogy, in English verse a line of six stresses. See **hexameter.**

allegory (Greek "saying otherwise"): saying one thing (the "vehicle" of the allegory) and meaning another (the allegory's "tenor"). Allegories may be momentary aspects of a work, as in **metaphor** ("John is a lion"), or, through extended metaphor, may constitute the basis of narrative, as in Bunyan's *Pilgrim's Progress*: this second meaning is the dominant one. See also **symbol** and **type.** Allegory is one of the most significant **figures of thought.**

alliteration (from Latin "litera," alphabetic letter): a **figure of speech.** The repetition of an initial consonant sound or consonant cluster in consecutive or closely positioned words. This pattern is often an inseparable part of the meter in Germanic languages, where the tonic, or accented **syllable,** is usually the first syllable. Thus all Old English poetry and some varieties of Middle English poetry use alliteration as part of their basic metrical practice. *Sir Gawain and the Green Knight*, line 1: "Sithen the sege and the assaut was sesed at Troye" (see vol. A, p. 204). Otherwise used for local effects; Stevie Smith, "Pretty," lines 4–5: "And in the pretty pool the pike stalks / He stalks his prey . . ." (see vol. F, p. 733).

*This appendix was devised and compiled by James Simpson with the collaboration of all the editors. We especially thank Professor Lara Bovilsky of the University of Oregon at Eugene, for her help.

allusion: Literary allusion is a passing but illuminating reference within a literary text to another, well-known text (often biblical or **classical**). Topical allusions are also, of course, common in certain modes, especially **satire.**

anagnorisis (Greek "recognition"): the moment of **protagonist's** recognition in a narrative, which is also often the moment of moral understanding.

anapest: a term of **rhythm.** A three-syllable foot following the rhythmic pattern, in English verse, of two unstressed (uu) syllables followed by one stressed (/). Thus, for example, "Illinois."

anaphora (Greek "carrying back"): a **figure of speech.** The repetition of words or groups of words at the beginning of consecutive sentences, clauses, or phrases. Blake, "London," lines 5–8: "In every cry of every Man, / In every Infant's cry of fear, / In every voice, in every ban . . ." (see vol. D, p. 141); Louise Bennett, "Jamaica Oman," lines 17–20: "Some backa man a push, some side-a / Man a hole him han, / Some a lick sense eena him head, / Some a guide him pon him plan!" (see vol. F, p. 860).

animal fable: a **genre.** A short narrative of speaking animals, followed by moralizing comment, written in a low style and gathered into a collection. Robert Henryson, "The Preaching of the Swallow" (see vol. A, p. 523).

antithesis (Greek "placing against"): a **figure of thought.** The juxtaposition of opposed terms in clauses or sentences that are next to or near each other. Milton, *Paradise Lost* 1.777–80: "They but now who seemed / In bigness to surpass Earth's giant sons / Now less than smallest dwarfs, in narrow room / Throng numberless" (see vol. B, p. 1514).

apostrophe (from Greek "turning away"): a **figure of thought.** An address, often to an absent person, a force, or a quality. For example, a poet makes an apostrophe to a Muse when invoking her for inspiration.

apposition: a term of **syntax.** The repetition of elements serving an identical grammatical function in one sentence. The effect of this repetition is to arrest the flow of the sentence, but in doing so to add extra semantic nuance to repeated elements. This is an especially important feature of Old English poetic style. See, for example, Caedmon's *Hymn* (vol. A, p. 31), where the phrases "heaven-kingdom's Guardian," "the Measurer's might," "his mind-plans," and "the work of the Glory-Father" each serve an identical syntactic function as the direct objects of "praise."

assonance (Latin "sounding to"): a **figure of speech.** The repetition of identical or near identical stressed vowel sounds in words whose final consonants differ, producing half-rhyme. Tennyson, "The Lady of Shalott," line 100: "His broad clear brow in sunlight glowed" (see vol. E, p. 149).

aubade (originally from Spanish "alba," dawn): a **genre.** A lover's dawn song or lyric bewailing the arrival of the day and the necessary separation of the lovers; Donne, "The Sun Rising" (see vol. B, p. 926). Larkin recasts the genre in "Aubade" (see vol. F, p. 930).

autobiography (Greek "self-life writing"): a **genre.** A narrative of a life written by the subject; Wordsworth, *The Prelude* (see vol. D, p. 362). There are subgenres, such as the spiritual autobiography, narrating the author's path to conversion and subsequent spiritual trials, as in Bunyan's *Grace Abounding.*

ballad stanza: a **verse form.** Usually a **quatrain** in alternating **iambic tetrameter** and **iambic trimeter** lines, rhyming abcb. See "Sir Patrick Spens" (vol. D, p. 36); Louise Bennett's poems (vol. F, pp. 857–61); Eliot, "Sweeney among the Nightingales" (vol. F, p. 657); Larkin, "This Be The Verse" (vol. F, p. 930).

ballade: a **verse form.** A form consisting usually of three stanzas followed by a four-line envoi (French, "send off"). The last line of the first stanza establishes a **refrain,** which is repeated, or subtly varied, as the last line of each stanza. The form was derived from French medieval poetry; English poets, from the fourteenth to the sixteenth centuries especially, used it with varying stanza forms. Chaucer, "Complaint to His Purse" (see vol. A, p. 363).

bathos (Greek "depth"): a **figure of thought.** A sudden and sometimes ridiculous descent of tone; Pope, *The Rape of the Lock* 3.157–58: "Not louder shrieks to pitying heaven are cast, / When husbands, or when lapdogs breathe their last" (see vol. C, p. 518).

beast epic: a **genre.** A continuous, unmoralized narrative, in prose or verse, relating the victories of the wholly unscrupulous but brilliant strategist Reynard the Fox over all adversaries. Chaucer arouses, only to deflate, expectations of the genre in *The Nun's Priest's Tale* (see vol. A, p. 344).

biography (Greek "life-writing"): a **genre.** A life as the subject of an extended narrative. Thus Izaak Walton, *The Life of Dr. Donne* (see vol. B, p. 976).

blank verse: a **verse form.** Unrhymed **iambic pentameter** lines. Blank verse has no stanzas, but is broken up into uneven units (verse paragraphs) determined by sense rather than form. First devised in English by Henry Howard, earl of Surrey, in his translation of two books of Virgil's *Aeneid* (see vol. B, p. 141), this very flexible verse type became the standard form for dramatic poetry in the seventeenth century, as in most of Shakespeare's plays. Milton and Wordsworth, among many others, also used it to create an English equivalent to **classical epic.**

blazon: strictly, a heraldic shield; in rhetorical usage, a **topos** whereby the individual elements of a beloved's face and body are singled out for **hyperbolic** admiration. Spenser, *Epithalamion*, lines 167–84 (see vol. B, p. 495). For an inversion of the **topos,** see Shakespeare, Sonnet 130 (vol. B, p. 736).

burlesque (French and Italian "mocking"): a work that adopts the **conventions** of a genre with the aim less of comically mocking the genre than of satirically mocking the society so represented (see **satire**). Thus Pope's *Rape of the Lock* (see vol. C, p. 507) does not mock **classical epic** so much as contemporary mores.

caesura (Latin "cut") (plural "caesurae"): a term of **meter.** A pause or breathing space within a line of verse, generally occurring between syntactic units; Louise Bennett, "Colonization in Reverse," lines 5–8: "By de hundred, by de tousan, / From country an from town, / By de ship-load, by de plane-load, / Jamaica is Englan boun" (see vol. F, p. 858), where the caesurae occur in lines 5 and 7.

canon (Greek "rule"): the group of texts regarded as worthy of special respect or attention by a given institution. Also, the group of texts regarded as definitely having been written by a certain author.

catastrophe (Greek "overturning"): the decisive turn in **tragedy** by which the plot is resolved and, usually, the **protagonist** dies.

catharsis (Greek "cleansing"): According to Aristotle, the effect of **tragedy** on its audience, through their experience of pity and terror, was a kind of spiritual cleansing, or catharsis.

character (Greek "stamp, impression"): a person, personified animal, or other figure represented in a literary work, especially in narrative and drama. The more a character seems to generate the action of a narrative, and the less he or she seems merely to serve a preordained narrative pattern, the "fuller," or more "rounded," a character is said to be. A "stock" character, common particularly in many comic genres, will perform a predictable function in different works of a given genre.

chiasmus (Greek "crosswise"): a **figure of speech**. The inversion of an already established sequence. This can involve verbal echoes: Pope, "Eloisa to Abelard," line 104, "The crime was common, common be the pain" (see vol. C, p. 529); or it can be purely a matter of syntactic inversion: Pope, *Epistle to Dr. Arbuthnot*, line 8: "They pierce my thickets, through my grot they glide" (see vol. C, p. 544).

classical, classicism, classic: Each term can be widely applied, but in English literary discourse, "classical" primarily describes the works of either Greek or Roman antiquity. "Classicism" denotes the practice of art forms inspired by classical antiquity, in particular the observance of rhetorical norms of **decorum** and balance, as opposed to following the dictates of untutored inspiration, as in Romanticism. "Classic" denotes an especially famous work within a given **canon**.

climax (Greek "ladder"): a moment of great intensity and structural change, especially in drama. Also a **figure of speech** whereby a sequence of verbally linked clauses is made, in which each successive clause is of greater consequence than its predecessor. Bacon, *Of Studies*: "Studies serve for pastimes, for ornaments, and for abilities. Their chief use for pastimes is in privateness and retiring; for ornament, is in discourse; and for ability, is in judgement" (see vol. B, p. 1223–24).

comedy: a **genre**. A term primarily applied to drama, and derived from ancient drama, in opposition to **tragedy**. Comedy deals with humorously confusing, sometimes ridiculous situations in which the ending is, nevertheless, happy. A comedy often ends in one or more marriages. Shakespeare, *Twelfth Night* (see vol. B, p. 741).

comic mode: Many genres (e.g., **romance, fabliau, comedy**) involve a happy ending in which justice is done, the ravages of time are arrested, and that which is lost is found. Such genres participate in a comic mode.

connotation: To understand connotation, we need to understand **denotation**. While many words can denote the same concept—that is, have the same basic meaning—those words can evoke different associations, or connotations. Contrast, for example, the clinical-sounding term "depression" and the more colorful, musical, even poetic phrase "the blues."

consonance (Latin "sounding with"): a **figure of speech**. The repetition of final consonants in words or stressed syllables whose vowel sounds are different. Herbert, "Easter," line 13: "Consort, both heart and lute . . ." (see vol. B, p. 1258).

convention: a repeatedly recurring feature (in either form or content) of works, occurring in combination with other recurring formal features, which constitutes a convention of a particular genre.

couplet: a **verse form**. In English verse two consecutive, rhyming lines usually containing the same number of stresses. Chaucer first introduced the **iambic pentameter** couplet into English (*Canterbury Tales*); the form was later used in many types of writing, including drama; imitations and translations of **classical epic** (thus *heroic couplet*); essays; and **satire** (see Dryden and Pope). The *distich* (Greek "two lines") is a couplet usually making complete sense; Aemilia Lanyer, *Salve Deus Rex Judaeorum*, lines 5–6: "Read it fair queen, though it defective be, / Your excellence can grace both it and me" (see vol. B, p. 981).

dactyl (Greek "finger," because of the finger's three joints): a term of **rhythm**. A three-syllable foot following the rhythmic pattern, in English verse, of one stressed followed by two unstressed syllables. Thus, for example, "Oregon."

decorum (Latin "that which is fitting"): a rhetorical principle whereby each formal aspect of a work should be in keeping with its subject matter and/or audience.

deixis (Greek "pointing"): relevant to **point of view.** Every work has, implicitly or explicitly, a "here" and a "now" from which it is narrated. Words that refer to or imply this point from which the voice of the work is projected (such as "here," "there," "this," "that," "now," "then") are examples of deixis, or "deictics." This technique is especially important in drama, where it is used to create a sense of the events happening as the spectator witnesses them.

denotation: A word has a basic, "prosaic" (factual) meaning prior to the associations it connotes (see **connotation**). The word "steed," for example, might call to mind a horse fitted with battle gear, to be ridden by a warrior, but its denotation is simply "horse."

denouement (French "unknotting"): the point at which a narrative can be resolved and so ended.

dialogue (Greek "conversation"): a **genre.** Dialogue is a feature of many genres, especially in both the **novel** and drama. As a genre itself, dialogue is used in philosophical traditions especially (most famously in Plato's *Dialogues*), as the representation of a conversation in which a philosophical question is pursued among various speakers.

diction, or **"lexis"** (from, respectively, Latin *dictio* and Greek *lexis*, each meaning "word"): the actual words used in any utterance—speech, writing, and, for our purposes here, literary works. The choice of words contributes significantly to the style of a given work.

didactic mode (Greek "teaching mode"): **Genres** in a didactic mode are designed to instruct or teach, sometimes explicitly (e.g., sermons, philosophical **discourses, georgic**), and sometimes through the medium of fiction (e.g., **animal fable, parable**).

diegesis (Greek for "narration"): a term that simply means "narration," but is used in literary criticism to distinguish one kind of story from another. In a *mimetic* story, the events are played out before us (see **mimesis**), whereas in diegesis someone recounts the story to us. Drama is for the most part *mimetic*, whereas the novel is for the most part diegetic. In novels the narrator is not, usually, part of the action of the narrative; s/he is therefore extradiegetic.

dimeter (Greek "two measure"): a term of **meter.** A two-stress line, rarely used as the meter of whole poems, though used with great frequency in single poems by Skelton, e.g., "The Tunning of Elinour Rumming" (see vol. B, p. 39). Otherwise used for single lines, as in Herbert, "Discipline," line 3: "O my God" (see vol. B, p. 1274).

discourse (Latin "running to and fro"): broadly, any nonfictional speech or writing; as a more specific genre, a philosophical meditation on a set theme. Thus Newman, *The Idea of a University* (see vol. E, p. 64).

dramatic irony: a feature of narrative and drama, whereby the audience knows that the outcome of an action will be the opposite of that intended by a **character.**

dramatic monologue (Greek "single speaking"): a **genre.** A poem in which the voice of a historical or fictional **character** speaks, unmediated by any narrator, to an implied though silent audience. See Tennyson, "Ulysses" (vol. E, p. 156); Browning, "The Bishop Orders His Tomb" (vol. E, p. 332); Eliot, "The Love Song of J. Alfred Prufrock" (vol. F, p. 654); Carol Ann Duffy, "Medusa" and "Mrs Lazarus" (vol. F, pp. 1211–13).

ecphrasis (Greek "speaking out"): a **topos** whereby a work of visual art is represented in a literary work. Auden, "Musée des Beaux Arts" (see vol. F, p. 815).

elegy: a **genre.** In **classical** literature elegy was a form written in elegiac **couplets** (a **hexameter** followed by a **pentameter**) devoted to many possible topics. In Ovidian elegy a lover meditates on the trials of erotic desire (e.g., Ovid's *Amores*). The **sonnet** sequences of both Sidney and Shakespeare exploit this genre, and, while it was still practiced in classical tradition by Donne ("On His Mistress" [see vol. B, p. 942]), by the later seventeenth century the term came to denote the poetry of loss, especially through the death of a loved person. See Tennyson, *In Memoriam* (vol. E, p. 173); Yeats, "In Memory of Major Robert Gregory" (vol. F, p. 223); Auden, "In Memory of W. B. Yeats" (see vol. F, p. 815); Heaney, "Clearances" (vol. F, p. 1104).

emblem (Greek "an insertion"): a **figure of thought.** A picture allegorically expressing a moral, or a verbal picture open to such interpretation. Donne, "A Hymn to Christ," lines 1–2: "In what torn ship soever I embark, / That ship shall be my emblem of thy ark" (see vol. B, p. 966).

end-stopping: the placement of a complete syntactic unit within a complete poetic line, fulfilling the metrical pattern; Auden, "In Memory of W. B. Yeats," line 42: "Earth, receive an honoured guest" (see vol. F, p. 817). Compare **enjambment.**

enjambment (French "striding," encroaching): The opposite of **end-stopping,** enjambment occurs when the syntactic unit does not end with the end of the poetic line and the fulfillment of the metrical pattern. When the sense of the line overflows its meter and, therefore, the line break, we have enjambment; Auden, "In Memory of W. B. Yeats," lines 44–45: "Let the Irish vessel lie / Emptied of its poetry" (see vol. F, p. 817).

epic (synonym, *heroic poetry*): a **genre.** An extended narrative poem celebrating martial heroes, invoking divine inspiration, beginning in medias res (see **order**), written in a high style (including the deployment of **epic similes;** on high style, see **register**), and divided into long narrative sequences. Homer's *Iliad* and Virgil's *Aeneid* were the prime models for English writers of epic verse. Thus Milton, *Paradise Lost* (see vol. B, p. 1495); Wordsworth, *The Prelude* (see vol. D, p. 362); and Walcott, *Omeros* (see vol. F, p. 947). With its precise repertoire of stylistic resources, epic lent itself easily to **parodic** and **burlesque** forms, known as **mock epic;** thus Pope, *The Rape of the Lock* (see vol. C, p. 507).

epigram: a **genre.** A short, pithy poem wittily expressed, often with wounding intent. See Jonson, *Epigrams* (see vol. B, p. 1089).

epigraph (Greek "inscription"): a **genre.** Any formal statement inscribed on stone; also the brief formulation on a book's title page, or a quotation at the beginning of a poem, introducing the work's themes in the most compressed form possible.

epistle (Latin "letter"): a **genre.** The letter can be shaped as a literary form, involving an intimate address often between equals. The *Epistles* of Horace provided a model for English writers from the sixteenth century. Thus Wyatt, "Mine own John Poins" (see vol. B, p. 131), or Pope, "An Epistle to a Lady" (vol. C, p. 655). Letters can be shaped to form the matter of an extended fiction, as the eighteenth-century epistolary **novel** (e.g., Samuel Richardson's *Pamela*).

epitaph: a **genre.** A pithy formulation to be inscribed on a funeral monument. Thus Ralegh, "The Author's Epitaph, Made by Himself" (see vol. B, p. 532).

epithalamion (Greek "concerning the bridal chamber"): a **genre.** A wedding poem, celebrating the marriage and wishing the couple good fortune. Thus Spenser, *Epithalamion* (see vol. B, p. 491).

epyllion (plural "epyllia") (Greek: "little epic"): a **genre.** A relatively short poem in the meter of epic poetry. See, for example, Marlowe, *Hero and Leander* (vol. B, p 660).

essay (French "trial, attempt"): a **genre**. An informal philosophical meditation, usually in prose and sometimes in verse. The journalistic periodical essay was developed in the early eighteenth century. Thus Addison and Steele, periodical essays (see vol. C, p. 462); Pope, *An Essay on Criticism* (see vol. C, p. 490).

euphemism (Greek "sweet saying"): a **figure of thought**. The figure by which something distasteful is described in alternative, less repugnant terms (e.g., "he passed away").

exegesis (Greek "leading out"): interpretation, traditionally of the biblical text, but, by transference, of any text.

exemplum (Latin "example"): an example inserted into a usually nonfictional writing (e.g., sermon or **essay**) to give extra force to an abstract thesis. Thus Johnson's example of "Sober" in his essay "On Idleness" (see vol. C, p. 732).

fabliau (French "little story," plural *fabliaux*): a **genre**. A short, funny, often bawdy narrative in low style (see **register**) imitated and developed from French models, most subtly by Chaucer; see *The Miller's Prologue and Tale* (vol. A, p. 282).

farce (French "stuffing"): a **genre**. A play designed to provoke laughter through the often humiliating antics of stock **characters**. Congreve's *The Way of the World* (see vol. C, p. 188) draws on this tradition.

figures of speech: Literary language often employs patterns perceptible to the eye and/or to the ear. Such patterns are called "figures of speech"; in classical rhetoric they were called "schemes" (from Greek *schema*, meaning "form, figure").

figures of thought: Language can also be patterned conceptually, even outside the rules that normally govern it. Literary language in particular exploits this licensed linguistic irregularity. Synonyms for figures of thought are "trope" (Greek "twisting," referring to the irregularity of use) and "conceit" (Latin "concept," referring to the fact that these figures are perceptible only to the mind). Be careful not to confuse **trope** with **topos** (a common error).

first-person narration: relevant to **point of view,** a narrative in which the voice narrating refers to itself with forms of the first-person pronoun ("I," "me," "my," etc., or possibly "we," "us," "our"), and in which the narrative is determined by the limitations of that voice. Thus Mary Wollstonecraft Shelley, *Frankenstein*.

frame narrative: Some narratives, particularly collections of narratives, involve a frame narrative that explains the genesis of, and/or gives a perspective on, the main narrative or narratives to follow. Thus Chaucer, *Canterbury Tales*; Mary Wollstonecraft Shelley, *Frankenstein*; or Conrad, *Heart of Darkness*.

free indirect style: relevant to **point of view,** a narratorial voice that manages, without explicit reference, to imply, and often implicitly to comment on, the voice of a **character** in the narrative itself. Virginia Woolf, "A Sketch of the Past," where the voice, although strictly that of the adult narrator, manages to convey the child's manner of perception: "—I begin: the first memory. This was of red and purple flowers on a black background—my mother's dress."

genre and mode: The **style,** structure, and, often, length of a work, when coupled with a certain subject matter, raise expectations that a literary work conforms to a certain **genre** (French "kind"). Good writers might upset these expectations, but they remain aware of the expectations and thwart them purposefully. Works in different genres may nevertheless participate in the same **mode,** a broader category designating the fundamental perspectives governing various genres of writing. For mode, see **tragic, comic, satiric,** and **didactic modes.** Genres are fluid, sometimes very fluid (e.g., the **novel**); the word "usually" should be added to almost every account of the characteristics of a given genre!

georgic (Greek "farming"): a **genre.** Virgil's *Georgics* treat agricultural and occasionally scientific subjects, giving instructions on the proper management of farms. Unlike **pastoral,** which treats the countryside as a place of recreational idleness among shepherds, the georgic treats it as a place of productive labor. For an English poem that critiques both genres, see Crabbe, "The Village" (vol. C, p. 1019).

hermeneutics (from the Greek god Hermes, messenger between the gods and humankind): the science of interpretation, first formulated as such by the German philosophical theologian Friedrich Schleiermacher in the early nineteenth century.

heroic poetry: see **epic.**

hexameter (Greek "six measure"): a term of **meter.** The hexameter line (a six-stress line) is the meter of **classical** Latin **epic;** while not imitated in that form for epic verse in English, some instances of the hexameter exist. See, for example, the last line of a Spenserian stanza, *Faerie Queene* 1.1.2: "O help thou my weake wit, and sharpen my dull tong" (vol. B, p. 253), or Yeats, "The Lake Isle of Innisfree," line 1: "I will arise and go now, and go to Innisfree" (vol. F, p. 215).

homily (Greek "discourse"): a **genre.** A sermon, to be preached in church; *Book of Homilies* (see vol. B, p. 165). Writers of literary fiction sometimes exploit the homily, or sermon, as in Chaucer, *The Pardoner's Tale* (see vol. A, p. 329).

homophone (Greek "same sound"): a **figure of speech.** A word that sounds identical to another word but has a different meaning ("bear" / "bare").

hyperbaton (Greek "overstepping"): a term of **syntax.** The rearrangement, or inversion, of the expected word order in a sentence or clause. Gray, "Elegy Written in a Country Churchyard," line 38: "If Memory o'er their tomb no trophies raise" (vol. C, p. 999). Poets can suspend the expected syntax over many lines, as in the first sentences of the *Canterbury Tales* (vol. A, p. 261) and of *Paradise Lost* (vol. B, p. 1495).

hyperbole (Greek "throwing over"): a **figure of thought.** Overstatement, exaggeration; Marvell, "To His Coy Mistress," lines 11–12: "My vegetable love should grow / Vaster than empires, and more slow" (see vol. B, p. 1347); Auden, "As I Walked Out One Evening," lines 9–12: " 'I'll love you, dear, I'll love you / Till China and Africa meet / And the river jumps over the mountain / And the salmon sing in the street" (see vol. F, p. 813).

hypermetrical (adj.; Greek "over measured"): a term of **meter;** the word describes a breaking of the expected metrical pattern by at least one extra syllable.

hypotaxis, or **subordination** (respectively Greek and Latin "ordering under"): a term of **syntax.** The subordination, by the use of subordinate clauses, of different elements of a sentence to a single main verb. Milton, *Paradise Lost* 9.513–15: "As when a ship by skillful steersman wrought / Nigh river's mouth or foreland, where the wind / Veers oft, as oft so steers, and shifts her sail; So varied he" (vol. B, p. 1654). The contrary principle to **parataxis.**

iamb: a term of **rhythm.** The basic foot of English verse; two syllables following the rhythmic pattern of unstressed followed by stressed and producing a rising effect. Thus, for example, "Vermont."

imitation: the practice whereby writers strive ideally to reproduce and yet renew the **conventions** of an older form, often derived from **classical** civilization. Such a practice will be praised in periods of classicism (e.g., the eighteenth century) and repudiated in periods dominated by a model of inspiration (e.g., Romanticism).

irony (Greek "dissimulation"): a **figure of thought.** In broad usage, irony designates the result of inconsistency between a statement and a context that undermines the statement. "It's a beautiful day" is unironic if it's a beautiful day; if, however, the weather is terrible, then the inconsistency between statement and context is ironic. The effect is often amusing; the need to be ironic is sometimes produced by censorship of one kind or another. Strictly, irony is a subset of allegory: whereas allegory says one thing and means another, irony says one thing and means its opposite. For an extended example of irony, see Swift's "Modest Proposal." See also **dramatic irony.**

journal (French "daily"): a **genre.** A diary, or daily record of ephemeral experience, whose perspectives are concentrated on, and limited by, the experiences of single days. Thus Pepys, *Diary* (see vol. C, p. 86).

lai: a **genre.** A short narrative, often characterized by images of great intensity; a French term, and a form practiced by Marie de France (see vol. A, p. 160).

legend (Latin "requiring to be read"): a **genre.** A narrative of a celebrated, possibly historical, but mortal **protagonist.** To be distinguished from **myth.** Thus the "Arthurian legend" but the "myth of Proserpine."

lexical set: Words that habitually recur together (e.g., January, February, March, etc.; or red, white, and blue) form a lexical set.

litotes (from Greek "smooth"): a **figure of thought.** Strictly, understatement by denying the contrary; More, *Utopia:* "differences of no slight import" (see vol. B, p. 47). More loosely, understatement; Swift, "A Tale of a Tub": "Last week I saw a woman flayed, and you will hardly believe how much it altered her person for the worse" (see vol. C, p. 274). Stevie Smith, "Sunt Leones," lines 11–12: "And if the Christians felt a little blue— / Well people being eaten often do" (see vol. F, p. 729).

lullaby: a **genre.** A bedtime, sleep-inducing song for children, in simple and regular meter. Adapted by Auden, "Lullaby" (see vol. F, p. 809).

lyric (from Greek "lyre"): Initially meaning a song, "lyric" refers to a short poetic form, without restriction of meter, in which the expression of personal emotion, often by a voice in the first person, is given primacy over narrative sequence. Thus "The Wife's Lament" (see vol. A, p. 123); Yeats, "The Wild Swans at Coole" (see vol. F, p. 223).

masque: a **genre.** Costly entertainments of the Stuart court, involving dance, song, speech, and elaborate stage effects, in which courtiers themselves participated.

metaphor (Greek "carrying across," etymologically parallel to Latin "translation"): One of the most significant **figures of thought,** metaphor designates identification or implicit identification of one thing with another with which it is not literally identifiable. Blake, "London," lines 11–12: "And the hapless Soldier's sigh / Runs in blood down Palace walls" (see vol. D, p. 141).

meter: Verse (from Latin *versus,* turned) is distinguished from prose (from Latin *prorsus,* "straightforward") as a more compressed form of expression, shaped by metrical norms. **Meter** (Greek "measure") refers to the regularly recurring sound pattern of verse lines. The means of producing sound patterns across lines differ in different poetic traditions. Verse may be **quantitative,** or determined by the quantities of syllables (set patterns of long and short syllables), as in Latin and Greek poetry. It may be **syllabic,** determined by fixed numbers of syllables in the line, as in the verse of Romance languages (e.g., French and Italian). It may be **accentual,** determined by the number of accents, or stresses in the line, with variable numbers of syllables, as in Old English and some varieties of Middle English alliterative verse. Or it may be **accentual-syllabic,** determined by the numbers of accents, but possessing a regular pattern of stressed and unstressed syllables, so as to produce regular numbers of syllables per line. Since Chaucer, English verse has worked primarily within the many possibilities of accentual-syllabic meter. The unit of meter is the **foot.** In English verse the number of feet per line corresponds to the number of accents in a line. For the types and examples of different meters, see **monometer, dimeter, trimester, tetrameter, pentameter,** and **hexameter.** In the definitions below, "u" designates one unstressed syllable, and "/" one stressed syllable.

metonymy (Greek "change of name"): one of the most significant **figures of thought.** Using a word to **denote** another concept or other concepts, by virtue of habitual association. Thus "The Press," designating printed news media. Fictional names often work by associations of this kind. Closely related to **synecdoche.**

mimesis (Greek for "imitation"): A central function of literature and drama has been to provide a plausible imitation of the reality of the world beyond the literary work; mimesis is the representation and imitation of what is taken to be reality.

mise-en-abyme (French for "cast into the abyss"): Some works of art represent themselves in themselves; if they do so effectively, the represented artifact also represents itself, and so ad infinitum. The effect achieved is called *"mise-en-abyme."* Hoccleve's *Complaint*, for example, represents a depressed man reading about a depressed man. This sequence threatens to become a *mise-en-abyme.*

monometer (Greek "one measure"): a term of **meter.** An entire line with just one stress; *Sir Gawain and the Green Knight*, line 15, "most (u) grand (/)" (see vol. A, p. 204).

myth: a **genre.** The narrative of **protagonists** with, or subject to, superhuman powers. A myth expresses some profound foundational truth, often by accounting for the origin of natural phenomena. To be distinguished from **legend.** Thus the "Arthurian legend" but the "myth of Proserpine."

novel: an extremely flexible **genre** in both form and subject matter. Usually in prose, giving high priority to narration of events, with a certain expectation of length, novels are preponderantly rooted in a specific, and often complex, social world; sensitive to the realities of material life; and often focused on one **character** or a small circle of central characters. By contrast with chivalric **romance** (the main European narrative genre prior to the novel), novels tend to eschew the marvelous in favor of a recognizable social world and credible action. The novel's openness allows it to participate in all modes, and to be co-opted for a huge variety of subgenres. In English literature the novel dates from the late seventeenth century and has been astonishingly successful in appealing to a huge readership, particularly in the nineteenth and twentieth centuries. The English and Irish tradition of the novel includes, for example, Fielding, Austen, the Brontë sisters, Dickens, George Eliot, Conrad, Woolf, Lawrence, and Joyce, to name but a few very great exponents of the genre.

novella: a **genre.** A short **novel,** often characterized by imagistic intensity. Conrad, *Heart of Darkness* (see vol. F, p. 73).

occupatio (Latin "taking possession"): a **figure of thought.** Denying that one will discuss a subject while actually discussing it; also known as "praeteritio" (Latin "passing by"). See Chaucer, *Nun's Priest's Tale*, lines 414–32 (see vol. A, p. 353).

ode (Greek "song"): a **genre.** A **lyric** poem in elevated, or high style (see **register**), often addressed to a natural force, a person, or an abstract quality. The Pindaric ode in English is made up of **stanzas** of unequal length, while the Horatian ode has stanzas of equal length. For examples of both types, see, respectively, Wordsworth, "Ode: Intimations of Immortality" (vol. D, p. 348); and Marvell, "An Horatian Ode" (vol. B, p. 1356), or Keats, "Ode on Melancholy" (vol. D, p. 981). For a fuller discussion, see the headnote to Jonson's "Ode on Cary and Morison" (vol. B, p. 1102).

omniscient narrator (Latin "all-knowing narrator"): relevant to **point of view.** A narrator who, in the fiction of the narrative, has complete access to both the deeds and the thoughts of all **characters** in the narrative. Thus Thomas Hardy, "On the Western Circuit" (see vol. F, p. 36).

onomatopoeia (Greek "name making"): a **figure of speech.** Verbal sounds that imitate and evoke the sounds they denote. Hopkins, "Binsey Poplars," lines 10–12 (about some felled trees): "O if we but knew what we do / When we delve [dig] or hew— / Hack and rack the growing green!" (see vol. E, p. 598).

order: A story may be told in different narrative orders. A narrator might use the sequence of events as they happened, and thereby follow what **classical** rhetoricians called the *natural order*; alternatively, the narrator might reorder the sequence of events, beginning the narration either in the middle or at the end of the sequence of events, thereby following an *artificial order.* If a narrator begins in the middle of events, he or she is said to begin *in medias res* (Latin "in the middle of the matter"). For a brief discussion of these concepts, see Spenser, *Faerie Queene*, "A Letter of the Authors" (vol. B, p. 249). Modern narratology makes a related distinction, between *histoire* (French "story") for the natural order that readers mentally reconstruct, and *discours* (French, here "narration") for the narrative as presented. See also **plot** and **story.**

ottava rima: a **verse form.** An eight-line stanza form, rhyming abababcc, using **iambic pentameter;** Yeats, "Sailing to Byzantium" (see vol. F, p. 230). Derived from the Italian poet Boccaccio, an eight-line stanza was used by fifteenth-century English poets for inset passages (e.g., Christ's speech from the Cross in Lydgate's *Testament*, lines 754–897). The form in this rhyme scheme was used in English poetry for long narrative by, for example, Byron (*Don Juan*; see vol. D, p. 669).

oxymoron (Greek "sharp blunt"): a **figure of thought.** The conjunction of normally incompatible terms; Milton, *Paradise Lost* 1.63: "darkness visible" (see vol. B, p. 1497).

panegyric: a **genre.** Demonstrative, or epideictic (Greek "showing"), rhetoric was a branch of **classical** rhetoric. Its own two main branches were the rhetoric of praise on the one hand and of vituperation on the other. Panegyric, or eulogy (Greek "sweet speaking"), or encomium (plural *encomia*), is the term used to describe the speeches or writings of praise.

parable: a **genre.** A simple story designed to provoke, and often accompanied by, **allegorical** interpretation, most famously by Christ as reported in the Gospels.

paradox (Greek "contrary to received opinion"): a **figure of thought.** An apparent contradiction that requires thought to reveal an inner consistency. Chaucer, "Troilus's Song," line 12: "O sweete harm so quainte" (see vol. A, p. 362).

parataxis, or coordination (respectively Greek and Latin "ordering beside"): a term of **syntax.** The coordination, by the use of coordinating conjunctions, of different main clauses in a single sentence. Malory, *Morte Darthur*: "So Sir Lancelot departed and took his sword under his arm, and so he walked in his mantel, that noble knight, and put himself in great jeopardy" (see vol. A, p. 539). The opposite principle to **hypotaxis.**

parody: a work that uses the **conventions** of a particular genre with the aim of comically mocking a **topos,** a genre, or a particular exponent of a genre. Shakespeare parodies the topos of **blazon** in Sonnet 130 (see vol. B, p. 736).

pastoral (from Latin *pastor,* "shepherd"): a **genre.** Pastoral is set among shepherds, making often refined **allusion** to other apparently unconnected subjects (sometimes politics) from the potentially idyllic world of highly literary if illiterate shepherds. Pastoral is distinguished from **georgic** by representing recreational rural idleness, whereas the georgic offers instruction on how to manage rural labor. English writers had classical models in the *Idylls* of Theocritus in Greek and Virgil's *Eclogues* in Latin. Pastoral is also called bucolic (from the Greek word for "herdsman"). Thus Spenser, *Shepheardes Calender* (see vol. B, p. 241).

pathetic fallacy: the attribution of sentiment to natural phenomena, as if they were in sympathy with human feelings. Thus Milton, *Lycidas,* lines 146–47: "With cowslips wan that hang the pensive head, / And every flower that sad embroidery wears" (see vol. B, p. 1472). For critique of the practice, see Ruskin (who coined the term), "Of the Pathetic Fallacy" (vol. E, p. 386).

pentameter (Greek "five measure"): a term of **meter.** In English verse, a five-stress line. Between the late fourteenth and the nineteenth centuries, this meter, frequently employing an iambic rhythm, was the basic line of English verse. Chaucer, Shakespeare, Milton, and Wordsworth each, for example, deployed this very flexible line as their primary resource; Milton, *Paradise Lost* 1.128: "O Prince, O Chief of many thronèd Powers" (see vol. B, p. 1499).

performative: Verbal expressions have many different functions. They can, for example, be descriptive, or constative (if they make an argument), or performative, for example. A performative utterance is one that makes something happen in the world by virtue of its utterance. "I hereby sentence you to ten years in prison," if uttered in the appropriate circumstances, itself performs an action; it makes something happen in the world. By virtue of its performing an action, it is called a "performative." See also **speech act.**

peripeteia (Greek "turning about"): the sudden reversal of fortune (in both directions) in a dramatic work.

periphrasis (Greek "declaring around"): a **figure of thought.** Circumlocution; the use of many words to express what could be expressed in few or one; Sidney, *Astrophil and Stella* 39.1–4 (vol. B, p. 593).

persona (Latin "sound through"): originally the mask worn in the Roman theater to magnify an actor's voice; in literary discourse persona (plural *personae*) refers to the narrator or speaker of a text, whose voice is coherent and whose person need have no relation to the person of the actual author of a text. Eliot, "The Love Song of J. Alfred Prufrock" (see vol. F, p. 654).

personification, or **prosopopoeia** (Greek "person making"): a **figure of thought.** The attribution of human qualities to nonhuman forces or objects; Keats, "Ode on a Grecian Urn," lines 1–2: "Thou still unvanish'd bride of quietness, / Thou foster-child of silence and slow time" (see vol. D, p. 979).

plot: the sequence of events in a story as narrated, as distinct from **story,** which refers to the sequence of events as we reconstruct them from the plot. See also **order.**

point of view: All of the many kinds of writing involve a point of view from which a text is, or seems to be, generated. The presence of such a point of view may be powerful and explicit, as in many novels, or deliberately invisible, as in much drama. In some genres, such as the **novel,** the narrator does not necessarily tell the story from a position we can predict; that is, the needs of a particular story, not the **conventions** of the genre, determine the narrator's position. In other genres, the narrator's position is fixed by convention; in certain kinds of love poetry, for example, the narrating voice is always that of a suffering lover. Not only does the point of view significantly inform the style of a work, but it also informs the structure of that work.

protagonist (Greek "first actor"): the hero or heroine of a drama or narrative.

pun: a **figure of thought.** A sometimes irresolvable doubleness of meaning in a single word or expression; Shakespeare, Sonnet 135, line 1: "Whoever hath her wish, thou hast thy *Will*" (see vol. B, p. 736).

quatrain: a **verse form.** A stanza of four lines, usually rhyming abcb, abab, or abba. Of many possible examples, see Crashaw, "On the Wounds of Our Crucified Lord" (see vol. B, p. 1296).

refrain: usually a single line repeated as the last line of consecutive stanzas, sometimes with subtly different wording and ideally with subtly different meaning as the poem progresses. See, for example, Wyatt, "Blame not my lute" (see vol. B, p. 128).

register: The register of a word is its stylistic level, which can be distinguished by degree of technicality but also by degree of formality. We choose our words from different registers according to context, that is, audience and/or environment. Thus a chemist in a laboratory will say "sodium chloride," a cook in a kitchen "salt." A formal register designates the kind of language used in polite society (e.g., "Mr. President"), while an informal or colloquial register is used in less formal or more relaxed social situations (e.g., "the boss"). In **classical** and medieval rhetoric, these registers of formality were called *high style* and *low style*. A *middle style* was defined as the style fit for narrative, not drawing attention to itself.

rhetoric: the art of verbal persuasion. **Classical** rhetoricians distinguished three areas of rhetoric: the forensic, to be used in law courts; the deliberative, to be used in political or philosophical deliberations; and the demonstrative, or epideictic, to be used for the purposes of public praise or blame. Rhetorical manuals covered all the skills required of a speaker, from the management of style and structure to delivery. These manuals powerfully influenced the theory of poetics as a separate branch of verbal practice, particularly in the matter of style.

rhyme: a **figure of speech.** The repetition of identical vowel sounds in stressed syllables whose initial consonants differ ("dead" / "head"). In poetry, rhyme often links the end of one line with another. *Masculine rhyme*: full rhyme on the final syllable of the line ("decays" / "days"). *Feminine rhyme*: full rhyme on syllables that are followed by unaccented syllables ("fountains" / "mountains"). *Internal rhyme*: full rhyme within a single line; Coleridge, *The Rime of the Ancient Mariner*, line 7: "The guests are met, the feast is set" (see vol. D, p. 448). *Rhyme riche*: rhyming on **homophones**; Chaucer, *General Prologue*, lines 17–18: "seeke" / "seke." *Off rhyme* (also known as *half rhyme*, *near rhyme*, or *slant rhyme*): differs from perfect rhyme in changing the vowel sound and/or the concluding consonants expected of perfect rhyme; Byron, "They say that Hope is Happiness," lines 5–7: "most" / "lost." *Pararhyme*: stressed vowel sounds differ but are flanked by identical or similar consonants; Owen, "Miners," lines 9–11: "simmer" / "summer" (see vol. F, p. 163).

rhyme royal: a **verse form.** A **stanza** of seven **iambic pentameter** lines, rhyming ababbcc; first introduced by Chaucer and called "royal" because the form was used by James I of Scotland for his *Kingis Quair* in the early fifteenth century. Chaucer, "Troilus's Song" (see vol. A, p. 362).

rhythm: Rhythm is not absolutely distinguishable from **meter.** One way of making a clear distinction between these terms is to say that rhythm (from the Greek "to flow") denotes the patterns of sound within the feet of verse lines and the combination of those feet. Very often a particular meter will raise expectations that a given rhythm will be used regularly through a whole line or a whole poem. Thus in English verse the pentameter regularly uses an iambic rhythm. Rhythm, however, is much more fluid than meter, and many lines within the same poem using a single meter will frequently exploit different rhythmic possibilities. For examples of different rhythms, see **iamb, trochee, anapest, spondee,** and **dactyl.**

romance: a **genre.** From the twelfth to the sixteenth century, the main form of European narrative, in either verse or prose, was that of chivalric romance. Romance, like the later **novel,** is a very fluid genre, but romances are often characterized by (i) a tripartite structure of social integration, followed by disintegration, involving moral tests and often marvelous events, itself the prelude to reintegration in a happy ending, frequently of marriage; and (ii) aristocratic social milieux. Thus *Sir Gawain and the Green Knight* (see vol. A, p. 204); Spenser's (unfinished) *Faerie Queene* (vol. B, p. 249). The immensely popular, fertile genre was absorbed, in both domesticated and undomesticated form, by the novel. For an adaptation of romance, see Chaucer, *Wife of Bath's Tale* (vol. A, p. 300).

sarcasm (Greek "flesh tearing"): a **figure of thought.** A wounding expression, often expressed ironically; Boswell, *Life of Johnson*: Johnson [asked if any man of the modern age could have written the **epic** poem *Fingal*] replied, "Yes, Sir, many men, many women, and many children" (see vol. C, p. 844).

satire (Latin for "a bowl of mixed fruits"): a **genre.** In Roman literature (e.g., Juvenal), the communication, in the form of a letter between equals, complaining of the ills of contemporary society. The genre in this form is characterized by a first-person narrator exasperated by social ills; the letter form; a high frequency of contemporary reference; and the use of invective in **low-style** language. Pope practices the genre thus in the *Epistle to Dr. Arbuthnot* (see vol. C, p. 543). Wyatt's "Mine own John Poins" (see vol. B, p. 131) draws ultimately on a gentler, Horatian model of the genre.

satiric mode: Works in a very large variety of genres are devoted to the more or less savage attack on social ills. Thus Swift's travel narrative *Gulliver's Travels* (see vol. C, p. 279), his **essay** "A Modest Proposal" (vol. C, p. 454), Pope's mock-**epic** *The Dunciad* (vol. C, p. 555), and Gay's *Beggar's Opera* (vol. C, p. 659), to look no further than the eighteenth century, are all within a satiric mode.

scene: a subdivision of an **act,** itself a subdivision of a dramatic performance and/ or text. The action of a scene usually occurs in one place.

sensibility (from Latin, "capable of being perceived by the senses"): as a literary term, an eighteenth-century concept derived from moral philosophy that stressed the social importance of fellow feeling and particularly of sympathy in social relations. The concept generated a literature of "sensibility," such as the sentimental **novel** (the most famous of which was Goethe's *Sorrows of the Young Werther* [1774]), or sentimental poetry, such as Cowper's passage on the stricken deer in *The Task* (see vol. C, p. 1024).

short story: a **genre.** Generically similar to, though shorter and more concentrated than, the **novel;** often published as part of a collection. Thus Mansfield, "The Daughters of the Late Colonel" (see vol. F, p. 698).

simile (Latin "like"): a **figure of thought.** Comparison, usually using the word "like" or "as," of one thing with another so as to produce sometimes surprising analogies. Donne, "The Storm," lines 29–30: "Sooner than you read this line did the gale, / Like shot, not feared till felt, our sails assail." Frequently used, in extended form, in **epic** poetry; Milton, *Paradise Lost* 1.338–46 (see vol. B, p. 1504).

soliloquy (Latin "single speaking"): a **topos** of drama, in which a **character,** alone or thinking to be alone on stage, speaks so as to give the audience access to his or her private thoughts. Thus Viola's soliloquy in Shakespeare, *Twelfth Night* 2.2.17– 41 (vol. B, p. 758).

sonnet: a verse form. A form combining a variable number of units of rhymed lines to produce a fourteen-line poem, usually in rhyming **iambic pentameter** lines. In English there are two principal varieties: the Petrarchan sonnet, formed by an octave (an eight-line stanza, often broken into two **quatrains** having the same rhyme scheme, typically abba abba) and a sestet (a six-line stanza, typically cdecde or cdcdcd); and the Shakespearean sonnet, formed by three quatrains (abab cdcd efef) and a **couplet** (gg). The declaration of a sonnet can take a sharp turn, or "volta," often at the decisive formal shift from octave to sestet in the Petrarchan sonnet, or in the final couplet of a Shakespearean sonnet, introducing a trenchant counterstatement. Derived from Italian poetry, and especially from the poetry of Petrarch, the sonnet was first introduced to English poetry by Wyatt, and initially used principally for the expression of unrequited erotic love, though later poets used the form for many other purposes. See Wyatt, "Whoso list to hunt" (vol. B, p. 121); Sidney, *Astrophil and Stella* (vol. B, p. 586); Shakespeare, *Sonnets* (vol. B, p. 723); Wordsworth, "London, 1802" (vol. D, p. 357); McKay, "If We Must Die" (vol. F, p. 854); Heaney, "Clearances" (vol. F, p. 1104).

speech act: Words and deeds are often distinguished, but words are often (perhaps always) themselves deeds. Utterances can perform different speech acts, such as promising, declaring, casting a spell, encouraging, persuading, denying, lying, and so on. See also **performative.**

Spenserian stanza: a verse form. The stanza developed by Spenser for *The Faerie Queene*; nine **iambic** lines, the first eight of which are **pentameters,** followed by one **hexameter,** rhyming ababbcbcc. See also, for example, Shelley, *Adonais* (vol. D, p. 856), and Keats, *The Eve of St. Agnes* (vol. D, p. 961).

spondee: a term of **meter.** A two-syllable foot following the rhythmic pattern, in English verse, of two stressed syllables. Thus, for example, "Utah."

stanza (Italian "room"): groupings of two or more lines, though "stanza" is usually reserved for groupings of at least four lines. Stanzas are often joined by rhyme, often in sequence, where each group shares the same metrical pattern and, when rhymed, rhyme scheme. Stanzas can themselves be arranged into larger groupings. Poets often invent new **verse forms,** or they may work within established forms.

story: a narrative's sequence of events, which we reconstruct from those events as they have been recounted by the narrator (i.e., the **plot**). See also **order.**

stream of consciousness: usually a **first-person** narrative that seems to give the reader access to the narrator's mind as it perceives or reflects on events, prior to organizing those perceptions into a coherent narrative. Thus (though generated from a **third-person** narrative) Joyce, *Ulysses*, "Penelope" (see vol. F, p. 604).

style (from Latin for "writing instrument"): In literary works the manner in which something is expressed contributes substantially to its meaning. The expressions "sun," "mass of helium at the center of the solar system," "heaven's golden orb" all designate "sun," but do so in different manners, or styles, which produce different meanings. The manner of a literary work is its "style," the effect of which is its "tone." We often can intuit the tone of a text; from that intuition of tone we can analyze the stylistic resources by which it was produced. We can analyze the style of literary works through consideration of different elements of style; for example, **diction, figures of thought, figures of speech, meter and rhythm, verse form, syntax, point of view.**

sublime: As a concept generating a literary movement, the sublime refers to the realm of experience beyond the measurable, and so beyond the rational, produced especially by the terrors and grandeur of natural phenomena. Derived especially from the first-century Greek treatise *On the Sublime*, sometimes attributed to Longinus, the notion of the sublime was in the later eighteenth century a spur to Romanticism.

syllable: the smallest unit of sound in a pronounced word. The syllable that receives the greatest stress is called the *tonic* syllable.

symbol (Greek "token"): a **figure of thought.** Something that stands for something else, and yet seems necessarily to evoke that other thing. In Neoplatonic, and therefore Romantic, theory, to be distinguished from **allegory** thus: whereas allegory involves connections between vehicle and tenor agreed by convention or made explicit, the meanings of a symbol are supposedly inherent to it. For discussion, see Coleridge, "On Symbol and Allegory" (vol. D, p. 507).

synecdoche (Greek "to take with something else"): a **figure of thought.** Using a part to express the whole, or vice versa; e.g., "all hands on deck." Closely related to **metonymy.**

syntax (Greek "ordering with"): Syntax designates the rules by which sentences are constructed in a given language. Discussion of meter is impossible without some reference to syntax, since the overall effect of a poem is, in part, always the product of a subtle balance of meter and sentence construction. Syntax is also essential to the understanding of prose style, since prose writers, deprived of the full shaping possibilities of meter, rely all the more heavily on syntactic resources. A working command of syntactical practice requires an understanding of the parts of speech (nouns, verbs, adjectives, adverbs, conjunctions, pronouns, prepositions, and interjections), since writers exploit syntactic possibilities by using particular combinations and concentrations of the parts of speech.

taste (from Italian "touch"): Although medieval monastic traditions used eating and tasting as a metaphor for reading, the concept of taste as a personal ideal to be cultivated by, and applied to, the appreciation and judgment of works of art in general was developed in the eighteenth century.

tercet: a **verse form.** A stanza or group of three lines, used in larger forms such as **terza rima,** the **Petrarchan sonnet,** and the **villanelle.**

terza rima: a **verse form.** A sequence of rhymed **tercets** linked by rhyme thus: aba bcb cdc, etc. first used extensively by Dante in *The Divine Comedy*, the form was adapted in English **iambic pentameters** by Wyatt and revived in the nineteenth century. See Wyatt, "Mine own John Poins" (vol. B, p. 131); Shelley, "Ode to the West Wind" (vol. D, p. 806); and Morris, "The Defence of Guinevere" (vol. E, p. 560). For modern adaptations see Eliot, lines 78–149 (though unrhymed) of "Little Gidding" (vol. F, pp. 679–81); Heaney, "Station Island" (vol. F, p. 1102); Walcott, *Omeros* (vol. F, p. 947).

tetrameter (Greek "four measure"): a term of **meter.** A line with four stresses. Coleridge, *Christabel*, line 31: "She stole along, she nothing spoke" (see vol. D, p. 468).

theme (Greek "proposition"): In literary criticism the term designates what the work is about; the theme is the concept that unifies a given work of literature.

third-person narration: relevant to **point of view.** A narration in which the narrator recounts a narrative of **characters** referred to explicitly or implicitly by third-person pronouns ("he," she," etc.), without the limitation of a **first-person narration.** Thus Johnson, *The History of Rasselas.*

topographical poem (Greek "place writing"): a **genre.** A poem devoted to the meditative description of particular places. Thus Gray, "Ode on a Distant Prospect of Eton College" (see vol. C, p. 994).

topos (Greek "place," plural *topoi*): a commonplace in the content of a given kind of literature. Originally, in **classical** rhetoric, the topoi were tried-and-tested stimuli to literary invention: lists of standard headings under which a subject might be investigated. In medieval narrative poems, for example, it was commonplace to begin with a description of spring. Writers did, of course, render the commonplace uncommon, as in Chaucer's spring scene at the opening of *The Canterbury Tales* (see vol. A, p. 261).

tradition (from Latin "passing on"): A literary tradition is whatever is passed on or revived from the past in a single literary culture, or drawn from others to enrich a writer's culture. "Tradition" is fluid in reference, ranging from small to large referents: thus it may refer to a relatively small aspect of texts (e.g., the tradition of **iambic pentameter**), or it may, at the other extreme, refer to the body of texts that constitute a **canon.**

tragedy: a **genre.** A dramatic representation of the fall of kings or nobles, beginning in happiness and ending in catastrophe. Later transferred to other social milieux. The opposite of **comedy;** thus Shakespeare, *Othello* (see vol. B, p. 806).

tragic mode: Many genres (**epic** poetry, **legend**ary chronicles, **tragedy,** the **novel**) either do or can participate in a tragic mode, by representing the fall of noble **protagonists** and the irreparable ravages of human society and history.

tragicomedy: a **genre.** A play in which potentially tragic events turn out to have a happy, or **comic,** ending. Thus Shakespeare, *Measure for Measure.*

translation (Latin "carrying across"): the rendering of a text written in one language into another.

trimeter (Greek "three measure"): a term of **meter.** A line with three stresses. Herbert, "Discipline," line 1: "Throw away thy rod" (see vol. B, p. 1274).

triplet: a **verse form.** A tercet rhyming on the same sound. Pope inserts triplets among heroic **couplets** to emphasize a particular thought; see *Essay on Criticism,* 315–17 (vol. C, p. 497).

trochee: a term of **rhythm.** A two-syllable foot following the pattern, in English verse, of stressed followed by unstressed syllable, producing a falling effect. Thus, for example, "Texas."

type (Greek "impression, figure"): a **figure of thought.** In Christian allegorical interpretation of the Old Testament, pre-Christian figures were regarded as "types," or foreshadowings, of Christ or the Christian dispensation. *Typology* has been the source of much visual and literary art in which the parallelisms between old and new are extended to nonbiblical figures; thus the virtuous plowman in *Piers Plowman* becomes a type of Christ.

unities: According to a theory supposedly derived from Aristotle's *Poetics,* the events represented in a play should have unity of time, place, and action: that the play take up no more time than the time of the play, or at most a day; that the space of action should be within a single city; and that there should be no subplot. See Johnson, *The Preface to Shakespeare* (vol. C, p. 807).

vernacular (from Latin *verna,* "servant"): the language of the people, as distinguished from learned and arcane languages. From the later Middle Ages especially, the "vernacular" languages and literatures of Europe distinguished themselves from the learned languages and literatures of Latin, Greek, and Hebrew.

verse form: The terms related to **meter** and **rhythm** describe the shape of individual lines. Lines of verse are combined to produce larger groupings, called verse forms. These larger groupings are in the first instance **stanzas.** The combination of a certain meter and stanza shape constitutes the verse form, of which there are many standard kinds.

villanelle: a **verse form.** A fixed form of usually five **tercets** and a **quatrain** employing only two rhyme sounds altogether, rhyming aba for the tercets and abaa for the quatrain, with a complex pattern of two **refrains.** Derived from a French fixed form. Thomas, "Do Not Go Gentle into That Good Night" (see vol. F, p. 833).

wit: Originally a synonym for "reason" in Old and Middle English, "wit" became a literary ideal in the Renaissance as brilliant play of the full range of mental resources. For eighteenth-century writers, the notion necessarily involved pleasing expression, as in Pope's definition of true wit as "Nature to advantage dressed, / What oft was thought, but ne'er so well expressed" (*Essay on Criticism*, lines 297–98; see vol. C, p. 496–97). See also Johnson, *Lives of the Poets,* "Cowley," on "metaphysical wit" (see vol. C, p. 817). Romantic theory of the imagination deprived wit of its full range of apprehension, whence the word came to be restricted to its modern sense, as the clever play of mind that produces laughter.

zeugma (Greek "a yoking"): a **figure of thought.** A figure whereby one word applies to two or more words in a sentence, and in which the applications are surprising, either because one is unusual, or because the applications are made in very different ways; Pope, *Rape of the Lock* 3.7–8, in which the word "take" is used in two senses: "Here thou, great Anna! whom three realms obey, / Dost sometimes counsel take— and sometimes tea" (see vol. C, p. 515).

B: Publishing History, Censorship

By the time we read texts in published books, they have already been treated—that is, changed by authors, editors, and printers—in many ways. Although there are differences across history, in each period literary works are subject to pressures of many kinds, which apply before, while, and after an author writes. The pressures might be financial, as in the relations of author and patron; commercial, as in the marketing of books; and legal, as in, during some periods, the negotiation through official and unofficial censorship. In addition, texts in all periods undergo technological processes, as they move from the material forms in which an author produced them to the forms in which they are presented to readers. Some of the terms below designate important material forms in which books were produced, disseminated, and surveyed across the historical span of this anthology. Others designate the skills developed to understand these processes. The anthology's introductions to individual periods discuss the particular forms these phenomena took in different eras.

bookseller: In England, and particularly in London, commercial bookmaking and -selling enterprises came into being in the early fourteenth century. These were loose organizations of artisans who usually lived in the same neighborhoods (around St. Paul's Cathedral in London). A bookseller or dealer would coordinate the production of hand-copied books for wealthy patrons (see **patronage**), who would order books to be custom-made. After the introduction of **printing** in the late fifteenth century, authors generally sold the rights to their work to booksellers, without any further **royalties.** Booksellers, who often had their own shops, belonged to the **Stationers' Company.** This system lasted into the eighteenth century. In 1710, however, authors were for the first time granted **copyright,** which tipped the commercial balance in their favor, against booksellers.

censorship: The term applies to any mechanism for restricting what can be published. Historically, the reasons for imposing censorship are heresy, sedition, blasphemy, libel, or obscenity. External censorship is imposed by institutions having legislative sanctions at their disposal. Thus the pre-Reformation Church imposed the Constitutions of Archbishop Arundel of 1409, aimed at repressing the Lollard "heresy." After the Reformation, some key events in the history of censorship are as follows: 1547, when anti-Lollard legislation and legislation made by Henry VIII concerning treason by writing (1534) were abolished; the Licensing Order of 1643, which legislated that works be licensed, through the Stationers' Company, prior to publication; and 1695, when the last such Act stipulating prepublication licensing lapsed. Postpublication censorship continued in different periods for different reasons. Thus, for example, British publication of D. H. Lawrence's *Lady Chatterley's Lover* (1928) was obstructed (though unsuccessfully) in 1960, under the Obscene Publications Act of 1959. Censorship can also be international: although not published in Iran, Salman Rushdie's *Satanic Verses* (1988) was censored in that country, where the leader, Ayatollah Ruhollah Khomeini, proclaimed a fatwa (religious decree) promising the author's execution. Very often censorship is not imposed externally, however: authors or publishers can censor work in anticipation of what will incur the wrath of readers or the penalties of the law. Victorian and Edwardian publishers of **novels,** for example, urged authors to remove potentially offensive material, especially for serial publication in popular magazines.

codex: the physical format of most modern books and medieval manuscripts, consisting of a series of separate leaves gathered into quires and bound together, often with a cover. In late antiquity, the codex largely replaced the scroll, the standard form of written documents in Roman culture.

copy text: the particular text of a work used by a textual editor as the basis of an edition of that work.

copyright: the legal protection afforded to authors for control of their work's publication, in an attempt to ensure due financial reward. Some key dates in the history of copyright in the United Kingdom are as follows: 1710, when a statute gave authors the exclusive right to publish their work for fourteen years, and fourteen years more if the author were still alive when the first term had expired; 1842, when the period of authorial control was extended to forty-two years; and 1911, when the term was extended yet further, to fifty years after the author's death. In 1995 the period of protection was harmonized with the laws in other European countries to be the life of the author plus seventy years. In the United States no works first published before 1923 are in copyright. Works published since 1978 are, as in the United Kingdom, protected for the life of the author plus seventy years.

folio: the leaf formed by both sides of a single page. Each folio has two sides: a *recto* (the front side of the leaf, on the right side of a double-page spread in an open codex), and a *verso* (the back side of the leaf, on the left side of a double-page spread). Modern book pagination follows the pattern 1, 2, 3, 4, while medieval manuscript pagination follows the pattern 1r, 1v, 2r, 2v. "Folio" can also designate the size of a printed book. Books come in different shapes, depending originally on the number of times a standard sheet of paper is folded. One fold produces a large volume, a *folio* book; two folds produce a *quarto*, four an *octavo*, and six a very small *duodecimo*. Generally speaking, the larger the book, the grander and more expensive. Shakespeare's plays were, for example, first printed in quartos, but were gathered into a folio edition in 1623.

foul papers: versions of a work before an author has produced, if she or he has, a final copy (a "fair copy") with all corrections removed.

incunabulum (plural "incunabula"): any printed book produced in Europe before 1501. Famous incunabula include the Gutenberg Bible, printed in 1455.

manuscript (Latin, "written by hand"): Any text written physically by hand is a manuscript. Before the introduction of **printing** with moveable type in 1476, all texts in England were produced and reproduced by hand, in manuscript. This is an extremely labor-intensive task, using expensive materials (e.g., **vellum,** or **parchment**); the cost of books produced thereby was, accordingly, very high. Even after the introduction of printing, many texts continued to be produced in manuscript. This is obviously true of letters, for example, but until the eighteenth century, poetry written within aristocratic circles was often transmitted in manuscript copies.

paleography (Greek "ancient writing"): the art of deciphering, describing, and dating forms of handwriting.

parchment: animal skin, used as the material for handwritten books before the introduction of paper. See also **vellum.**

patronage, patron (Latin "protector"): Many technological, legal, and commercial supports were necessary before professional authorship became possible. Although some playwrights (e.g., Shakespeare) made a living by writing for the theater, other authors needed, principally, the large-scale reproductive capacities of **printing** and the security of **copyright** to make a living from writing. Before these conditions obtained, many authors had another main occupation, and most authors had to rely on patronage. In different periods, institutions or individuals offered material support, or patronage, to authors. Thus in Anglo-Saxon England, monasteries afforded the conditions of writing to monastic authors. Between the twelfth and the seventeenth centuries, the main source of patronage was the royal court. Authors offered patrons prestige and ideological support in return for financial support. Even as the conditions of professional authorship came into being at the beginning of the eighteenth century, older forms of direct patronage were not altogether displaced until the middle of the century.

periodical: Whereas journalism, strictly, applies to daily writing (from French *jour,* "day"), periodical writing appears at larger, but still frequent, intervals, characteristically in the form of the **essay.** Periodicals were developed especially in the eighteenth century.

printing: Printing, or the mechanical reproduction of books using moveable type, was invented in Germany in the mid-fifteenth century by Johannes Gutenberg; it quickly spread throughout Europe. William Caxton brought printing into England from the Low Countries in 1476. Much greater powers of reproduction at much lower prices transformed every aspect of literary culture.

publisher: the person or company responsible for the commissioning and publicizing of printed matter. In the early period of **printing,** publisher, printer, and bookseller were often the same person. This trend continued in the ascendancy of the **Stationers' Company,** between the middle of the sixteenth and the end of the seventeenth centuries. Toward the end of the seventeenth century, these three functions began to separate, leading to their modern distinctions.

quire: When medieval manuscripts were assembled, a few loose sheets of parchment or paper would first be folded together and sewn along the fold. This formed a quire (also known as a "gathering" or "signature"). Folded in this way, four large sheets of parchment would produce eight smaller manuscript leaves. Multiple quires could then be bound together to form a codex.

royalties: an agreed-upon proportion of the price of each copy of a work sold, paid by the publisher to the author, or an agreed-upon fee paid to the playwright for each performance of a play.

scribe: In **manuscript** culture, the scribe is the copyist who reproduces a text by hand.

scriptorium (plural "scriptoria"): a place for producing written documents and manuscripts.

serial publication: generally referring to the practice, especially common in the nineteenth century, of publishing novels a few chapters at a time, in periodicals.

Stationers' Company: The Stationers' Company was an English guild incorporating various tradesmen, including printers, publishers, and booksellers, skilled in the production and selling of books. It was formed in 1403, received its royal charter in 1557, and served as a means both of producing and of regulating books. Authors would sell the manuscripts of their books to individual stationers, who incurred the risks and took the profits of producing and selling the books. The stationers entered their rights over given books in the Stationers' Register. They also regulated the book trade and held their monopoly by licensing books and by being empowered to seize unauthorized books and imprison resisters. This system of licensing broke down in the social unrest of the Civil War and Interregnum (1640–60), and it ended in 1695. Even after the end of licensing, the Stationers' Company continued to be an intrinsic part of the **copyright** process, since the 1710 copyright statute directed that copyright had to be registered at Stationers' Hall.

subscription: An eighteenth-century system of bookselling somewhere between direct **patronage** and impersonal sales. A subscriber paid half the cost of a book before publication and half on delivery. The author received these payments directly. The subscriber's name appeared in the prefatory pages.

textual criticism: Works in all periods often exist in many subtly or not so subtly different forms. This is especially true with regard to manuscript textual reproduction, but it also applies to printed texts. Textual criticism is the art, developed from the fifteenth century in Italy but raised to new levels of sophistication from the eighteenth century, of deciphering different historical states of texts. This art involves the analysis of textual **variants,** often with the aim of distinguishing authorial from scribal forms.

variants: differences that appear among different manuscripts or printed editions of the same text.

vellum: animal skin, used as the material for handwritten books before the introduction of paper. See also **parchment.**

watermark: the trademark of a paper manufacturer, impressed into the paper but largely invisible unless held up to light.

Geographic Nomenclature

The British Isles refers to the prominent group of islands off the northwest coast of Europe, especially to the two largest, **Great Britain** and **Ireland**. At present these comprise two sovereign states: **the Republic of Ireland**, and **the United Kingdom of Great Britain and Northern Ireland**—known for short as the **United Kingdom** or the **U.K.** Most of the smaller islands are part of the **U.K.** but a few, like the **Isle of Man** and the tiny **Channel Islands**, are largely independent. The **U.K.** is often loosely referred to as "**Britain**" or "**Great Britain**" and is sometimes called simply, if inaccurately, "**England.**" For obvious reasons, the latter usage is rarely heard among the inhabitants of the other countries of the **U.K.**—**Scotland, Wales,** and **Northern Ireland** (sometimes called **Ulster**). England is by far the most populous part of the kingdom, as well as the seat of its capital, London.

From the first to the fifth century C.E. most of what is now **England** and **Wales** was a province of the Roman Empire called **Britain** (in Latin, **Britannia**). After the fall of Rome, much of the island was invaded and settled by peoples from northern Germany and Denmark speaking what we now call Old English. These peoples are collectively known as the Anglo-Saxons, and the word **England** is related to the first element of their name. By the time of the Norman Conquest (1066) most of the kingdoms founded by the Anglo-Saxons and subsequent Viking invaders had coalesced into the kingdom of **England,** which, in the latter Middle Ages, conquered and largely absorbed the neighboring Celtic kingdom of **Wales.** In 1603 James VI of **Scotland** inherited the island's other throne as James I of **England,** and for the next hundred years—except for the two decades of Puritan rule—**Scotland** (both its English-speaking **Lowlands** and its Gaelic-speaking **Highlands**) and **England** (with **Wales**) were two kingdoms under a single king. In 1707 the Act of Union welded them together as **the United Kingdom of Great Britain. Ireland,** where English rule had begun in the twelfth century and been tightened in the sixteenth, was incorporated by the 1800–1801 Act of Union into **the United Kingdom of Great Britain and Ireland**. With the division of Ireland and the establishment of **the Irish Free State** after World War I, this name was modified to its present form, and in 1949 **the Irish Free State** became **the Republic of Ireland,** or **Éire**. In 1999 **Scotland** elected a separate parliament it had relinquished in 1707, and **Wales** elected an assembly it lost in 1409; neither Scotland nor Wales ceased to be part of the **United Kingdom.**

The **British Isles** are further divided into counties, which in **Great Britain** are also known as shires. This word, with its vowel shortened in pronunciation, forms the suffix in the names of many counties, such as **Yorkshire, Wiltshire, Somersetshire**.

The Latin names **Britannia (Britain), Caledonia (Scotland),** and **Hibernia (Ireland)** are sometimes used in poetic diction; so too is **Britain**'s ancient Celtic name, **Albion**. Because of its accidental resemblance to *albus* (Latin for "white"), **Albion** is especially associated with the chalk cliffs that seem to gird much of the English coast like defensive walls.

The **British Empire** took its name from **the British Isles** because it was created not only by the **English** but also by the **Irish, Scots,** and **Welsh,** as well as by civilians and servicemen from other constituent countries of the empire. Some of the empire's **overseas colonies**, or **crown colonies**, were populated largely by settlers of European origin and their descendants. These predominantly white **settler colonies,** such as **Canada, Australia,** and **New Zealand,** were allowed significant self-government in the nineteenth century and recognized as **dominions** in the early twentieth century. The **white dominions** became members of **the Commonwealth of Nations**, also called **the Commonwealth, the British Commonwealth**, and **"the Old Commonwealth"** at different times, an association of sovereign states under the symbolic leadership of the British monarch.

Other **overseas colonies** of the empire had mostly indigenous populations (or, in the Caribbean, the descendants of imported slaves, indentured servants, and others). These **colonies** were granted political independence after World War II, later than the **dominions**, and have often been referred to since as **postcolonial** nations. In South and Southeast Asia, **India** and **Pakistan** gained independence in 1947, followed by other countries including **Sri Lanka** (formerly **Ceylon**), **Burma** (now **Myanmar**), **Malaya** (now **Malaysia**), and **Singapore**. In West and East Africa, the **Gold Coast** was decolonized as **Ghana** in 1957, **Nigeria** in 1960, **Sierra Leone** in 1961, **Uganda** in 1962, **Kenya** in 1963, and so forth, while in southern Africa, the white minority government of **South Africa** was already independent in 1931, though majority rule did not come until 1994. In the Caribbean, **Jamaica** and **Trinidad and Tobago** won independence in 1962, followed by **Barbados** in 1966, and other islands of the British West Indies in the 1970s and '80s. Other regions with nations emerging out of British colonial rule included Central America (**British Honduras**, now **Belize**), South America (**British Guiana**, now **Guyana**), the Pacific islands (**Fiji**), and Europe (**Cyprus, Malta**). After decolonization, many of these nations chose to remain within a newly conceived **Commonwealth** and are sometimes referred to as **"New Commonwealth"** countries. Some nations, such as **Ireland, Pakistan**, and **South Africa**, withdrew from the **Commonwealth**, though **South Africa** and **Pakistan** eventually rejoined, and others, such as **Burma** (now **Myanmar**), gained independence outside the **Commonwealth**. Britain's last major overseas colony, **Hong Kong**, was returned to Chinese sovereignty in 1997, but while Britain retains only a handful of dependent territories, such as **Bermuda** and **Montserrat**, the scope of the **Commonwealth** remains vast, with 30 percent of the world's population.

British Money

One of the most dramatic changes to the system of British money came in 1971. In the system previously in place, the pound consisted of 20 shillings, each containing 12 pence, making 240 pence to the pound. Since 1971, British money has been calculated on the decimal system, with 100 pence to the pound. Britons' experience of paper money did not change very drastically: as before, 5- and 10-pound notes constitute the majority of bills passing through their hands (in addition, 20- and 50- pound notes have been added). But the shift necessitated a whole new way of thinking about and exchanging coins and marked the demise of the shilling, one of the fundamental units of British monetary history. Many other coins, still frequently encountered in literature, had already passed. These include the groat, worth 4 pence (the word "groat" is often used to signify a trifling sum); the angel (which depicted the archangel Michael triumphing over a dragon), valued at 10 shillings; the mark, worth in its day two-thirds of a pound or 13 shillings 4 pence; and the sovereign, a gold coin initially worth 22 shillings 6 pence, later valued at 1 pound, last circulated in 1932. One prominent older coin, the guinea, was worth a pound and a shilling; though it has not been minted since 1813, a very few quality items or prestige awards (like the purse in a horse race) may still be quoted in guineas. (The table below includes some other well-known, obsolete coins.) Colloquially, a pound was (and is) called a quid; a shilling a bob; sixpence, a tanner; a copper could refer to a penny, a half-penny, or a farthing (¼ penny).

Old Currency	New Currency
1 pound note	1 pound coin (or note in Scotland)
10 shilling (half-pound note)	50 pence
5 shilling (crown)	
2½ shilling (half crown)	20 pence
2 shilling (florin)	10 pence
1 shilling	5 pence
6 pence	
2½ pence	1 penny
2 pence	
1 penny	
½ penny	
¼ penny (farthing)	

Throughout its tenure as a member of the European Union, Britain contemplated but did not make the change to the EU's common currency, the Euro. Many Britons strongly identify their country with its rich commercial history and tend to view their currency patriotically as a national symbol. Now, with the planned withdrawal of the United Kingdom from the EU, the pound seems here to stay.

Even more challenging than sorting out the values of obsolete coins is calculating for any given period the purchasing power of money, which fluctuates over time by its very nature. At the beginning of the twentieth century, 1 pound was worth about 5 American dollars, though those bought three to four times what they now do. Now, the pound buys anywhere from $1.20 to $1.50. As difficult as it is to generalize, it is clear that money used to be worth much more than it is currently. In Anglo-Saxon times, the most valuable circulating coin was the silver penny: four would buy a sheep. Beyond long-term inflationary trends, prices varied from times of plenty to those marked by poor harvests; from peacetime to wartime; from the country to the metropolis (life in London has always been very expensive); and wages varied according to the availability of labor (wages would sharply rise, for instance, during the devastating Black Death in the fourteenth century). The following chart provides a glimpse of some actual prices of given periods and their changes across time, though all the variables mentioned above prevent them from being definitive. Even from one year to the next, an added tax on gin or tea could drastically raise prices, and a lottery ticket could cost much more the night before the drawing than just a month earlier. Still, the prices quoted below do indicate important trends, such as the disparity of incomes in British society and the costs of basic commodities. In the chart on the following page, the symbol £ is used for pound, s. for shilling, d. for a penny (from Latin *denarius*); a sum would normally be written £2.19.3, i.e., 2 pounds, 19 shillings, 3 pence. (This is Leopold Bloom's budget for the day depicted in Joyce's novel *Ulysses* [1922]; in the new currency, it would be about £2.96.)

circa	1390	1590	1650	1750	1815	1875	1950
food and drink	gallon (8 pints) of ale, 1.5d.	tankard of beer, 5d.	coffee, 1d. a dish	"drunk for a penny, dead drunk for two-pence" (gin shop sign in Hogarth print)	ounce of laudanum, 3d.	pint of beer, 3d.	pint of Guinness stout, 11d.
	gallon (8 pints) of wine, 3 to 4d.	pound of beef, 2s. 5d.	chicken, 1s. 4d.	dinner at a steakhouse, 1s.	ham and potato dinner for two, 7s.	dinner in a good hotel, 5s.	pound of beef, 2s. 2d.
	pound of cinnamon, 1 to 3s.	pound of cinnamon, 10s. 6d.	pound of tea, £3 10s.	pound of tea, 16s.	bottle of French claret, 12s.	pound of tea, 2s.	dinner on railway car, 7s. 6d.
entertainment	no cost to watch a cycle play	admission to public theater, 1 to 3d.	falcon, £11 5s.	theater tickets, 1 to 5s.	admission to Covent Garden theater, 1 to 7s.	theater tickets, 6d. to 7s.	admission to Old Vic theater, 1s. 6d. to 10s. 6d.
	contributory admission to professional troupe theater	cheap seat in private theater, 6d.	billiard table, £25	admission to Vauxhall Gardens, 1s.	annual subscription to Almack's (exclusive club), 10 guineas	admission to Madam Tussaud's waxworks, 1s.	admission to Odeon cinema, Manchester, 1s 3d.
	maintenance for royal hounds at Windsor, .75d. a day	"to see a dead Indian" (quoted in The Tempest), 1.25d. (ten "doits")	three-quarter length portrait painting, £31	lottery ticket, £20 (shares were sold)	Jane Austen's piano, 30 guineas	annual fees at a gentleman's club, 7 to 10 guineas	tropical fish tank, £4 4s.

circa	1390	1590	1650	1750	1815	1875	1950
reading	cheap romance, 1s.; a Latin Bible, 2 to £4; payment for illuminating a liturgical book, £22 9s.	play quarto, 6d.; Shakespeare's *First Folio* (1623), £1; Foxe's *Acts and Monuments*, 24s.	pamphlet, 1 to 6d.; student Bible, 6s.; Hobbes's *Leviathan*, 8s.	issue of The *Gentleman's Magazine*, 6d.; cheap edition of Milton, 2s.; Johnson's *Dictionary*, folio, 2 vols., £4 10s.	issue of *Edinburgh Review*, 6s.; membership in circulating library (3rd class), £1 4s. a year; 1st edition of Austen's *Pride and Prejudice*, 18s.	copy of the *Times*, 3d.; illustrated edition of *Through the Looking-glass*, 6s.; 1st edition of Trollope's *The Way We Live Now*, 2 vols., £1 1s.	copy of the *Times*, 3d.; issue of *Eagle* comics, 4.5d.; Orwell's *Nineteen Eighty Four*, paperback, 3s. 6d.
transportation	night's supply of hay for horse, 2d.; coach, £8; quality horse, £10	wherry (whole boat) across Thames, 1d.; hiring a horse for a day, 12d.; hiring a coach for a day, 10s.	day's journey, coach, 10s.; coach horse, £30; fancy carriage, £170	boat across Thames, 4d.; coach fare, London to Edinburgh, £4 10s.; transport to America, £5	coach ride, outside, 2 to 3d. a mile; inside, 4 to 5d. a mile; palanquin transport in Madras, 5s. a day; passage, Liverpool to New York, £10	15-minute journey in a London cab, 1s. 6d.; railway, 3rd class, London to Plymouth, 18s. 8d. (about 1d. a mile); passage to India, 1st class, £50	London tube fare, about 2d. a mile; petrol, 3s. a gallon; midsize Austin sedan, £449 plus £188 4s. 2d. tax
clothes	clothing allowance for peasant, 3s. a year	shoes with buckles, 8d.	footman's frieze coat, 15s.	working woman's gown, 6s. 6d.	checked muslin, 7s. per yard	flannel for a cheap petticoat, 1s. 3d. a yard	woman's sun frock, £3 13s. 10d.

labor/incomes

shoes for gentry wearer, 4d.	woman's gloves, £1 5s.	falconer's hat, 10s.	gentleman's suit, £8	hiring a dressmaker for a pelisse, 8s.	overcoat for an Eton schoolboy, £1 1s.	tweed sports jacket, £3 16s. 6d.
hat for gentry wearer, 10d.	fine cloak, £16	black cloth for mourning household of an earl, £100	very fine wig, £30	ladies silk stockings, 12s.	set of false teeth, £2 10s.	"Teddy boy" drape suit, £20
hiring a skilled building worker, 4d. a day	actor's daily wage during playing season, 1s.	agricultural laborer, 6s. 5d. a week	price of boy slave, £32	lowest-paid sailor on Royal Navy ship, 10s. 9d. a month	seasonal agricultural laborer, 14s. a week	minimum wage, agricultural laborer, £4 14s. per 47-hour week
wage for professional scribe, £2 3s. 4d. a year + cloak	household servant 2 to £5 a year + food, clothing	tutor to nobleman's children, £30 a year	housemaid's wage, £6 to £8 a year	contributor to *Quarterly Review*, 10 guineas per sheet	housemaid's wage, £10 to £25 a year	shorthand typist, £367 a year
minimum income to be called gentleman, £10 a year; for knighthood, 40 to £400	minimum income for eligibility for knighthood, £30 a year	Milton's salary as Secretary of Foreign Tongues, £288 a year	Boswell's allowance, £200 a year	minimum income for a "genteel" family, £100 a year	income of the "comfortable" classes, £800 and up a year	middle manager's salary, £1,480 a year
income from land of richest magnates, £3,500 a year	income from land of average earl, £4,000 a year	Earl of Bedford's income, £8,000 a year	Duke of Newcastle's income, £40,000 a year	Mr. Darcy's income, *Pride and Prejudice*, £10,000	Trollope's income, £4,000 a year	barrister's salary, £2,032 a year

The British Baronage

The English monarchy is in principle hereditary, though at times during the Middle Ages the rules were subject to dispute. In general, authority passes from father to eldest surviving son, to daughters in order of seniority if there is no son, to a brother if there are no children, and in default of direct descendants to collateral lines (cousins, nephews, nieces) in order of closeness. There have been breaks in the order of succession (1066, 1399, 1688), but so far as possible the usurpers have always sought to paper over the break with a legitimate, i.e., hereditary, claim. When a queen succeeds to the throne and takes a husband, he does not become king unless he is in the line of blood succession; rather, he is named prince consort, as Albert was to Victoria. He may father kings, but is not one himself.

The original Saxon nobles were the king's thanes, ealdormen, or earls, who provided the king with military service and counsel in return for booty, gifts, or landed estates. William the Conqueror, arriving from France, where feudalism was fully developed, considerably expanded this group. In addition, as the king distributed the lands of his new kingdom, he also distributed dignities to men who became known collectively as "the baronage." "Baron" in its root meaning signifies simply "man," and barons were the king's men. As the title was common, a distinction was early made between greater and lesser barons, the former gradually assuming loftier and more impressive titles. The first English "duke" was created in 1337; the title of "marquess," or "marquis" (pronounced "markwis"), followed in 1385, and "viscount" ("vyekount") in 1440. Though "earl" is the oldest title of all, an earl now comes between a marquess and a viscount in order of dignity and precedence, and the old term "baron" now designates a rank just below viscount. "Baronets" were created in 1611 as a means of raising revenue for the crown (the title could be purchased for about £1,000); they are marginal nobility and have never sat in the House of Lords.

Kings and queens are addressed as "Your Majesty," princes and princesses as "Your Highness," the other hereditary nobility as "My Lord" or "Your Lordship." Peers receive their titles either by inheritance (like Lord Byron, the sixth baron of that line) or from the monarch (like Alfred, Lord Tennyson, created 1st Baron Tennyson by Victoria). The children, even of a duke, are commoners unless they are specifically granted some other title or inherit their father's title from him. A peerage can be forfeited by act of attainder, as for example when a lord is convicted of treason; and, when forfeited, or lapsed for lack of a successor, can be bestowed on another family. Thus in 1605 Robert Cecil was made first earl of Salisbury in the third creation, the first creation dating from 1149, the second from 1337, the title having been in abeyance since 1539. Titles descend by right of succession and do not depend on tenure of land; thus, a title does not always indicate where a lord dwells or holds power. Indeed, noble titles do not always refer to a real place at all. At Prince Edward's marriage in 1999, the queen created him earl of Wessex, although the old kingdom of Wessex has had no political existence since the Anglo-Saxon period, and the name was all but forgotten until it was resurrected by Thomas Hardy as the setting of his novels. (This is perhaps but one of many ways in which the world of the aristocracy increasingly resembles the realm of literature.)

The king and queen	(These are all of the royal line.)
Prince and princess	
Duke and duchess	(These may or may not be of the royal
Marquess and marchioness	line, but are ordinarily remote from the
Earl and countess	succession.)
Viscount and viscountess	
Baron and baroness	
Baronet and lady	

Scottish peers sat in the parliament of Scotland, as English peers did in the parliament of England, till at the Act of Union (1707) Scottish peers were granted sixteen seats in the English House of Lords, to be filled by election. (In 1963, all Scottish lords were allowed to sit.) Similarly, Irish peers, when the Irish parliament was abolished in 1801, were granted the right to elect twenty-eight of their number to the House of Lords in Westminster. (Now that the Republic of Ireland is a separate nation, this no longer applies.) Women members (peeresses) were first allowed to sit in the House as nonhereditary Life Peers in 1958 (when that status was created for members of both genders); women first sat by their own hereditary right in 1963. Today the House of Lords still retains some power to influence or delay legislation, but its future is uncertain. In 1999, the hereditary peers (then amounting to 750) were reduced to 92 temporary members elected by their fellow peers. Holders of Life Peerages remain, as do senior bishops of the Church of England and high-court judges (the "Law Lords").

Below the peerage the chief title of honor is "knight." Knighthood, which is not hereditary, is generally a reward for services rendered. A knight (Sir John Black) is addressed, using his first name, as "Sir John"; his wife, using the last name, is "Lady Black"—unless she is the daughter of an earl or nobleman of higher rank, in which case she will be "Lady Arabella." The female equivalent of a knight bears the title of "Dame." Though the word knight itself comes from the Anglo-Saxon cniht, there is some doubt as to whether knighthood amounted to much before the arrival of the Normans. The feudal system required military service as a condition of land tenure, and a man who came to serve his king at the head of an army of tenants required a title of authority and badges of identity—hence the title of knighthood and the coat of arms. During the Crusades, when men were far removed from their land (or even sold it in order to go on crusade), more elaborate forms of fealty sprang up that soon expanded into orders of knighthood. The Templars, Hospitallers, Knights of the Teutonic Order, Knights of Malta, and Knights of the Golden Fleece were but a few of these companionships; not all of them were available at all times in England.

Gradually, with the rise of centralized government and the decline of feudal tenures, military knighthood became obsolete, and the rank largely honorific; sometimes, as under James I, it degenerated into a scheme of the royal government for making money. For hundreds of years after its establishment in the fourteenth century, the Order of the Garter was the only English order of knighthood, an exclusive courtly companionship. Then, during the late seventeenth, the eighteenth, and the nineteenth centuries, a number of additional orders were created, with names such as the Thistle, Saint Patrick, the Bath, Saint Michael, and Saint George, plus a number of special Victorian and Indian orders. They retain the terminology, ceremony, and dignity of knighthood, but the military implications are vestigial.

Although the British Empire now belongs to history, appointments to the Order of the British Empire continue to be conferred for services to that empire at home or abroad. Such honors (commonly referred to as "gongs") are granted by the monarch in her New Year's and Birthday lists, but the decisions are now made by the government in power. In recent years there have been efforts to popularize and democratize the dispensation of honors, with recipients including rock stars and actors. But this does not prevent large sectors of British society from regarding both knighthood and the peerage as largely irrelevant to modern life.

The Royal Lines of England and Great Britain

England

SAXONS AND DANES

Egbert, king of Wessex	802–839
Ethelwulf, son of Egbert	839–858
Ethelbald, second son of Ethelwulf	858–860
Ethelbert, third son of Ethelwulf	860–866
Ethelred I, fourth son of Ethelwulf	866–871
Alfred the Great, fifth son of Ethelwulf	871–899
Edward the Elder, son of Alfred	899–924
Athelstan the Glorious, son of Edward	924–940
Edmund I, third son of Edward	940–946
Edred, fourth son of Edward	946–955
Edwy the Fair, son of Edmund	955–959
Edgar the Peaceful, second son of Edmund	959–975
Edward the Martyr, son of Edgar	975–978 (murdered)
Ethelred II, the Unready, second son of Edgar	978–1016
Edmund II, Ironside, son of Ethelred II	1016–1016
Canute the Dane	1016–1035
Harold I, Harefoot, natural son of Canute	1035–1040
Hardecanute, son of Canute	1040–1042
Edward the Confessor, son of Ethelred II	1042–1066
Harold II, brother-in-law of Edward	1066–1066 (died in battle)

HOUSE OF NORMANDY

William I, the Conqueror	1066–1087
William II, Rufus, third son of William I	1087–1100 (shot from ambush)
Henry I, Beauclerc, youngest son of William I	1100–1135

HOUSE OF BLOIS

Stephen, son of Adela, daughter of William I	1135–1154

HOUSE OF PLANTAGENET

Henry II, son of Geoffrey Plantagenet by Matilda, daughter of Henry I	1154–1189
Richard I, Coeur de Lion, son of Henry II	1189–1199
John Lackland, son of Henry II	1199–1216
Henry III, son of John	1216–1272
Edward I, Longshanks, son of Henry III	1272–1307
Edward II, son of Edward I	1307–1327 (deposed)
Edward III of Windsor, son of Edward II	1327–1377
Richard II, grandson of Edward III	1377–1399 (deposed)

HOUSE OF LANCASTER

Henry IV, son of John of Gaunt, son of Edward III	1399–1413
Henry V, Prince Hal, son of Henry IV	1413–1422
Henry VI, son of Henry V	1422–1461 (deposed), 1470–1471 (deposed)

HOUSE OF YORK

Edward IV, great-great-grandson of Edward III	1461–1470 (deposed), 1471–1483
Edward V, son of Edward IV	1483–1483 (murdered)
Richard III, Crookback	1483–1485 (died in battle)

HOUSE OF TUDOR

Henry VII, married daughter of Edward IV	1485–1509
Henry VIII, son of Henry VII	1509–1547
Edward VI, son of Henry VIII	1547–1553
Mary I, "Bloody," daughter of Henry VIII	1553–1558
Elizabeth I, daughter of Henry VIII	1558–1603

HOUSE OF STUART

James I (James VI of Scotland)	1603–1625
Charles I, son of James I	1625–1649 (executed)

COMMONWEALTH & PROTECTORATE

Council of State	1649–1653
Oliver Cromwell, Lord Protector	1653–1658
Richard Cromwell, son of Oliver	1658–1660 (resigned)

HOUSE OF STUART (RESTORED)

Charles II, son of Charles I	1660–1685
James II, second son of Charles I	1685–1688

(INTERREGNUM, 11 DECEMBER 1688 TO 13 FEBRUARY 1689)

HOUSE OF ORANGE-NASSAU

William III of Orange, by	
Mary, daughter of Charles I	1689–1701
and Mary II, daughter of James II	–1694
Anne, second daughter of James II	1702–1714

Great Britain

HOUSE OF HANOVER

George I, son of Elector of Hanover and	
Sophia, granddaughter of James I	1714–1727
George II, son of George I	1727–1760
George III, grandson of George II	1760–1820
George IV, son of George III	1820–1830
William IV, third son of George III	1830–1837
Victoria, daughter of Edward, fourth son	
of George III	1837–1901

HOUSE OF SAXE-COBURG AND GOTHA

Edward VII, son of Victoria	1901–1910

HOUSE OF WINDSOR (NAME ADOPTED 17 JULY 1917)

George V, second son of Edward VII	1910–1936
Edward VIII, eldest son of George V	1936–1936 (abdicated)
George VI, second son of George V	1936–1952
Elizabeth II, daughter of George VI	1952–

Religions in Great Britain

In the late sixth century C.E., missionaries from Rome introduced Christianity to the Anglo-Saxons—actually, reintroduced it, since it had briefly flourished in the southern parts of the British Isles during the Roman occupation, and even after the Roman withdrawal had persisted in the Celtic regions of Scotland and Wales. By the time the earliest poems included in *The Norton Anthology of English Literature* were composed (i.e., the seventh century), therefore, there had been a Christian presence in the British Isles for hundreds of years. The conversion of the Germanic occupiers of England can, however, be dated only from 597. Our knowledge of the religion of pre-Christian Britain is sketchy, but it is likely that vestiges of Germanic polytheism assimilated into, or coexisted with, the practice of Christianity: fertility rites were incorporated into the celebration of Easter resurrection, rituals commemorating the dead into All-Hallows Eve and All Saints Day, and elements of winter solstice festivals into the celebration of Christmas. The most durable polytheistic remains are our days of the week, each of which except "Saturday" derives from the name of a Germanic pagan god, and the word "Easter," deriving, according to the Anglo-Saxon scholar Bede (d. 735), from the name of a Germanic pagan goddess, Eostre. In English literature such "folkloric" elements sometimes elicit romantic nostalgia. Geoffrey Chaucer's "Wife of Bath" looks back to a magical time before the arrival of Christianity in which the land was "fulfilled of fairye." Hundreds of years later, the seventeenth-century writer Robert Herrick honors the amalgamation of Christian and pagan elements in agrarian British culture in such poems as "Corinna's Gone A-Maying" and "The Hock Cart."

Medieval Christianity was fairly uniform, if complex, across Western Europe—hence called "catholic," or universally shared. The Church was composed of the so-called "regular" and "secular" orders, the regular orders being those who followed a rule in a community under an abbot or an abbess (i.e., monks, nuns, friars and canons), while the secular clergy of priests served parish communities under the governance of a bishop. In the unstable period from the sixth until the twelfth century, monasteries were the intellectual powerhouse of the Church. From the beginning of the thirteenth century, with the development of an urban Christian spirituality in Europe, friars dominated the recently invented institution of universities, as well as devoting themselves, in theory at least, to the urban poor.

The Catholic Church was also an international power structure. With its hierarchy of pope, cardinals, archbishops, and bishops, it offered a model of the centralized, bureaucratic state from the late eleventh century. That ecclesiastical power structure coexisted alongside a separate, often less centralized and feudal structure of lay authorities, with theoretically different and often competing spheres of social responsibilities. The sharing of lay and ecclesiastical authority in medieval England was sometimes a source of conflict. Chaucer's pilgrims are on their way to visit the memorial shrine to one victim of such exemplary struggle: Thomas à Becket, Archbishop of Canterbury, who opposed the policies of King Henry II, was assassinated by indirect suggestion of the king in 1170, and later made a saint. The Church, in turn, produced its own victims: Jews were subject to persecution in the late twelfth century in England, before being expelled in 1290. From the beginning of the fifteenth century, the English Church targeted Lollard heretics (see below) with capital punishment, for the first time.

As an international organization, the Church conducted its business in the universal language of Latin. Thus although in the period the largest segment of literate persons was made up of clerics, the clerical contribution to great literary writing in vernacular languages (e.g., French and English) was, so far as we know, relatively modest, with some great exceptions in the later Middle Ages (e.g., William Langland). Lay, vernacular writers of the period certainly reflect the importance of the Church as an institution and the pervasiveness of religion in the rituals that marked everyday life, as well as contesting institutional authority. From the late fourteenth century, indeed, England witnessed an active and articulate, proto-Protestant movement known as Lollardy, which attacked clerical hierarchy and promoted vernacular scriptures.

Beginning in 1517 the German monk Martin Luther, in Wittenberg, Germany, openly challenged many aspects of Catholic practice and by 1520 had completely repudiated the authority of the pope, setting in train the Protestant Reformation. Luther argued that the Roman Catholic Church had strayed far from the pattern of Christianity laid out in scripture. He rejected Catholic doctrines for which no biblical authority was to be found, such as the belief in Purgatory, and translated the Bible into German, on the grounds that the importance of scripture for all Christians made its translation into the vernacular tongue essential. Luther was not the first to advance such views— Lollard followers of the Englishman John Wycliffe had translated the Bible in the late fourteenth century. But Luther, protected by powerful German rulers, was able to speak out with impunity and convert others to his views, rather than suffer the persecution usually meted out to heretics. Soon other reformers were following in Luther's footsteps: of these, the Swiss Ulrich Zwingli and the French Jean Calvin would be especially influential for English religious thought.

At first England remained staunchly Catholic. Its king, Henry VIII, was so severe to heretics that the pope awarded him the title "Defender of the Faith," which British monarchs have retained to this day. In 1534, however, Henry rejected the authority of the pope to prevent his divorce from his queen, Catherine of Aragon, and his marriage to his mistress, Ann Boleyn. In doing so, Henry appropriated to himself ecclesiastical as well as secular authority. Thomas More, author of *Utopia*, was executed in 1535 for refusing to endorse Henry's right to govern the English church. Over the following six years, Henry consolidated his grip on the ecclesiastical establishment by dissolving the powerful, populous Catholic monasteries and redistributing their massive landholdings to his own lay followers. Yet Henry's church largely retained Catholic doctrine and liturgy. When Henry died and his young son, Edward, came to the throne in 1547, the English church embarked on a more Protestant path, a direction abruptly reversed when Edward died and his older sister Mary, the daughter of Catherine of Aragon, took the throne in 1553 and attempted to reintroduce Roman Catholicism. Mary's reign was also short, however, and her successor, Elizabeth I, the daughter of Ann Boleyn, was a Protestant. Elizabeth attempted to establish a "middle way" Christianity, compromising between Roman Catholic practices and beliefs and reformed ones.

The Church of England, though it laid claim to a national rather than pan-European authority, aspired like its predecessor to be the universal church of all English subjects. It retained the Catholic structure of parishes and dioceses and the Catholic hierarchy of bishops, though the ecclesiastical authority was now the Archbishop of Canterbury and the Church's "Supreme Governor" was the monarch. Yet disagreement and controversy persisted. Some members of the Church of England wanted to retain many of the ritual and liturgical elements of Catholicism. Others, the Puritans, advocated a more thoroughgoing reformation. Most Puritans remained within the Church of England, but a minority, the "Separatists" or "Congregationalists," split from the established church altogether. These dissenters no longer thought of the ideal church as an organization to which everybody belonged; instead, they conceived it as a more exclusive group of likeminded people, one not necessarily attached to a larger body of believers.

In the seventeenth century, the succession of the Scottish king James to the English throne produced another problem. England and Scotland were separate nations, and in the sixteenth century Scotland had developed its own national Presbyterian church, or "kirk," under the leadership of the reformer John Knox. The kirk retained fewer Catholic liturgical elements than did the Church of England, and its authorities, or "presbyters," were elected by assemblies of their fellow clerics, rather than appointed by the king. James I and his son Charles I, especially the latter, wanted to bring the Scottish kirk into conformity with Church of England practices. The Scots violently resisted these efforts, with the collaboration of many English Puritans, in a conflict that eventually developed into the English Civil War in the mid-seventeenth century. The effect of these disputes is visible in the poetry of such writers as John Milton, Robert Herrick, Henry Vaughan, and Thomas Traherne, and in the prose of Thomas Browne, Lucy Hutchinson, and Dorothy Waugh. Just as in the mid-sixteenth century, when a succession of monarchs with different religious commitments destabilized the church, so the seventeenth century endured spiritual whiplash. King Charles I's highly ritualistic Church of England was violently overturned by the Puritan victors in the Civil War—until 1660, after the death of the Puritan leader, Oliver Cromwell, when the Church of England was restored along with the monarchy.

The religious and political upheavals of the seventeenth century produced Christian sects that de-emphasized the ceremony of the established church and rejected as well its top-down authority structure. Some of these groups were ephemeral, but the Baptists (founded in 1608 in Amsterdam by the English expatriate John Smyth) and Quakers, or Society of Friends (founded by George Fox in the 1640s), flourished outside the established church, sometimes despite cruel persecution. John Bunyan, a Baptist, wrote the Christian allegory *Pilgrim's Progress* while in prison. Some dissenters, like the Baptists, shared the reformed reverence for the absolute authority of scripture but interpreted the scriptural texts differently from their fellow Protestants. Others, like the Quakers, favored, even over the authority of the Bible, the "inner light" or voice of individual conscience, which they took to be the working of the Holy Spirit in the lives of individuals.

The Protestant dissenters were not England's only religious minorities. Despite crushing fines and the threat of imprisonment, a minority of Catholics under Elizabeth and James openly refused to give their allegiance to the new church, and others remained secret adherents to the old ways. John Donne was brought up in an ardently Catholic family, and several other writers converted to Catholicism as adults—Ben Jonson for a considerable part of his career, Elizabeth Carey and Richard Crashaw permanently, and at profound personal cost. In the eighteenth century, Catholics remained objects of suspicion as possible agents of sedition, especially after the "Glorious Revolution" in 1688 deposed the Catholic James II in favor of the Protestant William and Mary. Anti-Catholic prejudice affected John Dryden, a Catholic convert, as well as the lifelong Catholic Alexander Pope. By contrast, the English colony of Ireland remained overwhelmingly Roman Catholic, the fervor of its religious commitment at least partly inspired by resistance to English occupation. Starting in the reign of Elizabeth, England shored up its own authority in Ireland by encouraging Protestant immigrants from Scotland to settle in the north of Ireland, producing a virulent religious divide the effects of which are still playing out today.

A small community of Jews had moved from France to London after 1066, when the Norman William the Conqueror came to the English throne. Although despised and persecuted by many Christians, they were allowed to remain as moneylenders to the Crown, until the thirteenth century, when the king developed alternative sources of credit. At this point, in 1290, the Jews were expelled from England. In 1655 Oliver Cromwell permitted a few to return, and in the late seventeenth and early eighteenth centuries the Jewish population slowly increased, mainly by immigration from Germany. In the mid-eighteenth century some prominent Jews had their children brought up as Christians so as to facilitate their full integration into English society: thus the nineteenth-century writer and politician Benjamin Disraeli, although he and his father were members of the Church of England, was widely considered a Jew insofar as his ancestry was Jewish.

In the late seventeenth century, as the Church of England reasserted itself, Catholics, Jews, and dissenting Protestants found themselves subject to significant legal restrictions. The Corporation Act, passed in 1661, and the Test Act, passed in 1673, excluded all who refused to take communion in the Church of England from voting, attending university, or working in government or in the professions. Members of religious minorities, as well as Church of England communicants, paid mandatory taxes in support of Church of England ministers and buildings. In 1689 the dissenters gained the right to worship in public, but Jews and Catholics were not permitted to do so.

During the eighteenth century, political, intellectual, and religious history remained closely intertwined. The Church of England came to accommodate a good deal of variety. "Low church" services resembled those of the dissenting Protestant churches, minimizing ritual and emphasizing the sermon; the "high church" retained more elaborate ritual elements, yet its prestige was under attack on several fronts. Many Enlightenment thinkers subjected the Bible to rational critique and found it wanting: the philosopher David Hume, for instance, argued that the "miracles" described therein were more probably lies or errors than real breaches of the laws of nature. Within the Church of England, the "broad church" Latitudinarians welcomed this rationalism, advocating theological openness and an emphasis on ethics rather than dogma. More radically, the Unitarian movement rejected the divinity of Christ while professing to accept his ethical teachings. Taking a different tack, the preacher John Wesley, founder of Methodism, responded to the rationalists' challenge with a newly fervent call to evangelism and personal discipline; his movement was particularly successful in Wales. Revolutions in America and France at the end of the century generated considerable millenarian excitement and fostered more new religious ideas, often in conjunction with a radical social agenda. Many important writers of the Romantic period were indebted to traditions of protestant dissent: Unitarian and rationalist protestant ideas influenced William Hazlitt, Anna Barbauld, Mary Wollstonecraft, and the young Samuel Taylor Coleridge. William Blake created a highly idiosyncratic poetic mythology loosely indebted to radical strains of Christian mysticism. Others were even more heterodox: Lord Byron and Robert Burns, brought up as Scots Presbyterians, rebelled fiercely, and Percy Shelley's writing of an atheistic pamphlet resulted in his expulsion from Oxford.

Great Britain never erected an American-style "wall of separation" between church and state, but in practice religion and secular affairs grew more and more distinct during the nineteenth century. In consequence, members of religious minorities no longer seemed to pose a threat to the commonweal. A movement to repeal the Test Act failed in the 1790s, but a renewed effort resulted in the extension of the franchise to dissenting Protestants in 1828 and to Catholics in 1829. The numbers of Roman Catholics in England were swelled by immigration from Ireland, but there were also some prominent English adherents. Among writers, the converts John Newman and Gerard Manley Hopkins are especially important. The political participation and social integration of Jews presented a thornier challenge. Lionel de Rothschild, repeatedly elected to represent London in Parliament during the 1840s and 1850s, was not permitted to take his seat there because he refused to take his oath of office "on the true faith of a Christian"; finally, in 1858, the Jewish Disabilities Act allowed him to omit these words. Only in 1871, however, were Oxford and Cambridge opened to non-Anglicans.

Meanwhile geological discoveries and Charles Darwin's evolutionary theories increasingly cast doubt on the literal truth of the Creation story, and close philological analysis of the biblical text suggested that its origins were human rather than divine. By the end of the nineteenth century, many writers were bearing witness to a world in which Christianity no longer seemed fundamentally plausible. In his poetry and prose, Thomas Hardy depicts a world devoid of benevolent providence. Matthew Arnold's poem "Dover Beach" is in part an elegy to lost spiritual assurance, as the "Sea of Faith" goes out like the tide: "But now I only hear / Its melancholy, long, withdrawing roar / Retreating." For Arnold, literature must replace religion as a source of spiritual truth, and intimacy between individuals substitute for the lost communal solidarity of the universal church.

The work of many twentieth-century writers shows the influence of a religious upbringing or a religious conversion in adulthood. T. S. Eliot and W. H. Auden embrace Anglicanism, William Butler Yeats spiritualism. James Joyce repudiates Irish Catholicism but remains obsessed with it. Yet religion, or lack of it, is a matter of individual choice and conscience, not social or legal mandate. In the past fifty years, church attendance has plummeted in Great Britain. Although 71 percent of the population still identified itself as "Christian" on the 2000 census, only about 7 percent of these regularly attend religious services of any denomination. Meanwhile, immigration from former British colonies has swelled the ranks of religions once uncommon in the British Isles—Muslim, Sikh, Hindu, Buddhist—though the numbers of adherents remain small relative to the total population.

PERMISSIONS ACKNOWLEDGMENTS

TEXT CREDITS

Annie Besant: "The White Slavery of London Match Workers" from STRONG-MINDED WOMEN by Janet H. Murray. Copyright © 1982 by Janet H. Murray. Reprinted by permission of the Markson Thomas Literary Agency.

Ada Nield Chew: Extract from THE LIFE AND WRITINGS OF A WORKING WOMAN by Ada Nield Chew. Published by Virago Press, London. Reprinted by permission.

Gerard Manley Hopkins: Selections as indicated from THE JOURNALS AND PAPERS OF GERARD MANLEY HOPKINS, edited by Humphry House and Graham Storey (1959). Reprinted by permission of Oxford University Press on behalf of the Society of Jesus.

"Poverty Knock" from FOLK SONG IN ENGLAND by A. L. Lloyd (1967). Reprinted by permission of Lawrence & Wishart Ltd.

Christina Rossetti: "Cobwebs," "In an Artist's Studio," "Promises Like Piecrust," "In Progress," and "Cardinal Newman" from THE COMPLETE WORKS OF CHRISTINA ROSSETTI edited by R. W. Crump. Copyright © 1990 by Louisiana State University. Reprinted by permission of the Louisiana State University Press.

George Bernard Shaw: *Mrs Warren's Profession*, copyright © 1898, 1913, 1926, 1930, 1933, 1941 George Bernard Shaw, copyright © 1957, The Public Trustee as Executor of the Estate of George Bernard Shaw, © 1970 The Trustees of the British Museum, The Governors and Guardians of The National Gallery of Ireland and Royal Academy of Dramatic Art. Reprinted by permission of The Society of Authors on behalf of The Estate of Bernard Shaw.

Flora Thompson: From chapter 11 "School" from A LARK RISE TO CANDLEFORD by Flora Thompson. Copyright © 1939 by Oxford University Press. Reprinted by permission of Oxford University Press.

Oscar Wilde: *De Profundis* from THE LETTERS OF OSCAR WILDE, edited by Sir Rupert Hart-Davis and Merlin Holland. Letters © 1962 by Vyvyan Holland, © 1985, 1990, 2000 by Merlin Holland. Editorial matter © 1962, 1985 by Rupert Hart-Davis, © 2000 by Rupert Hart-Davis and Merlin Holland. Reprinted by permission of HarperCollins Publishers Ltd.

IMAGE CREDITS

Pp. 2–3: Manchester City Art Gallery, Manchester, UK; p. 6: GRANGER / GRANGER. All rights reserved; p. 9: Public Domain; p. 11: Yale Center for British Art, Paul Mellon Collection, USA / Bridgeman Images; p. 15: GRANGER / GRANGER. All rights reserved; p.17: Everett Historical / Shutterstock; p. 151: Culture Club / Hulton Archive/ Getty Images; p. 263: from Charles Dickens, *A Christmas Carol*, 1843 Edition. Illustration by John Leech. Scanned image by Philip V. Allingham. Courtesy Dickens collector and bibliophile Dan Calinescu, Toronto. The Victorian Web www.victorianweb.org/art /illustration/carol/gallery.html; p. 272: from Charles Dickens, *A Christmas Carol*, 1843 Edition. Illustration by John Leech. Scanned image by Philip V. Allingham. Courtesy Dickens collector and bibliophile Dan Calinescu, Toronto. The Victorian Web www.victorianweb.org/art /illustration/carol/gallery.html; p. 277: from Charles Dickens, *A Christmas Carol*, 1843 Edition. Illustration by John Leech. Scanned image by Philip V. Allingham. Courtesy Dickens collector and bibliophile Dan Calinescu, Toronto. The Victorian Web www.victorianweb.org/art /illustration/carol /gallery.html; p. 289: from Charles Dickens, *A Christmas Carol*, 1843 Edition. Illustration by John Leech. Scanned image by Philip V. Allingham. Courtesy Dickens collector and bibliophile Dan Calinescu, Toronto. The Victorian Web www.victorianweb.org/art /illustration/carol/gallery.html; p. 291: from Charles Dickens, *A Christmas Carol*, 1843 Edition. Illustration by John Leech. Scanned image by Philip V. Allingham. Courtesy Dickens collector and bibliophile Dan Calinescu, Toronto. The Victorian Web www.victorianweb.org/art /illustration/carol/gallery.html; p. 304: from Charles Dickens, *A Christmas Carol*, 1843 Edition. Illustration by John Leech. Scanned image by Philip V. Allingham. Courtesy Dickens collector and bibliophile Dan Calinescu, Toronto. The Victorian Web www.victorianweb.org/art /illustration/carol/gallery.html; p. 314: from Charles Dickens, *A Christmas Carol*, 1843 Edition. Illustration by John Leech. Scanned image by Philip V. Allingham. Courtesy Dickens collector and bibliophile Dan Calinescu, Toronto. The Victorian Web www.victorianweb.org/art /illustration/carol/gallery.html; p. 319: from Charles Dickens, *A Christmas Carol*, 1843 Edition. Illustration by John Leech. Scanned image by Philip V. Allingham. Courtesy Dickens collector and bibliophile Dan Calinescu, Toronto. The Victorian Web www.victorianweb.org/art /illustration/carol/gallery.html; p. 520: Fogg Art Museum, Harvard University Art Museums / Bequest of Grenville L. Winthrop / The Bridgeman Art Library; p. 547: Private Collection / Bridgeman Images; p. 607: Alamy; p. 610: Public Domain / Wikipedia; p. 620: British Library, London / British Library Board. All Rights Reserved / The Bridgeman Art Library; p. 623: Public Domain / Wikipedia; p. 634: 1842–43 Children's Employment Commission; p. 644: The Granger Collection, NY; p. 649: Pannemaker, pub. 1872 (engraving), Gustave Doré (1832–1833) / Private Collection / The Stapleton Collection / The Bridgeman Art Library; p. 650: The Granger Collection, NY; p. 657: Allom / A. L. Dick / www.fromoldbooks.org; p. 667: Delaware Art Museum, Wilmington / Samuel and Mary R. Bancroft Memorial / The Bridgeman Art Library; p. 671: London Stereoscopic Company / Hulton Archive / Getty Images; p. 681: Courtesy of Dover Books / *Victorian Fashions & Costumes from Harpers Bazar 1867–98*; p. 684: The Granger Collection, NY; p. 690: Hulton Archive / Getty Images; p. 703: © Look and Learn / Illustrated Papers Collection / Bridgeman Images; p. 706: Yale University / Beinecke Library. *Boys of the Empire, A Journal in Colours of Fun, Instruction and Romance*. Edited by Edwin J. Brett; p. 710: The Granger Collection, NY; p. 760: The Granger Collection, NY.

COLOR INSERT CREDITS

Index